To all the social psychologists and students who, through their research, theories, questions, and criticisms, have contributed to the ideas and efforts of the authors

Preface

Although social psychology textbooks have been published for nearly 70 years, most of the development in the science has occurred in the last quarter century. This rapid development has been somewhat helter-skelter. Research efforts have typically been devoted to examining single hypotheses based on the intuitions of investigators rather than on well-elaborated theories; and, as a result, the various areas of research seem to have no relationship to one another. Most of the recent textbooks march from area to area with little connection between chapters. Our belief that an integration of much contemporary social psychology can be achieved by using the basic concepts of social influence theory was a major factor in our decision to write this book. Because of this attempt at integration, the chapters of the text tend to be cumulative and probably should be read in order. However the attempt to integrate did not result in such a tightly woven fabric that a snag in one part brings about a total unraveling; instructors might, therefore, skip some chapters or change the order of a few if they provide the student reader with necessary transitional material.

The decision to write a textbook brings with it many other choices. We decided that we wanted to present and examine the major theories in social psychology so that the introductory student could have an appreciation of the issues occupying the attention of contemporary researchers. This emphasis on theory made it necessary to be selective in presenting supporting research, since it would be impossible to incorporate all of the available research. In our selection we tried to be fair to all views. Classic studies are usually presented for their historical importance in the development of the field of social psychology. Experiments are generally chosen over less controlled research such as field studies, surveys, or correlational findings because experiments represent the best tests of hypotheses. Samples of nonexperimental studies are found throughout, however, for their instructional value and occasionally for their real-world relevance. Moreover, when we considered a theory important and there was little experimental work available by which to evaluate it, we presented other kinds of research.

Because social psychologists usually focus on the interaction of no more than a few people, it may appear that they are avoiding or evading the real world in all of its complexity. But, content with the knowledge that most neurophysiologists would not discuss problems of social conformity or of leadership on the grounds that such phenomena are outside their purview, we take the same stand with respect to more complex processes. Of course political, economic, sociological, and cultural phenomena have important psychological aspects to them; but the social psychologist usually overreaches himself and his expertise when he attempts to apply his theories to such complex events. This point is briefly demonstrated in the last part of Chapter 14.

The situation within which people interact has important effects on their actions. Any social psychological principle can be violated given the right set of circumstances, and until we understand the effects of all describable sets of circumstances on the behavior under study, we can say only that the principle holds, *ceteris paribus* (other things being equal). Sometimes it is the convention in scientific works to include the disclaimer *ceteris paribus* wherever appropriate. It should be assumed to hold in the case of every social psychological principle in this book.

Writing the textbook has confirmed our conviction that social psychologists have raised a great many interesting questions and have been extraordinarily creative in designing research to answer them. We have tried to capture some of the excitement that is felt about the contemporary issues occupying the attention of social psychologists. Despite the inherent interest of many of the issues addressed and despite our attempts to define sharply the theoretical controversies that give substance to the field of social psychology, we realize that the book is not an easy one to read. Few science books are. This book is not geared for a course in applied psychology or the psychology of adjustment; it is designed for the serious student of social psychology as a science. We have assumed an intelligent and critical reader who is motivated to learn about a field that is rapidly growing and contains enduring challenge. For many instructors the text will be most suitable for an upper division course. It is appropriate also for a first-year graduate course in social psychology if the students are not assumed to be well grounded in social psychological theory.

The text is written in five parts. In Part 1 we present the view that science is a way of thinking—a way of thinking that is illustrated throughout the book by the questions asked and answered. The first chapter describes the level of analysis considered appropriate for the social psychologist as well as many of the assumptions and values that permeate any social science discipline, including the belief in determinism. Some instructors may find this opening chapter expendable, but we have found that students find the material interesting; it also lays bare the assumptions underlying our approach. Chapter 2 deals with the logic of scientific inquiry, methods used by social psychologists, the social psychology of the psychological experiment, and questions of ethics in performing research with human beings.

Part 2 examines the individual person in the context of social stimuli. He or she is described as a sensor in the midst of many stimuli. The person as an information processor is attentive to only some of the available stimuli. With the intervention and help of other persons, he transforms information into his own way of interpreting events. He develops perspectives, attitudes, values, and habits that affect his interactions with others. Information processing, person perception, beliefs and attitudes, and socialization are the subjects of Chapters 3–6.

Part 3 shows the individual in interaction with others and describes the processes of influence by which they affect one another. The elements of influence, including the source, the mode of influence, and the target, represent a system in which numerous factors can operate to affect the consequences to either party. In Chapters 7, 8, and 9 we consider what causes the individual to comply with influence attempts, what determines who will be chosen as a target, which mode of influence will be used, why and under what circumstances coercion will be utilized to achieve dominance over others, how people reach bargains with one another, and who will form partnerships or coalitions to achieve their interpersonal objectives.

Part 4 focuses on positive and negative interactions between people. When are people kind, helpful, and willing to intervene to provide aid during emergency situations? And when do they stand aloof and coldly watch while others suffer? What causes people to like or dislike one another? How does friendship differ from love? Under what conditions will a subject in the laboratory harm other people? Does watching violent television programs act as a catalyst in stimulating a viewer to attack others? In Chapters 10, 11, and 12 a rather critical view of the research and theory concerning prosocial behavior, interpersonal attraction, and aggression is provided. These have been untidy areas of research, mainly because of the complexity of the phenomena under study and the lack of powerful theories to guide us. We have attempted to be fair in representing the field as it exists but have not resisted the temptation to offer our own theories as potential integrative conceptions of the available evidence. We hope that our own conceptions are sufficiently provocative to have a stimulating effect on the future development of fundamental theory and research in social psychology.

Part 5 shows the individual in the context of larger groups. Here he is confronted with the problems of being compared with others and with pressures to conform. To be productive in solving collective problems, groups have to organize their talents and efforts through the development of structure and the emergence of leadership. Individuals make decisions and solve problems differently when in a group than when alone. These topics may help the many practically minded people who want to know what makes an efficient leader. In addition to these topics, Chapters 13 and 14 contain discussions of decision making during political crises, and such social phenomena as crowds, panics, riots, and revolutions. Attention is given to some psychological factors relevant to social deviance and problems of economic development.

So many people have been helpful in bringing this textbook to completion that we are sure to forget to acknowledge someone. Peg Tedeschi has probably put more hours into the production of the book than anyone else save the authors—she critically read the manuscript in several versions, helped in copyediting the final manuscript, assembled and checked all of the references, drew many of the graphs, and indexed the entired text. Alexander Morin's questions were penetrating and insightful, and for a nonpsychologist he was quite sophisticated in suggesting alternative explanations to those offered by researchers. M. Brewster Smith was stimulating as a source of many intelligent criticisms of the manuscript.

Innumerable other colleagues and students have read one or more chapters and corrected errors of fact and interpretation. At the risk of forgetting someone, we wish to acknowledge the help given by Jack Arbuthnot, Jane Becker, Russ Bennett, Thomas Bonoma, Sue Foster, Gerald Gaes, Norm Greenfeld, Bob Helm, Joann Horai, Joanne Joseph, Thomas Kane, Bruce Layton, Danny Moates, Bob Mogy, Pete Nacci, Stuart Oskamp, Alba Rivera, Barry Schlenker, Pat Sloan, Pat Smith, Rick Stapleton, Fred Tesch, Marc Wayner, and Robert Zajonc.

The strain placed on the secretarial staff and certain undergraduate students in the production of the manuscript was sometimes quite strong. We owe a debt of thanks to Al Diamond, Irene Farruggio, Lili Hsu, Sandy Johnson, Donna Petronis, Terry Stapleton, Barbara Steere, Ann Tedeschi, Louise Tornatore, Mary Lou Tucker, and Sue Volks for the work they did in putting all of this together.

JAMES T. TEDESCHI
SVENN LINDSKOLD

Albany, New York
Athens, Ohio
September 1975

Thomas Bellew Ph.D.

Social Psychology

Social Psychology

INTERDEPENDENCE, INTERACTION, AND INFLUENCE

James T. Tedeschi
State University of New York at Albany

Svenn Lindskold
Ohio University

A WILEY-INTERSCIENCE PUBLICATION

JOHN WILEY & SONS, New York • London • Sydney • Toronto

Library of Congress Cataloging in Publication Data

Tedeschi, James T
  Social psychology.

  "A Wiley-Interscience publication."
  Bibliography: p.
  Includes indexes.
    1. Social psychology. I. Lindskold, Svenn, joint author. II. Title. [DNLM: 1. Psychology, Social.

HM 251 T256s]
HM51.T43   301.1   75-38883
ISBN 0-471-85017-9

Printed in the United States of America

10 9 8 7 6 5 4 3 2

Contents

PART 1

Social Psychology: Orientation and Methods

What do social psychologists study? It may be interesting for you to stop and think about what it is you expect to learn from this book. Do you expect to find solutions to important social problems, such as racial conflicts or wars? What kinds of preconceptions about man's social behavior do you bring to your study of social psychology?* Do you believe that men are governed by instincts or by unconscious forces? Do men have free will and are they basically selfish? Chapter 1 provides an orientation to how social psychologists typically answer these questions. We will see that the basic focus of social psychology is the individual—how he affects and is influenced by other people. Of course social psychology overlaps with and borrows from other social and biological sciences, but it has a set of special interests and problems not studied by the other disciplines. In order to provide an orientation to social psychology, it is necessary to understand what is distinctive about the science and how it differs from the other sciences of man.

A central assumption of all sciences is that the events of interest have discoverable causes. This assumption of determinism is the subject of much controversy particularly when it is applied to human behavior. Much of the argumentation has been based on faulty conceptions of what determinism implies about the nature of man. Since determinism is basic to any scientific study of man, a full discussion of the assumption is provided in Chapter 1.

Long before the development of the social sciences philosophers conjectured about the nature of man. Very different basic assumptions concerning man have emerged over the centuries. It will be worthwhile to examine several of the prominent contemporary views of man because the kinds of questions asked and the types of answers proposed by social psychologists are often based on the assumptions they make about the nature of man.

*The conventional uses of "man" and "he" throughout this text refer to both sexes. We apologize to our readers for the awkwardness of the English language.

How the social psychologist studies his subject matter is just as important as its content. Social psychology is a science and hence there are rules governing the acquisition of knowledge about social psychological phenomena. One could not appreciate or fully understand social psychology without understanding the logic used in formulating hypotheses and the methods used in testing them. Consider how much you would enjoy games such as football, baseball, bridge or chess if you did not understand the rules of play. In Chapter 2 the logic of scientific inquiry and the particular methods employed by social psychologists will be examined. Social psychologists have some special problems because their experimental situation, consisting as it does of both human participants and a human experimenter, is itself a social situation. Also, each human participant is an amateur psychologist who knows that he is under observation by a professional psychologist. By systematically investigating the social psychology of the experiment, the social psychologist has tried to develop methods to overcome these difficulties. In addition, research undertaken with humans raises certain ethical issues that are irrelevant when one studies physical events. A mastery of the material in Chapter 2 will provide analytic tools with which you can critically evaluate the work of social psychologists as it will be presented throughout the remainder of the text.

CHAPTER 1

An Orientation to Social Psychology

CHAPTER PREVIEW

Social psychology is the scientific study of interdependence, interaction, and influence among persons. Interdependence reflects the fact that most of the things a person desires cannot be obtained without the collaboration of other people. Think for a minute about something you would like to do or have. If there were no other people in the world could you obtain your objectives? Food, clothing, shelter, love, security, and many other necessities of life depend upon the behavior of many other people—the farmer, grocer, carpenter, brick layer, plumber, mother, policeman, and so on. This interdependence of people provides the basis for cooperation or conflict between them.

People interact with one another because they are interdependent; they need one another. In the course of interaction, influence is exerted. The individual's view of the universe and the values he has, the impressions he forms of other people and of himself, and the friendships he establishes emerge out of his interaction with other people. Any time the actions of one person affect the outlook, values, or actions of another person, social influence has been exerted. Much influence occurs without either party intending it or even noticing it. On the other hand, influence is often deliberate, as when persuasive arguments are made or threats are issued.

Political scientists, sociologists, economists, and anthropologists are also interested in social influence and power. Although the boundaries between the social sciences are not firm or fixed, there are distinct differences in what is studied by each of them. Similarly, we will point out how social psychology differs from individual psychology. One commonality in all of these sciences is the assumption that social behavior is caused by discoverable natural events. If this assumption of determinism is not made, there is little reason to undertake scientific investigations. In the first part of this chapter we will undertake to differentiate among the social sciences, and in the second part we will examine in some detail the implications of accepting the principle of determinism.

In the third part of this chapter we will briefly consider several views regarding the nature of men that have influenced the directions taken by social psychologists in their study of social behavior. Everyone has a conception of the nature of man, although some have a clearer and more integrated picture than others. Man has been curious about himself from the time of earliest recorded history, and many weird and wonderful descriptions of his nature have been developed through the ages. Man has been viewed as a selfish pleasure-seeking organism, as an animal governed by instinctive urges, as a machine, and as a free and creative child of God. Concepts borrowed from some of these orientations play an important part in contemporary social psychology. These pre-scientific assumptions about man are seldom directly testable by scientific methods, but their general usefulness is indirectly evaluated by the scientific enterprise.

I. THE SOCIAL SCIENCES AND THE STUDY OF MAN

The construction of a building benefits from the collaboration of workers possessing many different skills, from the architect to the electrician, carpenter, and plumber. In a similar way, the development of knowledge about man and his social behavior is a cooperative enterprise. The division of labor is reflected in the departmental structure of universities. Each group of experts concentrates on gathering knowledge about a part of the complex world that exists outside the ivy-covered walls. Political, economic, cultural, and organizational features of human activities are the focus of study by different groups of experts. Claims are sometimes made that this or that social science discipline is *the* most important or most central for understanding man's behavior. But science is not a contest; one social science does not set out to vanquish the others in a race to explain man's social behavior. Rather, each provides a piece of the puzzle and each contributes to a full portrait of man.

The search for full knowledge of any particular human process or activity often carries the investigator into specialized areas outside his own. For example, the experimental psychologist interested in visual perception may need to learn about physical optics, neurophysiology, and biochemistry in order to track down the answers to his questions. Similarly, the social psychologist who studies social conflict may find himself studying personality theory, economic and political organization, social structure, and international relations. This interdisciplinary mingling is increasingly apparent in the universities. It is no longer unusual for an individual trained in one specialty to become a professor in a department representing a different field. For example, social psychologists may be found in departments of nursing, sociology, political science, economics, education, cultural anthropology, business administration, and criminal justice.

There are two ways in which the social sciences may be differentiated from one another—by their level of conceptual analysis and by their predominant methods used in investigation. The basic concepts of the scientist have a major impact on what he chooses to study. The economist may be concerned about supply and demand and their effects on the price structure, but he is seldom interested in what individuals think, do or say. The social psychologist may completely ignore economic factors in trying to explain the varying social responses of individuals. The method of investigation used will depend on the level of analysis chosen by the scientist. The economist cannot undertake experiments to ascertain the nature of supply and demand, but he can take careful measurements of events as they unfold in the economic process. The social psychologist

is much more apt to rely on experiments since he can study how individuals interact with one another in controlled laboratory conditions.

The boundaries between the social sciences can be understood in terms of the different levels of analysis that serve as the focus of activity within each field of study. There are those who argue that human behavior can be completely understood in terms of the level of analysis used in their particular discipline. For example, Marx theorized that human conflict (and most other human behavior) is fundamentally a function of economic processes. Some psychologists (e.g., Freud) have viewed war (and most other social behavior) as caused by man's instinctive motivations.

Our own view is that each social science is necessary but none is sufficient for understanding human behavior. To explicate further the concerns of social psychologists, we will consider the problems of levels of analysis, social science boundaries, reductionism, and the relationship of social psychology to its closest neighbors, individual psychology and sociology.

A. Levels of Analysis, Reductionism, and Social Science

Dividing social scientists into compartments labeled psychology, anthropology, sociology, economics, and political science may seem silly or even obstructive to a unified approach to the study of man. Concern for solving important social problems led to the development of interdisciplinary programs at some of our most prestigious universities in the 1960s. Unique centers and institutes were formed to study the problems of war and peace, poverty, and racial conflicts. These interdisciplinary efforts have usually turned out to be failures, and many have been abandoned. Differences in levels of analysis and research techniques have proved to be so significant that they cannot be overcome by merely bringing different social scientists together. Nevertheless, it is important that these interdisciplinary efforts continue, since they tend to provide a more encompassing view of man than do the separate sciences.

1. Units of Study and Reductionism

The phenomena studied by scientists may be characterized as molecular (i.e., small and detailed) or molar (i.e., large and general) in nature. The events of interest to scientists may be as molecular as the neural impulse or as molar as international warfare. It is doubtful whether discoveries made by the physiological psychologist will have much bearing on understanding the causes of war. The political scientist therefore has little interest in the work of neuropsychology. Thus the answers garnered by one social science often have little relevance to the questions posed by specialists in another social science. Some examples of the levels of analysis used in the various social sciences are summarized in Table 1.1.

The attempt to explain molar phenomena by reference to simpler concepts and units of study is referred to as *reductionism*. An extreme and systematic reductionist might argue in the following way about the causes of revolutions: revolutions result from mob violence, which, in turn, is the product of the discrete behavior of the individuals who make up the mob; each individual's behavior is comprised of muscular responses triggered by neural impulses; hence, revolutions are ultimately explainable at the level of analysis of neurophysiology.

The reductionist position does not take into account factors that are unique to each level of analysis. In studying nerve impulses the neuro-physiologist does not need to account for the distribution of natural resources in the world, economic competition, military preparedness, and other factors that must be considered by a political scientist who studies war. Since the physiologist does not take into account these many factors, it is

Table 1.1 Some examples of the levels of analysis and units of study typically used by the various social sciences

Social science	Level of analysis	Units of study
Anthropology	Culture, technology	Tools, laws, manners.
Sociology	Institutions, classes, norms, deviance	Social organization, characteristics of group members.
Economics	Production and allocation of goods and services	Supply, demand, wages, prices.
Political Science	Nations, elites, power	Alliances, lobbies, military organizations.
Social Psychology	Interpersonal influence, interaction, interdependence	Persuasion, conformity, leadership.
Psychology	Learning, motivation, perception, personality	Needs, reinforcement, stimuli, traits.
Biopsychology	Physiological bases of behavior, nervous system, endocrinology	Neuronal activity, blood chemistry, anatomical structure.

difficult to see how he could explain the very complex phenomenon of war. Of course a political scientist might find that neurophysiology has something to do with the events he studies. For example, President Wilson suffered a coronary thrombosis and became so incapacitated that his wife virtually ran the government of the United States during the last 18 months of his term of office. The failure of Wilson's brain to function properly does not tell the whole story, however. Why did Wilson's wife take over the reins of government? Why not the Vice-President or the Secretary of State? The answers to these questions are not to be found by studying the functioning of neurons.

Psychocentrism is the tendency to explain all social phenomena by the concepts or theories of psychology. There have been attempts to explain wars in terms of the instincts, motives, and personalities of individuals. This form of psychological reductionism ignores many of the factors (geography, natural resources, etc.) that political scientists consider crucial for understanding the causes of war. While psychological processes may constitute part of the explanation for armed conflicts between nations, there are nonpsychological factors to consider as well.

It is generally accepted that each social science must find explanations for the phenomena it studies at its own level of analysis. Although there is some overlap between the social sciences, each discipline is unique. We can better understand the nature of social psychology by examining the boundaries between it and the other social sciences.

2. Levels of Analysis, Units of Study, and Disciplinary Boundaries

The focus of social psychology is usually on the individual in face-to-face interactions with other people. The other social sciences tend to be concerned about the products or actions of groups or collections of people.

The economist is interested in the buying habits of a single consumer only in order to examine and explain the relations among aggregations of such behavior as production, employment levels, supply and demand, price structure, and the international balance of payments. The details of a specific interaction between a supervisor and a worker or between a shopkeeper and a customer is not something an economist would wish to study. The social psychologist, on the other hand, would be interested in what causes conflicts between supervisors and workers and how a shopkeeper and a buyer reach agreement about their exchanges. Thus the social psychologist seldom has any reason to examine the units of study of the economist.

It sometimes appears as though two separate social sciences are seeking answers to the same question. For example, both psychologists and anthropologists have investigated the causes of ethnic prejudice. Psychologists have found that prejudices are learned and that they satisfy certain needs of the individual, such as self-aggrandizement, the release of pent-up frustration, and the expiation of guilt. Leslie White (1949), a cultural anthropologist, has asserted that psychological explanations of prejudice are fallacious. He finds no significant biological or psychological differences among the peoples of different human societies, but the kinds of prejudices held are quite variable.

According to White, only a cultural analysis can provide an explanation of the occurrence of a particular form of prejudice within a society. Prejudice will occur if certain sociocultural conditions obtain: (1) if one group is competing with another for possession of territory, for jobs, or for other economic advantages, or (2) if a minority attempts to preserve its own subculture and resists the effort of the larger society to assimilate the group. Thus, prejudice represents an attempt to exclude certain groups from economic competition and to maintain the dominance of a majority culture. Whichever minority groups exist in a society under the conditions specified by White will be the targets of prejudice.

Despite White's arguments, it can be shown that psychologists and anthropologists are actually asking quite different questions. The anthropologist wonders what causes prejudice to appear and flourish in a society, while the psychologist asks why a particular individual human being is prejudiced. The concepts used by White include minority and majority groups, economic competition, and shared ethnic values. In our example, the psychologist's level of analysis deals with the individual's attitudes and values. Of course different questions require different answers and so the two disciplines have little direct relevance for solving each other's problems. If White believes that psychologists cannot provide answers for the kinds of questions he asks, he is probably right; but neither can he provide solutions for the problems that occupy the attention of psychologists. This difference in direction was captured in a short interchange in Lewis Carroll's *Alice in Wonderland:* "Would you tell me, please, which way I ought to go from here?" asked Alice. "That depends a good deal on where you want to get to," said the cat.

Interdisciplinary boundaries are permeable and much borrowing occurs between the social sciences. It is helpful to know something about the sister sciences since they may suggest variables that can contribute to solving social psychological problems. Maintaining a broad perspective will also prevent the social psychologist from mixing levels of analysis and making fallacious reductionist errors.

B. Individual Psychology and Social Psychology

To obtain a clearer orientation toward the problems studied by social psychology it will be helpful to distinguish it from individual psychology and (in the following section) from sociology. Two psychologists working on separate and specialized problems may share fewer concepts and have less in common than each has with members of other disciplines. A biopsychologist is closer to a biologist than he is to a social psychologist, and the latter has more in common with a sociologist or political scientist than with a biopsychologist. What all psychologists have in common is an interest in studying the individual person. The distinctiveness of the social psychologist within the discipline of psychology is attributable to his use of somewhat different concepts and units of study, the identification of social rather than physical causes of behavior, and a concern for reconstructing the individual's view of the world in terms of beliefs, attitudes, and values

1.   Units of Study and Social Psychology

Psychologists vary in the strategies they adopt in studying behavior. Some take a molecular view and assume that an understanding of simple responses, such as blinking an eye or pressing a bar, will yield laws of behavior applicable to more complex responses. This strategy assumes that once the laws of learning simple responses are fully understood, the laws of combining them into more complex behavior can also be discovered. A more molar view of behavior assumes that problem-solving or goal-oriented responses are not reducible to elementary laws. For example, in order to understand what maintains the behavior of a medical student through almost ten years of formal higher education, the psychologist is not likely to isolate all of the discrete little responses the student makes and attempt to show that they are responses to identifiable physical stimuli. The molar view assumes that the more complex the event to be studied, the more complex the causes are likely to be.

The molecular-molar controversy is an old one in the history of psychology. John Stuart Mill in the 19th century addressed this issue and argued that there are emergent properties at more complex levels that are not implied at simpler ones. This argument has often been expressed by the statement that "the whole is greater than the sum of its parts." Actually, this is an inadequate way to express the core idea, which is that the whole may not be adequately characterized as the sum of its parts nor may its properties be wholly predictable from part properties. Mill illustrated the problem facing the molecular psychologist with an analogy from chemistry. The compound, water, is qualitatively different from its component elements, hydrogen and oxygen. Water is a liquid, whole hydrogen and oxygen are gases. The qualitative difference of the compound from its component elements cannot be understood as a simple addition of the two gases but rather is an emergent property of a specific and peculiar relationship between the two elements.

A similar process occurs when a concert pianist performs. He moves his fingers more quickly than mere stimulus-response chaining can account for. The patterning of the pianist's responses are very complex and occur at great speed. In fact, the quickness with which his fingers depress the keys is faster than the speed of neural impulses, which makes it difficult to believe that one finger waits until it gets feedback from the brain that another finger has done its job. Furthermore, the concert pianist does not play in exactly the same way at each performance of a particular composition. This variability indicates he has organized his responses in various patterns and that such organizations are not reducible to simple laws of conditioning.

Understanding social behavior requires an analysis of the relationships between people and cannot be understood by knowing the elementary bases of a single individual's responses. In social psychology the individual's behavior is always assumed to have implications for his social relationships. The concepts at the social psychologist's level of analysis refer to these social relationships and are always formulated within the context of interaction, interdependence, and social influence.

2. Physical and Social Causes of Behavior

Traditionally, psychologists have emphasized the study of various internal processes of the organism, including learning, perception, motivation, emotion, and memory. These processes have usually been examined as they are affected by physical events. In learning, animals and humans are taught to make or withhold responses when presented with physical stimuli. The study of motivation has typically involved depriving the organism of food or water. The main reason for this emphasis on physical factors is that they are well defined and can be accurately measured.

Although the social psychologist may also be interested in learning, perception, motivation, emotions, and memory, he desires to relate these processes to the social environment. The principles developed by psychologists with reference to physical stimuli are not always directly applicable to the way an individual responds to social stimuli. For example, the critical features of the visual perception of physical space include color, brightness, shape, and texture. The perception of other people, as we shall see in Chapter 4, is organized around inferences made about their intentions, attitudes, and feelings. The physical attributes of persons may also be important in forming impressions of them, but social factors add to the complexity of the process.

The dimensions of the social environment have not been reduced to precise measurement and are therefore not well defined. Much of the activity of the social psychologist is directed toward identification of the important attributes of the social environment that affect the behavior of persons in interaction with one another. The concern for relating behavior to the social environment adds a dimension to the task of the social psychologist beyond those considered by most other psychologists.

Two strategies for defining the social environment have generally been used: (a) directly analyzing social situations, and (b) asking people how they "see" social situations. An example of the first approach is the ingenious work of Roger Barker (1968). Social situations are identifiable by the expectations people have of the kinds of behavior considered appropriate within them. Rules are learned about how to conduct oneself in particular kinds of settings. Barker has referred to distinctive social situations as *behavior settings*.

Consider the classroom in a school. It may be described as having a location in space and time, a boundary that is self-generated and that changes with the size of the class and the nature of the class's activities, rules governing who will speak and when, and a class of behavior objects, such as paper, pencils, blackboards, desks, and chairs. People within the boundaries of this behavior setting may be changed or replaced with very little change in observed behavior.

In much the same way, Boy Scout meetings, cocktail parties, and funerals are behavior settings that significantly determine what kinds of behavior are typically displayed in their contexts. Behavior settings often appear to control the behavior of people more than their individual motives and perceptions or differences in their learning histories. Movie-time at summer camp elicits different behavior from campers than does free time at the swimming hole.

The second approach to defining the social environment is to determine how the individual describes it to himself. If it can be ascertained how the person perceives his world, what kinds of discriminations he makes and what he thinks is important,

then some progress can be made in understanding why he acts as he does. For this reason many social psychologists have devoted their efforts to finding out how the individual cognitively structures his world—what kinds of beliefs, attitudes and values he has. When aspects of these cognitive structures have been measured (by using questionnaires and observing the kinds of judgments people make in experimental situations), attempts can be made to associate them with the person's integrative view of the world. This strategy for defining the social environment (treated in Chapters 3 and 5 of this text) has been most often manifested in the study of attitudes. Because the individual psychologist seldom concerns himself with defining the social environment, he usually shows little interest in the measurement of attitudes or beliefs. The learning theorist is mostly involved in the question of process (i.e., how), while the social psychologist gives somewhat more emphasis to the question of content (i.e., what is learned).

C. Sociology and Social Psychology

The sociologist studies social systems and attempts to relate various aspects of social structure to patterns of human behavior. One of the basic concepts at the sociological level of analysis is the institution, which may be defined as a pattern of conduct by interdependent human actors whose behavior is regulated by a set of rules (Berger & Luckmann, 1966). The church, slavery, and the public school system are examples of institutions. Rules can be formally or informally acknowledged in a society and are referred to as *norms*. Within each institution there is a differentiation of function so that actors undertake different specialized tasks. Much like a drama, each actor has a role prescribed for him in the institution. A *role* refers "to the functions a person performs when occupying a particular characterization (position) within a social context"

(Shaw & Constanzo, 1970, p. 326). Knowledge about the norms and roles associated with an institution helps the sociologist account for regularities in human behavior.

1. Norms

Norms prescribe how persons in various social situations should or should not act. Gouldner (1960) has called attention to the norm of reciprocity, which he considers to be universal. The *positive reciprocity norm* specifies that a man should help those who help him and the *negative reciprocity norm* specifies doing harm for harm. If someone invites you to dinner, then you are obligated to return the favor; if someone strikes you, then you should hit him back. A great deal of human behavior seems to conform to these reciprocity norms. But there are many exceptions to these rules, also. For example, when an American man is struck by a woman, usually he will not strike her back. The sociologist explains this kind of exception by another norm: males should not hit females.

Sanctions (i.e., rewards and punishments) are associated with conforming to norms or deviating from them. Much of the regularity of human behavior can be accounted for by knowing the norms and sanctions in a particular society. For example, knowledge of traffic regulations and their enforcement allows the sociologist to predict that the large majority of motorists will stop at red lights. He does not need to consider how people perceive colors, learn to push brake pedals, or decode symbolic communications. Sociologists have been able to associate different rates of crime with various features of the social structure such as the ethnic identity of human groups, educational level, socio-economic status, and location in rural, suburban, or urban communities. In these examples the purpose of the sociologist is to assess the incidence of behavior in a given group or class under conditions imposed by a special set of social circumstances.

2. Roles

A role is defined for the individual by the shared expectations of people around him. The administration of a university expects a college professor to perform a number of different activities: teach classes, counsel students, engage in creative scholarly work, serve on departmental and university committees, and participate in town-and-gown activities. Students also have expectations about how a college professor should behave. They expect organized and interesting lectures, fair examinations, availability of a professor during office hours for information and counsel, and so on. Most professors attempt to conform to these multiple expectations. Much of the professor's behavior can therefore be predicted by knowing how his role has been defined by others. Knowledge of both norms and roles provides the sociologist with units of analysis that can be used to explain uniform patterns of human conduct.

The social psychologist finds the sociologist's descriptions of the social structure helpful in understanding the behavior of individuals. However, the social psychologist's focus is on the individual.

Historically, social psychology emerged as a subfield in both psychology and sociology at about the same time. Sociological social psychology is organized around the concepts of roles and norms, and may examine how the individual perceives them. But the emphasis is on the impact of the individual on the group or the larger system. Psychological social psychology is concerned with how individuals influence one another and the impact of the group on the individual. The latter view is the one adopted by this book.

D. Summary of the Social Sciences and the Study of Man

There is no subject matter as complex as the human being. Just as the natural scientists have divided up their task of trying to understand the physical universe, so the social scientists have specialized in studying different aspects of human behavior. Each social science uses a level of analysis that is difficult to translate into that of the others. Although there is much borrowing between them, each of the social sciences must deal with its phenomena at its own peculiar level of analysis. There is nothing superior about any particular level of analysis; each simply raises different questions and requires its specific techniques of study. Interdisciplinary activities are seldom successful because of significant differences in concepts, units of study, theories, and research methods. Although it is often difficult for one social scientist to communicate easily with another because of their language differences, interpenetration and cross fertilization are common in bringing about major scientific advances.

Social psychology is unique because of its emphasis on the individual in social contexts. Individual psychology tends to ignore the social context of behavior and seldom refers to interactions in terms of influence, power, and conflict. Sociology relates social structure to patterns of actions by groups of people and tends to ignore individual variability in behavior. Social psychology stands between individual psychology and sociology, borrows units of study and theoretical concepts from each field, but supplements both with added factors necessary to explain the actions of individuals as they interact with one another.

II. THE PRINCIPLE OF DETERMINISM

Despite the differences between the social sciences, they all assume that the causes for the phenomena they study can be discovered. All of the social sciences accept the principle of determinism. In its simplest form this principle is that there are discoverable causes for every event. Most edu-

cated people accept determinism when it refers to the physical or nonhuman animal world. There is little dispute about whether there are natural causes for earthquakes and volcanoes or for the migration of birds. It is also generally accepted that there are natural causes for various forms of human physiological phenomena, such as hunger, the formation of blood clots and succumbing to disease. However, there is greater controversy when the principle of determinism is applied to all human behavior.

Many people dislike the notion that all human behavior is capable of explanation in terms of ascertainable causes. Four basic arguments have been made against this assumption: (1) each person has the stubborn feeling that he is often free of external constraint; (2) there are many kinds of human behavior that are inherently unpredictable; (3) man, unlike other organisms, has free will; and (4) no system of moral responsibility for regulating human conduct could be devised if all behavior was strictly determined. Let us examine each of these arguments in more detail.

A. Perceived Freedom

Each person feels that he can discriminate between situations in which he is constrained and others in which he is free to choose between alternative actions. Should you stop to think about it, you feel you can keep on reading this book, put it away, or throw it across the room. The determinist would reply that people have feelings of freedom but there are causes for them; that whatever you do with this book is capable of strict causal explanation. Just because a person is unaware of the causes of his own behavior is no reason to assume there are no causes. If primitive peoples are ignorant of the cause of pregnancy, does that mean there is no cause? The determinist would ask the question, what causes the individual's feelings of freedom? We do not always feel free. There are times when we feel trapped by events and believe we have no choice about what we can do. Perceived freedom has become an important area of research in social psychology (cf. Steiner, 1970; Chapter 4).

Besides ignorance of the causes of his own behavior, the individual's stubborn feeling of freedom is based on the fact that his orientation is generally toward the future rather than the past. Most people are too preoccupied with planning how to achieve future goals to stop and analyse the causes of their past behavior. This future orientation is crucial for man's continual adjustments to his environment, since the past cannot be changed, but the future can be. Nevertheless, in more reflective and contemplative moments people do develop hypotheses about why they did one thing or another. At such times they dwell on the causes of their own actions or the actions of other people. The very fact that each of us spends much time and effort in influencing the behavior of other people implies a belief that at least some human behavior is determined and that one can act as a cause of another's behavior.

The individual generally feels free when he can perceive no external constraints on his behavior (Bem, 1967a). Political and economic freedoms are often defined in terms of constraints. If a person wants to see a pornographic movie and the standards of obscenity in the community will not permit its showing, he is not free to see that particular movie. Nor would he be free to see the movie if he did not have the price of admission. But if the movie is at the theater and he has sufficient funds, he feels free to go to see it or to forego the opportunity.

There are also internal psychological constraints on the individual's behavior. Perhaps he does not go to the movie because he would feel embarrassed if anyone saw him there or because his own sense of morality inhibits such behavior. These internal constraints are themselves assumed by psychologists to be caused and in turn are viewed as causes of the subsequent behavior of the individual. The person tends to perceive behavior stemming from such internal causes as a sign of his freedom. Thus, a belief in freedom is not incompatible with a belief in determinism, and the phenomenological experience of freedom is not a strong argument against the principle of determinism.

B. Prediction and Determinism

Many people find determinism repugnant because of the implication that when psychologists have gained sufficient knowledge, all of a person's behavior, thoughts, and feelings can be predicted and controlled—perhaps by a malevolent dictator. This kind of reaction is captured in such cautionary anti-utopian tales as Huxley's *Brave New World* and Orwell's *1984*. Think how drab the world would be if everything we might do in the future could be predicted ahead of time. Our lives would be reduced to acting out predetermined roles, and our conversations would be no more spontaneous than voices recorded on a tape. The world would be reduced to a stale routine in which surprise, novelty, and spontaneity would be banished and individual feelings of uniqueness, originality, and creativity would no longer exist. But even if this implication of determinism were accurate, which it is not, we should remember that the world does not conform to our likes and dislikes. Simply because we do not like to believe something does not mean it is not true.

Determinism and predictability are not synonymous. The principle of determinism can be maintained even if human behavior cannot be predicted. Consider such creative products as a poem, a painting, an invention, or a sculpture. The specific creation is inherently unpredictable. The psychologist may be able to predict who will be creative and may understand some of the causes of creativity, but he is not likely ever to predict the specific product of the creative process (Barrett, 1958). We may be able to predict the continuation of work by a sculptor because of our knowledge of the environmental and intrapersonal factors that cause his behavior. What is not predictable is the precise form or size of his next work. The artist himself may have only a very hazy notion of what he wants to do and shapes his work as he goes along; it emerges from the creative act.

Modern man lives in a largely man-made environment, which is a product of the creative acts of many people—architects, carpenters, artists, inventors, scientists, legislators, etc. No society is completely static, and modern industrialized societies have experienced rapid and accelerating changes. The difficulty of predicting the creative products of man's activities is illustrated by the attempt of a distinguished group of American scientists, who met in 1937 to predict the scientific breakthroughs they expected in the ensuing decade (Millis & Real, 1963). They failed to foresee the development of radar just four years later, nor did they anticipate the development of antibiotics, the jet airplane, the atomic bomb, or the rocket. There is little doubt that these creative products served to change the lives of men. Some illustrations of the unpredictable effects of technological changes on the social conditions of life are provided in Box 1.1.

Since we cannot predict the exact form of future creative acts, we cannot know what tomorrow's environment will be. If man's behavior is partly determined by the environment he lives in, then we will not be able to predict what he will do in the future. It may be concluded that we will never be able fully to predict man's behavior.

The principle of determinism is the assumption that all events have causes, not that all events can be predicted. The historian examines the past for explanations of present events. Similarly, the scientist can also look for the causes from his knowledge of effects that have already occurred. For example, Coleridge woke up one morning and wrote the poem, *Kubla Khan,* after "experiencing" it in a dream. No one could

have predicted he would write that exact poem, not even Coleridge. Yet investigation has revealed that he had been studying explorers and mariners intensely prior to his dream. Thus unpredictability does not imply that an event has no causes, and a belief in determinism does not imply a disbelief in the spontaneity, creativity, or novelty of life.

C.   Free Will and Determinism

A hypothesis contradictory to determinism is founded on a belief in free will. The opposite of determinism is *indeterminism* or the belief that all events are random and chaotic and have no causes. What is meant by free will is not always clear, but it apparently is not the same as indeterminism. The scientist's work would be meaningless in an indeterminant universe. A social scientist who does not take a deterministic view regarding human behavior would be setting out on a hopeless voyage for he could hope to learn nothing at all if behavior is random and unlawful.

One definition of free will is that the individual can make choices regardless of the constraints of the external environment. In other words, he can always do as he wishes at any particular moment in time. This concept of free will is completely compatible with a determinist position. The individual's decision-making can be viewed by the determinist as stemming from internal causes, such as values, attitudes, and perceptions. Furthermore, these internal factors may themselves have been determined by the prior learning and experiences of the individual. The belief that many human decisions are self-determined does not contravene the principle of determinism.

A second definition of free will denies that internal determinants of behavior are themselves caused. The assertion is that the values or desires of people are spontaneously formed, meaning that they are uncaused. In this form, the free will

Box 1.1 TECHNOLOGY AND LIFE

The inventiveness of man has produced machines and social organizations that have changed the very conditions of life. These technological products become part of the man-made environment which shapes the attitudes and behavior of men. Of course the attitudes, ideologies and social organizations of men also help determine what kind of technologies will be developed. For example, the U.S. government spends considerable sums on developing nuclear energy and weapons of war—the expenditure for defense in 1976 by the United States amounted to approximately $15 million per hour—this presumably reflects a dominant value of our society.

As the technology of agriculture becomes more sophisticated, fewer and fewer people are engaged in farming. The moldboard plow was invented about 100 A.D. Considerable power was required to pull it, and the peasants pooled their oxen for ploughing. Horses were not widely used because the neck-yoke developed for oxen tended to strangle a horse. It was not until the ninth and tenth centuries that the horse collar, tandem harness, and iron horseshoe were invented (Cottrell, 1955), and these inventions made the horse much more efficient than the ox.

A revolution in agricultural technology has taken place in the past 100 years. The tractor, reaper, cotton gin, and many more machines, together with the application of soil physics and chemistry, hybrid plants and animals, the control of pests, and irrigational engineering have made it possible for a few people to produce the food needed by many. As a consequence, there has been a great shift in population from the farms to giant urban centers and associated suburban communities. These structural changes in society have contributed to changes in the size and nature of the family unit and have produced a need for different forms of government. An agricultural society has much less need than does urban civilization for police forces, firemen, zoning boards, recreation departments, traffic regulations, building inspectors, welfare workers, and so on.

Not only is the scientist unable to predict what inventions are likely to occur in the future, he usually cannot foresee the overall effects they will have on social life. It is doubtful that anyone could have predicted the consequences of the printing press and gunpowder for the growth of nations and the development of democracy. The inability to make these kinds of projections implies that scientists will never be able to predict human behavior very far in advance. The prophesies of books like *Future Shock* (Toffler, 1970) must therefore be treated rather skeptically.

hypothesis is similar to the indeterminist position and does contradict the principle of determinism. A test of its truth is impossible since spontaneous events, by definition, are unpredictable. Also it is impossible to demonstrate that there are *no* causes for any events because every possible cause must be discounted before accepting the indeterminist's position. When faced with two contradictory hypotheses, a choice must be based on which seems most reasonable given the available evidence. Every time the social scientist finds a new cause-effect relationship, he finds support for the principle of determinism and weakens the hypothesis of free will (as spontaneity). Just because we do not know the causes of behavior, we are not justified in asserting there are no causes. If it is impossible to show that there are no causes for behavior, the free will hypothesis cannot be confirmed and the principle of determinism cannot be disconfirmed. We leave it to the reader to decide whether he would rather believe a deterministic principle that can be supported by evidence or a free will hypothesis that can only be weakened by evidence of causal relationships.

D. Moral Responsibility and Determinism.

Objections to the principle of determinism have been raised on the ground that no system of moral responsibility could be devised if all behavior is strictly determined. After all, if a person is pushed and pulled by a combination of biological and environmental forces, he cannot help doing what he does. How can he be praised or blamed for the good things he does or the wrongs he commits when he could not have done otherwise? The individual must have a moral choice or else he cannot be held responsible for his actions. A person who forges a check at the point of a gun cannot be found guilty of violating the law; his action was performed under coercion or duress.

If this notion of moral responsibility is incompatible with the assumption of determinism, it is just as reasonable to seek a redefinition of responsibility as it is to reject the principle of determinism. For example, praise or blame could be assigned to persons according to whether the consequences of their behavior were good or bad. If a person commits murder, he may be blamed not because he freely chose to kill, but because he is viewed as dangerous to society *whatever the causes of his behavior.* Of course, the moral precepts of a society are themselves important determinants of human conduct.

American jurisprudence reflects both a deterministic view and a system of moral responsibility. The basic concern of our legal system is to protect society from persons who violate certain rules of conduct. Penalties are meted out for two purposes: (1) as a deterrent to others who might consider similar activities, and (2) to reduce the probability that the convicted person will engage in a similar act again in the future. But there are certain classes of causes for behavior that are recognized as beyond the control of the individual, for example, accident, coercion, provocation, and insanity. Should a defendant be able to show that his behavior was caused by any of these, his responsibility is diminished in the eyes of the law. Questions about the subjective state of the person when he committed the action are relevant in a criminal trial. Attorneys may legitimately explore what the accused knew, believed, or foresaw; whether he was subject to coercion or provoked into passion; or whether he was prevented by disease or temporary disability from controlling his actions.

The individual's legal responsibility is diminished by these excusing conditions. It is assumed he is unlikely to repeat his illegal actions. For example, if a person were coerced into performing an illegal action it would be presumed that he would be unlikely to repeat the behavior when the coercion was removed. These judgments are obviously based on a deterministic view of man. It must be concluded, therefore, that a system of moral responsibility not only can be devised to be consistent with the assumption of determinism, but that in fact our system has already done so.

E. Conclusion

One view of determinism is that it implies a materialistic basis (either biological or environmental) for all human behavior, denies the individual's feelings of freedom, has as its undesirable goal the possibility of controlling human behavior, contradicts a belief in free will, and promotes moral anarchy because the individual cannot be held responsible for his conduct. These notions of determinism are categorically rejected by contemporary social scientists. The perception of freedom by individuals is not denied, rather it is studied to ascertain its causes and consequences. Behavior is seen as having both social and material causes. Social science has the goal of understanding events; the prediction and control of human behavior are only important for testing hypotheses, not for pursuing political ideals or policies. The contemporary view of determinism does not reject free will (in the self-determination sense) nor is it incompatible with systems of moral responsibility. Modern determinism is consistent with ideas of freedom and morality, makes no commitment with respect to materialism, and has no manipulative goals.

Determinism is considered an *assumption* because it is not a principle that can be tested like other scientific hypotheses. Consider the dilemma of trying to prove the principle of determinism. If everything we think and believe is determined, then anything we say is caused. Hence, what we believe to be true is beyond our control. How can a person assert that what he says is really true under such conditions, unless he claims he is an exception to the universal principle? Either he is determined to say the principle of determinism is true or else

he is not determined to say it is true. So the assertion that determinism is true can tell us nothing about the actual epistemological status of the principle. Nevertheless, it is a methodological commitment made by the scientist to look for causes.

The social scientist assumes the principle of determinism because if he did not there would be no reason to search for the causes of human behavior. The determinist takes heart each time a scientific finding shows that the universe, including human behavior, is lawful. But his faith is not shattered when a prediction of a lawful relationship is unsupported by experimental findings. Instead, he assumes his hypothesis was wrong and undertakes investigation of alternative hypotheses.

III. ASSUMPTIONS REGARDING THE NATURE OF MAN

Man has been reflecting about his own nature for many millenia. Although the questions asked are extraordinarily complex, there has been a distinct tendency to provide simple answers. A central trait or characteristic is treated as if it were the basic and fundamental aspect of man. Man has been viewed as an animal, as a machine-like processor of inputs and outputs, as tormented by inner unconscious urges that must be controlled for the good of society, as a pursuer of pleasure, and as a unique creature capable of developing a symbolic world and inhabiting it. In describing these complexities of man Gottschalk (1969) noted that "as a thing, he has a physics and a chemistry. As an animal he has an ancestry, a physiology, and a psychology. As a human being, he has institutions, situations, traditions, and aspirations, and is subject to both inward and outward psychological urges and pressures" (p. 240).

Social scientists often fall victim to the temptation of developing simplified models of man. The resulting narrow perspective may actually be a necessary step to posing questions that can be answered by scientific means. Instead of starting out with an inquiry into the nature of the universe and working toward more simple questions, scientists usually begin with manageable problems and develop more elaborate schemes and theories from the answers they receive from the earlier investigations. While narrowing the focus of inquiry may be an expedient step in the pursuit of knowledge, we must be careful to remember that each perspective has its merits and that none can be proven to be better than another.

It will be helpful in presenting our orientation to contemporary social psychology to examine some of the central assumptions that have been made regarding the nature of man. Each assumption is in part the product of the intellectual spirit of a particular time in history (often called a "Zeitgeist"). An exciting intellectual current would sweep over contemporary thought causing a remolding of the prevailing image of man. Thus a hedonistic view of man originated in the Golden Age of Greece. Darwin's theory of biological evolution made the treatment of man as an animal both permissible and popular. Freud created an integrative view of man in psychoanalytic theory, which links man's animal ancestry with his unique attributes. Technological advances led to the adoption of the analogy of man as a machine. Reactions to Freudian and mechanistic views has led to the new popularity of a humanistic perspective that has been prevalent in philosophy and literature for centuries. We will look briefly at each of these speculative images of man's nature and will indicate what is acceptable and what is not to the present-day social psychologist, who is committed to a scientific approach to the acquisition of knowledge.

A. The Hedonistic Nature of Man

The hedonistic principle is that man acts in order to maximize his pleasure and to minimize his pain. Down through the ages three versions of the principle have been formulated. *Hedonism of the present* assumes that all persons act in a manner calculated to obtain the maximum possible immediate gratification here and now. "Eat, drink and be merry, for tomorrow we die," was Shakespeare's way of stating this form of hedonism. Whatever truth may be in the belief that men always follow a hedonism of the present in their conduct, there are so many restrictions imposed by society that hardly anyone would characterize the life of modern adults as always seeking the satisfaction of momentary urges. Even Freud postulated that the impulses of the id were inhibited or rechanneled by the ego and the superego; the pleasure principle is curbed by the reality principle.

Hedonism of the future is the principle that each person acts now to maximize his future pleasure or minimize his future pain. This way of behaving requires anticipation, purpose, expectation, and decision making—processes that are emphasized in Freud's reality principle. People work during the week for a paycheck at the end of the pay period, undergo the inconvenience and suffering of hospitalization and surgery for future health, and deny themselves momentary pleasures to obtain larger or more enduring ones. Hedonism of the future is an important characteristic of contemporary social learning theory, which emphasizes both the acquisition of patterns of behavior through observation of the behavior of others and the development of expectations regarding the future based on the consequences of past experiences (see Chapter 6).

Hedonism of the past explains present behavior in terms of the consequences of past behavior. If a certain response in the past led to pleasurable outcomes or to the avoidance of pain, the response is apt to be repeated again under similar conditions in the future. This is a fundamental tenet of reinforcement theory (Thorndike, 1905) and has had a profound impact on 20th century psychology. Skinner's (1953) theory of operant behavior is an elaborate and consistent explanation of all human behavior in terms of reinforcement histories.

1. Are Men Invariably Hedonistic?

The question raised by those who object to all forms of hedonism is whether man is essentially acquisitive and selfish, seeking only to maximize his own pleasure and minimize his own pain. Do all men agree with Gunn's (1961) conclusion that "there are two ways to be happy: want less or get more" (p. 50). Many Americans believe that the profit motive, which is central to our Western capitalistic economic system, is a basic characteristic of all men. History and crosscultural research fail to support this view, however. Although it is true that the rich were envied in Biblical times, the average person did not enter the struggle for wealth. Heilbroner (1961) reminds us that "In the Middle Ages the Church taught that 'No Christian ought to be a merchant,' and behind that dictum lay the thought that merchants were a disturbing yeast in the leaven of society. In Shakespeare's time the object of life for the ordinary citizen, for everybody, in fact, except the gentility, was not to advance his station in life, but to maintain it. Even to our Pilgrim forefathers the idea that gain might be a tolerable——even a useful—goal in life would have appeared as nothing short of a doctrine of the devil" (p. 12).

From his anthropological study of tribes of the Melanesian New Guinea archipelagos, Malinowski (1922) reported that the objective of the tribes' economic activities was to assist the chief and promote the welfare of the entire community. Work was not performed for personal profit. Based on this evidence, Malinowski argued vigorously against the doctrine of hedonism.

Hedonism, however, need not imply that all men are selfish. A distinction can be made between selfish behavior and action taken by the individual in his own enlightened self interest. A person may engage in philanthropic activities because of the gratitude and love he receives in return or because his own values dictate that he should help others. Whereas a selfish person disregards the interests of others, a person acting in his enlightened self interest may be said to be practicing the Hindu principle of Karma, which states that doing good for others will eventually bring good back to the doer—as you sow, so will you reap. In this way, a person can be both hedonistic and oriented toward helping others. Of course if a person derives pleasure from intangible social rewards or by exercising a personal sense of moral responsibility, he may be said to be acting hedonistically. This way of defining hedonism comes close to asserting that any determinant of behavior can be interpreted as maximizing pleasure or minimizing pain. Whether it is useful to do so in developing scientific understanding of human behavior is a matter of dispute. We will have more to say about this issue in Chapter 10.

2. Hedonism and Values

Aristotle clearly recognized the implications of the hedonistic doctrine for ethics when he said, "it is on account of pleasure that we do bad things, and on account of the pain that we abstain from noble ones" (McKeon, 1947, p. 334). During the 19th century Jeremy Bentham was the major proponent of the ethical doctrine of psychological hedonism. According to him a society should praise as good behavior that which yields the greatest good to the greatest number of people. He argued, for example, that sweat shops ought not to be regulated by government or considered as evil because they made good clothing available cheaply to the populace. Hence, the benefits to the masses outweighed the suffering of a relatively few children (Allport, 1968, pp. 11-12).

How does one measure the suffering of a

few children or the pleasures gained by the many who had new clothing to wear? Bentham's answer was that a calculus of values must be developed. A hedonistic calculus must recognize that pleasures differ with respect to duration, intensity, certainty, proximity, the amount of pain involved, and the number of people who experience them. The amount of pleasure is the important factor to take into account, not the quality of it. Pleasure derived from wealth is neither superior or inferior to pleasure derived from imagination, love, relief, or power.

Bentham did not succeed in perfecting a hedonistic calculus, and contemporary social scientists are still wrestling with the problem of measuring values. One obvious standard of value is money, and a measure of how much something is worth to a person is how much he would be willing to pay to obtain or avoid it. But money is not equally valued by all people. A dollar may be more valuable to a beggar than a millionaire. Also, many things of apparent value, such as sunsets, beaches, enjoyment of art, friendship, and philosophy cannot be given a price tag. Instead of measuring objective value, it is necessary to assess the subjective value—called "utility" by economists—of specific activities and commodities to the particular individual.

One way to measure utility is to have an individual put his preferences in order of their importance to him. He may be given a choice among a bunch of bananas, a Marlon Brando movie, and a game of pinochle and be asked to rank them in terms of how much he values each of them. Once a wide range of a person's preferences are known, his choices from among them may be predicted. Whenever the person must make decisions among alternative actions, it may be assumed he will act to maximize the utility available to him under the circumstances. While the attempt to measure individual utilities has encountered serious difficulties, a hedonism of the future which views man as a rational decision maker who

acts to maximize his utilities is a prominent assumption of current social psychological theories.

B. The Biological View of Man

Darwin's theory of evolution has had a revolutionary impact on the way man views himself. Man turns out to be an animal and not a unique and special creature. He is now conceived as possessing a number of fundamental biological properties in common with other animals. Critical to the evolutionary process is the role of genetic factors. Genes transmit complex behavior patterns from parent to offspring in the form of instincts, and man came to be considered the possessor of some of the same instincts as other animals. The fields of ethology and behavior genetics have been developed to study the various effects of inherited characteristics on the behavior of organisms.

The assumption of biological continuity among species encouraged psychologists to undertake comparative studies. The scientist interested in man can observe other animals in order to explore early or imperfect forms of man's behavior. It may be presumed that the way a rat or chimpanzee learns new behavior is not fundamentally different from the process of learning in man. Though man is obviously more complex than other animals, the differences may be considered more a matter of quantity than quality.

The theory of evolution, perhaps more than any other scientific theory, has penetrated every realm of thought. Philosophers discuss the evolution of ideas, the astronomer ponders the evolution of the stars, the biochemist traces the evolution of inorganic materials, and so on. Of particular interest to the social psychologist is how the emphasis on the biological nature of man has been applied to rationalize social philosophies, such as fascism and colonialism. Although social Darwinism is not very popular today, extrapolations of biological principles to social phenomena are still to be discerned in modern thought.

1. Instincts

An instinct is an unlearned complex behavior pattern specific to an entire species that is triggered by environmental stimuli and amplified or inhibited by internal biochemical factors within the organism. A baby is born with many simple reflexes, including sneezing, coughing, sucking, and regurgitating. An instinct is differentiated from a reflex by the amount of time it takes to perform the response, its complexity, and its goal orientation. A reflex is completed in a very short time interval, while an instinct is a complex pattern of responses that unfolds over time. Exposing the eye to an air puff will cause a person to blink and the entire stimulus-response sequence occurs within a split second. It takes a good deal of time for a beaver to build a dam or for a bird to fly south for the winter. A reflex is a single all or none response, while an instinct consists of a sequential pattern of responses. The temporal dimension is ordinarily sufficient for discriminating between reflexes and instincts.

By definition, instinctive behavior is automatically elicited by environmental stimuli. A male stickleback fish—which has a large red stomach—will defend his breeding territory by attacking any invading object that also appears to have a large red stomach, including such objects as a cardboard silhouette that in all other respects does not look in the least like a fish (Tinbergen, 1953). However, not all automatic behavior is instinctive. When a person first learns to drive an automobile, he has difficulty executing the proper sequence of responses, but as he gains experience, driving becomes semi-automatic. Driving habits are learned; an instinct is an unlearned behavior pattern.

This is the crucial identifying characteristic of an instinct: it is innate, not learned. The sexual behavior of the rat appears to be instinctive. It is a complex behavior pattern and is automatically performed when the male is presented with a female in estrus. Furthermore, male rat pups who are isolated from other rats at birth, and therefore have no opportunity to learn sexual behavior from other rats, perform copulatory responses just as adequately as do more experienced Don Juan rats. The pattern of sexual behavior is species specific (i.e., all male rats manifest the response) and is affected by internal biochemical factors (hormones).

In the first social psychology textbook written by a psychologist, McDougall (1908) tried to explain all social behavior in terms of instincts, either singly or in combination. If men fight one another and engage in destructive warfare, it is because they have an instinct of pugnacity. The love and care given by mothers to their offspring is attributable to a maternal instinct. Religious behavior is a complex blend of the instincts of curiosity, fear, and self-abasement, as well as a reflection of the instinct to love one's parents. McDougall's procedure was first to observe a social behavior and then invent an instinct or blend of instincts to fit the case. His bag of instincts was always sufficiently full to explain any behavior in this way. If a unique bit of behavior was observed, a new instinct could always be invented to explain it.

McDougall's approach to understanding social behavior soon came under strong attack. His reasoning was exposed as circular in nature. For example, if it is observed that a child imitates his father, the behavior is not explained by stating that the child has "an instinct to imitate." The behavior that needs explanation is renamed an instinct, but the causes of the behavior have not thereby been uncovered. The misconception that one has explained something by giving it a name is referred to as the *nominalistic error*. This type of thinking has the unfortunate effect of causing the scientist to look no further for the causes of what he is investigating, since he believes he has solved the problem.

The application of the biological view of man to the nature of social behavior was further undermined by the work of anthropologists and other social scientists. Very few human behavior patterns could be discovered that were species-specific. Cultural anthropologists have found pacifist peoples who neither fight nor understand what is meant by war (Montagu, 1968). Sexual behavior is quite variable across cultures. For example, studies of many different cultures revealed that of seven coital positions, no one is preferred by a clear majority of societies (Ford & Beach, 1952). What is considered "normal" in one society is not so considered in another. Unlike the sexual behavior of the rat, learning is crucial for human sexual conduct.

Social scientists have discarded the belief that the social behavior of men can be explained by reference to biological urges or instincts, although maturation of abilities may be considered as based on genetic coding (see Chapter 6). Many scientists still maintain the belief that man is a basically aggressive animal, as we shall see in Chapter 12. Typically, these biological interpretations of man's behavior are tied to important ideologies. The ideology that a capitalistic economic system is superior to any alternative is often rationalized in terms of man's acquisitive instinct. Recent attempts to extrapolate to human behavior the results obtained from studies of subhuman behaviors (such as the brilliant work of modern ethologists like the Nobel prize winners, Lorenz [1966] and Tinbergen [1953]), may titilate many readers, but they advance our understanding little, if at all.

2. Behavior Genetics

Behavior changes can be produced within members of a species by selective breeding. In a classic study of behavior genetics Tryon (1940) bred rats based on their ability to learn a maze. "Bright" males were bred with "bright" females and "dull" males were bred with "dull" females. After 12 generations all the "bright" offspring learned better than all the "dull" offspring. In another study McClearn and Rodgers (1961) bred mice according to their preference for alcohol or for water, producing generations of tipplers and teetotalers. These behavior changes have different survival values in the evolutionary process. Brightness should enhance survival, while a fondness for alcohol should reduce the chances of survival.

Behavior genetics has also been applied to the study of social behavior among subhuman animals. Beagles have been bred to get along with one another in packs, while fox terriers, young and old, male and female, are bred to be fighters (Scott & Fuller, 1965). Guinea pigs have been bred to be differentially responsive to sexual stimulation, various strains of hens differ in broodiness, and rabbits differ in maternal care practices (Scott, 1969). To illustrate genetically determined behavior which is truly defeating of survival prospects, male mutants have been produced in fruit flies who are unable to disengage after the usual 20 minute copulation period; a second type of male mutant pursues males as persistently as he does females; and a third practices coitus interruptus—disengaging from copulation in about half the usual time and without ever producing offspring (Benzer, 1973).

The role of genetic factors in human social behavior is probably minor. Human behavior is less stereotyped and is much more modifiable by experience than the behavior of subhuman organisms. It is difficult to separate the effects of early experience from those of innate dispositions on the later behavior of mature humans. The role of genetics in human social behavior remains unclear because there is no superman experimenter who can live for 12 generations to carry out a breeding study and examine changes in behavior as a function of genetic factors. Studies of identical twins can provide important information about the role of inheritability of certain traits and abilities, but have yet to make a strong contribution to social psychology.

Man's behavior is limited by the biological capacities he inherits. But the fact that a man has the anatomical apparatus to speak or the theory that man is born with a template guiding the way he learns language (Chomsky, 1968) gives us no explanation for what he says. Social psychologists have been persuaded by over 75 years of accumulated evidence that the role of experience and learning is much more important for understanding the variability of human social behavior than are biological determinants.

3. Comparative Social Psychology

Darwinism implied that every human process or behavior has its origins lower in the phylogenetic scale. The operation of sensory mechanisms or of learning processes could therefore be studied in lower organisms. There is little doubt that a comparative approach to psychology has been a rich source of knowledge about man. In a similar way medical research with lower organisms has disclosed much about human disease. Comparative social psychologists have also attempted to find analogues of human behavior among lower organisms. For example, recent research on animals has been done to study altruism (Krebs, 1970), crowding (Calhoun, 1962), and aggression, sexual behavior, and social organization (Scott, 1969).

Comparative work is most relevant to understanding processes that have a particular anatomical locus and serve specific biological functions. Social behavior has neither. Melville's comment (in *Moby Dick*) that "hell is an idea first born on an undigested apple-dumpling; and since then perpetuated through the hereditary dyspepsias nurtured by Ramadans" is amusing, but is not supported by scientific evidence. It is difficult to conceive of a biological basis for a person's views of justice, freedom, or religion. For these kinds of social phenomena we know of no equivalents among subhumans and hence they can be studied only in human beings.

Comparative social psychology started with the hope that the doors to understanding the nature of man would be unlocked by studying lower forms. Today, interest in the social behavior of animals is a topic that stands or falls as an independent area of study and not for what it can tell us about humans. Despite contemporary fascination with "the naked ape" and "the human zoo," the differences between man and his nearest relatives are much greater than the similarities (Huxley, 1953). We will have more to say about these differences when discussing the humanistic view of the nature of man.

4. Social Darwinism

Central to the biological theory of evolution is the notion of natural selection. Those organisms which are best equipped to survive in a particular environment are those that survive and reproduce, and those that are less able to adapt are not perpetuated. Natural selection refers to variations among individuals that lead to the origin and survival of a species and does not provide any basis for evaluating the "fitness" of individuals. Nevertheless, catch-phrases such as "struggle for existence" and "survival of the fittest" have been applied by some social philosophers to competitive behavior within the human species. In order to make the analogy of biological evolution applicable to ideological concerns the time dimension must be contracted to fit the day-by-day behavior of men instead of a process usually involving changes in countless individuals over several millenia.

Taken out of its biological context the law of natural selection has been applied in justifying the success of robber barons, colonialism, class and racial struggles, and the national suppression of minorities. The very fact of survival is interpreted as indicating the possession of superior traits. The social philosophy of fascism was constructed on the foundation of this distortion of the biological model of man. In contemporary America, the success of caucasians in accumulating wealth and power has sometimes been interpreted as indicating their biological superiority as compared to other races. Although social Darwinism has been discredited by social science, traces can still be found in the thinking of nonscientists as they speculate about the "natural" functioning of economic, international, and human affairs.

5. Conclusion

The biological view reminds the social scientist that men differ from one another and that man differs from other species. Two men may differ in innate intelligence and a monkey cannot speak because he does not have the proper kind of larynx. Knowledge of these biological factors can be useful, but they are not sufficient for understanding the complex social behavior of men. Human beings are not dominated by instincts, and while some of the variability of human behavior may be understood through behavior genetics, there are definite limits to this approach. Comparative social psychology tells us more about the animals studied than about man. Popular versions of social Darwinism are based on distortions of the biological theory of evolution and serve ideological or entertainment purposes, but they do not provide valid scientific explanation of human behavior. As we shall see in Chapter 12, the remnants of Darwinism are most strong in discussions of human aggression.

C. Psychoanalytic Theory

Freud's psychoanalytic theory represented a synthesis of many strands of knowledge applied to the development of a comprehensive picture of personality. Although men were considered able to make rational decisions, much human behavior was attributed to unconscious impulses stemming from primitive animalistic instincts. The individual was seen as developing through a series of stages of childhood during which a number of inevitable intrapsychic conflicts are faced and resolved. Freud borrowed ideas from the plays of Sophocles, the Greek philosophers, the Jewish mystics and the physical science of his day in formulating his processes of development, including the oedipus and electra complexes, the superego, and the building up and release of psychic energy. Most contemporary social scientists view psychoanalytic theory as a myth rather than a scientific theory. Nevertheless, it has left a legacy of fertile ideas that have had a permanent impact on psychology.

1. Instincts, Hedonism, and Repression

The source of all human energy, according to Freud, is the *id*. The primitive urges of the id consist of instincts inherited in the evolutionary processes from lower animals. There are two basic groups of instincts: life instincts *(libido)* and destructive instincts *(thanatos)*. The sexual impulses associated with the libido are inhibited and rechanneled into constructive activities by social constraints as the individual evolves through oral, anal, and phallic stages of development. Freud added the notion of thanatos to his theory after witnessing the senseless slaughter of World War I. He found himself in essential agreement with Hobbes, who considered men to be savages who are kept in check by society; without society, life would be "solitary, poor, nasty, brutish, and short." Thanatos reflected Freud's horror of war and helped him to account for the otherwise unexplainable tendency of men to destroy one another.

The impulses arising from the id, both sexual and destructive, have to be repressed, and the development of internal inhibitions within the individual is attributed to the growth of the *superego*. Men are not able to control their animalistic impulses, particularly since these primitive urges are unconscious. Parents serve as the agents of society and punish children when they engage in "natural" primitive behavior. Through this process children learn conscience, guilt, and pride. Though primitive urges still prompt the socialized individual's behavior, he seeks socially accepted ways to satisfy his needs; dancing may satisfy sexual urges and playing football may gratify destructive urges. This change in the control of behavior from id to ego represents a shift from a hedonism of the present to a hedonism of the future and a change from acting on unconscious impulses to rational decision making.

The psychoanalytic model of man is strictly deterministic. Freud believed that every experience and behavior of man was caused by natural events. Every human activity was subjected to analysis, including dreams, slips of the tongue, and humor. Man was considered to be basically amoral, but controllable by appropriate social constraints. Some people have wrongly interpreted the puritanical Freud as being an advocate of "free sex" and asserting that frustrations and inhibitions are detrimental to mental health. Psychoanalysis assumes that when the unconscious becomes conscious, when the irrational becomes rational, when a man is not motivated by guilt or pride but acts according to the reality principle (i.e., hedonism of the future), then he will be fulfilled. As Ogden Nash expressed it, "There is only one way to achieve happiness on this terrestrial ball, and that is to have either a clear conscience or none at all."

2.   The Legacy of Psychoanalysis

In his biography of Bernard Shaw, Lord Chesterton commented that "psychoanalysis cannot be a science; it is too popular." Whatever its merits as a scientific theory, psychoanalysis as a myth has penetrated every aspect of popular culture. Freudian concepts and symbols can be found in the great literature of the West, including the novels of André Gide, Alberto Moravia, and William Faulkner. American theater during the 1950s was dominated by Tennessee Williams and served as a make-believe, public clinic to observe the psyches of various characters. Abstract expressionism in art was avowedly an attempt to explore the inner self and to make the unconscious conscious. Paul Tillich (1952) constructed a theology on the cornerstone of psychoanalysis.

Freud was an authentic genius, but may be considered a mythmaker, moralist and philosopher rather than a scientist. As Hall and Lindzey (1970) conclude in their well known text on personality: "Freud, of course, was not a social scientist, and when he turned his attention to social phenomena, it seems to have been with the intention of indicting society for its deleterious influences on personality. The view of society that one gets from neurotic patients is not likely to be a favorable one, and it was probably difficult for Freud, as a practicing psychiatrist, to maintain a dispassionate attitude toward society (p. 273)." What Freud objected to in society were those influences that created strong superegos in individuals and interfered with the development of the ego.

The psychoanalytic model of man has had a significant impact on the development of social psychology. Freud's view of intrapsychic conflict, posing man as torn between inner urges demanding immediate gratification and social pressures internalized in the form of conscience, duty, and respectability, has been largely rejected as it was originally stated. But it has been reformulated by contemporary social psychologists as the study of norms, obligations, and self-control. The psychoanalytic concept of the ego has led to research on the individual's self-concept and its effect on his behavior. The idea of developmental stages has its counterpart in contemporary theories of intellectual and moral development. These legacies of Freudian thought are discussed in Chapter 6.

D. Man as a Machine

Machine analogies of man have changed as the sophistication of technology has developed. The earliest machines were made of cogs, wheels, levers, and other moving parts. After electricity had been harnessed and the telegraph and telephone had been invented, more complex sets of operations could be performed by machines. Computer technology has brought about a machine that can plan, calculate and make decisions. In the wake of these technological developments have come the mechanistic, learning machine, and cybernetic views of man.

1.   The Mechanistic View of Man

The achievements of Johann Kepler and Tycho Brahé in astronomy and Galileo and Newton in physics seemed to reveal a machine-like universe which operated according to principles that could be expressed in the form of mathematical equations. In the 19th century, the astronomer Sir George Biddell Airy defined the entire universe as "a perpetual-motion calculating machine whose gears and ratchets are an infinite system of self-solving differential equations." The great mathematician La-Place went one step further. He inferred that just as the existence of a watch implies a watchmaker, so does the existence of the more complex machine-universe imply a maker. LaPlace envisioned God as a master mathematician who devised the formulae governing the universe.

The mechanistic view of the universe was expressed in the ideas of social philosophers. Descartes devised a mechanistic view of man that was probably stimulated from watching moving statues in the French royal gardens which were constructed so that certain members (an arm, the head, etc.) could be put into operation. These movements were effected by regulating water pressure in pipes built into the statues. Hidden valves controlled the water pressure.

Descartes considered the nerves of the human body as hollow tubes through which vital spirits flowed to cause movements of the limbs. The vital spirits were directed by the mind—by ideas. While the body was material, the mind was immaterial. A perennial problem for philosophers has been to explain how the immaterial mind can influence the material body—the mind-body problem. Descartes settled the issue for himself by postulating that the two substances interact with each other in the pineal gland, a small structure deep in the brain. A number of other answers have been given to the mind-body problem (cf. Boring, 1950), including that there is no problem. The materialist argues that all is matter and the idealist argues that all is mind.

Modern materialists have taken the position that there is nothing to the mind other than the brain, which operates according to physical laws. Experiments have confirmed that the destruction of certain portions of the brain is accompanied by losses in sensory, perceptual, cognitive, and motor abilities. It can be reliably demonstrated that the skeletal muscles of the body can be activated by electrically stimulating the appropriate site on the brain. Specific memories can be elicited in the same way. The extreme position of the mechanist-materialist implies reductionism. It entails the belief that all human behavior can be understood given sufficient knowledge of anatomy, the nervous system, biochemistry, and biophysics.

2.   Man as a Learning Machine

The view of man implicit in modern behavioristic theory is basically that of a learning machine. To understand man's behavior it is necessary to uncover the laws of learning. Pavlov and Thorndike, a Russian physiologist and an American psychologist, developed the basic principles of two kinds of learning: classical and instrumental conditioning.

Ivan Pavlov was a mechanistic-materialist. For him the mind was nothing more than the physical processes of the brain. As part of his Nobel Prize-winning (1904) work on the physiology of digestion, Pavlov launched into the study of the classical conditioned reflex. His first demonstration focused on the salivary reflex. Dogs salivate when meat powder is presented to them. If a bell is sounded just an instant before the meat is presented, and this occurs a number of times, the salivary reflex will be conditioned to the bell. The result is salivation by the dog when the bell sounds, even when no meat is forthcoming. Learning is a matter of transferring a reflex that is associated with one stimulus (salivating in response to meat powder) to a new stimulus (salivating in response to the bell).

After discovering laws governing the phenomena of inhibition, extinction, stimulus generalization, discrimination, and higher-order conditioning, Pavlov came to believe that animals, including man, were basically physical systems which operate according to a law of stimulus substitution. Reference to such "mystical" concepts as ideas, consciousness, or expectations was considered unnecessary to understand learning and performance. Man was a learning machine and nothing more.

Edward Thorndike developed a different conception of man by invoking the analogy of a telephone switchboard. When sense receptors are activated by stimuli, a chain of neural impulses is transmitted along the affector neurons to the main switchboard (the brain), where connections are made to outgoing effector neurons, which in turn cause skeletal muscle movements. Although some of the connections between affectors and effectors may be innate, most of them are acquired by a process of reinforcement and punishment which stamps them in or stamps them out of the organism in the course of its trial and error behavior.

When presented with a stimulus the organism may randomly try out a number of responses. If a response is reinforced (i.e., produces pleasant consequences), the central connection between the affector and effector in the brain is strengthened, increasing the probability that the next time the same stimulus occurs, the same response will occur. If a response does not lead to reinforcement, then the connection is weakened. Thus connections and the responses they mediate follow a law of natural selection as well as the hedonistic principle of utility. Learning is a matter of acquiring the correct response out of all the responses that could be performed with respect to any particular stimulus. While for Pavlov classical conditioning involved the performance of the same or similar responses to different stimuli, Thorndike conceived of instrumental conditioning as the selection of one of a number of alternative responses performed in the presence of the same stimulus. Modern theories of learning generally include both processes and have abandoned the switchboard analogy. In contemporary social learning theories man is generally presumed to be an information processing decision–maker who plans much of his behavior according to his expectations for the future. Many social psychologists apply the principles of learning to understanding complex social phenomena, including imitation, moral development, friendship and aggression (see Chapters 6, 11, and 12).

3. The Cybernetic Conception of Man

The advent of the computer proved that a machine could perform many operations previously denied to man by behavioristic theories, such as comparing, rejecting, evaluating, and decision-making. Computers are based on cybernetic systems of information processing. Cybernetic machines can follow a plan for the future and hence can be said to be purposive. The belief that future events can affect the present is referred to as *teleology* and has been rejected as absurd by mechanistic materialists. However, "once a teleological mechanism could be built out of metal and glass, psychologists recognized that it was scientifically respectable to admit they had known it all along" (Miller, Galanter, & Pribram, 1960, p. 43).

A cybernetic model conceives of man as an information processing, purposive machine. Computers are capable of sorting, choosing, chess-playing, and problem-solving. The nervous system, like the elements of the computer, is thought to consist of a sequence of binary (off-on) switching devices. Memory is the equivalent of storage capacity and the analogue to the computer tape is the biochemical trace left in the brain. Both the computer and man have sensory capacity to take in information from the environment and both have programs or plans for how to utilize the information taken in or stored. Not only do both make decisions, but each can change its program or plan as a function of past decisions (i.e., learn and change goals). Changes in and regulation of decision-making requires feedback loops so that new information can be related to old information. A man, for example, keeps a record of the tensions and positions of his muscles as he walks along, and if he trips, this new information is used to quickly adapt to the change in equilibrium and prevent him from falling. A thermostat regulating the heat from a furnace operates in much the same way.

Science fiction writers, philosophers, and psychologists have speculated that in principle there are no fundamental differences between cybernetic machines and humans. An artificial being, an *android*, might be constructed in the future. How would it be different from a human? Suppose it could program itself, reproduce itself, and report

feelings of pain, love, and fear under the appropriate conditions? If it is argued that machines cannot program themselves, the answer is that humans don't either—they have a genetic program that has arisen during the process of evolution. This materialist position is a matter of faith and has by no means been established by scientific evidence.

E. The Humanist's View of Man

There are those who find the view of man as a machine repugnant. The behavioristic conception of love as the connection between a pleasant sensation and a stimulus object is hardly the glorious phenomenon that moves the sensitive poet. However, if there is more to man than has been dreamt by all the world's philosophers, it is necessary for scientific purposes to state what that something more is. This is what the humanists have attempted to do.

The humanistic conception of man is best understood as a revolt against a now antiquated scientific view of man. The humanistic psychologist can accept that the hedonistic, biological, psychoanalytic, and mechanistic views each capture some aspect of the human experience, but man is considered to be more than the sum of these parts. Man is an active and spontaneous organism and not merely passive and reactive. The consciousness, the inner experience, of man is his primary reality. He reacts to a subjective reality and not to a physically described, objective world. The principal experiences in human life are those of freedom and choice, growth and self-actualization, and love. The humanistic psychologist is inclined to assume the basic goodness of man, who is motivated to develop his unique capacities and to be creative and altruistic. If men do not actualize these innate capacities, it is because of the interference of environmental factors.

Man is basically a symbol user. He develops concepts of himself and of his world as placed within the stream of time. An orientation to the future provides the basis for planning his activities. No other organism is remotely similar to man in these respects. Comparative psychology can reveal very little of significance about man. Of course rats and men acquire habits in much the same way, but who ever heard of a religious rat, a juvenile delinquent rat, a nationalistic or warlike rat, or a rat who lived life for art's sake? The humanist holds that we will never be able to understand man by studying other animals. Instead of ratifying man, we need to rehumanize him. Some humanists believe that the unique human experience is too complex ever to be understood by the methods of science.

1. Symbols

The humanist is certainly not the only one who stresses that man's unique abilities depend on his ability to create symbols. A school of sociological social psychologists called "symbolic interactionists" bases its entire conception of society on man's symbolic constructions, and a major area of study in modern psychology is psycholinguistics. There is unequivocal proof in any museum, concert hall, library, or theater that man has the capacity to symbolize his sensory experience. He can even create synthetic images of things he has never experienced, such as unicorns, angels, ghosts, and flying saucers. Images are malleable. For example, an image of an elephant can be changed from large to small or from pink to green. His imaginative capacity makes man a dreamer, artist, scientist, mythmaker, and nationalist. Man can imagine the existence of ghosts and then be frightened by them. Archeologists can reconstruct the beliefs, values, habits, and intentions of men from inspecting artifacts of a long-dead culture.

Each man constructs his own symbolic way of representing the universe. In order to understand human behavior, it will be necessary for the social psychologist to gain an understanding of each man's unique constructions. The effects on his experience of man's capacity to create symbols is eloquently stated by Cassirer (1944):

"Man has, as it were, discovered a new method of adapting himself to the environment. Between the receptor system and the effector system, which are to be found in all animal species, we find in man a third link which we may describe as the symbolic system. This new acquisition transforms the whole of human life. As compared with the other animals, man lives not merely in a broader reality; he lives, so to speak, in a new dimension of reality . . . Man cannot escape from his own achievement. He cannot but adopt the conditions of his own life. No longer in a merely physical universe, man lives in a symbolic universe. Language, myth, art, and religion are parts of this universe. They are the varied threads which weave the symbolic net, the tangled web of human experience. All human progress in thought and experience refines upon and strengthens this net. No longer can man confront reality immediately; he cannot see it, as it were, face to face. Physical reality seems to recede in proportion as man's symbolic activity advances. Instead of dealing with the things themselves, man is in a sense constantly conversing with himself" (p. 42–43).

2. Future Orientation

Man's ability to anticipate the future and to conceive of it in the present is the basis of modern learning theories and of the cybernetic conception of man, but has received strong emphasis by the humanists. The ability to conceive of the future provides the basis of technological invention. Animals use some simple tools, but only humans seem capable of devising a tool to be applied to remote anticipated problems. There is little evidence that any subhuman animal can plan activities as far as an hour in advance; yet a high school boy may plan to become a physician and act accordingly through ten years of school. Furthermore, a person can meditate about his past behavior, and by so doing, change his conceptions of the past, present and future. Psychoanalysis was founded on the assumption that patients would restructure their views of themselves after exploring their past with the analyst. In a similar way religious conversion can change a person's life.

Man's experience of himself as an entity, together with his impression of his own continuity over time, allows him to compare his own conduct with that of other people and to develop standards of morality and law. A self-concept is probably a necessary factor in the development of a social order, since a recognition of rules of conduct is predicated upon the individual's belief in the continuity and consistency of his own and others' behavior. Only man of all living creatures is aware of his mortality, and his knowledge of impending death has implications for how he lives. Eschatological systems have been created to integrate death into the reality of social existence.

3. The Social Imbeddedness of the Individual

A humanistic viewpoint more than any of the others presented in this chapter implies a social psychological analysis of behavior. According to the humanist, one of the most significant problems facing each person is his existential loneliness. The person must confront his ultimate uniqueness and separateness from all others. The suffering of aloneness may also occur as a result of being separated from a loved one, or may be due to a pathological and unbreakable sense of isolation (Severin, 1973, p. 52).

The materialistic conceptions of man as a machine or an animal lead people to view each other as objects to be manipulated or controlled. The humanist emphasizes love of self and of others. Genuine self-love allows the individual to view others on their own terms. Instead of treating others as objects, the humanist emphasizes a sharing

of experiences, an openness toward others, and mutual support for self-actualization. Man cannot live in aloneness; we are all connected to one another and none can grow independent of others. While there are actually many different humanistic outlooks one is captured by Robert Ingersoll's (1968) short poem:

Justice is the only worship.
Love is the only priest.
Ignorance is the only slavery.
Happiness is the only good.
The time to be happy is now.
The place to be happy is here.
The way to be happy is to make others so.

IV. CHAPTER SUMMARY

Social psychology is the scientific study of the individual human being in a social context. The basic level of analysis focuses on interdependence, interaction, and the social influence process—how the individual affects others and what influence they have on him. Most social psychologists are antireductionist and believe that each science must be understood at its own level of analysis.

Social psychology is distinguished from individual psychology by the fact that the former focuses on the social environment and interaction between persons, while the latter is primarily concerned with processes within the individual that link him to the physical environment. The sociologist attempts to relate social structures to the regular patterns of behavior of groups of people, while the social psychologist is more concerned with the face-to-face interaction of individuals and with the variability of behavior. Social psychology stands between and overlaps with both individual psychology and sociology, but borrows concepts from other social sciences as well.

All of the social sciences assume a principle of determinism. There would be little reason to investigate the causes of human behavior if it could not be assumed that there were discoverable causes. Determinism does not imply that all human behavior is predictable, not does it deny that men make free choices or that they are morally responsible for what they do. A determinist need not be a materialist, but may instead believe that much human behavior is elicited by social or symbolic causes.

Research and thought about the nature of man has developed under the influence of major intellectual or technological developments. According to Hollander (1971), the study of social behavior has progressed through three stages. The oldest stage, dating back to antiquity, is the stage of social philosophy and is characterized by speculation and logic. The second stage, social empiricism, began in the 19th century and emphasized data gathering and description of the social environment. The third stage, social analysis, involves a search for causal relationships and the development of scientific theories.

The hedonistic, biological, and psychoanalytic views of man reflect varying social philosophies. The early work of sociologists and anthropologists consisted of descriptions of presumed relationships between aspects of social structure, such as the relationship between religion and capitalism (Weber, 1958). The machine conception of man is an application of social philosophy to the methods of social analysis. Although humanism represents a partial retreat to the first stage of social philosophy, social psychology is basically a science that operates at the level of social analysis.

Each view of man has had its impact on the formulation of theories and research in social psychology. Traces of each will be found throughout this text. But contemporary social psychologists are apt to believe that each model paints with too broad a stroke. Assertions that man is "basically" anything are too broad and indefinite to put to scientific test. Questions asked about human behavior must be specific, recognizing that man's behavior is contingent on his social situation and his past experience. The only limitations on man's behavior are imposed on him by his biological inheritance and his environmental circumstances.

The conception of man that will emerge in this book is of an information processing, future-oriented, decision-making organism caught up in a web of interactions that produce the opportunity for love and cooperation or for hate and conflict. Man is capable of killing his fellows and he has often been seen to act altruistically, without anticipation of gaining anything for himself. In general, the biological model of man is rejected on the grounds that social behavior is not explainable by (or reducible to) biological factors. Psychoanalytic theory is generally rejected also; though important directions of research were first suggested by Freud; but as a decision maker, man is considered to be more rational than psychoanalytic theory would suggest.

Now that we have provided an orientation to what the social psychologist studies and some of the assumptions he makes, we are ready to examine the methods used. The methods of scientific inquiry used by the social psychologist are logically similar to those employed by the natural sciences. However, as we shall see, there are some persistent problems of performing social psychological research which are unique to the discipline.

SUGGESTED READINGS

Birney, R. C., and Teevan, R. C. (Eds.) *Instinct.* Princeton, N. J.: Van Nostrand, 1961. A collection of classic studies and theoretical statements regarding animal and human instincts.

Brenner, C. *An elementary textbook of psychoanalysis.* New York: Doubleday Anchor, 1955. An exceptionally clear account of Freud's thought for the introductory reader.

Hilgard, E. R. and Bower, G. H. *Theories of learning.* (4th ed.) Englewood Cliffs, N.J.: Prentice-Hall, 1975.

Provides systematic descriptions and evaluations of modern learning theories from Pavlov and Thorndike to modern mathematical and neurophysiological accounts of behavior. For the serious student of psychology.

Hook, S. (Ed.) *Determinism and freedom in the age of modern science.* New York: Collier, 1961. Papers which include arguments by philosophers for and against the assumption of determinism.

Nash, P. *Models of man.* New York: Wiley, 1968. An examination of the many conceptions of man that have been held throughout history, including many not mentioned in this chapter.

Wiener, N. *The human use of human beings: cybernetics and society.* Boston: Houghton-Mifflin, 1950. A classic account of some of the ethical and sociological implications of conceiving of man as a cybernetic system.

CHAPTER **2**

Methods of Social Psychology

CHAPTER PREVIEW

Social psychology is a science. What characterizes any discipline as a science is its approach to knowledge. The word "science" may evoke images of test tubes, microscopes, shiny instruments, and strange and complex machinery. But it is neither the particular instruments used or what is known about a particular subject that identifies a field as a science. The scientific method constitutes a way of thinking about problems. Science consists of a set of logical and methodological steps devised to answer questions and to resolve disputes concerning nature.

Epistemology is the area of philosophy concerned with how man acquires and evaluates knowledge. Social psychology can be said to be a science that studies the epistemologies of different people—how they come to believe as they do, acquire the values they have, and resolve the differences between them. Science is only one way of acquiring knowledge. In order to understand the strengths and weaknesses of the scientific method, it is necessary to examine both the ways in which the nonscientist acquires his knowledge and the intricacies of the logic of scientific inquiry. A major tool of the scientist is the experiment, but a whole set of nonlaboratory techniques are also available to supplement the experiment. In the first three sections of this chapter we will examine informal approaches to knowledge, the logic of scientific inquiry, and nonlaboratory methods of social psychology.

A set of peculiar problems arises for the social psychologist when he conducts his research. The social psychologist observes people and they react in a variety of ways to being observed. People generally know they are participating in an experiment, and this knowledge affects how they respond to the situation. For example, if a person discovers the experimental hypothesis, he can choose to confirm or disconfirm it. For these reasons the social psychology of the experiment has itself been studied. In addition, there are a series of ethical problems associated with conducting experiments with people. The social psychology of the experiment and the ethics of research will constitute the two final topics of this chapter.

I.   INFORMAL APPROACHES TO KNOWLEDGE

The average college student has innumerable beliefs and opinions about other people, institutions, nations, and events, and probably many are false. Of course each person considers all of his beliefs to be true; otherwise, he would correct his beliefs to fit the truth. Yet who would claim to be infallible? Such perfection is reserved for the gods. But once it is accepted that each of us is fallible the question arises: which of our beliefs are true and which false? This immensely complicated question has been the subject of philosophical inquiry for at least 2000 years.

One way to evaluate beliefs is to examine the methods by which they are acquired. The diversity of beliefs both within and among cultures has convinced contemporary social scientists that all knowledge is acquired by the individual during his lifetime. Beliefs are not transmitted genetically. At conception the human infant has no ideas, and what he comes to know about the world is gathered through the course of experience in his physical and social environment.

Charles Sanders Peirce (1877) provided an analysis of four basic methods by which the average person gathers information in formulating and assessing his beliefs: authority, direct experience (a priori methods), tenacity, and science. The values learned by the individual have an effect on how he assesses the beliefs acquired from each of these sources of knowledge. We will briefly examine each of the nonscientific sources of knowledge as a prelude to a longer and more detailed discussion of the scientific method.

A. Method of Authority

Probably the most common way of developing beliefs is by accepting them secondhand from authorities. It is certainly an easy way. An authority is someone who has some basis in age, experience, popularity, prestige, or power to claim that what he says should be heeded. A parent, religious functionary, educator, politician, scientist, physician, or journalist may be considered an authoritative source of information. Peirce differentiates between two general types of authority: dogmatic and expert. A *dogmatic authority* presents no empirical evidence for his assertions, nor is there any way in which they could be checked. An *expert authority* relies on factual evidence which can be independently checked by anyone who has sufficient means or skill to do so.

Dogmatic authorities generally promote beliefs leading to the adoption of values. Religious myths about the creation of man, the existence of gods, and life after death cannot be independently checked by any known methods and hence, whatever values they contribute to the way men live, they must be treated as dogmatic assertions.

Whether an individual believes dogmatic assertions depends more upon his trust in the authority than his ability to evaluate independently the information provided. Disagreements among dogmatic authorities are usually settled by means of superior persuasive skills, bribery, censorship of opposing opinions, and coercion. The nagging question persists, however, as to where the dogmatic authority got his information and how reliable it is. Clever rhetoric does not establish the truth of an assertion, nor does might make right.

Expert authorities may possess great prestige and may use their persuasive skills or power to get their views adopted. However, the information they present can be independently checked. If an automobile mechanic provides a diagnosis of why a car is malfunctioning, the owner can learn the appropriate skills to verify the information. However, most of us depend on expert authorities without checking them because we do not have enough time or sufficient interest to do so. We may gather information from other people about their opinion of the mechanic or we may occasionally take our car to another garage to get a second expert judgment before having it repaired.

Even the most trustworthy, prestigious, and credible expert must be checked—at least occasionally. His information may be out of date, or his personal and political biases may interfere with the objectivity of his reports. Consider what would happen if a municipal government decided to cut expenses by replacing salaries for judges with a commission system; each judge would be able to keep 15% of each fine that he levies against defendants. Who would want to be tried by a judge who has a vested interest in the guilt of each defendant? In a similar manner each person's judgments are subject to the distorting effects of his own values and interests. This is why it is considered unwise for an attorney to try his own case; he lacks the necessary objectivity to make the best case for his point of view.

We place great reliance upon expert authorities. Although we seldom check the information they provide, it is very important that we can do so. Sooner or later someone somewhere may challenge the reports, methods, or evidence of the expert. In this way the information he provides must stand the test of independent evidence gathered over time by other observers.

B. A Priori Methods

Beliefs acquired through direct experience seem to be obviously true. Such knowledge does not depend on the word or experience of others. The methods of direct experience are called *a priori* (loosely translated as "in the first place") because the beliefs acquired seem to need no further substantiation—they are considered self-evidently true. *A priori* methods include revelation, miracle, commonsense, and intuition.

1. Revelation

A revelation is defined as a direct communication from some supernatural source to an individual. When the recipient of a revelation informs a second person of the information, the latter is not experiencing a revelation. The report of the revelation is a statement from a dogmatic authority, because it is not possible to find out if he really did receive the communication.

The person who believes he has experienced a revelation cannot be certain that he has. Psychological research has shown that hallucinations can be produced in a variety of ways. Persons who are classified as mentally ill occasionally claim to be in contact with gods, demons, and a variety of spiritual and extraterrestrial beings. Hallucinations can be stimulated by drugs, fasting, continual pain, and stimulus deprivation. It is not possible to independently establish that a reported revelation was not a hallucination. One man's prophet is always another man's kook.

Prophets and seers often claim to make their predictions on the basis of special revelatory information available only to them. Their prophesies are usually annoyingly vague. Names, dates, times, and events are seldom detailed, or, if they are, the predictions are based on fairly evident grounds and are no more mysterious than guesses made by any intelligent observer. No special revelation would have been necessary to predict in January, 1972, that Richard Nixon would be re-elected President in November that year. A prophet can improve his batting average by including among his predictions some which could be made by anyone else. When Jeanne Dixon makes her yearly prophesies no one keeps account of how accurate she is, but if one or two of her predictions are interpreted as correct, her devotees are convinced of her occult powers. When a prophesy is so specific that even a sceptic would be satisfied that events could confirm or disconfirm it, the sceptic is usually in a position to make a prediction that is just as accurate. In any case, revelation is an unreliable basis for the development and assessment of beliefs.

2. Miracles

Miracles are defined as contradictions of natural laws and are attributed to supernatural causes. The witness to a miracle may conclude that a sign is being given to him by a supernatural being. Of course, it is up to the witness to interpret the meaning of the sign and to verify the event as a miracle. When a person witnesses what he interprets as a miracle, it must be asked whether he was fooled or tricked, and whether his initial expectations affected the way he perceived the event. Men not only can be tricked, they delight in being fooled. A magician who cannot fool the observer is considered inept. Men like to believe in such exotic things as abominable snowmen, flying saucers, and the Loch Ness monster. In the next chapter, we shall see how initial expectations affect the individual's interpretations of events.

Scepticism regarding miracles is also based upon the changing state of our knowledge. Modern lifesaving procedures make it possible for a drowning or heart-attack victim to be restored to life after apparent death. Medical science has produced any number of "miracle" drugs. What may have been interpreted as a miracle hundreds of years ago may be understood as a natural law today. Relatively few miracles are reported these days, probably because of widespread literacy and the increased ability of science to explain natural phenomena. When a report of a miracle is received, the recipient must ask himself whether it is more likely that the event occurred or that the witness was mistaken, fooled, or a liar.

3. Commonsense knowledge

Nothing seems as convincing as the direct perception of events. Reliance on perception for the development of beliefs is manifested in such sayings as "seeing is believing" and "show me, I'm from Missouri." Yet history teaches us that we cannot trust our senses. It seemed obvious to the layman in prescientific times that the earth was flat, did not move, and was orbited by both the moon and the sun. Galileo was made to confess his heresy about the movement of the earth both because it violated the doctrines of the church and because it seemed obvious from direct experience that the earth did not move at 1000 miles per hour.

Commonsense experiences are generally shared by a large number of people. When they compare their experiences, the meaning of events seems so obvious and reliable that no question arises about the validity of their collective knowledge. Even when a person does not directly experience a particular phenomenon, the reports of others may fit in with what he has experienced and hence may seem obviously true. For example, it makes perfectly good sense that workers who have fewer promotion opportunities would have lower morale than those who have many opportunities for advancement. Stouffer, Suchman, DeVinney, Star, and Williams (1949) found just the opposite pattern among members of the military service of the United States during World War II. Although the military police provided fewer promotional opportunities than almost any other branch of the Army, the MPs felt much less frustrated about their chances for promotion than did men in the Air Corps, where the promotion rates were quite high. Once presented with this evidence, good after-the-fact commonsense might say: sure, if a man had not been promoted and many of his buddies had been, he would be more dissatisfied than if few of his peers were promoted.

What is considered commonsense shifts over time, particularly with changes in technology and science. Commonsense is often supported by independently gathered scientific information. The problem is to determine when commonsense can be trusted and when it leads to a reasonable but wrong assumption about the nature of things. Although science begins with commonsense, like expert authority it must be checked by independent and different methods, and cannot be assumed to be an infallible method of acquiring knowledge.

4. Intuition

A flash of insight, a feeling from within, or a conception drawn from an analogy are referred to as intuitions because they do not seem to depend on any direct sensory experience. Intuition is quite personal and may not be shared by other people. It is characterized by the absence of any supporting evidence. But the individual who has the experience is quite certain that he has apprehended an important truth which no amount of evidence can controvert. Intuitions represent matters of faith—beliefs without support from information gained through the direct perception of external events.

Intuitive knowledge plays a strong role in human affairs. It has contributed to the development of great religions, the humanities, and political ideologies, as well as to many of the assumptions made by social scientists (e.g., hedonism and determinism). Anyone who believes that intuitions should not be taken seriously is reminded by Polanyi (1966) that, like all other knowledge, they are indirectly derived from experience and should be considered as hypotheses worthy of further investigation. Nevertheless, without further investigation we could not determine how much credence to place in such knowledge. Crackpot ideas would have to be considered just as valid as those supported by substantial independent evidence.

5. Conclusion

No method of acquiring knowledge could wholly abandon commonsense and intuition. However, all of the *a priori* approaches to knowledge are unreliable in varying degrees. Any viewpoint that refuses to reexamine beliefs acquired through *a priori* methods is at best naive and uncritical, and at worst deceitful and dogmatic. The scientist values *a priori* methods because they are the sources of his hunches and hypotheses; but he insists on further testing these tentative ideas so he can better discriminate those that can stand critical examination from those that cannot.

C. Method of Tenacity

As Peirce defined it, tenacity is more a way of holding beliefs than of acquiring them. A person may tenaciously cling to a belief despite evidence against it. There is an old psychiatrist's story about a patient who insisted he was dead. The psychiatrist thought for a few moments and then asked, "Do dead people bleed?" The patient replied, "Certainly not"; whereupon the psychiatrist pricked the patient's finger with a needle and triumphantly drew blood. The amazed patient stared at the blood, paused, and then confessed, "Doc-

tor, I was wrong. Dead people do bleed."

A well-known case of tenacity was reported by Festinger, Riecken, and Schachter (1956). These social psychologists had infiltrated an end-of-the-world group. Group members believed that the North American continent would be inundated because of God's anger at the sinfulness of the people there. The flood was predicted by the Guardians, residents of another planet, who would rescue the group just prior to the flood and carry them off in a flying saucer. The saucer did not arrive at the appointed time and date, and the small group of believers who had gathered together to be saved were temporarily crestfallen. Several hours later the group's leader received another revelation from the Guardians. The "message" said that because the members had proven to be true believers and were willing to subject themselves to ridicule and make sacrifices to support their beliefs, one final chance was to be given man. The flood was postponed, whereupon the members left the gathering to actively recruit new believers and to save man from himself.

Festinger et al. have suggested that tenacity is characteristic of people with strong beliefs. "A man with a conviction is a hard man to change. Tell him you disagree and he turns away. Show him facts or figures and he questions your sources. Appeal to logic and he fails to see your point . . . But man's resourcefulness goes beyond simply protecting a belief. Suppose an individual believes something with his whole heart; suppose further that he has taken irrevocable actions because of it; finally suppose that he is presented with evidence, unequivocal and undeniable evidence, that his belief is wrong: what will happen? The individual will frequently emerge, not only unshaken, but even more convinced of the truth of his beliefs than ever before. Indeed, he may even show a new fervor for convincing and converting other people to his view" (p. 3).

Both the psychiatric patient and the

end-of-the-worlders displayed tenacity by persisting in their beliefs despite contradictory evidence. Another kind of tenacity consists of holding on to a belief because there is no evidence against it. A person may believe in ghosts, gremlins, or angels because no one can prove they do not exist. But there is no way to prove that what does not exist does not exist. This is the reason why philosophers of science insist that the burden of proof is on the holder of a belief. When there is neither evidence for or against a belief, it is difficult to know how seriously to take it. Possibly the belief is correct. However, given our present inadequate understanding of nature, too many absurd things are possible. We do not act on the basis of what is merely possible, but instead seek out the most probable explanation, proposition, or belief.

Tenacity occurs because the individual likes the implications of a particular belief. Fortunately, the universe is not governed by our individual likes and dislikes. Our ideals may never be realized and our worst fears may be confirmed. Nevertheless, as we shall see in Chapters 3 and 5, values affect the way an individual processes information. What gains his attention, the kinds of questions he will ask, and the acceptability of answers are all shaped by the values he holds.

II. THE LOGIC OF SCIENTIFIC INQUIRY

As an alternative approach to knowledge, the scientific method constitutes an attempt to overcome the weaknesses of the informal ways of acquiring and assessing beliefs. There is reason to admit frankly at the outset that it may not be possible to free the scientist of his values (Gouldner, 1964; Vallance, 1972), but he has an obligation to carefully outline his values and assumptions so that what he says can be evaluated in the appropriate context. The scientific method is an attempt to pose questions to nature as the final arbiter of disputes among men. This goal can only be approximated when great care is taken in following the rather rigorous standards and procedures dictated by the logic of scientific inquiry.

The beginning point of all inquiry is observation. From planned and controlled observations come facts. A *fact* is an observation that has been consistently reported by independent investigators. Scientists attempt to find regularity in the relationships between facts. *Theories* are linguistic or mathematical structures designed to explain sets of regularities between facts. In order to pose his questions and answers with clarity, the scientist must be precise in the language he uses to describe his observations and to state his theories. The cycle of relationships between theories and observations, the discovery of functional relationships between facts, the construction of theories, and the concern for precision of language are the critical ingredients in the logic of scientific inquiry.

A. The Cycle of the Scientific Method

A *hypothesis* is a proposition that asserts a relationship between facts. The process by which a hypothesis is generated is called *induction* and is based on intuition. A hypothesis must be subjected to rigorous empirical test, and usually this can be done in a number of alternative ways. The process of making a specific prediction from a hypothesis is referred to as *deduction*. Observations, induction, hypotheses, deduction, predictions, verification, and back to observations constitute the cycle of the scientific method (see Figure 2.1). As can be seen, observation is the basic foundation of the scientific method, since the cycle both begins and ends with the direct perception of the scientist.

The cyclical nature of the scientific method can be illustrated by an example from research carried out to study interpersonal attraction. What is the basis of friendship? No one likes everybody; each

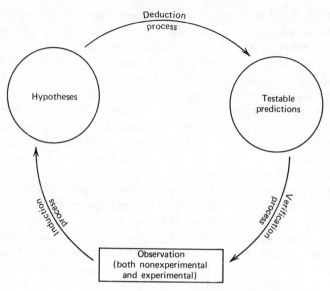

Figure 2.1.   The cycle of the scientific method.

person is selective in his choice of friends. One possible hypothesis to explain attraction(—reached by intuition—) might be that persons who share similar attitudes and values will like one another. This suggests a relationship between two possible observations—the existence of liking and of a similarity of attitudes.

What predictions can we deduce from this hypothesis? First of all we might predict that friends are more likely to belong to the same political party than nonfriends. A test of this prediction would require gathering certain facts. Friends and nonfriends could be compared to ascertain whether friends more often share the same political affiliation than nonfriends. If the prediction is supported, confidence in the hypothesis would be strengthened. It could not be said that the hypothesis was proved, however, because only one prediction among the many which could be deduced from the hypothesis was tested.

Hypotheses that are properly constructed are general enough to allow a very large, perhaps infinite, number of specific predictions to be deduced from them. For example, the attitude similarity hypothesis also leads to the deduction that one's liking will be greater for someone who shares

one's view of himself. A person who has a positive self-image will like someone who shares this positive view, while a person with a negative self-image will be attracted to someone who shares this negative view. Or it might be deduced from the hypothesis that people who like one another will belong to the same socioeconomic class. The greater the number of predictions from a single hypothesis hat are confirmed by subsequent empirical tests, the more confidence one can place in it. A single failure to predict may not seriously damage a hypothesis, because the test may have been carried out under inappropriate circumstances or the experimenter may have committed some error in his attempted verification. However, confidence in a hypothesis will be seriously damaged by repeated failures to confirm the predictions deduced from it.

The major weakness of the scientific method is that it never yields certainty of knowledge. Evidence can only lend greater or lesser credibility to a hypothesis. Knowledge acquired from authority or from a priori methods provides the comfort of certainty, but lacks the correction for error built into the cycle of the scientific method. To the scientist a hypothesis that cannot be disproved is meaningless; if it cannot be subjected to test, it has no established credibility and is not to be trusted.

B. Functional Relations and Experimental Laws

We have stated that hypotheses propose relationships between facts. It is often assumed that these relationships specify causes and effects. However, particularly in the social sciences, the identification of cause-effect relationships is extraordinarily difficult. According to Nagel (1961, p. 74) a causal relationship can be established when four conditions are satisfied: (1) the relationship is invariable; when the cause is present, the effect always occurs; (2) the two events are spatially contiguous; there can be no action at a distance; (3) the cause must precede the effect and the two events must be temporally contiguous; the events must occur sequentially and must be close to each other in time; and (4) the relation-

ship is not reversible; if X causes Y, then Y cannot cause X.

Because of the difficulties involved in isolating and controlling the occurrence of the events that are studied, these four criteria are seldom met in social psychological research. In practice, various magnitudes or degrees of an antecedent event are arranged by the experimenter and observations are then made to ascertain whether concomitant variation occurs in a consequent event. In the language of the psychologist, the experimenter varies the independent variable and assesses the effects on a dependent variable. A regular relationship found between two variables is referred to as a *functional relationship*.

Most social psychological research is directed toward finding functional relationships. For example, it has been found that the degree of similarity of the attitudes of two people (independent variable) is positively related to how much they like one another (the dependent variable). Figure 2.2 depicts the relationship found by Byrne

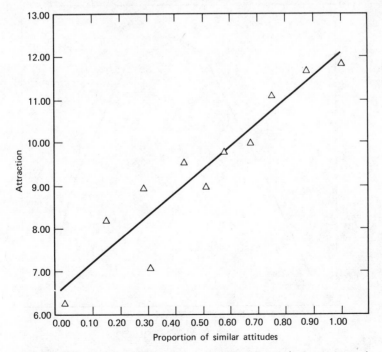

Figure 2.2. Attraction toward a stranger as a linear function of proportion of similar attitudes; Δ's indicate actual observations. (After Bryne and Nelson, 1965, p. 661.)

(1969). As can be seen, an increment of similarity leads to a roughly proportional increase in liking. The regularity of the function yields a straight line and is called a positive linear function, indicating that any increase in similarity results in an approximately proportional increase in liking.

Functions may take many different forms. Using the same example, suppose that a certain degree of similarity of attitudes maximized liking but that either less or more similarity decreased liking. This relationship would be curvilinear (see Figure 2.3), taking the form of an inverted U. This function would appear if persons did not like others who were either very similar to or very different from themselves.

When a functional relationship has been demonstrated many times, preferably by many different observers, the function comes to be called an *experimental law*.

C. Scientific Theories

The entire scientific enterprise is directed toward the construction of theories which systematically organize a group of experimental laws. A theory serves an explanatory purpose. By *explanation* is meant that from the basic concepts and relationships specified by the theory, experimental laws can be deduced. If it is assumed that the expression of attitudes similar to his own comforts the listener or gives him pleasure, the direct linear relationships between the proportion of similar attitudes and liking could be deduced from reinforcement theory (Byrne, 1971). As we shall see in Chapter 11, a number of other experimental laws regarding interpersonal attraction can be deduced from reinforcement theory. A theory is considered powerful when known facts can be deduced from it

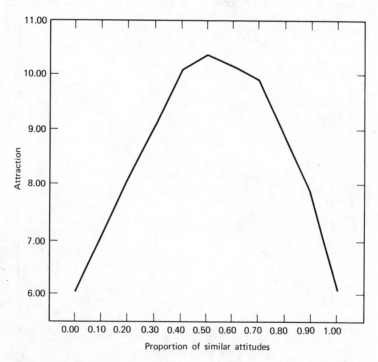

Figure 2.3. Hypothetical curvilinear function between attitude similarity and interpersonal attraction.

and when it leads to the discovery of new experimental laws. The interpretation of attraction in terms of reinforcement theory suggests a number of hypotheses that might not otherwise be considered; for example, the number of candies an adult gives to a child should be related to how much the child likes the adult.

The facts of social psychology are not easily organized into broad general theories. Social psychological theories tend to be closely tied to restricted sets of phenomena. There are theories of attraction, conformity, social influence, and so on, but there are few attempts to develop a general theory of social behavior from which the facts observed in all of these problem areas could be deduced. Most social psychologists argue that general theories cannot be constructed until a secure baseline of facts and experimental laws has been established and perhaps not even then. General theories, such as relativity in physics or biological evolution, are found infrequently in any of the sciences. The typical scientific theory is "middle range"—that is, it is designed to explain a restricted range of phenomena.

D. Language and Science

The scientist cannot afford to be painstaking in his observations and careful in the logic of his deductions but imprecise in his use of language. Clear predictions cannot be deduced from ambiguous hypotheses. The preferred language of science is mathematics because it eliminates the vagueness and emotion of everyday language. Much of the language used by social psychologists is borrowed from common sense and intuition. As will be seen in Chapter 11, some of the confusion in explaining interpersonal attraction arises because a precise definition of liking is seldom given. The development of a precise language is the mark of a mature science.

The cycle of the scientific method requires an articulation between theoretical concepts and the measurements carried out to test predictions. The actual measurement made is referred to as an *operational definition* of the theoretical concept. Only when two or more independent operations can be coordinated to a concept is there sufficient generality to include the concept in scientific theories. For example, the concept of interpersonal attraction may be very complex in meaning, and many different operations may measure part of the meaning. A paper-and-pencil scale may be one empirical approach, in which people can be asked to indicate how much they like another person by marking the appropriate part of a scale anchored at one end with "not at all" and at the other with "very much." Another way of measuring attraction might be to determine how close physically two people stand to one another. A third method might be to time the amount of eye contact between the two. Each of these operations presumably measures some aspect or dimension of the subject under study.

The adequacy of different operational definitions of the same concept may be assessed by whether they yield the same empirical functions. If paper-and-pencil, physical proximity, and eye contact measures are all linearly related to attitude similarity, we gain confidence in both the generality of the function and the equivalence of the operational definitions used. Because agreement between different operations provides convincing evidence for a theory, the same basic prediction deduced from an hypothesis may be tested in a number of different ways. A lack of agreement between two measures of the same theoretical concept may indicate that the measures do not in fact represent the same concept; the result is apt to be a narrowing and sharpening of the concept. It may also indicate that two investigators who believe they are studying the same phenomena were in fact studying different ones.

In conclusion, the scientist is confronted

with three major problems: (1) the deter- mination of significant facts, (2) the con- struction of theories, and (3) the matching of facts with theories. The cycle of the scientific method reflects the processes of induction and deduction as the scientist moves from fact to theory and back to fact. A hypothesis suggests an association bet- ween two or more facts. Consistent func- tions established between facts are referred to as experimental laws. Theories are ling- uistic or mathematical structures devised to explain experimental laws. Theoretical concepts must be explicitly defined and op- erations must be devised to measure them. In Figure 2.4 is an ideal representation of the induction process. Scientists often reach conclusions about facts and generate theories without consciously following this chain of inference. Insights are often achieved on the basis of keen observation and intuition.

Much of the excitement of science is gen- erated by contention between competing theories. Schlick (quoted in Frank, 1961) suggests one way of evaluating theories: "Every theory is composed of a network of conceptions and judgments and is *correct* or *true* if the system indicates the world of facts uniquely" (p. 39). When there are significant facts that cannot be explained by a theory, it is considered inadequate and scientists are stimulated to develop a new theory to fit the entire universe of known facts. Science is a never-ending process of discovering new facts, developing new theories, which predict more new facts, and so on.

We have reviewed some of the aspects of the logic of scientific inquiry, but the details of how the investigator actually acquires his facts have been left somewhat vague. The most powerful method available to the sci- entist is the experiment. An understanding of the logic, problems, and design of exper- iments will provide a more secure basis for the critical analysis of social psychological research.

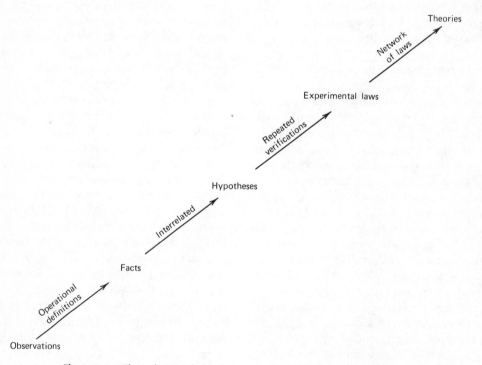

Figure 2.4. The inductive chain of reasoning from observations to theories.

III.   THE CONDUCT OF RESEARCH IN SOCIAL PSYCHOLOGY

Experiments are tests of hypothesized functional relations between events. The logic of experimentation requires that events be separated or isolated so that relationships can be established without the disturbance or interference of other (extraneous) events. In order to find the relationship between attitude similarity and attraction, other factors that might also be associated with liking—such as physical appearance or kindliness—cannot be allowed to interfere with the results of the research. If, for example, a person who has attitudes similar to yours also is very helpful to you, then it could not be determined if your liking for him is a function of similarity or a function of kindliness, or both.

An experiment that succeeds in eliminating the influence of all of the extraneous events and establishes a relation between the two or more events of critical interest is considered to be *internally valid*. An experiment must be carefully planned if it is to have internal validity. There are a variety of basic experimental designs available to the social psychologist. These designs differ in the amount of protection provided against the intrusion of extraneous variables into the experimental situation. It is impossible to eliminate all sources of error that can occur in an experiment, but statistical methods allow the scientist to estimate the amount of error and to take the estimate into account when assessing his results.

Every experiment is conducted in a specific setting and with a particular group of subjects, but the scientist is concerned with finding general functional relationships. The degree to which it is appropriate to extrapolate from the results of specific experiments to assert an experimental law is referred to as the *external validity* of experiments. Whether the experimental law will apply to the world outside the highly controlled conditions of the laboratory constitutes the problem of *ecological validity*.

The conduct of research in social psychology is an extraordinarily complicated activity. Training in the logic of experimentation, research design, and statistics are crucial to the whole enterprise. It would be impossible to conduct sophisticated research without these intellectual tools. Furthermore, without an understanding of the problems encountered in conducting research and the methods invented to solve them, the reader would lack the ability to evaluate critically the work of the social psychologist. It will be worthwhile, therefore, to examine in greater detail some of the problems encountered in conducting research.

A.   Logic of Experimentation

Science begins with observations. Suppose you are interested in some event, X; and you want to determine what antecedent event is functionally related to X. A careful appraisal of the situation as it was immediately before X occurred might reveal that a number of events preceded X. Let's suppose it is plausible to believe that any of four of the preceding events (A,B,C, and D) could be functionally related to X. If these four events can then be produced in a controlled laboratory setting and if X then occurs, one or more of them must be functionally related to X. But which one(s)?

A hypothesis may be advanced to suggest that D is invariably related to the occurrence of X. An appropriate test would require eliminating D from the pattern of antecedent events, so that two situations would be produced: (1) ABCD, and (2) ABC. If X occurs in situation (1) but not in situation (2), the hypothesis would be supported. If X occurs in both situations, D alone could not be responsible for the occurrence of X. A, B, and C might then be considered through a similar process of comparing differences between conditions. Of course, it is also possible that some combination of factors, such as both A and D, is required to bring about X. Sooner or later, if the right factors were originally identified as worthy of consideration, all possible comparisons should uncover the event that is functionally related to X.

This account of the *method of difference* was proposed by the 19th century British philosopher, John Stuart Mill. Although the method is quite persuasive in the abstract, it fails to recognize that very few real-life situations differ from each other in only one respect. When the event set ABCD is compared with set ABC, the presumption is that any difference in consequences is attributable to the presence of D in the first set and its absence from the second. However, if there are still other factors present in one condition but not in the other, no clear assessment of a functional relation can be made. These other, unplanned factors in experimental situations are called *extraneous variables*.

The purpose of *controls* is to neutralize the effects of extraneous variables so that differences between experimental situations cannot be attributed to their presence. One way to gain control over extraneous variables is to eliminate them from the experimental situation. If it is known that E is present, precautions can be taken to remove it. In studying the effects of attitude similarity on the liking between two strangers, the possibility that either person can help or reward the other may be eliminated so that kindliness (i.e., reinforcement) cannot affect the relationship under study. Another way to control the presence of an extraneous variable is to make sure it occurs equally in all of the conditions of the experiment. If we are comparing ABCD with ABC and E is also present, we can still find out if D is the critical factor in determining X by including E in both conditions (ABCDE and ABCE). For example, the sex of the experimenter might make a difference in how subjects respond if a male experimenter is used in one condition and a female in the other. It may not be possible to eliminate the experimenter from the situation, but the variable of sex can be con-

trolled. That is, it can be arranged that the experimenter is always a female or always a male in every condition of the study.

An extraneous variable needs to be controlled in an experiment only when its presence can affect the event under study. Which extraneous variables need to be controlled and which can be ignored can be determined by three means: (1) existing theory; (2) past research; and (3) the investigator's hunches. Theories usually specify more than one antecedent condition for any one effect. Liking may be functionally related to attitude similarity, reward mediation, physical attractiveness, and many other factors. When studying any one of these antecedent conditions, theory alerts us to the necessity of controlling the others. Familiarization with existing theory is therefore a prerequisite for undertaking research.

An experimenter should be well versed in the research already conducted on his problem. Prior research may have uncovered relationships not considered by current theories. These empirical relationships may suggest the need for controls that otherwise would go unrecognized. Even after he has carefully read the available literature, the experimenter can usually profit from performing a small pilot investigation just to become familiar with the setting and the specific procedures to be used in the experiment proper. The hunches developed from these preliminary explorations may lead the investigator to institute further controls in the major study.

From the above considerations we can define an *experiment* as a test of a hypothesized functional relationship in which two or more contrasting conditions are observed and all of the relevant variables except those of interest are controlled. The antecedent factors manipulated in an experiment are referred to as *independent variables*. The subsequent observed events are referred to as *dependent variables*. Thus, an experiment attempts to establish a functional relationship between an independent variable and a dependent variable.

B. Internal Validity of Experiments

An *experimental design* is a plan for an experiment. It considers which manipulations of the independent variables will be performed, what controls should be instituted, and the kinds of operational definitions to employ. The merit of a particular experiment depends upon how well it is designed. When the results of an experiment can be clearly attributed to the manipulation of the independent variable, the experiment possesses internal validity (Campbell, 1957). Many different kinds of designs have been developed in social psychology, and Campbell and Stanley (1963) have analysed them in terms of how well they control for various kinds of extraneous variables. These designs can be classified as non-experimental, experimental, and factorial, and vary in their internal validity. In discussing these designs, we will adopt the terminology of Campbell and Stanley. The independent variable will be represented by "X" and measurements or observations made by the experimenter will be represented by "O."

1. Non-experimental Designs

Two designs, neither of which are true experiments because there are no contrasting conditions, involve only one group of subjects. The *one-shot case study* (X - O) exposes subjects to the independent variable and then their behavior is observed. Although there is little difference between this simple design and the method of common sense, scientists sometimes are tempted to draw hasty conclusions from this type of situation. Suppose a group of people engage in a three-day encounter group experience (X) and afterward they are asked how they feel about their fellow men (O). If they say they believe that all men are basically good, can

this optimistic outlook be attributed to the encounter group experience? Perhaps optimistic people are apt to join an encounter group anyway, so they would have said the same thing prior to their experience. There is no way of knowing if the experience made a difference because there is no contrasting condition with which to compare it.

A *one-group pretest-posttest design* (O_1-X - O_2) provides for "before" and "after" measures. Before the encounter group experience the people may express a less favorable opinion of others (O_1) than they do after the experience (O_2). Is this not evidence that the experience has had an effect on their views of other people? Campbell and Stanley point out that four kinds of extraneous variables (history, maturation, testing, and measurement error) may provide alternative reasons for the results obtained.

History refers to events that occur during the same time period as the independent variable and may also affect the dependent variable. Perhaps during the three days of the group encounter session, it was announced over the radio that a peace treaty had been signed or an arms control agreement had been reached. These historical events may buoy up the spirits of the participants in the group. Their greater optimism about the nature of man at the end of the session may be due to the historical events or to the encounter experience or perhaps both; but there is no way of separating these factors within the research design employed.

Maturation refers to internal changes within the person, such as fatigue, boredom, development or loss of capacities, and so forth. A person who has been working day and night for weeks and is very tired or bored may find a three-day encounter session relaxing and a sufficient change of pace to relieve him of his boredom. Any other escape from his job might have had an equal effect in making him more cheerful and optimistic. Hence it cannot be concluded that the encounter group experience is the critical factor in changing his attitudes.

The very process of *testing* may affect the reactions of people. For example, it is difficult for many people to remain "natural" when a camera is pointed in their direction. Testing an individual's attitudes before an encounter session may activate thought processes about the issues in question that contribute to the change observed during the second test. If testing at O_1 elicits processes apart from the encounter group experience which contribute to the effects observed at O_2, the change cannot be attributed to the encounter group experience alone.

Finally, *measurement* error may also affect the dependent variable. Differences in the way observations are measured at two separate times may account for the changes observed from O_1 to O_2. Suppose the experimenter is more friendly or more interested in the respondents as people while taking observations at O_2 than he was at O_1. Or suppose two forms of the attitude measuring instrument have been developed to minimize the possibility that respondents would merely repeat their answers on the second testing. If the two forms are not actually equivalent, the change in attitudes could be attributable to the measurement device itself and not to the encounter group experience.

2. Experimental Designs

Three basic experimental designs frequently used in social psychological research are shown in Figure 2.5. The *static group comparison* adds to the one-shot case study by providing a contrasting condition; the independent variable (X) is present in one condition but not in the other (see Figure 2.5a). The condition in which subjects experience the independent variable is referred to as the *experimental group*, while the group that does not experience the independent variable is called the *control group*. Whenever there are contrasting conditions, the effects of history, maturation, test reac-

tivity, and errors in measurement are equally present in all conditions and hence cannot contribute to the differences found between conditions. Unfortunately, in a static group comparison we cannot be sure that the two groups were the same before the experiment. The way subjects are selected for the two groups might be related to the differences subsequently found between them. Suppose the encounter group subjects were volunteers from a psychology class and the control group subjects were obtained from an engineering class. The attitudes expressed toward people may reflect initial value differences in these two groups and may not be attributable to the unique experience of the experimental subjects.

X O_1 O_1 X O_2

O_2 O_3 O_4

(a) Static group   (b) Pretest—posttest
    comparison   control group design

O_1 X O_2

O_3 O_4

X O_5

O_6

(c) Solomon four-group design

Figure 2.5.   Three experimental designs described by Campbell and Stanley (1963).

One way the subject selection problem can be controlled is by randomly selecting subjects for experimental groups. *Random sampling* of subjects assures that each subject has as much chance of being placed in one condition as another. If 20 people are to be in the experiment, their names could be placed in a hat and the first name drawn would be assigned to group one, the second to group two, the third to group one, and so on. This random process is assumed to avoid any systematic selection of subjects that could produce initial differences between groups in an experiment. When the two groups in the static group comparison design are randomly selected from the same population the resulting design is referred to as the *post-test only control group design*.

Random sampling is also used to ensure that the subjects who participate in the various conditions of an experiment are representative of a larger population. The more representative they are, the more general the results of the study may be assumed to be. Since almost all college students take an introductory psychology course, experiments which use such subjects may be considered to represent what would happen if other college students had been used. However, populations with different characteristics might not act in the same way as these highly literate, mostly white, mostly middle class students.

Random sampling of the potential subject population is seldom achieved in practice. Most experiments are carried out with college students, who, it is said, are the most experimented-upon organism other than the white rat. In most universities, students in introductory psychology courses are required to participate in research, but can choose between alternative studies. Some students may be attracted to an experiment labeled "learning," while others may prefer one labeled "encounter group." Such a "self-selection" effect will bias the sampling process and make the subjects in any experiment somewhat unrepresentative of the general college population.

The *two-group pretest-posttest design* shown in Figure 2.5b ensures the equivalence of two groups of subjects with regard to various criteria before the independent variable is introduced into the situation. Suppose a study is designed to evaluate the effects of reinforcement upon learning a complex task. The intelligence of all subjects can be initially measured and then

their assignment to groups can be carried out so that the average intelligence in both conditions is approximately equal. In this way it can be assured that differences in intelligence between the two groups (O_1 and O_3) cannot account for the findings (O_2 and O_4).

The initial intelligence measurements may have an effect on how the subjects respond to the task given them, however. If they believe the task is intended to reflect their intelligence, they may be more highly motivated to perform well than if they had not been initially tested. Their performance would then be a joint function of the initial testing and the effects of reinforcement. Such multiple effects are referred to as *interactions*. Whether an effect is due mainly to the independent variable *(main effect)* or is a function of an interaction cannot be ascertained within the two-group pretest-posttest design.

The *Solomon four-group design* shown in Figure 2.5c controls for all of the types of extraneous variables considered above and provides for an assessment of interaction effects. Compare the first (O_1 - X - O_2) and third (X - O_5) groups. Both experience the independent variable, but only the first group is pretested. If there is no difference between O_2 and O_5, then pretesting cannot have had any effect on the dependent variable, and it may be concluded that no interaction effect occurred. If O_2 and O_5 are different, the difference may be attributable to the pretest, but this single comparison does not establish an interaction. The results from all four groups must be examined to determine whether an interaction occurred. If O_2 and O_4 are about the same, then X did not produce a main effect. A comparison between O_4 and O_6 will establish whether testing alone produced a difference between these two groups. Only O_2 experiences both pretesting and the independent variable; if there is an interaction effect, O_2 will have to be different from all of the other observations (O_4, O_5 and O_6).

3. Factorial Designs

In the designs discussed so far only one independent variable has been treated, and the problem of assessing the interaction of a pretest with the treatment has been considered. Experiments may be designed which test for the interaction of two or more independent variables on the dependent variable. If we think of the pretest as a second treatment, then the Solomon four-group design can be arranged in the form shown in Figure 2.6a.

	Pretest	No pretest
Treatment X	O_2	O_5
No Treatment X	O_4	O_6

(a) Solomon four-group design

Intent of Donor	Value of reward	
	Low	High
Intentional	O_1	O_2
Unintentional	O_3	O_4

(b) A 2 × 2 factorial design

Figure 2.6. Experimental designs that permit the examination of interactions between factors.

Human behavior is complex and only occasionally reflects the effects of a single antecedent factor. Simple functions can be established under highly controlled laboratory conditions, but the individual is usually exposed to multiple factors outside the laboratory. For this reason, social psychologists are interested in exposing subjects to several independent variables at once.

Consider the hypothesis that the greater the value of reward given a recipient the more he likes the donor. This is an interesting hypothesis and many predictions derived from it can be tested. But it might also be asked whether the relationship between reward magnitude and liking would hold if the donor had not really intended to reward the recipient—if his action was (or the recipient perceived it as) accidental.

An experiment can be designed employing both independent variables (low vs. high value of reward and intended vs. accidental behavior). A *factorial design* represents each possible combination of the independent variables (factors) under study. Reward magnitude is one factor and there are two levels (high and low). The second factor is intentionality (yes and no). As can be seen in Figure 2.6b, each level of each factor has been combined to form a 2 × 2 matrix.

The main effects of both factors and their interaction can be assessed with a factorial design. If high reward produces more attraction than low reward, $O_2 + O_4$ should be greater than $O_1 + O_3$ (the column totals). If subjects like an intentional donor more than an unintentional donor, then $O_1 + O_2$ should be greater than $O_3 + O_4$ (the row totals). Let us suppose that the actual results of the experiment are represented in Figure 2.7. Increases in the value of the reward lead to less liking for the intentional donor, but promote more liking for the unintentional donor. These results represent an interaction effect; liking depends upon a particular combination of the two factors.

Many different interpretations might be given to our hypothetical finding. Since the experiment was not designed to evaluate a specific interaction hypothesis but only a hunch that both factors might affect liking, any explanation after the facts are obtained *(post hoc explanation)* must be treated as a hypothesis yet to be tested. The reason is that it is much easier to come up with an explanation for facts already obtained than

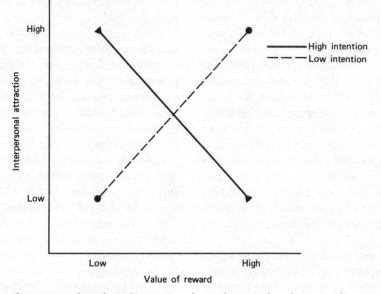

Figure 2.7. A hypothetical interaction of reward magnitude and intentionality on interpersonal attraction.

it is to predict facts never observed before. Also, more than one *post hoc* explanation can always be found for any result. Another such explanation might be that the intentional giving of a highly valued reward arouses suspicion about the donor's motives and, hence, lowers attraction, while such suspicions are not aroused when the donor accidentally mediates a large reward. A second study can then be done in which measurements of suspicion are included to establish a relationship between suspicion and attraction. Filling in the network of evidence may require a number of separate experiments. The scientific method of acquiring knowledge is often a slow and laborious process.

Both the number of factors and the levels assigned to each can be indefinitely expanded in complex factorial designs. A 2 × 4 × 3 design contains three factors with two levels of the first, four levels of the second, and three levels of the third. However, more than three factors are seldom investigated in a single experiment. Social psychological theories are usually not specific enough to make predictions involv-

ing the simultaneous interaction of more than three factors. In addition, unexpected interactions of three or more independent variables are extremely difficult to interpret meaningfully.

4. Groups, Measurement Error, and Statistics

The focus of interest in social psychology is the individual as he affects and is affected by other people. Why then are experiments conducted with groups of subjects rather than with a single individual? There are two reasons why this is so: (1) the variability of subjects' behaviors in complex situations, and (2) measurement errors. Both of these threats to internal validity can be illustrated by a learning experiment. A well-accepted principle of psychology is that learning is a direct linear function of the magnitude of reward the individual receives for making correct responses. To test this principle, it would be possible to place one person in a small reward condition and a second person in a large reward condition. Would this be a reasonable test of the hypothesis? The answer is clearly no. The person in the low reward condition might have more experience relevant to the task and hence be able to perform better than the person in the high reward condition. Motivational differences between the two subjects might also exist. Suppose the person in the large reward condition understands the task perfectly well but resents the requirement to participate in the experiment. If the person in the small reward condition believes his participation is valuable and gives his full commitment to it, his higher motivation may lead to better performance than is displayed by the subject in the large reward condition.

Measurement error can occur in many ways. The experimenter may inadvertently give slightly different instructions to the two subjects, or one of them may misunderstand the directions. A recording error may be made either at the time of observation or else when the data are transferred to computer cards or other records. These and many other sources of error would make it difficult to interpret whether differences in performance between the two subjects are attributable to reward magnitude or experimenter error.

In order to handle the problems of subject variability and measurement error, the social psychologist chooses a number of persons who are either matched on pretests or assigned to experimental conditions randomly. Subject differences are then either controlled by equivalence in assignment or by chance, so it is probable that the subjects in the various conditions are comparable for all relevant characteristics. For example, if some subjects have more experience with the task then others, there should be just as many experienced subjects in one condition of the experiment as in another; hence, any differences found in performance cannot be attributed to the variability of the subjects. Similarly, measurement errors are likely to be distributed randomly across experimental conditions if

there is a sufficient number of subjects in each group.

It is not always easy to determine whether a difference has been found in an experiment. In order to make comparisons it is necessary to find the average score of the measures obtained from all of the subjects within each experimental condition. Comparisons are then made between these averages. However, the scores reflect the variability due to subject-related factors and measurement error, as well as the effects of the particular condition experienced by the subjects in the experiment. The variability of the individual scores of subjects around the average score in a particular condition provides a basis for estimating all of the sources of error involved in a study. Statistical techniques have been developed to help the experimenter make a decision about whether differences between average scores are attributable to error in the experiment or can properly be considered a reflection of the effects of the independent variable. A thorough knowledge of statistics is essential to the conduct of social psychological research. The training of psychologists places heavy emphasis upon acquiring statistical skills.

C. External Validity of Experiments

An experiment has *external validity* when the same results are found using different research procedures, subject populations, or measuring instruments. The greater the generalizability of an experimental finding, the stronger the external validity of the study. According to Campbell and Stanley, internal and external validity are inversely related. Internal validity requires precise controls over all sources of extraneous variables, and the use of many controls creates a situation unlike most other (less controlled) situations. The uniqueness of the highly controlled, internally valid experimental situation makes it less likely that results can be generalized to other situations. For this reason it is usually necessary that a particularly well done experiment must be replicated by using different methods and subjects in order to establish an experimental law.

D. Ecological Validity

Experiments are usually artificial situations of minimal complexity. They are characterized as much by what is not allowed to happen (control) as they are for what does happen (manipulation of independent variables). Most social situations, on the other hand, are complex, and many factors simultaneously influence a person's behavior. Therefore it is almost always imprudent to apply directly a principle uncovered in a carefully controlled experiment to a complex social situation.

Ecological validity refers to the generalizability of scientific knowledge to the world of affairs, while external validity concerns the consistency of results of different experiments (Bjorkman, 1969). Ecological validity is achieved through the application of scientific theories. Kurt Lewin, one of the founders of modern social psychology, once remarked that the most practical thing in the world is a good scientific theory. He meant that theories deal with a large number of relationships and variables, while experiments typically involve only two or three specific variables. Experiments are tests of hypotheses and not attempts at building models of the real world; theories do provide models of the world. The problem of ecological validity raises questions regarding the relevance of scientific research and the moral responsibility of the scientist.

1. Relevance

How relevant a science is for solving practical problems depends on how well developed its theories are. Only sophisticated theories can account for processes and events as they occur within the context of a set of complex factors in the natural environment. The attempt to generalize from a limited set of research findings obtained under highly controlled conditions fails to consider the probability that the added factors in the natural setting would interfere with or obscure the process of interest. The powerful theories of the physical sciences have had an impact on the practical world of our day. The same cannot be said of social psychology. Social psychological theories do not encompass a wide range of principles that are applicable to a large number of situations and kinds of behavior. Although social psychologists are making great strides in isolating functional relationships, the construction of grand theories of social behavior is not possible with the relatively few principles now understood. It is often remarked that the most relevant thing a social scientist can do is to carry on with his pure research to develop theories that can later be applied to the solution of social problems. The student seeking relevance and prescriptions for social reform from the knowledge available in social psychology will often be disappointed.

Technological advance can occur without the help of scientific theory. Thomas Edison, for example, worked as a technologist, not as a scientist. Knowledge of scientific work can stimulate technological innovations. Applied psychologists have developed techniques from laboratory research that apparently work in treating autistic children, in helping make personnel decisions, and in marketing consumer products. Usually, the principles learned from laboratory research must be applied cautiously and with careful assessment of the success of the innovative program. The attempts throughout this book to generalize from social psychological principles to contemporary or historical events are made with the foreknowledge that the degree of error involved is probably high.

The assessment of new programs can be carried out by those skilled in the use of scientific method. Too often when policy makers are committed to a policy, such as a crackdown on speeders to cut highway deaths or innovations in the classroom to enrich learning, they are reluctant to assess its success. Failure of a program may imply wasted public funds and hence may be detrimental to a politician's future career. But a fair evaluation of an innovation requires the same careful and rigorous methods that are taken to establish the internal validity of an experiment (Campbell, 1969). The applied social scientist can make a direct and relevant contribution to social change and policy making through his expertise in evaluating the effects of new and old programs. From these evaluations will naturally come recommendations for how to improve existing programs. This contribution of social psychologists to the assessment and modification of social reforms will probably grow as more community programs of social relevance are established by public and private agencies.

2. Science and Moral Responsibility

As citizens, scientists have the same moral responsibilities with respect to social issues as anyone else. Scientists are particularly concerned with maintaining freedom to pursue their quest for knowledge unhampered by political considerations or ideological interference. The special responsibilities of the scientist have been outlined by Edel (1964): "The most obvious commitment he has as a scientist is of course to the dominant value of truth in his enterprise. This means that if he speaks out on a question of his discipline, he is committed to stating what he knows as a scientist. . . . A second obligation is to maintain the conditions of his scientific enterprise. If he is committed to the pursuit and extension of truth, he is committed to maintaining and extending the conditions requisite for scientific work. . . . A social scientist can op-

pose McCarthyite (Senator Joseph) guilt by association and restrictive military secrecy in science, not just as a citizen, but as a scientist, if the evidence is clear enough that these are conditions which hinder scientific development" (p. 231–232).

Too much concern for the relevance of his work may interfere with the clear and precise development of the social psychologist's research. Poor experiments often result from trying to find out too much rather than too little. As Kaplan (1964) has warned, "You get what you pay for, and bargains are as much to be distrusted in research as anywhere else" (p. 158). Social problems are very complex and typically involve economic, political, and sociological factors, as well as social psychological ones. The researcher is usually overwhelmed by the enormity of trying to resolve racial issues, problems of war and peace, or discrimination against women. Any experiment requires that some aspect of the total problem be isolated for purposes of study. Research directed toward solving large scale social problems is likely to raise more questions than it solves, and a series of new problem areas, each with competing theories, develops. As a result the social psychologist finds himself removed from the practical concerns that originally motivated his research and totally immersed in purely scientific questions regarding the construction of theories, the design of experiments, the development of operational definitions of concepts, and so on. Naturally, he hopes the knowledge he accumulates will eventually be useful in serving the welfare of all mankind. Only when the scientist is confident of his theories can he properly make policy recommendations based on his scientific knowledge. Some facts and relationships that are not well integrated by theory may be gathered by the scientist for use by policy makers who consider evidence acquired from a number of scientific and nonscientific sources.

E. Correlational Research

Relationships between events can be studied without doing experiments. The astronomer cannot manipulate gravitational forces, orbits, or stars, nor can he control all the extraneous variables that may impinge on the events under his observation. Careful observation is used to establish a set of facts which are then related to each other through the use of powerful mathematical and statistical techniques. These relationships, once established, permit predictions, which can be tested by subsequent observations.

One statistic that provides a measure of the relationship between two sets of measurements is the *correlation coefficient*. Two simple examples will illustrate what a correlation is. There is evidence that interpersonal attraction is a symmetrical relationship. The degree of liking between two people is roughly the same for each (Newcomb, 1961). To test this hypothesized relationship, suppose we take pairs of people who know one another and ask each individual to indicate how much he likes his partner by checking a point along a scale that ranges from 0 (dislike very much) to 100 (like very much).

Assume we obtain the scores shown in Table 2.1. It can be seen that some individuals like their partner a great deal while others do not. Obviously, there is a strong relationship between the scores of persons A and B. In fact, it would be possible from these data to predict B's liking for A if you knew how much A liked B. The better one set of scores predicts the second set, the higher the correlation is; the coefficient of correlation for the scores shown in Table 2.1 is +.98. Perfect correlation (i.e., complete predictability) is 1.00. A correlation of 0 indicates no systematic relationship between the pairs of scores. There might be a zero correlation between how much persons like one another and how close they sit together in a classroom if the seating is as-

Table 2.1   Hypothetical Measures of Liking Between Pairs of Persons.

Pair number	Person A	Person B	Person C
1	92	97	50
2	87	89	70
3	81	79	30
4	75	69	50
5	63	67	12
6	54	61	60
7	48	53	70
8	41	38	45
9	24	19	80
10	15	11	68

signed by the teacher in alphabetical order.

A positive correlation tells us that as the scores in one set become larger, so do those in the second set. The same amount of predictability exists with a negative correlation as with a positive one. Recall our earlier example of the relationship between promotional opportunities and morale in military units (Stouffer, et al, 1949). This relationship could be examined by obtaining a measure of the proportion of men who are promoted each year in each branch of the service (e.g., MPs, Air Force mechanics, Navy Signal Corps). Then selected samples of men in each unit could be given questionnaires that include a measure of their degree of satisfaction regarding promotion opportunities. Assume the measure of satisfaction ranged from a low score of 0 to a high of 100. An average of the scores of the men in each unit could then be paired with the appropriate promotion opportunity scores, as in Figure 2.8. It can be seen that in this hypothetical study the greater the opportunity for promotion, the less satisfied the men in a unit were. A perfect negative correlation would have a coefficient of −1.00; the correlation in our hypothetical example is −.99. The prediction of scores can be made in either direction. If promotional satisfaction is known, opportunity for promotion can be predicted; if promotion opportunity is known,

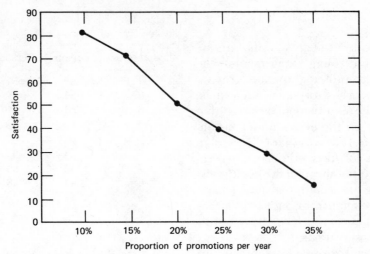

Figure 2.8. Hypothetical negative relationship of actual promotional opportunity and satisfaction with promotional opportunity.

satisfaction can be predicted. Of course the relationship between scores is seldom as apparent as in our hypothetical examples. The correlation of −.39 between the scores of persons B and C in Table 2.1 is not ascertainable from a simple scanning of the data.

Correlational research has two important limitations: (1) it does not establish a time sequence between two events, and (2) it does not demonstrate that one event affects the other. The first limitation is often not serious because it is easy enough to infer what the time sequence probably is. For example, it is unlikely (though possible) that promotion opportunity in a military unit is caused by the average level of satisfaction of the men. But the second limitation makes it impossible to infer causation from the fact that two events are highly correlated. The degree of liking between two persons may be symmetrical, but this does not mean that the degree of liking of A for B is *determined* by B's degree of liking for A. Attitude similarity, a third factor, may account for both the degree and the symmetry of liking.

The lack of control of extraneous variables and the failure to manipulate independent variables make correlational research inferior to experiments in demon-

strating and testing functional relationships. On the other hand, a functional relationship does imply a correlation between two factors. A failure to find a correlation provides evidence against a hypothesized functional relationship. If there is no correlation in the expressed liking between pairs of persons, then attitude similarity cannot be a cause of attraction.

What has been stated about the inability to draw inferences regarding causation from correlations is true of virtually all available social psychological research using the correlation statistic. However, procedures have recently been developed to permit the testing of models of causal relations with correlation procedures (Blalock, 1963). These procedures are too complex to present here. In brief, they involve diagramming the causal relations assumed to exist among a network of variables, testing whether or not correlations exist where they should, and, more importantly, testing whether or not they do not exist where they should not. If in theory variable B is a function of A, C is a function of B, but A has no effect on C, then there should be no correlation between A and C (if the shared effects of B are statistically removed by partial correlation). The virtue of partial correlation, path analysis, and other multivariate correlational analyses is that they permit the testing for functional relations in data that has been collected through surveys, examination of archives, and other nonexperimental and nonlaboratory approaches. Though these techniques have been much heralded for their promise (McGuire, 1967, 1973), they have been seldom applied by social psychologists.

Simple correlational research is often carried out to explore possible relationships between a large number of variables. It is an efficient way of summarizing a large amount of data and identifying relationships. If we were to start from scratch in exploring how personality affects social behavior, we might begin the research program by giving a large number of people a battery of personality tests and by observing and coding their behavior in a variety of social situations. All of the dependent variables (personality and behavior scores) could then be correlated with one another. Correlation coefficients should indicate which personality characteristics are related to each example of behavior. Experiments could then be designed to examine further the relationships identified by the correlational study. This research strategy is a more efficient way to proceed than carrying out a large number of experiments to examine each possible relationship of all the variables under consideration.

The interpretation of experiments in which subjects are chosen on the basis of their scores on personality, intelligence, or other tests is limited in the same manner as other simple correlational studies. A relationship between the subject-related factor and the dependent variable in the experiment cannot be established as a causal one. For example, if one group of subjects who scored high on a test of authoritarianism behaved differently from those who scored low, it could not be said that authoritarianism caused the difference in behavior. Many other factors may be associated with authoritarianism which could account for the behavior, and until these other extraneous factors are ruled out by control procedures the relationship between the scores on the authoritarian measure and the dependent variable should be treated as a correlation. This kind of experiment is quite different from one in which the difference between subjects is manipulated, such as when high and low self-esteem are caused by manipulating their success or failure experiences. In the latter case, subjects are assigned to conditions randomly and it may be assumed that they are alike at the beginning of the study. Hence, manipulated self-esteem should not be systematically correlated with any other differences that existed between the groups prior to the experiment, and causal interpretations may be made.

IV. METHOD OF OBSERVATION

The social psychologist has developed a variety of tools that can be used to make observations outside the laboratory. Each of these nonlaboratory methods has its own set of peculiar problems. Reliable observation and the establishment of facts can result from careful use of paper-and-pencil tests, content analysis, clinical interviews, surveys, natural observations, or natural and field experiments. We will briefly examine each of these methods.

A. Paper-and-Pencil Measures

The social psychologist is often interested in how the characteristics of individuals affect the course of social interaction. If he had enough time to observe a single person in many different settings, he could probably provide a sound judgment of the intelligence, attitudes, abilities, and personality attributes of that person. However, as we have seen, experiments usually involve a sizeable number of people; there would not be enough time to follow each person around before undertaking a study. As a substitute procedure, paper-and-pencil tests have been constructed as a way of estimating the characteristics of individuals. These instruments now number in the thousands and include measures of intelligence, attitudes, self-esteem, motivations, interpersonal attraction, and hundreds of other factors.

Paper-and-pencil tests are not useful unless they are both reliable and valid. The *reliability* of an instrument refers to its consistency in measurement. It is not usually expected that the enduring characteristics of an individual will fluctuate widely over time. For this reason a test can be considered accurate or reliable if persons tested score about the same when retested at a later time. A test is *valid* if it measures what it purports to measure. Several ways to establish test validity have been devised.

If the test score is a good basis for predicting future behavior, it has *predictive validity*. If person A is identified by a test as an introvert and person B is identified as an extrovert, then it should be predictable that A will talk less in a group discussion than B. Confirmation of the prediction increases our confidence in the validity of the original test.

Personality variables are theoretical constructions, not facts that are obvious and readily observed. A personality construct usually consists of a network of behavior which goes to make up the trait being proposed. For example, a person with low self-esteem is assumed to be more strongly concerned with the social approval of others than is a person with high self-esteem. If persons who score low on a self-esteem test are found to be more concerned with social approval, *construct validity* for the test is said to be established. The greater the network of relationships *(nomological net)* implied by a construct and supported by evidence, the greater the confidence that the test measures what it purports to measure.

An unreliable test is always invalid; scores cannot be used even to predict future scores on the same test and, hence,

cannot yield consistent relationships with other measures. A reliable test is not necessarily a valid one; it may reliably measure something other than what it was intended to measure. In such cases neither predictive nor construct validity can be established. If the introversion test reliably measures something other than introversion it would be of no use in predicting behavior theoretically associated with introversion.

B. Content Analysis

Any communication serves as a record of the thoughts, perceptions, and purposes of its source. Content analysis represents an attempt to make inferences about the characteristics of a person by systematically investigating the form, style, or content of his communications. The projective techniques used by clinical psychologists exemplify the content analysis approach. For example, in the Thematic Apperception Test a series of somewhat ambiguous drawings of persons in various settings is shown to the respondent who then tells a story about what he sees in the picture. The psychologist then scores the story for themes relating to needs for achievement, affiliation, failure, or power. The general assumption underlying the use of projective tests is that the individual must provide interpretations of the ambiguous stimuli presented to him from his own background, experience, and needs.

A systematic approach must be taken in content analysis. The investigator must decide what it is he is chiefly interested in assessing and what units he will count in order to make his assessment. For example, will he use themes, the frequency of particular words, or measures of writing style?

The researcher's purpose may dictate his choice of units for analysis. Counting the frequency of particular words, for example, may establish the author of a communication. The dispute over whether Madison or Hamilton was the author of certain of the Federalist papers was apparently settled by counting the frequency of 265 words such as "whilst" and "upon" (Mosteller & Wallace, 1964). Sentence length was of no use in distinguishing between the two authors because Madison averaged 34.59 words per sentence in undisputed writings and Hamilton averaged 34.55 words.

The usefulness of new techniques must be evaluated in the light of other available evidence. The settling of authorship disputes apparently cannot be achieved solely on the basis of content analyses. Ellison (1965) used a procedure for discriminating style, which was presumed to be reliable, in studying James Joyce's difficult book, *Ulysses*. The indicators were sentence length; frequency of the definite article; third-person pronouns; all parts of the verb, *to be*; and the words *and, but,* and *in*. Ellison concluded that *Ulysses* was written by six different persons, none of whom wrote Joyce's earlier novel, *Portrait of the Artist as a Young Man*.

Content analysis is used for government intelligence purposes, to examine the relationship between public attitudes and the content of the mass media, to analyse dreams, to assess motives and perceptions, and for many other purposes. As a research tool, it is still in an exploratory stage of development. The computer has reduced much of the drudgery associated with the technique. At the present time efforts are being primarily devoted to constructing computer dictionaries and categories of analysis. Although content analysis looks very promising, more explorations of the reliability and validity of the technique will determine how useful it will be to the social scientist.

C. Clinical Assessment Methods

Clinical methods are distinctive in that individual subjects are observed and evaluated over a period of hours, days, or months by a variety of techniques, including observation, interviews, and testing. Considerable effort is devoted to learning as much as possible about a single person. Detailed, in-depth information about the social behavior of a few individuals can be very useful in forming hypotheses to guide experimental research. Clinical methods have been employed to study marihuana use (Becker, 1963), alienation among young people who "dropped out" of the cultural mainstream (Keniston, 1965), and the effects of vasectomy operations on psychological functioning and marital adjustment (Ziegler, Rodgers, & Prentiss, 1969).

Clinical methods suffer from a lack of control over extraneous variables. Furthermore, the investigator's own biases may color his interpretations of the data, particularly since his subjective judgments play an important role in the observations made. Nevertheless, clinical methods are quite valuable for exploratory purposes and serve to generate valuable hypotheses meriting further study.

D. Survey Techniques

Surveys have become part of our daily culture. The results of the Gallup and Harris polls may be read each week in the newspaper. Television programs prosper or fold based on surveys assessing their popularity among viewers. The results of important elections are predicted with considerable accuracy from survey data several days before the voters go to the polls.

Surveys are often carried out because of the investigator's interest in the values, habits, or opinions of persons in a particular population. If the number of people in the population is small enough, each individual might be interviewed. This is usually impractical, however. The survey researcher therefore draws a *representative sample* from the population and interviews the people who are selected. It is presumed that the distribution of characteristics in the sample are very similar to those in the larger population. If they are not, the sample is said to be biased and the results of the survey invalid. An historical example of poor sampling technique was the Literary Digest Poll in 1936 that predicted Landon would defeat Franklin D. Roosevelt in the presidential election. Questionnaires were sent by mail to persons whose names were obtained from automobile registration lists and from telephone directories. This sample did not accurately represent the entire population of people who were likely to vote for two reasons: (1) people who owned automobiles and had telephones were predominantly upper middle class, a group that traditionally leans toward the Republican party candidates; and (2) during the Depression of the 1930s the people most likely to respond to a questionnaire sent in the mail were those who were dissatisfied with the state of affairs and tended to be opposed to the incumbent (Roosevelt).

Surveys differ from clinical methods in that they are usually restricted to relatively limited aspects of the respondent's personal history, attitudes, or habits. Comparatively little time is spent with each respondent. McClosky (1958), for example, was able to interview over 1200 persons in Minneapolis and St. Paul regarding their political attitudes. He divided respondents into four groups according to their scores on a measure of conservatism. Despite the brevity of the interviews much was learned, as is indicated by McClosky's conclusions:

The extreme conservatives are easily the most hostile and suspicious, the most rigid and compulsive, the quickest to condemn others for their imperfections and weaknesses, the most intolerant, the most easily moved to scorn and disappointment in others, the most inflexible and unyielding in their perceptions and judgments . . . The extreme emphasis on order and duty; the elaborate affection for the tried and familiar; the fear of change and the desire to forestall it; the strong attachments to the symbols and rituals of the ingroup culture; the hope for a society ordered and hierarchical in which each is aware of his station; the unusual concern for law, authority, and stability—all of these can easily be understood as doctrinal expressions of a personality pattern which has a strong need for order and tidiness . . .

When a survey involves more than one sample from different populations, it has the appearance of an experiment. For example, Whittaker and Watts (1969) administered a personality inventory to 151 persons in a non-student "fringe" group in Berkeley in 1965 and compared their responses with those of a comparison group of students from the University of California. The fringe possessed a stronger intellectual disposition, sought more self-gratification, experimented more with life, placed a higher value on self expression as contrasted to rule adherence, and had higher estheticism scores than did the students. While these findings are interesting and provocative, it must be remembered that the researcher did not institute controls or manipulate an independent variable; the data are essentially correlational in nature and cannot demonstrate causal relationships. Nevertheless, the results are heuristic because they suggest hypotheses that can be investigated by more rigorous experimentation.

Budding social scientists are often eager to set out with some hastily devised questionnaire to find out how their peers feel about some issue of burning relevance. But conducting a survey requires a considerable amount of technical skill and careful preparation. There are problems associated with constructing questionnaire items that are reliable and valid, training interviewers, and selecting a sample of respondents. Should questions be direct or indirect, to what extent should they be leading, how does the answer to one question affect the respondent's reaction to succeeding questions? Should the interviewer be black or white, male or female? Should the questions be of the yes-no type or should a scale be devised; if the latter, what kind of scale should it be? How should the data be coded and what statistical procedures should one apply to analyse the data?

Survey methods suffer the weaknesses of all correlational methods. They can establish relationships between sets of observations, but since there is no control over extraneous variables, functional relationships cannot be established unless complex models of causal relations are systematically evaluated. Surveys are valuable in describing characteristics of the population investigated, and their results may stimulate experimental research by disclosing relationships which suggest new hypotheses to the investigator.

E. Natural Observations

People-watching from the comfort of the front porch or the sidewalk cafe is a time-honored custom. The social psychologist does not confine himself to a laboratory, a library, or to testing and interviewing. He often observes social behavior as it takes place in the natural environment. However, unlike the layman, the social psychologist plans his observations and systematically selects settings, procedures, and measurements before venturing into the field.

A recurrent problem in field studies is the awareness of the subject that he is under observation. His reaction to being observed is often referred to as the *Hawthorne effect* because it was first noticed in a study by Roethlisberger and Dickson (1939) at the Hawthorne Works of the Western Electric Company. They were interested in making environmental changes to improve production on a small parts assembly line. Unexpectedly, they found an increase in production whether they improved or worsened lighting and temperature and whether hours of work and rest periods were lengthened or shortened. Apparently, the jobs performed by the workers

were so dull that any change or any sign of personal interest in them resulted in increased output.

Subjects may give the appearance of becoming unaware of video filming or tape recording, but it is reasonable to believe they remain aware of these devices and react to them. Soskin and John (1963) had a married couple wear radio transmitters during the entire period of a two-week vacation. After the first day, the couple made few comments indicating self-consciousness about the public nature of their behavior. However, it is probable that their awareness of the monitoring device affected what they said and did during the observation period. Ethical problems are raised when the social scientist considers means of recording the private and personal activities of people without their awareness. Hiding under beds in college dormitories (Henle & Hubble, 1938) may eliminate the Hawthorne effect, but the insensitivity to ethics in committing such an invasion of privacy needs little comment in a post-Watergate era.

Ethical problems are raised even when the observer gains permission from his subjects. How much responsibility should be attributed to WNET-TV of New York City for the dissolution of the marriage of the William C. Louds? The Loud family was under observation for a period of seven months by a national television audience, and television personnel lived in their Santa Barbara home during the filming of "An American Family." It would be surprising if the family's interactions were not disturbed by the everpresent cameras. Legally, of course, the family's consent absolved the producer of responsibility for any consequences.

Webb, Campbell, Schwartz, and Sechrest (1966) reviewed a variety of methods for collecting data unobtrusively. For instance, the number of whiskey bottles found in trash cans may be an indicator of the liquor consumption in a town, or the amount of wear on tile floors in a museum may be used to evaluate the attractiveness of an exhibit. Unobtrusive measures were obtained by Wrightsman (1969) in a study of the committed electorate just prior to the 1968 presidential election. Law and order was the basic theme of Alabama governor George Wallace in the campaign. Wrightsman took advantage of the fact that a new law required an automobile tax sticker to be displayed on all vehicles. The law took effect on November 1, 1968, a few days before the election. He identified committed voters by going to parking lots and looking for cars with candidate bumper stickers. According to the results, Wallace supporters were less law-abiding at least in this one respect than either voters who supported other candidates or people who were uncommitted (no candidate sticker). It was not necessary to interview or directly observe the subjects in this field study.

The real world has certain disadvantages from the scientific observer's point of view. Many phenomena of great interest occur only rarely; other phenomena of little interest occur with great and tiresome regularity. One tactic the observer can use to increase the frequency of occurrence of a rare behavior is to manage the environment so as to elicit the behavior of interest. If one wishes to observe competitive behavior among boys, the creation of a short supply of valued activities and objects may be an appropriate tactic to use (Gump, Schoggen, & Redl, 1957).

The major disadvantage of the natural observation from the perspective of science is the lack of control exercised over the situation. It is difficult to acquire unbiased samples of subjects, to obtain measures of dependent variables, and to control a complex set of extraneous variables. Nonetheless, there are many kinds of behavior that cannot be studied in the laboratory. Natural observation, when supplemented by experimental research, may yield a significant body of data and provide infor-mation about the ecological validity of scientific theories.

F. Natural Experiments

A natural experiment consists of observations of contrasting conditions in the field. The manipulation of the independent variable is engineered by nature, not the researcher. Social psychologists have occasionally studied the effects of naturally occurring events on the attitudes and behavior of people. For example, Lieberman (1956) examined the attitudes of employees toward management and their union. More than a year later he returned and readministered his questionnaire to 23 employees who had been promoted to foremen, 35 workers who had been elected as union stewards, and a control group of workers who had not experienced any change of position. Lieberman did not control the promotions and union elections, but he did assess their effects on the attitudes of the affected workers. Newly elected foremen were more favorable to management than they had been before promotion, while newly elected union stewards were more favorable toward the union than they had been.

Nature smiled on Lieberman for the company had increased in size, having secured a number of government contracts, and the number of promotions was unusually numerous in the year of the study. Eventually, the government contracts were exhausted, the work staff was cut, and some of the new foremen were bumped back to worker status. After this second manipulation by nature, Lieberman returned and found that the demoted foremen were now less favorable to management and had reverted to their initial positive views of the union.

Natural experiments are valued because they occur under real conditions and without any meddling by the experimenter. There are three difficulties with them, however. First, the investigator may patiently wait for an experiment that never happens. When events are predictably frequent, planning and preparation can lead to systematic data collection, but if the events occur only rarely and unpredictably, natural experiments are impractical. Second, the experimenter has no choice in managing just how the independent variable is manipulated. He cannot control when it is introduced or its magnitude or complexity and must accept the particular variation produced by nature. Lieberman, for instance, might also have been interested in the attitudes of newly elected union stewards who lost their positions through the contraction of the company's business. But the reduction in the work force produced demotions of foremen without affecting the union's staff.

Finally, and probably most important, the assignment of subjects to conditions was not randomized. Subject-related factors may be confounded with the dependent variable. It could be assumed that positive attitudes toward management would be related to receiving the rewards given to supervisors as well as to the status of membership in the supervisory group.

G. Field Experiments

The field experiment is an attempt to take the laboratory out into the complex world. A design is planned and the experimenter manipulates an independent variable. One justification for the field experiment is our inability to study many kinds of behavior of interest in the laboratory. It would be difficult to study the behavior of taxicab drivers in a laboratory, and if the experimenter was interested in doing so, he could sacrifice some control over extraneous variables and move into the field.

Feldman (1968) explored the hypothesis that cab drivers overcharge their passengers particularly when they are easily identified as strangers to the city. Feldman had individuals hail cabs in Paris, Athens, and Boston. Half the time the passenger

was a compatriot and half of the time he was a foreigner. No differences in fares were observed in Athens or Boston, but the American foreigners were charged more than the Frenchmen in Paris. The Parisian cab drivers employed a wide variety of ruses to overcharge the Americans, including giving the wrong change, not changing the meter from the previous fare, misreading the meter, and taking a long way around to the destination.

McMartin (1972) reversed these roles by having the experimenter act as the cabbie, while the passengers served as unsuspecting subjects. The cab was dispatched to two types of sites to pick up passengers: places that served alcoholic beverages, and private residences and shopping centers. After picking up his passenger, the cabbie indicated he had been reading a book, either on the topic of alcoholism or on psychiatric insurance. These two manipulations (dispatching sites and topic of book) provide a 2 × 2 factorial design. The driver initiated no further conversation with his passengers, although he responded pleasantly and neutrally to any comments they made. The dependent variable was the size of tip received by the cabbie-experimenter. Bar passengers were big tippers when the driver's comment was innocuous, but when the cabbie mentioned alcoholism, tips were small. Apparently, the bar passengers perceived the driver as making negative evaluations of them and retaliated by reducing the amount of the tip. The tipping practices of passengers picked up at the control sites were unaffected by what the driver said he had been reading.

Field experiments have popular appeal because they partake of real life. They may often be faulted because their focus tends to be on applied and sometimes trivial matters, rather than on contributions to the refinement of theories of social behavior. The study of the French taxicab driver who overcharged his passengers may be of interest to American tourists, but it cannot be said to make any real contribution to scientific social psychology. No principles were discovered, no hypotheses of any generality were tested, and no functional relationships were found. Yet the field experiment is intriguing, and we will have occasion to report many of them throughout this book. The current mood of social psychologists appears to strongly encourage the use of field experiments. The great imagination of researchers in conducting field experiments is represented in several recent collections (Bickman & Henchy, 1972; Evans & Roselle, 1973; Swingle, 1973).

V. THE SOCIAL PSYCHOLOGY OF THE EXPERIMENT

The experiment may be considered a social situation in which experimenter and subject interact with one another. The behavior of subjects is apt to be affected by their perception of what the experimenter expects and by their awareness that they are under observation by a psychologist. Rosenzweig (1933) was one of the first to recognize that subjects are likely to approach an experiment with a questioning attitude: "A subject who acts in this way commits what we shall call the 'opinion error': he entertains opinions about the experiment—what its purpose is and what he may reveal in it—instead of simply reacting in a naive manner. The causes of the opinion-error are usually certain motives, such as curiosity and pride" (p. 343). To control for opinion error, social psychologists have commonly used deception to conceal the true purposes of the experiment from inquisitive and reactive subjects.

Rosenzweig also considered the experimenter as a potential source of extraneous variables that could undermine the internal validity of an experiment. Biosocial factors such as sex, race, and attitudes of the experimenter can have important effects on how subjects respond. Male subjects may respond differently in the presence of a female experimenter than they would with a male experimenter. The experimenter may tip off his hypothesis by an unguarded word or suggestive emphasis while giving verbal instructions or by the way he reacts to a subject's questions. Friedman (1967) sarcastically characterizes the researcher who ignores his own effects on subjects as subscribing "to the democratic notion that all *experimenters* are created equal; that they have been endowed by their graduate training with certain interchangeable properties; that among these properties are the anonymity and impersonality that allow them to elicit from the same subject identical data which they then identically observe and record" (p. 3–4).

The artificiality of laboratory situations, the need to involve subjects in experimental tasks, the power relationship that exists between experimenter and subject, and experimenter and subject effects on responses are major problems that have been the focus in the last decade of a major effort to study the social psychology of the experiment. When these sources of extraneous variables are understood, their effects can be brought under systematic control. Hyman (1954) views this process as a mark of an advanced state of a science: "All scientific inquiry is subject to error, and it is far better to be aware of this, to study the sources in an attempt to reduce it, and to estimate the magnitude of such errors in our findings than to be ignorant of the errors concealed in the data. One must not equate ignorance of error with lack of error. The lack of demonstration of error in certain fields of inquiry often derives from the nonexistence of methodological research into the problem and merely denotes a less advanced stage of that profession" (p. 4).

A. Artificiality of Laboratory Experiments

It has been argued that experiments are useless in telling us how people act in the course of their daily lives because of the artificiality of laboratory situations. It should be remembered that the primary value of a laboratory experiment derives from the possibility of manipulating independent variables precisely, controlling extraneous variables, and measuring dependent variables. The cost associated with these assets is artificiality.

Critical processes and events might never be understood if only naive and unaided observations were made. A profusion of extraneous events may interfere with identifying processes or critical factors may be invisible to the eye, as are electrons, genes, and attitudes. No one would think of criticising a biologist because he examined chromosomes under a microscope rather than observing them while animals roam freely in the wilds.

Experimental situations are not models of the real world, nor are they intended to be. The laws of classical conditioning were discovered by Pavlov in a highly artificial situation. He placed dogs in a harness, soundproofed the chamber, eliminated the presence of observers by automating the measurement of salivary responses, and standardized preexperimental handling procedures. Until these controls were introduced, making the situation very unlike the everyday world encountered by the animals, the conditioned reflex could not be reliably elicited. Within the framework of Pavlov's conceptual interests, the constraints imposed on each dog were successful because they enabled him to select from nature and test his hypotheses. Questions about the realism of experimental situations are misplaced because they confuse the issues of internal and ecological validity. Internal validity is a matter of control in experiments, while ecological validity refers to the application of scientific knowledge to natural situations

B. Mundane and Experimental Realism

Aronson and Carlsmith (1968) consider two types of realism—mundane and experimental—to be important in affecting the behavior of subjects in the laboratory. *Mundane realism* refers to the degree that what happens in the laboratory is likely to happen in the outside world. Reading a newspaper has mundane realism, while putting round pegs in square holes does not. Many of the tasks given subjects do not resemble anything they have ever experienced before. The more abstract and unreal the task, the more danger there is that it will not involve the subject. He may not take such tasks very seriously, and therefore his performance may not reflect what the experimenter is interested in studying. But there are many real-world tasks that are boring and uninvolving; so similarity to the real world is no guarantee of subject involvement.

Experimental realism refers to those features of the experimental situation that strongly motivate the subject to react to independent variable manipulations. That is, the subject responds as intended by the experimenter to those aspects of the environment that are crucial to the purpose of the research. Without experimental realism the subject may be disinterested, bored, and possibly inattentive to or contemptuous of instructions. While both mundane and experimental realism contribute to subject involvement, a high degree of experimental realism may eliminate the need for mundane realism. Some degree of mundane realism may be built into experimental procedures as part of the effort to establish experimental realism.

Subjects are generally unenthusiastic about filling out questionnaires, nor do they get very involved when asked to imagine themselves in hypothetical situations. If an experiment consists of playing a game with another person for points, a subject may be less involved than he would be if the stakes were money. The many studies reported throughout this book typically involve procedures intended to establish experimental realism and engage the subjects' motivation. Nevertheless, there are serious limitations on the kinds of manipulations that can be used. Extreme conflict, hostility, need, and so forth cannot be readily or uniformly manipulated in the laboratory. As Freedman, Carlsmith, and Sears (1970) have said, "The subject cannot be terrified; he cannot be made terribly sad; he cannot be made hysterical with laughter. In most cases this simply means that the effects are less strong than they would be if the variables were more extreme but that the basic relationships are the same. However, it is a serious weakness when there is reason to believe that high levels of a variable would produce different effects from intermediate ones" (p. 431).

C. The Power of the Experimenter

The very use of the word "subjects" implies a power differential in the experiment. Tedeschi and O'Donovan (1971) reminded psychologists of the early political meaning of the term. A king had divine rights, and his subjects were subservient. A later meaning of the word is closer to current usage; a subject is a cadaver dissected for anatomical study or used for exhibition purposes. Both the political and medical meanings are retained today, as we can see by analyzing an experiment from the subject's point of view.

The subject enters the realm of the experimenter (the laboratory) and is given directions about what he must do. The relationship is impersonal because the experimenter must treat all subjects in exactly the same way; sometimes the entire situation is automated with instructions and responses electronically recorded. The experimenter has planned the situation and carefully followed a prepared script. He is not discourteous (since he does not want to start a rebellion), but he usually attends to only those responses of subjects which are relevant to his manipulations and measurements. Only a fraction of what the subject does may be perceived by the experiment-

er. From the subject's point of view, he might just as well be anonymous; each subject is considered an average person who is of interest only for the period of time necessary to record a predetermined portion of his behavior. It will be remembered that experiments are done with groups of subjects and that average scores, rather than individual responses, are of primary interest. The identity and uniqueness of the individual is irrelevant and unimportant in most experiments. So it must have been with the king and his subjects.

The experiment is usually sanctioned as part of the activity of a prestigious institution such as a university. The subject therefore grants legitimate authority to the experimenter and submits to his direction. The subject is not told what aspect of himself or his behavior is under examination. Orne (1962) has shown that under such conditions the subject usually suspends his own judgment and is willing to do whatever he is told. Orne asked some of his acquaintances if they would do him a favor and, when they agreed, he asked them to do five push-ups. Invariably, he was asked the question, "Why?" But when he got a similar group of people to agree to participate in an experiment and asked them to perform the five push-ups, the question was, "Where?" When a request is made in the context of an experiment the subject considers it legitimate, and it is accepted that the experimenter need not inform subjects about his purpose.

The "quasi-magic" of science helps to establish experimental realism and motivates subjects to persist even in absurd tasks. Frank (1944) supplied subjects with a marble and a steel ball and informed them they were to balance one upon the other—an impossible task. Nevertheless, the subjects persisted as long as the experimenter gave the impression the task was not yet finished. This strongly cooperative attitude of subjects produces a problem of control. If subjects are strongly motivated to please the experimenter, their behavior may not be strictly a function of the independent variable, but rather an interaction of both the presence of a powerful experimenter *and* the independent variable.

D. Demand Characteristics

Subjects are said to be hypothesis-generating organisms. While the investigator does his best to conceal the purpose of the experiment, the subject makes use of whatever information and cues are available to guess what the hypothesis is. The subject may say to himself, "although he won't tell me what he expects me to do in this situation, I'll bet he hopes I do so-and-so. Therefore, in order to help him, I will do it." Sometimes the subject will be right, but often his guesses will be wrong. As a consequence of this problem-solving approach to experiments, the subjects' responses may not reflect the effects of the independent variable but instead may be due to other cues in the situation. Orne has referred to any cues in the situation which generate nonplanned hypotheses by subjects as *demand characteristics*.

Demand characteristics may be interpreted as tacit or implicit commands from an experimenter (the authority) to subjects (subordinates). The tacit messages conveyed by environmental arrangements, procedural details, and response limitations may sufficiently support one another to communicate clearly the experimenter's expectations to most subjects in a given condition. For example, Orne observes that in an experiment in which the same questionnaire is administered both before and after some events occur, even the dullest subject is aware that some change is expected. To be cooperative, the subject need only guess the direction of the desired change and on what items of the questionnaire to express it.

A recent controversy further illustrates the problem of demand characteristics. Berkowitz and LePage (1967) paired subjects with an experimenter's confederate and asked each of the two parties to list publicity ideas. The two were then separated and the confederate evaluated the subject's ideas by delivering shocks to the latter's fingers. One shock indicated an excellent performance, while ten shocks indicated a very poor performance. In one condition subjects received one shock; in another condition they received seven shocks. All subjects were then asked to evaluate their moods. Next, they were given an opportunity to "evaluate" the confederate's list of ideas. Some of the subjects in each condition found a revolver and shot gun near the shocking key; others found nothing next to the key. Although the experimental design was actually more complex than this, the main finding showed that subjects who received seven shocks retaliated with more shocks than subjects who had received only one shock. In addition, more shocks were delivered in the seven-shock condition when weapons were nearby than if there were no weapons. This weapons-eliciting effect on the degree of retaliation was not found in the one-shock condition.

Page and Scheidt (1971) contended that the weapons were a dead giveaway of the experimenter's hypothesis in the seven-shock condition. If subjects generally do not expect a peer to deliver many shocks, then the receipt of seven shocks may elicit some suspicion about the purpose of the experiment. Then the subjects were asked about their mood—including anger. Finally, subjects in the weapons condition must have believed that these objects were somehow involved in what was going on. Putting all these cues together might well suggest to subjects that they were expected to be more "aggressive." Thus the weapons-eliciting effect may be the manifestation of the subjects' attempts to cooperate with the experimenter and behave as he apparently wanted them to. Page and Scheidt twice failed to replicate the weapons-eliciting effect with naive subjects, but found that more sophisticated upper classmen showed a weak weapons-eliciting effect. They argued that sophisticated undergraduates were better able to decode the cues provided to them.

We encourage you to read Berkowitz' (1971) reply to the criticism. The dispute is by no means settled. Criticisms of research in terms of demand characteristics are often flip and careless. Conjectures about the presence of demand characteristics must be tested just like any other hypothesis. Even if subsequent research should demonstrate the effects of demand characteristics, the results from the original experiment may still be theoretically interesting. Berkowitz and LePage, for example, may have demonstrated that subjects will deliver an increasing number of weak shocks to a peer if they decode cues as indicating this type of behavior is desired by the high status experimenter. This is in itself an exciting finding. It is one thing for an authority to demand obedience to his commands to harm others, but it is another for subordinates to harm others in anticipation that it will please their superior.

The investigator may attempt to discover the presence of demand characteristics by thorough post-experimental interviews with subjects. However, as Orne (1969) has pointed out, a "pact of ignorance" may interfere with the frankness with which subjects will reveal their awareness of cues. The subject "knows that if he has 'caught on' to some apparent deception and had an excess of information about the experimental procedure, he may be disqualified from participation and thus have wasted his time. The experimenter is aware that the subject who knows too much or has 'caught on' to his deception will have to be disqualified; disqualification means running yet another subject, still further delaying completion of his study. Hence, neither party to the inquiry wants to dig very deeply" (Orne, 1969, p.153). Nevertheless, carefully structured interviews may reveal a great deal about how the subjects viewed the situation.

Since most experiments allow only one

factor to vary across different conditions, the cues available to subjects are much the same in all conditions. The presence of demand characteristics is more likely to conceal a real difference between conditions than to produce a difference. The exception to this rule is when the independent variables interact with situational cues. Systematic manipulation of situational cues would be required to demonstrate whether such an interaction occurs. Demand characteristics can be detected, minimized, or eliminated by careful pilot studies, post-experimental interview procedures, and experiments to check for the interaction of situational variables with independent variable manipulations.

E. Experimenter Effects

The experimenter may unintentionally affect the results he obtains from his research. He may introduce bias either by directly influencing the subject's behavior or by inaccurately recording and analyzing the data. Rosenthal (1969) has classified experimenter effects into three categories: (1) *biosocial*, which includes those experimenter characteristics that relate to his identity, such as age, physical appearance, sex, or race; (2) *psychosocial*, which refers to the personality characteristics of the experimenter, such as anxiety level or authoritarianism; and (3) *situational*, which includes the experimenter-subject interaction and the appearance of the laboratory.

Biosocial factors often have no effect on the results of an experiment. When they do, the effect is usually specific to the nature of the situation. For example, Summers and Hammonds (1966) found that the presence of a Negro experimenter had a considerable effect in decreasing the amount of anti-Negro prejudice reported by white subjects. On the other hand, Womack and Wagner (1967) found no effect of race on patients' responses to professional interviewers. The presence or absence of biosocial effects on the responses of subjects must be tested, like any other hypothesis, when it is plausible to expect their occurrence.

A psychosocial factor such as friendliness or aloofness can affect the way subjects respond to a situation. For example, in an experiment in which subjects were asked to make up sentences and were approved for using certain pronouns, subjects were more responsive to the approval when the experimenter was liked than when he was disliked (Berkowitz & Zigler, 1965). One way to eliminate systematic psychosocial effects is to utilize a rather large number of experimenters and make sure each of them runs an equal number of subjects in all conditions of the experiment. In this way, psychosocial effects can be assumed to be equally present in all conditions and the experimenters can be confident that no systematic differences can be caused by them.

Perhaps the most important situational factor that may undermine the internal validity of an experiment is the investigator's knowledge of his hypothesis. He may unintentionally bias his procedures and maximize the probability of obtaining results supporting his hypothesis. Experimenter-expectancy effects were found by Rosenthal and Fode (1963). Twelve students in an experimental psychology class were divided into two groups and were asked to train rats in a T-maze that had white and grey arms. There was food in the correct side (either white or grey) and the detachable arms were shifted from right to left over the trials. Half the student-experimenters were told their rats had been bred to be good maze learners (maze-bright) and half were told their rats were maze-dull. The information given to students apparently affected the way they ran the rats. The rats arbitrarily identified as bright performed better than those falsely identified as dull. The difference in performance was not a function of the genetics of the rats, but apparently of the expectations of the experimenters.

Rosenthal (1969) has reported a series of studies showing experimenter-expectancy effects. These studies have been criticized on several grounds. The student-experimenters, who presumably had a vested interest in completing the class-assigned experiment as fast as they could, were not checked for cheating (Barber & Silver, 1968). Perhaps they provided Rosenthal with the results he clearly expected. The studies were carried out with untrained undergraduate students. It is not obvious that trained and experienced scientists would make the same kinds of errors. Despite these criticisms, Rosenthal's work has led social psychologists to take precautions to control for experimenter-expectancy effects. Experimenters may be kept "blind" to the hypotheses under study or many experimenters may be used and randomly distributed so that each runs an equal number of subjects in all conditions. These procedures should reduce the probability of these effects.

F. Subject Effects

Pre-experimental attitudes and motivations of subjects may affect how they react to the research setting. Four types of subject attitudes have been identified as important in experiments: cooperative, apprehensive, faithful, and negativistic. We have already referred to Orne's view of subjects as cooperative and eager to confirm the experimenter's hypotheses. Subjects may be apprehensive because the experimenter is a psychologist. Many naive people believe (wrongly) that a psychologist has the ability to uncover their deepest and most secret motives and that this keen insight is focused on them. *Evaluation apprehension* may motivate a subject to present himself in a manner calculated to produce an image of a normal or average, adjusted, mature, and emotionally adequate person (Rosenberg, 1965). As a consequence, the subject does not act spontaneously or as he would in a nonexperimental situation.

Fillenbaum (1966) has characterized

some subjects as *faithful* and concerned in a docile way with following the instructions given to them. They may be uninvolved and apathetic and do as they are told (and no more) because it is the simplest way to complete participation in the study, or they may take their commitment seriously and attempt to act as they normally would. The faithful subject does not try to guess the experimenter's hypothesis and does not attempt to undermine the purposes of the study.

Masling (1966) emphasizes the "screw you" attitude of subjects who resent the experimenter's attempts to control their behavior or who react against an obnoxious experimenter or some undesirable element in the situation, such as electric shock. The *negativistic subject* may try to disrupt the experimenter's plans or to disconfirm the experimenter's hypothesis. Even though the negativistic subject may not correctly guess the hypothesis, his actions are motivated by factors other than the experimental situation.

Weber and Cook (1972) recently reviewed the research evidence regarding subject roles in experiments and concluded that the various roles all tend to lead to the same kind of response. A cooperative subject is faithful and will present himself in a favorable way. Even the behavior of the negativistic subject can be interpreted as motivated by a concern for "looking good." For example, a negativistic subject may stubbornly maintain his independence in a study of conformity, but since conformity is negatively valued, favorable self-presentation requires the adoption of an independent (and negativistic) role.

Evaluation apprehension is probably quite prevalent among subjects. It is therefore necessary to disguise from subjects what kinds of behavior are "correct," "good," and "normal." But evaluation apprehension can also contribute to experimental realism because it promotes attention to instructions and involvement in tasks. Concern for self-presentation is not unique to experiments, but is characteristic of everyday life. The available evidence indicates that evaluation apprehension does not introduce bias into experiments unless demand characteristics are also present (Rosenberg, 1969).

VI. THE ETHICS OF RESEARCH

The social psychologist faces some tough ethical questions in carrying out his research. Subjects are sometimes observed without their consent or they may be coerced in a variety of ways to participate in experiments. Research may involve invasion of privacy, deception, or procedures entailing physical and psychological discomfort or pain. Subjects may be treated as objects rather than as human equals of the experimenter. Virtually all investigators would prefer to avoid these practices, but they must balance their concern against the importance of carrying out their scientific enterprise. The American Psychological Association has developed ethical guidelines (see Box 2.1) to assist the investigator in resolving his dilemmas.

A. The Dilemma of Informed Consent and Effective Research

The investigator ought to obtain the informed consent of his subjects. That is, not only should the subject freely agree to participate, but he should know exactly what it is he is agreeing to do. Yet the experimenter cannot tell the subject what the research design and hypotheses are because such knowledge would constitute a demand characteristic and would destroy the internal validity of the experiment. The investigator must either forgo doing his study or must misrepresent the purposes of the research. Usually the subject is willing to place himself in the hands of the social psychologist. The experimenter-subject relationship may be interpreted as a contractual bond. As part of the contract, it is ac-

Box 2.1
ETHICAL PRINCIPLES IN THE CONDUCT OF
RESEARCH WITH HUMAN PARTICIPANTS

Ad hoc Committee on Ethical Standards
in Psychological Research

Published by
American Psychological Association, Inc.
1200 Seventeenth Street, N.W.
Washington, D.C. 20036

THE ETHICAL PRINCIPLES

The decision to undertake research should rest upon a considered judgment by the individual psychologist about how best to contribute to psychological science and to human welfare. The responsible psychologist weighs alternative directions in which personal energies and resources might be invested. Having made the decision to conduct research, psychologists must carry out their investigations with respect for the people who participate and with concern for their dignity and welfare. The Principles that follow make explicit the investigator's ethical responsibilities toward participants over the course of research, from the initial decision to pursue a study to the steps necessary to protect the confidentiality of research data. These Principles should be interpreted in terms of the context provided in the complete document offered as a supplement to these Principles.

1. In planning a study the investigator has the personal responsibility to make a careful evaluation of its ethical acceptability, taking into account these Principles for research with human beings. To the extent that this appraisal, weighing scientific and humane values, suggests a deviation from any Principle, the investigator incurs an increasingly serious obligation to seek ethical advice and to observe more stringent safeguards to protect the rights of the human research participant.

2. Responsibility for the establishment and maintenance of acceptable ethical practice in research always remains with the individual investigator. The investigator is also responsible for the ethical treatment of research participants by collaborators, assistants, students, and employees, all of whom, however, incur parallel obligations.

3. Ethical practice requires the investigator to inform the participant of all features of the research that reasonably might be exptected to influence willingness to participate and to explain all other aspects of the research about which the participant inquires. Failure to make full disclosure gives added emphasis to the investigator's responsibility to protect the welfare and dignity of the research participant.

4.   Openness and honesty are essential characteristics of the relationship between investigator and research participant. When the methodological requirements of a study necessitate concealment or deception, the investigator is required to ensure the participant's understanding of the reasons for this action and to restore the quality of the relationship with the investigator.

5.   Ethical research practice requires the investigator to respect the individual's freedom to decline to participate in research or to discontinue participation at any time. The obligation to protect this freedom requires special vigilance when the investigator is in a position of power over the participant. The decision to limit this freedom increases the investigator's responsibility to protect the participant's dignity and welfare.

6.   Ethically acceptable research begins with the establishment of a clear and fair agreement between the investigator and the research participant that clarifies the responsibilities of each. The investigator has the obligation to honor all promises and commitments included in that agreement.

7.   The ethical investigator protects participants from physical and mental discomfort, harm, and danger. If the risk of such consequences exists, the investigator is required to inform the participant of that fact, secure consent before proceeding, and take all possible measures to minimize distress. A research procedure may not be used if it is likely to cause serious and lasting harm to participants.

8.   After the data are collected, ethical practice requires the investigator to provide the participant with a full clarification of the nature of the study and to remove any misconceptions that may have arisen. Where scientific or humane values justify delaying or withholding information the investigator acquires a special responsibility to assure that there are no damaging consequences for the participant.

9.   Where research procedures may result in undesirable consequences for the participant, the investigator has the responsibility to detect and remove or correct these consequences, including, where relevant, long-term aftereffects.

10.   Information obtained about the research participants during the course of an investigation is confidential. When the possibility exists that others may obtain access to such information, ethical research practice requires that this possibility, together with the plans for protecting confidentiality, be explained to the participants as a part of the procedure for obtaining informed consent.

---

knowledged that the experimenter possesses information not available to the subject. The subject expects his interests to be protected by the experimenter and abdicates responsibility for what will take place.

The degree of trust vested in the experimenter by subjects has been shown by Orne and Evans (1965). Subjects, who were told they were unhypnotized controls in a hypnosis study, were told to handle poisonous snakes or place their hands in acid, and without hesitation they did as they were told. Apparently, subjects assume the experimenter will not allow them to be harmed.

Whenever physical or psychological discomfort could result from the subject's participation in a research project, he is said to be at risk. He must be informed prior to participation about the nature of the risk. For example, if electric shocks are to be administered or received by the subject, he must be given the option of refusing to participate. Whether a subject should be placed at risk is a question that requires weighing the magnitude of the risk against the merits of the research. The difficulty of making this decision can be illustrated by a recent study designed to simulate actual conditions in prison (Zimbardo, Haney, Banks, & Jaffe, 1972).

Twenty-one volunteers were recruited through a newspaper advertisement and were paid fifteen dollars a day for participating. Pretesting and depth interviews were conducted to select from the original 70 volunteers those who were emotionally stable and in the normal range of the psychological characteristics measured. Half of the subjects were randomly assigned as prisoners and the other half were designated as guards.

Each prisoner was picked up at his home by a city policeman in a squad car. The prisoner was frisked, handcuffed, and taken to the station house, where he was fingerprinted and booked. He was then blindfolded and taken to a simulated jail on the Stanford University campus which was identified with an indoor sign as the Stanford County Jail. Each prisoner was then stripped, deloused, issued a uniform and a number, and placed into a six-by-nine windowless cell with two other prisoners. Minimum toilet facilities were in a nearby location. Access to the toilet was denied after ten o'clock at night and buckets were placed in the cell for use during the night. As punishment, the guard sometimes denied any use of the toilet facilities, with the

result that the cell sometimes had a foul smell.

The guards were given nearly absolute power over the prisoners. Billy clubs, handcuffs, whistles, and keys were provided, and the guards were told to enforce the prison rules rigidly. Some of the guards made up their own rules and treated the prisoners in a brutal fashion. The abuse of power by the guards was described by Zimbardo et al.: "They made the prisoners obey petty, meaningless, and often inconsistent rules, forced them to engage in tedious, useless work such as moving cartons back and forth between closets and picking thorns out of their blankets for hours on end. Not only did the prisoners have to sing songs or laugh or refrain from smiling on command, but they were encouraged to curse and vilify each other publicly" (p. 10).

Three prisoners had to be released in the first four days because of severe psychological reactions; after six days of the planned two weeks of the study, the simulation had to be terminated. By this time four of the prisoners had suffered severe emotional disturbance, and one had developed a rash over his entire body. Intervention was also necessary because some of the guards had become so brutal as to endanger the physical welfare of the prisoners.

A number of ethical questions can be raised about this study of prison life. The researchers have said they did not anticipate the degree of brutality that occurred and terminated the study as soon as it became evident how great the risks were to the subjects. When it was clear after three days that four subjects had to be terminated, why did the researchers continue the study for three more days? Did the merit of the study justify the risks to the subjects? What was learned? Or, more precisely, what hypotheses were tested? Did the simulation really mirror life in prison, or did it merely reflect the prejudices and stereotypes of college students about how prison guards behave? Did the experimenters violate the trust subjects placed in them? Questions of this kind should be raised and answered before, not after, a study is conducted. The ethics involved could have been explored with prison officials, psychiatrists, and lay citizens. Fortunately, most research in social psychology does not present the complexity of ethical issues raised by this study.

Epstein, Suedfeld, and Silverstein (1973) examined the subject's view of the "contract" with the experimenter. Respondents to a questionnaire revealed their expectations. "Over 85% of the subjects expect to be respected by the experimenter, to have information about them kept confidential and to deal with a competent experimenter. ... Between 70 and 85% of the subjects expected that they would be given clear instructions, that they would not be told the purposes of the experiment, that embarrassing information about them would not be shown to others who were participating at the same time, that the experimenter would be punctual, and that the experiment would be enjoyable" (p.217). The respondents also acknowledged the appropriateness of two undesirable events: the use of electric shock and deception. They believed these features of the experiment constituted a legitimate part of the procedures they accepted when they agreed to participate. It can be said that social psychologists generally fulfull all these expectations in the way they conduct research.

B. Recruitment of Subjects

Although college students represent only three percent of the population, they are the subjects in from 70 to 85 percent of the published research in social psychology. This bias in the selection of subjects reflects the fact that social psychologists must use the resources available to them in conducting their research. College students may not adequately represent the general population, however. They differ in terms of age, intelligence, verbal skills, socio-economic background, and a host of other characteristics. If college students behave differently from the noncollege population, generalizations of research findings must be restricted until further studies increase the heterogeneity of the population sampled.

The use of volunteer subjects may further complicate the problem of generalizability. About seven percent of the human subjects used in university research are volunteers (Jung, 1969). It is known that volunteers are different from nonvolunteers in a number of respects. Rosenthal and Rosnow (1969) have reviewed the relevant research and conclude that volunteers are more intelligent, have stronger needs for approval, and are less authoritarian than nonvolunteers. Thus volunteers add further bias, but there are far too few volunteers available to conduct the amount of research done with human subjects. In order to solve these problems, many psychology departments require that introductory psychology students participate in experiments.

Several justifications have been given for requiring students to participate in research. Most introductory science courses (biology, chemistry, physics) require students to take a laboratory section to complement lectures. Because psychology courses are so popular, it is impossible to provide the laboratory space, supervisory personnel, and equipment to give so many students laboratory experience. By participation as a subject, the student gains some idea of what the research psychologist does. The student also gains an opportunity to contribute to the development of knowledge, which is a major function of a university. A strong ethical obligation is placed on the investigator to provide sufficient information to the students so they can learn from their experiences as subjects. This can be done in immediate debriefing following the experiment, a guest appearance in class, or by sending students a written account of the study.

C. The Problem of Deception

Social psychological experiments are generally concerned with how persons interact with one another. A common practice is to employ confederates who are presented to subjects as peers. Confederates act out a preplanned role in the experiment. Subjects may also be deceived about the purpose of a study, may be provided with false or misleading information about the meaning of various procedures, and may even be deceived about when the experiment has terminated. These deceptions are perpetrated in the belief that subjects would act differently if they were told the truth.

Kelman (1967) has been among the most vocal of those who are concerned about the long-run effects of deception on the credibility of psychologists. He sincerely doubts that a social psychology can be founded on the basis of lies. The questions raised by Kelman are researchable. Will subjects come to expect deception, and will trust and respect for psychologists be undermined? In two separate studies (Fillenbaum, 1966; Cook, Beam, Calder, Frey, Krevetz, & Reisman, 1970), the subjects who participated in an experiment were told in debriefing about the deceptions that had been used. These same subjects then participated in one or more subsequent experiments and were compared with subjects who either had not been or did not know they had been deceived in previous experiments. No effects of previous deception on behavior or attitudes were found. However, Fine and Lindskold (1971) found that repeated deceptions may produce some minor effects on behavior and evaluation apprehension.

Deception in advertising and politics is a common feature of life. There are two differences from everyday life in the use of deception by experimenters. There is no attempt to exploit the subjects, and all of the deceptions are revealed after the experiment is over. Experimenters should make a serious effort to find ways of doing research that do not require deception, but failing to find such an alternative, they should remain aware that the subject has a right to know. If in debriefing, the experimenter divulges the reasons for his deceptions and does not act smug about his cleverness, most subjects will not be offended and will have learned something from the experience.

A particularly objectionable form of deception occurs when subjects are told an experiment is over when it is not. In studies of helping behavior, subjects are sometimes deceived into believing they have broken equipment or spilled a box of alphabetically arranged index cards. After the experiment is allegedly terminated, a confederate may leave with the subject and ask him for help or ask for a contribution to a worthy cause. The amount and frequency of helping is then taken as a dependent measure. The problem with this procedure is that the subject has given his consent only for the duration of the experiment. Therefore, his post-experimental behavior is observed without his knowledge or consent.

Kelman has suggested role-playing as an alternative to deception. Subjects can be asked to tell the experimenter what they would do in a particular situation. A statement of intentions by subjects about what they would do is referred to as a *behavioroid measure*. Unfortunately, as we shall show throughout this book, what subjects say they would do is often not related to what they actually do (cf. Freedman, 1969). It is too easy for subjects to say whatever they think will bring a positive evaluation from the experimenter. A second type of role-playing consists of asking subjects to pretend that a setting is real and act out a particular part in the situation (like the guards in the prison study). This kind of role-playing is analogous to extemporaneous acting on the stage and may be more informative about the subjects' biases and prejudices than about the simulated situation. Of course, research could be carried out to establish when role playing can be used to study particular processes and when it cannot. However, at the present time it does not appear that role-playing is an adequate substitute for deception experiments in many areas of social psychological research.

D. The Ethics of Field Experiments

Three major ethical problems are associated with field experiments: informed consent, debriefing, and invasion of privacy. A failure to obtain informed consent from subjects in many field experiments is justified by the fact that the behavior under observation is public and open to observation by anyone. Debriefing is usually avoided because being informed may create anger or distress in the subjects; the principle followed is that ignorance is less disturbing to the individual, and that a full debriefing would bring him very few if any benefits. Protection of the anonymity of subjects and the nature of their public behavior blunts the charge that their privacy has been invaded.

There are occasions when considerable distress may be created for subjects in field studies. A pedestrian can be "shook up" by observing a confederate feign a heart attack or a motorist may be distracted by a contrived event and run into something. These are of course remote possibilities, but the social psychologist must consider the risks involved to subjects before he enters the field and intervenes in their lives.

VII. CHAPTER SUMMARY

Informal methods of acquiring and assessing knowledge involve a number of uncertainties. To rely on a dogmatic authority requires vesting total trust in him since there is no way to check what he says. Reports of revelations and miracles amount to communications from dogmatic authorities. Furthermore, direct revelations cannot be distinguished from hallucina-

tions, even by the person experiencing them. An event may be considered a miracle because of the witnesses' preconceptions and expectations or because they were fooled. Self-evident truths often turn out in the cold light of history to be delusions, and the common sense beliefs of prior generations may be considered fantastic by the present one. Without independent verification the informal methods of intuition, revelation, miracle, common sense and authority cannot be trusted.

The scientist insists on engaging in a complex and laborious process of inquiry in an attempt to control his own biases and values. The scientific method involves a cycle from observation of facts to the construction of hypotheses and theories and back to controlled observations, preferably through experiments. A hypothesis must be testable, but it can never be proven. In uncovering functional relationships and building and evaluating scientific theories, the scientist is confronted with the task of operationalizing his concepts and developing rigorous and systematic methods.

Experiments must be designed and carried out to minimize the impact of extraneous variables on the dependent measure. An experiment is internally valid when the results may be attributed to the effects of the independent variable. Errors due to subject variability and faulty measurement may be controlled through random assignment of subjects and appropriate statistical analyses of the data. The external validity of the experiment depends upon how generalizable the findings are to other experimental settings in which the same functional relationship is investigated and different subjects, procedures, or operational definitions are used. Ecological validity refers to the generalizability of scientific principles to the practical world of affairs and is a more appropriate demand to be made of theories than of specific experiments.

Social psychologists have developed a number of measurement techniques and nonlaboratory methods for studying social behavior. The correlation statistic provides a method for measuring the strength of association between two sets of scores. Predictions and hypotheses can be developed from correlation results but they require further evaluation. A single correlation is not evidence of a functional relationship between events because the effects of extraneous variables are not controlled. However, more sophisticated correlational techniques are being devised which allow evaluations of causal models of social processes.

Paper-and-pencil tests have been devised to assess attitudes, motives, and personality characteristics. These tests must have empirically established reliability and validity. A test must be reliable to be valid, though the reverse is not always true. Content analyses of communications can be used for a variety of purposes, but the reliability and validity of this promising technique have yet to be firmly established.

Clinical methods focus upon single individuals; observations usually occur over a considerable period of time, during which tests and interviews may be conducted. Surveys consist of structured interviews of a sample of persons representative of a larger population. Nonlaboratory methods, including natural observations and natural and field experiments, provide a rich source of hypotheses regarding social behavior. However, the lack of control inherent in these methods precludes drawing firm conclusions from them until experiments which are uncontaminated by extraneous variables confirm the functional relationships hypothesized.

Many special problems arise in conducting social psychological research. The artificiality of the laboratory may make it necessary to use procedures that reflect mundane realism in order to establish experimental realism. Experiments are not intended to be simulations of the real world. The chief criterion of a good experiment is internal validity. Demand characteristics can undermine the internal validity

of an experiment, but proper debriefing and the use of additional controls can detect or minimize the problem. Biosocial, psychosocial, and situational factors can all adversely affect results. Though these experimenter-effects have probably been overemphasized by some social psychologists, precautions must be taken to avoid them.

Subjects may play good, faithful, negativistic, or evaluatively apprehensive roles in the research setting. In general, subjects are aware they are under observation and present themselves in a manner designed to elicit positive evaluation from the experimenter. It is therefore important that evaluative cues are not provided and that subjects are kept uncertain about what constitutes "correct" behavior in the situation.

The subject in psychological experiments expects to be treated professionally and trusts the experimenter to protect his rights and welfare. The subject must be informed if his physical or psychological well-being are at risk in the research setting. Even when informed consent is obtained from subjects, the investigator must make a judgment about whether the risks involved are outweighed by the importance of the study. The drafting of students for research purposes has been justified as a learning experience relevant to the understanding of psychology in introductory courses and constitutes a contribution to the university's task of developing new knowledge.

Deception is often a necessary procedure in social psychological research in order to disguise the purposes of the investigation from the subjects. Deception is considered undesirable by subjects, but they accept it as a legitimate part of research. The experimenter has an ethical responsibility to minimize the use of deception and to inform subjects that deceptions are used in his research. The public nature of behavior in field settings relaxes some of the ethical obligations of social psychologists to gain informed consent, to conduct debriefings, and to provide information about the deceptions used.

SUGGESTED READINGS

Adair, J. G. *The human subject: The social psychology of the psychological experiment.* Boston: Little, Brown, 1973. A very readable and succinct account of the social psychology of the experiment.

Jung, J. *The experimenter's dilemma.* New York: Harper & Row, 1971. A lengthy survey of the problems associated with social psychological research including a discussion of the ethics of research. Additional readings are provided in the form of a dozen papers.

Kemeny, J. *A philosopher looks at science.* New York: Van Nostrand, 1959. A sophisticated yet readable treatment of the philosophy of science and scientific method.

Kuhn, T. S. *The structure of scientific revolutions.* Chicago: University of Chicago Press, 1962. A brilliant analysis of the evolutionary and revolutionary changes that occur in basic scientific concepts.

Lindsey, G., and Aronson, E. (Eds.) *The handbook of social psychology.* Vol. 2. (2nd ed.). Reading, Mass.: Addison-Wesley, 1968. Essential reading for all social psychology majors. Includes sections on experimentation in social psychology, data analysis, attitude measurement, systematic observational methods, interviewing, content analysis, and problems associated with cross-cultural research.

Rosenblatt, P. C., and Miller, N. Expermental methods. In C. G. McClintock (Ed.), *Experimental social psychology.* New York: Holt, Rinehart, & Winston, 1972. A detailed discussion of the aims of experimental design which gives some additional designs not discussed in this text.

PART 2

Defining the Social Situation

Why do you believe as you do? Consider the many beliefs you have accumulated. Where did they come from? Among the sources you would probably list experience, common sense, teachers, parents, the clergy, scientists, propagandists, newspapers, magazines, books, radio, and television. How do you sample these sources and are they reliable? How much of what you believe is really true? Do people tend to agree with one another? What happens when you publicly adopt a controversial point of view and defend it against a majority opinion? Chapter 3 will focus on what the social psychologist has learned about these kinds of questions. We will see that other people play a strong role in building an individual's picture of the world; they filter information, distort it and censor it. Each of us has a need for information, and we are dependent on each other for ways of interpreting and categorizing our experiences. Of course the way an individual responds to a situation depends on how he defines it. Understanding how each person constructs his own theory about the nature of reality is therefore an important part of studying his social behavior.

Other people make up a very significant part of our world. The characteristics attributed to others, such as personality traits, emotional states, attitudes, and trustworthiness, allow us to predict what they are apt to do in various situations. As we shall see in Chapter 4, recent research and theory concerned with person perception conceives of the perceiver as an amateur scientist who attempts to uderstand the causes of the behavior of others and of his own. At the same time he attempts to integrate specific bits of information to achieve consistent overall impressions of others. The principles which govern attributions, judgments, and impressions constitute the focus of contemporary research dealing with person perception.

What the person learns about his physical and social environment is represented in his beliefs, values, and attitudes. The relationships among these cognitive elements have been the subject of a number of attitude theories. Also, it has generally been assumed that there should be a consistency between a person's attitudes and his subsequent behavior. However, evidence has not strongly supported this relationship. On the other hand, it has been found that there is a strong tendency for people to maintain consistency between their behavior and the subsequent expression of their attitudes. These issues are discussed in Chapter 5.

The development of the individual and his views of the world are greatly influenced by socialization agents. The child adjusts his attitudes and his behavior to gain the approval of those around him and to avoid their disapproval. Although many of the child's lessons are learned through teaching and experience, he also profits from merely observing the behavior of others. He imitates models who are successful and whom he likes or respects. Intellectual development apparently takes place in a sequence of stages and affects the way the person makes moral judgments. His moral behavior reflects both personal characteristics and situational factors. As the individual develops, he forms a concept of himself and adopts a particular style of interacting with other people. These developmental processes will be discussed in Chapter 6.

The material in Part 2 emphasizes the manifold ways in which the individual is influenced by those around him. The way he constructs his version of reality, his subjective experiencing of emotions, the values he holds, and his conception of himself are all products of his interactions with other people. At the same time the individual is an active agent who reciprocally influences other people in many of the same ways. As Comte has observed, it is a paradox that man both creates society and is molded by it. Clearly, as the poet John Donne expressed it, "No man is an Iland, intire of itselfe. . ."

CHAPTER **3**

Information Dependence

CHAPTER PREVIEW

Men are basically curious about their environment and seek information in order to gain better predictability and control over it. An individual's view of the world and of himself is constructed out of information gained from direct experience and from other people. What is good or bad, beautiful or ugly, true or false, reality or fantasy is more often a matter of social consensus than of evidence gained from "objective" sources. Just as "the forest fashions the tree" (Gide, 1927, p.256), the human group serves as the reference for the individual's conception of reality. His dependence on other people for information is manifested particularly when he has an incomplete or unstable view of reality and turns to others for help in interpreting events.

Information about the world is screened through social and personal filters and is subject to many distortions before it is finally processed by the individual. Gatekeepers of information, typically represented by the mass media and educational institutions, are important social filters. Deliberate attempts to affect the individual's view of reality are made by propagandists. The individual's attention, selectivity in his memory, and the language he uses in classifying or labeling events serve as personal filters which bias his perception of the information.

The persons with whom an individual associates most regularly have the most influence on his conceptual structuring of the world. Social comparisons are made to seek confirmation of his opinions and values. When persons are in a state of uncertainty about impending events or about what actions might be taken, as is often the case during crises or when the individual is afraid, the need to affiliate with other people becomes increasingly important. Brainwashing is a particularly striking example of the dependence of individuals on the group for information.

Recent research suggests that persons not only interpret the outer world in the context of comparisons with others, but also look for social cues in interpreting their own emotional experiences. A two-factor theory of emotion views emotional states as consisting both of physiological arousal and of the cognitive label applied by the individual to his experience. The same physiological arousal state can be identified by the experiencing individual as either anger or pleasure, depending on the social cues provided to him in the immediate environment.

While all individuals are subject to the biasing of information through social and personal filters and are reliant on comparison others for interpreting both outer and inner events, individuals differ in the ways in which they process information. Some are more open-minded and others are more dogmatic. Open-minded people tend to make many distinctions regarding the world which are represented by many conceptual categories; their world is cognitively complex. Dogmatists represent the world with relatively few conceptual categroies and tend to view events in terms of polarities; their world is cognitively simple.

I. INFORMATION SEEKING

The study of motivation has tended to focus on those needs which must be satisfied with material rewards. Laboratory animals are deprived of water, food, or social contact, and satiation is made contingent on various responses specified by the psychologist. The tendency has been to overgeneralize and suppose that only material reinforcements motivate behavior. Recently, however, it has become rather clear that both men and other animals are motivated to seek information about their environment.

Charles Sanders Peirce viewed information seeking in motivational terms a century ago. He argued that men strive to attain beliefs. We find doubt to be a stressful and irritating state of mind and attempt to avoid or escape it. Peirce believed doubt was uncomfortable because a man in such a state does not know how to act. Only when a person has formed beliefs about the nature of things and people can he act. If it is known that a train will depart at a particular time for a desired destination, a traveler can plan on being at the station. Ignorance or doubt about the train schedule is not a good basis for planning actions. Doubt stimulates the individual to seek information that can serve as the basis of beliefs. According to Peirce, "as soon as a firm belief is reached we are entirely satisfied, whether the belief be true or false" (1951, p. 60).

A. Exploratory Drives

Research has demonstrated a strong exploratory drive in animal and human subjects when they are presented with novel stimuli or are deprived of stimuli. Even when they are hungry or thirsty, rats will pass up food and water to explore a new environment (Welker, 1961). Butler (1954) observed that monkeys worked long and hard to get a little window open in a barren cell so they could look out and watch a toy train going round and round. Similarly, men will undergo discomfort to satisfy their curiosity. Eloquent historical accounts of man's need to explore are associated with the actions of Sir Edmund Hillary, Thor

Heyerdahl, Scott, Amundsen, Magellan, and thousands of others. Although the statement may be apocryphal, Hillary supposedly said he climbed Mt. Everest, "Because it was there." Perhaps the most important motivation for the pursuit of knowledge in the sciences and humanities is man's native curiosity.

White (1959) postulated an effectance motive to explain exploratory, information-seeking behavior. Clearly, knowledge about the environment has important survival value for organisms that are not completely controlled by instincts. Men must adapt to their environment to gain nourishment, provide themselves with shelter, and preserve their safety against a multitude of dangers. The more understanding the individual has of his environment, the more predictable the outcome of his own behavior is likely to be. The knowledgeable person should attain more rewards and avoid more punishments than a person who lacks information. Curiosity, as Peirce implied, has an important function in making the individual more effective in exchanges with his environment.

Observations of children reveal a strong exploratory drive. An infant who is satiated with food, rest and other creature comforts is not simply a passive organism; instead, he engages in active transactions with his environment, uncovering novelty and finding out how to manipulate and change the environment by his own actions. According to Berlyne (1960), as the child grows older, he becomes more and more selective in his exploratory behavior. Specific needs for information replace a more indiscriminate curiosity. The impetus to seek information regarding a specific topic is related to three factors: (1) the amount of uncertainty, (2) the value of the information sought for the decision to be made, and (3) the probability that there is useful information available (Berlyne, 1965). A mature person will not be inclined to engage in information-seeking behavior if he is fairly certain about an issue, if he thinks the available information will be of little help in making decisions, or if he is convinced that no useful information can be found.

B. Physical and Social Reality

Festinger (1954) was among the first to point out the social psychological importance of the distinction between physical and social reality. Physical reality can be confronted directly and is perceived by one or another of man's senses—vision, audition, pain, taste, etc. The natural sciences and engineering have developed many ways of reliably measuring aspects of physical reality. It is relatively easy for a person raised in one part of the world to learn about the physical reality of another region. For example, a visitor from the tropics can learn about the attributes of snow rather quickly. He can test its coldness by touch or through the use of a thermometer; he can discover that it reduces to water by placing some in his pocket or in a pan on a stove. His beliefs about the coldness and wetness of snow can be repeatedly tested and the evidence of his senses will allow direct confirmation of his beliefs. The visitor's beliefs about snow can be formulated without the aid of other humans; in fact, he is likely to be quite resistant to any attempts by others to convince him that snow is not cold or not reducible to water.

Social reality is not directly available to the senses. Halle (1965) exemplifies the differences between the existential (physical) and conceptual (social) worlds by comparing a house to a nation: "The house is, clearly, a reality of the existential world; you can touch it, you can see it, you can photograph it; it has physical being. But you cannot see the United States of America as such, any more than you can see religious freedom as such. You cannot see the state or touch it, as you can see and touch the house. There is physical territory which we identify with the United States of America. There are woods and fields, houses and roads, cities and towns—but these are not the state. They were there before the state was created and would still be there if the state were abolished tomorrow. Not being, in itself, a physical entity, the state does not, like the house, belong to the existential world. It belongs to the conceptual world" (p.42).

A newcomer to our culture can readily test some aspects of social reality. It would not take long to learn that one does not talk loudly in a library or at a funeral and that eating with one's fingers at a fancy restaurant will bring quick signs of disapproval from others. However, the more intriguing parts of social reality are those that are not so readily or directly tested. How can a belief be tested that the U.S. government's friendly foreign policy toward the fascist government of Spain is injurious to its image as a defender of democratic ideals? Which religion is true? How does one go about deciding whether he is a good golfer? Are you physically attractive or ugly?

Festinger (1954) proposed that persons answer such questions about social reality by making social comparisons with others whose opinions are valued. That is, the individual approaches others who are similar and respected in order to gain consensual validation about his beliefs concerning social reality. His belief about the effects of U.S. foreign policy toward Spain is strengthened if others agree and shaken if they do not; there is little "objective" evidence to consult on the matter. Belief or disbelief in particular religions appears to be mostly a result of gegraphical accident—a person is likely to be a Hindu if born in India, a Catholic in Spain, a Moslem in Iran, and so on. Self-confidence about one's golf game depends upon whether comparisons are made with top professionals or pals at the local country club. The actions of others serve as social mirrors and the reflections give the individual a sense of his physical attractiveness (see Chapter 11 for more on this topic).

The individual's need to attain stable beliefs about social reality is what makes him truly dependent upon other people for information. A person may depend on experts as sources of knowledge about physical reality, but if he wishes to acquire the proper training and make the relevant tests, it would be possible to gain such knowledge from "hard" evidence obtained on his own. In contrast, social reality is a matter of agreement or social consensus.

Radloff (1961) demonstrated the need people have for consensual information. College students were asked to give their opinions concerning the financing problems of higher education. They were then provided with consensual validation in the form of a summary of the opinions of one of three other groups of persons: experts, peers, and high school students. Next, the subjects were asked if they would like to join a discussion group on the topic. Subjects who had been given the validating opinions of inferiors (i.e., high school students) indicated a stronger desire to join a discussion group than those who received validation from either peers or experts. The opinions of high school students were apparently not acceptable as a source of consensual validation.

Radloff also included a control group in his study. These subjects had not given their own opinions prior to being offered an opportunity to join a discussion group. These control subjects showed less interest in discussion than any of the three experimental groups. They had not committed themselves to an opinion, their competence was not under challenge, hence they had no need to seek validation of their opinions.

II. SOCIAL FILTERING

Most of what a person believes about the world is not learned firsthand. Consider some common beliefs of American college students: subatomic particles exist; there are craters on the moon; there is a nation called China, which has a leader named Mao Tse Tung; George Washington was the first president of the United States; the

Democratic National Headquarters at the Watergate was burglarized by a group of men hired with money raised to re-elect the president of the United States; there was a poet named Chaucer; and so on. You are unlikely to have any direct knowledge of any of these events, yet the truth of these beliefs is accepted because none has been strongly contradicted by reliable experts. Writers of textbooks, newspaper reporters, television commentators, and other people are gatekeepers of the information that reaches us. As we shall see, each of these gatekeepers acts as a filter through which information is screened.

Much of the distortion that occurs in the transmission of information is inadvertent, but a great deal is deliberately distorted as a way of producing a calculated effect on the target person. Propaganda messages may be completely accurate, however. The Oxford dictionary defines propaganda as "an association or scheme for propagating a doctrine or practice." A gardener propagates plants, and a propagandist propagates beliefs. As Hitler's propaganda chief, Goebbels, said, "We do not talk to say something, but to obtain a certain effect" (cited in Ellul, 1965, p. X).

The propagandist has many techniques to employ in his attempts to satisfy both the information dependence of his audience and his own interests. The ordinary person is not only the target of the information directed at him by thousands of gatekeepers and propagandists, but is also a victim of censorship and secrecy. A person's view of the world is shaped by what he knows and also by what he does not know. We will direct our attention to the role of gatekeepers, propagandists, and censors in developing our beliefs concerning physical and social reality.

A. Gatekeepers of Information

A source of information about events outside the direct experience of the individual is a *gatekeeper*. A great variety of persons serve gatekeeping functions for us. Our knowledge of the world outside our small area of direct experience is monitored by friends, co-workers, relatives, tourists, expatriates, military personnel, traveling businessmen, novelists, news reporters, and scholars. Beliefs about history and expectations regarding the future are also mediated in the same way.

In Chapter 2 we warned about the dangers of accepting knowledge from authoritative sources. In a society that is relatively free of censorship much of the information provided by gatekeepers is conflicting and contradictory. As a consequence, the individual must analyse the credibility of the sources, and a judgment must be made about which group of witnesses is most trustworthy. If the President of the United States and his military advisers inform the American people that the war in Vietnam is being won, while news accounts and editorial comments indicate that the war is unwinnable, who is one to believe? If a third-grade student learns in school that George Washington never told a lie, and his parents tell him that all men, including George Washington, tell lies, who is the student to believe? The person must consider factors such as the plausibility of the communication or its internal consistency and the credibility, trustworthiness, expertise, and status of the gatekeepers. We will examine these factors in considerable detail in Part III of this book.

To illustrate the problem of reconstructing events through the information provided by gatekeepers, we will take the example of learning about a foreign nation. What do we believe about China and how did we come to believe as we do? Very few Americans have been to China in the last 25 years. Some recent tourist might provide us with accounts of his packaged tour of a model collective farm, fine restaurants, museums, the Great Stone Wall, historical sites, new buildings, and the Peking Opera. Few tourists actually speak the Chinese language or have systematically studied the culture or history of the country before visiting it. The tourist, after all, is not usually interested in doing an anthropological field study; he is trying to have a good time, and his views of the country are apt to be quite superficial.

There are many Chinese expatriates in this country who can tell us about what China was like when they were last there. However, an expatriate is likely to be biased. He may have left the country because of lack of success, ill health, or political difficulties. A Chinese expatriate would no doubt find it difficult to be dispassionate and objective in his description of Mao's China. While the expatriate may be quite expert in some aspects of the culture he left, it would be an error to rely upon him as the sole source of information about China. Consider what you would be able to tell a foreigner about the United States. How confident are you about your ability to describe events here? Are draft resistors living in Sweden for the past five to ten years good gatekeepers of information about the United States?

Military personnel and businessmen often spend protracted periods in foreign countries. As outsiders, they ought to be more objective than the expatriate. But military personnel are often treated in a distinctive way by the population in the host country, and few go much beyond tourism and sensation-seeking in their travels outside their home country. Top-level military officers and businessmen often live in a native-language compound in the host country and this segregation tends to insulate them against the local culture. In the case of China, we have neither military personnel or businessmen maintaining residence in the country.

On an everyday basis our information about events is most likely to be obtained from the press, scholarly books, and influential persons in the community. In general, these three types of gatekeepers do their best to represent events accurately. But, as we shall see, they seldom succeed.

1. The press

Reporters are trained to be objective and to be careful in checking details when gathering their stories. Nevertheless, a reporter must rely heavily on informants since he cannot always be on the scene to observe the happening he reports. The material in a news story is not only chosen by the reporter, it is also selectively reported to him by his news sources. A reporter's view of China may be a blend of what some persons wanted him to believe, the limits of his capacity to inspect personally the country in detail, and his own biases and preconceptions. You are probably aware that news of events taking place in your own community is often incorrectly reported by the local newspaper.

Working newsmen must report to an editor. The editors of the mass media decide what is and what is not news. As Cater (1959) has pointed out, "the press decides which of these words and events shall receive the prompt attention of millions and which, like timber falling in a deep and uninhabited forest, shall crash silently to the ground" (p.14). The criterion for selection is often the presumed interests of readers rather than the importance of the event. The editor may choose to print stories on cultural events in China while ignoring information regarding industrial development. Great attention may be given to the bogus love lives of Hollywood stars while important debates and scientific happenings go unreported or are buried in the back pages of great cosmopolitan newspapers.

Competition among news media for exclusive stories and the stress on timeliness in reporting events provide opportunities for those who seek political, economic, or social advantage to stage events, "leak" information to reporters, or provide public or background interviews to bring attention to specific information and issues. William White (1958), an experienced reporter, observed that the "leak or exclusive story is rarely an example of a reporter's persistence and skill. More often it is simply an evidence of the harassed necessity of some official to put a situation before the public with a spurious sense of drama in order to gain attention for it" (p.79). Desire for revenge or recognition may motivate the disclosure of secrets by government insiders. But Cater (1959) asserts that "the primary cause for the almost constant revelation of behind-the-scenes episodes of government is the power struggle that goes on within the government itself or among the governments doing business in Washington" (p. 125).

One of the most important struggles between competing factions in any society is to propagate and control a particular version of reality. In some countries ruling elites do not depend on the mass media being made available to them only when they manage happenings correctly; instead, they directly control the mass media, censor opposing views, and imprison political dissenters who attempt to make their criticisms public.

2. The Scholar

The books, memoirs, diaries, and other documents produced by scholars, diplomats, and social critics provide a rich source of data, theory, and conjecture regarding the past, present, and future. The writings of a Gunnar Myrdal, a George Kennan, a J. Kenneth Galbraith, a Paul Goodman, or a Paul Ehrlich may shape the image of social reality held by great numbers of people and, eventually, may shape the social policies of nations. A knowledge industry involving a complex system for the production of expertise has developed in most modern societies. This system of expertise is based on the fact that no one can know everything. In fact, there are contrary scholarly views on almost every topic. As Berger and Luckman (1966) point out, part of our education is learning how the socially available stock of knowledge is distributed and "whom I can turn to for information on what I do not know, and generally which types of individuals may be expected to have which types of knowledge" (p.46). A person who has little information about Chinese society may rely upon the analysis and descriptions provided by Sinologists.

3.   The "Influential"

Most people seldom go to the trouble of seeking out expert sources of information in order to formulate a belief or opinion. Information is more often obtained from friends and acquaintances through face-to-face interaction. Katz and Lazarsfeld (1955) found a two-step flow of communications. A few influential people sample the mass media and pass on the information gained to their associates. Influentials tend to specialize in the type of information they gather and disseminate. *Cosmopolitan influentials* tend to buy national magazines and out-of-town newspapers to acquire a broad perspective on key issues of national and international politics. *Local influentials* tend to buy a number of community newspapers and magazines and make efforts to keep abreast of community politics and social affairs (Merton, 1949). Some people specialize in movies or the arts, while others are well informed about the prices at the supermarkets.

Eisenstadt (1952) studied the effectiveness of influentials among a group of immigrants to Israel. The influentials were usually teachers or rabbis who interpreted and legitimized communications from official agencies. The special expertise of the influentials consisted of knowledge about traditions, the right ways to behave, and how to make arrangements to get what was needed by the newcomers. But the more experience they gained about their new home the less dependent the immigrants were upon the influentials. As the strangeness of the new setting melted into familiarity and the immigrants developed their own beliefs regarding the system, the usefulness and desirability of the influentials dwindled.

4.   Conclusion

When one considers all of the events that occur in the world, the limitations on what a single individual can directly experience are rather obvious. Information about foreign countries, the school system, the local government or county police is usually obtained second hand. Furthermore, we are dependent on others for definitions of social reality because it often can be determined only by consensual validation. How does one determine what makes a good marriage? Examples are provided by one's parents and models in literature, the movies and television, and additional criteria are offered by local influentials through word of mouth. Thus, the person's construction of reality and his standards of judgment are firmly rooted in the pattern of his social relationships. To the degree that the gatekeepers of information serve as biased filters, the individual's view of reality will be a distorted one.

B.   Propaganda

The use of information to achieve a calculated effect on the listener is referred to as propaganda. At least in principle there are important differences between propaganda and education. The propagandist's arguments are often false, misleading, or unsound, and he stands to profit from the responses he seeks to elicit from his audience. The educator's aim is to provide alternative points of view to the student, along with ways of analysing information, so the student can arrive at his own conclusions.

Propagandists are not restricted to the manipulation of information (i.e., persuasion). Ellul (1965) has pointed to several other spheres of activity of the propagandist:

"Psychological warfare: Here the prop-

agandist is dealing with a foreign adversary whose morale he seeks to destroy by psychological means so that the opponent begins to doubt the validity of his beliefs and actions;

Re-education and brainwashing: Complex methods of transforming an adversary into an ally which can be used only on prisoners;

Public and human relations: These must necessarily be included in propaganda . . . because they seek to adapt the individual to a society, to a living standard, to an activity. They serve to make him conform, which is the aim of all propaganda" (p.xiii).

According to Ellul, much of modern propaganda depends on what passes for education. He considers education a form of "pre-propaganda" which conditions minds to be receptive to subsequent persuasive communications. People in the United States are generally taught that socialism and communism are inferior to capitalism and democracy, while citizens of the Soviet Union learn just the opposite pattern of preferences. As we shall see in Chapter 8, persuasive communications are more effective if they are congruent with existing beliefs and if propaganda is labeled and accepted as education. Of course education can also provide the capacity to recognize propaganda techniques and to evaluate arguments critically for their logic and to expose their underlying intent.

1.   Propaganda ABC's

In order to achieve success the propagandist must capture the attention of his audience and relate his message to its needs. The propagandist attempts to create information dependence with his opening thrust. The ABC's of propaganda include an *appeal,* a *bond,* and a *commodity.* The appeal is the attention getter, the headline, the lead item. A successful appeal entices the target to seek more information in order to ascertain whether his own values or interests may be involved. The perceived connection between the appeal and the forthcoming commodity is the bond, which may consist of a subheading, a warning, or an offer of good things to come. The commodity is the idea, product, institution, person, or nation that the propagandist is promoting.

2.   Propaganda techniques

The propagandist is skilled in the use of words. If he wishes to produce a negative reaction or destroy the audience's perception of a person's credibility, trustworthiness, or expertise (all of which make a communicator influential; see Chapter 8), the propagandist can resort to *name-calling.* Calling someone a liar, cheat, coward, Yankee, Gook, Nigger, Wop, or even "manipulator" can damage that person's image in the eyes of the audience. Only recently has the People's Republic of China been referred to by its proper name in the American press; heretofore it was called Red China or Communist China. *Glittering generalities* are used to achieve the opposite effect. A commodity may be given positive names to elicit favorable attitudes toward it by the audience. For example, a person may be called fair, forthright, 100% American, a man of courage, a keen analyst, and so forth.

The propagandist may attempt to *transfer* a positive or negative response of the target from one commodity to another by associating the two. Because sex is so highly valued in American society, almost every commercial product is advertised in association with a seminude female at one time or another. Females are draped over new automobiles, are fascinated by strangers who offer them little cigars, kiss those who use a particular mouth wash, and chase men who wear a certain aftershave lotion. The propagandist portrays his enemies as closely associated with subversive or criminal elements or as having reprehensible opinions or morals. The propagandist has many ways of promoting virtue or guilt by association.

In their studies of the classical conditioning of attitudes Staats and Staats (1958) illustrated the effectiveness of the transfer technique. Subjects were exposed to repeated pairings of the names of nationalities with positive or negative words (e.g., happy, gift, or failure, ugly). When subjects were subsequently asked to rate the positivity or negativity of their feelings toward the nationalities, transfer was displayed. Nationalities paired with good words were rated positively, and those paired with bad words were rated negatively.

A popular advertising technique is to have a movie star or professional athlete give *testimony* in behalf of a commercial product or political candidate. A negative form of testimony (boomerang effect) may also be used by the propagandist, as when a generally disliked person is revealed as supporting a competing commodity. An opponent of a national health plan may cite the support of a communist party leader for the legislation. Whether testimony is effective as a propaganda technique is not really known. Celebrities are not typically viewed as experts regarding the products they recommend and most adults are aware that their testimonials are often given for monetary gain. Nevertheless, testimony is a good way of gaining the audience's attention, without which persuasion is impossible (McGuire, 1969).

Band wagon techniques are appeals to the audience to fall in step with the crowd. Statements such as "All *good* housewives use Grayday detergent," or "Thinking men smoke Mindos" are attempts to exert pressure to conform (see Chapter 13). The propagandist hopes to elicit responses from target persons based on their need to be accepted by particular groups or on their fear of rejection for deviant conduct.

Politicians often attempt to use *plain folks* techniques by kissing babies, drinking a glass of beer at a Labor Day picnic, or mildly cursing in an appropriate place. The image is created of a candidate who is similar to the voter and is, therefore, believed to understand and support the voter's interests.

Card-stacking involves the production of facts to be used subsequently as the basis for a propagandistic message. Packard (1957) used a fictional illustration of a new fountain pen company which sent sales representatives to visit all circuit court judges in the United States and presented them with Scratcho fountain pens suitably decorated with the judge's initials in gold leaf. Several weeks later the judges were visited by someone taking a survey which included a question about the brand of pen they used. A two-page spread in a national magazine followed which announced that seven of ten circuit court judges in the United States use Scratchos. Card stacking is also accomplished through the selective use of facts, distortion (e.g., brand X advertising), and faulty reasoning.

C. Censorship

Some information about physical and social reality is simply unavailable. The depths of space, the ocean, and the arctic core are largely inaccessible, even to the best equipped and most daring explorers. Some information is deliberately withheld or carefully restricted to a few privileged persons. The activities of the Central Intelligence Agency are carefully guarded secrets and are not disclosed even to most senators and congressmen. During the Vietnam War, correspondents were willing to risk their lives to bring back first-hand stories, but the military command made many areas off limits to newsmen. Bombing missions were kept secret from high Pentagon officials through the falsification of required reports. The extent to which information is withheld from the public is enormous. Representative Moss (Democrat of California), chairman of the House Government Operations Committee, was quoted in 1962 as saying that each week a stack of documents equivalent in height to the Empire State Building is stamped with one or another security classification that restricts its circulation.

Censorship is not necessary when the truth of a matter is known; it is invoked only when the truth is uncertain. Sexual matters may be censored for fear an established standard of morality will be undermined, and military secrets are kept in order to maintain public support for current policies. Censorship is a form of silent propaganda and often follows the dictum that what you don't know can't hurt the propagandist.

Censorship is not always condemned as wrong or evil. There is general agreement that the police would be less effective in their pursuit of fugitives if they disclosed all of the information available to them. Government units usually keep secret their future plans to purchase land since such information would be likely to foster speculation and an inflation of prices. Hence, censorship is widely practiced even in the most democratic nations.

III. HUMAN INFORMATION PROCESSING

The amount of information reaching the individual through social filters is almost limitless, yet there are limitations on how much of the available information he can attend to at any given time. A number of factors determine how the individual selectively samples information. His values, his cognitive categories developed through experience, the labels his language provides, and his memory processes serve as personal filters through which information must pass and which further distort and bias his representations of events.

A. Attention

Consider the startling estimate that there are 7,295,000 discriminable colors (Nickerson & Newhall, 1943). The child customarily begins by discriminating and labeling the primary colors—red, yellow, green,

and blue. Only later do finer distinctions develop for which labels are sought. There are cross-cultural differences in the way adults make color discriminations (Bornstein, 1973), probably because of variations in the labels provided by languages, a topic we will turn to shortly. Within our culture, occupational and avocational interests (artist, interior decorator, etc.) are associated with the degree of attention paid to the finer discriminations of color. Most persons probably develop fewer than 50 color names or categories.

Selectivity in processing information from the environment is referred to as *attention*. The individual is naturally interested in information that is potentially useful to him. His values act as selective filters which serve to include or exclude information. There are also certain features of the stimulus situation that attract the attention of observers. Selectivity always occurs in perception because of the limited information capacity of the organism. We will examine more carefully each of these factors as they affect the attention of the human information processor.

1. Values and Attention

However the individual's values or preferences are developed, whether through the adoption of culturally shared beliefs or through idiosyncratic learning experiences, reality is structured around them. James (1892) noted that "millions of items of the outward order are present to my senses which never properly enter into my experience. Why? Because they have no interest for me . . . Only those items which I notice shape my mind—without selective interest, experience is an utter chaos. Interest alone gives accent and emphasis, light and shade, background and foreground—intelligible perspective, in a word" (p.403).

The selectivity of the individual in scanning the environment is based on his plans, objectives, and values, as well as certain stimulus conditions. When a person wishes to mail a letter, he may notice a number of mail boxes along his way that he never noticed before, even though he has traveled the same path many times. Or a person who suspects a source of communication as trying to manipulate him may be selectively attentive to the propaganda techniques being employed.

Holzner (1968) suggests that an individual is like a cartographer in developing his representation of reality. In designing a map of a geographical area, the cartographer does not attempt to reproduce all aspects of reality. He ignores the type of architecture used in the construction of buildings, the type of fish in the rivers, and the hunting lodges and ski runs in the mountains. He abstracts those aspects of the situation that most interest him or are most useful to him. Rules of scale and projection and the type of symbols used constrain and determine the information that will be processed in making his maps. Similarly, the human observer adopts one of many possible perspectives in approaching any particular situation, and what he "sees" will be determined by his interests and the categories and classification techniques available to him.

The individual's image of reality is not a photographic representation of the actual, perceivable world, but is rather a personal *construction* in which certain events are selectively noticed and categorized. Each of us is something of a nonrepresentational artist, painting a picture of the world that expresses our view of the meaning and significance of events. As Krech, Crutchfield, and Ballachey (1962) conclude, "There are no impartial facts. Data do not have a logic of their own that results in the same cognitions for all people" (p.24). To perceive the world is not a passive process but one in which the individual actively contributes to his images of reality.

2. Stimulus Factors and Attention

How is a person's attention caught and held? Many stimulus factors may attract attention. A single black person in a group of white people may be the focus of an observer's eyes, and the speaker in a group will get more attention than his audience. Change or movement in the environment may catch the eye of an observer, as when a fish jumps out of the water or a person stands up in the middle of a seated group. The apparent movement associated with the pattern of flashing lights on a movie marquee is more likely to gain the attention of a passerby than is a uniformly illuminated sign.

Television commercials are typically louder than the rest of the program. It is assumed that more intense stimuli attract more attention. Bright colors are used for the product, while the color of the background is more subdued. Repetition also gains attention. The politician repeats his main points, the singing commercial is played incessantly, and the lecturer (and textbook writer) makes the same point in several different ways.

The direction of gaze of other people may also focus the attention of the individual on a particular aspect of the environment. Milgram, Bickman, and Berkowitz (1969) demonstrated the effect that a crowd can have upon the individual. Groups of various sizes strolled out on a New York City street, paused, and gazed up at a sixth-floor window across the street. The larger the size of the original stimulus group, the greater the number of passersby who looked up (see Figure 14.1).

It is usually difficult to hold a person's attention for any great length of time. Cameron, Frank, Lifter, and Morrissey (1968) investigated the cognitive functioning of students in a psychology lecture course. Although the students thought the lectures were quite good, they were really not listening close to two-thirds of the time. Instead, they were daydreaming—much of the time about romantic and sexual matters. The master lecturer is like the neighbor who offered to help a farmer train a stubborn mule. The first thing the neighbor did was to hit the mule right between the ears with the butt end of an ax. When asked by the farmer what he was trying to do, the neighbor replied that before he could teach the mule anything he had to gain its attention. The lecturer is mindful of the many ways of attracting the students' attention and manipulates the environment to maintain it.

3.   Limits to Attention

There is a limit to the amount of information the individual can process at any time. According to Miller (1956), the span of attention is the "magical number seven plus or minus two." Only that many chunks of information can be attended to at once and registered in short-term memory. A person on a subway can attend to his fellow passengers, the signs posted in the car, the litter on the floor, but he cannot attend to more than about seven stimuli simultaneously. If a person is exposed to a list of names or numbers for a few seconds, he will be able to remember about seven of them after the list is removed from view. Perhaps this is the reason telephone numbers have a limit of seven digits. The limitation of our ability to process information requires selectivity in our perceptions.

Miller suggests that a person can "chunk" information. For example, a stereotype represents chunking. A person may form a picture in his head of the characteristics possessed by all members of a particular ethnic group, and a *cognitive category* (Bruner, 1957) is formed to represent the entire group. Should the observer see a person who has any of the relevant characteristics, he may be assigned to the appropriate cognitive category. Events, objects, and persons may be assigned to various categories as the individual tries to impose order and meaning on his world. If you are at a picnic and you catch a glimpse of a white object coming toward you, you must decide to duck or catch it. If you categorize the object as a fresh egg, you will probably duck; but if you categorize it as a soft rubber ball, you may put out your hand to catch it.

Information can be chunked by formulating principles or schemata representing the relationships between events. A *schema* may be considered a rule of thumb formulated by the individual as a basis for predicting the future; it is a belief in a particular relationship between events. As a rule of thumb automobile insurance companies have found that young male drivers are greater risks than older drivers. It may be the case that driving experience, which is of course correlated with age, is really the critical factor associated with accident risk (Riker, 1974), but for the purpose of the insurance company, the age schema works well enough. An understanding of multiplication and the knowledge that the square of a number is that number times itself allows an individual to reproduce an entire table of squares. The principle allows the individual to chunk a great deal of detailed information in a simple rule. Learning the rule concerning squares of numbers is much easier than memorizing the table of squares. In interpersonal relations a schema that persons who are similar to one another get along better may cause a person to try to make himself appear similar to someone he wants to like him.

B.   Cognitive Selectivity

When a person is faced with ambiguous stimulus conditions his values, cognitive categories, and schemata determine how he defines the situation. These cognitive factors act to provide structure to an otherwise ill-defined stimulus situation. Two basic processes have been proposed as operating when the individual is faced with a fleeting or blurred stimulus: perceptual vigilance and perceptual defense. *Perceptual vigilance* refers to the increased accessibility of certain categories, which, in effect, leads the individual to see what he expects to see. *Perceptual defense* refers to the inaccessibility of certain cognitive categories, which interferes with the individual's ability to identify stimuli correctly.

1. Perceptual Vigilance

Wispé and Drambarean (1953) presented words to subjects by a tachistoscope, which is a device similar to a slide projector except that it allows control over the time of exposure to a small fraction of a second. A series of neutral words and words related to food and water were exposed for very brief periods of time. The procedure followed was to expose the stimulus word for such a brief time that it was just a blur and then to increase the time of exposure incrementally until the subject could correctly identify the word. The exposure time at which the subject could first correctly identify the stimulus word is called the *recognition threshold.*

The subjects were deprived of food and water for various periods of time. Perceptual vigilance was demonstrated by the finding that recognition thresholds were lower for food and water words as deprivation increased, but the identification of neutral words was unaffected by hunger and thirst. Under these ambiguous stimulus conditions the subjects would glimpse the word and then guess what it was. One interpretation of the results is that drive states, such as hunger and thirst, make certain cognitive categories more readily available to the individual. As a result, his guesses or interpretations of ambiguous stimuli are affected by his needs. It might also be argued that the experimental procedure of deprivation furnished a demand characteristic that increased the subjects' readiness (set) to perceive words related to food and water. However, this set should be the same whatever the length of deprivation and, therefore, does not adequately account for observed differences based on deprivation period.

Postman, Bruner, and McGinnies (1948) found an association between the values held by a person and his recognition thresholds. A paper-and-pencil scale (the Allport-Vernon Scale of Values) was administered to all subjects. The scale measures the religious, aesthetic, social, economic, theoretical, and political values of subjects. Words related to each of these areas of values were then presented to the subjects by tachistoscopic exposure. As can be seen in Figure 3.1, the results showed lower recognition thresholds for words that were related to the individual's strongest values.

There are hundreds of other studies of perceptual vigilance. One carried out by Lazarus, Yousem, and Arenberg (1953) is representative of a somewhat modified procedure. They photographed a number of food and nonfood objects, including a bunch of grapes, pancakes, a cigarette lighter, and a typewriter. These photographs were made into slides and presented via a tachistoscope. After subjects had been deprived of food for varying numbers of hours, they were asked to identify the slides with whatever words came to mind. In general, it was found that the hungrier the person, the more likely he was to recognize food objects.

The effects of hunger on recognition thresholds found in the laboratory are corroborated by reports of behavior in concentration camps during World War II. Cohen (1953) was a physician who spent several years in a German concentration camp. He reported that the prisoners reverted to animal-like behavior with respect to food, fighting for extra scraps and practically killing one another in order to lick up a spot of soup on the floor. Much of the conversation in the concentration camp was about food, meals that the men had eaten in the past, special meals they would eat when they were freed, and so on. Furthermore, there was a sharp decrease in sexual concerns, a decline in sociability, and an increase in the incidence of dreams about food and food-related themes. Keys, Brozek, Henschel, Mickelsen, and Taylor

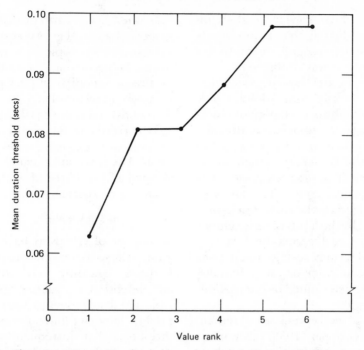

Figure 3.1.   Recognition thresholds as a function of value rank of the stimulus
words. (After Postman, Bruner, and McGinnies, 1948.)

(1950) found much the same kind of "food neurosis" among conscientious objectors who volunteered to be subjected to a prolonged period of semi-starvation on a diet of less than 1600 calories per day.

Perhaps the withdrawal of food had such profound effects on the prisoners and CO's because they had been accustomed to an adequate diet before being deprived. Do the many people in the world who live constantly on the verge of starvation have food neuroses? Holmberg (1946) reported that the Siriono of Bolivia, who live in a climate making food storage very difficult and are therefore constantly in search of food, frequently worry and daydream about it. They also make food a major focus of their magic.

In conclusion, the evidence generally supports the principle that cognitive categories become more accessible when values, needs, or expectancies important to the individual are activated. As a consequence, persons with differing sets, values, or cognitive structures are apt to make quite different interpretations of objective reality. Selectivity in perception and the interpretation of events explains why witnesses at a courtoom trial may honestly report very different versions of the same event. During the Senate Watergate hearings in the summer of 1973 this principle became known as Ervin's Law when Senator Sam Ervin noted that contradictions in the testimony of witnesses did not necessarily imply that one of them must be committing perjury.

2.   Perceptual Defense

In an early study of perceptual defense, McGinnies (1949) had a female experimenter tachistoscopically present sets of taboo and neutral words to male subjects. Among the taboo words were whore, penis, and the like. The reasoning behind the study was that subjects would be threatened or would become anxious by seeing taboo words and would defensively avoid seeing them. The prediction that taboo words would have higher recognition thresholds than neutral words was confirmed.

Subsequent research has suggested that both perceptual vigilance and defense may be attributable to the expectations of observers. For example, subjects in the McGinnies study may not have expected taboo words to be presented to them in the context of a scientific research project and by a female experimenter. The kinds of guesses the subjects make about words may be determined by the kinds of expectations they have. Perceptual sets may be elicited by environmental factors, such as instructions from the experimenter or other stimulus cues, or may be determined by internal values and needs.

In a study of perceptual set, Postman, Bronson, and Gropper (1953) forewarned half of their subjects that taboo words would be included among those presented to them. The other half were not forewarned. When subjects expected taboo words, their recognition thresholds for them were lower than for neutral words, but when taboo words were not expected, the neutral words were more readily recognized. Bitterman and Kniffin (1953) found that subjects gradually reduced their recognition thresholds for taboo words even when they had not been forewarned, if they were given a sufficiently large number of trials. When they had been presented with enough taboo words they developed their own set and the category accessibility of the words was increased.

Freeman (1954) carried this line of research one step further. He followed the procedure of either forewarning or not forewarning subjects that taboo words would be presented to them. However, he did not include any taboo words in his list; instead there were words such as hiss, shut, and muck, which have a close resemblance to familiar taboo words. The forewarned subjects made the obvious errors in misidentifying these as taboo words.

Bruner and Postman (1949) demonstrated set and category accessibility clearly with a tachistoscopic task not involving words. Subjects required much longer exposures to identify correctly playing cards that were miscolored (e.g., red clubs, black diamonds). With the passage of trials, subjects correctly reported the incongruous cards at lower exposure times than regular cards. The set of incongruity had been developed and superseded the set generated from prior experience with playing cards.

3. Critical Discussion

A number of criticisms have been raised about these research procedures and findings regarding perceptual vigilance and defense. For example, it has been established that frequently used words in the English language have lower recognition thresholds than infrequently used words (Howes & Solomon, 1951; McGinnies, Comer, & Lacey, 1952). Taboo words have a relatively low frequency (at least they used to have, in a formal university setting). On the other hand, persons probably often encounter words related to their prominent values. A theology student is more familiar with religious than economic words, while the reverse is true of the business student. Howes and Solomon (1950) also suggested that taboo words may have high recognition thresholds in studies of perceptual defense because of the embarrassment the subject might suffer by identifying them under the very ambiguous conditions of tachistoscopic presentation. Indeed, Nothman (1962) found lower recognition thresholds for taboo words when the subjects reported their guesses in writing rather than orally.

Despite these criticisms, Erdelyi (1974) in a recent review of the literature concluded that there is a substantial residue of evidence of cognitive bias attributable to the emotional or value content of stimuli. Cognitive selectivity does operate to determine how the individual will interpret complex and ambiguous events.

In a classic study, Hastorf and Cantril (1954) demonstrated the effects of cognitive selectivity in a real-life situation. Subjects were shown a film of a particularly rough football game in which Dartmouth upset previously unbeaten Princeton in the last game of the year. Princeton's star, Dick Kazmaier, had to leave the game with a broken nose, and a number of other injuries occurred to both teams. Princeton students judged the game as "rough and dirty," predominantly attributed the origin of the rough play to the Dartmouth players, and "saw" the Dartmouth team make over twice as many infractions as the Princeton team. While the Dartmouth students believed the number of infractions was approximately equally distributed, they "saw" their own team make only half the number of infractions the Princeton students "saw." Box 3.1 reports a study of John Foster Dulles, a former U.S. Secretary of State, in which cognitive selectivity may have had a significant impact on world affairs.

Box 3.1 COGNITIVE DYNAMICS AND IMAGES OF THE ENEMY

During the presidency of Dwight Eisenhower, John Foster Dulles was U.S. Secretary of State. Dulles had a powerful effect on American foreign policy during his tenure at the State Department. The way he conceptualized the world and attributed causes to the policies (i.e., intentions) of other nations presumably had a strong impact on world events during a period when the United States was indisputably the world's most powerful and richest nation. Finlay, Holsti, and Fagen (1967) attempted to reconstruct how Dulles viewed the Soviet Union by analysing the content of all of the publicly available statements made by Dulles from 1953 to 1959, including 122 press conferences, 70 addresses, 67 appearances at Congressional hearings, and 166 other documents. This material was supplemented by newspaper stories, memoirs written by those who worked in the State Department, and questionnaires sent to a number of Dulles' closest associates.

Finlay, et al stated that "of the many attributes in Dulles' belief system it is perhaps his theological world view that was most germane to his conception of the enemy. It is clear that the Soviet Union represented the antithesis of the values that were at the core of his belief system. . . . The distinction between moral and political bases for evaluating the Soviet Union was blurred, if not totally obliterated" (p.22). Compromise and coexistence, which are the essence of both domestic and international politics, was out of the question with respect to the Soviet Union. One can not trust atheists to keep their word, one cannot compromise with the Devil, and evil is not to be tolerated but must be destroyed. Dulles' numerous statements indicated that he viewed Russian foreign policy as an instrument of an international communist ideology rather than of national interest, and that he believed the Soviet people provided little support to their leaders. Though he realistically respected the technological and military capabilities of the Soviet Union, he believed the nation was in imminent danger of economic collapse.

The inability of Dulles to view any action by the Soviet government as a genuine gesture of good will toward the United States was evidenced in 1957. The Soviet Union unilaterally pulled all of its troops out of Austria. The occupation forces were in Austria legitimately following an agreement reached between the victors at the end of World War II. At the time these troops were withdrawn serious disarmament talks were under way at the United Nations and the Soviet Union had accepted a French-British proposal which the United States had endorsed. Instead of interpreting the Soviet action as signaling their sincerity in the disarmament negotiation, Dulles stated that he thought it would have been much better for the Russians to use their men for guard duty in Austria than to send them home and place them in factories to build weapons for an attack on the United States. It might be added that the United States withdrew its endorsement of the proposal accepted by the Soviet government. Presumably, if the enemy accepted our proposal it couldn't possibly be in American interests to be a party to the agreement.

Of course the Soviet Union was the major threat to the United States during the 1950's and a Secretary of State who ignored the dangers that did exist would not have been realistic. On the other hand, history might have been different had Secretary Dulles developed a more complex view of Soviet conduct. As Kennan (1947) has said, "it is an undeniable privilege of everyman to prove himself in the right in the thesis that the world is his enemy; for if he reiterates it frequently enough and makes it the background of his conduct, he is bound eventually to be right" (p.569).

State Department policy seems still to be based on "worst case analysis"; that is, judgments are made about the technological and military capabilities of other nations on the basis that they will acquire or make operational the maximum number of weapons. Our response to this assumption is to be fully prepared for every contingency, which of course makes similar worst case analysis by adversary nations necessary.

C. Selective Memory

Memory is usually considered a complex process involving three stages (Broadbent, 1958). *Iconic* or *echoic memory* refers to a momentary stage, lasting perhaps half a second, during which the individual has a fading replica (a sensory store) of the stimulus experienced through the sensory apparatus. *Short-term memory* involves a period of 15 to 30 seconds during which the individual may continually attend to a capacity of 7 ± 2 bits or chunks of information. *Long-term memory* consists of information placed in relatively permanent storage.

We have discussed short-term memory under the headings of attention and cognitive selectivity. The information that enters long-term memory is more responsive to deliberate cognitive activities, such as repetition and rehearsal. Although you may be able to repeat a telephone number 15 seconds after hearing or seeing it, you cannot do so 15 minutes or 15 days later unless you engage in some cognitive effort. Failures of short-term memory are the result of decay or inattention, while failures of long-term memory are usually the result of some kind of interference or distortion caused by competing memories.

The processes of storage and retrieval of information in long-term memory are affected by the emotional state of the observer, his values and interests, and the cognitive categories and schemata available to him. Selective forgetting also occurs as a function of systematic changes in stored information. These systematic changes are well illustrated in the study of rumors, as we shall see.

1. Values, Emotions, and Memory

The utility of information helps determine whether it will be stored in long-term memory. A waiter in a restaurant may remember exactly what each person at several tables ordered until he has written the final checks; thereafter he will forget the information rapidly as new and competing information is acquired. Zeigarnik (1927) found that subjects who had not been allowed to complete a task remembered it better several hours later than did subjects who had been given the same task but were allowed to finish it. When an individual cannot finish a task because he is interrupted, the challenge remains interesting, but when the task is completed, its interest value is typically exhausted. Leaving five words incomplete in a puzzle maintains an interest in finishing it, but a person loses interest in a puzzle he has completed.

Momentary states of emotion apparently reduce a person's capacity to transfer information to long-term memory. One of the authors (JTT) carried out a classroom demonstration familiar to most social psychologists, to illustrate the unreliability of courtroom testimony concerning emotionally charged circumstances. A person dressed in a sweat suit entered the classroom during a lecture and shouted, "That's enough of your god damn theories, take that," and shot the professor with a starter's pistol. The professor collapsed behind the podium, while the startled students jumped up or froze in their seats. (It should be added that even though the professor knew the event was staged, he generated a good deal of adrenalin in himself nevertheless.) The professor immediately rose from the floor, smiling, and the class began to engage in anxious laughter. Before any real information could be exchanged, the students were asked to take out paper and pencil and respond to a series of questions posed by the professor acting in the role of district attorney.

The descriptions of what occurred and of the assailant did not yield information that would have been clear to any law enforcement officer. The assailant was described as anywhere from 5'4" to 6'5" tall; 145 to 215 pounds; having blue, green, and brown eyes; brown, black, red, and blond hair fixed in a variety of styles; and wearing all kinds of apparel. Though only one shot had actually been fired, students reported anywhere from one to three shots, and from all kinds of weapons. Very few students could recall what the assailant said, and the curse words were most often forgotten.

Intense states of emotion create a type of tunnel vision, in which attention to environmental stimuli contracts to a very few dimensions. The narrowing of focus may be due to the individual's internal search for categories which tell him how to react to the crisis. A diver whose oxygen is cut off while deep under water is not apt to notice the coral formations and the type of fishes that are swimming by him; his attention will be riveted on his breathing apparatus and his orientation in space so he can plan his move to the surface.

2. Categories and Long-Term Memory

If an individual does not have storage categories for new information and is unable to translate the information into an existing category, then short-term memories will not reach long-term memory. The conversion of information into categories typically makes the remembered versions of events shorter and more coherent than the actual events. Some parts of the original experience will drop out for lack of coding into a category—a process called *leveling*—and the resulting recollection is often disjointed and fragmentary. The individual fills out his recounting of the event by adding elements and smoothing out his story to make it more comprehensible—a process called *assimilation*. In the reconstructed event reported from memory, the individual tends to emphasize details consistent with his own values and not because they were actually prominent in the referent event—a process referred to as *sharpening*.

Thus, leveling involves the elimination of details that cannot be coded into long-term memory, sharpening is the process of giving emphasis to those details that are congruent with expectations and values, and assimilation involves adding details and bringing discrepant details into agreement with existing schemata. Bartlett (1932) found evidence for all three of these processes in a study in which subjects were asked to recall a North American Indian folk tale after they had read it twice. The tale was a rather disconnected account of a supernatural event, but it was dramatic enough to evoke visual imagery from readers. The successive reproductions of the tale by readers became increasingly concise and coherent; inconsistent elements dropped out completely. The special interests of some subjects were reflected in the interpretations they made of mysterious events in the story.

Variations among persons in coding information into categories for storage in long-term memory are often great, especially for people living in different cultures. Bartlett (1932), in his classic studies of memory, reported anecdotal information regarding the memory of Swasi herdsmen. In the Swasi culture cattle play a prominent role, being central to both economic and ritualistic practices (such as dowries). Since his life is focused around his valuable cattle, the Swasi herdsman develops a much more complex set of categories for cattle than would someone who has lived all his life in New York City or even than a cattle rancher in North America. The ability of a herdsman to remember in great detail the characteristics of individual cows he saw but once in a commercial transaction taking place years before was astonishing. He had apparently taken note of, categorized, and stored many details about the cow which would have little significance to a person from a culture where cows had less meaning and consequence.

3. Rumor Transmission

A particular communication that is carried through a chain of people, requiring recollection and retelling by each person in the chain, is referred to as *serial reproduction*. Bartlett reported evidence that "serial reproduction normally brings about startling and radical alterations in the material dealt with. Epithets are changed into opposites: incidents and events are transposed; names and numbers rarely survive intact for more than a few reproductions; opinions and conclusions are reversed—nearly every possible variation seems as if it could take place, even in a relatively short series. At the same time, the people in the chain may all be very well satisfied with their efforts, believing themselves to have passed on all important features with little or no change" (p.175). These changes in serial reproduction are similarly involved in the transmission of rumors.

Rumors occur during times of crisis when the individual seeks explanations to reduce or justify his intense emotional involvement (Allport & Postman, 1947). When there is high interest in an event and the stimulus situation is ambiguous and difficult to interpret, rumors are born and are likely to circulate through the entire population of people who share the common concern. Allport and Postman proposed a formula to indicate that rumors will occur only if interest and ambiguity are present:

Rumor Intensity = f (interest × ambiguity)

Without ambiguity there is no information dependence and no need to gain cognitive clarity; and without interest the individual is unlikely to attend to or transmit the content of a communication.

Ernie Pyle (1945), a famous foreign correspondent during World War II, reported the abundance of rumors that circulated on a troop ship sailing with a convoy across the Atlantic Ocean: "Of all the spots on earth where rumors run wild, I think a convoy trooper must lead, hands down. Scores of rumors a day floated about the ship. We got so we believed them all, or didn't believe any. . . . The rumor-mongering got so rife that one officer made up a rumor to the effect that we were going to Casablanca, and timed it to see just how long it would take to encircle the ship. It came back to him, as cold fact right from the bridge, in just half an hour" (p.708). The possibility that they might be going to battle combined with a lack of information about where they were headed was sufficient to generate a great deal of rumor intensity and rumor frequency among the troops. Similar observations of rumors promulgated in a primitive society are presented in Box 3.2.

Box 3.2   RUMOR IN TIKOPIA

An anthropologist, Raymond Firth (1956) has reported on the function of rumor in a primitive society on the island of Tikopia in the Western Pacific. Residents of Tikopia seem always eager to receive news; the usual greeting includes an inquiry about new events on the island or from the outside world. They have no word for rumor, but they do differentiate "speech of the crowd" from verified events. They frequently ask whether the news is true or false. Children, who often go around in gangs, are widely blamed for creating and spreading rumors; but analyses of their content clearly indicate that the rumors are originated by adults.

Observation supported the theory proposed by Allport and Postman that interest and ambiguity dictate the content of rumors. One of the major events for the Tikopia is the arrival of a ship. Many rumors of such arrivals circulate although only one or two arrivals occur each year. Rumors are often elicited by such ambiguous stimuli as a cloud which may look like smoke from a steamer. During one of Firth's stays there was a famine; this background condition stepped up the production of rumors. Another time there was a shortage of tobacco and several rumors circulated that Firth or his assistant was going to travel to a distant island to buy some. Rumor activity also grew intense when a group left the island to work as plantation laborers and word circulated that they had met with some undefined disaster. Many of the rumors related to the selfish use by the anthropologists of a radio-telephone for business conversation without trying to find out what had happened to the laborers.

Rumors may be deliberately planted by a person as a means of achieving certain goals. For example, a man of rank in Tikopia may allow it to be inferred from his actions that he is preparing to take his canoe and go on a voyage—to survive or die as the fates will have it. As the rumor spreads public opinion may be mobilized against the action. Steps may then be taken to correct the situation that the man of rank originally found objectionable. Such tests of public opinion ("trial balloons") are commonplace in contemporary Washington, D.C. Deliberately planted rumors serve as a social instrument to firm up the position of a leader and to secure an improvement in his status.

Schachter and Burdick (1955) have carried out an experiment on the social psychology of rumors. In four of six classes at a girl's preparatory school, the principal interrupted the normal work and asked one girl to get all her things because she would be gone the rest of the day. The two then left the classroom without any further explanation. Later, girls from two of the classes from which a girl had been removed and from the two control classes were interviewed about their progress in school. During the interviews, the teacher remarked, "By the way, some examinations have been taken from the office. Do you happen to know anything about this?"

Later in the day all of the girls in all six classes were interviewed by a team of 20 interviewers. Because of the opportunity for communications during lunch period, gym classes, and recess the rumor about the missing examinations had reached all the girls in all six classes. According to Allport and Postman, the propagation of a rumor concerning the lost examinations should occur where there was cognitive ambiguity about the removal of the girls. Although all the girls had heard the rumor, twice as many reported passing on the rumor in the classes where the girl had been removed *and* the teacher had asked a question about missing examinations.

When the size of an object is associated with its value the individual's memory of the object is distorted. *Perceptual accentuation* refers to the tendency to exaggerate or overestimate the size of valued objects. Actually, the effect is not due to perception, but is attributable to processes of memory. In a representative study, Carter and Schooler (1949) asked children to adjust a circular spot of light so that it matched the size of a penny, nickel, dime, quarter, and half dollar. When the children were allowed to see the coins while adjusting the size of the spot, they made relatively accurate size estimates, but when they had to turn away from the coins to make adjustments, and thus had to depend on their memories, they overestimated the size of the coins. The degree of accentuation was proportional to the value, but not the actual size, of the coins. For example, although a nickel is larger than a dime, the children overestimated the size of the dime more than they did the size of the nickel.

Distortions in rumors and in fish stories may be a function of the perceptual accentuation of stored information. Distortion may also serve an important social function, as when a person relates how big the bully was who pushed him around. Similarly, an evangelist may exaggerate the size of the crowd which attends his revival meeting. The maintenance of a positive self-image and the promotion of one's interests are obvious sources of exaggerated reports, but the persons involved may not be consciously or deliberately conveying what they know to be falsehoods. According to Jacobs (cited in Milgram and Toch, 1969, p.533) the police often overestimate the size of the crowds they must handle at parades and demonstrations; it is in their interest to emphasize the amount of work they have to perform to gain public support for increasing the size of the force.

D. Language

Language is a means of codifying, storing, and transmitting information. There are certainly other means of processing and communicating. Children can obviously learn, store, retain, retrieve, and communicate information long before they acquire language. Similarly, subhuman organisms have non-linguistic ways of representing their past experiences. Kellogg and Kellogg (1933) raised a female chimpanzee along with their son and found that the chimpanzee understood more directions at the age of eight months than the boy did at the age of two months. However, as the boy learned language, he soon left the ape far behind. Though the chimpanzee learned to respond to over seventy verbal commands, she could not use language to transcend the limitations of her simian capabilities.

Language provides the individual with a culturally shared set of cognitive categories that can be used for coding information and interpreting events. It thus provides the person with a great capability to process information. These linguistic categories or labels also have an important effect on the individual's reproduction of past events, as can be seen from Figure 3.2. Children were shown the middle stimulus figures and then were provided with either the left or right word to label the particular figure. When the children were later asked to draw the figures they had been shown earlier, their drawings showed the effects of the initial labelings. Furthermore, a stimulus that is labeled is more likely to be stored and retrieved from memory than one that is not so readily interpretable in terms of language (Brown & Lenneberg, 1954).

The communication functions of language provide for a greater range of possible interactions and relationships between people than can occur between subhumans. Part 3 of this book will be almost totally devoted to the types of influence language makes available to people. Here, we will concentrate on three basic aspects of lan-

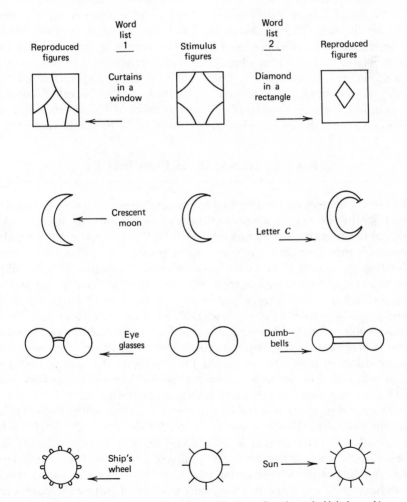

Figure 3.2. Ambiguous symbols are reproduced to reflect the verbal labels used in storing them in memory. (After Carmichael, Hogan, and Walter, 1932.)

guage: (1) the differences between signs, signals, and symbols; (2) the relativity of languages; and (3) the denotative and connotative meanings associated with language.

1. Signs, Signals, and Symbols

To understand the functions of language it is necessary to distinguish between signs, signals, and symbols. A *sign* is an environmental stimulus that leads the organism to expect certain associated events. In Pavlov's classical conditioning study, a dog was taught to salivate to a bell that had frequently preceded the presentation of meat powder. Presumably, the dog came to anticipate that he would receive meat powder when he heard the bell. The conditioned stimulus (i.e., the bell) can be considered a sign. A sign is related to the event to which it refers in a direct and inflexible way. The bell is always and only a sign of meat powder in the conditioning experiment. If the bell is dissociated from the expectation of

meat powder through experimental extinction and, instead, the dog learns that the bell precedes electric shock, then its significance is changed—it has become a different sign.

A *signal* is a sign produced by a living organism, such as a threat posture by a rhesus monkey, the mating call of the bullfinch, raised eyebrows by a human, or an electronic display engineered by human technicians (see Box 3.3). The Kellogg's chimpanzee showed that she could discriminate among the verbal commands (i.e., signals) of a human trainer. Wilson (1972) notes that "by human standards the number of signals employed by each species of animal is severely limited. One of the most curious facts revealed by recent field studies is that even the most highly social vertebrates rarely have more than 30 or 35 separate displays in their entire repertory. . . . The number ranges from a minimum of 10 in certain fishes to a maximum of 37 in rhesus monkeys" (p.32).

Box 3.3   SIGNAL DETECTION THEORY

Electronic devices are used by men to monitor events, and men are used to identify the presence or absence of the referent events. Scanning a radar screen for aircraft is such a task. If very few blips occur, the trained radar operator may have difficulty maintaining his vigilance; if nothing occurs for hours it is easy to become distracted and inattentive. If many blips occur, fatigue may interfere with accurate identification. A *false positive* identification refers to reporting an aircraft when none is approaching, and a *false negative* is a failure to identify an aircraft that is approaching. The problem for the scanner is to avoid both types of error and identify the appropriate signals from the background of competing signals or noise (random interference) on the radar screen. The task is similar to that performed by an inspector on an assembly line who scans the products moving along to pick out those that are defective.

Signal detection is affected by the rewards and penalties experienced by the operator. The rewards for accurate detection are likely to be minimal, since the person is only doing his job, but the penalty for reporting many false negatives may be loss of job or transfer to a different job. A false positive identification may lead to sounding an alarm, which can have great consequences for many persons including the operator's superiors at high levels, especially in times of war or international crisis. Since there is no referent aircraft in the case of a false positive, the preparatory action is wasted and the scanner's superiors may be severely embarrassed. Frequent false positives place the scanner in the position of the boy who cried wolf too often; but since he cannot just be ignored in a critical situation, he is replaced. When the penalties for false positives are high, the probability of false negatives goes up (Swets, 1961).

Persons in the Washington bureaucracy frequently act in fear of making false positive identifications (Fisher, 1969). One does not like to "bother" superiors with unexpected or unpleasant news or to be the instigator of a major false alarm. The penalties for this kind of conduct in the bureaucracy are either some form of disciplinary action or consignment to insignificance, with less hope of gaining a position of greater influence. It appears that some of these considerations were present in the Committee to Re-elect the President in the 1972 Watergate scandal.

deRivera (1968) applied signal detection theory in analysing the inappropriate response of the United States to signals concerning the impending invasion of South Korea by North Korea on June 23, 1950. In early June, the U.S. Ambassador to South Korea sent a cable to the State Department in Washington describing a heavy buildup of troops and materiel just north of the 38th parallel, which divided the two political entities of Korea. The cable was routed to the Assistant Secretary for Far Eastern Affairs. Because the Ambassador had recently been in Washington to argue for an increase in the military equipment furnished to South Korea, the Assistant Secretary interpreted the cable as simply a "scare tactic" used as a supporting argument for the Ambassador's request. As deRivera points out, periodic reports of border fighting in Korea and rumors of Soviet troop movements in the Balkans also produced noise in the communication system. The Assistant Secretary was of course cautious about sounding a major false alarm. He therefore made a false negative interpretation of the Ambassador's signal and buried the cable in the files rather than notifying others who might take counter measures. Therefore the U.S. was unprepared for the invasion by North Korea when it occurred.

Premack (1971) has shown that the recognition and use of human signals by a chimpanzee can be greatly increased by intensive training. Sarah was taught 128 words, including a different name for each of eight individuals (both human and chimpanzee), and signs representing colors, foods, adjectives, and adverbs. Sarah's use of these signals was quite rigidly tied to concrete situations and is light years away from the language possessed by a normal human child, who communicates what happened yesterday and what he would like to happen next week. The ape can only signal within an existential time frame.

A *symbol* is a representation of a referent that is shared by a group of people. Various groups may use different symbols to represent the same event. For example, either "chair" or "stuhl" may represent the same object. The meaning of a symbol depends on the social consensus of the group; symbols become detached from the physical world. The referents of symbols may be material or nonmaterial, such as books and radios or father (a relationship), goodness, and God. Not only words, but flags, insignias, trademarks, sculptures, and paintings are symbols. Combinations of words into metaphors and parables can also be symbols. For example, "he stood his ground as sturdily as a rock" symbolizes something more than simply the person's strong appearance.

Symbols differ from signs in three ways. Whereas signs are used to predict other events, symbols stand for the thing symbolized. Unlike signs which are restricted to co-temporal events, symbols usually refer to events only remotely associated with one another in time or space. Finally, while signs cannot be detached from the events they signify without involving some process of re-learning such as experimental extinction, symbols can be "freed" of direct physical referents without disrupting the "connection" between them.

The communication of apes is restricted to the use of signals. They cannot communicate their plans or goals for more than a very short future, while men can make plans for years and even decades ahead. Apes cannot communicate their past experiences; but men can. The signs used by apes refer to their own internal states (e.g., hunger) or to external environmental stimuli. Symbols may have no exact existential or physical referents, but may have meaning for how a person behaves. Symbols have a profound effect on human behavior; belief in God, patriotic devotion to one's nation, or concern for the inevitability of death depend on the ability to use them.

Only man uses symbols. Other animals engage in behavior that is often misinterpreted as indicating an ability to use symbols. For example, the honey bee engages in a complicated dance to communicate the location of honey. Bowing movements indicate the direction to travel relative to the sun and the number of turns made in a dance per unit of time indicates the distance to be traveled (Von Frisch, 1955). However, this ability to communicate about a distant referent event is apparently a signaling system genetically built into the honeybee. Their inability to communicate

where there is no honey makes it clear that the transmission of signals through dancing is not language (Terwilliger, 1968). In contrast, the movements made by Edward Vilella and Patricia McBride of the New York City Ballet have all the ingredients of symbolic communication.

Symbols may be used to aggregate phenomena into classes or categories. Thus, the class of foods may represent a large number of referent objects, including some which have never been seen before. Clearly what is considered "food" differs among and within cultures. The class of citrus fruits is a subset of the more general category "food," while oranges serve to identify a subclass of the category "citrus fruits." A particular word or label may be used in a number of different cognitive categories. For example, orange may refer to a citrus fruit, a color, the name of a county, or anything else a group of humans agrees upon. Such multiple classifications provide the human with immense flexibility in interpreting and responding to events. The associations made possible through the linguistic manipulation of symbols provide a basis for human creativity. The ability to abstract from physical reality and to share meanings with other people gives the individual an ability to associate events that are separated in time and space. As a consequence the individual can develop theories regarding the causes for a chain of events and communicate them as history.

2. Linguistic Relativity

In Chapter 1 we quoted Cassirer to the effect that language transforms the quality of human life creating a symbolic universe that is not tied to the physical environment, except in an indirect way. Whorf (1956) proposed a linguistic-relativity hypothesis which argues that a person's construction of reality is a product of the particular language he has learned. As a student of American Indian languages, Whorf could find no direct translation of some of their terms into English. Some of the Indian languages he studied made no distinction between nouns and verbs, had only one category for the colors gray and brown, and blurred the distinction among past, present, and future. Thus each language represents a different set of symbols that serve as the basis for the categories the individual uses in interpreting physical and social reality. In addition, Whorf has argued that variations in the rules of syntax of languages result in different modes of thought.

Hertzler (1965) has stressed the importance of language as a gating mechanism through which the person apprehends his world: "Our given language, through the habits of identification and categorization which it develops in us, determines what we, the speakers, perceive in our environment—that is, what we notice, what we are conscious of, what is important to us, what can be ignored. We perceive the objects, events, conditions of being and relationship of our experience only through types of knowns, as particularly represented by nouns, verbs, and adjectives. The symbols *alert us* to what is for us 'real,' to what has existence and distinction of kind of detail among 'things' and 'action,' 'states' and 'qualities.' These words function as spectacles for us, as we look out upon our world, and also as molds of and frameworks for comprehension" (p.41).

Some indication of the filters that linguistic symbols provide is shown by the fact that the Masai, who possess a good memory for details of their livestock, have 17 terms for cattle. Thomas (1937) reports the astonishing fact that there are 6000 Arabic words for camel, including 50 describing phases of pregnancy in camels. Navaho Indians utilize three different words for rough; one for rough ground, one for a rough object, and a third for rough skin; but they have only one word for flint, metal, and knife (Kluckhohn & Leighton, 1946).

Language also provides the basis for developing and stabilizing the individual's conception of himself. The ability to trans-

cend the existential moment and associate remote events with one another provides the basis for perceiving a continuity of experience. Berger and Luckmann (1966) suggest that "men must talk about themselves until they know themselves" (p.38). Conceptions of masculinity, femininity, national and religious identifiction, race, and so on are symbolic categories that the individual uses to define himself. These categories are often socially or culturally determined and the emotional and evaluative meanings associated with them determine the individual's self-esteem.

3. Denotative and Connotative Meaning

Words have both denotative and connotative meaning. *Denotative meaning* points to a referent of a word; dictionary definitions are usually denotative in character. *Connotative meaning* refers to the feelings that the user associates with the word as a symbol. Two words which have the same denotative meaning, such as "party-girl" and "whore", have different connotative meanings; the latter produces a stronger negative reaction than the former. For some words the connotative meaning is more important for determining human responses than the denotative meaning. For example, many people have only the fuzziest comprehension of the denotative meanings of such abstract words as "justice" and "freedom," but they have strong feelings for them.

Osgood, Suci, and Tannenbaum (1957) explored the dimensions of connotative meaning by presenting subjects with a series of concepts and having them rate each concept on a set of scales made up of bi-polar adjectives, such as safe-dangerous, honest-dishonest, good-bad, strong-weak, wise-foolish, and so on. The large amount of data collected was then examined by the sophisticated statistical method called factor analysis. This method permits the investigator to find out what principal dimensions were used by the subjects in filling out the rating scales. Connotative meanings were found to possess three basic dimensions or factors: evaluation, potency, and activity. The *evaluation dimension* refers to the good or bad, right or wrong, positive or negative quality that the referent word has for the individual, and is the most prominent aspect of connotative meaning. The *potency dimension* refers to the degree of strength or weakness the person associates with a concept or event. The *activity dimension* refers to how active or passive the individual considers the referent event, concept or word to be.

In principle, every cognitive category can be rated on the E, P, and A dimensions. Osgood et al. developed a *Semantic Differential Scale* which has been frequently used to measure connotative meanings. For example, in Figure 3.3, a subject has rated the concept "comfort" on a modified Semantic Differential Scale. Each pair of bipolar adjectives are known to measure one of the connotative meaning dimensions. On the potency dimension, hard, rash, and severe are strong, while soft, cautious, and lenient are weak. On the evaluative dimension, honest, wise, and kind are good, while dishonest, foolish, and cruel are bad. On the activity dimension, progressive, changeable, and excitable are active, while regressive, stable, and calm are passive. Each scale

is scored from +3 to −3, with the strong, active, and good sides of the scales given the positive numbers.

The appropriate scales can be added together to obtain an overall measure for each dimension. For example, the Potency score for the subject in Figure 3.3 is obtained by adding the hard-soft (−3), cautious-rash (−2), strong-weak (−1), and severe-lenient (0) ratings, for a total of −6. The scores for the evaluative and activity dimensions can similarly be obtained (+8 and −9, respectively). "Comfort" has a connotative meaning for our hypothetical subject as good, weak, and passive. "War" would probably be rated as bad, strong, and active. Although individuals may rate the same concept differently, cross-cultural studies in several dozen societies with different languages have established that the same three connotative meaning dimensions are used by people all over the world (Osgood, 1964).

Problems of communication between people may develop as a function of differences in either the denotative or the connotative meanings given to symbols. While one person may define work positively as a means of realizing his abilities and fulfilling his life's ambitions; another person may view the same work negatively, and as limiting his personal growth. Although both

COMFORT

P (+3)	Hard	___	: ___	: ___	: ___	: ___	: ___	: X	Soft	(−3)
P (−3)	Cautious	___	: X	: ___	: ___	: ___	: ___	___	Rash	(+3)
E (−3)	Bad	___	: ___	: ___	: ___	: ___	: ___	: X	Good	(+3)
A (+3)	Active	___	: ___	: ___	: ___	: ___	: ___	: X	Passive	(−3)
E (−3)	Dishonest	___	: ___	: ___	: ___	: X	: ___	___	Honest	(+3)
A (+3)	Progressive	___	: ___	: ___	: ___	: X	: ___	___	Regressive	(−3)
A (−3)	Stable	___	: X	: ___	: ___	: ___	: ___	___	Changeable	(+3)
P (−3)	Weak	___	: ___	: X	: ___	: ___	: ___	___	Strong	(+3)
A (−3)	Calm	X	: ___	: ___	: ___	: ___	: ___	___	Excitable	(+3)
E (−3)	Foolish	___	: ___	: ___	: ___	: ___	: X	: ___	Wise	(+3)
E (+3)	Kind	___	: X	: ___	: ___	: ___	: ___	___	Cruel	(−3)
P (+3)	Severe	___	: ___	: ___	: X	: ___	: ___	___	Lenient	(−3)

Figure 3.3   A hypothetical subject's ratings of the concept "comfort" on a Semantic Differential Scale.

persons may believe they are talking about the same thing, what each means by the word is not the same. The slogan "law-and-order" may have positive connotative meaning for one person and negative meaning for another; although both might agree that the slogan denotatively refers to close governmental regulation of deviant social conduct, they may have different values about such regulation and connotatively define the slogan in opposite ways. As can be seen in Box 3.4, these semantic problems of communication can have a very significant impact on human affairs.

Box 3.4 THE SEMANTIC DILEMMA

White (1966) has reported the results of interviewing over 5,000 people from four major West European countries and the U.S. These citizens of Great Britain, France, West Germany, and Italy were asked to place the United States on a scale extending from "completely capitalistic" to "completely socialistic." Though Europeans perceived the U.S. as extremely capitalistic, Americans rated themselves as moderately socialistic. Interestingly enough, the Europeans predominantly chose moderate socialism as desirable for their own countries. Most of the respondents were strongly opposed to Communism and made a sharp distinction between socialism and Communism. Americans often use the two terms interchangeably, as paradoxically, do Communists.

Wedge (1965) has reported that visitors from developing countries supported by State Department "leader grants" are in many instances startled by the extent of American socialism (i.e., social welfare and government regulation of industry). Although U.S. intellectuals do not do so, the intellectuals from European and the developing countries proudly identify themselves with socialism. When asked about their definition of socialism, the Europeans indicate that it refers to government regulation of industry and to the development of extensive welfare legislation. Americans tend to think of socialism as a system of government ownership and control of all major industries and resources, requiring a central authority to decide how to allocate wealth. Thus, the Europeans actually agree with the Americans about the undesirability of government ownership and control and about government regulation and welfare legislation.

The semantic dilemma here does not stem from disagreement from about what type of economic system is desirable but from what to call it. The Voice of America and Radio Free Europe broadcasts insist on calling the U.S. a capitalistic society and attempt to convert others to that ideology. Yet the listeners are apt to be opposed to what they conceive to be capitalism, which harks back to the Robber Baron days of American history and the writings of Charles Dickens and Upton Sinclair. On the other hand, the listeners would probably approve of much of the reality of what these media call "capitalism." Hence, the name is more important than the reality, because the name *is* the reality for the person who hears it. Humpty Dumpty may have said to Alice that words can mean whatever he wants them to mean, but it is not likely that he would get others to agree with him.

Kuhlman, Miller, and Gungor (1973) have experimentally examined the role of denotative and connotative differences in the reduction of interpersonal conflict. The subjects were first required to rate the concepts "state control" and "elections" on a series of ten semantic differential scales in order to assess the connotative meaning of the two terms. Subjects who were either markedly different or very similar in their ratings were then formed into pairs. Next, the subjects were given training to establish the denotative meaning of the same two terms insofar as they were useful in predicting the level of democracy in a series of hypothetical nations. Some subjects learned that the level of democracy in a nation could only be predicted from knowledge concerning the amount of state control; the other subjects learned that only information about the degree of elections in a nation was useful in predicting the level of democracy in the nation. Thus, 4 different conditions existed for pairs of subjects: they had similar or different connotative meanings and were given either similar or different denotative training for the critical terms.

The subjects were informed that during the experimental trials they would be working in pairs and would be making judgments about the level of democracy in real nations. They were told that these judgments would be more difficult than the ones they had made during training on the hypothetical nations and that they might have disagreements. Information was provided about the amount of state control and the degree of elections in each of the nations to be judged. Each subject first made an independent judgment of the level of democracy for each nation and then presented it to his partner. They then discussed their judgments until they arrived at a mutually acceptable decision. Twenty test trials were carried out and the degree of conflict or agreement among pairs of subjects was observed.

Of course the similar subjects had no conflict to resolve and readily agreed on mutual decisions. Subjects who were similar in connotative meanings but different in denotative meanings had early difficulty in reaching mutual decisions; however, they demonstrated a reduction in conflict over trials. The greatest conflict occurred between pairs of subjects who were connotatively different, whether or not they were denotatively similar. Kuhlman et al. concluded: "The effects of connotative and denotative differences on cognitive conflict may be summarized as follows: (1) differences in denotation are the primary determinants of the amount of conflict during the *initial* stage of the interactive sequence; (2) these differences are reduced during the interactive sequence; and (3) during the *latter* half of the sequence, connotative differences inhibit the further reduction of conflict and may lead to an increase in the amount of conflict experienced. In short, after conflict due to denotative differences undergoes some resolution, differences in connotations persist and become major determinants of the level of cognitive conflict" (p.235).

Apparently, some agreement must be reached between parties on denotative meanings before connotative differences become a major source of conflict. Disagreements between persons often occur because neither really understands what the other means denotatively. Once agreement and understanding is reached on denotative meanings, their conflict will be resolved if their values and emotions regarding the referent are similar, but their conflict will sharpen if they are connotatively dissimilar.

4. Conclusion

Language is a building block of most human culture. Human institutions require an articulation of roles and behavior, and without language to help coordinate their activities, human groups would be reduced to primitive organizations dependent on signs and signals like every other form of life known to us. The institution of law could not exist without codes of law, theories of jurisprudence, legal language, and the legitimation of the codes by the ethical, ideological, and religious systems of thought predominant in the society. Without language there would be none of the marvelous symbolic achievements of man.

IV.   DEPENDENCE ON GROUPS FOR INFORMATION

The individual's construction of reality is heavily dependent on the information provided to him by other people. By making social comparisons with others he may replace doubt with belief and ambiguity with clarity. Groups provide normative information about right and wrong conduct, as well as validation of the nature of reality. The information dependence of the individual is heightened by environmental conditions which produce fear and he may seek affiliation with others to find solace, comfort, or clarity of interpretation. Any type of crisis produces a need for information. The process of brainwashing is probably the most dramatic demonstration of the individual's information dependence on the group.

A.   The Social Comparison Process

The individual is more dependent on others for his construction of social reality than for information about physical reality. According to Festinger (1950): "An opinion, a belief, an attitude is 'correct,' 'valid,' and 'proper' to the extent that it is anchored in a group of people with similar beliefs, opinions and attitudes" (p.272). Once the individual adopts the values and beliefs of a particular group, he uses the group as a reference for *comparative appraisals* in forming new judgments about reality.

Sherif (1936) demonstrated how an individual's judgment of an ambiguous stimulus situation is affected by other peo-

ple. Subjects were first asked to make judgments while alone about the amount of movement of a spot of light projected on a screen in a dark room. Under these conditions, although the light does not actually move, observers report its movement and disagree on how far it does move. The apparent movement of the light is an illusion called the *autokinetic effect*. After making a number of judgments about how far the spot of light moved, the subjects typically developed a standard range, say 4 to 6 inches. After they had developed their standards, each individual was seated together with a confederate of the experimenter who had been instructed to make judgments within a different range. Both the subject and the confederate then made judgments within the presence of each other. As Sherif expected, the subjects shifted their range of judgments in the direction of those made by the confederate. Furthermore, when the subject subsequently made judgments while he was once again alone, he continued to use the modified range. The judgments of others have a relatively lasting effect on the individual in ambiguous stimulus situations. The more confused or ambiguous the situation, or the more vague the criteria for assessing the nature of reality, the more effective is this kind of informational influence (Luchins, 1945; Walker & Heyns, 1962).

A number of experiments have generally supported Festinger's assumption that persons will not seek consensual validation from just anyone, but will turn to persons who are similar to themselves (e.g., Gruder, 1971; Samuel, 1973; Wheeler, Shaver, Jones, Goethals, Cooper, Robinson, Gruder & Butzine, 1969). The typical procedure in these studies is to have subjects complete a personality test and then provide them with false feedback indicating either that their tests had not yet been scored or that they had received "middle range" scores. Subjects are provided an opportunity to compare their scores with others, but they must choose among comparison others. In support of Festinger's hypothesis, subjects usually prefer to make comparisons with similar others.

However, there is also a tendency to compare with those who make high positive scores. Learning about someone who possesses favorable characteristics may be more informative than learning about a person with less desirable traits. Also, making comparisons with a valued other person is self-enhancing and may reflect an aspiration to be like the referent person. On the other hand, it might be negatively reinforcing (i.e., self-disparaging) to be constantly compared to superior other people. For this latter reason, as we shall see in more detail in Chapter 11, similarity appears to be more important than expertise, status, or prestige in choosing comparison others.

B. Normative Versus Informational Influence

In their analysis of the functions that groups play in the formation of an individual's conception of reality, Deutsch and Gerard (1955) differentiated between normative and informational influence. The enforcement of group standards and judgments through rewards and punishments constitutes *normative influence*, while social comparison reflects *informational influence*. A similar distinction was made by Thibaut and Strickland (1956), who refer to the means of maintaining group membership as *group set* and the need to attain cognitive clarity about the environment as *task set*. The individual is considered to be dependent on others as "mediators of facts" in the case of task set, while concern about achieving or maintaining positive relationships with others is the basis of group set. The group often punishes deviance from accepted beliefs and standards of conduct. The desire to gain rewards and avoid punishments and the information dependence of the individual ties him to reference groups.

1. Punishment for Deviance

Schachter (1951) studied the reactions of a group toward a member who maintained a deviant opinion. Group discussions were held concerning the recommended treatment for Johnny Rocco, a juvenile delinquent. Subjects were asked to indicate their recommendations on seven-point scales ranging from lenient treatment, emphasizing love and affection, to very severe punishment. The subjects generally took a middle position on the scale, advocating some mixture of love and punishment. Three confederates were planted in each group, each of whom played a different role in the discussion. The *deviate* advocated extreme punishment and maintained his position throughout the discussion. The *slider* also advocated extreme punishment at the beginning of the discussion, but shifted and adopted the prevailing moderate view midway in the discussion. The *conformist* adopted the moderate opinion from the very beginning and maintained it throughout the discussion.

Analysis of the communications showed a rather uniform level directed toward the conformist throughout the discussion, a tendency to reduce communications to the slider as he fell in line, and a tendency to direct frequent communications toward the deviate until near the end of the discussion, when there was a sharp decline, providing the group members were attracted to one another and the discussion was relevant to a group goal. Most members in these groups eventually gave up on the deviate but only after trying very hard to bring him into line. Gerard (1953) and Festinger and Thibaut (1951) found that the amount of communication directed toward a deviate was greater the more extreme his position. In both of these latter studies there was a sharp drop in communications toward the deviate at the end of the discussion. The subjects' desire to persuade the deviate to conform may be due to the doubt that his conflicting opinion produces in the group.

Another way to accomplish the objective of maintaining group consensus is to eject the deviate from the group. Measures obtained in Schachter's study revealed that subjects were in favor of ostracizing the deviate. They were in general agreement to eliminate him from future discussions in the event the group size had to be reduced, and in making nominations for various committee assignments the group relegated him to unimportant committees.

2. The Reference Group

It is difficult for a person to publicly adopt an opinion that his friends and loved ones consider wrong or repugnant. For many people friendship is far more important than an abstract concern for "the truth." The implication is that the individual's *reference groups,* the groups of people with whom he makes social comparisons or comparative appraisals, maintain a conservative hold on him. Fear of disapproval or rejection may make him unwilling to examine or accept new ideas.

As persons shift reference groups, they also revise their ways of looking at the world. Newcomb (1943) has shown that a profound change may occur among college students who shift reference groups during their educational experience. His classic study was carried out at Bennington College in Vermont. The typical freshman at this all-girl school in 1935 came from a wealthy New England family embracing conservative political opinions. An attitude survey revealed a pattern of attitudes among freshman students similar to the opinions held by their families, which constituted the students' reference groups at this time. Most of the faculty at Bennington were young and liberal in political orientation. Presumably their biases, beliefs, and values were communicated to students in lectures, informal discussions, and reading materials. Newcomb took samples of students from all classes and found that the longer the student had been at Bennington, the more liberal were her political opinions.

Seniors were more liberal than juniors, juniors were more liberal than sophomores, and sophomores were more liberal than freshmen.

Girls who maintained close contact with their parents and home community through frequent visits and communications retained their conservative opinions. They indicated their discontent with many of their classmates with statements such as, "I wouldn't care to be intimate with those so-called 'liberal' student leaders;" "The things that I really care about are mostly outside the college;" and so on (Newcomb, 1958). For these students the college community was a *negative reference group.*

Students who fully participated in the college community, as indicated by membership in clubs and sororities or by working in campus politics or on the college paper, adopted the liberal views of the faculty and the upperclassmen. These students were often not close to their families, as indicated by such statements as, "I accepted liberal attitudes here because I had always secretly felt that my family was narrow and intolerant, and because such attitudes had prestige value," and "I came to college to get away from my family who never had any respect for my mind. Becoming a radical meant thinking for myself and, figuratively, thumbing my nose at my family" (Newcomb, 1958, p.272–273). For these students the college community was a *positive reference group.*

Thomas Wolfe, in his autobiographical novel *You Can't Go Home Again,* portrayed the difficulty of ever reestablishing the relationships of youth after one had been a student at college, traveled widely, and learned something about the ways of the world. Could the Bennington girls return home again? Interviews conducted with nearly the entire graduating class of 1939 some 20 years later found that the changes that occurred in college had persisted in the lives of the once conservative freshmen of 1935 (Newcomb, Koenig, Flacks, & Warwick, 1967). The Bennington alumni who had adopted liberal attitudes in college married men with similar opinions, thereby maintaining a reference group at odds with their parents and their more conservative peers.

Cartwright (1951) has described how deeply imbedded an individual is in his groups: "how aggressive or cooperative a person is, how much self-respect and self-confidence he has, how energetic and good he is, what he loves or hates, and what beliefs and prejudices he holds, all of these characteristics are highly determined by the individual's group memberships" (p.388).

Of course a person may be a member of a group without using it as a reference group; that is, he may maintain beliefs that are idiosyncratic in his particular membership group because he does not use it as either a positive or negative reference group. Furthermore, a person may adopt a reference group of which he is not a member. For example, a person may express a set of ideals advocated by a geographically remote group, the members of which are unaware of his existence. Lewin (1947a, 1947b) recognized the degree to which the individual is tied to groups and suggested that producing change in an individual requires change in his group's view of reality. Such change involves three stages: (1) unfreezing the attitude or behavior under consideration from the group standard, (2) modifying the attitude, and (3) refreezing the newly developed patterns by attaching them to new group standards.

Unfreezing the group norm is usually a very difficult task, and failure to do so works against the propagandist or social change agent. While an influential source may persuade or dissuade a target person temporarily, when the target takes the new opinions and views back to his reference group he may find himself subject to verbal arguments, social rejection, and censure until he is willing to give up the objectionable new ideas. Most people are pragmatists who are concerned with having beliefs that gain them acceptability and rewards, and

they are not motivated to take stands that produce rejection and punishments. Because the individual's opinions are strongly anchored to reference groups, Lewin (1958) suggested that it might be easier to change the entire group than to change a single member. If the entire group can be persuaded, each member can reinforce the other's new opinions and behavior, a process which constitutes refreezing.

Schein and his co-workers (Schein, 1958; Schein, Schneier, & Barker, 1961) pointed out that a breakdown in firm group relationships may lead to unfreezing. Isolation from friends, removal of self-defining titles or status, breakdown of hierarchical authority, substitution of value-incongruent information, and the engineering of feelings of guilt can lead to the unfreezing of fixed opinions and remove resistance to change. Significant shifts in group membership and a concomitant change in norms and informational inputs is often a powerful means of unfreezing old attitudes and behavior and provide the basis for refreezing new patterns. Alienated or marginal men lack firm social anchors and hence are often caught upon the winds of change and are recruited to social and ideological movements (Hoffer, 1951). It was no accident that the Austrian ex-soldier Adolph Hitler held his first meetings and attracted his first adherents in the beer halls of Germany.

If the many strands that connect an individual with his past are rooted in his continuing memberships in groups, then the more dissociated a person is from reference groups, the more influenceable he should become. Presumably, a small residential college should have more impact on a person than a large community college or high school. The separation of the individual from his groups often occurs in a highly mobile, industrialized, urban society in which there has been a breakdown of the influence of the family and the church. The urban dweller often lacks roots in either a geographical place or a social tradition. To a degree previously unknown in history the individual is required to think about matters on his own; he must judge everything for himself. Ellul (1965) concluded that "in theory this is admirable. But in practice what really happens? The individual is placed in a minority position and burdened at the same time with a total, crushing responsibility. Such conditions make an individualist society fertile ground for modern propaganda. The permanent uncertainty, the social mobility, the absence of sociological protection and of traditional frames of reference—all these inevitably provide propaganda with a malleable environment that can be fed information from the outside and conditioned at will. The individual left to himself is defenseless, the more so because he may be caught up in a social current, thus becoming easy prey for propaganda" (p.92).

C.   Fear and Affiliation

When danger lurks but its exact nature or intensity is not known, a person may seek out others to make social comparisons about the feared event. After a particularly tough examination students are likely to spend a great deal of time in post mortems to try to assess how well they may have done. The anxiety of waiting several days for their grades encourages them to find out how others fared. Those individuals who have the highest fear may be expected to affiliate more than those with less fear.

In a series of imaginative studies Schachter (1959) tested the relationship between fear and affiliation. In the original study, subjects were aggregated into groups of from five to eight and met in a laboratory containing electrical equipment. The experimenter, who was dressed in a white lab coat, identified himself as a professor of neurology and psychiatry. He said the purpose of the experiment was to study the effects of electric shocks on human responses.

In a high fear condition, subjects were told they would receive rather intense shocks that would be quite painful but would not do permanent damage. In a low fear condition, the instructions indicated that the shocks would be quite mild and would resemble a tingle more than anything unpleasant. Thus subjects in both conditions anticipated shocks, but half were induced to expect a painful and frightening experience and half were led to expect a mild and nonthreatening experience. Self-report measures indicated that the manipulation worked. Subjects who were given the painful shock instructions reported more fear than did subjects who were given the mild shock instructions.

The experimenter said he would need about ten minutes to prepare the equipment and told the subjects they could wait alone, if they wished, in one of a number of rooms that contained comfortable chairs and reading materials. He also said that some subjects preferred to wait with other people and indicated the availability of a group waiting room. Subjects were asked whether they would like to wait alone, wait with others, or were indifferent about where they waited. No shocks were actually administered to subjects. The results showed that high fear subjects preferred to wait with others while low fear subjects generally had no preference.

In a supplementary finding, birth order was found to be associated with the desire to affiliate with others under conditions of high fear. First and only children displayed a stronger need to affiliate than second-born children, the latter showed a stronger affiliation tendency than third-born, and so on. Since it is widely believed that first-born children gain more attention and social support from their parents while growing up than later born children, it may be conjectured that first-born children seek more solace and protection from others when they are afraid. Hence one explanation for this finding is that the cause of affiliation is a desire to reduce fear.

Subsequent research has found that the

major cause of affiliation under high fear is a need for social comparison about the impending danger and not a desire for social comfort. For example, in the above study Schachter (1959) found that high fear subjects had less preference for waiting with others when informed that no discussion of the impending experiment would be allowed. In a second study, Schachter offered half his high fear subjects the alternative of waiting together with other subjects in the experiment; the other half were given the option of waiting with persons who were not part of the experiment but were just waiting to be advised by a professor. These subjects preferred to wait with someone who shared their fate rather than with people who were not in the same boat.

In a similar study Zimbardo and Formica (1963) found a stronger desire to affiliate with other subjects who were waiting to participate in the experiment than with subjects who had completed their participation. One might think that veteran subjects could tell the naive person about the nature of the shock, how painful it was, and so on. But naive subjects preferred persons who had not yet experienced the shocks, people who were apprehensive and emotionally aroused like themselves. Apparently the subjects wanted to make comparisons about the degree of fear others were experiencing. As Schachter summarized these findings, "Misery doesn't just love company, it loves similarly miserable company."

Gerard and Rabbie (1961) provided evidence to clarify further the fear-affiliation relationship. Subjects were told that electrodes attached to their finger and head would register the degree of emotionality they were experiencing on a dial placed in front of them. On a scale from 0 to 100 the dial indicated a rather high level of emotionality; each subject's rating was contrived to read 82. In one condition of the experiment, each subject was informed that three other subjects were being tested in other rooms and he could see their emo-

tionality ratings on three separate dials displayed before him. These bogus dial settings were 79, 80, and 81. In a second condition subjects received feedback only about their own scores. In a third condition no information was given the subject about his own or any other emotionality scores. Subjects were then provided an opportunity during a waiting period to affiliate with others. When subjects already had information about the emotionality experienced by others, which should have satisfied their need for social comparison, they showed a much weaker desire to affiliate with others than when they were permitted to see only their own score or had no information at all.

In a follow-up study Gerard (1963) provided either clear or ambiguous feedback to subjects about the emotionality experienced by others who were waiting to be shocked. In the High Clarity condition stable dial settings allowed the subject to see the emotionality scores of the others. In the Ambiguous Feedback condition the needles on the dials fluctuated wildly, permitting little certainty about the level of emotionality experienced by the others. As would be expected from a social comparison hypothesis, subjects who had only vague and ambiguous information about the emotionality of others expressed a stronger desire to affiliate than did those who possessed clear information.

D. Information Dependence During Crisis

A crisis may be defined as a situation in which great harm may occur and quick decisions must be made. Typically, persons are disoriented at such times and are not sure what they should do. The lack of a personal frame of reference or schema makes the individual informationally dependent on any person who acts decisively and seems to know what to do. Killian (1964), in a field study of disasters such as hurricanes, explosions, and fires, found that people often grant autocratic authority to a single individual such as a sheriff or civil defense director and readily respond to his demands, orders, requests, and suggestions.

A similar effect occurs during such national crises as war, depression, and commodity shortages. National leaders are given unusual powers, sometimes to the extent of the virtual elimination of civil liberties. Unusual power is presumably necessary so the leader can effectively muster the resources necessary to deal with the crisis and bypass the usually time-consuming legislative and judical processes. Citizens are usually responsive to their leadership under crisis conditions. For example, during the energy crisis in the winter of 1973-74 American citizens responded to the appeals of their leaders to reduce voluntarily their fuel consumption by lowering their thermostats, curtailing the amount and speed of automobile travel, and other fuel saving responses.

Rapid social change may take place during a crisis because accepted ways of doing things may no longer be possible. Hamblin (1958) attempted to simulate conditions of rapid social change in the laboratory by changing the rules of a game after groups of subjects had learned the procedures necessary for success. The rule change made success impossible for the experimental groups, while in a control condition other groups experienced no such rule changes. The group leader was highly influential in making suggestions in the ambiguous "crisis" condition, whereas his influence in the control groups diminished over time. Dependence on the leader in the crisis situation was underscored by the observation that several of the crisis groups changed leaders because of the inability of the prior leader to come up with a solution. This is reminiscent of the athletic coach who is fired if his team cannot seem to find its way out of the doldrums and start winning again.

E. Brainwashing

Schein, Schneier, and Barker (1961) have adopted the term "coercive persuasion" to characterize a situation in which complete control is maintained over the information and the administration of rewards and punishments received by an individual. In popular parlance, these techniques are called "brainwashing."

Ellul (1965) suggests that there are three major aspects of brainwashing: (1) cutting the individual off from his reference groups (i.e., friends, relatives, news sources, etc.) and disrupting old habits by frequent interruptions of his sleep, reducing opportunities for physical exercise, and maintaining irregular hours for meals; (2) exposing the individual to the opinions and slogans of guards, radio programs, books, magazines and fellow prisoners who have already been converted; and (3) providing "democratic" discussions in which uncertainty and guilt are created in the target person. Guilt plays upon the person's system of morality and ties the actions of his old reference groups to wrongs done to humanity. Explanations are then provided which eliminate guilt, give meaning to the slogans, and provide him with new reference groups. These three techniques are associated with "unfreezing" the person from his former standards of reference, providing him with new beliefs through propaganda, and then "refreezing" him into new reference groups.

The process of brainwashing may be illustrated by the treatment of some American prisoners of war held by the Chinese during the Korean War. Written accounts (Lifton, 1961; Schein, 1958) show that the Chinese followed the steps of isolation, propaganda, and "democratic" discussions in their attempts to gain collaboration from the POWs. Upon capture the American POWs were greeted by a young Chinese who congratulated them on their liberation. After long marches to far distant POW camps, during which the men were exposed to extreme hardships, the men were given adequate quarters.

The unfreezing process was begun immediately. The men were segregated by rank, race, and nationality. This segregation was intended to break down military discipline and to promote ethnic hostilities. Group meetings were prohibited in order to prevent the formation of informal group structures. Distrust was fostered among the men by interrogating them repeatedly about the activities of the others. Small acts of informing on one's fellows were carefully and consistently rewarded by the prison camp officials. Approximately one out of every four men provided some kind of information to the enemy—for example, that someone failed to share with his buddies, did not properly dispose of cigarette butts, or some other insignificant action. The person informed on was then subjected to harassment by his fellows, who generally were more advanced in the brainwashing process, and was asked to confess his guilt. This process was at first resisted and resented, but gradually these reactions gave way to the prisoner's belief that he was in fact guilty and deserved to be punished. Resistance by a prisoner was met by placing him in chains, making him stand or squat for long periods of time in small spaces, and preventing him from sleeping.

Contacts with the home environment were either severed or poisoned by control over the mail. Mail was generally withheld from prisoners unless it was bad news, such as a wife informing her husband that she had started divorce proceedings. If no mail was delivered the captors suggested that the POW had been abandoned by his friends and his loved ones. Mass media inputs were hand picked by the Chinese; only Communist movies, radio broadcasts, newspapers, and magazines were available. While compulsory lectures were crudely propagandistic and unsuccessful, voluntary seminars drew more attention from POWs. The seminars were set up to study various topics; attendance was voluntary, but since the prisoners had little else to do and were eager to gain whatever information they could, there was little difficulty in getting them to volunteer. These seminars would often build upon a criticism of historical events familiar to the prisoners. For example, beginning with a discussion of the ruthless business practices of the robber barons in 19th century America, generalizations would then be made to the contemporary exploitation of steel workers in Pittsburgh. The less education a POW had, the more susceptible he was to such propaganda.

The POWs were forced to write autobiographies which were then discussed in order to point out how the soldiers' misfortunes and difficulties were the product of the American capitalistic system. Self-criticism for the most trivial offenses was required. Confession and collaboration were rewarded while resistance was punished. The reading of communist literature, the expression of the "correct" opinions, and the criticisms of former reference groups by the prisoners was consistently rewarded. Support from "teachers" and prisoners who were more advanced in their indoctrination served the function of trying to refreeze the individual into a new reference group.

By and large the Chinese attempt to resocialize American soldiers failed in its basic aim of engendering political beliefs and values similar to those held by the Chinese themselves. Some POW's were converted, some were bent toward conversion, but most resisted or played it cool until they were released. Many of the men suffered relatively permanent psychological scars from the experience, however. Their distrust of other men, built up through the system of informing, and the deep humiliation associated with making confessions in front of fellow prisoners left a deep residue of reserve towards people in general and, in many cases, led to a genuine misanthropy. The Chinese failure to be fully successful in achieving their aims is testimony to the effectiveness and strength of the socialization processes that created identity in the men as "Americans" and then as "American soldiers." Lambert and Lambert (1964) view brainwashing as an everyday technique to which all of us are subjected to some degree. The specific techniques of social control are simply more noticeable when they are used to convert adult men from one conception of social reality to a totally different one.

V. EMOTIONAL LABELING

Common sense tells us that our emotions are our own private experiences and that we enjoy them or suffer them as spontaneous reactions to events. Until very recently most scientists believed that humans were born with a ready assortment of emotions that are elicited under the appropriate environmental circumstances. New and compelling evidence has been gathered, however, which indicates an entirely different view of the emotions. Just as we construct a picture of the outer world by making social comparisons with referent others, environmental and social cues provide a basis on which we make inferences about general states of arousal we feel. Whether we feel angry or happy in a particular situation which produces a sense of arousal depends to some degree upon the social cues that indicate which feeling state is most appropriate in the situation. Internal physiological cues are not sufficient to allow a person to identify his emotional state.

The concept of emotion has never been very well articulated or defined. We will briefly examine the problem of definition to show why the study of emotions has been a very complex matter. We will then discuss the new view of emotion propounded by Schachter (1964), which is referred to as a "two-factor theory" because it takes into account both the physiological arousal states of the human organism and the choice of cognitive labels he makes in identifying

those states. The choice of labels is dependent on past experience and present cues in the environment. The dependence of the individual on social cues for identifying his own emotional states lays a basis for misattributing the causes of his own feelings. If a person can be led to believe his depression is due to certain environmental factors and not a chronic characteristic of his personality, his depression might be alleviated by a change in the situation. That is, a person's emotions can then be manipulated by varying the social cues that are associated with physiological arousal states.

A. The Concept of Emotion

For many years physiologists and psychologists have searched unsuccessfully for the underlying biochemical or neurological cues that allow us to discriminate the emotions we experience. Mandler (1962) concluded that the available evidence reveals that emotional reactions involve general, global, and diffuse conditions of arousal. The only reliable distinguishing feature of emotional states that can be tied to physiological factors is general arousal, in the form of increased heart rate, sweating of the palms, constriction of the blood vessels, and other activities controlled by the autonomic nervous system. But separate emotions are *not* related to distinctive neuronal or hormonal factors.

One problem that has plagued the study of emotion is a lack of clarity about the definition of the concept. According to Mandler, there is little consistency in the way investigators study the problem. Some researchers have attempted to establish a relationship between certain types of environmental events and visceral responses, others have studied the association of visceral and skeletal responses, and still others have focused on the phenomenological reports of subjects regarding their feeling states. A separation of environmental events, physiological factors, phenomenological reports, and skeletal responses is seldom accomplished because of the insistence on referring to all of them as "emotions."

B. The Two-Factor Theory of Emotions

Schachter's two-factor theory of emotions is an attempt to understand how the individual does identify his own emotional states. If the emotions are not discriminated from one another on the basis of physiological processes, how does the individual know what emotion he is experiencing? Apparently, the number and types of emotions that a person experiences are culturally determined, like his language. Just as an Eskimo may have many different names for snow and a pygmy none, so there are large differences in the emotional vocabulary among cultures.

The identification of emotions must be learned during the socialization process. When physiologically aroused, the person must learn to label his emotions according to the cues available. He learns to identify which conditions are associated with which emotional labels. Physiological arousal is often a learned reaction to stimulus conditions; thus, at one time in history viewing a lady's ankle was quite arousing, while at another time nothing less than a glimpse of a thigh would produce arousal.

In a succinct statement of his theoretical position, Schachter (1964) considered an emotion to be "a function of a state of physiological arousal and of a cognition appropriate to this state of arousal. The cognition, in a sense, exerts a steering function. Cognitions arising from the immediate situation as interpreted by past experiences provide the framework within which one understands and labels his feelings. It is the cognition which determines whether the state of physiological arousal will be labeled 'anger,' 'joy,' or whatever" (pp.50–51). Figure 3.4 is a pictorial view of Schachter's theory. Both physiological arousal *and* past experience or environmental cues must be present if the individual is to find a label with which to identify his feeling state. When one or the other component is missing he will not be able to report an identifiable emotion.

Schachter and Singer (1962) reported an early study by Marañon (1924) in which patients were injected with adrenalin, a drug which induces physiological arousal, and then were asked to report their reactions to the drug. The majority reported

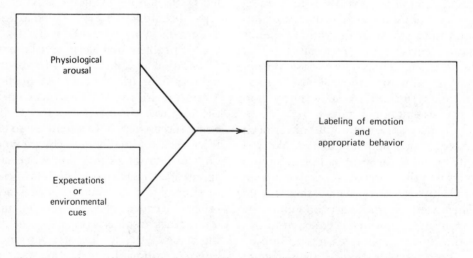

Figure 3.4. The two-factor theory of emotion. The individual invokes a label to associate his sensed arousal with either his expectations regarding arousal or environmental factors that seem appropriate to the sensed arousal.

whatever physical effect they noticed, such as headaches, tension, and so on. But 29 percent of them said they felt *as if* they were afraid or expected some happy event. These "as if" emotions were recognized by the patients as probably not real and were referred to by Marañon as "cold" emotions. However, a few of these patients were reminded of their sick children or dead parents—comments which did not arouse emotions before the injections—and reported what they described as real emotions. Apparently, to generate genuine emotion it was necessary to produce physiological arousal by an artificial stimulant and also to provide social cues that would allow the patients to use an appropriate label to identify their feeling states.

To test this hypothesis, Schachter and Singer (1962) told subjects in a laboratory situation that the experiment was concerned with examining the effects of a vitamin compound (given the fictitious name "Suproxin") on vision. After obtaining their permission, half of the subjects were given injections of epinephrine, which activates the sympathetic nervous system to produce the general arousal which is characteristic of emotion; the other half were given a placebo, a saline solution that produces no known physiological effects. Epinephrine takes effect in three to five minutes and produces heart palpitations and other signs of arousal for 10 to 15 minutes. Thus some subjects were aroused and some were not.

The information provided to the subjects injected with epinephrine was manipulated to provide three experimental conditions. In the Informed condition the subjects were told to expect certain side-effects from Suproxin, such as tremors, pounding heart, and perhaps some flushing of the face, which would last from 15 to 20 minutes. In the Misinformed condition, subjects were told to expect transitory side-effects consisting of numbness of the feet, some itching, and a slight headache. In the Ignorant condition, subjects were told that Suproxin was a mild and harmless substance that had no discernible side-effects. According to Schachter's theory, subjects in the Informed condition should be able to attribute their arousal states to the effects of receiving Suproxin, but subjects in the Misinformed and Ignorant conditions would have no ready explanation for their reactions and would seek cues from their environment in order to label their epinephrine-induced arousal states. Subjects in the Placebo condition were given only the Ignorant instructions.

The subjects were next provided with social cues from another person with whom they could make comparisons about their feeling states. While a subject was waiting the approximately 20 minutes supposedly necessary for Suproxin to take hold, the experimenter brought in a stooge and told the subject: "Both of you have had the Suproxin shot and you'll both be taking the same test of vision. . . . When we are certain that most of the Suproxin has been absorbed into the bloodstream we'll begin the tests of vision" (Schachter & Singer, 1962, p.384).

The stooge's behavior was manipulated to express euphoria or to reflect anger. In the Euphoria condition the rehearsed behavior of the stooge included doodling on scratch paper, crumbling paper into balls and shooting them into a waste basket, making paper airplanes and flying them, playing with one of two hula hoops in the room, making verbal comments indicating positive feelings, and inviting the subject to join in by tossing him a paper ball, an airplane, and a hula hoop.

In the Anger condition the experimenter left identical questionnaires for the stooge and the subject to fill out. The questionnaire started out with innocuous questions but soon asked rather personal and offensive ones like, "With how many men (other than your father) has your mother had extramarital relationships?" The stooge made increasingly hostile comments about the questions and finally said he would no longer participate, ripped up the questionnaire, threw it on the floor, stomped out of the room, and slammed the door.

Half of the subjects in the Informed, Ignorant, and Placebo conditions were exposed to the euphoric stooge and the other half were exposed to the angry stooge. The Misinformed subjects were exposed only to the euphoric stooge. Observers scored the subjects' behavior while they waited with the stooge. Following each subject's observation of the extraordinary behavior of the stooge, he was asked to fill out a self-report of his mood state. The results consisted of the observers' ratings of the subjects and the subjects' self-reports of their own feeling states. Subjects who were physiologically aroused by epinephrine injections but had no adequate explanation for the arousal (i.e., the Misinformed and Ignorant conditions) reported their emotional state more in accord with the stooge's behavior than did subjects who had been provided with a ready explanation for their arousal states (i.e., Informed condition). The observers' ratings of the subjects' behavior while they were waiting with the stooge reflected the same pattern of either euphoria or anger as the self-report data. Thus, the two-factor theory of emotions was supported.

In a second test of the two-factor theory of emotions Schachter and Wheeler (1962) injected subjects with epinephrine, a saline solution (placebo), or chlorpromazine (a sympathetic depressant or "tranquillizer"). All subjects were told the drug was Suproxin and were informed there would be no side-effects. During a waiting period the subjects viewed a 14-minute excerpt from a Jack Carson film entitled *The Good Humor Man*, which focused on a slapstick chase scene. A judge observed the subjects and recorded the number of smiles, grins, laughs, and belly laughs emitted during the film.

The epinephrine subjects showed more amusement, especially in the form of laughs and belly laughs than did the placebo subjects, and the chlorpromazine subjects revealed the least amount of amusement. These findings are consistent with the theory, since the most intense emotions were expressed when the individual was aroused and was presented with environmental stimuli that could be used to identify emotional states. The epinephrine-aroused subjects, who had no readily available explanation for their arousal, behaved as though the movie was extremely funny. The same movie had relatively little effect on subjects whose arousal systems had been dampened by a tranquillizer. Since arousal had been elicited artificially by drugs, it could be said that subjects had been led to misattribute their arousal states, because without the drug they believed the film to be less funny. A series of studies have established that subjects can be caused to attribute (or misattribute) emotions to drugs, the environment, or to another person. As indicated in Box 3.5, such self-attributions are not restricted to emotions but may also refer to such internal states as hunger and thirst. Obesity, for example, may reflect a problem in the cues an individual uses in making self-attributions about hunger.

C. Re-Attributions of Emotions and Other Internal States

The two-factor theory of emotions implies that one can change the individual's attributions of the causes of his feeling states. This implication has potentially important applications for studying the so-called psychosomatic illnesses. For example, if a person believes his discomfort is attributable to an internal physiological dysfunction, he may be resigned to interpreting his arousal states in terms of discomfort; but if he can attribute the cause of his discomfort to external stimuli, he can presumably re-attribute the arousal states he feels when those external stimuli are absent, removed or replaced.

Box 3.5   HUNGER, AFFILIATION AND OBESITY

Most people in the United States eat three or more times a day. To go without food for 20 or more hours should create intensified visceral cues related to hunger but should be so unfamiliar that the individual may seek additional consensual information through social comparison with similar others. Schachter (1959) manipulated the hunger of subjects who were informed that the purpose of the experiment was to ascertain the effects of food deprivation on visual and auditory perceptions. A High Hunger group missed breakfast and lunch, a Medium Hunger group missed only lunch, and a Low Hunger group was fed prior to the experiment. During an adaptation period the subjects were permitted to wait with another person or could choose to wait alone. Subjects in the High Hunger condition chose to affiliate during the waiting period more frequently than subjects in either of the two other conditions. Going without lunch, as did the subjects in the Medium Hunger condition, was apparently not sufficiently strange to induce them to be more eager to compare themselves with others than those who had just eaten.

Schachter (1967) subsequently developed the hypothesis that overweight individuals may be more reliant on external cues about their state of hunger than normal persons, who are more responsive to "internal" physiological cues about hunger and satiety. Generalizing from his findings about the misattribution of emotions, Schachter reasoned that obese individuals may develop eating habits based on food-related cues in the environment rather than on nutritional needs. Schachter and Gross (1968) found that overweight people eat more when the clock indicated that it was mealtime. Schachter, Goldman, and Gordon (1968) determined that overweight persons do not increase their food intake after increases in food deprivation, nor do they eat more when they are afraid. In all of these respects overweight people respond differently than normals. Furthermore, overweight people are more willing to fast for religious purposes and report less discomfort from doing so than normal people. These findings suggest that if the obese person can remove himself from food-related environmental cues, his food intake will go down. Weight-watcher groups may also be quite beneficial in providing social comparison information to help him regulate his food intake to normalize his body weight.

The re-attribution process was examined by Nisbett and Schachter (1966) in another pioneering study. Subjects were asked to undergo a series of electric shocks of increasing intensity and to tell the experimenter when they became too painful to tolerate. Prior to experiencing the shocks the subjects were given a placebo pill. Half of the subjects were told to expect arousal symptoms, while the other half were told that the pill would cause some physical effects not related to emotional arousal. The rationale behind these procedures was that when subjects were led to misattribute some of their discomfort to the pill rather than to fear or the pain associated with shocks, they would be able to tolerate higher shock intensities. When they expected no arousal or discomfort from the pill, their self-attributions would more clearly be associated with the shocks and they would tolerate less intense shocks. Consistent with this reasoning, the results showed that arousal-instructed subjects tolerated four times the shock amperage accepted by the subjects not instructed to expect arousal from the placebo pill. The expectations of the person affect how he responds to noxious stimulation from the environment. Presumably, when a person feels blue, bad news may not be so upsetting as when his spirits are more positive. As the old saw has it, "when you get so far down, the only way you can go is up."

Ross, Rodin, and Zimbardo (1969) showed that subjects can be led to misattribute emotional reactions to stimuli without the intervention of pills or injections. All subjects received a bombardment of noise for a period of three minutes. Half the subjects were told to expect increased palpitations of the heart, flushed face, and "butterflies" in the stomach as a result of exposure to the noise. The remaining subjects were instructed to expect several symptoms not connected with arousal, such as dizziness, headache, ringing in the ears, and weariness. After the subjects had been exposed to the noise, they were given an opportunity to work on one of two puzzles. If they chose to work on one of the puzzles they could win money for a correct solution and if they chose to work on the other they could escape a shock. In attempting to gain money, subjects had to accept a shock; but if they worked to avoid the shock, they could not win any money.

Subjects who were told to expect arousal in reaction to the exposure to noise more often chose to solve the puzzle to gain money. The subjects who could not misattribute to the noise their arousal arising from their fear of shock more often worked to avoid the shocks. Ross et al. suggested the possible clinical application of this reattribution process in alleviating maladaptive emotional states. An externalization of the cause of irrational fear or anxiety might

relieve a chronic mental patient of these emotional feelings and allow him to function adequately without psychological support from professionals.

Storms and Nisbett (1970) applied the reattribution hypothesis to the treatment of students who reported suffering from insomnia. Presumably a person has trouble going to sleep because of a high level of tension, alertness, and mental activity. The more he tries to go to sleep, the greater his tension and mental activity. If an insomniac could be induced to misattribute his arousal at bedtime to an artificial source, such as a placebo pill described as a drug producing arousal, then his cycle of increasing tension can be broken. He no longer needs to worry about what causes him to remain awake; he can attribute his alertness to the pill. On the other hand, if a person expects the placebo he has taken to reduce his tension, which of course it does not, he must assume that his problem is even worse than he thought it was. In the latter case, the insomniac might say to himself something like, "If I feel as aroused as I do now, when a drug is operating to lower my arousal, than I must be very aroused indeed" (Storms & Nisbett, p.320).

Led by this reasoning, the researchers gave all of their insomniac subjects a placebo pill to take before bedtime. Half the subjects were told that the pill would cause arousal symptoms, and the remainder were told to expect to be relaxed and calmed by the pill. As predicted, the subjects who received the arousal information went to sleep sooner than they had previously, and those who received the relaxation information had even more difficulty getting to sleep than before. Once the insomniacs could attribute their arousal state at bedtime to an external cause, they could relax and go to sleep. Because these results are contrary to common sense expectations, it is not too surprising that the exact opposite findings have also been reported (Kellogg & Baron, 1975).

In summary, the experience of unexpected physiological arousal places the individual in a state of information dependence. The aroused person seeks information from his own experiences (i.e., memory), other people, or impersonal environmental cues in order to construct a causal schema associating the external cues and the internal arousal state. The individual can then apply a cognitive label to his experience. By managing the kind of information made available, the experimenter or therapist can create misattributions and control the kind of label the person applies to his experience. As can be seen in Box 3.6, the two factor theory may also contribute to our understanding of the effects of some drugs.

The task of learning the conditions and language of emotions is very subtle and complex. Those who have failed to learn the socially approved emotional language well and who misidentify their emotions (in terms of the norms of appropriateness in their reference groups) may feel unhappy or experience concern about their mental health. For example, arousal in the presence of a parent may be misidentified and given a label more appropriate to a lover, bringing distress to the person who "experiences" it. Failure to experience arousal may also cause the individual a great deal of concern, as when a wife does not feel about her husband as she believes she should. The potential for solving these problems through the process of reattribution is an exciting one for clinical psychology.

VI. INDIVIDUAL DIFFERENCES IN INFORMATION PROCESSING

Some persons are open and receptive to new information, while others resist and

---

Box 3.6   THE TWO-FACTOR THEORY OF EMOTIONS AND THE USE OF MARIHUANA.

Howard Becker, (1970) a sociologist and former professional jazz musician, interviewed a number of marihuana users to determine what led them to become users. Of course the first step was learning how to inhale the smoke. The next step was learning to recognize the symptoms that the "high" is supposed to produce. An experienced user may inform the novice that smoking intensifies hunger and sexual pleasure, slows the experience of time, and yields a good feeling state. First-time users seldom feel that they have been "high." However, Becker found that "with increasing experience, the user develops a greater appreciation of the drug's effects; he continues to learn to get high. He examines succeeding experiences closely, looking for new effects, making sure the old ones are still there. Out of this grows a stable set of categories for experiencing the drug's effects whose presence enables the user to get high with ease" (p.386). The final step requires learning to enjoy the sensations induced by smoking. They are not automatically pleasurable any more than is a person's first cup of coffee or first glass of scotch. Dizziness, thirst, and perhaps a vague sick feeling require social definition as pleasant in order to be experienced as pleasant. Fear reduction, social approval and social support are necessary in learning to make the experience of smoking marihuana pleasurable. Many one-time users may never use marihuana again if they find it to be a "bomb-out" or experience unpleasant sensations. Thus, the experiences of the smoker are not determined by the marihuana itself.

avoid information that challenges what they already believe. These differences are a product of the experiences of people, including child-rearing, education, travel, and so on. The closed-mindedness or open-mindedness of a person in responding to information contrary to his beliefs can be assessed by paper-and-pencil scales of authoritarianism and dogmatism. Persons also differ in the complexity of their cognitive constructions of reality. While some people develop a very complex set of cognitive categories concerning the world, others have relatively few. The latter view the world in terms of the simplicities of black and white, while the former perceive everything as complex and shaded in grays.

Not only are there characteristic and stable differences between persons in cognitive structuring and information processing, but there are also speaker-listener differences in cognitive tuning. Speakers tend to be more rigid and less receptive to new information than listeners. Although too little is known to permit wide generalizations about the effects of these differences in social interactions, some interesting hypotheses concerning authoritarianism, dogmatism, cognitive complexity, and cognitive tuning have been examined.

A. Authoritarianism and Dogmatism

A group of researchers with a distinctive Freudian orientation to psychology undertook an investigation of anti-Semitism in the late 1940s (Adorno, Frenkel-Brunswick, Levinson, & Sanford, 1950). They discovered that anti-Semites generally shared a whole set of attitudes or orientations to the world. They tended to be prejudiced against blacks, chicanos, and other ethnic minorities, were extremely deferent to authority but hostile to subordinates, were rigid and conventional in thought, were conservative on political and economic issues, revealed exaggerated concern with sexual "goings-on" in society, and projected their own forbidden im-

pulses onto others. Through testing and depth interviews it was concluded that this pattern of authoritarianism was based on child-rearing practices. Harsh discipline, the subordination of the child's needs to those of the parents, and the promulgation of conventional goals and values characterized the homes of those identified as authoritarians.

Since these attitudes and values were characteristic of many Germans during World War II, the researchers identified authoritarians as fascists and developed a scale to measure this personality trait. The California F Scale has often been used to identify subjects in studies as authoritarians or egalitarians—usually these labels are applied to those who score very high or very low on the F scale. Authoritarianism has been found to be negatively correlated with intelligence (Christie, 1954), years of education (Hyman & Sheatsley, 1954), and socio-economic class (MacKinnon & Centers, 1956). In general, those who score high on the F Scale are considered narrow-minded, bigoted, and reactionary.

These conclusions must be tempered by the many criticisms leveled at the original study by Adorno, et al. and the F Scale. Biased sampling of subjects, lack of standardized procedures of interviewing, and many other problems make it difficult to draw any conclusions from the Adorno, et al. exploratory study (Hyman & Sheatsley, 1954). Christie and Jahoda (1954) found a methodological problem with the F Scale. Agreement with all items would yield a high score. As a consequence, any person who had a simple tendency to agree (i.e., acquiescence set) would be assessed as authoritarian. Although it is simple enough to correct this error in procedure, the interpretation of specific items remains equivocal. Significant changes in social attitudes have occurred in America since the 1940s. In the forties authoritarianism was indicated by agreement with items such as "Nowadays more and more people are prying into matters that should remain personal and private" and "Someday it will probably be shown that astrology can explain a lot of things." In the 1970s agreement with these items would suggest an egalitarian liberalism in politics, rather than an authoritarian conservatism.

What the F Scale is really measuring has not been firmly pinned down. The antequated Freudian theory that was used as a rationale for the F Scale can no longer be accepted as an interpretation of its validity. Kelman and Barclay (1963) suggested that the F Scale measures the breadth of perspective the individual has developed. Those who have limited psychological capacities or have had narrow social opportunities may score high in "authoritarianism." A person with low intelligence is psychologically prevented from developing a broad perspective, while a person who has not been exposed to others who have differing values, opinions, manners, and morals may view these differences as threatening or dangerous. Kelman and Barclay reported data which showed that capacity and opportunity made independent contributions to F Scale scores of subjects.

The concept of authoritarianism is not independent of political beliefs. Rokeach (1968) believed that liberals could be just as dogmatic as conservatives and hence set out to measure "narrow-mindedness" independent of political ideology. In devising his theory Rokeach defined a belief as a cognition, expectancy or hypothesis held and considered to be more or less true by an individual. Beliefs are differentiated into parts, and the greater the articulation of the belief into categories or schemata, the greater is the degree of differentiation. For example, a person may judge an object purely in terms of color or color or weight (its physical attributes) or he may evaluate it also by its potential uses (as a tool, as a nutrient, etc.). Of course a person often considers alternatives before adopting one as a belief, and what he disbelieves may be as differentiated as what he believes. The beliefs of a dogmatic individual are more differentiated than are his disbeliefs. This difference in the two kinds of cognitions is presumed to render the dogmatist more closed-minded in receiving new information contrary to his existing beliefs; he has fewer categories available for processing incongruent information. The non-dogmatic person is more responsive to new inputs because of his ability to accept conditions, variations, and shades of gray for an opposing position. To examine these theoretical differences between people, Rokeach developed a paper-and-pencil test to measure dogmatism.

Jamias and Troldahl (1965) used the dogmatism scale to investigate the effects of cognitive structure and social conditions on responsiveness to innovation. They identified farmers in terms of their degree of dogmatism in two types of rural townships in Michigan. One township was identified by county agricultural agents as containing people who were generally willing to adopt new practices, while people in the second township were considered resistant to innovative suggestions. Both dogmatism and the progressiveness of the community were shown to affect the willingness of the farmers to accept innovation. Dogmatic persons were willing to adopt the agents' suggestions when the community was generally receptive to change, but were resistant to the new information when they lived in a conservative township. Less dogmatic persons frequently adopted the recommendations of the agents regardless of the type of community in which they lived.

The resistance of the dogmatic individual to contrary arguments or evidence causes others to perceive him as opinionated. Dogmatic beliefs are often accepted from authorities rather than through the processes of examining all the available alternatives, logical reasoning, and independent assessment of the evidence. The susceptibility of dogmatic individuals to authority figures was demonstrated by Vidulich and

Kaiman (1961). Dogmatic and nondogmatic subjects were asked to make 30 judgments of the autokinetic phenomenon while alone. They were then given reports of the judgments allegedly made by another person, who was identified either as a college professor or a high school student. Subsequently, subjects once again made 30 judgments while alone. The second set of judgments made by dogmatic subjects showed a greater shift in the direction of the high than the low status person. Nondogmatic subjects, on the other hand, tended to be more influenced by the judgments of a low status person, possibly indicating resistance to information provided by the high status authority.

There is some evidence that dogmatism can affect bargaining behavior. Persons relatively low in dogmatism are better able to work out agreements than persons high in dogmatism (e.g., Druckman, 1967). The resolution of bargaining conflicts requires a fair degree of willingness to accept the fact that the other party may be equally justified in maintaining a strong bargaining position. As we will report in more detail in Chapter 9, some degree of openness, willingness to compromise, and mutual trust are important to reaching solutions in negotiation. The impact of dogmatism in other social situations has not been thoroughly examined.

B. Cognitive Complexity

The cognitive categories developed by the individual may be associated with each other by a number of relations and rules, such as rules of exclusion and inclusion and cause-effect relations, to create various schemata. The greater the level of cognitive complexity, the more personal and unique is the perspective of the individual. At a low level of complexity an individual is relatively rigid and his schemata are constructed with very simple rules. Few dimensions are used to represent objects, persons, works of art, social situations, or other aspects of physical and social reality.

Streufert and Fromkin (1972) report that less than 15% of the population is cognitively complex and that complexity is not correlated with intelligence. In addition to differences between persons in their level of cognitive complexity, differences may also occur within the same individual (Schroder, Driver, & Streufert, 1967). A person may be cognitively complex in the way he perceives some events and simple in his view of others. He may be a connoisseur of art and able to detect many nuances and styles and yet be totally imperceptive when it comes to the intricacies of machines.

Situational variations may affect the complexity of information processing. For example, cognitive processes tend to be simple and stereotyped under conditions of stress. We noted this type of tunnel vision earlier in discussing information processing when a person is experiencing strong emotions. Frank (1967) and deRivera (1968) have reported how the image of an enemy during prewar crises becomes a very simple and malevolent one with no room for the real complexities of the opponent's perceptions, motivations, and problems.

Persons may develop any one of a variety of cognitive styles. For example, Kagan, Moss, and Sigel (1963) found that persons adopted one of three styles of describing pictures. When asked to talk about the similarities between pictures, persons with a *descriptive* style focused on details. Those with an *inferential* style tried to impose a classificatory scheme, and individuals with a *relational* style looked for functional relations between objects in the pictures. Our understanding of the ways that persons organize schemata and use them in making judgments and decisions is only rudimentary. Some of the dynamics involved in structuring cognitions will be examined in the next two chapters.

C. Cognitive Tuning

Zajonc (1954) suggests that there are characteristic differences between speaker and listener in the complexity of information processing. A communicator must focus on the elements of his message; his attention to his own communication makes him more rigid and polarized in thought than he normally is. That is, a person "tuned" for transmission worries about the coherence and structure of what he is saying and becomes less able to focus on other perspectives or viewpoints. The listener, on the other hand, is more relaxed, and although he receives the general perspective being transmitted he may not attend to all of its details. The listener therefore remains free to restructure the information into complex cognitive categories as he searches through his stored information for relevant comparisons and evidence. We typically praise the individual who retains sufficient cognitive complexity while speaking to be able to "think on his feet."

Cohen (1961) found evidence that cognitive tuning affects the complexity of information processed. Subjects were directed either to transmit information describing a stimulus person to a third person or simply to form an impression of the stimulus person, and were then offered an opportunity to obtain additional information about the stimulus person. Cohen reasoned that if transmitters experience more difficulty in cognitive tuning, process less information, and use fewer dimensions to represent external events, then they would be more satisfied with the information they already possessed and would not seek new information. Nontransmitters, on the other hand, should be able to make a finer cognitive tuning with regard to the stimulus person, should process more information, and should be open to enriching their complex picture of the person by asking for further information. This reasoning was supported by the data. Transmitters desired less new information than did subjects who merely made quiet observations of the stimulus persons.

VII.   CHAPTER SUMMARY

Everyone seeks information enabling him to acquire a stable set of beliefs about the nature of physical and social reality. A person's need for information about his world is just as strong as his needs for physical comforts. He needs to be competent and knowledgeable in order to predict and control his environment. The individual needs to acquire reliable information because as a decision-maker, he cannot make intelligent choices when he is locked in doubt. A Hamlet is paralyzed by indecision.

Physical and social reality represent two realms of experience—the direct perceptions of the senses and the mediated information that cannot be separated from social consensus. The needed consensual validation of the individual's view of social reality is sought from attractive or valued reference groups and not just from any other person. The individual is selective about his choice of comparison others. Nevertheless, sources of information act as filters that select, omit, and change what had been available for transmission.

Persons in a social system are dependent on others for information about social and physical reality. Both the stability and accuracy of beliefs formulated depend on the fidelity of the gatekeepers of information. Tourists, newsmen, and scholars provide us with information that cannot be obtained firsthand. For various reasons the reports of gatekeepers are incomplete, inaccurate, and biased. Propagandists filter information with the objective of co-opting the target audience. They manipulate what their message contains and the way it is presented in order to maximize its planned impact on the audience. Censors attempt to manipulate beliefs or behavior by shutting off access to facts or theories which are considered as potentially detrimental to their interests.

The individual's world is incredibly complex and he is bombarded with far more information than he can possibly process. Of the great mass of stimuli impinging on his sensory apparatus, the individual must be selective in sampling information. There are limits to how much a person can attend to even though he chunks information into categories to increase his processing capabilities. What he attends to depends on the categories he has available, his interests and values, and stimulus factors which serve to attract his attention. Perception is an active process. Gating mechanisms such as perceptual vigilance and defense operate to determine cognitive selectivity. These intrapersonal information processing factors—gating, cognitive set, categories, and schemata—tend to distort information and lead to misperceptions and/or disagreements about the nature of reality.

The individual relies heavily on his past experiences in interpreting events. Memory is a highly selective process and is affected by existing cognitive categories, schemata, mnemonic devices, chunking, and competing information. The person's values and connotative meaning system may determine what is remembered or forgotten, and emotional states may interfere with his being a reliable witness to past occurrences. Memory loss causes leveling, assimilation, and sharpening of information. Serial reproduction demonstrations and the transmission of rumors emphasize the distortions that occur in storing, retrieving and transmitting information. Rumor intensity is a function of interest and ambiguity. A person's values seem systematically to distort his recollection of size, number, and perhaps extremity of valued objects and events.

Words, symbols, or labels have both denotative and connotative meanings. While denotative meaning points to the referents of symbols, connotative meaning refers to the emotional responses of persons to symbols. Connotative meaning is three dimensional. Research has shown that the Evaluative, Potency, and Activity dimensions are apparently universally used. Semantic differences can be a source of conflict and disagreement between men. Thus, while language is probably the most important factor in making the great cultural achievements of man possible and is responsible for freeing man of his total dependence upon the physical environment, it also serves as a source of disharmony and acrimony between men and societies.

Dependence on others for information regarding social reality leads the individual to make social comparisons. Comparative appraisals are made with others who share similar values and attitudes with the individual. Conformity with the beliefs, opinions, and behavior of the reference group is facilitated by punishments for deviance and rewards for conformity. Persons may shift reference groups as a result of important experiences such as living within a college community, extensive travel, or a major shift in occupation. Apart from such shifts in reference groups, unfreezing the group norms, influencing group members, and re-freezing new patterns are required in order to produce stable changes in people. It may be easier to change an entire group than it is to permanently change one member of the group.

When a person is dissociated from his past and from the consensual validation provided by reference groups, he is especially susceptible to the influence of others in redefining social reality. Conditions of fear, uncertainty, and crisis cause persons to rely heavily on others for definitions of their own states of stress and for information regarding actions they might take to relieve the stress and deal with the crisis. Brainwashing represents an attempt to achieve a total separation of the person from social reality as he has come to know it and to substitute an entirely new social reality. Control over both the information and the reinforcements available to the individual, isolating him from his reference groups, disrupting his routine habits, and subjecting him to propaganda constitute the techniques employed in brainwashing.

The individual is also informationally dependent on others for interpreting his own inner experiences. The two-factor theory of emotions proposes that the individual's cognitive categories, schemata, expectations, and the social and environmental cues to which he is exposed serve as the bases for his interpretations of his emotional experiences when he is physiologically aroused. The learning of emotions is a very complex and subtle process. Recent experiments show how easy it is to make misattributions about the causes of one's own arousal states. Misattributions about emotional states may cause the individual a great deal of psychological distress. Mental health professionals may apply techniques to get the individual to re-attribute the causes of his emotional states and thereby relieve his distress.

The study of individual differences in the way that persons organize categories and schemata and utilize them in making judgments and decisions is still in a very early stage of development. People vary in the degree to which they are generally open to information that contradicts their beliefs. Dogmatists tend to form complex categories and schemata for their own points or view, but tend to oversimplify alternative viewpoints. Dogmatists tend to be susceptible to the influence of authority figures and may be open to change when general approval for such innovation is expressed by significant other people. The disbeliefs of nondogmatists tend to be as cognitively complex as their beliefs and they remain open to new information and change.

Both interpersonal and intrapersonal differences exist between people both in cognitive complexity and cognitive styles. Situational factors, such as stress or crisis, reduce the information processing-capacity of the individual. In interpersonal interactions the cognitive tuning of the speaker is focused on his own communications, while the listener may stay attuned to the gist of the conversation and, at the same time, search for additional information either from memory or other aspects of the environment that can be used to interpret or rebut the speaker's point of view. The ramifications of these cognitive differences between people as they affect interpersonal interactions and social influence are not yet well understood.

SUGGESTED READINGS

Brown, J. A. C. *Techniques of persuasion: from propaganda to brainwashing.* Baltimore, Md.: Penguin Books, 1963. An examination of what is known about changing beliefs, attitudes, and behavior through the use of information.

Festinger, L. A theory of social comparison processes. *Human Relations,* 1954, **7,** 117–140. The classic statement about the interdependence of people in development of beliefs about social reality.

Pettigrew, T. F. Social evaluation theory: convergences and application. In D. Levine (Ed.), *Nebraska Symposium on Motivation.* Lincoln: University of Nebraska Press, 1967. Reviews the many applications of the social comparison process in human relationships.

White, R. K. *Nobody wanted war: misperception in Vietnam and other wars.* New York: Doubleday Anchor, 1970. A case study of misperception and its tragic impact on the lives of millions of people.

Valins, S., and Nisbett, R. E. Attribution processes in the development and treatment of emotional disorders. Morristown, N.J.: *General Learning Press,* 1972. This learning module presents a recent review of the research and theory regarding the clinical application of attribution theory.

CHAPTER 4

Person Perception

CHAPTER PREVIEW

Everyone is an amateur psychologist. Each of us forms impressions of other people: how they feel, what they are thinking, what they are likely to do next, and what causes them to act the way they do. This information is important in helping us decide how we should behave with other people. We may avoid a person who we think angry and approach one who is believed to be happy. How we react to a person may depend on our causal analysis of the reasons for his actions. We may not feel grateful to someone whose actions accidentally benefit us; we give credit only when the action is perceived as deliberate or intended. Each of us develops an unsophisticated theory of personality, which we apply to form stable and unified impressions of other people. In this chapter we will examine three major problems of person perception: how the average person goes about making causal analyses of human behavior, how he makes attributions about the internal states of other people, and how he forms overall impressions of others.

There are three major differences in the way we perceive people as compared to how we perceive physical objects. First, it is assumed that people experience internal states and that objects do not. Because we all have the ability to introspect, to experience feelings and to make plans, we assume that other people can do the same. Although some primitive peoples and young children may attribute feelings to inanimate objects, most mature adults make such attributions only to animate beings.

A second difference is that persons, but not objects, are perceived as first causes. If a rock rolls down a hill and hits you on the foot, you do not usually shout at it, retaliate against it or blame it for striking you. You are apt to look up the hill for the cause of the rock falling. On the other hand, if a person steps on your foot, you will try to ascertain whether it was done deliberately or accidentally—that is, whether the behavior originated in the internal plans of the other person or whether there were environmental causes (crowding) or accidental causes (stumbling) for his behavior. If the behavior can be attributed to the internal states of the other person, he will be perceived as a first cause and held responsible for his conduct.

Third, persons unlike objects, can deliberately manipulate and exploit the perceiver. We can manipulate objects, but the reverse cannot happen without the intervention of a human planner. Since persons can act as origins or first causes, they are perceived as capable of manipulating both objects and other people. As a consequence, it is important for the individual to develop causal schemata that allow him to predict the probable actions of other people. Such predictive schemata provide him with a stable basis for planning his own actions.

The use of the word "perception" may be somewhat misleading regarding the problems to be considered in this chapter. We are not referring to the size, color, or texture of persons as stimuli, but rather to the presumed internal states of a stimulus person which are *inferred* from perceptual cues. However, we are not usually aware of an inference process. The image we form of a person is so direct and immediate that it appears to result from the perception of external stimuli. Very much the same kind of experience is associated with seeing a red apple as "good to eat." Obviously, since the apple has not yet been tested, this interpretation is a function of a previous schema relating bright redness with good flavor and is not a property of the object being perceived. But the image resulting from the stimulus *and* the interpretation provided from past experience (i.e., a schema drawn from memory) are so integrally related that they produce a single experience. In the same way we directly perceive the internal states of other people (Asch, 1952). People "look" angry or happy to us. How the individual makes inferences regarding the causes of a stimulus person's actions and internal states, and the way overall impressions (with both denotative and connotative aspects) are formed constitute the basic problems of person perception.

I. PERSONS AS CAUSAL AGENTS AND THE ATTRIBUTION PROCESS

Perceivers view events as caused. Something caused the rock to roll down the hill, and something caused person A to step on person B's foot. The development of causal schemata regarding persons and events allows the perceiver to structure reality and predict the future course of events. Causal schemata provide the basis for comprehending a stable and somewhat controllable environment. If the observer did not attribute causes to events, his world would be chaotic and unruly, frightening and unpredictable, and he could make no plans because he could anticipate no regularity in the environment. The scientific study of how people attribute causality to events is an attempt to understand the processes of causal analysis used by the ordinary person. As a consequence, this area of study is often called common sense or naive psychology (Heider, 1958).

The observer attempts to arrive at an answer to the question, "Why did the stimulus person act as he did?" and is satisfied when he finds *sufficient* reason for the person's behavior. By sufficient reason Heider means that a workable explanation is accepted by the ordinary person, who probes no further into the matter. For example, if a person walks across the street and enters a drug store, the naive observer would probably be satisfied with the explanation that he wanted to make a purchase of some kind. A sufficient reason would usually not be enough to satisfy a scientific psychologist, who would want to probe deeper in order to discover the exact causes of behavior and to rule out alternative possible explanations. A thoroughgoing inves-

tigation might reveal, for example, that the person crossed the street and entered the drug store in order to avoid someone he saw approaching him on the sidewalk.

The naive observer makes a fundamental distinction between personal and environmental causes for behavior. He may believe that there are sufficient environmental pulls or pushes to cause the stimulus person to act as he does, or he may attribute the cause to the plans and intentions of the actor. Persons may be perceived as "pawns" moved about by environmental forces that are too strong to resist or as "origins" (first causes) of their own actions (deCharms, 1968). According to Heider, observers routinely search the environment for possible causes of an actor's behavior. When an environmental cause cannot be found, a personal attribution is apt to be made. A student's presence in a classroom may be attributed to a strict teacher who routinely takes attendance and imposes penalties upon absentees. But if the student is observed in the classroom listening to a visiting lecturer's talk when attendance is voluntary, the observer may attribute the student's presence to his interest in the lecture. The observer's causal analysis may be wrong, of course; the student may attend the lecture because a friend asked him to accompany her. But the assumption is a reasonable one, and from the observer's vantage point, sufficient to account for the student's presence when it is not required. As can be seen in Box 4.1, whether the observer makes an attribution to personal or environmental causes is important in determining his reactions to other people.

The naive observer's causal analysis consists of an inference process that starts with the effects produced by an actor's behavior. Of course, not all the effects of a given behavior are always perceived as intended by the actor. Consider what happens in a murder trial. A man may be charged, tried, found guilty, and sentenced based on what the judge and jury perceive his intentions to have been. Did he or did he not intend to

Box 4.1 ATTRIBUTIONS AND SOCIAL PROBLEMS

A social problem may be defined as a departure from social ideals. If most people in a society believe that all able-bodied persons should participate in productive activities, unemployment will be considered a social problem. Staines (1972) asserted that "the attributional diagnosis of a social problem largely determines what is done about that problem. A person-blame diagnosis may generate an attempt to change the individuals involved whereas a system-blame diagnosis may facilitate structural changes" (p. 2). A person-blame diagnosis explains the social problem in terms of the characteristics of the actors and would, for example, focus on lack of motivation or genetic inferiority in intelligence as the causes of unemployment among certain ethnic groups. A system-blame diagnosis might focus on monetary and fiscal policies that result in a specific level of unemployment.

Caplan and Nelson (1973) have argued that the work of social scientists has been used to displace blame from the system and onto individuals as a means of preserving the status quo. In a speech to a group of correctional psychologists, Judge David Bazelon (1972) suggested that consideration of fundamental system changes is unnecessary if social problems can be solved by social scientists through the latest therapeutic or behavior-change techniques. He asked his audience to consider "our motives for offering you a role . . . (and) consider how much less expensive it is to hire a thousand psychologists than to make even a minuscule change in the social and economic structure" (p. 61).

Person-blame diagnoses free the government and cultural institutions from blame for a problem and from responsibility for doing anything about it. If an institution does provide help, it can be credited with being exceedingly humane, while simultaneously gaining influence over those helped. Beefing up police forces and providing treatment facilities in prisons and mental hospitals are attempts to control troublesome members of society. Such actions also distract attention from more fundamental causes of disapproved behaviors. Caplan and Nelson conclude that "person-blame interpretations reinforce social myths about one's degree of control over his own fate, thus rewarding the members of the great middle class by flattering their self-esteem for having 'made it on their own.' This tendency for patting itself on the back increases public complacency about the plight of those who have not 'made it on their own.' The major conclusion that can be drawn . . . is that person-blame interpretations are in everyone's interests except those subjected to analysis" (p. 210).

It is possible to agree with these arguments but not with their conclusion. Myths serve important functions for a society, serving as social cement to weld large groups of people together so they can share experiences and rationalize their cooperation with one another. A myth is not just a false conception of reality for those who believe in it. What is a myth to one person *is* reality to another. To the extent that myths are important for motivating individuals by instilling certain values in them, they help people to take responsibility for their own problems and lead to constructive actions. An important dilemma may therefore face the policymaker.

If he attributes social problems to the system, he provides individuals with rationalizations that leave them dependent on system changes; but if he attributes problems to persons, the necessary system changes may not be implemented. How to maintain attributional complexity that includes both system and person factors is a problem that faces the social change agent in all societies.

---

kill the victim? The defense attorney may admit that his client's action caused the death of the victim, but he may claim that the effect was incidental or accidental; that is, the death occurred as a consequence of carrying out other intentions and was not premeditated or was determined by forces outside the control of the defendant. Suppose the defendant's car went up on the sidewalk and struck and killed a pedestrian. The death may have been intentional—a murder. The death may have been incidental—the driver could be charged with manslaughter on grounds of failing to keep his vehicle under control or in safe operating condition. The death may have been accidental—the defendant may have been sideswiped by another car, which caused him to lose control of his own automobile. Thus, the same effect can be brought about from a set of different causes.

Assigning the locus of causation to the actor requires that the observer attribute intent to the actor. Intent refers to a deliberate plan to bring about behavioral consequences that are satisfying or rewarding to some motive or need of the actor. The logic followed by the naive observer, according to Heider, is that an actor cannot be perceived as having intent unless he could foresee the effects produced by his behavior and had the ability to produce those effects. Lack of knowledge would prevent him from planning effects and lack of ability would prevent him from carrying out the plan.

When the observer decides that the locus of causation is in the actor and not the environment, the question remains: What about the actor caused him to act in such a

fashion? The observer therefore looks behind the plan to see what motivated it. Establishing a motive in a murder trial is an attempt to find out why the defendant would commit homicide. Perhaps he was attempting to acquire wealth or to wreak revenge. If no sufficient reason can be found, the act may be attributed to insanity.

The inference process works backwards from observations of effects and behavior, as shown in Figure 4.1. The observer attempts to find an environmental cause for the behavior, but if one cannot be found, he is apt to consider the person as the locus of cause. The observer must believe it is plausible that the actor both had knowledge about the effects before emitting the behavior and that he had the ability to produce the effects. If the actor can be presumed to have both knowledge and ability then his behavior may be perceived as intended, and the observer may attempt to discover the motivation or values that led to the plan implemented by the actor. Sometimes this inference chain is quite simple and direct. For example, when a person takes a drink of water, it may be assumed that he is the origin of his action (he intended it) and that the motive underlying the intent is thirst. At other times, the inference chain is complex and difficult to construct, requiring the observer to make repeated observations of the actor in similar circumstances or to analyse the complex information obtained from a single observation.

The actor is an observer of his own behavior and makes inferences about the causes of his own conduct. How many times have you stopped after doing something and said to yourself, "Now why did I do

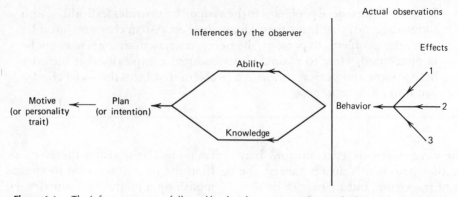

Figure 4.1. The inference process followed by the observer in attributing the locus of cause to the actor. (After Jones and Davis, 1965.)

that?" As we shall see, causal analysis leading to self-attributions is carried out in much the same way as attributions about other people. It is not always easy to determine whether one's reactions to events are attributable to the properties of external events or to internal mood states. For example, we may laugh at a joke told by a television comedian. Was it because the joke was really funny or was it because we were in an especially good mood? We would have to engage in a causal analysis of our response to arrive at a satisfactory answer to this question.

The attributions others make about the actor and the attributions he makes about himself are often divergent. The actor tends to attribute his behavior to environmental factors, while other observers tend to attribute the same behavior to the actor's intentions. These divergent perceptions can be the cause of much misunderstanding and conflict. When one person is perceived as having caused a second person's behavior, the first person is perceived as having power over the second. There are often divergent perceptions of who exercises power in any given situation.

We will now examine in more detail how an observer draws inferences from multiple observations of a stimulus person's behavior, how he makes a causal analysis based on a single observation, and how he assesses the knowledge and ability of an actor. The process of self-attribution, the divergent perceptions of actor and observer, and attributions of power will also be considered. Although these processes may not always operate independently of one another, we will discuss them one at a time.

A. Inferring Causation from Multiple Observations

Kelley (1967) has developed a model that accounts for the inferences persons make regarding the causes of behavior. Basically, the problem is to predict whether cause for behavior will be attributed to the person or to the environment. Suppose John saw the movie, *Jesus Christ, Superstar,* and reports that he liked it very much. Is his response due to the fact that the movie was actually a good one, or is his evaluation a function of his mood at the time he saw it, or does he like all the movies he sees? That is, can we attribute John's response to the external event (the movie) or to some peculiar internal state? If we know that John's response to the movie is *distinctive* because he usually does not like movies, we still do not have a full answer to our question, although lack of discrimination on John's part would be ruled out. If we know that he has seen the play on which the movie is based and has seen the movie twice, once at a theater and once on cable television, and that he *consis-*

tently liked it, his temporary moods must be ruled out as a possible cause. Finally, if a number of other people provide *consensus* for John's opinion of the movie, we may feel confident that *Jesus Christ, Superstar* is really a good movie and that the cause of John's positive report was the quality of the film and not something peculiar about him. According to Kelley, observers consider these three criteria—distinctiveness, consistency, and consensus—in making attributions about the causes of another's behavior.

Figure 4.2 summarizes Kelley's attribution model. The "entities" refer to environmental stimuli or events that are considered as possible explanations for a stimulus person's behavior. In our example, entities refer to the various movies that John has seen in the past, one of which is *Jesus Christ, Superstar*. The more distinctive the entity in producing a particular re-

sponse, the more likely it is that the environment and not the person will be perceived as the cause of the response. John liked *Jesus Christ, Superstar* but he usually does not like movies. The time-modality dimension refers to the number of occasions on which the person experienced a particular entity and the variety of ways in which he experienced it. John saw *Jesus Christ, Superstar* three times, once as a play, once as a movie on a big screen, and once as a movie on television. The consistency of John's responses over time and modalities leads an observer to attribute his behavior to environmental causes—the entity. The persons dimension refers to the number of people who are exposed to a particular entity and whose reactions are known. The degree of consensus in response to the entity is directly related to the likelihood that the reactions are attributable to environmental causes.

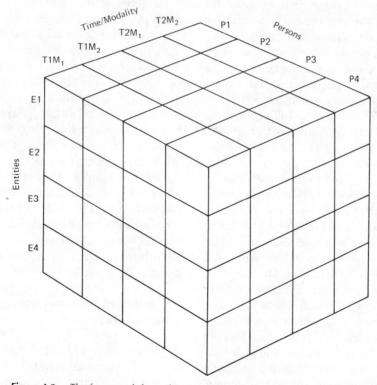

Figure 4.2. The framework for making causal attributions about environmental entities. (After Kelley, 1973.)

McArthur (1972) experimentally investigated Kelley's attribution theory by presenting statements about a particular person's response to an entity, with additional information regarding consensus, distinctiveness, and consistency. For example, one statement read, "John laughs at the comedian." A consensus statement either indicated that almost everyone who hears the comedian laughs at him or that hardly anyone laughs at him. Consistency information indicated that John almost always or almost never laughs at this particular comedian. Distinctiveness information indicated that John laughs at all comedians or almost never laughs at any other comedian. Thus, with each statement presented to the subjects one of eight combinations of high or low consensus, consistency, or distinctiveness was provided.

The subjects were asked to attribute the described act to one of four causes: (1) something about the person caused him to make the response, (2) something about the entity caused the response, (3) something about the particular circumstances caused the response, or (4) some combination of these three factors caused the response. As predicted, attributions to the person were more frequent when the subjects were presented with low rather than high consensus information, with low rather than high distinctiveness information, and with high rather than low consistency information. For example, a strong personal attribution can be made to John when he laughs at the comedian and hardly any one else does (low consensus). when he laughs at all comedians (low distinctiveness), and when he almost always laughs at this particular comedian (high consistency). On the other hand, a strong attribution can be made to the entity (the comedian) when John and almost everyone else laughs at the comedian (high consensus), John almost never laughs at other comedians (high distinctiveness), and he almost always laughs at this particular comedian (high consistency).

Certain combinations of information led to inferences regarding an interaction of the person and the entity. "If Ralph trips over Joan's feet while dancing and (a) hardly anyone else who dances with Joan trips over her feet (low consensus), (b) Ralph does not trip over almost any other partner's feet (high distinctiveness), and (c) in the past Ralph has almost always tripped over Joan's feet (high consistency), then what seems to have caused the event to occur is that Ralph and Joan do not groove together on the dance floor. On the other hand, if (a) almost everyone else who dances with Joan trips over her feet (high consensus), (b) Ralph also trips over almost every other partner's feet (low distinctiveness), and (c) in the past Ralph has almost always tripped over Joan's feet (high consistency), then what seems to have caused the event to occur is that (a) Ralph is a clod, and (b) Joan is a clod. The cause is both the person and the stimulus" (McArthur, 1972, p. 181).

In general, distinctiveness and consistency information played a greater role in the causal attributions made by subjects than did consensus information. That is, the information about the actions of the central person in the situations was given more importance than information about the behavior of other persons. These findings support Kelley's (1967) assumption that information about physical reality takes precedence over social reality. The results also support Heider's (1958, p. 54) assumption that an actor's behavior is central and engulfs the field in which it occurs. The subject's attention was directed to the central person's behavior, and the actions of other persons provided only background information.

B.　Inferring Causation from Single Observations

When an observer has information regarding only an isolated instance of behavior by an actor, a number of cues can be assessed in making a causal analysis of the origins of the behavior. The observer usually has a store of rules-of-thumb (schemata) about human behavior that can be searched for an appropriate attributional interpretation. Suppose the observer has a schema incorporating the principle that a person is usually more willing to comply with requests made by liked than by disliked others. How would this affect the observer's attributions? An answer to this question was found by deCharms, Carpenter and Kuperman (1965). They had subjects read stories about a person who was persuaded to do something by a liked or disliked other person. The subjects perceived the compliant person to be more of an origin of his action when he liked the source of influence than when he did not. In the latter case, the central person was considered more of a pawn—forced by his environment rather than freely and willingly offering help. Other kinds of interpersonal schemata that observers have developed will be considered later in the chapter when we discuss stereotypes and implicit personality theories.

When an observer does not have a ready-made schema to apply to a single observation, he will engage in causal analysis until a sufficient explanation of the actor's behavior is found. Observers apply a number of general principles in making causal attributions to persons rather than to environmental forces, including the augmentation principle, the discounting principle, the principle of hedonic relevance, and personalism. We do not mean to imply that these principles are consciously applied during the attribution process; however, the evidence we will review supports the view that observers do apply them with some generality.

1. The Augmentation Principle

The more pain, embarassment, penalty, or criticism an individual is willing to risk in order to act as he does, the more the observer believes he knows about the actor's

motives and values. Performing a socially undesirable or extraordinary act communicates more about the intentions of the actor than does performing a socially desirable or typical action. When an individual does what most other people would do under the same circumstances, strong attributions about his personal characteristics or intentions are not possible; about all one can say is that he is like most other people. The rule of thumb applied is that the more the effects of an actor's behavior deviate from what the average person would attempt, the more accurately and confidently can the observer make attributions about his intentions and motives. More formally, the augmentation principle states that "when there are known to be constraints, costs, sacrifices, or risks involved in taking an action, the action once taken is attributed more to the actor than it would be otherwise" (Kelley, 1973, p. 114). As Confucious once said, you can tell more about a man's character from knowing who his enemies are than by knowing his friends.

Doing what most other people would do in a given social situation may be considered *in-role behavior*. So long as persons perform their roles appropriately it can be expected that they will be approved and rewarded; but once they disobey the demands and expectations associated with their roles, they are apt to be disapproved, rejected, and otherwise punished. In-role behavior provides little unique information about a person; but when he willfully disregards the standards of proper conduct in his group, the observer can be confident he must have a powerful reason for behaving in such a deviant fashion. In-role behavior is expected of everyone and if all conform, little can be discovered about the personal characteristics of any of them. *Out-of-role behavior* is unexpected and is presumed to be expressive of the "true" nature of the person and his values or motives. When the national anthem is played at a sports event, most people stand, and little can be gleaned about their patriotism. However, those who do not stand convey strong feelings regarding the ceremony and what it implies; their behavior is out-of-role.

Jones, Davis, and Gergen (1961) have demonstrated the high information value of out-of-role behavior. Subjects were given the task of listening to a taped interview of an individual seeking a job as either a submariner or an astronaut. The first part of the tape provided a description by the interviewer of the ideal characteristics desired of a job applicant. The desirable traits of a submariner, who has to work in cramped quarters with others for long periods of time, were described as friendliness, obedience, cooperativeness, and gregariousness ("other-directed"). The ideal characteristics associated with the astronaut position (in those days they traveled alone) were described as resourcefulness, thoughtfulness, and independence from the need for company or the help of other people ("inner-directed").

Subjects next heard a tape recorded version of the applicant presenting himself for the job. He sought a position either as a submariner or an astronaut and presented himself in the interview as either an inner-directed or other-directed person. Thus, half of the subjects heard the applicant present himself in a role-appropriate way and half heard a role-inappropriate presentation. After listening to the taped interview, subjects rated the applicant on a series of trait dimensions and also indicated the degree of confidence they had in their ratings.

Some of the results are shown in Table 4.1. The two in-role applicants (astronaut position—inner-directed and submariner position—other directed) were rated as moderately affiliative and conforming, but the subjects in these two conditions indicated relatively low confidence in their judgments. Since the in-role applicants knew the requirements for the job and then presented themselves accordingly, little could be said about what they were really like. Were they posing for the purpose of getting the job or were they genuinely as they presented themselves to be?

When the applicant for the position of submariner, which required a sociable, obedient, and cooperative person, presented himself in an inner-directed manner, subjects rated him as independent and nonaffiliative, and indicated strong confidence in their ratings. A strong impression was also formed of the applicant who presented himself as other-directed in the interview for the astronaut position (which required an inner-directed type of person). In the latter case, subjects rated the interviewee as conforming and affiliative, and did so confidently.

When the applicants chose to act out of role, the subjects must have viewed them as choosing to violate the obvious job specifications for some reason. What better reason than that they were actually as they

Table 4.1   Mean Ratings by Subjects of Interviewees on Measures of Affiliation, Conformity, and Candor.[a]

Trait rated	Experimental conditions			
	Astronaut interview		Submariner interview	
	Other-directed	Inner-directed	Other-directed	Inner-directed
Affiliation	15.27	11.12	12.00	8.64
Conformity	15.91	13.09	12.58	9.41
Candor	12.42	9.68	10.09	12.08

[a] After Jones, Davis, & Gergen, 1961, p. 9.

presented themselves and refused to manage impressions of themselves or "put the interviewer on" just to get the job? One reason to violate the expectations of others is to affirm what one really is in a defiantly truthful manner. The ratings of candor given in Table 4.1 suggest that this is exactly how the subjects perceived the out-of-role applicants. The augmentation principle applied because of the obvious potential costs associated with presenting oneself as lacking the characteristics required for the job in question. A personal attribution was made to the out-of-role applicants and an environmental attribution made it difficult for subjects to feel confident about the personal characteristics of in-role applicants.

2. The Discounting Principle

An observer may consider a number of hypothetical causes for an actor's behavior. When a particular causal hypothesis seems to lack plausibility and other causes seem more likely, the observer discounts or rejects the less plausible hypothesis. As Kelley (1973) states the discounting principle, "the role of a given cause in producing a given effect is discounted if other plausible causes are also present" (p. 113). We may discount the hypothesis that a speaker's message reflects his own views if we also know that he is engaging in a school debate or that he is merely playing a designated role as the experimenter's confederate. Knowledge of some of the conditions under which a single action is observed to occur allows the observer to discount a number of hypotheses about the degree to which the behavior reflects the personal characteristics of the actor.

The status relationships of two persons may serve as information about whether an action is environmentally caused or attributable to personal factors. In an experiment carried out by Thibaut and Riecken (1955a), subjects were asked to persuade two people to give blood to the Red Cross. The subjects were provided information about the accomplishments and back-grounds of the two target persons, who were actually confederates of the experimenter and alternated which role they played. The target person was described as either a professor or another student. Both eventually agreed to give a pint of blood to the Red Cross. The subjects believed they had been successful in persuading the student to give blood (environmental cause), but believed the professor had volunteered because he was a "nice guy" (personal cause). Low status provided a reason for discounting personal causes and high status allowed the discounting of environmental causes.

When the observer believes external pressures are placed on an actor by other people, what the actor says may be discounted as not reflecting his real attitudes. Jones and Harris (1967) have shown this kind of discounting effect. Subjects were asked to infer a stimulus person's real attitude toward Fidel Castro after hearing him deliver a speech either opposing or favoring the Cuban Prime Minister. The stimulus person was introduced as a debater from a nearby university who had written his own speech. The subjects were also informed either that the debater had been assigned one side of the issue or that he had been allowed to choose which side of the issue he wanted to defend.

As might be expected, the position taken in the written speech played an important part in the subjects' inferences; the stimulus person was perceived to be more pro-Castro when he wrote a favorable speech than when he wrote a speech attacking Castro. The speaker who had a choice was perceived as more extreme in his true opinion than the speaker who had been assigned the position he advocated. Assignment did not totally discount the possibility that the pro-speaker really was favorable toward Castro. The assigned pro-Castro speaker was viewed as more in favor of Castro than the assigned anti-Castro speaker. Apparently, subjects believed that a debater should refuse a position with which he personally disagrees, or should, at least, write a rather poor speech for a repugnant position. Since the writer of the pro-Castro speech in the assignment condition did neither, he was assumed really to be favorable toward Castro.

A similar effect has been reported by Jones, Worchel, Goethals, and Grumet (1971). A person who expressed a rather weak but favorable opinion when he was under strong pressure to express a strongly favorable opinion was believed by observers actually to have an unfavorable attitude. This also reflects the augmentation principle, since a failure to heed pressure could reflect some willingness to accept costs by the stimulus person.

Steiner and Field (1960) have also found clear evidence for the discounting principle. Groups of three students were asked to discuss desegregation of schools and to attempt to reach agreement on the issue among themselves. In half the groups a confederate was openly assigned the role of "a typical Southern segrationist." The other groups were encouraged to take into account the viewpoint of a member of a civil rights group, a Northern clergyman, and a Southern segregationist; but no one was actually assigned to any of these roles. In both types of groups a confederate promoted identical segregationist views. Afterwards, the subjects were more confident about the confederate's actual attitudes about segregation when he had not been openly assigned the role of advocating it. The role assignment (environmental cause) allowed the subjects to discount a personal locus of cause for his expressed opinions.

Consider the problem of discriminating between true admiration and false flattery. As Jones (1964) has pointed out, Americans generally disapprove of flatterers who attempt to ingratiate themselves through giving false praise. How do we discount the possibility that praise is meant to be ingratiating? In an empirical examination of this question, Dickoff (cited in Jones, 1964) arranged for a graduate student to either compliment or criticize a subject. The graduate student either was attempting to recruit the subject as a volunteer for an experiment or had no particular ax to grind. In general, the complimenter was liked better than the critic. However, when the complimenter was not interested in getting the subject to participate in an experiment, she was better liked than when she had something to gain. The compliments were discounted when there was an apparent external cause to explain them.

In summary, inferences about a person's wishes, intentions, attitudes, and likeability are made from his actions. These inferences to personal factors are weakened when there are other, external, causes available as apparent explanations for the behavior. Although the presence of such external causes leads the observer to discount hypotheses about personal causes, there maybe a constant bias to attribute the cause of an action to the actor than to environmental factors.

3.   Discounting, Noncommon Effects, and Choice Behavior

An actor usually considers alternatives before deciding on the course he will take. When an observer knows which alternatives were considered and also knows what choice was made, an attribution may be made about the actor by comparing the differences in outcome (or effects) associated with the alternatives (Jones & Davis, 1965). The observer does this by discounting the effects that are common to the alternatives and by making inferences about the actor from the noncommon effects realized from the alternative actually chosen.

Suppose an actor is a high-school senior who has been accepted for admission to two universities, X and Y. Suppose both universities are state-supported, have similar academic standing, athletic programs, and cultural programs and are equally supportive of fraternity and sorority life. With only this information, together with the knowledge that the actor chose University Y, the observer would be unable to make any attribution regarding the cause of the actor's choice, since the effects of either choice are the same. But if University X is in an urban setting while University Y is in a rural setting, the noncommon effect of choosing University Y would be to live in a rural community. Therefore, the observer would discount the common effects and attribute the choice to the actor's desire to live in a rural setting (or to avoid an urban university). The observer might be wrong, of course; the senior's real reason may have been to go to the same school as a friend. But without added information, the observer may make his inference on the basis of the single noncommon effect associated with the choice made by the actor.

4. Hedonic Relevance

When an actor's behavior effects the observer's outcomes, the behavior is hedonically relevant to the observer. Hedonic relevance affects the attributions made by the observer. According to Jones and Davis (1965), an observer is more likely to attribute the cause of an act to the intentions of the actor when the observer's outcomes are positively or negatively affected by the actor's behavior than when the actor's conduct has no effects on the observer's outcomes.

Jones and deCharms (1957) illustrated the principle of hedonic relevance in a study in which a confederate was the only group member to fail on a task. The confederate's failure either prevented the entire group from receiving a reward or had only the effect of preventing the confederate from receiving a reward. The first condition involved the common fate of the entire group, while the second involved only the individual's fate. Subjects rated the confederate as less dependable, competent, and favorable in the common-fate situation than in the individual fate condition. Al-

though the confederate's performance was identical in both the consequences for the subjects were quite different. When the confederate's behavior had hedonic relevance for the subjects, they were more likely to attribute bad characteristics to him than when his behavior had no consequences for them.

5. Personalism

When an action is hedonically relevant to the observer, he must decide whether the behavior was uniquely determined by the knowledge that he was affected by it and whether he was the specific target of the other's action. When the observer believes that the actor has affected his outcomes, as distinct from other possible targets, the observer will be more confident in making attributions to personal causes (Jones & Davis, 1965). If an employer provides a handsome across-the-board raise to all of his employees, he may be considered to be trying to maintain high morale and productivity; but if he gives a raise only to you on the basis of your meritorious performance, you will be more apt to attribute his behavior to benevolent intentions.

C. Attributions of Knowledge and Ability

Heider (1958) was among the first to note that an attribution cannot be made to the intentions of an actor unless he can foresee the effects of his behavior and has ability to bring about those effects. When a baby is just learning to crawl and pulls out a lamp cord, causing a lamp to fall off a table, we do not attribute malevolent or harmful intentions to him because we do not believe he is aware of the connection between his action and its consequences. Similarly, when a person launches into a discussion of the effects of cancer and one member of the audience begins to weep, we do not hold the speaker responsible for the effect unless he knows that the person weeping has just lost her sister because of cancer. Young children are seldom prosecuted for criminal actions because they are not believed capable of understanding the consequences of their actions.

If an actor is believed not to have the ability or skill to achieve certain effects, he will not be perceived as intending them. Suppose it is known that a person is playing poker for the first time and lacks the skills of an experienced player; and yet he wins. His success may be attributed to luck (an environmental cause). On the other hand, if a person has played poker every Wednesday night for ten years and wins on any given night, his success is apt to be attributed to his skill (a personal cause).

How much ability an observer attributes to an actor will depend to some degree upon the perceived difficulty of the task. If it is easy, an actor's success conveys little information about his ability; almost everyone would be successful. Similarly, failure at a very difficult task allows little assessment for almost everyone would be expected to fail. Maximum information about an actor's ability is obtained by knowledge of his success or failure on moderately difficult tasks.

It is possible for a person to have a lot of ability and still fail at a moderately difficult task if he does not try. The reason for an actor's failure may be attributed either to lack of ability or failure to try by an observer. Presumably, the more difficult the task and the less the ability of the actor, the more likely success will be attributed to effort or luck.

Weiner, Frieze, Kukla, Reed, Rest, and Rosenbaum (1971) have developed a model based on Heider's theory of how observers make attributions from knowledge of an actor's success or failure. They note that ability and effort are personal factors, while task difficulty and luck are external or environmental factors; and they have applied Kelley's principles of consistency and consensus to generate predictions about attributions to the four causal factors of abil-

ity, effort, task difficulty and luck. Consistent success or failure over time and over various kinds of tasks (modalities) would allow an unambiguous attribution regarding an actor's ability.

In a systematic study of attributions of ability, task difficulty, luck, and effort, Frieze and Weiner (1971) provided subjects with past performance information that specified the degree of success a hypothetical person experienced in the past at a specific task (100, 50, or 0 percent). Consistency information on similar tasks was also given, specifying the degree of success the same person had encountered in similar tasks in the past; and consensus information indicated the percentage of other persons who had succeeded in solving the specific task.

Consistency information relating to past performance on the specific task produced a number of interesting effects. Attributions to luck were reported when the hypothetical person succeeded after having always failed the task in the past, or when he failed after a history of repeated successes. When he succeeded after a consistent history of successes, strong attributions of ability were made; or else attributions were made regarding the ease of the task. When he failed and had failed consistently in the past, observers attributed his failures to the difficulty of the task or to his lack of ability. Consistency information on similar tasks had similar effects with the exception that there were no significant differences in attributions to task difficulty.

Consensus information also affected the attributions made by subjects. When the hypothetical person succeeded and others had failed, or when he failed and others had succeeded, observers attributed his performance to ability and effort. But when the person's performance was consistent with that of others, his success or failure was attributed to the task. Finally, success was more likely to be attributed to the internal factors of ability and effort than was failure (see Figure 4.3), while task

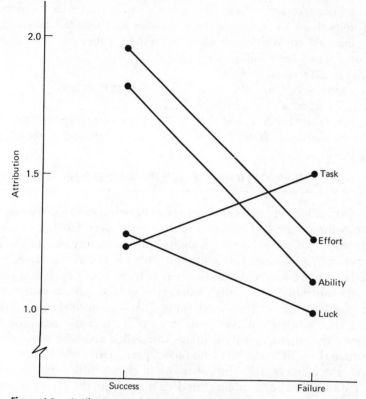

Figure 4.3. Attributions to ability, effort, task, difficulty, and luck as a function of success or failure outcome. (From J. Frieze and B. Weiner, Journal of Personality, 39. Copyright 1971 by Duke University Press.)

difficulty was most often perceived as the cause of failure. Thus, while success leads to attributions of ability, failure may not lead observers to infer lack of ability.

Jones, Rock, Shaver, Goethals, and Ward (1968) found the pattern of success and failure over time to be an important determinant of ability attributions. Subjects were paired with a confederate and each member of a pair was asked to solve a series of special tests that included difficult and even insoluble items. The solutions to the 30 items were sufficiently ambiguous as to allow the experimenter to announce success or failure at the end of the item regardless of the response made by either the subject or confederate, without arousing suspicion on the part of the subjects. The experimenter reported 10 random successes for the subject on the 30 items attempted. The

confederate's success was manipulated in one of three ways: (1) he was successful on early items, but failed on later ones; (2) he randomly achieved successes on the 30 items; or (3) he failed on early items, but showed increasing successes on the later items. The actual number of successes achieved by the confederate was fifteen in all three conditions.

Ratings of the confederate by the subjects were obtained. He was perceived as more intelligent when he had early successes than when he achieved only random or later successes. The pattern of early successes conveyed the impression of an intelligent person who could solve the items when he tried, and the pattern of later successes left the subjects with an impression of the confederate as a slow learner. The maximum performance observed on prior occasions is used by observers as a basis for making attributions about an actor's ability (Rosenbaum, reported in Weiner, *et al.*, 1971). Early success and later failure suggests high ability but decreasing effort.

Attributions made about the ability or effort exerted by an actor can have important effects on both the observer and the actor. How such attributions affect the be-

havior of supervisors towards their subordinates and the effectiveness of teachers with their students is described in Box 4.2.

D. Self-attributions

The same principles that allow an observer to make attributions about other people

---

Box 4.2   SOCIAL IMPLICATIONS OF ABILITY AND EFFORT ATTRIBUTIONS

Causal attributions of ability and effort can have important consequences for social interactions. A teacher may become very frustrated with a student who is judged to have high ability but lacks motivation, but he may work patiently and long with a student with less ability who tries hard. Similarly, as will be seen also in Chapter 8, there is evidence that supervisors are more likely to punish workers who have poor attitudes than those who have underdeveloped skills. Lanzetta and Hannah (1969) showed that students playing the role of supervisor administered stronger punishments to subordinates who failed and who were of high ability than those of low ability who failed, particularly when the task was difficult. Punishment, therefore, is more likely when the attributions to the person are that he has ability but does not put out the effort necessary to succeed.

A *teacher-expectancy effect* has been shown by Conn, Edwards, Rosenthal, and Crowne (1968) and Rosenthal and Jacobson (1968). When teachers were provided (false) information that a group of pupils in their classes were late bloomers who could be expected to show unusual intellectual gains during the school year, the identified children did show more gains than a matched group of pupils about whom this attribution of blossoming ability had not been implanted. A similar finding was obtained in a Head Start program (Beez, 1968) and with swimming classes in a summer camp (Burnham & Hartsough, 1968). Meichenbaum, Bowers, and Ross (1969) found that the teacher-expectancy effect with institutionalized adolescent female offenders was associated with increasing positive behavior by some teachers and decreasing negative behavior by others. Thus a self-fulfilling prophecy occurs when teachers are led to expect good performances from students. The expectency of good performance leads the teacher to interact more positively with "special" students, giving them more feedback regarding their performance, providing more opportunities for them to respond, and attempting to teach them a greater amount and more difficult material (Rosenthal, 1974). This behavior of the teacher leads to a positive cycle of fulfilled expectations—the students perform better, reward the teacher for his behavior, eliciting more positive expectations and behavior from him, which (to end the circle) reward the students for their improved performance.

apply to attributions he makes regarding himself. As Bem (1972) states, "Individuals come to 'know' their own attitudes, emotions, and other internal states partially by inferring them from observations of their own overt behavior and/or the circumstances in which this behavior occurs. Thus, to the extent that internal cues are weak, ambiguous, or uninterpretable, the individual is functionally in the same position as an outside observer, an observer who must necessarily rely upon these same external cues to infer the individual's inner states" (p. 2). In the last chapter we reviewed evidence in support of this statement when we considered Schachter's two-factor theory of emotional labeling and the process of social comparison. When the individual lacks past experience as a basis to interpret his own internal states, he uses social cues and comparison others as a basis for making self-attributions.

1. Self-attribution from single observations

Bem (1970) has developed a theory of self-attribution which considers the actor's inferences about himself as a function of observing his own behavior. The actor attributes the causes of his behavior to himself when it is perceived as free from environmental pressures. When it can be attributed to environmental circumstances, he will not interpret it as reflecting his own internal states. According to Bem, a person who always chooses brown rather than white bread at dinner will say he likes brown bread because he has so often observed himself eating it. His behavior serves as the basis for attributing the attitude to himself. If he could be steered into choosing white bread, his attitude would presumably change. He would say to himself, "The reason I am now eating the white bread is that I have come to like it better than the brown bread; why else would I have chosen to eat the white bread?" The way to change a person's attitudes is to get him to change his behavior in a way that allows him to view

his new behavior as freely chosen. Box 4.3 provides some illustrations of emotional disorders suffered by persons who mistakenly attributed their behavior to internal causes when environmental causes were actually responsible.

The tendency to attribute attitudes to oneself consistent with one's own behavior is illustrated in a study performed by Bandler, Madaras, and Bem (1968). Subjects were induced to choose to accept electric shocks or to terminate shocks by pushing a button. According to Bem's theory, the former should believe the shocks were not painful, while the latter should believe the shocks were quite painful. Each subject received a series of shocks to the hand. After each shock one of three colored lights was illuminated on a box set in front of the subject. In the red light (escape) condition, the subject was instructed to push the button in his hand when the red light came on, but "if the shock is not uncomfortable, you may elect to not press the button. The choice is up to you." In the green light (no escape) condition, the subject was told not to press the button when the green light was illuminated "unless the shock is so uncomfortable that you feel you must. . . . The choice is up to you." In these two conditions the subjects were induced to follow the preferences of the experimenter, but allowed to believe they did so of their own free choice. In the yellow light (reaction time) condition, the subjects were asked to press the button as soon as the the yellow light was illuminated and were told that the shock might or might not terminate as a consequence; it actually did terminate half the time.

Although all of the shocks were of equal intensity, the subjects rated them as more uncomfortable when they escaped them than when they endured them. When they had no choice to endure or escape the shocks (reaction time condition), they did not attribute more discomfort to the shocks they escaped than to those they endured. Observations of their own choice to endure

PERSON PERCEPTION

Box 4.3 MISATTRIBUTIONS AND EMOTIONAL DISORDERS

Valins and Nisbett (1971) have discussed the ways in which an understanding of self-attributions can lead to understanding and treatment of anxiety-related emotional disorders. Recognizing the need of persons to rely on others for consensus information with which to construct social reality, they argue "that the failure or inability to use social consensus to check shameful evaluations can lead to self-ascriptions of mental abnormality and personal inadequacy that can be profoundly debilitating. We also argue that under conditions in which no one else shares the individual's experiences he is apt to distrust other people, and left alone he may develop incorrect and seemingly bizarre interpretations of his experiences. In the absence of social consensus, unusual feelings or events may be explained by delusional systems—a symptom characteristic of the paranoid schizophrenic" (p. 2).

Valins and Nisbett report a case study by Neale in which a 25-year-old, unmarried male came to therapy because he thought he was homosexual, and this led to anxiety and deep depression. His belief was based on three factors: sexual intercourse was unsatisfactory, he often found himself looking at the crotch area of other men, and he believed he had an abnormally small penis. The therapist began by convincing him that his penis was within the normal range of size and urged him to use a mirror to view himself, because the law of optics is such that objects in the same plane as the line of vision appear foreshortened. The therapist then explained the crotch-gazing behavior as the result of normal curiosity resulting from his concern about penis size. The patient's shame led him to avoid simple social comparisons that would be possible, in, say, locker rooms. Third, the therapist explained his lack of sexual satisfaction as due to normal concern about inadequacy, which was compounded by his homosexual fears. In this simple way, the therapist modified the social and physical reality of the shamed patient who, thereafter, no longer considered himself homosexual and experienced less depression and anxiety.

Valins and Nisbett also cite a *Time* magazine report in which army psychiatrists noted a large number of emotional disorder casualties among new men going to battle in Vietnam. The typical reaction of the seasoned veterans to a new man in a combat unit was strong suspicion and hostility. The negative reaction of his peers, together with apprehension about battle and ignorance of the unwritten rules of the new unit, created a stress-provoking situation with which many new men could not cope adequately. The remedy was simple. Field commanders were instructed to prepare the new men in advance for their reception. When the new men knew they were receiving the typical "fucking new guy" treatment, they could discount their own inadequacy as a cause for the negative reactions.

the shocks allowed the subjects to attribute less pain to them while self-attributions of greater pain were made when they had terminated the shocks. A similar finding was obtained by Corah and Boffa (1970), who used the same basic procedures, using aversive bursts of noise instead of shocks as stimuli.

An alternative, impression management, explanation for the above findings is that the subjects were simply justifying their behavior to the experimenter. Although the experimenter left the choice of response up to the subjects, he also made it clear what he would like the subjects to do. When they chose to terminate the shocks, they might look foolish if they then rated them as mild; therefore, they said they were painful. On the other hand, when they chose to tolerate the shocks, they might have looked foolish if they said they were very painful. The results can be understood as attempts by the subjects to manage the experimenter's impressions of them as reasonable persons (Goffman, 1959). The consistency of attitudes with behavior noted by Bem may be interpreted as attempts by the individual to rationalize his behavior to observers. Only future research will allow us to evaluate these competing interpretations of the behavior-attitude relationship.

2. Self-attributions from Multiple Observations

The principles of distinctiveness, consistency, and consensus—components of Kelley's model of attribution—are just as applicable to self-perception as they are to perceptions of other people. A student who does consistently well in math courses but barely manages to pass his English courses will judge his own abilities according to the consistency and distinctiveness of his performances. In addition, he will make social comparisons with his peers to obtain consensus information. For example, persons predict higher future performance levels

for themselves when they are provided with information that their past performances were below those of someone to whom they attributed low ability (Chapman & Volkmann, 1939; Festinger, 1942).

The degree to which a person attributes success or failure in solving tasks to his own ability or to luck depends on his initial expectations of success. Feather (1969) reported that when subjects were initially confident about their ability to solve anagram problems, they attributed success to ability and failure to bad luck. But when they were initially lacking in confidence, they attributed success to good luck and failure to lack of ability.

Feather and Simon (1971) investigated the effects of consistency and consensus information on self-attributions of ability. Subjects worked together in pairs, though each was asked to solve lists of anagrams independently. The self-confidence of the subjects was manipulated by having them consistently succeed or consistently fail during practice test sessions. Each subject was asked to predict the probability of his own success and that of his partner prior to the critical test sessions. The subjects were more confident that their partner would succeed than they were of their own likelihood of success. They believed they would be more successful in the critical test session if they had been consistently successful during the practice trials than when they had often failed in practice. During the critical test session a deception procedure was employed to induce both members of the pair to succeed, both to fail, or one to succeed and the other to fail. The subjects were then asked to make attributions regarding the performance of the other subject working in parallel with them and to assess their own performance.

Attributions to good or bad luck were made for both self and other when an unexpected outcome occurred. If success was confidently expected and failure occurred, or if failure was expected and success occurred, the subjects made attributions to an environmental cause (luck). When performance was consistent with expectations, the subjects made attributions both to luck and ability. However, the other person's success was more often attributed to ability than the subject's own success, and the other's failure was more often attributed to bad luck than the subject's own failure. Feather and Simon warn that their results can also be interpreted in terms of an impression management hypothesis. A person who publicly and confidently predicts his own success may appear more humble by attributing more ability to another person and may appear more understanding if he attributes the failure of the other person to bad luck. The subjects' responses may not have been genuine attributions of causation, but instead may have been attempts to present themselves favorably (as humble, generous) in order to gain social approval from the experimenter.

A study by Schneider (1969) confirms the probable contamination of self-attribution studies with self-presentation considerations. Subjects failed or succeeded on a task and were subsequently interviewed by a trained interviewer who was to assess their social sensitivity. Half the failure subjects and half the success subjects were told that the interviewer would reveal his evaluation of their ability to them; the remainder of the subjects did not expect an evaluation. Only those subjects who expected to have their abilities evaluated by the interviewer should have been concerned with managing impressions of their abilities to him. Subjects who failed were more positive about themselves when they expected evaluation than when they did not, while subjects who had been successful were more modest when they expected evaluation than when they did not. In general, when subjects believed they could affect the interviewer's subsequent evaluation, they presented themselves in a favorable light.

E. Divergent Perceptions of Actor and Observer

Jones and Nisbett (1971) note a "pervasive tendency for actors to attribute their actions to situational requirements, whereas observers tend to attribute the same actions to stable personal dispositions" (p. 2). Observation suggests that such divergent perceptions are often expressed in casual conversations. For example, when negatively evaluated acts are performed by another person we tend to find fault with his character; but when we perform negative acts, we find excuses or justifications for why we could not do other than we did. Think of Lucy in the Peanuts comic strip when she strikes out in a baseball game, saying: "the ball is too small; the bat is too thin; dust got in my eye." The actor perceives his own behavior as constrained by environmental forces, while the observer views the other person's actions as originating from internal forces. These divergent perceptions are important in the layman's tendency to personify history (see Box 4.4).

An empirical study of divergent perceptions was reported by McArthur (cited in Jones & Nisbett, 1971). Subjects who agreed to participate in a survey explained their cooperativeness as due to the importance of the survey (an environmental cause). Observers attributed the participation of the volunteers to their cooperative nature (a personal cause), with only secondary importance given to the value of the survey. In a similar study, Nisbett, Caputo, Legant, and Maracek (1973) asked each subject to write paragraphs to explain his choices of a college major and a girl friend. The subjects were also asked to furnish reasons for similar choices made by their best friend. The content of the paragraphs was analysed to identify the kinds of attributions made. The reasons were classified as person causes ("I want to make a lot of money;" "I like warm girls") or environmental causes ("Chemistry is a

Box 4.4   PERSONIFICATION OF HISTORICAL FORCES

History books and political conversations are filled with accounts of heroes and villains. The attribution of responsibility for wars, economic depressions, victories and defeats often centers on a particular individual. The great biographer and essayist, Thomas Carlyle, proclaimed that all factors in history are due to the acts of great men. On the other hand, Tolstoy, Marx, and many others advocated an historical determinist position that great men are the products of their times. Trotsky (1932) summed up the view that great historical events have an inevitability that ignores the personal peculiarities of the actors: "To a tickle, people react differently, but to a red-hot iron, alike. As a steam-hammer converts a sphere and a cube alike into sheet metal, so under the blow of too great and inexorable events resistances are smashed and the boundaries of 'individuality' lost" (p. 93). Hence the discovery of America by Columbus or Leif Ericson was inevitable, given the technological developments in navigation; and if Columbus had never lived, America would have been discovered by someone else. Similarly, the Renaissance, the industrial revolution, and the rise of capitalism represented sweeping historical forces and did not depend on the actions of single individuals. In a letter to A. C. Hodges on April 4, 1864, Abraham Lincoln wrote: "I claim not to have controlled events, but confess plainly that events have controlled me" (cited by Duchacek, 1971, p. 214).

The role of the individual in history probably depends on a complicated set of factors, including his position in the system, his particular skills and weaknesses, and the constraints that impinge on him (Greenstein, 1969). The more ambiguous the situation, the less precedent there is, and the more alternatives available to the individual, the greater his impact on history can be. Hook (1955) distinguishes between the event-made man and the event-making man on the basis of choice points created by the cross-currents of historical forces, which provide the individual personality with an opportunity to change the course of events.

A national leader cannot simply manipulate domestic and foreign policy according to his own prejudices and ideology. Even a powerful dictator is limited by his nation's geographic location, its resources, history, traditions, and the habits of the people. Smith (1962) analysed the constraints on an American president in developing foreign policy. The internal structure of the government and the division of powers fragments responsibility so that an agricultural committee of Congress can take an action (say, setting tariffs for cotton) which would undermine the patient development of positive relations with a foreign country. Policy must be pursued for a long period of time to accomplish its objectives but a president must be re-elected if he is to have as long as eight years to accomplish his purposes.

In his memoirs, George Kennan's (1972) chief complaint about foreign policy decisions was that they are made primarily for domestic political purposes rather than in pursuit of rational foreign policy objectives. Public opinion and the support of various business and professional groups are vital factors for a president to consider before taking new policy initiatives. Government agencies, such as the Departments of Commerce, Agriculture, and Interior are highly responsive to special interest groups. Representatives of these Departments then bring pressures to bear that act as restraints on the State and Defense Departments (cf. Pruitt, 1964). Finally, there are the external constraints of the balance of power in the world, commitments made though alliances, and principles established by the United Nations. While the ordinary citizen perceives a president as quite powerful and able to do as he chooses, the president in office feels hemmed in, frustrated, and tied to outmoded policies that he cannot change. While the actor attributes his behavior to the environment, the observer attributes cause to the actor.

high-paying field;" "She's a very warm person"). The results are shown in Table 4.2. As can be seen, subjects gave more external reasons for their own choices than they attributed to their best friends.

One reason given for divergent perceptions is that the actor and observer are attentive to different aspects of the situation. The actor does not attend to his own behavior so much as he does the environmental cues and goals that elicit, guide, and end the behavior sequence. The observer focuses on the actor's responses and tends to ignore or minimize the influence of situational factors in constraining behavioral opportunities. These tendencies were shown in a clever experiment performed by Storms (1973).

Two previously unacquainted subjects sat across from one another at a table and engaged in a five-minute getting-acquainted conversation; they fulfilled the role of actors. Two other subjects, in their role as observers, sat at the far end of the table; each was asked to watch closely a different actor. Video cameras were also focused on each of the actors. At the end of the getting-acquainted conversation the experimenter explained that one of the cameras had not produced an adequate videotape; the videotape of the other actor was viewed by both actors and observers. The result was that one actor and one observer viewed a replay of the second actor, who they had watched earlier (same orientation condition), while one actor saw himself and one observer viewed an actor he had not watched earlier (different orientation condition). In a control condition, the experimenter reported that both cameras failed to function and no viewing occurred.

All subjects were then asked to answer items on a questionnaire. Actor subjects responded to questions about themselves,

Table 4.2   Number of External Causes and Personal Causes Given By Subjects as Explanations of Their Own and Their Best Friend's Choices of Girlfriend and College Major.[a]

	Causes for liking girlfriend		Causes for choosing major	
Explanation	Personal	External	Personal	External
Own behavior	2.04	4.61	1.83	1.52
Friend's behavior	2.57	2.70	1.70	.43

[a] After Nisbett, Caputo, Legant, & Maracek, 1973.

while observer subjects answered questions about the actor they had been assigned to watch. The stimulus person's friendliness, talkativeness, nervousness, and dominance were rated and the degree to which they were attributed to personal or external factors was assessed. The results are shown in Table 4.3. As can be seen, the usual actor-observer difference occurred in the control condition (no videotape) and in the same-orientation condition. In both of these conditions the actor viewed his own behavior as less determined by personal factors than did observers. However, in the new orientation condition in which actors were made outside observers of their own behavior, they made strong personal attributions about themselves. Observers in the new orientation condition attributed their assigned actor's behavior relatively more to external factors after watching the other actor on videotape.

A close examination of the data revealed that changes occurring in the new orientation condition were due to a re-evaluation of external factors rather than shifts in attributions to personal factors. This supports the view that the divergent perceptions of actors and observers stem from the observer's failure to pay attention to situational factors affecting the actor's behavior.

Jones and Nisbett offer another reason why actors and observers have divergent perceptions. The actor has a greater continuity of observations of his own behavior than does any observer. An observer may note a particular response, but he may be ignorant of the events that instigated the behavior. Hence, what looks like an action to the observer is perceived as a reaction by the actor. An actor who strikes another person may appear irrational and aggressive to an observer until he finds out that the attack was instigated by some prior (unobserved) behavior of the person who was struck. Despite the reasonableness of this explanation for divergent perceptions, there is little empirical support for it. In any case biases in making attributions to personal causes or external causes are important in understanding social behavior, as we saw in Box 4.1.

F. Attributions of Power

In this final section on causal attributions, we will consider two parties interacting where one is perceived as having influence over the other. The attribution of power is a special case of assigning causes of an actor's behavior to external factors; here the external cause is another person. Attributing power to person A involves a judgment about how much change in the behavior of person B was caused by A. According to Schopler and Layton (1974), power attributions derive from changes made by observers in the probabilities assigned to various kinds of behavior by actors. That is, observation of B's behavior may lead the ob-

Table 4.3   Ratings of Personal Factors Minus Ratings of External Factors Totaled Over All Four Traits.[a]

	Experimental Conditions		
Attribution	Same orientation	No videotape	New orientation
Actor's attributions of own behavior	.15	2.25	6.80
Observer's attributions of assigned actor's behavior	4.90	4.80	1.60

[a] After Storms, 1973, p. 169.

server to expect similar behavior in the future when similar circumstances occur. If B, when interacting with A, substantially surprises the observer by doing the unexpected, B's behavior may be attributed to the influence of person A. For example, if B seldom attends invited lectures on campus but the observer sees him accept an invitation from A, the observer will attribute the acceptance to A's ability to influence B's behavior.

If the observer is one of the two persons in interaction, a systematic bias occurs in the way he makes attributions about power. The observer tends to take credit for causing the behavior of the other person when positive outcomes result, but he seldom takes the blame for causing negative behavior. Thus, the observer attributes power to himself only when the behavior of the other person leads to desired outcomes.

1. Surveillance and interpersonal causation

Teachers, supervisors, and others of high status may attribute performances of high quality by their subordinates to the maintenance of surveillance over the latter's activities. If it is assumed that workers tend to goof off when not monitored, then it is not unreasonable for superiors to view themselves as external causes for a subordinate's performance. The subordinate is presumably concerned about the rewards and punishments that a person of high status controls. In a test of the surveillance-power attribution relationship, Strickland (1958) had subjects serve in the role of supervisors. Over the first set of trials the subjects monitored the performance of one worker much more than they did a second worker. At the end of this first set of trials the subjects were informed that both workers performed equally well. During the second set of trials the supervisor was given an opportunity to monitor performance of either worker. The subjects chose predominantly to maintain surveillance over the same worker closely supervised in the first set of trials. In

response to a questionnaire, they indicated more trust of the nonmonitored worker than the worker they kept under heavy surveillance. They perceived their presence as necessary to the performance of the heavily monitored worker's performance (external cause) but attributed the other worker's performance to the personal quality of trustworthiness. Kruglanski (1970) found essentially the same results. In this manner close supervision provides its own justification.

2. Bias Due To Outcomes

The tendency to attribute power to self for the desired outcomes associated with another person's behavior and to disclaim influence when the other person's behavior has undesirable outcomes has been studied by Johnson, Feigenbaum, and Weiby (1964). Subjects were asked to play the role of teacher in a simulated teacher-student situation. Each "teacher" was asked to instruct two fictitious elementary school students on multiplication problems prior to each of two work sessions. One of the students was uniformly successful; the second student either performed poorly during both sessions or performed poorly at first but improved during the second session. The subjects believed their effective teaching was responsible when a student improved, but they attributed a uniformly poor performance to internal qualities of the student.

In a study with similiar procedures, Beckman (1970) varied the pattern of performance of the second fictitious student over a series of four sessions: (1) uniformly poor performance, (2) low initial and high final performance, or (3) high initial but low final performance. In addition to the subjects who acted the role of teachers, other observer subjects were asked to read a description of one of the three conditions and were also asked to make attributions about the causes of the student's performance. A divergence in attributions was found. When the student showed improvement over time, the teachers attributed the cause to their skills, while observers tended to give more credit to the student. When the student always performed poorly or showed a decrement in performance over time, both teachers and observers attributed the failure either to the environment (e.g., problems too difficult) or to the student's lack of motivation.

II. ATTRIBUTIONS OF INTERNAL STATES

A traditional concern of social psychologists has been the accuracy with which people attribute emotional states and personality traits to other people. Some of this interest derives from the professional concerns of clinical psychologists and psychiatrists. It is generally believed that successful therapy depends on the therapist's skill in discerning the feelings and moods of his patients. In fact, Truax et al. (1966) consider accurate empathy, the ability to share in the emotions experienced by the patient, to be one of the most important factors in psychotherapy. Of course, accuracy in attributing internal states to other people is also very important in day-to-day social interactions.

The way the observer chunks information about stimulus persons has implications for the accuracy of his attributions. In order to facilitate the processing of information about other persons and the attribution of personality traits to them, the observer classifies people into groups, based on religion, nationality, race, or other criteria. All members of the group are then assumed to share common characteristics. These *stereotypes* prevent the observer from making accurate attributions about other people because they rarely describe particular actual persons adequately. Errors in judgment about other people also occur because observers tend to assume a greater

similarity between themselves and others than is usually the case.

As we shall see, there are important methodological problems in studying the accuracy with which observers make specific attributions regarding the internal states or personality traits of other people. After discussing some of these problems, we will examine the types of stereotypes commonly developed about other people and the role that assumed similarity plays in the perception of persons.

A. Attributing Emotions to Other People

Research on perceived emotions has been strongly influenced by Darwins's theory of biological evolution. According to Darwin, man's emotions are innate, rather than learned; his emotional responses are considered to be deeply rooted in his phylogenetic history. For example, Darwin believed that facial expressions provide reliable cues about the states of emotion experienced by a person. Just as a wolf draws his lips back to bare his fangs, a man's lips tend to tighten when he is angry. If invariable and characteristic responses accompany each specific emotion, then observation of another person's face should be sufficient to allow the observer to make an attribution about the stimulus person's emotional state. To test the accuracy of observers, the experimenter must establish some sort of objective criterion for assessing emotional states against which comparisons can be made. This methodological problem has not been satisfactorily solved.

1. Criterion Problems

A number of techniques have been employed in an attempt to produce stimulus faces which could be said objectively to portray specific identifiable emotions. Artists have been asked either to paint faces which express particular emotions or to touch up photographs in order to idealize emotional expressions. Accuracy is then judged by whether subjects' attributions match the labels applied by the artist to his drawings. Alternatively, trained actors portray various emotions, photographs of their faces are made, and the ability of subjects to identify the emotions is assessed. Motion pictures and tape recordings of voices have also been used as media through which stimuli can be presented to subjects for identifying emotions. The inadequacy of these methods for assessing accuracy in the perception of emotions is best examined in the context of studies which use them.

Charles Darwin (1872) was one of the first to study the accuracy question. He obtained photographs representing a number of emotions and asked 20 judges to identify them. The judges were able to agree with Darwin's labeling of several of the photographs, but there was little or no agreement on others. Rather than concluding that the observers were poor judges, Darwin assumed that the photographs did not adequately portray the emotions.

Langfeld (1918) used a set of 105 pictures taken of a male actor, which were retouched and somewhat idealized by an artist. The most successful subject provided 58 percent agreement with the emotional labels used by the artist; the least successful subject displayed only 17 percent agreement. Langfeld presented each picture again, this time providing an emotional label for each one, and asked subjects whether they agreed with the label or not. For half the subjects an incorrect label was provided; correct labels were provided for the other subjects.

The results can be summarized as follows: (1) when asked to provide emotional labels for pictures, the subjects showed only 38 percent agreement with the labels provided by the artist; (2) when the artist's labels were furnished to them, they found these acceptable about 70 percent of the time; and (3) when erroneous labels were presented with the pictures, subjects found them acceptable 43 percent of the time.

Hence, providing labels for observers does reduce their information processing problem. Langfeld's study suggests that providing such cognitive categories improves the observer's ability to identify emotions from facial expressions. Perhaps observers accepted the artist's label whenever the picture was not incongruent with it because of the influence of an expert's judgment.

Perceptions of emotions are certainly not governed only by cues provided in facial expressions. Carmichael, Roberts, and Wessel (1937) took both still and moving pictures of the hands of an actor portraying various emotions. The ability of subjects to recognize the emotions portrayed in these photographs was just about as good as for facial expressions. Furthermore, still pictures provided as much information for observers as did motion pictures. Inflections of the voice also convey the speaker's feelings. Dusenberry and Knower (1938) presented a recording of someone reading the letters of the alphabet in different emotional tones. Listeners were able to recognize the intended emotions from the vocal expressions about as well as they did from observations of facial expressions.

2.   Schlosberg's Model of Facial Expressions

Clearly, observers can make some inferences from facial, gestural, and vocal cues about the emotional states of the actor. Although fine discriminations cannot be made among specific emotions, such as between disgust and contempt, observers can make judgments along several broad dimensions. Schlosberg (1952; 1954) has proposed a two dimensional model to represent the way observers classify facial expressions. Faces are described along pleasant-unpleasant and attention-rejection dimensions. In the context of the concern of the observer to predict how the actor will respond (so he can plan his own responses), these two dimensions may serve his purposes very well. When the stimulus person is perceived as attentive and in a pleasant mood, he is approachable, but when he is perceived as being in an unpleasant emotional state and as rejecting, the observer will try to avoid an encounter.

3.   Are Facial Expressions Of Emotions Universal?

Darwin, of course, believed that all men produce the same pattern of muscular changes in their faces when they experience the same emotion. Research on the perception of emotions has thrown doubt on this assumption of universality. In a classic study of Chinese literature, Klineberg (1938) reported that the descriptions of facial expressions by Oriental authors indicate important cultural differences. While a smile may reflect a pleasant emotional state to the Western observer, it typically conveys anger in Chinese literature. Birdwhistle (1963) and many others have concluded that anecdotes from visitors to other cultures, including anthropologists, indicate a lack of universality in facial expressions.

Recent research has revitalized the Darwinian position. Ekman and Friesen (1971) compared the descriptions of emotions depicted in photographs given by Westerners and by tribesmen in New Guinea. The latter had virtually no exposure to the mass media or other cultural products of the Western world. The photographs used represented six emotions—happiness, sadness, anger, surprise, disgust, and fear—which had been correctly identified by more than 70 percent of the Western judges. The tribesmen were presented with two or three of the photographs and a translator described a situation to them (e.g., "His friends have come, and he is happy"). The nonliterate observers were asked to identify which of the stimulus faces was most appropriate to the situation described.

The results indicated a generally high level of "correct" choices (64 to 100 percent) by the tribesmen. Confusion occurred most often when a face showing surprise was chosen for a fear story. Ekman and Friesen concluded that the association between particular facial expressions and emotion is universal and not strictly a cultural product. On the other hand, Izard (1969), using somewhat different methods, found rather large differences betweeen cultures in their ability to identify the emotions associated with various facial expressions. While the evidence provided by Ekman and Friesen is sufficient to re-open the controversy, methodological differences make any conclusions premature.

The recognition of emotions from facial expressions is further complicated by the fact that in everyday life people often try to control their emotions or feign emotions they do not feel. There are many socially important nuances in expression that have not been considered in studies of accuracy. For example, a person may smile in a sarcastic or deprecating manner; when this happens one observer may catch the actor's meaning while others naively assume the smile represents genuine pleasure. A person who is afraid may keep a stiff upper lip and attempt to hide his fear from others. It is well known that military men under fire often engage in horseplay and exchange witticisms; this has sometimes been called gallows humor.

In everyday life facial, gestural, and vocal expressiveness occur together within a specific situation. Given that the actor often labels his own emotions according to both arousal states and social-environmental cues (see the discussion of Schachter's two-factor theory of emotions in Chapter 3), it would be reasonable to expect closer agreement between actor and observers and finer discriminations of emotional attributions by observers when they possess information about the situational context within which the actor's behavior occurs. The effects of context were demonstrated by Pudovkin (1954), who showed subjects three different film strips containing the same passive facial close-up of a well-known actor. The film strips created varying backgrounds by showing a bowl of soup, a child playing with a toy bear, or a dead woman in a coffin. As might be expected, the actor was judged as pensive, happy, or sad, respectively.

B. Attributions of Personality Traits to Other Persons

When considering the accuracy of attributions made by observers regarding the personality traits of stimulus persons, the criterion problem is even more intractable than in the perception of emotions. There is some doubt about whether persons actually possess personality traits or whether "traits" are merely cognitive categories invented by observers in their attempts to develop stable images of other people. In the science of psychology, the concept of *personality* has been used to refer to the unique or idiosyncratic aspects of the person which (at least to some extent) help to explain the consistency of his behavior over time and situations. As we have seen, idiosyncratic personal factors, such as dogmatism and cognitive complexity, may also be used to account for why one actor behaves in completely opposite ways to another in similar situations. As Allport (1937, p. 102) has put it, "The same fire that melts the butter hardens the egg."

The prevalent approach to the scientific study of personality has been to identify a set of traits, such as trust, authoritarianism, need-achievement motivation, and dogmatism; to develop paper-and-pencil tests of the traits; and then to attempt to predict the individual's behavior based on the trait measurement and knowledge of the specific experimental situation. In a recent review of personality research, Mischel (1968) reported that only a small part of behavior can be accounted for on the basis of personality traits. With the possible exception of certain abilities (e.g., intelligence, perceptual-motor skills, etc.), no traits have been found that provide a good basis

for predicting the behavior of persons in known situations. Mischel concluded that there is little objective evidence for theories of personality and suggested the possibility that traits exist only in the cognitive structures of observers. If Mischel is correct, then the accuracy question can never be settled, since there can be no objective standard against which to compare an observer's attributions regarding the personality of an actor.

Why then do people make attributions regarding another's personality if psychologists are not certain there is an objective basis for them and such attributions do not provide a good basis for predicting the other's behavior? It is possible that naive observers use different information than psychologists and are better predictors. But why do psychologists persist in testing personality theories? Mischel suggests four possible answers: (1) a belief that all the data are not yet in and it is premature to draw conclusions; (2) a belief that better measures of personality traits can be developed to provide a firm basis for predicting behavior; (3) a belief that the "correct" traits have not yet been identified; and (4) a belief that traits exist only in the eye of the beholder. Whatever the answer may be, observers do perceive constancy in the behavior of stimulus persons and develop naive (often implicit) personality theories about other people.

In fairness, it needs to be said that social psychologists tend to be sympathetic to the criticisms of trait theories of personality. Social psychologists focus on the study of situational influences on behavior and perhaps as a consequence seldom find much effect of personality factors. However there are a number of personality theorists (e.g., Alker, 1972) who are firmly convinced that there is ample evidence to support trait theories. An emerging interactionist perspective contends that both traits and social situations are crucial for explaining consistency of behavior (Bowers, 1973; Carson, 1969).

1. The Perception of Behavioral Constancies

A number of constancies occur in our perception of the physical world. For example, although the size of an object on the retina of our eyes may shrink or expand as we move further away or closer to it, we tend to perceive the object as remaining the same size, whatever our distance from it. Similarly, the brightness, color, and shape of objects tend to remain perceptually constant regardless of wide variations in environmental conditions. Brunswick and Kamiya (1953) have noted the functional utility of such physical constancies in providing the individual with a stable environment in which events can be predicted. Given an organized, stable, and predictable environment, the individual can plan his activities in a way that can maximize his satisfactions and minimize unpleasant consequences.

Observers also try to maintain organized, stable, and predictable perceptions of the social environment, and particularly of other people (Heider, 1958). We try to find some constancy in the behavior of other people. Because an actor's behavior is almost infinitely variable, we attempt to discover some underlying, stable dispositions that can account for the variety. If the actor joins a fraternity, seeks political office on campus, and applies to law school, an observer may assume an underlying need for power or dominance over other people. In this way the variety of responses can be integrated (or chunked) into a single stable "disposition."

Observers tend to assume that people will act consistently over time. This assumption of constancy was demonstrated by Nisbett, Caputo, Legant, and Maracek (1973). Observers watched another subject and two confederates interact with the experimenter, who asked the three of them whether they would volunteer to help the University host a visit from prospective financial backers for a research institute.

The experimenter indicated that the University needed hostesses for conducting tours, holding receptions, and to help in other activities. The two confederates were asked first and both agreed to help; pressure to conform was therefore brought to bear upon the subject. About half the subjects volunteered. Both actor and observer subjects were then asked to estimate the likelihood that the actor would volunteer to perform a future service task (canvassing for the United Fund).

Among subjects who had been asked to serve as University hostesses, there was no difference between those who agreed to do so and those who did not in their estimations of the likelihood of their helping the United Fund. But observers who saw an actor volunteer believed it was more likely the actor would help the United Fund than did observers who saw the actor refuse to volunteer. Furthermore, observers of volunteers perceived them as more likely to help the United Fund in the future than did the volunteers themselves. Thus, observers assumed a constancy of behavior that actors did not assume about themselves. This divergence of perceptions of actors and observers is one we have already noted. The actor views his behavior as mostly environmentally caused (hence yielding little information about how he would act under other circumstances), while the observer views the actor's behavior as reflecting personal characteristics that should be constant in other situations.

The tendency of observers to discount environmental factors may produce an impression of consistency in an actor's behavior for another reason. We observe most people in only a few roles. We see the grocer at the store, the doctor in his office, Walter Cronkite every evening on the television news, and the minister every Sunday at church. To the extent that a person is behaving according to the requirements of a particular role, his behavior is situationally determined. If an observer always saw the same person acting in the same basic role, the actor would appear to be consistent over observations and a person attribution would be made. Most students only see a college professor in a few places—in the classroom, in his office, at the library, or elsewhere on campus. The professor's style of dress may be consistent, and he may appear sincere, intellectual, and self-confident at all times. Outside his role at the college, however, the professor may shout for blood at prize fights, run around home in a pair of ragged shorts, seldom shave except when he must go to school, and booze it up every weekend. It is only because the student has a limited number of observations of the professor as he enacts the requirements of a single role that he appears to be consistent over time.

An impression of consistency is fostered by the fact that a person appears physically continuous and expresses similar mannerisms over time (Mischel, 1968). Because the actor looks the same, has the same vocal quality, wears characteristic clothes, and has some pet verbal expressions, the observer assumes that there is also consistency in his behavior. The illusion of consistency is also fostered by the labels provided by language. The person has a name that does not change and labels are available in the culture to characterize both his behavior and his underlying traits. For example, if an act is considered aggressive by an observer, he is apt to assign a rather stable trait of aggressiveness to the actor. This type of correspondence between acts and dispositions has been noted by Jones and Davis (1965). An observation of a particular act, which is labeled, is used as a basis for predicting similar behavior from the actor in the future.

The actor is more attentive to situational forces and has many more observations of himself to draw on than do other observers; hence, he is not apt to categorize himself in terms of traits. As Jones and Nisbett (1971) state, "When the actor steps back to view himself, he is probably inclined to emphasize not the superficial topography of behavior but the underlying purposes mediated by the behavior. The actor is consequently more likely to conceive of his personality as a configuration of values and strategies than as a collection of response dispositions. When the actor compares himself to others, we might expect him to believe that he differs chiefly in the priorities that he assigns to his goals and in the particular means he has devised to achieve them" (p. 13).

2.   Implicit Personality Theory

The traits assigned by an observer to an actor are tied together in implicative form. Certain traits are seen as rather inevitably going together. Therefore, if an actor is perceived to possess a particular trait, the observer will immediately infer that the actor also has all of the associated traits. For example, Bruner, Shapiro, and Tagiuri (1958) described a stimulus person to subjects and asked them to rate the stimulus person on some other traits. The kind of question addressed by these investigators was: if an intelligent person is considered to be responsible while an inconsiderate person is believed to be irresponsible (because these traits happen to "go together"), then how responsible would subjects rate a person who was both intelligent and inconsiderate? According to the data, the answer is "moderately responsible," and is predictable on the basis of how strongly each of the two known traits is associated with the trait of responsibility by the observer. For the subjects of this experiment, intelligence implied responsibility more strongly than inconsiderateness implied irresponsibility.

The various clusters of traits the observer carries around as schemata which can be used to make attributions about other people make up his implicit personality theory. Each observer develops a different set of interrelated traits to describe actors (Cronbach, 1955), and these implicit theories are applied equally to friends and strangers (Hakel, 1969; Norman, 1963;

Passini & Norman, 1966). Thus, the observer may not only make an error by assigning a particular trait to an actor but may compound the error by assigning an entire collection of traits which he believes goes along with the initial trait.

Kelly (1955) cautions against assuming an equivalence in the perceptions of two observers simply because they label an actor in the same way (e.g., as "kind"). Not only may kindness have different implications for other traits for the two observers, but the construct "kind" may not mean the same for both of them. If the opposite of "kind" is "cruel" for one observer but "selfish" for the other, the dimensions they are using are different. Thus, the same linguistic label may have different meanings and may refer to different associated traits, and these differences in coding can create difficulties in communication between observers.

The impressions formed of actors may be more a function of the implicit personality theories of observers than of any "actual" traits they possess. This possibility was suggested by a study carried out by Dornbush, Hastorf, Richardson, Muzzy, and Vreeland (1965). They asked children at a camp to provide descriptions of two other campers. In analyzing the content of the descriptions, the researchers measured the overlap in the descriptions of one person by two different observers, the overlap in the descriptions of two persons by one observer, and the overlap in descriptions of two persons by two observers. The results are pictorially presented in Figure 4.4. There was a 57 percent overlap when one observer described two other campers, a 45 percent overlap when two observers described the same third person, and only 38 percent agreement when two observers described two other campers. A single observer apparently applies similar categories in describing all other persons, while different observers use different categories in describing the same person.

Can people be taught to lay aside their implicit theories of personality and to become more objective in perceiving others? Presumably, training in psychology should help the student reduce his subjective biases. Kremers (1960) had students majoring in psychology, the natural sciences, and classical literature listen to a person give a speech on the topic of labor relations. The subjects were then asked to predict what the speaker would do in a number of different situations. An accuracy criterion was established by asking the speaker and some of his close friends to predict how he would behave. Only those speakers who were consistent in predicting their own behavior and whose close friends provided consensual validation were used in the experiment. Accuracy in predictions by the subjects were quite low in general and the psychology students were no more accurate than the other students. Also, a mature psychologist-experimenter was found by Deutsch (1960a) to be a poorer judge of a

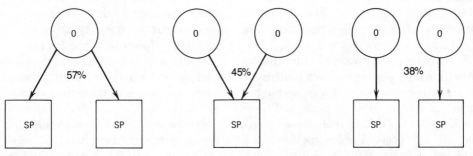

Figure 4.4. Percentage overlap in descriptions by observers (O) of stimulus persons (SP). (After Dornbush, et al, 1965.)

student's reactions to an experience of failure than were other students. It can be presumed that familiarity with the norms and standards of peers led to the greater accuracy of the students. Thus, the available evidence provides little reason to believe that psychologists are any better judges of personality than anyone else.

C. Stereotypes

A stereotype is a cluster of traits that is attributed indiscriminately to all members of a group. The group may be identified in terms of race, class, religion, occupation, age, nationality, sex, or any number of other criteria. Although an individual may have a *personal* set of stereotypes, a *social* stereotype represents the consensus of the majority of a given group of judges.

Stereotypes of national, ethnic, and racial groups among Princeton University students were studied in the early 1930s (Katz & Braly, 1933); they were examined again after World War II (Gilbert, 1951), and once again in the late 1960s (Karlins, Coffman, & Walters, 1969). Table 4.4 illustrates the changes that occurred over this period of more than three decades. As can be seen, some of the more negative traits assigned to groups, particularly to Negroes, have softened over time. Nevertheless, 67 percent still agree that Americans are "materialistic," 59 percent agree that Germans are "industrious," and a majority agree that Chinese are "loyal to family ties." Groups are sometimes characterized by terms that are denotatively similar but connotatively opposed. For example, Americans are generally considered intelligent and the Chinese are sly.

A stereotype is a means of chunking information. If a person believes Italians are musical and passionate, he will react to any particular Italian as if he possessed those characteristics. The fact that many Italians may not appreciate Verdi's operas or that some suffer from sexual inadequacies may be ignored. The evidence regarding stereotypes is marred somewhat by the procedures used. Most studies ask subjects to rate the traits that best represent a group of persons. As a consequence, subjects must base their ratings on the most typical person of the group to be rated. The nature of the task requires that the judge ignore individual differences between group members. Hence, just because a person indicates that he shares a stereotype of a group of people does not imply an inability to distinguish between representatives of the relevant group when confronted with them on a face-to-face basis.

Present-day awareness of the prejudicial aspects of stereotyping may have induced the reduction in negative traits assigned to Negroes and Jews in the Princeton study. Especially in a college environment, censure is invited if one acts like a bigot. But it is difficult to judge whether these negative stereotypes have really changed or whether the student's willingness openly to acknowledge them has changed. Sigall and Page (1971) found evidence for the latter hypothesis. One group of subjects was asked to evaluate on paper-and-pencil scales how typical a set of traits was in describing Americans and Negroes. The subjects in a second group were wired up to bogus physiological recording equipment that was described to them as an experimental model of a new machine called an electromyograph. The machine was said to be capable of detecting fine gradations of emotional responses from the measurement of implicit muscle movements, and was more sensitive than the most advanced lie detector machine. This mock apparatus has been called the "bogus pipeline'" (Jones & Sigall, 1971).

Subjects in the paper-and-pencil condition would not be apprehensive about being detected for faking their responses in order to "look good," but subjects in the bogus pipeline condition should have believed they would be detected if they faked their responses. As expected, the latter expressed more negative attitudes toward

Table 4.4   Percent of Students Assigning Traits to Selected Ethnic and National Groups.[a]

Trait	Checking trait (%)			Trait	Checking trait (%)		
	1933	1951	1967		1933	1951	1967
Germans				**Negroes**			
Scientifically minded	78	62	47	Superstitious	84	41	13
Industrious	65	50	59	Lazy	75	31	26
Stolid	44	10	9	Happy-go-lucky	38	17	27
Intelligent	32	32	19	Ignorant	38	24	11
Methodical	31	20	21	Musical	26	33	47
Extremely nationalistic	24	50	43	Ostentatious	26	11	25
Progressive	16	3	13	Very Religious	24	17	8
Efficient	16	—	46	Stupid	22	10	4
Social	15	—	5	Physically dirty	17	—	3
Aggressive	—	27	30	Pleasure loving	—	19	26
Arrogant	—	23	18				
Italians				**Jews**			
Artistic	53	28	30	Shrewd	79	47	30
Impulsive	44	19	28	Mercenary	49	28	15
Passionate	37	25	44	Industrious	48	29	33
Quick tempered	35	15	28	Grasping	34	17	17
Musical	32	22	9	Intelligent	29	37	37
Imaginative	30	20	7	Ambitious	21	28	48
Very religious	21	33	25	Sly	20	14	7
Talkative	21	23	23	Loyal to family ties	15	19	19
Revengeful	17	—	—	Persistent	13	—	9
Pleasure loving	—	28	33	Aggressive	12	—	23
				Materialistic	—	—	46
Americans				**Chinese**			
Industrious	48	30	23	Superstitious	34	18	8
Intelligent	47	32	20	Sly	29	4	6
Materialistic	33	37	67	Conservative	29	14	15
Ambitious	33	21	42	Tradition loving	26	26	32
Progressive	27	5	17	Loyal to family ties	22	35	50
Pleasure loving	26	27	28	Industrious	18	18	23
Alert	23	7	7	Meditative	19	—	21
Efficient	21	9	15	Reserved	17	18	15
Aggressive	20	8	15	Very religious	15	—	6
Straightforward	19	—	9	Ignorant	15	—	7
Practical	19	—	12	Deceitful	14	—	5
Sportsmanlike	19	—	9	Quiet	13	19	23
Individualistic	—	26	15	Courteous	—	—	20
Conventional	—	—	17	Extremely nationalistic	—	—	19
Scientifically minded	—	—	15	Humorless	—	—	17
Ostentatious	—	—	15	Artistic	—	—	15

[a] Adapted from Karlins, Coffman, & Walters, 1969.

Negroes and were more positive toward Americans than were the former. Still, the stereotype expressed by bogus pipeline subjects was not as negative as among the Princeton students in 1933. Sigall and Page conclude that the changes in the stereotype of Negroes over the last three decades represents "a little fading, and a little faking."

There is often a grain of truth in a stereotype. Many human groups share values that affect their behavior. For example, many poor people drop out of school and do not acquire the requisite skills to obtain jobs; they may maintain many superstitions and may appear to be lazy. Given that a disproportionate number of Negroes in America are poor, they may be stereotyped as superstitious and lazy. Bayton, McAlister, and Hamer (1956) found a stereotyping of lower class Negroes that did not apply to upper class Negroes. Perhaps the fading of negative stereotypes over recent years is due to the changes taking place in education and the job market as many racial and ethnic barriers have gradually been taken down.

A person may hold stereotypes because they serve to boost his self-concept. He may attempt to protect himself from feelings of inferiority by making comparisons with groups of persons he considers worse than himself (Katz, 1960). If a boss does not provide good wages for his employees, he may consider them fortunate not to be working for a member of some other ethnic group. In addition, stereotypes emphasize the perceiver's uniqueness. People in American society generally place a high value on being different from the masses; their distinction provides an identity for them.

In summary, stereotypes serve to organize perceptions of groups of people and provide a basis for predicting what strangers will do. They provide orientation to social situations, especially when other cues are ambiguous or absent, so the perceiver is prepared to approach or avoid individuals who can be classified as members of the stereotyped group. Whatever their social

validity in representing the cultural values and behavior patterns of groups of people, they are never adequate for describing any particular person. Stereotypes may be self-enhancing since they serve to point out the uniqueness of the observer and bolster his sense of status and superiority through the comparisons he makes with the stereotyped groups.

D. Assumed Similarity as a Factor in Person Perception

In a stable social world it is usually safe to assume that most other people react to situations the same way you do. If you laugh at a cartoon or are repelled by a grotesque painting of war, you generally assume that your friends and associates will have the same reactions. Generalization from your own experiences and feelings leads you to attribute similar internal states to others.

According to Newcomb (1950) "the self is the ground against which others are perceived." The individual's self-concept influences his perceptions of other people. A person with a positive self-concept may assume that he is much like most other people and therefore assumes similarity in making attributions to them. However, a person with low self-esteem may assume he is worse in many ways than other people and may not assume similarity. Support for these hypotheses was found by Bramel (1962). Self-esteem was manipulated by providing male subjects with false information about their performances on a series of personality tests; half of the subjects were provided favorable feedback (i.e. high self-esteem) and half were given negative feedback (i.e. low self-esteem). The subjects were then paired with one another, each pair containing a high and a low self-esteem person. Electrodes which feigned physiological measurements of emotional reactions were placed on the subjects. The subjects were then shown photographs of nude males. The experimenter told the subjects that the degree of physiological arousal produced by the photographs provided a measure of latent homosexuality. False scores were given to the subjects, indicating either high or low latent homosexuality. After each subject received his score in response to a particular photograph, he was asked to estimate the other subject's score.

When high and low self-esteem subjects received low latent homosexuality scores, they guessed that their partner also received a low score. Assumed similarity was also manifested by high self-esteem subjects who received high homosexuality scores; they estimated that their partner also received a high score. However, low self-esteem subjects who received high homosexuality scores did not assume their partner also received a high score; they were apparently willing to believe they were different from other people and in a way that was unfavorable to themselves.

Bramel's study has been criticized for allegedly overstepping the bounds of ethics in placing subjects at risk. Some subjects were presented with a bogus negative evaluation by a psychologist regarding their performance on a number of personality tests and then were provided with false information regarding their latent homosexuality. Despite the fact that the experimenter revealed all of his deceptions at the end of the study and also spent a good deal of time reassuring the subjects who might have been made anxious by their experience, a question remains about whether the post-experimental debriefing procedures adequately compensated for the anxiety produced. As we indicated in Chapter 2, this ethical question is a matter of judgment which weighs the risk to the subjects against the merits of the scientific investigation. It would probably be helpful if nonpsychologists served on a committee to assist the sometimes over-eager psychologist in making these ethical decisions.

A belief that others are similar to oneself can serve an ego-defensive purpose. The perceiver can assume that he is no worse than other people and is in fact at least average in most ways. If this is the case, then experimental observers should not project attributions of similarity when another person is known to be worse than average in some respect. Bramel (1963) found that similarity is assumed only to occur with respect to other average people. He paired subjects with a partner who was identified either as a student or a chronic criminal and carried out the procedures described above. The subjects assumed similarity in latent homosexuality scores only when they were paired with another student. Subjects who received high or low scores guessed that their student-partner would receive similar scores. There was no relationship between the subjects' own scores and their estimates of the criminal's scores.

The cognitive label by which a person identifies his own emotional states is a form of category accessibility which may readily be applied in attributing emotions to other people. The basis of the bias toward assumed similarity may be the increased accessibility of relevant cognitive categories when the observer is emotionally aroused. Feshbach and Singer (1957) provided some evidence for this point of view. Mildly painful shocks were administered to half of a group of subjects while they watched a film of an actor demonstrating a manual skill; the other half were not shocked. The subjects were than asked to rate the actor in the film on a series of adjective scales both "in this situation" and "in general." There were no differences in the ratings of the actor "in this situation," but the shocked subjects rated him as more fearful "in general" than did the non-shocked subjects. These results are consistent with those of Dornbush et al. (reported earlier), which showed that campers' evaluations of one another were affected strongly by implicit theories of personality. The accessible cognitive categories of the perceiver, whether of an enduring nature or affected by temporary emotional states, may produce a bias toward assumed similarity in person perception.

In summary, an observer must draw upon his own cognitive categories and schemata in making attributions about other persons. His own experiences and feelings provide a basis for making inferences about similar internal states of others. Unless he has specific information regarding his dissimilarity or that of the other person, the similarity of reactions by others to events will be assumed. Most of the research on assumed similarity has concentrated on negatively evaluated traits or unpleasant emotional states; hence, the subjects' responses may reflect concern for managing an impression of being no worse than other persons rather than an honest report of attributions. It is not clear whether a person would assume similarity in making attributions when the internal states involved do not reflect so strongly a positive or negative evaluation of the perceiver.

III. FORMING OVERALL IMPRESSIONS OF PERSONS

Until now we have considered how observers make attributions about the causes of behavior and the specific attitudes, abilities, emotions, traits, and motives of other people. In everyday life the perceiver obtains complex bits of information about a stimulus person over time, and some of this information may be contradictory. Yet the observer usually manages to arrive at an organized and stable impression of the stimulus person. The study of impression formation is primarily concerned with how the observer processes information he receives either from direct interactions or through reports from third parties. The information processing problem for the perceiver may be somewhat different when he gains information from a single observation than when it is gathered over a series of occasions.

Global impressions of stimulus persons include both denotative and connotative content (see the discussion of language in Chapter 3). In most laboratory studies, the subject is presented with adjectival descriptions of hypothetical persons or with restricted information about a stranger. Adjectives more often represent evaluative judgments than they do denotative characteristics. It is not surprising, therefore, that observers appear to rely more heavily on *connotative* factors in forming impressions under laboratory conditions.

Early research on impression formation suggested that observers tend to organize their impressions around some central trait or characteristic of the stimulus person. More recently, a series of mathematical models has been developed to represent the way observers combine various bits of information. Although these models usually represent information gathered in a single observation period, they have been extended to account for findings regarding "order effects" in person perception. The relative importance of first impressions and of later information constitute these order effects, referred to as primacy and recency effects, respectively. As we shall see, the evidence shows that impressions organized along the Semantic Differential (connotative) dimensions of evaluation and potency may allow the individual to predict the future behavior of a stimulus person.

A. Central and Peripheral Traits

In forming an overall impression of a person, the observer does not give equal importance to all the information he receives. This was demonstrated in a series of classic studies by Asch (1946). He described a stimulus person to one group of subjects by the adjectives: intelligent, skillful, industrious, warm, determined, practical, and cautious. A second group of subjects was presented with an identical list of traits, except for the substitution of cold for warm. The subjects were asked to write a paragraph describing the stimulus person and then to chose the traits that best fit him from pairs of opposite traits.

The warm-cold difference in the list of adjectives produced differences in the paragraph written by subjects. The warm person was described as "A person who believes certain things to be right, wants others to see his point, would be sincere in an argument and would like to see his point won," and as "A scientist performing experiments and persevering after many setbacks. He is driven by the desire to accomplish something that could be of benefit." In contrast, the cold person was described as "A very ambitious and talented person who would not let anyone or anything stand in the way of achieving his goals. Wants his own way, he is determined not to give in, no matter what happens," and "A rather snobbish person who feels that his success and intelligence set him apart from the run-of-the-mill individual. Calculating and unsympathetic" (p. 263).

The response traits chosen as representative of the stimulus person also reflected the warm-cold difference. While the warm person was overwhelmingly viewed as generous, wise, happy, and good-natured, the cold person was described by the opposite traits. Some traits, such as reliable and important, were not affected by the warm or cold descriptions.

When polite or blunt were used to describe the stimulus person (in place of warm or cold), little difference occurred in the impressions formed by observers. Asch concluded that some traits are central and serve as the foundation around which images are formed, while other traits are peripheral and have less impact on overall impressions. The same trait may be central or peripheral in forming impressions, depending on the context of adjectives provided to the observer. For example, Asch was able to counteract the positive image generated by the adjective "warm" when he imbedded it in an unrelentingly negative set of adjectives (obedient, weak, shallow, unambitious, and vain).

Wishner (1960) reasoned that certain traits may be central in organizing impressions because they have high information value. In Asch's procedure a hypothetical person was described in terms of a set of stimulus traits and subjects were asked to select from a list of response traits to further describe him. Stimulus traits that are highly correlated with one another but not with response traits provide little basis for predicting the response traits. But a trait that is not correlated with other stimulus traits and is correlated with response traits would yield a high amount of distinctive and predictive information.

Wishner had 214 students rate their instructor on a set of 53 traits and then correlated the ratings with each other. When the adjective traits that had been used in Asch's study were isolated and examined, two interesting findings emerged: (1) the trait warm-cold was relatively uncorrelated with the other stimulus traits used in Asch's study (see Table 4.5) and the other stimulus traits were moderately correlated with one another; and (2) warm-cold did correlate with the response traits used in Asch's study (again, see Table 4.5), but the other six stimulus traits were not strongly correlated with the response traits.

The next step was to show that any trait could be made central by following a few simple rules of selecting stimulus and response traits: (1) choose a designated trait so that it is not correlated with other stimulus traits but is correlated with the response traits, and (2) choose the other stimulus traits in such a way that they correlate with each other but not with response traits. Wishner demonstrated the effectiveness of his information hypothesis by taking humane-ruthless, a peripheral trait in Asch's study, and by following his two rules, converting it into a central trait. Of course this demonstration does not detract from the importance of Asch's work, but it does remove the mystery associated with it.

Acquaintances sometimes arrange for their friends to meet one another, often

Table 4.5   Correlations Between Warm-Cold, Other Stimulus Items and the Most Affected Response Items Used by Asch (1946). [a]

Trait	Correlation coefficient
Stimulus list	
Unintelligent-Intelligent	−.07
Clumsy-Skillful	−.10
Industrious-Lazy	.26
Determined-Indecisive	.34
Practical-Unpractical	.25
Cautious-Impulsive	−.00
Response list	
Ungenerous-Generous	−.33
Irritable-Good natured	−.57
Humorous-Humorless	.24
Sociable-Unsociable	.70
Popular-Unpopular	.50
Self-centered-Altruistic	−.30
Unhappy-Happy	−.54
Humane-Ruthless	.34
Imaginative-Unimaginative	.48

[a] After Wishner, 1960, p. 101.

providing preliminary verbal information so that each develops some expectation of what the other will be like. Publicity often precedes a lecture or speech given by a visitor to a university. Do these initial verbal introductions affect the reactions of the people involved when they meet one another face-to-face? Kelley (1950) found a positive answer to this question when the verbal introduction included central traits. Written introductions of a guest speaker were passed out to students in a psychology class at M.I.T., referring to the speaker's institutional affiliation and area of expertise and including several trait adjectives. Although the students were not aware of it, two slightly different introductions were handed out; in one the adjective "warm" was included, while "cold" was substituted in the other. The visitor then led a 20-minute discussion in the class.

The students who had received the "warm" introduction participated more in the discussion and rated the guest lecturer more positively on a set of traits when the class was over. This might be called the student-expectancy effect to contrast it with the teacher-expectancy effect referred to in Box 4.2. A teacher's prior reputation among students may be quite important in determining his later effectiveness in class.

Denotative contradictions or inconsistent connotations may make the task of forming a unified impression more difficult. The observer may resolve inconsistencies by discounting aspects of the information and by applying his implicit theory of personality to integrate the contradictions. Haire and Grunes (1950) demonstrated these processes. Students were presented with the following description of a stimulus person: "Works in a factory, reads a newspaper, goes to the movies, average height, cracks jokes, intelligent, strong, and active." A second group of students received an identical description, except for the omission of the adjective "intelligent."

It was obvious from the descriptive paragraphs written by the students that the word "intelligent" was incongruous with the other factors. For example, one student discounted the incongruous factor by stating, "He is intelligent, but not too much so, since he works in a factory." Another student applied his implicit personality theory by stating, "He is intelligent, but doesn't possess initiative to rise above his group." Still another tendency was to deny that the person was an ordinary factory worker by promoting him to a position as foreman. Some students maintained the inconsistency by indicating "the traits seem to be conflicting. Most factory workers I have heard about aren't too intelligent."

The word "intelligent" is clearly not congruent with the stereotype of a factory worker held by college students. Describing a particular factory worker as intelligent makes him somewhat special. He is therefore perceived as lacking motivation, lacking money to get an education, having emotional problems, deciding to be a social drop-out, being influential in union activities, or he is promoted to a management position. This one bit of information was sufficiently central to undermine the applicability of the stereotype to the particular person.

B. Information Processing Models of Impression Formation

Heider (1958) stated that there are really only two things others may do which are important to the individual: they can either benefit him or harm him. A favorable impression may allow the observer to predict positive behavior, while an unfavorable impression may allow the prediction of negative behavior. The effects of generalizing such impressions have long been known by personnel officers. A *halo effect* occurs whenever a general evaluative impression carries over to subsequent judgments of the referent person. A supervisor may rate a very productive employee as also obedient to safety regulations, friendly and cooperative, and creative and resourceful, even when the employee is really mediocre in these nonproductive aspects. The positive evaluation of one major activity is carried over to bias the rater's judgments in other situations.

A number of mathematical models have been constructed to represent how observers combine bits of information about a stimulus person in developing overall evaluative impressions of him. Suppose an observer is given four adjectives—two positive and two negative—to describe a hypothetical person. How will these four bits of information be combined? Will the positive and negative bits cancel each other out and leave the perceiver with a completely neutral impression? To answer this kind of question, a list of adjectives has been scaled in terms of their favorability or unfavorability. If, for example, the Semantic Differential scoring system described in Chapter 3 were used, a particular adjective would have a scale value from $+3$ to -3, depending on the average judgment of a sizable sample of raters. A hypothetical person would then be described by a set of adjectives with known scale values, and the observer's overall evaluation can then be obtained. Research using this method can assess and help develop models of information processing. We will describe and evaluate the summation, averaging, and weighted-averaging models of information processing.

1. Summation Model

Triandis and Fishbein (1963) proposed a summation model to account for the way observers arrive at an overall evaluation of stimulus persons. This model assumes that the observer merely adds together the scale values of the component items of information and uses the total as the basis for his impression. For example, a stimulus person might be described in terms of his nationality, religion, race, and occupation, as in the sentence "a Black American bank manager

of a different religion from the observer."
Suppose the component information had
been previously rated on seven-point scales
from "dislike very much" (0) to "like very
much" (7) by a subject and the results were:
Black (2), American (7), bank manager (5),
and different religion (2). The sum of these
values is 16. When they compare the evaluation of this person with the ratings of other
hypothetical persons described in different
ways, Triandis and Fishbein found the
summation model to be a fairly accurate
predictor of the subjects' overall evaluative
ratings. Thus, a description formed of elements summing to 16 will lead to a more
positive evaluation than a description
formed with information that sums to a
lower value (e.g., Black (2), Turkish (1),
used car salesman (2), and different religion (2), yielding a total value of 7).

2.   Averaging Model

Anderson's (1962) averaging model predicts that an overall evaluative impression
will be a function of the average evaluation
of the component descriptive elements. According to Anderson, the observer adds the
elements, as in the summation model, but
then divides the total by the number of
elements processed:

$$E = \frac{S_1 + S_2 + S_3 \ldots + S_n}{n}$$

where E represents the overall impression,
S is a descriptive adjective, and n indicates
the number of adjectives used in the description.

The summation and averaging models
sometimes (though not always) make opposing predictions. If a new piece of positive information is provided to the observer, the summation model predicts an
increment in likableness; but the averaging
model may predict no change, an increase,
or a decrease, depending on whether the
added information was greater or lesser in
scale value than the average of the prior
elements. As an example, consider what

would happen if we added to the description of the Black American bank manager
by including the information that he was
male, which has a scale value of 4. The
summation model would predict an even
higher overall evaluation of the stimulus
person because the total would now be 20
rather than 16. However, the averaging
model would predict no change, since adding an element of the weight 4 does not
change the average. Before the additional
bit was added to the description, the average of the elements was:

$$E = \frac{\begin{array}{c} 2 \text{ (Black)} + 7 \text{ (American)} + 5 \text{ (bank} \\ \text{manager)} + 2 \text{ (religion)} \end{array}}{4 \text{ (Number of Adjectives)}} = \frac{16}{4} = 4$$

Adding another adjective with the scale
value of 4 does not change the average, and
hence no change in overall evaluative impression should occur.

3.   Weighted-averaging Model

As might be expected from Asch's findings
regarding the effects of central and
peripheral traits, not all elements of information can be treated as if they have the
same weight. In the course of comparing
summation and averaging models, Anderson (1965) found it necessary to modify his
assumptions and to develop a weighted-
averaging model. He presented subjects
with two or four traits to describe a stimulus
person, each of which represented a particular evaluative rating as scaled by subjects prior to the descriptions. The values of
the traits were low (L), moderately negative
(M−), moderately positive (M+), or high
(H). The summation model predicts that
adding M+ to an H will increase the posi-
tiveness of the rating of the stimulus person, but the averaging model predicts that
the same addition of elements will result in
a decrease in overall evaluation. In support
of the averaging model, Anderson found
that a stimulus person who was described
by two highly positive traits (HH) was

rated more favorably than one described by two highly positive and two moderately positive traits (HHM+M+).

The various other combinations examined by Anderson revealed inadequacies of prediction by the averaging model. For example, an HHHH stimulus person was rated more favorably than an HH person. Since the added elements for the stimulus person described by four traits did not change the average obtained from the two traits, there should have been no difference in subjects' ratings. To account for these unexpected differences, Anderson generated a weighted-averaging model. Although the mathematics of this model are too complicated for us to pursue here, a verbal description can be given. Two major modifications distinguish the weighted-averaging from the averaging model: (1) each trait may be given a different weight, aside from its scale value; and (2) the addition of congruent bits of information affects the average. Each additional consistent adjective adds less than the preceeding one; thus, HHHH yields a higher average than HH, but the tenth H added to the list might add little or nothing to an overall impression.

4. Conclusion

Information processing models have been constructed to represent the way observers combine bits of information about stimulus persons in forming overall evaluative impressions. The summation, averaging, and weighted-averaging models have all been somewhat successful in predicting the evaluative responses of subjects to hypothetical persons described by a list of adjectives. The weighted-averaging model does remarkably well in predicting the overall impressions formed by observers under these restricted conditions. Critics (e.g., Cook, 1971) have argued that observers seldom obtain information about other persons in the form of trait descriptions and that the artificial laboratory conditions

used to study impression formation are so unlike everyday circumstances as to yield little knowledge of value.

Whatever the merits of this criticism (see the discussion of experimental realism in Chapter 2), the various kinds of information obtained by an observer about other people have to be processed in some way. There is little doubt that observers do form organized and stable perceptions of other people, particularly in terms of evaluative impressions. It would be a curious phenomenon indeed if the subjects processed information in one way in the laboratory and in another in the nonlaboratory world. On the other hand, the focus on easily measured adjective descriptions of fictitious persons by proponents of mathematical models of information processing may omit significant factors involved in person perception. For example if denotative as well as connotative information is used in forming stable overall impressions, models developed to understand only how connotative information is processed will necessarily be inadequate in describing information processing more generally. Furthermore, information is acquired at different points in time, and modification of the models is necessary to account for temporal order effects.

C. Order Effects in Person Perception

Two major kinds of order effects have been found when an observer is provided with information about a stimulus person sequentially over time. *Primacy effect* refers to the situation when the observer gives more weight to initial than to later information in forming overall evaluative impressions, and *recency effect* refers to the situation in which later bits of information are given more weight. Research has established that the primacy effect occurs frequently when observers are given a series of descriptive adjectives.

Asch (1946) exposed one group of subjects to a list of traits, such as intelligent, industrious, impulsive, critical, stubborn, and envious, and presented these adjectives in exactly the reverse order to a second group of subjects. A more positive impression of the stimulus person was created when "intelligent" and "industrious" came first in the order than when they came last. Asch attributed this primacy effect to a change in meaning of the later traits as a result of the context provided by the earlier traits . According to this *trait-context interaction theory*, the connotative meanings of adjectives or trait descriptions do not have fixed scale values, but vary according to the context within which they appear.

The first impression of a person may have a disproportionate impact on the observer's persisting evaluation of him. Context is also provided by the relationship of the judged person to other persons in the environment. Bieri, Orcutt, and Leaman (1963) presented written sequences of fictitious cases of patients in psychotherapy in such a way that a case of moderate pathology was preceeded by two cases of either low or high pathology. The degree of pathology of the first two patients affected the observer's judgment of the third. Subjects judged the moderate case to be less pathological when presented in the context of two patients with extreme pathology than in the context of patients with slight pathology.

Asch's trait-context interaction theory has been challenged by Anderson (1965), who argues that the primacy effect is explained by the weighted-averaging model of information processing. Observers give less weight to later than to earlier information in forming overall impressions because they tend to "tune out" or discount information contradicting the impressions they already have. Anderson and Barrios (1961) found that the influence of a particular adjective decreases systematically with its position in the order of the set provided the observer. Subjects were presented with sets of six adjectives scaled for their evaluative ratings (e.g., HHHLLL or LLLHHH); over

sixty combinations were used in describing hypothetical persons. Whether the changes in value within sets were gradual or abrupt, and no matter how much practice the subjects had in making judgments, strong primacy effects were found.

Anderson and Jacobson (1965) found evidence of discounting when subjects were presented with contradictory information over time, which produced a primacy effect. Subjects were presented with adjective lists that contained both connotative and denotative inconsistencies. For example, honest-deceitful-gloomy consists of one positive (honest) and two negative (deceitful-gloomy) connotative adjectives, and honest-deceitful form a contradictory denotative pair. A set of adjectives such as honest-considerate-gloomy contains a connotative inconsistency since the first two are evaluatively positive and the last is negative, but there is no denotative contradiction.

The subjects were asked to judge 36 sets of three traits, which contained denotative and connotative inconsistencies. Before making an overall evaluative rating of the stimulus person, they were given one of three types of instructions: (1) imagine that each word in the set was contributed by a separate person, that all three informants know the stimulus person equally well, and that each word is equally valid; (2) imagine that three people have provided one word each in the description, but they are not equally good judges of the stimulus person; or (3) imagine that each word in the description was given by a different informant, but one of the words does not actually describe the stimulus person. The first instruction was intended to produce information processing that would use all the words equally, hence facilitating an averaging effect. The second and third instructions were intended to produce a discounting effect because the subjects were given a reason to ignore the contradictory information.

Although no primacy effect was expected in the instructional conditions where all elements were to be equally weighted by the subjects, one was found, and evidence for discounting was found in the other two instructional conditions as well. The subjects tended to accept the first trait description and ignore the antonym in forming an overall impression of the stimulus person. According to Asch's trait-context interaction theory, the meanings of the later adjectives were changed by the context provided by the earlier ones, but Anderson and Jacobson argue for the weighted-averaging model. Both theories can account for the data, and it is possible that both are correct. Evidence presented earlier has shown how perceptual set or category accessibility, leveling, sharpening, and assimilation bias information processing, so that the cognitive structure of the perceiver acts as a context within which his perceptions are given meaning. On the other hand, the effects of discounting have also been widely acknowledged as important in the attribution processes.

Once an observer forms an impression of a person he may become less attentive to additional information about that person. Primacy effects have been erased when subjects were instructed to pay equal attention to each item in a list of adjectives or when equal attention was assured by having the subjects read each word out loud (Anderson & Hubert, 1963; Hendrick & Constantini, 1970). Further evidence for an *attention decrement* hypothesis was found by Stewart (1965). He asked subjects to give their impressions of a stimulus person after receiving each adjective rather than after receiving all the information. They were thus forced to pay equal attention to all the elements of the description, and no primacy effect was found.

When the conditions that favor attention decrement or discounting are eliminated from experimental procedures, and subjects are made dependent on all the information as the result of one or another instructional set, primacy effects tend to disappear. In fact, a number of factors have been identified that increase subjects' dependence on later information, producing a recency effect.

Luchins (1958) discovered that when an observer is given information about a hypothetical person, is required to put his impressions in writing, is then provided with inconsistent information, and is asked once again to give his impression, a recency effect is obtained. Subjects who did not write their impressions between the two blocks of information did not display a recency effect. The first impression may, therefore, create an expectancy in terms of which later information is processed. When the expectancy is violated by contrary information, the observer gives greater weight to the most recently acquired information.

Another interpretation is that the recency effect found by Luchins was an artifact of his experimental procedures. The subjects were asked to give their impressions of the same hypothetical person twice within a rather short interval of time. Interpolated between the two impressions they received new information from the experimenter. Lana (1969) has reported evidence that this kind of procedure leads subjects to believe they should modify their opinions or attitudes. Why else would the experimenter be giving them new information? The fact that the second impressions provided by the subjects were more responsive to the latest information they had received therefore would not be surprising. Whether recency effects occur in impression formation has yet to be unequivocally established.

D. Connotative Impressions and Interpersonal Interactions

Osgood et al. (1957) have found that persons tend to apply evaluative and potency dimensions (as measured by the Semantic Differential; see Chapter 3) in their connotative ratings of other people. The favorability ratings in most person impression studies probably correlate highly with the evaluative dimension of the Semantic Differential. A series of studies have shown that a person who is consistently rewarding is perceived as good and impotent and a person who is consistently punishing is perceived as bad and potent. Komorita and Brenner (1968) found that a bargainer who yields the most is viewed by his opponent as good but weak, while a bargainer who yields the least is perceived as bad but strong. As we shall see in Chapter 9, bargainers often try to convey an image of firmness or strength as a strategy to enhance their effectiveness.

Tedeschi and his associates (Faley & Tedeschi, 1971; Helm, Bonoma, & Tedeschi, 1972; Lindskold & Tedeschi, 1971a; Schlenker, Brown, & Tedeschi, 1975) have found similar reactions to persons who use threats and promises. A threatener is perceived as bad and potent if he consistently punishes defiance by the target, but he is viewed as good and impotent if he seldom punishes defiance. On the other hand, a promiser is perceived as good and impotent if he consistently rewards compliance, but he is viewed as bad and potent if he seldom rewards compliance. In these studies of social influence, subjects seldom developed images of others as bad-impotent or good-potent.

There is little intuitive difficulty in understanding why punishments are associated with badness and rewards with goodness, and it makes sense that a harm-doer is perceived as potent if he is willing and able to administer punishment for defiance. The perception as impotent of a promiser who consistently does as he will, however, is not quite so expected. Schopler and Layton (1974) suggest an explanation: "If A is using rewards to obtain conformity, he must make another response when B conforms, that is, A must reward B. It may be that from B's point of view conformity exerts some control over A and lessens A's attributed power. In the extreme case in which conformity is always

followed by a reward, B can easily invert the power relationship. It is like the situation depicted in a well-known cartoon a number of years ago. A rat in his home cage is saying to his cagemate, 'I've really got this psychologist conditioned; every time I press the bar, he gives me a pellet of food.' The use of punishment, in contrast, requires A to do nothing if B complied. In this sense, B can exert some control if he does not conform and thus requires A to make a response. B can only increase his sense of control, and lower A's attributed power, by conforming to rewards and not conforming to punishment" (p. 52).

If harm-doing causes an observer to view the actor as bad and potent, does the reverse also occur? That is, would a bad and potent person be expected to do harm? And if rewarding behavior creates a good and impotent image, would such an impression lead the observer to expect rewarding behavior? These questions suggest that the formation of impressions along the two connotative dimensions of evaluation and potency may be sufficient to allow observers to predict the future behavior of the referent person.

In two separate studies Brown, Smith, and Tedeschi (1974) manipulated subjects' impressions of a confederate and then had them predict whether he would punish or reward them. The subjects were asked to rate themselves on a set of polar adjectives on a Semantic Differential. Under the guise of studying impression formation, the experimenter had the subject and a confederate exchange their self-ratings. The confederate's self-ratings were manipulated to be either good and impotent or bad and potent, as shown in Figure 4.5. As a manipulation check the subjects were then asked to rate the confederate on a set of different polar adjectives.

The subjects were then paired with the confederate. Through a sham drawing the confederate was given the role of Operator and the subject was assigned the role of Estimator. In the first experiment, the con-

Self Impression Scale

NAME _____ John Smith _____ SEX __ M ____

Give your frank overall impression concerning yourself on the scales below by placing a check in one of the spaces between each pair of adjectives. Place the check on a space between the adjectives where you feel it most accurately describes you. Please do not be careless; your true impressions are most important to this study.

Hard	____ : O : ____ : ____ : X : ____ : ____	Soft
Cautious	____ : ____ : ____ : X : ____ : O : ____	Rash
Bad	____ : O : ____ : ____ : ____ : ____ : X	Good
Dishonest	____ : ____ : ____ : XO : ____ : ____	Honest
Weak	____ : ____ : X : ____ : ____ : ____ : O	Strong
Harmful	____ : ____ : O : ____ : ____ : X : ____	Beneficial
Kind	X : ____ : ____ : ____ : O : ____ : ____	Cruel
Severe	____ : O : ____ : ____ : X : ____ : ____	Lenient

Figure 4.5. Self-rating scale of the "other person" given to subjects in the Brown, Smith, and Tedeschi (1974) study. Subjects who received a scale filled in as indicated by the X's perceived the confederate as good and impotent, while subjects who received a scale filled out as indicated by the O's perceived him as bad and potent.

federate could give a point to the subject each time a light came on to signal such an option. Between trials the subjects were asked to estimate the likelihood (from 0 to 100 percent) that the confederate would give them a point the next time the light came on. The points were given value by making them exchangeable for extra experimental time to fulfill a course requirement for participation in psychological research. The confederate actually gave the point to the subjects either 2 or 18 times out of 20 opportunities. In the second experiment, the confederate was provided with ten opportunities to deliver an electric shock to the subjects' fingers, and the subjects were asked to estimate the probability that they would be shocked before each trial. No shocks were actually administered.

The initial impression of the confederate affected the subjects' estimates of the probability of receiving benefits or harm. Subjects who perceived the stranger as good and impotent had a stronger initial expectancy of receiving a benefit, while subjects who perceived the stranger as bad and potent estimated their chances of receiving a benefit at about 50-50. Also, the bad-potent impression of the confederate led subjects to make a higher initial estimation of receiving a shock than did a good-impotent impression. In each study, after some interaction experience was gained by the subjects, their estimates of whether they would receive benefits or harm conformed to the actual behavior of the confederate and first impressions no longer affected their predictions.

Smith, Brown, and Tedeschi (1974) have found that good-impotent and bad-potent impressions allow the perceiver to make predictions about a wide range of behavior. Students were presented with Semantic Differential scales and were told the protocols represented the self-ratings of subjects in an experiment undertaken in the prior semester. Each protocol had masking tape over the name, allegedly to protect the anonymity of the person who had filled it out. Students received a Semantic Differential which was faked to convey either a bad-potent or good-impotent image, exactly as shown in Figure 4.5. A questionnaire was then passed out to all the students which asked them to indicate along a six-point scale from "always" to "never" whether this person would fulfill his threats, keep his promises, lie to protect a friend, help a stranger in trouble, and so on; they were to answer the questionnaire as they believed the person who originally filled out the Semantic Differential would have done.

An impression of a good-impotent person led the subjects to predict lack of resolve in backing up threats, consistent fulfillment of promises, unwillingness to lie for a friend, and readiness to help strangers; a bad-potent image led to just the opposite predictions. Apparently, when persons have little denotative information to use, they form impressions along the connotative dimensions of evaluation and potency, from which benevolent or malevolent intentions can be inferred. Subsequent predictions about the probable behavior of the stimulus person can then be made.

IV. OBSERVER CHARACTERISTICS AND PERSON PERCEPTION

In Chapter 3 we discussed individual differences in needs for information and in the way information is processed. The related personality factors referred to as authoritarianism, dogmatism, and cognitive complexity might also be expected to affect person perception. The authoritarian individual generally is intolerant of ambiguity, is highly motivated to attain cognitive clarity, and is very attentive to status relationships; authoritarians may therefore be prone to see others in terms of absolutes (good or bad, kind or cruel) and be resistant to change. The dogmatic individual is generally resistant to inconsistencies in information and may display a strong primacy effect. The cognitively complex individual is apt to have a greater number of cognitive categories and schemata to apply in his perceptions of persons and, as a consequence,

should be better able to process contradictory bits of information than a cognitively simple person. The implications of these individual differences in processing information have received experimental attention.

A. Authoritarianism and Dogmatism: Cooperators and Competitors

Authoritarians are less well informed, more certain of their information, and less able to differentiate on perceptual and sensory tasks than are egalitarians (Bookbinder, 1963; Kaplan & Singer, 1963; Powell, 1962). Because authoritarians apparently have a strong need to minimize anxiety in social interaction, they tend to assume similarity in others; egalitarians tend to perceive more differences (Crockett & Meidinger, 1956). If persons are all about the same and their actions are predictable and unsurprising, then an observer need be less anxious about what they will do. When the observer has more tolerance of ambiguity and a low need for cognitive clarity, he is not likely to be fearful of people who are different from him.

A series of studies (Crockett & Meidinger, 1956; Scodel & Freedman, 1956; Scodel & Mussen, 1953) has shown a tendency by authoritarians to assume that others are also highly authoritarian, while egalitarians tend to view others as moderately authoritarian. In several of these studies (Jones, 1954; Kates, 1959; Lipetz, 1960), the subjects listened to recordings of interviews involving either a high- or low-authoritarian person. The subjects were then asked to complete a questionnaire, which included items from a measure of authoritarianism, as they thought the interviewee would have done. Regardless of the type of interviewee observed, high authoritarian subjects assumed a high degree of similarity between themselves and the stimulus person. Egalitarians viewed the stimulus person as somewhat different from themselves and as moderately authoritarian.

Authoritarians also demonstrate an intolerance of trait inconsistencies in impression formation. Warr and Sims (1965) found a tendency for authoritarians to form strongly positive or strongly negative impressions of persons from a set of inconsistent trait descriptions, while egalitarians form more complex images that contain both positive and negative connotations. Steiner and Johnson (1963) found a similar intolerance of trait inconsistencies by authoritarians.

Dogmatism, which is of course correlated with authoritarianism, has similar effects on impression formation. Compared to high dogmatic subjects, open-minded subjects are more responsive to detail and form more complex impressions of persons (Foulkes & Foulkes, 1965; White, Alter, & Rardin, 1965), engage in more information search and more often utilize additional information (Long & Ziller, 1965), and use less stereotyped and conventional schemata in their thinking (Plant, Telford, & Thomas, 1965). Although Jacoby (1971) did not find a difference between high and low dogmatists in the amount of similarity to themselves that they attributed to a stimulus person, low dogmatic subjects were more accurate in attributing dogmatism to others.

Kelley and Stahelski (1970a, b, c) note the similarity between persons who fall along the authoritarian-egalitarian dimension and persons they identify along a competitor-cooperator continuum. Competitors expect others to be predominantly competitive in interaction and view their own competitive behavior as a necessary defensive strategy. Cooperators, on the other hand, view the world as more complex and as containing both cooperators and competitors. A cooperator is apt to accurately perceive the cooperative or competitive behavioral orientations of other people, and although he would prefer to cooperate with them, he may defensively compete with a competitor. The competitor's expectations lead him to take self-fulfilling actions. He perceives others as competitive; consequently, he behaves competitively himself, and his competitive behavior forces even a cooperative opponent to assume a competitive stance. The competitor is therefore always right; everyone with whom he interacts does act competitively. J. William Fulbright (1966) has noted many examples of the competitor's way of perceiving and reacting in international relations.

Kelley and Stahelski examined their hypotheses by identifying subjects as cooperators or competitors. This was done by asking them how a partner would probably respond in a game which could be played either cooperatively or competitively (see a fuller description of the Prisoner's Dilemma game in Chapter 7). The subjects were also asked how they would play the game themselves. Those who expected their partner to compete and intended also to compete were identified as competitors; those who both expected their partners to be cooperative and intended to cooperate themselves were identified as cooperators. Then pairs of subjects actually played the game. Three combinations of pairs were formed: cooperator-cooperator, competitor-competitor, and cooperator-competitor. The results confirmed the hypotheses: cooperators often cooperated with each other; cooperators competed against competitors; and competitors were competitive with one another and with cooperators.

Differences observed in the behavior of authoritarians and egalitarians parallel those of competitors and cooperators. Intolerance of ambiguity, a characteristic of authoritarians, has been related to protracted conflict and refusal to accept compromises (Druckman, 1967; Pilisuk, Potter, Rapoport, & Winter, 1965; Teger, 1970). Authoritarians are less trusting, less trustworthy, and more competitive than egalitarians in games where two people can choose to cooperate or compete with one another (Bixenstine & O'Reilly, 1966;

Deutsch, 1960b; Wrightsman, 1966). A person's nationalistic perspectives as measured along an Isolationism-Internationalism Scale is considered similar to and is highly correlated with the authoritarianism scale. Isolationists are characterized by distrust of other countries, an inability to see the point of view adopted by other nations, and strong ethnocentrism; internationalists are characterized by the opposite tendencies. Furthermore, internationalists cooperate more than isolationists in cooperative-competitive games (Lutzker, 1960; McClintock, Gallo, & Harrison, 1965; McClintock, Harrison, Strand, & Gallo, 1963).

These similarities suggest the equivalence of viewpoints and behavior tendencies of authoritarians, isolationists, and competitors, who expect others to be hostile and competitive and act in a defensively competitive fashion themselves. Egalitarians, internationalists, and cooperators apparently view the social world in a more complex way. Perceiving that others may be cooperative or competitive, they prefer to be cooperative themselves but are prepared to compete with those who are contentious.

B. Cognitive Complexity and Person Perception

A cognitively complex person is one who has acquired a relatively large number of conceptual categories and schemata to represent his world. Bieri (1955) demonstrated this judgmental difference between cognitively complex and simple subjects. The subjects were asked to compare three stimulus persons and to indicate the number of ways in which two of them resembled each other and to enumerate the ways in which both differed from the third person. Each subject made a series of such judgments. Cognitively complex subjects used more categories in describing similarities and differences among the three stimulus persons than did cognitively simple subjects.

Cognitively simple people do not have sufficiently complex integrating schemata to process inconsistent information and hence are more likely to apply discounting to arrive at a consistent overall impression of persons. Discounting is displayed by persons who show either a primacy or a recency effect; in either case, they are ignoring part of the information provided to them. It can be predicted, therefore, that cognitively simple people will be more likely than complex people to display these effects. Some support for this hypothesis has been found by Crockett and his associates (Crockett, 1965; Mayo & Crockett, 1964; Rosenkrantz & Crockett, 1965). Subjects identified as simple or complex by paper-and-pencil tests were presented with two contradictory blocks of information about a stimulus person. The procedure followed was modeled after the one developed by Luchins (1958), which reliably produces a recency effect. The subjects were asked to commit themselves to an impression of the stimulus person after receiving the first block of information; they next received the second block of information; and then were asked once again to give their impressions.

Cognitively simple subjects displayed a strong recency effect, forming their final impressions from the second block of information and discounting the first. The impressions of cognitively complex subjects contained a balance from both blocks of information, discounting neither. Leventhal and Singer (1964) also have found that cognitively simple observers change their initial impressions more with disconfirming evidence.

V. CHAPTER SUMMARY

Observers attribute the causes of an actor's behavior either to environmental forces (i.e., the situation or other persons) or to personal factors (i.e., intentions, motives, attitudes, or personality traits). When attributions are made on the basis of multiple observations, distinctiveness, consistency, and consensus allow the assignment of cause to external factors, while lack of distinctiveness, inconsistency, and social disagreement imply a personal locus of causation.

An observer may invoke an available schema in order to "understand" the responses of an actor. Clues gleaned from a single observation may also allow the observer to undertake a causal analysis of the actor's behavior. According to the augmentation principle, the greater the discomfort, risks, punishments, or costs associated with the performance of a particular behavior, the more likely the observer is to attribute cause to the actor rather than to the environment. According to the discounting principle, the role of any particular cause is considered less important whenever other plausible reasons for the actor's behavior are present in the situation. The observer may attempt to reconstruct the actor's decision alternatives and attribute the choice made to noncommon effects associated with the chosen alternative; effects that are common to all the alternatives are discounted by the observer. The greater the hedonic relevance and personalism of the actor's behavior, the more likely it is that the observer will make attributions to some personal aspect of the actor.

The attribution process is based on a reconstruction of events. The observer first notices the effects and then looks at the responses that produced them. An inference cannot be made that an actor intended or planned the effects caused by his behavior unless the observer believes he had prior knowledge of the probable consequences of his action and the ability to produce its effects. If no environmental reason can be found for the actor's behavior, and he is believed to have both knowledge and ability, a causal attribution will be made to personal factors.

In making attributions regarding the causes of their own behavior, current theories suggest that actors employ the same general rules used in making attributions about other people. However, the results of research on self-attributions are just as plausibly explained by impression management theory. There appear to be clear divergences between perceptions of self and attributions made by other people. Observers focus on the actor's behavior and tend to make personal attributions regarding him, while the actor tends to focus on the environmental restraints that limit his behavior. Although there are a number of plausible reasons for such divergent perceptions, the difference in information attended to by actor and observer appears to be the major reason.

Attributions regarding interpersonal power represent a special case of assigning cause to the environment. Actor A's behavior may be attributed to the external influence of actor B when the behavior in question would be considered improbable in the absence of actor B. When the observer is one of the two interacting parties, his self-attributions of power appear to be biased by the outcomes associated with the other person's behavior. He is likely to take credit for influencing the other person's behavior when the outcomes associated with it are desirable and likely to deny having influence and to place blame on personal characteristics of the other party when undesirable outcomes occur.

Once a causal attribution is made to personal factors, a specific internal state must be inferred as responsible for the actor's behavior. Accuracy in perceiving the inner states of others has been thought to be important because inaccuracies are believed to lead to misunderstandings, conflicts, and miscalculations. However, no adequate criteria have been developed for measuring accuracy of attributions. Interpersonal agreement between the perceiver and the stimulus person is the best standard of accuracy available. Characteristic gestures and expressions along with knowledge of the social context within which they occur provide the best information about the internal states of others. However, the concern people display for managing impressions of themselves often makes outward appearances quite deceiving about inner realities.

Perceivers attempt to develop organized and stable impressions of other people and therefore look for underlying constancies to explain the variety of observed behavior. Stable perceptions allow the observer to predict the course of behavior likely to be followed by the stimulus person in given situations. Implicit personality theories are developed by observers; when a stimulus person is observed to possess a particular trait, he is assumed to possess the entire cluster of traits which the perceiver associates with the observed trait. Persons differ in their implicit personality theories; as a consequence, they may experience difficulty in communicating to each other.

The constancies associated with a person may be the result of a number of factors, which may not reflect the actual inconsistency in his behavior over situations and time. The perceiver may observe the actor in only a few situations, in which behavioral consistency is a reflection of role demands or situational constraints rather than personality traits. Constancy in physical appearance, mannerisms, speech, and name may create the illusion of behavioral consistency.

The judgments made of strangers may be governed by stereotypes and the assumption of similarity. Social stereotypes provide a cultural template which includes cognitive categories and schemata that can be readily applied to members of human groups. A stereotype gives the individual some basis for predicting the behavior of total strangers. When making attributions about the internal states of others, the perceiver's best source of information is his own reactions to the situation. Unless he views himself or the stimulus person as atypical, an assumption of similarity will be made in attributing to the stimulus person internal reactions similar to his own.

Observers process the various bits of information they obtain about stimulus persons and combine them into organized impressions. Some of the traits of a person are central in organizing an overall impression and others are peripheral. The traits that are given the most weight appear to be related to the connotative dimensions of evaluation and potency, and are important in their implications for interpersonal behavior. The polar dimensions of warm-cold and humane-ruthless, for example, can be converted into connotative meaning dimensions and can be used to predict the future behavior of the stimulus person.

Several theories have been devised to explain or predict the overall evaluative impressions formed by subjects from the processing of multiple bits of information about a stimulus person. The trait-context interaction theory suggests that the meaning of subsequent information is modified by the context provided by earlier information. Summation, averaging, and weighted averaging models suggest various ways in which observers may process information.

The order in which the observer receives information affects his overall impression of a stimulus person. The first information received is often given more importance, resulting in a primacy effect. The trait-context interaction theory and the weighted-averaging model predict primacy effects. The latter theory assumes attention decrement and discounting to be the processes responsible for producing the primacy effect. Special instructions or procedures, which require the observer to pay equal attention to all the information given him and give him little reason to discount information, eliminate the primacy effect. When particular attention is directed to later information or when observers are made dependent upon it, a recency effect can occur.

An observer can make predictions about the future behavior of an actor on the basis of impressions formed along the connotative dimensions of evaluation and potency. A good-impotent person is expected to be rewarding, honest and kind, while a bad-potent person is expected to be punishing, deceitful, and cruel. Apparently, benevolent intentions are attributed to a good-impotent person and malevolent intentions are attributed to a bad-potent person.

Authoritarian personalities tend to form simple positive or negative impressions of other persons, while egalitarians tend to form more complex impressions. Authoritarians, isolationists, and competitors view others as hostile and competitive and tend to anticipate this behavior by acting in a competitive manner themselves. Egalitarians, internationalists, and cooperators tend to view the world as made up of friendly and cooperative as well as hostile and competitive people, and prefer to be cooperative themselves, though they will compete if provoked by the actions of others. Both authoritarians and dogmatists assume others to be like themselves, while egalitarians and open-minded individuals tend to view others as moderately authoritarian or dogmatic. Cognitively simple people engage in less information search, do more discounting of information, and use fewer cognitive categories to describe other people; cogni-tively complex people can form impressions composed of inconsistent bits of information because they have more complex schemata with which to integrate the information. As a consequence of these individual differences, cognitively simple people show a stronger recency effect than do cognitively simple people.

SUGGESTED READINGS

Heider, F. *The psychology of interpersonal relations.* New York: Wiley, 1958. A classic work in social psychology, rich in insights. The basis of most of the contemporary work in attribution theory.

Hastorf, A. H., Schneider, D. J., and Polefka, J. *Person perception.* Reading, Mass.: Addison-Wesley, 1970. An overview of the three aspects of study in the area of person perception—causal attributions, attributions of internal states, and overall impression formation. Often used as a supplementary text in social psychology courses.

Jones, E. E., Kanouse, D. E., Kelley, H. H., Nisbett, R. E., Valins, S., and Weiner, B. *Attribution: perceiving the causes of behavior.* Morristown, N.J.: General Learning Press, 1972. An important collection of theoretical papers on the lively new topic of attribution theory.

Weiner, B. *Achievement motivation and attribution theory.* Morristown, N.J.: General Learning Press, 1974. A collection of readings on this new orientation to the study of achievement motivation.

CHAPTER 5

Beliefs, Attitudes, and Behavior

CHAPTER PREVIEW

As we have seen in the last two chapters, persons are information-processing organisms who actively seek to construct a comprehensible view of a predictable world. Cognitive categories, causal schemata, linguistic labels, implicit personality theories, and other selective, sorting, and combinatorial mechanisms are used in organizing information. It is reasonable to expect that how the individual views the world will be reflected in the actions he takes. The study of beliefs, values, and attitudes attempts to link the individual's view of the world to the way he behaves.

Consider the difficulties involved in a scientific reconstruction of the individual's cognitive representation of reality. The basic elements of cognition must first be defined, and then the ways in which they interact or combine must be described. This theoretical reconstruction must be done without ever directly observing its elements; beliefs, attitudes, and values can never be seen. Finally, the effects of these unobservable elements must be related to observable behavior.

As you might expect, many different approaches to these difficult problems have been taken. Theories of cognitive structure tend to focus on different aspects of the problems outlined above. A *structural approach* concentrates on the effects that beliefs have on one another. A *means-ends approach* views attitudes in terms of the individual's expectations and values. *Behavioral intentions theory* considers the expec-

tations and values of the individual and his beliefs about the normative requirements of the situation as they affect his verbal commitments regarding future behavior. *Social judgment theory* is basically concerned with the acceptance or rejection of persuasive arguments as a function of how similar or different the arguments are from the individual's original beliefs. Each of these approaches considers the person as a somewhat logical (or rational) information processor.

Several theories have been developed that stress the tendency of people to seek emotional or affective consistency among their attitudes. This kind of emotional psychologic often produces decisions and behavior that are contrary to the rules of philosophical logic. According to these *evaluative consistency theories,* the individual seeks an emotional balance among his attitudes. After explaining these theories and reviewing some of the evidence, we will provide a general critique of current thinking regarding the attitude-behavior relationship.

Finally, we will consider the behavior-attitude relationship and some of the social consequences associated with the verbal expression of one's attitudes. Given certain specified conditions, persons strive to give the appearance of possessing a logically consistent set of attitudes. A *theory of cognitive dissonance* has been advanced, which assumes that people have a need for both logical and emotional consistency in their behavior and attitudes. This theory has provoked much research and many controversies. It has also stimulated the development of a series of alternative theories.

I. ATTITUDES, BEHAVIORAL INTENTIONS, AND SOCIAL JUDGMENTS

An *attitude* may be defined as a belief combined with a relevant value. A *belief* is a complex cognition that relates two or more cognitive categories which do not define each other (Jones & Gerard, 1967). For example, the statement "higher education is too costly" is a belief because neither "higher education" nor "too costly" defines the other. The statement merely relates the two cognitive categories. Many beliefs refer to causal relations between categories, as in "Those who work hard and go to church on Sunday will be rewarded by being sent to Heaven for eternity." A person's confidence in a belief can be expressed by a probability value that indicates its strength. Full certainty is represented by a probability of 1.0 (or 100 percent), uncertainty is about .5 (perhaps so, perhaps not), and complete disbelief is 0.0.

The assignment of a positive or negative connotative meaning to a cognitive category constitutes a *value*. According to Jones and Gerard, "Any singular state or object for which the individual strives, or approaches, extols, embraces, voluntarily consumes, incurs expense to acquire, is a positive value. Anything that the individual avoids, escapes from, deplores, rejects, or attacks is a negative value" (p. 158). If a person declares, "Peace is glorious," he is expressing one of his positive values. Suppose he also states his belief that General X likes war. The value and belief may be related in a form very much like a syllogism:

> General X likes war.
> Peace is good.
> Therefore, General X is bad.

The conclusion of the syllogism is an attitude consisting of a combination of a belief and a value. Attitude theorists refer to the belief as the *cognitive* (or thinking) component of an attitude and the value as its *affective* (or emotional) component.

Beliefs are not maintained entirely separate from each other. The individual tends to organize beliefs into sets of structures, and as a consequence, one belief often affects the strength of others. The precise way in which the individual structures his beliefs and values has been the subject of much research, particularly in trying to predict the behavioral intentions of the actor toward a relevant object or a specific attitude. The beliefs and values of the individual are also important in determining the kinds of social judgments he will make about the opinions of other people. We will examine each of these processes in more detail.

A. Structuring Beliefs

Zero-order beliefs serve as unquestioned assumptions upon which many other beliefs depend (Bem, 1970). For example, an important zero-order belief is that we can rely on our sensory experience to inform us about the nature of reality. Another is that there is order and constancy in our environment. The furniture in a room is assumed to be there even when there is no one to observe it; we expect it to be present in the same state when we return and again perceive it. The shape, size, color, and texture of the furniture is also expected to remain constant. Still another example of a zero-order belief, held particularly by children, is that authorities are infallible. The unquestioned assumption that mother always tells the truth and that the Bible is literally true are zero-order beliefs because the person who holds them does not feel any need to provide proof or engage in further empirical investigation to establish their truth value. Such beliefs are accepted as certainly true (1.0 probability).

A zero-order belief may serve as a basic premise for establishing the truth of derived first-order beliefs. Suppose a person considers whether or not there is life in the hereafter. If he has zero-order faith in the Bible, he may reason in the following syllogistic manner:

Problematic belief: The Bible says there is life in the hereafter.
Zero-order belief: The Bible is true.
First-order belief: Therefore, there is life in the hereafter.

In reading this syllogism, the middle statement is considered the major premise because it contains the zero-order belief—the basis for drawing a conclusion that the first-order belief is true. The "middle term" allows the transfer from the minor to the major premise. In our example, the middle term is "the Bible" since it appears in both the major and minor premises. The "minor term" refers to the phrase that is transferred from the minor premise to the conclusion—"there is life in the hereafter." Syllogistic reasoning suggests that beliefs have a vertical hierarchical structure. We shall see that they also have a horizontal structure.

1.   The Vertical Structure of Beliefs

Beliefs are less certain when they are not founded on unquestioned assumptions of zero-order beliefs. Consider the following example:

The President says we can have peace only if with honor.
The President knows best.
Therefore, we can only have peace if it is with honor.

Unless "the President knows best" reflects the individual's belief in an infallible authority, the major premise depends on other, lower-order beliefs. These may include such beliefs as: any person in the presidency has access to more and better information than anyone else in the society, the President has proven himself in the past

to be an astute decision-maker in matters of foreign policy, one's most reliable friends have vouched for the President's judgment, and so forth. Hence, the conclusion in this syllogism rests on a vertical structure of beliefs that leads to a major premise. Moreover, two persons holding the same higher-order belief may have different underlying vertical structures. One person may believe the President knows best because of his proven successes, while another may hold to the same basic premise because he believes the American electoral system unfailingly chooses the best man for the job. The type of argument that will cause an individual to change his mind about a higher-order belief should depend on its vertical underpinning.

The vertical structure of beliefs may allow the individual to derive 2nd, 3rd, 4th, and still higher-order beliefs from those of lower orders. The resistance of a belief to change depends on the strength of the lower level beliefs that support it. Also, the higher the vertical structure, the more vulnerable a derived belief should be to counter-arguments; that is, the more supporting beliefs there are, the greater the likelihood that one of them will be vulnerable to attack, resulting in a toppling of the entire structure.

2.   The Horizontal Structure of Beliefs

Jones and Gerard (1967) suggest that a horizontal structure may also support or detract from the strength of a particular belief. Consider a patriot's belief that the President knows best, which may be based on a lower-order belief that the American system works well and the best men are always elected to high office. The patriot's faith in the President may be bolstered by the knowledge that radicals, who are derisive about patriotism, severely question the President's judgment on almost every issue. These same "wrong" people may deride the idea of peace with honor. In addition, external "enemies" may also question the wisdom of the President, providing further support for the patriot's belief that the President knows best. The psycho-logic followed by the patriot is that what an enemy says automatically is wrong.

In our example, a belief that the President knows best is supported at the next lower order by three horizontal beliefs: (1) the American system works well; (2) nonpatriots question and deride the President's judgment, and (3) external enemies are critical of the President's decisions. These three beliefs represent premises that lead to the same conclusion. The more horizontal structure there is among lower-order beliefs for a derived higher-order belief, the more certain the individual is likely to be about the higher-order belief.

The strength and resistance to change of a higher-order belief is a function of the number of vertical and horizontal structures supporting it. A belief that has a broad supportive structure is strongly embedded in the individual's belief system and may become the basis for many higher-order beliefs. Bronfenbrenner (1961) has suggested that basic assumptions often underlie beliefs regarding foreign nations. He carried out opinion surveys in both the Soviet Union and the United States during the height of the Cold War. Two basic beliefs were expressed by citizens of both countries: (1) each believed in the fundamental dedication of his own country to peace. The vast majority in each nation were not crusaders for causes and would not risk war in order to impose their ideology on others; (2) Citizens of the United States and the Soviet Union were afraid of each other and each viewed the other as their strongest adversary in international affairs. As is explained in greater detail in Box 5.1, Bronfenbrenner noted that the beliefs of Americans and Russians were mirror-images of each other.

Box 5.1   MIRROR IMAGES IN SOVIET-AMERICAN RELATIONS

On a visit to the Soviet Union in 1960 Urie Bronfenbrenner, a Russian-speaking psychologist from Cornell University, carried out an informal survey of attitudes of Russian citizens toward the United States. He was shocked to find that the most salient attitude was one of fear that the United States would launch a first-strike nuclear attack against the Soviet Union. The Russians viewed Americans as aggressive and reckless in their foreign policy and as ruled by a small elite that monopolized politics, education, the communications media, and economic privilege. Americans were considered aggressive because of the many military bases maintained around the world, their intervention in countries such as Lebanon, Korea, the Congo, Cuba, Nationalist China, and Vietnam, and their alliance with West Germany, all of which were interpreted as attempts by capitalism to maintain or expand sources of raw materials and markets for American business firms. The recklessness of American policy from the Russian view was demonstrated by the U-2 flights which violated the sovereign territory of the Soviet Union for almost five years, an act that in other times would have provoked war.

These policies were presumed to be designed by a small elite which controls both the Democratic and Republican parties and which offers Americans a choice between indistinguishable candidates at election time. This small industrial-military elite, through its control of the educational system and the means of mass communication, has deluded the populace about communism and the Soviet Union, and if the average American knew what really was occurring in the Soviet Union, he would choose a socialist way of life.

Noting that Americans view the Soviet Union as aggressive, reckless, and controlled by a small elite, Bronfenbrenner questioned the images of both peoples: "What frightened me was not so much the facts of Soviet reality as the discrepancy between the real and the perceived. At first, I was troubled only by the strange irrationality of the Soviet view of the world. Slowly and painfully it was forced upon me that the Russian's distorted picture of us was curiously similar to our view of them—a mirror image. But of course our image was real. Or could it be that our views too were distorted and irrational—a mirror image in a twisted glass?" (p. 46).

Angell, Dunham, and Singer (1964) found very similar images in a content analysis of items taken from the mass media in both countries. Each attributed the goal of the other to be aggressive expansion including, if necessary, a first-strike attack on the other. Foreign aid was perceived as a technique of economic penetration when the other provided it, but as altruistic when their own nation offered aid. An interesting departure from these reciprocal mirror images was the finding that although the Soviets believe international policies to be generally predictable, they also believe American foreign policy to be haphazard and unpredictable; on the other hand, Americans generally believe that international relations are unpredictable, but consider Soviet foreign policy to be predicated on masterful long-term views of events. As Frank (1967) concluded, "It is hard to know whether it is more alarming to view each move of an aggressive, powerful, and treacherous enemy as part of a deep-laid plot or as wild and unpredictable behavior" (p. 119).

President John F. Kennedy was sufficiently impressed with the social psychological data with respect to images of the enemy that he made an appeal to the American people to re-examine their attitudes toward the Soviet Union in a speech at American University on 10 June 1963: "It is discouraging to read a recent authoritative Soviet text on military strategy and find, on page after page, wholly baseless and incredible claims-—such as the allegation that 'American imperialist circles are preparing to unleash different types of wars . . . that there is a very real threat of a preventive war being unleashed by American imperialists against the Soviet Union . . . (and that) the political aims of the American imperialists are to enslave economically and politically the European and other capitalist countries . . . (and) to achieve world domination . . . by means of aggressive wars.'

"Truly as it was written long ago, 'The wicked flee when no man pursueth.' Yet it is sad to read these Soviet statements—to realize the extent of the gulf between us. But it is also a warning—a warning to the American people not to fall into the same trap as the Soviets, not to see only a distorted and desperate view of the other side, not to see conflict as inevitable, accommodation as impossible, and communication as nothing more than an exchange of threats . . . Let us not be blind to our differences, but let us also direct attention to our common interests and to the means by which those differences can be resolved."

According to White (1965), the way each national group interprets international affairs depends on the fundamental major premise that its own nation is peace-loving. He asked each American to consider "if he were a Soviet citizen and *if he literally had complete faith in Soviet peacefulness,* how would he be likely to interpret American bases on his borders, its nuclear arms overshadowing his own country's, its U-2 flights over his head, and its alliance with the Germans who had attacked his country in 1939" (p. 245).

Each side can maintain its basic belief in its own peacefulness, despite engaging in the arms race, issuing threats to the other side, and supporting clients in power struggles in various areas of the world, on the ground that such policies are only defensive reactions to the aggressive actions of the enemy. Numerous horizontal beliefs support the major premise for each group, making a belief in the peaceful intentions of one's own nation resistant to change. Thus, many Americans may believe the Vietnam War was unwise, unsuccessful, and costly in numerous ways, but they also believe the action was motivated by defensive and benevolent intentions. Some people consider that thinking otherwise is un-American.

In his novel *1984,* George Orwell introduced the notion of *doublethink* to refer to the ability of a person to interpret identical responses by himself and another person in opposite ways. Oskamp and Hartry (1968) found a double standard in the responses of college freshmen to questionnaire items dealing with belligerent and conciliatory actions that had been taken by both the United States and the Soviet Union. For instance, both countries had increased their military budgets, both had sent artists to perform in the other country, and so on. Nevertheless, the students viewed the American actions more positively than they did identical actions by the Soviet Union.

B. Beliefs and Values

A central proposition of cognitive learning theory is that organisms develop expectations about the future based on the sequence of events they have experienced in the past, and their behavior depends on their expectations and values. Contemporary attitude theories have tended to use cognitive learning theory as a model and have attempted to ascertain how the individual combines his beliefs and values so as to develop behavioral dispositions.

1. Cognitive Learning Theory

Tolman (1932) proposed that learning is the development of expectations regarding the connections that exist between cues, acts, and outcomes. In any given situation a person makes a particular response and receives a reward, a punishment, or nothing. After experiencing such a chain of events, the presentation of the same or a similar cue arouses an expectancy that if he makes the same response as last time, he will receive the same outcome. Of course, the connection between events is only probable. A particular outcome may occur only 40% or 75% of the time following a response to a specific cue. These probabilities represent the strength of the expectancy (or belief). The outcomes associated with an expectancy are more or less valued by the organism. Hence, the basic components of an expectancy are the probability of cue-response-outcome connections and the value of the outcome.

Each organism is considered to be a decision-maker who constructs a *belief-value matrix* representing his alternative courses of action. This matrix consists of a list of means, each of which is associated with an outcome that has a particular value for the individual. An example is shown in Table 5.1. Albert is considering who to ask for a date, the probability that his offer will be accepted, and the value of each possible alternative date. Rosemary represents the most preferred value for Albert, with Sally second, and Patricia the least preferred of the girls considered.

According to Tolman (1955), the decision-maker determines the preferred

Table 5.1   Components of a Belief-Value Matrix. Probability of Achieving the Outcome, the Value of the Outcome, and the Product of Probability Times Value Are Shown

Means to outcome	Evaluation of decision alternatives		
	Probability of success	Value of outcome	Probability X value
Ask Sally after class	.5	50	.5 × 50 = 25
Phone Sally tonight	.2	50	.2 × 50 = 10
Ask Patricia after class	.8	10	.8 × 10 = 8
Ask Rosemary in cafeteria	.1	100	.1 × 100 = 10

means by multiplying the probability of the several means leading to the desired outcome and the value of the outcome. In our example, Albert believes the probability that Rosemary will accept an offer of a date is only .1 (i.e., 10 percent). If we arbitrarily set the value of a date with Rosemary at 100 units, then the product of the probability and value would be 10. Albert believes the probability that Sally will accept a face-to-face offer of a date is greater than the probability she will accept an offer over the telephone. He believes that Mary is most likely to accept his offer, but she is also the least preferred of the alternatives considered. The decision-maker will choose that alternative which maximizes the product of the probability associated with the means and the value of the outcome. In our example, Albert should ask Sally for a date after class; the probability of acceptance is believed to be .5 and the value is 50 units (i.e., .5 x 50 = 25). A reconstruction of an actor's belief-value matrix would be necessary to predict what he will decide to do.

2.   Rosenberg's Means-Ends Theory

Rosenberg (1956) extended Tolman's theory by suggesting that the means used to bring about an outcome may take on the same value as the outcome. If a particular person, policy, or institution is believed to be associated with (or believed to mediate) an outcome the actor considers bad, he will acquire a negative value for the means by which the outcome is mediated. Conversely, positive value is placed on means that lead to desired outcomes. Any particular means may lead to a number of different and contradictory outcomes—at one time a person may mediate rewards, and at another time the same person may mediate punishments. To determine the individual's attitude toward an object, person, or policy requires an analysis of all the probabilities and values of the outcomes associated with it.

In a demonstration of his theory, Rosenberg gave subjects 35 cards, each containing a statement relating to such goals and values as the importance of protecting the market-value of private property, keeping promises, providing equal rights to everyone, and so on. The subjects were asked to sort the cards according to how negatively (down to − 10) or how positively (up to + 10) they rated each statement. They were then asked to estimate the probability that each of two actions would facilitate or hinder the attainment of each of these 35 values. The two actions were: (1) granting free speech to communists, and (2) integrating Blacks into American society. For example, the subjects were asked to estimate the probability that granting free speech to Communists would contribute to equal rights or that integrating Blacks into American society would deleteriously affect the value of private property.

The attitudes of the subjects toward the two proposed actions should be predictable from knowing how these actions would affect their values. The probability estimates made by a subject with regard to whether an action would facilitate or hinder the attainment of each of the 35 values were multiplied by each of the rated values, and these products were summed. For example, if granting free speech to Communists was viewed as having a .5 probability of promoting equal rights, and equal rights was valued at +8, a +4 (.5 × 8 = 4) was added to the total score associated with granting free speech to Communists. The sums obtained were then used to predict the attitudes of the subjects toward free speech for Communists and integration of Blacks, which had been directly measured three to five weeks earlier. There was significant agreement between the predictions and the attitudes of the subjects stated earlier. Thus, attitudes toward means are predictable from the subject's beliefs regarding the probabilities that the means will lead to given ends and the values he places on those ends.

It is implied by Rosenberg's theory that attitude change can be produced by deliberately associating means with ends. If a person has a negative attitude toward integrating Blacks into American society, a more positive attitude might be engendered by showing him that the action will maximize outcomes he values. Carlson (1956) found that the association of means with new ends through persuasive communication could lead to attitude change toward the means. Subjects were first asked a question regarding their attitude toward Blacks moving into all-white neighborhoods. The subjects were then asked to rate the values of 25 statements, such as "being broadminded" and "high international

prestige for America." Four of these statements were used four weeks later as major premises in persuasive communications directed toward the subjects indicating that the values in the statements would be enhanced by integrated housing. Hence, integrated housing was associated with making people more broadminded or as enhancing the international prestige of America. Measurement of the subjects' attitudes was made three weeks after they had been exposed to the persuasive communications. The experimental subjects who had weak initial attitudes toward the issue became more positive in their attitudes toward housing desegregation than did either those with initially strong positive or negative attitudes or control subjects who did not receive the persuasive communications.

3.   Fishbein's Summation of Traits Model

Fishbein (1963) proposed that a person's attitude toward an object is predictable from a knowledge of his beliefs that certain characteristics or traits are possessed by the object and of the values he places on those characteristics. The probability that a particular trait is possessed by the object is multiplied by the value of the trait. A sum of all of the products for all traits associated with the object would be the basis for predicting his attitude toward it.

In a test of this model, Fishbein presented subjects with the attitude object "Negroes." First, the subjects evaluated ten traits such as athletic, dark skin, and lazy, on a Semantic Differential scale. Second, they were asked to estimate the extent to which they believed Negroes possessed each of the ten traits, on scales providing probability values from 1.0 (possess the trait) to 0.0 (do not possess the trait). Finally, the subjects indicated their general attitudes toward Negroes on evaluative semantic differential scales.

A product was obtained for each of the ten traits by multiplying the subject's estimate of the probability that Negroes possessed the trait and the value he assigned to the trait. The ten products were then summed. According to Fishbein's theory, the higher this sum the more positive the subject's attitude toward Negroes should be; and the results supported this prediction. Furthermore, the summation of traits model was a significantly better predictor of attitudes than was a consideration of either values or beliefs alone.

Fishbein's attitude theory is very similar to the summation model that was developed to study overall evaluative impressions of persons (see Chapter 4, III, B, 1). However, it is important to note that the study of attitudes incorporates the probabilities associated with beliefs, while person perception studies tend to focus entirely upon connotative values. Nevertheless, the effects of order of presentation and the differential weightings of traits found in studies of person perception suggest that similar effects can be expected in the study of attitudes. For these reasons a summation model may be inadequate as a predictor of attitudes. In anticipation of these problems, Anderson (1971) has recently applied his averaging and weighted-averaging models to the assessment of attitudes. There is too little research available to evaluate the merit of these new approaches.

C. Beliefs, Values, and Behavior Intentions

Beliefs and attitudes are considered important in understanding social behavior because of their *conative* component, representing an acquired behavioral disposition, "a readiness to respond, ... exerting a directive and/or dynamic influence on behavior" (Allport, 1954, p.63). Advertising and other forms of propaganda are predicated on the assumption that changes in attitudes lead to changes in behavior. This assumption has held sway among social psychologists who maintain an active concern with solving social problems. For example, a social psychologist may believe that discrimination against blacks and racial conflict can be eliminated by changing or ending the prejudicial attitudes of both whites and blacks.

Obviously, a decision to act is qualitatively different from an attitude toward an object. It is one thing to state verbally a positive attitude toward civil rights; it is quite another to commit time, money, and effort to the task of ensuring civil rights for minority groups. A distinction between verbal commitment and actual behavior should also be kept in mind. A person can pledge a sizeable donation to the cancer fund without keeping his commitment. Ajzen and Fishbein (1969) assert that statements of intentions will be highly correlated with actual behavior when the verbal commitment is quite specific rather than general and the lapse of time between the two is very short. A long time interval between a verbal statement of intentions and the occasion when behavior is to occur provides an opportunity for intervening events to change the actor's mind.

Ajzen and Fishbein propose that a verbally expressed intention to act in a particular way is a function of four factors: (1) attitude toward the act, (2) personal normative beliefs regarding whether one should perform the act, (3) perception of the normative expectations of other people, and (4) desire to comply with what others consider to be appropriate conduct. The verbal intention to act may be better predicted from knowledge of all four of these factors than from the individual's attitude toward the object alone. Suppose a restaurant owner has a negative attitude toward the act of serving orientals and also has a personal belief that the races should be kept separate. If he is asked to fill out a questionnaire in the privacy of his office, he may well state his intention not to serve orientals. However, when he is faced with orientals seeking service, other customers witness the act and he must consider their expectations about how he should behave. If he believes his customers would disapprove his refusal to serve the orientals, and he is strongly motivated to conform to the expectations of his customers, he may very well serve his unwelcome guests.

In a classic study, LaPiere (1934) provided some support for this scenario. He traveled widely across the United States in the company of a Chinese couple. They stopped at 66 sleeping places and 184 dining facilities and were refused service only once. In many instances they recorded that service was well above average. At the conclusion of the trip, questionnaires were mailed to each of the proprietors of the establishments that had been visited, asking whether he would serve "members of the Chinese race as guests in [his] establishment." Over 90 percent of the 128 respondents said they would not serve Chinese people. As Dillehay (1973) noted, there is strong doubt that the person who filled out LaPiere's questionnaire was the same person who served the customers. Nevertheless, Kutner, Wilkins, and Yarrow (1952) found supporting evidence in an investigation of the willingness of restaurants to take written or telephone reservations for "colored" guests. They found the same disparity between stated intentions and actual behavior reported by LaPiere.

The four-factor model for predicting intentions was systematically evaluated by Ajzen and Fishbein in a questionnaire study. Three of the four factors (motivation to conform was not measured) were separately assessed for a number of different kinds of behavior, such as going to a party, going to a concert, playing a game of poker, and reading a mystery novel. The subjects were asked to make the following ratings: (1) an evaluative rating of the object of the activity (i.e., concert or party) on a semantic differential scale; (2) an evaluative rating of the act ("going to a concert on Friday night"); (3) the degree to which the person believed he should engage in the activity ("I personally think I should go to a party on a Friday night"), rated on a seven-point scale anchored at the ends with "probably" and "improbably;" (4) the same kind of probability rating for social normative beliefs ("my friends expect me to go to a party on Friday night"); and (5) three measures of behavioral intentions:

On a Friday night I would go to
A party ————— A concert

and

On a Friday night
I would ———————— I would not
Go to a party.

and a ranking was secured of the eight Friday night activities included in the study in terms of the order of the likelihood that the subject would engage in them.

By a formula that resembles a weighted-averaging model, the three factors of attitude toward the act, personal normative beliefs, and the normative expectations of other people were combined and related to the stated intentions of the subjects. The combined weighting of all three factors predicted intentions better than any single factor. Personal normative beliefs provided the strongest single association.

Schwartz and Tessler (1972) have offered three criticisms of the Ajzen-Fishbein study. First, they suggest that Friday night activities are a regular experience of the subjects, and their past experience may have been the primary determinant of their reports of attitudes, beliefs, and intentions. As a consequence, stated intentions merely reflect what the subjects have done in the past rather than what they might do in the future. Second, the positive correlations between measures may simply reflect the fact that the kinds of objects chosen for the experiment virtually required certain acts specific to them. Novels are read, movies are viewed, and poker is played. Thus, if one is positive toward the object, presumably one would also be ready to respond positively toward it. Finally, it was suggested that normative beliefs might be better defined in terms of obligation rather than with scales anchored by "probably" and "improbably." The likelihood of an action does not communicate its moral character.

In a study designed to avoid these problems, Schwartz and Tessler investigated attitudes, obligations, and intentions toward being a kidney, heart, or bone marrow donor—actions presumably not part of the past experience of most subjects. Personal normative beliefs were measured by asking subjects whether they would feel a moral obligation to be a transplant donor under various circumstances. For example, they were asked if they would feel obligated to be a donor if a close relative needed a transplant and they were suitable donors. This measure was a 7-point scale identified at the end points by "obligation not to donate" and "strong obligation to donate." Attitudes toward the transplant activity were measured on a 5-point scale indicating how rewarding, bad, or pleasant the act was expected to be. Finally, social normative beliefs were measured by asking subjects to estimate whether people whose opinions they valued would think the particular donation was something they ought to do, regardless of their own views. Clearly, each of the measures was obtained in a different way.

All three components of the model studied—attitude toward the act, personal normative belief, and social normative belief—significantly contributed to the subject's statement of intentions. Just as in the Ajzen and Fishbein study, personal normative beliefs (now measured by felt obligation) was the single best predictor Both studies found that the three factors considered could predict with about 50 percent accuracy the tendency for subjects to state the intentions they did. However, other factors were also found to contribute to their statements, including age, occupation, religion, and willingness to accept responsibility for negative personal consequences.

Perhaps the most important finding of the Schwartz and Tessler study was obtained in a follow-up three months later when the subjects were asked if they would actually volunteer to go on file as potential bone marrow donors. Personal normative beliefs alone were just as predictive of actual volunteering as were statements of behavioral intention. People often do not follow through by acting in a manner consistent with their verbal statements of intention. Of course, the time lag could have led to changes in any of the factors of the the model, and the magnitude of the consequences may have lowered the relationship between verbal statements of intention and actual volunteering.

The fourth factor in the Ajzen-Fishbein model, motivation to conform to other people's expectations, has not been evaluated. The evidence gathered to date reveals that predictions of intentions and associated behavior cannot be made accurately with only assessments of beliefs and values. Nevertheless, it does appear that assessments of the beliefs and values associated with an act, personal norms, and social norms provide a much better basis for predicting behavior than does the simple assessment of attitude toward the object.

D. Beliefs, Values, and Social Judgments

When faced with new information relevant to his beliefs and values the individual must decide to accept, reject, or ignore it. In the Carlson study (described on p. 193) subjects who held extreme positive or negative views toward housing integration were unaffected by persuasive communications favoring integration. Those who held extremely positive views did not change because they already had favorable attitudes, and those who held extremely negative views rejected the new information as too inconsistent with their own strongly held beliefs and values. Only those subjects who held moderate views were susceptible to persuasion.

A basic tenet of social judgment theory is

that a person's existing attitudes form anchors for classifying new information. New information that is similar to a person's anchor will be *assimilated* and will be interpreted as being closer to his own view than it really is. New information that is sufficiently dissimilar from the person's own attitude will be *contrasted* and will be classified as more different from his own attitude than it actually is. The range of positions toward a given object or issue that is assimilated forms a *latitude of acceptance,* and the range of positions that is contrasted forms a *latitude of rejection.* There is also a set of positions that constitutes a *latitude of noncommitment* or a neutral zone. Hence, the structure of the individual's attitudes is a determinant of his receptivity to persuasive communications.

In a test of social judgment theory, Hovland, Harvey, and Sherif (1957) selected subjects holding three different views (internal anchors) on the issue of selling alcoholic beverages. The study was carried out in Oklahoma following a referendum which resulted in the approval of prohibition by a small margin. A group of "drys" was selected from the Salvation Army, strict denominational colleges, and the Women's Christian Temperance Union. A group of "extreme wets" was selected from acquaintances of the experimenters. An additional group of unselected subjects was defined as "moderate wets."

In the first experimental session, the subjects were asked to read nine statements and underline the one that came closest to their own attitude. They then indicated which other statements were acceptable to them and also indicated which were unacceptable. In this way, their latitudes of acceptance, rejection, and noncommitment for the nine statements were measured. Extreme subjects, whether dry or wet, had broader latitudes of rejection than acceptance, much as dogmatic personalities do. The rejection category was wider for extreme than for moderate subjects, that is, extreme subjects rejected more statements than did moderate subjects.

At a second session the subjects listened to a 15-minute tape-recorded communication carrying one of three types of messages: pro-wet, pro-dry, or moderately pro-wet. Subjects were asked to rate the theme of the communication, how favorably they viewed it, and their own current attitude toward the prohibition issue. Similar effects were found on all three measures. Subjects with attitudes similar to the communication judged it accurately, were favorable to it, and had no need to change their attitudes. Contrast effects were most marked when subjects rated the moderately pro-wet communication. Those with extreme pro-wet attitudes viewed the moderate communication as supportive of the dry position, while the extreme pro-dry subjects viewed the same communication as strongly pro-wet.

1. Ego-involvement

The more important an issue is to a person—that is, the greater the value he places on it—the more ego-involved he is said to be. According to social judgment theory, the more ego-involved a person is the narrower his latitude of acceptance and the broader his latitude of rejection. Ward (1965) confirmed these hypotheses by studying subjects who held extremely favorable attitudes toward Negroes. Forty of the subjects had spent several months picketing local movie theaters in protest against segregation policies, while other subjects holding similar attitudes had not made an equivalent behavioral commitment to civil rights. Subjects in the "pickets-salient" condition were told they had been contacted because of their membership in the picketing group; and before they filled out a questionnaire, the experimenter led a brief discussion on the importance and value of their activities. In the "pickets-nonsalient" condition, members of the picketing group were brought out of the classroom and told they had been selected on a random basis. In the "nonpickets" condition, subjects with strong pro-Negro attitudes who did not belong to the picketing group were selected.

All the subjects were asked to judge 40 statements about the social position of the Negro, which ranged from asserting that the Negro is held in a position of inferiority in American society to the opposite position that the Negro holds a position of superiority. Other statements regarding militarism and pacifism were rated by all subjects, and each was asked to complete a questionnaire regarding the Cuban revolution. The results revealed that judges with strongly favorable attitudes and strong personal involvement, reflecting their intense value position, viewed the Negro as suffering most from an inferior position in American society. Those in the pickets-salient conditions judged the social position of the Negro as least favorable, the judgments of the pickets-nonsalient group were intermediate, and nonpickets viewed the position of the Negro most favorably. Thus, the more ego-involved the subject the greater his latitude of rejection for opposing opinions. Furthermore, this biasing effect did not occur in judging statements about militarism and pacifism or with regard to questions about the Cuban revolution; only information relevant to the subjects' specific area of ego-involvement was affected.

2. Social Judgment and Attitude Change

The evidence is predominantly favorable to social judgment theory with regard to assimilation and contrast effects in the classification of information. However, the evidence is more equivocal with respect to the implications of these processes for attitude change. We are concerned not only with which statements a person views as similar or different from his own, but how he changes his position when exposed to contrary opinions. On the positive side, Atkins, Deaux and Bieri (1967) and Peterson and Koulack (1969) have provided evidence supporting the prediciton of social judgment theory that statements at the

boundaries of the latitudes of acceptance and rejection produce the most attitude change.

However, a recent study by Eagly and Telaak (1972) suggests that social judgment theory may be an inadequate theory of attitude change. They presented subjects with a series of statements related to birth control and, based on the judgments made, determined the latitudes of acceptance and rejection for each subject. Unbeknown to the subjects, only those favoring birth control were retained for the next phase of the study. These subjects had narrow, medium, or wide latitudes of acceptance for discrepant information. The subjects were then paired, and asked to write a communication expressing their opinions about birth control; they then exchanged their communications. Actually the experimenter intervened in the exchange and substituted a prepared communication for the one the subject wrote. The bogus communication had been pre-scaled by other subjects and was either slightly, moderately, or strongly discrepant from the subject's own, previously assessed position.

As it turned out, the slightly discrepant message was within the latitude of acceptance for all the subjects who received it, and the strongly discrepant message was in the latitude of rejection for all but two of the 37 subjects who received it. Of principal interest was the reaction of the subjects to the moderately discrepant message, which was in the latitude of rejection for all of the narrow latitude of acceptance subjects; it was in the latitude of noncommitment (42 percent) or the latitude of rejection (58 percent) for the medium latitude subjects; and in the latitudes of acceptance (38 percent), noncommitment (38 percent), or rejection (25 percent) for the wide latitude subjects.

It was predicted from social judgment theory that a small amount of attitude change in the direction of the slightly discrepant message would occur; no change would occur to the strongly discrepant message; and varying change, depending upon the latitude of acceptance, would result from the moderately discrepant message. However, the results did not support these predictions. Persons with a wide latitude of acceptance changed their attitudes in response to all three types of messages, and persons with medium or narrow latitudes of acceptance did not change at all. In interpreting these findings, it might be argued that persons with a wide latitude of acceptance are more broad-minded on the issue and hence more acquiescent, or that they are uncertain and ambivalent and consequently more informationally dependent on communications from others than are persons with narrower latitudes of acceptance. Whatever the reason for the differences obtained, they are not consistent with social judgment theory.

Other factors in addition to the denotative consistency of opinions are influential in determining agreement with the communication of another person. Obviously the value importance of the topic is one of these factors as the ego-involvement results have indicated. A great deal of research has been devoted to the question of whether persons act so as to maintain evaluative consistency in the attitudes they express.

II. EVALUATIVE CONSISTENCY AMONG ATITUDES

Most mature persons feel discomfort when they are caught in inconsistency among their clearly stated beliefs. A person would not want to say in the same breath, "A college education is a valuable asset" and "I agree with those who declare college to be worthless." Such contradictory statements would reveal him as illogical. It is of course possible for a person to organize his attitudes so that what appears illogical to others may not seem at all illogical to him. It may not seem inconsistent to believe that "Peace is the most important value for men to achieve" and "We must wage war against our enemies," if the individual views war as necessary to achieve "a generation of peace."

Logical inconsistencies between beliefs involve denotative meanings. Attitudes also contain a value component. There is evidence that people require their attitudes to be consistent in terms of value (the evaluative component of connotative meanings). In fact, the need to maintain consistency of values often seems to be more important to an individual than his concern for denotative consistency. Consider the following example of persistence in maintaining evaluative consistency:

"MR. X. The trouble with Jews is that they only take care of their own group.

MR. Y. But the record of the Community Chest shows that they give more generously than non-Jews.

MR. X. That shows they are always trying to buy favor and intrude in Christian affairs. They think of nothing but money; that is why there are so many Jewish bankers.

MR. Y. But a recent study shows that the percent of Jews in banking is proportionately much smaller than the percent of non-Jews.

MR. X. That's just it, they don't go in for respectable business. They would rather run night clubs" (Allport, 1954, pp.13-14).

This kind of "psycho-logic" (Abelson & Rosenberg, 1958) has been intensively investigated, and several theories of evaluative consistency among attitudes have been developed. We will consider two major consistency theories: balance and congruity theories.

A. Balance Theory

Heider (1958) laid the foundation for balance theory, although there have been a number of refinements and variations of it since his first statement. Balance theory is primarily concerned with the relationships between cognitive elements; that is, it attempts to explain how a single individual may nonlogically organize his cognitions and how the various cognitions affect one another. Two kinds of relationships are assumed to exist between cognitive elements: unit and sentiment relations. A *unit relation* between elements indicates some kind of tie or belongingness between them, such as ownership, kinship relations, ethnic group membership, and so on. A *sentiment relation* indicates an emotional tie between them, as expressed by such verbs as like, dislike, approve, disapprove, adore, condemn, and so on.

Unit and sentiment relations can be either positive or negative in nature. A person can belong to a group or be an outcast and he can like or dislike the group. It will be convenient to use a kind of shorthand notation in referring to the relations between cognitive elements. Let p refer to a person and x refer to an object. p U x expresses a unit relation between p and x, such as that a person owns the object (x belongs to p). Let o refer to another person. p L o is a symbolic way of expressing the sentiment relation that p likes o; and p DL x is translated to mean that the person dislikes a particular object x.

1. Balanced Relations

It seems consistent for something someone owns or has a positive unit relation with to be liked by the person. As we shall see in Chapter 11, there is a great deal of evidence that people do tend to maintain consistency between unit and sentiment relations. However, here we will ignore unit relations and focus on Heider's statement that a person prefers harmonious or balanced sentiment relations among his attitudes. Two relations are balanced if both are positive or if both are negative. If p L o and o L p, the relations are balanced. Similarly, p DL o and o DL p are balanced, but p L o and o DL p are imbalanced. A state of imbalance among cognitive elements is assumed to be discomforting and a person will change one or more of the relations among cognitive elements to maintain or restore balance (consistency). In the case of p L o and o DL p, it is likely that p will learn to dislike o (or o

will learn to like p) and hence bring about a balance in the sentiment relations between them. In each of these examples, it should be clear that the symbols represent the beliefs and attitudes of the individual (p), including his belief about whether o likes or dislikes him. p's beliefs about o's sentiment relations could, of course, be wrong.

Any number of cognitive elements can be related to one another. Consider the triadic relationships shown in Figure 5.1. Solid lines indicate positive sentiment relations between elements, and broken lines indicate negative sentiment relations. The triads shown in Figure 5.1a,b,c and d are balanced, while e, f, g, and h are unbalanced. People generally expect those they like to like what they like (5.1a), and to dislike what they dislike (5.1b). People also expect those they dislike to dislike what they like (5.1c) and to like what they dislike (5.1d). For example, if the United States dislikes the Soviet Union and the Soviet Union likes India, it makes psycho-logical (though not logical) sense for the United States to dislike India. Conversely, as Aronson and Cope (1968) have experimentally demonstrated, a person displays a more favorable attitude toward his enemy's enemy (5.1c) than towards his enemy's friend (5.1d).

2. Attributions About Sentiment Relations

Suppose you are told that Paul and Mary both like George and that Paul and Mary know one another. What sentiment relation would you attribute to Paul and Mary? According to Heider, you would make attributions about sentiment relations so as to maintain a balanced state among the cognitive elements considered. In an early test of balance theory, Jordan (1953) presented subjects with a series of sets of hypothetical statements, such as "I dislike o; I like x; o dislikes x." The subjects were instructed to assume the role of "I" and to rate each set of statements in terms of the degree of pleasantness or unpleasantness associated with

Balanced relations

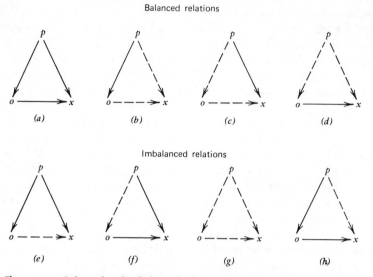

Imbalanced relations

Figure 5.1. Balanced and imbalanced relations. (Note that an even number of negative relations results in balance, and an odd number of negative relations results in imbalance.)

it. A number of unit and sentiment relations were expressed in the 64 sets presented for ratings.

Balanced relations were generally rated as more pleasant than unbalanced relations; and, when the relationship between p and o was positive, imbalance (as represented by either p Lx and o DLx or p DLx and o L x) was rated as unpleasant. However, contrary to balance theory predictions, when the relationship between p and o was negative, both balanced and unbalance states were rated as unpleasant. Price, Harburg, and Newcomb (1966) found essentially the same results when subjects were asked to rate hypothetical situations which included their best friends and people they strongly disliked as o's and p's.

Newcomb (1968) reviewed the available evidence and concluded that only configurations involving positive relations between two persons should be interpreted as balanced or imbalanced. When the relation between two persons is negative, all triadic relations among cognitive elements should be considered *non*balanced. Newcomb also pointed out that if two men loved the same woman (p L x and o Lx), balance theory would predict they would like one

another—an outcome apparently at variance with commonsense observation. However, a consideration of unit relations makes it understandable why p and o would not like one another in Newcomb's example. Love may imply a need for possession or ownership and hence inplies a positive unit relation (p U x and p L x). When another person (o) also claims possession of x (o Ux), negative sentiment relations occur between p and o (p DL o and o DLp). Thus, under certain conditions of contradictory unit relations, p and o can like the same things but dislike each other.

A *positivity bias* has been displayed by subjects when they are asked to infer the relation between two elements. They are more inclined to assume a positive than a negative sentiment relation between two people (Rubin & Zajonc, 1969; Zajonc, 1968a). Possibly this bias is a result of the average person's everyday experience. He likes more people than he dislikes and observes the same tendency in others. The positivity bias could lead to fortuitous confirmations of balance theory. For example, when a subject is presented with the hypothetical set of relations p Lx and o Lx and is asked to infer p's attitude towards o, his positivity bias (p L o) would confirm the balance theory prediction of a preference for balanced over unbalanced states. Also, in the hypothetical situation p DL x and o DL x, a positivity bias would produce apparent balance (p L o). Wyer and Lyon (1970) found that when the positivity bias was prevented from occurring, subjects did not make inferences displaying a preference for balanced over imbalanced states.

A *similarity bias* has also been shown to affect the way subjects make inferences about sentiment relations (Zajonc & Sherman, 1967). Subjects tend to assume that a third relation has the same affective quality as the other relations in a set when all of the sentiment relations are the same. For example, when two known relations are both negative or both positive, the subject infers that the third relation is the same. If given information that p DL x and o DL x, then subjects are apt to infer that p DL o—a relation that creates an imbalanced rather than a balanced state.

The evidence gathered from the attributions made by subjects has not shown that they have a clear preference for balanced states and an aversion to unbalanced states. Apparent support for balance theory sometimes results from the positivity and similarity biases of the subjects. Some cognitive structures are neither balanced nor unbalanced, but instead are considered to be nonbalanced.

3.   The Restoration of Balanced States

According to Heider, whenever a person has a set of cognitive elements that are in an unbalanced state, one or more sentiment relations will change and a balanced state will be brought about. Evaluative consistency is therefore maintained among a person's beliefs and attitudes. Suppose that Bill likes Nixon (p L x), Bill likes Sue (p L o), and Bill believes that Sue dislikes Nixon (o DL x). The inconsistency among sentiment relations creates an imbalance among Bill's cognitions, and to restore balance, he must

change one or more of them. He can change his attitude toward Nixon, or he can change his attitude toward Sue, or he can attempt to persuade Sue to like Nixon. That is, balance can be achieved by making two relations negative or by making all three relations positive. It is generally assumed that whichever sentiment is strongest in an imbalanced state will determine which change will occur to restore balance. If Bill likes Sue more than he likes Nixon, then he will either change his mind about Nixon or else will attempt to persuade Sue to like Nixon, but he will not change his sentiment toward Sue.

When a balanced state can be restored by either changing one sentiment relation or by changing two, Rosenberg, et al. (1960) predicted that people would usually prefer to make the simplest change. To test this hypothesis, they asked subjects to choose among three alternatives, each of which would restore balance to an imbalanced triadic set of cognitive elements. Two of the alternatives required the subjects to change two sentiment relations and the other required a change in only one relation.

Subjects were asked to assume the role of a department-store owner. In a hypothetical situation, they were provided with three bits of information: (1) Fenwick, the manager of the rug department, has increased sales in the past; (2) Fenwick plans to display modern art in the rug department; and (3) modern art displays reduce sales. The subjects were then told to assume certain sentiment relations toward sales, Fenwick, and modern art. For example, one-third of the subjects were informed they should be positive toward both sales and Fenwick, but negative toward modern art. These unit and sentiment relations constitute an imbalanced state. They are depicted in Figure 5.2.

Three different communications were then presented to the subjects, which argued that: (1) Fenwick did not actually plan to put up a display of modern art, (2) Fen-

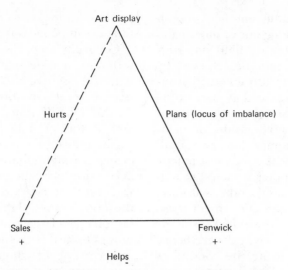

Figure 5.2. Subjects' cognitive structure. Imbalance arises because Fenwick (+) who helps sales (+) is planning a display of modern art (−) which hurts sales. (After Rosenberg, et al., 1960, p. 128.)

wick had not maintained sales in the past, and (3) a display of modern art would increase sales. The subjects were asked which of the three communications they found most acceptable in the context of their role as owner of the store and given the attitudes assigned to them by the experimenter. Acceptance of the first communication would restore balance simply by dissociating the unit relation between modern art and sales. Acceptance of the second communication would not restore balance unless the subjects also changed their sentiment toward Fenwick. It would not be consistent to both like Fenwick and to believe that he had not maintained sales in the past. That is, the second communication provided a basis for balance but only if both a unit and a sentiment relation were changed. Acceptance of the third communication changed the unit relation from "hurts" to "helps" but would not restore balance unless the negative sentiment toward art was also changed. The findings confirmed the hypothesis that subjects would choose the simplest means of restoring balance to the set of cognitions; they

predominantly found the first communication to be most acceptable.

The Rosenberg, et al. study may be criticized on the same grounds as other role-playing experiments. Subjects' predictions regarding a store owner's preference for information (or balancing operations) may be more representative of their stereotypes about store owners than the way owners really think or the way subjects would think in a real life situation. More important, Rosenberg, et al. found that the predictions of balance theory were not always supported. For example, the store owner should have experienced a restoration of cognitive balance following his opportunity to rate the communications. Measurements of the subjects' attitudes toward sales, modern art, and Fenwick revealed no reduction of imbalance following the receipt and rating of the three communications.

4.   Critique of Balance Theory

There are a number of ways by which a person can attain balance among cognitive elements: changing unit, sentiment or both types of relations among one or more pairs of elements. Newcomb (1959) has suggested that balance may be achieved by changing inter-entity attraction, disconnecting unit relations so that an attitude toward an object is perceived as irrelevant to an interpersonal relationship, derogating an object as unimportant or trivial, changing one's attitudes to be consistent or inconsistent with another person's, changing one's perceptions of the other's attitude toward an object, and so on. Any of these adjustments should reduce the tension of imbalance. Unfortunately, balance theory does not always indicate the conditions under which a particular balancing operation will occur.

The evidence for balance theory is at best equivocal. Research has typically not gone beyond asking subjects to make ratings about the pleasantness of various hypothetical situations or asking them to infer a relation from a knowledge of other relations provided by the experimenter. The significance of balanced and unbalanced cognitive states in affecting actual social behavior has not been clearly delineated.

B. Congruity Theory

Osgood and Tannenbaum (1955) have developed a theory of congruity, which combines some of the features of balance theory with aspects of social judgment theory. Congruity theory is concerned mainly with attitude change in situations in which the person receives a communication from an identifiable source. Unlike balance theory which concerns itself with unit and sentiment relations, congruity theory presents a quantitative model that attempts to measure degrees of positive or negative evaluation. It is not only concerned with the sign (positive or negative) of a relation, but with its strength as well. By using evaluative semantic differential ratings made on seven-point scales (+3, +2, +1, 0, −1, −2, −3), as shown in Figure 3.4, the degree of

positivity or negativity of an individual's attitudes can be measured.

Congruity theory is basically concerned with how an individual changes his evaluation of the source and the object of a persuasive communication when there is a measurable difference in attitudes toward both factors prior to the communication. Again, unlike balance theory in which one or more relations may change when imbalance exists, according to congruity theory whenever there is a discrepancy between the attitudes toward the source and the object of a persuasive communication, the attitudes toward both will always change.

According to congruity theory, communications or assertions by the source are either associative or dissociative. When the source indicates a positive attitude toward the object of his communication, the relationship is *associative*. When the source asserts a negative attitude toward the object of his communication, the relationship is *dissociative*. The individual's reaction to a persuasive communication will be determined by his evaluation of the source, his attitude toward the object, and the associative or dissociative relationship of the source to the object of communication.

Suppose a person evaluates a source as strongly positive (+3), the object of communication as mildly positive (+1), and the source-object relationship is associative. The target of the communication will change his evaluations of both the source and the object by reducing the disparity of his evaluations of them. The amount of the changes depend on the intensity of the pre-persuasion evaluations. An extreme attitude should change less than a moderate one because it is more strongly embedded in the person's belief system. In our example the object (+1) is less polarized than the evaluation of the source (+3); hence, the object will gain more in value than the source will lose. The precise formulae devised by Osgood and Tannenbaum for calculating the degree of change to be expected in this case predict that the post persuasion evaluation of the object would be +2½ and the evaluation of the source would be +2½.

The theory makes different predictions for a dissociative assertion by a source. In this case changes are predicted to occur so that the evaluations of the source and the object are equidistant from zero, but on opposite sides of the zero point of the scale. For example, suppose the person has a strong negative attitude toward the source (−3) and a mildly favorable attitude toward the object of the assertion (+1), and the source makes a negative assertion regarding the object. In this case the individual will dislike the source somewhat less after hearing him state an agreeable opinion, and will be even more positive toward an object that even his enemies favor. Again, as in the associative relationship, the more extreme evaluation will change less than the moderate one. According to the precise formulae of the theory, the individual will achieve congruity by making post assertion evaluations of the source and object as −2½ and +2½ respectively.

In a representative study of congruity theory, Tannenbaum and Gengel (1966) first measured subjects' attitudes toward three well-known psychologists and toward teaching machines. The subjects were then presented with statements allegedly made by the psychologists regarding teaching machines, and positive, negative, and neutral assertions were associated with the three sources. Two weeks later the subjects were provided with "a copy of an Associated Press article on a 'comprehensive report on teaching machines from the U.S. Office of Education'" (p.301). This article presented either a favorable or unfavorable view of teaching machines. The subjects' evaluations of the three psychologists and of teaching machines were once again measured.

According to congruity theory, if the individual's attitude toward teaching machines is changed through the acquisition of new information (the newspaper article), a change in evaluation of the psychologists who made assertions about the machines should also occur. If the new information should make the subjects more favorable toward the machines, their evaluation of the psychologist who made a positive assertion about them should be enhanced and their evaluation of the psychologist who made a negative statement should become less positive. Just the opposite predictions are made when the new information causes the subject to have a more negative attitude toward teaching machines. When the psychologist made a neutral statement, intermediate changes in evaluation should occur. The actual results of the experiment tended to confirm these predictions. However, contrary to congruity theory, there were no negative attitude changes toward the psychologists; the relative changes in attitudes toward the psychologists after receiving additional information were due entirely to changes in a positive direction.

Tannenbaum (1967) has reinterpreted a good deal of evidence from various studies of persuasive communications and attitude change and found it to be generally favorable to congruity theory. However, important disconfirmations of the theory have also been found. For example, a persuasive communication affects a person's attitudes toward the subject of the message more than it does his evaluation of the source. And although the theory is often able to predict qualitative changes in evaluation, attempts to predict the precise degrees of attitude change by using mathematical formulae have seldom been successful.

A number of suggestions have been made to improve congruity theory. For example, Rokeach and Rothman (1965) suggest a measure of the importance of an attitude, which may not be reflected in ratings on the semantic differential. Osgood and Tannenbaum (1955) have recognized the need to measure characteristics of communications, which may be more or less complex and contain varying degrees of positive or negative evaluation of various issues or objects. Jones and Gerard (1967) point out that in congruity theory "an attitude is identified only in terms of its evaluative direction and intensity, not in terms of the beliefs that support it. Two persons can have the same negative attitude toward Negroes and yet one may believe them to be passive and weak, whereas the other may see them as strong and powerful" (p.169). Revisions in the theory may take these and other factors into account.

III. EVALUATION OF THE ATTITUDE-BEHAVIOR RELATIONSHIP

The basic reason social psychologists have attempted to reconstruct an individual's definition of a situation from his beliefs and attitudes is their desire to obtain a better understanding of social behavior. Implicit in the study of attitudes is an assumption that there is consistency in a person's behavior in different situations, which is a consequence of his enduring values and beliefs. A contemporary issue in social psychology concerns how much correspondence there actually is between attitudes and action.

Wicker (1969a) reviewed 46 studies in which verbal and overt behavioral responses to attitude objects were measured in separate situations. In most of these experiments, attitudes were found to be unrelated to behavior, and, where there was a relationship, it was typically very weak. According to Wicker, there is "little evidence to support the postulated existence of stable, underlying attitudes within the individual which influence both his verbal expression and his actions" (p.75).

Notwithstanding the lack of encouragement provided by the available evidence, a stubborn intuition derived from everyday observation persists that a person's attitudes do affect his behavior. Attitude theorists are aware that there are many problems associated with measuring attitudes and that many other factors aside from attitudes may govern behavior; but they are convinced that it would be impossible to understand human interactions without some theory of cognitive structure. Kelman (1974) notes that nonlaboratory studies tend to show systematic relationships between racial and religious attitudes and the behavior of voting for or against political candidates and of affiliating with members of certain groups. The laboratory may be an unnatural place for the average person and may interfere with the attitude-behavior relationship. In a laboratory the behavioral alternatives available are carefully controlled by the experimenter and are limited in range. One feature of the field surveys of attitudes and behavior is that they focus on behavior that is freely chosen by the person—how he votes in the privacy of the election booth, what groups he joins, and so on.

The demonstrated inconsistencies between attitudes and behaviors have provoked a penetrating and critical reanalysis of the entire problem. Two fundamental approaches have been taken toward finding solutions: (1) reexamination of the methods used to obtain a "pure" measure of attitudes, uncontaminated by other factors; and (2) the inclusion of other factors, which, in association with attitudes, determine behavior.

A. Measurement and Control Problems

No one has seen or ever will see an attitude. It is a hypothetical construct (as are genes in biology and subatomic particles in physics), which because of the properties it is assumed to possess allows the scientist to organize a set of data that otherwise do not fit coherently together. Consider the difficulties involved in devising the attitude construct and then measuring it. In genetics, selective breeding yields regular and predictable manifestations of genes in terms of blood type, eye color, certain behavior of fruit flies, and so on. Thus, a rather clear inference can be made backward from the manifestation (phenotype) to the underlying factor believed to cause it (genotype). But the basis for inferring an attitude is the verbal or motor behavior of an individual; and, from our present knowledge, these manifestations may be a result of many factors other than attitudes, such as attention, perception, information processing, memory, and so on. The problem is to sort out which verbal or motor acts represent attitudes and which do not. Only when this sorting is done can confidence be placed in inferences drawn about a person's attitudes from his behavior.

1. Difficulties in Measuring Attitudes

By far the most frequent method of measuring attitudes is to ask subjects to divulge their beliefs about an object and how they feel toward it or how they do or would behave toward it. This kind of measure assumes a direct relationship between attitudes and statements about them. Unfortunately, self-report measures are very susceptible to distortion. Cook and Selltiz (1964) have noted the tendency of subjects to manage the impressions others have of them: "The purpose of the instrument is obvious to the respondent; the implications of his answers are apparent to him, and he can consciously control his responses. Thus, a person who wishes to give a certain picture of himself—whether in order to impress the tester favorably, to preserve his own self-image, or for some other reason—can easily do so". (p.40).

To compensate for this susceptibility, attempts have been made to disguise the purpose of the questions and to avoid items that require answers which are obviously socially desirable or undesirable. Direct questioning about moral responsibility, experiences of failure, or social hostility or thoughtlessness is unlikely to produce frank answers on the paper-and-pencil tests typically given as part of a course requirement to participate in experiments. The validity of a self-report may be improved by assuring respondents of their anonymity, stressing the importance of honest answers for the validity of scientific research, and telling subjects that wide variations in responses are expected and there are no right or wrong answers. Although these procedures may reduce the effects of impression management it would be too optimistic to believe that when they are employed we can accept a respondent's self-report as a reflection of his "true" attitude.

A recent attempt to avoid the biases associated with paper-and-pencil tests is the development of the bogus pipeline procedure, which was used by Sigall and Page (1971) in their study of faking stereotypes (see Chapter 4, II, C). The validity of the procedure depends on the willingness of subjects to believe the experimenter's claims regarding the working of the apparatus. Such trust may be uncharacteristic of subjects who have any sophistication in psychology or who are wary of the social psychologist's laboratory "tricks."

There have been several attempts to develop behavioral measures from which clear inferences about attitudes can be made. DeFleur and Westie (1958) identified those white students in introductory sociology classes who scored high or low on a self-report measure of prejudice toward Negroes. These students were taken to a laboratory and asked to observe a series of pictures portraying Negroes and whites of both sexes, shown singly and in all possible pairs. Physiological reactions to the pictures were measured by galvanic skin responses and changes in finger blood volume; both of these measures indicate physiological arousal and emotional response. The subjects were then shown a series of pictures of pairs of male and female, white and Negro young adults, who were seated beside one another in separate chairs in a portrayal of cordiality but not romance. The subjects were asked to give projective interpretations of what was happening between the persons in the photographs.

Following this interpretative task, the subjects were told that another group of pictures was needed for a future experiment. They were asked if they would be willing to be photographed with a Negro of the opposite sex, the purposes of which were indicated in a photograph release agreement, including: (1) laboratory experiments, (2) publication in a technical journal, (3) experiments in which a few dozen University students would see the photographs; (4) teaching aids to be viewed by hundreds of students, (5) the student newspaper, as part of the publicity about the research, (6) the student's hometown newspaper, and (7) a nation-wide publicity campaign advocating racial integration. The subjects were asked to sign their names next to each use they would permit of the pictures taken of them.

The self-report measure of prejudice was positively correlated with physiological arousal in response to the photographs; also, subjects identified as more prejudiced on the paper-and-pencil test did more often avoid being photographed with a Negro than did nonprejudiced subjects. Yet some prejudiced subjects signed the agreement for all seven uses of the photographs without hesitation, while some nonprejudiced subjects were unwilling to permit any use. In fact, fully one-third of all the subjects displayed behavior patterns in opposition to their stated attitudes. In response to a question about whether they had thought of any particular person or group when contemplating giving permission to use the photographs, the subjects invariably indicated they had and also considered whether the person or group would approve of their decision. Thus, some relationship was found between self-report, physiological, and behavioral measures of attitudes but the correlations were not very strong and significant departures from expectations occurred. To some extent, the subjects' concern about the approval or disapproval of significant others disturbed the expected consistency between attitudes and behavior.

Warner and DeFleur (1969) found that concern for how others will view a subject affects the relationship between his attitude and behavior. Students who had been previously identified as prejudiced or nonprejudiced in terms of their responses to an attitude questionnaire, were mailed requests to sign statements about whether they would interact with Negroes in a number of situations varying in social intimacy. The visibility of the behavior was manipulated by informing the subjects either that their statements would be kept confidential or that they would be published in the student newspaper. The study was conducted in a border state and the perceived social constraints were against integration. In this social context, prejudiced subjects more often refused to interact with Negroes when their statements would be made public than when they would remain anonymous. Hence, prejudiced students showed more attitude-behavior consistency when their behavior was to be publicized. Nonprejudiced subjects, on the other hand, revealed more attitude-behavior consistency when their statements were to remain anonymous than when they were to be made public; that is, they were less willing to interact with Negroes when this attitude-consistent behavior would be made public. Thus, behavior was consistent with attitudes when it was likely to produce positive approval from relevant others, or when it was anonymous and would not evoke disapproval. It is easier to be consistent when rewarded for it, but more difficult when it brings costs.

2. Verbal versus Motor Behavior

Verbal and motor behavior often serve different purposes, and as a result, consistency between them cannot always be expected. Verbal behavior, from which attitudes are usually inferred, may also be used to feign future conduct, to threaten, to promise, to lie, or to rationalize and justify past or present actions. To some extent verbal behavior is under different reinforcement contingencies than motor responses. One may not be punished for a verbal statement of refusal to obey one's parents as long as one's actual behavior is obedient. Similarly, when making a threat or a promise, a person may intend to back up his attempt at influence with punishment or reward, but when the actual time comes to put up or shut up, he may well shut up because of the costs that would be incurred by actually following through.

Verbal behavior is used as a tactic in interpersonal relationships and may serve to disguise the person's attitudes rather than reveal them. To penetrate a person's public presentations and gain a glimpse of his "true" self may or may not be possible. Thomas Wolfe once likened the person to an onion. As you peel off one layer after another and finally reach the center, he said, you find . . . nothing! Perhaps the person is nothing more than all of the presentations he makes of himself. There may be no true self or true attitudes to discover. Detractors of attitude research and personality theory suggest that the focus of our attention should be on the relationship of verbal and motor behavior without reference to any mediating attitudes and that attempts should be made to relate each type of behavioral system to the set of reinforcements typically administered by relevant persons or groups. Such an approach would conceive of the individual as completely expedient and never acting on the basis of prior principle. The limitations of attitude theory do not seem to warrant such an extreme position. Rather, the emphasis might be placed on examining other factors, which along with attitudes, determines what the individual does.

B. Inclusion of Other Factors in Predicting Behavior

Although attitude theories have been somewhat successful in predicting statements of attitudes and intentions, social judgments, and reports of sentiments, they have been less successful in predicting specific instances of overt behavior, except possibly, the study of voting behavior (Kelman, 1974). It seems clear that simple assumptions that behavior can be predicted from the individual's attitude toward an object or act are not adequate.

The remedy does not require that social psychologists completely give up trying to develop a theory of behavior that incorporates the concept of attitudes. Instead, additional factors may be added to any theory of behavior to improve its predictive power. For example, the theory of behavioral intentions developed by Ajzen and Fishbein takes into account the individual's attitude toward an act but also considers normative constraints and his need for social approval. Wicker (1969a) has suggested that the following additional factors might be considered in attempts to make predictions of overt behavior: (1) other relevant attitudes; (2) competing behavior; (3) competing motives; (4) generality of attitude and specificity of behavior; (5) personal behavioral capacity; (6) costs; and (7) deliberate deception.

1. Other Relevant Attitudes

More than one attitude may be associated with any particular behavior. For example, in a study of voting in the 1956 presidential election, it was found that positive attitudes toward Eisenhower correlated only .52 with reported voting for him (Campbell, Converse, Miller, & Stokes, 1960). When attitudes toward Stevenson, both parties, and the platforms of both parties were added to the attitudes toward Eisenhower, the correlation increased to .71. Examination of other relevant attitudes may also weaken the relationship between attitudes and behavior. Insko and Schopler (1967) suggested that a person who has favorable attitudes toward the civil rights movement may not contribute money to support the cause if he also has attitudes favoring a good credit rating, paying his bills on time, and providing a minimum level of comfort for his family.

Rokeach and Kliejunas (1972) contend that if all the relevant attitudes (and their relative importance) in a situation are known, behavior can be consistently and accurately predicted from that knowledge. They predicted which students would cut classes from their knowledge of the students' attitudes toward the professor and toward class-cutting. Prediction was more accurate when the two weighted attitudes were considered together than when they were either considered separately or were left unweighted. Presumably, even better predictions could be made if other attitudes were also considered, such as attitudes toward classmates, the teaching assistant, the room in which the class was held, the long walk from the dormitory to the classroom, going out on rainy, cold, or snowy days, and so on.

2. Competing Behavior

If more than one attitude can be relevant to any particular behavior, it is also possible for one attitude to be associated with several kinds of behavior. When one response interferes or competes with another, an inconsistency between attitudes and behavior is likely to result. Suppose a person contributes money to the civil rights movement and a little later is asked to participate in a mass rally in Washington. He may refuse to attend the rally because the money he has already contributed has left him finanically unable to travel so far from home. People who are unaware of his prior contribution and his financial problem may consider him a hypocrite for failing to join the demonstration.

3. Competing Motives

Attitudes are often considered to motivate behavior. However, attitudes and motives may clash or they may be consistent with each other. Consider a person who has a strong need for achievement but who has not been very successful recently. Although he may have proper ethical attitudes, if his motive to achieve is more potent than his ethical attitudes, he may act unscrupulously to gain his objectives. Corey (1937) found that the number of questions a student missed on an examination was a better predictor of cheating than was his attitude toward cheating. When he was not well prepared, his concern for passing the examination was greater than his scruples. Well-prepared students did not need to cheat in order to pass; hence, their trustworthy behavior was consistent with their ethical attitudes.

4. Generality of Attitude and Specificity of Behavior

The global attitudes of a person may be a poor basis for predicting related but specific actions. In considering stereotypes in the last chapter, we noted that a person's attitude toward a group may not tell us how he will act toward any member of that group. For example, American college students hold a generally low opinion of Turks (Karlins, et al., 1969), yet we would not be in a very good position to predict a student's behavior toward any particular Turk, especially if the latter does not outwardly conform to the stereotype. A person's general attitude toward certain public issues may appear inconsistent with his behavior. Many people who sincerely believe in integrating the races in American society have opposed mandatory school busing to achieve integration. While maintaining the general principle, these people resent busing because it interferes with other values they hold. They might very well support other ways of achieving integration.

5. Personal Behavioral Capacity

According to Wicker, low intelligence or ability may make it difficult for a person to translate his attitudes into appropriate actions. A lack of social skills may inhibit or hamper the exercise of interpersonal persuasive tactics in support of his attitudes. A person with a high energy level may take many actions that are consistent with his attitudes, while one with a low activity level may engage in few such actions. Thus an individual's abilities and skills may facilitate or detract from the consistency between attitudes and behavior.

6. Costs and the Attitude-Behavior Relationship

The costs of not acting may cause an individual to behave in a manner that is contrary to his attitudes. For example, during the 1960s young men were concerned about being drafted into the army and sent to Vietnam. These perceived costs may have produced an anti-war attitude among young people, especially since there were no perceived gains to be achieved by the war. For instance, if a potential army draftee held an anti-war attitude and also felt negatively about engaging in political activity, the potential costs of doing nothing may be great enough to cause him to join in political protests. Changes in a person's circumstances may cause him to act in a manner that is contrary to his previously held attitudes. Wicker suggests that even if a person's attitude toward public housing is negative, a sudden drop in his income may result in his application to live in a public housing project. In general, people maintain attitudes that are consistent with rewarding behavior; attitudes and behavior that are associated with costs are inhibited or changed.

7. Deliberate Deception

We have already considered the possibility that stated attitudes may not reflect the individual's "true" beliefs and values but instead are tactics of impression management and social influence. Naturally, attitude-behavior consistency could not be expected if in fact attributions about a person's attitudes are incorrect. It is likely that statements obtained in the laboratory and in formal interviews more often reflect an individual's concern for "looking good"

or presenting himself as "normal" than his "true" or "private" cognitions.

C. Conclusions regarding the Attitude-Behavior Relationship

The available evidence reveals little consistency between a person's attitudes and his subsequent behavior. There is no one-to-one relationship between the way a person views the world and his responses to it. Predictions of behavior are improved by ascertaining an individual's attitudes toward a number of relevant objects and acts, his motives and abilities, and the costs and gains believed to be associated with each of the available response alternatives. To some degree the lack of consistency between attitudes and behavior may be attributed to a tendency to predict specific behavior from global attitudes and to the deliberate deception practiced by persons who manage impressions of themselves and seek to influence other people.

The low consistency between attitudes and actions does not indicate that people do not act in accord with their beliefs and values. They may or may not. Behavior is obviously based on more than just the person's beliefs and attitudes. Nevertheless, as Kelman (1974) has said, "It is very difficult to imagine a social psychology without a construct designed to capture the conceptions of social objects and events that people bring to their interactions with each other and with their social institutions and that they share, to varying degrees with other members of their diverse groups, organizations, and communities" (p.316).

While it makes sense to propose a construct which links a belief with a value, there is no justification for maintaining that any piece of verbal behavior invariably represents an underlying attitude. To hold such an assumption after all of the work of the past 50 years is simply naive. The future work of many social psychologists will undoubtedly be devoted to building theories of behavior which include those factors considered important by attitude theories of today as well as other factors needed to predict more consistently and accurately the behavior of persons in social interaction.

IV. COGNITIVE DISSONANCE

When Peirce (1877) argued that doubt is an uncomfortable or irritable state, he stated that it motivates a person to seek new information in order to resolve the doubt and reach a state of belief. One of the conditions that produces doubt is the discovery that two or more beliefs are contradictory to one another. To remove the doubt caused by contradictory beliefs, it is necessary to determine which are false (or at least which are less useful). Contradictions may be experienced by a person when there are evaluative inconsistencies among his attitudes (i.e., psycho-logic) or when there are logical inconsistencies between denotative cognitive elements. The motivating character of these contradictory (or dissonant) relations is the basis of Festinger's (1957) theory of *cognitive dissonance*.

As we shall see, dissonance theory has stirred a great deal of controversy among social psychologists, but it has also stimulated a great amount of very imaginative research. Many of the hypotheses drawn from the theory are intriguing because they fly in the face of common sense. Cognitive dissonance theory is distinctive from the consistency or balance theories considered earlier because (1) it is stated in less formal terms, (2) the propositions are more broadly stated to include behavior as well as cognitions, (3) it deals with both connotative and denotative properties of cognitions, and (4) it is concerned with the question of how behavior affects attitudes rather than how attitudes influence behavior.

According to Festinger, cognitive elements are bits of knowledge consisting of beliefs about oneself, the environment, and one's behavior. These cognitive elements may form one of three types of relations——consonant, dissonant, and irrelevant. Festinger stipulates that "two elements are in a dissonant relation if, considering these two alone, the obverse of one element would follow from the other. To state it a bit more formally, x and y are dissonant if not-x follows from y" (1957, p.13). Furthermore, "If, considering a pair of elements, either one *does* follow from the other, then the relation between them is consonant. If neither the existing element nor its obverse follows from the other element of the pair, then the relation between them is irrelevant" (p.15). These relations among cognitive elements are based on formal logic, cultural norms, the past experience of the individual, and the context afforded by a larger, more inclusive set of cognitions.

A person who smokes cigarettes and maintains the belief that smoking causes lung cancer or heart disease would be in a state of dissonance, assuming, of course, that he desires a long and healthy life. His belief about the deleterious effects of smoking are contradictory to his knowledge about his own behavior. To give up smoking is consonant with the belief that it causes health problems. Before the Surgeon General's Report was released outlining its hazards, smoking was not dissonant with a concern for good health; the relationship was one of irrelevance.

Dissonance is assumed to produce tension or an unpleasant state which the organism seeks to reduce. Tension can be reduced by bringing dissonant cognitions into a consonant relationship or by severing the connecton between cognitive elements (rendering them irrelevant to one another). Hence, dissonance theory is sometimes characterized as primarily a theory of motivation. Festinger clearly acknowledges that no one can completely eliminate all dissonance from his cognitions however much he may strive to do so. However, tension will be minimized by dissonance-reducing or dissonance-avoiding behavior. The origins of the tension produced by dissonance are left unspecified. It is not known whether it occurs because of innate biological mechanisms or whether it is acquired through socialization experiences.

Festinger has enumerated various dissonance-reducing strategies that may be employed. A person may retain contradictory cognitions without tension if one of the elements is suppressed in the unconscious. Dissonance may be reduced by decreasing the importance of the cognitions or by adding new cognitions that alter the relationship between existing elements. Dissonance may also be reduced by modifying behavior that is linked with a dissonant cognitive element or by distorting one or both of the dissonant cognitions. Of course, a person may simply give up one of these contradictory beliefs. The theory does not specify the conditions under which these processes will occur, leaving it to research to find the limiting conditions in each case.

We can illustrate these dissonance-reducing processes by reference to our cigarette smoker. One way for him to reduce his dissonance is to question the evidence relating smoking to various diseases. For example, a report of an experiment in which rats were forced to smoke the equivalent of two packs of cigarettes a day with the result of an increased rate of lung cancer might lead the person to conclude that rats should not smoke, but to deny any generalization of this observation to human beings. Of course, another way to reduce dissonance would be to give up the smoking habit. The third element, his desire for good health, could also be changed; he might indicate his preference for a short, relaxed, and happy life rather than a long, anxiety-ridden, and tormented life, and might conclude that everyone must die sometime; after all, 100 percent of the people who eat tomatoes also die.

If none of these dissonance-reducing mechanisms is satisfactory, a person may search for additional information that pro-

vides a context in which the formerly contradictory cognitions can be retained without too much discomfort. For example, he may learn that smog in the city is more injurious to his health than heavy smoking. Since he is endangered whether he smokes or not, giving up the habit will not improve his chances of good health. The new cognitive element reduces the importance of cigarette smoking as it relates to health.

Four basic areas of research have been stimulated by Festinger's theory: (1) insufficient justification, (2) effort justification, (3) post-decision dissonance, and (4) selective exposure to new information. Dissonance is generated when a person engages in behavior without sufficient justification for doing so, exerts a lot of effort to attain something that proves to have little value, and makes a decision to choose one of two equally attractive alternatives. In each case he has acted and subsequently needs to find a good explanation for his actions. He should therefore be observed to avoid dissonance-producing information and to be receptive to dissonance-reducing information.

A.   Insufficient Justification

Dissonance may occur between inconsistent beliefs, between a belief and one's awareness of contradictory behavior, or as a result of knowledge of two contradictory kinds of behavior. When a person performs an act that goes counter to his previous attitudes, beliefs, and behavior, and he cannot attribute the act to external or environmental forces, he lacks sufficient justification for his behavior and dissonance is aroused. On the other hand, if he can attribute his behavior to environmental forces, no dissonance is aroused because it need not be viewed as flowing from, or contradictory to, his personal beliefs, attitudes, or behavioral dispositions. If a nonsmoker who believes in the connection of smoking to cancer is forced to smoke a cigarette by his army sergeant, no dissonance results because he realizes that he was coerced by external pressures and his smoking was not a voluntary action expressing his inner beliefs.

The arousal of dissonance by counterattitudinal behavior performed without sufficient justification is illustrated in an early experiment by Festinger and Carlsmith (1959). Male subjects spent one hour performing two extremely dull manual tasks. Each subject was then asked if he would act as an experimental accomplice in place of a confederate who had failed to appear in the laboratory as scheduled. Most subjects agreed to tell a waiting female subject (actually a confederate) that the experiment was interesting and enjoyable. Half the subjects were paid $1 and half were paid $20 for their services. According to Festinger and Carlsmith, the cognition associated with actually performing the task ("the task was boring") should be dissonant with the cognition of the subsequent statement about it ("I said the task was enjoyable"). Receiving payment provided some justification for the counterattitudinal behavior of saying the task was enjoyable. Presumably, the less money paid to subjects, the greater the resulting dissonance should be. One way of reducing this dissonance would be to alter one's evaluation of the task; if the task were believed to be actually enjoyable, no dissonance would result from telling someone it was interesting.

As would be expected from this line of reasoning, when the subjects were asked during an alleged departmental survey of experiments whether they found the task interesting and enjoyable, how important they believed the experiment was, and if they would volunteer to be in another similar experiment, those in the $1 condition responded more positively than did those in the $20 condition. The results are shown in Table 5.2. Presumably, receiving $20 provided sufficient justification for lying to a second person ("I was paid a lot of money and that made me tell a lie") but $1 was not ("I had little monetary reason to lie"). To reduce dissonance, subjects in the $1 condition distorted their evaluations of the task ("I didn't really lie, because the task was actually somewhat enjoyable"). Hence, insufficient justification for a counterattitudinal behavior produced the nonobvious result of behavior changing an attitude.

Zimbardo, Weisenberg, Firestone, and Levy (1965) tested the insufficient justification hypothesis by having a person who was identified as a military doctor ask for volunteers from a group of college students and Army reservists to eat fried grasshoppers. The doctor was presented either as unattractive, by his gruff manner in chastising an assistant in front of the subjects, or as an understanding, sympathetic and attractive person. Over 50 percent of the subjects in both the attractive and unattractive

Table 5.2 Average Ratings on Interview Questions for Each Condition.[a]

Questions on interview	Experimental conditions	
	One dollar	Twenty dollars
How enjoyable tasks were (rated from −5 to +5)	+1.35	− .05
Scientific importance (rated from 0 to 10)	6.45	5.18
Participate in similar experiment (rated from −5 to +5)	+1.20	− .25

[a] After Festinger and Carlsmith, 1959, p. 207.

conditions ate the grasshoppers (which when fried, taste something like popcorn). When asked to rate how much they liked the food, those subjects who had volunteered to do so for the unattractive doctor were more favorable than those who had volunteered for the attractive doctor. Apparently, doing a favor for a nice guy was sufficient justification for engaging in counterattitudinal behavior. But when subjects volunteered to eat the grasshoppers at the behest of an unattractive person, they were left with insufficient justification for doing so. They presumably reasoned that "If I ate the grasshoppers, it must be because they were good because I surely didn't do so as a favor to that creep!"

Aronson and Carlsmith (1963) proposed that dissonance may also be aroused when a person has insufficient justification for *not* doing something he desires to do. Small children were asked to rate their preference for five toys. The second most preferred toy was then placed on a table and the remainder were set on the floor. Before leaving the child alone in the room with the toys, the experimenter told the child not to play with the toy on the table. Accompanying this prohibition was either a mild or a severe threat regarding the consequences of disobedience.

The children were then observed through a one-way mirror while alone with the toys; very few of them played with the forbidden toy. Following this free-play period, the children were once again asked to rate their preferences for the toys. Changes in the ratings of the prohibited toy were expected, depending on the reason the children had for *not* playing with it. When severe punishment was threatened, it would be consonant for the child not to play with a toy he likes, and he should maintain his original evaluation of it. But when the threat was very mild, consisting of only slight disapproval, the child had little external justification for abstaining from playing with the forbidden toy. He must therefore assume that the reason he did not play

with the toy is because he really did not like it very much.

The results supported the predictions. The children in the mild threat condition did tend to derogate the forbidden toy by rating it as less desirable following the play period than they had before. This effect is similar to a sour-grapes rationalization whereby an individual who does not engage in behavior he desires to perform denies that he wanted to do so. Children in the severe threat condition tended to rate the forbidden toy as even more desirable after than before the play period. The concern displayed by the experimenter about the forbidden toy may have suggested to the children that it must be very valuable.

Although several other studies (Freedman, 1965a; Pepitone, McCauley, & Hammond, 1967) have replicated these findings, Lepper, Zanna, and Abelson (1970) found that when children were told prior to a temptation period that other children had not played with the forbidden toy (i.e., had obeyed the experimenter), those in the mild-threat condition did not devalue the toy. To account for this anomalous finding, it is possible to reason that the consensual information concerning the obedience of other children provided the subjects with sufficient external justification for obeying the experimenter; hence, no dissonance was aroused. An additional finding by Lepper et al. was that the mild-threat children derogated the toy when the consensual information was provided after rather than before the temptation period, and this can be handled by similar post-hoc reasoning. It may be assumed that when the child had not received consensual information prior to the play period, dissonance was aroused and that dissonance reduction (derogation of the prohibited toy) had already occurred. The flexibility of dissonance theory, which enables it to explain almost any result, stems from the possibility of inventing new cognitive elements on a post-hoc basis to generate dissonant or consonant relationships as required by the particular results. This is, of course, an undesirable feature of any scientific theory, since it makes it impossible to find evidence against the theory.

B.   Effort Justification

According to dissonance theory, the amount of effort expended in achieving an objective will affect the value placed on it. It would be inconsistent for a person to believe both that he worked hard or endured hardships to attain a goal and then to dislike the goal. The more worthless, unappealing, uninteresting, or counterattidinal the outcome, the greater the need for effort justification.

Suppose your professor sometimes gives pop quizzes, but it is difficult to predict when they will be given. Further suppose that last night you studied very hard and your classmate did not. It would be inconsistent for you to study hard and to believe that there would be no pop quiz; therefore, you are likely to believe that one will occur. Similarly, in order to maintain consonant cognitions, your roommate should be inclined to assign a low probability to the event.

Yaryan and Festinger (1961) performed an experiment that approximates this scenario. They first informed female high school students that half of them would be required to take an IQ test, but which of them would take the test was not revealed. Half the girls were induced to learn a long list of definitions that would allegedly be helpful in taking the test. The remainder of the girls were asked to read over the list, but were assured that it would be available to them should they be asked to take the test. All the girls were then asked to estimate the probability they would be selected to take the IQ test. Girls in the high effort condition considered it more likely they would take the test than did those in the low effort condition. Presumably, knowledge that they had worked hard in preparation for the test led the girls to exaggerate the probability they would be required to take it, while lack of effort was consistent with a belief that they would not be selected.

Submitting oneself to hardship, pain, or embarrassment in order to achieve a goal would be dissonant with a belief that the goal is worthless. For example, a person may voluntarily submit himself to an initiation ritual in order to join a group. If he is admitted without any difficulty at all, it is consonant for him to believe the group lacks attractiveness. After all, it should be difficult to join a really valuable group. If he suffers through a severe initiation ritual in order to join it, it would be inconsistent for him to believe it to be worthless and unattractive. This kind of reasoning is illustrated by Groucho Marx' statement that "any club that would admit me as a member is a club I don't want to be a member of."

Aronson and Mills (1959) investigated the effects of severity of initiation upon an individual's attitude toward a group. Female subjects were informed they would have an opportunity to join a group that was discussing the psychology of sex. One of the original members had allegedly dropped out, making room for a new member. Because it was important for group members to be able to talk freely about sex, the subjects were told they would be given a brief embarrassment test to screen out those who would not be compatible with the group. In a severe initiation condition, the test involved reading aloud twelve obscene words and two lurid passages from current fiction. In the mild initiation condition, the subjects were asked to read aloud several words that were related to sex but would not ordinarily be considered obscene. In both conditions, the reading was done in the presence of a male experimenter. A control group for which no initiation was required was also included in the study.

The subjects were then allowed to hear a group discussion covering parts of the book, *Sexual Behavior in Animals;* but since they had not read the book, they were not allowed to participate in the discussion. They were informed that each discussant was seated in a separate booth with a microphone for transmitting and a headphone for receiving communications. This procedure was rationalized as minimizing embarrassment for all the participants. The subjects' microphones were turned off because they were not to contribute to the discussion, and they then listened to a tape recording of a standard discussion that had been prepared before the experiment. The taped discussion was very dull and confused; the discussants spoke haltingly and often did not finish their sentences. When asked to rate how interesting and worthwhile the discussion was and how attractive they believed the group to be, subjects in the severe initiation condition rated both the discussion and the group more positively than did the subjects in the other two conditions.

Critical examination of the procedures of this study raises the possibility that the severe initiation was not embarrassing and negative to the girls, but instead was sexually stimulating. It is also possible that listening to the discussion following the severe initiation provided relief from the sexual anxiety it aroused. Either of these alternatives would lead to a prediction of more favorable ratings by the severe initiation subjects. To establish that severe initiation produces dissonance independently of these possible contaminating factors, Gerard and Mathewson (1966) replicated the Aronson and Mills study but substituted electric shock as the initiation ritual. Subjects were given either severe or mild shocks as a test of their emotional stability before being admitted to a discussion group. The topic of the dull (taped) discussion was cheating on examinations. Consistent with dissonance theory and the Aronson and Mills results, the subjects in the severe shock condition rated the discussion as more interesting than did those in the mild shock condition.

C. Post-decisional Dissonance

When a person chooses between two or more alternatives, some dissonance is probably aroused. Seldom is a choice so clear that there are no good aspects to the unchosen alternative and no negative features to the one chosen. The perceived positive features of the rejected alternative and the negative factors associated with the chosen alternative are dissonant with whatever decision is made. The more important the decision and the more similar the alternatives considered, the greater the dissonance should be. Following decision–making, therefore, an individual may derogate the rejected alternative and may enhance the value of the one chosen as means of reducing postdecisional dissonance. The result is a *spreading* apart of the decision alternatives in support of the alternative actually chosen.

Post-decisional effects are exemplified by the results obtained by Brehm (1956). His female subjects rated the attractiveness of eight commercial products such as a toaster, a radio, and a stopwatch. The subjects were then given their choice of one of two of the items as a gift. The two items provided for choice were neither the subject's most preferred nor least preferred products, but were either two that had been rated very similarly (high dissonance) or two between which the subject had expressed a clear preference (low dissonance). After they received the gift of their choice, they were asked once again to rate the eight products. Compared to the first ratings, the chosen product increased in attractiveness and the rejected item decreased in attractiveness. In support of dissonance theory predictions, these enhancement and derogation effects were stronger in the high than in the low dissonance condition. These changes in ratings were not simply a result of receiving a gift, but required an active decision by the subject. A control group of subjects were given a gift without prior choice and their ratings did not change from the first to the second rating period.

Knox and Inkster (1968) demonstrated post-decisional dissonance reduction in the real-life setting of a race track. In two separate field experiments, bettors were approached either on the way to make a $2 win bet or just after leaving the $2 win window. They were asked to estimate, on a seven-point scale (or on a 23 centimeter scale in the second experiment), the chance their horse had of winning the race. In both experiments the bettors leaving the window were more certain about their horses winning than were those who were on their way to place their bets. Of course, it is possible that people changed their bets from long shots to favorites as they approached the window and that their post-decision confidence reflected this change. This possibility was ruled out in the second experiment by making certain that bettors leaving the window had not changed their minds regarding their wagers as they approached it.

Festinger (1964) acknowledged that a person may experience a moment of doubt following a decision about whether he has made the right choice. This may occur early in the post-decisional period, but as dissonance reduction proceeds, the usual spreading of the alternatives through enhancement and derogation takes place. Some evidence for the experience of *post-decision regret* was found by Walster (1964). Through the cooperation of the Human Resources Research Office of the U.S. Army, she was able to use recruits as the subjects of her experiment. These recruits first rated their preferences among 10 occupational specialties and then were given a choice between two of them. They believed they were making real choices that would commit them to the occupation chosen for the following two years. After his choice, each recruit again ranked all ten occupations, but these post-decisional ratings were obtained at different times: immediately afterward, four minutes later, fifteen minutes later, or ninety minutes later. Walster did not really know when to expect the post-decisional phases of regret and spread to occur; the time periods were chosen arbitrarily.

The measure used to indicate regret or spreading effects was the amount of change in attractiveness of the two occupations between the first and the post-decisional rating. A decrease in the attractiveness of the chosen alternative accompanied by an increase in attractiveness of the rejected one would indicate post-decsional regret, while the reverse pattern of change would reveal a dissonance-reducing spreading effect. Walster found that regret occurred four minutes after the decision was made and that spreading occurred 15 minutes after the decision. However, neither effect occurred immediately or 90 minutes after the decision. Since dissonance effects have been found both immediately and after long spans of time, her failure to find spreading after very short or moderately long time intervals is puzzling.

Post-decisional dissonance or regret presumably occurs because one candidate for choice was rejected and any benefits to be derived from the nonchosen alternative are therefore lost to the decision-maker. But suppose a person chooses between alternatives and believes he will be able to obtain the rejected alternative later on. Under these conditions there is no need to derogate the rejected alternative, and little dissonance should be aroused. The favorable aspects of the nonchosen alternative may be acknowledged without implying any inconsistency with the choice made, since he expects to eat his cake and have it too. The negative features of the chosen alternative need not arouse dissonance either, since it is normal not to expect perfection in anything so long as one has not chosen the worst of the available alternatives. Under these circumstances, research shows there is no dissonance effect (Allen, 1964; Jecker, 1964).

D. Selective Exposure to Information

A person who suffers from post-decisional dissonance should welcome new information that reflects positively on his choice or further derogates the rejected alternative. In fact, he may be expected to seek such information on a selective basis as a way of reducing dissonance. A person who has just purchased a Volkswagen may read material favorable to Volkswagens and avoid material favorable to Toyotas, his non-chosen alternative. Ehrlich, Guttman, Schonback, and Mills (1957) investigated the readership of automobile advertising following the purchase of a new car. Advertisements for the type of car purchased were read more than advertisements for other cars. However, the buyers apparently did not *avoid* reading advertising about cars they considered buying but had rejected; there was no difference between reading advertisements about the rejected cars and those that had never been considered.

Canon (1964) proposed that the chief determinant of selective exposure to information is its potential usefulness and not dissonance. Information extolling the virtues of a rejected alternative may be welcomed by the decisionmaker when it is believed to have future usefulness to him. In a study to examine this view, Canon also considered the effects of self-confidence on selective exposure. A confident and self-assured person may be more willing to expose himself to contradictory information, if it is useful, than a less confident and more easily threatened person.

In a test of these hypotheses, Canon first attempted to induce high or low self-confidence in his subjects. They were asked to read case histories in business, and each subject was asked to indicate which of

two or three alternative courses of action he thought was the best solution for the problem in each of the first three cases. In the high-confidence condition the subjects were told they got all three cases right and that most of the other subjects got them wrong. In the low confidence condition, the subjects were told they had been correct in only the first case and that most of the other subjects had got all three cases right.

After the fourth case, the subjects were not told how they had done. Instead, they were asked to write a brief essay defending their solution. Half the subjects in each confidence condition were told that their essay was in preparation for a debate in which they would be expected to rebut opposing arguments. The other half of the subjects were not led to anticipate opposing arguments.

At this point, and *before* the subjects wrote essays, they were told that it might be helpful to them to see other people's responses to the same cases. Because there were allegedly a limited number of copies, the subjects were asked to indicate how much they would like to read each of five papers. The title of these papers indicated that two supported the subject's position, two opposed it, and one was neutral. The subjects rated the five papers on a scale ranging from 0 (not at all interested) to 100 (maximally interested) and then ranked them from 1 to 5 in order of preference. A measure was also obtained of the subject's confidence in his decision on the fourth case. Since these dependent variables completed the study, the subjects were not required to write the essay.

The results supported Canon's predictions. The subjects who believed they would need to know opposing arguments for purposes of debate had a distinct preference for information contrary to their own decisions. Highly confident subjects had a stronger preference for contradictory but useful information than did those who lacked self-confidence. Subjects who did not anticipate having to know opposing arguments preferred consonant information; those who lacked self-confidence had a stronger preference for consonant information than did highly confident subjects. When Freedman (1965b) followed almost the same procedures as Canon, he found the same preference for useful information but no differences between high and low self-confidence subjects was found. No reason for this discrepancy was offered, but the results provide consistent support for the hypothesis that the utility of information determines its selection. Despite the fact that information may be dissonant with an individual's beliefs or decisions, he will choose it if he believes it will be useful to him in the future.

V.　CONTROVERSIES REGARDING DISSONANCE THEORY

Despite its common sense persuasiveness, there are problems with cognitive dissonance theory. The assumption that inconsistency among cognitions produces tension has not been adequately substantiated. The opposite of dissonance effects has also been found in research on insufficient justification. An *incentive effect* has been demonstrated in which an individual shows more attitude change when he receives large rewards than small for his counterattitudinal behavior. In other words, this effect reveals more cognitive change as a result of behavior that is sufficiently justified than from behavior that is not. These contradictory results have made salient the failure of dissonance theory to specify the conditions under which various effects should occur.

Imagine the law of acceleration of falling bodies being applied without regard for the prevailing environmental conditions. The law states that a falling body will accelerate in speed at a constant rate of increase. It might be expected from a knowledge of this physical law that if a feather and a bowling ball were dropped from the Leaning Tower of Pisa at exactly the same time, they would hit the ground simultaneously. But, of course, this would not occur because both the mass of the body and the resistance of the medium must be taken into account. That is, until the specific conditions are specified (i.e., dropping the objects in a vacuum), it is not possible to make accurate predictions from knowledge of the physical law.

The conditions for reliably obtaining a dissonance effect in laboratory studies have been gradually delimited. The individual must believe he has free choice to engage in counter-attitudinal behavior, this behavior must be public, and it must have negative consequences for others or for the actor. A series of alternative theories have been developed to explain why these special conditions are necessary for producing dissonance, including theories of self-perception, self-esteem, responsibility, and impression management.

A.　Tensions Aroused by Dissonance

According to Festinger (1957), "dissonance acts in the same way as a state of drive or need or tension" (p.18). He compares the drive properties of dissonance with those of hunger, which is associated with active or energetic behavior. Rats, for example, run more in activity wheels when hungry than when satisfied with food. The analogy has led a number of researchers to attempt to show the energizing effects of dissonance on behavior (e.g., Cottrell & Wack, 1967; Pallak, 1970; Waterman, 1969; Waterman & Katkin, 1967). Although all of these studies found support for dissonance theory, the procedures used in each case can be criticized for arousing anger, embarrassment, or anxiety—each of which, independent of any dissonance, may be associated with energizing effects (Spence & Spence, 1966).

The assumption that organisms are

motivated to reduce tensions was prevalent at the time dissonance theory was formulated. However, accumulated research on lower animals and humans shows that organisms often seek novel and tension-increasing information in their environment (Berlyne, 1966; see also Chapter 3, I). Many dissonance theorists are among the first to criticize a simple tension reduction model of behavior (e.g., Zimbardo, 1969a). Thus, not only is there no rigorous demonstration of the energizing effects of dissonance, but there is also reason to question the assumption that tension automatically leads to behavior directed toward tension reduction. In any case, "tension" and "energizing" are highly metaphorical terms that have no specific denotative meaning.

B. Incentive vs. Dissonance Effects

Studies of insufficient justification brought about a controversy between cognitive and reinforcement theories of attitude change. A reliable finding obtained in research on learning is that performance is facilitated by increases in incentive value. Other things being equal, an employee in an industrial training program will learn faster and perform better if he is given liberal salary increases than if he is awarded an embossed certificate of achievement. When applied to attitudes, reinforcement theory implies that unpleasant tasks should become more attractive the greater the incentive for performing them. Yet the Festinger and Carlsmith study of insufficient justification found that a small incentive ($1) produced greater liking for a boring task than did a larger incentive ($20).

Rosenberg (1965) explained the inconsistency between incentive and dissonance predictions of attitude change as owing to the arousal of evaluation apprehension among subjects who were offered large incentives (see Chapter 2, IV). The subject who is given $20 for telling a small lie in the context of a legitimate scientific study may wonder why he is being offered so much to

do so little. He may become suspicious that his integrity is under observation and "may be led to hypothesize that . . . his autonomy, his honesty, his resoluteness in resisting a special kind of bribe, are being tested" (p.29). By insisting that the task was boring and uninteresting following his lie, the subject in the high incentive condition can demonstrate his integrity and, hence, thinks he can gain the positive approval of the experimenter.

Rosenberg tested his hypothesis by asking Ohio State students to write essays in favor of banning the Ohio State football team from playing in the Rose Bowl, presumably a counter-attitudinal behavior. A small or large incentive was offered for writing the essays. Subsequent measurements of the subjects' attitudes toward the issue were obtained in the context of what was represented as an entirely different experiment. This separation of dissonance arousal from the measurement of attitude was intended to remove evaluation apprehension as a factor. A simple incentive effect was indeed found. Subjects were more opposed to participation in the Rose Bowl when they received larger rather than smaller rewards for writing essays taking this counter-attitudinal position.

C. Perceived Freedom and Self-Attribution Theory

One necessary condition for obtaining a dissonance effect is the perceived freedom of the individual to engage in counter-attitudinal behavior (Brehm & Cohen, 1959; Brock & Becker, 1967). Linder, Cooper, and Jones (1967) obtained a dissonance effect when their subjects believed they had free choice in deciding whether or not to write a counter-attitudinal essay and obtained an incentive effect when the subjects were given no choice but were simply told to write the essay.

Bem (1967a) has proposed that perceived freedom is required because the process involved is self-attribution (see

Chapter 4, I, D). The person who acts freely asks himself why he acted as he did. If he can attribute his counter-attitudinal behavior to environmental factors, he need not infer that his attitudes are reflected in his behavior. But if there is insufficient justification in terms of external causes, he may say to himself, "I must really believe the task is interesting, since I am saying that it is, and there is no external pressure requiring that I say so." Similarly, children who resist the temptation to play with a forbidden toy when a very mild threat is issued to them are more apt to attribute their inhibition to their lack of interest in the toy than children who can attribute their inhibition to a severe external threat.

According to Bem, whenever internal cues are weak, ambiguous, or uninterpretable, the actor's behavior provides him with information about what his attitudes must be. Under these conditions the actor is in the same position as an outside observer. One implication of Bem's formulation is that observers who are provided with descriptions of a dissonance experiment should be able to make accurate attributions about the subject's attitude change. Some "interpersonal simulations" of dissonance experiments have confirmed Bem's self-attributional analysis (Bem, 1965; 1967b, 1968; Bem & McConnell, 1970) but others have not (Jones, Linder, Kiesler, Zanna, & Brehm, 1968; Mills, 1967).

Bem has argued that the failure to find support for self-attribution theory in interpersonal simulation experiments is due to imperfect information provided to observers. When observers are given information about the attitudes of actors prior to counter-attitudinal behavior and asked to predict attitude change, they are unable to predict results consistent with a dissonance effect. But when they are not provided with information about prior attitudes and are simply asked to infer the actor's attitude from their observation of his counter-attitudinal behavior, their predictions are consistent with Bem's hypothesis (Piliavin, Piliavin, Loewenton, McCauley, & Ham-

mond, 1969). The controversy boils down to the question of what information should be presented to observers to best capture the exact experience of the actor so that the observer is in the same position and has the same information as the actor.

Jones et al. (1968) believe it is "untenable to hold that a subject is bereft of knowledge of his own (initial) attitude" (p.266). Aronson (1969) has posed the issue as an empirical one: "What must be established in future experiments is whether or not the subject's behavior (writing a counter-attitudinal essay) becomes so very salient that it overwhelms his memory about his original position . . . The question remains an open one" (pp.15-16). Bem (1972) has answered his critics by restating the self-perception position: "Bem and McConnell (1970) . . . demonstrated that subjects in dissonance experiments cannot, in fact, recall their initial attitudes at the time of the final attitude assessment, that they see their post-manipulation attitudes as the same attitudes which motivated them to comply in the first place, and that they do not experience any attitude change phenomenologically. Hence, initial attitudes are not salient for involved subjects, and should thus not be made salient for observers in the simulations" (pp.30-31).

Bem (1972) has argued that when the individual is reminded of or is asked to think about his initial attitude, change of attitude in the insufficient justification situation should diminish or disappear. According to Bem, dissonance theory would state that making the initial attitude salient should cause the individual to become more aware of cognitive conflict and hence should increase the amount of attitude change.

Synder and Ebbesen (1972) tested these competing predictions in a design which included asking subjects to think about their initial attitudes toward the critical issue prior to writing counter-attitudinal essays; subjects in a nonsalient condition were not given these instructions. Freedom of choice was also manipulated.

Choice to write the counter-attitudinal essay was given to half of the subjects, but not to the remainder. The results tended to support Bem's position. Subjects in the choice-salience condition showed less attitude change than subjects in the choice-nonsalience condition. Unexpectedly, and contrary to both self-perception and dissonance theories, subjects showed the greatest amount of attitude change in the no choice-salience condition. This finding has yet to be explained.

Another attempt to test the effects of salience was performed by Ross and Shulman (1973). They actually showed subjects in the salience condition the pretest scales and asked them to look at the item referring to the issue relevant to the counter-attitudinal essay. Subjects in the non-salient condition where not shown their pretest protocols. In addition, subjects either were or were not given choice to write the counter-attitudinal essays. This experiment found unequivocal support for dissonance theory. Subjects in the choice-salience condition showed more attitude change than those in the no choice and no salience conditions. These findings have been replicated by Green (1974).

Bem (1972) has expressed skepticism that any experiment can make a crucial test between dissonance and self-perception theories. The two theories are each capable of claiming some territory not covered by the other. Where they overlap, they tend to predict exactly the same results. Dissonance theorists have attempted to isolate such elusive phenomena as post-decisional regret and selective exposure, while self-perception theory is silent on these phenomena. Dissonance theory, on the other hand, has not dealt with the self-perceptions of persons.

D. Public Commitment, Responsibility, and Self-Esteem Theory

A second necessary condition for obtaining a dissonance effect is that the subject's counter-attitudinal behavior must be public rather than anonymous or private in nature. Carlsmith, Collins, and Helmreich (1966) replicated the findings of the Festinger and Carlsmith study when the subjects told the confederate in a face-to-face encounter that the boring task was enjoyable, but they obtained incentive effects when the subjects made their statements in an anonymous essay; the results are shown in Figure 5.3.

According to Carlsmith et al., when the subject's counter-attitudinal behavior was private or anonymous, no dissonance was aroused because he was aware that his expressed attitude was not accepted by the experimenter as representing his "true" attitude. Anonymyity re-affirmed the role-playing nature of the counter-attitudinal behavior, and role-playing is consistent with the subject's cognition that the experimenter is aware of the reason for his behavior—his concern to cooperate with the experimenter. In the public condition, the subject's counter-attitudinal statement is apparently believed by the confederate, who cannot know why he is saying the task is interesting. Hence, the subject is left with the question of why he is making such a statement, and in the 50¢ condition, he has insufficient justification for his actions.

Three basic explanations have been offered for the effects of the private-public manipulation of counter-attitudinal behavior: (1) public behavior commits a person to the position expressed by his counter-attitudinal behavior; (2) public behavior, unlike private conduct, reflects upon his self-concept and is therefore more apt to produce cognitive conflict; and (3) a person is more apt to be held responsible for his public actions than his private ones.

1. Commitment

The public-private distinction has led to the view that the degree of commitment associated with performing counter-attitudinal behavior is a factor in arousing dissonance. It may be assumed that the greater the gain from performing a behavior,

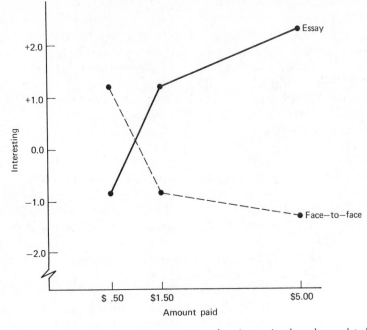

Figure 5.3.   Responses to posttest question on how interesting the task completed was. (After Carlsmith, Collins, and Helmreich, 1966.)

the less is the perceived personal commitment of the actor. On the other hand, the greater the costs incurred, the stronger the perceived personal commitment. The concept of commitment is another way of stating Kelley's (1973) augmentation principle in attribution theory (see Chapter 4, I, B). Consistent with both dissonance theory and Bem's self-attribution theory, the augmentation principle assumes that the attribution of personal cause to the actor from an observation of counter-attitudinal behavior is stronger the less the actor gains or the more he loses by performing the behavior. In the Carlsmith et al. study, the subject presumably had more to lose in making a false presentation in public than he did in conforming to the experimenter's request in the private condition. There was a pact between the experimenter and the subject in the private condition, but there was no pact between the subject and the confederate in their face-to-face encounter. Therefore, the subject perceived himself as more committed in the latter case. The stronger

an individual's commitment to his counter-attitudinal behavior, the greater the dissonance produced between it and his prior attitudes.

Helmreich and Collins (1968) have found evidence supporting the commitment hypothesis. Prospective subjects were asked if they would help to produce communications designed to change the attitudes of introductory psychology students and were offered either $.50 or $2.50 to do so. This procedure stressed the freedom of the subject to participate or to refuse. The subjects were then asked to prepare a communication advocating government regulation of family size to control the population explosion. All the subjects had been pretested in the classroom (with no apparent connection to the experiment), and the experimenters knew that advocating government control was counter-attitudinal for the subjects chosen.

In the public condition, each subject presented his communication on videotape, stating his name, home town, class, major, and then his arguments. In a second (video takeback) condition, the subjects were allowed to make a second videotape on which they could explain why they had made the first arguments and the purpose of the experiment; these subjects were told that the second videotape would also be viewed by the introductory psychology students. In a third (anonymous audio) condition, the subjects presented their arguments on audio tape and did not identify themselves.

The greatest commitment by subjects should have been in the video- $.50 condition since they had publicly identified themselves and were paid very little for making a counter-attitudinal speech. The least commitment would presumably be found in the audio-anonymous- $2.50 condition, since the subjects did not identify themselves and were given a high incentive for performing the counter-attitudinal behavior. Video-takeback subjects should have been committed to an intermediate degree, but more committed when they had less to gain ($.50) for performing the counter-attitudinal behavior than when they had more to gain ($2.50).

An incentive effect was found in the audio-anonymous condition; the subjects changed their attitudes more in the direction of the counter-attitudinal communication when they received $2.50 than when they received only $.50. A dissonance effect occurred in the two commitment (public) conditions. As can be seen in Figure 5.4, the video subjects showed a stronger dissonance effect than did the lower commitment, video-takeback subjects.

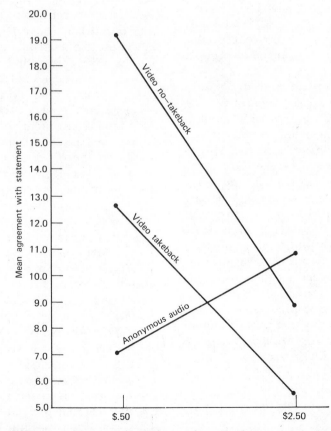

Figure 5.4. Posttest scores. Higher numbers represent a more favorable attitude. (After Helmreich and Collins, 1968.)

2. Self-concept

Aronson (1969) attributes the effect of public commitment on dissonance to its implications for self-concept: "at the very heart of dissonance theory . . . we are not dealing with any two cognitions; rather, we are usually dealing with the self-concept and cognitions about some behavior. If dissonance exists, it is because the individual's behavior is inconsistent with his self-concept" (p.27). It would not be dissonant for a subject in the Festinger and Carlsmith study to believe the task was boring and to tell someone else it was interesting if he also believed himself to be a liar. But to lie would be inconsistent with a concept of oneself as a decent and honest person. Similarly, working hard or suffering hardship to obtain an objective (in effort justification studies) would not be inconsistent with believing the objective is worthless if a person had a concept of himself as a "schnook." It is because most people have positive self-concepts that negative behavior and outcomes produce dissonance.

Aronson's refinement of dissonance theory to include the self-concept is an attempt to account for individual differences in tolerance for dissonance and in preferred modes of dissonance reduction. Differences in self-concept also help to explain why what is dissonant for one person is consonant for another. There is evidence that some personality characteristics associated with self-esteem may affect dissonance. Individuals who are classified as highly anxious demonstrate behavior in accord with dissonance predictions, while those who are low in anxiety behave according to incentive theory predictions (Steiner & Rogers, 1963). Similarly, persons high in their need for social approval display more dissonance than individuals with low need for social approval (Rosenberg, 1969).

3. Responsibility for Negative Consequences

In addition to perceived freedom and public commitment, it is also necessary for a person to anticipate that negative consequences will result from his counter-attitudinal behavior (Cooper & Worchel, 1970). In the Festinger and Carlsmith study of insufficient justification, the confederate would soon discover that the task was boring and the subject would be exposed as a liar. What would happen if he should meet the confederate on campus on a later occasion? Counter-attitudinal advocacy that leads another person to adopt "the wrong position" should be viewed by the actor as a negative consequence.

Cooper and Worchel demonstrated that negative consequences are implicated in the dissonance effect. They offered subjects either 1/2 hour or one hour extra credit for participation in their experiment if the subjects would tell a waiting "person" that the boring task they had just completed was interesting. Half the subjects learned they had succeeded in persuading the naive person and half learned that he did not believe them, but maintained his conviction that the task would be dull. Only those subjects who received a small incentive for engaging in the counter-attitudinal behavior *and* believed they had brought about the undesirable consequence of misleading the waiting person showed significant attitude change in the direction of the counter-attitudinal statement. The subjects who had sufficient justification for their behavior (a large incentive) or who believed they had not succeeded in convincing the waiting person that the task was interesting did not change their attitude.

Perceived freedom to perform counter-attitudinal behavior and public commitment to it are important for producing dissonance effects because these are the conditions under which a person feels responsible for actions that have negative consequences. Of course, it is possible to feel responsible even when actions are private or anonymous in character. If no one knew it was you who left the roller skates on the stairs, you would presumably still feel responsible if someone tripped over them and fell down the steps. Collins (1969) has proposed that an individual will experience dissonance if his overt behavior produces aversive consequences either for himself or for his audience, regardless of whether the act is counter-attitudinal or pro-attitudinal.

Hoyt, Henley, and Collins (1972) tested the responsibility hypothesis by asking subjects to write private counter-attitudinal essays strongly arguing against the practice of brushing teeth. All the subjects were told that both pro and con essays were being written for the experiment, but that enough of the pro essays had already been obtained from previous subjects. High-choice subjects were asked if they would be willing to help the experimenter by writing a con essay, but it was stressed that the final choice was strictly up to them. Low-choice subjects were simply assigned the task of writing a con essay. The subjects were informed that their essays would be read by junior high school students. Half the subjects in the free choice condition and half in the no choice condition were told that negative consequences would occur to the students, who would be persuaded by the essay. Their dental hygiene would deteriorate, and they would suffer an increase in cavities and other dental problems. The remainder of the subjects were told that the students would also read pro essays written by the Opinion Research Institute and the con essays written by the subjects would have little or no detrimental effect.

A dissonance effect was found only in the high choice, negative consequences condition and was manifested in a more negative post-behavior attitude toward toothbrushing by these subjects compared with those in any of the other three conditions. This shift of attitude toward the view expressed in the counter-attitudinal essay was obtained from subjects seated in the classroom and presumably represented an anonymous or private action, suggesting that even a private behavior may generate dissonance given the right set of conditions. However, the subjects were asked to place their essays under their seats; and they may

not have believed their actions were private. Furthermore, their attitudes toward toothbrushing were obtained on a so-called medical questionnaire, and since they all wrote con essays, their "real" opinions could be seen to be more or less consistent with their essays by the experimenter. It is therefore questionable whether the condition established was actually private. The description of procedures in the research report by Hoyt et al. are not sufficiently detailed to judge the probability of these suspicions.

Dissonance theory emphasizes an intrapsychic view of cognitive events according to which inconsistent cognitions arouse tension and motivate the individual to act to reduce the dissonance. Recent evidence, recounted above, suggests a very different view of the phenomenon. The necessary conditions for obtaining a dissonance-like effect are freedom of choice in performing a counter-attitudinal behavior, public commitment, and negative consequences resulting from the behavior. These conditions are associated with self-attribution of attitudes, self-esteem and anxiety, sense of responsibility, and a concern for social appearances. Cognitive dissonance has become less and less a topic of concern for individual (cognitive or motivational) psychologists and more and more a concern for social psychologists. An impression management theory has been proposed that attempts to provide an interpretation of cognitive dissonance experiments in purely social psychological terms.

E. Impression Management Theory

It is curious that men should only want to be consistent when they believe they have freely and publicly committed themselves to an action that has negative consequences. Why should tension be aroused by contradictory cognitions only under these conditions? Is the need for consistency innate or is it learned? These and many other questions about the phenomenon of dissonance led Tedeschi, Schlenker, and

Bonoma (1971) to devise an impression management theory in an effort to provide coherent answers to these questions. Essentially, it is assumed that subjects in dissonance experiments are engaged in managing the impressions of consistency that the experimenter forms about them; this concern is an aspect of evaluation apprehension, a factor known to be prevalent in psychological experiments.

Ralph Waldo Emerson, in his famous *Essay on Man,* reflected upon man's apparent overconcern with appearing consistent to those around him. He considered such a concern to be as foolish as worrying about your shadow on the wall and to be the "hobgoblin of little minds"; he pointed to geniuses as unafraid to contradict themselves in public. Dollard (1949) propounded the contrary view, that consistency is an important factor in everyday life: "Consistency between words and deeds enables men to participate in organized social life with good confidence that others will do what they say they will do. . . . Every man is under compulsion to keep his promises, to make his acts correspond with his verbal expressions. He constantly watches others to see they do likewise" (p.624). If a person follows an inconsistent pattern in his words and deeds, his credibility will be lowered and his ability to influence others will be undermined. These social reactions might not bother a preoccupied and confident genius, but the average man would be severely disturbed by them.

Consider what would happen to a person who was completely indifferent to consistency. Suppose he told you one day his name is George, but the next day he told you his name is Frank, and the following day that his name is Ernest. Suppose he told you he likes person A or object X and just as vehemently informed others that he hates both A and X. According to apparent whim, he also tells you at different times that he is a janitor, college professor, policeman, and accountant. Not only would such a person be considered mentally unsta-

ble (Asch, 1946), but his statements would surely not be believed and he would lack any ability to influence others effectively.

1. Socialization of Consistency

Concern for self-esteem should exist even when the individual is alone. However, Collins (1970) has stated "that an individual in our culture is not much concerned with the silly and foolish things he does while locked in a dark closet" (p. 212). Impression management theory views the behavior-attitude consistency shown in dissonance studies as a manifestation of the individual's attempts to rationalize or justify his counter-attitudinal behavior in order to avoid social punishment or disapproval for the negative consequences he has caused; to gain rewards and approval for being reliable, consistent, and predictable; and to maintain credibility for purposes of social influence.

According to Tedeschi et al., individuals learn they must have "reasons" for their behavior. Teachers, parents, supervisors, and friends ask the child to justify his actions to them. If his behavior is considered "bad" and he cannot offer sufficient justification for it, he may be punished; but if he can justify his behavior as desirable or at least necessary, he may escape punishment.

"Good" behavior does not need to be rationalized or justified by the actor. Even if his positive action is known by observers to be counter-attitudinal and, hence, contradictory, he need not engage in impression management to repair his image. He will generally be viewed positively by others, although he may be perceived as having reformed or as "changing his ways." On occasion he may gain even more credit for a positive behavior when it is known that it violates his beliefs. When there are no discernible environmental reasons impelling his behavior, and his principles are known to be contrary to what he is doing, his behavior may be perceived as truly altruistic and motivated entirely by a desire to help the target person.

In summary, the individual is taught to engage in verbal rationalizations to avoid punishment for the negative consequences he may bring about by his conduct. These rationalizations have been interpreted as dissonance-reducing behavior. Of course, they are only necessary when the actor can be held responsible for the consequences of his behavior; that is, when his behavior is freely undertaken and publicly known. The behavior-attitude consistency brought about by such rationalizations has been interpreted as cognitive consonance. The individual is also actively concerned for appearing consistent to avoid being stigmatized as "crazy" and to maintain a reputation as a credible person. Hence, dissonance-reduction is really a form of rationalization of behavior that serves two purposes: (1) justification of counter-attitudinal behavior as a means of avoiding retribution or punishment; and (2) restoration of the person's reputation as honest, reliable, and credible. Impression management theory denies that the individual has any internal need to be consistent and assumes that he would be unconcerned about contradictions between cognitions and behavior known only to himself.

2. Impression Management Interpretations of Dissonance Experiments

According to impression management theory, counter-attitudinal behavior is recognized as such by actors. They are neither confused nor ignorant regarding their "true" attitudes as implied by Bem's self-attribution theory, nor is any dissonance-like tension the necessary consequence of performing contradictory behavior. The actor is assumed to be aware of his prior attitude and his subsequent counter-attitudinal behavior. His concern is for how others will perceive the inconsistency and whether his action will lead to good or bad impressions of him because those percep-

tions are related to the reinforcements and punishments he receives from others.

Commitment and apparent freedom of choice are exactly the conditions that lead an observer to make an attribution to the person rather than the environment. When a subject in an experiment is first asked about his attitude toward an issue, and then chooses to make a counter-attitudinal statement under conditions providing little external incentive, an observer (the experimenter) may make two contradictory attributions: (1) that the subject says he believes X, but (2) that the subject freely commits himself to the position that he believes not-X. Under these conditions and when the subject's counter-attitudinal behavior has negative consequences, he has a problem of managing the impressions others have of him. He must mend his image so that he is not considered bad or inconsistent.

In the Festinger and Carlsmith study of insufficient justification, the subjects were not asked how interesting they considered the task to be until after they had informed a waiting person that it was very interesting. The actual measurement was obtained by someone other than the original experimenter. To avoid leaving the impression with the experimenter that they were lying to the waiting person, the subjects in the $1 condition said the task was interesting. Of course, the experimenter might believe the task was really boring but it would not be completely implausible for the subject to find it at least moderately interesting. What choice does the subject have? The experimenter has placed him in a situation where he must either admit that he finds a boring task interesting or that he lied to another person. As Walster, Berscheid, and Barclay (1967) have suggested, the subjects caught up in this interpersonal dilemma choose that mode of dissonance reduction that is least likely to the challenged by future events. Actually, Festinger and Carlsmith made the choice easy for subjects by remarking that "Most of our subjects tell us afterward that they found it quite inter-esting" (p.206), just before the ratings of the task were obtained. Subjects in the $20 condition were more willing to admit telling a lie because because they had suf-ficient justification for their behavior. It could be assumed that almost any college student would do the same thing for the same amount of money. The "lie" could be attributed to the money (an external factor) rather than the subject's true char-acter (a personal factor).

The conditions which attribution theory proposes as leading to a person attribution rather than an environmental attribution are the same as the conditions empirically demonstrated as necessary for producing dissonance effects. We have already noted the similarity between the necessary condi-tions for obtaining a dissonance effect and the augmentation principle. Commitment to negative behavior under low incentive conditions allows an observer to make an attribution to personal causes. Attribution theory also assumes that a person must have knowledge of the probable conse-quences of his actions before he can be held responsible for their effects (Heider, 1958; see Chapter 4, I, C). According to impres-sion management theory, dissonance ef-fects should not be obtained when the per-son does not have foreknowledge of the consequences that will follow his counter-attitudinal behavior. The individual will not need to rationalize his behavior under such conditions because others will not be able to hold him responsible for its effects. Freedman (1963) found that when subjects were not informed about the consequences of their counter-attitudinal behavior until *after* it had been performed, no dissonance was aroused.

Insufficient justification experiments may be interpreted as studies of the verbal rationalizations of counter-attitudinal be-havior used by subjects to create a positive impression of themselves for the experi-menter. Effort justification may be similarly explained. After being induced to work

hard or to suffer much to obtain an objec-tive, a person might very well be evaluated as a fool if he told the observer the objective was not worth the effort. Effort justifica-tion is an attempt by subjects to rationalize their behavior as merited by the value of the objective sought. It is reasonable and laudable to work hard or endure hardships for something really worthwhile.

Research on post-decisional dissonance demonstrates that subjects will extol the vir-tues of their decisions to other people; to do otherwise would require that they admit to making stupid or wrong decisions. Suppose someone decided to buy a Toyota after seriously considering the alternative of a Datsun and you asked him about the rela-tive merits of the two types of automobiles. What would you think of him if he told you he preferred the Datsun? By emphasizing the value of his choice and derogating the nonchosen alternatives, he creates the im-pression that he has good values and sound judgment. According to impression man-agement theory, the spreading effect that occurs following decision-making is a man-ifestation of the individual's rationalization of his choice.

3. Evidence for Impression Management Theory

Several recent experiments have pitted the predictions of impression management theory against those of alternative theories of dissonance phenomena. Schlenker (1975) reinterpreted the grasshopper study of Zimbardo et al. It may be recalled that subjects said they liked the grasshoppers better when they had volunteered to taste them for an unattractive doctor, and re-ported liking them less when they had vol-unteered at the request of an attractive doc-tor. Zimbardo et al. interpreted this effect as due to dissonance because the volunteers in the unattractive source condition had insufficient reason for eating the grasshop-pers, and as a result of the need to reduce dissonance created by their contradictory behavior, enhanced their value. It would be consistent to have volunteered if the food was tasty. This interpretation emphasizes the evaluation of grasshoppers by subjects in the unattractive source condition, but Schlenker points out that the difference between the two experimental groups may derive from the subjects in the attractive source condition. Referring to the grasshoppers as a survival food implies they are not very tasty; otherwise they might be referred to as a delicacy or staple. Subjects who volunteered for the attractive doctor expressed more dislike for the food because they were prone to agree with the implied evaluation held by the doctor. The so-called dissonance effect here may only be an instance of one of the best-known principles in social psychology: a liked source of influence will be more effective than a disliked source (see Chapter 8).

If Schlenker's interpretation is correct, the subjects in this study would have rated the grasshoppers in exactly the opposite way had the attractive doctor implied that the food was a delicacy. Subjects tend to agree with an attractive source because they want to create a favorable impression of themselves, but they are relatively unconcerned about the impression an unattractive person forms of them. Schlenker asked students to volunteer for an experimental sensitivity group. Each subject was required to go through an initiation procedure involving shock that was alleged to be a test of emotional stability. The attractiveness of the experimenter was manipulated; he either treated the subjects in a friendly and courteous fashion, smiling frequently and maintaining a good deal of eye contact, or he was rude and unfriendly, indicating disdain for the value of working with undergraduates. The attitude of the experimenter toward sensitivity groups was also varied; whichever demeanor he displayed toward the subjects, he either indicated that he had bet the project director the sensitivity groups would be productive and worthwhile or that he had made the opposite bet.

Thus the experimental design consisted of an attractive or unattractive experimenter who either did or did not believe in the value of sensitivity groups.

Following the initiation ceremony, the subjects were assigned to a sensitivity group that had already met once. Since all sessions were tape-recorded they were permitted to listen to a 20-minute segment of the first meeting of their assigned group. The tape contained a boring series of disconnected statements made by several male and female voices and was filled with long pauses. The subjects were told that the tape segment was entirely representative of the first meeting and were asked to fill out a questionnaire that had been completed by the other members of their group.

What predictions would dissonance theory make about how such subjects would like their groups? All of them had gone through a noxious experience to join the group, and they had heard a boring group discussion. They had little external reason to continue in the experiment when they were given the option to discontinue before being shocked, especially when the experimenter indicated an unfavorable attitude toward sensitivity groups. Subjects in the unattractive experimenter condition would have the least reason for staying in the experiment and hence should have suffered more dissonance when they heard the boring group discussion than subjects in the attractive experimenter condition (cf. Zimbardo et al.) Dissonance theory thus would predict a more favorable rating of the group by subjects who disliked the experimenter than by those who liked him. As can be seen in Figure 5.5, this prediction is clearly disconfirmed. According to impression management theory, these subjects should have been unconcerned about the impression the disliked experimenter had of them, while they should have rated the group in a manner consistent with the opinion expressed by the liked experimenter. The results shown in Figure 5.5 confirm these predictions.

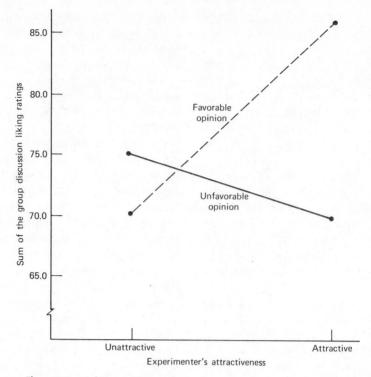

Figure 5.5.   Subjects ratings of the boring group discussion on a 100-point scale. (After Schlenker, 1975.)

Gaes, Rivera, and Tedeschi (1975) employed the same essay-writing paradigm for studying insufficient justification that was used by Hoyt, et al. (i.e., anti-toothbrushing essays to be given to junior high school students). All subjects experienced the conditions of free choice and negative consequences. Half of the subjects had to identify themselves publicly with their counter-attitudinal essays, while the remainder wrote anonymous essays. The subjects' subsequent attitudes towards toothbrushing were measured by one of two methods: the usual paper-and-pencil scale or a bogus pipeline measure (see description in Chapter 4, II, C). While paper-and-pencil tests can be used by subjects to "fake good," they should be restrained from such "faking" in the bogus pipeline condition because of the belief that the lie-detecting character of the bogus pipeline would reveal their lack of candor, making them look bad. A dissonance-like effect was found

only in the public, paper-and-pencil condition of the experiment in which subjects indicated more agreement with the statement that "toothbrushing is harmful." Why did a bogus pipeline erase the effect? The obvious implication is that subjects knowingly lie to the experimenter in the paper-and-pencil condition, but they do not lie in the bogus pipeline condition because they believe they will be discovered. These results support the interpretation that subjects consciously attempt to manipulate the experimenter's evaluation of them. It is interesting to note that subjects in the paper-and-pencil condition rated themselves as more consistent than did those in the bogus pipeline condition. The former were actually more consistent when the essay writing required a public commitment, but they were rather inconsistent when they remained anonymous. Apparently, subjects will even fake self-reports of consistency when they cannot be discovered, but do not engage in this form of impression management when their self-reports are gathered by a bogus pipeline technique.

Goethals, Reckman, and Rothman (1973) found that subjects displayed a consistency of attitudes as a way of managing impressions of themselves. Subjects' attitudes toward a consumer boycott were assessed in their residence rooms purportedly as a part of an economics project. Several weeks later, they were asked to participate in a psychology experiment in which the experimenter was a different person. Subjects were asked to deliver a speech opposing boycotts, a position that was known to be counterattitudinal because of the earlier survey. The usual practice of giving the subjects a choice of giving a pro speech that was not needed by the experimenter was followed. After the speech a second assessment of attitudes toward boycotts was made. Subjects showed a significant change in the direction of the counterattitudinal speech from their pre-experimental attitudes—an effect that resembles dissonance reduction. A number of days later the attitudes of subjects were obtained for a third time—half by the economics project surveyor and half by the psychology experimenter. The attitude expressed by the subjects was dependent on who was asking the question. When the third assessment was made by the psychology experimenter, subjects maintained the attitudes expressed after giving the speech; but when it was made by the economics surveyor, subjects reverted back to their pre-experimental attitudes. Thus, both groups maintained consistency at the third assessment, but the consistency was with the attitudes they had formerly expressed to the person who was now questioning them.

VI. CHAPTER SUMMARY

An attitude is a combination of a belief with a value. Beliefs are organized into vertical and horizontal structures, and lower order beliefs may serve as a basis for higher order, derived beliefs. Beliefs usually involve expectations of response-outcome contingencies. The expectations of the person are held with a greater or lesser degree of confidence. The outcome associated with a belief has a particular value for the person. Independent assessments of the probabilities associated with beliefs and of the values associated with outcomes have enabled researchers to predict a person's attitudes.

Rosenberg's means-ends theory asserts that the means used to attain valued ends acquire value in themselves. The value of an instrumental act can be determined by assessing the probabilities and values associated with all its outcomes. The sum of the products of the probabilities and values yield a reasonable estimate of the individual's attitude toward the instrumental act. A person's attitude toward an object may be predicted from the probability that the object or person has a particular trait and the value rating of each such trait.

Ajzen and Fishbein have developed a theory of behavioral intentions which includes attitudes toward an act, personal norms, perception of social norms, and the need to conform to social expectations. These four factors are combined to predict the person's verbal commitments to act. While this theory has been reasonably successful in predicting verbal statements, it has been less successful in predicting actual behavior.

A persons beliefs and attitudes serve as anchors for making social judgments and agreeing or disagreeing with statements or opinions regarding various issues. Assimilation and contrast effects occur based on the anchor of existing attitudes and the latitudes of acceptance, rejection, and non-commitment associated with the strength of the anchors and the ego-involvement of the subjects.

Balance theory proposes that individuals seek evaluative consistency among related attitudes. Congruity theory deals with the affective consistency among a source, an issue, and the source's communication. Whenever related cognitions are unbalanced or incongruous, the affective values of the relations among elements and of the elements themselves are thought to change to restore balance or achieve congruity. But the evidence for these theories is not convincing; biases related to positivity and similarity often occur.

It has become apparent from the evidence that the assumption of a direct relationship between attitudes and behavior is incorrect. A number of reasons has been offered for the failure to find consistency. Assessing attitudes is difficult, and measured responses are susceptible to faking and impression management by respondents. As a result, the stated attitudes of subjects may not reflect their "private" or "true" attitudes. The verbal behavior of the individual often serves different functions and operates under different reinforcement schedules than his motor behavior. There is no necessary connection between the two response systems and little reason to expect much consistency between them.

The beliefs and values of the individual are of paramount importance in determining his behavior. However, no single cognitive element, such as an attitude, may be sufficient for successfully predicting the behavior he will emit in any given social situation. The ability to predict behavior from knowledge of an attitude may be improved by a consideration of: (1) other relevant attitudes held by an individual, (2) whether his attitudes lead to contradictory or competing responses, and (3) his motives. In addition, global attitudes provide a poor basis from which to predict specific behavior. Lack of ability or skills may also make a person appear hypocritical if he is unable to produce those responses that would be consistent with his attitudes. A potential for costs and gains may cause an individual to shift either his attitudes or his behavior or both, hence disturbing the consistency between his prior attitudes and his subsequent behavior. Finally, the individual's need to influence others and to manage his image often requires him to feign attitudes he does not hold. These and other factors will most probably be incorporated in future attitude theories designed to predict overt behavior.

Cognitive dissonance theory has been primarily concerned with cognitions regarding the actor's own behavior. Pairs of cognitive elements may be dissonant, consonant, or irrelevant. The presence of dissonance motivates the individual to reduce tension by changes in behavior, changes in cognitions, and integration of the dissonant elements into a larger set of cognitions. These dissonance-reducing mechanisms restore consonance to the cognitive elements or render them irrelevant to one another.

Dissonance results when an individual has insufficient justification for his counterattitudinal behavior, when great effort or hardship is undergone for outcomes of little worth, or when difficult choices between alternatives are made. In each of these cases, changes in attitudes follow changes in behavior. Other theories of cognitive structure attempt to predict behavior from attitudes; dissonance theory predictions are in the other direction. Although there may be little consistency between attitudes and behavior, there apparently is a good deal of consistency between behavior and attitudes.

The original assumption that contradictory cognitions automatically produce dissonance-reducing behavior has been considerably modified as we have come to understand the limiting conditions for finding dissonance-like effects in the laboratory. Generally, counterattitudinal behavior must be freely chosen (or else the subjects must believe the experimenter or observer thinks it was freely chosen), the person must have publicly committed himself to the behavior, and it must have negative consequences either for the self or for another. These limiting conditions have spawned alternative theories of these phenomena, including self-attribution, self-esteem, and impression management theories. These alternative theories serve as the basis for much of the contemporary research on dissonance-like phenomena.

SUGGESTED READINGS

Feldman, S. (Ed.) *Cognitive consistency*. New York: Academic Press, 1966. Summary review of research and critical discussion of the major theories of cognitive consistency for the more advanced reader.

Festinger, L., Riecken, H. W., and Schachter, S. *When prophecy fails*. Minneapolis: Univ. of Minnesota, 1956. A very readable account of the original study from which dissonance theory emerged.

Goffman, E. *The presentation of self in everyday life*. New York: Doubleday Anchor, 1959. A fascinating and path-breaking book concerning the methods and problems of impression management.

Insko, C. A., and Schopler, J. *Experimental social psychology*. New York: Academic Press, 1972. The first five chapters offer a very thorough exposition of attitude-behavior and behavior-attitude relationships for the introductory reader.

CHAPTER **6**

Social Learning and Development

CHAPTER PREVIEW

So far in Part 2 we have concentrated on the cognitive and social processes that are involved in the way the individual perceives, interprets, and structures physical and social reality. Although these factors affect everyone, observations reveal astonishing cross-cultural differences in the way persons view the world and act toward it. Social habits, normative standards, kinds of reinforcements, languages, and much else vary from one society to another. These cultural variations are not based on genetic differences between human groups, but are due to the socialization of the individual in his society. *Socialization* may be defined as "the whole process by which an individual develops, through interaction with other people, his specific patterns of socially relevant behavior" (Zigler & Child, 1969, p. 474). Socialization is a life-long experience involving continual adjustments to change, including childhood, adolescence, adulthood, and marriage, parenthood, old age, and so on. In this chapter we will focus on the socialization of the child.

Some wag once defined a newborn infant as a long alimentary canal connected to a loud noise at one end and a lack of responsibility at the other. The infant does not have a language, a self-concept, beliefs, attitudes, or values, and is totally dependent on others for survival. He cannot even distinguish himself as separate from his environment and eventually takes obvious delight in discovering his own hands and feet. Although the infant has a set of potentialities provided by his genetic endowment, there is nothing inevitable about what kind of social being he will be.

The early social experiences of the individual are inestimably important to subsequent development. Cases of *feral* children, who were abandoned in the wilds and later captured, suggest the importance of socialization. A wild boy was found in the woods of Aveyron in France in 1799. He was about eleven years of age and was given the name of Victor. He was naked and "a disgustingly dirty child affected with spasmotic movements and often convulsions who swayed back and forth ceaselessly like certain animals in a menagerie, who bit and scratched those who opposed him, who showed no sort of affection for those who attended him; and who was in short, indifferent to everything and attentive to nothing" (Itard, 1962, p. 4).

Victor was nearly a deaf-mute, but he learned to dress himself and to sleep without wetting his bed. However, he never learned to walk upright. He preferred a crouching shuffle, using his hands to help himself along, somewhat like a chimpanzee. Itard spent five years trying to train Victor to understand a few words. Itard would point out a word and Victor would hunt for the referent object. Victor also developed some human emotional responses, such as grief and affection. Yet Itard observed that an affectionate greeting after an absence (Victor often ran away) was less a function of how long Victor had been gone than of how much suffering he had endured while he was gone and the advantages he received when he returned. His emotions were egocentric rather than truly social; he could not feel empathy for another person. The relationship between Victor and Dr. Itard was sensitively portrayed in Trufaut's classic motion picture "The Wild Boy."

We do not want to draw hasty conclusions from the observation of a few feral children. Perhaps they were originally abandoned because of a physical or mental deficiency. Some genetic factor might be responsible for their peculiar behavior and their inability to learn the habits of their culture. Nevertheless, these few cases do provide striking examples of the thesis, generally accepted by social psychologists, that infants must be socialized into human beings.

Two major theoretical approaches have been taken in the study of the socialization process. A *learning approach* emphasizes the adaptive response of the child to his experiences. An extreme reinforcement view of learning was promulgated by John Watson, who claimed he could make a child into anything at all—lawyer, thief, or indian chief—if he were given total control over the rewards and punishments the child experienced. Particularly important in socialization are the social reinforcements provided by significant others. A non-reinforcement view of learning has been proposed by Bandura (1969), who has convincingly demonstrated that observation of a model's behavior may elicit imitative responses from the observer. The child learns a wide variety of responses through the observation of models, many of which probably could not be learned in any other way.

The *developmental approach* to socialization assumes that certain critical periods or stages occur, during which the child is maximally prepared to acquire emotional attachments, language, and motor skills. Most influential among developmental theories is Piaget's (1952) theory of cognitive organization. He views the child as an active, information-seeking organism who has certain basic response capabilities. Through interactions with his environment, the child develops cognitive structures (schemata) which relate means (his actions) and ends (outcomes of his actions). The modes of thought of the individual are presumed to evolve through a series of qualitatively different stages as he matures and gains more experience. This cognitive development is believed to influence the individual's moral judgments and his transgressive behavior, as well as his self-concept.

The learning and developmental approaches often conflict with one another, but can also be interpreted as complementary views of socialization. The basic conflicts between the two approaches are sharpest when considering moral development, transgression behavior, and the formation of self-concept. We shall examine some of the basic arguments and relevant research evidence.

I. SOCIAL REINFORCEMENT AND DEPENDENCE ON APPROVAL

An empirical definition of reinforcement is that it is anything the organism will approach and maintain and will do nothing to avoid or escape. A punishment is something the organism will avoid or escape and will do nothing to maintain or bring about. Psychologists have clearly demonstrated the importance of material reinforcement in determining behavior. We take it as axiomatic here that food, water, comfort, sexual pleasure, money, and so forth, are rewarding; while starvation, water deprivation, sleep deprivation, shock and bodily injury are punishing. In general, organisms repeat responses that are reinforced and suppress responses that are punished.

People are not only motivated to achieve material reinforcement, but also to seek signs of social approval from relevant others. One person may succeed in influencing another's behavior by bestowing praise and approval or by assigning blame and disapproval. Sometimes just a smile or a frown will have a telling effect on performance. Because they are often uncertain about the appropriateness of their behavior, children often rely on the judgments and evaluations of others as behavioral cues more than adults do. Reassurance, confirmation of opinions, affection, approval, and nurturance are various forms of social reinforcement that play an important role in the child's structuring of social reality and in determining his actions.

The effectiveness of social approval has been convincingly demonstrated in the laboratory. However, there appear to be individual differences among persons in the degree to which they are responsive to or dependent on social approval. Also, states of relative deprivation or satiation in the amount of social approval experienced by a person makes him more or less susceptible to the influence of social reinforcement. Lack of self-confidence or anxiety seem to be implicated in dependence on approval. An emerging social influence view of social reinforcements is that they provide information or cues that can be used by the actor to determine what the source wants him to do. Whether the actor will behave in a manner calculated to please the source depends on a large number of other factors.

A. The Effectiveness of Social Reinforcement

People communicate verbal approval to each other by saying "fine," "good," "excellent," "un-huh," "right." Greenspoon (1955) has demonstrated that these verbal communications may act as reinforcements in increasing the frequency of a particular behavior emitted by an actor. His subjects were asked to tell the experimenter all the nouns they could think in a period of 50 minutes. During the first 25 minutes no

experimental manipulations were performed, and a record was kept of the relative frequencies of singular and plural nouns emitted by the subjects. In the second 25 minutes one of five different conditions was created. In the first, plural nouns were positively reinforced by the experimenter, who said "mmm-hmm" after each one. In the second, plurals were negatively reinforced or disapproved by saying "huh-uh." In the third and fourth conditions, singular nouns were similarly approved or disapproved, and in the fifth or control condition, the experimenter said nothing. Pairing "mmm-hmm" with behavior had effects similar to those produced by material reinforcement; "huh-uh" produced effects similar to those found with material punishment. "Mmm-hmm" increased the production of plural nouns in the first group and singular nouns in the third group, while "huh-uh" decreased the number of plural nouns in the second group. No change in the use of plural and singular nouns occurred in the control group.

In less artificial, non-laboratory settings, Verplanck (1955) had 17 student experimenters converse with friends at various places around the campus. Of course, the friends were not aware that they were under careful observation. The experimenters deliberately reinforced statements of opinions either by indicating agreement ("uh-huh") or by restating the opinion. These tactics served to increase the number of opinions emitted by the students. Verbal approval may also affect the kind of clothes people choose to wear. Calvin (1962) had the 24 members of his psychology class walk around the campus of a small college and compliment other students on the color of their clothing. The number wearing blue increased with social reinforcement from 25 to 38 percent in five days, and was reduced to 27 percent when reinforcement was discontinued. Likewise, the wearing of red was increased from 13 to 22 percent in a period of five days.

B.   Individual Differences in Approval Dependency

Crowne and Marlowe (1964) developed a scale to measure the degree to which individuals need social approval from others. Crowne and Strickland (1961) used this scale to identify subjects who were relatively high or low in approval dependence. The subjects were subsequently asked to emit nouns, as in the Greenspoon study, and were either positively ("mmm-hmm" and a head nod) or negatively ("uh-uh" and a head shake) reinforced for plural nouns. The subjects who scored high on need for approval responded by producing more plural nouns when positively reinforced and fewer when negatively reinforced. Those who scored low in approval dependency did not respond differentially to the reinforcement conditions; their production of plural nouns was very similar to that of subjects in nonreinforced control groups (see Figure 6.1). Apparently, there are in-

dividual differences in the degree to which persons are influenced by the social approbation of others.

C.   States of Deprivation and Satiation

The value of material reinforcements, such as food and drink, vary with the state of deprivation or satiation of the organism. A rat's performance in a maze or Skinner box will be facilitated by food or water rewards when he has been prevented from eating or drinking for 24 hours; but these rewards are ineffective when he has had free access to an abundant supply just before he is placed in the experimental situation (Hull, 1952).

Gewirtz and Baer (1958) have shown that the need for social approval has motivational characteristics similar to those resulting from material reinforcement; deprivation and satiation effects occur with social reinforcement as well. Their experiment was conducted in an elementary school with

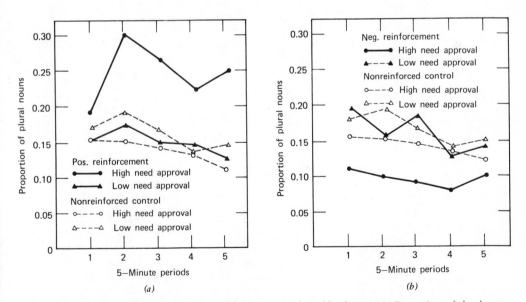

Figure 6.1.   Conditioning of verbal behavior. (After Crowne and Strickland, 1961.) *(a)* Proportions of plural nouns given by high and low need approval groups under positive reinforcement and nonreinforced control conditions; *(b)* Proportions of plural nouns given by high and low need approval groups under negative reinforcement and nonreinforced control conditions.

children 6 to 9 years old. In a deprivation condition, each child was escorted from his classroom to a room used for the purposes of the study; the experimenter maintained a quiet and professional manner toward the child and then left him alone in a room for 20 minutes "because the game he was to play was in use." In a satiation condition the experimenter was pleasant toward the child during the walk. During the 20-minute waiting period, the child was allowed to play with drawing materials and the experimenter stayed in the room, directing a steady stream of friendly conversation toward him, including statements of praise and admiration whenever he made references toward himself during conversation. In a (third) non-deprivation condition, the experimenter was quiet and professional during the walk down the hall, but there was no 20-minute wait; the child was put right to work on the experimental task.

All the children were asked to play a game that consisted of dropping marbles into one of two holes in the top of a box; the marbles returned to an open trough at the bottom of the box. During the first four minutes, a record was kept of the number of times the child attempted to start a conversation with the experimenter, who restricted herself to brief but friendly answers. During the fourth minute the experimenter observed how many marbles were dropped in each of the two holes, thereby determining which of the two the child preferred. Beginning with the fifth minute, ten minutes of social reinforcement ("good," "mmm-hmm," "fine") were administered each time the child dropped a marble into the nonpreferred hole.

The effects of verbal reinforcement on the deprived and satiated children are shown in Figure 6.2. Children in the deprivation condition made a greater shift to

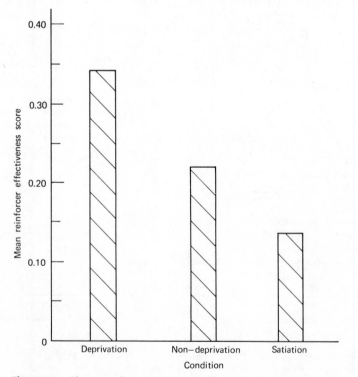

Figure 6.2.   The means for social approval effectiveness for the three conditions. (After Gewirtz and Baer, 1958, p. 169.)

their nonpreferred hole than did children in the non-deprivation control condition, who, in turn, were more responsive than were children in the satiation condition. The frequency of their attempts to initiate conversation with the experimenter reflected a similar pattern; deprived children made more attempts to talk than non-deprived children. These deprivation and satiation effects may not be restricted to children. How often have you sensed a need for social interaction after long periods of private study or social isolation, and how often have you longed for privacy and seclusion after a particularly intense round of social interaction?

D. Anxiety and Approval Dependency

The deprivation procedure of placing a small child in a room by himself for twenty minutes may cause him to be anxious. The subsequent effectiveness of social approval may therefore be attributable to a need for reassurance created by an anxiety-provoking situation, rather than to social deprivation. Walters and Ray (1960) examined the relationship of anxiety to verbal reinforcement, creating isolation and satiation conditions similar to those used by Gewirtz and Baer. Half the subjects in both conditions were made anxious by having them wait in a room containing mysterious equipment, and half were not. In the low anxiety condition, the child was given a warm and reassuring explanation of what was going to occur.

There was greater responsiveness to reinforcement on the marble-dropping task by anxious than by nonanxious children and the responsiveness was greatest in the condition involving both isolation and anxiety. The reassurance value of social approval was indicated by the anxiety results. Approval dependence, like information dependence, is greater when the structure of the situation is ambiguous.

While situational factors may create transient states of anxiety, people also vary in the amount of anxiety they chronically display. Taffel (1955) found a strong positive relationship between an individual's level of chronic anxiety and his responsiveness to social reinforcement. Psychiatric patients were identified as high or low in chronic anxiety by the way they responded to a paper-and-pencil test. The subjects were then given the task of making up sentences. On each trial they were presented with a list of the same six pronouns (I, he, she, we, you, they) and a verb and were instructed to use one of the pronouns and a verb in constructing a sentence. Whenever the subject used the pronouns "I" or "we" in making up a sentence, the experimenter said "good" or "mmm-hmm." High anxiety patients emitted more first person pronouns in forming their sentences than did low anxiety patients. These findings were replicated by Sarason (1958); but Buss and Gerjuoy (1958) and Spielberger, DeNike, and Stein (1965) found just the opposite relationship between measured chronic anxiety and the effectiveness of social reinforcement. These contradictory findings suggest that chronically anxious persons are reassured by the social approval of others in some situations, but may be made even more anxious by the presence of others in other situations. Clarification of these relationships awaits further research.

E. Social Reinforcement, Information, and Influence

Dulany (1962) has questioned the view that social reinforcements automatically and incrementally change a person's behavior without awareness of what is transpiring. Instead, the person is considered as an active decisionmaker, who interprets social reinforcement as tacit communication. "Mmm-hmm" and "good" not only provide reassurance but also present information relevant to solving tasks and interpersonal problems. For example, in Taffel's task each subject was asked to create sentences. He learned over the trials that the experimenter emitted a social reinforcer only when a certain pronoun was used. Once the subject discovered this, he could either provide the response the experimenter appeared to want or he could withhold the response.

In confronting tacit communication of this kind the target is faced with a decoding problem; he must discover the contingency relating his behavior to the social reinforcement emitted by the source. Presumably, the repeated association of a reinforcer with the same type of response allows the target to decode the "rule" governing the response-reinforcement connection.

Page (1970) has interpreted the verbal reinforcement paradigm of Greenspoon and Taffel as presenting the subjects with three tasks: (1) discovering the connection between their own responses and the verbal reinforcement of the experimenter; (2) discovering what the experimenter wants them to do; and (3) deciding whether to comply or not to comply. The verbal reinforcement provides information about the "correct" responses, the desires of the experimenter, and the consequences of the subject's actions. For example, in Taffel's procedure the experimenter transmits the tacit promise, "If you use the pronouns 'I' or 'we' in constructing sentences, I will indicate my social approval by saying 'good'." According to Page's analysis, verbal reinforcement studies involve aspects of both social perception and social influence.

Early research on social reinforcement emphasized the operant conditioning nature of the effects obtained. Subjects were assumed to be unaware of the way in which experimenters were shaping their behavior. In fact, any subjects who reported awareness of the response-reinforcement contingency were dropped from the experiments. For example, approximately 11 percent of the subjects were dropped from the Crowne and Strickland study reported above because of their awareness. A major dispute has been raging for years about whether subjects who do not report "aware-

ness" really are unaware and whether a subject must be conscious of the contingency before his performance is affected by it. The controversy boils down to the question whether subjects blindly respond to the clever manipulations of an experimenter or easily decode the experimenter's wishes and then deliberately decide whether to cooperate.

In a test of the awareness hypothesis, DeNike (1964) asked subjects to write down their thoughts about the experiment after each block of 25 trials. The subjects who could articulate the response-reinforcement contingency were considered to be aware and those who could not were considered to be nonaware. The aware subjects displayed responsiveness to verbal reinforcement, whereas unaware subjects showed no change in their performance over the trials. Furthermore, the subjects displayed no increase in the frequency of the critical responses until they were able to report the contingency.

Subsequent investigations have questioned DeNike's results. We will skirt the many contradictory experiments that have been reported and the complicated theoretical and methodological issues that have arisen concerning the meaning and measurement of "awareness." Bandura's (1969) conclusion can be endorsed: "The overall evidence would seem to indicate that learning can take place without awareness, albeit at a slow rate, but that the symbolic representation of response-reinforcement contingencies can markedly accelerate appropriate responsiveness" (p. 577).

Both the need for social approval and social influence interpretations of social reinforcement suggest that the characteristics of the person administering it will be important to their effectiveness. As we shall see in Chapter 8, two important characteristics that enhance influence effectiveness are the attractiveness and expertness of the source. A target person is more apt to be persuaded by a friend than an enemy and is more influenced by the arguments of an expert than of a fraud. In tests of an influence theory of social reinforcement, Sapolsky (1960) and Brown, Helm, and Tedeschi (1973) manipulated the attractiveness of the experimenter, who then administered social reinforcements in a Taffel task. Significant increases in reinforced responses occurred among subjects who liked the experimenter, but not for an unattractive experimenter. It is difficult to say whether these results were due to differences in attentiveness and decoding by subjects or whether they were simply differentially compliant to the tacit requests of the experimenter.

Helm, Brown, and Tedeschi (1972) found a similar effect of experimenter expertness. Half their subjects were greeted by a nicely dressed young man who introduced himself as a graduate student and told them that the experiment was his dissertation project. The other half were greeted by the same young man dressed in blue jeans and T-shirt; he introduced himself as a sophomore who was fulfilling an experimental psychology course requirement. Post-experimental questionnaires established that the Ph.D. student was perceived as more intelligent and was more respected than the sophomore. Subjects produced more "I's" and "we's" in the Taffel task for the former than for the latter. The subjects were therefore more compliant to the tacit requests of the more prestigious person.

F. Age and the Effectiveness of Social Reinforcers

Children are more dependent on others than are adults. The child constantly seeks candy, cookies, and toys, is perpetually asking questions and receiving instructions or orders, and is subjected to many expressions of approval and reassurance or disapproval and correction. The verbal reinforcement administered by relevant others plays an important role in the socialization process. Praise, agreement, and ad-

monishments provide information about the socially acceptable judgments, evaluations, and responses he needs to acquire as he learns about his social world, his place in it, and the normative structure of his social groups.

There is considerable evidence that the rewarding or inhibiting effects of simple verbal expressions of approval or disapproval vary with the age, sex, social class, and race of the child (Stevenson, 1965). Social reinforcers tend to decrease in effectiveness with age, and are more effective with females than males, with lower class than middle class children, and with blacks than whites. Praise ("good" or "fine") is more effective with lower class children, while information cues ("right" or "correct") are most effective with middle class children. According to Gewirtz (1954), the effectiveness of praise and approval diminishes with maturity and the information value of social reinforcement becomes more important with age. This change in the basis of social reinforcement from praise to information as a function of age reflects a shift from a dependency on the evaluation of others toward a concern with self-appraisals and learning socially appropriate behavior.

II. MODELING AND IMITATION

At the beginning of the 20th century the theories of Edward Thorndike and John Dewey produced a revolutionary impact on American education. The basic idea behind these theories was that practice and rehearsal of actual behavior was critical for learning; their new teaching plans incorporated the principle of "learning by doing." But practice was not considered to be enough. Correct responses had to be rewarded and incorrect responses were either to be ignored or punished. The view that learning is a process involving the selective reinforcement of responses was challenged by Edward Tolman, who believed that rats can symbolically represent environmental events without making any responses and without receiving any reinforcement at all. According to Tolman, learning can occur as the result of mere observation of events, but behavior is regulated by expected rewards and punishments.

Anyone who has seen an infant learn to wave "bye-bye" or to emit a simple verbal response like "dada" is aware that children imitate the behavior of adults. A 19th century French sociologist, Tarde (1903), considered imitation to be the most important factor in socialization. Cultural and linguistic habits were believed to be transmitted through imitation, a kind of hypnotic state during which a photographic image of a model's behavior formed in the observer's mind. Innovations, wars, and arguments were believed to be products of the imitation of contradictory models. For example, the invention of the plow could be interpreted as the consequence of trying to imitate both the digging of a hole in the ground with a stick or shovel and the evisceration of a slain animal with a knife.

McDougall (1908) was also impressed with the pervasive tendency of people to imitate habits, fads, and fashions. He considered imitation to be an inborn tendency, an instinct. Criticisms of McDougall's view point to the fact that hypothetical innate tendencies do not account for why observers imitate some models and not others, or why some people maintain independence while others are strongly influenced by the actions of those around them.

Miller and Dollard (1941) took an important first step in explaining the process of imitation in terms of the concepts of learning theory. They proposed that a model's behavior serves as a cue for the responses of an observer. When an observer's responses happen to match those of the model and are rewarded, a tendency to imitate the model is learned. The process is termed *matched-dependent behavior*.

It has become clear that matched-dependent behavior constitutes only a lim-

ited form of imitation. Over the last decade, Bandura (1969, 1971, 1973) has established that learning may occur even when an observer is not allowed to match a model's behavior immediately after observing a model and even if neither the model nor the observer are rewarded for their behavior. Bandura has been careful to distinguish between learning behavior and performing it. His research has been focused primarily on the effects of reinforcement on the performance of imitative behavior. Characteristics of the model have been shown to be important in determining the probability of imitative responses by observers, and recent research suggests an interpretation of modeling in terms of social influence. In any case, the range of behavior that may be learned through modeling is virtually unlimited and includes much that probably cannot be learned in any other way.

A. VICARIOUS LEARNING THROUGH OBSERVATION

Bandura's theory of vicarious learning assumes that observers acquire symbolic representations of modeled activities. The model's behavior and its outcomes provide the observer with information about the causal structure of the environment and the incentives that may exist for performing various kinds of behavior. We have referred to the individual's encoding of such information as *schemata*. The observer develops beliefs about what behavior leads to which outcomes in unfamiliar situations by watching what happens to the model. In effect, the model tacitly communicates his experiences in the situation and the observer profits from them (Tedeschi, Bonoma, & Schlenker, 1972). This social influence approach to modeling views the observer as engaged in three essential tasks: (1) decoding the communication to understand the causal contingencies transmitted; (2) determining the relevancy and appropriateness of the information received for his own course of action; and (3) performing an imitative response.

Some behavior is easily decoded for subsequent storage in memory; more complex behavior patterns may be difficult to decode. Flanders and Thistlethwaite (1970) found greater imitation on an easy task than on a complex concept formation task in which the correct solution required the use of three stimulus dimensions (brightness, number, and position on the display card). However, when the model provided verbalizations of the reasons for his choices, making decoding unnecessary for the observer, more imitative responses occurred than when decoding was not provided.

Interference with symbolic decoding and encoding during observational learning decreases the amount of imitation. Bandura, Grusec and Menlove (1966) had children watch a filmed model engage in a series of complex responses. One group of children was simply asked to pay close attention to the film; a second group was asked to verbalize the model's behavior as it occurred; and a third group was asked to count rapidly while watching the film. When children had been encouraged to develop symbolic representation of what they saw (the second group), they produced more matching responses than when they had been simply asked to attend closely to the film. The children who were instructed to engage in counting, which produced competing symbolization, performed the least number of imitative responses.

B. Reinforcement and Imitation

Observers may symbolically encode the behavior-outcome contingencies experienced by the model but not imitate his behavior. There is no automatic connection between learning the causal structure of the environment by observing another's behavior and actually performing that behavior. Learning without imitation was shown in a study by Hamilton, Thompson,

and White (1970). College students observed a verbal reinforcement task enacted by the experimenter's confederate. Subsequently, those observers who could articulate the contingency between the "correct" responses and the experimenter's "mmm-hmm" showed significantly better performance in the verbal reinforcement task than did observers who could not articulate the contingency. However, some of the "aware" subjects did not display improved performance. When asked why, they indicated that they knew the correct contingency but did not want to imitate the model. Symbolic representation occurred but did not produce a subsequent impact on behavior.

Many studies of vicarious learning have been designed to investigate the conditions under which an observer will imitate a model. While learning involves only observation and symbolic representation, performance is importantly affected by the rewards received by the model. Positive reinforcement for his behavior. In the absence of tangible rewards, the model may display that an observer will perform imitative behavior. Walters, Leat, and Mezei (1963) provided evidence for this proposition by exposing kindergarten children to one of three child models. The models had an assortment of attractive toys physically available to them but had been forbidden to play with them. In every case the model transgressed by playing with the forbidden toys. In a punishment condition, the model was verbally rebuked by his mother for his transgression. In a reward condition, the child's transgression was followed by a very positive nurturant interaction with his mother. In a control condition, the model was neither punished nor rewarded.

After observing one of these models, each observer was placed in a room with the toys for a period of 15 minutes and was told not to play with them. The children who had seen the rewarded model displayed more transgressions than those who had seen the punished model, while control children displayed an intermediate amount of resistance to temptation.

Imitation of a model may occur even when he does not receive material reinforcement for his behavior. In the absence of tangible rewards, the model may display emotions suggesting intrinsic satisfaction with his activities or he may transmit fear or anxiety. These representations of the model's subjective experience of reward or punishment have the same effects on the observer's performance as do material reinforcements. Aronfreed and Paskal (1966) found that children often imitated self-sacrificial behavior by giving up a share of their rewards to others when an adult female model had emitted expressions of joy and provided hugs following her own self-sacrificial behavior.

The observer may empathically share the emotions expressed by the model. Berger (1962) has shown that observers display a physiological reaction when a model is punished in their presence. Conversely, Geer and Turteltaub (1967) found a reduction of fear toward snakes, as indicated by approach behavior, when observers had seen a model act calmly with snakes. The clinical application of modeling for reducing the phobic reactions of patients has now become widespread (see Box 6.1).

The amount of reward received by a model is directly related to the probability

Box 6.1   PHOBIC REACTIONS AND MODELING THERAPY

A phobia is an irrational fear that may be associated with almost anything, from open spaces to butterflies. The individual may panic when faced with the feared object or situation. For example, a person may be afraid of all snakes, although of course there are many species that are quite harmless. It is difficult to teach people to overcome their irrational fears. If a person could be induced to face the feared situation so he could discover that it is harmless, then he might learn to overcome his fears. Modeling has been used as a therapeutic technique to help people rid themselves of phobias.

Bandura and Menlove (1968) worked with a sample of children who were fearful of dogs. The children were shown a film of a model who engaged in a graduated sequence of ever more vigorous (and to the viewers, more threatening) interactions with a dog. The model gave every appearance of enjoying the dog. Simultaneously, the experimenter provided descriptive comments on the filmed events to sustain attention and to assist in decoding. The children were subsequently observed to approach and interact with live dogs.

Bandura, Blanchard, and Ritter (1969) obtained similar results with snake-phobic adults. The subjects were shown a 35-minute film which they could individually control; they could stop it or reverse it whenever the events shown were too anxiety-provoking, and they could take all the time they wanted to view the entire film. This procedure allowed the subjects to view the film without intense emotional arousal. The content of the film included children and adults handling snakes, letting them crawl over their bodies, etc. After viewing the film, most of the subjects were willing to touch and hold a snake and one-third permitted a snake to crawl in their laps while they held their hands at their sides. Another group of subjects observed a live model through a one-way mirror and then were guided through a sequence of approaching and handling a snake. When helped by the live model, 92 percent of the phobic subjects permitted a snake to crawl in their laps.

Perhaps people isolate themselves from each other because of fear. O'Connor (1972) has shown that modeling may promote socializing among children who are social isolates. Subjects were shown one of two films: (1) a 23-minute film containing 11 scenes of graduated activity in which a model joined in social interaction with other children, including joining and talking with a single child who had been reading a book and joining a group of several children who were vigorously tossing large paper blocks about the room; (2) a film about dolphins that was approximately the same length and of the same interest as the modeling film, but with no humans shown. Observations made several weeks later showed that the subjects who viewed the modeling film engaged in as much social interaction as the non-isolates, while the subjects who viewed the control film showed no change in the amount of their socializing. Furthermore, O'Connor found that the modeling film was more effective in promoting social interactions than was a two-week program consisting of five hours of social reinforcement (praise and attention) for engaging in such activities.

---

that an observer will engage in imitative behavior. Kanareff and Lanzetta (1958) demonstrated a positive relationship between the proportion of rewards received by a model and imitative behavior by observers. Subjects were asked to identify which of two tones had the higher pitch. Actually, the tones were identical 80 percent of the time. Feedback indicated to observers that the model's judgments were correct 84, 60, or 36 percent of the time. The subjects imitated the judgments of the model to the degree that he was correct.

The model's own commitment to a set of values is obviously stronger when he performs behavior directed toward implementing his values than when he merely verbalizes his intention to do so. Adults often resort to exhortation in their efforts to mold the behavior of their children. But the old adage that "children do as you do and not as you say" has been substantiated by Grusec and Skubiski (1970). Prior to serving as a model, an adult female acted in a positive, socially reinforcing, and nurturant way toward a child or else maintained a neutral, objective, non-nurturant relationship. The child then either heard the model say that sharing rewards is a good idea or saw the model actually share with charity some of the rewards gained from playing a game. The observer children were then provided with a similar opportunity to engage in charitable behavior. The actual performance of sharing by the model was imitated by the children, but in general, exhortation did not elicit sharing behavior. Girls who observed a nurturant model did, however, heed the words alone. The difference between the imitative behavior of girls and boys may be because girls develop verbal facility more rapidly than boys.

Many factors contribute to an observer's tendency to act on the basis of the causal structure of the environment communicated tacitly by the actions of a model. The observer's desire to be different and not to conform may negate the model's effectiveness, and cause him to act in an opposite manner. Rebellious youth may murder the English language as a way of showing their defiance of the established order, in which social and political leaders use well-turned phrases and urbane speeches to promote ends that are distasteful to youth. A model's behavior shows an observer what can be done in a situation and what the results are likely to be. When the results are rewarding, imitation is likely, but when the outcome for the model is punishing or unrewarding, his action is not apt to be imitated.

C. The Model as a Source of Influence

According to a communications interpretation of modeling, the model's behavior informs the observers about the causal structure of the environment. His behavior may be decoded as a general rule of the form: "If you make response X, you will receive reward Y." Since the model displays a behavioral commitment to his stated beliefs, his sincerity is beyond dispute, although his wisdom is judged in terms of the outcome as perceived by the observer. When positive outcomes frequently follow modelled behavior, the observer may gain confidence in the general rule that is tacitly (and perhaps inadvertently) communicated and imitate the response in the hope of attaining similar rewards for himself. Hence, a model's behavior may serve the same function as a persuasive communication in influencing an observer's behavior. Source and target characteristics known to enhance the effectiveness of persuasive communication (as we shall see in Chapter 8) have also been shown to facilitate the imitation of a model.

1. Model Characteristics

As stated earlier the attractiveness of a source is positively related to his effectiveness in influencing a target person. A number of experiments have shown that a nurturant model, one who spends a period of time with a child in a warm and supportive relationship, is imitated more than a non-nurturant model (Bandura & Huston, 1961; Staub, 1971). However, the type of behavior displayed by a nurturant model affects the degree of imitation. It is connotatively consistent for a nurturant model to engage in positive behavior, but inconsistent for him to display negative or aggressive behavior. On the other hand, it is consistent with an observer's impression of a non-nurturant (cold) model for him to perform negative behavior and inconsistent for him to perform positive actions.

Yarrow and Scott (1972) addressed the question of how observers react to the inconsistent behavior of an attractive model. They found that children imitated the positive behavior of a nurturant model, but not his negative behavior; they imitated a non-nurturant model's negative behavior but did not imitate his positive behavior. Apparently, these inconsistencies of the model undermined the credibility of his tacit communication about appropriate conduct. The model's behavior in the inconsistency conditions was contradictory and conveyed competing cues regarding the appropriateness of the modeled behavior. In these conditions, the observer may become confused about which pattern of responses to imitate.

In addition to attraction or nurturance, Bandura, Ross and Ross (1963a) found that a model's control over resources that can be used to reward or punish others contributes to his effectiveness in eliciting imitative responses. A child was placed in a situation with two adults. In one condition the first adult provided rewards for the second adult in the form of attractive toys and snacks, and both ignored the presence of the child who was left to play with a few unattractive toys. In the second condition, the adult who controlled the resources rewarded the child and ignored the second adult. In subsequent modeling sequences, the children more often imitated the adult model who displayed a reward capability than the one who had been rewarded (a rival) or the one who had been ignored.

Grusec and Mischel (1966) manipulated the perceived power of the model in another way. An adult model was introduced to nursery school children either as their new permanent teacher or as a temporary teacher. A permanent teacher possesses greater future control over rewards and punishments than a temporary teacher. Children who observed the behavior of the more powerful permanent teacher displayed more imitative behavior than did those who observed the less powerful temporary teacher.

From the point of view of a child, an adult is very powerful and possesses great status. It might be expected, therefore, that a child would be more likely to imitate adults than other children. Dorr and Fey (1974) found confirmation for this hypothesis. They pretested young children aged from 5 to 11 on a moral judgment test and identified two groups: (1) children who made moral judgments based on the damage done (i.e., objective judgments), and (2) those who judged on the basis of the attributed intentions of the actor (i.e., subjective judgments). Both groups were then asked to make a series of moral judgments and alternated with a model who was not physically present but whose judgments were read by a narrator on videotape. The narrator identified the model as an adult to half the children and as a peer to the remainder. The judgments of the model were opposed to the typical mode of moral judgments made by the child; objective subjects heard about the subjective judgments of the model and subjective subjects received feedback about his objective judgments. As can be seen in Figure 6.3, the more powerful adult elicited more imitative judgments from the children than did a peer; however, the latter was also effective in eliciting moral judgments opposed to the children's typical mode of making judg-

ments, as was apparent in comparison which a no-model control condition.

2. Observer Characteristics

As we shall document in Chapter 8, some persons are more persuasible and otherwise susceptible to interpersonal influence than others. Similar findings have been reported in studies of modeling. For example, subjects who are low in self-esteem (deCharms & Rosenbaum, 1960), who are incompetent at the experimental task (Kanareff & Lanzetta, 1960), or who show a great deal of dependence by accepting help on tasks that they are able to handle on their own (Jakubczak & Walters, 1959), are especially susceptible to the influence of a model. People with these characteristics also tend to be informationally dependent and hence are responsive to the tacit communication of a model.

D. The Scope of Learning from Models

Children imitate the use of language, learn vicariously to impose stringent criteria on self-rewards, copy the altruistic behavior of others, and adopt the moral codes of important models. There is apparently little limitation to what can be learned through modeling. Some behavior probably can not be learned in any other way. If children had no opportunity to hear others use speech, for example, they would have great difficulty developing linguistic skill, as observations of deaf children indicate.

Liebert, Odom, Hill, and Huff (1969) demonstrated grammatical modeling by exposing children to a model who constructed sentences according to the rule, "preposition-article-noun," such as "The boy went *to the house*," or according to the rule "article-noun-preposition," such as "The boy went *the house to*." Whichever rule the model used, the observer children tended to adopt the same rule, though more imitation was observed among

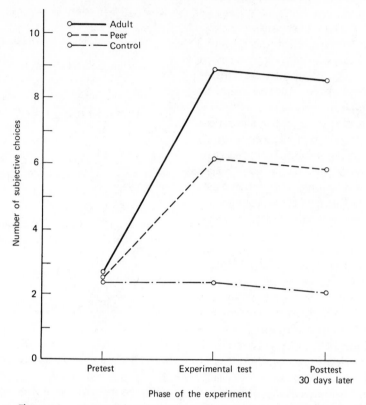

Figure 6.3. Mean number of subjective moral judgment responses produced by objective children on each of the three test periods for each of the experimental conditions. (After Dorr and Fey, 1974.)

14-year-old children than among 6- and 8-year-old children. Though the older children can be presumed to have had a better knowledge of grammer, they also may have performed more imitative erroneous grammatical constructives as a way of ingratiating themselves to the experimenter. The work of Chomsky (1968) and Lenneberg (1967) suggests, however, that there may be a genetic basis to language (and grammatical) usage.

Social learning theory does not assume that the individual is completely guided by external reinforcement and the examples provided by models. If behavior were determined only by such external influences, it would shift as sand in a strong wind, always adjusting to the environment. People would never act according to principle and

would not deliberately incur costs in making a stand. Social learning theory stresses that persons learn to monitor their own reinforcement contingencies, to generate expectancies, to judge the adequacy of their own behavior, and often to discount the opinions of others even when to do so is costly (Bandura, 1971). Self-evaluation and self-criticism are considered essential in the development of autonomy (Hilgard, 1949). An individual manifests self-control by regulating his own reinforcements according to his own criteria for self-approval and by delaying the gratification associated with immediate rewards in order to achieve greater future rewards. These processes of self-control require the adoption of internal standards or values.

According to Bandura (1971), there are

three major scientific problems associated with the study of self-reinforcement: (1) understanding how self-monitoring reinforcement systems are learned; (2) determining how effective these systems are in regulating behavior; and (3) discovering what maintains the standard of self-reinforcement the individual adopts. Direct material and social reinforcement for adopting either stringent or lenient internal standards of self-reinforcement have been shown to be effective in establishing self-evaluative judgments of performance (Kanfer & Marston, 1963). Modeling also plays an important role. Bandura and Kupers (1964) had children observe a model who rewarded herself sparingly and only when she achieved superior performance on the task. Another group of children observed a model who rewarded herself frequently for low achievement. Subsequently, the children adopted the standard set by the model they observed.

Presumably, parents serve as models for their children for standards of self-evaluation and self-reinforcement. When parents express satisfaction and reward themselves for low levels of performance, their children may do so also. When parents display high standards of achievement and seldom indulge themselves with favorable self-evaluations, applying high standards for rewards, their children may be more exacting in establishing standards for their own performance.

It is difficult for an individual to accept and maintain stringent criteria for self-evaluation because, at least at first, he must reject reinforcement he could readily secure. Once he learns that high achievement can bring greater rewards later on, he may adopt and sustain high standards. Mischel (1966) has reported positive relationships between a preference for delayed but more valued rewards and measures of social responsibility and achievement motivation.

American culture is supportive of an individual who adopts high achievement standards. Excellence often brings both material rewards and social acclaim. While the system of reinforcement in society may sustain high criteria for self-evaluation, it may also produce psychological distress for those who cannot meet high standards. Even competent persons may experience depression because they cannot attain the lofty goals they set for themselves. The college professor in the School of Music who gains the plaudits of students for his performances on campus may be unhappy because he has dreamed of, and practiced for, the concert stage.

III. INTELLECTUAL AND MORAL DEVELOPMENT

The contributions of Jean Piaget (1926, 1952; Piaget & Inhelder, 1956) have dominated the cognitive-developmental view of socialization. Piaget does not deny the importance of social learning, but he emphasizes the cognitive capabilities of the human organism which are manifested as he interacts with and gains experience in his environment. Intellectual development is considered to center around changes in the cognitive processing of information rather than the acquisition of specific responses or skills through reinforcement or modeling. As the child matures, qualitative changes occur in the way information is processed; and what the child is able to learn depends on the stage of cognitive development he has reached.

Praise and blame, reward and retribution, are means of showing approval or disapproval of another person's behavior. Making moral judgments about another is a matter of person perception; such judgments depend on attributions of cause. A person can be held responsible for his actions only when they reflect free choice. The stage of intellectual development of the observer has been found to play a significant role in the way he makes attributions, particularly when the actions under scrutiny are relevant to moral codes. Piaget and Kohlberg have proposed theories of moral development that have provided the basis of most current research on the topic.

A. Piaget's Theory of Intellectual Development

According to Piaget, the child begins to form schemata regarding space, time, matter, and causality from his earliest interactions with the environment. *Schemata* refer to patterns of coordination developed by the individual in adapting to the environment. For example, a child may acquire spatial schemata through his attempts to turn a long, narrow toy in a vertical position in order to push it between the bars of his playpen. By manipulating objects in the environment, he learns about gravity; when objects are dropped, they do not float upward or sideways; instead, they fall down. Because the individual is curious and continually explores his environment, he constantly encounters new stimulus events and therefore is constantly forming new schemata to represent and incorporate his experiences.

A person's cognitive state is in equilibrium when his sensory inputs are consistent with his previously acquired knowledge—when he has sufficient cognitive categories to handle the new information. When new experiences are encountered, they may be incorporated into existing schemata—a process referred to as *assimilation*. When these new inputs do not fit or are incongruous with existing schemata, the person's equilibrium is disturbed. The revision of existing schemata to adapt to new or surprising sensory inputs is referred to as the process of *accommodation*.

We can illustrate these processes by the actions of a child. Suppose he has acquired a schema for grasping, which relates his capacity for closing his fingers to having an object in his possession. If he closes his fingers around a cord dangling over his playpen, he may assimilate the experience into his grasping schema. But if the cord is attached to a bell and grasping it produces a ringing noise, the grasping schema will not enable him to assimilate the new experience and a disequilibrium will result. In order to accommodate the new experience, he would have to develop a new schema or adjust the grasping schema to include cord-pulling and bell-ringing.

Cognitive development occurs as newly formed schemata permit the assimilation of more complex aspects of experience. Environmental changes are always forcing the individual to process new information, causing cognitive disequilibrium and requiring accommodation through the development of new schemata. The child moves from states of equilibrium to disequilibrium and back again as the processes of assimilation and accommodation are constantly cycling during his intellectual development.

The very young child is *egocentric* in several important respects. He often fails to differentiate between the subjective world of thought, feelings, and dreams and the external world of physical things. Dreams, for example, may be treated as if they were part of the external environment—as real happenings. Similarly, physical objects and events are often endowed with psychological attributes such as consciousness, feelings, and intentions. This type of thinking is demonstrated by a child who describes a fallen object as "hurt." Not until he reaches the age of 10 or 11 does he completely abandon such animistic ideas and attribute psychological states solely to animals and people.

An important feature of egocentrism is an inability to play the role or take the point of view of another person. The very young child assumes that others perceive and experience events in exactly the same way he does. Piaget and Inhelder (1956) seated children aged 4 and 11 so they faced a scale model of three mountains and tested their ability to describe how the mountains would appear to an observer looking at them from various positions around the model. The four-year-old children were much less able to take the perspective of others than were eleven-year-old children.

Role-taking is based on an ability to make attributions about another's capabilities, traits, expectations, feelings, and potential reactions. Flavell (1968) found that children do not usually develop these skills until the ages of 8 to 10. Presumably, the egocentric thinking of young children is modified through experiences as they are continually challenged by other people and must accommodate their schemata to the different points of view they encounter.

The transition to intellectual maturity requires that the individual be able to de-center by acquiring role-taking skills. *Decentering* refers to the individual's ability to adopt the viewpoint of another person, and apparently takes place through play activities, the imitation of significant models, the use of language as a means of interpersonal learning, and accommodations in schemata occasioned by the fact that other persons control significant reinforcements.

The way a child responds to rules appears to develop through a sequence of stages also. At first the very young child accepts the rules provided by adults as immutable and unchangeable. At this stage the child may resist any attempt to change the rules of a game even though his egocentric pattern of behavior causes him frequently to violate the rules. Later on the world appears more dynamic and arbitrary to the growing individual; an understanding and appreciation of the origins of rules and their social functions is achieved. Changes in rules can be accepted when a democratic consensus for doing so exists in the social group. At the highest stage of intellectual development the person may adopt abstract principles of conduct that may not be consistent with the rules adopted by others.

In summary, Piaget's theory of intellectual development proposes that the child's adaptation to the external world is a function of the quality of his thinking. Through the processes of assimilation and accommodation the individual develops complex schemata to represent his world. His ability to form certain types of schemata is dependent on his stage of intellectual development. Teaching and experience may speed or slow development, but they cannot alter the sequence of intellectual stages. The stages and their sequence depend on organizing tendencies in combination with an individual's particular experiences with the environment. Each stage is not merely more or less complex than the others; each is qualitatively different from the others. Clear changes from concrete to abstract, egocentric to decentered, and fixed and unalterable to dynamic and relative, occur during intellectual development.

B. Piaget's Theory of Moral Development

Factors associated with intellectual development, such as egocentrism and decentering, should affect the way the individual makes moral judgments. Piaget (1966) devised a method of systematically examining the relationship of intellectual development and moral judgment. He asked children between the ages of four and thirteen to judge the "naughtiness" of the characters in a series of ten pairs of stories dealing with clumsiness and stealing. For example, in one story of a pair, a little boy was called to dinner; on opening the dining room door, he unwittingly knocked over a chair on which rested a tray with 15 cups on it; the cups fell to the floor and broke. In the second story of this pair, a boy attempted to reach some forbidden jam positioned high in the cupboard while his mother was absent from the house. While reaching for the forbidden jam, he knocked over a cup and it crashed to the floor and broke. Children were asked to say which of the boys is the naughtier and why. A judgment that the boy who broke 15 cups is the naughtier reflects an *objective orientation,* since the main determinant of the moral judgment is the number of cups broken or the amount of damage done. A judgment that the second boy was naughtier would represent a subjective orientation, because the intentions attributed to the actor take precedence.

1. Stages of Moral Realism and Moral Independence

The objective orientation is characteristic of the stage of moral realism, which, according to Piaget, lasts until the age of 7 or 8. During this stage, behavior is evaluated in terms of its physical consequences; right and wrong are matters of absolute judgment, and an act is considered bad because it is punished rather than because it breaks a rule or harms others. In the story pair described above, younger children considered the boy who broke the 15 cups naughtier than the boy who broke one cup because they focused on the material consequences of the action rather than on the subjective intentions of the actor. When a character in a story pair is punished or will be punished for his actions, children at the stage of moral realism consider him bad, irrespective of the circumstances involved.

In the subsequent stage of moral independence, moral judgments reflect a subjective orientation, taking into account the intentions and motivations of the actor, the moral rules that are applicable in the situation, and the degree of harm done by a transgressor. Thus, more mature children judge the boy who broke a single cup in his illicit attempt to get the jam as more naughty than the boy who accidentally broke 15 cups.

2. Types of Punishment

Younger children (moral realists) believe that an actor should be made to suffer (*expiatory punishment*) for his transgressions. The degree of suffering should be proportional to the degree of harm. The forms of expiatory punishment considered appropriate including spanking, depriving the

transgressor of his allowance, and denying him the use of toys.

Older children (moral independents) attempt to fit the punishment to the crime so that the transgressor will gain a sense of the wrongness of his action. *Reciprocity punishment* is used in an attempt to reform the sinner and make restitution to the damaged party. Having the boy buy his mother a cup would be one way of administering reciprocity punishment; he would need to spend his allowance in making restitution and the mother's cup would be replaced.

The key to differences between younger and older children in the making of moral judgments is considered to be the degree of egocentrism characteristic of their thinking. An inability to take the role of another person prevents the morally realistic child from considering the subjective intentions of the actor. Egocentric thought does not permit a relativistic stance that admits of a diversity of views regarding what may be considered right or wrong. When a child begins to decenter and to view rules as relativistic, he begins to enter the stage of moral independence and takes a subjective orientation toward moral judgments.

The individual's concept of justice also changes as he evolves through the stages of intellectual development. Piaget has observed that the younger child believes in *imminent justice*, a belief that misdeeds can be punished by naturally occurring events. If a child does something bad and then accidentally falls off a chair and hurts himself, the moral realist will assume that the two events are associated with each other; natural events somehow brought about just punishment to the actor for his misdeeds. Children capable of more abstract thought no longer believe in imminent justice; they would view an accident following a transgression as merely coincidence and not as an administration of just punishment.

3. Rules Regarding the Distribution of Rewards and Punishments

The transition from the stage of moral realism to moral independence is a function of both intellectual development and the changing character of the child's social interactions. At first, the child is governed by powerful adults who make up the rules and control the rewards and punishments. Because he has neither the intellectual resources nor the power to challenge his parents or guardians, he accepts the world as he finds it and adopts an absolute and authoritarian ethic. As he grows older he begins to enter into interactions with his peers and acquires a schema regarding the value of cooperation with others and adopts a more relativistic and democratic ethic.

The development and codification of rules now becomes essential both for regulating behavior and for allocating the rewards achieved through group effort. An *equality norm,* which stipulates that rewards should be equally distributed among all members of the group, is usually adopted by early adolescence. Later on an *equity principle* is adopted, which stipulates that rewards should be commensurate with the efforts, contributions, and circumstances of each individual in the group. Thus, in Piaget's view, there are three stages in the development of ideas regarding distributive justice—parental authority, equality, and equity.

4. Research Evaluation

Central to Piaget's theory of the development of moral judgments is a shift from an egocentric, realistic perspective, in which the individual is the center of his own world, to a relativistic perspective, in which the "decentered" individual can attribute independent intentions to others. Most empirical research carried out to test Piaget's theory has focused on this shift.

In a review of non-experimental, cross-cultural evidence, Kohlberg (1969a) found a shift in the basis of moral judgment from a consideration of the gross consequences of an act toward a regard for the actor's intentions. Such differences as a function of age were found in several American Indian cultures (i.e., the Atayal, Hopi, Zuni, Papago, and Mayan) as well as in the indus-

trialized societies of America, Switzerland, Taiwan, and Turkey. However, variables other than age were found to be related to the shift. Intelligence was positively correlated with the maturity of moral judgments, and middle-class children referred to the intentions of others at an earlier age than lower-class children. Nonetheless, the transition specified by Piaget occurred in all the societies studied.

Bandura and McDonald (1963) challenged Piaget's theory by demonstrating that children can be taught to adopt either the perspective of moral realism or of moral independence. Children from 5 to 11 were pretested on a set of story pairs from which they were identified as having objective or subjective orientations. Morally realistic (objective) children were exposed to a model who made subjective judgments, while morally independent (subjective) children were exposed to a model who made objective judgments. The model was always given social reinforcements after making his judgments. Half the subjects were given social approval for agreement with the model and half were not. A third group of children observed no model but were reinforced whenever they made the "correct" response, which was a moral judgment opposite to the predominant orientation of the child. The children always changed their orientation to make moral judgments in agreement with the model, but did not change merely as a result of being reinforced when no model was present. The data for the originally subjective children are shown in Figure 6.4.

Cowan, Langer, Heavenrich, and Nathanson (1969) improved on the procedures used by Bandura and McDonald in testing Piaget's theory. They had the children make judgments about story pairs different from the ones judged by the model, whereas Bandura and McDonald had observers and models make judgments about the same story pairs. Not only did Cowan et al. replicate the earlier results, but they found that the effects of modeling on the moral judgments of the children persisted

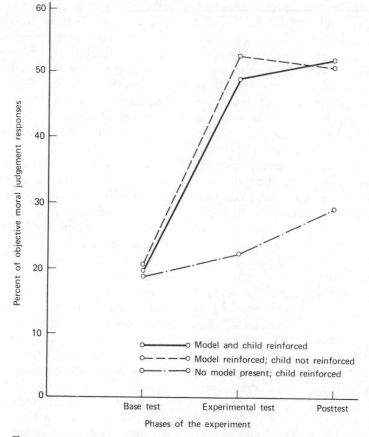

Figure 6.4. Mean percentage of objective moral judgment responses produced by subjective children on each of the three test periods for each of three experimental conditions. (After Bandura and McDonald, 1963.)

two weeks later. Dorr and Fey (1974) further modified the procedures but once again the same results were found (see Figure 6.3), and the effects endured for 30 days.

Although these modeling studies show that children can be taught to use a particular schema in solving a two-choice concept formation problem (i.e., which is naughtier?), there may be some question about whether they demonstrate the adoption of a general orientation toward moral judgments. For example Crowley (1968) has shown that training alters specific responses without affecting the level of cognitive operations. He trained first-grade children, who were predominantly objective in their orientation toward moral judgments

on a pretest, by rewarding them for making judgments based on attributions of intent. There were four training conditions: (1) moral stories were presented and identifications of the naughtier child were tangibly rewarded, while incorrect identifications were corrected by the trainer; (2) the same, except that the children also participated in a discussion of the story pairs in which intent was emphasized; (3) nonmoral stories were presented and the subjects were asked "Which was better?" (e.g., "Who was the better hunter?"); (4) the same, except that competence was discussed (e.g., one hunter killed the deer accidentally and the other did so because of his skill); and (5) a control group did not receive training. All children were then tested on 12 moral story pairs 18 or 19 days after the end of the two-week training period.

As can be seen from a summary of the results in Table 6.1, direct training in moral judgment clearly affected the kind of judgments the children made. However, training the children to attend to subjective factors on nonmoral materials produced only a slight (though statistically significant) transfer effect to moral judgments as compared to the control subjects. Discussions of the subjective characteristics of the actions judged did not affect the moral judgments of the children. Crowley concluded that: (1) the "subject's uniformly excellent performance on the training task indicates that objectivity does not betoke inability to grasp intention, but rather failure to focus on intentions when a competing cue (size of damage) is introduced" (p. 232); (2) informal observations indicated that subjects trained to use a principle did no better than subjects who were provided only with a verbal discrimination response; and (3) "subjects trained on nonmoral stories did not consistently 'carry over' the concept of intentionality to moral stories in posttesting" (p. 231).

The available evidence shows that young children can make attributions of intent and can be taught to use them in making moral judgments, but they normally attend to the objective consequences of the behavior of others in making moral evaluations. The failure of children to attend to the intentions of actors may be due (at least in part) to the methods employed by experimenters. A re-examination of Piaget's story pairs reveals that both consequences and intentions may vary between the comparison stories. For example, in the pair illustrated above, it may be noted that the breaking of cups in both scenarios was accidental, although the boy who was trying to reach the jam inadvertently broke the cup while engaging in a transgression. Children may consider the latter boy as more naughty because he disobeyed his mother and not because he broke the cup. The subjective orientation, therefore, may not be a matter of attributions but a recognition of norm violations.

Armsby (1971) has shown that very young children do make attributions of intent to characters in story pairs if sufficient information is presented to clearly distinguish between accidental and purposeful acts.

In summary, most of the available research has examined the shift from objective to subjective orientations in making moral judgments. Learning theorists have shown that children can be taught to take either orientation in situations very similar to two-choice discrimination tasks. Although the controversy between the cognitive-developmental and learning theory approaches to the study of moral judgment has not been firmly settled, the evidence to date does not convincingly contradict the developmental view that an individual's moral reasoning evolves from a focus on concrete consequences to subjective attributions of intentions.

C. Kohlberg's Theory of Moral Development

Kohlberg (1963, 1968) has offered a somewhat complex elaboration of Piaget's

Table 6.1 Mean Number of 12 Stories Answered in a "Subjective" Fashion.[a]

Training Received	Mean
Nonmoral stories with corrections only	4.4
Nonmoral stories with correction and discussion	3.3
Moral stories with correction only	11.0
Moral stories with correction and discussion	10.9
Control	1.5

[a] After Crowley, 1968.

theory of moral development. According to Kohlberg, there are three levels of moral reasoning, each of which is considered to include two stages. These six stages (shown in Table 6.2) are assumed to develop in sequence, and a later stage cannot be reached without going through the earlier ones. Not all persons reach the higher and more mature stages. Fixation may occur at any stage simply because the individual is not faced with sufficient conflict or disequilibrium in his social interactions to cause him to seek new accommodations in his existing schemata; hence, the evolution of moral reasoning depends on both intellectual development and social experience.

1. The Preconventional Level

At the preconventional level of moral development the child judges right and wrong in terms of the consequences of actions or as a function of the authoritarian pronouncements of powerful adults. This level includes two stages: *punishment and obedience orientation* (stage 1) and *instrumental relativistic orientation* (stage 2). During stage 1, whatever action results in the avoidance of punishment or shows deference to power is considered good behavior. The soldier who carries out his orders without question is a stage 1 moralist.

Stage 2 is a basically hedonistic one during which the individual acts in a pragmatic way to satisfy his own needs, although at times he may also consider the needs of others. A "what's in it for me" attitude is prevalent. Elements of fairness and equity appear, but with a pragmatic interpretation, as suggested by the phrase, "You scratch my back and I'll scratch yours." Loyalty, gratitude, and justice are absent. The ends justify the means. A stage 2 moralist might approve of a grafting politician who helps pass a piece of pork-barrel legislation. Mercy killing may be approved because "it puts the person out of his misery."

2. The Conventional Level

The second level represents a morality of conventional role-conformity in which concern for the approval of significant others supercedes strivings for sensate or hedonistic gains. The individual devotes himself to meeting the expectations of his family or group. The two stages of Level II are: *interpersonal concordance* (stage 3) and *law and order orientation* (stage 4). During stage 3 a good-boy, nice-girl orientation is adopted, and being considered good or nice by others becomes very important. Now moral judgments are based on intentions rather than on consequences or authority. Yet the individual remains conventional in the

Table 6.2   A Summary of Kohlberg's Stages of Moral Reasoning.

Level	Stage	Characteristics
I. Preconventional	1. Punishment and obedience	Authoritative, concern for sanctions
	2. Instrumental relativistic	What's the payoff?
II. Conventional	3. Interpersonal concordance	Good intentions, meet others' expectations
	4. Law and order	Doing duty, maintaining social order
III. Postconventional	5. Social-contract legalistic	Changing law through democracy to improve society
	6. Universal ethical principles	Principles above society

sense that he rarely challenges the existing group consensus about right or wrong. Whatever the group's values, they appear to be normal and natural; the person is more concerned about approval than he is about the origins of moral rules. One who conforms to the majority is a stage 3 moralist.

A stage 4 moralist is a person who is committed to established authority and the rules of the social order. A good person is the one who shows respect for authority, and right behavior consists of doing one's duty. It is believed that social order should be maintained for its own sake. Stage 4 law and order morality became a watchword among political rightists in the United States during the late 1960s and early 1970s. Political candidates, particularly those who ran for mayoral offices in large cities, were often elected on the basis of the single issue of maintaining law and order on the streets.

3. Postconventional Level

The third and highest level of moral reasoning is the morality of self-accepted principles. The mature individual generates a set of moral rules that are apart from the particular authorities over him or the groups to which he belongs. There is a clear awareness that moral principles are always relative and are adopted by group consensus. The two stages at this level are: *social-contract legalistic orientation* (stage 5) and *orientation of universal ethical principles* (stage 6). Stage 5 moral reasoning recognizes individual differences in values and opinions and hence emphasizes democratic procedures for reaching consensus. In contrast with the blind acceptance of legal authority that characterizes a law and order orientation, the legalistic orientation respects the law but may seek to change it in the interests of improving society. The United States Constitution exemplifies stage 5 moral reasoning.

Stage 6 represents the highest level of moral development. The person who reaches stage 6 thinking adopts a set of moral principles in accord with his own conscience. Abstract universal principles of justice and human rights held by the individual may be in conflict with the moral rules shared by his groups or his society. The principled actions of a person like Martin Luther King, Jr. exemplify the morality of individual conscience.

4. Assessing Stages of Moral Development

Kohlberg has constructed a set of stories that pose a series of moral dilemmas for the respondent. Typically, an opposition is set up between a legal rule, a social norm, and a human need. For example, in one story a man visited a druggist to purchase a drug that might save his wife, who was suffering from a rare kind of cancer and was near death. The druggist asked ten times the cost he paid for the drug and the man could not raise the purchase price, so he broke into the drug store one night and took the drug for his wife. The respondent is then asked a series of questions about this episode, such as whether the robbery was justified, whether the druggist was right to charge as much as he did, and so on. An explanation is obtained from the respondent for each of his answers.

Kohlberg (1964) reported examples of answers considered to be appropriate to different levels of moral reasoning. In reaction to the story, a ten-year-old boy provided a stage 2 response: "Why should the druggist give the drug to the dying woman when her husband couldn't pay for it?" This response reflects the hedonistic orientation of "What's in it for him?" A 16-year-old boy produced a stage 6 response: "By the law of society he was wrong but by the law of nature or of God the druggist was wrong and the husband was justified. Human life is above financial gain." Although robbery is against the law, abstract principles regarding the worth of human life supercede materialistic considerations and legalistic principles.

5.   Research Evaluating Kohlberg's Theory

According to Kohlberg, the individual advances through a fixed sequence of stages as he develops more mature modes of moral reasoning. One implication of this theory is that an individual should be better able to understand, learn, and utilize the orientation of the next higher stage than that of a stage two steps higher. In addition, since growth is upward, he should prefer the next higher stage of reasoning to the one just below his own. Turiel (1966) examined these hypotheses by first identifying 12 and 13-year-old children who were predominantly at stages 2, 3, and 4. These subjects were asked to role-play one of the characters in each of three of the Kohlberg stories. After the story was read, the subject played the main character and was told to seek advice from two friends about his moral dilemma. The experimenter played the part of both friends and gave advice.

In one condition, the reasoning presented by the experimenter was one stage below the subject's pretested dominant stage (−1 treatment); the second condition exposed the subjects to reasoning that was one stage above (+1 treatment); and, in a third condition, the reasoning was two stages above (+2 treatment). The following is an example of stage 3 reasoning regarding the druggist story, which was presented by the experimenter (posing as a friend) to a stage 2 subject in the +1 treatment condition: "You should steal the drug in this case. Stealing isn't good, but you can't be blamed for doing it. You love your wife and you are trying to save her life. Nobody would blame you for doing it. The person who should really be blamed is the druggist who was just mean and greedy" (p. 615). This advice shows concern for social approval or disapproval; what is good or bad depends upon the judgments of others and is characteristic of stage 3 moral reasoning.

A week following their role-playing experiences, the subjects were again tested on the Kohlberg stories. The results are shown in Table 6.3, which includes a no role-playing control group. As can be seen, the +1 treatment was the most effective in increasing the level of moral judgments of the subjects, while the +2 treatment was more effective than the −1 treatment. Turiel concluded that the attainment of the next higher stage of thought "involves a reorganization of the preceding modes of thought, with an integration of each previous stage with, rather than an addition to, new elements of the later stages" (p. 616).

Subsequent studies by Tracy and Cross (1973) and Glassco, Milgram, and Youniss (1970) have shown that training is effective in advancing subjects to the next stage of moral development, but only for subjects at the lowest stages. Perhaps this is because training affects decentering rather than the formal operations of thought. While decentering would allow the individual to change from an objective to a subjective orientation toward moral judgment, it would not bring about a transition from a type 4 mode of reasoning to a type 5 mode or a shift from type 5 to type 6.

Kohlberg has been criticized for introducing value judgments into his theory. The "highest" stages seem to reflect a liberal political view, while the middle stages appear to represent a conservative political philosophy. Also, the higher stages are more consistant with Kantian than situational ethics. It is reasonable to ask on what

Table 6.3   Mean Proportions of Usage of Concepts at the Stages One Below, the Same As, One Above, and Two Above the Pretest Dominant Level. [a]

Stage level relative to dominant stage in pretest	Treatments			
	Control	−1	+1	+2
−1	.24	*.34*	.18	.21
0	*.40*	.28	.35	.37
+1	.12	.13	*.27*	.15
+2	.09	.06	.10	*.10*

[a] Italicized numbers are of primary interest to the hypotheses tested (After Turiel, 1966).

basis a law and order orientation can be considered less mature than a morality of individual conscience? One possible answer by cognitive-developmental theorists is that the evidence predominantly shows an invariable sequence of stages: persons simply do not move from stage 2 to stage 6 without going through the intermediate stages. Kohlberg (1969a, p. 385), however, has speculated that stages 4, 5, and 6 may be alternative or parallel forms of mature moral reasoning rather than sequential stages.

Hogan and Dickenstein (1972) have collapsed mature moral reasoning into the two parallel stages of the *ethics of responsibility* and the *ethics of conscience*. The former is related to principled rule compliance, belief in the instrumental value of law, and a tendency to attribute injustice to the actions of individuals. The latter is related to principled disobedience, doubt concerning the value of law as a means of promoting human welfare, and a tendency to attribute social injustice to institutions rather than to individuals.

A series of reports (Haan, 1972; Haan & Block, 1969; Haan, Smith, & Block, 1968) has revealed that the majority of students who participated in the 1964 Free Speech Movement sit-in at Berkeley were either preconventional or post-conventional on measures of moral development. Presumably, the two types of activists participated in radical political behavior for different reasons. Persons at the preconventional stage of moral reasoning may have perceived the movement as a means of hedonistically improving their status through conflict. The postconventional students, on the other hand, may have been focusing on the principles involved in the conflict rather than on their own status within the system they were opposing.

The specific relationship of stages of moral reasoning to political ideology was investigated by Fishkin, Keniston, and MacKinnon (1973). Preconventional college students tended to approve violent radical slogans, while conventional students preferred conservative political slogans. Postconventional students disagreed with both conservative and radical slogans; their "radicalism" was more a rejection of conservatism than an espousal of radical ideology. Fishkin, et al. concluded: "Preconventional and postconventional subjects have in common the fact that they have experienced and rejected Stage 4 reasoning (either by a 'regression' from Stage 5 back to Stage 2 or by a development to postconventional reasoning). The psychodynamics of anticonservatism today seem to parallel the quest for moral structures more adequate than law-and-order reasoning" (p. 118).

In conclusion, the available evidence has tended to support the theory of a sequential development of moral reasoning, at least through the first four stages. Recent studies suggest that Kohlberg's "higher" levels of moral reasoning (stages 4 through 6) may represent parallel political philosophies. The relationship between political behavior and ideology suggests that persons at different stages of moral reasoning may engage in exactly the same activities. Just as it is not possible to predict behavior precisely from a knowledge of a person's attitudes, it may not be possible to predict morally-relevant behavior from knowledge of a person's level of moral reasoning. Before Kohlberg's theory can be accepted more substantial evidence is needed and some methodological questions must be satisfactorily answered.

IV. MORAL BEHAVIOR

Morality refers to rules of conduct dealing with the impact of one person's behavior on the rights and needs of others. The moral code of a society is designed to promote justice (however defined in a particular society) in human relationships. Persons who conform to the moral code are considered good, right, and virtuous, and are often praised and rewarded. Those who defy the code are considered bad, wrong, and sinful, and are often condemned and punished. *Moral rules* take the form of abstract and general principles of conduct. It is therefore often difficult to determine how a rule applies in a particular situation. Killing may be considered wrong, but killing in self-defense or in time of war may be praised. While rules against theft and murder are often clear, there are many other kinds of behavior, such as abortion and adultery, where there may be much dispute about the validity of the rule.

Social norms and standards prescribe positive forms of social behavior. We will postpone a consideration of these positive actions until Chapter 10; here we will focus on the violation of rules or standards of conduct. An important part of socialization is learning to resist temptation and not to transgress against accepted rules. Some research has been directed toward answering the question whether there is a general disposition for people to be moral or to be defiant of rules. Some of the factors that have been discovered to affect transgressions are the anxiety and self-control of the individual, the costs and gains associated with behavior in a particular situation, the amount of injustice that is felt and the prior history of the individual.

A. The Empirical Search for a Moral Disposition

If a person cheats, will he also lie and steal from others? If he would cheat in one situation (on an examination), is he also likely to cheat in a second situation (on his income tax return)? In a classic study covering a five-year period and including over 10,000 school children, Hartshorne and May (1928) tried to answer these questions. The children were tempted to act in some immoral way in the classroom, at parties, at church, and in other places. For example, after making copies of students' test papers, the experimenters asked the students to grade their own papers. The changes made on the papers in order to correct an answer provided a measure of cheating. No consistencies were found between cheating, stealing, and lying. The data indicated that transgressions are specific to a situation rather than a manifestation of a general disposition of the individual.

The data analyses carried out by Hartshorne and May were limited because sophisticated statistical techniques had not yet been developed. A reanalysis of their data by Burton (1963) revealed some rather weak evidence for an individual disposition of honesty, which was relatively independent of situational factors.

It might be expected from cognitive-developmental theories of moral reasoning that persons at different stages would behave differently in various situations. Krebs (1967) found that 12-year-old children who had been identified on pretests as having reached Kohlberg's level of principled morality (stages 5 and 6) cheated less than children who had been identified as preconventional and conventional (stages 1 through 4). Some question could be raised about this finding because there were only five children at the higher level and 118 at the lower levels. However, Brown, Feldman, Schwartz, and Heingartner (1969) found essentially the same results with college students. Somewhat related is the finding reported by Kohlberg (1969b) that postconventional subjects were least compliant to an experimenter's commands to deliver aversive electric shocks to another person.

Information regarding the individual's history of transgressions and his level of moral reasoning provides some basis for predicting his future moral behavior, but these predictions are not very accurate. The restrictions placed on the researcher because of ethical considerations has limited the kinds of transgressions studied principally to cheating and lying. As a consequence, it is not really known whether some kinds of moral behavior may be closely related to others. Nevertheless, a number of personal and situational factors are known to bolster the individual's ability to resist the temptation to transgress against moral rules.

B. Self-Esteem, Intellectual Maturity, and Self-Control

It seems intuitively sound to suppose that a person who has a positive self-concept would be less likely to engage in "bad" behavior than someone who has a negative self-concept. One reason for having a positive self-concept is precisely the knowledge that one does not engage in "bad" behavior. A positive self-concept should therefore be associated with an individual's ability to exercise self-control and resist temptation to transgress against moral rules, while a negative self-concept should lead to greater willingness to transgress.

In a complex study Mussen, Rutherford, Harris, and Keasey (1970) found positive relationships of self-concept, intelligence, and the child-rearing attitudes of mothers with measures of self-control. Twelve-year-old children were asked to rate each other on a questionnaire regarding moral behavior. Among the items were: "Which boys (girls) are most likely to follow the rules even when the teacher is not around? Which boys (girls) are willing to share things with other children? Which boys (girls) would never copy another person's answers on a test?" The children were asked to name the three classmates who would be most likely to do what the question asked. Self–esteem and intelligence tests were also given to the children. Through personal interviews, information was gathered about the mother's attitude toward her child, her perception of the child's relationships with peers, and the promulgation of values, the enforcement of rules, and the amount of nurturance displayed toward the child.

The children were observed in two tasks. A ray-gun game provided a temptation to cheat. The children were offered an attractive prize for obtaining a designated score with the gun, but the game was rigged so that the score was impossible to achieve. The experimenter left the subject alone and asked him to keep his own score. Any child who reported a score sufficiently great to win the prize was known to be cheating. The second task was a game played with a peer in which a child could choose to be cooperative (altruistic) or competitive (selfish).

The results reflected the different socialization experiences of boys and girls in American culture and suggest two general patterns of moral behavior: conformity to rules and concern for the welfare of others. Girls are typically socialized to be more obedient and conforming, while boys are expected to be less concerned with rules and to be independent in thought and action. Successful socialization into either of these sex-role patterns is associated with a positive self-concept and with having a warm, positive, and nurturant relationship with the mother. Thus, while resistance to temptation in the ray-gun game was positively related to the honesty ratings of peers for both sexes, girls who departed from the typical female pattern and cheated were apt to have negative self-concepts and to have mothers who were non-nurturant and punitive. The boys who cheated, however, were more likely than those who did not to have positive self-concepts and to have mothers who were warm, easy-going, permissive, supportive, and who encouraged their son's independence and achievement orientation. Behavior on the second task indicated that parental emphasis on the achievement of goals and the acceptance of personal responsibility was associated with altruism in both sexes.

The ability to delay gratification in order to achieve a greater reward is a form of self-control and has been shown to be related to an individual's ability to resist temptation to transgress. Mischel and Gilligan (1964) exposed subjects to a temptation to cheat, and a month later offered them choice between a small immediate reward and a larger, deferred one. Resistance to temptation and ability to delay gratification were positively related. The ability to defer rewards requires a mature time perspective; similarly, an ability to resist temptation may depend on the individual's consideration of the long-range consequences of his actions. Indirect support for this line of reasoning is the finding by Brock and Del-Giudice (1963) that subjects who resisted the temptation to steal a small sum of money also wrote imaginative stories spanning longer periods of time than did children who yielded to temptation.

C. Anxiety Reduction and Self-Control

Punishment is anxiety-producing, and to reduce anxiety is reinforcing. Whenever anxiety reduction can be associated with resistance to temptation, the individual will learn self-control. The effectiveness of punishment in teaching self-control depends a good deal on the timing of its application. Aronfreed and Reber (1965) point out that when punishment is administered at the time the transgression is performed, the anxiety that is aroused will be associated with the available cues and will be aroused on subsequent occasions *before* the transgressive act is performed. Resistance to temptation is assumed to reduce anxiety about being punished. If punishment is delayed so that it is not administered until after the transgressive behavior is completed, then anxiety will not occur during the temptation period in future similar situations, but will be aroused only *after* the act is completed. Punishment too long delayed does not contribute to self-control and resistance to temptation.

In a test of their hypothesis, Aronfreed and Reber asked fourth and fifth grade children to choose one of a pair of toys and describe it. The children were told that some of the toys were only for older boys. One of the toys in each pair was always

more attractive than the other, and the children were presented with a series of choices. On the first nine choices, whenever a subject chose the more attractive toy in a pair he was told, "No, that's for the older boys." Punishment in the form of this verbal admonition was administered either (1) at the moment the child extended his hand toward a toy but before he touched it, or (2) after the child had chosen the toy and held it in his hand for two or three seconds. Boys in the control group were simply told that the more attractive toy in each pair was for the older boys and were not permitted to handle any of the toys.

The experimenter said nothing to the children on the tenth trial but simply watched to see what they would do. Those children who received punishment on completion of their behavior during training and the control subjects frequently chose the more attractive toy, but those who had experienced punishment at the initiation of the forbidden response during training resisted the temptation. While these results are intriguing, interpretative questions remain. Can the statement that some of the toys are for older children be considered a moral rule? Can choosing the more attractive toy be considered a transgression? Was the verbal admonition experienced by the child as punishment? Was anxiety aroused at all? Until these questions are answered by future research, Aronfreed and Reber's hypothesis about the relationships between timing of punishments, anxiety arousal and reduction, and self-control, must be cautiously applied to moral behavior.

D. Costs and Gains

Just as personality traits and attitudes are generally poor predictors of behavior, so the disposition to resist temptation, self-esteem, and self-control are probably less important for understanding moral behavior than are situational factors. Two important situational factors are the probability of detection and the degree of penalty that would follow detection.

A number of studies support the general principle that the greater the probability of detection for transgressing, the more resistance to temptation is shown by the individual. Kanfer and Duerfeldt (1968) asked children in one condition of their experiment to silently keep track of how often they were correct in guessing numbers (from 1 to 100) drawn from a box. Children in another condition were asked to write their guesses on slips of paper. Although the latter children were told that their slips of paper would be thrown away without anyone looking at them, it can be assumed that the risk of detection for lying about the number of correct guesses was greater when the guesses had been written down than when they were not communicated in any form. Whenever a child's accuracy in guessing numbers was better than chance, he was considered to have cheated; while in every case this may not have been true, in the great majority of cases it would be. Children in the written guess condition cheated less than children who kept their guesses to themselves. Hill and Kochendorfer (1969) also found that the amount of cheating decreased as the risk of detection increased, and Rettig and Pasamanick (1964) found an inverse relationship between subjects' estimates of the probability of censure and cheating.

An individual may weigh the possible gains to be achieved from transgression against the potential costs. In general, the greater the incentive for transgression, the less resistance to temptation is shown by the individual. In support of this principle, Mills (1958) found more cheating the greater the amount of money that could be gained by transgression. Of course, an inability to acquire the gain by legitimate means is a factor in producing a temptation to transgress. Hill and Kochendorfer (1969) found cheating among children on an achievement test when two conditions were met: (1) the children were anxious

about their school achievement, and (2) they were each informed that it was unlikely they could perform as well as their peers.

A cost-gain analysis suggests that anyone is susceptible to temptation. When a particularly important value is at stake and no legitimate means to achieve it is likely to succeed, almost anyone can be tempted into moral transgression. Bernard Shaw told a story about asking a beautiful lady whether she would go to bed with him for one million dollars. After some hesitation, she replied in the affirmative. Shaw is then alleged to have said that since they had established the basic principle, they could now haggle about the price. As some cynics say, any man (or woman) has his (or her) price.

One does not need to agree with the cynics to recognize the power of incentives to produce temptations. Some incentives consist of the approval and social reinforcement provided by other persons. Piliavin, Hardyck, and Vadum (1968) found juvenile delinquency to be related to an individual's concern about the approval or disapproval of significant adults. Eleventh and twelfth grade boys in a working-class community were identified as delinquents (they had been apprehended by the police for committing some transgression in the past) or as nondelinquents. All the boys filled out scales measuring their concern for the approval of their fathers, mothers, and school teachers. Subsequently, a confederate attempted to induce the subjects to cheat on a task in order to earn a monetary reward. Boys who did not care about the disapproval of adults cheated more than boys who were concerned about adult approval. Delinquent boys cheated more than did nondelinquent boys. In a second study frequently delinquent boys were shown to be less concerned with approval than were boys who were seldom or never delinquent (Piliavin, Vadum, & Hardyck, 1969).

Piliavin, Hardyck, and Vadum interpreted their results in terms of anticipated costs: "Police contact may lead to the reali-zation that the costs actually incurred for delinquency are much lower than those previously anticipated. Consequently, on subsequent occasions where the opportun-ity is avilable, the likelihood of engaging in crime is increased" (p. 231). Fear of the unknown is usually greater than fear of the known. When the delinquent boys found that little harm or enduring censure had befallen them, the anticipated costs of fu-ture transgressions were reduced. This di-munition of anticipated costs may be an important factor in criminology. (A discus-sion of deterrence will be presented in Box 8.1.)

E. Felt Injustice

An individual may engage in transgressions against other persons when he can justify his actions as directed toward rectifying an injustice. Nye (1958) established that delin-quent children view their parents as unjust and inconsistent. The kinds of discipline used by their parents and severity of punishment were not related to the inci-dence of delinquent behavior, but the per-ceived fairness of discipline was. The characteristic inconsistency of the discip-line used by the parents of delinquent chil-dren produces confusion about what is right and what is wrong and makes it difficult to discriminate how punishments and rewards are associated with an ability to resist temptation. Nevertheless, there is lit-tle difference between the expressed moral beliefs of delinquent and nondelinquent children (Hill, 1935; Stein, Sarbin, Chu, & Kulik, 1967).

Stephenson and White (1968) manipu-lated injustice in a laboratory study and ex-amined its relationship to moral behavior. Fourth grade boys were assigned to one of four experimental conditions: (1) absolute deprivation, in which their job was to pick up cars when they came off the track of a model electric racing car game and give them to the boys who raced the cars; (2)

privileged, in which the boys were the operators of the cars; (3) relative depriva-tion, in which boys picked up cars for adult operators; and (4) equity, in which boys retrieved cars and then switched roles with the operators. All the boys were then temp-ted to cheat in order to win model cars.

Cheating was more frequent in the absolutely-deprived than in the relatively-deprived condition, and it occurred more often in the relatively-deprived than in the equity condition. The subjects' perceptions of the injustice of the situation followed the same pattern. Although the boys consi-dered the situation to be unjust when they had to pick up cars for another person, they did not believe it was unjust when they had the privilege of operating the car. Boys in both the privileged and equity conditions showed a greater tendency to resist tempta-tion than did those in the other two condi-tions. Thus, transgressions occurred when the subjects perceived the situation as un-just, but resistance to temptation was dis-played when the situation was perceived as equitable.

F. Post-Transgression Behavior

When a person is tempted to transgress against a moral rule, there are consequ-ences for him no matter what he does. If he resists temptation, he may feel pride in his own moral character; yielding to tempta-tion may produce guilt feelings. The reac-tions of a person to his own behavior are presumably learned, like most other be-havior. Pride may represent anticipation of the approval the individual usually gains from others for displaying self-control, while guilt may represent the anticipation of disapproval or censure from others for a failure to resist temptation.

Aronfreed (1964) has suggested that self-criticism is a learned avoidance re-sponse. When a parent punishes a child for misconduct, verbal criticism may be con-tinued after the physical punishment ter-minates. Criticism is thereby associated with the termination of punishment and, as a consequence, is reinforcing. The process is presumed to be similar to the effects found by Sandler and Quagliano (1964), who trained monkeys to administer less painful shocks to themselves in order to avoid more painful ones. Although the intensity of the self-administered shocks was gradually increased until they were as great as the shocks to be avoided, there was no reduction in the frequency of pressing the lever that brought about self-administered shocks. Even when the shock to be avoided was discontinued, the monkeys continued to punish themselves with shocks of an intensity they had originally worked hard to avoid.

Punishment arouses anxiety and the termination of punishment reduces anxiety. If verbal criticism occurs after physical punishment, then criticism becomes associated with or conditioned to the pleasant state of anxiety reduction. The individual may emit oral self-critical responses in order to reduce anxiety. Moreover, oral self-criticism ordinarily induces the parent to reduce the magnitude of punishment or even to forego punishment altogether. In this manner, a mechanism (self-criticism) originally established to reduce anxiety also serves as an effective influence tactic to mitigate the punishments that produce the anxiety. Schwartz, Kane, Joseph, and Tedeschi (1975) found that expressions of remorse for harmdoing softened the negative impressions observers had of the harmdoer and decreased the degree of punishment considered appropriate for his transgression.

If a transgression is considered serious enough, an individual may develop a great deal of anxiety about the consequences he can expect for himself. Self-punishment may relieve the intolerable anxiety. It is a case of better get it over with than wait. In this way, the individual may learn to engage in intropunitive or self-destructive behavior. As indicated earlier, Aronfreed considers the timing of punishments to play

a critical role in the development of resistance to temptation; punishments timed to occur at the initiation of a transgression are associated with the development of self-control. Now we see that punishments that occur *after* a trangression produce guilt, remorse, self-criticism, and self-punishment.

Most parents probably socialize their children to develop a semblance of resistance to temptation, some self-control, and a tendency to emit post-transgression responses of guilt and self-punishment. As a result, there tend to be positive correlations among these factors. MacKinnon (1938) found that subjects who resisted temptation reported stronger guilt feelings than yielders. Furthermore, many delinquents are notably lacking in self-critical or guilt-related responses. Because self-control and guilt tend to be associated with each other, some theorists (notably Freud) have placed them in a causal relationship, stating that the conscience of the individual is responsible for his resistance to temptation. But the evidence is not persuasive that there exists any *necessary* connection between guilt reactions and moral restraint.

Children of very permissive parents may not learn to be self-critical because they are so seldom punished for misbehavior, and children of very strict parents may not learn guilt because misconduct is punished without regard for how the child feels about his own behavior afterward. In the former case, self-criticism is not associated with the avoidance of punishment, and in the latter case, self-criticism does not work effectively to mitigate punishment. Of course, permissive parents would not be effective in teaching resistance to temptation. Strict parents, depending on the timing of their punishments, would probably teach a strong resistance to temptation.

Another consequence of harmdoing is that the actor becomes more likely to do the victim a favor, if the two parties remain in contact with one another. As we shall see in Chapter 10, attempts to make restitution are particularly likely when it is not clear that the harm-doer intended to produce harm. By doing the victim a favor, the harmdoer affirms his benevolent character and signals that his behavior was accidental. When it is clear to everyone that his behavior was motivated by malevolent intent, he may rationalize his behavior by derogating the victim and conveying the notion that he deserved what he got (Lerner & Matthews, 1967).

Making reparations and expressing remorse are responses to transgression that tend to mitigate retributive punishment. These post-transgression actions suggest to onlookers that the individual is sorry for what he did and would like to undo the harm done. Observers may assume that the self-critical, remorseful, and reparative harmdoer is much less likely to repeat his transgression than is someone who fails to display these responses. The punishment does not fit the crime so much as it does the criminal. The nonpenitent, antisocial harmdoer is considered incorrigible and is subjected to more severe punishment than is the self-critical, remorseful individual who wants to make reparations for the harm he has done. The latter is considered either rehabilitated or susceptible to rehabilitation. The effects of post-transgression responses on others is not lost on those recidivists who, when they are in court for the fourth or fifth time, express remorse for their actions and swear to the judge they will never do it again. Expressions of guilt or remorse may reflect true inner feelings, or they may simply be influence tactics used by persons to forestall, diminish, or avoid punishments or both.

V. THE DEVELOPMENT OF SELF-CONCEPTS

Philosophers have long speculated about man's ability to reflect on himself as an object, as a causal agent, and as the possessor of thoughts and feelings. At the end of the 19th century William James (1890) argued that an individual develops many conceptions of himself. As his *material self,* he experiences his own body, his possessions, his family, and other objects that surround him. The *spiritual self* refers to his awareness of his own internal states of feeling and the very process of thinking. The *social self* includes his awareness of how others view him, including the reputation he has established, his status and prestige. According to James, a person has as many social selves as there are significant others who recognize him. Changes in the display of self have been observed by most parents who have watched their domesticated child suddenly change into an untamed stranger when a friend visits the home. Every man has many faces, and many masks.

The social origins of the self-concept were emphasized by the sociologists Cooley and Mead. Cooley (1902) considered the social self as a system of concepts derived from the individual's interactions with other persons. The individual gathers information about how others judge him and from this social mirror a "looking-glass self" emerges. To form his looking-glass self, a person must be capable of (1) imagining his own appearance, (2) imagining the other person's evaluation of that appearance, and (3) some sort of self-feeling such as pride or mortification. If the wrong impression is created by his behavior, then an actor's pride may cause him to modify his behavior to elicit a favorable impression from other people. A mature person can usually anticipate the reactions of others and is able to produce consistently favorable impressions.

The most significant others are primary, intimate, face-to-face groups such as the family, the peer groups, and the neighborhood to which an individual belongs. Cooley concluded that in primary groups "human nature comes into existence. Man does not have it at birth; he cannot acquire it except through fellowship, and it decays in isolation" (1909, p. 30). Try to imagine the concept you would have of yourself if you had grown up as a feral child on a desert island in total isolation from other people.

Mead (1934) emphasized communication and role-playing as the most important factors in the development of the self-concept. Symbolic communications convey the reactions that others have toward an individual, who then imitates the responses of others toward himself. He learns to take the role of others in their interactions with him and to perceive himself as others do. In play activities, the child rehearses many roles, including mother, policeman, milkman, and so on. Various aspects of these roles are adopted by the child in his patterns of speech, attitudes, values, and behavior. The person develops multiple perspectives about himself as an actor (I) and as an object that others perceive and evaluate (me); when he can eventually integrate these multiple perspectives, he is able to view himself from the perspective of the "generalized other" and can fully participate in the role relations of complex society.

Contemporary views have added to these older ones. Epstein (1973), for example, believes each person develops a self-theory that includes his self-attributions, the cognitive categories and schemata by which he describes himself, his inferred inner self (attitudes and values), and his moral self. As we have seen, the individual is constantly processing new information, making attributions, assigning responsibility for behavioral consequences, making social comparisons, and learning new responses. The great variety of concepts he has about himself are probably not integrated into a consistent hierarchical structure. There are many self-beliefs and self-attitudes and they are applicable in many different situations. While being carefree and gay may be appropriate conduct with respect to your girl or boy friend, being serious and responsible may be appropriate behavior toward your professor. Pressures toward maintaining an image of consistency make it necessary to develop a self-theory. Just as scientific theories change with new evidence, so does the self-theory change as each naive scientist adapts his theory to new situations and new information.

The scientific study of the self does not assume a unitary, hypothetical construct called "self." Rather, research has been concerned with the various processes used by an individual in developing self-relevant categories, schemata, and attributions. Among the most important processes in the development of self-concepts are reflected appraisals, the evaluation of one's own abilities, the development of self-esteem, and identification with models.

A. Reflected Appraisals

There is a subtle but important distinction between comparative and reflected appraisals. An individual examines his own opinions and abilities as compared to those of other people by comparative appraisals (see Chapter 3). *Reflected appraisals* are an individual's beliefs about the impressions that others have of him. To determine whether one is a slow reader it may be useful to know how many words a minute others read; this kind of *comparative appraisal* uses others as a standard for making judgments about the self. But in reflected appraisal, the individual seeks information about whether others believe he is a slow reader. He may tell a friend that he reads 350 words a minute and ask if that rate is slow, or he may read aloud to his mother and look for cues about her reactions to his speed. In a cohesive group, a person may be hesitant to express deviant opinions because of the likelihood of a negative appraisal of him by the other members. He does not ordinarily want attractive others to reflect back to him an impression that he is weird, which would represent a threat to his self-esteem.

An interesting case of a self-concept that

depended almost entirely on the opinions of a single other person is revealed in the *Autobiography of John Stuart Mill.* John was under the strict tutelage of his father, James Mill, and did not engage in play with peers. He learned Greek and Latin by the time he was three and calculus soon after, and he edited his father's history of India before entering his teens. Yet he had no conception that any of this was out of the ordinary. He had no standards against which to compare himself, and his father treated his achievements as unexceptional.

Harry Stack Sullivan (1953), a psychiatrist, argued that an individual's self-concept is a reflection of his relationships with a few significant other people, primarily his mother. To minimize fear of rejection and to gain the approval of these few significant others, the individual adopts their standards and values. Concepts of "good me" and "bad me" are formed and serve as a basis for his behavior. Wylie's (1961) review of the relevant research reveals support for Sullivan's theory. The self-concepts of children are very similar to the impressions they believe their parents have of them. Particularly important is the child's perception of the attitudes of his or her parent of the same sex. Maladjusted children believe that their parents hold contradictory views about them.

Black children and members of other minority groups may be taught self-hatred through the reflected appraisals of people of the majority culture. An indication of this process was found by Clark and Clark (1958). They gave three- to seven-year-old black children a choice between playing with a white or a brown doll. About two-thirds of the children preferred the white doll. Over 50 percent of the children evaluated the brown doll negatively ("looks bad"), while only 17 percent stated that the white doll "looks bad." Preference for white or light skin over black by black children has been demonstrated repeatedly (Greenwald & Oppenheim, 1968; Morland, 1966; Stevenson & Stewart, 1958).

A series of important black writers, including James Baldwin, Franz Fanon, Malcolm X, Eldridge Cleaver, and Ralph Ellison, have participated in creating a new sense of pride in being black. In a television interview, Baldwin reflected on the appraisal of blacks that has been displayed by a majority of whites. He said that if he were white, wore a beard, long hair, jeans, a polo shirt, and boots, collected unemployment compensation and rode a motorcycle, he might be disliked and rejected. If he wanted to be accepted he could shave, get a haircut, change his clothes, obtain a job, and trade the bike in for a small automobile. But as a black he is rejected because his hair is too kinky, his lips too thick, his skin too dark, and his nose too flat, none of which he could change. Although some blacks formerly straightened their hair by painful procedures or lightened their skin with various creams in the hope of "passing," most were doomed to rejection and feelings of ugliness. Once the black American rejected white standards and accepted his own standards of beauty and worth, a new sense of pride and positive evaluation developed. The rapidity of this change among today's black adults suggests that child rearing may not have as permanent an effect on the development of self-concept as many psychologists have supposed.

Reactions to positive or negative evaluations from others have been investigated in many social psychological experiments. Positive evaluations may lead to doing favors and interpersonal attraction. Negative evaluations may lead to dislike, anger, and harmdoing. Sometimes information that others see him as weak may cause an individual to engage in coercive behavior designed to restore "face." Indications that he has failed to meet the expectations of others may lead him to try harder or to give up altogether. The specific conditions under which these transitory threats to self-esteem lead to each of these reactions will be explicated in later chapters.

B. Achievement Motivation and Control Orientation

Children are faced with a series of tasks in the home, in school, and at play. The history of successes and failures experienced by the child, the degree of responsibility and encouragement provided to him by his parents and teachers, and his comparative and reflective appraisals will all contribute to his assessment of his own abilities. The aspirations of an individual and the degree of control he believes he exercises over his environment are dependent on his task-related experiences.

1. Level of Aspiration

Success in solving tasks produces self-confidence and encourages the individual to attempt even more difficult tasks. Failure produces anxiety, withdrawal, and a lowering of aspirations. Hoppe (1931) showed these effects of success and failure in a ring-toss game. Children were asked to estimate how many of 16 rings they thought they could toss over moving pegs. The children had no prior experience with the task and, hence, could have no realistic appraisal of how well they might do. Most started by making cautious and low estimates of their probable success. These estimates were called the subject's level of aspiration (LA). Over a series of trials it was found that LA generally was raised after success and lowered after failure.

A child may receive praise for successful performance or he may suffer disapproval for failure. Standards of excellence are often stressed by significant others, and both social and material reinforcements may be made contingent on achieving high standards. Privileges or gifts or praise may be provided for getting good grades at school or for getting a good batting average in softball games. An individual may develop an aspiration for achievement with respect to the kinds of tasks emphasized as important by those who control his reinforcement. McClelland, Atkinson, Clark, and Lowell (1953) refer to the development of an internal standard of excellence (LA) as a *need for achievement*. Some children may aspire to achieve high performance in athletics, others in intellectual or artistic tasks, and still others in economic activities.

According to Crandall, Katkovsky, and Preston (1960), achievement behavior is directed toward gaining approval for competence in performance on tasks for which standards of excellence are relevant. Birney, Burdick, and Teevan (1969) have focused on the opposite side of the coin. Children who continually experience failure try to avoid disapproval by attempting only easy tasks or by setting such unrealistically high levels of aspiration that success is almost impossible and failure is not likely to bring disapproval.

2. Internal and External Control Orientation

Rotter (1954, 1966) has applied the basic principles of learning theory to personality development and particularly to feelings of mastery or control. An individual acquires beliefs or expectancies as a result of his experiences in a variety of situations. He learns that he is effective in gaining reinforcement for himslf or that he is not. This *generalized expectancy* regarding his control over the outcomes of his behavior defines the dimension of internal or external control and refers to "the degree to which the individual believes that what happens to him results from his own behavior versus the degree to which he believes that what happens to him is the result of luck, chance, fate, or forces beyond his control" (Rotter, 1967a, p. 128). In other words, a person with a *internal control orientation* typically attributes his outcomes to his own behavior, while a person with a *external control orientation* attributes the causes of his outcomes to chance, fate, or the acts of others. Whether outcomes represent success or failure is not the issue; what is important is the expectancy that one can do things to produce desired effects. The person with an external orientation does not view himself as able to influence what happens to him; he does not expect rewards for solving tasks or performing well, nor does he expect punishment and disapproval for failing; whatever happens happens, and he believes he has no control over events. Rotter (1966) and Crandall, Katkovsky, and Crandall (1965) and others have developed paper-and-pencil measures of I-E control.

As might be expected, "internals" have been found to be more achievement-oriented than "externals" (cf. Lefcourt, 1972). Internals set more realistic LAs for themselves on the basis of success and failure feedback than do externals (Phares, 1957; Rotter, 1966). These differences are not attributable to intelligence. Although internals score scholastically at a higher level than externals, there is only a moderately positive correlation between intelligence and internal control orientation (Crandall, Katkovsky, & Preston, 1960). Even when IQ scores are controlled, internals have higher grade point averages in college than do externals (Lessing, 1969).

A person who believes he can control his own destiny would display more self-control than someone who believes his life is controlled by outside forces. Walls and Smith (1970) did find a positive correlation between internal orientation and delay of gratification as indicated by the choice of a delayed, larger reward over an immediate, smaller reward. Externals are less able to delay gratification and exercise less self-control than internals. Internals, for example, have been found to be more successful in quitting cigarette smoking than externals (James, Woodruff, & Werner, 1965).

Internals actively seek out information that will help them solve particular problems. In a study of inmates at a prison, Seeman (1967) found that those prisoners who were internally oriented learned more about rules, parole laws, and long-range economic facts than did externals. Presumably, this kind of information had instrumental value in obtaining release from prison and in facilitating rehabilitation once released. Internal control orientation has also been shown to be related to taking action for social causes (Gore & Rotter, 1963; Strickland, 1965).

3. Ecological Factors, Achievement Motivation , and Control Orientation

Environmental circumstances may provide an individual with inept models, lack of opportunity for success or control, and little approval for achievement. Lower-class children tend to be external, while middle-class children tend to be internal in their orientation toward control; and blacks are more external than whites, especially in the lower classes (Battle & Rotter, 1963).

A person may learn helplessness or hopelessness from a history of failures and an inability to control his own outcomes. Infrahuman animals have been shown to learn helplessness in laboratory experiments. In a typical study (Carlson & Black, 1960; Dinsmoor & Campbell, 1956; Overmier & Seligman, 1967; Seligman & Maier, 1967) the organism is exposed to a series of inescapable shocks. For example, a rat may be confined to a box with an electrified floor or a dog may be strapped in a harness and cannot escape shocks. After a relatively brief exposure to inescapable shocks, the previously helpless organism is given an opportunity to learn avoidance responses, such as pushing a bar or jumping out of the compartment. These responses are readily learned by organisms who have not been exposed to noncontingent and inescapable punishments, but the previously helpless animals are completely unable to learn an avoidance response. Instead, they crouch, take their punishment, and make little or no effort to escape. In a "therapy" study of helpless dogs, the investigators finally taught them avoidance responses, but only after the dogs had been physically dragged from the shock compartment to a safe compartment 30 to 50 times (Seligman, Maier, & Greer, 1968).

Fear of failure and external control orientation produce behavior that is similar to the learned helplessness of animals. There is no motivation to learn anything new even when new responses would be instrumental in bringing about rewards or removing punishments. The therapy study of Seligman et al. suggests that great patience and extensive training will be required to change these patterns of learned helplessness. Such remedial programs may not be geared specifically to producing success experiences, but may be directed toward providing an individual with the realization that he can control his own outcomes; he must be given a sense of control or power over his environment. Once he develops enough confidence to take initiatives, specific training to correct errors and reduce the probability of failures can follow. This kind of remedial program may also be required in the rehabilitation of prisoners. As can be seen in Box 6.2, the incarcerated individual may lose confidence in his ability to "make it" outside prison walls.

Box 6.2   LEARNED HELPLESSNESS AND THE GERMAN CONCENTRATION CAMP

Bruno Bettelheim, now a leading child psychiatrist, spent the year 1938-39 in German concentration camps at Dachau and Buchenwald. Prisoners in these camps were required to perform hard labor and suffered malnutrition, torture, and strict regulation of every moment of their time. The Gestapo ran these camps for four reasons: to break down the inmates as individuals, to spread terror among the outside population, to provide training to Gestapo members, and to provide the Gestapo with an experimental laboratory. In a general way, the camps were designed to brainwash the prisoners and rehabilitate them as citizens of the Nazi state. Bettelheim partially protected himself from the effect of the camp experience by informally carrying out his profession of psychiatrist through observing, interviewing, and collecting data. He was distinguished from almost all the other prisoners by being in this way able to maintain some continuity between his former life and the extreme life of Dachau.

Bettelheim (1958) observed differences between new prisoners, those in the camp less than one year, and old prisoners, those who had been there three years or more. The new prisoners detached themselves mentally from the most brutal aspects of camp life; it somehow never seemed real—the brutalities happened to them as objects but not to them as persons. What was real was their contact with the outside world and their hopes and daydreams about their return to their "real" life. For the old prisoners, however, the outside life was remote and inaccessible and camp life was accepted as their everyday world. The old prisoners schemed to get a better place in the camp rather than trying to stay in contact with the outside world. They were now detached from their families, had little hope of ever rejoining them, and for the foreseeable future, their lives required adjustments to the contingencies of the concentration camp.

The Gestapo attempted to eliminate the individuality of the prisoners by treating them as groups, working them in groups, and punishing every member of the group for an individual transgression. The prisoners were forced to assume a childlike dependence on the guards since permission had to be obtained to use the latrine. They were forced to address one another with the German "thou," which is used only among young children, while they were required to give full deference to the guards in addressing them. They were forced to perform childish and stupid labor like carrying rocks from one place to another and then back again, and digging holes with their hands when tools were readily available.

The older prisoners adopted the values and behavior of the guards. When they were in charge of a group of fellow prisoners they were often more brutal and cruel than the guards. They sometimes helped the Gestapo in getting rid of troublesome prisoners. They even tried to get pieces of the guards' uniforms to wear, or they altered their camp garb to match the fashion of the uniforms. They copied the guards' game of hitting each other to see who could stand being hit the longest without a complaint, and they prided themselves in standing well at attention during the count formations. They obeyed nonsensical rules made up by the guards even after the guards themselves had forgotten about them. This blind obedience to and emulation of the guards were fostered by the helplessness and dependence of the prisoners in the concentration camp.

Child-rearing practices have been shown to be important in the development of both achievement motivation and fear of failure. Winterbottom (1958) examined the stories written by 8 to 10-year-old male children for the use of themes related to achievement needs. This measure of achievement motivation was then related to responses about their child-rearing practices obtained in interviews with the mothers of the children. Children with strong achievement motivation had greater demands placed on them to be independent, were given more responsibility at an earlier age, and were consistently rewarded for fulfillment of parental demands; they apparently learned that they could control their own reinforcements by accepting high standards of performance in the kinds of situations stressed by their parents. A follow-up study of the same children six years later found that the independence training reported by the mothers was still predictive of the boys' achievement scores (Feld, 1959).

The importance of rewarding success is emphasized in a study reported by Teevan

and McGhee (1972). They modified the Winterbottom questionnaire to examine the development of fear of failure in children. The mothers of high fear-of-failure children used many of the same child rearing practices as did the mothers of children with high achievement motivation; they stressed independence and achievement behavior, and they punished unsatisfactory behavior. However, they did not reward their children for successes. The mothers of low fear-of-failure children characteristically rewarded their sons following their satisfactory behavior.

Self-attributions of power or control are obviously related to achievement motivation, fear of failure, and learned helplessness. In terms of the structure of society it is only natural that lower class, disenfranchised, and alienated people should feel unable to control their own lives. For the most part they are simply being realistic. The social scientist must be careful to recognize the value bias associated with a middle-class notion of control orientation. The standards of excellence or task ef fectiveness that are usually employed in research on control orientation reflect the values of the middle-class world. But consider what would happen to the person who scores high on a paper-and-pencil measure of internal control when he is left to fend for himself in a back alley of a slum neighborhood late on a Saturday night. He is not likely to feel in control of his own outcomes. On the other hand, the ghetto resident may feel more confidence and competence in the world to which he is accustomed.

Whether a person feels powerful or powerless may depend upon the nature of the situation. A recent study indicates that the paper-and-pencil measure of internal-external control may, in fact, measure four different factors: the difficult-easy world, the just-unjust world, the predictable-unpredictable world, and the politically responsive-unresponsive world (Collins, 1974). Thus, internal control may reflect a person's expectations of success in a difficult (complex problem-solving) and just (effort and ability payoff) world. The same person may display an external control orientation with regard to political matters because he considers local, national or international events to be unpredictable and policy to be unresponsive to his efforts and skill. Future research on control orientations will probably place more emphasis on behavior in complex non-laboratory settings.

Relating expectations to specific types of situations recognizes the multifaceted and complex nature of the individual's self-concept. A person who feels graceful on the football field may consider himself clumsy on a dance floor. One who is convinced of his ability and vigor in pursuing his goals may feel impotent in trying to change his political situation. As we have seen, the origins of such diverse self-impressions are the reflected appraisals of others, successes and failures in achieving levels of aspiration, and the individual's experience of his ability to affect the reinforcements he receives.

C. Identification

Identification refers to the relatively permanent adoption by an individual of the attributes, behavior, fashions, values, or demeanor of a model or a class of models. This imitative behavior may be considered to be internalized by the individual. Although at first the adopted characteristic may be deliberately and consciously imitated, it eventually becomes a stable feature of his self-concept and life style. For example, a little boy or girl is typically informed by others of the appropriate behavior associated with his or her sex identity. The child may then view the characteristic, trait, or behavior as appropriate and expected and therefore begin to display it. Before long the characteristic becomes part of the individual's definition of himself.

Identification may occur through social learning and the imitation of important social models. Bandura and Huston (1961) have shown that children imitate both the task-relevant and the incidental behavior of a model; they may take on many of the characteristics of models in addition to specific instrumental behavior. Particularly important for determining who the child will identify with is the perceived power of the model in terms of his control over resources and his ability to influence others. The effectiveness of these power-related capabilities in facilitating identification is sometimes explained in terms of *status envy*. Because the child wants to be powerful, he identifies with those who are perceived to possess power; if he does what powerful people do, then he may become powerful also. Oscar Wilde captured the essence of this process when he observed that "imitation is the sincerest form of flattery." The behavior of the concentration camp prisoners described in Box 6.2, can be interpreted in terms of status envy.

Parsons (1955) stressed the importance of parental power in the process of identification, as have more recent studies of modeling and imitation. Hetherington (1965) hypothesized that children of either sex would identify with the more powerful or dominant parent. During the first years of life, children have few other models and are relatively unaware of any conflicting social norms regarding conduct appropriate to their sex. Hetherington separately interviewed parents about how they would handle 12 hypothetical problems involving child behavior. Then both parents were brought together and asked to discuss each problem until they reached agreement. By comparing the interview responses with those accepted by both patents in discussion, it was possible to determine which of the parents was dominant. The degree of masculinity or femininity of the children was also measured. Finally, the parents were separately used as models to ascertain how much imitation they elicited from their children.

Parental dominance did affect imitation, but only for boys, for whom the dominant parent was more often imitated. Which parent was dominant was not related to the sex-role behavior of girls. Boys were affected by inversions from the conventional male-dominant pattern in the home. Boys from mother-dominated homes displayed more feminine characteristics than those from father-dominated homes. These effects of parental dominance were present at ages 4-5 and were sustained through ages 9-11.

Sex-role identification has a profound impact on the development of the child; it governs the attitudes, values, and skills one is expected to have and is reflected in the clothes one wears and the occupation one chooses, in tastes, hobbies, courting practices, manner of walking and sitting, and in speech. Recent concern with "sexism" has created an awareness that many people hold stereotypes of persons because of their gender. A new interpretation of the Virgin Mary by the Vatican attempts to bridge the gap between traditional and liberated views of women (see Box 6.3).

The child clearly learns the concepts "male" and "female" before the age of five (Hartup & Zook, 1960; Kagan, Hosken, & Watson, 1961). The prevailing sex-role stereotypes about masculinity and femininity in a given culture are adopted rapidly by its children. It is interesting to note that there are significant differences among cultures in the ideal characteristics attributed to each sex. Block (1973) asked respondents in six countries to provide a description of the "kind of person I would most like to be" by checking the appropriate adjectives on a list. As can be seen in Table 6.4, the stereotypes for men and women in the United States are sharply different, much more so than in Denmark and Sweden.

Children are rewarded for meeting the cultural expectations of behavior appropriate to their sex. Preschool boys are aware of the kinds of behavior expected of them, while girls learn these expectations more slowly (Brown, 1956, 1958). Not only are more stringent demands made of boys (and at an earlier age), but these demands are more strongly enforced. More stress is placed on inappropriate behavior for boys than on what they should do. Adults tell them that boys don't cry and don't play with dolls, etc. Perhaps this is why many boys evidence anxiety about their masculinity and avoid behavior that might be considered feminine and invite anxiety-provoking reflected appraisals from significant others. In American society, to display emotion is distinctly feminine (see Table 6.4). Consistent with this stereotype are the reports by children of the amount of affection displayed toward them by their parents. Seventh grade girls receive more affection than boys, and both report more affection from their mothers than from their fathers (Droppleman & Schaefer, 1961).

Box 6.3 POPE PAUL DESCRIBES MARY AS "FAR FROM SUBMISSIVE"*

Vatican City (AP)

Pope Paul VI, in an attempt to modernize the image of the Virgin Mary, describes her as "the new woman" who took an active role in the early Christian church and championed the rights of the weak against the powerful.

"The modern woman will note with pleasant surprise that Mary of Nazareth . . . was far from being a timidly submissive woman," the Roman Catholic pontiff writes in the fourth document he has issued on Mary in his 10 years as pope.

In a 95-page "Apostolic Exhortation for the Right Ordering and Development of Devotion to the Blessed Virgin Mary," issued today the Pope conceded that "that picture of the Blessed Virgin presented in a certain type of devotional literature cannot easily be reconciled with today's life style, especially with the way women live today."

But he proposed Mary as an example to be imitated for the way in which "she fully and responsibly accepted the will of God."

To "the modern woman anxious to participate with decision-making power in the affairs of the community, Mary will appear not as a mother exclusively concerned with her own divine son but rather as a woman whose action helped to strengthen the apostolic community's faith . . . ," he wrote.

"She was a woman who did not hesitate to proclaim that God vindicates the humble and the oppressed, and removes the powerful people of this world from their privileged positions."

"Mary, the new woman, stands at the side of Christ, the new man," Pope Paul said.

He said devotion to Mary was something that Catholics shared with the Orthodox churches and with the Anglicans, and he expressed concern about the impact that a false approach to devotion of the Virgin Mary would have on efforts to bring Christians of all denominations closer together.

*From *The Messenger,* Athens, Ohio, Sunday, March 24, 1974.

Grusec and Brinker (1971) have shown that young children are selectively attentive to the sex-appropriate incidental behavior of adult models. Five- and seven-year-old boys and girls were shown movies of male and female adult models performing a variety of simple actions. The children were later better able to recall the behavior of the adult of the same sex.

The problems associated with learning sex-appropriate behavior are different for boys and girls. Girls have more contact with a sex-appropriate model than do boys in American society, because the mother interacts more with the children than the father, who often works or plays for long hours outside the home. A little girl can imitate the behavior of her mother, but a

Table 6.4 Sex Differences in Adjective Ideal Self-Descriptions Among Students in Six Countries. X Indicates That Males and O Indicates That Females Use More Often.[a]

	Country					
Adjective	United States	England	Sweden	Denmark	Finland	Norway
Practical, shrewd	X	X	X	X	X	X
Assertive	X	X		X	X	X
Dominating	X	X	X		X	X
Competitive	X	X	X			X
Critical	X	X			X	X
Self-controlled	X	X			X	X
Rational, reasonable	X				X	
Ambitious	X		X			
Feels guilty				X		X
Moody		X				
Self-centered		X		X		
Sense of humor					X	
Responsible					X	
Fair, just						
Independent						X
Adventurous						X
Loving, affectionate	O	O	O	O	O	O
Impulsive	O	O	O		O	O
Sympathetic	O	O	O		O	O
Generous	O		O	O		O
Vital, active	O					O
Perceptive, aware	O					O
Sensitive	O	O	O			
Reserved, shy	O	O				
Artistic					O	O
Curious		O				
Uncertain, indecisive					O	O
Talkative		O			O	
Helpful		O				
Sense of humor		O				
Idealistic				O		
Cheerful						O
Considerate						O

young boy often must develop a more abstract conception of his masculine role through information provided by his mother, the mass media, his peers, and trial-and-error learning.

According to Lynn (1962), "The little girl acquires a learning method which primarily involves: (a) a personal relationship and (b) imitation rather than restructuring of the field and abstracting principles. On the other hand, the little boy acquires a different learning method which primarily involves: (a) defining the goal; (b) restructuring the field; and (c) abstracting principles" (p. 558). Lynn believes these differences in learning sex roles have important implications for many other aspects of the lives of males and females in our society. Females develop a concern for affiliating with others for social comparison purposes, which makes them more socially dependent than males. Because of their focus on abstract reasoning in sex-role identification, males tend to surpass females in problem-solving skills and develop a greater concern for abstract internalized moral standards.

Sex differences are consistently found in psychological experiments which use adult subjects. Females are more preoccupied with affiliation (Lansky, Crandall, Kagan, & Baker, 1961), are more conforming (Tuddenham, 1961), are less able to perform well on problem-solving tasks that require creative thinking (Sweeney, 1953), and are more responsive to the standards of others (Douvan, 1957) than are males. On the other hand, boys tend to be more independent and deviant, as indicated by the fact that delinquency rates strongly favor young males and that boys are more likely to be referred to child guidance centers (Schwartz, 1949; Gilbert, 1957; Ullman, 1957). Thus the sex-related stereotypes held by members of the culture get translated into actual behavior through socialization.

Learning to identify with a role is a very complex process. A role involves a set of actions that are learned in a variety of situations, from a number of different people, and by numerous means. A child learns his or her sex role at home, in school, and at play from parents, teachers, relatives, and friends, through modeling, symbolic communications, and trial-and-error behavior. Another method, central in the theories of Mead and Piaget, is role-playing. Direct "rehearsals" provide an individual with the opportunity to integrate the disparate elements he has learned into a single role.

Role learning is not confined to gender identification. A person may identify himself in terms of his job or profession, his ethnic group, his religion, or through association with important national symbols. Not only may a person perceive himself as a social psychologist, but he may also conceive of himself as an Italian or Scandinavian, a Catholic Protestant, Jew, or atheist, and as a white or black American citizen. The ability of Jews to survive 5000 years of pogroms, wars, and extermination rests largely on their strong self-identification as Jews. Until recently a sense of Jewishness was based on religion and the rejection of others. Today the nation of Israel serves as a source of identification.

The importance of these multiple identifications for self-concept can be illustrated with reference to American blacks. Negroes were stripped of much of the basis for self-identity when they were shipped from Africa to America. They were given non-African names, their religions were systematically eliminated, and their families were destroyed by the arbitrary trading of husbands, wives, and children. While most white Americans can trace their ancestry to specific countries in Europe, most black Americans are unable to trace their genealogy to particular African nations. The recent emphasis on identification with African culture, including learning Swahili, wearing African dress, and taking African names, is part of the re-identification process among American blacks. The rediscovery of Africa is interesting because it has had to cut through the image created of a Dark Continent infested with savage and wild primitive tribes, as shown in Tarzan movies. The peoples of Africa have had great civilizations and have contributed greatly to Western culture. For example, African sculpture stimulated the artistic experimentation by Picasso and Braque called Cubism, which was one of the most important developments of modern art. The pendulum is now swinging the other way and American blacks have gained a sense of pride through their identification with a sometimes idealized view of Africa.

D.   Psychosocial Development and Identity Crisis

Erikson (1950) has posed a theory of development that focuses on the way a person copes with other people and the concept he forms of himself. Based on naive and uncontrolled observations and biographical analyses of historical figures (e.g., Martin Luther), Erikson speculates that psychosocial development involves eight stages, each of which poses a conflict for the individual. Adequate resolution of each conflict in succession permits continual personal growth and increasing social maturity. Failure to resolve a conflict can produce despair and interpersonal ineffectiveness. The identity (stage 5) and intimacy (stage 6) crises pose major problems for young adults. The eight stages and conflicts proposed by Erikson are as follows:

1.   Trust Versus Mistrust

The question that must be resolved here is whether the environment is orderly and predictable or chaotic and unpredictable. This conflict is encountered in the first year of life. The resolution of the conflict depends on the quality of care and nurturance received from other persons, particularly the mother. The child learns whether he can or cannot rely on other people.

2.   Autonomy Versus Doubt

This crisis occurs in the second and third years of life and requires the child to determine if he is adequate or ineffective in dealing with his environment. Excessive criticism and restraint on exploration can cause shame or doubt. Rewards and approval may give the child a sense of independence. There is a strong similarity between autonomy-doubt and Rotter's concepts of internal and external control.

3.   Initiative Versus Guilt

This crisis is met at the age of four or five. Its resolution will depend on the parents. Will their responses to the child create a sense of freedom and initiative or of guilt and ineptitude?

4.   Industry Versus Inferiority

Does the person learn to handle tools and develop skills that can be used in the environment outside the home or does he develop a sense of inferiority from the reflected appraisals of others? This is the crisis of the early school years (ages 6-11).

5.   Identity Versus Role Confusion

Can the person define himself and his roles and values adequately? Is he accepted by others or is he considered an outsider? Problems concerning adult ideologies are confronted during this crisis at 12-18 years of age, as the individual ponders religion, politics, and utopian ideas.

6.   Intimacy Versus Isolation

Once the individual resolves his identity crisis, he must determine whether it can be fused with another person or whether he must suffer isolation. This is the crisis of early adulthood. Intimacy demands a commitment to others and requires the ethical strength to abide by the commitment despite costs, sacrifices, and compromises. Sometimes two persons can form a partnership with one another in isolation from the rest of the social world.

7. Generativity Versus Stagnation

This adult crisis pits responsibility to the younger generation against the self-indulgences of the individual. Early physical or psychological invalidism may produce sufficient self-concern to resolve the crisis in favor of self-indulgence.

8. Ego Integrity Versus Despair

How will the person view his own life in retrospect? Will he look back with satisfaction and pride at the way he has resolved the crises of his life or will he despair that he has no more time to build a life of integrity? This is the crisis of maturity.

There is little or no evidence other than clinical observation to support Erikson's theory of psychosocial development. There is some question about whether it is even testable. However, the keen observations of this sensitive psychiatrist are worthy of note. They are remarkably similar to scientific concepts developed after his theory was formulated, including achievement motivation, internal-external control orientations, and independence training.

VII. CHAPTER SUMMARY

An individual is born with certain capacities for learning and development, but he actualizes these potentialities only in relation to other people. Without the aid of others, the child is essential to his successful integration into the social world. Socialization agents provide the growing child with material, informational, and social reinforcement when he performs desired, appropriate, and approved responses. Social reinforcements are particularly effective with children, who are dependent on adults for approval and love. Approval dependence varies with conditions of deprivation and satiation, the anxiety of the individual, and the ambiguity of the situation. Social reinforcements may serve as tacit communications that prompt the target person to act in a manner to please the source.

Bandura's social learning theory of development conceives of the individual as an information-processing organism capable of symbolically representing the causal structure of the environment from information obtained through observations of the behavior of other people. The actions of models produce effects and outcomes, and may be interpreted as tacit communications that an observer can symbolically decode for their information value. If the decoding process is hampered by competing cognitive activity or by inconsistencies or ambiguities in the behavior of the model, imitation will not occur.

After decoding the tacit communication associated with a model's behavior, the observer must decide whether he should also perform the behavior. The relevance of the model's behavior to the observer's course of conduct may be increased by similarities between them and by the particular situations both experience. A boy may be more likely to imitate a male peer than an adult female, particularly when the situation the boy faces is similar to the one in which the model successfully acquired rewards. The degree of success and the value of the rewards gained by the model are directly related to the amount of imitation displayed by observers. Expressions of joy, comfort, fear, or anxiety emitted by the model that reflect subjective states associated with rewards and punishments may also elicit or inhibit imitation.

Observational learning can be interpreted as a special case of social influence in which the model is the source and the observer is the target of tacit communications. By the example of his own behavior, the model-source transmits the tacit message to anyone who may be observing that "If you do as I do you will receive the same outcome." The heuristic value of interpreting modeling in terms of social influence is that it alerts the social psychologist to the possible effects of source and target characteristics on imitation. Consistent with findings in other areas of social influence, the attractiveness, expertness, and power of the model and the lack of confidence, low self-esteem, and information dependence of the observer increase the probability that the observer will imitate the behavior of the model.

Both direct reinforcements and vicarious learning determine standards for self-evaluation and self-reinforcement. The individual learns high standards for self-evaluation because of their association with greater future reinforcements. The middle-class culture of American society serves to bolster high standards of performance (need-achievement motivation) and stringent criteria for self-reinforcement.

While some understanding of how an individual learns has been gained through recent research along these lines, the manner in which rewards and punishments affect patterns of social interaction is not well understood at present. Bandura (1971) has illustrated how reciprocal reinforcements may operate in a parent-child interaction: "On most occasions children's mild requests go unheeded because the parent is disinterested or preoccupied with other activities. If further bids also go unrewarded, the child will generally display progressively more intense behavior that is increasingly aversive to the parent. At this stage in the interactive sequence, the child is exercising aversive control over the parent. Eventually the parent is forced to terminate the troublesome behavior by attending to the child, thereby reinforcing obstreperous responsiveness. Since the child gains parental attention and the parent gains temporary peace, the behavior of both participants is rewarded, although the long-term effects benefit neither" (p. 41).

The intellectual development of the child involves qualitative changes in the way information is processed. According to Piaget's theory of intellectual development, the individual evolves through a sequence of stages as he acquires language, develops the ability to take the roles and perspectives of other people (decenters), and shifts from concrete and simple to abstract and complex modes of thinking. Intellectual development is intertwined with all other aspects of socialization.

The theory of moral development proposed by Piaget has emphasized the effects of cognitive factors on the individual's moral judgments. Early intellectual functioning which involves egocentrism, absolutism, and concrete thinking are associated with an immature form of moral reasoning, while decentering, relativism, and abstract thinking are associated with more mature levels. Assignment of responsibility implies a willingness to impose punishments. The kind of punishment advocated is associated with the level of moral maturity; expiatory punishment is considered appropriate by the moral realist, while reciprocity punishment is advocated by the more mature morally independent person. Similarly, the principle by which rewards should be allocated to members of groups is assumed to shift from reliance on parental authority to an equality principle and then to an equity norm.

Kohlberg has elaborated on Piaget's basic theory by suggesting that there are three general levels of moral reasoning, with two stages within each level. While subsequent research has generally supported the sequential development of the individual from the two stages of the preconventional level through the two stages of the conventional level, stages 4 through 6 may represent parallel political philosophies of conservatism and liberalism ("postconventional" morality).

Both personal and situational factors affect the individual's ability to resist temptation to transgress against moral rules. The notion of levels of moral reasoning or a general disposition to transgress account for very little of moral behavior. A person who has positive self-esteem, has received sex-appropriate training from his or her parents, and has a well-developed time perspective, is apt to possess self-control and will most probably be able to resist temptation. The timing of punishments by socialization agents may be important in creating self-control. Punishments that occur at the time transgressive responses are initiated produce self-control because of the reduction of anxiety that accompanies resistance to temptation. Punishments that occur after the misbehavior may create guilt in the individual.

The probability and costs of detection are inversely related to transgressions. When a person has a strong incentive for transgressive behavior and cannot achieve what he desires by legitimate means, transgression is likely to occur. A person may also be motivated to transgress if he feels he has been wronged and believes his behavior will redress the injustice.

There are consequences for an individual whether or not he resists temptation. He may experience either pride or guilt. Pride may be the learned anticipation of social approval for displaying self-control. Guilt may involve a number of post-transgression actions, such as self-criticism, remorse, and restitution. These responses may reduce anxiety and influence others to reduce or eliminate restitutive punishment. It is difficult to know whether these guilt-related responses truly represent an internal conscience or superego or whether they are simply learned strategies directed toward avoiding punishment.

In the course of socialization each person forms a self-concept consisting of a complex set of attitudes toward himself as an object. Self-definition occurs as a function of comparative and reflected appraisals, evaluations of one's abilities, attitudes, and physical appearance. A person with a history of success tends to increase incrementally his level of aspiration, and one with a history of failure may set a very low or an unrealistically high level of aspiration. Internalization of standards of excellence with respect to certain tasks reflects an achievement orientation. A person who learns that he can effectively manipulate his environment and produce his own reinforcements develops an internal control orientation, while a person whose reinforcements are not contingent on his responses but instead appear to be capricious develops an external control orientation. Achievement orientation is associated with internal control and fear of failure is related to external control.

Ecological factors and child-rearing practices determine the motivations and control orientations of children. Lower class children tend to feel powerless, have a history of failure experiences in school (which has a middle-class orientation), and live in a highly unpredictable environment. They tend also to develop external control orientations. A sense of helplessness, which is very difficult to reverse, is learned among disadvantaged children. Independence training, assignment of responsibility at an early age, and consistent reinforcement of performance that meets parental expectations is associated with high achievement motivation. The same constellation of factors may cause the individual to have a high fear of failure if his successful performances go unrewarded.

An individual tends to adopt the characteristics, traits, attitudes, and behavior of others. He may imitate powerful models, learn appropriate behavior through symbolic communication or through trial-and-error, and persuade himself through role-playing activities. Self-identity is complex, involving identification with gender and with a multitude of other roles. A person's theory about himself is not a hierarchical and organized structure, but a set of situation-oriented and sometimes contradictory attitudes and kinds of behavior. A person's self-concept is constructed out of his sense of identification with other people, rules, religious beliefs, historical events, and the norms of his society.

SUGGESTED READINGS

Bandura, A. *Social learning theory.* New York: General Learning Press, 1971. A review of the literature on modeling and social learning in a looseleaf modular form.

Clausen, J. A. (Ed.) *Socialization and society.* Boston: Little, Brown, and Company, 1968. A collection of papers dealing with problems and processes of socialization through the life cycle. For the more advanced student.

Danziger, K. *Socialization.* Baltimore: Penguin Books, 1971. A review of the field of study for the introductory student.

Gordon, C., and Gergen, K. J. (Eds.) *The self in social interaction.* New York: Wiley, 1968. A collection of some of the most important theoretical and empirical papers written on the topic of self-concept during the twentieth century.

Hamachek, D. E. *Encounters with the self.* New York: Holt, Rinehart and Winston, 1971. A broadranging introduction to the self-concept literature.

Wright, D. *The psychology of moral behaviour.* Baltimore: Penguin, 1971. A presentation of what is known about moral judgments and conduct written for the introductory student.

PART **3**

Interdependence and Influence

Most of the things you want in life depend to some degree on the actions of other people. A desire for good health makes most of us dependent on practitioners of medicine. Our need for food cannot be fulfilled in an urban society independently of supermarkets, wholesale food distributors, processing and packaging firms, farmers, and the federal Food and Drug Administration. Policemen, firemen, educators, journalists, bus drivers, and many others provide services that are essential to us. Our friends and co-workers provide us with information, approval or disapproval, and rewards and punishments. The interdependence between people is the basis for cooperative relations and also produces conflicts among them. We seek to control our interactions so we can gain positive outcomes from ourselves and avoid unpleasant outcomes. We must find ways of influencing other people to do what we want them to do.

The interdependence of people makes the processes of social influence basic to the understanding of their behavior. Chapter 7 provides an analysis of the forms that interactions can take and of the influence tactics that can be employed by individuals as they attempt to get their way with others. Within the context of a particular pattern of interaction, an individual may attempt to manipulate features of the environment, reinforcement, and information to influence others. The influence tactics described in Chapter 7 will be important for understanding the remainder of this book.

Chapter 8 is concerned with the factors that contribute to the success of the various modes of influence. The characteristics of the source, the history of past interactions, the type or content of communication, the gains and costs of yielding and of resistance, and the personality of the target all play a part in determining his reaction to influence attempts. As we shall see, social psychologists have also explored the factors that encourage the individual to resist influence.

A different set of questions is posed in Chapter 9. Here we are concerned with what causes an influence agent to choose to influence a particular target and how he arrives at the decision about the kind of influence tactic he should employ. Special emphasis is given to coercive influence as we try to understand why men harm one another and engage in violent actions. In addition, social interaction will be viewed as a dynamic bargaining process that involves tactics used to gain advantage or compromise from others. When three or more persons find themselves in conflict with one another, they may form alliances or coalitions. How coalitions form and the rules which govern the distribution of their winnings are presented in Chapter 9.

Although the next three chapters concentrate on the manipulative nature of human interactions, it would be a mistake to conclude that men are basically Machiavellian. In our own times to be "Machiavellian" means power-mongering and plotting to gain advantage over others. Deceit and treachery are advised at the expense of ethical principles, and selfish gain is emphasized to the exclusion of a generous altruism. An expression of concern for ethics or religion is merely for the purpose of enhancing power and should not be confused with a true sense of moral responsibility. Although these tactics are often employed by most of us, we are not always consciously aware of some of the more subtle ways by which we influence one another. We are not eternally scheming to delude or exploit others. As will be seen in Part 4, men are quite capable of giving more than they receive, of being altruistic and concerned about the welfare of others, and even of giving their lives for abstract principles and ideals. But when viewed in the context of social influence, the machiavellian aspect of man's behavior is naturally emphasized.

CHAPTER 7

Patterns of Social Behavior

CHAPTER PREVIEW

Every human interaction has a structure. Organization settings, cultural norms, and other social factors provide a context within which the structures of interactions take shape. People bring different interests, plans, values, and goals to an interaction. These initial individual factors provide the structure within which subsequent behavior emerges. The direction that behavior will take can be importantly affected by the type of interdependence that exists between persons. If neither person has anything the other desires, it is unlikely that any influence will be attempted by either of them. If one of the parties needs expert help the other can provide, and has resources that are valuable to the other, an exchange can probably be worked out. Whether the goals of the two persons are compatible or in conflict will determine how amiable or hostile their interaction will be. The possession of superior power or the availability of other persons with whom he can interact profitably provides one individual with an advantage in a two-person influence relationship. Hence, as a prelude to examining the various modes of influence available to individuals, the first part of this chapter will deal with the anatomy of interdependency.

Modes of influence can be classified into three basic types: ecological control, reinforcement control, and information control. *Ecological control* refers to the manipulation of the physical or social environment in order to produce specific changes in a target individual. For example, a grocer may place certain "impulse" items in a prominent place in his store to increase the probability that shoppers will buy them. *Reinforcement control* refers to the use of rewards and punishments (or promises of rewards and threats of punishments) as tactics of social influence. Many different kinds of reinforcement may be used by a source of influence, including salaries, fines and bonuses, grades in school, and social

approval or disapproval. *Information control* includes gatekeeping, censorship, and persuasion as methods for trying to change the beliefs, values, and decisions of a target person. Candidates for political office employ information control to persuade people to vote for them.

People are not restricted to language when influencing one another. Nonverbal modes of communication are probably as important for understanding human interaction as the more explicit verbal modes. Birdwhistell (1966) has developed a coding system for "body language," which he refers to as *kinesics*. Various postures and gestures convey meaning and help to regulate human interaction. Hall (1959) coined the term *"proxemics"* to refer to the use of interpersonal space and eye contact in social interaction. Proxemics reveal the attitudes that individuals have toward each other. Although the experimental study of kinesics and proxemics is relatively new in social psychology, we will see that some interesting results have been found.

An account of the individual's exploration of his social environment to gain information about the goals, resources, and intentions of others will conclude the chapter. In making such probes the individual may disclose something about himself as an inducement to the other person to make a reciprocal self-disclosure. The use of humor may make inoffensive and acceptable a probe that otherwise would be considered tactless and inappropriate. In addition, people exchange information about third parties and themselves during rap sessions or through ordinary gossip. The information gathered helps them decide whom to influence and how.

I. THE ANATOMY OF INTERDEPENDENCE

An understanding of the anatomy of interdependence between two persons must take five factors into account: the responsiveness of each party to the other, the amount of conflict arising from incompatibility of their goals, the power relationship between them, their aspirations and how well the interaction satisfies them, and the exchange relationship they may work out between themselves.

Although our focus is on the interaction between two principal parties, its course may be indirectly affected by other parties not immediately involved. This may happen when one party is totally dependent on the other because he knows of no other person with whom he could interact to obtain what he seeks; under these circumstances he is likely to maintain the interaction, even if the other person may cause their relationship to be often unpleasant and frustrating. On the other hand, if many people have what an individual wants, he is not likely to persist in a relationship with someone who is unpleasant or reluctant to provide the outcome desired.

A. Responsiveness in Interaction

Jones and Gerard (1967) have distinguished four classes of two-person interactions based on whether each merely carries out a preestablished plan, whether each has no plan and only reacts to the behavior of the other, or whether each has a plan but is responsive to the other so that his plan is modified to accommodate the other.

1. Pseudocontingency

A pseudocontingency interaction has the appearance of an interaction, but there exists the very minimum of responsiveness. In a two-person pseudocontingency each person's behavior is primarily determined by his pre-established plan. An appearance of interaction is created because each person must dovetail the details of his plan with a series of actions by the other. Each emits a series of timing cues to which the other responds.

Consider as an example two actors on a stage who are reading their parts. Think of them as actors, not as the characters they are playing. Each has come on stage with the pre-established plan of playing his part as well as he can. In order to do so he must act on the cues contained in the speech and action of the other actor. Each is in no way responsive to what the other does; each merely times his actions to the actions of the other.

People participating in rituals, such as weddings and inaugurals, are in pseudocontingency interactions. Jones and Gerard point out that many routine social interactions are pseudocontingencies; the waitress and customer and the doctor and patient each may read their lines rather mechanically according to what they are there to achieve. The customer is there to give an order, and the waitress is there to take one.

2. Reactive Contingency

A reactive contingency is, in a sense, the opposite of a pseudocontingency interaction. In a reactive contingency neither person has a plan; instead, each of their actions is determined by the preceding action of the other. Two novices at chess, knowing only the basic rules and how the pieces can be moved, make their moves based on what their opponent last did; they have no planned strategy. Two persons engaging in a casual and spontaneous conversation in a waiting room are interacting reactively; their interaction is unplanned.

3. Asymmetrical Contingency

An asymmetrical interaction combines the pseudo and reactive classes of interaction. One person's actions are determined by a plan and the other's actions are unplanned and responsive to the first person's behavior. For example, in a structured interview, the interviewer has a set of questions he will ask in order, timing the asking of each in accord with the time required by the respondent for answering the preceding one. The interviewer does not depart from his list of questions nor does he ask the questions out of sequence. The respondent comes with no plan other than to answer the questions put to him. The primary characteristic of an asymmetrical interaction is that one person has had a better opportunity to work out the details of the projected encounter beforehand.

4. Mutual Contingency

The most interesting and most common class of interaction is one of mutual contingency. Here each person enters the interaction with a plan; however, each is responsive to the actions of the other and modifies his plan as a result. An expert in chess will open with a strategy, but he will alter that strategy if the moves of his opponent dictate a change. Two disputants may arrive at a compromise so they can pool their resources, accommodate each other, and both achieve some measure of mutual success. Both have contributed to and both have taken something away from the exchange.

Thibaut and Kelley (1959) have defined interaction as that state of affairs in which people emit behavior in the presence of each other. The four classes of interaction described above suggest that an understanding of social behavior may be facilitated by knowing the structure of interdependence. However, there is clearly more to the matter than the responsiveness of two individuals to each other's behavior. Social behavior almost always produces consequences both for the individual emitting it and for the other person. The interdependence of two people in producing reinforcements and outcomes for each other provides opportunities for conflict and cooperation. The kind of conflict existing between persons is another facet of the anatomy of interdependence.

B. The Structure of Conflict

The goals of two persons in interaction are frequently incompatible. Two politicians running for the same office, two children after the last piece of cake, and two motorists approaching an intersection at a 45° angle are instances of interpersonal competition or conflict. Deutsch (1969) suggests that the term "conflict" should denote incompatible activities, while the term "competition" may refer to an "opposition in the goals of the interdependent parties such that the probability of goal attainment for one decreases as the probability for the other increases" (p. 8).

Conflict may occur even when the parties have compatible goals; the conflict may be over means, not ends. Two parents may share the goal of correcting their son's behavior problem, but they may be in conflict about how to do it. Deutsch's distinction suggests that competition can be reduced only through attempts to modify the goals of one or both of the interacting persons. Those conflicts that are not based on underlying goal incompatibilities may be resolved by reaching agreement on how to coordinate actions.

While this distinction between conflict and competition can be useful, the analysis of the structure of conflict has focused on the degree of concordance of goals between persons and the scarcity of resources that fosters competition between them. Interdependence may range from one of pure conflict to pure coordination, but usually some mixture of both elements exists.

1. Pure Conflict and Pure Coordination

Pure conflict exists whenever two or more persons have incompatible goals and no compromise can be reached; that is, one person can achieve his objectives only at the expense of the other(s). Students of conflict have found game analogies helpful; to illustrate the case of pure conflict, suppose that two persons, P and O, can each choose one of two colors, green or red. A rule of this game is that both persons must choose simultaneously so that neither knows what the other will choose in advance of his own choice. If both choose green, P wins $5 and O loses $5. If both choose red, P wins $10 and O loses $10. If P chooses green and O chooses red, P loses $10 and O wins $10. Finally, if P chooses red and O chooses green, P loses $15 and O wins $15. This game is shown in matrix form in Figure 7.1a. By convention the row player's (P) outcome is always the first payoff in each cell and the column player's (O) outcome is shown second. Notice that whatever one player wins, the other player must lose. Further, the amount won always equals the amount lost; the sum of the two entrees in any one cell equals zero. This is why pure conflict situations are called *zero-sum games*.

Only rarely is pure conflict found outside of parlor games. In most such games, as in the case of wars between nations, common interests among the participants can almost always be found. For example, a gentleman's agreement prevails in playing cards that no one will cheat. Nations involved in war often tacitly agree to limit the amount of violence or the type of weapons that will be employed. During the Korean war China and the United States maintained a tacit agreement that the former would not prevent the use of port facilities in South Korea and the latter would not bomb north of the Yalu River. Agreements or rules such as these suggest that some area of agreement and some coordination of interests are usually present in human interaction.

Pure coordination exists whenever each

	O	
	Green	Red
Green	+5,−5	−10,+10
P		
Red	−15,+15	+10,−10

(a)

	O	
	Green	Red
Green	5,5	10,10
P		
Red	10,10	−5,−5

(b)

	O	
	Green (cooperative)	Red (competitive)
Green (cooperative)	+4,+4	−5,+5
P		
Red (competitive)	+5,−5	−4,−4

(c)

Figure 7.1. Three types of interdependence: (a) pure conflict situation, (b) pure coordination situation, and (c) mixed-motive situation.

person in an interaction can achieve his best outcome only when all other parties also achieve their best outcomes. In the game shown in Figure 7.1b, P and O are given a choice between two response alternatives, green and red. It can be seen that the best outcome for both persons occurs when they choose opposite colors; when one chooses red and the other green they both win $10. The problem for the persons in a simultaneous choice situation is to coordinate their behavior so that both can receive their most preferred outcomes.

Schelling (1960) illustrated the problem of a pure coordination interaction with the example of two people cut off during a telephone conversation that both want to continue. If both call back immediately, both will find the line busy (i.e., both lose). If neither calls back, both lose. The problem centers about getting it together; one must call while the other waits. Pure coordination situations are exceedingly rare, however. It is not very difficult to uncover covert areas of disagreement between persons even when their interaction appears on the surface to be one of pure coordination. Although members of an athletic team may display extraordinary coordination of their behavior in carrying out plays, closer observation may uncover jealousies among players and competition on the field for starting positions on the team.

2. Mixed-Motive Situations

Mixed-motive interactions lead to mutual outcomes that are not perfectly correlated; both individuals stand to profit if they coordinate their responses in a given manner, or one can gain at the expense of the other, or both can lose if they attempt to exploit each other. Such an interaction is shown in Figure 7.1c. Both can win $4 if both choose green, and both can lose $4 if both choose red. Of course, both persons may settle for mutual cooperation and a profit of $4. Yet in accordance with the objective of the game, both would prefer $5 to $4 and are therefore tempted to choose

red in the hope that other will choose green. The green response is usually termed the *cooperative* response; the red response is termed *competitive*.

This form of interaction is described as "mixed-motive" not because the parties lack clear objectives but because of the ambivalance of their relationship (Schelling, 1960). Their interests are partly coincident and partly in conflict. They may perceive each other as opponents at one moment but an instant later may view each other as partners. In both mixed-motive and pure coordination situations the outcomes found in all the cells of the payoff matrix do not add up to zero and hence they are referred to as *nonzero-sum*.

Many different laboratory games have been invented to study the cooperative and competitive behavior of subjects in mixed-motive situations. Two such games that will be often referred to in the following chapters are the Prisoner's Dilemma and the Trucking Game. The essential features of Prisoner's Dilemma are described by Luce and Raiffa (1957):

"Two suspects are taken into custody and separated. The District Attorney is certain that they are guilty of a specified crime, but he does not have adequate evidence to convict them at a trial. He points out to each prisoner that he has two alternatives: to confess to the crime the police are sure they have done, or not to confess. If they both do not confess, then the D.A. states he will book them on some very minor trumped-up charge such as petty larceny and illegal possession of a weapon, and they would both receive minor punishments; if they both confess, they will be prosecuted, but he will recommend less than the most severe sentence; but if one confesses and the other does not, then the former will receive lenient treatment for turning state's evidence, whereas the latter will get 'the book' slapped at him" (p. 95).

Figure 7.2 depicts some numerical outcomes corresponding to the alternatives the D.A. has posed for the two prisoners. P

must consider whether he will or will not confess. If *O* does not confess it is clearly to *P*'s advantage to confess, since he will then receive no punishment (rather than one year in jail should he not confess). If *O* confesses it is again in *P*'s interests to confess, for then he will receive only 5 years in jail rather than the 10 years he would receive by not confessing. Thus, irrespective of what *O* may do it is in *P*'s best interests to confess. *O* should follow the same logic and also confess. However, if each chooses his own best strategy and confesses, then both will spend five years in jail and are worse off than if they had trusted each other and not confessed

Laboratory versions of the Prisoner's Dilemma use monetary payoffs, or the subjects play for points. The experimental game is usually played many times by a pair of subjects. The number of cooperative choices by one player can be controlled and manipulated by having a confederate act as one of the subjects. It is generally found that subjects are quite competitive even when a confederate plays a predominantly or even unconditionally cooperative strategy (Bixenstine, Potash, & Wilson, 1963; Solomon, 1960). This basic laboratory game can be enriched by allowing the subjects to exchange communications during play. For example, an experimenter's confederate may send notes to the subject that say that he promises to cooperate on the next play of the game. Examples of this line of research will be reported in the next two chapters.

The Trucking Game is an attempt to enrich laboratory games by building into them a greater correspondence to the real world. Deutsch and Krauss (1960, 1962) constructed the game that is illustrated in Figure 7.3. Two subjects are given the roles of owners of trucking companies (Acme and Bolt). Their task is to transport products from their starting points over a stretch of road to their final destinations. On each trial each player receives a fixed sum of money from which the costs of delivery are subtracted. These costs are a direct function of the time spent en route; therefore profits are maximized by making the trip in as short a time as possible. Each trucker has a choice of two routes to his destination: a short route that maximizes speed of delivery but contains a one-lane stretch of road through which only one truck at a time may pass, and a longer alternate route that takes much more time to traverse but has no comparable impasse.

On any trip a trucker can profit only by taking the shorter route; the longer route results in a slight loss of money. However, if both players attempt to profit and take the shorter route they will meet head-on in the one-lane road, and both will lose money because of the time lost through confrontation and backing up. The only way both players can make a long-run profit is to coordinate their responses over the trials

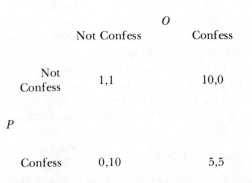

Figure 7.2. Mixed-motive games. The Prisoner's Dilemma, with the outcomes given in years in prison.

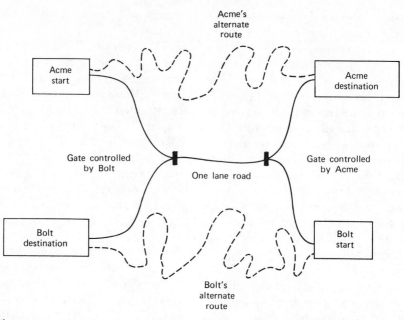

Figure 7.3. Subjects' road map in the Trucking Game. (From Deutsch and Krauss, 1960)

and alternate in taking the one-lane route. Any other strategy will result in one person's attempting to exploit the other for his own advantage. Naturally, if both players adopt competitive strategies, they both suffer. The mixed-motive character of the game should be apparent.

To complicate matters further, one or both players can be provided with gates to block the other from using the one-lane route. The possession of gates has the effect of providing the subjects with the power to punish each other. Deutsch and Krauss (1960) found that subjects earn more for their trucking companies when they do not possess gates and earn least when both parties are armed with punishment capability. But even when gates are not introduced into the game, the subjects frequently fail to coordinate their actions and end in a stalemate with neither party willing to back up to permit the other to pass. Mixed-motive conflicts are not easy to solve either in the laboratory or in real life.

3. Scarcity of Resources and Conflict

The scarcity of available resources creates a potential for competitive interaction. If

three billion people want oxygen to breathe, they are not in conflict with one another. Despite pollution, there is more than enough air in open spaces for each person to breathe and what one person inhales does not in any way affect what is available for another person. Scarcity involves a relationship between the available supply of a commodity and the human desire for it. The greater the demand relative to the supply, the more competition and conflict there is likely to be. There are only so many acres of lake front property, paintings by Jackson Pollock, and persons with a certain skill in the labor pool. The greater the demand for these commodities, the more valuable they are and the more competition there will be to acquire them.

Time is often a factor in determining whether conflict will occur over available resources. If a family has only one automobile and the parents wish to use it for travel from their country home to the theater while the son has planned to take his best girl to a dance, a conflict situation involving incompatible goals is potentially aroused. If the parents had matinee tickets, there would be no conflict over the use of the automobile since they could use the car in the afternoon and their son could use it at night. Similarly, conflicts may occur on a highway because two motorists contend for a right of way or battle for a single parking space, though each actually would save only a small amount of time by "winning." Thus demand may exceed supply because of matters of timing. Scarcity, whatever its basis, is directly related to both the existence and the intensity of social conflict (Kuhn, 1963).

C.   Control Features of Interaction

The structure of outcomes associated with the choices of persons in interaction may indicate the type and amount of power each has over the other. Thibaut and Kelley

(1959) have distinguished between two types of interpersonal control: fate control and behavior control.

Fate control is characteristic of a situation in which one party has unilateral control of the other's outcomes; the controlling party can determine what the dependent party receives irrespective of the latter's behavior. It is possible for each person in an interaction to have fate control over the other, usually in different forms. For example, a wife may have complete control over what her husband will eat, but the husband may control when and how the wife will receive sexual gratification. In Figure 7.4a, P has fate control over O because P can either choose green and give O one point or choose red and give O four points. What O does has no effect on these

		O Green	O Red
	Green	10, 1	0, 1
P			
	Red	10, 4	0, 4

(a)

		O Green	O Red
	Green	1, 1	4, 4
P			
	Red	4, 4	1, 1

(b)

		O Green	O Red
	Green	1, 1	4, 1
P			
	Red	4, 4	1, 4

(c)

Figure 7.4.   Types of interpersonal control (After Thibaut and Kelley, 1959): (a) Mutual fate control; (b) Mutual behavior control. (c) Fate control of P over O and behavior control of O over P.

outcomes. However, O also has fate control over P, since O can choose to give P either ten points or nothing. In such instances, each party has an incentive to give the other the larger of the possible outcomes to induce reciprocity.

The amount of power that each person has can be measured by the extent to which each can affect the range of outcomes for the other. The wider the range of outcomes one person can mediate for another, the greater the power of the first over the second. In our example the range of outcomes through which P can move O is three (i.e., 4 − 1 = 3), while the range of outcomes O controls is ten (i.e., 10 − O = 10). Thus O is more powerful than P, although both have absolute control over the other's outcomes.

Behavior control is a mutual contingency relationship in which the choice of the most desirable behavior of one person depends on the behavior chosen by the other. A wife may attempt to please rather than displease her husband at meal time as a way of inducing him to please her at bedtime. As can be seen in Figure 7.4b, if P makes the green choice, O should want to make the red choice in order to receive four points; conversely, if P makes the red choice, O should want to make the green choice in order to receive four points. Assuming that P wants O to make the green choice (thereby maximizing the payoffs to P), P should choose red every time; then O can maximize his own profit only by choosing green. Thus, P can control O's behavioral choice, but O also has behavior control over P.

Some interactions represent a mixture of fate and behavior control. Figure 7.4c depicts a situation in which P has fate control over O, while O has behavior control over P. If P makes a green choice, O will receive one point no matter what O does; if he makes a red choice, O will receive four points. O can make it desirable for P to make a red choice by making the green choice, since if both choose green, P will receive only one point rather than the four points that he could make by choosing red. A similar situation

exists in the case of an employer who controls employment and an employee who produces profit for the firm. The control that each party has over the other permits an exchange to occur that is in both of their interests.

D. Exchange and Satisfaction in Interaction

Exchange theory is a model proposed to account for an aspect of social interaction the boundaries for which have yet to be discovered and specified. In developing it, Homans (1961) has applied some of the elementary principles of economic exchange to social interaction. Just as a buyer and seller exchange money for commodities, one person may give approval in exchange for desired behavior on the part of another. A person may grant higher status to another in exchange for the other's expert assistance in solving a problem. In a sense, Homans sees each individual as a capitalist who invests his resources, talents, energy, and time in exchanges with other people to reap a profit. But the profit need not be material; it may consist of approval, love, or self-respect. Homans refers to the investments an individual makes as "costs" and the positive outcomes he receives in interpersonal exchanges as "gains." Each person is assumed to act in a manner calculated to maximize his profits in social interaction, where a profit is defined as the total gains minus the total costs associated with a given action.

Just as in marketplace decisions, each person in social interaction must find a solution to the exchange problem: how much help is worth how much status? Therefore much social behavior takes the form of bargaining, as occurs openly when a buyer and a seller haggle about prices in a marketplace.

The more important status is to a person the more he should be willing to work to achieve it, and the more valuable help is to a recipient the more willing he should be to grant status to the helper. Scarcity affects the value of behavior in exchange relationships. A person who is sparing in his praise will find that his approval is highly valued, while another who uses praise abundantly may find that his approval is worth very little. Thus supply and demand are important factors in social exchange. A person's expertise may be worth more when the supply of his particular skills is scarce and many others desire his help than when those skills are plentiful and few people need them.

An individual may be regarded as a frugal shopper who surveys all the available sources of a commodity that he wants and tries to get it at the lowest cost. He examines all the possible exchanges he can make with others and enters into that relationship he believes will yield the greatest profit. Any particular relationship may be maintained or discontinued depending on the alternatives he believes are available to him. Thibaut and Kelley (1959) define the individual's *comparison level for alternatives* (CLalt) as the lowest level of outcomes a person will accept from a particular exchange, given his available alternatives. If the CLalt is high compared to the rewards he can get from his current interaction, he will discontinue the relationship and enter into an alternative one, but if the CLalt is low, he will stay in his current interaction. CLalt indicates how dependent an individual is on another person. The more preferred outcomes that can be mediated by an actor for another person, compared to all possible alternative social relationships, the more dependent the person will be on that actor. Another way of saying the same thing is that the lower the CLalt, the higher the individual's dependence on the person who controls the relevant reinforcements.

The degree of satisfaction a person derives from a particular relationship depends to some extent on his expectations. Drawing on level-of-aspiration theory, Thibaut and Kelley (1959) define *comparison level* (CL) as the average amount of reward a person expects and feels he deserves from any social exchange. An optimistic and self-confident individual should have a generally high CL, and a pessimistic and anxious person should have a generally low CL. Hence the latter should be satisfied with much less than the former. If a person is dissatisfied with the outcomes he receives, he may either leave the relationship or exert influence to increase his gains. In this way the CL may be used as a rough index of the likelihood that an individual will exert influence. On the other hand, if outcomes only just meet his expectations, he may resist any attempt by his partner to extract more from him in the exchange relationship by threatening to terminate it.

Within most social interactions there is a great deal of give and take that cannot be understood by simply knowing the anatomy of the relationship. Each person can choose among a wide variety of influence tactics to obtain more favorable outcomes. The use of influence is so prevalent in human relationships that social psychology has often been defined as the study of social influence (Aronson, 1972; Collins, 1970; Hollander, 1971). In achieving a fundamental understanding of social behavior it is important to supplement the structure of interdependency with the modes of influence that are used in interaction.

II. ECOLOGICAL CONTROL

When one person has the ability to alter critical aspects of the environment so as to bring about a desired change in another person's behavior, the powerful party may be said to possess *ecological control* (Cartwright, 1965). There are three types of ecological control: roundabout control, cue control, and non-decision-making. *Roundabout control* refers to the manipulation of general aspects of the environment, which in turn produce general behavioral effects (Dahl & Lindblom, 1953). *Cue control* is the "actor's provision of stimuli that elicit pre-established habit patterns in another" (Jones & Gerard, 1967, p. 529). *Nondecision-making* refers to deliberate inaction on the part of an actor that is intended to influence a target person by maintaining the status quo. These three tactics are probably most effective in such institutional settings as prisons, hospitals, and schools.

A. Roundabout Control

The general goals of roundabout control include shaping an individual's value prefer-ences, his general outlook on the world, his perception of social roles or norms, and his agenda of decisions. Parents may attempt to affect the development of their wayward son by placing him in a military school. Roundabout control may also be exercised by putting a person in a prison, mental institution, half-way house, university, or many other institutional settings that place constraints on him and presumably help shape his future values and behavior. A particularly interesting historical example of roundabout control is recounted in Box 7.1.

Box 7.1 ROUNDABOUT CONTROL CHINESE STYLE

There are many instances in history when foreign dignitaries have been carefully treated by the host country in order to create or maintain good will. Wendell Willkie, who opposed Franklin Roosevelt for the presidency of the United States in 1940, was sent on a round-the-world good will tour during 1942 as a special envoy of his successful rival. On the itinerary was a trip to China. Chiang Kai Shek's government was anxious to secure as much aid from the United States as possible to contain the Japanese invaders. Tuchman (1971) describes the preparations made for Mr. Willkie:

"There was to be an unbroken schedule of banquets, receptions, reviews, dinners, visits to schools, factories, girl scouts, arsenals. He was to be installed in a Chinese guest house as the guest of the Chinese Government rather than in the American Embassy, much to the annoyance and disapproval of Ambassador Gauss. The arrangement ensured that Willkie would see and hear only what his hosts wanted him to . . . In a spasm of face-making for the occasion, the police of Chungking tore down paupers' shacks, herded the more wretched beggars beyond city limits, and ordered the poorest and shabbiest shops to close during the visit. Streets were decked with banners and welcoming wall slogans; schoolchildren, waving and shouting, lined the eleven-mile route from the airport; and the populace was ordered to buy Chinese and American paper flags from the police" (p. 332).

Willkie wrote about his experiences in ten newspaper installments and in a bestselling book entitled *One World* when he returned home. The picture he portrayed of wartime China was almost precisely the one arranged for him by his hosts through the roundabout control they exercised over his experiences. As Tuchman concluded her account: "The Chinese could not have made a better investment" (p. 333).

The environment has many effects on the general tone of a person's life. The size of a home can minimize or maximize conflicts among its inhabitants. If two adults and five children occupy a four room apartment, there will be little privacy, more interaction, and greater conflict than if the same people lived in a house with five bedrooms and two family rooms. Thus, the federal government may directly effect the life styles of the poor by the type of housing it provides for them. Similarly, the style and colors used by an artist may reflect his physical environment. A patron who provides the artist with travel funds and a stipend is exercising roundabout control over his future development.

Methods of ecological control are usually Machiavellian in character. The source typically attempts to prevent the target from becoming aware of the intent to influence or control his behavior. When influence is characterized by an attempt to hide the source's intentions, we speak of *manipulation*. Because roundabout control involves manipulation of general features of the environment, its use cannot always be hidden from view. However, the source who uses roundabout control may attribute the environmental changes to a third party or may rationalize its use in terms that stress the benefits to the target person.

B.   Cue Control

By the systematic application of reinforcements during the learning process, trainers build up in their animal proteges a series of responses to discriminative stimuli. When, for example, a dolphin's trainer raises both arms high above his head, the dolphin jumps out of the water and is promptly rewarded with a fish. After the habit has been thoroughly learned, anyone who provides the appropriate cue (raising both arms) will be able to elicit the jumping behavior. What is required is knowledge of the cue-response association and the ability to produce the cue.

An observant person may notice or learn from an intermediary that another person has habitual responses, which can be elicited through cue control. On April 1 each year children and adults alike attempt to elicit habitual responses from each other and, when they are successful, gleefully shout "April fool!" Cue control is used frequently in competitive sports where feints and deception are designed to deceive an opponent by getting him to commit himself in the wrong direction. People who know each other very well can often elicit anger, laughter, or tears almost at will. A person may be able to affect his own outcomes by eliciting responses from a target person through cue control.

This is an inexpensive means of influence since no resources other than those necessary to bring about the cue are required. No exchange is involved; the cue controller does not have to "pay" for the outcomes he receives. If the use of cue control is discovered by the target, he may seek something in exchange from the source. To minimize the costs of using cue control, the source may attempt to prevent the target from discovering its use or else may deny the value of any benefits derived from the target's habitual response pattern. March (1955) and Jones and Gerard (1967) have emphasized the importance of cue control as a means of social influence, but almost no research has been carried out to examine the technique.

C.   Nondecision-Making

Two political scientists, Bachrach and Baratz (1963), have noted that both the legislative and executive branches of government can affect the course of events in the country by deliberate nondecisions—by pigeon-holing bills in committees, filibustering, and failing to provide or expend funds for particular purposes. If John F. Kennedy was right in saying that "political behavior is only an exaggeration of everyday life," then it may be presumed that nondecision making is also used as a mode of influence in daily interactions. For example, a child may ask if he can have something when walking through a store with one of his parents, and the parent may simply ignore his request. The parent may not want to say no to the child because of the clamor that could result; on the other hand, he doesn't want to say yes for other reasons. The way out of the dilemma is to delay, postpone, or otherwise fail to make a decision. Of course, this nondecision affects the child's outcomes. Nondecision-making, as this example illustrates, often helps to avoid sharp conflicts, while implementing the preferences of the deciding party.

D. Conclusion

Ecological control methods involve indirect influence because the target is not specifically directed to perform any specific action and no influence communication is transmitted in interaction. Ecological control often takes a great deal of time to accomplish and may not bring about the specific effects desired by the source. The source may not have sufficient resources for producing roundabout control, the target may not possess habits that can be elicited by cue control or his habits may not be relevant to the source's needs, or the source may not play a role that allows him to exercise much control by nondecision making. Control over immediate reinforcements provides opportunity for eliciting specific responses from a target person. By the use of threats and promises and by the mediation of punishments and rewards, the source can gain control over a target's behavior.

III. REINFORCEMENT CONTROL

The possession and selective mediation of significant reinforcements with and without communications allows an individual to shape the behavior of others. Parents and teachers are important in child development because of their many opportunities to reward acceptable behavior and punish objectionable behavior. Rewards strengthen and punishments inhibit or weaken responses. Although reinforcements are sometimes administered following behavior, it is more typical of social interaction that individuals provide incentives for each other by communicating threats of future punishment or promises of future rewards. The use of threats, promises, punishments, and rewards are techniques of reinforcement control that may be used for purposes of social influence. We will provide definitions of these forms of influence now and postpone discussion of the available research until the next chapter.

A. Threats

A threat is a communication from a source that he will punish the target if the latter does not comply with the former's demands. A threat may be contingent or noncontingent. A *contingent threat* takes the form: "If you don't do X, I will do Y," where Y is an action, the withholding of an action, the production of a punishment, or the removal of a positive reinforcer, all of which can be perceived by the target as detrimental, punishing, and costly. A *noncontingent threat* simply asserts "I will do Y." While a contingent threat gives the target the opportunity to comply with demands and avoid punishment, a noncontingent threat merely announces that punishment is forthcoming and provides the target with no opportunity to avoid it. A contingent threat does not merely convey an intent to do harm, but is focused on the goal of gaining a compliant action from the target.

Schelling (1966) has suggested that contingent threats may be either compellent or deterrent in nature. *Compellent threats* require that the target perform specific actions to avoid the threatened punishment.

A parent may inform his daughter that unless she receives all passing marks on her report card, she will be "grounded." *Deterrent threats* are communications ordering the target not to do something. In international relations the United States has clearly indicated to the Soviet Union that an invasion of Western Europe would bring swift and devastating retaliation. Hence, compellence requires specific actions, while deterrence forbids particular behavior. Compellent threats are perceived as more hostile and constraining because the target must make a particular response and forgo all other responses, while deterrent threats forbid a single action but allow the target to do almost anything else.

If the threatener is vague in making his demands or in stating what he will do should the target fail to comply, he is not likely to get his way in interaction. Fisher (1969) has suggested that for the best results a threat should be stated as a "Yesable proposition." It should be clear to the target what is desired so he can decide whether to comply or not. In order to be successful a threatener must make the costs associated with noncompliance (i.e., punishment) outweigh the costs of compliance. Ambiguous threats may be deliberately used by a source because of his desire to avoid a crisis that would result from making a specific commitment to a punishing action. The purpose of such ambiguous threats may not be to gain compliance but to indicate to the target that he should be more cautious about future actions that encroach on the prerogatives of the source. Politicians and diplomats have perfected the art of ambiguity in their utterances, as anyone can determine for himself by watching a news interview on television any Sunday afternoon.

B.   Promises

A promise is a communication that offers a reward to a target. Promises, like threats, may be contingent or noncontingent. A *contingent promise* requires that the target perform or not perform some action as a condition for receiving the promised reward. It takes the form: "If you do X for me, I will do Y for you," where Y is an action, the withholding of an action, the provision of a commodity, or the removal of a punishment, any of which may be considered beneficial or rewarding by the target. A *noncontingent promise* is a communication in which the source offers to do something the target desires. It takes the form "I will do Y." A contingent promise represents a specific offer of exchange on a take-it-or-leave-it basis. Presumably, the target will comply with the source's request if the terms of exchange are acceptable. A noncontingent promise may be used to state an intention to fulfill an obligation, to generate good will, or to convey a positive impression of the source's benevolence.

C.   The Importance of Threats and Promises in Social Life

Many social phenomena may be interpreted as threats or promises. For example, money may be viewed as a promise. When money was first invented as a substitute for barter, releasing men from temporal and geographical limitations to trade, it had intrinsic value. That is, it consisted of gold or ivory or some other commodity that was valuable in itself. In our time, paper money is widely used, and it may be asked why a person would be willing to give up something valuable in trade for a slip of paper. Of course, the recipient believes that he can exchange the paper for something of value at a later time. Thus paper money is interpreted as a promise that the person who holds it can gain something of worth in exchange with other persons. Having confidence in the dollar simply refers to the belief the person has in his government's ability to make the promise good. Money is a form of credit, like an IOU. As Bazelon (1963) says:

"Money is a contract—the freest, most

gorgeous contract of them all. Money is somebody else's promise to pay, to give me what I want, when I want it. What a magnificent conception! . . . Whatever else history may ultimately record of the Western bourgeoisie, this honor most certainly must be accorded them: *They perfected modern money, which is a contract with parties unknown for the future delivery of pleasures undecided upon*" (p. 73, emphasis his).

Other economic artifacts may also be interpreted as complex promises. A credit card is a promise to pay money (usually in the form of a check, itself a promise) at some specified later time. All contracts, including treaties in international relations, consist of mutual promises regarding future conduct and exchange. Property is a contractual relationship that delegates rights and obligations to various parties. If a person holds a mortgage on his home, he has certain rights regarding access to and use of the property, but so does the bank that provides the financing, the Federal Housing Authority that guarantees the loan, the municipal government that holds rights of way, and so on. A person does not have the right to do anything whatsoever with his property. He cannot burn down his home, for example. The rights and obligations of people are backed by a legal system, which consists of threats and punishments against violators.

The use of threats and force in international relations is all too familiar. Particularly important in the modern era of nuclear weapons is the concept of deterrence that presumably has so far prevented World War III. The nuclear superpowers have held each other at bay, even when each took actions that in other times would have led to war, because of their mutual fear of unleashing calamity on all mankind. Persons involved in weapons development and deployment and diplomacy are constantly concerned about maximizing the effectiveness of the deterrent threat of nuclear weapons. Box 7.2 pro-

Box. 7.2   PROBLEMS OF NUCLEAR DETERRENCE

The possession of large numbers of deliverable nuclear weapons provides both the Soviet Union and the United States with the ability to destroy each other and most of the nations of the world. The new military technology provides the context within which international relations are conducted. Each nuclear power justifies the acquisition of its weapons systems on the grounds that they are intended to deter hostile actions by the other nation. Kahn (1962) has discriminated between three types of deterrent threats involving nuclear weapons. Type I is a threat of retaliatory destruction should the other side initiate a large scale attack on the military forces or the population of the defensive nation. Type II threats are intended to prevent provocative actions short of an attack on the homeland, such as a Russian invasion of Western Europe or an American military intervention in Czechoslovakia. Type III deterrence consists of implicit threats meant to influence the course of diplomatic negotiations and is often discussed as bargaining from a position of strength—a kind of nuclear blackmail.

Deterrence will not succeed if the target does not believe the source will or can carry out his threat. Weapons systems have been designed to maximize the probability that deterrent threats will be believed. If Type I

deterrence is to be believed, it is necessary that the enemy not be able to destroy the retaliatory capability of the threatener in a first strike attack. There are two ways to eliminate this possibility. Weapons systems can be made invulnerable to a sneak attack by placing them underground in hardened sites or by making them mobile and difficult to detect, as with nuclear submarines. Another way of assuring a second strike capability is to possess a greater number of weapons than the other side and spread them out over the earth so they cannot all be destroyed in a single attack.

Type II deterrence is more difficult to believe than type I. If neither side can with a first strike eliminate the probability of retaliation, neither is likely to risk self-destruction on the behalf of third parties. Would the United States be willing to risk the destruction of its great metropolitan centers by attacking the heartland of the Soviet Union in response to the latter's invasion of West Berlin? In response to this problem of making Type II threats believeable the superpowers have taken the advice of deterrence theorists (e.g., Kissinger, 1957; Snyder, 1961) by devising graduated and controlled responses that fit the punishment to the crime. Instead of directly attacking the Soviet Union, for example, small tactical nuclear weapons could be employed to destroy the guilty military forces without directly attacking the heartland of the enemy. Escalation may be deterred since both sides still have the incentive of protecting their heartlands. In this way the type II deterrence threat has achieved a modicum of believeability. While type III deterrence may have possessed some believeability when the United States was the only nation that controlled nuclear weapons in the late 1940s and early 1950s, it is not likely that it plays much part in negotiations today.

The problems of nuclear deterrence are much more complex than can be pursued here. Nearly all the current discussions of the topic focus on various strategies that can be employed to enhance the believeability of deterrent threats, to prevent crises during which the threats must be invoked, to remove the incentives to third parties for acquiring superpower status, and to ensure that no accidental or unauthorized action takes place that would trigger the use of the weapons. In addition, much concern is expressed about how to achieve arms control measures that would preserve the virtues of deterrence, while reducing the stockpiles and costs of the two superpowers.

---

vides more details about the intricacies of nuclear diplomacy and mutual deterrence.

Sociologists have stressed that human behavior is importantly affected by shared expectations of group members (i.e., their norms). Norms specify what is permissable and what is not. Deviant behavior in violation of norms may be punished, and conformity with group expectations may bring approval or other rewards. Norms are often imprecise and hence allow for much leeway of interpretation. For example, the rule that "friends should help one another" is only a crude guide to behavior because it does not indicate what kind of help should be provided or under what circumstances. Nevertheless, norms may be interpreted as nonspecific promises and threats that originate in the group and are sanctioned by its members. Because of the ambiguity of norms, an individual must test the limits of propriety himself or must learn by observing others. Lord Byron captured this process in his line, "the way to moderation is the road of excess." As Cohen (1966) has pointed out, "By providing an occasion for the clarification of a rule, the deviant may render an important service to the other members of the group; they come to know more clearly than before what they may and may not legitimately do" (p. 8). One of the chief functions of legal institutions, especially of an appellate court, is to reduce the ambiguity of social rules, a continuing process necessitated by changing conditions to which the law must be applied.

D. Direct Mediation of Reinforcements

It is possible to establish control over a target's behavior by the direct use of rewards and punishments and without the prior communication of either promises or threats. Skinner (1938, 1950) has been relentless in acquiring knowledge about the effects of various schedules of reinforcement on behavior. The development and use of behavior modification techniques in therapeutic settings and in schools have had some success in changing undesirable behavior and replacing it with more acceptable conduct. Skinner has argued strongly that in the long run direct punishment does not effectively control behavior. However, recent evidence (cf. Johnston, 1972) indicates that punishments may have effects complementary to rewards. A particularly effective means of controlling behavior is to punish an undesirable response while providing an opportunity for a more acceptable one that is immediately rewarded. Such a carrot-and stick policy can quickly modify behavior.

Skinner acknowledges that punishment can be effective in changing behavior when it involves removing the negative reinforcement in exchange for a compliant response. This form of control has been referred to as "distress relief" by Kuhn

(1963). The source produces a need for relief in the target and then offers to satisfy the need. Parents sometimes put children under "room arrest" until they display penitence for having done something "wrong." When the correct behavior is emitted, the punishment is terminated. The creation of needs and the deprivation of rewards lowers the target's resistance to subsequent promises of rewards by the source.

E. Conclusion

The use of threats and punishments as modes of social influence is often referred to as *coercive power*, while promises and rewards are classified as forms of *reward power* (French & Raven, 1959). Coercive power places greater control in the hands of the source than reward power because the former makes a demand and the latter merely makes a take-it-or-leave-it offer. Whether a target responds to promises or rewards is up to him and no negative consequences follow from failure to take up the offer except for possible loss of good will. But a threatener does not merely make a this or that offer; instead he seeks compliance and commits himself to punish the target should the latter fail to comply.

There are a number of disadvantages associated with this kind of reinforcement control. In order to apply rewards and punishments selectively or to enforce threats and fulfill promises, it is necessary for the source to keep the behavior of the target under surveillance; otherwise, he would not know whether the appropriate response has occurred. Such surveillance may be costly, inconvenient, or impossible to carry out. In addition, the side-effects of using reinforcement control can detrimentally affect the relations between the interacting parties. A target learns to dislike a source who employs coercive power. The target may also object to reward power if he considers the reward as a form of bribery compromising his integrity. To avoid the problems associated with surveillance and the long term negative aspects of employing reinforcement control, a source of influence may choose less direct methods of information control to affect the decisions made by the target.

IV. INFORMATION CONTROL

People are information-processing and decision-making organisms. They assess the available behavioral alternatives in terms of goals and values and behave in a manner calculated to produce the best possible outcomes for themselves. Because their assessment of situations is often inadequate or incorrect, they do not always succeed in achieving their goals. Information conveyed by others may significantly effect the individual's decisions. A source of influence may therefore attempt to affect the decisions made by a target person through persuasion, activation of commitments, or by ingratiation.

Persuasion is an attempt to change the goals or attitudes of a target person through the use of argument, propaganda, and special knowledge. *Activation of commitments* refers to an appeal to normative values to cause a reassessment by a target of what he *ought* to do in a given situation; it involves exhortation or moral suasion (Parsons, 1963). *Ingratiation* is an attempt by a source to increase his personal attractivenss or value to a target in the hope of gaining something of value in return (Jones, 1964). Each of these methods of affecting the decisions of a target consists primarily of information control and does not depend on the exercise of reinforcement control.

A. Persuasion

A source may attempt to affect directly the decisions of a target by communicating persuasive arguments. The target's preferred alternative may be shown to have a low probability of success or to involve unforeseen costs. Other more attractive alternatives may be shown to be available or a nonpreferred choice may be shown to lead to a positive outcome not initially considered. Another way of affecting the target's decision is to change his estimate of the value of various goals, as when a source provides information about the appraised value of a diamond ring or a used automobile. In short, a source can gain control over the behavior of a target by manipulating the elements of his decision, including his perceived alternatives, his probability assessment of means-ends relations, and the values of the ends he has in mind (March, 1955, 1957).

There are at least two clearly discriminable types of persuasive communications: recommendations and warnings. The word persuasion means "to sweeten." Communications that provide the lure of better alternatives by informing the target of future possible rewards are *recommendations*. A tout at a race track who provides a tip on a horse is communicating a recommendation, as is a person who informs a fellow employee that the time is propitious for talking to the boss about a raise. A *warning* is a communication that predicts harmful consequences should the target decide on a particular course of action. Warnings are sometimes referred to as fear-arousing communications because of the predictions of harm that are associated with them.

An important difference between persuasion and threats and promises is the degree of control the source has over the consequences associated with his communications. The source of persuasive communications does not control the positive or negative consequences that he predicts; he merely acts as a forecaster of events. Clearly, a threatener or promiser is assumed to control the punishments and rewards associated with his communications. This distinction is not always clear to the target of persuasive communications, who must wonder about the real intentions of the source and whether he really has influence over the events he foretells. Is the source being helpful or manipulative? Are his recommendations and warnings really promises and threats?

Both recommendations and warnings may predict consequences that stem from nature (hurricanes) or from other human beings (robbery). Persuasive communications, like threats and promises, may be contingent or noncontingent. For example, a source may warn a target that failure to brush his teeth will cause cavities. This contingent warning specifies both the undesirable behavior and the harmful consequences associated with it. A noncontingent recommendation merely predicts positive consequences without specifying any connection to any behavior of the target or other antecedent conditions. Warnings and recommendations are not always discriminably different. The dental hygiene warning could be interpreted as a recommendation, since it is implied that brushing one's teeth will prevent cavities. Often the source will communicate his message both ways: fail to brush your teeth and you get cavities; brush after every meal and you avoid cavities.

B. The Activation of Commitments

Still another form of information control is the *activation of commitments,* which involves an appeal to the normative values of the target to cause him to reassess what he ought to do in a given situation. This form of exhortation or moral argument asks the target to consider the standards of conduct that are important to his group or society when making his decisions. The source may refer to important documents, such as the Ten Commandments, the Constitution, the law, or other norms of the group, to substantiate his appeal. The target is asked to consider what effects his actions will have on others before undertaking them and, perhaps, to give up his selfish interests that conflict with moral standards. The source is attempting to activate in the target the latter's commitment to certain values by showing how they are relevant to his current or proposed behavior.

A subtle implication of communications directed toward activating commitments is that the target will receive social approval or rewards for choosing certain actions or that he will receive disapproval or punishment for deviating from normative standards. These communications may therefore represent tacit forms of promises, recommendations, threats, or warnings. When a beggar appeals to the conscience of a rich man to get money for a cup of coffee, the potential benefactor may view the costs as a way of blunting the possibly unpleasant consequences associated with refusal. Hence, he may interpret the appeal as a tacit threat. On the other hand, the rich man may believe in a generalized norm of reciprocity, similar to the Hindu notion of Karma, that the good things he does will eventually bring rewards to him. A belief in a just world may lead the rich man to interpret the appeal as a recommendation: "Do good for me and someday you will receive compensation."

C. Ingratiation

Ingratiation consists of deliberate manipulative tactics employed by a source to increase his attractiveness in the eyes of a powerful target in the hope of reward. This is one of the few modes of influence available to those who would otherwise have no influence at all. Their threats may not be believed because they are too weak to back them up; their lack of resources may deny them the ability to make exchanges with others; they may be ineffective at persuasion because of their lack of competence. Given this perspective, the behavior of the groveling junior executive or the shuffling Negro on a southern plantation saying "yassah" becomes easier to understand. Yet the person's very powerlessness makes his use of ingratiation tactics suspect. As a consequence, he must adopt very subtle techniques to avoid being unmasked.

Jones (1964) has described the

"ingratiator's dilemma" as arising from the fact that the greater the source's stake in making himself attractive to the target, the more sensitive the target is apt to be to this form of deception. As the need for ingratiation increases, the probability of successful influence decreases. Jones, Gergen, and Jones (1963) found evidence that ingratiation must remain concealed if it is to be successful. Subjects were asked to evaluate a stimulus person who was either dependent or not dependent on a third person, and who either agreed closely or did not agree with the third person. The subjects evaluated the stimulus person more negatively when he was dependent and agreed with the third person than when he agreed but was not dependent. Thus the ingratiator's need for guile, cleverness, and concealment becomes more essential the more powerful the target and the more dependent the source.

Ingratiation is usually directed toward a powerful person and can be accomplished in several ways, including conforming to his opinions, complimenting him, and publicizing one's own good traits (Jones, 1964). Each of these tactics is intended to project a favorable impression of the source as a likeable, benevolent, and intelligent person. The source wants to be liked because experience teaches him that friends provide help and rewards, whereas enemies do neither and may do harm (Bramel, 1969). Almost everyone uses ingratiation tactics to some degree, in flattering the boss, extolling the virtues of the neighbor's daughter, or complimenting a friend's wife on her purchase of an atrocious hat. We will examine each of the ingratiation tactics in the context of the available research.

1. Conformity Ingratiation

Similarity of attitudes and values is known to induce interpersonal attraction between peers (Byrne, 1969). The distinction between ingratiation tactics and other behavior that creates interpersonal attraction is that the former are hypocritical and in-

sincere, while the latter may be presumed to represent the true attitudes of the source. Conformity with another's statements of opinion is meant by the ingratiator to induce liking for him. An awareness by the ingratiator that similarity produces attraction is an important factor in a relationship.

Jones, Gergen, Gumpert, and Thibaut (1965) have shown that people use conformity ingratiation tactics only when the target has discretionary power to affect their outcomes. Subjects were asked to rank order a series of advertising slogans in terms of their effectiveness in increasing sales. At the same time, the subjects were told they could win a substantial sum of money by doing well in a business game, but during practice trials they were given feedback indicating that their performance was poor. After the practice trials, they were given an opportunity to overhear a set of beliefs and values expressed by a supervisor during an interview. The supervisor either stressed the importance of getting along with others in accomplishing group goals or emphasized getting the job done rather than concentrating on group morale and cooperation. Finally, the subjects were told either that the supervisor would have discretionary power to evaluate their performance or that he would merely rate their judgments according to predetermined criteria. They were then given opinion questionnaires to fill out, but never did complete playing the business game.

When the supervisor did not have discretionary power the subjects did not reveal conformity with his attitudes on the opinion questionnaire. When he did have discretionary power and extolled the virtues of group cooperation and stressed the importance of morale, the subjects indicated agreement with him. When he similarly had discretionary power but stressed independent and autonomous behavior, the subjects showed the least conformity to his views, since only by being independent in their opinions could they act in a manner consistent with his values. Thus, only when the supervisor had discretionary power did the subjects use the tactic of conformity ingratiation.

2. Complimenting Others

Flattery and compliments (other-enhancing communications) are used in the expectation that the target will be obliged to return the favor with a rewarding act of his own. The ingratiator relies on the principle of exchange and the norm of reciprocity when he displays open approval of the target. Kipnis and Vanderveer (1971) have provided evidence that other-enhancing communications can be effective in gaining rewards. Subjects were asked to take the role of an industrial supervisor and oversee the work of four persons in a simulated factory setting. They were asked to do their best to increase the productivity of the workers. The subject-supervisor could communicate to the workers (who were simulated) through an intercommunications system, and the experimenter had the "workers" send back written notes to the "supervisors". To control the workers' behavior the subjects could employ a variety of influence tactics: they could promise or reward the workers with 10¢ raises; they could threaten or punish the workers with 10¢ fines; they could threaten to transfer or actually transfer the workers to more boring jobs; or they could fire a worker.

The subjects were provided with information about the productivity of the four workers. Two of the workers were average, a third was clearly superior, and a fourth was a problem either because he was inept or because he had negative attitudes and lacked motivation. One of the average workers sent ingratiating notes to the subjects, including such messages as: "Count on me for help—what can I do?" "If you want me to go faster, let me know;" and "I was afraid that a college kid would boss me around, but your assistant (a messenger working for the experimenter) is a real nice guy and you seem to be too" (pp. 282–283).

As can be seen in Table 7.1, the subjects gave the ingratiating worker more promises and more raises than the other average worker, although their productivity was the same. In addition, when the subjects were asked to evaluate the quality of performance of the workers, the ingratiator was evaluated as favorably as the superior worker and much more favorably than the other average worker. The results clearly demonstrate that the ingratiator was successful in changing the subject-supervisor's attitudes and behavior toward him and that ingratiation under these conditions paid off.

3. Self-Enhancing Communications

Ingratiation may take the form of publicizing the communicator's positive traits to create an impression of worthiness. If these self-enhancing communications are successful, the target may be led to respect the opinions of the source so that subsequent persuasive communications become more effective. The target may also become convinced that the source merits greater rewards than he has received. If the ingratiator is associated with persons who are

Table 7.1 Number of Promises and Pay Rises Given to Workers by the Thirty Subjects in the Kipnis and Vanderveer (1971) Study.

Type of reward power	Superior worker	Average worker	Ingratiator
Promises of pay raises	38	26	35
Number of pay raises given	36	21	28
Total exercise of reward power	74	47	63

disliked by the target, self-enhancing communications may take the form of emphasizing how the source is different from the undesirable others.

Cooper and Jones (1969) found that subjects changed their opinions as a way of dissociating themselves from an obnoxious other person. All subjects had their attitudes measured in a mass testing session in their regular classroom. Several days later they participated in an experiment with a confederate who was either obnoxious or sympathetic in his behavior toward the experimenter. By arranging for the subjects to see the confederate's attitude questionnaire, they were led to believe that he was either similar or dissimilar to them in background and attitudes. The confederate's dress also was similar or dissimilar. Afterwards, the subjects were asked to complete a similar questionnaire. A comparison was then made between the opinions expressed in the classroom with those made in the experimental situation. Only those subjects who participated with the similar and obnoxious confederate changed their opinions in order to appear different from him. These subjects manipulated the information provided to the experimenter in a deceitful manner to create a favorable impression of themselves.

When powerful persons want to create positive impressions of themselves among subordinates, they may use the reverse tactic of revealing some of their inadequacies. Jones, Gergen, and Jones (1963) found that when high status subjects were told to make themselves liked by their subordinates, they tended to advertise their minor faults. Fallibility tends to enhance the likeableness of powerful and able persons (Aronson, Willerman, & Floyd, 1966).

D. Conclusion

Recommendations, warnings, the activation of commitments, and ingratiation tactics are methods of information control that are used to affect the decisions made by a target person. Sometimes these influence tactics are used for specific and immediate rewards and sometimes they are used to generate good will, favorable impressions, obligations, and interpersonal attraction (which may enhance the effectiveness of subsequent influence attempts). Strictly speaking, other-enhancing communications may be considered social reinforcements and therefore are combinations of information and reinforcement control. The defining characteristic of information control is a reliance on verbal communication to the exclusion of other incentives or punishments to bring about a change in the target person. However, people also communicate in nonverbal ways to influence one another, though these more subtle behavioral techniques are typically used less deliberately and with less awareness than verbal modes. Nevertheless, nonverbal communications can be effective as modes of influence.

V. NONVERBAL MODES OF COMMUNICATION

Visual contact, gestures, body orientation, and the use of interpersonal space help to regulate social interaction, serve as substitutes for verbal communication, provide a context within which to interpret verbal communication, and convey attitudes between persons. Wiener, Devoe, Rubinow, and Geller (1972) have cautioned about interpreting these kinds of behavior as communications. A distinction must be drawn between signs and the use of a symbolic code that is shared by the interacting parties (see Chapters 3 and 5 for full discussion of this distinction). Any behavior may be interpreted by the observer as a sign of something else, such as the intentions or attitudes of the actor. But true communication requires that the actor encodes a message and that the observer respond systematically to a decoding of the message.

The equivocal nature of most nonverbal communication makes both encoding and decoding difficult and hence may produce misunderstandings between actor and observer. For example, a voice inflection may be interpreted as sarcasm or irony by a listener, though the speaker may not be aware of encoding his message in that fashion.

Birdwhistell (1966, 1967) has developed a coding system for the body movements that accompany social interaction. Included in his system of kinesics are eye contact and aversion, gestures, body orientations, and facial expressions. Though Birdwhistell's work in anthropology has not had much direct impact on social psychology, he has helped focus attention on "body language." Perhaps more important to social psychology is Hall's (1959) examination of cultural differences in postures, physical contact, and the use of interpersonal distance. For example, Spanish Americans tend to stand close to each other during conversation and North Americans tend to stand farther apart. Hall gives the example of a Spanish American continually edging closer to a North American who finally backs into a wall. The former is uncomfortable when interpersonal distance is too great, while the North American attempts to increase spatial separation because proximity makes him uncomfortable. Hall refers to the study of interpersonal space as "proxemics."

Kinesics and proxemics focus on the functions of bodily movements in social interaction. Goffman (1971) has said that one of the most interesting problems of sociology is how two people walking toward one another on a sidewalk manage to avoid a collision. Analogously, the *regulation of a conversation* is at least equally difficult. How do people know when to talk, listen, repeat themselves by rephrasing a statement, or interrupt one another? In addition to regulating conversations, body movements serve a *pantomimic function;* gestures can substitute for verbal language in communicating specific information to the

target individual. Nonverbal behavior also conveys *attitudes of attraction and status* between persons. Although nonverbal behavior serves other functions as well, like providing contextual cues for interpreting the meaning of verbal communication, most of the available research focuses on the three functions that have been emphasized here.

A. The Regulation of Conversations

A focused interaction is typically begun by a period of eye contact between parties who face each other in rather close proximity (Goffman, 1963). Once a conversation is under way, the parties continue to look at each other, though direct eye contact is only intermittent. The person listening spends more time looking than the person doing the talking (Exline & Winters, 1965; Kendon, 1967; Nielsen, 1962). The dynamic synchronization of behavior in a conversation depends on eye contact and pauses. The source looks at the listener during pauses for cues about how he is responding to what is said. The listener may respond in one of four possible ways during these pauses: (1) he may raise his eyes upward without speaking, thereby indicating that he is thinking, and the speaker will usually wait until he is ready to respond; (2) he maintains a blank expression without speaking, thereby manifesting a lack of understanding of what has been said, and the speaker will usually repeat his message in another way; (3) he maintains eye contact while nodding his head in a slow rhythmic manner, evincing understanding, and the speaker continues the conversation; or (4) he maintains eye contact and smiles, signifying that he understands but has nothing to add, and the speaker may continue (Wiener, et al., p. 208).

A listener may emit other forms of nonverbal behavior that affect the speaker during a conversation. A raised eyebrow or a frown may be interpreted as disagreement and may encourage the speaker to repeat, correct, or elaborate his message. A sudden intake of breath in conjunction with a slight opening of the mouth as if to speak, often accompanied by a forward shift in posture, may indicate that the listener has something to say; the speaker may end his message and take on the role of listener or he may continue his speech at a higher pitch or rate to prevent interruption. He may also raise his hand with palms facing the listener as if to say "wait until I'm finished." A listener may signal an end to the conversation by not looking at the speaker and shifting his position away from him, or by uncrossing his legs, rising from a sitting to a standing position, etc.

The orientation of the body also has an impact on interaction. Moscovici (1967) found that subjects who faced each other, even when separated by a screen, used typical spoken language, while those seated side by side or back to back used language in a manner more appropriate to written communication. Moscovici interpreted these findings as implying the loss of gestural and postural signalling ability in the nonfacing situation. Argyle and Kendon (1967) found that a more conversational and cooperative atmosphere prevailed in a discussion conducted over the corner of a table than in one carried out across a table. Thus heads of state meet across a table when negotiating the details of a treaty, but they pose side by side in front of news cameramen to suggest progress and good will.

B. The Pantomimic Functions of Nonverbal Communications

Gestures may take the place of words, serve to act as modifiers (like adjectives and adverbs) of the content of a message, or communicate the speaker's confidence in his own messages (Efron, 1941; Ekman & Friesen, 1969; Krout, 1935; Saitz & Cervenka, 1962; Wiener, et al., 1972). Some gestures are universally recognized and invariantly decoded by observers, and thus serve the same function as speech. Examples include waving goodbye, nodding the head to denote "yes" or "no," forming a circle with index finger and thumb to indicate "okay" or "perfect," depicting the shape of a well-proportioned female, and giving someone "the finger." Gestures may be improvised during speech to emphasize a particular point and have meaning only in the particular situation and with respect to the specific content of what is said.

The clarification of verbal meaning may also occur through gestures. A finger pointing at the listener clarifies that "you" is being used in the specific rather than in the general sense. The orientation of the palms of the speaker's hands signifies the degree of confidence he has in what he is saying. Holding the palms floorward reflects his certainty about what he is communicating and that the issue is not open to question. Palms up expresses uncertainty and is equivalent to "I think" or "It seems to me." The richness of nonverbal communication has not been fully unraveled, but anyone who appreciates dance or mime will understand that there is much more to be learned about its use.

C. The Nonverbal Communication of Attitudes

Body postures, eye contact or aversion, and proximity may reveal the degree of liking or hostility and the power relation between persons. Goffman (1959) has pointed out that prolonged visual contact may communicate a desire to pursue the development of a relationship with a stranger. Demure young ladies soon learn to drop their eyes under the gaze of flirtatious young men. Poets have written about the power of looking into the eyes of a lover. Rubin (1970) found that couples who were romantically involved gazed into each other's eyes more than did couples who were less involved. Mehrabian (1969) concluded that the available research shows that a high percentage of eye contact between persons is typically associated with mutually positive attitudes.

Physical proximity also signifies the degree of attraction between persons. Rosenfeld (1965) asked subjects to seek approval or avoid disapproval from a confederate and found that approval-seeking subjects sat closer to him. Mehrabian (1968) reported that subjects inferred that the less the spatial distance between persons, the more they like each other.

Touching is the most intimate of senses and is associated with the strongest of human emotions. Men and women develop initial impressions of one another on the basis of a handshake. Concern about bodily harm or pain and the impulse to deliver bodily harm to another are associated with the emotions of fear and anger. Profound feelings are associated with precoital petting and love-making. The social significance of being touched is learned during the early years of life, and particularly during the courtship years.

Garfinkel (1964) recounted the reactions of students to an exercise performed in class. Each student was asked to choose an acquaintance to talk to and, during the conversation, to bring his face up to the other person's face, acting as if nothing unusual was happening. The reactions to these intrusions on intimate space consisted of avoidance, bewilderment, and acute embarrassment, especially between pairs of males. The person approached almost always attributed sexual intent to the intruder, and the intruder usually had a hard time restoring the situation by explaining that it was only an experiment. Each subject wanted to know why he or she in particular had been chosen. Spatial proximity and touch are so bound up with intimacy and sex that it was difficult for the subjects to quiet their automatic reactions to the situation.

Visual contact may be interpreted as threatening. Enemies often try to stare each other down and the dropping of a gaze may reveal cowardice. Gaze aversion is characteristic of the subordinate of two animals

and is an expression of submission (Altmann, 1967). Exline and Winters (1965) showed that subjects avoid looking at a hostile interviewer. Ellsworth and Carlsmith (1968) found that eye contact was differently interpreted depending on how positive or negative an interviewer was. An interviewer was either critical or acted positively toward subjects and maintained either frequent or infrequent eye contact during the interview. The subjects then rated the interviewer. The critical interviewer was rated more negatively when he maintained frequent eye contact, while the positive interviewer was better liked when he made frequent eye contact.

The prolonged gaze of a stranger may cause fear and an avoidance reaction by the person observed. Ellsworth, Carlsmith, and Henson (1972) had male and female experimenters on motor scooters pull up alongside automobiles stopped at a red light at a busy intersection. The experimenter either stared at the driver or did not. The driver sped faster across the intersection when the light changed to green when he was stared at than when no staring occurred. Recognizing the possibility that the drivers may have interpreted the stare as a challenge to a drag race, the experimenters carried out a second study. This time the experimenter stood at an intersection of a one-way street and either stared at the driver of an automobile stopped by a red light or did not stare. Again, it was found that staring produced greater speeds in crossing the intersection. The results of these two experiments are shown in Table 7.2. These flight reactions to staring indicate that prolonged gazing is perceived as threatening by the observed person.

Spatial distance between a source of communication and his target may be an important factor in the effectiveness of influence attempts. Lott and Sommer (1967) reported that an intermediate distance between persons enhanced the perceived status of a speaker. Protocol often dictates that persons of high status take a

Table 7.2 Average Time to Cross the Intersection in the Ellsworth, et al (1972) Study of the Effects of Staring on Drivers.[a]

Experiment	Average time scores (secs)	Stare				No stare			
		Male experimenter		Female experimenter		Male experimenter		Female experimenter	
		Male driver	Female driver	Male driver	Female driver	Male driver	Female driver	Male driver	Female driver
Scooter	Taking into account the sex of both E and driver	5.2	5.9	4.8	5.3	8.0	6.5	6.1	5.9
	Ignoring the sex of the driver	5.6		5.0		6.9		6.1	
	Ignoring the sex of both driver and E		5.3				6.5		
Street corner	Taking into account the sex of both E and driver	5.9	6.3	4.9	4.8	6.7	7.5	6.1	6.8
	Ignoring the sex of the driver	6.1		4.8		7.0		6.4	
	Ignoring the sex of both driver and E		5.5				6.7		

[a] Adapted from the original source. E = experimenter.

middle position in a group or sit at the head of the table at dinners or committee meetings. In addition to spatial arrangements that foster the perception of power differences between persons, the sheer frequency of nonverbal activity exhibited by a source directly affects the target's perception of his persuasiveness (Mehrabian & Williams, 1969).

VI. EXPLORING THE SOCIAL ENVIRONMENT

In Part 2 of this book the processes of information gathering, organizing, and evaluating were emphasized. People receive information from many sources, including gatekeepers, acquaintances in face-to-face interactions, and models under observation. Impressions of others are formed and serve as a basis for predicting their future behavior, allowing one to devise strategies that maximize his chances of receiving rewards in interpersonal exchanges. But an individual does not simply sit back and passively wait for information. He actively explores his social environment for information that may be useful to him in interaction. Social communications that appear on the surface to have no ostensible purpose, like gossip and "rap" sessions, are probing tactics to discover information about other people. Though the individual is concerned about the impressions he creates, he may disclose something about himself to elicit reciprocal self-disclosures from others that may be used for subsequent influence purposes. Humor is especially well suited for social exploration because it promotes a positive image of the person using it, at the same time allowing the humorist to find out information about others. Probes, self-disclosure, and humor are often combined in social exploration, but for purposes of exposition can be examined separately.

A. Probes

Much social interaction takes the form of curiosity. The individual makes forays into his social environment to reconnoiter and discover who has what he values, who values what he has to offer in exchange, who will offer resistance to influence, and who will be the best person to influence and who should be avoided. We saw earlier in this chapter when discussing interdependence that what constituted the best choice of a behavioral alternative in interaction depends on what the other person chooses. For this reason much social interaction consists of attempts to probe the other person to ascertain how he views his response alternatives and the values he assigns to outcomes. Probes are information-gathering activities that may be used to predict what others will do. If an actor could accurately predict the behavior of others, presumably he could increase his profits by choosing astutely among his own behavioral alternatives.

Gossip, "small talk," and "rap" sessions provide information about absent third parties. The more relevant third parties are to the goals and values of a person, the more likely it is they will be the subject of conversation. Such conversations may present an opportunity for an individual to seek advice about his personal problems and to test his attributions to and impressions of others. Social comparisons and the consensus of others makes it less probable that he will miscalculate in his appraisals of others. Feedback about his own impression management strategies can help him evaluate and improve his own performances. Although probes provide information to the person that may be critical for future interaction, there has been almost no scientific study of these "trivial" aspects of social behavior.

B. Self-Disclosure

When a person obtains a loan from a bank he usually must put up some form of collateral. If he fails to repay the loan, the bank can then cash-in the collateral and recover its investment. A similar process occurs in everyday transactions between persons.

When an individual tells someone about his most secret and intimate experiences and desires, the discloser makes himself vulnerable because the listener could deliberately employ the information to do harm to him. For example, if the discloser is married but reveals an extra-marital affair, the listener could use that information to cause future difficulties for him. From an interpersonal power viewpoint, a relationship may be more firmly cemented when both parties have secret and intimate information about the other, since each would be inhibited by fear of retaliation in using the information against the other. Thus, disclosure is a way of placing one's fate to some degree in the hands of a listener. This display of confidence builds trust and provides safety for the second person to make reciprocal self-disclosures. The depth of reciprocal self-disclosures has been found to be positively related to the degree of liking between persons (Fitzgerald, 1963; Jourard, 1959).

A large number of studies have shown that self-disclosure is an effective means of eliciting reciprocation from a listener. In a representative study, Ehrlich and Graeven (1971) paired male subjects with a male confederate and asked them to engage in a conversation about themselves. Each person took two-minute turns and each had four turns. Visual contact between subject and confederate was prevented; they sat at opposite ends of a table divided by a partition. The confederate spoke first in all cases and either revealed a high degree of intimacy in his statements or kept the conversation on an impersonal level. For example, in the high intimacy condition he revealed that he wanted to marry a warm, sensitive woman and that it was not important whether she was a virgin; that he did not want children right away and that with the aid of birth control pills, it would be relatively easy to plan his family. In the low intimacy condition, the confederate said he would like to marry a woman who was a good cook, would like her to work for a couple of years, and indicated a preference for an apartment over living in a house.

Two trained judges analysed the content of the subjects' communications for the degree of intimacy of their disclosures to the confederate. They made more intimate self-disclosures when the confederate also revealed intimate information. However, there was no relationship between the intimacy of disclosure and their liking of the confederate. According to Ehrlich and Graeven reciprocal self-disclosures will induce attraction only when such information reveals that the two parties are similar to each other. Finding out that another is a clandestine cannibal is not apt to promote a liking for him. Self-disclosure elicits reciprocal intimacies but the result of the exchange is just as apt to be revulsion and dislike as it is affiliation and attraction.

Refusal to reciprocate self-disclosure may imply distrust or indicate that the listener is not sufficiently attracted to the other person to divulge confidential information. Lack of reciprocity may therefore be interpreted as a sign of refusal of friendship. Research has shown that violation of a mutually established rate of disclosure exchange does result in a termination of the relationship between pairs of persons (Fitzgerald, 1963; Jourard, 1959, 1964).

Levinger and Snoek (1972) view the development of attraction between persons as occurring through increasingly more intimate self-disclosures. It is possible to deter a relationship by disclosing too much too fast. A total stranger who begins an interaction by disclosing much intimate information about himself may be considered to be maladjusted or "weird." Cozby (1972) found that subjects rated a low discloser as having better mental health and considered an intimate discloser as more maladjusted. Furthermore, intimate self-disclosures by a stranger on first meeting produced less liking than did a stranger who disclosed fewer intimate details about himself.

Self-disclosure can also have the goal of revealing something the source wants the other to know about himself. Recounting past experiences may reveal that the discloser has always resisted any type of coercion and may be intended to discourage the listener from the future use of coercion. Disclosure may be an impression management strategy meant to convey the source's alleged sincerity, honesty, benevolence, or any number of other factors important to render future influence attempts more effective.

C. Humor

Humor is a unique human phenomenon and may be used for a variety of purposes. As a probing tactic telling jokes and stories can be quite effective. An employee may jokingly probe his boss's evaluation of him by laughingly asking whether a huge increase in salary is being considered. If the boss merely laughs, the prospects may appear poor, but the boss may smile and then seriously remark that the employee is likely to receive a salary adjustment in the near future. Humor provides an opportunity to either or both persons in interaction to back off from a question or to reveal information without much danger to either party. An interesting demonstration of this process has been reported by Davis and Farina (1970).

A female experimenter was either dressed and acted in a sexually provocative manner or was presented in an unattractive way to male subjects. The subjects were asked to rate three kinds of jokes for how funny they were. One class of jokes was sexual in nature. The subjects either made their ratings privately on sheets given them for the purpose or else made their judgments orally to the female experimenter. When subjects reported their evaluations directly to the attractive female, they rated the off-color jokes as most humorous, but when they made their judgments privately or publicly to an unattractive female, the sexual jokes were not rated as funnier than the other two types.

Davis and Farina interpreted the behavior of the subjects in the attractive female public-rating condition as demonstrating the use of humor as a "come-on" or probe. These males were apparently communicating to the female experimenter that she was considered to be a desirable sexual partner. Little could be lost by this kind of behavior, since it was perfectly legitimate within the instructions given for the experiment. If the female experimenter did not respond to their interest, nothing was lost and no embarrassment would result for anyone. Humor as a probing tool communicates the values of the humorist, and the strength of the listener's response (a weak smile, a frown, or hearty laughter) indicates his values and his willingness to talk about them with the humorist.

VII. CHAPTER SUMMARY

No one is entirely self-sufficient and capable of gaining what he desires without the aid of others. Social interactions are characterized by interdependence. What one person obtains in the way of gains and costs from his interactions depends not only on what he does but also on what the other person does. The anatomy of interdependence reveals that each individual may be more or less responsive to the other person's behavior during interaction. Interactions may take one of four forms: pseudocontingency, reactive contingency, asymmetrical contingency, or mutual contingency. The interpendence of persons also presents the possibility that they may have complementary or incompatible goals. Hence the interaction may be one of pure conflict, pure coordination, or mixed-motive in character. Control over the outcomes of interaction may give one or both parties to interaction power over the behavior of the other. Fate control or behavior control may provide an individual with important incentives that can be used to control another's behavior.

Typically, an exchange of values or rewards will occur during interaction, but both parties will attempt to gain as much for themselves as they can. There are many influence tactics available to entice or compel another person to do as the source wants; the modes of influence are summarized in Table 7.3. Manipulation of features of the environment through roundabout or cue control may produce value changes or elicit habitual responses from the target person. Nondecision making may maintain the status quo and prevent an altercation that might occur if a negative decision were made explicit. Reinforcement control techniques, involving the issuance of threats and promises and the mediation of punishments and rewards, may bring compliance with the source's demands or requests and may help to shape the kinds of behavior the source wants the target to emit.

Because persons are decision-makers and can choose to help or hinder the outcomes desired by others, informational forms of influence may be used to affect decisions that are made. Persuasive communications, which include warnings, recommendations, techniques of ingratiation and the activation of commitments, may change a target's perception of his alternatives and his probability associations between means and ends or may cause him to re-evaluate the values of his perceived outcomes. These explicit verbal forms of information control are supplemented by non-verbal modes of communication. Gestures, eye contact, body orientations, and proximity in interpersonal space (kinesics and proxemics) help to regulate communications, provide a context for verbal communications, provide a context for the meaning of verbal statements, and transmit attitudes of persons toward each other. To maximize the effectiveness of future influence attempts, people explore their social environment through probes, induced self-disclosures, and humor. The information gathered may reveal the values, motives, resources, and susceptibility

Table 7.3 An Outline of the Modes of Influence and Information-Gathering Activities Used by Individuals in Social Interaction.

A. Ecological control
  1. Roundabout control
  2. Cue control
  3. Nondecision making

B. Reinforcement control
  1. Promises
    a. noncontingent
    b. contingent
  2. Mediation of rewards
  3. Threats
    a. noncontingent
    b. contingent
  4. Mediation of punishments

C. Verbal means of information control
  1. Warnings
    a. noncontingent
    b. contingent
  2. Recommendations
    a. noncontingent
    b. contingent
  3. Ingratiation
    a. opinion conformity
    b. other-enhancement
    c. self-enhancement
  4. Activation of commitments

D. Nonverbal means of information control
  1. Kinesics
  2. Proxemics

E. Probes
  1. Self-Disclosure
  2. Gossip
  3. Humor

to influence of other people. In the next chapter we will examine how these influence techniques are used and what factors contribute to their effectiveness.

SUGGESTED READINGS

Altman, I., & Taylor, D. A. *Social penetration: The development of interpersonal relationships.* New York: Holt,

Rinehart, & Winston, 1973. A wide ranging discussion of many of the topics in this chapter with emphasis placed upon the patterns of behavior associated with intense interpersonal relationships.

Fisher, R. *International conflict for beginners.* New York: Harper & Row, 1969. An entertaining and illuminating discussion of policy formation and the problems of communication in the conduct of foreign relations.

Mehrabian, A. *Nonverbal communication.* Chicago: Aldine, 1972. The language of the body, behavior, interpersonal space, and the implicit meanings that are associated with explicit verbal messages are thoroughly discussed in this interesting book.

Rapoport, A. *Two-Person game theory.* Ann Arbor: University of Michigan Press, 1966. The basic ideas of game theory are clearly presented. For students who are interested in applications of game-theoretic models to the understanding of social conflicts.

CHAPTER 8

Yielding to Influence from Others

CHAPTER PREVIEW

The way an individual views the world, his attitudes and values, and the actions he takes are significantly affected by the presence of other people. These social influences are often inadvertent. Gatekeepers of information may not be aware they are shaping the individual's view of the world, and models seldom intend to elicit imitation from observers. An individual is also the target of deliberate influence attempts and may be persuaded to change his attitudes or values or yield to demands or requests. Among the factors that affect the success of influence attempts are the characteristics of the source, the type of influence message used, the manner by which the message is presented, and the receptivity of the target.

The target plays an active role in the influence process. He must assess the truthfulness of a source before deciding how to react to warnings, recommendations, threats, or promises. As a decision-maker, he must weigh the gains and costs associated with choosing to obey or yield to the source of communication against those that may be incurred by taking the opposite course.

The target's acquiescence is related to the perceived reputation of the source. Does he view the source as an expert, as a person with legitimate status, as an attractive or benevolent person? In addition, he may be swayed by the way the source presents a persuasive argument. Is a rational appeal superior to an emotional appeal? Is an argument more effective when the source draws the conclusion for the target, or is it better to let him draw his own conclusion? Will he be more persuaded by an argument that treats both sides of a question, or should the source ignore opposing points of view in making his pitch?

The past experience and personality characteristics of the target may affect his readiness to yield to specific types of influence attempts. Targets differ from one another in intelligence, education, personal histories of success and failure, self-esteem, respect for social norms, and readiness to trust others. These target-related factors play an important role in the influence process.

The entire constellation of source, presentational, and target characteristics operate simultaneously in the influence process. However, for purposes of scientific study it is necessary to isolate each of these variables to establish the effects of each on the target's reactions to specific types of influence messages. The practical problems associated with both experimentation and the need to maintain strict controls over all variables not being manipulated focus attention on short-term effects. In addition the impression is created that resistance to change is less characteristic than it actually is in everyday life. We will first examine the effects of source credibility and the value consequences for the target of influence messages. Then we will turn to presentation factors, source attributes, target characteristics, and, finally, some special determinants that produce resistance by the target to influence attempts.

I. CREDIBILITY, VALUE, AND INFLUENCE

Credibility is defined as the objectively determined truthfulness of a source of communication. For example, consistent failure to back up threats or to fulfill promises results in low credibility, but a source who always does what he says he will has high credibility. When a source uses warnings or recommendations, his credibility is based on his record of accuracy in foretelling events over which he has no control.

Believeability is the target's perception of the probability that the consequences and contingencies stipulated in a specific message will occur. The distinction between credibility and believeability is important and is clarified in Figure 8.1. Credibility is associated with the source and reflects the

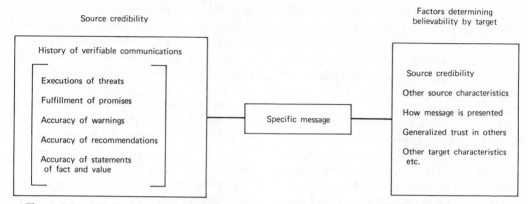

Figure 8.1. Factors affecting the credibility of a source and the believeability of a message to a target.

reliability of his communications in the history of his interactions with the target. A current message has no credibility because the events it foretells have not yet had a chance to occur, and the target may or may not believe it. In general, the higher the source's credibility, the more likely the target is to believe his current message.

A particular message may not be believed even though the source has established high credibility in the past. A child may know that his father consistently punishes disobedience in the home, but may disbelieve his father's threats in the grocery store or at grandmother's house. Thus credibility may be perceived as relevant only to particular situations. Conversely, the target may believe the communication of a low credibility source under certain circumstances. If a source of threats appears emotionally overwrought or desperate, he may be believed despite a poor record of enforcement in the past. We shall see that presentation strategies, source characteristics, and the personality of the target all contribute to the degree of believeability he assigns to a message.

A source's credibility is never easy to measure. Some messages cannot be verified. Propagandists are fully aware of the danger of developing a "credibility gap" and are careful to hedge many of their statements in a way that prevents a listener or reader from ascertaining whether their communications are true or false. For ex-

ample, it is often heard in time of war that our enemy does not desire peace (though of course we do). What the enemy secretly desires is not open to verification, and the propagandist need not fear contradiction. Even if commonsense suggests that the enemy always desires peace on his terms, the credibility of the propagandist is not endangered.

When a message cannot be verified, its assertion does not add to or subtract from the source's credibility. By definition, credibility refers to known relationships between messages and their referents. It should not be concluded that nonverifiable messages are always disbelieved, however. A person may believe a nonverifiable message because of the past credibility of the source, because he lacks any other source of information and grasps at any straw, or for any number of other reasons. The statement that the enemy does not desire peace may be believed because the enemy is hated and the source has great prestige (e.g., the President of the United States).

Influence messages generally communicate contingencies between behavior and outcomes to the target. When making decisions about his future course of action, the target takes into account the subjective probability he assigns to a message (its believeability) and the value of the consequences it stipulates. He may believe the message and yet not make the decision advocated by the source. For example, an engineering firm's president might offer the governor of a state a bribe in exchange for contracts to build highways and bridges. The governor may believe the source's promise, but the offer may be refused because of the many costs associated with such criminal activity.

The value of the reinforcements predicted by a message contributes to the effectiveness of an influence attempt. Threats and promises are forms of reinforcement control. They are used to encourage the target to make certain decisions. Threats attempt to make compliance less costly than noncompliance; promises are intended to reward a particular course of action so the target will consider compliance his best choice. As informational modes of influence, warnings and recommendations predict punishments and rewards. These persuasive communications should affect the target's decision when the values of the contingent reinforcements are sufficiently great. We will consider how the credibility of the source and the values associated with each type of message affects the decision of a target to yield to or resist influence attempts.

A. Magnitude of Punishment and Credibility of Threats

Public concern about the amount of crime in the United States has led many political candidates to advocate increases in penalties for various offenses. When he was governor of New York Nelson Rockefeller initiated legislation to require a penalty of life imprisonment for selling large quantities of drugs. Will this new law, which constitutes a threat of high magnitude, decrease the amount of drug peddling? The amount of penalty cannot be divorced from the credibility of the authorities when it comes to carrying out the threat. What are the chances of being caught for selling drugs illegally? Even if the probability of detection and conviction are high and the penalty is great, the potential criminal may not

be deterred. Suppose he is an addict and pushes drugs to feed his own habit; under these circumstances he is not likely to obey the law. Laboratory studies of threats are undertaken in simple situations and do not consider the many factors that may be important in considering complex social issues, such as the effectiveness of capital punishment in deterring homicides (see Box 8.1 for a discussion of crime and punishment).

In order to investigate scientifically the effects of threats on a target, it is necessary to operationalize the relevant factors. How can we measure source credibility? We must reconsider how threats are defined and the conditions under which the threatener's credibility is established. A contingent threat, as defined in the last chapter, demands compliance and states the penalty for noncompliance. The credibility of the source in using threats in the past can be determined only on those occasions when the target refused to comply with the threatener's demands. Successful threats do not enable the source to carry out punishment because the target does what he is told. Only when the target refuses to comply is the credibility of the source put to the test.

Threat credibility is measured by the proportion of times the source actually punished noncompliance to his demands over his entire history of interactions with the target. Suppose the source had threatened the target 15 times; if the target complied five times, the source's credibility depends on how often he punished the target after the ten unsuccessful threats. If on those ten occasions, the source punished noncompliance every time, his credibility would be 100 percent; if he never backed-up his threats, the source's credibility would be 0 percent; if he punished noncompliance five out of ten times, his credibility would be 50 percent; and so on.

Consider the decision of the person who has been threatened. Compliance is usually given reluctantly because the target incurs

Box 8.1   CRIME AND PUNISHMENT

There are competing theories about the prevention and control of criminal activities. One view is that violations of the law have complex determinants based in the structure of a society. People who are well integrated into society and are given opportunities to acquire material satisfactions are not likely to be tempted to go outside the law to acquire what they want. Crime rates are much higher among the poor and disadvantaged than among other classes of society. The remedy for high crime rates, then, is to change the conditions under which poor people live so they can acquire the skills, jobs, and opportunities now denied to them.

An alternative view suggests a reliance on the law enforcement and judicial agencies of society to prevent crime. This theory emphasizes increasing the efficiency of the police in apprehending criminals, and providing sufficient penalties to deter would be criminals from violating the law. The statistics of crime indicate that the less the probability of detection and the smaller the penalty, the higher the incidence of particular criminal activities. Larcenies, which involve stealing valuables without breaking and entering homes and places of business, are less often solved than robberies. Similarly, proportionately fewer robbers are apprehended and convicted than murderers.

Some evidence in favor of the deterrence theory of crime prevention has been found. Gibbs (1968) developed a scale for measuring the severity of punishment and the probability of conviction for homicides in 48 states in 1960. He found that the greater the punishment and the higher the probability of conviction, the lower the homicide rate. In a field study, Chambliss (1966) found an inverse relationship betwen the frequency of parking violations on a college campus and the severity and certainty of punishment. The uncontrolled nature of these studies suggests caution in accepting their conclusions at face value. No differences in the incidence of homicides were found when comparisons were made between states which had a capital penalty and those that did not (Katzenbach, 1968). Also, there has been no change in the homicide rate in the United States over the past two decades (Beattie & Kenney, 1966), despite the fact that the use of capital punishment declined to zero during that time. In cross-national comparisons the United Nations Department of Economic and Social Affairs (1962) found no relationship between the rates of particular classes of crimes and the degree of their punishment. Capital punishment for robbery apparently has no more deterrent value than a year or two in prison.

Of course deterrence is not the only problem to be considered when discussing capital punishment. It is a penalty that cannot be reversed and seldom can we be 100 percent certain of anyone's guilt. A person often spends years on death row while appeals are made through higher courts. No one would want to interfere with his right to exhaust his opportunities to show he is innocent, and yet it is cruel to keep him facing death for a long period of time. Most homicides occur among acquaintances, one of whom has been drinking alcoholic beverages. Homicide is often a crime of passion. Under such conditions no abstract threat of punishment is likely to be considered by the individual before he plunges the knife or fires the bullet. Also life in prison may be every bit as much a penalty as death and nine out of ten homicide cases are brought to conviction. Therefore, it is doubtful that more deterrent value can be squeezed from the justice system than is already in effect. However, the removal of all punishments would probably increase crime rates.

---

costs by giving in to the demands of the source. There would be no need to threaten him if compliance already were his preferred response. But if the target refuses to comply, he risks the punishment threatened. The target is therefore in the unenviable position of facing a least-of-evils choice—comply and incur costs, or defy the threatener and risk being punished. He will make his decision based on how he calculates the probabilities, costs, and punishments associated with each of his alternative responses. He will act in a manner calculated to minimize his costs. If the penalty threatened is smaller than the costs of compliance, the threatener will be unsuccessful in gaining compliant behavior.

The higher the credibility of the source and the greater the magnitude of punishment threatened for noncompliance, the more probable it is a target will comply to the demands made on him. This proposition has been confirmed many times in a research paradigm developed by Horai and Tedeschi (1969). Subjects were pitted against a confederate in repeated trials of the Prisoner's Dilemma game (see Chap. 7.B.2). Occasionally the confederate sent the subject the threat: "If you do not make Choice 1 on the next trial, I will take n points away from your counter." Choice 1 was the cooperative choice and the amount of punishment was either 5, 10, or 20 points. The credibility levels used in the experiment were 10, 50, and 90 percent.

On those occasions when he sent threats, the confederate always made Choice 2. The subject was therefore placed in a least-of-evils situation. If he complied by making Choice 1, he would lose 5 points and the confederate would gain 5 points (see Figure 7.1c). If he made Choice 2 he would lose only 4 points (as would the confederate), but he also risked the possibility of punishment for noncompliance. The results indicated that both the magnitude of punishment and the credibility of the source affected the decisions made. Compliance increased as a direct function of both independent variables (see Figure 8.2). Thus, when only one participant had the ability to threaten, the most effective strategy for him to use was to maintain high credibility and transmit high magnitude threats.

It may be argued that the behavior of subjects in a trivial laboratory game tells us little about how people act in real life. The game of life is not played for points or trivial sums of money and people are not always cooly examining their alternatives but may be genuinely angry or emotionally overwrought. This criticism is justifiable only to the degree the scientist overgeneralizes his findings. The most careful statement that can be made is: holding all else constant, there is a direct relationship between punishment magnitude and source credibility and compliance with threats.

B. Magnitude of Rewards and Credibility of Promises

When a source promises a reward in exchange for some action by a target, his credibility is tested only when the target makes himself eligible for the reward by complying. If the target ignores the promise, the source is not called upon to deliver the reward and the target gains no information about his credibility. The credibility of a promise is measured by the proportion of

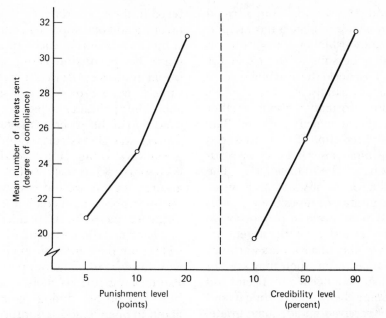

Figure 8.2. The effects of punishment and of credibility on the degree of compliance. (After Horai and Tedeschi, 1969.)

times the source kept his word in the past by rewarding compliant responses by the target.

In making his decision about whether to comply with a given promise, the target must consider both the credibility of the source and the value of the promised reward. The reward offered must be sufficiently large to offset the costs of compliance and make compliance more profitable to the target than any alternative responses open to him. The greater the credibility of the source and the higher the value of the reward offered, the more probable it is a target will comply with a source's requests.

These relationships were demonstrated in the context of a Prisoner's Dilemma game by Crosbie (1972). Subjects were offered either high or low amounts of reward and, in the latter case, the source's credibility was controlled to be high or low. As predicted, subjects were more compliant when rewards were more valuable or when the credibility of the promisor was high.

There is some evidence that targets evaluate a promise by multiplying the credibility of the source by the value specified

in the current promise. Zipf (1960) asked subjects to provide written estimates of the probability that a promisor would reward compliance and the value of the rewards they would receive for complying. Compliance was a function of the product of the two factors (i.e., probability x value). Lindskold and Tedeschi (1971a) found that subjects would comply with the promises of a low credibility source when the product of the credibility and the value of the reward promised exceeded the product associated with not complying. A source can compensate for low credibility by offering greater rewards and a highly credible source can gain compliance by offering less in exchange. High credibility is a valuable resource that reduces the costs and maximizes the success of influence attempts, at least in the long run. Honesty is the best policy and truth is power.

C. Credibility and the Value of Warnings and Recommendations

To determine the credibility of a source of warnings, a target will have to find out if the predicted relationship between behavior and outcome is accurate. If a student receives a contingent warning from a friend that a professor will not like a term paper, he will not know whether the warning is accurate unless he submits the paper for evaluation. To check the credibility of a noncontingent warning the target needs only to obtain information about whether the event predicted actually occurred. The weatherman's prediction of a hurricane can be tested by simple observation or by reading the newspaper the following day. The credibility of a source of warnings is measured by the number of times the warnings are found to be accurate in proportion to the total number tested by the target.

The believeability of a source's warnings may be enhanced even when they are not tested. If the student heeded his friend and rewrote his paper before submitting it, and subsequently received an adequate grade, he might attribute his success to the helpful advice. In this case, enhanced believeability is not a result of an increase in the credibility of the source, which was not tested, but rather is a consequence of the target's rationalization of the cause of his own behavior.

When a target is faced with contradictory communications from two different sources, he should be most affected by the one with a reputation of greater credibility. In a test of this hypothesis Ference (1971) gave subjects the task of predicting whether 20 applicants to the freshman class at Carnegie Institute of Technology would subsequently graduate. Each subject examined the high school records of twenty applicants who allegedly had been admitted to CIT in previous years. Some of the applicants were said to have graduated and some had failed, and the subject's task was to determine which was which.

Included in the information provided to subjects regarding the applicants were letters of recommendation from the same two persons—a high school principal and a college admissions officer who had interviewed all 20 applicants. For 16 of the 20 applications reviewed, the two sources differed in their recommendations, with one favoring and one opposing admission. The subject considered each applicant and made his prediction about whether he would graduate. After each prediction, the subjects were provided with information about the applicant's college record; in one condition of the experiment one of the two sources was always correct and the other was always wrong. In a second condition, each source was equally credible. When the accuracy of the two sources was different, the one who was most credible had the most influence over subjects' predictions.

There may be occasions when a target will rely on the communications of a source with lower credibility. Suppose Ms. Hope Pandora was curious about a box that had been left on her dining room table, was about to open it, and was informed by one room-mate that it was probably a corsage while a second room-mate said it looked just like the description of a box containing a bomb that had exploded in a downtown office last week. Even if the latter source were considered less credible than the former, the value consequences of the warning are so great that Ms. Pandora may be reluctant to open the box. Decisions are made not only on the basis of an estimation of the believeability of a message, but also on its value consequences.

Many studies that have manipulated the magnitude of harm conveyed by warnings, while holding source credibility constant, have established a direct relationship between "fear arousal" and the degree of yielding to influence by target persons. *Fear arousing communications* warn an individual about accidents or disease, bodily harm or death, or threats to security and property. Typically, they include recommendations about what the target can do to avoid the harm predicted.

In a representative study Dabbs and Leventhal (1966) gave subjects one of two communications about the danger of tetanus. The low-arousal material described the infrequent incidence of tetanus and informed the subjects that bleeding from a wound usually flushed the poison-producing bacilli out of the body. The high-arousal material stated that tetanus was contracted very easily and often led to death. Included with each communication were specific instructions about how to obtain inoculations from the University Health Clinic. The subjects exposed to the high fear-arousing warnings more often stated their intentions to obtain tetanus shots and in fact more often did visit the Health Clinic to obtain inoculations. Similar findings have been reported when the persuasive communications concerned dental hygiene (Haefner, 1956), safe driving practices (Berkowitz & Cottingham, 1960), cigarette smoking (Insko, Arkoff, & Insko, 1965), tuberculosis (DeWolfe & Governale, 1964), viewing the sun during an eclipse (Kraus, El-Assal, & DeFleur, 1966), and the use of handrails for safety on stairways (Piccolino, 1966).

Impressed by the consistency of the relationship between the magnitude of harm stated in warnings and successful persuasion, Leventhal, Singer, and Jones (1965) suggested that "fear functions as a drive which promotes the acceptance of recommended actions, and, regardless of the absolute level of fear arousal used in any study, the communication which arouses the more fear will be more persuasive" (p.20).

It has become increasingly clear that fear arousal may produce statements of a target's intention to take remedial action without necessarily inducing action. For example, a person who smokes cigarettes may fear cancer and may express his desire to stop smoking—but he may nevertheless continue smoking. While fear arousal invariably produces changes in verbal behavior, the conditions under which stated intentions or desires are manifested in remedial or preventive action need to be spelled out. Leventhal (1965) proposed two reasons for inconsistencies between stated intentions and subsequent behavior by targets exposed to fear-arousing communications: (1) their lack of assurances that protective actions can be taken, and (2) their lack of specific instructions about how to carry out such actions.

When these two conditions are met, the inconsistencies between statements of intention and subsequent behavior are eliminated. Leventhal et al. (1965) exposed subjects to high or low fear arousing communications about the dangers of tetanus and either provided or withheld instruction about how to obtain inoculations. All the subjects were given a general recommendation to obtain a tetanus shot, but only half of them also received a map of the campus showing where the Health Center was located and a list of typical student activities that occurred close to the Center. More of the students who received these specific instructions actually obtained tetanus shots, both in the low and in the high fear-arousal conditions.

An inconsistency between stated verbal intentions to stop smoking and actual smoking behavior was eliminated by Leventhal, Watts, and Pagano (1967). High fear-arousing communications produced more verbal statements of a desire to quit smoking than did low fear-arousing communications. However, the subjects modified their actual behavior only when they received specific instructions about how to stop smoking. Thus, the larger the magnitude of harm specified in a fear-arousing communication, the greater the fear reported by targets and the stronger their stated desire to take protective action; but action occurs only when fear-arousal is combined with knowledge about how to reduce the danger.

If a fear-arousing communication informs an individual that there is nothing he can do to avoid harm, he may do nothing, and simply wait to see if he will be lucky or will suffer the fate predicted. Rogers and Thistlethwaite (1970) showed subjects either high or low fear-arousing movie sequences depicting the case history of a man with lung cancer. The subjects included some who smoked cigarettes and some who did not. After viewing the film, the subjects read a 500-word essay presenting some of the evidence linking smoking to lung cancer. The subjects were then asked to read one of two additional 250 word essays, one of which indicated that the chances of getting lung cancer would be effectively reduced by giving up cigarette smoking, while the other argued that there was no evidence to show that changing smoking habits would improve a smoker's chances. Smokers indicated their intentions to stop only when doing so would improve their chances of avoiding cancer.

The credibility of a source of recommendations—messages predicting rewards—is established in the same way as with warnings. Surprisingly little research has been carried out to examine explicit recommendations. More interest might be expected in this form of influence, since commercials in the mass media so often employ messages suggesting the connection between products and outcomes such as sexual conquests or happy homes. Despite the lack of evidence, it is reasonable to assume that both the credibility of a source and the value of the positive consequences associated with a recommendation will be directly related to successful influence. Indirect support for this generalization can be drawn from our interpretation of modeling as social influence (see Chapter 6, IIB and IIC).

D.   The Generalization of Credibility

It is not really known whether a target develops an overall estimate of a source's credibility or whether he maintains a separate index for each type of message. Presumably, if the source's warnings have been accurate, the target should also believe the source's recommendations. But suppose the source backs up his threats; will the target believe his subsequent promises? If the source keeps his promises, will the target believe subsequent threats?

Heilman (1974) provided female high school students with information that the person with whom they were to interact had sent either a threat or a promise to a prior subject and had either kept her word or not. In this way the confederate's reputation was manipulated. Whichever type of message the confederate allegedly had sent to the prior subject, she sent the opposite message to the subject. Measures of believeability were obtained. The students believed the threats of the confederate when she had kept her previous promise, but there was no transfer of credibility from threats to promises whether or not the previous threat had been fulfilled.

Schlenker, Nacci, Helm, and Tedeschi (1974) found almost identical results when compliance measures were obtained in the context of a Prisoner's Dilemma game. In the first of two experiments a confederate transmitted five noncontingent promises of cooperation to subjects and either always kept his promises or never did. During the second half of the game the confederate sent intermittent threats and punished noncompliance either 0 or 100 percent of the time. Subjects were more compliant to the threats when the confederate had first established a high credibility for promises.

In the second experiment, threats of 0 to 100 percent credibility were sent to subjects during the first phase of the game and noncontingent promises of cooperation were transmitted during the second phase. The credibility of the promises was either 0 or 100 percent. As compared to the 0 percent credibility condition, the confederate who always punished noncompliance to threats received less cooperation from the subjects when he shifted to promises. However, this initial inverse effect of threat credibility was weak and was counteracted by the credibility of the subsequent promises. That is, the source gained more cooperation from the subjects in the second phase of the study when the promises were 100 percent credible than when they were 0 percent credible.

Clearly there is no simple generalization of credibilities from threats to promises. On the other hand, the effects of promise credibility are strong and do affect how target persons respond to threats. It is certainly not common sense to discover that a threatener can enhance his credibility just as much by making unilateral and benevolent promises as he can by continually demonstrating his willingness to enforce threats. Conciliatory behavior does not undermine the perception of a source's readiness to utilize coercive power; instead, it enhances his reputation for credibility in using both reward and coercive power.

II. PRESENTATION FACTORS AND INFLUENCE

The believeability of a source's message is a subjective estimate about its truth value and is affected by many factors other than the source's credibility. How the source presents his persuasive communication may contribute to the effectiveness of his influence attempts. Given that he cannot in the short run change his reputation or credibility are there ways of presenting his message or argument that will enhance its believeability? Whatever response he wants to elicit from a target, there are many different persuasive arguments he can use for the purpose. According to the attitude theories of social judgment and congruity presented in Chapter 4, he might search for arguments that are congruent with the preconceptions and beliefs of the target. Persuasive communications that are too discrepant from what the target believes may be automatically disbelieved and rejected.

The degree of confidence a source expresses in his own communications can be expected to affect the target's response. Why should the target believe something the source communicates but apparently does not believe? The source might consider making an emotional appeal or might decide to present a carefully planned logical argument. Which is apt to be more persuasive? If the latter, should the conclusion be drawn for the target or should he be allowed to draw the conclusion for himself? Perhaps drawing the conclusion will appear too manipulative and will undermine the effectiveness of the attempt at persuasion. Should the source present his thesis without considering alternative arguments or should he present both sides of the issue? If more than one side of an issue is to be presented, does the order of presentation make any difference? The answers to these questions are important, not only to professional propagandists but to the everyday man as he engages in interpersonal politics.

A. Congruity of Persuasive Communication

The lack of congruity of a message with the existing "knowledge" of the target undermines its effectiveness. There are several lines of evidence to support this general principle. Brigham and Cook (1970) asked liberal and conservative students to rate the degree to which they agreed or disagreed with arguments for or against interracial marriage, minority rights, speeding up desegregation, and so on. The subjects were then asked also to rate the arguments on a scale ranging from very effective to very ineffective. As might be expected, the more favorable the subjects were toward a particular argument, the more effective they rated it. Waly and Cook (1965) and Selltiz and Cook (1966) also found that people consider an argument with which they agree to be more plausible and effective than one with which they disagree. One implication of these findings is that people who share beliefs and values can present arguments to one another more effectively than can those who initially disagree with one another.

Incongruity may explain the results of the very few studies that have not found the usual direct relationship between degree of fear arousal and the effectiveness of warnings. Janis and Feshbach (1953) designed three illustrative lectures on dental hygiene to arouse different levels of fear. The low fear-arousing lecture said little about the negative consequences of not brushing teeth. The moderate warning pointed out the dangers of tooth decay, bad breath, and other associated problems. The strong warning, which was illustrated with slides, stated that "if you ever develop an infection of this kind from improper care of your teeth, it will be an extremely serious matter, because these infections are really dangerous. They can spread to your eyes, or your heart, or your joints and cause secondary infections which may lead to diseases such as arthritic paralysis, kidney damage or total blindness" (p.79). Also included in the latter lecture was a warning that poor dental hygiene may lead to gangrene of the jaws in old age.

Measures of attitudes two weeks after the lectures revealed that the students had been most influenced by the low and moderate lectures and least influenced by the high fear-arousing lecture. Katz (1960) has suggested that the latter must have seemed implausible to high school students. While the consequences portrayed must have aroused some fear in the subjects, the believeability of the message must have been low. Thus the effectiveness of a warning is a function both of its believeability and the value consequences it predicts. No matter how great the harm predicted, if the warning is assigned a low probability of truth little influence will be exerted. The low and moderate messages were much more believeable because they were congruent with the knowledge already possessed by the subjects and the magnitude of harm predicted was sufficiently high to arouse concern. "Scare" tactics may not curtail the use of drugs by college students because of the incongruity of the arguments with prior knowledge. If college students are told they will have defective children and will develop gangrene of the jaws in old age because they smoke marijuana, the chances are the warning will be ignored. The source will have no effect except to arouse laughter for making foolish statements.

Congruity of a communication with a target's beliefs may overcome a source's lack of credibility. Suppose a person had read somewhere that 78 percent of the American people are opposed to capital punishment and is later told by an acquaintance that a majority are opposed to it. Even if the acquaintance has low credibility, the target is apt to find his communication believeable; but in the absence of prior information about the attitudes of the American public, he would probably disbelieve it.

B. Confidence Expressed by the Source

A source's confidence in what he asserts is probably communicated by nonverbal as well as by verbal means. Pauses in the flow of conversation or other signs of hesitation, lack of eye contact at a critical phase of the interaction, wavering of the voice, and postural cues may suggest lack of confidence and hence undermine the believeability of his communications. The degree of confidence of the source about what he asserts may be expressed as a specific probability: "I'm about 75 percent sure." Mehrabian (1972) has found that head-nodding and smiling indicate lack of self-confidence and detract from a person's ability to persuade others. In general, the less confidence the source conveys about his own statements, the less believeable the target will find them.

C. The Style of the Message

Unsystematic, common-sense observation suggests that a source may be disbelieved if there are internal contradictions in his communication or if he is inconsistent over time. However, there is no scientific basis for believing that a supremely logical argument will be more effective than a more inconsistent one. Future research may well reveal the functions of logic in persuasive communication. Certainly there is a great deal of evidence that people are quite concerned about appearing consistent over time (see Chapter 5, V).

After comparing logical and emotional appeals, McGuire (1969, p.202) concluded that the evidence weakly supports the superiority of emotional appeals. Unfortunately, this kind of research seldom controls the magnitude of consequences to make sure the values associated with logical and emotional appeals are the same. Emotional arguments, almost by definition, imply that the consequences to the target are apt to be great. Thus the slight superiority in effectiveness of emotional appeals may be due to their greater apparent consequences rather than a reflection of a valid difference in responses to logical and emotional influence attempts.

A source's style in presenting his message may effect its believeability. The communicator may be dynamic or lethargic and may pepper his communications with wit and humor or may maintain a sober monotone. John F. Kennedy was noted for his style as a charismatic leader, though historians disagree about the achievements of his presidency. It would be surprising if style had no effect on the influence process, but the matter has not been studied. The available evidence suggests that an intense and dynamic presentation is considered propagandistic and is less successful than a more methodical one (Bowers, 1963; Dietrich, 1946). On the other hand, Bowers and Osborn (1966) have found that speeches using metaphorical conclusions were considered more effective than speeches using literal conclusions.

The stereotyped afterdinner speaker generally begins his talk with a story or joke, the purpose of which is to relax the audience and foster a positive attitude toward him. Windes (1961) reported that the campaign speeches of Adlai Stevenson when he ran for the presidency of the United States in 1956 were more effective when they were introduced with a humorous story than when they were not. Unfortunately, lack of control precludes accepting this conclusion. The speeches that were analysed varied in many ways, and some

other factor may have produced the differences reported in effectiveness. Gruner (1965) and Lull (1940) found no effects of humor on the persuasiveness of a speaker.

Style is often considered a prominent characteristic of dynamic, popular, and heroic leaders. Gerth and Mills (1953) suggested that attraction toward a heroic leader (i.e., charisma) occurs when people are disoriented because of crises and are informationally dependent for guidance. In other words, charisma is as much a function of the needs of the target as it is of the style of the person he chooses as a leader. Perhaps this is why in classical Greece, when Cicero stopped speaking the people said, "How well he spoke," but when Demosthenes finished speaking the people said, "Let us march."

D. Drawing Conclusions

Among the many things Americans like to believe about themselves is that they are independent in their thinking. They do not want others to tell them what they should believe. Freud observed the same tendency among his Viennese patients. He found that a patient was more apt to work through his unconscious problems if the therapist assisted him in discovering them than if the therapist merely told him what his problems were. This observation is debatable; other therapists (e.g., Ellis, 1958) argue that clear direction is more efficient.

Hovland and Mandell (1952) presented statements to students in the form of radio transcriptions. One program discussed the economic conditions under which currency should be devalued and stated that such conditions currently existed in the United States. A second group of students were presented with an otherwise identical program which also drew the logical conclusion that the dollar should be devalued. There was more verbal agreement with the persuasive communication when the conclusion was drawn for the audience than when it was not. The effectiveness of drawing a conclusion was not affected by the tested intelligence of the subjects.

Cooper and Dinerman (1951) reported that the intelligence of the audience was a factor in determining whether drawing conclusions would be effective. New York City Catholic and Protestant high school students were shown an army film which concerned the attacks on religious groups of the Nazi regime in Germany. For some students a conclusion was drawn about ethnic and religious prejudice and hatred. Other students did not have a conclusion drawn for them. The film was more effective in eliciting verbal statements of reduced prejudice from the more intelligent students when no conclusion was drawn; less intelligent students were more persuaded when a conclusion was drawn for them.

The inconsistency between these two studies may be partly resolved by noting the difference in content of the persuasive communications. While college students presumably do not have much knowledge about the relatively abstract issues of economics and dollar devaluation, the film about prejudice was concerned with a social phenomenon all of the subjects had personally experienced and about which relatively strong opinions were held. But why familiarity and strong opinions on an issue should combine with intelligence to produce different reactions to drawing conclusions has not yet been answered.

E. One-Sided Versus Two-Sided Communication

By ceding a few points to the opposition, considering its arguments and refuting them, a communicator may appear less biased, less propagandistic and less ill informed, than by ignoring contrary viewpoints. But the presentation of both sides of an issue may backfire. If a target is ignorant, exposing him to the opposition's arguments may detract from the source's ability to persuade him. As part of the military

effort in World War II, Hovland, Lumsdaine, and Sheffield (1949) investigated the effectiveness of one-sided and two-sided arguments on the attitudes of U.S. servicemen. After the German army had surrendered and the focus of the war shifted to the Pacific theater of operations, there was official concern that American soldiers might be too optimistic. What would happen to morale if the war were prolonged?

A persuasive communication was constructed as a propaganda tactic to create the belief that the war with Japan might be long and tough. Two radio broadcasts were prepared, both of which argued that it would take at least two years to defeat Japan. A one-sided program lasted fifteen minutes and detailed the logistical problems of fighting so far from the North American continent, the size and fighting ability of the Japanese army, and the resources still possessed by the enemy. The two-sided program contained all the information of the one-sided program and added four minutes of negative information, pointing out the superiority of the U.S. navy and air force and indicating the increased effort that could be made against the Japanese because of the German surrender. After soldiers listened to one or the other of the two programs, measures of their attitudes toward the war in the Pacific area were obtained.

The two programs had different effects depending on the initial opinions and educational backgrounds of members of the audience. The two-sided program produced more change toward believing the war would be prolonged among servicemen who had at least a high school diploma. When the audience lacked a high school education and was initially in favor of the position advocated, a one-sided communication was more effective. Perhaps a poorly educated audience that already agrees with the position to be communicated does not know the contrary arguments; when exposed to a two-sided communication the new contrary information interferes with the effectiveness of the propagandist's message. It may be concluded that a communicator must know his audience—what they believe and how educated they are —before deciding whether to present a one-sided or two-sided argument.

F. The Order of Presentation of Arguments

Debates and jury trials require that first one speaker presents his argument and then a second speaker presents an opposing view. In jury trials the prosecuting attorney sums up his case first, and then the defense attorney is provided his opportunity. Which side has the advantage? A *primacy effect* occurs when being first provides an advantage in persuading an audience. A *recency effect* refers to the case where the second person has the advantage.

Hovland, Campbell, and Brock (1957) have provided evidence that when a person publicly commits himself to an opinion after he hears the first argument but before he hears the second one, a primacy effect occurs. If the second argument is a two-sided communication, the advantage for the first speaker is eliminated, however. Apparently, a two-sided argument provides more justification for a listener to change his mind even if he had committed himself before hearing it, because such a communication seems to be more fair and objective.

A primacy effect may occur if a listener only expects a single presentation. The order of presentation will not be crucial for opinion change if the listener expects to hear two sides of an issue and does not commit himself before hearing both of them (Hovland, 1958). In debates and jury trials the members of the jury expect to hear both sides of the question; hence, the order of presentation should not give an advantage to either side.

Miller and Campbell (1959) applied a learning theory analysis to primacy and recency effects. The first argument heard by a person should have more impact than the second because it had "prior entry." On the other hand, the first argument is subject to more "memory decay" than the more recent one. Prior entry should be more important than memory decay when two arguments are presented to a listener in a short time period, and a primacy effect should occur. But when the arguments are separated by sufficient time, the memory loss for the first communication should more than offset the advantage of prior entry and a recency effect should occur. Miller and Campbell found experimental support for their hypotheses. Nonetheless, matters are apparently more complicated than can be accounted for by learning theory. Several investigators have failed to find a primacy effect when two messages were presented right after each other (Insko, 1964; Thomas, Webb, & Tweedie, 1961).

A source may be concerned about the internal order of presentation of his persuasive communication. A parent or teacher may want to convince children of the need to take care of their teeth. The children might be warned about the problems associated with poor dental hygiene habits and specific information might be offered about appropriate preventive actions. Should the recommendations be given last or should they be interspersed with the fear-arousing communication? Leventhal and Singer (1966) addressed this question by exposing subjects to high or low fear-arousing communications about the consequences of poor dental hygiene. The subjects were also provided with detailed information about how to reduce dental disease. The recommendations were placed either before, after, or interspersed with the fear-arousing communication. The subjects were asked to report how much fear was aroused and to state whether they intended to change their dental habits.

The placement of the recommendation had different effects on reported fear and stated intentions. In the high fear-arousal condition, the subjects reported less fear when the recommendation was given prior to the warning and most fear when it was presented after the warning. Just the reverse pattern was found in the low fear condition; prior exposure to the very detailed recommendations created more anxiety than the mild warning. As should be expected, the subjects more often stated their intention to change their dental habits when they had heard the high rather than the low fear arousing communication. The placement of the recommendations had no effect on their stated intentions to change their dental habits. Thus, while placement of a recommendation may affect the degree of fear aroused in subjects, it has little effect on gaining acquiescence to a persuasive communication.

III. SOURCE CHARACTERISTICS

Who a source of influence is, what he is like, what resources he possesses, and the intentions attributed to him by a target all affect the success of influence attempts. Source characteristics may be considered bases of power because they contribute to the believeability of influence communications. Political scientists and social psychologists have long speculated about the characteristics of the source that add to his power. Empirical work has provided support for the view that expertise, status, control over resources, perceived trustworthiness, and attraction are the critical dimensions. The specific contribution that each makes to the influence process depends on which mode of influence is considered. For example, liking for the source may enhance the believeability of his promises but may undermine the effectiveness of his threats.

The problem of associating particular bases of power with specific forms of influence becomes even more complicated when the various combinations of source characteristics are examined. Will a source who is an expert, disliked, and perceived as trustworthy be more believed when trans-

mitting persuasive communications than one who is inexpert, liked, and trustworthy? The answers to such combinatorial questions are less readily available than answers to questions about the specific and separate effects of each source characteristic.

A. Bases of Social Power

Political scientists have identified a number of source characteristics as important to an effective exercise of power. In a study of an American community, Dahl (1961) observed that power was based on a person's wealth, social standing, popularity, control over jobs and information, and access to the legal apparatus. Lasswell and Kaplan (1950) viewed political behavior as an exchange process. Power is possessed by those persons who control the resources or values desired by others; these bases of power provide the potential to influence others. Eight fundamental values were considered. Those values that emphasize deference include power, respect, rectitude, and affection, and those that emphasize welfare include wealth, well-being, skill, and enlightenment. These base values are considered exchangeable. For example, wealth may be traded for respect or skill may be bartered for wealth.

The theory of Lasswell and Kaplan had immediate impact on a group of social psychologists at Yale University. Hovland, Janis, and Kelley (1953) identified two source characteristics as significant in enhancing the believeability of his persuasive communications—his *expertise and his trustworthiness*. A person was considered to be an expert if he had special training or experience, relevant education, a history of success in solving problems, seniority, or social background. Trustworthiness refers to the extent to which a source's communications are considered to be objective and are preceived as furthering no vested interest of his own. Hovland et al. postulated that the more expert or trustworthy a source, the more believeable and effective are his persuasive communications.

A typology of the bases of social power was proposed by French and Raven (1959). They identified five types: reward, coercive, legitimate, referent, and expert power. *Reward* and *coercive power* refer to the use of promises, rewards, threats, and punishments and hence are not source characteristics but constitute modes of influence. *Legitimate power* is based on a particular position or office held by a person that is recognized by others as giving him authority. This recognition is rationalized by a set of symbols, documents, and rules that define the scope of the authority provided to the occupant. The constitution of the U.S. defines the power of the President and a table of organization typically provides job descriptions for the managers of a corporation. A person who complies with a source because he feels he ought to may be responding on the basis of the source's legitimacy. Such deference is not directly dependent on coercive or reward power and may occur even when the target dislikes or lacks respect for the source. Alienated people, marginal men, and revolutionaries may not show deference to society's constituted authorities because they do not view the "system" or its set of rationalizing symbols and rules as legitimate. Even those who consider the system legitimate and ordinarily show deference to an authority may consider certain of his requests as outside his scope. A private may disobey a sergeant's order to trade in his automobile for a new model because the command is considered beyond the sergeant's legitimate power.

The desire of a target to be perceived as similar to, liked, and accepted by a source provides the latter with *referent power*. A concern for a source's approval may lead a target to adopt values, attitudes, and behavior similar to those displayed by the source. The target's desire to be accepted is not manifested merely by ingratiation tactics but consists of genuine change toward similarity with the source. Such acquiescence corresponds to identification with the source and represents an internalization of his values.

Raven (1965) distinguished between *expert power* and *informational influence*. Influence may occur simply as a result of information provided to a target, independent of the characteristics of its source or his credibility. The information may be logically persuasive, as in the case of a theorem in mathematics, or it may be congruence with the prior beliefs of the target and therefore appear convincing to him. Expert power derives from the reputation of the source, while in informational in;uence "it is the content of the communication that is important, not the nature of the influencing agent" (Raven, 1965, p.372).

Jones and Gerard (1967) have emphasized the degree to which persons are informationally dependent on others for descriptions of the environment, the meaning of events, and the planning of future actions (as we have shown in Part II). A person who lacks stable perceptions of the world may become anxious and unusually susceptible to information providing him with such perceptions (Kelley & Thibaut, 1969). Informational influence may therefore occur because of its internal logical coherence, a lack of competing information, congruency with the existing beliefs of the target, and the stability it provides for the target's perceptions.

The control of the source over material resources provides him with the ability to back up his threats, make good his promises, and acquire knowledge and skills. A target will not comply with a threat if he perceives the source as incapable of enforcing it. A beggar's promise to give you $1,000 is not apt to be believed because presumably he does not possess that much money. The possession of resources may contribute to the amount of resolve the source is perceived to have in seeking influence. Morgenthau (1969) has defined *prestige* as the perception that a source has both the ability and the intention to use his resources to exercise influence. The greater a source's prestige, the more probable it is that the target will yield to his influence attempts.

It is one thing to speculate about a list of the possible bases of social power and quite another to obtain evidence identifying the independent characteristics of the source that affect the influence process. In general, research has supported the leads provided by theoretical speculation.

B.   Factor Analytic Studies of Power Bases

A statistical technique known as factor analysis has been used in a series of studies to identify those characteristics of a source that affect the course of social interactions. Factor analysis provides information about whether two or more traits or attributes are so closely associated as to yield basically the same effects and hence should be treated as a single characteristic. Do the attractiveness of the source and his expertise produce separate and independent effects on the responses of target persons? Factor analysis is particularly suited as a technique to answer this type of question.

Marwell and Schmitt (1967) asked subjects to choose between sixteen influence modes they would employ to gain compliance from others in job, family, sales, or room-mate relationships. The modes provided included threats, promises, recommendations, aversive stimulation, social reinforcements, and appeals to moral or normative standards. Factor analysis revealed five basic types of power: reward, punishment, approval or disapproval of the target's behavior, moral appeals, and expertise. These factors were interpreted as consistent with the power bases identified by French and Raven as reward and coercive power, referent power, legitimate power, and expert power.

Lemert (1963) asked college students in both Canada and the United States to rate news sources on a set of bipolar adjectives, such as good-bad, frank-reserved, and so on. The sources rated were newspapers and men who were often in the public eye. Most of the communications were in the form of warnings, recommendations, and statements of fact. Sometimes the message was associated with a specific source and sometimes not; hence, the source characteristics could be separated from pure informational influence.

Factor analysis disclosed three principal clusters of adjective ratings, identified as *safety, qualification,* and *dynamism.* Safety reflected the perceived intentions of the source, as was indicated by the cluster of adjectives: good, gentle, fair, friendly, reasonable, and unselfish. Qualification referred to the expertise of the source, by the use of the following adjectives: skilled, informed, educated, trained, experienced, and intelligent. How active or powerful the source was perceived to be was reflected by the dynamism factor and included such adjectives as strong, forceful, active, emphatic, and aggressive. Safety and dynamism appear to be similar to the two components of prestige (intentions and capability), while qualification clearly is identical to expertise. In a follow-up cross-cultural study involving raters in Brazil, the Far East, and Canada, Berlo, Lemert, and Mertz (1966) found the same three factors. A fourth factor of sociability was identified by Lemert (1969) when the source was known to the subjects and was not identified with any particular communication. Sociability represented the attractiveness of the source to the raters.

From these and other factor analytic studies we may conclude that there are six dimensions relevant to a source's impact on a target: expertness, reliability (credibility), legitimate power, dynamism (capability), intentions, and personal attractiveness. Table 8.1. summarizes the theory and evidence regarding these dimensions of the

Table 8.1   Summary of Source Characteristics.

Theories regarding bases of social power

Lasswell & Kaplan	French & Raven and Hovland, *et al.*	Factor analytic results	Source characteristics
Enlightment Skill Well-being (success)	Expertise	Expertise Qualification	*Expertise*
Power Respect	Legitimate	Moral appeals	*Legitimate status*
Wealth	Reward/coercive	Reward Punish Dynamism	*Resource control*
Rectitude	Trustworthy	Safety	*Trustworthiness*
Affection	Referent	Approval Disapproval Sociability	*Attractiveness*

source, excluding his credibility. We can now ask what specific effects each of these characteristics has on the influence process.

C.   Expert Power at Work

Undoubtedly one of the strongest principles in social psychology is that an expert is superior to a nonexpert in gaining conformity to his persuasive communications. Expert power enhances the effectiveness of warnings, appraisals of values, and recommendations. Johnson and Izzett (1969) reported that a radiologist was more effective than a quack in persuading subjects that X-rays are dangerous. Miller and Hewgill (1966) found more opinion conformity to a professor of nuclear physics about the consequences of nuclear war and natural disasters than to the same communications of a high school sophomore.

The perceived quality or value of literature is significantly affected by the judgment of expert critics. Aronson, Turner, and Carlsmith (1963) asked subjects to read and evaluate a set of obscure poems before they read an evaluation of one of the poems. The evaluation was attributed either to the great American-British poet T.S. Eliot or to another student. The greater the discrepancy between the subjects' first evaluations and those attributed to Eliot, the more the subjects changed their rating of the poem. The evaluation of another student had no effect on their critical evaluations. Finally, Aronson and Golden (1962) exposed sixth grade children to recommendations about the benefits obtainable from a thorough knowledge of arithmetic. The communication was attributed either to an engineer or to a dishwasher. The children's subsequently expressed verbal attitudes toward arithmetic were more favorable when the recommendations were attributed to the expert.

Several reasons why expertise should contribute to the effectiveness of influence have been offered. Bandura (1969) suggested that "A competent or prestigious communicator is generally more influential than a less competent one because the former's behavioral recommendations, if executed, are more likely to result in favorable outcomes" (p.600). A source's reputation for expertise apparently leads a stranger to assume that his credibility is high, since it would be difficult to acquire such a reputation if his recommendations and predictions were almost always wrong. Expertise provides a basis of power particularly when a target is dependent on the superior information or skills possessed by the source. For example, a person who has little knowledge of automobiles is often completely dependent on a garage mechanic's recommendations about repairs.

The scope of influence of an expert is usually assumed to be confined to his area of competence. However, the pronouncements of scientists on public policy, the apparent influence of movie stars in the political arena, and the frequent television commercials made by professional athletes raise the issue of whether expertise in one area extends the influence of the source to matters outside his known competence. Although there is no definitive scientific answer to this question, Lemert (1969) found evidence that the expert's scope of influence is confined to his specialty. He had two fictitious news stories set in type and presented them to California State College students in the form of clippings. One story dealt with municipal income taxes and the other was about rezoning downtown portions of "our city." The clippings were attributed either to the St. Louis *Post-Dispatch,* pre-rated by students as a highly competent newspaper, or to the Connersville, Indiana, *News-Examiner,* pre-rated as a less competent newspaper. When the scope of the issue was national, the *Post-Dispatch* was considered more authoritative, but when the story was local in scope both papers were rated as equally authoritative. If the expert's sphere of influence does not go beyond his area of competence, why do so many television commercials use testimonials by celebrities? Celebrities may elicit attention to the messages or candidates they support without substantially influenc-

ing positive or negative reactions to their communications (McGuire, 1969).

Experts can be found who differ in their recommendations and evaluations on almost any significant issue. One way a person can decide whose advice to follow is to determine the consensus of the experts. Weiss, Weiss, and Chalupa (1967) presented persuasive speeches to subjects which were said to be endorsed by 0, 25, 50, 75, or 100 percent of a group of experts. A measure of believeability was obtained from the subjects, who were asked to rate the probability of the truth of the message. The believeability of the message was directly related to the proportion of experts endorsing the position.

Consensus is clearly not the whole answer to what a person does when confronted with conflicting recommendations by experts. People appear to attribute expertise to others not only on the basis of their objective credentials but also according to shared values. One man's expert is another man's fool! In a test of the hypothesis that people choose their experts according to an assumed correspondence of values and interests, McGinnies (1968) presented Taiwanese students, most of whom were favorable toward U.S. intervention in the Indochina war, with a persuasive communication antagonistic to American participation. The communication was attributed either to a prominent Japanese newspaper or to a group of American college professors and senators. The American source was more persuasive than the Japanese source.

The effect of similar orientations of the values of sources and targets has also been shown by Weiss (1957). All subjects received a communication opposing fluoridation of the water supply. Half the subjects had heard a prior communication from the source on the topic of academic freedom which agreed with the subjects' position. Thus, half the subjects heard the fluoridation speech from a *co-oriented source* and half heard it from a stranger whose other values were unknown. The co-oriented source was more effective in persuading subjects to agree. The view that people's attitudes are easily changed, that they are sheep to be led by any shepherd, is not consistent with these findings. People give a great deal of weight to internal standards and values when evaluating the communications of others. The degree of expertise attributed to a source is a function of his competence and the co-orientation of his values with those of the target.

The expert's reputation is based on his accuracy or truthfulness in describing events and recommending and evaluating actions. Expertise enhances the believeability of persuasive communications, but does it affect the believeability of threats and promises? If an expert is perceived as concerned with transmitting truthful messages of whatever form, his threats and promises may also be believed by a target. Tedeschi, Schlenker, and Bonoma (1975) found that an expert source did receive more compliance to threats of low credibility than did a nonexpert source. However, the expert's area of competence was in the use of controlled violence (karate) and was directly relevant to enforcing threats. There is little reason to assume that a carpenter's or psychology professor's threats and promises should be believed more than those issued by anyone else.

D. Legitimacy and Status

Human groups and institutions often formalize role positions as a way of coordinating activities and distributing authority. The person's perception that another has legitimate authority is referred to as status. Status may be considered a resource or power base given to a person in exchange for his significant contribution to achieving group goals. A target's perception that a source's requests are legitimate increases the probability of his compliance with influence attempts. A target may engage in behavior he otherwise would consider unethical or unwise in compliance to the requests or commands of a high status source. Obedience transfers the responsibility for action from the actor to the authority.

1. Formal Status

In all societies children are taught a set of rules regarding how they should behave in a variety of situations. Learning to identify symbols of authority and to defer to the legitimate requests of persons holding positions of authority are included in the socialization process. The individual is taught to suspend his own judgment when obeying an authority. History attests to the power of monarchs and dictators to control their subjects. Subordinates have been known to commit suicide on orders from their chief. An early dictator of Haiti, Henri Christophe, is said to have flaunted his power by ordering soldiers to march over the edge of the citadel cliff (Frank, 1967).

The assumption made by lower status persons is that an authority can provide adequate reasons for what he requests (Friedrich, 1963). Given enough time, a surgeon can elaborate all the reasons why a nurse should obey each of his commands during an operation, but it would be inappropriate for the nurse to request an explanation before she complies. This kind of suspension of judgment in deference to authorities was shown in a study of Hofling, Brotzman, Dalrymple, Graves, and Pierce (1966). They found that 21 out of 22 nurses complied with an order by an unknown doctor to administer an "unauthorized" medication that was excessive in dosage.

Field studies have established that there is a strong relationship between role positions of authority in formal organizations and influence. Bass and Wurster (1953a,b) observed the influence effectiveness of individuals in small leaderless discussion groups. The individuals were drawn from the supervisory personnel at different levels of management of a large oil refinery. In general, the higher the individual's status in the organization, the more influence he wielded in the discussion. However, when the topic was relevant to company matters, the status of the source had more impact than when the topic was extraneous to the legitimate business of the corporation. French and Snyder (1959) and Bass (1954) reported a similar effect of status in military organizations. Higher ranked officers had more influence in group discussions than men of lower rank.

The power of legitimate and formal authority has also been demonstrated experimentally. Torrance (1954) assembled Air Force bomber crews into three-person groups and asked them to reach unanimous decisions about four ambiguous problems. Each triad was composed of a high status pilot, an intermediate status navigator, and a low status gunner. The navigator and gunner generally accepted the pilot's suggestions even when they were mainly incorrect. The hierarchical nature of status in the Air Force was shown by the fact that navigators, although not as influential as pilots, gained more acquiescence than did the low status gunners.

2. Symbols of Authority

Various symbols are associated with those who hold positions of authority. The presidential seal, the American flag, and the strains of "Hail to the Chief" often accompany the public appearances of the President of the United States. Generals have stars placed on their official automobiles, and men of rank in the military services wear insignia identifying their positions. Priests and policemen wear distinctive modes of dress. Such symbols serve to identify authority and may induce deference from total strangers.

The effects of mode of dress in eliciting obedience have been demonstrated by Bickman (1971a). The experimenter ap-

proached subjects in a telephone booth at Grand Central Station in New York City and asked them if they had found a dime, which he had left in the booth a few minutes earlier. When the experimenter was dressed as a person of high status (i.e., suit and tie) 77 percent of the subjects returned the dime. However, when he was dressed in work clothes and carried a lunch box or folding ruler, only 38 percent of the subjects returned the lost money. While it may not be true that clothes make the man, the kind of clothes a person wears does affect the reactions of others to him. Shakespeare was aware of this and had one of his characters advise a traveler:

"Costly thy habit as thy purse can buy;
But not expressed in fancy; rich not gaudy;
For the apparel oft proclaims the man!"

3. Status and Modes of Influence

Rosenbaum and Levin (1968) considered the status of the source in relation to the use of recommendations and warnings about a third person. Subjects were presented with descriptions of a third person by either a high or low status source. Status was operationalized in terms of occupation. The subjects evaluated the third person as "better" when positive adjectival descriptions had been provided by a high status communicator than when the message was attributed to a low status source. When negative adjectival descriptions were provided by a high status source, the subjects rated the third person "worse" than did the subjects receiving the same warning from a low status source. Tedeschi, Schlenker, and Bonoma (1973) interpreted these effects of status as due to the enhanced believeability of communications associated with a high status source.

High status also contributes to the effectiveness of threats. Faley and Tedeschi (1971) recruited high and low status ROTC students and gave them the role of the target of threats in a Prisoner's Dilemma game. Low status cadets believed they were playing either another low status cadet or a high status cadet. High status cadets believed they were playing a status equal or a status inferior. The threatener's credibility and the magnitude of punishment threatened were also manipulated in the experiment. Three major findings were obtained: (1) low status targets were more compliant when the source was of high rather than low status, and high status targets were defiant of threats sent by a low status source; (2) the higher the credibility of the threat, the more compliant the subjects; and (3) the greater the magnitude of punishment threatened for noncompliance, the more compliant the subjects were.

A fourth finding was somewhat unexpected. High status targets were just as compliant to a status equal as were low status targets to the threats of a high status source. The old saying that rank has its privileges was confirmed not only vertically but also horizontally. High status equals were quite compliant with each other's demands. This horizontal effect was not found among low status equals, who resisted the threats of their peers.

Public manifestations of mutual respect among those of high status is often found in state and federal legislatures. Senators who are known to despise one another privately display an exaggerated public courtesy toward each other. They never know when they will need the support of others on legislative issues, and they must maintain courteous relationships for future logrolling purposes. Persons of high status have too much to lose by maintaining hostilities, and they have much to gain from each other. One high status person may conform to the wishes of the other as a way of creating obligations for future exchange. Each is willing to give in on something the other strongly desires in exchange for similar reciprocal deference in the future. This may be why threatening to resign from a high status position can be a significant threat to

others of high status: debts may go unpaid. Low status persons are not in a position to control significant future rewards and hence are unwilling to place themselves under obligation to each other.

High status protects an individual from open criticism and the disapproval of inferiors. Thibaut and Riecken (1955b) had a confederate play the role of an Air Force reservist from a different unit than that of their subjects. The confederate held a rank just above or below the rank held by the subjects. The confederate communicated by telephone rather verbose, inexact, and self-contradictory instructions to the subjects about the placement of military positions on a map. The subjects were then given an opportunity to criticize directly the confederate's performance. Analysis of the criticisms revealed that more were proffered for the low than for the high status confederate. It is difficult not to be a "yes man" to persons with authority.

4. Status, Obedience, and Responsibility

Authority is always rationalized as furthering the long term interests of those asked to accept it as legitimate. An individual may be asked to make sacrifices, to risk his life, or to undertake behavior that otherwise he would consider immoral. For example, to kill another man is objectionable to most people under ordinary circumstances, but to do so in time of war is considered a heroic action. No one blames an executioner for administering capital punishment under the authority of the courts.

In a controversial series of experiments Milgram (1963) has shown that American males (aged 20 to 50, from a variety of occupations, and across several educational levels) obey an authority's commands to harm others. Subjects were instructed to deliver a shock to a confederate whenever he made an error in a learning task. The study was rationalized to the subjects as being about the effects of punishment on the learning process. The confederate was strapped into a chair in a separate cubicle and had an electrode attached to his wrist. The subjects were provided with a bank of 30 switches showing shock intensities from 15 to 450 volts, consecutively labeled Slight Shock, Moderate Shock, Strong Shock, Very Strong Shock, Intense Shock, Extreme Intensity Shock, Danger-Severe Shock, and XXX. Of course the confederate did not actually receive shocks, but the subjects were not aware of the deception. The subjects were asked to raise the shock intensity level after each error made by the confederate and were asked to state out loud the level of shock used to make sure they attended to what they were doing. At the 300 volt level and again at 315 volts the confederate banged on the wall. At higher levels of shock intensity the confederate maintained silence.

At various points during the procedure the subjects indicated disorientation, nervousness, and unwillingness to continue. When the confederate banged on the wall, they often turned questioningly to the experimenter, but were merely told to continue to give shocks for incorrect responses. Whenever they indicated a reluctance to go on, the experimenter authoritatively demanded they continue and prodded them with a series of commands: (1) "Please continue" or "Please go on"; (2) "The experiment requires that you continue"; (3) "It is absolutely essential that you continue"; and (4) "You have no other choice, you *must* go on." These remarks were always made in sequence with the more intense command being used when a more gentle prod failed. If prod 4 did not succeed in gaining compliance from a subject, the experiment was discontinued.

All the subjects gave up to 300 volts (Painful Shock) and 65 percent continued to the end of the series by adminstering shocks clearly labeled as Dangerous-Severe. Nine of the 14 subjects who discontinued did so at 300 or 315 volts when the confederate banged on the wall. In another condition of the experiment, subjects were not required to deliver the shock directly to the confederate. Instead they were asked to perform only one step in the process, such as throwing a master switch that permitted someone else to deliver the shock. Over 90% percent of the subjects were willing to continue until the end of the series under these more indirect conditions of participation.

There was some evidence of a reluctance to continue harming a victim when subjects were exposed to feedback about the pain he suffered. Milgram (1965) followed this initial observation by manipulating victim feedback in the same type of situation: (1) the confederate banged on the wall as in the first experiment; (2) the victim made verbal protests when the shock reached the 300 volt level and could be heard through the wall; (3) the victim was placed about one and one-half feet from the subject and in the same room, so the subject could see and hear his expressions of pain; or (4) the victim was required to put his hand on a shockplate and when he balked the subjects were required to force his hand onto the plate.

The greater the proximity of the victim and the more feedback given the subjects about the pain he experienced, the more probable it was that the subjects would refuse to continue. The results are illustrated in Figure 8.3. It is obviously easier to harm someone who cannot be seen or touched. Killing thousands of people by aiming bombs through the bombsight of an airplane should be much easier to do than to strangle the same people with one's bare hands. It is one thing to hear a victim's cry of pain and see the agony on his face; it is quite another to view an entire city through a bombsight. A cold and calculating decisionmaker at a minuteman missile site may be more dangerous to potential victims than an angry man who directly confronts them.

Baron (1971a) has found that pain cues from a victim will deter even an angry attacker. He had subjects write short essays,

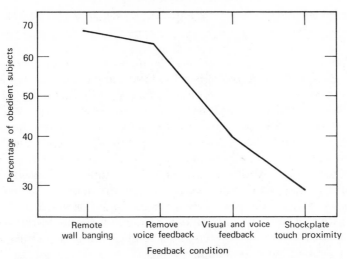

Figure 8.3. The effect of proximity to a victim on willingness of subjects to obey commands to harm him (After Milgram, 1965.)

which a confederate then evaluated by delivering shocks to them. Few shocks indicated a positive and many shocks reflected a negative evaluation. Presumably the subjects receiving many shocks would be angered. In the poor essay/anger condition the confederate administered nine shocks to the subjects and in the excellent essay/no anger condition the confederate delivered only one shock. The subjects and the confederate then reversed their roles and the subjects were asked to give shocks for all learning errors made by the confederate. Although the subjects were required to shock all errors, they could decide on both the intensity and the duration of the shocks administered.

The subjects were provided with a meter that allegedly integrated physiological measures of heart rate, respiration, and blood pressure to produce an objective index of the amount of pain suffered by the confederate. The subjects were asked to keep a careful record of the pain meter readings throughout the learning task. In the low pain conditions, the meter was manipulated to point to the labels "None," "Mild," and "Moderate" when the subject chose shock intensities 1-3, 4-6, and 7-10, respectively. In the high pain condition, the use of shock intensities in the same three

ranges was associated with meter readings of "Moderate," "Strong," and "Very Strong."

The subjects delivered higher shock intensities when they had been angered, but administered lower shocks in the high pain then in the low pain condition. The inhibiting effects of high pain cues were reflected by the fact that non-angry subjects delivered higher shocks in the low pain condition than did angry subjects in the high pain condition. Harmdoers are usually inhibited in retaliating against another if high pain cues from the victim are perceived.

A person who is obedient to the commands of an authority not only suspends his own judgment but shifts the burden of responsibility for his actions to the authority figure. Adolf Eichmann defended himself at his trial by stating that he was merely following orders in carrying out the extermination of millions of Jews. Lt. Calley similarly seems to have no sense of responsibility or remorse for his role in the tragedy of Mylai 4 in South Vietnam. The complexity of this issue is discussed briefly in Box 8.2.

Tilker (1970) manipulated the degree of responsibility subjects had for harming a victim, as well as feedback about the pain he suffered. Two collaborators of the experimenter acted the roles of teacher and

Box 8.2   THE TRAGEDY OF MYLAI—MONSTERS OR OBEDIENT MEN?

The type of warfare conducted in Indochina has been described in the Pulitzer Prize-winning books of Browne (1965) and Halberstam (1965). It was not a conventional battle of military forces where each side was easily identified by uniforms and fixed positions. Browne (pp.161–162) described an incident that characterized the war. He was riding in an armored car when two figures were spotted in the distance. One of the two persons was wounded and both were captured. They were two brothers, 8 and 9 years of age, who were carrying detonating wire and grenades. When questioned by a Vietnamese officer and threatened at the point of a gun, they stoically maintained their silence. These were hardened guerillas. Old women, young children, old men, and peasants working in the field by day, all might be the enemy at night. The friendlies could not be distinguished from the enemies.

It was in this context that three platoons of American troops, one led by Lt. William Calley, Jr., entered the small village of Mylai 4 on March 16, 1968. After groups of villagers had been rounded up, Lt. Calley ordered his men to push the people into a ditch. The captives were frightened and some attempted to get out of the ditch. Calley then ordered his men to shoot the prisoners. One of the American soldiers described the action: "I began shooting them all. So did Mitchell, Calley . . . I guess I shot maybe twenty-five or twenty people in the ditch . . . men, women, and children. And babies." He remembered that "the people firing into the ditch kept reloading magazines into their rifles and kept firing into the ditch and then killed or at least shot everyone in the ditch" (Hersh, 1970, p.63). No one knows exactly how many people were killed, though the best estimate is between 450 and 500.

Lt. Calley was subsequently tried and convicted for his part in the massacre. He defended his actions as carried out in the line of duty and he has shown no signs of remorse for the mass killings. The conviction of Lt. Calley was not popular and groups of sympathizers demonstrated in his behalf. President Nixon announced that he would ultimately review the conviction. Two months after Calley's conviction, Kelman and Lawrence (1972) carried out a national survey of the reactions of adult Americans to the incident. At the beginning of the interview the respondents were given a hypothetical situation: "Soldiers in Vietnam are ordered to shoot all inhabitants of a village suspected of aiding the enemy—including old men, women, and children." The respondents were asked what they believed most other people would do and what they would do in this situation. Sixty-seven percent replied they thought most people would follow orders and fifty-one percent said they would shoot if ordered to do so.

The reactions to Lt. Calley's trial were predominantly negative. Fifty-eight percent of the respondents disapproved of the trial and 34 percent approved. The reason given most frequently for disapproval was that "it is unfair to send a man to fight in Vietnam and then put him on trial for doing his duty." Respondents approving of the trial usually supported their position by saying that "even a soldier in a combat situation has no right to kill defenseless civilians and anyone who violates this rule must be brought to trial." In late 1974 a federal judge overturned Calley's conviction and ordered his release because he had been denied his full civil rights during the course of his trial.

The Nuremburg trials at the end of World War II established the principle that an individual maintains his responsibility for engaging in crimes against humanity even when ordered to perform such actions by the legally constituted authority of his nation. But the fine line that separates an act of conscience from disobedience or a justifiable act of war from an atrocity is a matter of interpretation. Science cannot solve this kind of problem. This is a matter for religion, philosophy, morality, and individual conscience.

---

learner. The teacher was to administer shocks whenever the learner made errors in performance. The teacher could decide on the intensity of the shock he administered. The subjects' responsibility for harm-doing was varied: (1) one group was given an opportunity to advise the teacher, though the final decision was always made by the teacher (No Responsibility Condition); (2) another group was told to discuss anything they wished with the teacher and to resolve all differences between themselves (Ambiguous Responsibility Condition); or (3) a third group was given clear responsibility for decisions about the conduct of the study (Responsibility Condition).

Three subgroups were formed within each responsibility condition: (1) subjects who had no visual or auditory contact with the learner; (2) subjects who were provided with auditory feedback, consisting of increasing levels of verbal protest from the learner; (3) subjects who received both auditory and visual feedback about the learner's reactions, including verbal protests and seeing the victim through a one-way mirror arching his back and struggling to get free of the chair in which he was strapped.

The more feedback received about the pain experienced by the victim, the greater the number of verbal protests the subjects made about shocking him. The more responsibility they had for administering shocks, the more they protested using shock and the more often they stopped the experiment. The most striking finding was that when the subjects had total responsibility and were provided with maximum feedback regarding the pain suffered by the victim, all of them stopped the experiment and did so earlier than the subjects in other conditions who also stopped the experiment. It is easier for a person to witness or even participate in harming others when responsibility is attributed to someone else.

When a person is ordered to carry out unpleasant actions, he may be disobedient when not under surveillance by the authority. Milgram (1963) found three times as much obedience when the experimenter was present than when he was absent during the administration of shocks by subjects. A great deal of work done in large organizations is not challenging and hence is unpleasant. This is why authority must be distributed throughout large organizations—when the cat is away, the mice will play. In addition to surveillance, the degree of legitimacy attributed to a high status person affects the degree of obedience given to his commands. When Professor Milgram conducted a study at his former home base, Yale University, he gained more obedience than when he carried out the same experiment with non-college students in a somewhat rundown, though respectable, office building in the down town shopping area of Bridgeport. Nevertheless, even without the prestige of Yale University, he obtained complete obedience from 48 percent of his subjects.

Statistics obtained at the end of World War II revealed that only 15 to 25 percent of American soldiers in combat had ever fired their weapons. This unwillingness to fight was demonstrated in both the European and Pacific theatres of operation (Marshall, 1947). The low level of obedience displayed by the soldiers is probably at least partially due to the factors isolated experimentally by Milgram. The close contact during fighting provides feedback about the pain and anguish of victims, the authorities are often not able to keep soldiers under surveillance during actual engagements, and in some cases there is a de-legitimization of the officers in command. Fragging, the deliberate killing of their own officers by soldiers, was a problem for American military authorities in South Vietnam. Obedience is much higher among bomber crews probably because there is no feedback from the victim and actions are part of a team effort, providing continual surveillance and diffusion of responsibility.

The language used by soldiers implies a need to make the enemy into an evil and abstract symbol rather than to perceive him as of flesh and blood. The enemy consists of Reds, Gooks, Cong, Rebels, Yankees, Huns, or Nazis and is dehumanized in a manner enabling the justification of violent retributive behavior. Apparently, these attempts to dehumanize the enemy work less well when he can be seen than when he cannot. If an authority can induce men to kill others, it can also be a powerful influence in producing obedience to the rules of society and a reduction in the amount of violence that occurs. Status systems allow groups to allocate responsibility for decisions and to coordinate behavior so that collective goals can be achieved.

E. Resource Control of the Source

If a source's threats and promises are to be effective in gaining compliance, he must be perceived as possessing the resources required to administer the relevant punishments and rewards. A young child may threaten to thrash his father or a jester may threaten his king, but the ability to carry out these actions is lacking. As a consequence, such threats will not be believed and may produce derisive laughter. Sometimes, people may attempt to promote the impression they have resources when they do not. For example, in a game of poker a player may bet strongly on a poor hand, causing players with better hands to drop out of the game. Bluffing, when combined with secrecy about the resources possessed by the source, may promote the perception of greater power than the source actually possesses.

In a study supporting Theodore Roosevelt's admonition to "speak softly and carry a big stick," Lindskold and Bennett (1973) had a confederate transmit twenty noncontingent promises of cooperation to subjects during play in a Prisoner's Dilemma game. In one condition the source could employ only a promise. In a second condition, he also had a contingent threat available, which he used only once. The confederate (source) who possessed both a promise and a threat had more influence on the target than the source who had only a promise available for influence purposes. The subjects were more cooperative with a promisor who could also threaten them.

In a different context, Bennis, Berkowitz, Affinito, and Malone (1958) found that control over resources facilitated obedience to authorities. Interviews of nurses in hospitals were conducted to assess the effectiveness of their supervisors. Supervisors who controlled more rewards and punishments were perceived as more effective in gaining compliance to directions. The greater the resources controlled by the source, the more influence he has over a target's behavior.

While control over resources may be sufficient to elicit believeability for a source's communications, if these reinforcements are not relevant to the values or interests of a target, compliance will not occur. In making his decisions the target takes both the probability and the value of the influence communication into account. A pertinent experiment was reported by Bass (1963), who assigned ROTC cadets to five-man groups. Some of the cadets were enthusiastic about potential military service and some were not. The degree to which each person contributed to an evaluation of the performance of other members of the group was manipulated. If a person had a weight of two and another person possessed a weight of one, the evaluation of the first was given twice as much weight in an overall evaluation report. The evaluations were presumed to be important in determining the ratee's eligibility for candidacy for advanced ROTC training. Three distributions of weights were created: (1) all five members of the group possessed equal weight; (2) the relative weights were 3-2-1-1-1; (3) the weights were 4-1-1-1-1. Subjects were asked to rank the frequency with which five adjectives are used by people in everyday life. Group discussions were then held, and individual judgments were obtained once again when the discussions were concluded.

When the cadets were uninterested in continuing the ROTC program, the weight of group members had no impact either on their attempts to influence others during group discussion or on their own individual judgments. However, when the cadets wanted to pursue further military training, the higher the weight of a cadet's evaluations, the more influence he attempted and the more he successfully exerted over

others. These results suggest that unless the values the source possesses or can mediate have utility for the target, those resources he does control will not facilitate influence.

F.   Attributions of Trustworthiness to A Source

A trustworthy source is one who is perceived by the target as intending to communicate valid statements about the causal structure of the social and physical environment (Hovland, et al., 1953). An untrustworthy source is one who is perceived as insincere, dishonest, and possessing selfish motives. When a source's self-interest can obviously be furthered by acquiescence to his persuasive communications, a target will discount what is said. Just as a lawyer would be foolish to defend himself because he is emotionally involved and cannot be objective about his case, so a target is well advised to suspect the reliability of communication from a source whose self-intrest is involved in the views expressed.

Powell and Miller (1967) manipulated the perceived selfishness of a source of influence. Subjects were exposed to tape-recorded persuasive messages advocating the donation of blood to the Red Cross instead of selling it to a private agency. The message was attributed to an anonymous source, a disinterested physician, or a chairman of a blood donor recruiting team of the Red Cross. The subjects were asked to rate the source on a number of factors following the communication. The physician was rated as most trustworthy and was perceived as more disinterested than the Red Cross chairman. Furthermore, the verbal expression of opinions changed in the direction of the advocated position when the source was perceived as trustworthy.

In a similar study, Walster, Aronson, and Abrahams (1966) presented arguments in favor of giving more or less power to the courts to punish criminals. The attributed source was either a prosecuting attorney or a criminal. Subjects rated the source as more honest and influential when he argued against his own presumed interests. The prosecuting attorney was perceived as more trustworthy when he argued for giving less power to the courts, and the criminal was rated more honest and influential when he argued for giving them more power. When the subjects' opinions were measured, it was found that the criminal had been more influential when he argued against his own best interests, but the prosecutor was equally effective whatever position he took. Since the prosecutor is a trained person who is supposed to serve the public interest without bias, he may be presumed to be trustworthy no matter what position he advocates (Collins, 1970). Scientists, philosophers, and other experts prefer to be perceived as disinterested; it is an image they cultivate about themselves, partly because it yields them additional influence and power. It is in the interest of persons who seek influence to appear disinterested.

When a person is interviewed by a personnel officer, how much of what he says can be considered honest and reliable? He obviously wants to create a good impression so he can win the job. An answer was provided to this question by the Jones, Davis, and Gergen (1961) study of in-role and out-of-role behavior of men interviewing for jobs as astronauts and submariners (see Chapter 4,I,B). Consistent with the augmentation principle of attribution theory the subjects believed they had a clearer impression of the interviewee's true personality when he presented himself in a manner opposite to the characteristics considered desirable for the job. When the person sacrificed potential rewards in the situation, he appeared more trustworthy than when he acted in a manner consistent with his own apparent interest. Jones, Gergen, and Jones (1963) also found that agreement

with a powerful source was perceived as less sincere than disagreement.

A speaker who presents a position on an issue to a hostile audience may be perceived as trustworthy. Mills and Jellison (1967) had students listen to a tape-recorded speech attributed to a political candidate for the state legislature, which advocated the passage of a bill tripling the licensing fees of tractor-trailers. The students were told the speech had been given either before a group of railway men or before a truck drivers' union. The unpopular speech implied the sincerity or trustworthiness of the source because a politician could lose many votes by offending truckers and could gain nothing by doing so. When the students were asked to state their opinions about the proposed legislation, there was a greater shift in their opinions to agree with the persuasive communication when the source was perceived as making an unpopular speech than when the audience was believed to have consisted of railway men who would be pleased by his statement.

There are times when a person overhears communications directed toward someone else. If a message is not directed toward him, he should not perceive any attempt to manipulate his opinions or behavior and the absence of perceived manipulative intentions might lead the target to perceive the source as trustworthy. Walster and Festinger (1962) arranged for subjects to overhear a warning associating cigarette smoking with lung cancer. In a second condition the same warning was directly communicated to them. Smokers were more persuaded by the overheard communication, though nonsmokers were not. Apparently both the trustworthiness of the source and the receptivity of the target contribute to the effectiveness of overheard communications.

If a communication is not considered relevant or important, the target will not be influenced by it even if the source is perceived as trustworthy. A test of this hypothesis was carried out by Brock and Becker (1965). Female college students were told that, following a color perception task, they would be asked to fill out a survey of their opinions. While the subjects wore black goggles over their eyes (and hence could not see), the telephone in the laboratory rang. The experimenter told the caller he was busy and would call back. A little later the phone rang once again. Although the experimenter tried to put the caller off, he was "forced" to talk. The experimenter either continued the phone call in the presence of the subject or else had a second experimenter take over while he took the call on another phone. The subjects could still overhear the conversation even when the experimenter took the call in another room. While a phone conversation in a lab might cause subjects to suspect that it is part of the experiment, shifting the call to another room should have removed their suspicions.

In the phone conversation the experimenter advocated a particular point of view on an issue. There were three communications: (1) advocacy of the resumption of ROTC obligations for all physically fit male students—an issue not relevant to female subjects; (2) advocacy of the reduction of tuition from $99 to $33 per quarter; and (3) advocacy of tripling tuition from $99 to $297. The latter two messages should have been of interest to the female students; presumably they agreed with reducing tuition fees and were opposed to increasing them. Following the phone conversation, during which the first experimenter provided details supporting his position, and after he had returned to the lab, the phone rang again. This third caller was put off until later. The subjects then finished the bogus task and were asked for their opinions on a number of issues, including compulsory ROTC and tuition fees. When the content of the overheard conversation was congruent with the subjects' opinions (i.e., to

reduce tuition), it was more effective in changing opinions than was the phone conversation held in the laboratory. The location of the conversation did not affect the subjects' opinions when they were either not interested in the issue or disagreed with the position taken by the experimenter.

Perceived trustworthiness may enhance the believeability of warnings, recommendations, and promises, while exploitative and selfish intentions contribute to the effectiveness of a threatener. The more important a goal is for a source, the more believeable his threat of punishment for noncompliance should be to a target. The kind of threat issued by a source may affect the degree of hostile or exploitative intentions attributed to him (Schelling 1966). Compellent threats, which specify actions the target must perform, should be perceived as more hostile, coercive, and exploitative than deterrent threats, which specify an action the target must not perform. Compellent threats should be perceived as offensive because they change the status quo; deterrent threats, on the other hand, are usually rationalized as defensive actions to maintain the existing state of affairs. If Schelling is correct and perceived exploitativeness contributes to a target's belief that a source will back up his threats, then more compliance should be tendered to compellent than to deterrent threats.

In a test of this hypothesis, Schlenker, Bonoma, Tedeschi, and Pivnick (1970) placed subjects in the position of targets of one of two kinds of threats in a Prisoner's Dilemma game: (1) a compellent threat that demanded a cooperative choice from subjects, or (2) a deterrent threat that told subjects not to make the competitive choice. It will be recalled that in the Prisoner's Dilemma game, a player can only make one of two choices, so telling him to make the cooperative choice and not to make the competitive choice amounts to the same thing. Nevertheless, subjects evaluated the compellent threatener more negatively and complied with his threats more often than to the deterrent threatener. It may be tentatively concluded that perceived hostility and exploitativeness does contribute to the effectiveness of threats.

G. Attractiveness of the Source

Attraction between persons is based on a history of rewarding interactions. People who like one another tend to share significant attitudes and values. A person should perceive a friend as more trustworthy, benevolent, and reliable than a stranger or an enemy. Given a choice between the promises of a friend or identical promises from an enemy, even if both sources have identical credibilities, a target should find his friend's promises more believeable. Similarly, a friend's persuasive communications should more often be perceived as in the target's interests, while the influence attempts of a nonfriend should more often be perceived as manipulative in character. Attraction serves as a power resource in interactions with others, since a person who is liked is also more influential.

According to a study done by Rittle and Cottrell (1967), the relationship between influenceability and liking is a matter of common knowledge. Male subjects were asked to make judgments about the degree of liking between people based on information about their influence relationships. When told a target liked a source, the subject considered it highly probable the target would be influenceable by the source. When told a target was influenced by a source, the subjects considered it probable the target liked the source.

The difficulty of recruiting pairs of friends for laboratory experiments has stimulated social psychologists to invent ways of inducing liking or disliking between strangers. For reasons we will examine in more detail in Chapter 11, the manipulation of perceived similarity or dissimilarity of attitudes, opinions and interests has been a reliable technique for inducing different states of liking. Subjects can be asked to give their opinions on a series of issues and it can be contrived that they see the faked attitude scale of a confederate. The faked opinions can be made similar or dissimilar to the attitudes expressed by the subjects.

Perceived similarity causes a target both to like a source and to infer his sincerity and trustworthiness. When a speaker and his audience have similar values, his communications are more effective in causing opinion change than when they differ. Empirical support for this association of value similarity and influence was provided by Mills and Jellison (1968). Subjects read a speech allegedly given before an audience of either engineering or music students. The source of the speech was said to have been either an engineer or a musician. The content of the speech was favorable to general education for all students. The opinions of the subjects regarding general education were subsequently obtained. They were more influenced by the speaker when he and the audience had similar rather than dissimilar values.

Perceived similarity mediates compliance with a source's recommendations. Brock (1965) employed students working in the paint section of a department store as experimenters. They attempted to persuade customers to purchase a brand of paint which was either less or more expensive than the kind the customers requested. In his persuasive communication, the salesman said he had used the recommended paint with excellent results on a job similar or dissimilar to the one the customer faced. More customers purchased the recommended paint, irrespective of the price involved, when the saleman had used it for a job similar to the one they faced.

A target is also more apt to believe warnings communicated to him by a liked source than by a disliked source. Indirect support for this proposition was produced by Weiss (1957) in a study reported earlier in this chapter. Differences in liking were probably induced by having a communicator either make preliminary remarks agreeing with the subjects' positions on academic freedom or make no such remarks. The source then communicated a warning to the subjects regarding the dangers of fluoridation of public reservoirs. When the warning was issued by a confederate with whom the subjects had earlier agreed, they were more strongly influenced by the communication than when the source had not indicated a similar view earlier.

The degree of contact between people who are attracted toward one another may determine the amount of influence each has on the opinions and behavior of the other. Janis and Hoffman (1971) obtained a direct measure of natural attraction between pairs of people working together on a newly developed method to curtail cigarette smoking. In this clinical setting the degree of liking between pairs was positively related to both the amount of change in verbal attitudes toward smoking and the actual decrease in the number of cigarettes smoked. Both liking and attitude change were greatest within pairs when the persons interacted frequently between weekly visits to the clinic.

Opinions expressed by an unattractive source may produce negative influence or a *boomerang effect*. Balance and congruity theories (see Chapter 5) predict that a positive statement by a disliked source will cause a target to take a more strongly opposite position on an issue. Abelson and Miller (1967) confirmed this prediction in a field study. An experimenter posed as a newspaper reporter and interviewed individuals seated on park benches in Washington Square in New York City. Each interviewee was asked his opinions about Negro protests against job discrimination. After an initial opinion had been expressed, a confederate, who was seated nearby, took exception to the interviewee's opinion.

In one condition the confederate only indicated his disagreement. In a second condition he prefaced his contrary opin-

ions with an insult directed toward the interviewee, such as "That's ridiculous," "That's obviously wrong," "No one really believes that," or "That's the sort of thing you'd expect to hear in this park." When the subject had been insulted, he became a more extreme advocate of his initial opinion than when he had been merely contradicted. Walster and Abrahams (1972) commented on this study by concluding, "Shouting wins enemies, not votes" (p. 230).

Sampson and Insko (1964) found a boomerang effect in a laboratory study. A trained confederate engaged subjects in either pleasant or insulting interactions prior to the critical phase of the experiment. The confederate and a subject were then paired and orally communicated their judgments of perceptual stimuli to the experimenter. The subjects' judgments were found to converge toward the dissimilar judgments of the liked confederate and to diverge from the dissimilar judgments of the disliked confederate. People apparently apply a rule of thumb which says "Bad people are always wrong."

A target's response to a source's threat depends to some extent on the quality of their relationship. The target may believe that a friend will be reluctant to harm him, but may be all too ready to believe that a foe will relish an opportunity to administer punishment. Based on these assumptions, Tedeschi, Schlenker, and Bonoma (1975) expected to find more compliance to the demands of a disliked threatener. They induced high or low attraction for a confederate and then provided him with coercive power in a Prisoner's Dilemma game. The confederate sent threats intermittently during the course of the game and punished noncompliance either 10 or 90 percent of the time.

The results are shown in Figure 8.4. The subjects who disliked the source complied equally often whether the threats were low or high in credibility. Even when they had evidence from the source's past actions of

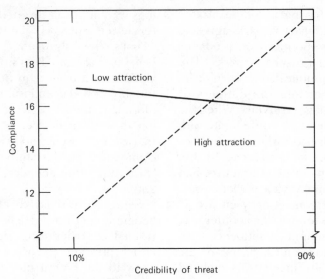

Figure 8.4. The effects of attraction and threat credibility on the frequency of compliance of target subjects. (After Tedeschi, Schlenker, and Bonoma, 1975.)

his reluctance to backup threats, they complied frequently. However, when they liked the source, they apparently did not underestimate the probability of being punished; instead they were realistic in their appraisal of the situation and complied more often to the high than to the low credibility threats.

Dislike is a form of power when threats are used as the mode of influence, but positive attraction has no effect on a target's reactions to coercive power. When a source of threats does not have any intention of punishing noncompliance (either because of the costs involved or due to his lack of resources) he can still be effective in gaining compliance if he can incur the target's dislike. Much of the verbal hostility that is expressed when threats are made has the effect of inducing the target to believe them. The emotion of anger may be a substitute for a more stable form of dislike between persons, enhancing the source's power in a coercive relationship.

H. Combining Source Characteristics

For purposes of scientific study, social psychologists have isolated the effects of single dimensions of the source. But what happens when a number of source characteristics are varied to form different complex combinations? While the evidence is still very sparse, it appears that attraction and expertise may be relatively independent of one another. Snyder and Rothbart (1971) found that an attractive source produced more opinion change than an unattractive one, but measures of postexperimental impressions revealed no difference in the perceived expertise of the two communicators. Horai, Naccari, and Fatoulah (1974) manipulated both the expertise and the attractiveness of a source and found significant but separate effects on the subsequent attitude change of target subjects.

Whether expertise and attractiveness of a source will have independent effects or interact with one another may depend on the nature of the situation. A person's expertise, if it induces dependency by other group members, may detract from his attractiveness; for example, the individual who initiates the most ideas during group problem solving is usually not the most liked member of the group (Bales, 1958). In addition, persons nominated to be leaders are seldom the best liked members of a group (Hollander & Webb, 1955; Radloff & Helmreich, 1968). Lack of expertise has been found to detract from the perceived legitimacy of an authority's position; Evan and Zelditch (1961) found that a supervisor who was perceived as incompetent was covertly disobeyed.

The perceived power of a source is a function of both his control over resources and the intentions attributed to him by a target. Singer (1958, 1963) has proposed a model of international relations in which he defines prestige as a multiplicative function of source capability and intentions. Japan is not usually perceived as a great world power although it is the third wealthiest nation on earth. The reason is the absence there of a large military force and their apparent reluctance to intrude into the political affairs of other nations. In other words, Japan is not perceived to have strong intentions of influencing others. China, a nation controlling fewer resources than Japan, is often perceived as powerful by those who attribute hostile intentions to her.

Similar perceptions occur in interpersonal affairs. Pepitone (1949) varied both control over resources and the intentions of a source of influence. High school students were told they would be interviewed by three people from a university who were interested in soliciting student opinions about sports. The panel was said to possess either highly valued tickets to a college basketball game or tickets to "some high school game." The interviewees judged to have the most sophisticated opinions were to be given free tickets. In addition to the value of the tickets, the demeanor of the judges was also manipulated. In one condition the panel members were basically either friendly or neutral while conducting the interview. In a second condition, one member of the panel was friendly, a second was neutral, and the third was hostile. Following the interview the students were asked to estimate the amount of power possessed by each of the three interviewers. Panel members who possessed the more valuable tickets were perceived as more powerful than those who possessed a less valuable reward. Also, the friendly member of the panel was perceived as the most powerful individual in both resource conditions. Hence, a source who had greater control over rewards is perceived as more powerful if the intentions attributed to him are benevolent and friendly. Schlenker, Bonoma, Tedeschi, and Pivnick (1970) found that a cruel and hostile threatener is perceived as more powerful than a reasonable and patient one. Attributed benevolence adds to reward power and perceived malevolence enhances coercive power.

Source characteristics combine to enhance or detract from influence effectiveness. Little is known about the precise effects of various combinations on the reactions of targets to different modes of influence. Practically speaking, this constitutes a very complicated area of research. Source characteristics are usually so mixed it is impossible to unravel them for experimental purposes. Imagine trying to create a disliked, expert, and high status source, who possesses very few resources and is untrustworthy. In everyday life such combinations do occur, but infrequently enough to make it difficult to undertake systematic field study. Until this technical problem is solved, social psychologists will probably examine source characteristics in combinations of two or three at a time. It is worth noting that this problem exists in all areas of social psychology and is one reason we earlier cautioned about generalizing directly from experimental findings to everyday life (see the discussion of relevance and ecological validity in Chapter 2).

IV. THE PERSONALITY OF THE TARGET AND HIS INFLUENCEABILITY

Throughout this chapter we have tried not to underplay the target's contribution to the influence process. He is certainly not a passive recipient of power imposed on him by others. We have emphasized that rewards must be meaningful to the target or he will not be responsive to influence attempts. The reputation of the source is not an objective part of the environment, but rather is partly determined by the perceptions, motives, and values of the target. As Victor Hugo expressed it in *Les Miserables:* "Be it true or false, what is said about men often has as much influence upon their lives . . . as what they do." Thus, the target recognizes only those experts who share significant values with him and he may or may not view authorities as legitimate. The perceived power of a source depends to some extent on the intentions attributed to him by the target.

Some persons are more susceptible to influence than others. Among the characteristics of a target identified as related to his susceptibility are self-esteem, interpersonal trust, authoritarianism, internal or external control orientation, and sex role identification. The study of personality is always treacherous and difficult because of problems with basic theoretical concepts and measurement devices. Nevertheless, some consistent and interesting data appear when personality differences are considered in the context of the social influence process.

A. Self-Esteem

An individual's evaluation of himself indicates his bias regarding his own expectations of rewards and punishments. High self-esteem persons generally believe they should and will be approved and rewarded by others, while low self-esteem persons expect few rewards and many punishments. Cohen (1959) has stressed how these expectancies affect behavioral styles. High self-esteem persons tend to avoid punishing or dangerous situations and to ignore, deny, or repress unpleasant experiences. Because of their pessimistic expectations, persons low in self-esteem cannot simply

ignore other people; they believe others will harm them and hence must be active in self-defense. In sum, high self-esteem persons act constructively in solving problems and are optimistic about reinforcements, and low self-esteem persons act destructively and are pessimistic about outcomes.

If low self-esteem persons are defensive and pessimistic about the intentions of others, they should be resistant to persuasive communication. It is also possible that they are less intelligent or educated and, as a consequence, less capable of comprehending subtle and complex messages. Consistent with this reasoning, a number of studies have found a positive relationship between self-esteem and persuasibility (Cox & Bauer, 1964; Gelfand, 1962; McGuire & Ryan, 1955; Silverman, 1964). But it is just as plausible to expect low self-esteem targets to be more yielding to influence. They are less certain of their beliefs and attitudes and more informationally dependent on others. High self-esteem persons are confident about what they believe and should be harder to change. This negative relationship between self-esteem and persuasibility has also been frequently found (Berkowitz & Lundy, 1957; Cohen, 1959; Janis & Field, 1959; Lesser & Abelson, 1959; Mausner, 1954).

These apparently contradictory findings can be understood by taking three factors into consideration: (1) the education or intelligence of the target; (2) the complexity of the information communicated; and (3) the differences between high and low self-esteem targets in their relative perception of what constitutes expertise or competence in another person. The first two factors have already been discussed; we will here consider the third.

A low self-esteem person may be more willing to acknowledge the superior expertise of others than would high self-esteem persons due to his negative evaluation of himself. There is no reason why the former should respect obvious quacks, nor will the latter deny the competence of a very expert person. But when the source of influence is only moderately expert, low self-esteem targets may perceive him as more expert than will high self-esteem persons and therefore be more influenceable. When these three considerations are taken into account, the available evidence indicates that low self-esteem people are quite persuasible when a persuasive argument is simple, direct, and unambiguous, particularly if the source is only moderately expert. When communications are complex or subtle, high self-esteem persons are more susceptible to persuasive influence.

High self-esteem persons may very well comply with promises because they are optimistic about gaining rewards anyway, but they may also comply with threats if doing so is clearly in their interests. Low self-esteem persons may not believe a source's promises because of their pessimism about receiving rewards, and they may resist a threatener even when to do so will be counter-productive. For the latter, the world is a hostile place and they are actively concerned with defending themselves against others. Lindskold and Tedeschi (1971b) found that high self-esteem children were more compliant to both promises and threats than low self-esteem children under conditions where compliance led to better outcomes than did defiance.

B. Interpersonal Trust

The individual has much information available to him in evaluating the reliability of communications from acquaintances, but how does he decide whether or not to believe communications from a total stranger? Someone who believes everything he is told by strangers is very gullible, and a person who is suspicious of all strangers is considered paranoid. Rotter (1967b) has referred to the tendency to believe or disbelieve the communications of strangers as *interpersonal trust* and has developed a paper-and-pencil measure of this disposition. Theoretically, high trust persons should yield more to the influence attempts of strangers than low trust persons.

The available research using Rotter's measure has yielded contradictory results. Schlenker, Helm, and Tedeschi (1973) provided a confederate with the ability to deliver noncontingent promises of cooperation or to transmit contingent threats of punishment to high and low trust subjects in a Prisoner's Dilemma game. Although the confederate possessed the ability to use both reward and coercive power, he actually sent only the promises and kept his word either always or never. Both groups of subjects were more cooperative when the source was credible than when he was not, but high trust subjects were somewhat more cooperative in response to promises than low trust subjects.

High trust persons may not respond to a source's noncontingent promises with reciprocal cooperation when he does not also possess the ability to use coercive power. In the above study, the source always sent promises, but from the point of view of the targets he could at any time have shifted to using threats. Cooperative responses to his promises may have been tendered because the subjects did not want to anger him. Monteverde, Paschke, and Tedeschi (1974) provided a source with only an ability to transmit promises of noncontingent cooperation in the Prisoner's Dilemma game. After the interaction was over, the subjects were asked to rate the confederate on a series of polar adjectives. High trust subjects rated the confederate as more trustworthy than did low trust subjects. Nevertheless, high trust subjects were somewhat more competitive in response to the source's promises than were low trust subjects.

These results support Rotter's contention that the Interpersonal Trust Scale identifies persons who believe or disbelieve the communications of strangers; furthermore, it is clear that high trust does not imply gullibility. When the source possessed coercive power, high trust subjects were cooperative because they didn't want to anger their more powerful opponent, but when he made himself vulnerable by committing himself to noncontingent promises and did not possess coercive power, they tried more often to take advantage of him.

C. Authoritarianism

Authoritarianism has been characterized as an exaggerated submissiveness to authorities, a disrespect for weakness, an intolerance of deviations from socially prescribed behavior, and a tendency to use coercive power against those of lower status. Egalitarians consider themselves less bound by social rules of conduct, show less deference to authority, and are apt to use more persuasive means to influence persons lower in the status system. Although it is not clear what socialization experiences are responsible for these personality differences, there is some evidence of their importance in the influence process. Izzett (1971) took class attendance on October 15, 1969—a national Moratorium Day devoted to protest against American participation in the Vietnamese war. Students who attended class scored higher on a measure of authoritarianism than those who observed the moratorium and cut the class. Some indication that respect for authority may be related to compliance with requests was found by Forte, Haake, Schmidt, and Lindskold (1973). Subjects who were more favorable toward the president of the United States (Mr. Nixon) were more compliant with the investigators' requests for answers to questions that were virtually impossible to answer, such as which side was responsible for the failure of Henry Kissinger's prediction in October, 1972, that "peace is at hand."

D. Internal and External Control Orientations

The Internal-External locus of control conception of personality (see Chapter 6, VI, B2) has obvious implications for social influence. The external person should rely on others because he believes reinforcements depend on them and not on himself, while the internal person should rely on himself and resist the attempts of others to influence him. There is evidence supporting these hypotheses. Gore (1962) asked subjects to view a series of pictures of people in ambiguous situations and to write stories about what they were doing, what led up to the present scene, and so on. In a subtle attempt to motivate the subjects to write longer stories, the experimenter smiled frequently and used warm voice intonations during his instructions. In a second condition the experimenter did not make such overtures. Externals wrote longer stories than internals only when the tacit influence attempts were made by the experimenter. Johnson, Ackerman, Frank, and Fionda (1968) employed a similar task; the stories written by the subjects were content analysed. The main characters in the stories written by internals more often resisted temptation to violate social norms than did those in the stories written by externals. Two other studies (Hjelle, 1970; Biondo & MacDonald, 1971) found more opinion conformity by externals.

Phares (1968) reported that internals are more responsive to information when it is useful for solving problems. An earlier study, carried out by James, Woodruff, and Werner (1965), examined the I-E scores of people who had read and believed the U.S. Surgeon General's report on the relationship of cigarette smoking and serious health problems. More internals quit smoking than externals. Platt (1969) found internals to be more susceptible than externals to role-playing techniques engineered to encourage people to quit smoking, particularly among those who believed that harmful effects are caused by smoking.

I-E control orientations may affect the weight given to source characteristics by an individual when he is the target of influence. Ritchie and Phares (1969) presented subjects with questions on governmental budgeting after each had read a persuasive communication. The communication was attributed to either a high or low expert source. Externals showed more opinion conformity, particularly when the source was expert, than did internals. In both conditions, internals did change slightly toward the position of the communicator. Hence, internals are more susceptible to informational influence and externals are responsive both to the source's level of expertise and to informational influence.

E. Sex Role Identification

According to the available evidence, females in our society are more conforming (Crutchfield, 1955), persuasible (Tuddenham, 1958), and compliant with promises (Lindskold, Bonoma, Schlenker, & Tedeschi, 1972) than are males. Women also score higher on measures of social desireability (Crowne & Marlowe, 1964), are more sensitive to interpersonal factors (Cook, 1971, p. 46), and are more concerned with social appearances than males. These sex differences must be interpreted cautiously, however.

Experimental social psychology has until recently been dominated by males, and most of the research has been conducted by male experimenters. Comparisons between male and female subjects often ignore the fact that there is an important uncontrolled factor—the sex of the experimenter. Perhaps females are concerned with appearing to behave consistently with the sex role stereotype presumably held by the male experimenters. As will be seen in the next chapter, males project an impression of strength and masculinity and engage in face saving behavior when observed by male experimenters. The relation of the sex of a person to his influenceability is probably based on a number of uninvestigated factors, such as the mode of influence used, the content of the information transmitted, the relevance of sex role identification to the interaction, and so on. At a time when definitions of sex roles are under reexamination and are undergoing rapid change in American society, it is particularly unsafe to draw conclusions about sex differences in persuasibility.

V. RESISTANCE TO INFLUENCE

Throughout this chapter we have focused on variables affecting the target's acquiescence to social influence. We will now entertain questions about the other side of the coin. What social psychological factors cause a target to turn aside attempts at influence? Does he treasure his independence and freedom from control? Is it important for him to stand his ground once he has committed himself to a defensible position? As we saw in Chapter 3 a person is embedded in his social groups and is generally quite resistant to change. Our concern here is for the individual's resistance to influence when he is alone, as is usually the case in laboratory experiments.

It is commonly believed that appeasing a tyrant only encourages him to make ever-increasing demands. This belief was wittily expressed by Heywood Broun when he said. "appeasers believe that if you keep on throwing steaks to a tiger, the tiger will become a vegetarian" (cited by Yutang, 1942, p. 268).A person must not appear too docile and compliant or he will gain the reputation of a patsy. In addition to encouraging others to make demands on him, such docility in the face of influence attempts may also make him appear less resolute and thus undermine the effectiveness of his own influence attempts.

The target's docility would be emphasized if he were to change his behavior to comply with an influence attempt after he publicly committed himself to a contrary but reasonable position. The importance of maintaining an impression of consistency and credibility may lead him to maintain a previously announced position even when he has been convinced of the merit of opposing arguments. When a person can anticipate the contrary position that will be adopted by a source, a shift of attitudes in the direction of the impending challenge may occur before the persuasive message is received. This anticipatory change can preserve the target's self-presentation of consistency when he might have trouble defending his private position.

Finally, and quite independently of the target's concern about the impression his actions convey to others, it is important to consider how his resistance to influence can be bolstered. If the findings of the social psychology of influence were to be applied, they would aid the manipulators more than the manipulated. How can a target be trained to be resistant? One method is to develop an immunity to contrary arguments through exposure to the opposing point of view. Being informed about all positions on an issue may provide an individual with the ability to maintain his independence in the face of opposition.

A. Maintaining Freedom Through Reactance

Brehm (1966) has developed a theory based on the notion that people want to reestablish their threatened independence and freedom. People display a concern for independence by resisting the attempts of others to manipulate their freedom of decision. Brehm argues that *psychological reactance* is a motivational state directed toward the reestablishment of whatever freedom has been threatened. Most often a person can reestablish freedom by choosing the opposite behavior to what is desired by a

manipulative source. A refusal of compliance or actual behavior opposite to what is requested serves to demonstrate to the source (or to third parties) that the target will not submit to influence attempts.

Brehm (1966) demonstrated reactance in a simple two-choice situation. Subjects were informed they would have a choice of trying to solve one of two problems (A or B). Before making his choice, each subject was handed one of two notes from another subject (actually a confederate): (1) "I choose problem A," or (2) "I think we should both do problem A." While the first note merely expressed the confederate's personal choice, the second attempted to control the choices of both persons. When the note indicated an attempt to control the subjects' decisions, 60 percent chose problem B, but when the note did not attempt to exercise control, 70 percent chose problem A. Though the effect was weak, some reactance by subjects did occur. Under the conditions of the experiment the costs of displaying autonomy were low. According to Brehm, a threat to free behavior enhances its value. An alternative interpretation is that a display of reactance is meant to discourage a source from attempting to manipulate the target again in the future. In effect, reactant behavior may be a tactic of counter-influence.

Despite the fact that numerous experiments have shown reactance-like effects in the laboratory, there are problems with the notion. For example, Brehm has argued that reactance should be greater as the importance of the threatened behavior increases and as the magnitude of the threat increases. In order to test these hypotheses, it would be necessary to produce more than two levels of reactance as a function of importance or magnitude of threat. However, manipulations of the degree of importance (Brehm & Mann, 1975; Wicklund, 1970) and the magnitude of threat (Brehm, Stires, Sensenig, & Shaban, 1966; Sensenig & Brehm, 1968) have failed to produce corresponding increments of reactance. This failure to support Brehm's hypotheses suggests that some other factor causes the boomerang effects observed in reactance experiments.

An alternative impression management interpretation of the reactance findings is suggested by a study conducted by Cooper and Jones (1969). They found that subjects changed their attitudes away from a position advocated by a highly similar other when the latter's behavior was obnoxious. This result was interpreted as an effort by subjects to avoid being miscast as being similar to the obnoxious person. This is a manifestation of an attempt to present a positive identity to the experimenter. Similar interpretations can be made in most other reactance studies in which subjects are told they are being evaluated for leadership or intellectual abilities, for example, and are then faced with an effort by a confederate to choose what task both of them will work on.

B. Public Commitment and Resistance

Prior public commitment is effective in producing target resistance to subsequent influence attempts (Cohen, Brehm & Latané, 1959; Deutsch & Gerard, 1955; Hovland, 1958). An individual's concern for creating an impression of consistency makes it difficult for him to act in a manner contrary to a position he has previously expressed. The individual's concern for his public image has been shown by Rosenbaum and Franc (1960) and Rosenbaum and Zimmerman (1959). Each subject was either told that people believed he had a particular attitude on an issue, or he was not told that anyone was aware of his public commitment. The subjects were then exposed to a persuasive communication attacking the position to which half of them had been committed. Those whose public image was at stake were more resistant to influence than those whose image was not under attack.

When told to expect a persuasive com-

munication, a target person becomes more resistant to change. A forewarning implies that the prospective source has informed others about his scheme to influence the target. If the source has planned his influence ahead of time, it may be assumed that he has manipulative or exploitative intentions. Hence, he would be considered untrustworthy and his persuasive communication would not be believed. In an investigation involving warnings, Freedman and Sears (1965) introduced a speaker to high school students as Dr. Vernon Allen, a noted expert on automobiles, highway administration, and driving. Only one of two groups of students were given a forewarning in the form of the title of the speech to be heard—"Why Teenagers Should Not Drive." The forewarned students were more resistant to Dr. Allen's persuasive communications. Similar findings have been reported by Kiesler and Kiesler (1964) and McGinnies and Donnelson (1963).

C. Anticipatory Attitude Change

One way to avoid "face" problems when forewarned is to change one's beliefs voluntarily *before* receiving an influence communication. In this way a target can tender verbal agreement without giving the impression of having relinquished his freedom to choose. A number of experiments have shown that when subjects are forewarned and are given a chance to express their opinions prior to hearing the communication, they change their opinions in the direction of the anticpated message (Cooper & Jones, 1970; McGuire &Millman, 1965; McGuire & Papageorgis, 1962). Hedging on his beliefs may prevent a person from eating as much a crow as he might if he were to be proved wrong in a subsequent argument. Once involved in an argument, most people are reluctant to admit they are wrong and become quite resistant to change. This "bull headedness" is probably an attempt to maintain credibility and a reputation for competence, which, as we have seen, are powerful resources for influencing others.

A person's reputation may not suffer much if he loses an argument to an expert opponent, but losing an argument to a peer or a nonexpert opponent may be considered detrimental. Concern about losing an argument to a nonexpert opponent may be greater among high self-esteem than among low self-esteem persons, who may not expect to do very well in arguments in any case. Following this line of reasoning, Deaux (1972) predicted that high self-esteem subjects would display greater anticipatory opinion change in the direction of a persuasive communication after forewarning than would low self-esteem subjects, but only when high self-esteem subjects could suffer a maximum loss of face—that is, when the anticipated message was to come from a nonexpert source. High and low self-esteem subjects were led to expect that their beliefs would be attacked either by a high expert or a low expert source. The results confirmed Deaux's hypothesis. High self-esteem subjects displayed greater anticipatory opinion change than low self-esteem subjects only when the source was not an expert.

In addition to the consistency and self-esteem explanations of anticipatory attitude change, a moderation hypothesis has been proferred (Cialdini, Levy, Herman & Evenbeck, 1973; Haas, 1975). What usually happens in this kind of study is that subjects move to a neutral point along the attitude scale. Cialdini, et al. suggest that this movement does not reflect a real attitude change; instead it represents a suspension of judgment until after the persuasive communication is heard. Thus, measurements of subjects' attitudes after they have been forewarned of an impending persuasive communication but prior to actually hearing it, should show a movement toward the neutral point on the scale, regardless of whether the speaker's position is expected to be more extreme in the same direction as, or opposite to, the positions of the subjects. Cialdini, et al. found that subjects did moderate even when anticipating a persuasive argument from someone on the same side of the issue; that is, subjects shifted their attitudes away from a position with which they initially agreed when they expected to hear an argument supporting their own view.

Consistency and self-esteem explanations suggest that subjects will always shift their attitudes toward the expected position of a persuasive communicator, while moderation theory proposes that subjects move away when the source's position is proattitudinal. Haas (1975) attempted to test these competing predictions. Subjects were led to expect persuasive communication that would be counterattitudinal, proattitudinal, or where only the topic was identified. A fourth group merely provided their attitudes on the issue without expectation of hearing any persuasive communication. While the topic only and counterattitudinal groups showed a moderation effect relative to the control group (as all three theories predict), the subjects in the proattitudinal position did not change their attitudes; the latter result disconfirmed the moderation hypothesis. Haas argued that moderation effects may be found in proattitudinal conditions only when the issue is nonemotional and the subjects' topic knowledge and commitment are low.

D.   Inoculation

The results of an experiment by Lumsdaine and Janis (1953) suggest that people can be immunized against persuasive communication. One-sided and two-sided arguments were constructed to support the view that the Russians would not be able to produce an atomic bomb for five years (note that this study was undertaken before the Russians actually produced their first atom bomb). The two-sided argument also included a few opposing points: atomic bomb factories were being built in the Soviet Union and there were large uranium mines in Siberia. After hearing one or the other of these arguments, the subjects were presented with a counter-argument supporting the view that the Soviet Union would have atomic bombs in less than five years. The subjects who first heard the two-sided argument were less persuaded by the counter-argument than were those who had heard the one-sided argument.

McGuire (1964) proposed an analogy to a medical model of disease in developing a theory of inoculation. He observed that people develop many beliefs that are generally accepted in the culture and are seldom examined and almost never challenged. For example, the belief that one should brush his teeth is seldom a matter of argument. These cultural truisms may be considered vulnerable in the same sense that a person living in a germ-free environment is highly susceptible to disease. A person in such an environment may not build up antibodies to protect himself from disease because they are developed only as a response to the disease-causing germs. A person is best protected against smallpox when he is given a small dose of the disease. Similarly, cultural truisms may be made more resistant to challenges if an individual is made aware of the arguments against his beliefs.

Two forms of inoculation were tried out by McGuire and Papageorgis (1961). Subjects were provided with supportive and refutational defenses for cultural truisms. A *supportive defense* involved reading a truism, followed by four supporting arguments. A *refutational defense* involved reading a truism, followed by four arguments against the truism, and a paragraph refuting the attacking arguments. Each subject received a supportive defense for one truism and a refutational defense for another. Several days later each subject was presented with three persuasive communications attacking three cultural truisms, the two that had been inoculated and one that

had not. A refutational defense was clearly superior to a supportive defense in protecting the individual's beliefs against counterarguments. A supportive defense did strengthen the subjects' beliefs before the counter message was received, but provided only very weak protection against attacks on cultural truisms.

Inoculation may produce resistance to influence only when cultural truisms are attacked—but almost as a matter of definition, they are seldom the object of verbal attack. At the present time there is little evidence to support any generalization of inoculation effects to the more controversial opinions and issues that serve as the content of most persuasive communication in everyday life.

VI. CHAPTER SUMMARY

A target will yield to influence attempts when he stands to maximize his gains or minimize his losses by so doing, and he will resist influence when it is in his best interest to do so. In deciding what is in his best interest, he must evaluate the believeability of a source's communication. In making decisions about acquiescence or defiance, he considers both the believeability of the source's messages and the value consequences of yielding or resisting.

The credibility of the source, established over past interactions, is important for eliciting believeability for his messages. The higher the credibility of threats, promises, warnings, and recommendations, the more the target yields to influence attempts.

The manner in which a source presents his persuasive communications may determine the reaction of the target. Choosing a message that is congruent with the target's belief as well as displaying confidence in the message transmitted increases the likelihood that the target will believe what is communicated. A dynamic presentation peppered with humor may not be any more effective than a more humdrum statement, and the relative merits of logical and emotional appeals are not well understood. Drawing explicit conclusions may produce equal and opposite effects, depending on the content of the message and the intelligence of the audience.

One-sided arguments are more persuasive when the audience is uneducated and already agrees with the source; otherwise, two-sided arguments are more effective. The order in which speakers are presented may produce a primacy effect when the listener does not expect to hear the second argument or when he commits himself to an opinion before hearing a second speaker. A recency effect occurs when two opposing views are heard at widely separated times and may be due to memory decay for the first communication.

A number of source and target characteristics affect the target's evaluation of the believeability of influence communications. Targets will assess persuasive messages and promises as more believeable if their source is an expert, an authority, attractive, trustworthy, and possesses great resource capability. A threatener will be more believed when he is an expert, possesses great ability to do harm, has high status, is disliked, and is perceived to be untrustworthy. A target's self-esteem, trust of strangers, sense of control over his own reinforcements, and degree of authoritarianism have complex effects on the influence process, which depend on the conditions of specific interactions and the personality factor involved.

An active motivation to resist influence often stems from an individual's concern for how others will perceive him. He may engage in demonstration behavior to show others that he cannot be manipulated or coerced. He may resist influence because he wishes to maintain the impression that he is a credible and consistent person. An individual's reputation is an important basis of his future power to influence others, and he does his best to protect and enhance it. When the arguments of others can be anticipated, a person tends to hedge on issues and show some anticipatory opinion change to minimize the degree of conflict and possible loss of face that could occur from losing an argument.

SUGGESTED READINGS

Champlin, J. R. (Ed.) *Power.* New York: Atherton, 1971. A set of papers by scholars from a wide range of disciplines devoted to analyzing the concept of power.

Parsons, T. *Sociological theory and modern society.* New York: The Free Press, 1967, pp. 297–383. The two essays in this collection dealing with the concepts of political power and social influence are classics. They provide profound insights into the basis of legitimate power and factors important to social influence.

Schelling, T. C. *Arms and influence.* New Haven: Yale University Press, 1966. A fascinating analysis of how to maximize the effectiveness of threats in international relations.

Tedeschi, J. T. (Ed.) *The social influence processes.* Chicago: Aldine, 1972. A collection of papers that provide excellent reviews of theories and research relating to interpersonal influence.

CHAPTER 9

Tactics of Social Power and Conflict Resolution

CHAPTER PREVIEW

People are interdependent. The values, commodities, love, approval, and skill possessed by other people must be sought in order for an individual to acquire satisfaction and avoid disappointment. Often there are many different people who can provide the desired outcome for an individual and therefore, he has to choose between alternative targets of influence. Who will he choose? An individual can also choose between a number of modes of influence to gain his objectives. Will he attempt to persuade, to threaten or to bribe the target? Factors contributing to the decisions of who and how to influence will occupy our attention in the first part of this chapter.

Much of human interaction takes the form of bargaining. Any situation in which two persons contend for values and neither can have what he most prefers may be considered a bargaining problem. A father may tell his little boy to eat all of his breakfast cereal and the little boy may seek a compromise after each bite by saying, "Is that enough now, daddy?" Each party will develop a set of tactics in order to gain the best possible solution for himself. Bargainers may attempt to influence one another directly or they may enlist a third party to act as a mediator. In the second part of this chapter we will examine the process of bargaining.

The final topic to be considered is the formation of alliances in groups of three or more people (n-person groups). In a three-person group, for example, two persons may form a coalition against the third. There are many social scientists who agree with Simmel (1950) that the process of coalition formation is the building block of all group activities. A person who is too weak to achieve his objectives by himself will often seek out allies so their combined strength may be used to maximize their chances for success in influencing others.

A mother may seek the help of her children to persuade her husband about the type of vacation they should plan for the summer, and the children may seek an alliance so that mother will protect them from father. We will see that the resources and relationships of group members and the kinds of bargains they can strike among themselves are crucial for determining which coalitions will form.

I. THE DECISION TO INFLUENCE

Although an individual does not always choose the person with whom he will interact, he can often manage to avoid or arrange to meet others. Who will the person choose as a potential target of influence? Suppose you had the job of selling encyclopedias from door to door. Would you select the potential customers in any systematic way? You might avoid the sections of town in which the income level is low because the inhabitants could not afford to buy your product. You might also avoid small apartment units because their lack of space for a large set of volumes would produce customer resistance. You would presumably choose to make your pitch to people who have sufficient income to buy the product and who live where the prospects of success in exercising your influence are good.

Another consideration is the cost involved in attempting influence. In our example there are costs of time, effort, and transportation. We shall see that there are a number of other potential costs that must be considered by a potential source of influence before he chooses a target or mode of influence. In sum, three factors contribute to the source's choice: (1) the values controlled by the target; (2) the estimated probability of success of influence attempts; and (3) the potential costs of attempting influence. The target who is expected to yield the greatest net profit will be selected. If there is no target available who will yield a net profit (or minimize a loss), no influence will ordinarily be attempted.

Some people are assertive and frequently attempt influence, while others are more passive and avoid the conflicts potentially associated with interpersonal relationships. The frequency with which a person will attempt influence and his choice of tactics are determined by his prior history of success in exercising power and by the power bases he controls. The possession of great resources, status, or expertise may encourage an individual to attempt influence frequently. How much the source and target like each other may encourage or discourage them from interacting and may determine which modes of influence are used when they do interact.

Of particular interest to students of social conflict are the conditions under which coercive power will be offensively employed by interacting persons. Why do people threaten and harm one another? This is a complex question for which there are many possible answers. The nature of a particular conflict may be a determining factor; if two men love the same woman, neither persuasion nor bribery are apt to solve their problem. Intense conflicts involving significant and opposing values tend to be perceived as zero sum in character (pure conflict). Since there must be a winner and a loser and neither wants to lose, each attempts to force the other to give up his claim. We shall see that conflict intensity, lack of self-confidence, concern for establishing a masculine self-identity or for saving face, challenges to authority, and shortness of time perspective are all related to the use of coercion.

A. Decision Criteria of Costs and Gains

Sometimes there is only one other person who has what a potential influencer wants. For example, a person may love and desire to be loved by a single other person. The problem is not the choice of target but rather how to bring about the desired result. More usually, many others possess what a person wants. Both questions, *who* and *how*, occupy the individual who must choose one of a population of targets, all of whom possess the value desired. He must estimate his chances of success in influencing the target and gaining what he wants, and these expected gains must be compared to the probability and value of the costs that will be incurred in the influence attempt.

A source must consider three types of costs before making a decision to attempt influence. *Fixed costs* are known prior to exercising influence and are voluntarily incurred by the source. For example, if a company decides to persuade people to buy its product, it will place advertisements in newspapers and buy time on television. The cost of securing communication opportunities can often be determined before influence attempts are made. Costs that may be incurred but are contingent on the target's reactions to influence attempts are referred to as *opportunity costs*. (Harsanyi 1962). The source retains a choice whether to incur opportunity costs, but he cannot make this decision until he knows the target's reactions. If threats are successful, there is no need to punish the target; but when noncompliance occurs, the source must decide whether to incur the costs of imposing punishment. Finally, *target imposed costs* are directly administered by the target, and may take the form of resistance, retaliation, or counterinfluence. The greater the probability and value of the expected costs of exercising influence, the fewer attempts the source will make.

1. Fixed Costs

A source may incur fixed costs for obtaining access to channels of communication and for maintaining adequate surveillance of the target. A source who makes a threat or promises a reward must be in a position to know whether the target actually performs the desired behavior; otherwise, the target may go unpunished for his failure or may claim an undeserved reward. There is need to maintain adequate surveillance whenever modes of reinforcement control are used by the source (Kelley & Ring, 1961; Ring & Kelley, 1963).

A source may need to acquire resources that can serve as the power basis for an influence attempt. If a nation wants to use high-magnitude international threats, it must weigh the cost of developing nuclear capability against the possible gains from having such a power base. For many nations the costs would far outweigh the potential gain. Similarly, a person may buy an automobile or a gun to enhance his ability to influence a particular target. Investments made for power resources are fixed costs because the source may choose to incur them without knowing what the prospective targets may do.

2. Opportunity Costs

Some of the costs voluntarily incurred by the source are dependent on the reactions of the target. The prudent person estimates the probability and value of these opportunity costs before initiating influence attempts. If a target were to resist a threat, the source must put up or shut up, and punishment is costly in time, effort, resources, and decreased liking and legitimacy. When a threat fails, incurring the costs of punishing the target cannot recover the compliance already forgone; the source may therefore be tempted not to punish. However, if he anticipates future interactions with the target or is concerned about his reputation with third parties, he will expend the necessary resources to enhance his credibility for future influence attempts. Absorbing the costs of administering punishment is an investment in maximizing the effectiveness of future threats.

Similarly, if a target complies with a con-

tingent promise of reward, the source may be tempted not to provide what is promised. For example, you may promise to play with a child later if he will let you finish reading. Afterward you may be tempted to try and avoid the commitment. Why incur the costs in time and effort when you have already received what you wanted. Of course, you may consider how disappointed the boy will be and anticipate the costs of some retaliatory action such as future interruptions of reading. The temptation not to fulfill promises is usually offset by anticipated costs in reputation, loss of attraction or legitimacy, and possible retaliation by the target.

Successful threats and unsuccessful promises do not require expenditures for punishments and rewards. A source would appear irrational if he punished a target for doing as demanded or provided a reward even when the target did not fulfill his part of the bargain. It can be seen that promises cost more when they succeed, while threats cost more when they fail. Increasing the size of a promised reward enhances the probability of compliance from a target and increases the opportunity costs to the source. Decreasing the magnitude of threatened punishment lessens the probability of gaining compliance and increases opportunity costs. Threats hold out the possibility of having your cake and eating it too—compliance without opportunity costs. Both Kite (1964) and Schlenker and Tedeschi (1972) have shown that subjects who possess unilateral power in conflict-of-interest situations do perceive threats as more powerful and prefer to use them rather than promises.

Tedeschi, Horai, Lindskold, and Faley (1970) investigated the effects of opportunity costs on the behavior of subjects who were provided with the ability to use threats. Robot targets were programmed to defy all the threats sent to them by subjects in a Prisoner's Dilemma game. When the robot target failed to make the response demanded by a threat, the subjects were given an option to administer punishment by taking 10 points away from the robot's score. Some subjects were not charged for using their punishment power, one group was charged 5 points, and another group was charged 10 points for each use. The subjects established high credibility for their threats in all conditions, but they transmitted fewer threats when the opportunity costs were higher. Apparently, they took into account the cost of exercising power before deciding to send threats, but once threats were communicated, they felt themselves committed to backing them up.

3. Target-Imposed Costs

A potential source of influence must take into account the costs that can be imposed upon him by his chosen target. He can minimize target-imposed costs by choosing positive modes of influence, such as persuasion or promises. The use of threats elicits resistance and counterthreats (Deutsch & Krauss, 1960) and the implementation of punishment often brings retaliation. Moreover, the exercise of coercive power detracts from the source's attractiveness and undermines his legitimacy. These target-imposed costs counteract the advantages of threats that appear when only opportunity costs are considered.

The loss of attraction and legitimacy (see Chapter 5) that a source of coercive power provokes are damaging to his ability to exercise influence over the long run. The ability to influence without surveillance depends on the very bases of power lost by a source who habitually uses coercion. This is why Talleyrand, the great French diplomat who served under Napolean, once remarked that we can do almost anything with bayonets except sit on them. There are clearly limits to what can be achieved through coercive power, although it may not appear that way to either sources or targets in the short run. One cannot educate a child merely by threats of terrible punishment. Resentment and hatred of the

educational process are apt to result and the source will lose rather than gain control over the child's behavior. Nevertheless, the short-term advantages of coercive power encourage its frequent use.

In summary, successful threats minimize opportunity costs but bring about a decrease in attractiveness and legitimacy in the eyes of the target. Unsuccessful threats challenge the source to back up his words with punishing deeds and leave him with the choice of losing credibility or risking retaliation from the target. These relationships between threats and promises and opportunity and target-imposed costs are summarized in Table 9.1. The source's estimation of the probabilities of incurring costs is related to his estimate of the probability of success in influencing the target. His confidence in his ability to influence others is determined by a number of factors, to which we now turn.

B. Source Factors and the Exercise of Influence

One of the principles of performance we can borrow from individual psychology is that rewarding a response will increase its subsequent frequency. A similar relationship exists between success and frequency of influence attempts. Lippitt, Polansky, Redl, and Rosen (1952) observed the behavior of boys at a fresh-air camp in Michigan after first identifying the most influential boys on the basis of peer ratings. Those identified as influential did attempt more influence than the others. The greater a person's prior success in influencing others, the more often he exercises influence.

As we saw in the last chapter, a number of characteristics of a source contribute to his success in influencing a target. The material resources he possesses, his status, expertise, and attractiveness are related to how often he attempts influence and partly determine which mode of influence he uses. A source's estimate of the probability

Table 9.1   Relationships Between Costs and Success or Failure in Using Threats and Promises.

Success or failure of threats and promises	Opportunity costs	Target-imposed costs
Successful threats	No	Yes
Unsuccessful threats	Yes	Yes
Successful promises	Yes	No
Unsuccessful promises	No	Yes

of success is to some degree a function of his control over the relevant bases of power. The more confident he is about his ability to exercise effective influence, the more probable it is he will attempt it.

1.   Material Resources

The possession of material resources gives an individual the ability to reward and punish others. The greater his resources, the more confident he is about his ability to influence others, particularly by modes of reinforcement control. Money, weapons, control over the target's income, and physical strength and prowess can be displayed before a target in an effort to secure his compliance. The possession of great resources reduces one's expectation of target resistance and decreases the probability of incurring target imposed costs such as retaliation.

Smith and Leginski (1970) investigated the relationship between capability and the use of coercive power. Subjects participated in a bargaining game against a confederate, in which they were given a printed table that presented three "issues" to negotiate, each containing twenty possible levels of agreement. Each outcome level carried opposing point values for the subject and the confederate; as the points for one increased, the points for the other decreased, and vice versa. The interests of the subjects and the confederate were therefore directly opposed. Their task was to reach agreement on a contract value for each of the three issues. The subjects were limited to

passing notes to the confederate announcing their own offers or their agreement to offers from their opponent. They were also given the ability to send threats of a fine and actually to impose fines on their opponent. The magnitude of the fine was varied among groups and could be 20, 50, 90, or 140 points. The subjects could impose a fine in a precise or an imprecise fashion. Precise power allowed a subject to fine the confederate any amount from one point up to the maximum for their group, while imprecise power required them to exercise their full power (the maximum fine) whenever they used threats or fines.

As can be seen in Figure 9.1, subjects in the precise power condition used threats more frequently, the greater the magnitude of power they possessed. They also threatened greater punishments and imposed more fines, the greater their capability. Exactly the opposite pattern was found in the imprecise power condition. Subjects with precise power could respond flexibly to the responses of their opponent, making threatened punishment contingent on the undesireability of the confederate's offer of a contract. Imprecise power tied the subjects to an inflexible use of punishment and placed them in the same situation as a man who tries to kill mosquitoes with an elephant gun or, more realistically, to an attempt by a superpower to deter revolutions with nuclear threats. These results support the hypothesis of a direct relationship between source capability and frequency of influence attempts, as long as the source can flexibly use his punishment power.

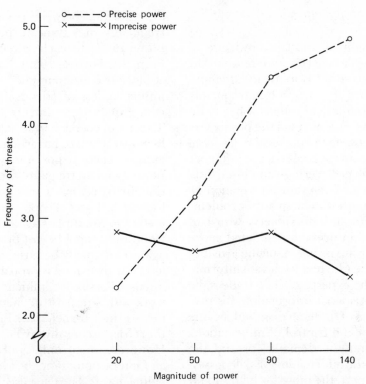

Figure 9.1. Relationship between magnitude of power possessed by subjects and the frequency with which they used threats. (After Smith and Leginski, 1970.)

2. The Status of the Source

A person of high status assumes he will receive deference from those over whom he possesses legitimate authority. This expectation makes him confident of his ability to wield influence successfully. A number of studies have found a positive relationship between the status of a person and the degree of security he feels in his position of authority (Cohen, 1958; Heinicke & Bales, 1953; Kelley, 1951). Persons high in status have been observed to speak more frequently in group discussions than persons of lower status (Hurwitz, Zander, & Hymovitch, 1968). In a laboratory study (reported in more detail in Chapter 8) Torrance (1954) found that officers in the Air Force exerted influence on each other in direct relationship to their ranks. High status leads a source both to anticipate and to gain compliance with requests, persua-

sion, and commands. Status is directly related to the frequency with which a source attempts to influence others.

A person who holds high office in an organization may have access to information and resources not available to other members. He may maintain secrecy, exercise censorship, or deliberately engage in nondecision making as methods of manipulatory influence. Blau (1964), Homans (1961), and Hollander (1964) have postulated that the approval of a high status person is worth more than the approval of a low status person. If this hypothesis is true—and it does seem plausible—it can be expected that high status persons will come to recognize the significance of their social approval and employ this very inexpensive and effective means of social control. Thus, the higher the individual's status the more tempted he is to use manipulatory forms of influence.

3. The Expertise of the Source

The possession of special knowledge or skills increases a source's confidence in the probable success of his influence attempts, and confidence encourages him frequently to attempt to influence others. Shevita (in Hemphill, 1961) confirmed the positive relationship between the possession of special information and the frequency of influence attempts. Subjects were given either task-irrelevant or task-relevant information by an experimenter in a group problem-solving situation. The subjects who had task-relevant information initiated more changes in group problem solving activities than did those who had irrelevant information. Since the expert's stock in trade is the possession of special information, his preferred mode of influence should be the manipulation and control of information.

The greater the demand for and the more scarce the information or skill possessed by an expert, the more his help should be sought by others. The less knowledge a target has, the more informationally dependent he is on an expert. The effectiveness of an expert in influencing others increases as the difficulty, complexity and ambiguity of a task or problem increases (Coleman, Blake & Mouton, 1958; Luchins, 1945). If it can be assumed that a source will choose a target who is susceptible to influence, we can summarize as follows: the greater the complexity or ambiguity of the situation, and the more informationally dependent the prospective target, the higher the probability of an influence attempt by an expert source.

4. Interpersonal Attraction

A source of influence anticipates a cooperative interaction with persons he likes and a hostile and exploitative relationship with disliked persons. He expects his persuasive communications and his promises to be more successful when directed at a liked rather than a disliked target. The higher the attraction between persons, the more frequently they transmit persuasive communications to each other (Back, 1951; French & Snyder, 1959).

Since friendship implies susceptibility to influence, loss of friendship means a decrease of future influence (and rewards). The use of coercion against a friend results in a decrement of attraction. While the exercise of coercive power may produce temporary short-term gains, the loss of attraction involved leads to more permanent long-term losses. People are generally reluctant to use threats against their friends. Good will cannot be lost by using coercion against an enemy because there is none to lose, but retaliation is probable and may be intense. Persuasive influence is not apt to work with a distrustful enemy, and promises will not be believed. Enemies should therefore generally avoid one another. However, when conflicts of interests arise and interaction cannot be avoided, an individual may feel he must use threats or force to gain his objectives.

Krauss (1966) investigated the relationship between interpersonal attraction and the exercise of threats and punishments. Pairs of subjects were induced to like or dislike one another prior to playing the trucking game. During the game the subjects were provided with gates to block each other's access to the shorter and more profitable of the routes to the destination (see Figure 7.3 on the trucking game). When the subjects liked one another they threatened and used the punishing gates less often than when they disliked one another.

Friendship implies equality in power bases—expertise, possession of resources, and status. Differentials in expertise make it difficult for people to share significant attitudes and values. Disparity in the possession of resources or status interferes with the development of attraction because friendly overtures by the weaker party may be interpreted as ingratiating. These considerations led Henry Adams to remark that a "friend in power is a friend lost" (1931, p.108).

C. The Offensive Use of Coercion

In most societies individuals are taught to defend themselves against the attacks of other persons. A man would seldom be disapproved for striking someone who assaulted him and generally would not be held legally reaponsible if he killed another person in self-defense. It is less understandable to most of us why a person should attack someone who has done him no harm. Why cannot people be reasonable and find peaceful ways to settle their interpersonal problems? We have seen that there are many ways of exercising influence besides coercion. But despite the old adage that honey will attract more bees than vinegar, almost everyone at one time or another uses coercion as a means of getting his way in interaction with others. The factors that cause a person to use coercion offensively are different from those that elicit its use defensively. The latter will be discussed in Chapter 12.

1. Intensity of Conflict

The degree of conflict between two persons has important effects on the modes of influence each will direct toward the other. When their goals are incompatible and interdependent and each considers his goal important to attain, there is a perceived need to solve the conflict by compelling the other person to give way. Intense conflict breeds suspicion and reduces the effectiveness of more peaceful modes of influence, such as promises, persuasion, or the activation of commitments. Miller and Butler (1969) have shown experimentally that when intensity of conflict is low and the cooperative nature of a situation is salient, subjects prefer to use rewards rather than punishments in their interactions with one another.

Intense conflict undermines the perceived trustworthiness of the adversary and decreases the effectiveness of persuasive communications. Expertise and status, which normally add to a source's ability to influence, no longer serve as power bases when conflict is intense. Conflict with an authority reduces the perceived legitimacy of his status and the deference shown by the individual of lower status. Former friends may become enemies and every initiative may be interpreted as a trick in a competition for advantage. Threats are easier to believe than promises. Each person views himself as defending against the intrusions of the other and a cycle of increasing hostilities may sometimes escalate out of control (Pruitt, 1965).

Deutsch, Canavan, and Rubin (1971) manipulated the intensity of conflict by varying the length of the one-lane road in the trucking game. When the road was short (small conflict), it was easy to let the other truck go first and then proceed through; but when the road was long (great conflict), it took more time to back up to let the other person through, hence increasing the cost of being unilaterally cooperative. Twenty, 50, or 90 percent of the main route was declared one-lane for different pairs of subjects. When the size of conflict was large, fewer trials had positive outcomes, more trials resulted in subjects receiving the maximum possibile negative payoffs, and the gates were more often used to threaten and punish the opposing player.

Scarcity of resources is the basis of many conflicts. Rights to hunting or fishing areas, control over territories considered important for defense, rivalry for a mate, control over which television program will be viewed, and many other situations present people with conflicts of greater or lesser intensity. In such situations the individual has only three choices: (1) withdraw and allow the other person to have what he wants; (2) seek resolution through compromise; or (3) attempt to make the other person withdraw. The more intense the conflict, the more probable it is that coercive power will be exercised.

Paradoxically, the use of coercion results from the felt powerlessness of a source to do anything else. His actions may be carried out in desperation or despair rather than from sadistic delight or a sense of power. It has been said that Kaiser Wilhelm of Germany entered World War I with full knowledge of the likelihood of defeat, and Emperor Hirohito is quoted as saying prior to the Japanese attack on Pearl Harbor that sometimes there is no alternative to leaping off a tower. The issues at stake were sufficiently important for these national leaders to cause them to initiate offensive military actions against other nations (Kahn, 1960; Tuchman, 1962).

2. Self-Confidence

Among the factors important for gaining influence over others by noncoercive means are being liked, being trusted, possessing skills, abilities or special education, and being able to to communicate effectively with others. Many people either do not possess these requisites for successful noncoercive influence or do not believe they do. Feelings of powerlessness and inadequacy, lack of self-confidence, and low self-esteem make it more likely that an individual will rely on coercive means of influencing others. When a person uses coercion, there is a decrease in his ability to successfully employ other means of influence. He earns the enmity and distrust of the target and of others who observe or hear about his coercive actions, making it even more likely he will need to employ coercion again to achieve his goals. When a person with low self-esteem gets caught up in this kind of vicious cycle, there is little he can do to extricate himself without the aid of others.

Lower class people often lack interpersonal skills used in the larger society and develop attitudes associated with a disposition to use coercive power. Fannin

and Clinard (1965) observed differences between the self-images of lower- and middle-class delinquents. Unlike the middle-class boys, the lower-class boys viewed themselves as tough, powerful, and fierce, and they had aspirations to perpetuate these self-images. The success of coercion is promoted by an image of toughness. A person who frequently resorts to coercive influence believes he cannot be successful by any other means. People who feel isolated and powerless are perceived by those who know them as more aggressive than are integrated and self-confident persons (Ransford, 1968). As we will see in Chapter 12, a person is perceived as aggressive when he uses coercive power in an offensive way against others, but is not perceived as aggressive when he uses coercion for justifiable defensive reasons.

Where there are large economic differences in a society and there is little mobility permitting a person to escape the class of his birth, some individuals are prevented from enjoying the same level of living as others. Those who believe they are excluded from pursuing legitimate avenues to achievement may seek access to rewards by recourse to illegitimate means, which may involve doing harm to others.

Fear may motivate attack when an individual can see no other way of saving himself. For this reason it has sometimes been argued that fewer people would be killed in the course of trying to enforce the law if the police were not permitted to carry guns. When a policeman fires at a suspect, a shootout may occur because the target believes either he or the policeman must die. The "Bobbies" of England do not ordinarily carry guns, and the number killed in the line of duty is far less than among policemen in the United States. Of course one must be careful in interpreting this difference. The reason why the "Bobby" doesn't carry a gun and why there are fewer killed in the line of duty may be deeply rooted in English values and social structure.

A person who is chronically self-confident has a history of success in working out problems and has often developed expertise, achieved some status, and acquired material resources. In experimental situations these power bases can be eliminated and the effects of self-confidence on the social influence process can be isolated and separately examined. A sense of power and feelings of self-confidence are related to internal and external control orientations. Internals characteristically believe they control their environment and can effectively manipulate their own rewards and punishments, while externals believe they are controlled by their environment and that rewards and punishments are capriciously determined by chance, luck, or fate. Thus, internals view themselves as powerful and externals perceive themselves as powerless (Minton, 1972).

Goodstadt and Hjelle (1973) divided subjects into two groups on the basis of whether they scored high or low on Rotter's measure of internal-external control orientation. The subjects were given the role of supervisors and had the task of improving productivity among their workers. They could choose between a variety of influence modes in achieving their production goals. The total frequency of influence attempts was not affected by the personality of the subjects, but the mode of influence chosen was. Persons high in internal control clearly preferred persuasion and promises, while those high in external control predominantly chose to use threats and punishments as means to influence the workers. Those who lack self-confidence do not believe the gentle or positive forms of influence will succeed and, hence, prefer coercive power.

Lindskold and Tedeschi (1970) more directly tested the relationship between self-confidence and preference for influence modes. After receiving instructions about how to play a Prisoner's Dilemma game, subjects were asked how successful they thought they would be. Two groups of subjects were identified from these initial self-predictions as either high or low in self-confidence. The subjects were then provided with opportunities to employ either noncontingent promises of cooperation or threats demanding a cooperative response from a confederate player. More influence attempts were made by self-confident subjects. Furthermore, subjects who lacked confidence displayed a strong preference for threats over promises, while self-confident subjects more often sent promises as a means of resolving the conflict of interests between themselves and the confederate.

Uncontrolled observations outside the laboratory are consistent with these experimental findings. Raser (1966) has reported a biographical analysis of the personalities of totalitarian and democratic leaders. The latter were found to be more secure in their private lives, while the former were insecure and lower in self-esteem. Of course this kind of study fails to separate the style of leadership from the type of social system. Nevertheless, the implication is that insecurity and lack of confidence dispose individuals with access to power resources to use coercive and manipulative forms of influence. Kipnis (1974) has observed that people who appear to be passive and timid in their private lives may be transformed into severe taskmasters when given access to institutional power resources (i.e., status and authority). To some extent this transformation from sheep to wolf may be attributable to the individual's attempt to win respect and to bolster his own self-image.

3. Self-Presentation and Identity

Fanon (1963), whose ideas were important among black intellectuals in America during the turbulent 1960s, argued that colonized peoples in Africa could regain their self-identity and self-respect only by extracting a pound of flesh from those who had subjugated them and distorted and changed their native cultures. Only by a violent act of revolution could colonized peoples purge themselves of the submissive habits they developed under foreign domination. Following some of the property riots in the United States, during which blacks burned down white-owned stores and tenaments in the ghettos, television interviews and newspaper pictures revealed that a substantial number of young blacks felt an increased sense of pride and manhood. One young black in Memphis said to a television interviewer the day following a property riot, "At least, today I am a man."

An individual's self-image is developed within the context of cultural values that are typically transmitted to him through the various socialization agencies of his society, including the family, the school, and the mass media. The cultural definition of what it means to be masculine probably has an important effect on the way a man will present himself to others. In an examination of 30 different cultures, Textor (1967) found a relationship between personal crime and the glorification of the military. Where there was a strong emphasis on killing and torturing one's enemies, and where military glory was extolled, there was a high incidence of personal crime. Less emphasis on these martial values is associated with a lower rate of crime. Balinese society (before the Indonesian attacks on the overseas Chinese) stressed esthetic values in the world of art, music, and dance. Until quite recently, this gentle society was almost devoid of any kind of violence.

In certain subcultures physical forms of coercion are the accepted mode of solving interpersonal conflicts (Wolfgang & Ferracuti, 1967). Reluctance to fight may be considered to reflect a lack of masculinity. Toch (1969) has suggested that an advertised willingness to fight is a way of promoting a tough and masculine self-image. The promoter acts to provoke others into fighting him by insulting them and stepping on their toes. To demonstrate masculinity it is not necessary for a person to win all his fights; the important thing is to display courage and a willingness to fight anybody. The image desired is of a man who has "guts." This behavior can be functional, since even though a possible opponent may believe he can defeat the promoter in a fight, the latter's reputation indicates that the fight cannot be won cheaply. Unless the goal is worth the effort, the strong may back down before a courageous weaker person.

The promoter of a tough self-image builds a reputation that adds to the believability of his threats and enhances the effectiveness of his coercive influence attempts. A problem arises for him in a sub-culture of violence, however. Many of the targets he attempts to coerce have their own reputations to defend, and the result may be that they band together in gangs to dampen conflict among themselves, or that they try to avoid one another. In some cases, as in a movie western where young gunslingers seek out the "fast gun," self-image promoters may deliberately provoke one another. It is important to precipitate incidents to keep their reputations fresh in the memories of observers.

4. Face-Saving Behavior

Goffman (1959) has argued that there is a pervasive need to maintain face in American society which motivates people to avoid situations where they would be embarassed before others. Each person desires to maintain an image of strength and ability, or dignity in his status position, and of competence in solving problems. The culture may prescribe that a person must gain revenge for harm deliberately done him by another, generating feuds like those described in Greek tragedies and in Shakespeare's *Hamlet*. Failure to extract measure for measure may well cause an individual to be humiliated in the eyes of those around him. A person will often make great sacrifices to restore his self-respect.

Brown (1968) found American males to be quite ready to resort to exploitation and coercion, even at cost to themselves, to save face. In a trucking game, a confederate was given control over a gate for the first half of the experiment and the subject was given the threatening and punishing ability during the second half. When the confederate had the power advantage, he exploited subjects, used the gate quite often, charged subjects high tolls to pass through the gate, and ended up with a much larger profit than the subjects. To make their defeat even more ignominious, the subjects were told they had been observed through a one-way mirror by a group of peers.

Midway through the experiment, and before the subjects gained the power advantage, they were given feedback about how their peers evaluated their performance. One group was informed that their fellow adolescents viewed them as "weak," as "suckers," and as "pretty bad." A second group was told that all things considered they "looked good" because they "tried hard and played fair." Presumably, only the subjects in the first group needed to save face during the second half of the game; the subjects in the second group had not had their images damaged by the confederate's exploitative play.

After receiving the bogus evaluations, the subjects were given the power to choose from a toll schedule exactly how much they wanted to charge the confederate for passing through the gate. The schedule included low or moderate tolls that cost little to administer and high tolls that cost a great deal to administer. Half the subjects were told that the confederate knew their costs for administering the tolls and half believed the confederate did not know their cost schedule.

The results revealed that the subjects who felt they had looked foolish earlier charged much higher tolls than did those who believed they had looked good, despite the fact that charging high tolls meant they incurred prohibitive costs. Such self-damaging retaliation was more frequent when the confederate allegedly did not

know the subjects' costs than when they were known. The opponent's awareness of the harm that subjects were doing to themselves in order to gain revenge suppressed the use of self-damaging tolls. Thus, subjects accepted costs and used coercion when they could repair their damaged self-images by so doing. In a similar way, a person may retaliate when subjected to insults and name-calling. Retaliation to insult compensates for a damaged self-concept, in addition to gaining revenge and demonstrating a strong resolve to resist coercion by others.

In two experiments Holmes (1971) found that men may submit to pain or engage in great effort to display their masculinity. In the first study, the instructions informed subjects of the task they would perform. Half were told they would suck on four objects: a baby's rattle, a rubber nipple on a baby's bottle, a pacifier, and a breast shield. The other half of the subjects were told they would feel various kinds of surfaces, such as sandpaper and a piece of cloth. Both groups were shown the relevant objects while the experimenter busied himself with readying instrumentation to measure their physiological reactions. The subjects were then told that in a second part of the study they would experience electric shocks, but since some people were afraid of shocks, the experimenter wanted them to indicate how great a shock intensity they would be willing to accept. The subjects who anticipated an embarassing experience indicated they would be willing to accept higher shock intensities than did those who anticipated more neutral experiences. One interpretation of these results is that men who expected to engage in sucking behavior wanted to avoid two possible self-damaging impressions—that they enjoyed the sucking and hence were immature or infantile or else they had homosexual needs for oral-genital contact. Their choice of high shock intensities was meant to present themselves as tough, courageous, masculine types.

In the second study the initial expectations of the subjects were the same, but this time Holmes told them the second phase of the experiment involved squeezing a hand dynamometer, an exercise device which measures the pressure of a grip response. He asked them to indicate how many times they would be willing to squeeze the dynamometer. The subjects who anticipated a humiliating experience indicated a willingness to expend more of this masculine effort than did those who did not anticipate embarrassment. In both studies, college males indicated a willingness to accept costs to compensate for an anticipated loss of face.

5. Maintenance of Authority

A person of high status typically does not depend on coercive means of influence, but when his authority is challenged swift coercive action may be taken. A subordinate who is perceived as willfully defying a high status person's commands may be severely punished. Punishing disobedience serves notice to other subordinates that authority cannot be flouted with impunity, restores the high status person's sense of power, and either causes the recalcitrant subordinate to submit to authority or removes him from a position where he can continue to defy authority.

Kipnis and Misner (1972) found disobedience to be an important cause for the arrests of male offenders on a charge of disorderly conduct. This charge allows police officers wide latitude in deciding whether a violation of the law has taken place. Thirty police officers were asked to describe the most recent incident in which a male offender was arrested for disorderly conduct, and another 30 policemen described a similar incident where no arrest was made. Analyses indicated that the kind of incident (e.g., street corner disturbances, domestic fights, traffic violations, etc.) did not differentiate between whether an arrest would be made or not. Rather, the clear determinant of an arrest was resistance by the offender to the police officer's orders at the scene.

In a study of assaults against police officers, Toch (1969) found that escalation of violence often follows a sequence in which a person is asked to "move on" and refuses to follow the policeman's order. The person may believe he has a right to be on the street and may not accept the policeman's order as legitimate. The officer then becomes belligerent and threatens arrest. The offender, in turn, becomes even more defiant because he perceives the actions of the officer as arbitrary. This cycle continues until a physical confrontation takes place.

Challenges to the authority of supervisors have been observed in work settings by Kipnis and Consentino (1969). Supervisors were more likely to use coercive means against workers who lacked motivation than against those who lacked the skill to do a good job. When a worker's resistance to the supervisor's attempts to get better production were attributed to motivational causes ("I refuse") rather than lack of ability ("I don't know how"), the supervisor relied on threats and punishments to lower the worker's resistance to performing the desired behavior.

This type of supervisory behavior is contrary to knowledge available from learning theory about how to improve an individual's performance. Threatening a poorly motivated person is only apt to cause him to have even more negative attitudes. On the other hand, if a person does not have aptitude for a task, no amount of rewarding or persuading is apt to lead to good performance. The supervisors' choice of influence modes was not effective if their goal was to increase production. However, they may have had other objectives in mind. Piqued by willful resistance to their authority, supervisors may become more concerned with saving face than with achieving organizational goals. They therefore punish behavior that challenges their authority and reward obedient behavior even at the cost of organizational efficiency.

6. Attention-Seeking and Affirmation of Self

An ineffectual individual may be driven to an extreme and uncharacteristic action to prove to himself and others that he is important, courageous, and manly. Megargee (1970) has discovered many cases of extreme assault that involve rather passive persons with no previous history of violence. For example, in one case "a 21-year old man from Colorado who was accused of the rape and murder of two little girls had never been a discipline problem and, in fact, his stepfather reported, 'when he was in school the other kids would run all over him and he'd never fight back. There is just no violence in him.' " (p.110).

Presidential assassins are characterized by a need to bring public attention to themselves. A National Commission on the Causes and Prevention of Violence (Kirkham, Levy, & Crotty, 1970) found an extraordinary similarity among these men. They were all white, rather short and slender, had experienced an absence or disruption of normal family relationships, were loners and had difficulty making friends of either sex, especially had difficulty in establishing lasting relationships with women, were unemployed for two or three years before the assassination attempt, and had delusions of the importance they would have in world history. Two examples are described in Box 9.1.

Cultural values may affect the nature of an assassination attempt. On December 7, 1973 an attack took place against Mrs. Imelda Marcos, the wife of the President of the Philippine Republic. The assassin mounted a public platform wielding a foot-long bolo knife and leaped at his victim. Although he slashed Mrs. Marcos on the arms causing injuries requiring 75 stitches he failed to kill her before he was subdued. If he wished to be sure of killing Mrs. Marcos, why didn't he use a gun? It is interesting to note that in the Philippine culture warriors of great courage wield knives, not guns; although the gun is the symbol of masculinity in America, the knife is the equivalent symbol in the Philippines. A speculative possibility is that the assassin was concerned with his own masculinity and self-worth and that his action was mainly directed toward affirming his identity to himself and to others.

A similar process may be involved in the assaultive behavior of children in schools. Consider the child who is dominated by his parents in the home and derogated or ignored by his teachers and peers. Friendless and alone, full of self-doubt and anxiety, viewing the world as hostile, and believing that no one is aware of or concerned about his very existence, the child lashes out and assaults a victim. Now he may be punished, but he will not be ignored. In much the same way a child after bedtime may risk a spanking rather than stay in bed and not be noticed by visitors to his home.

7. Time Perspective

There are two ways in which time may determine whether a source will use coercion against others. Where compliance by a target is required quickly and other means of influence are deemed too slow, coercion may be used. When a child is told to take out the trash right away because the collectors are down the street and he dillydallies, his parent may use coercion and not sweet persuasion as the means of obtaining compliance. When a source wants to control the timing of a target's responses, something that cannot be done with modes of influence, such as promises and persuasion that leave the decision of how and when to act up to the target, coercive power is likely to be used.

A source's behavior is also affected by his time perspective. Failure to consider future consequences of an action may make a person reckless. Melges and Harris (1970) identified three conditions that predispose

Box 9.1   POLITICAL ASSASSINATIONS

Taylor and Weiss (1970) described the behavior of John Schrank, who tried to assassinate Theodore Roosevelt: "On the night of McKinley's assassination John Schrank had a vision. He saw the dead President rise from his coffin and accuse Theodore Roosevelt, the incoming President, of arranging his death. Eleven years later, chronically unemployed and wandering from place to place in the Bowery of Manhattan, Schrank reexperienced this vision, which he interpreted as a divine mandate to avenge McKinley's death. . . . After twenty-four days of travelling more than two thousand miles in eight states, Schrank had succeeded in putting himself in the same city at the same time with Roosevelt on only three occasions. . . . Outside a hotel in Milwaukee Schrank stood up in the back of the crowd and fired a shot into the candidate's chest. Before the bullet could enter the right lung, it had to pass through a metal eyeglass case and a folded fifty-page speech. It spent its final force in cracking a rib. After the unsuccessful assassination attempt police found among Schrank's personal papers a note which read: "Theodore Roosevelt is in conspiracy with European monarchs to overthrow the Republic . . . We want no king. We want no murderer. The United States is no Carthage. We will not yield to Rome' " (p.296).

Arthur Bremer's attempt to assassinate Governor George Wallace of Alabama did not seem to be politically motivated. It did not seem to matter to him whether he killed George McGovern, Richard Nixon, Hubert Humphrey, or George Wallace. The continual smirk on his face during the entire affair and even afterward seemed to indicate the satisfaction Bremer gained from his new notoriety. On the way to jail Bremer is said to have asked how much the officers thought he would receive for his memoirs.

---

a person to ignore costs and to attack those who appear responsible for his inability to achieve his goals: (1) a felt need to take some action quickly; (2) a focus on the present to the exclusion of the future; and (3) an egocentric view of the situation that precludes empathy and dehumanizes the opponent. All these conditions are likely to occur during very intense conflicts or in crisis situations.

Various kinds of drugs are known to concentrate a person's time perspective on the present and to produce an egocentric focus. The excessive use of alcohol produces these effects and is known to be associated with violence. In a careful five-year study of 588 homicides in Philadelphia, al-

cohol was found to be present in either the offender or the victim in 64 percent of the cases (Wolfgang & Strohm, 1956). The prevalence of alcohol in suicide cases has also been documented (Palola, Dorpat, & Larson, 1962). Furthermore, Guze, Tuason, Gatfield, Steward, and Picken (1962) found that 43 percent of 223 convicted felons were diagnosed as alcoholic. The alcoholic is often economically disadvantaged and has low self-esteem. He is often predisposed to use coercion even when sober. Lack of a future time perspective prevents him from being deterred by threats of future punishment. Thus, strong laws against driving while drinking have not prevented the offense from occurring.

Drinking has been implicated in over 50 percent of traffic fatalities (United States Dept. of Transportation, 1968).

Along with a marked decrease in his ability to delay responses the user of amphetamines develops an increased awareness of many previously unnoticed sensory cues. As a consequence, he may experience himself as a unique personal recipient of environmental information. When the amphetamine user "comes down" he experiences discomfort and becomes irritable, and at this point he becomes prone to assaultive behavior (Tinkleberg & Stillman, 1970).

When a person's time perspective contracts, he fails to consider the consequences of his actions. The risk of retaliation, or social disapproval, or of transgression of ethical standards fail to deter him from taking extreme action in behalf of short-term objectives. Combined with low self-esteem, feelings of powerlessness, and the interpretation of cues from others as signs of hostility, the use of certain kinds of drugs can lead to assaultive and criminal behavior. Eighty-two percent of murders occur in situations where the motives appear to be short-lived and ambiguous or impulsive, often involving arguments over domestic matters, such as money, children, and alcohol. Zimring (1968) found that a majority of murder victims were friends, lovers, or relatives of the murderer.

The availability of guns is important, since ready access encourages their use during intense arguments when an angry or fearful person's time perspective does not extend beyond the moment. Guns are about five times more likely to kill the victim than knives, the next most commonly used murder weapon. Figure 9.2 shows the rate of deaths by gunshot wounds in the United States from 1913 to 1966. Even though more people were attacked with knives than guns, more people died from gun attacks. In 1967 about 63 percent of all homicides were shootings (FBI, 1968). It should not be surprising that in this country

in which there are 115 million privately owned guns and over 9 million alcoholics and drug addicts, we have such a high homicide rate.

8. Acquiring Influence Styles

Common observation suggests that there are marked differences between persons in means they use in influencing others. Some people seem unflappable as they patiently and quietly try to persuade those who disagree with them. Others seem to have short fuses and are quick to find insult and threats to their self-esteem; they may prefer to use coercion as a means of resolving disputes. Some people appear timid and avoid social interactions, while others assert themselves constantly in their attempts to manipulate those around them.

Preferences for influence modes are acquired through modeling, instrumental learning, role taking, and identification—processes discussed in Chapter 6. Children from conflict-filled homes soon learn that coercion is the prevalent and ultimately successful means of settling disputes. Children whose parents frequently resort to corporal punishment learn that what is effective in gaining compliance from them in the home can be employed to influence others outside the home. In both lower-class (Glueck & Glueck, 1950) and middle-class (Bandura & Walters, 1959) groups, the antisocial person is one who emerged from an environment characterized by punitive discipline, family conflict, parental rejection, and inconsistent reinforcement contingencies.

Parents who have a history of negative reinforcements from their interactions with others may lead the child to view the world as hostile and dangerous. The child may, therefore, react "defensively" to others and may appear to be quite aggressive. McCord, McCord, and Howard (1961) found that children of mildly deviant, irresponsible, and escapist parents were likely to use coercion as often as children socialized by punitive parental models.

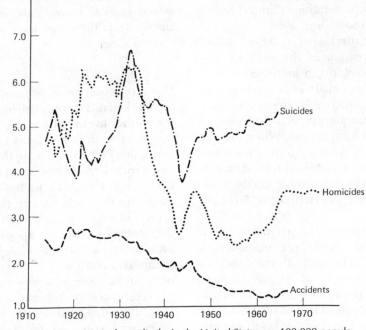

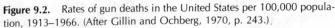

Figure 9.2.   Rates of gun deaths in the United States per 100,000 population, 1913–1966. (After Gillin and Ochberg, 1970, p. 243.)

It may be assumed that learning an influence style would follow much the same principles as learning any other responses. However, more specific questions need to be answered. For example, is a person who learns to use verbal insults or to spread vicious gossip about enemies also more likely to do physical harm to his enemies? How does one learn to bluff, and under what conditions? If children learn to use coercion in order to defend themselves, will they also employ coercive tactics offensively against others? If a person fails to keep his promises, will he also fail to back up his threats? These and related questions have not yet received the attention of social psychologists.

A number of cultural factors have been associated with the general tendency to use coercion in a society. In cross-cultural comparisons among 30 societies, Bacon, Child and Barry, (1963) and Textor (1967) found three consistent correlations between child-rearing practices and the incidence of violent crime: (1) Adults stress taking of responsibility for one's actions and teach children to be self-reliant; these practices emphasize an individualistic rather than a group-oriented view of society and are more likely to occur in nations which espouse a capitalistic rather than a socialistic ideology. (2) Children are expected to adopt achievement-related goals of success for their lives; as a consequence, a great deal of anxiety is generated by failure to achieve the expected successes. (3) There are prolonged periods of father-absence, either physically or psychologically, from the home. Those children who cannot meet cultural (or parental) expectations may develop low self-esteem and become prone to use culturally disapproved methods to achieve their goals. These illegitimate means often involve doing harm to others through robbery, blackmail, and assault.

II.   BARGAINING

Webster's New World Dictionary defines a bargain as "an agreement between parties settling what each shall give and receive in a transaction between them." Bargaining thus refers to an interaction between two or more persons in which potential agreements are sought about how each will behave in the future. Such transactions conjure up images of outdoor markets in Africa, tobacco auctions in South America, contract negotiations between management and labor unions, and treaty talks among the representatives of nations. However, many informal social exchanges can be conceptualized as bargaining. When children discuss which programs they want to watch on television, one may offer a time slot to the other in return for agreement that he can later watch his own favorite program.

While much can be learned about the exercise of power by looking at the decision criteria evaluated by a potential source, interaction with others is not usually a one-shot affair in which a single influence mode is directed from one party toward another. The first attempt at influence may not succeed and the target may react by using some form of counter-influence. The first attempt may be predictable from the source's characteristics or his relationship with the target. But as the interaction between two persons becomes more complicated and each tries to seek advantage through various tactics and counter-influence techniques, the dynamic nature of the relationship takes on the characteristics of bargaining.

The course of bargaining will depend to some degree on the structure of the situation. Communication between bargainers serves four major purposes: (1) a discovery function designed to secure information about the preferences and values of the other party; (2) attempts to disguise the communicator's own preferences and values; (3) a manipulative function involving the use of influence tactics to affect the opponent's behavior; and (4) attempts to alter the basic relationship between the bargainers, such as the degree of trust or attraction each invests in the other (Smith, 1968). We will first describe the structure of

bargaining situations and then examine each of the functions that communication plays in the bargaining process.

A. The Structure of Bargaining Situations

Deutsch and Krauss (1960) have succinctly described the essential features of a bargaining situation: "(1) Both parties perceive that there is the possibility of reaching an agreement in which each party would be better off, or no worse off, then if no agreement was reached. (2) Both parties perceive that there is more than one such agreement that could be reached. (3) Both parties perceive each other to have conflicting preferences or opposed interests with regard to the different agreements that might be reached" (p. 101). Bargaining behavior typically consists of tactics that each party uses to induce his opponent to make maximum concessions, while conceding as little as possible himself. Each party is usually motivated to achieve an agreement that maximizes his own gains or advantages.

Walton and McKersie (1965) have distinguished between two types of bargaining situations—distributive and integrative. In *distributive bargaining* anything gained by one party is lost by the other. For example, a buyer who comes up $2 in price "loses" that $2 to the seller. In *integrative bargaining* the parties, by working together, can increase the total product that can be divided between them. For example, two small businessmen might agree to merge their firms and share the increased profits of the larger organization.

Many bargaining situations have both distributive and integrative aspects. Consider a hypothetical situation involving a college faculty and the college administration. Suppose the negotiating team for the faculty made a concession on a salary increase in return for changes in administrative policies that would strengthen academic freedom on campus. The concession is a distributive issue since the faculty loses in income and the college gains funds to use for other purposes. Strengthening academic freedom would presumably improve the quality of education in the college, and this is an integrative issue since the result will benefit both the faculty and the administration. It benefits the administration because high quality colleges can usually attract more funds from agencies and alumni and charge higher tuition fees. The increased financial security of the college should make it possible to provide better salaries for the faculty in the future.

Most research in social psychology has focused on the type of pure distributive bargaining illustrated by a transaction on a used car lot (see Table 9.2). Suppose a salesman has an investment of $2000 in an automobile and, given his overhead and a minimal profit, he will not accept less than $2200 for the car. The minimum price the seller will accept is referred to as his *resistance point*. Suppose the potential buyer is enamored with this particular car and is secretly willing to spend as much as $3000 to buy it. The maximum the buyer is willing to spend constitutes his resistance point.

Neither the buyer nor the seller want the other to know his resistance point and each wants to locate the resistance point of the

other. If the seller is successful he will receive the maximum price the buyer is willing to pay ($3000); if the buyer is successful he will be able to purchase the car at the minimum price the seller will take ($2200). The distance between the two resistance points is referred to as the *bargaining range*. No bargain can be reached outside these limits. Of course the bargainers seldom know what the bargaining range is. Much of bargaining behavior is directed towards finding out what the resistance point of the opponent is.

Each bargainer attempts to reach an agreement as near the other's resistance point as possible. The value the bargainer realistically seeks is referred to as his *level of aspiration*. In the example given in Table 9.2, the buyer's level of aspiration is to obtain the car for $1800 and the seller's level of aspiration is to sell the car for $3000. Given the bargaining range, it is possible for the seller to gain his level of aspiration, but it is impossible for the buyer to achieve his. If no bargain is reached between parties, each leaves the interaction with the resources he had before bargaining began—*the status quo point*. The seller still has the car and the buyer still has his $3000.

Table 9.2 The Structure of a Bargaining Problem.[a]

Seller profit	Sales price of car	Buyer savings
1200	3400	−400
	Bargaining range	
800	3000	0
400	2600	400
0	2200	800
−400	1800	1200
−800	1400	1600

Seller's asking price = $3400
Seller's level of aspiration = $3000
Seller's resistance point = $2200
Buyer's initial bid = $1400
Buyer's level of aspiration = $1800
Buyer's resistance point = $3000
Status quo point = no agreement, The seller has the car, the buyer has $3000.

[a] After Tedeschi, Schlenker, & Bonoma, 1973, p. 127

The range of critical bargaining points for a particular actor, including the status quo point, resistance point, and level of aspiration, is referred to as his *utility schedule.* The process of distributive bargaining is characterized by the tactics employed by each party to discover the other's utility schedule.

B. Discovering the Adversary's Utility Schedule

The possession of information about the utility schedule of an adversary is commonly believed to provide an actor with a bargaining advantage. If the seller in our example knew the buyer was willing to spend $3000 on the car and the buyer did not know the seller's resistance point, the seller could set his price at $3000 and hold firm until the buyer agreed. To gain this advantage, each bargainer devotes much effort to gathering information about the status quo point, resistance point, and level of aspiration of the adversary. If both bargainers had complete information about each other's utility schedules, the bargaining process would take on a different character. The bargainers would no longer need to discover each other's utility schedule, and tactics meant to deceive the adversary about the actor's preferences would no longer serve a useful purpose.

Initial offers and the rate and kinds of concessions made are used as probes to gather information about an adversary's resistance point. The information gathered also has an important role in allowing an actor to set a realistic level of aspiration for himself. When the actor has prior knowledge of his adversary's resistance point, his level of aspiration will be set at the maximum he knows the adversary is willing to take. But when he has no information about the adversary's resistance point, his level of aspiration may be importantly affected by the kinds of offers he receives early in the bargaining process.

Liebert, Smith, Keiffer and Hill, (1968) suggested that most of the tactics involved

in bargaining are directed toward developing realistic levels of aspiration, which are based to some degree on the adversary's resistance point. In the absence of complete information, the bargaining range may be inferred from the adversary's initial bid and his subsequent concession rate. Liebert et al. placed subjects in the role of an automobile seller opposing a programmed confederate posing as another car dealer who wanted to buy an automobile. Each subject was told he could not accept less than $2,500 for the car; that is, his resistance point was set at $2,500. Half the subjects knew the buyer could pay as much as $3500, the other half did not know the buyer's resistance point. The buyer (confederate) opened the bidding with an initial offer that was favorable ($3050) or unfavorable ($2615) to the subject.

When the subjects had complete information about the buyer's resistance point, his initial bid had no effect on the final outcome. The subjects knew the bargaining range and could hold out for what they perceived as a fair contract. However, when they had no information about the buyer's resistance point, they made greater profits when the confederate started out with a favorable rather than an unfavorable bid. Apparently when a bargainer does not have complete information about his opponent's resistance point, he becomes dependent on his opponent's bids and concessions in selecting his own level of aspiration.

Schelling (1960) questioned the assumption that discovery of an adversary's utility schedule always provides an advantage to the informed bargainer. Knowledge of the bargaining range may cause a bargainer to temper his own demands according to what he knows to be a fair solution for both parties. The uninformed adversary cannot judge the fairness of the offers and hence perceives the concessions as a sign of weakness. Hence the informed bargainer finds himself at a bargaining disadvantage.

Harnett and Cummings (1968) examined the effects of asymmetrical information in a three-person bargaining situation. Two subjects acted as sellers (A and B) and one as a buyer (C). They were asked to reach a single agreement binding on all of them. Each bargainer had a different utility schedule; that is, each earned different amounts depending on the contract agreed upon. Seller A found himself in a conflict of interest with seller B and buyer C. In all conditions of the experiment seller A had complete information about the utility schedules of B and C. B and C were given either full or no information about A's schedule. When B and C knew A's utility schedule they yielded more concessions over the bargaining session than when they were ignorant of it. Thus, when a bargainer negotiated a single agreement with two opponents, he concluded a more profitable agreement with completely informed adversaries than with uninformed ones. The uninformed bargainers usually began with high initial bids, took longer to reach agreement, and gained more in their negotiations with A than did the informed bargainers.

The kinds of communication that were exchanged between bargainers were also very much affected by the amount of information each possessed. Two informed bargainers frequently resorted to threats, promises, and appeals to norms of fairness. However, an informed bargainer dealing with an uninformed adversary generally did not make such demands, but rather tried to use his information as a basis for encouraging his ignorant adversary to make a reasonable offer. Two competing, uninformed bargainers did not seek information, as if they were aware that such knowledge would weaken their position. The evidence suggests a surprising conclusion. An actor should not depend on competitive information as a means of increasing profit, and if he should acquire full information about his adversary's utility schedule, it might be wise to reveal his own utility schedule. However, it is more typical that neither bargainer has such information, and each devotes a great deal of effort

to conceal his preferences from his adversary.

C. Disguising One's Own Utility Schedule

A bargainer is aware that his offers, counter-offers, and concession rates may tacitly communicate his utility schedule to his adversary, and this awareness affects his behavior. Most subjects in bargaining experiments start out with high initial demands. They first "feel out" their opponent and then begin to scale down their demands to more realistic levels of aspiration. They often shift their levels of aspiration more than once as they acquire new information about their adversary. A bargainer who sets a high level of aspiration makes increasing demands and few concessions and frequently uses bluffs to create an image of "toughness."

Tough strategies have contradictory consequences for the bargaining process (Bartos, 1970). On the one hand, toughness decreases the chances of reaching agreement. On the other hand, if the tough strategy is successful, the bargainer will enhance his own outcome. A strong, unyielding bargainer presents his adversary with two negative choices: (a) make large concessions, thereby presenting himself as weak, or (b) drop out of bargaining, foregoing the chance of reaching any agreement and accepting the status quo point.

Tough bargaining strategies give rise to the *bargainer's dilemma*. Attempts to appear strong in order to gain a bargaining advantage interfere with a flexible strategy and lower the chances of reaching an agreement. But yielding encourages the opponent to take a tough bargaining stance. If both parties make concessions, agreement may be reached and both may achieve their objectives; if neither makes concessions, no agreement is possible. If one bargainer makes concessions and the other does not, then a bargaining solution will surely favor the tough bargainer. These relationships were found in a bargaining study reported by Bartos (1966). The fewer the concessions made by a bargainer, the less often an agreement was reached, but if a solution did occur, the bargainer who made the fewest and smallest concessions attained the greater profit.

Why not just be honest in bargaining? Cannot a bargainer make a genuinely "fair" offer, and then hold to his position? Komorita and Brenner (1968) found that this apparently reasonable strategy is not effective. They also reported what happened when a bargainer made regular, noncontingent, and consistent concessions; his adversary perceived him as weak and came to expect even more concessions. The adversary only needed to hold firm and wait for the bargain to sweeten. Consistent concessions have no effect on the size or rate of an adversary's concessions (Liebert, et al., 1968; Pruitt & Drews, 1969). When a bargainer makes irregular or unpredictable concessions, he is perceived as strong and tough and elicits concessions from his adversary (Chertkoff & Conley, 1967; Pruitt & Johnson, 1970).

A bargainer may attempt to create the impression that he has made his final concession by communicating his commitment to a particular offer. Schelling (1960) has characterized this strategy as follows: "In bargaining, the commitment is a device to leave the last clear chance to decide the outcome with the other party, in a manner that he fully appreciates; it is to relinquish further initiative, having rigged the incentives so that the other party must choose in one's favor" (p. 37). The bargainer who adopts such an inflexible posture must be careful not to commit himself to an untenable position. Making a commitment requires him to hold to his position whatever the consequences. An irrevocable position, if it is taken, should be made as close to the adversary's resistance point as possible. If the commitment is made outside the bargaining range, no agreement will be possible unless the commitment is withdrawn. The loss of credibility associated with failing to keep a commitment makes it difficult

for a bargainer to move back from an untenable posture.

Commitment can be illustrated in the context of the game of chicken. Shubik (1968) has described this adolescent game: "Consider two leather-jacketed California high school dropouts, each armed with a souped-up old car, driving toward each other on a superhighway, each with one pair of the wheels of his car on the line in the middle of the road. The first one to veer from the collision course is deemed to be "chicken" (presumably a derisive term) and loses the game. Of course, if neither veers, they crash and may both lose their lives but maintain their honor" (p. 85). Either of these adolescents may attempt to convince the other that under no conditions will he veer from the collision course. If this commitment is believed, then the only rational alternative left to the other person is to swerve and avoid the inevitable collision. Kahn (1965) suggests that a player might insist the game be played at night, show up drunk and wearing dark glasses, refrain from turning on the car lights, and when under way throw the steering wheel out the window. These tactics might communicate the irrationality of the actor, but in these conditions apparent irrationality is the most rational strategy to use if one wants to win (Schelling, 1966).

In a study of commitment and bargaining in the trucking game, Deutsch and Lewicki (1970) told subjects that if their trucks met head-on in the one-way lane, they would both lose money on that trial. A commitment device, which allowed a player to lock his truck in forward gear and head down the one-way lane, was given to both, only one, or neither of the players. A light on each player's panel informed him when his adversary had commited himself to an irrevocable course by turning on the "lock-in" device. Most subjects never used the commitment device, but when it was used *and* a crash did not occur, the person using the lock-in device increased his profits.

Time pressures sometimes have important effects on the course of bargaining. A union may commit itself to a strike if a new contract is not signed by a given date, or a star baseball player may hold out beyond the beginning of the regular season. When time limits exist, the actor must decide whether to maintain a tough bargaining posture and risk failure or to make one or more concessions and possibly be perceived as weak. Time pressures were found by Pruitt and Drews (1969) to lower levels of aspiration, lower demands, and reduce the frequency of bluffing during the first few minutes of bargaining. However, as the subjects became more involved in the bargaining task, they reverted to "normal" bargaining tactics and goals.

In summary, actors attempt to conceal or disguise their utility schedules from one another while establishing their own levels of aspiration. Tough bargaining strategies may be adopted, including the use of high initial demands, few concessions, and some form of commitment to an inflexible bargaining position. Such tactics increase an actor's outcome when agreement is reached, but when both parties employ them there is less chance of agreement. Early attempts to reach a "fair" agreement give the appearance of weakness and encourage an adversary to seek a solution more in his own favor. More lengthy and patient bargaining strategies which include irregular and contingent concessions are more likely to lead to agreements that are satisfactory to both parties.

D. Manipulating the Adversary's Bargaining Position

A number of influence strategies may be adopted in bargaining to gain advantage by manipulating an adversary's utility schedule. Three major influence tactics are used: (1) coercive power; (2) the employment of third-party mediators; and (3) the invocation of normative rules alleged to be relevant in the situation.

1. Coercive Power and Bargaining

Bargainers often threaten one another.

Representatives of management and labor may threaten lock-outs or strikes, or a child may threaten not to let his sister play with a toy if she won't accept a trade of television programs. Threats may be effective in bringing an adversary to agreement. Consider how threats affect a target's utility schedule. If he does not concede to the source's offer, he stands some chance of being punished; and if he is punished, he will be worse off than before the bargaining process started. Punishments lower the status quo point of the target. As a consequence, he should be more eager to reach agreement than before. Unless he can regain his losses through an agreement, he must leave the interaction with a net loss.

Subjects playing the trucking game employ coercion when given threat capability. Deutsch and Krauss (1960) provided gates that could be used to prevent access to the one-lane road to both players, only one player, or neither player. When neither player possessed gates, they achieved the highest joint profits of any of the three conditions; they evidently found it frequently possible to coordinate their interests. The subjects in both of the coercive power conditions suffered net losses. When both subjects possessed gates they lost more than pairs in which only one player possessed a gate.

Three conclusions were drawn from these results: (1) if either person in a dyad has a threat potential, it is better to be the person who has it; (2) if the other party already possesses threat capability, it is better not to have it; and (3) if neither party possesses threat capability, bargaining outcomes for the dyad are larger than otherwise. Apparently, if a person has threats, he will use them; and using threats produces counterthreats, hostility, and competition. Nevertheless, bargainers are not concerned about their *joint* payoffs; instead each is usually motivated to achieve the most he can for himself. A person who is willing to use threats may gain an advantage if his adversary relinquishes his opportunities to employ coercive power. When both bargainers use threats, the result is a conflict spiral that leaves both parties worse off than before bargaining began.

By failing to retaliate against a threat, an individual may leave the impression he is weak and compliant; thereby inviting further attacks. Even if a target is subjectively willing to accede to a powerful adversary's demands, he may still openly defy the threatener because of his fear that the threatener will only be encouraged to make even greater demands in the future. Appeasement consists of yielding to a threatener's demands to accept a change in the status quo. The role of appeasement in the development of World War II is described in Box 9.2

Resistance is not only a matter of momentary defense but may serve to deter future attempts at coercion. Though one cannot out-muscle a more powerful opponent, a target may threaten action of sufficient cost so that it is not worthwhile for his opponent to pursue his objectives by coercive means. Allowing a threat to go unchallenged also causes the target to lose self-esteem. We have already seen that subjects in the laboratory are willing to pay a price to save face. All of these considerations work against the success of coercion in bargaining situations.

When the size or intensity of conflict is sufficiently great, and an escalatory cycle of hostilities can be foreseen that provides no advantage for either side, one strategy for defusing the situation and limiting the areas of disagreement is to fractionate the issues (Fisher, 1964). Slicing up a big issue makes it possible to focus attention on each smaller issue, one at a time, or to trade off so one party gains an advantage on one issue and accepts a disadvantage on another. These "salami" tactics were instrumental in bringing about the current arms control negotiations in Geneva between the United States and the Soviet Union. In the history of such negotiations the Soviet Union has traditionally sought a comprehensive plan for total disarmament, while the United States has preferred to seek limited agreements. A series of limited treaties was negotiated, including a nuclear test ban treaty, a nonproliferation of nuclear weapons treaty, and an agreement not to place weapons in satellites. The Geneva talks have been concerned with limiting the acquisition of new weapons and restricting the deployment of operational weapons systems.

A disagreement may be arbitrarily defined as large or may be considered to be limited. For example, in 1962 Brazil expropriated a telephone company owned by an American firm. This action could have been defined as a serious breach of relations between the two countries, and some members of Congress suggested that U.S. economic aid to Brazil be cut off. President Kennedy chose to define the dispute as a limited one between the governor of a province in Brazil and an American corporation over how much compensation should be paid for the transfer of its ownership. In this way a potentially big issue was defined as a small one. Such tactics may backfire, however, if an adversary interprets them as a sign of appeasement.

2. Mediation

A mediator is a neutral third party whose function is to help the bargainers reach a fair and peaceful settlement. When bargaining has reached an impasse and neither party believes he can make further concessions, mediation may break the deadlock. An effective mediator may have a fourfold impact on the bargaining process: (1) he modifies the perceived meaning of concessions; (2) he causes both parties to shift their levels of aspiration; (3) he allows one or both parties to save face; and (4) he introduces norms of equity, fairness, and justice into the bargaining situation.

A concession made during mediation is not perceived as a sign of weakness or as an indication that future concessions can be expected. Podell and Knapp (1969) had subjects give their impressions of their bargaining opponent (a programmed confed-

Box 9.2   APPEASEMENT AND WAR

Historians tend to agree that the failure of his adversaries to resist Adolf Hitler's tactics of piecemeal conquest eventuated in a World War that no one really anticipated or wanted (Taylor, 1960). At the conclusion of the first World War Germany was forced to give up territory to France and Poland, and the Rhineland (adjacent to France) was made into a demilitarized zone. A series of small actions were taken by Hitler beginning in 1933. Germany withdrew from a European disarmament conference and, on 14 October, 1933 began to re-arm contrary to the existing agreements. Encouraged by Mussolini's successful invasion of Ethiopia and the failure of the League of Nations to act in the matter, Hitler's troops occupied the Rhineland on 7 March, 1936. Hitler had assured his nervous generals that he would withdraw at the first sign of French counteraction, but his belief that the French would do nothing was confirmed. On 13 March, 1938 Austria was annexed by Germany. The German-speaking portion of Czechoslovakia was obtained with the acquiescence of France and England in the Munich Pact, and then all of Czechoslovakia was occupied. Hitler presumably expected he could use the same piecemeal tactics in a war of nerves over Poland, which he finally invaded in September, 1939

At each point in this progression of events, France and England did their best to avoid war. The German demands did not sound so unreasonable. The people of the Saar region of the Rhineland held a plebiscite before the German reoccupation and in a genuinely democratic vote overwhelmingly expressed their desire to be joined to Germany. A similar expression of German nationalism was displayed in the Sudeten. Each step was a restoration of the lost territories of Germany and a unification of the German-speaking people of Europe. Hitler was encouraged to continue his tactics because he did not believe anyone would risk war to stop him.

Taylor's analysis suggests that Hitler did not expect England and France to intervene in Poland and that Germany was not prepared in 1939 for a major Europe-wide war. But England and France had given up so much that they had backed themselves into a corner. If they had discouraged Hitler at the very beginning and called his bluff, World War II might have been averted.

---

erate). When the opponent made concessions in the presence of a mediator who offered suggestions about a fair solution, the subjects rated their adversary as "less weak" than when exactly the same concessions were made in the absence of a mediator.

Not only are the perceptions of an opponent modified by the presence of a mediator, but so are the bargainer's self-perceptions regarding his own concessions. Pruitt and Johnson (1970) found that when bargaining occurred in the absence of a mediator, the subjects' perception of their own weakness was directly related to the size of their own concessions. However, when a mediator was present, the size of the individual's concessions was no longer related to perceptions of his own weakness. Bargainers generally want to avoid the appearance of weakness and this concern prevents them from making concessions during bargaining. When an impression of weakness can be avoided, it becomes easier for both parties to adopt a more flexible bargaining position. In the Pruitt and Johnson study, the subjects made more concessions when a mediator intervened than when he did not. These changes in bargainers' behavior in the presence of a mediator reflect adjustments in levels of aspiration because the emphasis is on a fair solution rather than on gaining maximum advantage.

Concessions made under the auspices of a mediator are perceived as a close approximation to the best solution of the bargaining problem. Since the mediator is an objective third party who has the information available to both sides in the dispute, the compromises he suggests are apt to be considered fair. Sometimes bargainers represent the interests of constituents who balk at making further concessions. In 1974 when Secretary of State Henry Kissinger shuttled between the capitals of the Middle East to find a settlement to the military turbulence in the area, he found Israeli demonstrators in the streets of Jerusalem who did not want their government to make concessions to the Arabs. Part of Kissinger's role as mediator was to make these concessions more palatable to Prime Minister Golda Meir's constituency.

3.   Norms

A mediator may appeal to standards of morality or to abstract concepts of justice as a basis for obviating the usual push-and-pull of selfish interests in a bargaining situation. Such social norms are rules that prevail in a group and govern what is acceptable conduct by members. Norms serve the interests of the group rather than the individual. The violation of normative standards often brings some form of punishment to the offender. Though the effectiveness of a norm may depend on the immediate social enforcement of conformity, its power ultimately depends on values internalized in individuals and the belief that the norms maintain and enhance those values. Homans (1961) states that "when we say that some people conform to a norm 'for its own sake' we mean that they are rewarded by the result that the norm itself, if obeyed, will bring" (p.116).

Equity norms refer to fair or just solutions to distribution or allocation problems, which constitute the core problems of bargaining. One interpretation of fairness is a *norm of equality*. As Pruitt (1972) has expressed it, such a norm proposes that "people should have equal basic rights, that they should begin a contest with equal resources, and that they should divide benefits equally" (p.144). Another rule of fairness is a *norm of equity*. The equity norm specifies that each individual should receive a share of the rewards based on the contribution he made toward acquiring the resources to be allocated (Adams, 1965).

The operation of norms on behavior is often implicit rather than produced by exhortation (the activation of commitment). People's understanding of what is fair is often a guide to their conduct. Morgan and Sawyer (1967) found that norms of fairness regulated the behavior of fifth and sixth grade boys. Pairs of boys faced each other across a bargaining board like the one shown in Figure 9.3. As can be seen, the boy on one side of the board possessed resources in the form of nickels. The pockets on the side containing nickels increased from none at one end of the board to six at the other end. For the second boy, the pockets contained from zero to six quarters but in exactly the reverse order.

Two boys were placed on either side of the bargaining board and were asked to come to an agreement consisting of the joint choice of a pair of directly opposite pockets. They made offers or counteroffers and engaged in discussion to arrive at

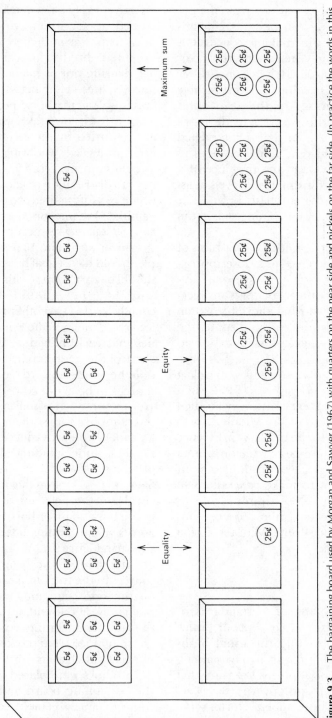

Figure 9.3. The bargaining board used by Morgan and Sawyer (1967) with quarters on the near side and nickels on the far side. (In practice the words in this figure do not appear on the board—only the coins themselves.)

an agreement. The boys were allowed to keep the money in the pocket associated with an agreement; one received nickels and the other quarters. If a bargain could not be struck, neither boy received anything. A further rule of play was that the boys could not make a side deal to split their winnings after the game was over.

What is a fair solution to this bargaining problem? Three possible outcomes could be considered most fair or reasonable under the circumstances. An argument could be made for making an agreement according to a norm of equality. The boys had been arbitrarily assigned their bargaining positions and both were of about the same age and experience. It would be reasonable to suggest a solution that would give each boy exactly the same amount of money: five nickels and one quarter respectively. An equity norm recognizes the fact that each boy has a different capability and suggests an outcome midway between the worst and best alternatives for each. According to the norm of equity one boy should accept three nickels and the other boy should accept three quarters. A third possibility is a *social welfare norm,* which would argue for an agreement that maximizes the amount involved in the bargaining solution, independent of the distribution of rewards to each player. Sometimes individuals may be asked to make sacrifices in order to maximize the outcome available to the group. The social welfare norm suggests an agreement in which one boy would receive the maximum outcome (6 quarters) and the other boy would receive nothing.

Actually, 18 of the 28 pairs of boys who participated in the Morgan and Sawyer study settled for 25 cents each (the equality solution). Of the ten other pairs, three settled for the social welfare outcome, one for the equity solution, and six compromised by making an agreement halfway between equity and equality. These agreements were not immediately obvious to the boys, as was indicated by the fact that they aver-

aged 17 offers and counteroffers and nine minutes to reach their agreements.

Competing norms or competing interpretations of the same norm make it difficult for bargainers to agree on what constitutes a fair solution. Considerable time in bargaining is often spent arguing about normative standards. Management may argue that their pay offer is proportional to the increase in production of the workers and hence their offer is fair. Labor may argue that profits for the corporation increased at a faster rate than productivity and hence pay increases should be tied to the rise in profits. Both sides argue for equity, but neither can agree about what is equitable.

Norms regulate the very process of bargaining, in addition to suggesting solutions. Robert's rules of parliamentary procedure may be adopted to facilitate communication and to ensure an orderly consideration of all issues. In formal bargaining situations, a concession must be carefully considered because once put forth it cannot be easily withdrawn. If offers could be used as deceitful tactics to elicit reciprocal concessions from an adversary and then quickly withdrawn, there would be little basis for continuing the bargaining process.

Rules also govern informal attempts to break deadlocks. Meetings over lunch or dinner may allow bargainers to explore alternatives that could not otherwise be discussed. In such informal meetings, each party may risk more open and specific overtures to find a compromise solution to their differences. If a proposal is made but spurned in an informal meeting, there is little danger of weakening the position of the formal negotiator since he can argue that he neither knew about nor authorized any such offers. The norms regulating informal meetings have been summarized by Pruitt (1971a): (1) what is discussed should be kept secret; (2) it is not necessary to hold to the rule about not withdrawing concessions; (3) statements about the flexibility of the bargainers' positions should be truthful; (4) each party should be willing to make a concession if the opponent does; and (5) agreements reached in informal meetings must be honored when the formal meetings reconvene.

Failure to live up to certain standards of conduct may disrupt the bargaining process and cause the contestants to distrust and dislike one another. Such negative relationships interfere with progress in bargaining. If the values at stake are sufficiently important, the bargainers may engage in tactics intended to improve their relationship. The building of trust and the development of more positive attraction make it easier to reach agreement.

E. Conciliation and Conflict Resolution

Solutions to bargaining problems will be facilitated when the bargainers are responsive to each other's needs and when they trust one another. Conflicts of interest often cause a deterioration of relationships between people. Recognition of the facilitating effects of liking and trust may lead an individual to build these positive relationships in the long-term interest of solving bargaining problems. Osgood (1962) has suggested a strategy called GRIT (*graduated reciprocation in tension reduction*) that is meant to produce gradual reduction in international tensions but that is equally applicable in interpersonal relations.

When individuals, groups, or nations are locked in intense conflict, many modes of influence lose their effectiveness and the likelihood of reliance on coercive power is increased. GRIT is a carefully announced strategy intended to promote a more positive atmosphere for bargaining. The GRIT strategy consists of a series of small, unilateral, conciliatory initiatives. Each intiative must be preceded by an announcement of the specific benevolent action to be performed. The strategist should not make his

unilateral gestures contingent on any act by the other party nor should he require reciprocation, although he invites it. In addition, deterrent power is resolutely used to discourage the adversary from perceiving the conciliatory gestures as signs of appeasement. Some examples of such initiatives are reported in Box 9.3.

Unilateral gestures may not be effective unless they are announced beforehand. Solomon (1960) had subjects play against a confederate in a Prisoner's Dilemma game without the possibility of communication. The confederate played either a 100 percent competitive strategy or a 100 percent cooperative strategy. The subjects were more competitive in their play against the unconditionally cooperative (pacifistic) confederate. Unilateral gestures that are not announced beforehand and do not require reciprocity merely invite exploitation.

In another study in which the requirements of GRIT were not fulfilled, Shure, Meeker, and Hansford (1965) had a confederate tell subjects he did not believe in shocking others and promised he would not shock them. In the context of the game he was playing with them, a promise not to use shocks constituted unilateral disarmament. Despite the fact that the confederate fulfilled his pledge, this form of pacifistic behavior did not prevent the subjects from engaging in competitive behavior, including the administration of shocks to the confederate. There are two reasons why the confederate's announcement and subsequent behavior did not fulfill the requirements of a GRIT strategy: (1) he announced an intention not to harm the subject, but did not promise to undertake any unilateral benevolent behavior; and (2) he permitted himself to be exploited. Unilateral initiatives should be taken while maintaining a firm stance with regard to any attempts by the adversary to exploit one's display of good will.

Gahagan (1969) had a confederate announce his unilateral cooperative intentions in a Prisoner's Dilemma game. As

Box 9.3   REAL-LIFE GRIT

Amitai Etzioni (1970) analyzed a series of foreign policy events occurring between June 10 and November 22, 1963. The sequence of events suggested the possibility that both the United States and the Soviet Union were deliberately implementing a GRIT strategy. Just a few months after the Cuban missile crisis, which almost erupted into World War III, President Kennedy made a "Strategy for Peace" speech at the American University on June 10, 1973. The speech was a public announcement of a sharp change in American foreign policy toward the Soviet Union—a prerequisite to any GRIT strategy. President Kennedy asked Americans to re-examine their attitudes toward the Cold War and toward the Soviet People. He warned against the self-fulfilling prophesy of believing war to be inevitable and advocated a reconstruction of foreign policy to make it in the Russian interest to agree to peaceful coexistence.

As a first unilateral initiative, Kennedy announced a cessation of all atmospheric nuclear tests; the resumption of testing was made contingent on subsequent tests made by the Soviet Union. The speech was enthusiastically received in the Soviet Union. It was published in *Izvestia* and *Pravda,* the Russian people lined up at newstands to buy papers, and the jamming of Voice of America broadcasts was stopped. A few days later Premier Khrushchev announced a halt in the production of strategic bombers—a reciprocation of Kennedy's first initiative.

Over the next few months a number of unilateral gestures were made by both sides. The Soviet Union removed its objections to having United Nations observers in Yemen; the United States removed its objection to restoring full member status to the Hungarian delegation at the U.N. The Soviet Union agreed to a communication link at Geneva, which had been proposed by the U.S. some months earlier; and both countries agreed not to conduct atmospheric tests of nuclear devices prior to signing a test ban treaty. President Kennedy, in a speech delivered before the U.N., proposed a cooperative venture with the Soviet Union in exploring space. The U.S. then announced the sale of 250 million dollars of wheat to the U.S.S.R. A formal pact, prohibiting the orbiting of nuclear bombs, was ratified. These initiatives manifestly lessened the hostility and reduced the tensions that existed between the two nations and laid the foundations for *detente.*

The initiatives fell somewhat short of Osgood's statement of the requirements of an effective GRIT strategy, since they were more psychological than real. The U.S. had so much data available from earlier nuclear tests in the atmosphere that it would take several years to fully analyse them. On the other side, the Russian strategic bombers were already scheduled to be phased out before Khruschev made his announcement. The pact to prohibit the orbiting of nuclear bombs came after tests had shown such weapons to be inferior to conventional air and missile systems. The wheat deal was not as large as it was first represented—only 65 million dollars worth was actually sold to the Soviet Union. Finally, there was a basic lack of communication on the part of the U.S. regarding coexistence, since all of the initiatives were justified to the domestic audience as tactics devised to produce an American advantage in the Cold War.

compared with subjects who received no communications, subjects who received promises cooperated more often. However, noncontingent promises apparently do not ameliorate conflicts between parties who are unequal in power. Tedeschi, Lindskold, Horai, and Gahagan (1969) placed subjects in strong, weak, or equal power roles with respect to a confederate in a Prisoner's Dilemma game. The confederate intermittently transmitted unilateral promises of cooperation and kept his word either 10, 50, or 90 percent of the time. The subjects in the powerful role ignored his initiatives and were least cooperative throughout the interaction. Weak subjects became more competitive as the credibility of the confederate's promises increased. Only in the equal power condition did the subjects show a conciliatory pattern of behavior, becoming more cooperative as the credibility of the confederate's promises in-

creased. As can be seen in Figure 9.4, these relationships are particularly clear when compared to control groups in which no messages were exchanged in the interactions.

Several implications flow from this examination of power relationships and the effectiveness of a GRIT strategy. Conciliation by a powerful party who has been consistently exploitative is likely to be exploited by the weak party; it is his chance to get even with the powerful party. An indication that restraint in the use of superior coercive power maximizes the effectiveness of conciliatory gestures comes from the Lindskold and Bennett study reported earlier (Ch. 8, III, E). Much more research is needed to gain further information about the circumstances, types of conflicts, and relationships between adversaries that may make a GRIT strategy effective in ameliorating conflict.

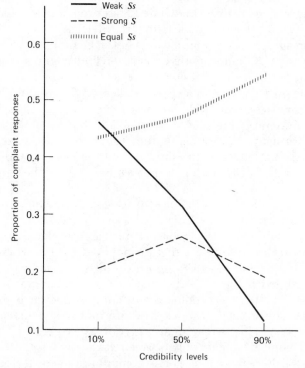

Figure 9.4. The cooperativeness of subjects in reaction to non-power than themselves (after Tedeschi, Lindskold, Horai, & Gahagan, 1969).

III. COALITION BEHAVIOR IN N-PERSON GROUPS

Conflicts between parties are not always restricted to two adversaries but may occur within larger groups. In groups of three or more persons (n-person groups), individuals may seek to form alliances or coalitions and use their combined strengths to gain their objectives. The factors determining how such alliances are formed and how persons within alliances solve their bargaining problems are the major issues addressed in the study of coalition behavior.

A *coalition* consists of two or more persons, groups, organizations or nations who band together to achieve their common objectives against the opposition of a competing party or parties. The minimum number of people involved in a coalition is two, but any larger number may be involved. Coalition behavior involves the formation of a group or subgroup whose intention is to employ mutual resources and skills to accomplish a common objective in a mixed-motive situation. The resources that can be pooled include material items such as money and votes and personal factors such as expertise, status, and special ability to influence other people. For example, a coalition may be formed by small manufacturers to obtain a contract from a large buyer. The coalition may be more effective if its membership includes individuals with enough money and material to fulfill a contract once it is obtained, an expert proficient at planning such deals, and possibly a trustworthy friend of the powerful buyer.

The rules adopted by groups about how to make decisions often encourage members to seek enough support to carry an issue within the group. Many groups adopt a majority rule that requires a minority to accept the decisions reached by vote of the membership. The decisions of a nine man Supreme Court, a legislative body, a board of trustees, and a student-faculty committee are usually made by a majority vote.

Even in authoritarian organizations, a number of vice-presidents may band together and sufficiently impress their powerful leader so he will agree to the coalition's recommendations. The study of coalition behavior involves understanding who joins with whom and for what reasons (Simmel, 1902).

Two basic theoretical approaches have been taken toward explaining coalition behavior. *Structural theories* focus on the material resources and abilities of the members of the group. For example, the distribution of money, power, and votes deliverable on election day plays a major role in predicting which coalition will form and how its members will allocate the outcomes they win. *Process theories* view coalition behavior in terms of decision-making processes and include consideration of the interpersonal relationships that exist within the precoalition group. The process of decision-making involves a calculation by each person about his potential gains or losses from choosing each possible coalition partner. The relationships between precoalition members of the group in terms of status, attraction, or trust are considered by process theorists to be important in the decision.

A. Structural Theories of Coalition Behavior

Three basic structural theories of coalition behavior have been proposed and evaluated by research. Caplow's (1956) *power theory* postulates that each member of a group will choose coalition partners in a manner calculated to maintain or enhance his power position. *Game theory* was proposed by Vinacke and Arkoff (1957) to fit the case where any coalition that forms in a group is certain to attain its objectives. In this case, coalition choices are assumed to be essentially random. Gamson's (1961, 1964) *minimum resource theory* considers each individual's choice of a partner as based on a calculation of how to obtain the most for himself in terms of the outcomes achieve-able through forming an alliance. First we will describe these three theories in more detail and then examine some of the evidence gathered to evaluate them.

1. Power Theory

Caplow's power theory is based on an analysis of the initial distribution of power among members of a group of three persons (a triad). Caplow sets forth his theory in the form of five basic postulates:

I. Members of a triad may differ in strength. A strong member can control a weaker member and will seek to do so.

II. Each member of the triad seeks control over the others. Control over two others is preferred to control over one other. Control over one other is preferred to control over none.

III. The strength of coalitions takes place in an existing triad, so there is a precoalition in each triad. Any attempt by a stronger member to coerce a weaker member in the precoalition condition will provoke the formation of a coalition to oppose the coercion (1956, p.490).

IV. The "chooser" in a triad seeks the max-

imum advantage or minimum disadvantage of strength relative to his coalition partner.

V. The "chooser" in a triad seeks to maximize the strength of the coalition in relation to the excluded members (1959, p.492).

When the amount of power possessed by members of a triad can be measured, power theory can predict which coalition will form. Different distributions of power in a triad and the predictions of power theory are shown in Table 9.3. Persons A, B, and C are assumed to possess measurable degrees of power, say in the form of money or votes. Each of the cases in Table 9.3 represents a different distribution of resources in the precoalition triad. Consider case number 5: A is more powerful than B, B is more powerful than C, but the combination of B and C in a coalition is more powerful than A by himself. In notation, this distribution of power is indicated as $A > B > C$ and $A < (B + C)$.

Caplow's analysis of case number 5 is based on the attempt by each person in the triad to form a coalition in a manner calculated to maximize his power. On a direct one-to-one basis, A is the most powerful

Table 9.3   Triad Types, Predictions From Various Theories, and Representative Results. [a]

Triad type	Coalitions predicted by Caplow	Coalitions predicted by game theory	Coalitions predicated by Gamson	Weights used by Vinacke-Arkoff	Results of Vinacke-Arkoff study (1957)
1. $A = B = C$	Any	Any	Any	1-1-1	Any
2. $A > B, B = C,$ $A < (B + C)$	BC	Any	BC	3-2-1	BC
3. $A < B, B = C$	AB or AC	Any	AB or AC	1-2-2	AB or AC
4. $A > (B + C),$ $B = C$	None	None	None	3-1-1	None
5. $A > B > C,$ $A < (B + C)$	BC or AC	Any	BC	4-3-2	BC
6. $A > B > C,$ $A > (B + C)$	None	None	None	4-2-1	None

[a] From Chertkoff, 1970.

person and has control over both other persons. C is the weakest member of the group and can enhance his power only by forming a coalition with either of the other two. It should be irrelevant to C whether he joins with A or B, since in either case he will be controlled by his coalition partner. Nevertheless, C should seek a coalition because if he succeeds, he gains power over the excluded group member. B can enhance his power only by gaining control over A and he can do so by forming a coalition with C. B can also maintain his power over C by forming a BC coalition. A should wish to form a coalition only as a precaution to prevent B and C from forming a coalition against him, but A should not care which partner he chooses. Whether A forms a coalition with B or C, he will maintain control over both the coalition partner and the excluded group member.

According to this analysis, A should be equally likely to choose B or C as a partner, C is similarly indifferent between A and B, while B clearly prefers a coalition with C. Naturally, no coalition can form unless a pair of persons reciprocate choices. If A chooses B, B chooses C, and C chooses A, no coalition will form. Caplow's power theory predicts that either coalition AC or BC will form because in both cases reciprocated choices are possible.

Chertkoff (1967) has refined power theory to take into account the probabilities of the choices of the three precoalition members. If in a case 5 triad, A and C are indifferent about a coalition partner and can choose between the other two, then the probability that each will choose one or the other as a coalition partner is 50 percent. Power theory suggests that B will always choose C as a coalition partner (100 percent probability). The exact probability that any particular coalition will form is a product of the probabilities of the reciprocal choices by members of the group. The probability of an AC coalition is the product of the probabilities that A and C will choose each other; hence this coalition should form 25 percent

of the time ($50\% \times 50\% = 25\%$). Given that B would never choose A as a partner, this coalition could never form ($0\% \times 50\% = 0\%$). The probability of a BC coalition forming is 50 percent; B will certainly choose C and C will reciprocate B's choice 50 percent of the time ($100\% \times 50\% = 50\%$). The probabilities of reciprocal choices are shown in Figure 9.5.

2. Game Theory

Caplow's power theory does not consider the bargaining process and the subsequent allocation of resources won by a coalition as important in predicting which coalition will form. But in many situations a fixed reward is at stake and any coalition that forms will automatically win it. A struggle may take place between three partners who control equal shares of a business and any coalition that forms will gain control. Members of the winning coalition will then need to bargain between themselves about how to distribute the power they share.

Vinacke and Arkoff (1957) believe the resources possessed by members of a precoalition group are irrelevant in the case where any coalition that forms is guaranteed to win. Their game theory analysis of case number 5 (Table 9.3), where $A > B > C$, $A < (B + C)$, illustrates the irrelevancy of power resources in making a coalition choice. Assume that the resource weights of the precoalition members are $A = 4$, $B = 3$, and $C = 2$. Any coalition that forms will win and hence each person in the alliance makes an equal contribution to winning. It does not matter whether B has resources of 3 and C has only 2; if they form a coalition, they will win, and the same is true of any other coalition that may form. The resource weights do not contribute to the possibility of winning. Each coalition member can claim an equal contribution since by agreeing to be a member he assures its victory. This theory of coalition behavior therefore predicts that each member of the precoalition group will be indifferent about

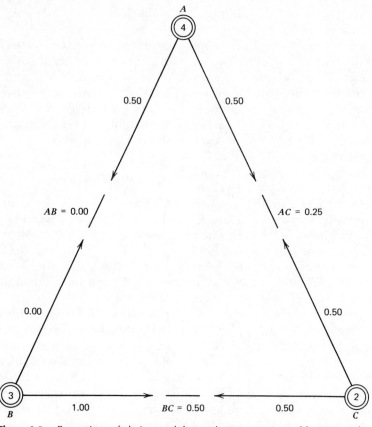

Figure 9.5. Proportions of choices and the resultant proportions of forming coalitions according to Chertkoff. (After Chertkoff, 1967, p. 175.)

his choice of a coalition partner and each member of a winning coalition should claim exactly half the winnings accrued by the coalition's efforts. Hence, every possible coalition is equally likely to form.

By applying Chertkoff's probability analysis to game theory predictions, the likelihood of each possible coalition can be determined. Every member of the precoalition triad has a 50 percent probability of choosing one of the other two members. The probability of reciprocal choices is therefore 25 percent (50% × 50% = 25%). It can be predicted that the *AB, BC,* and *AC* coalitions will each occur one-fourth of the time and that no coalition will form 25 percent of the time.

3. Minimum Resource Theory

The basic assumption of Gamson's minimum resource theory is that a "coali-

tion will form in which the total resources are as small as possible while still being sufficient to win" (1964, p.86). The members of a precoalition group consider both the contribution of their combined resources to the success of possible coalitions and the part their individual resources can play in later bargaining about how to share the coalition's winnings. Each group member is motivated to be in a winning coalition, but there may be a number of available coalitions he can join. Which one should he join? Gamson's answer is that each person will wish to be in a winning coalition in which his own resources entitle him to the largest possible share of winnings according to a norm of equity. He will use his relative resource weight as a basis for bargaining once the coalition attains its objectives and will therefore want to form a coalition with the weakest possible partner consistent with the objective of winning. As a consequence, the coalition with the minimum combined resources necessary for winning will form.

Consider a case 5 triad (Table 9.3) in which resources are distributed as follows: $A = 4, B = 3$, and $C = 2$. Miminum resource theory predicts a preference by A for C as a partner, although an AB coalition would also win. A's preference is based on his consideration of how winnings will be divided. According to the norm of equity, A can expect to be on the favorable end of a 4 to 2 split in an AC coalition, according to the ratio of the power weights of the two partners. A would receive only a 4 to 3 split in an AB coalition. It is clear that C cannot receive even half the winnings no matter which coalition he is in, but considering the applicability of an equity norm, C will prefer to be in a BC coalition. Here C will receive a 2 to 3 split, while in an AC coalition he will receive only a 2 to 4 split. Since both B and C will be better off in the BC coalition, they will always choose one another and A will always be excluded.

4. Empirical Evaluation of Structural Theories

The power, game, and minimum resource theories of coalition behavior have been investigated by rather simple research procedures. Vinacke and Arkoff (1957) employed the game of parchesi as a basis for studying the coalition process. On each play of the game, a single die is thrown and all the players simultaneously move their men the number of spaces shown on the die multiplied by a weight assigned to each person. The weights of the players (the multiplication factor) represent the power of the precoalition members. Players can form coalitions, and on the toss of a die, a coalition can move their men the number of spaces indicated by their added weights multiplied by the number thrown. Suppose the resource weights are $A = 4, B = 3$, and $C = 2$ and B and C form a coalition. If a 2 turns up on a toss of the die, A can move eight spaces

$(4 \times 2 = 8)$ and the BC coalition can move ten spaces $[(3 + 2) \times 2 = 10]$. The goal of the game is to be the first to reach the end point. The winner receives 100 points. If the winner is a coalition, the partners must bargain about how to divide their winnings.

In the Vinacke and Arkoff study the subjects drew a slip indicating their resource weights prior to the start of every third game of the 18 games played. Each person was assigned six different weights during the experiment. The weights distributed within the triads represented each of the six types shown in Table 9.3, where a summary of the results also appears (in the last column). Substantial support was found both for Caplow's power theory and for Gamson's minimum resource theory, though little encouragement was provided for game theory. In the only test of differential predictions by the power and minimum resource theories (the case 5 triad), the BC coalition predominated, supporting minimum resource theory. The finding that subjects actually do exclude the most powerful group member from coalitions gives rise to the paradox that "weakness is strength" and "strength is weakness," the so-called *power inversion effect* (Gamson, 1964). The presumably powerful A is continually excluded from winning coalitions and so continually loses, while the less powerful members form coalitions and share in the winnings. Sometimes the weakest person in a group is in a better position to reap rewards than is the strongest.

Kelley and Arrowood (1960) claimed that Vinacke and Arkoff created the illusion of the importance of resource weights by periodically changing the weights and thus calling undue attention to their apparent relevance to the solution of the experimental task. These critics conducted their own study and assigned to each subject in a triad a single weight that did not change. Only case 5 triads were created. The weights still had an effect on coalition behavior. The subjects perceived A to be the most powerful group member in the first few games played, excluded him from more coalitions, and allotted to him over half the winnings when he was included in a winning coalition. There was a decrease in the perception of A's power and in his exclusion from coalitions as the players gained experience. By the end of the experiment A was excluded from coalitions no more frequently than would be predicted on the basis of chance alone, hence providing some support for game theory. However, even after a considerable number of trials (up to 70 or more) there was still a significant tendency for subjects to perceive A as most powerful.

Vinacke, Crowell, Dien, and Young (1966) made a further attempt to cause subjects to ignore weights in making coalition choices. The subjects were specifically informed about the power and game theories of coalition behavior. They were told that some people viewed the weights assigned to players in a parchesi game as real bases of power and that other people viewed them as essentially meaningless when any coalition can win. The subjects were then assigned weights to form case 5 triads and played 24 games. BC coalitions formed most frequently. The subjects did not ignore the assigned weights in forming coalitions, and made their choices consistently with the predictions of minimum resource theory.

Komorita and Chertkoff (1973) view the bargaining process within coalitions in terms of the conflicting norms of equity and equality. It is in the interest of the more powerful party to argue for equity, since by so doing he will gain more for himself. Similarly, the weaker party can get more by arguing for an equal split of the winnings. If the coalition partners reach a compromise solution, they will adopt a *split-the-difference principle* (Schelling, 1960) and accept an agreement somewhere between the equity and equality solutions. In their reviews of the coalition literature Gamson (1964) and Chertkoff (1970) have noted that the allocation of winnings within coalitions typically follows these lines.

In an experiment illustrating the split-the-difference principle, Psathas and Stryker (1965) varied the resources assigned to players to form three precoalition distributions: 6-6-5, 6-6-3, and 6-6-1. The coalitions that were formed included one member of high power and one of low power, as would be predicted by both power and minimum resource theories. If the high power person were oriented toward an equity norm, he would claim less of the winnings the greater the power of his partner; i.e., he should claim less in a 6-5 coalition than in a 6-3 coalition and should claim most in a 6-1 coalition. On the other hand, if the low power member were oriented toward an equality norm, he would argue for an equal share of the winnings no matter what the power of his partner. The data clearly reflected the differences in norms applied by the powerful and weak members of coalitions. As the weight of the weak person increased, the counteroffers of a strong person for how the winnings should be shared became less demanding. The weights of the weaker persons had little effect on the offers they made during bargaining. Powerful people argue for equity in bargaining and weak people argue for equality.

Structural theories of coalition behavior apply to very simple situations. It is difficult to discern the similarity between a parchesi game played for points among strangers and cigar-smoking senators in a cloakroom working out a coalition to logroll a series of bills through a legislative committee. However, there is some suggestion from complex simulations of international relations and from historical observations that power resources are important in the formation of alliances among nations (see Box 9.4). But power considerations are not the whole answer to understanding coalition behavior. The friendships, abilities, and trust among persons in a precoalition group should have some bearing on which coalitions are likely to form. Seldom can a coalition be assured of winning merely because it has formed. The members of a group

Box 9.4 BALANCE OF POWER IN WORLD POLITICS

The balance of power refers to a particular configuration of alliances in the international system. Zinnes (1970) describes it as a configuration in which "the power of every unit in the system—state or alliance of states——is less than the combined power of all the remaining units in the system. Thus, a balance of power is a system in which no single state and no alliance of states has an overwhelming or preponderant amount of power with respect to the rest of the system" (p. 253). A state of balance is associated with world peace. From World War II until the 1960s the world took on a bipolar structure. Two great alliances existed, with the United States and the Soviet Union serving as the bases of the two coalitions. The motivation of Western European countries was fear of Soviet penetration so they formed an alliance with the United States as the protecting nuclear power. A similar alliance was formed on the other side of the Iron Curtain.

As France, England, and China have developed their own nuclear weapons they have become less dependent for protection on other nations. Brody (1963) hypothesized that the spread of nuclear weapons to nth countries would have the effect of breaking down alliances. In an international simulation, he had teams of subjects play the roles of the decision makers of fictitious nations. The subjects were provided with a history of their fictitious world, were given details of their economic and military power, and were then allowed to conduct relations with the other nations. They could trade, give aid, have international conferences, make treaties, form alliances or declare war on one another.

At the start of the simulation the world structure (among five nations) was bipolar; there was one nuclear power in each alliance. Brody then introduced nuclear capability first to one additional country and then to another. The data confirmed that after the experimentally induced spread of nuclear capability, intrabloc cohesion was reduced, perceptions of external threat were reduced, and significant changes in communication patterns took place. Communication between members of different blocs increased. In the binuclear system most of the communication was directed to the economic and military leader of the alliance, but in the n-nuclear system the less developed nations were as likely to direct their communications to a member of the other alliance.

The effects of resource bases on the fragmentation of alliances in a balance of power system is probably not this simple, but the remarkable resemblance of what has happened to world wide alliances to Brody's experimental findings suggests that a great deal can be learned in the laboratory about complex coalition processes.

must weigh the probabilities and values to be gained or lost through forming coalitions before entering them. The relationships among members of a precoalition group and the criteria used in choosing coalition partners are the major factors considered by process theories of coalition behavior.

B. Process Theories of Coalition Behavior

Structural theories of coalition behavior tend to ignore the relationships (aside from power) that exist among persons. Status differences, cliques of friends, animosities, and the distribution of expertise among group members are also important in the process of coalition formation. Joining a coalition against a superior may cost a subordinate his job, and excluding a friend from an alliance may break up the friendship. The concentration by structural theorists on the distribution of power in a group shifts attention away from the decision making criteria used by individuals in deciding whether they should form coalitions, and if so, who should be chosen as partners. An individual must decide what values he can gain by forming a coalition, what he can lose should it fail in its purposes, and the probability of success or failure. Process theories focus on the relationships among precoalition members and the criteria used in making coalition choices.

1. Relationships Among Precoalition Members

Anderson (1967) has presented a theory of coalition behavior that emphasizes the role of status in the formation of alliances. The inclusion of a high status person should contribute to the probability of success of a coalition. His authority and control over resources yields more influence for the partnership, and he can be expected to obtain deference from other group members, so his association with the coalition may

is also possible that he may retaliate against any group excluding him, thereby increasing the costs to "revolutionary" coalitions.

On the negative side of the ledger, a high status person may place a high value on his contribution and may therefore ask for a large share of the winnings. His adoption of an equity principle would decrease the rewards obtainable by other members of his coalition. A low status person may decide to form or join a coalition with a high status member only if the advantages of including him are believed to outweigh the disadvantages.

One step in deciding whether to join or oppose a high status person is to sound out the positions taken by other group members. The degree of disaffection of other low status persons was found by Michener and Lyons (1972) to be a critical determinant in the formation of revolutionary coalitions. The formation of a coalition against a person of high authority depended on the perception by low status persons of the degree of support given to the authority by the group. When group dissatisfaction was great, revolutionary coalitions frequently formed.

The inclusion of a particular person in a coalition may be considered desirable because he possesses special skills in planning goal-oriented activities, in attracting other members, or in solving group problems. If it can be foreseen that a coalition is likely to incur legal problems, the inclusion of a lawyer would be wise. An expert may contribute to the success of the coalition, but it can be expected that he will argue for equity in dividing the rewards obtained by the alliance. The expert produces an advantage by increasing a coalition's chances of success, but constitutes a disadvantage because his presence reduces the amount the other members can gain.

Hoffman, Festinger, and Lawrence (1954) investigated the impact of expertise on the coalition process. In one condition subjects were formed into groups and led to believe that one person in each group had a much higher intelligence than the others. In a second condition the subjects believed that all the members of each group were about equal in intelligence. The subjects could form partnerships in solving a task and were to be given rewards for success. In the first condition, more high I.Q. persons were included in coalitions than could be expected by chance. Furthermore, the member said to have the higher intelligence received a greater share of the winnings than his partner. The subjects were apparently willing to accept less reward in order to form a coalition with an expert person and thus assure their own success. It is better to win a little of something than to have an equal share of nothing.

Reciprocal choices must be made if a coalition is to form. A person may consider it more probable that a friend will reciprocate his choice than a nonfriend or an enemy. Also, a friend is apt to be an equal in status and expertise and may be expected to ask for no more than an equal share of the rewards earned. Helm, Nacci, and Tedeschi (1974) found attraction to be an important factor in coalition choices. Subjects were asked to read a description of the parchesi game in which players had weights of 4-4-2. They were then asked to take the role of the weak player and to indicate which of the other two parties, if any, would be chosen as a coalition partner. The subjects were given a choice between an attractive individual and a rather neutral person. The liked person was chosen more often as the desired partner and an equality solution to the bargaining problem was expected.

In a longstanding group, like a state legislature or a family, a person who frequently changes coalition partners may be viewed as someone who cannot be depended on. His loyalties seem to shift with the winds of immediate advantage. Lieberman (1964) has called attention to the development of *interest trust* between coalition partners. Interest trust reflects the reliability of an individual in sticking with a particular partner once a stable coalition has formed. Lack of interest trust would be a reason for excluding a person from a coalition. In order to earn the interest trust of others, one should be willing to sacrifice some small amount of immediate gain that might result from betraying his partner and joining another coalition. Lieberman (1962) has found some empirical support for this theory.

2. Precoalition Decisionmaking

Coalitions do not always gain their objectives. Mother and daughter may not be able to convince Dad to change their vacation plans, and a group of senators may not secure a majority vote for their legislation. Members of a precoalition group must therefore make decisions about their choice of a partner under conditions of uncertainty. Suppose the players take turns throwing the dice and moving their men in a Parchesi game. A lucky player who throws large numbers could defeat a coalition of two players who throw small ones. Ordinarily the amount of combined resources of coalition members is directly related to the probability of winning.

Gamson (1964) suggests that each player in a coalition game will choose a partner based on his expected value, which is calculated by multiplying the probability that a coalition will win by the amount that can be won. Suppose the probabilities of winning for various coalitions were: $AB = .8$, $AC = .6$, and $BC = .4$. Also assume that 100 dollars can be won and that the players have agreed to share on the basis of equity. The expected value of an AB coalition is the probability of its winning times the amount to be won or $80. The expected values of the AC and BC coalitions are $60 and $40, respectively. After determining the expected value of coalition with A, and A will prefer a coalition how much of the winnings he would get. In the AC coalition, A could expect to gain a 4 to 2 split (based on his weight) if he wins; hence the expected gain for player A in an

AC coalition would be $40 and the expected gain for *C* would be $20. Given that each player attempts to maximize his expected gains, both *B* and *C* will prefer to form a coalition with *A* and *A* will prefer a coalition with *B*. Therefore, the *AB* coalition will form most frequently. This prediction is contrary to power, game, and minimum resource theories for a case 5 triad (Table 9.3).

The expected value theory of coalition behavior was tested by Chertkoff (1966). He simulated a presidential nominating convention and divided delegate votes among three subjects on a 40-30-20 basis. Any coalition that formed had enough votes to nominate one of its members. However, before a coalition could form the potential partners were required to agree on how to divide the 100 jobs that would become available should the nominee win the presidency in a general election. The probability of a nominee winning the election was manipulated. In one group the nominee would automatically win the election (1.0 probability); in a second group, the subjects were informed that any nominee would have a 50 percent chance of winning. In the two remaining conditions *B* and *C* both had a 50 percent chance of winning the election if nominated, while *A* had either a 70 or a 90 percent chance. The outcome of the election (except in the automatic win condition) was determined by having the nominee draw a slip of paper from a box containing "win" and "lose" slips. The proportion of win and lose slips matched the candidate's probability of winning.

The total amount that could be won was 100 jobs and was constant across all conditions of the experiment. The decision about who to choose as a nominee therefore depended wholly on the probability of his winning the general election. Across three conditions of the study, player *A* could contribute to winning with a 50, 70, or 90 percent probability. The greater the probability that *A* would win the election, the grea-

ter the expected value of any coalition that included him and the more often he was actually chosen by *B* and *C*. When any player nominated could automatically win the election and probability of success was not a factor, the weakest players tended to form coalitions against the stronger player—a power inversion effect. Thus, under conditions of uncertainty the predictions of decision theory were supported, but under conditions of certainty the results were consistent with both power and minimum resource theories.

More complicated mathematical and computer models of coalition behavior are in various stages of development and evaluation (Friend, 1973; Komorita & Chertkoff, 1973; Ofshe & Ofshe, 1970; Tedeschi, Schlenker, & Bonoma, 1973). Each of these new models attempts to build on the expected value theory first proposed by Gamson (1964). The application of decision theory to coalition behavior looks very promising. Not the least important aspect of these new developments is the movement toward more enriched experimental paradigms for studying coalition processes. It must be admitted that the parchesi game and the political convention hardly reflect the subtleties and complications of an alliance system such as might occur between Southern Democrats and Northern Republicans in the Senate of the United States. To capture the complexities of coalition behavior as it occurs in everyday life will tax the ingenuity of social scientists for the foreseeable future.

IV. CHAPTER SUMMARY

In this chapter we have moved from simple one-way influence attempts by a single source to the more complex and dynamic processes of bargaining and coalition formation. A source's choice of target and mode of influence is determined by a complex set of factors. A source will direct an influence attempt to a target when the expected gains for doing so are greater than can be obtained by any alternative action. The mode of influence chosen will depend on the probable costs involved and the probability that the mode chosen will gain compliance from the target. In general, more influence will be attempted when: (1) the value of the rewards to be gained through influence increases; (2) the probability of success increases; (3) the amount of costs is small; and (4) the probability of incurring costs is low.

Self-confident people more often seek influence than people who lack self-confidence. The possession of great resources, status, and expertise builds an individual's self-confidence and encourages him to attempt influence frequently. The basis of an individual's power affects the mode of influence he is likely to use. A high status person generally chooses a subordinate as a target and prefers manipulatory tactics, such as the use of social reinforcements. An expert typically relies on persuasion and chooses targets who are informationally dependent. A person who possesses great resource capability prefers reinforcement control tactics. Finally, interpersonal attraction builds trust and facilitates implicit positive reciprocity and discourages the use of coercive power.

Intense conflict encourages the contesting parties to use threats and punishments because under such circumstances the effectiveness of persuasion and promises is undermined by hostility and distrust. A person who feels powerless, is low in status, and lacks expertise and self-confidence, is prone to use coercion, particularly when he desires to share the commodities available to other members of his group and cannot do so in any other way. Coercion is also apt to be used when a source wants to gain compliance quickly and when his time perspective is narrowed to the present moment.

A bargaining situation is defined as one in which two or more persons who are in disagreement over one or more issues at-

tempt to arrive at a mutually acceptable agreement. In lieu of the development of more sophisticated theory, the empirical literature has focused on the processes and goals of bargaining. Four major goals include: (1) discovering the opponent's utility schedule; (2) disguising one's own utility schedule; (3) manipulating the opponent's utility schedule; and (4) altering the relationship patterns between the contending parties.

A bargainer seeks to discover his opponent's resistance point through offers and counteroffers. In an attempt to disguise his own utility schedule, a bargainer's initial offers are typically greatly inflated. Scaling down his demands through a series of concessions is often inhibited by a fear of appearing weak and the consequent encouragement of the opponent to seek exploitative advantage. Paradoxically, an attempt to appear tough often backfires by placing a bargainer in an inflexible position and reduces the chances of reaching a settlement; but, if the tough strategy works, the bargainer will gain an agreement that is strongly in his own favor. Despite the advantages in discovering an opponent's utility schedule, it is again paradoxical that possessing such knowledge is sometimes disadvantageous to the holder. Evidence indicates that the knowledge holder will seek a fair solution since he knows what is fair and equitable, but the ignorant party may merely see such "fair" offers as a sign that his opponent is weak and thus may seek exploitative advantage.

Bargainers may seek to influence one another by the use of threats, the activation of norms, or mediation. If a bargainer has the ability to threaten his opponent he will be tempted to do so, but the result often is retaliation and the escalation of conflict, with the result that both parties are worse off. But if one party has more power than the other, the stronger may gain a bargaining advantage. Norms govern the very process of bargaining, and may be invoked as a basis for agreement. Norms of equity and equality are often in conflict and the basis for determining equity is often subject to disagreement. Powerful bargainers are apt to argue for a norm of equity, while weak bargainers most often support an equality norm. Mediators often help bargainers to save face in making concessions. Because of the full information a mediator has, he can more legitimately invoke norms of fairness in a particular bargaining situation. An indirect strategy for resolving conflicts is to build trust through unilateral initiatives, in tandem with a firm position that rebuffs exploitative initiatives by the other party. Similarly, informal, friendly relationships and high status can facilitate a solution to bargaining conflicts.

Structural theories of coalition formation focus on the distribution of power and resources in a precoalition group. Power theory views the choice of a coalition partner as based on an attempt by each individual to maintain or enhance his power position in the group. Game theory applies to situations in which any coalition that forms is certain of winning; this makes the initial distribution of power in the group irrelevant and the choice of a partner is essentially random. Minimum resource theory assumes that individuals will want to maximize their winnings by forming partnerships that have the minimum resources necessary to assure success. In this way each person can minimize the demands made by his partner during bargaining. Power theory ignores bargaining, game theory assumes an equality norm, and minimum resource theory assumes that coalition partners will agree to either an equity norm or a split-the-difference principle.

Process theories of coalition formation have concentrated on the relative degrees of status, expertise, and attraction among members of a precoalition group. Not enough research has been done to give us a very clear understanding of how these characteristics affect coalition behavior under varying circumstances. Decision theory takes the risks of coalition choices into account, as well as the costs and gains associated with choosing among alternative alliances. There has been no attempt to combine the effects of resources, interpersonal relationships, and decision criteria into a single overall theory of coalition behavior.

The available evidence shows support for all theories of coalition behavior and it may well be that they are complementary rather than contradictory. Given the right set of conditions, the predictions of each of the theories can be confirmed. This is an unsatisfactory state of affairs because social scientists would like to develop a single theory to organize all the available data and help us understand coalition behavior under more complex circumstances. The importance of this task is underscored by Simmel's (1902) observation that the formation of coalitions is a fundamental aspect of human social behavior.

SUGGESTED READINGS

Daniels, D. N., Gilula, M. F., and Ochberg, F. M.(Eds.), *Violence and the struggle for existence.* Boston: Little, Brown, 1970. A series of thoughtful papers by members of the Department of Psychiatry at Stanford University concerning the causes of human violence.

Groennings, D., Kelley, E. W., and Leiserson, M. (Eds.), *The study of coalition behavior.* New York: Holt, Rinehart & Winston, 1970. A set of papers summarizing the various theories of coalition formation and presenting historical and contemporary analyses of the effects of alliances on the political process.

Tedeschi, J. T., Schlenker, B. R., and Bonoma, T. V. *Conflict, power, and games.* Chicago: Aldine, 1973. An integrated presentation of many of the topics presented in Chapters 8 and 9 of this textbook, including experimental games, the responses to and exercise of various types of influence, bargaining, and coalition formation.

Walton, R. E. *Interpersonal peacemaking: Confrontations and third-party consultation.* Reading, Massachusetts: Addison-Wesley, 1969. A discussion of the role of the mediator and arbitrator in settling disputes concerning business organizations.

Walton, R. E., and McKersie, R. B. *A behavioral theory of labor negotiations.* New York: McGraw-Hill, 1965. A very readable and thorough analysis of bargaining.

PART 4

Positive and Negative Social Interactions

Kindness and cruelty, generosity and selfishness, love and hatred are labels that apply to various positive and negative kinds of interpersonal behavior. Observations of such behavior leave us with many unanswered and perplexing questions. Why, for example, do people risk their own lives to help total strangers? Have you ever personally struggled with the question of how to define love or why certain people form friendships? Of particular complexity is the study of aggression, which has been a subject for all the life sciences from biology to political science. The next three chapters will be devoted to what social psychologists have learned about altruism, loving, and aggression.

Chapter 10 examines prosocial (as distinguished from antisocial) behavior. Explanations of this positive form of behavior suggest that it is caused by obligations stipulated by social norms, by learning, and by such internal states as feelings of well-being, sympathy, empathy, and guilt. Emergency situations in which victims are physically endangered present passersby with opportunities to help—sometimes at great personal risk. We will examine what causes a passerby to intervene or to avoid responsibility in emergency situations.

Chapter 11 focuses on positive sentiments toward others that are referred to as attraction, liking, or love. Social psychologists have intensively investigated the antecedents of liking between persons. These include providing rewards, positive feeling states, positive expectations regarding future behavior, attitude and value similarity, a tendency toward cognitive balance, complementarity of needs, and physical attractiveness. People like to be liked by others because attraction serves as a power resource in obtaining outcomes that are controlled or mediated by others and provides a basis for effectiveness in influencing others.

The complement of love is hatred, and hatred leads to negative interaction. Man has demonstrated an immense capacity for cruelty throughout his history. Why do men kill, maim, and otherwise harm their fellows? To some extent we addressed this question in Chapter 9 when the use of coercion was examined. Here we will focus on those theories, approaches, and questions that have been typically associated with the study of aggression. Three basic approaches to the problem have been taken. The biological approach explores genetic, neurological, and biochemical bases for harm-doing behavior. A learning perspective assumes that men acquire or inhibit harm-doing responses just as they do any other behavior—according to their prior reinforcement history and through observing models. A social psychological approach interprets harm-doing as coercive power that can be used offensively or defensively against others. We will critically evaluate these approaches in Chapter 12. In addition, we will examine controversy concerning the question whether violence portrayed on television is causally related to the harm-doing of viewers. Finally, the conditions under which a person is labeled by observers as aggressive and the consequences of such labeling for the actor will be described.

In the three chapters of Part 4 we maintain the view that the actions taken by an individual are governed by his concern for being effective in interpersonal relationships. A basic concern of each person is to acquire those physical and social resources that make him successful in influencing others. Topics such as prosocial behavior, attraction, and aggression are value-laden. What is good or bad, altruistic or selfish, defensive or offensive, pacifistic or violent is often in the eye of the beholder and not an objective characteristic of the events described. At times we are quite critical of much of the theory and research dealing with these topics. Although we try to adopt a neutral moral stance with respect to these kinds of social behavior, our preferences are, naturally and normatively enough, in favor of prosocial behavior and love and against coercive behavior and hatred.

CHAPTER 10

Prosocial Behavior

CHAPTER PREVIEW

Prosocial behavior consists of actions that provide benefits to another person and do not appear to be motivated by the benefactor's desire to obtain immediate reinforcements for himself. The range of actions identifiable as prosocial is immense. Seldom does a day go by when we do not observe or perform a prosocial act. A blind man is helped across the street, a student helps a buddy with his homework, automobile drivers pick up hitchhikers, a donation is made to charity, blood is contributed to the Red Cross, and so on. Every individual has many opportunities to play the part of the good Samaritan.

If prosocial behavior is not directed toward immediate reinforcement, why do people ever assume the cost of helping others? Recent research has established that a number of cultural, social and personality factors are involved. The demands of cultural norms, the past learning or present internal states of the potential benefactor, his interpretation of the immediate situation, the presence of other people, and the characteristics of the person to be helped, have all been shown to facilitate or inhibit prosocial behavior. Most of the present chapter will be concerned with these determinants. A final section will consider the factors that lead observers to perceive and label prosocial behavior as altruistic. As we will see, not all prosocial behavior is considered in this light.

I. NORMS GOVERNING PROSOCIAL ACTS

In our society there are standards of conduct that serve to insure that people in need of help receive it. People are seldom now allowed to starve to death simply because they do not have the means to feed themselves. Victims of accidents and natural disasters are not left to die but are provided with help by those who are in a position to do so.

Societies differ in the amount of self-sacrifice demanded of the individual in behalf of the larger group. According to Parsons (1951), societies emphasize either an individualistic or a collectivistic orientation, although these general orientations—reflecting the competing concerns of self-fulfillment and social responsibility—exist to some extent in all societies. The United States may be said to have an individualistic orientation, but strong religious and humanistic traditions nevertheless exist that condemn the selfishness of King Midas and Scrooge. Admiration is expressed for people (legendary or real) who relinquish concern for worldly goods to devote their lives to the welfare of their fellow men. But cultural ideals may not affect our expectations about how ordinary men should behave and may differ from the social norms that govern everyday behavior. Theologians, moralists, and ethical philosophers may be concerned with how men *ought* to act, but social psychologists are interested in discovering what determines how men *do* act.

Three prominent social norms have been associated with prosocial behavior: reciprocity, social responsibility, and equity. The *positivive norm of reciprocity* stipulates that an individual should help those who help him (Gouldner, 1960). A student may help a peer with his homework to repay a past obligation rather than to obtain new reinforcements. The *norm of social responsibility* includes the ideals of the Good Samaritan, my brother's keeper, humanitarianism, and noblesse oblige. According to this norm, people who are powerful, wealthy, skillful, or have a special ability to help needy others should do so. The Hippocratic Oath of physicians expresses their special responsibility to preserve the lives of all men—whatever the cause of the health problem, whoever the patient may be, and irrespective of his ability to pay for the help received. The *norm of equity,* as we saw in Chapter 9, is a rule for distributing rewards fairly in a group. This norm may require that an individual who receives an unjustly large share of rewards give up part of them to those who received unjustly small rewards. The conditions under which these three norms facilitate prosocial behavior have been systematically studied.

A. The Positive Norm of Reciprocity

The norm of reciprocity may be universal. In every society a person has the duty of repaying favors done for him. An expectation that favors will be repaid encourages an individual to engage in prosocial behavior since it is in his own longrun interest. This norm fosters cooperative relationships and hence helps to create stable social organization.

The obligation to repay favors raises the question of how much to repay. In general, the norm says, a person should reciprocate enough to establish an equivalence of values in the exchange. However, Gouldner (1960) has pointed to a number of factors that affect the value of benefits received and, consequently, the degree of obligation incurred. The value of a benefit varies with: (1) the intensity of the recipient's need at the time the benefit was bestowed; (2) the resources of the donor; (3) the motives imputed to the donor; and (4) the nature of the constraints in the situation, such as status differences between the two parties. We will examine research bearing on each of these factors after first considering the function of the norm itself in social organization.

1. The Social Organization Function

The anthropologist, Westermarck, stated: "to requite a benefit, or to be grateful to him who bestows it, is probably everywhere, at least under certain circumstances, regarded as a duty" (1906, vol. 2, p.154). A similar principle can be found in the moral teachings of many if not all societies. For example, in Norse mythology (Clarke,

1923) it is said: "That friendship lasts longest—if there is a chance of its being a success—in which friends both give and receive gifts. . . . A man ought to be a friend to his friend and repay gift with gift. . . . Gifts ought to be repaid in like coin. . . . A gift always looks for recompense" (pp. 41–48 and 145).

The French anthropologist Mauss (1967) examined the functions of giftgiving. People are ordinarily constrained to accept gifts offered by others, except when specific norms prohibit such exchanges. A refusal of a gift implies the refusal of friendship, and receiving a gift implies an obligation to reciprocate. Studies of primitive societies suggest that people initiate gift-giving as a sign of friendship and as a means of forstalling hostile interaction with strangers. The customs of hospitality and cordiality to strangers serve these purposes. Gift-giving activities are therefore designed, not necessarily consciously, to place the recipient in a position of debt to the benefactor. Giving a gift implies trust and constitutes a form of credit, a basic feature of modern economies. Thus, "men could pledge their honour long before they could sign their names" (Mauss, 1967, p.36).

Providing alms and making sacrifices to the gods were informal contracts that early men initiated because "gods who give and repay are there to give something great in exchange for something small" (Mauss, 1967, p.15). How men behave depends on their conception of the universe. People may engage in prosocial behavior to avoid sin and to please Providence; much prosocial behavior is related to an individual's belief that his good work will give him entry into heaven or allow him to avoid the pain of the Inferno. A failure to exercise the responsibility of helping others may be considered a sin. According to Dante, the hottest places in Hell are reserved for those who, in a period of moral crisis, maintain their neutrality. Anticipated reciprocity from religious entities may account for many acts of martyrdom. Japanese

Kamakazi pilots could commit suicide by diving their planes into American warships during World War II because they believed they would be rewarded in heaven. It was an honor to die for the Emperor, who was believed to be the son of God.

Mauss' analysis suggests that a failure to repay courtesies, invitations, and gifts is demeaning to the man who accepts them, particularly when he accepts such benefits without intending to reciprocate. "Charity wounds him who receives, and our whole moral effort is directed towards suppressing the unconscious harmful patronage of the rich almoner" (p.63). Welfare demeans those who are forced to accept it if they have no way of repaying the debt. To maintain positive social relationships, the debtor should repay his benefactor more than he received, thereby placing the original donor in the position of debtor and providing a basis for continuing their social relationship. A person will not often sever a relationship with someone who owes him a debt, nor will the debtor ordinarily want to terminate the relationship until the debt is paid. The reciprocity norm therefore serves to bind men to one another in continuing social groups.

In hunting and food gathering societies mutual cooperation and the sharing of food is obligatory (Cohen, 1972). However, there is continual conflict among the hunters over who should gain credit for the kill. The argument is not about who acquires the food but rather over the right to give it away and gain the status that is associated with giving. Strict rules have been developed to determine who the owner of the dead animal is (Dowling, 1970). When a single individual contributes more to his group than can be repaid, he is often given status or authority in recompense for his help. The struggle over power may be manifested by competition over who can contribute most to his group.

In agricultural and industrial societies certain persons acquire crops, herds, and machinery. As a consequence of disparities in accumulated wealth, unequal oppor-tunities for giving are provided and unequal status and prestige emerge. For example, Cohen (1972) has noted that in northern Nigeria political leaders and wealthy men validate their status by giving more than others at tribal ceremonies. Ordinary people engage in reciprocal giving; they give to those who can be expected to repay and in amounts that can be reciprocated. People who seek upward social movement go to more ceromonies than the average person and give more than they would normally expect to receive. The upwardly mobile person expects, of course, to gain status through his redistributive giving. He might give away wealth without gaining status, if others give more than he does. Should the person fail to gain status, he is called a "ceremonies man," and is considered a spendthrift. These maneuvers to acquire power are quite open and aboveboard. Attempts to conceal them lead tribal members to view the individual as untrustworthy.

Gouldner (1960) considers that the norm of reciprocity not only serves a stabilizing social function, but also acts as a "starting mechanism." Particularly in mobile societies, individuals and groups are constantly brought together in new combinations. They tend to interact with one another when each possesses something of value to the other. There may be an initial tendency on the part of strangers to entertain the hope of gaining the resources of another person without relinquishing their own. Since each person may suspect the other of exploitative motives, a stalemate of suspicions may occur, blocking the development of positive exchanges and friendly relationships. The norm of reciprocity allows the relationship to begin. Suspicion and hesitancy to release one's own valuables is lessened because of the obligation stipulated by the norm. One can offer gifts with confidence that he will be repaid. The anticipation of reciprocity underlies the GRIT strategy of unilateral positive actions discussed in Chapter 9.

A rough scale of equivalence must be

applied in determining how much is owed to a benefactor. Although the benefits may not be identical in form, they should be equivalent in utility. Equivalence requires that the subjective outcome for each party in the exchange be approximately the same. However, it is difficult for individuals to know how much they owe and what constitutes equivalence. As a consequence, social ties are not easily broken. People are never completely certain whether they are debtors or creditors and hence maintain stable exchange relationships, unless they are convinced that the other person is not meeting his obligations in the relationship. The norm of reciprocity acts as a kind of moral cement in producing stable social relationships.

2.   Resources of and Costs to the Donor

According to Gouldner, the amount of debt created by a benefactor is inversely proportional to his ability to provide rewards for others. If a rich man and a poor man each give someone the same amount of money, the recipient will owe a larger debt to the man with fewer resources. Pruitt (1968) found experimental support for this hypothesis.

A confederate was given an envelope containing dimes in the amount of either one dollar or four dollars and was told to divide the money in any manner he wished between himself and a subject. The confederate gave away the funds according to one of three prearranged schedules: (1) 80% of $1 (80 cents); (2) 20% of $4 (80 cents); or (3) 20% of $1 (20 cents). In conditions 1 and 2, the amount given to the subject was the same (80 cents), but the resources possessed by the confederate were different ($1 vs. $4). In conditions 2 and 3 the percentage of resources given to the subject was the same (20%), but the absolute amounts given were different (80 cents vs. 20 cents).

After the confederate distributed the appropriate amounts to the subjects, the latter were given envelopes containing ten dimes to distribute. Before making an allocation the subject was told there would be a third go-round and that the confederate would once again be given an opportunity to allocate funds, this time either 50 cents or two dollars. This manipulation was introduced to determine if anticipation of future reciprocity as well as obligation for past benefits would affect the subjects' allocations of the ten dimes.

The results confirmed the hypotheses under investigation. The amount of money given to the confederate was directly related to the amount received by the subject; more was given to the confederate who gave 80% of $1 than to the one who gave 20% of $1. Second, the amount of money given by the subject was related to the confederate's generosity; more was given to the confederate who gave the subject 80% of $1 than to the one who gave 20% of $4 (the same absolute amount). Finally, the amount of money given to the confederate was directly affected by the amount of resources he would control on the third go-round; more was given when the subject expected the confederate to distribute $2 later than when he expected only 50 cents to be given away. People not only repay debts according to the past generosity of a benefactor, but attempt to create debt when they expect him to acquire future resources that can be used for exchange purposes. Although it is clear in this experimental study that overpayment was motivated by the possibility of future gains, similar behavior outside the laboratory may appear to lack selfish purpose and may be perceived as altruistic.

When the resources of both persons in interaction are about the same, equivalence of values rather than of generosity should be the basis of reciprocity. Wilke and Lanzetta (1970) found support for this hypothesis in a study in which each subject participated in a transportation game with a confederate. The task was to fill a sequence of 40 orders to transport cargo by various types of carriers. The subjects were seated in front of a communication panel that could be used to signal the completion of an order, to signal for help, and to receive offers of help and requests for help from the confederate. Over the first 20 trials the subjects received orders they could not fill by themselves on 10 occasions. Over the last 20 trials all orders could be filled without aid. During the first 20, the confederate offered to help the subject 0, 2, 4, 6, 8, or 10 times. Over the last twenty trials, the confederate requested help on 10 occasions. As can be seen in Figure 10.1, the amount of help offered by the subjects was a direct function of the amount of help received. Thus, a rough equivalence was found between help received and help given.

The effect on reciprocity behavior of the costs incurred by a benefactor has also been investigated. Tesser, Gatewood, and Driver (1968) studied gratitude rather than reciprocity. A recipient's gratitude for a be-

stowed favor was directly related both to the costs incurred by the benefactor and the value of the favor. In a survey conducted by Muir and Weinstein (1962), the size of social debt was considered by respondents to be proportional to the amount of sacrifice suffered by a benefactor. Greenberg, Block, and Silverman (1971) reported effects of both costs and amount of rewards on reciprocity behavior; however, the cost factor had less impact than did the magnitude of reward.

3. *Motives Attributed to the Donor.*

Credit for beneficial behavior cannot be given if it is believed to result from accidental, inadvertent, or coercive causes. A person can gain credit for benevolence only when his prosocial behavior is perceived as intended and when his motive for giving is seen as benefiting the recipient and not furthering his own interests. Helping be-

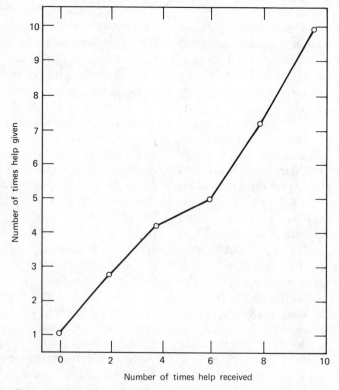

Figure 10.1. Amount of reciprocated help as a function of amount of help received. (After Wilke and Lanzetta, 1970.)

havior that is blatantly self-serving or environmentally determined is often resented by its recipient. The conditions that lead to internal or environmental attributions of causation were discussed in Chapter 4.

Several studies have shown that reciprocity will occur only when the benefactor's prosocial behavior is believed to be intentional. Nemeth (1970) paired each of her subjects with a confederate but gave them independent problems to solve. In different conditions of the experiment, the first one to finish either (1) was required to help the other person: (2) could chose to help the other person on a voluntary basis; or (3) was not allowed to help the other person. The confederate always solved his problem first. After completion of the first phase of the study, the subjects were asked to rate the attractiveness of the confederate. As might be expected, subjects liked the confederate who voluntarily provided help more than the confederate in either of the other two conditions.

When the experiment was allegedly terminated, the confederate asked the subjects to help collect data for a survey. More subjects volunteered to help when the confederate had voluntarily given them help than in either of the other two conditions of the experiment. Over all conditions there was no correlation between the degree of liking for the confederate and the amount of help volunteered by subjects. Schopler and Thompson (1968), Greenberg and Shapiro (1971), and Goranson and Berkowitz (1966) also found reciprocity behavior when benefits were voluntarily given but not when they were accidentally or inadvertently provided.

4. The Relationship Between the Parties

The amount of reciprocity given in exchange might be expected to be related to how much the parties like each other. But contrary to commonsense expectations, a number of studies have found no effect of liking on reciprocity.

Schopler and Thompson (1968) had a salesman interview female subjects in a formal or informal manner. At the conclusion of the interview the salesman either gave the subject a flower that was on the table or else did give her any gift. The subjects were then asked to rate the interviewer and were asked how many times they would be willing to wash a blouse the salesman was interested in testing for its wearability. They were willing to wash the blouse most often when their interview had been informal and they received a gift. Their willingness to wash blouses was no greater in the formal gift condition than in the formal and informal no gift conditions.

These results are difficult to interpret. It might be suggested that the interviewer's gift of a flower in the formal interview condition was considered inappropriate or incongruous; however, subjects were asked to rate the appropriateness of the gift and there were no differences across conditions. Subjects did rate the interviewer in the informal gift condition as more generous than in the other conditions. It is possible that the formality in the interview led the subjects to interpret the gift giving as an impersonal act, a bribe, or an attempt at ingratiation, and hence they gave the salesman no credit for generosity or concern for them as persons (see Chapter 4 IB5). As a consequence, they felt no obligation to repay the formal interviewer for the gift.

In a study that manipulated attraction through an attitude similarity–dissimilarity procedure, Stapleton, Nacci, and Tedeschi (1973) informed subjects that the purpose of the experiment was to study probability estimates. After a fake lottery, the subjects were assigned the role of estimator; and the confederate was assigned the role of point giver. The confederate was instructed to decide before each trial whether or not to give the subject two points. The subjects were given points on 1, 5, or 9 out of 10 trials by an attractive or an unattractive confederate. The subjects estimated before each trial the probability they would be given points. The points were convertible into extra experimental time for the subjects, who were required to participate in three hours of research for their introductory psychology course; this procedure was followed to give the points some real value.

The subjects then traded positions with the confederate and were given ten opportunities to give points to her. They displayed a concern for reciprocity by giving her a greater number of points, the more they had received. However, liking for the confederate had no effect on how many points they gave her. We may find this result encouraging since the power of the reciprocity norm to override dislike for other persons suggests that on the basis of a *quid pro quo* even disliked others may be treated fairly.

B. The Social Responsibility Norm

Much prosocial behavior is directed toward helping dependent persons—homeless children, starving beggars, the blind, the sick, and the old. Berkowitz and Daniels (1963) have proposed that such behavior is guided by a norm of social responsibility. Helping dependent others is unlike behavior undertaken to fulfill the norm of reciprocity because the donor does not expect to receive future benefits from the recipient. Many common words in the English language characterize the prosocial acts of a person who provides help to needy others at a sacrifice to himself: philanthropy, generosity, charity, altruism.

The degree of responsibility for providing help to another is related to the power of the potential donor and the dependency of the potential recipient. Whether help will be given or not will also be partly determined by how much it will cost the donor to provide it. Finally, the norm of social responsibility may not apply to all needy people, but may be specific to those with particular characteristics of sex, race, and socio-economic class. We will examine the research relevant to these three factors.

1. Power and Dependence.

Berkowitz and Daniels (1963) attempted to demonstrate the operation of a responsibility norm. The experimental situation was described to subjects as an evaluation of supervisory ability. A confederate enacted the role of supervisor and the subjects served as workers. The confederate sent notes about how to make paper boxes which the subjects were to construct. The dependence of the supervisor on the subjects was manipulated. In a high dependency condition the subjects were told that their productivity would be important in determining whether the supervisor would win $5. In a low dependency condition they were told their productivity would not affect the evaluation of the supervisor. Although other factors were also manipulated in the two experiments reported by Berkowitz and Daniels, the essential finding was that the subjects in the high dependency condition produced more boxes than did those in the low dependency condition.

Berkowitz and Daniels accepted their results as supporting the existence of a social responsibility norm. However, an alternative explanation is equally plausible. The subjects in the low dependency conditions were led to believe their productivity was not important for the purposes of the experiment (the evaluation of the supervisor). No reason was given to them for making paper boxes and there was no indication that either the supervisor or the experimenter would be interested in the quantity of their production. On the other hand, subjects in the high dependency condition were quite aware that the evaluation of the supervisor was directly related to how many boxes they made. By implication, then, they were also being evaluated—both the supervisor and the experimenter were interested in how many boxes they would produce. The difference between the two conditions can therefore be interpreted as reflecting the subjects' concern about gaining approval for themselves in the high dependency condition, rather than the existence of a sense of social responsibility.

Power and dependency are related concepts. Thibaut and Kelley (1959) defined person A's power over person B as the range of outcomes through which A can move B. The greater the amount of rewards and punishments controlled by A, the greater his power over B. Dependence is the reciprocal of power; the greater A's power, the more dependent is B. A rich man can very much affect an indigent person's life; he can provide him with wealth or have him arrested for vagrancy. There is little the indigent person can do to affect the rich man except perhaps praise or curse him. Frequently, a rich man fulfills a beggar's requests for money, and the norm of responsibility has been postulated as one reason for his prosocial behavior.

Schopler and Bateson (1965) reported three experiments that attempted to demonstrate that the amount of compliance to a partner's request for help is directly related to his degree of dependence. Subjects were informed they would be required to participate in a Ph.D. candidate's dissertation experiment, but were allowed to choose between two different conditions. They could spend 30 minutes in a chamber in which the temperature would be 75° or one in which it would be 125° Fahrenheit. All the students received a request from the candidate asking them to volunteer for the 125° condition. Dependency was manipulated by telling half the students that the candidate was desperate to finish his study in order to qualify in time for a job opportunity; in a low dependency condition the other half of the subjects were informed that he had an entire year in which to complete his dissertation.

Females were more willing to volunteer for the 125° chamber when the experimenter was dependent and males were more willing to help when the experiment-

er was not dependent (see Table 10.1). These sex-linked reactions cast some doubt about the operation of a general norm of responsibility. The responsiveness of females to a dependent person may reflect a socialization process in which they are taught to be nurturant as part of their roles as housewives and mothers. Males, on the other hand, may be more concerned about projecting an image of masculinity. They could demonstrate their courage by volunteering to sit in the hot chamber, but they may tend to avoid helping dependent males for fear their aid will be perceived as reflecting some unmasculine characteristic.

Table 10.1 Percentage of Subjects Who Complied to the Candidate's Request.[a]

Degree of dependence	Males (%)	Females (%)
Low	71	25
High	50	40

[a] After Schopler and Bateson, 1965, p. 248.

2. Costs and Gains

Schopler and Bateson designed two further experiments to eliminate courage as a factor in determining the subjects' responses and to include costs and gains as considerations relevant to behavior regulated by a responsibility norm. The greater the cost of performing a particular behavior, the less likely it is the person will choose to perform it. This proposition has been amply supported by the evidence reviewed in previous chapters. In their further experiments on prosocial behavior, Schopler and Bateson defined costs as the probability of losing future rewards. In a gambling situation, the outcomes for subjects and a confederate were made interdependent; as the chances of winning for one increased, the chances for the other decreased. The subject was given the role of supervisor, which allowed him to choose the bet and provided him with an advantage. The confederate, as the subordinate, could, prior to each trial, transmit his preferences, but the subject-supervisor was empowered to make an independent decision.

Two independent variables were manipulated. Costs were manipulated by varying the probability that subjects would lose their bet if they yielded to the subordinate's advice. This probability was conveyed to subjects before each trial by the experimenter. Dependency was varied by manipulating the range of outcomes associated with the bets. When the range of winnings was small and the subjects had less power over the amount of outcome he could receive, the confederate was less dependent. When the range of possible winnings controlled by the subjects was greater, the power of the subjects and the dependency of the confederate was greater.

As in the first experiment, sex differences were found. When their costs were low, females yielded more to the highly dependent person and males yielded more to the less dependent person. When costs were high neither males or females were likely to yield to the subordinate's requests, whatever his state of dependency. A third experiment confirmed these findings. When costs were low and a conflict existed between optimizing their own outcomes and helping a partner, females helped the dependent other and males more often helped a less dependent other.

Schopler and Bateson explain these consistent sex differences as due to the competitiveness of males and the lack of competitiveness of females. If the males yielded to the confederate in the high dependency condition, they would provide him with a large outcome and leave themselves with a smaller outcome; hence, the confederate would "win" and the subjects would "lose." In the low dependency condition, the differential between what the subjects and the confederate could gain was considerably smaller; hence, males could allow the confederate to gain occasionally without allowing him to win overall. Females are more

responsive to social factors and are socialized to be nurturant; they are not very competitive in the face of social pressures to be cooperative, and are responsive to the dependency of others.

Research to date does not convincingly demonstrate the operation of a general norm of social responsibility. Nevertheless, it is becoming increasingly clear that costs are inversely related to the willingness of people to engage in prosocial behavior. Schaps (1972) carried out a field experiment in which an adult female and male visited 64 exclusive women's shoe stores in Chicago. Dependency was manipulated by having the female enter the store with a broken heel and tell the salesman she could not walk any further, or by having her walk into the store without difficulty. Costs were manipulated in an ingenious way. In the low cost condition the experimenters entered the store only when there were one or no customers per salesman. More than one customer per salesman constituted the high cost condition. Shoe salesmen receive commissions for sales; when they can serve a customer with no one waiting, they can take their time, but when customers are waiting they may lose a sale by spending too much time with one customer. The experimenter was very demanding and required a considerable amount of time from the salesman (and she did not buy any shoes). Of course, the ethics of these procedures are questionable, since the experimenters made a nuisance of themselves, did not obtain permission from the store managers, and were not legitimate customers.

A composite helping score was tabulated by a male companion, consisting of the number of pairs of shoes shown by the salesman, time spent in serving, and the number of trips to the stockroom for more shoes. When costs were low the salesman provided more help for the dependent than for the nondependent customer; when costs were high, less help was provided and there was no difference between the dependency conditions. In considering these results and those of other studies Schaps concluded that "dependency is most likely to elicit helping when a dependent adult is female, is not disliked, and it is not costly to give aid. When dependent adults are male, or are disliked, or when giving help is costly, any social responsibility norm that facilitates helping may at best be weakened or at worst neutralized" (p. 78). Perhaps social responsibility in this situation was nothing other than chivalry displayed by males toward a female. If so, chivalry is displayed only when it is not costly. Also, it must be remembered that these findings may be restricted to middle class Americans and may not represent what would happen in other cultures.

3. Demographic Characteristics of the Dependent Other.

All this research suggests that helping behavior is elicited as a function of the type of situation and the sex of the potential benefactor and the dependent person. Wispé and Freshley (1971) examined the effects of both sex and race in an experiment in which a woman (a confederate) dropped her groceries through a hole she unobtrusively tore in her shopping bag when a bystander (the subject) approached her in a middle-class shopping center. The woman was either black or white and she stood before a store in which the customers were either predominately white or black.

As might be expected on the basis of chivalry, men helped the woman in distress more often than did women. Black and white men helped equally often and the race of the woman made no difference. Women, however, helped someone of their own race, but ignored the person in distress if she was of a different race. Understanding why help is offered to another person apparently requires knowledge of sex-role demands, how individuals are socialized, and the specific details of a situation.

Hence, these findings are surely culturally bound and are probably specific to American society. An overall norm of social responsibility is not a useful principle from which predictions about prosocial behavior can be made.

Hornstein (cited in Wispé and Freshley, 1971) reported strong socio-economic differences in helping. He dropped envelopes containing a wallet and a note indicating that a prior finder (thus providing a model) had been about to return it. To all appearances, the prior finder had also lost the wallet. The note clearly indicated that the prior finder was either black or white; in addition, credentials in the wallet revealed the owner to be either black or white.

Whites returned the wallets more often than blacks, regardless of the race of the model or the owner. If it can be assumed that blacks are generally of lower socio-economic level than whites, the costs to them of helping are different. There was a small amount of money in the wallet, and while a couple of dollars may not seem like much to a middle-class person, it may be worth more to a poor person. Thus there may have been greater cost to the blacks than the whites in returning the wallet intact. A similar study, also by Hornstein (1969), confirmed that socio-economic differences occurred between whites and blacks in returning wallets.

C. Equity and Prosocial Behavior

In Chapter 9 we saw that norms of distributive justice and equity are believed to be important in the processes of bargaining and coalition formation. Walster, Berscheid, and Walster (1973) have applied equity theory to the behavior of bystanders in emergency situations. Four basic assumptions are fundamental to the theory: (1) individuals try to maximize their outcomes; (2) groups develop and enforce equity norms to foster cooperation and maximize the probability of obtaining their goals; (3) individuals in inequitable relationships feel distress; and (4) they attempt to reduce their distress by behavior directed toward restoring equity.

Distress may lead an individual to engage in harmful or prosocial behavior, depending on the nature of the inequity. Giving compensation to someone who has been cheated or providing aid to a victim are attempts to reduce the inequity between the fortunate and the unfortunate. But another way of restoring equity is to derogate a victim and decide that his plight is justified; he suffers harm because he deserves it; equity has been maintained. A person may deny that he has produced inequity by denying responsibility for his behavior. In all these cases the actor's behavior is directed toward reducing distress through the restoration of equity.

Walster et al. generate a number of other possible predictions from their equity theory. However, the theory is recent and has not been subjected to empirical test. While equity appears to be important for the allocation of rewards in work groups and has been shown to be important in bargaining, we do not know if it motivates prosocial behavior.

D. Normative Explanations of Prosocial Behavior.

Several criticisms have been raised about normative explanations of prosocial behavior (Krebs, 1970; Latané & Darley, 1970). As noted in the discussion of moral development in Chapter 6, norms are very general in their prescriptions and their application to specific situations is always problematical. In any situation several conflicting norms may be applicable. For example, should a person intervene in a quarrel between a man and a woman? A norm of social responsibility may suggest intervention to protect the woman, but a norm of minding your own business may suggest staying out of the conflict. Further-

more, normative explanations often have the character of post hoc reasoning. If the expected behavior occurs, an investigator may say it was governed by the relevant norm; if it does not occur, the observer may claim the norm was not activated. Normative explanations must take into account the perceptions and values of the actor, the nature of the situation, and the characteristics of the dependent person to avoid such post hoc interpretations.

Berkowitz and Macaulay (reported in Berkowitz, 1972) conducted two studies in an attempt to examine the activation of a norm to help others. In the first study, two groups of women were interviewed at a shopping center, one group about helping behavior and a second group about their consumer practices. Near the end of each interview a college student confederate approached and requested 40 cents for bus fare because he had lost his wallet. Contrary to the hypothesis that an interview about "helping" would activate a social responsibility norm, there was no difference in the number of persons who provided help during either type of interview.

In the second study, women were interviewed on the topic of helpfulness. The interviewer consistently indicated approval either for prosocial or for selfish answers by the interviewees. Control subjects received no approval for their answers. A confederate then approached and made his request for 40 cents. Women who had received approval for prosocial answers were no more likely to provide the needed money than women in the control group. Women rewarded for selfish answers in the interview were least willing to provide help. It may be concluded that neither study demonstrated any activation of a social responsibility norm.

Schwartz (1973) has proposed a narrowing of focus in studying norms. Individuals differ with respect to the norms they consider relevant to a particular situation, and their personal norms are likely to be better predictors of behavior than more general norms. According to Schwartz, "What distinguishes a norm as personal is that sanctions attached to it are tied to the self-concept: anticipation or actual violation of the norm results in guilt, self-deprecation, loss of self-esteem; conformity or its anticipation result in pride, enhanced self-esteem, security" (p. 353)

For a personal norm to become relevant to a given prosocial act the individual must: "(1) become aware of consequences for the welfare of people in a situation; (2) hold personal norms enjoining action pertinent to the consequences; and (3) feel some capability to control the action enjoined and its outcomes—some personal responsibility" (p. 353) Schwartz also cautions that personal norms will not be activated when sufficient costs of time, effort, and loss of future gains are associated with a prosocial act. Denial of consequences and denial of personal responsibility are two ways by which an individual can justify his failure to engage in prosocial behavior. In chapter 5 we reported an investigation of bone marrow donors by Schwartz and Tessler (1972) which tends to support this conception of personal norms. In contrast to non-donors, bone marrow donors did not deny personal responsibility for the plight of victims who needed help.

II. LEARNING PROSOCIAL BEHAVIOR

Prosocial behavior may be considered to consist of learned habits. It has been argued that any response is a product of a person's reinforcement history and the current stimulus conditions. According to the basic law of reinforcement, any response that is rewarded is likely to be repeated when the circumstances eliciting it recur. Consistent failure to reward a learned response reduces the probability of its occurrence and may even lead to its extinction (the elimination of the response from the individual's behavior repertoire). Although we have defined prosocial behavior as action that benefits others and has no apparent instrumental purpose for the benefactor, it may be established through reinforcement and maintained by an inconsistent association with rewards. Thus, any particular instance of prosocial behavior that goes unrewarded may appear to an observer who is unaware of the actor's reinforcement history to be unrelated to selfish motivations.

In chapter 6 we saw that modeling is important in the acquisition of new behavior. The modeling of prosocial behavior has attracted the interest of many psychologists. The relationship between a model's verbal exhortations and the imitative behavior of an observer has been intensely investigated. Reinforcement and modeling theories of learning are complementary to each other and help to explain much of prosocial behavior.

A. Reinforcement Theory

A pigeon can be trained to press a lever to deliver rewards to a hungry pigeon in an adjoining Skinner box. The benefactor pigeon may be placed on a schedule of reinforcements that requires it to press the lever many times before receiving a pellet for itself. As long as sufficient reinforcements are provided to prevent extinction, the pigeon will perform the behavior. In much the same way, a person may be trained to be considerate of others or to engage in good deeds. Presumably, if his prosocial behavior frequently goes unrewarded or brings him punishments and costs, he will behave in this way less and less often.

An experiment carried out by Fischer (1963) illustrates the reinforcement approach. Marbles were given to four–year-old children who were then shown a picture of a small child who had none. The children were asked to donate some of their marbles to the less fortunate child. Children who were given bubble gum after sharing were more likely to continue to share than were control subjects who received no reward. There is certainly nothing surprising about this result, since it demonstrates a familiar principle in psychology. Some of the children were willing to exchange marbles for bubble gum, but few were willing to give up their marbles when they received nothing but verbal praise in exchange. These results actually reflect the order of the children's preferences: (1) bubble gum, (2) marbles, and (3) verbal praise. When given a choice, the children picked their preferred reward.

Verbal praise has greater value when given to an individual by someone who is liked than by a stranger or someone who is not liked. Midlarsky and Bryan (1967) paired verbal praise with an affectionate response by the reinforcing agent. Girls from the first through fourth grades were presented with two levers; one turned on a red light and the other dispensed an M & M candy. The experimenter tacitly indicated by her use of verbal praise that she preferred the child to turn on the light. When the lever turning on the light was pulled, the child received (1) verbal praise followed by a hug, (2) a hug followed by verbal praise, (3) only a hug, (4) only verbal praise, or (5) no reinforcement of any kind.

Following training, the children were asked to undertake a series of trials. Half the children in each reinforcement condition were verbally praised for pulling the light lever; the other half received no reinforcement at all during the trials. The results are shown in Table 10.2. Children who received verbal praise during test trials pulled the light lever more often than children who did not. More important, children who had been trained with both a hug and verbal praise (conditions 1 and 2) pulled the light lever more often than the candy lever. Children in all the other conditions pulled the candy lever more often than the light lever. If the children interpreted the hug as a display of the pleasure of the experimenter, it can be concluded that they valued giving pleasure more than the candy

Table 10.2 Number of light-lever (prosocial) responses by children.[a]

Conditions on training trials	Conditions on test trials	
	Rewarded	Not rewarded
Hug-Praise	26.38	17.63
Praise-Hug	24.63	17.88
Hug Only	16.88	14.88
Praise Only	16.75	14.81
Control	15.25	14.56

[a] After Midlarsky and Bryan (1967).

(Rosenhan, 1972). However, unless they *also* received praise, they did not display a preference for the light lever. When they received only a hug or only praise they preferred the candy lever.

Aristotle captured the essence of reinforcement theory when he stated that "most men wish what is noble, but choose what is profitable; and while it is noble to render a service not with an eye to receiving one in return, it is profitable to receive one" (cited in Blau, 1964, p. 88). Many charitable actions can be performed at little cost or effort to the donor, and he may receive much in exchange. For example, a rich man can afford to give a small percentage of his income to indigent people or to the arts and, in return, he may receive a tax reduction from the government and the admiration of many citizens. More material advantages may also accrue if others come to believe he is a desirable person with whom to do business. Since many of these reinforcements are indirect, the observer (and perhaps the donor himself) may view the charitable behavior as unselfish.

B. Modeling Prosocial Behavior

Observing a model's behavior may activate social norms for the observer, teach him new responses, and indicate the outcomes associated with various kinds of behavior. In chapter 6 we saw that a model who is rewarded for his behavior is imitated by observers. But will an observer imitate self-sacrificial behavior? Is it enough for a model to propound high principles or must he demonstrate his lack of hypocricy by doing good deeds as well? Will a model who accepts high costs to engage in prosocial behavior be imitated? These and other questions regarding modeling have been systematically investigated.

1. Imitation of Self-Sacrificial Behavior.

There is ample evidence to show that observers will imitate self-sacrificial behavior. Bryan and Test (1967) reported three field experiments in which a model was used to instigate prosocial behavior. The first study examined the willingness of automobile drivers to help change a flat tire and the other two observed the effects of a model on monetary contributions to charity.

In the first experiment a young woman was stationed by a car with a flat, left rear tire; a good spare was leaning against the side of the car. In the model condition another car was stationed about a quarter mile from the critical car; at that site a woman was watching a man changing a flat tire. Both sites were near two predominantly residential sections of Los Angeles. There were no intersections between the location of the model and the critical car, so all cars passing would have seen the model car. Two thousand cars were observed in the model and no-model conditions. When the model was present, 58 cars stopped to help; when there was no model, 35 cars stopped.

Why did the presence of a model have this effect? A number of possible explanations are plausible. Perhaps the model activated a social responsibility norm. Maybe the presence of the model slowed traffic and made it safer for drivers to stop at the critical car. Bryan and Test suggested that the model may have lowered inhibitions about trying to pick up a young woman. Many of the drivers who stopped did make pickup attempts.

A second experiment was conducted to eliminate these competing hypotheses and more carefully test the role of modeling. A Salvation Army kettle was placed in front of a store. In the model condition a whitecollar male walked out of the store and made a contribution; those persons who came out within 20 seconds, and therefore had ample opportunity to observe the model, were considered subjects. The no-model condition started 40 seconds after the model left the store and also lasted for 20 seconds. More donations were made in the model condition than in the no-model condition.

The bell-ringing Salvation Army solicitors were not permitted to maintain eye contact with shoppers and refrained from verbal pleas; however, they did thank donors, including the model. Social reinforcement could be considered significant in eliciting self-sacrificial responses in the modeling condition. A third experiment was carried out using basically the same procedures, except this time the solicitors did not thank the donors. Again, more donations were made when a model was present than when he was not. Although these experiments show a modeling effect, it is not clear why observing a model who engages in self-sacrificial behavior elicits imitative behavior on the part of some observers; in all these experiments the number of subjects responding in this way was quite small.

2. Do As I Say or Do As I Do?

Parents, teachers, and religious leaders often exhort us to act according to moral precepts even at some sacrifice to our selfish interests. Do words of high principle move people to perform good deeds? Grusec and Skubiski (1970) compared verbal and actual performance in a study of elementary school children. Each subject observed either a male or female adult model. In the performance condition the model played a bowling game and contributed one of every two marbles won to a charity for poor children. In the verbal condition, the model stood in front of the bowling game, mused about the score he expected to get, and said he hoped to give away one of every two marbles he won. Immediately after this speech and before he could play the game, the experimenter entered the room to explain that the model's boss had called to ask that he return to work. In both conditions the model left the room. The children then played the game and were observed to see how many marbles they gave to the poor children. The actual performance of sharing by the model produced more imitation by the children than did mere verbalization.

The old saying that children do as you do and not as you say is also supported by a survey by Rettig (1956). He questioned college students about the sources of their altruistic behavior and asked each of them to respond to a test of altruism. Correlational analysis established that the longer students had been in college the less significant religion was in motivating altruistic behavior and the more often students reported significant prior reinforcement as determining their prosocial acts. Scores on the altruism scale were positively correlated with the students' reports of altruistic behavior by their parents. Parental modeling was apparently an important factor in the degree of altruism they displayed on the paper-and-pencil test.

The interview and the paper-and-pencil test consisted of verbal responses and not actual prosocial behavior, however. Bryan and Walbek (1970) found that both verbal and behavioral responses may be learned by observing models. Elementary school children watched a film of an adult model with a little girl, both of whom were to play a game in which certificates could be won. Prior to playing the game, the model exhorted the watching girl to be either generous or selfish in contributing certificates to the March of Dimes. In a control condition, the model said nothing about contributing winnings to charity. Half the subjects in

each of these three conditions then saw the model act either generously or selfishly.

The children donated more when they had observed a generous model than when they had witnessed selfish behavior. The verbal exhortations of the model had no effect on their behavior. However, each subject was asked to make an exhortative statement to be transmitted to the next subject. When the subjects had heard an exhortation by the model, whether generous or selfish, they were more likely to advocate sharing to the next person than when they had heard no statement from the model. Apparently, these children already had learned the proper statements to make about sharing, and hearing a model's exhortations elicited verbal advocacy. This finding reveals that even an inappropriate model can activate verbal advocacy of personal and social norms of conduct.

It may not be enough to teach by example. According to the principles of learning theory, an elicited response must be reinforced or else it will extinguish. Bryan, Redfield, and Mader (1971) had a model either share or not share with charity his winnings from a game. The model also had made either a positive or a negative statement about sharing. Subsequently, the model either verbally reinforced the observer child's self-sacrificial responses in another type of situation or did not provide verbal approval. Models who preached and practiced charity, but did not reward similar responses by the child, elicited few self-sacrificial responses. Models who preached and practiced charity and also reinforced the child's similar behavior elicited many self-sacrificial responses. Thus the reinforcement of a self-denial response may be more important than the model's verbal and behavioral example.

3. Costs and Imitation

In most modeling studies carried out with children, self-sacrificial behavior consists only of sharing the winnings acquired in the course of an experiment, rather than giving up something the children possessed beforehand. The children come away from the situation better off than when they arrived, with a net gain from their experience. Under these conditions it may be easy to influence them to imitate a model. What would happen if it were costly?

Wagner and Wheeler (1969) varied three factors in studying the charitable behavior of Naval personnel: (a) a selfish or a generous model, (b) a high or a low need for aid, and (c) high or low costs of helping. In the high need condition, the subjects overheard a solicitor inform another person that $1,000 was needed to fly the parents and two sisters of a dying Naval Hospital Corpsman to his bedside in Vietnam; according to the solicitor's statements 40 people would be needed to contribute $25 each. In the low need conditions, the solicitor simply asked for a contribution to a local serviceman's fund. In the high cost condition, the donation would be taken as a lump sum from the serviceman's next pay check; in the low cost condition, $1 would be taken out of each pay check until the total pledge was fulfilled. A generous model gave $20 to the solicitor and a selfish model gave nothing.

Need had no effect on charitable behavior. More subjects were charitable when they overheard a generous model make a pledge than when they overheard a model refuse to make a donation, but only when the costs of giving were low. Fewer donations were made and modeling had no effect when costs were high. Costs inhibit prosocial action, whether it is chivalrous behavior by men toward ladies in distress or imitation of a generous model.

4. Conclusion

Observers will imitate the self-sacrificial behavior of a model. The exhortations of a model may elicit verbal statements by observers advocating generous behavior, but they do not affect actual behavior. Hypocrisy is not a factor in imitation—the observer does as the model does and not as he says. The strongest imitation of prosocial behavior occurs when a model emits generous verbal statements, engages in consistent prosocial behavior, and rewards the observer for making similar responses. The more costly it is to perform imitative prosocial behavior, the less effective a model is in eliciting them.

The research reviewed in Chapter 6 clearly indicated that liked models elicit more imitation when the behavior in question is rewarded. The degree of liking for a model has not been shown to be related to the imitation of self-sacrificial behavior (Grusec & Skubiski, 1970; Midlarsky & Bryan, 1967; Rosenhan & White, 1967). The effects of a model's status, expertise, and prestige on imitation of prosocial behavior have not been investigated.

Modeling effects have generally been shown to occur only within a short time and typically in the same mode of response. A person watches a model make a particular response and is immediately provided with an opportunity to make an identical response. Are his imitative responses specific to the situation? Do they lead to long-term changes in his disposition to act in a prosocial manner? In a study that only begins to address these questions, White (1967) had children either observe or rehearse charitable behavior or both and then observed them several days later. There was a decrease in the amount of their charity over time. Unless it can be shown that prosocial behavior learned by modeling will occur in other situations and long after the original learning, it is possible to interpret modeling effects as due to temporary states of the imitator or to specific features of the original modeling situation.

III. INTERNAL STATES OF THE BENEFACTOR

Do happy and successful people engage in more prosocial behavior than grumpy failures? Are sympathy and empathy for the plight of unfortunate people sufficient to move an individual to help? Will a person try to expiate his feelings of guilt through altruistic actions? How will concern about one's self-image affect one's willingness to undertake prosocial behavior? A series of recent studies have investigated the relationship of these internal states of the actor to acts of helping.

A. The Glow of Good Will

Temporary emotional states may induce an individual to perform negative or positive behavior. For example, an irritable parent may punish a child for misbehavior; but when the parent is feeling good, the very same behavior may go unpunished. This commonsense observation was checked by Berkowitz and Conner (1966). Subjects participated in a task and were given feedback of either success or failure or no feedback was provided. Subsequently, all the subjects were placed in a worker role vis-a-vis a supervisor-confederate. The procedures were identical to those described earlier for studies of the norm of social responsibility—the supervisor's evaluation depended on how many boxes the subject made. Those subjects who had experienced success in a prior task helped the dependent supervisor by constructing more boxes than those in either the failure or the no feedback conditions. Success apparently produced a "glow of good will" that spilled over as a greater disposition to help others.

A person who temporarily feels good may make a commitment to perform a benevolent act at some time in the future. Will he keep his commitment after the "glow" dissipates? In an attempt to answer this question Kazdin and Bryan (1971) told subjects they were either highly competent or not competent in performing a task, which was or was not related to the process of giving blood. Regardless of the relevance of the task, competent subjects more often

volunteered to donate blood than the noncompetent. These results were interpreted as supporting the "warm glow" hypothesis, since it was the evaluation of competence and not the relationship to bloodgiving ability that mediated the subjects' willingness to volunteer. However, followup information revealed that few subjects actually kept their commitment to donate blood. Apparently when the temporary "glow" of success had dissipated, their proclivity to engage in prosocial behavior also declined.

Failure should cause people to "feel bad," and it would be reasonable to expect a subsequent decrement in the probability that they will provide help to others. Yet in the two studies just described subjects who failed or were informed they were not competent helped just as much as the control subjects. People who fail may attempt to repair their image in the eyes of the experimenter by providing help to others, while success may motivate subjects to help so as to maintain the positive evaluation already elicited from the experimenter. Thus impression management rather than mood states may account for the association of success with helping behavior in the laboratory. Perhaps, failure would lead to significantly less prosocial behavior when the subject is not under continual surveillance.

Underwood, Moore, and Rosenhan (1972) attempted to manipulate mood states without associating them with success or failure. Second and third grade children were asked to participate in a test of some new hearing equipment and were paid 25 pennies for their 3½ minutes of time. After listening through earphones for the required time, the children were assigned to one of three conditions. They were asked to sit quietly for 30 seconds, during which they were to (1) think of a happy experience, (2) think of a sad experience, or (3) count slowly. The children in all three groups were then informed they could share some of their pennies, if they wanted to, by putting a contribution into a can marked "money for other children." The experimenter then left the children alone for 90 seconds.

Children in the positive mood condition made the most donations and children in the "sad" condition contributed less than control subjects. Of course, it is possible that the instructions to think of positive or negative experiences acted to prompt the behavior of the children. No independent evidence was provided by the researchers to establish that corresponding "good" or "bad" feeling states were actually aroused in the children by the experimental procedures.

In still another attempt to show an effect of the "glow of good will" on prosocial behavior, Isen and Levin (1972) carried out two field experiments. The first established a relationship between cookies and kindness. A confederate entered the carrel area in the university library and gave some of the occupants cookies. A few minutes later the students who had received a cookie and those who had not were approached and asked to serve as a confederate in a psychological experiment. They were provided with one of two kinds of information about the probable reactions of subjects to the confederate, either that the subjects would appreciate the confederate's role or that they would be annoyed by the behavior the confederate would be asked to manifest.

The willingness of students to volunteer depended both on whether they had received a cookie and on how they would be evaluated by their peers. Subjects who were presumably under the influence of a temporary "glow of good will" because they received cookies were more likely to volunteer than control subjects when it was expected that their participation would be appreciated, but less likely to volunteer when they believed that others would be annoyed by their participation. Thus good will increases the likelihood of prosocial behavior and decreases the probability of negative action.

Once again, however, these results may be attributed to factors other than mood states. Two events occurred within a short time for the students—a stranger gave them a cookie and a psychologist solicited their help–both of which were unusual, especially in the context of a library carrel. Isen and Levin found no evidence of suspicion in debriefing the subjects, but subjects are often reluctant to reveal their suspicion for fear of ruining an experiment (see the discussion of the pact of ignorance and of demand characteristics in Chapter 2). It does not seem unreasonable to suggest that the students associated the cookie with the experimenter's request. If they did, they would have been aware that they were themselves in a experiment, whereas the students who received no cookie would not be suspicious. The aware students would have to ask themselves why they were given a cookie and the answers to this question may have determined their responsiveness to the experimenter's request. Of course actual prosocial behavior was not examined, but only verbal commitments were obtained under conditions of direct solicitation.

The second field experiment reported by Isen and Levin was conducted in suburban shopping malls outside San Francisco and Philadelphia. In one condition, the experimenter entered a telephone booth, made an incomplete call, did not remove the dime from the coin return slot, and left the booth. In a second condition, no dime was left in the phone. The next person to use the phone was considered a subject. When the subject left the booth, a confederate dropped a manila folder full of papers in his path. The confederate was not aware whether the subject had received a dime. As can be seen in Table 10.3, 14 of 16 subjects who found a dime did help pick up the papers and only 1 of 25 subjects who did not find a dime volunteered to help.

The phone booth study is not susceptible to the criticisms made of the cookies and kindness study. It is unlikely that the subjects were aware they were being observed, and unsolicited prosocial behavior constituted the dependent variable. However, it

Table 10.3   Number of People Who Did and Did Not Help in the Phone Booth Study.[a]

	Females		Males	
Condition	Helped	Did not help	Helped	Did not help
Dime	8	0	6	2
No Dime	0	16	1	8

[a] After Isen and Levin, 1972.

would be too hasty to conclude that a pleasant internal feeling was responsible for this behavior. Internal states of the subjects were neither observed or measured. Alternative hypotheses therefore cannot be ruled out. Perhaps the subjects who received a dime felt a little guilty about taking the money and their subsequent display of helping served to expiate guilt. Or finding the coin may have sensitized the individual to a norm of social responsibility. In any case, experiences of success and gaining unearned benefits do have a direct if momentary impact on prosocial behavior. Because of the transient nature of this phenomenon, it has been attributed to temporary mood states of the actor.

B.   Sympathy and Empathy.

Sympathy refers to a disposition to relieve the distress of others, while empathy is a vicarious sharing of another person's emotional state. Aronfreed (1970) has proposed that sympathy is based on empathy. If an actor empathizes with a person in distress, he may actually vicariously experience distress himself. By helping, he may alleviate his own uncomfortable feeling state. A benefactor may vicariously share in the experience of relief or joy of the recipient and gain emotional reinforcement for prosocial actions; to give joy is to experience joy.

Empathy will not automatically elicit prosocial behavior, according to Aronfreed. A person must first learn what kinds of responses will reduce another's discomfort. In a very complex experiment, Aronfreed and Paskal (1966) attempted to teach seven- and eight-year-old girls empathy and also the prosocial behavior appropriate to a particular situation. The children were given the task of assigning toys to one of three classifications (appropriate for house, dog, or school) by pushing an appropriate lever. Actually the middle lever represented a category (dog) that the child perceived as inappropriate for any of the toys.

In the first phase of the experiment, both the child and the experimenter wore earphones. On six of twelve trials a noxious seven-second noise was heard by both of them. The child was told that the adult's noise was louder than her own. When the noise had been on for three seconds the adult began to emit obvious signs of distress by placing her head in her hands.

In the second phase of the study, the adult did not wear earphones but the child did. When the noxious noise occurred the adult could and did turn it off by pushing the middle lever (the one that was inappropriate for classifying the toys). Thus the adult chose a response that helped the child, but at the cost of making a wrong classification. In the third phase, the child could reduce the distress of another child who was also exposed to the noise by pushing the inappropriate lever.

Four control sequences were also carried out. In the first, the adult showed distress in the first phase, but not on the trials when the child heard the noxious noise. The second was exactly like the experimental sequence except that the noise heard by the child was mild; as a consequence, the sympathetic response of the adult during the second phase should have had little distress-reducing value to the child. In the other two control conditions the other child in the third phase either did not demonstrate distress or did not even wear earphones. A summary of the research design and the sequencing of events is presented in Table 10.4

Children in the experimental group showed a marked preference for the inappropriate lever during the third phase; they typically made this sympathetic choice four or five times out of the six trials on which the other child displayed distress. Children in the four control groups showed a stronger task orientation by classifying the toys appropriately during the third phase instead of making sympathetic responses.

Children in the first control group had the noxious noise turned off by the sympathetic behavior of the adult, but they never experienced the noxious noise at the same time that the adult displayed signs of distress. In the second control group they heard a very mild noise when the adult emitted distress and hence never developed empathy with her. In the third and fourth control groups, empathy was not aroused because the other child did not display any distress. Aronfreed and Paskal concluded that initial training in empathy and cues from another person that arouse empathy are both necessary for establishing sympathetic behavior.

A single experiment, even when it is as ingenious as this one, is not sufficient for establishing a theory (see Chapter 2). Alternative interpretations of the data are easier to devise for one study than for a series of tests of the predictions derived from a theory. For example, it could be claimed that only the children in the experimental condition had sufficient information to properly interpret "holding one's head" as a signal of need for help. A generalized reciprocity norm which essentially stipulates "do unto others as you would have them do unto you" could explain the "sympathetic" behavior of the children in this condition. Acceptance of a general obligation to help others may assure an individual that he will also receive help from others, if everyone is willing to accept similar responsibility. If the children had already learned this norm before participating in the study, the norm would be elicited only when it was obvious that someone needed help. Only further research can establish whether empathy does mediate sympathetic behavior.

C. Guilt and Restitution

In chapter 6 we saw that a variety of post-transgression responses may be performed by an individual, including self-criticism, intropunitive behavior, and expressions of remorse. Another response available to a person who has done something wrong or harmful is to make restitution to the injured party. Restitutive responses may be considered prosocial if they are not directed toward obtaining future rewards or avoiding future punishments. In psychoanalytic theory it is assumed that a person may condemn himself because of his internalized standards of conduct (his superego). Self-condemnation can produce distress that may be relieved by compensating "good" behavior.

An alternative view is that restitutive behavior is directed toward eliciting positive evaluations from other people. H. L. Mencken (1955) once said that "conscience is the inner voice which warns us that someone may be watching" (p. 231). If you do something that may throw question on your character, you may perform a prosocial action to demonstrate your essential goodness. Although most of the research on restitutive behavior has been generated by hypotheses concerning guilt, it can equally be interpreted in terms of impression management.

Wallace and Sadalla (1966) forbade subjects to touch an expensive machine and

Table 10.4 Experimental Design of Study by Aronfreed and Paskal (1966).

Sequence of events	Conditions experienced by groups					
	Experimental	Control #1	Control #2	Control #3	Control #4	
Phase #1	S^a and E hear noxious noise and E shows distress	S and E hear noxious noise but E shows distress only on trials when S does not hear noise	S and E hear mild noise, E shows distress cues	Same as experimental	Same as experimental	
Phase #2	S hears noxious noise and E turns it off	Same as experimental	Same as experimental	Same as experimental	Same as experimental	
Phase #3	S provided opportunities to reduce distress of another child who wears earphones	Same as experimental	Same as experimental	Other child does not show distress	Other child does not wear earphones	

$^a S$ = subject, E = experimenter.

432

then lured them into transgressing against the prohibition. The machine either did or did not break down when they operated it. Afterward, all the subjects were asked to volunteer for another psychology experiment. Those who broke the machine more often volunteered than did those who did not. In a similar study, Brock and Becker (1966) had subjects do a small amount of damage to a machine—a puff of smoke emerged when they manipulated a dial— or do a great amount of damage—the machine emitted a great deal of smoke and made a loud noise. More compliance to a request was obtained from the subjects who did "great" damage than those who did little.

The researchers interpreted the willingness of subjects to volunteer as motivated by guilt feelings generated by the harm done to the machine. But guilt requires that the individual attribute the harm to his own behavior; otherwise, he will not feel responsible for it. It seems likely that the subjects in these experiments would attribute the breakdowns to accidental failure rather than to their deliberate sabotage of the equipment. Nevertheless, they had an interpersonal problem. They may have attributed the equipment failure to accident, but how could the experimenter be sure they did not deliberately break the machine? The experimenter provided the subjects with a way of showing their generosity, and their display of prosocial behavior may have been an attempt to show that they were not the kind of people who would deliberately break the experimenter's machine. If this impression management strategy was successful, the experimenter would be led to attribute the machine failure to accident rather than to the deliberate intention of the subjects.

Konečni (1972) performed a field study of guilt, sympathy, and restitution on wet days when few pedestrians were on the streets of a middleclass neighborhood in Toronto. In (a) the control condition the experimenter walked toward a pedestrian

and "accidentally" dropped a folder containing 40 IBM cards when he was four yards in front of the pedestrian. The experimenter bent down to pick up the cards and said, loud enough so the subject could hear, "Please, don't step on them." In (b) the restitution condition, the experimenter walked up behind the pedestrian and, at the moment of passing, brushed the folder against the pedestrian's free arm and dropped the cards. Again, he asked the subject not to step on them. In (c) the sympathy condition, a confederate was hidden in a doorway or standing in a shop entrance. As a subject approached, the confederate briskly walked out of the doorway and bumped into the experimenter, who let the cards slip out of the folder. The confederate then walked away without apologizing or attempting to help. In (d) the generalized guilt condition, a confederate ran into the subject and dropped some books he was carrying on the pavement. Before the subject could help, the confederate picked up his books, muttering "they are not mine, and you have to do this (to me)." Following this incident and after the pedestrian walked another 50 to 70 yards, the experimenter then acted in the same manner as in the control condition.

As can be seen in Table 10.5, the subjects in the sympathy condition provided by far the most help. The restitution and guilt conditions produced more help than was obtained in the control condition. But before drawing firm conclusions from this study, we have to ask whether Konečni's manipulations actually produced the appropriate internal states of guilt or sympathy in the pedestrians—and there is no way of knowing. The pedestrians (all male) may have provided help in the restitution condition to placate the male experimenter so he would not cause an unpleasant scene. Impression management cannot be ruled out in this condition, since helping could establish that the pedestrian did not mean to bump into the experimenter. In the sympathy condition, the subjects could be

Table 10.5   Percentage of Subjects Helping and the Mean Amount of Help Per Subject by Experimental Condition.[a]

Condition	Percent of subjects who collected cards	Mean number of cards collected per subject
Control	16	1.29
Sympathy	64	8.61
Restitution	39	4.64
Generalized guilt	42	4.77

[a] After Konečni, 1972.

made to look especially good in comparison with the clumsy and obnoxious confederate. Although the results are provocative, they are difficult to interpret. In addition, interfering without consent in the lives of people on the streets must be considered questionable on ethical grounds.

In yet another study of guilt and restitution, Berscheid and Walster (1967) arranged to have women from church groups play a question-and-answer game to win trading stamps. The critical subject was asked to decide how many out of 10 questions she and her partner would answer correctly. If the two partners did not correctly answer the number of questions chosen, they did not win. When they succeeded, they won S & H green stamp booklets equal to the number of correct answers they provided. The subjects did not actually see their partner, and were told she really needed the stamps to get her child a birthday present. The game was contrived so the critical subjects caused their partners to lose; the partner answered questions correctly, but the subjects did not.

The subjects then played a second game either with the same or with a different partner, after which they were given an opportunity to award bonus stamps either to their partner in the second game or to a crippled boy. The number of stamps they could award was either insufficient, sufficient, or excessive to compensate the partner for the loss of stamps in the first game. Berscheid and Walster reported their observations of these women during interviews conducted after the first game. The women apparently expressed some sense of guilt and were upset about their responsibility for their partner's failure to win the needed stamps.

The subjects more often gave bonus stamps to their first partner than to another person; furthermore, compensation to the first partner occurred more often when exact restitution could be made than when it would be either insufficient or excessive. Berscheid and Walster concluded that although guilt motivated restitution, the subjects were more willing to provide compensation when it was equitable than when it was not.

Once again alternatives to the guilt-restitution hypothesis can be offered. First, it is clear that the subjects did not intentionally "throw" the first game to prevent their partner from winning although they did report a sense of responsibility and guilt. They may have had some need to demonstrate their good will as a matter of impression management when they had an opportunity to compensate their partner. Second, compensation did not cost the subjects anything, since they had to give away stamps in any case. Even if guilt did affect their behavior in this study, we should be careful not to generalize the guilt-restitution relationship to situations in which it would cost the guilty party some of his own resources to provide compensation.

Darlington and Macker (1966) had subjects participate with a confederate in a study in which both could allegedly win extra points toward a course grade. The points each could earn depended on the performance of the other. The situation was contrived so the confederate would solve the tasks and gain points for the subject, but the subjects would always fail to gain points for the confederate. In a control condition, it was made clear that the confederate did not need extra credit. All the subjects were then given an opportunity to engage in prosocial behavior in relation to a third party, who asked them to donate blood to the University Blood Bank.

More subjects agreed to make a donation in the experimental than in the control group. The experimenters interpreted their results as reflecting displacement of guilt. It is equally plausible to interpret the prosocial behavior of the subjects in the experimental condition as an attempt to reveal themselves as kind and benevolent and not as the type of person who would cause a peer to lose points because of lack of effort.

In summary, the guilt-restitution relationship has been studied only in situations in which people did not mean to harm anyone but where some harm occurred anyway. Under such conditions, a harmdoer will usually take some immediate affirmative action either toward the victim or toward a third person. We have emphasized the impression management interpretation of these results because, as we shall see in Chapter 12, research shows that when a person deliberately injures another, his reactions to the victim are seldom benign. Yet it is precisely when harmdoing is deliberate that guilt should be greatest.

D.   Concern for Self and Concern for Others

An egocentric person is not apt to be empathetic or sympathetic. His concern about himself, which may be based on low self-esteem or lack of self-confidence, makes him unlikely to give to others. Self-concern may be accentuated when a person is being evaluated on a characteristic he deems important. A frequently used experimental method to experimentally manipulate levels of self-esteem is to arrange for a subjects' success or failure on a task or to provide him with positive or negative feedback about his performance. Failure may induce low self-esteem and arouse self-concern, thereby making subjects less willing to engage in prosocial behavior.

Johnson, Hildebrand, and Berkowitz (reported by Berkowitz, 1972) directly examined the relationship between self-concern and prosocial actions. Subjects were shown a set of ten pictures of groups of persons. Their task was to identify the group leader and the attitude of the group toward the leader from viewing each picture. In one condition they were told the task measured "social sensitivity", and in another condition the task was identified as a measure of their "supervisory ability." To enhance their self-concern, the subjects were told they would be evaluated shortly after they completed the task. Before leaving to score the protocols, the experimenter asked the subjects to help him in scoring some other data.

Both men and women participated in the experiment. It was assumed that women would be more concerned with social sensitivity, while men would be more concerned about being evaluated for supervisory ability. The results supported the hypothesis that self-concern would inhibit prosocial action. Women helped less when they were waiting for a social sensitivity report, and men helped less when their supervisory ability was being evaluated.

In a follow-up study (Berkowitz, 1972), self-concern was or was not aroused in female subjects. All the subjects then listened to a tape recording of a conversation in which one person was complaining to another about a burdensome library assignment. Some heard the second person say she would not help with the assignment; others heard a tape in which help was offered and the recipient thanked the benefactor for the offer.

The results are shown in Table 10.6. Most help was given when the subject's self-concern was high and they had been exposed to a prosocial model who had been thanked. Thus self-concern can inhibit or facilitate prosocial behavior, depending on the particular circumstances. Berkowitz (1972) summarized these two studies as showing that "Self-concern apparently enhances only a selfishly motivated helpfulness, not true altruism" (p. 93).

Table 10.6 Mean Number of Pages Scored for the Experimenter During a 10-Minute Work Period.[a]

Overheard conversation outcome	Self-concern level	
	High	Low
Help and thanks	75.4	54.6
No help	56.8	57.8

[a] After Berkowitz, 1972.

IV. HELPING STRANGERS IN EMERGENCIES

In 1972 over 11 million Americans suffered nonfatal injuries and over 100,000 people died in various kinds of accidents, including motor vehicle collisions, falls, burns, drownings, firearms, machinery, and the ingestion of poisonous substances. In the same year there were more than 5 million arrests made on criminal charges, 18,880 homicides, and 24,280 suicides (Newspaper Enterprise Association World Almanac, 1974). Natural disasters, such as hurricanes, tornados, earthquakes, and floods, are unpredictable but occur frequently all over the earth. Any person may become a victim of any of these sources of danger. During times of emergency an endangered person often needs help from others to minimize harm to himself and his property. Journalistic reports of emergency situations (see Box 10.1) reveal acts of heroism on the part of bystanders, callous indifference and refusal to help victims, and even instances where bystanders encourage would-be suicides to jump.

In the past decade, social psychological research has been directed toward the question of what factors cause bystanders to intervene to help others in emergency situations. It is not always clear to bystanders that an emergency exists. If a passerby happens on an automobile accident and there are bodies strewn across the road, there is little difficulty interpreting that help is needed. However, if a man staggers and falls to the pavement, it is difficult to ascertain whether he is merely drunk or suffering a heart attack or seizure. If a man and a woman are having a violent quarrel, one may be reluctant to intervene because he may interpret the altercation as a domestic affair. How a bystander defines the situation is crucial in determining his subsequent reaction.

Consider the problem facing the bystander. The characteristic feature of any emergency is that it involves the threat of harm to life, well–being, or property. If he intervenes at all, he must usually do so quickly and without clear guidelines about how to proceed. He can look forward to few rewards for intervening and he may jeopardise his own well–being and perhaps even his own life by taking action. As Latané and Darley (1969) state: "The picture . . . is a rather grim one. Faced with a situation in which there is no benefit to be gained for himself, unable to rely on past experience, on the experience of others, or on forethought and planning, denied the opportunity to consider carefully his course of action the bystander to an emergency is in an unenviable position. It is perhaps surprising that anyone should intervene at all" (p. 247).

It is an undeniable fact that bystanders often do intervene to help extricate a victim from difficulty. Once a bystander defines a situation as an emergency, the likelihood he will intervene depends on the presence of other people, on who they are, on his own special competence to provide help, on the responsibility attributed to the victim for his own plight, and on other and competing

Box 10.1 BYSTANDER REACTIONS IN EMERGENCY SITUATIONS

The way bystanders respond to the plight of victims varies from apathy or indifference to outright callousness and pleasure or to sympathetic and heroic actions to provide aid and solace. Newspaper stories have described incidents in which all of these kinds of reactions occurred. For example, on March 13th, 1964, a little after 3:00 AM, Kitty Genovese returned to her home in Queens, New York City, after working late as a manager of a local bar. As she left her car she noticed a man lurking in the parking lot so she hurried nervously toward a police telephone box. Before she reached it the man caught up with her and attacked her with a knife. She screamed "Oh, my God, he stabbed me! Please help me! Please help me!" People in the apartment buildings along the street were awakened. The turning on of lights, opening of windows, shouting by one man to "Let the girl alone" frightened the assailant and he left the scene. However he returned soon after and resumed the attack, once again to be frightened away. Still a third time he returned to the attack, this time fatally wounding the victim. The entire sequence of events took 35 minutes, and 38 people witnessed the event. No one intervened or so much as called the police about the matter. This incident was so shocking that it made the headlines of newspapers around the country and raised questions about the loss of moral sensitivity of the American people. It also stimulated social psychologists to study prosocial behavior.

Some people try to take advantage of the helplessness of victims. On August 25, 1974 the Associated Press reported from Miami an account of "the world's most rotten robber". As a middle-aged man lay helpless in the street after being hit by a car, a witness to the accident pulled a gun and robbed him of his wallet. A similar well-known phenomenon is the likelihood of looting following natural or man-made disasters. Armed force is usually required to prevent the theft of all valuables after a city has been evacuated.

Of course, there are also many instances of heroism in which one person risks life or limb to help others. Communities usually organize ceremonies to recognize and reward these prosocial actions. An incident that occurred in Chicago in July of 1974 has the elements of both bystander apathy and heroism. A woman lawyer who had been struck with a heavy chain while riding a bicycle began to chase her assailant. She yelled for help but others in the crowded city park ignored her. Joggers, other cyclists, a man reading a newspaper, a bus full of people, guards taking down the flag at the Chicago Historical Society, a woman emptying her garbage—all said they watched the calls for help. Finally, a candidate for the state legislature, who was on his way to play tennis along with another unidentified man, chased, stopped, and held the alleged attacker until the police arrived on the scene. The woman lawyer's condition was described as very bloody, and she later needed ten stitches in her neck.

These observations have raised questions about why, when, and under what conditions passersby will intervene at risk to themselves to help a person in distress.

responsibilities demanded of him. Most of these factors have been examined in the laboratory, and field studies carried out during natural disasters have also contributed to our knowledge of intervention.

A. Analysing the Emergency Situation

Latané and Darley (1969) have provided an outline of the five major components of an emergency situation that affect a bystander's behavior: (1) gaining his attention; (2) interpreting the situation as an emergency; (3) deciding what form of assistance can be provided; (4) deciding what he can do in the situation; and (5) considering the rewards and costs of intervening and not intervening. The presence of other people at the scene affects each of these factors.

According to Latané and Darley, a bystander may look to others for cues about how to interpret an ambiguous situation. If others seem unconcerned, casual, and unresponsive, he is apt to suppress his original alarm and interpret the situation as a nonemergency. A second effect of the presence of others is on the degree of responsibility he feels. When others are on the scene, his help may not be needed and he is less apt to be blamed for not intervening; when no one else is around and help is clearly needed, he cannot avoid responsibility.

The effect of others on a bystander's interpretation of a situation and on his responsibility to intervene have been systematically investigated. In a representative study, which Latané and Darley (1970) entitled "Where There's Smoke, There's (Sometimes) Fire," subjects were placed in a cubicle either alone or with two other subjects to fill out preliminary questionnaires prior to an expected interview. When they had completed several pages of the questionnaire, the experimenter began to introduce smoke to the cubicle through a small vent in the wall. The clearly visible stream of whitish smoke was jetted into the room in puffs and by the end of the ex-

perimental period, it had produced ar acrid odor, interfered with breathing, anc obscured vision. The subjects' behavior was observed through a one-way mirror. If a subject left the cubicle to report the smoke, he was told that the situation "would be taken care of." If the subject did not report the smoke within 6 minutes from the time he was first observed to notice it, the experiment was terminated.

Seventy-five percent of the subjects who were alone reported the smoke to the experimenter. In only 38 percent of the three-person groups did at least one person report the smoke. The typical subject in the alone condition would notice the smoke, stare at it, walk over to the vent, and examine the situation very carefully. After some hesitation, he would then leave the cubicle calmly to report the emergency, typically within 2 minutes after first noticing it.

The subjects who did not report the smoke gave an astonishing variety of interpretations of the situation, most of which were associated with the experiment. They thought the smoke was steam or airconditioning vapors or smog purposely introduced to simulate an urban environment or a "truth gas" filtered into the room to induce them to answer the questionnaire honestly. Clearly, when the subjects were in groups they were less apt to interpret the situation as an emergency and consequently were less apt to report it.

It must be asked whether this experiment reproduced the basic components of an emergency situation as defined by Latané and Darley. If there was danger to anyone, it was presumably to the subjects and not to others. Any action they took could easily be interpreted as self-protective and not as an intervention to help others. Recognizing this possible criticism, Latané and Rodin (1969) created a different situation, in a study of the "fallen woman."

Subjects participated in the experiment singly or in unacquainted pairs. They were led to believe its purpose was to evaluate game and puzzle preferences for a market research organization. After providing them with questionnaires, the attractive female experimenter told them she would be working next door in her office for about 10 minutes. Four minutes after leaving, the experimenter turned on a tape recorder which produced the sounds of a loud crash, a scream, and a chair falling to the floor. The experimenter's voice then said: "Oh, my God, my foot . . . I . . . I . . . can't move . . . it. Oh . . . my ankle . . . I . . . can't get this . . . thing . . . off me." The entire episode took place in about 2 minutes.

Seventy percent of the alone subjects intervened in some manner, while in only 40% of the groups did one member intervene. Those who intervened claimed they did so because they believed help was needed or because the situation warranted investigation. Those who did not intervene either did not consider the situation serious or else believed that other people would or could help. Noninterveners did not feel they were lacking in responsibility, since their inaction was consistent with their perception of the situation. From these results, Latane and Darley concluded that the presence of other people affects the interpretation of an ambiguous situation as an emergency. When no one else is present, an individual is more apt at least to investigate and is not inhibited by the inaction of others. When bystanders see the inaction of others, they are apt to conclude that there is no emergency.

Goffman (1969) has suggested that a display of emotional responsiveness is a better cue to the internal state of other people than is behavior because actions are more controlled and less spontaneous than emotions. The subjects in the two studies just described were busy filling out questionnaires, and in the group condition may have missed the initial startled reactions of the others. The presence of others may actually facilitate intervention if an individual perceives the initial emotional responses of others.

Darley, Teger, and Lewis (1973) examined the affects of startle responses on helping behavior. Subjects were given the task of sketching from a model of a horse, which was alleged to be a test of perspective. They made their drawings under one of three conditions: (1) alone in a cubicle; (2) seated back-to-back with another subject; or (3) seated face-to-face and sketching from the same model as another subject. The experimenter left the room and said he would return in 10 minutes. Four minutes later a tape was played, portraying an accident to a construction worker in the adjoining room who injured his leg. The subject was considered as offering aid if he opened the door or shouted an inquiry.

Ninety percent of the alone subjects, 80 percent of the face-to-face subjects, and 20 percent of the back-to-back subjects offered aid. What happened to increase the amount of helping in the face-to-face as compared to the back-to-back situation? Of course it is possible to perceive the other person's startle response in the former condition, but only the other person's behavior would become noticeable in the latter. An alternative possibility is that the subject may have realized that he communicated his own definition of the situation by a startle response observed by the other party, and might then have felt more obligation to intervene. Whatever the mechanism turns out to be, it is clear that the presence of others does not always inhibit an individual from defining a situation as an emergency or from intervening to help the victim.

B. The Assumption of Responsibility in Emergency Situations

There may be a diffusion of responsibility within a group. Any single person is less apt to be blamed for not helping when many other persons are present than when he is alone. He may feel less responsibility when a person who has special competence to provide aid is available, and may feel more responsibility when he himself possesses special competence. Various relationships within a group may also be important in affecting the degree of responsibility the individual will assume, such as the presence of friends or authorities. We have already seen that the characteristics of a needy person may affect a potential benefactor's reactions. The responses of a bystander may be affected by still other variables when many people are endangered by a disaster. Once the situation has been unambiguously interpreted as an emergency an individual's willingness to assume responsibility is determined by all these special circumstances.

1. Diffusion of Responsibility

Darley and Latané (1968) tested the diffusion of responsibility hypothesis in an emergency in which all ambiguity about the nature of the situation was removed. Subjects were asked to participate in an in-depth discussion with strangers about the personal problems faced by college students in an high-pressure urban environment. To avoid embarrassment, they were to remain anonymous and to communicate with one another from individual cubicles via microphones and earphones. Each person took turns talking for two minutes, after which other members of the group commented on what had been said. The subject was led to believe that the discussion group consisted of: (1) two persons including herself, (2) three persons, or (3) six persons. All group members except for the subject were confederates of the experimenter.

In each group the future victim spoke

first; she mentioned that she was prone to seizures, particularly when under pressure. All other group members then took their turns. When it was the victim's turn again, she spoke calmly for a few minutes and then exclaimed in a loud and incoherent voice that she was experiencing a seizure and needed help. The major dependent variable was the amount of time it took before the subject left her experimental cubicle after the seizure took place.

The results are shown in Table 10.7. Both the percentage of subjects who helped and the speed with which they responded were directly affected by the number of people in the group. The larger the group, the less likely it was that subjects would offer help and the slower they were to respond. These differences cannot be attributed to ambiguity about whether help was needed. Darley and Latané assure us that the subjects believed there was an emergency and many were visibly shaken by the experience. Yet many subjects did not intervene, and many who finally did intervene delayed for a considerable period of time. While these results support the responsibility diffusion hypothesis, an alternative explanation is equally plausible. The subjects knew they were in an experiment and were under observation, particularly when other group members were in the immediate vicinity. They may have been reluctant to act because of a fear of looking foolish in the eyes of others if there was no real emergency.

Bickman (1971b) tested the diffusion of

Table 10.7   Effects of Group Size on Likelihood and Speed of Response.[a]

Group size	Percent of subjects responding by end of seizure	Average time of intervention (secs)
Two (subject and victim)	85	52
Three (subject, victim, and 1 other)	62	93
Six (subject, victim, and 4 others)	31	166

[a] After Darley and Latané, 1968, p. 380.

responsibility hypothesis by manipulating the distance between the subject and other group members. In an alleged study of extrasensory perception, subjects were to operate a panel designed to "send" symbols to another person (the alone condition) or to two other persons (the group condition). In the group condition, both of the other subjects were said to be nearby or else one was nearby and the second was in another building. During the experiment a nearby person was heard to fall off a chair and scream. When the subject was alone or when the other bystander was not able to help because she was too far away, most subjects reported the incident and did so quickly. When they believed there was another bystander nearby, fewer helped than in either of the other two conditions. Once again, both diffusion of responsibility and fear of embarrassment can explain the results.

Several studies have found that subjects fail to intervene in certain kinds of situations even when they are alone. Latané (1967) found that virtually all his undergraduate subjects failed to intervene on behalf of a child who was being assaulted. Kaufmann (1968) had subjects observe a teacher deliver increasingly severe and dangerous shocks to a learner. Despite the learner's pleas for help, only 11 percent of the subjects attempted to intervene. Perhaps they interpreted the teacher's actions as legitimate and were therefore inhibited from acting. This kind of interpretation might prevent a person from getting involved in what may appear to be a domestic argument. In such cases, somewhat like the Kitty Genovese murder described in Box 10.1, the bystander may consider the norm to mind his own business as most relevant for defining what he ought to do.

2. Special Competence

If a victim is believed to be injured and it is known that a person with medical competence is nearby, will a bystander be inhib-

ited from intervening? The answer may not be very obvious, since a person could be encouraged to assist by his lessened responsibility for any negative consequences to the victim. On the other hand, the presence of a competent bystander may absolve him from any further responsibility in the situation.

A complex study reported by Schwartz and Clausen (1970) attempted to provide an answer to this problem. They followed the procedure of having a confederate feign a seizure in the same manner as Darley and Latané. In addition to the seizure victim and themselves the subjects believed the discussion groups included (1) one other person; (2) four other bystanders, three females and one male, none of whom were known to have any special competence; or (3) four other bystanders, three females, and a male premedical student who worked three nights a week in the emergency ward of a local hospital. The male victim was first to take a turn in the discussion. For half the subjects in each of the three conditions, the victim, when mentioning his problem, provided specific information about how he should be helped in an emergency ("get medicine I keep in my pocket"). The other half of the subjects was not given specific information about how aid should be administered.

As can be seen in Figure 10.2, male and female subjects responded to the situation somewhat differently. When alone, females responded more quickly to help a male victim than did males. This result is difficult to interpret. Are females more nurturant than males in this type of situation or is the result due to heterosexual factors? Would males have responded more quickly if the victim had been female?

In the 6-person group males and females intervened at about the same time when none of the other bystanders was competent. However, females were slower to intervene when a competent male bystander was believed to be present. Male subjects responded in about the same way in all

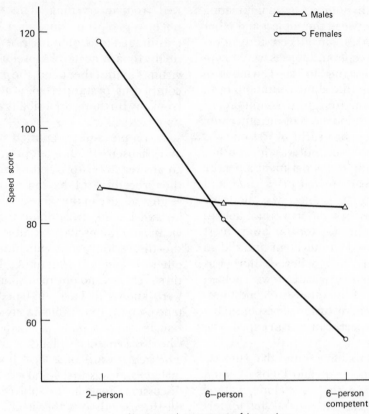

Figure 10.2.   Average speed of helping by male and female subjects in the three types of groups. The higher the score the faster the intervention of subjects. (After Schwartz and Clausen, 1970, p. 304.)

conditions of the experiment. Schwartz and Clausen suggested that males were largely unaffected by the experimental manipulations because the presence of female bystanders encouraged their enactment of role-appropriate behavior reflecting courage, strength and dominance. Finally, both female and male subjects responded more quickly when the victim had provided specific information about how to help him.

In Darley and Latané's study of responses to a victim's seizure, reported above, a comparison was also made of the responses of males and females when a competent bystander was present or absent in a three-person group. The presence of a competent bystander had no effect on the subjects' reactions to the plight of a female victim. The combined results of these two studies do not strongly support the diffusion of responsibility prediction that the presence of a competent bystander should allow an individual to absolve himself of responsibility.

3.   The Relationship of Bystanders To Each Other and To the Victim

The embarrassment hypothesis suggests that subjects in bystander intervention studies may be less concerned about appearing foolish to friends than to strangers. The experimental situations are unusual and to some degree unbelieveable. A person may intervene and take a chance of being mistaken in the presence of a friend, who is not likely to find fault with the actor simply because he made an error in judgment in a laboratory experiment. But a stranger may believe the actor has lost his "cool" when the circumstances do not clearly justify it. The responsibility diffusion hypothesis also suggests that subjects will more often intervene in the presence of friends than strangers, since responsibility can more easily be shifted to a stranger than to a friend.

Darley and Latané (1968) found support for these predictions. The seizure procedure was once again used. The subjects were run in groups of three (the victim, the subject, and a friend the subject brought with him). The results were compared with the earlier study in which a subject was paired with strangers. The subjects with a friend responded to a call for help just as frequently and as quickly as subjects who were alone, and significantly faster than subjects paired with strangers.

Commonsense suggests that bystanders will be more ready to intervene on behalf of persons they know and like than on behalf of total strangers. It would be particularly humiliating to meet someone you know after an incident in which help was needed and you did not provide it. A person has a special responsibility to help his friends. Some support for this commonsense belief was found by Darley and Latané. Subjects met and had a pleasant conversation with the future victim of a seizure, following which the usual procedures were followed in a subject/victim/four-stranger condition. When the victim had been personalized and was no longer just a strange voice, the subjects in the group conditions were just as likely to help as were those who were alone. A mild degree of attraction may have been fostered by the original encounter with the victim, thereby engendering more sympathy and a greater sense of responsibility for helping her in the emergency situation.

4. Victim Responsibility

Bystanders are reluctant to help a victim who is viewed as responsible for his own predicament. When a stranger falls to the street, a passerby is more likely to help if his distress is attributed to illness rather than drunkenness. This exact comparison was carried out by Piliavin, Rodin, and Piliavin (1969) in a field experiment. Teams of college students enacted emergency scenes on board commuter trains in New York City. The confederate who took the role of the victim was either a white or a black adult male between the ages of 26 and 35. The victim was portrayed as either drunk or sick. In the drunk condition he boarded the train reeking of liquor and carried a bottle wrapped in a brown bag. In the sick condition the actor appeared sober and carried a black cane.

After the train passed the first station, the victim staggered forward and collapsed, remaining supine until he received help either from a passenger or confederate. The confederate was directed to intervene in about one minute if no one else did; he was to act as a model. The number, speed of helping, sex, and race of all good samaritans were recorded by two other students on the train. Preliminary rides on the trains had revealed that on the average, 45% of the passengers were black and 55% were white.

On the 65 trains in which the sick role was enacted, the passengers helped the victim before the model intervened in 62 of the cases. The drunk received spontaneous help in only 19 of 38 cases. Over 90 percent of the good samaritans were male. Blacks and whites helped about equally often when the victim was sick, irrespective of his race. However, there was a distinct tendency for the samaritans to help only members of their own race when the victim was drunk. Contrary to the diffusion of responsibility hypothesis, there was no relationship between the number of bystanders and the speed of helping. Once again, as in so many of the field studies of prosocial behavior, the surreptitious intrusion in the lives of people in public places must be considered ethically questionable.

The difference between a laboratory situation and the very real emergency that faced passengers on the trains may account for the lack of support for the responsibility diffusion hypothesis. In laboratory studies, subjects do not usually confront a victim directly, there is some problem in interpreting the situation, and the response required is simply to report the incident verbally to the experimenter. On the commuter train, there was little ambiguity about the victim's need for help and the bystanders had ample opportunity to observe one another's startle reactions to the situation. When the victim's plight is not considered his own doing, no ambiguity exists regarding the emergency, experienced conflict becan directly perceive the victim, the presence of other bystanders apparently does not inhibit helping behavior.

5. Helping in Natural Disasters

A typical pattern of helping behavior has been observed following natural disasters. The Oklahoma Research Institute (reported in Cartwright & Zander, 1953) interviewed people who had been involved in one of four disasters—three tornadoes in Oklahoma and an explosion in the port of Texas City. The typical person who was separated from his family at the time of the disaster rushed to find and rejoin them, and much of the disorganization of the community was a result of these flights to the kinship group. Public servants, such as a policemen, fireman, and public utility workers, whose services were needed during the emergency, experienced conflict between doing their duty and rejoining their loved ones. Most chose to leave their posts to find their families. One exception to this rule were the refinery workers in Texas City, who stayed on the job, as they had been trained to do, until the refinery was safely shut down. It is questionable that these workers were motivated by loyalty to the refinery, however. The most direct and specific action they could perform to pre-vent the disaster from growing, with consequent damage to the entire community and their own families, was to contain it at the refinery.

Help was most often extended to strangers by persons who had special competence or prior experience in disaster situations and who knew their families were safe. For example, a police chief in Texas City stayed at his post for 72 hours and provided the leadership necessary for the reorganization of the community. According to his own report, he said he could give undivided attention to his duty because he knew that his family was visiting relatives in another community at the time of the explosion. Similarly, a fireman in a town struck by a tornado was at home when the storm occurred and no one in his family was hurt. Although he immediately went out to fight the fires caused by the storm, he reported that none of the other firemen showed up because of injuries to their family members.

Many of the rescue workers who provided help to strangers were drawn to the vicinity of heavy casualties because they believed members of their own family were in the area. For example, a man rushed to a movie theater before a tornado struck because of concern for his children who were in attendance. He prevented the frightened people in the theater from rushing out into the storm by holding the doors shut. When acclaimed as a hero later on, he said his only thought was for the safety of his children and denied taking any risk for the sake of strangers in the audience.

The differences in response of two company officials to the explosion in Texas City further suggests that some bond between people is associated with a tendency to provide help in an emergency. One plant official suffered a broken arm and multiple lacerations but nevertheless was actively involved in rescue operations. He reported having no concern at all for the property of the company; his only important concern was for the preservation of life. The second plant official had recently arrived in the community and hardly knew his coworkers or their families. His first reaction was to protect the company's property and to inform the company's president of the accident.

These isolated observations under uncontrolled conditions suggest that the strength of family ties is important in determining the responses of individuals during a disaster. Clifford (1956) found support for this conjecture in a study of a Rio Grande flood that struck two communities, one in Texas and the other in Mexico. The Mexican town of Piedras Negras was more strongly family-oriented than the nearby Texas town. Aiding victims and evacuation procedures were almost exclusively family-connected in the Mexican town but were primarily carried out by community and governmental organizations in the Texas town. In fact, the Mexican victims were quite likely to reject official aid from bureaucratic organizations such as the Red Cross.

Rural and small town communities are more integrated than large metropolitan centers; everything is more personalized and everyone knows everyone else. According to a personal bond hypothesis of helping in emergencies, it might be expected that people from centers with small population will be more likely to help than residents of large centers. There is some evidence that subjects from rural communities are more likely to intervene in experimentally-created emergencies in a laboratory than are subjects from large cities (Latané & Darley, 1969; Milgram, 1970).

Tourists visiting New York City for the first time are often shocked to see drunks lying in the streets with passersby simply walking around them apparently oblivious and indifferent to the distress of the victims. The anonymity of the large city may indeed reduce a sense of responsibility for providing help to others in emergency situations. In a small town there is no anonymity, and each resident may be held responsible for helping others when help is needed. Also, the New Yorker sees so many unusual events as a matter of course that what may appear to others as a crisis is perceived as an everyday occurrence by him.

Following a disaster, there is usually a convergence of people from a wide surrounding area on the stricken community. Some of these outsiders are relatives of residents, some are curiosity seekers, and some may be exploiters in search of profit. A number of the outsiders represent competent personnel organized to provide help to those who need it. These outside helpers, who are often specially trained and paid for their work, do not have the same conflicts between duty and family as do professionals within the community. Form and Nosow (1958) found that a high degree of technical competence and prior experience with disasters were among the most important characteristics of effective helpers in a community struck by a tornado. In a nationwide disaster, such as nuclear attack, outsiders may not be available to provide help (See Box 10.2).

V. PERCEPTION OF PROSOCIAL BEHAVIOR

Prosocial behavior was defined at the beginning of this chapter as the provision of help to others which does not *appear* to be motivated by the hope of gaining a reward. The benefactor may be fulfilling an obligation under a norm of reciprocity or social responsibility or may be seeking to maintain equity between himself and others. His behavior may be due to past learning, and though he may seek to achieve reinforcements, his failure to obtain them may lead an observer to believe his behavior was not selfishly motivated. An actor may provide help and give gifts as an offer of friendship, to obtain social approval, to convey an image of benevolence, as a sign of good will during negotiations, or to attain status. In other words, prosocial behavior is often directed toward influencing other people.

Box 10.2 BEHAVIOR FOLLOWING A NUCLEAR ATTACK

The small amount of social psychological knowledge we have about behavior during disasters can be used to project what would happen following a large scale nuclear attack. The Rand Corporation has estimated the following consequences of a 10,000 megaton attack upon the U.S. There would be approximately 124,000,000 casualties. Many millions of people would be suffering from radiation sickness, third degree burns, broken bones, and blindness induced by looking directly at nuclear explosions. The entire world would appear to be on fire. Automobiles, gas stations, refineries, inflammable houses and materials and dry forests would be consumed in huge firestorms. Water mains and sewers would burst, reservoirs would be demolished or contaminated by radiation. Hospitals, stores, and warehouses that serve as the sources of medical and food supplies would be destroyed.

The extent of the catastrophe would be unparalleled in human history. There are a few previous cases of society-wide disasters. For example, Paraguay lost about 60 percent of its population in a war with Uruguay over a five year period, and the Black Death killed over a third of the population of Europe. But both of these disasters took place over a period of years, while a nuclear disaster would take place within a matter of hours or days.

The Civil Defense plan is to get survivors to shelters as soon as possible. Even one hour of exposure to the likely radiation levels could be fatal. How would the survivors respond to the crisis? Suppose the attack took place during a working day. The father, mother, and children in a family would be distributed in work settings, the home, and school. Would these family members accept separation and uncertainty about each other's fate or would they refuse shelter and seek to reunite?

The evidence suggests that family members are often concerned less about their own lives than about their loved ones. If any roads can still be traversed, imagine the traffic jams as each person seeks shelter, attempts to leave the cities, and tries to reunite with his family; and what would trained personnel do? Physicians, nurses, policemen, firemen, ambulance drivers, and many others would either be confined to shelters or would abandon their duties to search for their families. Unlike many natural disasters, the national scope of the crisis would probably leave few intact communities from which secondary aid by competent and trained personnel could be expected by people in the stricken areas.

Conditions in the shelters would be abominable. Diabetics would be deprived of insulin. Many people would be vomiting from radiation sickness. There would be no refrigeration for food, no electricity for light or heat, little water, a major sewage disposal problem, and inadequate quantities of disinfecting agents. The filth would create the conditions for epidemic diseases. How would people get along with each other in the protracted period they would have to stay in the shelter (at least three weeks)? Would racial or ethnic conflicts occur? How would people react to their own government, which did not prevent such a disaster from happening? These questions are not pleasant to contemplate and few definitive answers can be given to them.

Reactions to benefactors are probably determined by the observer's perception of the cause of the prosocial actions. When a benefactor incurs costs in time, effort, and resources and assumes risks in order to help someone else (the augmentation principle), and no extrinsic reason can be found that would allow an attribution to selfish motives (the discounting principle), an observer will consider the actor to be altruistic. Altruistic acts involve sympathetic and helpful behavior that is freely chosen by a benefactor without regard for his own self-interest. Are men ever altruistic? Or does a perception of altruism always depend on ignorance of the benefactor's real motives?

A. The Altruistic Paradox

One view of man assumes his basic goodness and considers him to be capable of selfless action. But why should a person engage in self-sacrificial behavior? To help others? Why should he want to help others? The hedonist would be pleased with much of the research in social psychology, because an ultimately selfish reason is almost always found for prosocial behavior. How can some people be so convinced of the goodness of man if hedonism is correct? People do give their lives for great causes, in behalf of principle, and to save others. The hedonist does not deny the occurrence of such actions, but he is ready to suggest that some values are greater than life and a person may be ready to exchange a lesser value for a greater one. Thus, a selfish reason can be found for every prosocial behavior, but paradoxically, people clearly perceive others and themselves as capable of selfless behavior.

Neither philosophers nor psychologists are likely ever to satisfy either party to the above dispute. The term "prosocial" was adopted to avoid the controversy, not to solve it. The conditions under which prosocial actions are elicited are investigated, and no commitment is made beforehand about whether the behavior is altruistic or hedonistic. Who would deny a philan-thropist the internal pride or satisfaction he feels in providing funds to help develop a great university? He may be considered altruistic and be considered by many as deserving of their admiration. He is entitled to feel good for doing good works.

The scientific question of interest is not whether a benefactor is *really* altruistic, but rather what conditions lead observers to *believe* an actor is altruistic. The principles of person perception reviewed in Chapter 5 should be applicable to understanding when observers label prosocial behavior as altruistic.

B. Attributions of Altruism

Very little research has been done concerning the perception of altruism. Nevertheless, we can speculate about what conditions should lead an observer to label an actor as altruistic. These speculations should be considered hypotheses requiring empirical evaluation. It seems rather clear that an actor's behavior must be perceived as beneficial and intentional.

The invariance of favor-doing or beneficial behavior is a basis for inferring altruistic motives. The attribution of altruism will be stronger when the actor consistently provides benevolent behavior in spite of the fact that the recipient reacts to the benefactor in a variety of ways—selfishly, indifferently, lovingly, angrily, or whatever. The mediation of non-contingent rewards is perceived as more altruistic than contingent rewards. When the actor does stipulate a contingency for providing a reward, he may still be perceived as altruistic if the contingency is perceived as in the recipient's best interests.

Social comparisons may also promote the interpretation of an actor's prosocial behavior as altruistic. A comparison may indicate that he provides more favors and benefits than the average individual with whom the observer interacts. In addition, the social consensus of others may lay to rest suspicions about his intentions, reaffirm the observer's attribution of altruism, or help to interpret an actor's intentions when they are ambiguous. The observer's own philosophy and value system may affect his attribution. Some cynics always find a selfish motive to explain a benefactor's behavior, while idealists may see good intentions behind even the most dastardly act.

Does an actor ever view his own prosocial actions as altruistic? Generally, he is more likely to view his own behavior as caused by environmental factors than the behavior of other people (Jones & Nisbett, 1971). This tendency is modified when the outcomes of actions are classified as bad or good. A person tends to view his bad acts as strongly determined by the environment, but attributes good actions to his own volition. When you do something bad, you find reasons why nothing else could have been done; when you do something good, like giving to charity, you tend to overlook the social pressures that may have caused you to drop the quarter in the cannister.

The principles of attribution theory may help to answer the question of when prosocial behavior will be perceived as altruistic. The risks taken to provide the help and the time, effort, or other costs incurred allow the observer to make an attribution of altruism when the actor does not require compliance or reciprocation from the person helped. This represents the augmentation principle. An altruistic person's actions cannot be discounted as due to environmental causes because they appear to be freely undertaken and intentional. Of course it is easier to infer that a person is altruistic if his prosocial actions show consistency over time, situations, and persons. Several of these principles have been confirmed in studies of perceived altruism (Rivera, Gaes, & Tedeschi, 1975).

VI. CHAPTER SUMMARY

Prosocial behavior consists of beneficent actions that do not bring immediate and tangible rewards to the actor. A person may engage in prosocial behavior for many different reasons. The demands of social norms may prompt self-sacrificial action. Three norms have been considered as important for eliciting prosocial acts: (1) reciprocity, (2) social responsibility, and (3) equity.

The norm of reciprocity is considered universal to all societies. It serves both as a starting mechanism in encouraging people to interact with one another and as a type of moral cement in maintaining social relationships. Initiating interaction by generosity fosters friendship and incurs debt on the part of the recipient. Inability to repay a debt may be compensated for by giving the creditor additional status in a group. Failure to pay a debt brings shame on the debtor. In general, reciprocity requires equivalence in the utilities exchanged between the parties. However, the need of the recipient, the resources and generosity of the donor, and the possibility of future exchanges all affect reciprocity behavior. The personal relationship between the parties has no effect on the norm of reciprocity and its stipulation of equivalence in exchange. The expectation that others will meet their obligation to repay debts encourages an individual to initiate exchange by offering gifts or benefits. When people meet the demands of the reciprocity norm, a stable social organization can develop.

The evidence does not support a general norm of social responsibility. Instead, there are apparently situations in which females are encouraged to be nurturant and males are encouraged to reject the appearance of dependence on others. On the other hand, males tend to be chivalrous to females in distress, while females are less likely to help under such circumstances. The conditions under which a norm is activated or that make an individual feel responsible to render help are not well understood at present. One strongly supported principle has emerged from investigations of social responsibility: the greater the costs of prosocial behavior, the less likely it is it will be performed. Speculation suggests that prosocial behavior can also be motivated by attempts to reduce the distress associated with inequity. However, this conjecture has yet to be adequately tested.

Prosocial behavior is often learned; if it is seldom reinforced, it will undergo extinction. From an observer's point of view, an actor's prosocial behavior may not be perceived as motivated by an attempt to gain reinforcements because the actor is not obviously successful in achieving them. Observers also imitate the self-sacrificial behavior of a model, as long as the costs are not high for doing so. The performance and generalizability of modeling effects over time and varying situations are not known at present.

Research directed toward establishing relationships between internal states of the actor and his willingness to engage in prosocial behavior has uncovered some empirical regularities. It is much less certain whether it has revealed very much about the internal states of the individual that might account for the observed relationships. The following circumstances apparently elicit prosocial behavior: (1) the individual experiences success; (2) the individual receives some unearned benefit; and (3) accidental harm is done but the actor's motives may be in question. The behavior elicited by these circumstances occurs within a short time after the actor experiences them; there is no evidence of any long-term effects. Furthermore, most of the studies have imposed only a small cost on subjects for engaging in prosocial actions.

Hypotheses about a "glow of good will," sympathy and empathy, guilt, and self-concern have generated some interesting experiments and results have sometimes confirmed these hypotheses. However, there are too many other plausible explanations for the findings to have great confidence in any single one. Much prosocial behavior could be explained by an actor's concern for impression management.

A bystander must first interpret a situation as an emergency before deciding whether to provide help to a victim. He looks for cues from other people in making this interpretation. If others appear unconcerned and take no action, he is apt to decide that no emergency exists. On the other hand, startle responses and other signs that a crisis is at hand may cause him to take action. A bystander will be reluctant to intervene if he believes he is intruding in a legitimate conflict between others.

Fear of embarrassment for undertaking a foolish action and a belief that other bystanders will take the responsibility for action may inhibit an individual from offering help. A personal bond with other bystanders or with the victim encourages one to take responsibility. Most communities employ professionals who are trained to provide expert help during emergencies. Bystanders often confine their intervention to calling on expert professionals to provide what is needed.

The philosophical question of whether men are completely hedonistic and whether they are capable of altruistic action can probably never be solved by science. Whatever stance is taken on this issue, it is clear that even when benefactors view their own behavior as selfish, observers sometimes perceive them as altruistic (and the converse). The causes of prosocial behavior and the conditions that determine how an observer will perceive such actions are not identical.

We can speculate about the conditions that lead an observer, including the actor, to attribute prosocial behavior to altruistic motivation. Principles borrowed from attribution theory, such as consistency, consensus, and the augmentation and discounting principles, as well as social comparison information, can be used to predict the conditions under which altruistic motives will be inferred as the basis of prosocial behavior.

SUGGESTED READINGS

Gouldner, A. W. The norm of reciprocity: A preliminary statement. *American Sociological Review,* 1960, *25,* 161–178. A classic statement of the norm of reciprocity by a leading sociologist.

Latané, B. and Darley, J. M. *The unresponsive bystander: Why doesn't he help?* New York: Appleton-Century-Crofts, 1970. An account of a number of imaginative studies performed by the authors and a discussion of the major issues regarding research on intervention in emergency situations.

Macaulay, J., and Berkowitz, L. (Eds.) *Altruism and helping behavior.* New York: Academic Press, 1970. A series of papers that examine the situational determinants of helping, the socialization of altruism, and the function of social norms in promoting prosocial behavior.

Mauss, M. *The gift.* New York: Norton, 1967. An anthropologist's fascinating study of the forms and functions of prosocial behavior in different societies.

Smith, R. W. (Ed.) *Guilt: Man and society.* New York: Doubleday Anchor, 1971. A collection of papers examining the origins of guilt, its social manifestations, and its political significance.

Wispé, L. G. (Ed.) Positive forms of social behavior. *Journal of Social Issues,* 1972, *28,* 1–227. A special issue devoted to examining all facets of prosocial behavior.

CHAPTER 11

Interpersonal Attraction

CHAPTER PREVIEW

What do you mean when you say you like someone? What is love? Why do you love one person and not another? Poets, romantics, philosophers, and lovers have attempted for many centuries to answer these questions. Can scientists find the answers, or is studying love like trying to catch smoke? The more you try to grasp it, the more it eludes you? Only in very recent years have questions of the antecedents and consequences of interpersonal attraction been scientifically studied.

Social scientists have tended to skirt the problem of a conceptual definition of attraction by the operational expedient of asking people whether or not they like one another, and, if so, how much. Experimenters manipulate various independent variables in an attempt to ascertain their relationships to the verbal reports provided by subjects on a like-dislike scale. This trial-and-error procedure has uncovered some relationships that have provided the basis for theories of attraction and even of love.

Most of the hard evidence concerning the development, maintenance, and enhancement of attraction between people has been gathered in laboratory settings. The persons studied are usually total strangers who meet for the first time in the experiment. The question naturally arises whether these fleeting encounters throw much light on enduring relationships involving passionate love or hatred, the nurturant love of a mother for her child, or the loyalty of a deep and lasting friendship. To deal with this question, a series of field and case studies have been carried out. Basic agreement among the results obtained from divergent approaches provides us with strong reason to believe that fundamental knowledge about attraction is being garnered from this highly controlled scientific research.

A number of antecedent conditions have been associated with liking for another person. Someone who provides rewards is liked, particularly when the rewards are greater than expected by the recipient. When a person is feeling good, he is more friendly toward others. Because being rewarded makes an individual feel good, it is difficult to determine whether it is the reward itself or the positive mood associated with it that produces attraction. Other antecedent conditions for liking another person are similarity, proximity, self-esteem and physical attractiveness. An individual is more apt to like someone who has similar attitudes, beliefs, and values, who lives or works nearby, and who provides positive evaluations that bolster his self-esteem. Physical appearance is also an important factor in the development of attraction, particularly between persons of the opposite sex.

A number of alternative theories have been proposed to explain why particular antecedent conditions lead to attraction or disattraction. Theories of reinforcement, social comparison, cognitive balance, and exchange offer competing explanations. Each of these theories has been developed with respect to a particular set of antecedent conditions. For example, cognitive balance theory is most relevent to a consideration of similarity. We will examine each theory in the context of the most relevant antecedent condition.

Another way of viewing attraction is as a power resource. People who are liked are more influential than people who are not liked. Thus, a person may want to be liked because of the power it gives him. This perspective interprets the antecedent conditions of attraction in terms of their relevance to social influence. We will conclude the chapter by describing this social power theory.

I. REWARDS AND AROUSAL AS ANTECEDENTS OF ATTRACTION

Traditional learning theory suggests that any neutral stimulus which is consistently associated with a reinforcement will acquire reward value. This is the *principle of secondary reinforcement*. Primary reinforcements are generally considered to be those that satisfy some biological requirement, such as food or sex. The basic need of the human infant at birth is to be fed. Presumably, the child is not born loving his mother. If the mother is considered to be a neutral stimulus and is consistently associated with rewards (feeding the child), he will come to value his mother. That is, her presence will in itself be a pleasant state of affairs for the child.

Obtaining reinforcements is associated with positive arousal states. A person who gets what he wants may report being in a good mood. It is apparently difficult to dislike people when you are feeling good; the world looks rosy and you feel generous. As we saw in the last chapter, positive arousal states are believed to promote prosocial behavior. The reinforcement and arousal hypotheses are seldom clearly separable. When a person receives a reinforcement from a stranger, is the latter liked more because of the reward associated with him or because the recipient is in a pleasant state? We will examine this issue in more detail.

Still another view of the relationship between rewards and liking is in expectancy theory. People are said to develop a comparison level, an expectancy of the amount of reward they will receive from any particular interaction (Thibaut & Kelley, 1959). Increments or decrements in liking may depend on violations of expectancies. Contrary to the secondary reinforcement principle, expectancy theory suggests that it is possible for a decrease in attraction to occur even when rewards are given—if the rewards are less than were expected.

Secondary reinforcement, positive arousal states, and disconfirmation of expectations provide alternative conceptions of the effect of reinforcements on liking. While the theoretical disputes are unresolved, it is clear that persons generally do like others who provide rewards, regardless of the explanation given.

A. Reinforcement Theory

Lott and Lott (1972) have clearly stated a secondary reinforcement view of how attraction is developed: "Being in the presence of a discriminable person (or some symbolic representation of him) when one attains satisfaction of any drive or succeeds in reaching any desirable goal, regardless of whether the discriminable person has any instrumental relationship to this state of affairs, is a sufficient condition for the acquisition of liking for the contiguous person. Being in the presence of a discriminable person when one experiences pain or frustration is a sufficient condition to produce dislike for the contiguous person" (p. 112).

The secondary reinforcement view of attraction is somewhat different from Homans' (1961) theory of social exchange. According to Homans, we like those who help or reward us and we dislike those who hinder or harm us. The implication is that the other person must be instrumental in providing the reinforcements. In the theory proposed by Lott and Lott, the neutral person need only be present at the time a reward is provided to a target; whether or not he is instrumental in securing rewards, he will be liked by the target as long as he is present when they are received.

The evidence has clearly established that persons who willingly reward or otherwise facilitate the goal attainment of others are liked (Berkowitz & Levy, 1956; Kleiner, 1960; Myers, 1962). Conversely, persons who willingly punish others or impede their goal attainment are disliked (Burnstein & Worchel, 1962; Kipnis, 1958; Zajonc & Marin, 1967). Liking produces the expectation of rewards, which, in turn, encourages frequent interaction; and if the expected rewards are forthcoming, further growth of the relationship is probable. A positive cycle of increasing attraction is the result.

The person is rewarded, likes his benefactor, develops expectations of future rewards, is encouraged to increase the number of his interactions with the benefactor, and if the subsequent interactions are also rewarding, his degree of liking intensifies.

The studies cited were restricted to examining how a recipient of favors or harm evaluates the person who was instrumental in producing these outcomes. Lott and Lott (1960) tested a secondary reinforcement prediction by seating three children around a game board, with each playing independently of the others. If a child safely landed a rocket ship in the game, he was rewarded; the other children had nothing to do with his success or failure. Children who succeeded liked the other two children in their group more than did children who failed.

Two further predictions from learning theory were tested: (1) the more frequently a reinforcement is paired with a neutral stimulus, the greater the acquired (secondary reinforcement) value the neutral stimulus should have; and (2) the greater the delay between the presentation of the neutral stimulus and subsequent reinforcement, the less secondary reinforcement value the neutral stimulus should have. Using the same rocket game procedures, James and Lott (1964) found that children who had been rewarded frequently preferred their two companions more than did children who had been rewarded less frequently. Lott, Aponte, Lott, and McGinley (1969) had first-grade children play a different kind of game. The experimenter was instrumental in providing rewards and either gave them immediately or delayed them. The children were asked how much they liked the assistant to the experimenter, who was present but had not directly given any rewards. The assistant was liked better in the immediate than in the delayed reinforcement condition.

Two further experiments reported by Lott, Bright, Weinstein, and Lott (1970) produced some inconsistent results. In the first experiment children performed a task and were rewarded with either a highly preferred snack or a less desired snack—determined for each child by prior selections among types of crackers, chips or peanuts. The reward value of the snacks was also manipulated by testing half the children immediately before lunch and the other half right after lunch. The snacks should have been more reinforcing when the children were hungry than when they were satiated.

The snack was handed to a subject in a box that contained a photograph of a college student. The children were then asked to rate the attractiveness of the photograph. Consistent with learning theory, the photograph was rated as more attractive when it was associated with the preferred snack. The greater the primary reinforcement (snack), the more value was acquired by the secondary reinforcement (photograph). Contrary to predictions of learning theory, however, the degree of hunger of the children did not affect their ratings of the photograph.

In the second experiment, the subjects were college students who were identified as either high or low in their need for academic recognition. All subjects were asked to take an intelligence test and were given bogus feedback that they had either done well or poorly. The subjects were then asked to evaluate a person who was present when they received their scores. Subjects with a high recognition need expressed greater liking for the other person in the successful than in the poor performance condition. Subjects with a low need for academic recognition gave neutral ratings to the stimulus person whatever their performance had been on the intelligence test.

Why did need produce an effect in the second but not in the first experiment? One possible explanation is that there is something about concern for academic recognition that leads people to be more emotionally responsive to others. In other words, the separation of the subjects according to their high and low need for recognition may have simply identified people in terms of how responsive or friendly they are to other people. The same results may have been achieved even if the rewards and punishments used had no relevance at all to the presumed needs of the subjects. With respect to the first experiment it is reasonable to assume that snacks and lunches are separate reinforcers for children and that being satiated by eating lunch does not reduce the pleasure they experience by eating snacks.

B. Arousal and Attraction

A stirred-up emotional state may temporarily affect how an individual feels about other people. Several studies have shown that arousal is associated with positive and negative evaluations of other persons. Griffitt (1970) placed subjects in a chamber with a controlled temperature of either 90.6° or 67.5° Fahrenheit. The subjects in both chambers were given exactly the same information regarding an anonymous person and were asked to rate him. They liked the stimulus person less when the chamber was hot than when it was comfortably cool. Griffitt concluded, "It appears that when one is feeling good his responses to others will be more positive than when he is feeling bad" (p. 243). Although he referred to crime statistics that reflect an association between hot summer weather and the incidence of violent crimes in America, it is questionable whether temperatures rather than some correlated factors are responsible for the increase of crime in the summer. For example, teen-agers are out of school and workers have vacations providing both with more opportunity to get into trouble.

Griffitt and Veitch (1971) followed much the same procedure, creating hot or comfortable conditions in a chamber but in addition placing a small group (3 to 5 persons) or a large group (12 to 16 persons) in the small chamber. Subjects were asked how they felt while they were in the chamber and responded more negatively in the hot and crowded than in the cool and sparsely populated chamber. Furthermore, the more uncomfortable they rated themselves, the less they liked a stimulus person.

Several other experiments have also shown the arousal-attraction relationship. Izard (1964) had subjects observe an actress portray one of four roles: (1) a highly enthusiastic person; (2) a warm, friendly person; (3) an angry, hostile person; or (4) a fearful, anxious person. The subjects exposed to the two positive conditions rated themselves as feeling better and evaluated the actress more positively than did those in the two negative conditions.

Gouaux (1971) created different moods in subjects by showing them one of two movies, either *Good Old Corn* (Warner Brothers) or *John F. Kennedy 1917–1963* (20th Century Fox). The first film produced laughter and positive feelings, while the second was sad and produced depression. The subjects who watched the happy film rated a stimulus person as more attractive than those who watched the depressing film.

Positive emotional states may soften an individual's impression of a negative stimulus person. Landy and Mettee (1969) either had subjects witness an experimenter insult another subject or else the subjects themselves were insulted by the experimenter. They were then asked either to rate hostile and nonhostile cartoons or to engage in another kind of task. Finally, they rated the attractiveness of the insulting experimenter. The subjects who had been exposed to humor, and presumably had an opportunity to change their negative arousal state to a positive one, rated the experimenter as less unattractive than did those who had been given the task which did not involve humor. Many tense and hostile encounters have been defused by the deft humor of peacemakers.

Any event that arouses a negative emotional state may create a temporary dislike for whoever is nearby. When a person is given bad news, a negative emotional state is aroused and may be associated with the bearer. Tyrants have been known to cut out the tongues of messengers who brought them bad news. Rosen and Tesser (1970) found that subjects were reluctant to transmit bad news in a study of the "MUM" effect. When the subjects arrived at the laboratory, each was told that his discussion partner was late. A collaborator informed the experimenter of a phone call for the subject who was late. The message was to call home immediately because of some really good or bad news. The waiting subject had an opportunity to give the late arrival the message. The subjects were more willing to relay the good news than the bad. While almost all subjects mentioned the phone call, those in the good news condition also mentioned its quality, while those in the bad news condition kept mum about the quality of the message.

C.   Secondary Reinforcement and Attribution Theory

When a person gets a reinforcement, he feels good, and when he feels good, he likes those who are around him. If this chain of events is due to secondary reinforcement, the effects should be relatively lasting; if they are attributable to a transient emotional state, then the momentary positive evaluation should disappear after the state dissipates. Secondary reinforcement studies so far have required subjects to evaluate stimulus persons at the time of or shortly after receiving a reward; consequently, it cannot be determined if it is the association of reward with a neutral stimulus person that produces liking (secondary reinforcement) or whether the pleasant feeling of receiving a reinforcement causes a momentary warm feeling toward other human beings.

The secondary reinforcement theory assumes that all stimuli associated with prim-

ary reinforcement will take on positive value for the organism. It should not matter whether a benefactor provides rewards accidentally, under coercion, or voluntarily; he should be liked in any case because of his association with rewards. However, Pepitone and Sherberg (1957) found that subjects liked a person who insulted another with the good intention of stimulating adaptive behavior, but did not like a person who did the same thing with bad intentions. Pepitone and Kleiner (1957) reported an increase of attraction within competitive groups when a reduction in threat to the status of the group was causally attributed to members of the group. When the cause for the reduction of the threat was attributed to factors external to the group, no increase in attraction occurred.

In Nemeth's (1970) study of reciprocity behavior, reviewed in the last chapter, subjects liked a confederate who voluntarily helped them more than a confederate who helped because he was instructed to do so by the experimenter. According to secondary reinforcement theory, the motive for helping should not affect the degree of liking, but the attribution of motives apparently does matter. The results of these three experiments suggest that support of the secondary reinforcement theory is an artifact of the presence of momentary arousal states.

The issue is far from settled, however. Griffitt and Guay (1969) have found support for the secondary reinforcement hypothesis. They had subjects engage in a creativity task that was scored by a fictitious grader; a confederate sat just outside the room while they received good or poor scores. Half the subjects in each of the reinforcement conditions were asked to evaluate the grader and half were asked to evaluate the confederate who sat outside the room. The rewarding agent (the grader) and the neutral confederate were liked equally well when the subjects were rewarded with good scores and neither was liked very much when they received poor scores.

One possible explanation for why subjects liked the confederate when they received good scores is that he knew how well or poorly they had done on the creativity task. It could be presumed that an observer who saw them perform well would have some respect for them, and people tend to like those who respect them. Support for this alternative hypothesis was found by Stapleton (1975). As we saw in Chapters 8 and 9, esteem (perceived expertise) is a valuable power resource and it may be expected that any increment of power will be experienced as reinforcing.

D. Expectancy Theory

Thibaut and Kelley (1959) proposed that attraction develops as a function of disconfirmed expectancies. A person is assumed to develop an expectancy for what he will gain from each interaction with another person. His mean expectancy is referred to as his *comparison level* (see Chapter 8). When another person provides benefits that exceed the CL, the recipient should increase his liking for the benefactor. When benefits are less than the CL, a decrease in attraction should occur. The receipt of benefits consistent with expectations should not affect the degree of liking. Hence, pleasant surprise or disappointment—both of which result from disconfirmed expectations—are considered to be the bases of changes in liking for another person.

Stapleton, Nacci, and Tedeschi (1973) found support for the disconfirmed expectations theory. Subjects were induced to like or dislike a confederate of the same sex. The confederate was then given ten opportunities to reward the subjects and actually gave one, five, or nine rewards. According to reinforcement theory, the more rewards received by the subjects, the greater their liking should be for the confederate. The predictions of expectancy theory are a bit more complicated. High attraction should lead subjects to expect many benefits from the confederate, and low attraction should lead to a low CL. The receipt of many benefits should merely confirm the expectations of the high attraction subjects, but should exceed the expectations of the low attraction subjects; no change in liking should occur among the former, but a substantial increase should be observed among the latter. Just the opposite pattern of results would be expected when only one benefit was provided by the confederate. High attraction subjects should be disappointed and lower their liking for the confederate, while low attraction subjects should merely have their expectations confirmed and should not change their liking.

Measures of the degree of liking for the confederate were taken both before and after he mediated benefits to the subjects. Changes in attraction from pre- to posttests could reflect either a decrease (minus score) or an increase (plus score) in liking. The results shown in Table 11.1 clearly support expectancy theory and disconfirm the prediction of reinforcement theory.

Similar predictions can be derived from CL theory with regard to punishments. High attraction for another person should lead an individual to expect few punishments, and low attraction should lead to a

Table 11.1   Mean Changes From Pre-to-Post Ratings in Subjects' Liking for a Confederate, as a Function of Original Liking and the Frequency of Benefits Received.[a]

Pre-benefit attraction level	Frequency of benefits		
	One	Five	Nine
High	−2.20	−0.67	−0.20
Low	+0.20	+1.10	+2.30

[a] After Stapleton, Nacci and Tedeschi, 1973, p. 203. On a 2–14 point scale the pre-ratings of subjects in the high attraction conditions averaged 11.8 and those of subjects in the low attraction conditions averaged 6.5.

greater expectation of punishment. Changes in attraction for the agent should occur only when these expectations are disconfirmed. Stapleton, Nelson, Franconere, and Tedeschi (1974) had a liked or disliked confederate deliver one, five, or nine shocks (out of ten opportunities) to subjects. Changes in attraction once again supported the CL theory. Low attraction subjects increased their liking for the agent when they were shocked infrequently and high attraction subjects decreased their liking for him when they were shocked frequently. When high attraction subjects were shocked infrequently and low attraction subjects were shocked frequently, their expectations were confirmed and they did not change their level of liking for the agent.

II. SIMILARITY AND ATTRACTION

In the physical world particles with opposite charges attract one another; but, among people, like attracts like. Over 2000 years ago Aristotle observed, "And they are friends who have come to regard the same things as good and the same things as evil, they who are friends of the same people, and they who are enemies of the same people . . . We like those who resemble us, and are engaged in the same pursuits . . . We like those who desire the same things as we, if the case is such that we and they can share the same things together" (translated by McKeon, 1932, pp. 103–105). The keen observations of Artistotle have been confirmed by a great deal of scientific evidence.

Three basic theories have been proposed to explain why similarity of beliefs, attitudes, and values is an antecedent to interpersonal attraction: reinforcement, social comparison, and balance. The reinforcement and social comparison theories are based on an assumption that the individual has a need to develop a "correct" view of social reality (Festinger, 1954). White (1959) proposed that man has a drive to be competent in dealing with the environment (see also Chapter 3, I). Competence is associated with success, rewards, and power, as well as biological survival. White refers to the need for competence as the *effectance motive*.

Byrne (1971) has interpreted interpersonal agreements as reinforcing to the individual's need for competence. Balance theory, as was explained in Chapter 5, assumes that stable systems of attitudes are comforting, while inconsistent attitudes are associated with tension and discomfort. Persons who share similar attitudes like one another because of the cognitive comfort each derives from the relationship. We will see that these three theories make somewhat different predictions regarding the development of attraction between persons.

A need-complementarity theory proposes that opposites sometimes attract each other. If what one person needs prompts behavior that fulfills the needs of a second person, and vice versa, their opposite needs will complement each other. It is consistent with reinforcement theory that persons with complementary needs should like one another. After first reviewing the evidence with regard to theories of attitude similarity, we will examine the need complementarity hypothesis.

A. Attitude Similarity and Attraction

Numerous studies, using a variety of procedures and measures, have explored the relationship of attitude similarity and attraction. In a classic field study, Newcomb (1961) offered male sophomore and junior transfer students to the University of Michigan rent-free housing for a semester in exchange for their agreement to spend four or five hours a week filling out questionnaires. Transfer students were selected because they came from widely separated geographical areas, making it unlikely that they would be acquainted with one another prior to the study. The questionnaires asked about the students' attitudes regarding the world at large, their fellow roomers, and themselves. Newcomb assigned some men who were similar to each other and some who were dissimilar as roommates. Over the 16-week period, the development of friendships among strangers was carefully observed.

As might be expected, the students' perceptions of one another's attitudes and values became more accurate over time. Presumably, they had ample opportunity to interact, perhaps including discussions of items on the weekly questionnaires. At first the men were most attracted to their roommates or near neighbors in the rooming house, but these early friendships were not very stable. Attitude similarity turned out to be the most stable determinant of attraction between pairs of students. The men chose as friends those who were similar on a number of measures: political and religious views, rural or urban background, college major, and so forth. Furthermore, friends considered each other to be more similar in attitudes and values than they actually were, though they tended to become more accurate in their perceptions over time. The same tendency to overestimate similarity has been found with married couples (Byrne & Blaylock, 1963). Levinger & Breedlove (1966) also reported that the greater the satisfaction with marriage, the greater the similarity assumed by the partners.

Byrne (1962) attempted to induce attraction for a stranger among subjects by providing information about their degree of similarity. The subjects filled out an attitude questionnaire that asked them to check one of six alternatives, from strongly agree to strongly disagree, with regard to statements about issues of considerable interest, such as music, premarital intercourse, belief in God, drinking, and so on. After the subjects completed the attitude survey they were informed that the experiment was concerned with how people form impressions of one another when they have never met but have some information about each other's attitudes. They were then given questionnaires allegedly filled

out by another person, but which had in fact been prepared to reflect varying degrees of similarity to the subjects' own responses. This is sometimes called the "phantom other" technique, because subjects never see the stimulus person. Eight degrees of similarity were manipulated, ranging from no agreement to agreement on all seven attitude items. The subjects were then asked to make a series of judgments about the "other person" on a scale that included a measure of liking. As can be seen from Table 11.2, liking was a direct function of the degree of similarity between the attitudes of the subject and the stimulus person.

Byrne and Nelson (1965) asked whether the similarity-attraction relationship was based on the absolute number of similar attitudes or whether the proportion of similar to dissimilar attitudes was the critical factor. The design of their experiment is shown in Table 11.3. The prepared questionnaires given to subjects reflected 4, 8, or 16 similar attitudes. The number of dissimilar attitudes was varied from 0 to 32 in order to manipulate the proportion of similarity (i.e., from 1.00 to .33). Only the proportion of similar attitudes produced effects on liking; their absolute number had no effect.

Computer dating systems often attempt to pair up couples who have similar backgrounds and interests. How good is this method of arranging dates? Byrne, Ervin, and Lamberth (1970) assessed the attitudes of male and female college students and then arranged 30 minute coke dates between similar and dissimilar pairs. Similar pairs reported greater attraction for one another after these dates than did dissimilar pairs.

Byrne (1969) has empirically examined the importance of the issue involved in the similarity-attraction relationship and has concluded (p. 58) that topic importance is (as rated by the person) relevant in determining attraction only when there is an intermediate degree of similarity between the measured attitudes of two people. The re-

Table 11.2   Functional Relationship Between Attitude Similarity and Attraction.[a]

Experimental condition	Mean attraction response
7 Similar, 0 dissimilar	12.15
6 Similar, 1 dissimilar	11.15
5 Similar, 2 dissimilar	11.43
4 Similar, 3 dissimilar	9.07
3 Similar, 4 dissimilar	8.69
2 Similar, 5 dissimilar	8.47
1 Similar, 6 dissimilar	7.71
0 Similar, 7 dissimilar	7.00

[a] After Byrne, 1969. The scale measuring liking ranged from 2 to 14 (low to high).

sults of a study by Banikiotes, Russell, and Linden (1972) disagree with Byrne's conclusion. These investigators asked members of an undergraduate housing cooperative at a large Midwestern university to fill out an attitude survey like the one used by Byrne. A measure of how much each member of the group liked each of the other members was also obtained. The difference in attraction among pairs was attributable to a single item on political philosophy. However, because the pair-members were known to one another and not "phantom others," this study leaves open the possibility that there were many other differences in attitudes between most- and least-liked pairs which the experimenters did not measure.

B.   Social Comparison Theory

Why should attitude similarity be a basis of attraction? According to Festinger's (1954) theory of social comparison (see Chapter 3), each person strives to attain a true picture of reality, presumably because accurate perceptions are more apt to lead to rewards than faulty perceptions. When a person is unsure about his opinions, attitudes, values and abilities, he will seek out others to make comparisons and gain consensual validation for his views. Comparison others are chosen because of their known similarity to himself. People avoid dissimilar others because the information

they provide would produce cognitive dissonance (see Chapter 5). In sum, social comparison theory assumes a need to know about the world; consensus information is considered reassuring; and contradictory beliefs arouse dissonance, which is an uncomfortable tension state.

Social comparison theory suggests that similarity in attributes other than attitudes may also be important in the development of attraction. There is clearly a tendency for friendships to occur more often between persons of the same sex than between those of opposite sex. This sex preference has been found among nursery school children (Abel & Sahinkaya, 1962; Moore & Updegraff, 1964), elementary school children (Bonney, 1954; Gronlund, 1953; Koch, 1957), and teen-agers (Faunce & Beegle, 1948; Bjerstedt, 1958). Economic class is

Table 11.3   Experimental Design to Study Both the Number and the Proportion of Similar Attitudes of a Stranger, and Liking.[a]

Proportion of similar attitudes	Number of similar attitudes		
	4	8	16
1.00	4/0	8/0	16/0
.67	4/2	8/4	16/8
.50	4/4	8/8	16/16
.33	4/8	8/16	16/32

[a] After Byrne and Nelson, 1965, p. 660.

also an important factor in forming friendships. Byrne, Clore, and Worchel (1966) found people to be more positive toward strangers of the same rather than different economic status. If it is more likely that others of the same sex and economic circumstances share more of the interests and attitudes of a person, then for social comparison purposes it makes sense for him to choose them as friends.

The individual's need to know is greater when he lacks self-confidence. Consensual information may be more rewarding to the uncertain than to the confident person. Worchel and McCormick (1963) found more liking for an agreeing person when the subjects were uncertain rather than certain about their opinions. A similar finding was reported by Gerard and Greenbaum (1962).

The historical evidence indicates intense dislike of heretics by traditional thinkers. Unorthodox thinkers may produce doubt about the most sacred ideas of society. Heretical views from a member of one's own group may create more dislike than would the same views in an outsider. The outsider is not a comparison other and can be easily discounted as a relevant source of information, but the defection of an insider is sometimes very disturbing to group members.

Iwao (1963) followed this line of reasoning in a study of heretics among divinity school students. The students were presented with criticisms of their motives and values from another divinity student or from a law student, both of whom were actually confederates of the experimenter. As was predicted, the law student was rated as more pleasant, warm, and likable and was perceived as having more in common with the subjects than was the heretical divinity student.

The value of consensual information may be inversely related to its supply. When almost anyone can provide consensual validation for one's beliefs, its value will be low; but when few people have the knowledge or ability required to validate an individual's beliefs, their support may be considered valuable. Hence, an individual should like a person who provides scarce consensual information more than someone who can provide commonly available information.

Jellison and Zeisset (1969) have shown that the belief that one shares a scarce positive trait with another increased attraction. They informed female college students that the ability to make taste discriminations is genetic and is related to the presence or absence of phenylthio-renin (PTR) in their saliva. One group was told that most people had this ability and a second group was told that few people had it. Half the subjects in each group were informed that possessing PTR was desirable because it allowed a person to become a fine cook and a gourmet. The other half were told that PTR acted as a chemical desensitizer, that people possessing it could not make fine taste discriminations and hence could not become fine cooks and gourmets. Pairs of subjects were then given taste discrimination tests and both were informed they possessed PTR. In another phase of the experiment, the subjects were asked to rate the person with whom they were paired for the saliva tests.

When the PTR trait was considered desirable and it was scarce rather than plentiful, the similar other was liked most. However, when the PTR trait was believed to be undesirable, the subjects liked the similar other more when the trait was plentiful rather than scarce. It is nice to be a member of an elite group when the basis of similarity is desirable, but better to be safe with the majority when the basis of similarity is undesirable.

C. Reinforcement Theory

Byrne (1969) has borrowed from Festinger's theory and applied traditional reinforcement concepts to it. An effectance motive is postulated, which acts very much like hunger. Any stimulus that satisfies the motive can be considered a reinforcer and any stimulus that increases it can be interpreted as a punishment. When an individual is provided with information that his viewpoints are "correct" his sense of competence is reinforced; but when he is given data suggesting he is "wrong" his sense of competence is undermined. Some other person who expresses similar attitudes provides reinforcement, and, as we have seen, such persons are liked.

In general reinforcement theory and social comparison theory make identical predictions about the similarity-attraction relationship. Several studies have demonstrated that similar attitudes can be used as traditional reinforcers in a learning task. In a discrimination learning situation, attitude statements that were similar or dissimilar to those held by subjects were used as positive and negative reinforcers. The performance of subjects was better when their responses were followed by similar rather than by dissimilar statements (Byrne, Young, & Griffitt, 1966; Golightly & Byrne, 1964).

D. Balance Theory

Heider, Newcomb, and others have developed theories of cognitive balance (see Chapter 5) which have been used to explain the similarity-attraction relationship. We will restate the principles of balance theory as they apply to the study of interpersonal attraction and review evidence that both supports and disconfirms predictions derived from the theory. A particularly interesting controversy regarding the relative importance of race and beliefs as antecedents to liking has developed from tests of balance theory.

1. Fundamental Principles of Balance Theory

You may recall (from Chapter 5, II, A) that Heider's (1958) balance theory postulates two kinds of relationships between persons:

unit and sentiment relations. Persons and things form a positive unit (+U) when they are perceived as belonging together. A person and his products, actions, and partners form unit relations. Some observers are surprised and even irritated when they see a young black man sitting with a young white woman in a restaurant or bar; in such a case, the observer believes the two persons do not belong together (−U).

Sentiment relations refer to evaluations, including interpersonal attraction (+L or −L). If two people, P and O, belong together (+U) and both like the same things (+L), their relationship is balanced. If P and O do not belong together (−U) and one likes (+L) what the other dislikes (−L), their relationship is also balanced. In both of these cases, there is a consistency of cognitions within each individual—a friend (+U) should like (+L) what you like (+L), and an enemy (−U) should like (+L) what you dislike (−L). This consistency is psychological and not logical. It seems psychologically reasonable to believe that you should oppose what your enemy supports.

Heider assumes that each individual strains to achieve consistency among his cognitions and feelings. When a relationship is unbalanced, as when P and O belong together but P likes X and O dislikes X, there will be a tendency for it to change over time. Either P and O will change their relationship or else one of them will change his attitude toward X. In Iwao's study, the divinity students changed their sentiment relation with the heretical divinity student; there was not the same strong need to dissociate further from the heretical law student because he was not a unit member and his views could be inconsistent with those of the divinity students without creating imbalance.

2. Evidence Supporting Balance Theory

When persons find they like and dislike the same things, they should tend to form positive unit relations—to join the same clubs, form business partnerships, get married, and so on. Reciprocally, if positive unit relations are created between persons, they should tend to like one another.

Experimental support for the unit-sentiment relationship was provided by Darley and Berscheid (1967). College women were led to expect they would be involved in a discussion of sexual standards with another woman. Some preliminary information was given them about the personality of their future partner and another stranger with whom no contact was expected; both possessed equally desirable characteristics. In rating the two persons, the subjects reported a marked preference for their future discussion partner and indicated they would have chosen her (rather than the stranger) if a choice were given them.

A cooperative relationship is a positive unit relation, while a competitive or conflictful interaction is a negative unit relation. According to balance theory, a person should choose to interact with a dissimilar person in a competitive situation and a similar person in a cooperative situation. Lerner, Dillehay, and Sherer (1967) provided subjects, who anticipated a highly competitive interaction, with information about two potential opponents. The subjects preferred to participate with an opponent who was dissimilar rather than similar to themselves.

Perceived similarity affects the way persons see their unit relationships. Kaufmann (1967) induced attraction or repulsion toward a confederate by manipulating the similarity and dissimilarity of his attitudes with those of subjects, who were paired with him in a two-person mixed-motive game. The subjects who liked the confederate expected him to be cooperative (+U), while the disliked confederate was expected to be competitive (−U). Indeed, people who like one another actually do cooperate more than people who dislike one another (Oskamp & Perlman, 1966; Scodel, 1962; Tornatzky & Gewitz, 1968).

3. Evidence Disconfirming Balance Theory

A person may wish to stress the dissimilarity between himself and someone who is stigmatized because of physical or mental disability. The desire to dissociate oneself from a stigmatized other (−U) should lead a person to develop a negative sentiment relation (−L) toward him. When an individual and a stigmatized person are similar in many respects, the individual may stress his dislike in order to emphasize to third persons that he should not be similarly stigmatized. Novak and Lerner (1968) predicted that similarity would lead to repulsion under these conditions.

Subjects were asked to complete a short form providing information relevant to an experiment, including an open-ended item for any information not covered by the previous items. It was contrived that the subjects "accidentally" found a questionnaire completed by a confederate. In the normal condition, "None" was written in the space after the last item. In the emotionally disturbed condition, the following was written in response to the last item: "I don't know if this is relevant or not, but last fall I had kind of a nervous breakdown and I had to be hospitalized for a while. I've been seeing a psychiatrist ever since. As you probably noticed, I'm pretty shaky right now." All the subjects were then given a version of Byrne's attitude survey and exchanged their completed forms with the confederate. The confederate's responses were prepared to be either similar or dissimilar to the responses of the subjects.

In the normal condition, the subjects had no difficulty determining whether the confederate was similar or dissimilar to themselves. However, the subjects in the emotionally-disturbed condition perceived the confederate as dissimilar no matter which attitude survey they saw. Despite their tendency to view the emotionally disturbed person as different from themselves, they reported being more willing to interact with the similar than with the dissimilar person who was disturbed. Contrary to balance theory predictions, the subjects did not stress their dislike for the stigmatized person. In fact, they liked the other person more when he was similar whether or not he was emotionally disturbed, although they did tend to like the normal person more than the disturbed one.

We may conclude that people do not enjoy interactions with stigmatized people and probably avoid them. Nevertheless, the power of the similarity-attraction relationship is not negated by the mental or emotional condition of the referent person. Byrne and Lamberth (1971) have reported several replications of the Novak and Lerner experiment in which essentially the same results were found.

4. Race Versus Belief

A major controversy emerged during the 1960's concerning whether race or belief is more important in determining attraction. Rokeach (1961) argued that the rejection and segregation of racially different persons is based on the assumption that racial difference implies dissimilarity of beliefs and attitudes. According to Rokeach, racial prejudice is merely a special case of belief prejudice—we simply do not like people who are dissimilar to us in beliefs. This view is consistent with the principles of balance theory; segregation ($-U$) implies incompatible attitudes ($-L$).

Rokeach, Smith, and Evans (1960) performed two studies to test their hypothesis. In the first experiment, white subjects considered blacks who expressed similar attitudes on important issues as more socially acceptable than whites who expressed dissimilar attitudes. The same result was found whether the subjects were from the South or the North. In the second study, Jewish children accepted Gentiles who agreed with them more than Jews who disagreed with them.

If an individual avoids racially different people, he never learns what their attitudes

are. As a consequence, he is more apt to believe they have dissimilar attitudes. Stein, Hardyck, and Smith (1965) confirmed that both race and belief play significant roles in social acceptance. Race was important in the absence of information about beliefs, while beliefs were more important when both kinds of information were presented to subjects.

Strong legal and social restrictions on racial mixture have characterized American history. On matters of abstract beliefs or principles, racial differences might not be very important. But when social intimacy is involved, as among neighbors or in a social club, race may be more important than beliefs as a basis of social rejection (Triandis, 1961). Social prohibitions concerning socializing between the races are stronger in the South than in the North. Smith, Williams, and Willis (1967) found race to be more important than beliefs in determining social acceptance in the South, and beliefs to be more important in the North. Goldstein and Davis (1972) found belief similarity to be more important than racial difference in producing positive reactions by subjects in relatively casual encounters; but as intimacy increased, race became more important than beliefs in causing negative reactions.

The race versus belief controversy reveals the ambiguity of balance theory. How does one define a unit relation? Whites apparently like blacks with whom they share similar beliefs as long as their encounters are casual ($+U$); but whites reject blacks who have similar beliefs when their social relations become intimate ($-U$). What determines the sign of a unit relation or the point along a social distance scale where it changes from plus to minus?

E. Complementarity and Attraction

Two persons may get along better if their needs are not similar but rather, complementary and mutually supportive

(Winch, Ktsanes, & Ktsanes, 1954). For example, one person may have a strong need to dominate others, while a second may have a strong dependency need. On a dominance-submission scale, the two persons represent opposite ends of the same basic need dimension, and their opposite needs complement each other.

Consider what would happen if two dominant people formed a friendship or got married: a great deal of conflict may be predicted and a deterioration of the positive relationship would probably occur. If each person in a relationship is submissive, both may passively await the other's initiatives; the consequence may be that neither person ever gets from the other what he wants.

Although a dominant-submissive pair may appear to require the attraction of opposites, this type of complementarity may be considered as a special case of attitude similarity. If both parties agree that one should be dominant and the other submissive, their attitudes regarding their relationship are similar.

Complementarity may be considered a kind of symbiosis. For example, a sadistic person gains satisfaction by inflicting pain on others, and a masochistic person derives pleasure from being hurt. Such complementary people should be attracted to each other like the opposite poles of a magnet. From an exchange theory point of view, what one person can supply cheaply is valuable for the other. The reader may conjure up other complementary need pairs, such as nurturance-succorance and talkative-quiet.

The evidence for the complementarity theory is equivocal, but in general it is not supportive. One of the problems with the theory is that it presumes a reliable set of personality or motivational dispositions that can be measured accurately. Unfortunately, one can have little confidence in any of the available theories of personality or motivation and less in the measurement techniques that have been devised. In fact, there has been a growing consensus that little of the behavior of an individual can be attributed to his needs or personality traits (Mischel, 1968; see discussion in Chapter 4).

III. PROPINQUITY AND ATTRACTION

The closer together two people are in geographical space the greater the probability they will be either friends or enemies. We shall see that there is ample evidence in support of this proposition. Two basic explanations have been offered for the effects of propinquity, both of which focus on the more frequent interactions between people who live or work near to one another. According to reinforcement theory, people who interact frequently have more opportunity to reward or punish each other; hence, they develop stronger friendships or hatreds than people who interact less frequently. A second and perhaps complementary view is that people feel more comfortable among others whose behavior is predictable. People who are frequently observed are more predictable than those who are seldom observed. After reviewing these two theoretical explanations, we will briefly discuss the implications of the propinquity-attraction relationship on community design. Finally, the effects of propinquity on coercive actions will be examined.

A. Evidence of the Propinquity-Attraction Relationship

The effects of propinquity (sometimes referred to as proximity) on interpersonal relationships have been demonstrated by a multitude of studies. For example, clerks in a large department store and members of a bomber crew in the U.S. Air Force were more friendly toward those who happened to work next to them than toward others who worked even several feet away (Gullahorn, 1952; Kipnis, 1957; Zander & Havelin, 1960). Stronger friendships develop among college students who share classes, dormitories, and apartment buildings than among those who are separated by more space (Byrne & Buehler, 1955; Festinger, 1953a; Maisonneuve, Palmade, & Fourment, 1952; Willerman & Swanson, 1953).

Propinquity has been found to be associated with who marries whom. In a classic sociological study, Bossard (1932) examined 5,000 marriage licenses where one or both parties lived in Philadelphia before the wedding. In 12 percent of the cases, both parties already lived at the same address when they applied for a license. Another one-third of the couples lived within five or fewer blocks of each other. The percentage of marriages declined as the distance between the two parties increased. Of course this study was carried out before advanced transportation systems and high population mobility further changed the basis of life in urban America, but later evidence reaffirms the importance of propinquity as a factor in mate selection (Abrams, 1943; Katz & Hill, 1958).

B. Propinquity and Reward Exchange

Homans (1961) has pointed to a benign cycle associated with the frequency of interactions and rewards. People who are in close proximity have opportunities to mediate rewards for each other. When such rewards are mediated, the individuals seek out further interactions with each other. When an individual does not receive rewards, he restricts the amount of his future contact with the nonrewarding others, unless the demands of the situation—such as a job assignment—require the maintenance of contact. Hence, proximity provides opportunity for rewards, rewards encourage more frequent interactions and more rewards, and so on, as the attraction between the mutually rewarding persons grows. Punishments or failure to gain rewards lessen the contact between persons. Some-

times an individual will remain in interaction with a person who frequently punishes him because the only other alternative is to associate with persons who mediate even greater punishments (see discussion of CL$_{alt}$ in Chapter 7).

Reinforcement theory contradicts the old adage that absence makes the heart grow fonder. Physical separation usually means a cessation of reinforcements and lack of such continued support for a friendship typically cools the warmth felt between two persons. Parents who disapprove of a potential marriage partner may send their daughter off on an extended European vacation to dampen the ardor of the relationship. Driscoll, Davis, and Lipety (1972) found, however, that parental interference in love relationships between unseparated pairs resulted in a greater intensity of love feelings. Restrictions on the pair's freedom to relate presumably invoked reactance (see Chapter 8), with the effect of enhancing the perceived rewardingness of the romantic partner. The authors termed this the "Romeo and Juliet effect."

People who share the same space usually find it in their mutual interest to work out amicable relationships. Even when there are important racial or religious differences between them, they may overcome their prejudices when their proximity makes a resolution of conflict desirable for both of them. White people displayed less prejudice toward blacks when they lived in an integrated housing project (Deutsch & Collins, 1951), worked together in a meat packing plant (Palmore, 1955), studied together in a university classroom (Mann, 1959), and fought together in war time (Stouffer, et al., 1949). One implication of these findings is that racial prejudice is maintained by segregation in the schools or in housing. Without integration and associated interaction opportunities, it is virtually impossible for members of different races to exchange rewards (or punishments) with one another.

C. Propinquity and Familiarity

Familiarity is more apt to breed liking than contempt. Someone with whom one interacts frequently is more predictable than an outright stranger (Bramel, 1969). The norm of reciprocity, as was noted in the last chapter, may be partially responsible for instigating new relationships. This norm makes an individual optimistic about other people and encourages him to behave positively toward them. His positive actions usually elicit positive reactions from others. It probably does not pay to assume that others will be cantankerous, exploitative, or competitive, since such a misanthropic orientation may be self-fulfilling. Much more can be gotten through the use of honey than the use of vinegar.

Zajonc (1968b) demonstrated a relationship between familiarity and liking. Subjects were shown some pictures as many as twenty-five times and other pictures as few as one or two times. The subjects were then asked how much they liked each face and how much they would like the pictured person. The more frequently a picture had been exposed to them, the more liking they reported both for the pictured face and for the person represented by the photograph.

Freedman, Carlsmith, and Suomi (1969) extended the findings of Zajonc by demonstrating the familiarity effect with live people. Pairs of subjects were brought together, seated across from each other, and not permitted to talk to one another. They met three, six, or twelve times. When asked at the conclusion of the series of meetings how much they liked the other person, they reported stronger liking the more frequently they had met. Saegert, Swap, & Zajonc (1973) also found the familiarity effect in two experiments involving actual encounters. The effect occurred whether the situation involved pleasant or unpleasant consequences for the subjects. Why mere exposure should have this effect on attraction is not yet understood, although prop-

inquity and predictability seem to be involved.

D. Propinquity and Community Design

The design of a community, a housing development, and a building can have an important impact on who knows whom and who likes whom. Whyte (1956) carefully examined the social column in a suburban newspaper which reported information about who gave parties, who was invited and attended, and the pattern of friendships in a new housing development (Park Forest). Those who attended baby showers, eggnog parties, and otherwise formed friendships almost always lived quite close to one another.

The possible effects of architectual design on the pattern of human relationships was shown in a study by Festinger, Schachter, and Back (1950) of a large married students' housing development called Westgate West. The development consisted of seventeen two-story buildings, each containing five apartments on each floor (see Figure 11.1). The residents were asked to name the three people in the community they saw socially most often.

Social relationships occurred more often between residents of the same floor, and more often the closer the apartments of the residents. Forty-one percent of next-door neighbors, 22 percent of those two doors away, and 10 percent of those at the end of the hall were named by residents as social friends. In other words, the more probable it was that people would meet during their daily comings and goings, the more probable it was they would become friends, at least when the residents are from a homogeneous student population. Functional as well as physical distance brought people into brief encounters. For example, the position of the mailboxes and the stairways improved the social lives of the residents who lived near these heavily used locations.

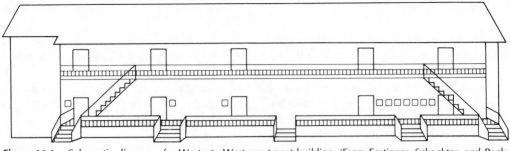

Figure 11.1. Schematic diagram of a Westgate West apartment building. (From Festinger, Schachter, and Back, 1950.)

Festinger (1951) also studied a small housing project in which all but ten of the houses faced toward a common court. The occupants of the ten end houses facing the street had only half as many friends in the community as did those who lived in the houses facing the court. Of course it must be recognized that persons buying the end houses may have done so because they were less socially inclined and sought more privacy than the others. Similarly, people in Westgate West may have rented apartments in the middle of a floor or near a stairway because they were more socially inclined than the occupants of the end apartments.

These early studies of the effects of space on human behavior certainly do not conclusively show the effects of propinquity on the formation of friendships. However, they have brought about some consciousness among architects of the behavioral impact of their constructions. In fact, a whole new specialty has developed in recent years around the topic of environmental psychology (see Proshansky, Ittelson, & Rivlin, 1970 and Downs & Stea, 1973).

E. Propinquity and Coercion

Physical proximity does not automatically ensure the development of positive attraction; it merely provides an opportunity for people to find common ground for mutually rewarding exchanges. Propinquity also provides occasions for conflict and competition. The exercise of coercive power will probably be directed also against proximate

others. The opportunity to harm another person is greater the closer he is to the source.

Hatred and harmdoing often occur between persons who are acquainted or close together. According to J. Edgar Hoover (*Time,* 1966), most cases of aggravated assault occur between intimately acquainted persons, and one-third of all murders occur within families, where feelings are intense and conflicts appear to be unresolvable by any other means.

Parents often are careful to instruct their children to beware of strangers, but the evidence reveals the parents to be more dangerous to their children than the strangers. Records of child abuse cases, though incomplete for many reasons (including the reluctance of neighbors to report incidents), clearly show that brutal beatings, torture, enforced starvation, and other cruelties are more often perpetrated by parents than by strangers.

The 1967 Annual Report of the Detroit Police Department provided statistics showing that the majority of thefts in the city were perpetrated by persons who were either related to or acquainted with the victim. There are good reasons why a thief should steal from someone he knows well. The thief is more apt to know about the existence of and the location of the valuables belonging to acquaintances. He is also privy to the movements of the victim. While the identification and apprehension of a thief may be easier when he victimizes a friend or relative, legal authorities are somewhat more lenient in dealing out penalties when there is an intimate relationship between the two parties. Then, too, relatives and friends may be more forgiving, may accept reparations, and may refuse to press charges.

IV. SELF-ESTEEM AND ATTRACTION

An individual is constantly being evaluated by other persons and often he is provided with positive or negative feedback from them. Parents, friends, teachers and others are not chary of telling an individual what his strengths and weaknesses are. Positive evaluations presumably enhance his self-esteem and may be considered reinforcing, while negative evaluations lower self-esteem and can be interpreted as punishing. Positive and negative evaluations should have important effects on the degree of attraction an individual feels toward the evaluator.

A person who has chronically low self-esteem may be more dependent on the evaluations of other people than a person who characteristically has high self-esteem. Dependence on others may increase the impact of evaluations in determining interpersonal attraction. The similarity-attraction relationship examined earlier suggests that an individual will like others who are similar to himself both in the way they evaluate themselves and how they evaluate him. Will a low self-esteem person like someone who provides a confirming negative view of him? Do low self-esteem people like other low self-esteem persons? Recent evidence has been gathered to provide answers to these questions.

Exchange theory suggests that the worth of approval or disapproval is inversely related to their supply. A person who profusely provides many positive evaluations soon loses his credibility, and hypercritical persons are soon ignored. The gains to self-esteem associated with approval may be greater when it comes from a person who has previously been critical. This idea

is behind the gain-loss theory of self-esteem and attraction. Dependence on others, similarity of self-evaluations, congruity of evaluations, and discrimination in making evaluations have been shown to be important determinants of attraction.

A. Self-Esteem and Dependence on Others

The dependence of an individual on members of a group is a function of the strength of his needs and the amount of gratification provided by the group. According to Dittes (1959), "the type of gratification that persons most commonly gain from membership in groups is that of social acceptance and the closely related rewards of support, recognition, security, and general esteem from other members of the group. The personal need that is gratified by acceptance may be variously designated and measured. It is assumed here that the need is best indicated by a person's level of self-esteem or general sense of adequacy. The lower the level of self-esteem ,the greater is a person's need for supports to self-esteem as provided by acceptance in a group" (p. 77).

In order to test his hypothesis, Dittes first measured the self-esteem of subjects with a paper-and-pencil questionnaire and then divided them into low and high self-esteem groups. The subjects met in groups of five or six and held discussions on several interesting topics. They were stopped several times so the experimenter could acquire ratings from them on the desirability of having each other member remain in the group. At an intermission halfway through the session, the experimenter showed each subject how the other group members allegedly rated him. In actuality the ratings were prepared to show half the subjects in each self-esteem condition that they were well below the average for the group, while the other half saw that they were average or above.

High self-esteem subjects were equally attracted to the other members of the group no matter which kind of evaluation they received. According to the need gratification hypothesis, the low self-esteem subjects should have been more strongly attracted to a group which gave them positive evaluations than the high self-esteem subjects. The results showed no difference between high and low self-esteem subjects in their ratings of the group when both received positive evaluations. However, low self-esteem subjects were strongly affected by negative evaluations and gave the group a low attraction rating. Consistent with reinforcement theory, subjects who received positive evaluations were more attracted to their groups than were those who received negative evaluations.

Jones, Knurek, and Regan (1973) found support for self-esteem theory by an experiment in which they asked subjects to indicate how much self-confidence they had in a variety of academic, social, and everyday situations. The subjects subsequently learned that their partner in the experiment either approved or disapproved of them. As can be seen in Table 11.4, they indicated greater liking for an approving than for a disapproving partner. More important, the low self-esteem subjects were more strongly affected by the evaluation of their partners than the high self-esteem subjects. People who lack self-confidence may experience approval as more reinforcing and disapproval as more punishing than self-confident people.

Table 11.4 Attraction as a Function of Self-Esteem and Approval from Others.[a]

Partner's evaluation	High self-esteem	Low self-esteem
Approval	5.36	6.67
Disapproval	4.33	3.55

[a] After Jones, Knurek, and Regan, 1973.

B. Self-Esteem, Similarity, and Attraction

Griffitt (1966) hypothesized that a person who is dissatisfied with himself will not like other low self-esteem persons. A high self-esteem person will like others who also evaluate themselves positively. In simpler terms, we like in others what we like in ourselves, and we dislike in others what we dislike in ourselves.

To test this intuition Griffitt had subjects fill out a paper-and-pencil test to measure their actual and ideal self-concepts. The subjects were then divided into low and high self-esteem groups, the former reflecting a large discrepancy between ideal and actual self, while small discrepancies were assumed to reflect high self-esteem.

The subjects were then asked to evaluate a stranger based on his self-concept inventory. His ideal self protocol was prepared to be 38 percent similar to the subject's score, but his actual self-concept score was either the same as the subject's or only 33 percent similar. The results showed that subjects liked the stranger better when he was more similar to themselves in actual self-concept, regardless of the level of their own self-esteem.

In a second study, Griffitt (1969) held the degree of similarity of actual self-concept to 40 percent and manipulated the similarity of ideal self-concept. Again, subjects liked the stranger more when he was more similar in ideal self-concept, and their own self-esteem had no effect. A person apparently likes another who has a similar actual or ideal self-concept, even when similarity means that both individuals have negative views of themselves.

Another empirical question is raised by a consideration of balance theory. Will a person with a negative self-concept like someone who negatively evaluates him? In such a case both persons hold similar attitudes about the referent person. For example, if a person performed poorly on a task, would he be attracted to a person who frankly gave him a negative evaluation (congruence) or would he prefer an evaluator who provided what was perceived as insincere positive feedback (incongruence)?

To test this question, Deutsch and Solomon (1959) arranged for subjects to either succeed or fail on a task and then provided them with positive or negative performance evaluations from others. As might be expected, the subjects who did well and were positively evaluated liked the evaluator more than the subjects who failed and were negatively evaluated. In addition, the subjects who did well liked a positive evaluator better than a negative one. However, the subjects who failed liked the evaluator more when he frankly indicated he thought they had performed poorly than when an inappropriate positive evaluation was received. Congruence between self and other evaluations may be more important for attraction than gaining indiscriminate positive feedback from others. This conclusion must be tempered by the possibility that the subjects were suspicious of the positive evaluation of a poor performance and may have rejected the evaluator as a hypocritical ingratiator.

Dutton (1967) provided additional evidence in favor of the congruence hypothesis. Subjects were induced to deliver a monologue on a political issue that went counter to their known attitudes and were led to believe they had given either a good or a poor performance. They then received evaluations from two other persons, one providing congruent and the other incongruent feedback. When the subject had done a good job, she liked the congruent and positive evaluator best, and when she had done a poor job, she liked the congruent and negative evaluator best.

A problem of interpretation arises because of the fact that the subjects argued a position counter to their own private beliefs. Consider the viewpoint of subjects who performed poorly in behalf of a position they privately believed to be wrong and then were told they had done well. The implication is that the evaluator must have already believed the position presented in order to evaluate a poor performance as good. This implied attitude dissimilarity would therefore serve as the basis for interpersonal rejection. While the subjects who performed well may have judged the

evaluator on his congruent view of the performance, the subjects who performed poorly may have rejected the positive judge because of an assumed dissimilarity of attitude concerning the topic at issue.

The attitude dissimilarity interpretation leads to the prediction that congruency effects will not be obtained when a subject presents his own viewpoint on an issue poorly and an evaluator provides negative feedback about the performance. When a person presents his own views he usually wants to influence others to agree with him. A negative evaluation of his poor performance would simply mean that the influence attempt failed, while a positive evaluation of a poor performance implies that the listener shared the view presented prior to the influence attempt. Attitude similarity and congruency hypotheses would lead to opposite predictions in this situation. A poor performance positively evaluated implies attitude similarity (but incongruency) and a poor performance negatively evaluated is congruent but constitutes a failure at influence and implies dissimilarity of attitudes.

Dutton and Arrowood (1971) followed this reasoning in designing a study to evaluate the similarity and congruency hypotheses. They had subjects argue either for their own position on an issue or in opposition to their own view. Half the subjects in each condition believed they had argued well and the other half believed they had argued poorly. Each subject was provided with feedback from four evaluators, two of whom agreed, whereas the other two disagreed with the position presented. One of the agreeing and one of the disagreeing evaluators thought the subject had argued well or badly in each case.

The results (shown in Table 11.5) supported an interpretation based on attitude similarity and social influence and disconfirmed the congruency hypothesis. When the subjects presented their own position on the issue, they liked the evaluators who agreed with them and were only secondarily affected by the evaluations of their

Table 11.5 Attraction Ratings of Each Evaluator. [a]

Subject's argument	Evaluator indicates agreement		Evaluator indicates disagreement	
	Evaluator praises performance	Evaluator critical of performance	Evaluator praises performance	Evaluator critical of performance
Own position-poor performance	66.6	61.6	43.4	50.4
Own position-good performance	81.8	63.8	55.0	29.8
Opposite position-poor performance	68.4	46.2	55.9	28.9
Opposite position-good performance	78.4	52.1	49.2	43.8

[a] After Dutton and Arrowood, 1971. High scores indicate greater attraction.

performance. When they presented a position opposed to their own, their liking depended primarily on congruency between their own and the evaluators' perceptions of how well or poorly they had presented the argument.

Least liked among the evaluators were those who either (1) disagreed with the subjects' true position and also negatively evaluated their performance, or (2) disagreed with the subjects' counterattitudinal argument (actually agreed with the subjects' private view) and evaluated a poor performance as a good one. The latter evaluator must have been puzzling for subjects, since he held the "correct" opinion but was not able to make a proper judgment about their skill in making the argument. Perhaps he could be persuaded to change his mind on the issue (adopting the "wrong" position) by a really good performance.

In summary, the more information provided to subjects that an evaluator agreed with their private opinions and the more resistant to change his similar opinions were perceived to be, the more the subjects liked him. Persuading someone to adopt a "wrong" position is not reinforcing.

C. The Gain-Loss Theory of Self-Esteem and Attraction

In everyday life an individual may be provided with a series of evaluations from a single other person over a period of time. A recipient of uniformly positive feedback (social reinforcement) should like the evaluator more than would a recipient of uniformly negative feedback (social punishment). Contrary to this common-sense view of the reinforcement-attraction relationship, Homans (1961) has argued that social approval is more valuable when it is reluctantly and sparingly given. Reluctance implies that the evaluator is hard to please. Praise from a discerning judge is more flattering than profusive and continuous approval from one who is nondiscerning. An A grade from a "tough" professor is worth more than an A from an "easy" professor.

The effect of a series of evaluations on liking was investigated by Aronson and Linder (1965). During the course of the experiment it was arranged for subjects to hear seven evaluations of themselves by a single confederate. The evaluations were either all positive, all negative, first positive and then negative, or first negative and then positive. The subjects liked the evaluator most when he shifted from negative to positive evaluations and liked him least when he shifted from positive to negative. Somewhat perplexing was the finding that the continuously negative and continuously positive conditions did not differ. A gain in esteem produced more attraction than steady positive esteem, while a loss in esteem generated more hostility than steady negative esteem.

Subsequent research has not always supported the gain-loss theory of esteem and attraction. Sigall and Aronson (1967) required subjects to give a series of speeches and the experimenter provided feedback about their performances in four conditions: $(++)$, $(+-)$, $(-+)$, and $(--)$. The experimenter was liked most when he provided uniformly positive evaluations and was liked least when he provided uniformly negative evaluations.

Mettee (1971) provided subjects with major or minor criticisms or approval of their written opinions on how to handle a rehabilitation problem with a juvenile delinquent. The subjects heard first one evaluation (major or minor) and then the other. The sequential evaluations (double signs indicating major evaluation) were $(++/-)$, $(--/+)$, $(+/--)$, and $(-/++)$. The results confirmed reinforcement theory, but disagreed with the predictions of gain-loss theory. After the initial feedback and again after the second evaluation the subjects liked the major positive-minor negative $(++/-)$ evaluator most and the major negative-minor positive evaluator

$(--/+)$ least; liking for the other two evaluators was intermediate.

The last two experiments differ in an important procedural respect from the original Aronson and Linder study. In the latter the subjects overheard the evaluations and the evaluator allegedly did not know they were listening; in the other two studies the evaluator presented feedback directly to the subjects. If presenting negative feedback to an individual you have never met before is considered rude and contrary to the rules of social conduct, the subjects would have two reasons to dislike an evaluator in the negative-negative condition: (1) the evaluator holds a negative opinion of the subjects, and (2) he is a rude and tactless person. When the evaluator shifted from a negative to a positive opinion, his lack of tact was sufficient to prevent the subjects from developing a strong liking for him. This interpretation suggests that a gain or loss of esteem would occur if an evaluator provided criticisms or approval directly to a person under conditions where it was socially appropriate to do so. A teacher or a parent may be able to give sequential evaluations directly to a student, including strong negative evaluations, without violating social norms.

V. PHYSICAL ATTRACTION

It is sometimes said that beauty is only skin deep. Nevertheless, it is quite clear that the desire to affiliate with another person is related to his appearance. Businesses that cater to the public and require encounters with customers hire people who are physically attractive. Airline stewardesses, receptionists, salesmen, and public relations personnel must have a pleasant appearance to get their jobs. Presumably, their appearance is related to advancing the interests of the firm through successful interpersonal encounters.

Why is a person considered beautiful or ugly? What standards do we have for judging the physical attractiveness of other people? Does everyone have a different standard or is there a great deal of agreement about the nature of beauty? Does beauty imply intelligence, goodness, and other positive traits? Does an individual judge his own appearance in the same way other people do? Do people match in terms of how beautiful they are when they date? And what value does physical attraction have for social interaction? Research has been directed toward answering all these questions.

A. Standards for Physical Attractiveness

Hochberg (1964) has remarked that "Except for some arbitrary beauty-contest conventions about 'ideal' female dimensions, we know less about attractive stimuli for man than we do about those for fish" (p. 112). Such ignorance does not prevent people from demonstrating an amazing amount of agreement about who is and who is not beautiful or handsome in their own society.

Height is one standard of beauty in America. A person's height is associated with his success in occupational and political life. Feldman (1971) cited a recent survey of University of Pittsburgh graduates which revealed that male students 6'2" or over received an average starting salary 12.4 percent higher than graduates who were under 6' in height. In a marketing survey at another university, college recruiters were presented with two job applicants who were equally qualified, one of whom was 6'1" tall and the other was 5' tall. Only 1 percent of the recruiters would have hired the shorter man. Feldman noted that "every American president elected since at least 1900 has been the taller of the two major political candidates" (p. 2). This observation must be amended because Senator McGovern was the taller candidate in the presidential election of 1972.

A cardinal principle of date selection, according to Berscheid and Walster (1974), is that the man must be as tall or taller than the woman. Given these preferences for height, it is not surprising that when adolescents worry about their height, the boys are concerned about their shortness and the girls fear they will grow too tall (Stolz & Stolz, 1951).

Agreement often occurs in judging head-and-shoulder photographs of people. Kopera, Maier, and Johnson (1971) found no differences between male and female college students' ratings of the attractiveness of photographs of 84 caucasian females. Similar consensus in rating the attractiveness of photographs has been found among fifth and eleventh grade boys and girls (Cavior & Dokecki, 1971). Consensus about beauty is much less when the age, sex, and racial characteristics of the judges and the judged are varied (Cross & Cross, 1971).

Observations across cultures reveal highly variable standards of beauty. You may have seen photographs of African tribesmen or women who deliberately inflict wounds on their faces, chests, or buttocks to produce scars or who place large wooden plugs into their lips to make them protrude. These devices are intended to make them more attractive, and Westerners are apt to be repelled by them. But there is always a generally agreed upon stereotype within each culture of who is to be considered beautiful or ugly.

B. The Meaning of Attractiveness

Marketing students are taught the importance of packaging in selling consumer products. This emphasis on packaging belies the old adage that "you can't judge a book by its cover." The time, effort, and money spent on cosmetics and fashion should be enough to convince the most profound skeptic that human packaging is very important in interpersonal relationships. A stranger's physical appearance may lead the observer to make a number of inferences about him. Dion, Berscheid, and Walster (1972) found that attractive people

of both sexes (as compared to less attractive people) were perceived to be more sexually responsive, kind, interesting, sociable, strong, of better character, more exciting on dates, and as having better prospects for prestigious occupations and happier marriages. To be beautiful is good.

Physical attractiveness may be more important in making social choices for men than for women. Surveys reveal that men consistently place more importance on physical attractiveness in making dating choices than do females. Intelligence is the most important characteristic determining female choices (Coombs, & Kenkel, 1966; Hewitt, 1958; Vail & Staudt, 1950). Physically attractive females report having more dates than unattractive ones, but no such relationship was found among men (Berscheid, Dion, Walster, & Walster, 1971).

If attractive women are more often dated and are considered more desirable by men, then, assuming that "sin" is proportional to opportunity, attractive females should be more sexually experienced than their less comely peers. This conjecture has been supported by evidence. Attractive college women say they have been in love more often, have experienced more noncoital petting, and are more likely to have had sexual intercourse than their less attractive peers (Kaats & Davis, 1970).

C. Self-Impressions of Attractiveness

Physically attractive people are presumably frequently told about their good looks, while unattractive people are not. Attractive children are more popular than their less attractive peers from grammar school right through their college years. Attractive people should therefore become convinced of their beauty through the social consensus they receive. Although there is a significant positive relationship between self-ratings of attractiveness and the ratings of others, it is much less than might be expected. Murstein (1972) and Stroebe,

Insko, Thompson, and Layton (1971) found very low correlations between the self and the external ratings of men and women.

Almost no correspondence was found between self and external ratings of physical attractiveness among fifth grade girls. Cavior (1970) reported that three-fourths of the girls studied ranked themselves as the least attractive girl in their class. Although these self-ratings may reflect extreme modesty, the girls tended to view one part or another of their anatomy as deficient and as detracting from their general appearance. A judge might see a girl as attractive, but she would see herself as having too large a nose, eyes set too far apart, protruding ears, as being overweight or too skinny, and so on. More maturity is apparently required to discount individual features and arrive at an overall impression. Younger children tend to poke fun at anything unusual in their classmates, which may reinforce negative self-impressions.

D. Matching and Dating

Goffman (1952) has interpreted a marriage proposal as an attempt by a man to convince a woman that they are equal in social desirability and hence can conclude a merger. But what constitutes social desirability? Some of its attributes are intelligence, social skills, access to material resources, and physical attractiveness. Do people tend to match up in terms of overall desirability?

According to Walster, Aronson, Abrahams, and Rottman (1966), a person seeking a partner of the opposite sex will make his choice on the basis of two criteria: (1) the social desirability (or value) of the other person, and (2) the probability that his choice will be reciprocated. This probability is considered to be dependent on the individual's view of his own social desirability. Though an average man may desire a beautiful woman, he will tend to choose an average one because he will estimate his chances of succeeding with a beautiful woman as poor.

The evidence for the matching theory is equivocal at best. Partial support was found in two experiments reported by Berscheid, Dion, Walster, and Walster (1971). In the first study, subjects bought tickets for a computer matching dance and were rated by judges at the time of purchase from 0 to 8 on a scale of physical attractiveness. Half the subjects believed they could date anyone they chose from a pool of eligibles; the other half were informed that the partner chosen could refuse the date and that in the past about 50 percent of the eligibles had rejected offers. Each subject was then asked to specify on a questionnaire how intelligent, considerate, physically attractive, popular, and reserved or outgoing in personality he wished his date to be. An index of social desirability was devised from the subject's description of the type of date he would like.

The subjects who had been rated by the judges as most attractive indicated preferences for more physically attractive, popular, and socially desirable dates than did the less attractive subjects. Contrary to the matching hypothesis, the probability of rejection did not affect the descriptions of the kind of dating partner preferred. Of course, the subjects may have been indicating an ideal rather than a real dating choice. The probability of rejection would not affect a person's fantasies and dreams. But if they were indicating ideal rather than real preferences, why do attractive men have more socially desirable ideal dates than unattractive men?

The second experiment attempted to manipulate the idealistic or realistic basis of social choice in a computer dating situation. Subjects were presented with six pictures of dating possibilities and asked to make only one choice among them. In the realistic condition the male subjects believed the eligible females were also making choices between six possible male dates. To ensure the greatest compatibility between pairs, a date would be arranged only when both persons chose each other, and the subjects could not be sure their choice would accept their offer. In the idealistic condition, each subject was told that the eligible females had agreed to go out with whoever chose them, so they could be certain that their first choice would accept their offer. Attractive subjects chose more attractive dates than did unattractive subjects, and the probability of reciprocated choice from the female eligibles had no effect.

This failure to find a relationship between the choice of a partner and the probability of reciprocated choice is damaging to the matching hypothesis. However, it is possible that the realistic-idealistic manipulation did not produce a difference between the groups of subjects in their estimates of reciprocated choice. Huston (1973) reexamined the hypothesis by asking subjects for their estimates of the probability of reciprocation. Male college students chose dates from pictures of eligible females. Half of them were told that each of the eligibles had agreed to accept a date with him, and the other half were led to believe that each girl would see their pictures and would then decide on whom she would date. The subjects were asked to rate their own physical attractiveness, to make a dating choice, and to estimate the probability they would be accepted by the female chosen.

Men clearly showed strong preferences for the most physically attractive females, particularly when they were certain their offers would be accepted. When they were not certain, they estimated the probability of reciprocated choice as lower when the women were very attractive than when they were only moderately attractive or unattractive. Furthermore, the men who viewed themselves as physically attractive estimated the probability of reciprocation higher than did those who viewed themselves as less attractive. Contrary to the matching hypothesis, however, was the finding that self-ratings of physical attractiveness did not correspond to the chosen date's attractiveness.

Walster (1970) tried still another method of testing the matching hypothesis by attempting to manipulate subjects' self-esteem. A person with a positive view of his own social desirability should choose a more desirable date than someone whose self-esteem has been undermined. Prior to receiving a psychiatric analysis of a personality test of self-esteem they had taken, the subjects were given a booklet containing pictures, brief autobiographies, and "objective" social desirability ratings for five persons of the opposite sex. These persons were extremely above average, fairly above, average, below, or extremely below average in social desirability. The subjects were asked how much they would like each stimulus person.

One-third of the subjects received a positive report from a psychiatrist (to raise their self-esteem), one-third received a negative report (to lower their self-esteem), and one-third received no report (the control group). The subjects were then given a second booklet describing five persons who, it was said, would be attending a get-acquainted party. They were asked to rate how much they would like each of these persons romantically. No relation was found between their actual self-esteem scores or the false psychiatric feedback and the subjects' preferences.

If matching does not occur between strangers, do more enduring relationships occur between couples of equal physical attractiveness? In an investigation of this question, Murstein (1972) assembled ninety-nine couples who were either engaged or "going steady" and asked them to rate themselves and their partners on a scale of physical attractiveness. Judges also rated pictures of the couples. The discrepancy between a subject's self-rating and the rating by his partner was then calculated and compared to the discrepancy scores of random pairs of subjects based on the judges' ratings. The similarity of two partners in physical attractiveness was greater than that between randomly matched pairs. Apparently, matching on physical attractiveness does play a role in more enduring heterosexual relationships, though the basis and conditions of matching are not well understood.

E. The Value of Physical Attraction

Why are stereotyped cultural definitions of physical beauty important in the formation and development of heterosexual relationships? Advertising, movies, and television have surely had an impact in fostering culturally shared views of who is physically attractive and who is not. Much as Pygmalion constructed and then fell in love with Galatea, the media and the fashion designers have developed and promoted a relationship between sexual arousal and physical attractiveness. It is commonly assumed that a physically attractive partner is desirable because of his or her arousal properties and esthetic qualities.

Veblen (1934) took a somewhat different view. He observed that attractive women "enable successful men to put their prowess in evidence by exhibiting some durable result of their exploits" (p. 34). A beautiful woman can be an important status symbol for a man (Waller, 1937). The marketing value of a lovely wife is well known in various occupations, including political office. Often a corporation will interview a wife before hiring her husband as an executive. Fromm (1956) has suggested that in our society, when wives become older and lose their youthful beauty (and their market value), they may, like older cars, be traded in on a new model.

For a man to be seen with a beautiful woman on his arm conveys to observers that he must be socially desirable. Sigall and Landy (1973) demonstrated the radiating effects of being seen with a beautiful woman. Subjects briefly met a young man who was sitting next to an attractive or an unattractive female. The woman paired with the man was said to be linked romantically to him or else was said not to be associated with him at all. The subjects were then asked to rate the man on a series of personality scales and to indicate how much

they thought they would like him. Being romantically associated with an attractive girl enhanced the man's desirability and association with an unattractive girl detracted from the overall impression the subjects had of him. Sitting next to attractive or unattractive girls did not affect the subjects' impressions of the man when the girl had no association with him.

The trading rules of interpersonal relationships in the United States generally require a man to provide security or prestige to a woman in exchange for her physical attractiveness. Coombs and Kenkel (1966) found the dating attitudes of male and female Iowa State undergraduates to reflect these trading rules. While males were more concerned with the physical attractiveness of their dates, females were interested in males who were intelligent, high in campus status, and socially skilled. Elder (1969) examined the marriages of women who had been rated on a scale of physical attractiveness when they were in high school. The more attractive girls married men of higher status than did their less attractive classmates. The relationship of fashion to attractiveness and status is illustrated in Box 11.1

Rubin (1973) points out that a man's wealth and a woman's beauty are not the only marketable attributes, though they may be prominent in America. Wealthy Jewish merchants in the small towns of Eastern Europe often married their daughters to poor but talented scholars. The woman's economic status in such cases was exchanged for the man's intellectual and spiritual qualities.

Since physical attractiveness has value in interpersonal relationships, it can serve as a power resource. An attractive female may be the object of ingratiation or impression management strategies by males who hope to gain a more intimate relationship with her. Landy and Sigall (1974) demonstrated the power of physical attraction. They asked male college students to evaluate an essay written by an attractive or an unat-

Box 11.1   MODES OF DRESS

The origin of clothing is not fully understood. Apparently, clothing was first developed in warm climates and was not introduced merely to protect the wearer against the cold. In fact, Australian aborigines, who live in a temperate climate, did not until recently wear any clothing. They received some measure of warmth from a glowing log that they carried. Some ornamental clothing was worn, however, such as a waist-string and flaps hanging down from it (König, 1973). It seems likely that clothing was first worn to protect against insect bites and to provide for pouches and slings for carrying weapons and game acquired from the hunt.

Clothing may reveal the wearer's station in life, increase his beauty, serve practical functions, heighten sexual eroticism, and serve as a sign of the power relations among people. These rich meanings of dress and manners are referred to as fashion. Fashions have often been characterized as evil, damnable, wanton, erotic, eccentric, and taboo. The Amish and Mennonites in our society consider modern fashions to be sinful. Of course many have also praised and zestfully pursued the latest fashions in society.

The decorative aspect of fashion is devoted to drawing attention to oneself. It also allows the person to present himself as distinctive from other people, perhaps as a member of a particular group, tribe, sex, or social class. The distinctiveness may emphasize rivalry. Charlemagne in 808 A.D. developed a set of dress regulations prescribing the dress appropriate to each social class. The function of dress as a sign of status is most evident in military circles. The kind of braid worn on the sleeve or the number of feathers worn in the hair may symbolize the individual's rank in his social group. The Mao jacket in China is a conspicuous denial of class distinctions among the people and is worn by both the head of state and the common worker. The mode of dress is often related to ceremonial behavior and etiquette, as at weddings and religious confirmations.

Fashions have often been characteristic of various historical periods, such as the Elizabethan era, the Renaissance, the age of Louis XIV in France, and the post-war periods of the 20th century. In modern times fashions have shifted quite rapidly. Widespread literacy, constant exposure to the mass media, greater affluence, and frequent contact with other people in urban societies probably causes a greater concern for being in fashion and allows clothing manufacturers to manipulate rapid changes for purposes of making larger profits. In our own time there has been a growing trend for men in Western society to become more fashion conscious. They wear more ornamentation than ever before. Blue jeans may be ornamented with a patch of either leather or bright fabric over the genital area—suggestive of the penis sheath and codpiece of former ages. Fashions of dress among women have long emphasized various parts of their bodies, including the buttocks, the breasts, the knees, thighs, ankles, shoulders, neck or whatever other area might have contemporary erotic value. According to Flugel (1930) the entire female body is attractive to men, but it is impossible to attend to all of the areas at once. Clothing draws attention to a particular part of the anatomy and when the appetite of men is satiated, a shift in emphasis takes place, and a new fashion is created.

---

tractive woman. Control subjects rated the same essay without knowledge of the writer's appearance. Half the subjects in each condition were given a poorly written essay and half were given a well written essay to evaluate. Estimates of the writer's ability and the evaluation of her work were highest when she was attractive and lowest when she was unattractive, regardless of the quality of her work; when the writer's physical appearance was unknown, the subjects responded to the actual quality of the essays.

Mills and Aronson (1965) found evidence that physical attractiveness may be an important resource for influencing others. A female made to look attractive was more effective in influencing a male audience when she told them that she wanted to influence them than when she did not directly indicate that desire. When the same female was made to appear unattractive, her expression of intentions had no effect on the audience.

It is understandable why employers look to hire attractive people for jobs that involve dealing directly with the public. Physical attraction leads to more influence and more positive responses in encounters with strangers. The lack of effectiveness of physically unattractive people was demonstrated by Sigall and Aronson (1969). An attractive or an unattractive female provided positive or negative evaluations to male subjects. When an attractive female provided a positive evaluation, she was liked most, but when she provided a negative evaluation, she was liked least. When the female was unattractive, the positive or negative nature of her evaluations did not affect the subjects' liking for her. Being accepted by a beautiful female is heaven, but being rejected by her is hell. More terres-

trial reactions occur toward an unattractive female, whatever her evaluations.

F. Attraction and the Attribution of Responsibility

Attributions of malevolence and benevolence may affect the degree of responsibility assigned to a person for harmdoing behavior. Attraction to a harmdoer may therefore cause an individual to soften the degree of punishment considered appropriate. Dion (1972) found support for the hypothesis that attraction mitigates responsibility. College students were given a written description of a child's action, which was accompanied by a picture of an attractive or unattractive child. The child was alleged to have attacked a dog or another child. In the mild attack conditions, the child either stepped on the tail of a sleeping dog or hit another child on the leg with a snowball, producing no more than a slight sting. In the severe attack conditions, the child threw stones at the dog and cut its leg or put a piece of ice in a snowball and cut another child's scalp by throwing it at his head.

Severe harm was considered more antisocial by the subjects than mild harm and harming the dog was considered just as reprehensible as harming another child. Nevertheless, the attractive child in the severe harm condition was perceived as less antisocial than the unattractive child. Furthermore, the observers predicted that the attractive child would be less likely to perpetrate harm again than the unattractive child. Independent of the amount of harm done, the unattractive child was perceived as more unpleasant than the attractive one.

The attractiveness of a defendant on trial

and his similarity with his jurors have been shown to effect judgments of how much punishment he should receive. Landy and Aronson (1969) provided subjects with a full description of an offender's crime, including the following incidents: the defendant spent three hours at a Christmas office party, was stopped for drunken driving and was escorted into a taxi by a policeman, returned to his car, ran a red light, and killed a pedestrian. In one version of the case, the defendant was described as a 64 year old man who had worked as an insurance adjustor for 42 years, whose wife had died of cancer a year earlier, and who had aggravated his war wounds in the accident. The less attractive defendant was described as a 33-year-old janitor, who was twice divorced and who had two misdemeanors on his criminal record in the previous five years—breaking and entering, and a drug violation. A neutral defendant was described as employed in the area and heading home when the incident occurred.

The subjects judged the defendant guilty of negligent homicide whatever his attractiveness. However, the sentence recommended by these role-playing jurors was three years less for both the neutral and the attractive defendant than for the unattractive defendant. One reason the neutral person may have been treated so leniently is that subjects viewed him almost as favorably as they did the attractive defendant. Middle class college students often display a positive bias toward strangers (Epstein & Hornstein, 1969); except when they are provided with specific negative information.

The degree of punishment assigned to defendants in court trials may be based on subjective predictions about how receptive they will be to rehabilitation. Attractive people are apparently considered less likely to perpetrate harm again and to need less punishment than unattractive people. Kalven and Zeisel (1966) asked judges to answer questionnaires about criminal jury trials over which they had presided. Each judge recounted the decision made by the jury, the decision he would have made in the absence of a jury, and the reasons for the disagreements between the two verdicts. Of the 962 cases in which the judges disagreed with the juries' decisions, 11 percent were attributed to positive or negative impressions formed by the jury of the defendant.

VI. ATTRACTION AND SOCIAL INTERACTION

The theories reviewed so far have concentrated on the antecedents or determinants of attraction and have given much less attention to the implications for social interactions of the affective relationships between persons. Moreover, these theories have typically been concerned with processes occurring within the individual, such as needs, arousal states, cognitive balance, and self-esteem. Tedeschi (1974) has proposed a theory of interpersonal attraction that is concerned with both antecedents and consequences of attraction. Although the internal states of the individual are not ignored, the emphasis is on attributions, implicit reciprocity, and social influence. Attraction is viewed as a power resource that makes it possible for persons to have smooth and successful interactions with one another.

Attraction is defined by Tedeschi as an attitude having cognitive, affective, and dispositional components. The cognitive aspect focuses on the beliefs or expectations of the individual which serve as predictors of the actions of other people. The affective component involves the variety and intensity of emotions that are associated with a liked person. The dispositional component refers to the readiness of an individual to act benevolently toward the other person.

A. The Cognitive Component

Attraction may be said to represent the expectation that the other person will unselfishly provide benefits or help of various types and values across a variety of situations over some period of time. This expectation is developed on the basis of past interactions, secondary sources of information, and attributions made. Tedeschi considers the belief that another's benevolent behavior is intentional and unselfish as crucial for the development of attraction. Ingratiators are not liked even though they offer positive evaluations because their intentions are perceived as insincere and manipulative. If a stimulus person is perceived as providing rewards because it is in his own interest to do so, the recipient cannot attribute the behavior to benevolent or altruistic intentions. Stable attraction will develop for a stimulus person only when the recipient is able to say: "He is rewarding me because he likes me and cares about my welfare." In general, the greater the range of values, the greater the variety of situations, the longer the expectation of noncontingent rewards, and the more confidence the individual has in his expectation, the stronger the attraction of the referent person.

Dislike refers to an expectation that another person will cause harm without provocation. The strength of dislike depends on the amount of harm involved, the number of situations across which the other person can be expected to cause harm, the length of time for which the expectations are relevant, and the degree of confidence the individual has in them. Like and dislike are not just opposite ends of a single continuum; they refer to different kinds of expectations. Hence, it is possible to both like and dislike the same person. A child may develop an expectation that his parent's ill humor can be expected in certain conditions to bring about punishments, but that in other situations generous and rewarding behavior can be expected. The child has an ambivalent relationship with his parent; he may both love and fear the parent.

The interpretation of attraction as an expectation provides a basis for differentiating among types of relationships. Man-man, woman-man, woman-woman, father-daughter, brother-sister relationships all involve expectations of unselfish behavior, but the specific actions expected are somewhat different. While it is appropriate to expect sexual gratification from a lover, such behavior is not expected from a parent. A mother may be expected to cook meals, wash clothes, and clean house, but a girl friend is not generally expected to provide these kinds of help. Naturally, there are overlapping expectations; both a mother and a girl friend might provide transportation to a school basketball game.

B. The Affective Component

Strong emotions require intense arousal states. A 19th century German psychologist, Adolf Horwicz, suggested that any intense emotional arousal may heighten the experience of love: "Love can only be excited by strong and vivid emotion, and it is almost immaterial whether these emotions are agreeable or disagreeable" (cited in Rubin, 1973, p. 6). Schachter's two-factor theory of emotion, discussed in Chapter 3, can be used to understand the development of passionate love (Walster, 1971). If one is in the market for romance, is in the company of a potential mate, and experiences arousal that he cannot attribute to features of the immediate environment, he may attribute it to the other person and label his own emotional state "love." Persons who experience chronic anxiety and self-doubt, or who are constantly subject to danger or other forms of excitement may continually fall in love with new people. This misattribution of arousal states to a strong affection for others is apt to occur during wartime, on vacations when traveling to new places, and on blind dates (where the label is ready even when the arousal is absent).

Nonromantic attraction may be temporarily created by good fortune. When a person is feeling good, he may become optimistic about the probability of receiving rewards from others. On the other hand, bad news may provide temporary dislike in terms of a pessimistic view of the likelihood that others will be harmful in the future. These temporary mood states may be created by pleasant daydreams during which attraction or even unrequited love may develop for the dream object (say, a movie star). Usually, the attraction or dislike will dissipate. Long-term attraction is dependent on the cognitive analysis of the relationship, while emotions flare up and die down more quickly.

C. The Dispositional Component

When the individual receives rewards from others he may experience positive arousal and develop expectations of future rewards. But what about the person who provides the rewards? From the viewpoint of self-perception theory (Bem, 1972; see Chapter 4) the very act of providing a benefit may enhance liking for the other. In effect the actor asks himself why he provided the reward, and if no environmental determinant can be found he will infer that he likes the person benefited. This belief would be strengthened, according to attributional principles, the longer the time and the greater the number of situations over which he continues to provide benefits. A positive cycle of attraction may be established. The more benefits provided, the more the actor likes the other person, and the more subsequent benefits he is apt to provide. This positive behavior reinforces the recipient's expectations of being rewarded, fosters his liking for his benefactor, and produces reciprocal altruistic actions, thereby supporting the benefactor's self-attributions of liking.

Schopler and Compere (1971) found that self-attribution of liking was associated with being kind or harsh. Subjects were asked to supervise a task performed by two other "subjects" (actually confederates).

The real subjects were asked to be quite complimentary to one of the confederates and to be quite harsh in criticizing the second. Each of the confederates was equally often the target of compliment and harshness and each performed the task equally well. The subjects rated the complimented confederate as more attractive than the one criticized. Thus, the subjects' own behavior apparently provided cues that allowed a self-attribution of liking. When the subjects were kind, they liked the referent person, and when they were harsh, they liked the referent person less.

A balance is maintained between the cognitive and behavioral aspects of attraction. If the liked person does not provide expected rewards when appropriate, the individual will modify the strength or range of his expectations and will also adjust downward his readiness to provide benefits in the future. A mother may do many favors for her child; but sooner or later when she is exasperated, she will say, "After all the things I have done for you, why can't you do the simple things I ask of you?" While people who like one another are not apt to think of their relationship as one based on reciprocity, the failure to meet obligations may bring the norm to conscious awareness.

D. The Social Consequences of Attraction

The relevance of attraction to social behavior has been mentioned many times in previous chapters. As we have seen, liking increases the effectiveness of social reinforcers, enhances imitation of a model, makes persons more influential, reduces the probability that coercion will be used, increases cooperation, and induces conformity to group judgments, norms, and demands. Given these considerable benefits, it is no wonder that people value being liked. A person may also like to be liked because of the benevolent intentions attributed to him. These attributions will lead others to view the person as impartial, truthful, trustworthy, and helpful, and little suspicion will exist that he is trying to manipulate or trick them. Only when our friends are obviously pursuing their self-interests will we withhold our trust from them.

Friendship obviously brings many benefits. Tedeschi (1974) has said, "A good friend is a social insurance policy that accrues cash value that can be borrowed at any time without collateral and for an unstated interest rate or premium payment. The timing and the nature of the repayment is up to the borrower. But if he waits too long or repays too little, he will lose credit for the future" (p. 205).

Given the amount of power and influence that may be achieved through the development of positive relationships with other people, it is not surprising that an individual will devote a great deal of time and effort to acquire the valuable interpersonal resource of attractiveness. Behavior which on the surface appears to have little meaning or significance for human interaction can be understood as efforts to acquire this resource. Gossip, small talk, chit-chat, recounting past experiences, self-disclosure, humor, and many everyday courtesies have the function of communicating benevolent intentions.

E.   Reciprocity and Attraction

Reciprocity, which plays such an important role in interpersonal behavior, has a special relationship to attraction. An increment in attraction will occur only when a source of benefits provides his favors with no strings attached. As Heider (1958) commented, "P will not feel grateful for a benefit and will not feel obligated when he accepts it, if he thinks that is was owed to him by O, that O ought to benefit him, that it was O's duty to benefit him" (p. 264).

Regan (1971) has provided evidence that attractiveness will cause persons to enhance the giving of benefits only when credit can be gained for selfless behavior. Subjects were induced to either like or dislike a con-

federate. During the course of the experiment: (1) the confederate left the room, returned with two cokes, and told the subject that he had been allowed to buy a coke and had brought one back for him; (2) the experimenter brought cokes for both the confederate and the subject; or (3) no favor was provided to the subject either by the confederate or by the experimenter.

When the experiment was allegedly terminated, the confederate asked the subject to help collect data for a survey. When the subject had been done a favor, he was more likely to volunteer than when no favor was received. Attraction did not affect the frequency or amount of help volunteered in the favor conditions; hence, a strict norm of positive reciprocity apparently was dominant in the subjects' prosocial behavior. However, when the subject was not obligated because he received no favors during the experiment, attraction did mediate compliance with the confederate's request for help—the more liking, the more compliance. To let liking affect behavior when no credit can be gained would be costly, since the investment is not apt to produce a profit. That is why attraction does not affect behavior when the actor is under specific obligation to provide benefits for someone he likes.

F.   Determinants of Attraction and their Resource Relevance

The antecedents of attraction, reviewed earlier in this chapter, can be interpreted in terms of their contribution to the power of the person. Similarity is important in several ways. Persons who share values are more apt to engage in benign exchanges and are less likely to become immersed in conflicts than are persons who have significant differences in values. Similarity of attitudes enhances the believeability of persuasive communications; coorientation is known to make a target more responsive to the source's influence attempts (see Chapter 8). When dissimilarity prevails, everything may be questioned: reference materials, scientific evidence, and the logic of the persuasive message.

Positive evaluations from others create liking not only because they raise the self-esteem of an individual but also because of the increment in power they imply for future interactions. Perceived expertise and status have been shown to be important bases of power in Chapters 8 and 9. Physical attractiveness apparently gains favors for the person and gives him an edge in dealing with both strangers and acquaintances. If the person is not physically attractive, he can associate with attractive friends and enhance his own social desirability by so doing.

Propinquity should be related to liking for three reasons associated with exercising social influence: (1) it is less costly to influence someone who is nearby than one who is far away; (2) the expectation of benevolence from another person is not likely to be very great if he is seldom around, and the disposition to provide benefits cannot be manifested easily at long distance; and (3) a positive cycle of mutual rewards and increasing attraction is most easily accomplished in face-to-face interactions. It is of course possible through the power of fantasy and the postal service to produce liking between people who have never met; but it is an extremely rare occurrence.

In conclusion, Tedeschi's (1974) theory has been developed inductively from a variety of social psychological theories and evidence. It is distinctive in that attraction is viewed as primarily cognitive rather than emotional, and as a dynamic two-way interpersonal system rather than as a passive reaction toward others. It links the antecedent conditions for attraction to the effects it has on interactions.

VII. CHAPTER SUMMARY

A number of theories have been proposed to explain why certain antecedent conditions produce attraction between persons. Rewards and punishments play a central role in all these theories. Persons like those who reward them and dislike those who punish them. Momentary arousal states also affect liking. When an individual feels good, he evaluates others positively, but when he feels bad, he evaluates others more negatively. The disconfirmation of expectations about the reward to be gained from an interaction may lead to a change in attraction for a person. When rewards are unexpectedly great, an increase in liking occurs, but when they are disappointingly small, a decrease in liking takes place.

Similarity of attitudes, beliefs, values, race, and socio-economic class has been found consistently to be related to liking of one person for another. Social comparison, reinforcement, and balance theories have proposed explanations for this relationship. Social comparison theory assumes that consensual information is comforting to the individual, who is selectively inattentive to dissonant information (see Chapter 5 for evaluation of this hypothesis). Comparison others are chosen to support the individual's beliefs, while dissimilar others are rejected.

Reinforcement theory postulates an effectance motive or a need of the individual to have "true" or "correct" beliefs. The similar attitudes of others are reinforcing because they affirm the individual's competence. Dissimilar attitudes are punishing because they undermine his confidence in his own abilities and knowledge. A person likes those who reward him and dislikes those who punish him.

Balance theory postulates an association between attitude similarity, sentiments, and unit relations. People who share similar attitudes should like one another and should also form positive unit relations. The opposite chain of events can also occur. Persons in a positive unit relation tend to like one another and assume they share similar attitudes. Dissimilarity, repulsion, and negative unit relations also represent a balanced relationship.

An impressive array of evidence has been produced to support both social comparison and balance theories. The application of reinforcement theory to the similarity-attraction relationship has not led to much noncommonsense, hypothesis-testing research, but it fares rather well in post hoc explanations of the available research. On the other hand, inconsistent data have been found for each theory and ambiguities have been uncovered in all of them. The controversy about the relative effect of race and beliefs has shown that social conventions and fear of social disapproval may be more important than either of these factors in determining the degree of attraction between persons. Similarity of beliefs is more important than race in producing social acceptance for casual social interactions, but race tends to be more important as the degree of intimacy intensifies.

People who live or work near one another tend to form more intense personal relationships than people who are separated by more geographical space. Propinquity affects interpersonal attraction because people who interact frequently have more opportunity to reward each other or to develop conflict. Familiarity and predictability are associated with frequent observations of another's behavior and lead to positive evaluations. Familiarity also breeds contempt and dislike. Proximity by itself tells us very little about the quality of the relationship between people.

Persons who provide positive evaluations and heighten self-esteem are generally liked. Dependence on others for positive evaluations is significantly increased when an individual has low self-esteem. Compared to high self-esteem persons, low self-esteem people are more strongly attracted to those who provide positive evaluations and have greater dislike for those who present negative evaluations. Evidence indicates that people are attracted to people who have similar real and ideal self-concepts, and they are not repelled by low self-esteem persons. The congruency hypothesis, which suggests that agreement between self-evaluation and evaluation by another person should produce liking, has been disconfirmed. Subjects are more concerned about agreement on issues than they are about evaluations of how well they present arguments about the issues.

The gain-loss theory of self-esteem and attraction has received mixed experimental support. A discerning evaluator is more attractive than a consistently positive one when his criticisms or approval are presented in a way that does not violate norms of social conduct. A stranger who provides negative evaluations is not liked even if he subsequently provides positive feedback because of the lack of tact shown in criticizing someone he does not even know.

It seems clear that within cultures there is a great deal of consensus about who is physically attractive and who is not. Although there are few objective criteria by which to judge beauty and it may rest in the eye of the beholder, people generally agree in their judgments. Persons who are judged as physically attractive do not always view themselves as attractive. The matching of attractiveness sometimes occurs in dating and mating. Stereotypes of beauty lead people to assume that the possessor has other socially desirable traits.

Attractive people do have more opportunities for affiliation with others. Beauty may lead to affiliation and liking because it produces sexual arousal, brings esthetic pleasure, and has market value. These rewards may be so powerful that even when the probability of success in attaining affiliative relationships with beautiful members of the opposite sex is small, people risk failure in attempting to achieve it. The failure of the matching hypothesis to explain dating choices may be due to the potent reward value of physical beauty.

Physical attractiveness has marketability as a resource in social influence. A male gains in perceived attractiveness when he is romantically linked with a beautiful woman. As has been noted by many great novelists, poets, and social commentators, feminine beauty is a source of power. Research has shown that physical attractiveness adds to the value of social reinforcers (or punishers), yields more social influence, and encourages male admirers to engage in ingratiation tactics. Physical beauty can be traded in the marriage market for status and security. Attractiveness also mitigates the degree of responsibility attributed to a harm-doer.

A recently developed theory interprets attraction as an attitude with cognitive, affective, and dispositional components. The ubiquitous cognition associated with liking is an expectation that the relevant other person will unselfishly mediate future benefits of varying values across situations and time. Affective arousal states and their accompanying emotional labels characterize the relations between persons and may regulate the momentary intensity of liking of one for the other. The more attractive the other person, the greater the readiness of the individual to altruistically provide benefits of varying values across situations and time.

Attraction is a complex and subtle relationship between persons and is delicately calibrated in terms of benefits given and received. Yet it is important that the reciprocal nature of the relationship be implicit rather than explicit. The power relevance of attraction must be muted phenomenologically or else it could neither be perceived nor displayed. If a person were always consciously aware of the function of his benevolent activities, he would be practicing ingratiation.

Because perceived altruism is assumed to be the basis of attraction, the instrumentality of beneficial actions must remain disguised to both the actor and the recipient. Attraction depends to a great extent on illusion and appearances, which make up the reality of the person. Just as in a play by Pirandello, it becomes difficult to separate reality from appearance. A person must believe that he gives without selfish intent and yet must maintain his expectations of reciprocity to come at some later time and in a form to be decided by the other party.

The social influence theory of attraction does not concentrate merely on receiving rewards but also views liking in terms of giving. There is in individuals an active disposition to be concerned about the welfare of a liked person and a responsibility to respond when needed. Furthermore, liking implies respect, defined as the absence of exploitation and the presence of mutual trust. Being liked gives an individual power, but it also requires that he relinquish power under certain conditions. Love is not completely altruistic because it depends on reinforcements. Love is not completely selfish, either, because it requires an individual to accept certain responsibilities toward the loved person. This give-and-take nature of attraction has so many positive consequences for the individual that it is no wonder it plays a central role in human affairs.

SUGGESTED READINGS

Berscheid, E., and Walster, E. H. *Interpersonal attraction.* Reading, Mass: Addison-Wesley, 1969. A small book providing an introduction to the scientific study of attraction.

Huston, T. (Ed.) *Foundations of interpersonal attraction.* New York: Academic Press, 1974. A collection of papers for the sophisticated reader on theories, methods, and evidence on the topic of attraction.

Murstein, B. I. (Ed.) *Theories of attraction and love.* New York: Springer, 1971. A collection of papers delivered at the Connecticut College Symposium on Theories of Interpersonal Attraction in the dyad. Includes cognitive balance, reinforcement, attributional, and power theories.

Rubin, Z. *Liking and loving: An invitation to social psychology.* New York: Holt, Rinehart, & Winston, 1973. A very readable and comprehensive review of ideas, theories, and research on attraction, including the author's story of his own early attempts to study romantic love.

CHAPTER 12

Coercion, Harmdoing, and Aggression

CHAPTER PREVIEW

Man's capacity for harming his fellows is unprecedented in the animal kingdom, except perhaps for the cannibalism observed among tropical fish. Richardson (1960) calculated that 59 million people died in wars, skirmishes, and murders between 1820 and 1945. In this 126-year period, a man was killed by another man on the average of one every 68 seconds. In the United States in 1967, someone was shot to death every twenty-five minutes; this grim statistic included 7,700 homicides, 11,000 suicides, and 2,800 accidents in which guns were involved. Comparisons with 13 other industrialized nations reveal that the United States has by far the highest rate of deaths due to firearms (Gillin & Ochberg, 1970). A typical comparison is between the United States and Japan. If the United States had the same gun homicide rate as Japan, there would have been 32 such homicides in 1966 instead of 6,855. Although there is a common belief that violence in America is greater today than ever before in our history, the rate of gun slayings in 1966 was far below the rates in the 1920s and 1930s.

Dramatic statistics like these have long impressed laymen and scientists as revealing something about the nature of man. Hobbes (1909), the 17th century English philosopher, characterized man as *Homo homini lupus*—a human wolf, a vicious and cruel animal with no compassion for its fellows. Hobbes believed that man, in a state of nature and without the restraints of civilized society, would employ any means to satisfy his desires and gain reputation. The life of a primitive man was believed to be nasty, brutish, and short. As a philosopher, Hobbes was merely speculating about the nature of man; he had never observed either primitive societies or the social behavior of wolves. Gorer (1968) notes that Hobbes' analogy is libelous to the wolf, which is a rather cooperative and gentle animal with his fellow wolves, though he is a relentless predator. It might be more

appropriate to rename man *Homo homini rattus*—a human rat, since rats do sometimes kill other rats. In the animal kingdom interspecific killing is rare.

Most of the harm that men do to each other falls short of homicide. Men may shout epithets, spread vicious gossip, damage property, hold back promised rewards, imprison and exile others, and in a multitude of ways harm other people. These effects have been classified, along with such animal responses as intra-species fighting and predatory behavior, in the general category of aggression. Theories of aggressive behavior have been devised, but as we shall stress, there are conceptual and operational difficulties with all of them. Three basic perspectives have been developed with respect to harmdoing behavior: biological, learning, and social psychological.

Biologists generally segregate the harmdoing responses of animals into two categories: *predatory* and *agonistic* (Scott, 1958). *Predatory behavior* refers to interspecies hunting and killing, which have a survival function for the species. *Agonistic behavior* refers to intraspecies conflict, usually in defense of territory, the establishment and maintenance of dominance hierarchies, and reflexive fighting in response to pain. Concerted attempts have been made to find neurological or hormonal bases for "aggressive" behavior. The psychoanalytic theory of Sigmund Freud rests on the biological premise that man has an instinct to be destructive to others and to himself. We will skeptically examine the evidence with regard to instincts in animals and men.

Learning theorists tend to explain harmdoing behavior in terms of cue-response-reinforcement sequences. When an organism experiences frustration, tension builds up, and an "aggressive" response serves to release the tension. Of course, if the frustrating condition is not removed by this response, the organism will learn to make some other response to the situation. Under certain circumstances the organism learns to inhibit "aggressive" responses because they lead to punishing consequences. Harmdoing responses may also be learned by observing the behavior of models. Learning theories focus on the acquisition or performance of responses by an individual as a function of past reinforcements or future incentives. We will emphasize the view that the social context and meaning of the coercive behavior are usually ignored or given only secondary consideration by learning theorists.

A distinctively social psychological approach to the study of harmdoing behavior attempts to replace the ambiguous concept of aggression with the more precise language of coercive power, which includes various kinds of threats and punishments that can be used by an actor. Coercive power may be used either defensively or offensively. A person is likely to retaliate when attacked and is likely to seek to restore equity when there are costs to be distributed among group members. The degree of harm that an individual inflicts in reciprocity against a provoker depends on the degree of attack, actor and target characteristics, the norms extant in the situation, and the degree of emotional arousal experienced by the person doing the retaliation.

The offensive use of coercion has been discussed in Chapter 6, when we briefly looked at the socialization of influence styles, and again in Chapter 9, when we looked at the factors that lead a source of influence to choose coercive means. We will focus in the present chapter on the defensive use of coercion and will try to put into perspective the current controversy about the effects of violence in the mass media on viewer behavior.

Not all persons who use coercion are labeled as aggressive by observers. The attribution of malevolent intent to an actor and the labeling of behavior as "bad" are preconditions for perceiving aggression. It is the values and norms of the observer, rather than the intrinsic characteristics of the actor's behavior, that lead to negative evaluations. Because the labeling of a person as aggressive often means that retribution will be sought, the actor ordinarily tries to justify his coercive behavior to observers. Failing this, he may emit any of a number of post-transgression responses, such as self-criticism, self-punishment, remorse, and attempts to make restitution to the harmed person.

The study of aggression is extremely complex, involving all of the biological and social sciences. The phenomena studied range from a female turtle protecting her young to international war. We will examine the social psychological aspects of harm-doing, which include the use of coercive power, the person perception processes involved in labeling coercive actors as aggressive, and the effects that the label of aggressiveness has on the responses of others toward the actor. All these processes are characteristic of face-to-face behavior among humans, but may not be relevant to subhuman behavior and may constitute an oversimplification when it comes to what underlies war between nations (see our discussion of the problem of level of analysis in Chapter 1). The reader is cautioned in advance that we take a skeptical view of most of the theories and research on human aggression. The reason for this skepticism will become apparent as the various points of view are described. In the course of this rather unorthodox exposition of the topic, we offer a new interpretation that we hope will provide a less confusing and more concise view of aggression than has been advanced to date by social critics and biological and social scientists.

I. BIOLOGICAL VIEWS OF HARMDOING BEHAVIOR

Biologists tend to look for structural factors that help to account for the behavior of the organisms they study. Some rather complex behavior patterns of animals seem to be instinctual, since members of the species may invariably perform them even without any opportunity for learning them. An instinct is a complex, automatic, innate, behavior, specific to members of a particular species, and based on genetic determinants and environmental releasing stimuli (see the discussion of instincts in Chapter 1, III, B, 1).

The view that aggressive behavior in men may be instinctive has generally been dismissed by modern biologists, but has been revived by the work of European ethologists and by two popular books: Lorenz's *On Aggression* (1966) and Ardrey's *The Territorial Imperative* (1966). We shall have occasion to examine the question whether men have instincts when discussing predatory and agonistic behavior and psychoanalytic theory. Most biologists concentrate their efforts in looking for brain centers or biochemical factors that are linked to "aggressive" behavior in men. The search for such physiological bases of "aggression" has produced some interesting findings and some questionable conclusions.

Biologists have provided evidence that the predatory and agonistic behavior of some species of animals is instinctual. However, the question of interest to the social psychologist is whether men have instincts, innate biological tendencies or propensities to inflict harm on one another.

A. Predatory Behavior

Predatory attacks among sub-human animals consist of approach, attack, and kill responses that serve the purpose of obtaining food. This type of interspecies behavior is not very common among mammals. Cats, dogs, hyenas, and bears—animals with claws and fangs—are predatory, but many mammals are herbivorous.

An extraordinary example of instinctual predatory behavior is found in Box 12.1.

It would be too great a theoretical leap to generalize from the behavior of insects or even wolves to the behavior of man. Careful development of the phylogentic evidence would require scrutiny of the predatory activity of man's nearest relatives, the apes. On rare occasion, an ape may kill a small animal for food (see Box 12.2), but normally these primates are vegetarians and do not prey on other animals. Of course, it is well known that man is a meat-eater and does kill other animals for food. But there is absolutely no evidence to support the conjecture that man's predatory behavior is biologically rooted. Actually, it is extraordinary how little predatory behavior is displayed by man. Despite the well known activities of hunters and fisherman, relatively few men ever kill anything larger than a fly or a mosquito, except by accident. Even cattle ranchers and hog farmers prefer (for economic reasons) to let the killing be done by professional slaughter houses. In primitive societies, roles are differentiated so that only some of the hunting party actually perform a kill, while most of the men serve to maneuver the prey so the hunters carrying spears and arrows can reach them.

Lorenz (1966) does not consider predatory behavior to be a form of aggression because animals engaging in such behavior do not display any emotion—there is no particular malice or anger involved in interspecies killing. The predatory animal is merely hungry and the prey is available. The job is carried out in a rather perfunctory and automatic way. The difference between predation and aroused attack is demonstrated by cats, who, when after prey, often display a great deal of patience, stalking the unwary victim, and then pouncing on it; but when emotionally aroused, the cat hunches its back, the fur on its neck stands up, its tail swishes back and forth, and it may hiss. Scott's (1958) distinction between predatory and agonistic behavior cautions us not to make the error of generalizing from the study of *interspecies* behavior to provide explanations for *intraspecies* behavior. The grim statistics that were cited

Box 12.1 PREDATORY BEHAVIOR OF THE PEPSIS

The digger wasp of the genus Pepsis engages in an extraordinary pattern of behavior in hunting the tarantula. Petrumkevitch (1955) has described the behavior of the mother wasp when she is prepared to lay her eggs: "To identify the species the wasp apparently must explore the spider with her antennae. The tarantula shows an amazing tolerance to this exploration. (The tarantula will normally kill a wasp of any other species.) The wasp crawls under it and walks over it without evoking any hostile response. . . . The wasp, having satisfied itself that the victim is of the right species, moves off a few inches to dig the spider's grave. Working vigorously with legs and jaws, it excavates a hole 8 to 10 inches deep and a diameter slightly larger than the spider's girth. . .

"When the grave is finished, the wasp returns to the tarantula to complete her ghastly enterprise. First she feels it all over once more with her antennae. Then her behavior becomes more aggressive. She bends her abdomen, protruding her sting, and searches for the soft membrane at the point where the spider's legs join its body—the only spot where she can penetrate the horny skeleton. From time to time, as the exasperated spider slowly shifts ground, the wasp turns on her back and slides along with the aid of her wings, trying to get under the tarantula for a shot at the vital spot. During all this maneuvering, which can last for several minutes, the tarantula makes no move to save itself. Finally, the wasp corners it against some obstruction and grasps one of its legs in her powerful jaws. Now at last the harassed spider tries a desperate but vain defense. The two contestants roll over and over on the ground. It is a terrifying sight and the outcome is always the same. The wasp finally manages to thrust her sting into the soft spot and holds it there for a few seconds, while she pumps in the poison. Almost immediately the tarantula falls paralyzed on its back. Its legs stop twitching; its heart stops beating. Yet it is not dead, as is shown by the fact that if taken from the wasp it can be restored to some sensitivity by being kept in a moist chamber for several months" (p. 6-7).

The digger wasp then lays its eggs in the spider's grave and the larvae use the tarantula as a food supply as they grow. This complex set of responses is not learned by the digger wasp, but is part of its genetic heritage.

---

at the beginning of this chapter referred to the intraspecies behavior of men harming other men. It seems clear from observation that men do not have a predatory instinct.

B. Agonistic Behavior

Intraspecies conflicts take the form of threats and fighting. Animals band together in herds, broods, schools, flocks, pods, prides, packs, and coveys. Within these groupings there are often conflicts regarding territory, mates, and access to food. Through fighting and the use of threat signals, dominance hierarchies may be set up. Agonistic behavior is often species specific and usually has at least some genetic underpinning. In addition, many animals display reflexive attacks against any source of pain. To determine whether the

Box 12.2   PREDATORY BEHAVIOR AMONG CHIMPANZEES

It has been known for a number of years that primates such as baboons and chimpanzees are occasional eaters of meat. Baboons have been observed killing and eating newborn antelopes, and chimpanzees have been known to sample a wide diet including insects, lizards, eggs, fledgling birds, young bushpigs, and monkeys.

Teleki (1973) has reported observations of the hunting, killing, and eating of baboons by chimpanzees. A victim is picked out by the chimps, stalked, pursued, and seized without provocation. This behavior often occurs after the chimpanzees have just feasted on a large amount of fruit; hunger is clearly not the motive and one would have to stretch the definition to call it strictly predatory.

Baboons and chimps have similar habits, travel similar trails, occupy the same feeding sites, and have been observed eating side-by-side, playing together, and grooming one another. Thus, the killing and eating is an approximation of intraspecific aggression in the sense that the two societies are overlapping.

Teleki suggests that the behavior fulfills some kind of social function. He has made particular note of the fact that the chase is a cooperative venture on the part of the chimpanzees. Without verbalizations or detectable gestures they coordinate their pursuit very effectively. This behavior is very analogous to hunting as a sport among men—like a fox hunt.

The eating stage of this behavior pattern is extremely social as well. Never has a single chimpanzee been observed killing and devouring his prey all alone. When the prey is caught, the hunter emits a cry that can be heard for a mile, and chimpanzees not involved in the chase gather at the kill site. After the carcass is divided among hunters and early arrivals (usually without dispute or hostility), other chimpanzees join in by picking up dropped scraps, by tearing off a piece, or by requesting food—which is accomplished by holding an upturned palm under the possessor's chin and softly vocalizing. Any of the chimps may carry out requests, from those of high status to juveniles, and they are refused roughly seventy percent of the time. The brain, however, is apparently a delicacy, because it is never surrendered by the killer.

---

study of agonistic behavior among animals tells us much about human "aggression," we need to look more closely at territoriality, dominance hierarchies, and reactions to pain.

1.   Territoriality

Tinbergen's (1955) experiments on the territorial behavior of a small fish called the stickleback won him a Nobel Prize. The male stickleback builds a nest, seduces a female to lay eggs in the nest by using elaborate swimming patterns, fertilizes the eggs, and guards them until they hatch and the brood moves on. During this mating period, the male changes from his usual dull color and develops a red belly that serves to attract females, much as a male peacock's feathers do. The male stickleback protects his nesting territory against invasion from other males who may be competitive for females. He will threaten any object that has a red underbelly, but only when he is in his mating phase. Most of his territorial behavior consists of threat displays rather than actual fighting. The evidence suggests that the animal is predisposed by hormonal changes to engage in this genetically determined, complex behavior when faced with a releasing stimulus—an ovalshaped red object.

Territorial behavior is common in various species of fish, birds, and mammals, particularly during their mating season. The behavior is usually restricted to threats by the defender and withdrawal by the intruder. In some species, a test of strength may be involved, as when two bull moose lock horns. These encounters seldom lead to the death of the loser, who either simply runs away or displays his surrender by a characteristic behavior such as exposing his soft underside to the victor. Specific signs of surrender and deference serve to inhibit fighting in some species. For example, according to Lorenz, a defeated wolf turns his head away from the victor in a fight, exposing its jugular. This behavior is a signal that automatically causes the fight to end and preserves the life of the loser.

The biological function of territorial behavior is to enhance survival by preventing overpopulation in relation to the food supply. Territoriality assures an appropriate distribution of animals over a habitable region and the selection of the "best" males for mating. Where there is a colorful display by males, as among sticklebacks and peacocks, mating is usually based on female selection of a partner rather than on territorial behavior. In such cases, beauty wins out over strength as a determiner of evolutionary developments.

If territorial behavior is defined as the defense of a fixed geographical area against intrusion by members of one's own species, the evidence indicates that among primates, the gibbon is probably the only truly territorial species (Boelkins & Heiser, 1970). Many primates travel in social groups and resist having outsiders join them. However, this form of defense against "foreigners" does not take place in a particular location but happens wherever the group finds itself. Nor is it clear that such closed groups always resist intruders or that this defensive behavior is genetically determined. Refusal to grant membership to strangers may be a learned behavior and may be culturally transmitted to the young.

The importance of private property or territory to men varies enormously among cultures. For example, among Eskimo societies there is no concept of defense of territory even in those cases where invasion of a hunting area by other groups may mean starvation and death for the original inhabitants (Montagu, 1968). In some modern societies (e.g., China), an individual has no right to private property, while in others (e.g., the United States), most men believe they have the right to kill intruders to defend their own property (Blumenthal, Kahn, Andrews, & Head, 1972). These extreme variations cannot be explained on the basis of some biological constant such as a territorial instinct.

2.   Dominance Hierarchies

In many species of animals there is a typical social structure that is usually called a *dominance hierarchy*. A ranking of individuals develops in which one animal is clearly superordinate to all the other members of the group. Each of the other members takes a clear position in the hierarchy. For example, among hens A, B, C, and D there may be a dominance hierarchy in which B, C, and D all show deference to A; C and D show deference to B; and D shows deference to C. Thus if A decides to feed in a particular spot, all the others will move to give her entry. Furthermore, if A pecks B, B will not peck back, though B may peck C. It is this type of behavior that led to the notion of a "pecking order."

Intricate dominance hierarchies are present in most primate groups. Southwick

(1967) demonstrated a complicated group structure among rhesus monkeys in a zoo in Calcutta. Observations established the baseline frequency of twenty kinds of behavior in a group of seventeen monkeys, including adults, juveniles, and yearlings of each sex. Then at various intervals new monkeys were added to the group. New juveniles were attacked by the resident juveniles but not by any of the resident adults; new adult females and males were attacked by residents of the same age and sex. Thus, each subgroup in the established colony exhibited vigorous agonistic behavior when its own status was disturbed by a newcomer.

The establishment of a dominance hierarchy produces stability in a group and actually minimizes the extent of fighting. Bernstein and Mason (1963) demonstrated this benign function by placing seven unacquainted rhesus monkeys in a 24' by 48' enclosure. In the first hour, over 50 percent of all interactions consisted of threats and attacks; the frequency of agonistic behavior was 20 times greater than in any subsequent hour of observation. The dominance hierarchy established during the first hour remained essentially unchanged during the remaining 75 days of the study. When there is a settled dominance hierarchy in a group, agonistic behavior consists mostly of threatening gestures or postures by superiors and complementary deference from subordinates. As a result, most conflict is maintained at a harmless level.

Superficial resemblances between primate dominance hierarchies and human status systems have fostered inappropriate assertions that they serve the same functions and have the same origins. Dominance hierarchies among primates are based on biological states. Whereas such hierarchies among primates are determined by size, strength, sex, and biochemical factors, social structures among men are determined by economic wealth, social skills, geographical location, and other nonbiological factors. In addition, human status hierarchies must be rationalized and legitimized if they are to be effective in regulating behavior. Among other primates a high position in a dominance hierarchy serves strictly selfish interests. Men award status to group members in exchange for contributions to group goals. Hence, biological factors are prominent in determining dominance hierarchies among primates, while social factors are major contributors to the formation of human status systems. There is no evidence to support the belief that men, like other primates, are genetically programmed to develop relations of super- and sub-ordination.

3. Pain and Attack Behavior

Superficial pain, as distinguished from deep somatic pain (like a belly-ache), is the most reliable single cause of attack behavior in subhuman animals. When an animal experiences pain, he attacks whatever is perceived as the source of the pain. Reflexive fighting in response to pain caused by electric shocks has been demonstrated by mice (R. Tedeschi, D. Tedeschi, Mucks, Cook, Mattis, & Fellows 1959), hamsters (Ulrich & Azrin, 1962), and squirrel monkeys (Azrin, Hutchinson, & Hake, 1963). In these studies, two animals were placed in a closed space and then one was given a shock. When the space was large, attack behavior did not occur, but when the space was small the shocked animal attacked the innocent bystander as if the latter had bitten him. Ulrich and Azrin (1962) also found that extreme heat can elicit fighting behavior. The intensity and duration of such behavior among monkeys has been found to be a direct function of the amount of shock delivered to them (Azrin, Hutchinson, & Hake, 1967).

Reflexive attack responses to pain have not been demonstrated to occur in man. In fact, superficial pain seldom elicits fighting among humans. More often, the individual who is hurt will withdraw from the source of pain, weep, seek solace or aid, and attempt to reduce the pain. A man who stubs his toe in a crowded elevator will not strike out blindly against other people. Situational factors that elicit fighting behavior from other animals may not elicit fighting from men.

C.   The Freudian View of Aggression

According to later psychoanalytic theory (Freud, 1950), men have two basic drives or sources of psychic energy, called *Eros* and *Thanatos*. The productive, creative, and positive energy (Eros) is believed to be in conflict with a destructive, death-seeking force (Thanatos) in each individual. These forces require expression and emerge in various forms of behavior, ranging from chewing food (which both destroys and is productive through anabolism) to making love. The forces are considered to be of biological origin and to accumulate, building up pressure like steam in a pot. If they are not expressed in small amounts, a psychological explosion may result. A Casper Milktoast may suddenly erupt and become a mass murderer.

Three earlier hypotheses had been proposed by Freud before he developed the concept of Thanatos that are still the focus of considerable controversy in social psychology: (1) Frustration is one factor that determines the target of aggression; an individual has a tendency to attack sources of frustration. (2) If an individual cannot attack the frustrating agent because it is unavailable or too powerful, a substitute target will become the victim of the attacker's pent-up anger. This *displacement* of aggression was intended by Freud to explain apparently irrational behavior, such as killing a total stranger for no reason. (3) If an individual expresses aggression toward a target, his fund of stored-up frustration will be momentarily expended and he will be less aggressive until further energy is accumulated. This *catharsis* of aggressive energy is exemplified by playing a football game; an individual should be less likely to

perpetrate harm after playing than before. Thus socially acceptable activities may drain off aggressive energy and provide substitutes for destructive behavior.

Freud's increasingly pessimistic view of man's nature was based on his observations of the wanton destruction and killing during World War I. He believed an instinct for destruction is part of human life. When this compulsion is turned inward, the individual acts in self-destructive ways. While it is now clear that men do not have an instinct to be "aggressive," we will need to examine the available physiological evidence about the existence of an aggressive drive of cumulated Thanatos. Are there any internal biological factors that compel harmdoing and destructive behavior by humans? After examining this physiological question, we will turn to learning theory and an examination of Freud's three hypotheses regarding frustration, displacement, and catharsis.

D.   The Physiological Bases of Aggression

Biologically based drives have characteristic deprivation and satiation cycles. For example, catabolism (the breaking down of tissues in the metabolic process) apparently provides signals to the brain, which, in turn, produce internal cues in the form of contractions of the stomach informing an animal that he is hungry. An animal in a food deprived condition usually becomes restless, searches his environment for food, or, if he knows where it is located, will immediately approach and consume it. Consummatory responses remove the internal signals of hunger and the animal terminates all behavior directed toward obtaining and eating food. He is said to be satiated. All known biological drives that are cyclic in nature have this go-and-stop, deprivation-and-satiation character. The go phase is generated primarily within the organism and by mechanisms that are genetically inherited, although various rhythms may be established by learning and various tastes may be acquired.

One line of physiological research has been to try to locate "go" and "stop" centers for aggression in the brain. Moyer (1971) has interpreted the available evidence as showing that there are innate neural circuits in the brains of animals and men which, when activated in the presence of certain stimuli, produce destructive behavior by the organism. For example, Sheard and Flynn (1967) found that electrical stimulation of the lateral hypothalamus of the brain induced cats to attack rats. Interpretative problems plague this kind of research, however. The fact that particular activities can be elicited by electrical stimulation of various brain regions does not prove that these neural circuits are innate. Once a pattern of behavior is learned and is stored in the brain, stimulation may elicit it whenever an appropriate (learned) environmental stimulus is also present.

Delgado implanted electrodes in the brain of a bull and by operating a remote control unit caused him to charge, stop, back up, or turn around, according to which electrode was activated. Telemetry systems allow the control of electrodes from a considerable distance without the use of wires that would inhibit movement. Delgado (1960) has also shown that aggressiveness in a monkey can be inhibited by the stimulation of particular points in the caudate nucleus of the brain. A monkey that otherwise could not be handled at all will not bite the experimenter even when given an opportunity, if the appropriate electrode has been activated. Delgado observed what happened when he placed the control lever for inhibiting threat and attack behavior inside the monkeys' cage. Other monkeys in the group soon learned that if they pressed the lever, the dominant animal of whom they were afraid would behave in a fearful and submissive manner.

Subhuman animals remain sensitive to the presence and behavior of other members of their social group even when undergoing brain stimulation. Existing friendships and hostilities remain effective even when the animal's behavior is being artificially controlled by the experimenter. On the other hand, dominance relationships can be changed by electrode stimulation of the brain. By telemetric stimulation, Robinson (1968) was able to cause a subordinate monkey to attack a dominant member of the group. The threat-attack responses of the monkey were reliably elicited by electrical stimulation and over a period of several days, the dominance relationship between the two animals was reversed and remained stable without further artificial stimulation for the several months of the study. However, Plotnik and Delgado (1968) caution that the interpretation of research involving electrode implantations of the brain must take into account that stimulation of the brain may activate pain receptors and that pain is known to elicit attack behavior among subhuman animals.

Among many species of animals there is a relationship between concentrations of sex hormones and agonistic behavior. The male gonadal hormone (testosterone) is associated with fighting among many animals, including rats, chickens, and monkeys. Horses and bulls are often castrated as a way of taming them. Although males are typically more aggressive than females, there are significant reversals in nature. For example, it is the female bee that carries a stinger and defends against predators. Whereas male mice engage in more threatening and fighting behavior than female mice, the opposite is true among hamsters. In most human societies men are more violent than women. However, this is not a universal characteristic of the two sexes. For example, Mead's (1935) description of the temperament of the two sexes among the Mondugumor of New Guinea reveals a reversal of the usual relationship. The often violent women are the providers and defenders of the group and the more pacifistic men serve domestic and artistic functions. In still other societies there is almost no aggression by either sex (e.g., the Zuni Indians of the Southwestern United States). We may conclude that the role of biochemical factors, if any, is much less important in accounting for the agonistic behavior of men than social factors.

Moyer's statement that "there is abundant evidence that man has innate, neural, and endocrine organizations which when activated result in hostile thoughts and behaviors" (p. 83) may be considered more a function of his initial assumptions than of strong inferences drawn from unambiguous and conclusive evidence. The evidence may show that monkeys can be stimulated to fight or inhibited from fighting, but it is quite a theoretical jump to speculate that throwing hand grenades, firing rifles , shouting epithets, and spreading vicious gossip are forms of behavior that are controlled by innate brain patterns.

The biological approach to the study of aggression has produced some very important evidence, however. Electrode stimulation and hormonal studies have shown that predatory and agonistic behavior can be elicited by use of changing physiological states, but only when appropriate external stimuli are present. Apparently, there is no innately generated biological energy that will invariably be manifested in aggressive behavior. Food deprivation will cause the animal to initiate activity to correct physiological deficit. There is no evidence of any comparable internal need to emit aggressive responses or of a requirement to discharge pent-up tension or energy. Internal states may intensify responses that are elicited by environmental stimuli, but they do not cause the behavior to occur.

E.   A Critique of the Biological View

Anthropomorphism is the tendency to attribute unique human characteristics to other forms of life. Owners often attribute human emotions or intellectual abilities to their pets. Ethologists like Lorenz appear to make the opposite fallacy of generalizing from animal characteristics to man. Despite the layman's fascination with subhuman animals and such popular books as *The Naked Ape* (Morris, 1967) and *The Human Zoo* (Morris, 1969), comparative research does not establish a clear continuity between the predatory and agonistic behavior of subhuman organisms and men. Inappropriate generalizations have usually involved circular reasoning of the following form: animals engage in behavior that is analagous to the actions taken by men; therefore, we can better understand human behavior by studying the causes of infrahuman behavior. Unfortunately, if the original analogy between animals and men is superficial and false, then the study of infrahumans may reveal nothing at all about the harmdoing behavior of men.

An example of this fallacious type of reasoning by analogy is the layman's tendency to associate large teeth in animals with the weapons used by man. Almost all primates except men have large teeth. Yet all but the baboons are predominately vegetarian. Large teeth may, of course, be used to bite one's fellows, but their primary biological function is for more pacific and pastoral purposes (Fromm, 1973). Interpreting large teeth as weapons proposes an analogy that is misleading; it certainly makes no contribution to an understanding of why men harm one another.

The added complexity of human behavior needs to be recognized. Contests for females, territory, and food among infrahuman species depend on bodily resources such as fangs, claws, and horns. Men use tools, such as knives, guns, and bombs, to settle disputes that often focus on symbolic goals like self-enhancement, freedom, religion, and nationalism. Men may seek revenge; we have no evidence that subhumans are capable of the future orientation required to plan such action. Most important, men have the ability to transmit an almost infinite number of wishes and intentions to others through language, while subhumans can transmit only a narrow range of information through gestures, facial expressions, and vocalizations. Because of their limited ability to communicate, the ritualized threat gestures and attack responses of subhumans can be easily identified, particularly since this behavior is always undertaken within a situational context in which the source of conflict is obvious. Men, on the other hand, are capable of insinuating by innuendo, of simulating an accident when harm is intended, and of perceiving sources of conflict that no one else perceives. Aggression among infrahuman species is almost never accidental and no reference to intention is required to explain it. One does not consider the possibility that a lion's harmdoing behavior may be accidental. Men are accident prone because of their ability to use sophisticated tools over which they have less control than do animals with their teeth and claws. These differences led Scott (1970) to conclude that because of "man's unique genetic composition, no direct analogies (of agonistic behavior) from any other species to man are justified" (p. 570). The evolution of man has created the need for culture. This development makes purely biological explanations for human behavior less satisfactory than theories that stress social factors.

Attempts to understand the complex behavior of men by recourse to the simpler agonistic behavior of subhuman animals is like trying to understand why the jet plane flies by studying simpler vehicles such as wheelbarrows (Boulding, 1968). Complex behavior is qualitatively different from simpler responses. This is not to say that there is nothing to be learned about human social behavior through studying other animals. The effect of the presence of other members of the same species on learning and performance has been furthered by animal research (Zajonc, 1965). However, the biological approach has failed to pro-

vide adequate explanations for the harmdoing behavior of men.

In conclusion our brief excursion into biology has exposed a shaky foundation for explanations of the uses of coercive power. All organisms are of course limited by their genetic endowments, but capacities, however biologically determined, do not provide an explanation for actual human behavior. The capacity to speak neither means that all men will speak nor does it explain or predict what men will say if they do speak. It may be concluded that there are compelling reasons for social psychologists to seek an explanation for conflict-related behavior at an exclusively social level of analysis.

II. LEARNING THEORIES OF HARMDOING

Three major theories have been proposed about how humans learn harm-doing behavior: (1) frustration-aggression theory, (2) instrumental learning theory, and (3) modeling theory. Frustration-aggression theory retains the assumption of an innate mechanism which requires that the person rid himself of pent-up tension and incorporates the processes of displacement and catharsis from early psychoanalytic theory. Instrumental learning theory avoids assuming such mechanisms and treats harmdoing, just like any other response, as learned through reinforcements and punishments. Of course, modeling theory assumes that an individual may learn harmdoing by observing the behavior of another person. While frustration-aggression theory focuses on tension reduction, instrumental learning theory views the organism's harmdoing behavior as directed toward the removal of the source of frustration or as retaliation and self-defense against attack. Modeling theory emphasizes the learning of harmdoing responses that are not induced by frustrating circumstances or by an attack by another person.

A. Frustration-Aggression Theory

A group of psychologists at Yale University wrote a famous and influential book entitled *Frustration and Aggression* in which they outlined a theory that still dominates this area of research (Dollard, Doob, Miller, Mowrer, & Sears, 1939). The basic principle of the theory is that frustration always leads to aggression. *Frustration* is defined as any event or act of others that prevents a person from obtaining a goal he is actively seeking. Some confusion exists about whether the aggressive response that is automatically elicited by frustration should be considered based on genetic or biological mechanisms or whether it is a learned association. An organism can learn to inhibit aggressive responses because of fear of punishment, but it is assumed that frustration builds up a fund of energy or tension, which must find an outlet in some form. Thus, when one form of aggression is suppressed or inhibited, the energy is apt to be displaced against a substitute target.

Figure 12.1 depicts a model of the frustration-aggression theory. On the independent variable side of the picture there is a set of events that are considered to be frustrating. These events cause a build-up of aggressive energy in the organism. The aggressive energy causes the organism to direct one of a set of alternative responses (labeled as "aggressive") either at the frustrating agent or at a substitute target. Any frustration will result in immediate, delayed, or displaced aggression because of the need to release tension. Which form of aggression will occur and when will depend on a set of conditions that inhibit or facilitate the expression of such responses. Any expression of aggressive behavior drains off the aggressive energy that accumulated through frustrating experiences; this draining off is termed *catharsis*. Catharsis should be observable after a person performs an aggressive response; he should be less aggressive immediately after engaging in harmdoing than before. This theory makes similar predictions to those of Freud with respect to frustration, displacement, and catharsis, albeit for different reasons.

When the organism directs an aggressive response at a frustrating agent and the response is successful in removing the barrier to goal attainment, aggression is rewarded. A rewarded response is more likely to recur the next time the organism faces a similar situation. Thus, instead of producing

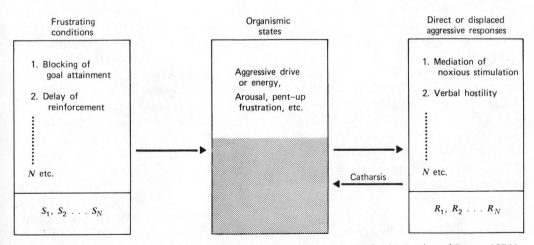

Figure 12.1. A pictorial model of the frustration-aggression theory. (After Tedeschi, Smith, and Brown, 1974.)

catharsis and reducing the probability of aggression, success is apt to increase the probability of harmdoing. Rewarding an individual for inhibiting an aggressive response or punishing him for emitting harmdoing behavior may teach him self-control. As a result of learned inhibition the aggressive energy either continues to build up in the organism or is expressed in indirect ways.

The empirical evidence does not consistently support the frustration-aggression theory. There is some difficulty in interpreting the evidence because clear conceptual and operational definitions of frustration and aggression have never been developed. When the independent and dependent variables of a theory are conceptually ambiguous, then any test of the theory will be equivocal. We will examine these conceptual problems and the evidence with respect to the processes of displacement and catharsis. We will also describe Berkowitz's cue-arousal theory as one attempt to modify frustration-aggression theory.

1. The Concepts of Frustration and Aggression

The vernacular use of the word "frustration" covers a multitude of meanings. As the scientific study of frustration has progressed, different sets of events, all of which may be considered as frustrating, have been found to have varying effects on behavior (Lawson, 1965). One way to operationalize frustration is to prevent an organism from performing a response leading to a reward and then see what happens; another way is to take away the reinforcement after the organism has made a learned response in order to reach it; still another way is to provide false norms and scores to a subject so he believes he failed in his attempts to achieve success. A great number of operational definitions of frustration have been developed that "fit" the conceptual requirement of blocking an individual's goal attainment. Actually, this variety of experimental procedures

is a desirable way of establishing the validity of a theoretical concept (see Chapter 2, II, D).

Unfortunately, no consistent relationship has been found between frustration and any particular class of responses by the organism. Frustration operationalized as task failure (Epstein, 1965; Gentry, 1970; Yarrow, 1948), failure to achieve a better scholastic grade (Buss, 1966), or time out from positive or token reinforcements (Gentry, 1970; Jegard & Walters, 1960; Walters & Brown, 1963) does not lead to aggression. Similar operationalizations have been associated with increases in nonaggressive behavior, such as regression, repression, fixation, and withdrawal (Sears, 1951). Because of these inconsistencies Lawson (1965) has concluded that the concept of frustration should be eliminated from the psychologist's scientific vocabulary.

The interpretation of responses as aggressive has been so global that it seems any response may be so labeled by experimenters. Aggression is sometimes defined as harmdoing behavior. However, this does not allow for accidents or for cases where an actor attempts to harm others but fails. A person who steps on another's toes may be considered clumsy but usually he is not perceived as aggressive. A sniper may fire at a potential victim and miss; the victim may be unaware of the action and hence suffer no physical or psychological harm, and yet an observer might well consider the sniper to be aggressive. These examples indicate that it may be impossible to devise a strictly behavioral definition of aggression. The problem of the actor's intentions is critical. Of course, intent is not behavior; it is an inference drawn from circumstances *and* behavior.

Laboratory studies of human aggression almost never establish the intentions of subjects. The experiments often rationalize harmdoing actions to subjects through "cover stories." These stories induce the subject to perform the behavior the experimenter has defined as aggressive. For example, subjects may be asked to deliver shocks as a way of improving the victim's (learner's) performance (Baron, 1971b) or as contributing to an important scientific investigation (Milgram, 1965; see Chapter 8, III, D, 4). The general failure to articulate operational with conceptual definitions of aggression is quite obvious when reviewing the research literature. Included among the dependent variables labeled as "aggressive" are: (a) delivering an electric shock to another person as a rating device for evaluating essays (Berkowitz & Green, 1962) or as a way of escaping electric shock in a competitive game (Epstein & Taylor, 1967); (b) sitting on or thumping a doll with a stick, paddle, or hand (Bandura, Ross, & Ross, 1961); (c) choosing to play with a doll rather than a ball (Lovaas, 1961); (d) recalling aggressive content presented in a film (the person who remembers most is considered the most aggressive (Maccoby & Wilson, 1957); (e) rating other persons negatively on measures of perceived intelligence, attraction, and so on (Berkowitz & Rawlings, 1963; Miller & Bugelski, 1948); (f) responding to TAT pictures with essays that are coded for "hostility" or "aggressiveness" by judges (Feshbach, 1955); (g) delay in asking the experimenter to stop popping balloons with a needle (Mussen & Rutherford, 1961); and (h) being late to school (Eron, Walder, & Lefkowitz, 1971). Thus behavior that neither does harm nor is intended to do harm has been labeled as aggressive by experimenters.

These problems can be illustrated by a recent experiment. Rule and Hewitt (1971) placed electrodes on subjects so their heart beats could be monitored. The subjects were asked to learn a list of nonsense syllables read to them by a peer, who acted as teacher and provided verbal feedback about their progress in learning. They received either an easy list with neutral comments from their peer ("Well, that's OK, let's do it again"), a difficult list with neutral comments, or a difficult list with derogatory comments ("God, at the rate you're going, we're never going to get finished."). The

experimenters interpreted these conditions as arousing low, moderate, and high frustration, respectively. Yet it is plausible to suggest that subjects with an easy list should expect to succeed at the task and should be frustrated when the neutral comments of a peer indicate they have not succeeded. Subjects with a difficult task may not be frustrated by failure if they do not expect to succeed anyway. When a peer insults them, they may be angered not by frustration so much as by the unprovoked verbal attack of a stranger.

In the second phase of the experiment, the subjects had an opportunity to "teach" the peer a list of syllables. Instead of providing verbal feedback, they were asked to indicate disapproval of the learner's progress by administering shocks, the degree of disapproval being indicated by varying the intensity or duration of the shocks. The subjects were told that the effect of reinforcement on the learning process was the phenomenon under investigation. They could interpret this explanation as indicating the beneficial effect of shocking the learner by contributing to science and improving his performance. When a subject used his ability to shock the learner, should he be considered aggressive? Or should he be considered altruistic for his contribution to the welfare of mankind? Baron and Eggelston (1972) using similar procedures, found that subjects interpreted their motivation in shocking the learner as an altruistic method of helping the student learn.

An analysis of cardiac responses showed that the subjects who had been insulted were aroused by their experience, but there was no difference in arousal between failing at simple and complex tasks. When the subjects were teachers in the second phase of the experiment, those in the neutral-comment, complex-task condition gave fewer shocks to the peer than did those in either of the other two conditions. The authors concluded that the results failed to support frustration-aggression theory because the low frustration condition produced less arousal but as much aggression as the high frustration condition. But if one wishes to interpret the easy task condition with neutral feedback as highly frustrating because of the subjects' expectation of success, then the aggression but not the arousal effects support frustration-aggression theory.

We have drawn out this critical discussion of the frustration-aggression theory because it is so widely accepted among social scientists. The Rule and Hewitt experiment is representative of the difficulty one has in interpreting the results of experiments when the concepts being tested are ambiguous and ill-defined. Buss (1966) has reviewed the research on aggression and has concluded that insult was the major antecedent of aggressive responses in laboratory experiments and that frustration by itself rarely leads to aggression.

2. Displacement

According to the frustration-aggression theory of Dollard et al., when an individual has accumulated aggressive tension and his initial response to a situation is inhibited or blocked, he will have a tendency to perform some other aggressive response as a way of releasing the tension. The major reason for considering under a single label such different responses as threats, expressions of anger, annoyance, or hatred, insults, punching, knifing, shooting, shocking, derogating, spreading gossip, and so on is that they have the same basic function—to relieve the pent-up tension brought about by frustrating conditions. If one response cannot occur, then any other from the set should serve the same function. Or when a response cannot occur with respect to the frustrating stimulus, it may be directed at a substitute stimulus. Instead of punching your boss in the nose for criticizing you, you may go to a bar and punch a total stranger in the nose. The labeling of responses as aggressive is therefore based on the availability of alternative responses to serve the same function of reducing aggressive tensions.

Looked at from a somewhat different viewpoint, any aggressive response should bring about catharsis and hence reduce the probability that any other response in the set of those identified as aggressive will occur. The processes of displacement and catharsis are crucial to the frustration-aggression theory and go to the heart of the definition of aggression. As Dollard et al. state the matter, "to the extent that the hypothesized unity is found, upon closer examination, to break down, the present use of the term 'aggression' will have to be modified or abandoned" (pp. 52-53).

More than three decades of research have failed to produce compelling evidence for the processes of displacement and catharsis. The classic study of displacement was done by Miller and Bugelski (1948). They asked young men to fill out an adjective checklist meant to assess attitudes toward various national groups, including Mexicans and Japanese. The men were promised that after dinner they could leave their CCC camp and go into town. The promise was violated and the men were given a large battery of tests instead, including another assessment of their attitudes toward Mexicans and Japanese. Because attitudes toward these groups were less favorable after than before dinner, the experimenters interpreted the subjects' response to the frustration as displacement of aggression onto Mexicans and Japanese.

Close examination of the data, however, casts doubt on a displacement interpretation. There was no increase in the number of negative adjectives checked by subjects; rather, there was a decrease in the number of positive items checked. Since it is quite likely that the men were hostile toward the experimenters for breaking their promise, it could be argued that they checked fewer total adjectives on the second test as a form of noncooperation. Unless it is accepted that the second attitude measurement truly represented their post-frustration attitudes toward the national groups, the responses must be interpreted as hostility directed at the experimenters.

Silverman and Kleinman (1967) carried out a study intended to find out if subjects are reacting to the experimenter or whether displacement really occurs when they are led to expect a positive outcome and then are frustrated. The subjects were given a variety of attitude measures in addition to an opportunity to displace their aggression onto minority groups following frustration. It was found that they reacted negatively to all attitude measures. Hence the replication data suggest that the frustration manipulation used produced a general negativism rather than a displacement of aggression. A similar interpretation can be made of other displacement studies (e.g., Berkowitz & Green, 1962).

In their review of the research on displacement, Nacci and Tedeschi (1975) have found support for the frustration-aggression theory only when the experiments allow for the operation of other social psychological processes, such as negative equity or social comparison, which produce (under the special conditions contrived) a displacement-like effect. For example, Holmes (1972) had subjects wait either 5 or 30 minutes for a second person (a confederate) to arrive before beginning an experiment. The longer the subjects had to wait, the more frustrated they were assumed to be. After the period of waiting the subjects were given an opportunity to either shock the person who was responsible for making them wait or someone else. The shock opportunity was provided in the context of producing stress during a learning task for which the confederate served as the learner. Subjects delivered more shocks in the 30-minute than in the 5-minute late conditions regardless of whether the other person had or had not been responsible for making them wait.

Holmes interpreted these findings in terms of displacement. However, it is equally plausible to explain them in terms of equity theory. Subjects had incurred the costs of waiting, while the confederate (whether responsible or not) had not. The longer subjects had to wait the greater the

inequity between them and the other person. The use of shocks by subjects may have had the purpose of reducing the negative inequity that existed in the situation by producing an amount of discomfort for the confederate equal to the amount suffered by them through waiting. Nacci (1975) found a very low rate of shocking by subjects in a 30-minute wait condition when the learner was believed to be someone who had also been waiting 30 minutes for an experimental partner who never appeared. Hence, inequity rather than displacement was the basis for behavior in both the Holmes and Nacci studies.

3. Catharsis

Catharsis refers to a discharge or purging of aggressive energy. Performing an aggressive response presumably results in some catharsis. Displacement effects would demonstrate that the great variety of responses labeled as aggression are similar in terms of psychological significance, because the inhibition of one response increases the probability that another in the set will occur. Catharsis would demonstrate the same similarity among responses, because the occurrence of one aggressive response makes another less probable.

Most of the research testing this hypothesis employs a confederate who either attacks or verbally insults subjects, and after an opportunity to act "aggressively" in another setting, the subjects are then provided an opportunity to harm the confederate. According to the hypothesis, they should be less apt to harm the confederate when they have already discharged their pent-up tension. For example, Thibaut and Coules (1952) gave half their subjects an opportunity to verbally attack someone who had insulted them; the other half was not given an opportunity to strike back. Those who had been given an opportunity to retaliate were less negative toward the confederate later on than were those who had not been able to express their hostility. Although at first glance these results appear to support the notion of catharsis, Thibaut and Coules carried out a content analysis which showed that the subjects who had been given an opportunity to strike back seldom did so; they made few hostile remarks to him. If no aggression was expressed, then catharsis could not have occurred. Thus the results indicate that a fair opportunity to "get even" reduced negative evaluation of the insulting other even though there was no overt aggressive response.

Mallick and McCandless (1966) followed a rather similar procedure in a well-known study of catharsis. They asked third graders to make constructions out of blocks. A sixth-grade confederate either frustrated the subjects by "clumsily" preventing them from completing any of their five tasks or helped them to complete their tasks. To heighten the amount of frustration, the children were promised a nickel for each task completed within a time limit; no promise of monetary rewards was made to those in the nonfrustration condition. All the children were then asked to indicate how much they liked or disliked the confederate. Presumably, this opportunity to express hostility against him should have drained off some of their aggressive energy.

In a second phase of the experiment, one group of frustrated and one of nonfrustrated subjects shot guns at a target on which was placed a picture of a child of the same age and sex as the confederate. A second pair of groups (one frustrated and one nonfrustrated) engaged in casual conversation with the experimenter. A third (frustrated) group was given a rationalization of the confederate's behavior by the experimenter, who explained that he was sleepy and upset and would probably have been more cooperative had they offered him a share of the nickels. All the subjects were then asked once again to rate how much they liked or disliked the confederate.

In a third phase of the experiment, the confederate was placed in another room and was allegedly given the task of making constructions with the blocks. The subjects were presented with a "response box" on which there were two buttons—one that could slow down the work of the confederate and one that could help him. The more often they pressed the slow-down button, the more aggressive they were considered to be.

The results revealed that frustrated subjects disliked the confederate more and were more aggressive toward him than nonfrustrated subjects no matter what transpired between the time of the frustration and the opportunities provided for hostility ratings or aggressive responses. A replication study by the same investigators produced essentially the same results. Thus there was absolutely no indication of any catharsis.

Feshbach (1955), however, found evidence in favor of the catharsis hypothesis. A lecturer insulted two introductory psychology classes. In one class the students were given an opportunity to express general hostility by writing stories related to four Thematic Apperception Test pictures. In a second class, the students were given a rather challenging intellectual task to perform. A third group, which was not originally insulted, also responded to the TAT pictures. All the students were finally given a paper-and-pencil questionnaire measuring the degree of hostility they felt toward the lecturer.

The insulted students expressed more general hostility in their TAT stories than did the control students, but they showed less hostility toward the lecturer on the questionnaire than the students who did not have a chance to express their "aggression" by writing fantasy stories. Furthermore, the more hostility the insulted students displayed in their stories, the less they expressed toward the lecturer.

Why did Feshbach find support for the catharsis hypothesis when so many other investigators have not? The answer may re-side in the procedures he employed. Writing fantasy stories about TAT pictures can be a constructive and creative enterprise, which is pleasurable and arouses positive affect. On the other hand, the demanding intellectual task given to the insulted non-fantasy group could have added to the resentment against the instructor. As we saw in Chapter 11, positive arousal states are associated with more liking for another person, while negative arousal states are associated with greater dislike. The more involved the students were in writing the TAT stories and the longer the stories written, the more likely it is they would include words codable as hostile or aggressive. Hence, Feshbach's study may only indicate that people are more generous in evaluating another person when they enjoy performing a task than when they do not. Whatever the merits of this reinterpretation, Hornberger (1959) failed to obtain similar results in a partial replication of the study.

A series of thorough reviews of the catharsis research (Berkowitz, 1962; Bramel, 1969; Weiss, 1969) have all concluded that there is very little support for the hypothesis. Thus there is almost no convincing support for one of the major processes assumed by a tension-reduction model of the frustration-aggression relationship.

4. Berkowitz's Cue-Arousal Theory

Berkowitz (1969) accepts the view that frustration creates arousal, but considers it unlikely that undifferentiated arousal will lead to specific and directed responses by the organism. These responses are guided by cues in the environment, while the intensity of the responses may be attributed to the degree of arousal experienced by the organism. Some cues may be inhibitory and restrain it from performing aggressive responses despite prior frustration and negative arousal; other cues may elicit aggressive responses.

In a representative study, Berkowitz (1965) paired subjects with a confederate who was introduced either as a physical education major interested in boxing or as a speech major. The confederate either insulted the subjects or behaved in a neutral and polite fashion. Half the subjects saw the fight scene from the motion picture *The Champion*, while the remaining subjects viewed a neutral film about canal boats. In the fight scene Kirk Douglas receives a terrible beating. The subjects who viewed the fight scene were given a preliminary statement by the experimenter indicating that Douglas deserved the beating he was about to receive. Finally, all the subjects were given an opportunity to evaluate the confederate's design of a floor plan for a house by shocking him from one to ten times (from excellent to poor).

Although the results were quite complex, they indicated that the confederate who was believed to be a boxer received more shocks then did the speech major even when no insult had occurred. The subjects probably assumed that a fighter would be more tolerant of pain and consequently were less reluctant to give him a poor score on his floor plan. Witnessing the fight scene, which presumably created more arousal in subjects than viewing the control film, did not automatically trigger off aggressive responses unless an appropriate external cue was present to elicit such behavior. Thus, when subjects were not insulted, there was no difference in the number of shocks they administered to the confederate regardless of which film had been viewed. But when they had been insulted by a boxer, witnessing the fight film did amplify their retaliatory behavior as compared to other conditions of the experiment.

Berkowitz interpreted his study as supporting a cue-arousal theory. The subjects had less inhibition against shocking a boxer, especially when aroused by frustration and witnessing filmed violence. That is, when aroused, the expression of aggressive responses occurs only when the appropriate cues are present; the subjects were not aggressive when they were aroused but no appropriate cue was available to elicit such behavior.

A simpler explanation may be that viewing a film about justified coercive behavior activated the negative norm of reciprocity (an eye for an eye) and indicated its appropriateness to the experimental situation in which the subjects had been insulted. The experimenter had also justified the beating received by Kirk Douglas, thereby legitimizing the reciprocity norm. The film also emphatically demonstrated the amount of pain a boxer can tolerate. The combination of factors (insult, salience of the reciprocity norm, and ability of the target to absorb pain) may have served to amplify the subjects' retaliatory behavior against an insulting person.

The cue-arousal theory is a modification of the frustration-aggression theory but also posits a system in which frustration produces a readiness to respond aggressively. However, without an appropriate cue, the arousal may not be given expression in aggressive behavior. Thus neither displacement nor catharsis occur; in Berkowitz's theory they are unnecessary concepts.

In conclusion, frustration-aggression theories suffer from two irreparable defects: (1) the definitions of antecedent and consequent terms are ambiguous, and (2) empirical evidence does not support major assumptions of the theory with regard to the functional equivalence of the class of responses labeled as "aggressive." There is little relationship between a conceptual definition of aggression as the intent to do harm and operational definitions in which harmdoing, irrespective of the subjects' motivations, is judged as aggressive. The fact that subjects are ordered to deliver shocks to confederates by an experimenter, are duped into believing the shocks will have an ultimately beneficent result, or are provoked into retaliatory action by attacks or insults, is given insufficient consideration by experimenters, who treat the subjects' actions as if they were unprovoked attacks on innocent parties.

B. Instrumental Learning of Aggression

Buss (1961; 1971) has attempted to provide a definition of aggression that avoids the problem of establishing intent to do harm. His "behavioristic" definition considers an action as aggressive whenever "one individual delivers noxious stimuli to another" (1971, p. 9). According to Buss, frustration is not invariably an antecedent of aggression, although attack by another person is likely to elicit retaliation. An individual's aggressive responses are learned like any other responses, through rewards and punishments. There are no innate factors involved, no automatic association between frustration and aggression, and no system of tensions. Emotions do not trigger off or motivate aggressive behavior, though anger may amplify a response that occurs.

A distinction is sometimes made between *angry aggression,* where the actor's response is rewarded by injury to the victim, and *instrumental aggression,* where any injury to the victim is simply a means by which the actor tries to attain other goals. Angry aggression is exemplified by crimes of passion or acts of revenge and is associated with decreased time perspective, alcohol consumption, and drug use (see Chapter 9, I, C, 7). Instrumental aggression is more apt to be planned in advance and is usually directed toward removing someone who blocks an individual's path toward a desired goal; however, the prime motivation is a desire for the goal and not for injury to another person.

Sears, Maccoby, and Levin (1957) proposed that angry aggression is learned in association with instrumental aggression. Because aggression often succeeds in getting the actor what he wants, and this rewarding circumstance is associated with signs of distress to other people, producing signs of distress becomes reinforcing in itself (a secondary reinforcement). An individual who experiences this sequence of events frequently enough will attempt to produce distress in another person through aggressive action; he has *learned* to be aggressive. Sears et al. interviewed 379 New England mothers and found that angry aggression in small children was associated with parental permissiveness for aggression and the use of physically punitive discipline in the home.

Rewards and punishments affect the frequency of aggressive behavior. Cowan and Walters (1963) rewarded small children for hitting a toy doll. Some of the children were placed on a continuous reinforcement schedule, while others were rewarded only intermittently for hitting the toy. In studies of other types of learning, this procedure has consistently shown a *partial reinforcement effect*—subjects who are rewarded part of the time for making a response display more resistance to experimental extinction than do subjects who are reinforced every time they make the desired response. When Cowan and Walters stopped reinforcing the children for hitting the toy, those in the intermittent reinforcement condition continued to hit the toy longer than did the continuously reinforced children. Thus aggressive responses, like other learned responses, are regulated by the partial reinforcement effect.

One way to eliminate an undesirable response, according to learning theory, is to reward a competing response. A rewarded response increases in frequency and will supplant a competing response that is not rewarded. Brown and Elliot (1965) used this technique to reduce the frequency of aggressive responses in children. They divided aggressive responses into two categories: physical (e.g., hits, strikes, teases, interferes) and verbal (e.g., disparages, threatens). A rater observed the 3- to 4-year-old children during free play periods at a nursery school and determined the frequency of aggressive reponses by each of them. A two-week period of special treatment followed during which the teachers provided social reinforcements to the children for cooperative and peaceful behavior and totally ignored aggressive behavior. A rating period of one week followed, a three week delay occurred, the treatment was then reinstituted for another two week period, and a final rating of aggressiveness was carried out.

The results are shown in Table 12.1. The reinforcement of cooperative and peaceful behavior dramatically decreased the amount of aggressive behavior among the children. During the three-week delay (follow-up) period, physical aggression recovered its pre-treatment level, but verbal aggression remained lower. A further decrease in both physical and verbal forms of aggression occurred during the second treatment period. Aggressive behavior apparently follows the general law of learning substitutive responses.

Punishment has the effect of inhibiting

Table 12.1 Average Number of Responses in the Various Rated Categories of Aggression by Children in the Brown and Elliott (1965) Study.

	Categories of aggression		
Times of Observations	Physical	Verbal	Total
Pre-Treatment	41.2	22.8	64.0
First treatment	26.0	17.4	43.4
Follow-up (delay period)	37.8	13.8	51.6
Second treatment	21.0	4.6	25.6

responses, at least temporarily. Chasdi and Lawrence (1955) found that punishment decreased the amount of aggression displayed by children. Nursery school children were divided into two groups. Both groups were allowed to play with dolls but only one group was given verbal reproofs for aggression displayed during play. The children who suffered reproofs displayed less hostility and aggression in their doll play than those who were not punished.

C. Modeling and Aggression

As we indicated in Chapter 6, there is substantial evidence that children can learn by imitating models. They imitate the use of language, vicariously learn to impose stringent criteria on self-rewards, copy the altruistic and self-sacrificial behavior of others, and adopt the moral codes of powerful and nurturant models. It is reasonable to suppose that a model's successful use of coercion will also be imitated by observers. There is a difference, however, in the performance of harmdoing and other forms of behavior that have been shown by research to be imitated by children and adults. Coercion, unless used in self-defense, is generally condemned by others as morally reprehensible, while learning instrumental skills and self-control are, of course, commendable. It is therefore not obvious that children will imitate the "aggressive" behavior of models.

The basic research paradigm used to study the imitation of an aggressive model employs an adult who engages in a series of responses, such as kicking, hitting, and tossing a large doll, shouting at the doll, tearing pages from books, shooting toy guns at dolls or humans, and so on. Observer children are then placed in a room with the same kinds of objects and toys and their behavior is observed. The inevitable result is that an aggressive model who has been rewarded for her behavior will be imitated, while models who are punished for their destructive behavior will not be imitated (Bandura, Ross, & Ross, 1961; 1963b).

There are interpretative problems with the typical modeling study. It is not clear that the children intend to do harm to the material objects, though they may intend to hit the doll or shoot the toy gun. The distinction is between intent to produce effects and intent to perform a particular response. Consider the sequence of events: (1) the child watches a model hit a doll, who does no discernible harm to it and is socially reinforced for the behavior; (2) immediately afterward, the child is presented with the same situation, in which the appropriate behavior appears to be one of hitting the doll; and (3) the child hits the doll. The child's behavior is labeled as aggressive by the experimenter. But why? It would be difficult to establish that the child had any intent to damage the doll and there are very few (if any) reports of damage done to five-foot vinyl clown dolls. The problem is that the operational definition of aggression (hitting the doll) is not consistent with the conceptual definition of aggression as a harmful action or an act intended to do harm; there is no evidence that either of these two conditions characterize the imitative responses of children in these studies. Perhaps the children merely perceive the situation as one in which certain play activity has been legitimized by the example of an adult performing various unusual responses (for an adult). The child may not perform the same behavior outside the play setting as he does in it; although he may hit the doll, he may not hit a human being.

Bandura (1969) has defended the original approach in this way: "A social-learning theory of aggression distinguishes the acquisition of instrumental reponses that have destructive or pain-producing potential from the conditions governing their subsequent performance. Aggressive response patterns are characteristically acquired under nonfrustrating conditions in the absence of injurious intent and often toward inanimate objects. Thus, for example, military recruits acquire and perfect combat skills through many hours of target practice and simulated skirmishes; boxers develop hurtful pummeling abilities by using punching bags and sparring partners whom they do not necessarily intend to hurt; and huntsmen acquire the basic rudiments of hunting by shooting at inanimate targets before they go out in search of game" (p.378).

There are a number of problems with Bandura's argument. If learning a skill that can be used to harm others is considered an aggressive response, there is little behavior that might not be considered aggressive. By this criterion one would be considered aggressive for learning a vocabulary that could be used to spread gossip, derogate other persons, and threaten others. Learning to drive an automobile would be considered aggressive since one could use the skill to deliberately run over a victim. The examples given by Bandura imply a knowledge, while the skills are being acquired, that they will be used to deliver harm in war, boxing, or hunting. His examples also refer to approved forms of harmdoing, such as self-defense in wars and boxing, and the acquisition of furs, food, and recreation in hunting. Actually, the major question is whether acquiring these skills makes anyone more likely to harm others. Buss, Booker, and Buss (1972) have found that subjects who had a great deal of experience in firing rifles delivered the same intensities of shocks to punish the errors of a confederate-learner as subjects who had no such experience. Bryan and Schwartz (1971), Singer (1971), and Weiss (1969) have all argued that the generalization of behavior from imitation in the play situation to real-life situations has never been empirically demonstrated.

In an attempt to demonstrate the imitation of aggression against live victims, Hanratty, Liebert, Morris, and Fernandez (1969) found that children emitted more "assaultive" behavior toward a person dressed as a clown after they had watched a film model "assault" an inanimate clown. Children who had not seen the film did not direct harm at the human clown. This "as-

saultive" behavior consisted of directing verbal insults at the clown, aiming and shooting a toy machine gun at him, and hitting him with a plastic mallet.

Interpretive questions are left unanswered by this study. Was harm intended by the children or did they perceive the situation as one of fantasy in which slapstick antics were appropriately directed at a clown? Can this behavior be generalized to any other situation? To any other target? The major question still to be answered by modeling studies is this: Will children imitate behavior that they clearly understand to be bad or wrong? It is known that when models are punished or reproved for their behavior they are not imitated.

Despite these criticisms, there is evidence (presented in Chapter 6) that coercive influence styles may be learned in conflict-ridden homes by children who observe that threats and punitive actions can be successfully used against other people. Generally in these circumstances, coercive tactics are considered normal and legitimate, rather than unusual, bad, or illegitimate. Consistent with other evidence that powerful models are more often imitated, Eron, Walder, Toigo, and Lefkowitz (1963) found that punitive high status fathers have more aggressive sons than punitive low status fathers.

D. Criticisms of Learning Theories of Aggression

Learning theories focus on how an individual learns to perform specific responses. When applied to the study of aggression, several problems arise for all such theories. For one thing, aggression is concerned with the intent of the actor and the effects of behavior rather than the specific responses that are performed. Consideration only of responses and not the plans and schemes of the actor robs the behavior of its social meaning. There is now general recognition that no adequate definition of aggression is available to the research scientist

(Bandura, 1973; Johnson, 1972; Kaufmann, 1970).

In order to study an entire class of responses labeled as aggressive, some relationship must be discernible among all members of the class. What makes a response aggressive? Does learning one type of aggressive behavior make it more likely that an actor will perform another aggressive response? For example, if an individual learns to make verbal threats, will he also be likely to engage in physical assaults? If he learns to use social punishments against others, will he also tend to use physical forms of punishment? Unless some connection can be demonstrated between these responses, there is no useful purpose in labeling them all as of the same type. As we have seen, belief that all aggressive responses have the common purpose of relieving aggressive energy has not been supported by the evidence regarding displacement and catharsis.

Buss's definition does not help matters. If we consider only those responses as aggressive that consist of attempts to deliver physically noxious stimuli to others, we cannot consider most agonistic behavior of animals (which consists mostly of threats and not of attempts to do physical harm) as aggressive, nor nonphysical means of harming the interests or ego of another person. Also, as Buss recognizes, there are times when a parent clearly intends to punish a child, and no one would consider him aggressive for carrying out his familial responsibilities. More important, we must ask whether learning one way of delivering noxious stimulation to another person makes it more likely we will also use other methods of harming him.

Undoubtedly, an individual learns to behave as he does. But learning theory may not provide the most adequate concepts for understanding harmdoing behavior. As we saw in Chapter 9, low self-confidence, inadequate time perspective, alcohol consumption, and drug use are associated with coercion and homicide. The degree of conflict existing between two parties is directly related to the probability that coercive means will be used to settle their conflict. Thus, while learning plays a role in behavior, many other factors associated with the individual and the situation may be more important in determining how an individual will act.

In conclusion, all learning theories have had difficulty defining what is meant by an aggressive response. Although several theories consider aggression as the intent to do harm, they never establish that subjects in laboratory experiments have any malevolent intent. More often the researcher tries to provide a legitimate excuse for subjects to harm another person for the "good of science," or to improve the victim's performance, or as an "objective rating procedure." Subjects are seldom observed to attack others in the laboratory unless they are provoked and then given an experimenter-sanctioned opportunity to retaliate. If we were to distinguish between offensive and defensive aggression, it would be clear that it is the latter that is most often studied by learning theorists.

A definition of aggression as the intent to do harm is not adequate. Role-sanctioned behavior—such as a policeman apprehending a resisting suspect or a fireman breaking down a door—and defensive actions are not usually considered to be aggressive. Thus a person can both intend to do and actually do harm and not be considered aggressive. The conceptual problem of defining aggression remains unresolved, and while the study of the subject goes on, no one seems able to define what it is they are studying.

III. SOCIAL POWER AND THE STUDY OF AGGRESSION

Tedeschi, Smith, and Brown (1974) have proposed that all of the types of action that have been labeled as aggressive by biologists, psychoanalysts, and learning theorists can be reconceptualized as different forms of coercive power. In Chapter 7 we discussed various kinds of distinctions that have been made between types of threats—contingent, noncontingent, explicit, tacit, compellent, and deterrent. A similar classification of punishments has been developed, including noxious stimulation, deprivation of existing resources, deprivation of expected gains, and social punishments.

Noxious stimulation is the application of unpleasant, painful, or biologically disruptive effects on the body of another person, which can range from putting an unpleasant-tasting substance on his tongue to placing him in an electric chair. *Deprivation of existing resources* refers to an action taking away something that a person has available. Court fines, robbery, destruction of property and the loss of love are forms of resource deprivation. *Expected gain deprivation* refers to the denial of rewards to a person in violation of a promise to provide them. Imagine the reaction of a young boy who mows a lawn in anticipation of payment when told afterward that the homeowner has changed his mind about the agreement. Expected gain deprivation occurs when points, money, candy, love and other valuables the target expects to gain are denied to him. *Social punishments* attack a person's self-concept or the impression he wants to maintain in the eyes of others. Expressions of dislike, name-calling, and social ostracism are examples of social punishment.

There are a number of advantages in viewing harmdoing behavior in terms of coercive power. For one thing, no assumption is made that because a person issues threats involving, say, social punishment, he necessarily is more likely to issue other kinds of threats (e.g., involving noxious stimulation) than anyone else. Nor is there any necessary relationship between the frequency of using one type of punishment and a propensity to use another type. A second advantage of this approach is that the phenomena are placed in the context of interaction, and responses are viewed in terms of their social meanings rather than as skeletal responses in the absence of any interpersonal context.

If a person cannot persuade, bribe, manipulate or otherwise induce another person to comply with his wishes, and compliance is sufficiently important to him, then his power may ultimately rest on his ability to restrain, transport, immobilize, injure, or destroy the target. To paraphrase Clausewitz' (1962) definition of war as the mere extension of diplomacy, it may be said that the exercise of coercive power is a means of gaining compliance that is used when other means fail. Of course, social psychologists want to know why, when, how, and against whom coercive means will be employed.

As we saw in Chapter 9, there are many reasons why people harm each other and there are many types of harm that can be employed. Besides seeking compliance or revenge and saving face, a person may harm another because he perceives his action as demanded by an authority (as in Milgram's studies) or as in the service of abstract or group goals (rather than personal ones). He may feel he must resist the coercive attempts of others so they do not view him as an "easy mark." If he doesn't face up to the challenges of forceful others, he may find himself continually subjected to coercive influence attempts. A person may also harm others because he is under the influence of alcohol or drugs and is oblivious to the future consequences of his actions. And a person may harm others because he has been taught to use coercion as a dominant influence style by his family or by other significant social models (see Chapter 6).

While the concern of most aggression theory has been focused on the offensive use of coercive power, most aggression research has involved the defensive use of coercion. Defensive coercion has been found to be elicited by the norms of reciprocity and equity and to be amplified by physiological arousal states in the actor. Other lines of investigation, on the effects of the mass media on the behavior of viewers, have led to a series of controversial conclusions, which we shall critically examine.

A. Negative Reciprocity and Restoration of Equity

The negative norm of reciprocity may be defined in terms of two minimal demands: (1) harm those who harm you, and (2) do not help those who harm you. This demand of an eye for an eye and a tooth for a tooth (*lex talionis*) gives an actor the right to retaliate for harm done to him. This is a defensive norm and requires the actor to make his response proportionate to the provocation.

A self-defense norm also exists and has been learned well, at least by American males. A national survey of attitudes toward violence revealed that more than 60 percent of American males considered it a right to kill to defend one's family, property, and self (Blumenthal et al., 1972). Americans believe strongly in a norm of self-defense and often stress this right in their child-rearing practices. Young boys are told to stand up to bullies and not to take any "guff" from others. Boys who refuse to stand and fight are often ridiculed and called sissies.

Antagonisms and hostilities may occur even when a person has not been intentionally harmed by another, if the first person feels an injustice has been done to him. Homans (1961) formulated a law of distributive justice (see Chapter 9, II, D, 3), from which may be derived a norm of equity. If punishments or costs or rewards are unfairly distributed in a group, the disadvantaged person may seek to restore equity by undertaking coercive action to impose costs on the advantaged members. This retributive behavior is very similar to a displacement of aggression, since the target of harm is often not responsible for the unfair distribution of costs within the group.

Traditional learning approaches to aggression can be re-interpreted in terms of the reciprocity norm. In his critique of frustration-aggression theory Buss (1961) was careful to distinguish frustration from attack. While blocking goals may lead to a large number of possible actions, many of which could not be called aggressive, attack is most likely to elicit retaliation and counter-attack. According to Buss, attack may not involve any thwarting or blocking, and, because it is easily observed, the ambiguities of the concept of frustration are avoided. Gentry (1970) has also argued that attack leads to anger and counter-aggression, independent of any frustration. The probability and degree of retaliation depends on the magnitude of the attack, the characteristics of the attacker and the victim and the degree of justification for the first attack. Physiological arousal states may contribute to the degree of retaliation meted out by the actor.

1.   Attack and Retaliation

Experiments have consistently shown that the degree of retaliation by subjects is proportional to the amount of provocation. For example, Berkowitz and Green (1962) paired a subject with a confederate and asked each to write a short essay about how to promote sales at a garage. They were then told to rate each other's essays. The scoring system required giving a minimum of one shock (the best possible score) and a maximum of ten shocks (the worst possible score). The confederate always rated the subject first. In one group the confederate delivered only one shock, but in a second group he delivered seven shocks. On a mood scale given to them immediately after being "rated," the subjects who were shocked most frequently indicated more anger. The subjects then rated the confederate's essay. Those who had received a single shock slightly overpaid by delivering an average of two shocks to the confederate, and those who had received seven shocks slightly underpaid by delivering an average of six shocks. Helm, Bonoma, and Tedeschi (1972), using a different research paradigm, found essentially the same results.

Taylor (1967) found that retaliation by matching the intensity of shocks delivered is also proportional to the degree of attack. In a reaction-time game, subjects were seated in front of identical task boards, like the one shown in Figure 12.2. Five buttons numbered one through five and labeled "shock setting" allow both parties to pre-set a shock intensity before the game is played. A second panel of five lights provides feedback to both players about the intensity settings made by the other player, but this information is not provided until a play of the game is completed and the loser has been shocked; the winner then finds out what shock intensity the loser had planned for him. Once each player has pre-set the shock intensity level, he presses a telegraph key until a signal light illuminates, at which time the person who releases the key first avoids the shock and the person with the slowest reaction time receives a shock of the intensity set by the other player.

In Taylor's study, the number of times the subjects lost and the shock intensity set-

tings of the confederate were prearranged. An escalation strategy was carried out in which the confederate began with low settings of 1 or 2 and gradually increased his settings over the trials until they reached levels of 4 and 5. The subjects lost on half the trials. Under these conditions, their shock settings followed the levels set by their opponent. However, the rate of escalation by the subjects was somewhat lower than that of the confederate.

In a similar study, Epstein and Taylor (1967) manipulated the degree of defeat by rigging the game so that the subjects lost on either 17, 50, or 83 percent of the trials. This manipulation could be considered as producing "frustration" in the subjects who presumably wanted to win the game. Half the subjects in each defeat condition faced a confederate who always chose minimal levels of shock intensities, and the other half faced an opponent who always set high levels (4 or 5).

Consistent with prior studies, the subjects calibrated their counter-attacks so that they matched the intensity of the confederate's attack. They did not try to compensate for losing; the proportion of defeats did not affect their shock settings. Perhaps this additional disconfirmation of the frustration-aggression hypothesis can be attributed to self-blame for losing. One can hardly blame an opponent for trying to

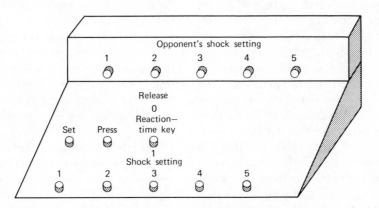

Figure 12.2. Reaction-time task board. (Drawn from description in Epstein and Taylor, 1967.)

escape the shock and the subject can blame himself for reacting too slowly and hence losing. The subjects could blame the confederate for setting high shock intensities, however. An attribution of responsibility must apparently be made before an actor feels justified in retaliating against a harmdoer.

A person often has difficulty deciding what establishes equivalence between himself and an attacker. In many experiments a confederate administers social punishment in the form of insults or negative evaluations and then the subjects are given opportunities to shock him (noxious punishment). The equivalence problem concerns how many shocks it takes to restore equity between the subjects and the confederate. McDaniel, O'Neal, and Fox (1971) addressed this question by having a confederate evaluate the performance of a subject by one of two modes, a point rating or the administration of electric shocks. Within each mode, the confederate gave the subject a positive rating of 2 (points or shocks) or a negative rating of 6. The subjects were then given an opportunity to retaliate by rating the confederate in either the same or in a different mode.

The subjects did more harm to the confederate when he had done more harm to them. However, they gave the confederate a more negative rating when they could retaliate in kind than when they were forced to retaliate in a different mode. Difficulty in deciding what constituted equivalence when counterattack was made in a different mode apparently led the subjects to err on the side of underpaying rather than overpaying the attacker. This was probably a wise decision, since overpayment would probably lead to further escalation of the conflict. A retaliator must take into account the probability that his opponent may exaggerate how much harm was done to him; underpayment may show a resolve not to let an attack go unanswered, but may also indicate a desire to end the conflict without further escalation.

A person may feel that justice is done even when someone else is the source of retaliation on an attacker. When a particularly heinous crime has been committed that has widespread effects on the community, the resulting anger may instigate a search for a scapegoat or may produce a demand for severe punishment of all wrongdoers. This restoration of justice by proxy was demonstrated in a study by Berkowitz, Green, and Maccaulay (1962). Angered subjects reported feeling better after hearing that their attacker had performed poorly on an assigned task than after learning he had performed well. This result suggests that even a severely angered man would gain satisfaction from observing the punishment of the object of the anger. For example, the person who cuts into your lane of traffic may make you angry, but your anger is assuaged when you see him stopped by a patrol car farther up the road.

2. Target Characteristics and Retaliation

The capability, attractiveness, and sex of a provoker affect the probability and degree of retaliation administered by his victim. Shortell, Epstein, and Taylor (1970) found that an opponent's ability to do great harm tempered the intensity of the subjects' retaliatory behavior in the reaction-time game. Half the subjects were placed in a "massive retaliation" condition in which both players had a shock intensity setting labeled 10 in addition to the usual settings of 1 to 5. The opponent never used this high level, however. In the second condition the subjects and the confederate possessed the usual settings of 1-5. In both conditions the confederate gradually raised his shock intensity settings over the trials. Although both groups of subjects increased their own settings as a direct function of the opponent's escalation rate, those in the massive retaliation condition set lower shock levels than those in the other condition. Apparently, they were concerned about provoking their opponent into delivering the level 10 shock.

One's degree of liking for an opponent does not affect the equitable return of harm for harm in the reaction-time game (Hendrick & Taylor, 1971). The relation of liking to retaliation may be affected by the type of situation in which an individual finds himself. Stapleton, Nelson, Franconere, and Tedeschi (1974) found a tendency of subjects to lower the level of retaliation against a liked person compared to a disliked person. A manipulated comparison of similarity and dissimilarity established high or low attraction for a confederate. In the first phase of the experiment, male subjects estimated the probability on each of ten trials that the confederate would shock them; he actually did shock them either one, five, or nine times. Then the roles were reversed and the subjects operated the shock apparatus while the confederate estimated the probability of being shocked. The number of shocks delivered by the subjects was approximately the same as they had received, but there was a tendency to give fewer shocks to the liked than to the disliked confederate. The effect of attraction on level of retaliation probably depends on a number of circumstances, such as the degree of responsibility assigned to the provoker for harm-doing, the legitimacy of the action, and the arousal state of the person attacked. Until future research establishes the effects of these factors, the relationship between liking and retaliation must remain problematical.

It is a norm, at least in American middle-class society, that men should not do physical harm to women. Buss (1966) found that college males gave less intense shocks to females in a teacher-learner paradigm than to other males. On the other hand, females gave intense shocks to males. What are the limits to this normative proscription against harming females? Will this type of one-sided chivalry hold true when a female attacks a male, or will he retaliate in kind? To answer this question, Taylor and

Epstein (1967) had male and female subjects compete against either a same-sex or an opposite-sex opponent in the reaction-time game. The opponent gradually raised his shock intensity settings over the trials. Both male and female subjects set higher shock levels for a male than for a female opponent; the women showed a greater increase in their shock intensity settings than the men, though in all cases the subjects' level of retaliation was lower than the level of attack.

The norm that a gentleman does not harm a lady is learned early in life, perhaps because those who are most influential in socializing children are women. Shortell and Miller (1970) modified the reaction time game to study sixth-grade children. Instead of using shocks, the loser was required to listen to a noxious loud noise. The opponent's provocation consisted of a gradual escalation of the intensity of the noise. Both boys and girls set higher levels of noise intensity against boy than against girl opponents; boys generally retaliated with greater intensity than did girls.

3. Individual Differences and Retaliation

People differ in their willingness to harm others. Pisano and Taylor (1971) identified subjects as high or low aggressors on the basis of their first trial shock settings in a reaction-time game. Low aggressors were identified as those who made low settings (levels one or two) on the first trial, while high aggressors were those who made settings of three or higher. The subjects faced a confederate who either adopted a punitive strategy consisting of only the highest intensity settings, or adopted a pacifist strategy consisting of only the lowest intensity settings. High aggressors retaliated at high levels of intensity whatever the strategy of the opponent, while low aggressors adjusted their retaliation to the level used by the opponent. Thus, high aggressors were not responsive to the level of provocation, while low aggressors were willing to keep the level of harm low when the opponent did.

How can a high aggressor be deterred? Two other conditions of the Pisano and Taylor study provide information about one viable strategy: (1) The opponent set on the succeeding trial a level of shock intensity similar to that set by the subjects on the previous trial; that is, he employed a tit-for-tat strategy. (2) High aggressors were offered more money, the lower the shock intensity they set on a trial, while the opponent always set high levels. Both strategies affected the behavior of high aggressors, but in different ways. The matching strategy slightly moderated their level of intensity settings. When offered money for low shock settings, they found a strategy that met both of their goals—to gain revenge and to gain money. They shifted from trial to trial, first giving a high level of shock to the opponent and then giving a very low level to gain the maximum financial reward.

4.   Justification and Retaliation

If a harmed person can be convinced that he deserves what happened to him—that the harm done to him was justifiable or legitimate—retaliatory behavior can be eliminated. Although a retributive law commands punishment for those who perpetrate evil, there are occasions when harmdoing is not considered to deserve punishment. A recognition of acceptable harmdoing is reflected in Pastore's (1952) distinction between arbitrary and nonarbitrary frustration. The former refers to an unjustified deprivation or blocking of a goal, while the latter refers to deprivation that can be rationalized to the frustrated party as legitimate or equitable.

Probably the most important factor in causing a person to become angry is a belief that he has been treated unfairly, and anger is associated with a tendency to retaliate against the person considered responsible for the inequity. Pastore found different reactions to arbitrary and nonarbitrary frustrations. Some subjects were provided with descriptions of arbitrary frustrations, such as "You're waiting on the right corner for a bus, and the driver intentionally passes you by." Other subjects were presented with examples of nonarbitrary frustrations, such as "You're waiting on the right corner for a bus. You notice that it is a special on its way to the garage." The subjects revealed more hostility in the arbitrary than in the nonarbitrary condition. Cohen (1955), using similar role-playing procedures, obtained similar findings.

In a behavioral study, Fishman (1965) had an experimenter unjustly criticize subjects and deny them a promised monetary reward for achieving success on a task (deprivation of expected gain). Another group of subjects experienced a nonarbitrary deprivation of the monetary reward; the experimenter justified his failure to provide it by informing them they had failed to complete the task adequately. All the subjects were then asked to fill out a "research evaluation questionnaire" which included a rating of the experimenter. They were led to believe that their evaluations would be used by a research supervisor in assigning a grade to the graduate student-experimenter. A poor rating by the subject therefore could bring about a poor grade (social punishment). The subjects who were arbitrarily harmed evaluated the experimenter more negatively than did those whose rewards were legitimately withheld. Retaliation occurred only when the subjects believed they had been treated unjustly.

Toch (1969) studied cases of assault against policemen and concluded that some incidents occur because a person is stopped on the street or ordered to move on from where he is standing and fails to comply with the patrolman's order. Toch describes the escalation process as follows: "When the man indicates his unwillingness to comply, the officer ignores his protests and thereby converts the situation (as the person sees it) into a confrontation between two hostile parties. The officer responds by placing the individual under arrest, thereby demonstrating his own authority and power. The person now feels his powerlessness and thus reacts by requesting that the officer encounter him on a 'man-to-man' basis. This type of incident is an almost inevitable consequence of the exercise of police authority in a context where its legitimacy is not granted" (p.48). In other words, the confronted individual views the patrolman's behavior as arbitrary in character and retaliates to each level of provocation, just as subjects do in the reaction-time game.

The law recognizes a distinction between justifiable and unjustifiable homicides. Killing is not always legally defined as criminal conduct or even as morally reprehensible. War and capital punishment are two examples where taking human life is considered a legitimate means of solving social problems. When an issue is sufficiently important to enough people, killing becomes socially justified as a means of making their interests prevail. Of course, each person must interpret this "ends justify the means" morality for himself. When an individual becomes convinced of the overwhelming importance of his cause and can find no other way of implementing it, he may decide that killing is a legitimate means. This kind of morality, along with man's ability to find malevolent intentions in others when there is no reason to suppose there are any, may lead men to kill because of a delusion that the victim meant to do them irreparable and arbitrary harm.

In conclusion, when people are attacked, they take socially sanctioned opportunities to retaliate. The degree of retaliation is intended to establish equivalence in the negative exchange. The restoration of equity provides no motive for either party to continue the conflict. While the retaliator may demonstrate his resolve to defend himself in order to deter future attacks, he does not wish to instigate an escalation of the conflict by producing an inequity in the exchange.

Characteristics of the attacker and the victim and normative factors in the situation will affect the probability and the intensity of retaliation. When an attacker has great but unused ability to do harm, retaliation is moderated, apparently as a precaution against inciting the powerful attacker to do even greater harm. This tactic is similar to that found by Pruitt with respect to the positive reciprocity norm (see Chapter 10, I, A, 2), where subjects repaid to benefactor more when they expected him to have the future ability to distribute greater rewards. In the case of the negative norm of reciprocity, it is also a wise tactic to leave the balance of inequity on the other fellow's side, to keep him in your debt. Nevertheless, as was shown in Chapter 9, failure to resolve conflicts can lead to escalatory attempts to coerce the other person when significant values are at stake.

B. Arousal and Harmdoing

In Chapters 10 and 11 we examined evidence that momentary positive arousal states produce altruistic behavior and positive evaluations of other people, and that negative arousal states are associated with refusals to help and negative evaluations of other people. What effect does arousal have on harmdoing? Will arousal states cause an individual to engage in unprovoked attacks on others? Will arousal affect the amplitude or intensity of a retaliatory attack? Many of the studies carried out to answer these questions were directed toward testing the learning theories of aggression, the processes of catharsis and displacement, and Berkowitz's cue-arousal hypothesis. These studies have looked at three basic ways of arousing subjects: (1) insult; (2) viewing violent films; and (3) other nonviolent means.

1. Insult, Arousal, and Retaliation

Hokanson and Shetler (1961) had a confederate insult subjects while they were engaged in an intellectual task. Measures of systolic blood pressure revealed an increase following the attack. Half the subjects were then given a socially sanctioned opportunity in a teacher-learning paradigm to administer shocks to the confederate. The remainder of the subjects were not given an opportunity to reestablish equity. The subjects who retaliated showed a dramatic decrease in blood pressure, while those who could not re-establish equity maintained a high blood pressure. Retaliatory behavior thus discharged arousal or tension, a catharsis-like effect.

Further studies by Hokanson and his colleagues have shown that arousal is not discharged through displaced attacks against a third party (Hokanson, Burgess, & Cohen, 1963) or by writing fantasies about TAT pictures (Hokanson & Burgess, 1962). Arousal is reduced only when the subjects have a chance to get even with their attacker. It should be remembered that arousal occurred in these experiments only after insult and was discharged through either retaliation or a negative evaluation of the attacker. Thus it could not be concluded that the arousal caused the retaliatory behavior. The attack may have simultaneously elicited arousal and the negative reciprocity norm, and the latter may have been the basis of retaliation.

2. Observing Violence, Arousal, and Retaliation

We still have not answered our question regarding the effect of arousal on harmdoing behavior. Hokanson's research tells us only about the effects of harmdoing on arousal states. There is evidence that arousal does increase the magnitude of retaliatory behavior. Hartmann (1969) had a confederate insult adolescent boys who were under court commitment to the California Youth Authority. The boys were then shown one of three short films: (1) two boys playing basketball; (2) two boys fighting, with the focus on the pain cues of the one being defeated; or (3) two boys fighting,

with the focus on the boy inflicting the pain. Presumably, the fight films created arousal but the rather dull basketball film did not. Despite the fact that many film-induced arousal studies fail to measure physiological arousal states, the assumption that arousal differences have been created by the experimental manipulation is usually plausible.

The boys were then given an opportunity to act as teacher and were required to shock all errors made by the confederate who had insulted them before they viewed the film. The subjects were given freedom to decide the duration and intensity of the shocks to be administered. The socially sanctioned retaliatory behavior of the subjects was more intense after they viewed the arousal films than after they viewed the neutral film. Whether the arousal films focused on the pain cues of the victim or the face of the attacker had no effect on their retaliatory behavior.

While most of the evidence indicates that a negative arousal state will not instigate unprovoked harmdoing by an individual, there is one study that does suggest such a possibility. Geen and O'Neal (1969) asked half their subjects to watch a seven-minute segment of a prize fight scene from the motion picture, *The Champion*. The other subjects viewed a control film showing baseball, tennis, and weightlifting action. The subjects then indicated their evaluation of a neutral confederate's essay by the number and intensity of shocks they delivered to him. While they were making their evaluations, some of the subjects were bombarded with noxious noise through head phones and some were not. The subjects who had watched the prize fight scene *and* listened to noxious noise during the evaluation delivered more harm to the confederate than did the other subjects. Although the confederate had not insulted or in any way attacked them, the combination of fight film and noxious noise which induced arousal caused these subjects to deliver more shocks than those who viewed the control film and were not bombarded with noise.

What is puzzling about these results (see Table 12.2) from the point of view of an arousal-aggression hypothesis is why subjects who had viewed the presumably arousing fight scene and did not experience the noise gave no more shocks than subjects who merely viewed the control film. Furthermore, the subjects who experienced the noise gave just as many shocks to the confederate whichever film they had seen. These data do not support the arousal-aggression hypothesis, but perhaps they support the view that subjects who experience negative inequity attempt to restore equity in experiments. When they were bombarded with unpleasant noise, they had a socially sanctioned opportunity to make the "other subject" uncomfortable also. Since both were participating in the experiment for the same reasons and the same rewards, it is reasonable to expect that the amount of effort, pain, or discomfort that each should contribute should be about the same. Since the subjects had control over how much discomfort the confederate would experience, they adjusted their harmdoing behavior to reestablish equity between themselves and the confederate. Unfortunately for the equity interpretation of the data, there is no difference between the noxious noise-fight film condition and the no noxious noise-fight film condition in the number of shocks delivered by subjects.

3.   Noncoercive Antecedents of Arousal and Retaliation

Evidence that any type of arousal may facilitate or amplify harmdoing responses was provided by Zillmann (1971). Subjects viewed one of three feature-length films: (1) *Marco Polo's Travels,* an educational, nonsensational report of the title figure's travels in China; (2) *Body and Soul,* the climax of which is a violent prize fight involving the main character (played by John Garfield); or (3) *The Couch,* an erotic film including female nudity and explicit scenes of a young couple engaged in intimate pre-coital behavior. Pilot research had established that *Body and Soul* and *The Couch* produced excitation and arousal in viewers as measured by a number of physiological indicators, and that *Marco Polo's Travels* did not produce arousal.

After the subjects had viewed one of the three films, they were asked to express some of their attitudes. In one condition, a confederate turned on a light any time he disagreed with the subjects' opinions; in a second condition, he shocked the subjects to signal his disagreement. Subsequently, the subjects acted as teachers and were required to shock all errors made by the confederate-learner. The intensity settings for the shocks were left to the discretion of the subjects.

The subjects who viewed *The Couch* gave higher intensity shocks to the confederate than did those who saw *Body and Soul*; the

Table 12.2   Average Number of Shocks Administered to the Confederate by Subjects in the Geen and O'Neal (1969) Study.[a]

Treatment while subjects were evaluating the confederate	Film viewed by subjects	
	Fight scene from *The Champion*	Control film
Noxious white noise	4.58[a]	3.50[ab]
No noxious stimulation	3.16[ab]	2.91[b]

[a] Note: only when two cells do not contain common alphabetical subscripts—*a* or *b*—are they statistically different from one another.

least intense shocks were administered by the subjects who saw *Marco Polo's Travels*. This raises the possibility that any type of arousal may amplify retaliatory responses by subjects. There is the clear implication that it is not the aggressive content of the film that stimulates subjects to engage in coercive behavior; rather, it is the degree of arousal that is responsible for intensifying the response, regardless of the source of the arousal. However, it is also possible that the contra-normative character of the film served as a cue that elicited harmdoing by subjects.

As is typical in teacher-learner studies, the subjects gradually increased the intensity of shocks over trials, suggesting that there is a general lessening of inhibition against harming a confederate. When the subject is *required* by the experimenter (the legitimate authority in the situation) to shock someone who earlier attacked him, the subject loses whatever qualms he may have had. The subjects also gave higher intensity shocks to the confederate when the latter used shocks rather than lights to signal his disagreement.

Instead of having subjects view a film, Zillmann, Katcher, and Milvavsky (1972) created arousal through physical exercise. Half the subjects were required to engage in strenuous bicycle pedaling; the remaining subjects were comfortably seated while they threaded nickel-sized discs drilled with off-center holes. Physiological measures established that the vigorous activity produced more arousal than the sedentary activity. The rest of the procedures followed those described above in the Zillmann study, including signaling by the confederate of his disagreement with the subjects' attitudes with either lights or shocks.

When the confederate signaled disagreement with lights (low attack), the intensity of shocks administered by the subjects was unaffected by their arousal states. But when he used shocks to signal disagreement, the subjects retaliated with more intense shocks when aroused than when they

had not been aroused by physical exercise. High arousal does not indiscriminately amplify harmdoing behavior independently of cognitive cues related to the target. High arousal amplified harmdoing only when the target "deserved" to be harmed.

In contradiction to previous research Baron (1974) has reported that sexual arousal serves to inhibit aggression. A confederate either did or did not insult subjects; half of each group was then shown a series of attractive, nude females from *Playboy* magazine and the other half was shown landscapes and abstract paintings. Subjects were asked to rate the attractiveness of the pictures and to state how aroused they would be if the object or person shown in the photograph was real. Subsequently, they were given a socially sanctioned opportunity to shock the confederate. The confederate was given the most intensive shocks in the insult-neutral pictures condition. Retaliation was apparently inhibited in the insult-erotic pictures condition.

As is so often the case when experiments yield contradictory results numerous interpretations are possible. An impression management explanation may be the simplest one. After the males had indicated they would be aroused in the presence of an attractive, nude female (to say otherwise would indicate abnormality) the delivery of low level shocks to the confederate constituted a display of their self-control. The subjects did not want to appear easily aroused under all conditions of the experiment because such consistency information might lead the experimenter to make a negative personal attribution about them. Subjects in the insult neutral pictures condition could look good in front of the experimenter only by behaving according to the social norm that was appropriate to the situation—the norm of reciprocity.

In summary, physiological arousal states, as induced by insult, attack, observation of physical violence, erotic stimuli, or physical exercise, do not cause an individual to launch unprovoked attacks on others. However, when an individual has been attacked or believes another person has arbitrarily and unjustifiably harmed his interests, arousal accumulated from all sources intensifies the degree of retaliation displayed. This effect of arousal may be interpreted in terms of Schachter's two-factor theory of emotions. A person labels his own arousal states in the context of the social cues in his environment. When he has been attacked or otherwise has experienced an inequity unjustly produced by another person, he has enough cues to label his emotional state as anger. The intensity of the anger may be a result of the degree of arousal the person is experiencing, whatever its source. Thus if a person has been aroused and then finds himself in conflict with someone, the arousal state may contribute to the degree of anger he experiences and he may manifest a greater use of force than can be accounted for by the level of provocation alone. In a fast-moving urban society, an individual is constantly bombarded with stimulation, which frequently produces arousal states that may be converted into angry counter-attacks instigated by minor incidents. The restrictiveness of arousal effects to the defensive or retaliatory use of coercion is reassuring. But before it is concluded that witnessing coercive actions by others does not elicit offensive coercive behavior, the specific effects of witnessing violence in the mass media need to be examined.

C. Television Violence and Modeling Coercive Actions

America is generally acknowledged to be a violent society. The rate of homicides, suicides, physical assaults, rapes, and other crimes against people is high compared to the incidence of such behavior in other societies. Naturally, there is concern for finding the factors that promote this high rate of harmdoing. A National Commission on the Causes and Prevention of Violence, congressional hearings, and reports by the Surgeon General's Office have all implicated television viewing as one cause of violence, particularly among youthful members of the audience.

By the age of three or four the American child is a regular television viewer, and will spend between two and three hours a day watching the tube (Liebert, Neale, & Davidson, 1973). By the time he graduates from high school, the average child has spent more time in front of the television than he has in the classroom. And what kinds of programs has he seen? Detective and police stories, murder mysteries, doctor and lawyer series which emphasize criminal activities, monster tales, fantasies like Superman or Batman, and cartoons that often involve mayhem (e.g., Popeye, Tom and Jerry, etc.). In addition, there are the news programs that bring wars, gang fights, and eyewitness accounts of murders, rapes, riots, atrocities, and other extraordinary events into one's home every night. In 1964 the National Association for Better Radio and Television estimated that approximately 200 hours per week were devoted to criminal scenes, including over 500 killings. The same organization has also stated that "the average child between the ages of 5 and 15 watches the violent destruction of more than 13,400 persons on TV" (cited in Liebert et al. 1973, p. 23).

It would be surprising, given the fact that almost 3 billion dollars is spent on advertising on television each year, if the content of programs has no effect on the viewers. A number of studies have attempted to find out if the amount of violence seen on television is related to subsequent aggressive behavior by the viewer. Two theoretically opposite positions have been taken on this issue, modeling and catharsis. The evidence we have already discussed suggests that children will imitate filmed models; hence, modeling theory assumes that watching models perform violent acts on television will encourage the viewers to imitate them. Aristotle first proposed a catharsis hypothesis more than 2000 years ago. Unlike learning theory in which catharsis is a discharge of built up tension accompanying aggressive responses, his view requires no behavior by the person for catharsis to occur. In his analysis of tragedy, Aristotle asserted that the audience identifies with the hero and by so doing purges itself in the final stages of the drama of pent-up emotions activated in the early parts. Feshbach (1971) has applied this theory to viewing television violence. When the viewer identifies with a character who commits an "aggressive" action, he releases aggressive energy; as a consequence, he will be less likely to commit an overtly aggressive act after watching television violence.

The effects of televised violence on the viewer may be more indirect than these theories suggest. Perhaps watching so much violence desensitizes a person so he no longer considers these actions to be morally repugnant. If the "good guys" seem to prefer violent means in apprehending or punishing the "bad guys" the way the viewer retaliates against future attackers may be affected. Violent behavior may be legitimized by the very fact that it seems to be so frequently performed by persons with outspoken grievances.

A great deal of research has been directed toward studying the relationship between television viewing and aggression, including tests of the modeling, catharsis, desensitization, and legitimization hypotheses. We will examine some of the major issues and problems associated with this research.

1. The Amount of Viewing and Aggression

Longitudinal and correlational studies have investigated the effects of viewing television violence on the behavior of children. The results obtained have been inconsistent. For example, Himmelweit, Oppenheim, and Vince (1958) found no relationship between the amount of time spent watching television and teachers' ratings of the aggressiveness of English children. Schramm, Lyle and Parker (1961) found that American children who viewed a great deal of television were more aggressive than children who spent little time watching it. On the other hand, they also found that Canadian children from homes that did not have television sets were more aggressive than children from homes with sets. These three results, showing direct, inverse, and no effects of viewing television, were obtained through survey questionnaires rather than direct observation.

McIntyre and Teevan (1972) interviewed 2300 junior and senior high school students from 13 schools in Maryland. A number of patterns were discovered. Young children watch more television than older children; females, blacks, and lower-class students reported watching more television than males, whites, and middle-class students. A violence index was applied to the single most favorite and the four most favorite programs of each student and then correlated with a self-report measure of fighting, threats of bodily injury, defiance of parents, petty delinquent acts resulting in damage to property and politcal activism. There was no correlation between the degree of violence associated with the single favorite program and self-reports of deviant conduct, but there was a very small correlation (+.10) between the violence index of all four favorite programs and the overall degree of aggressiveness reported by the students.

In a similar study, Robinson and Bachman (1972) surveyed 1500 twelfth graders. An overall index of the violence of their three favorite programs was used to divide the subjects into four groups, reflecting the degree of violence they like to watch on television: none, some, much, and a great deal. More of the students whose favorite programs contained a great deal of violence reported getting into serious fights than did students whose favorite programs contained no violence. However, it was also found that the education, race, and previous aggressive experience of the students' mothers were also related to the students' reports of aggressive behavior. The number of hours of television viewing was not correlated with aggressive behavior.

Both the viewing habits of children and their values may have been learned from their parents. Parents who frequently use coercive means to resolve family conflicts may also like to watch violent television programs. Dominick and Greenberg (1970) found a weak relationship between the amount of exposure to television violence and a readiness to use coercion, even when other factors associated with the home environment were statistically eliminated as contributing causes. Still, we cannot be confident that sufficient control was introduced to handle extraneous environmental factors. For example, a boy who constantly watches television may not have developed alternative interests (such as sports) and may be rejected by other boys in his peer group. Excessive watching of television may be a symptom of maladjustment rather than a cause of aggression. Despite the difficulty of interpreting these correlational studies, they often find weak positive relationships between the amount of exposure to television violence and aggressive behavior (McLeod, Atkin, & Chaffee, 1972; Eron, Walder, & Lefkowitz, 1971).

In an experimental attempt to link violence on television with aggressive behavior, Steuer, Applefield, and Smith (1971) observed ten preschool children from a Child Development Center during ten-minute play periods for ten days. A baseline level of fighting, hitting, pushing, kicking, and other forms of bodily contact was obtained for each child. Over the next 11 days, the children in an experimental group saw violent television programs immediately before being taken to the playroom, while children in the control group witnessed non-violent programs. More fighting was observed among the children who had watched the violent programs than among

those who had watched the nonviolent ones.

The small number of children involved in this study came from a specialized population (a Child Development Center), and it is therefore difficult to generalize their findings to the behavior of other children. No distinction was made between the defensive and offensive use of coercion nor between horseplay and actual hostilities; as a consequence, it cannot be ascertained whether the effects of watching the film were due to the arousal-retaliation relationship or whether the children were stimulated to engage in attack behavior. Much more research needs to be done before we can reach confident conclusions about the deleterious effects of television on viewers.

2. Modeling and Television Violence

According to social learning theory, only models who are rewarded are imitated by observers. It could be argued that TV villains always get it in the end and that punished models are not imitated. Jerome Frank (1967) pointed out that "The typical TV villain is abundantly rewarded until the very end, when he receives his just desserts, usually violent. Since young children do not grasp the story as a whole, they would be more likely to remember that violence is rewarded rather than that crime does not pay" (p. 72–73). Of course, the villain is not the only character to use coercion. The hero may also engage in fights and deception. The television screen is filled with coercive action taken in behalf of the innocent and good against those who are malevolent and evil. For example, in *Mission Impossible,* any illegal and underhanded behavior is justified as long as it is directed against the "bad" guys.

Earlier in this chapter we raised some questions about the interpretation of modeling studies of aggression. Nevertheless, Liebert (1972) has been sufficiently convinced by the available evidence to argue for stronger controls over the content of television programming before a congressional committee. One of the experiments he finds convincing was by Liebert and Baron (1972), in which children 5 to 9 years of age were provided an opportunity to watch television while waiting for the experiment. One group saw a short portion of *The Untouchables* that preserved the story line and presented a chase, fist fights, two shootings, and a knifing. The control group saw scenes from some rather unexciting sports events. After this viewing period, each child was led to a box containing a green and a red button, labeled "Help" and "Hurt." The experimenter explained that another child was operating a machine requiring the turning of a handle and that pushing the Help button made it easier to turn the handle and pushing the Hurt button made it more difficult to turn. The child who was allegedly operating the machine was not visible to the subjects. Finally, each child was placed in a room with nonaggressive toys (i.e., a "slinky" coil, a cook set, and a space station) and aggressive toys (a gun and a knife) for a play period. Children who had seen the violent film more often pushed the hurt button and played for a longer period with the aggressive toys.

One should be very cautious in advocating the abridgement of the first amendment rights of free speech and a free press to control the content of television, based on social psychological experiments of this kind. The children did not instigate conflicts with others, and they did not administer or attempt to inflict noxious stimulation or social punishment on innocent parties. The experimenter repeatedly *required* the children to push either the green or the red button. The degree of help or harm done by pushing the buttons could not be ascertained by the children since they could not see the alleged other child. Did making the handle harder to push really do anything except make the other child work a little harder? Did these very young children really understand what the

effects of pushing each button were? Being at an egocentric stage of intellectual development, they probably could not take the role of the "other child." Is choosing to play with a toy gun an aggressive act? What harm does it do? Is it true that children who play with guns are more likely to harm others than children who prefer "nonaggressive" toys? Earlier we saw that Buss, Booker, and Buss (1972) found no such relation between real guns and aggression.

The fear that children will imitate violent behavior seen on television may be unfounded. Seldom is a concern expressed that the children will perform exactly those actions displayed by television models; rather it is assumed that there is a class of responses all of which are "aggressive" and that when one is learned, it is more likely that other responses of the same sort are also learned. There is no evidence for this assumption of generalization across a class of "aggressive" responses. Also, as we have seen, studies of arousal indicate that watching violence has implications only for defensive or retaliatory behavior. Modeling appears most effective for defensive aggression. Baron and Kepner (1970) and Hicks (1965) have found that the attractiveness and capability of an aggressive model contribute to intensified retaliation against an attacker by an imitator. Thus, while modeling probably does occur with respect to television viewing, imitation is probably restricted to defensive aggression and redress for injustice (see below).

3. Catharsis and Coercion

According to Feshbach (1961), viewing television violence may either increase or decrease the aggressiveness of an observer's behavior, depending on his state of anger or arousal. An angry person can identify with a violent character and discharge his hostility. On the other hand, a violent film may artificially arouse a person who otherwise experiences no anger and hence may instigate greater aggressiveness.

Only one experiment has provided strong support for the catharsis hypothesis, so we will describe it in some detail.

Feshbach (1961) had an experimenter insult half his college subjects. Insulted and noninsulted subjects then viewed either a fight segment from the motion picture *Body and Soul* or a film about the effects of spreading rumors in a factory. Finally, all the subjects were asked to give a word association for eleven stimulus words, which included five considered to be "aggressive" (choke, massacre, murder, stab, and torture). Ten associations were obtained for each stimulus word. An overall score (from 0 to 50) was calculated for the number of "aggressive" associations the subjects emitted to the five stimulus words. Another experimenter entered the room and informed the subjects that the psychology department was evaluating the conduct of research. He asked them to fill out a questionnaire that included an evaluation of the previous experimenter, an evaluation of the experiment, and four other items. Each of the six items was scored from 1 to 6, from least to most aggressive, and a total aggression score was calculated, from 6 to 36.

The results are shown in Table 12.3. Insulted subjects who saw the fight film emitted fewer aggressive word associations and were more positive in their questionnaire ratings than insulted subjects who saw the neutral film. The subjects in the noninsult-fight film condition emitted just as many aggressive word associations as those in the insult-neutral condition and more than the subjects in the noninsult-neutral condition. However, only the insult-neutral film subjects answered the questionnaire in a way that produced scores on the aggressive side of the scale (more than 18).

Do these results provide a basis for inferring a process of catharsis? To make such an inference it would be necessary to know that the fight film (dealing with noxious stimulation) was actually experienced as more "aggressive" than the rumor film (dealing with social punishment). Feshbach provided no evidence that there was any difference between the two films in producing arousal or in their ability to produce catharsis. There was no manipulation check to ascertain the effectiveness of the experimenter's verbal insults. Were the subjects really angered or were their suspicions aroused about the purposes of the experiment? It is, after all, unusual to be insulted by an experimenter. Whatever the reasons for the findings obtained by Feshbach, similar experiments by Berkowitz and Rawlings (1963), Berkowitz, Corwin, and Heironimus (1963), and Hartmann (1965) have shown that sympathetic identification for the winning fighter in the film amplifies defensive retaliation instead of inhibiting or lowering it.

Feshbach and Singer (1971) carried out a very ambitious investigation of the effects of television violence, which they claim shows that catharsis results from viewing.

Table 12.3 Average Number of Aggressive Word Associations and Average Scores on the Aggression Questionnaire by Subjects in the Feshbach (1961) Study.

Dependent variable	Experimental conditions			
	Insult-Fight	Insult-Neutral	Noninsult-Fight	Noninsult-Neutral
Number of aggressive word associations	24.5	28.9	27.7	25.3
Score on the aggressive questionnaire	14.6	19.5	13.7	15.0

They manipulated the television diets of boys eight to eighteen years of age at seven institutions, including homes for boys and private schools. The boys could watch as many programs each week as they desired. One group watched only programs that portrayed violence, while a second group at each institution watched only nonviolent programs. The boys restricted to the nonviolent diet complained so strongly about their viewing fare that the experimenter added *Batman* to their approved list of programs. This difference in television diets was continued for a period of six weeks. During this time a behavior rating scale was completed on each subject by a house parent who was present during the television viewing periods, and the subjects in each group rated each other. These ratings were made at the end of each of the six weeks.

The boys who watched the nonviolent TV programs were twice as aggressive as those who watched the violent programs. This catharsis-like effect was pronounced in the boys' homes but did not occur in the private schools. This pattern suggests that television viewing affected lower class and not middle class boys. But do these findings support the catharsis hypothesis? An alternative possibility is that watching TV provided a frame of reference within which the everyday behavior of the boys looked relatively less aggressive than before. On the other hand, the subjects who were exposed to a constant diet of nonviolent programs may have perceived everyday behavior as relatively more aggressive than before. Hence, the behavior of the two groups may not have been affected by watching television; perhaps only the ratings given by the house parent and the boys changed over time. In any case, an attempt to replicate the Feshbach and Singer study has failed to reproduce their findings (Wells, 1972).

4. Desensitization and Television Violence

A medical student might feel squeamish the first time he cuts into a cadaver, but as he becomes more experienced, he loses this emotional reaction. Similarly, familiarity with war allows a soldier to disregard much of the blood and gore around him. This desensitization of the emotions may also occur in response to television. Continual viewing of murder, killing, fighting, and yelling may cause an individual to lose his moral sensitivity, his repulsion, and his outrage with respect to such actions. Alexander Pope warned about this desensitization to vice in a poem:

Vice is a monster of so frightful mien,
As to be hated need but to be seen;
Yet seen too oft, familiar with her face,
We first endure, then pity, then embrace.

Historical observation suggests that a blunting of moral sensitivity through familiarity does occur. In 1942 American military officials seriously debated moral principles before making a decision to begin the saturation bombing of Germany. By the time the atom bomb was dropped on Hiroshima and Nagasaki, American officials had become so accustomed to mass killing and firebombing entire cities that there was almost no governmental discussion of the moral aspects of the decision. It is hard to believe that there was an international conference in England in 1919 to outlaw a new and inhuman weapon that often killed civilians—the submarine. We have become accustomed to the use of technologically advanced weapons systems against any enemy.

Lazarus, Speisman, Mordkoff, and Davison (1962) exposed subjects to films of a bloody ritual performed on young males' penises by members of a primitive tribe. A number of physiological indicators indicated that subjects became increasingly less emotionally responsive with each successive exposure to this type of scene. According to a review of studies of physiological reactions to erotic stimuli, Zuckerman (1971) found a similar desensitization effect with repeated exposure. Earlier we saw how models could contribute to the desensitization of fear associated with phobic reactions.

There is only one somewhat flawed experiment examining the possible desensitization effects of watching violent programs on television. Cline, Croft, and Courrier (1973) identified boys from 5 through 12 who had watched television for either four hours or less per week for two years or more than 25 hours per week for two years. The physiological reactions of these boys to three films were measured: (1) a ski film; (2) a chase sequence from the W. C. Fields film, *The Bank Dick*; and (3) the fight scene from *The Champion*. Both groups showed greater arousal to the fight film than to the other two, but the boys who had been exposed to a great deal of television in the prior two years produced less of a physiological response than those who watched very little television. Unfortunately, there were a number of other differences between the two groups besides the number of hours spent in front of the television set. The high exposure children came from families in which the father had an occupation of lower status and less education than the children with low exposure. These are factors associated with child-rearing practices and general values that could account for the differences found in the study, quite apart from the television viewing habits of the children.

5. Grievances, Injustice, and Their Legitimate Redress

A person's identification with groups, nations, and symbols provides a basis for perceiving injustice even when no direct threat to him is involved. A television report of an attack against American citizens in another country may infuriate a viewer and cause him to advocate some form of retaliation by his government. Similarly, a filmed report of police and dogs attacking a group of black citizens may confirm a black viewer's feelings of injustice. Television also provides models for how a viewer might seek to redress injustice when he has a grievance.

In the 1960s, the spread of property riots in the large metropolitan centers across the country was almost certainly facilitated by the publicity given to them by television news programs. Thus, modeling of coercive behavior may well occur when an individual believes he has a legitimate grievance and television provides him with examples of how others with similar grievances seek redress.

Explicit reciprocity scenes on television have been shown to elicit more retaliatory behavior from viewers. Meyer (1972) asked subjects to write a five-minute essay on the importance of a college education. A confederate then rated each subject's essay by administering eight shocks (a negative evaluation, plus noxious stimulation). The subjects then watched one of three short film clips while the confederate was allegedly writing an essay: (a) a scene of South Vietnamese soldiers on a mission with American military advisors, in which a North Vietnamese prisoner is executed when a South Vietnamese soldier knifes him in the chest (the film was taken from "CBS Evening News with Walter Cronkite" and depicted an actual incident); (b) a fictional violent segment from the motion picture *From Here to Eternity*, in which Montgomery Clift kills Ernest Borgnine with a knife after a brief struggle; or (c) a nonviolent segment from the film *Corral*, which shows a cowboy saddling and riding a half-broken wild horse. In a fourth condition, control subjects viewed no film.

Commentary provided by the experimenter indicated to the subjects that the killings shown in the real and fictional film clips were either justified or unjustified. Two different voice tracks were recorded and played with the CBS film, and one of two explanations was provided to subjects prior to observing the scene in *From Here to Eternity*. For example, in a justification explanation, Montgomery Clift was said to have provoked the fight in seeking revenge for the death of his best friend, who had been beaten to death in a prison stockade by Borgnine, a cruel and sadistic man. In the unjustified explanation, Clift was said to be seeking revenge because he wrongly believed Borgnine had killed his friend. Similar explanations were given for killing the North Vietnamese soldier. Manipulation checks revealed that the subjects did view the violence as justified or unjustified according to the commentary provided to them.

All subjects rated the confederate's essay. They used the same scale of 1 to 10 shocks as had the confederate earlier, but they were also asked to select one of five levels of shock intensity, from slightly painful to extremely painful. The number and intensity of shocks delivered to the confederates are shown in Table 12.4. As can be seen, subjects in the justified violence conditions, as well as those who saw the fictional violence without prior commentary by the experimenter, delivered more shocks, and with greater intensity, than did the subjects in the other five conditions. Further analysis of the data showed that the subjects perceived the violence in the fictional film sequence as justified unless they were specifically told that it was not.

There was no difference between the subjects who had or had not watched a film, unless the film contained what appeared to be justified violence. In the justification condition, the film showed a violent action taken in revenge for an atrocity committed by the target individual. Even though viewing justified violence on film encouraged retaliation, the subjects still did not harm the confederate more than he had harmed them; retaliation was made equivalent to the provocation.

Models on television provide both an example and a legitimization of actions that can be taken by alienated people to redress perceived injustice. In addition, desperate people may gain ideas from the mass media about possible actions that can change their lives. Airplane hijacking is a good example. Hijackers are typically characterized as "mentally unstable," which means that they are persons who have had little success in their lives, have feelings of powerlessness,

and have problems with their self-concepts of masculinity and sexual adequacy. They are also often suicidal. These people are willing to gamble their lives on a single throw of the dice, and one example of a hijacker who succeeds in getting away with a large sum of money entices them to take a chance on succeeding also. It should be noted that these observational examples represent imitation of real-life rather than fictional models.

An analysis of television programs suggests that it teaches the same lesson taught by other institutions in American culture: when hit, a person has the right to hit back. Also, one can use coercive means to protect the weak and innocent, to preserve law and order, and to defend one's group and nation from external enemies. At the extreme, this morality is one in which the ends justify any means. Police heroes, private detectives, and cowboy sheriffs do not spend much time thinking of clever and nonviolent ways of preserving the lives of the bad guys. The most direct and violent route of dispensing with their legal tasks is taken without thought of moral alternatives. It is interesting to note that Chaffee and McLeod (1971) found almost no relationship between viewing violence and children's aggressive behavior, except in families that generally approved of coercive means of obtaining goals. Thus, when television teaches the norms of negative reciprocity and of coercive means to good ends, and parents support those values, viewing television violence is associated with aggressive behavior.

In conclusion, traditional attempts to show a causal link between viewing television violence and aggressive conduct have not produced convincing evidence. This is consistent with a statement from a recent report from the Surgeon General's Office (*Television and Growing Up: The Impact of Televised Violence,* 1972) that the results of the many studies are "neither wholly consistent nor conclusive." Perhaps too many kinds of behavior are being classified as "aggression" and a real relationship is con-

Table 12.4 Average Number and Intensity of Shocks Administered by Subjects in the Meyer (1972) Study.

Dependent variable	Experimental conditions							
	Fictional violence	Justified real violence	Justified fictional violence	Unjustified fictional violence	Nonviolent film	Unjustified real violence	Real violence	Control (no film)
Number of shocks	7.40	7.36	7.16	5.20	5.20	4.96	4.96	4.76
Intensity of shocks	3.52	3.48	3.40	2.72	2.64	2.36	2.28	2.16

cealed in the available data. Modeling research shows that subjects will imitate the defensive use of coercion, but there is no evidence that they imitate its offensive use.

The weight of the evidence is against the hypothesis that viewing violence on television will, by catharsis, reduce the probability of aggressive behavior by the viewer. Continual exposure to killings, fist fights, and other forms of coercion may desensitize an individual so he becomes accustomed to these forms of behavior, takes them for granted, and loses his moral repugnance for them. The consequent relaxation of moral standards may be one of the conditions that encourage people to use coercive influence tactics. Television may communicate information verifying and legitimizing a viewer's sense of injustice regarding some condition of his own life and may also provide models who show the aggrieved individual how to redress his injustice. The negative reciprocity norm and the norm of self-defense are strongly advocated in television programming, as they are by other institutions in America. In addition, people who are caught up in what they consider to be desperate life circumstances may imitate a deviant action seen on television in a last-ditch effort to change things for the better.

Perhaps the same effects occur from reading books, the socialization practices of parents and teachers, and ordinary conversation among acquaintances. Television may simply speed up the process, since it provides a flood of information about these matters. Also, television may be a particularly effective means of communicating values—though how one would compare a television program to a good book in terms of their effect on the consumer is difficult to determine.

IV. PERCEIVED AGGRESSION AND IMPRESSION MANAGEMENT

Whether or not the use of coercion will be perceived as aggressive depends on a number of factors. Threats and punishments may be used with benevolent intentions, and the source may not be considered aggressive. An action performed under one set of social conditions may be considered aggressive, while exactly the same response under other conditions may not be so labeled. The determinants of perceived aggression include attribution of intent to the actor, the norms that govern social interaction, and the values of the observer.

The process of labeling an actor as aggressive is associated with assigning responsibility to him, evaluating him negatively, and a willingness by the observer to undertake or support retributive punishment. The actor is usually aware of the relationship between being labeled as aggressive and suffering retribution, and so he tries various impression management strategies that are meant to justify his use of coercion to prevent observers from labeling him. He must attack one or more of the determinants of aggression if he is to avoid the negative label. He may try to change the observer's attributions, to rationalize the norms relevant to the situation in order to justify his conduct, or to challenge the values of the observer.

A. The Determinants of Perceived Aggression

In a national survey of adult American males, Blumenthal et al. (1972) found that the majority of the respondents labeled looting during a property riot, burning draft cards, and college demonstrations as violent behavior. But most of these men did not consider shooting looters or attacks by the police on college demonstrators as violent. A small minority of men, who could be characterized as alienated and as sympathetic to blacks and college students, took the opposite position. Apparently, what is considered violent, as with beauty and truth, is in the eye of the beholder. The very labeling of a behavior as violent or aggressive incorporates a judgment made by the observer. Thus, while revolutionaries label the system as violent, members of the "establishment" label the rhetoric and tactics of revolutionaries as violent (Pepitone, 1971).

A policeman who uses coercion in making an arrest may not be considered aggressive unless his actions seem arbitrary or unjustified. Lincoln and Levinger (1972) found differences in how a white policeman was evaluated depending on the context of his altercation with a black man. In all cases, the policeman performed exactly the same overt act: he was shown in a photograph as grabbing the shirt of a young black man. When the scene was described as a peaceful civil rights demonstration, he was evaluated negatively. However, when no cues were presented that would justify the victim's conduct, it was presumed that the policeman's action was legitimate and he received positive evaluations. Of course, the raters were young college students attending a liberal New England university. Segregationists might not have accepted the black man's right to demonstrate in the streets and hence might have rated the policeman positively in both conditions of the experiment. Whether an action is considered justified depends on the values and norms of the observer.

Brown and Tedeschi (1976) have shown that the offensive use of coercion is labeled by observers as aggressive, while the defensive use of coercion is not. Subjects viewed a live dramatization of a barroom scene. Each of four groups witnessed a different scenario and were asked to rate the actors on several Semantic Differential items, including aggressiveness. One man instigated an argument over a seat that was being saved by another man for his girl friend. The instigator either threatened the other man by asking "Are you looking for a shot in the mouth or something?" or else made the threat and attempted to use force by taking a swing (which missed). In two other conditions, the defensive man either made a counter-threat or used counter-force by striking the instigator hard in the stomach.

The results showed that the instigator was rated as aggressive in all conditions. However, the defensive use of force, where the only real damage occurred, was not perceived as aggressive. In fact, the actor in the latter condition was not perceived as any more aggressive than in a control condition where he was not involved in any altercation. While the defensive use of threats was meant to deter the instigator, the element of choice (other modes of influence could have been tried by the defensive actor) contributed to the mildly aggressive ratings given to him. When the defensive actor used force, he was already under attack by the instigator. Since it is difficult to use persuasion while someone is attacking you, the defensive actor was perceived to have little choice but to use counterforce against the instigator. The element of choice was important in producing a difference in the perceived aggressiveness of the two defensive actors. The fact that the most damaging action was perceived as least aggressive across all of the scenarios is a striking demonstration that the context of the action rather than the behavior as such determines how aggressive an actor will be perceived.

These studies suggest that an actor will be labeled as aggressive when three necessary conditions are met: (1) he is perceived as attempting to punish the target or to limit or constrain the target's behavioral alternatives and outcomes; (2) the effects of the actor's behavior are perceived as intentional, irrespective of his real intent; and (3) his action is considered by the observer to be antinormative, offensive, unprovoked, or disproportionate to the provocation.

B. Labeling, Retribution, and Impression Management

Labeling a person's behavior as aggressive is tantamount to blaming him for his actions. Blame focuses responsibility for illegitimate or unjustified actions. Retributive behavior is therefore justified against an aggressive actor (Pruitt & Gahagan, 1974). Only when a coercive behavior can be legitimized in the eyes of observers can an actor avoid blame. Commonsense observations, historical records, and scientific evidence all indicate that actors may take great pains to rationalize their use of coercive power as legitimate, defensive, and necessary.

This is just as true of nations as it is of individuals. For example, in 1939 elite German troops were dressed as Polish soldiers and simulated attacks on German radio stations and other minor targets along the Polish-German border. Concentration camp prisoners were also dressed as Polish soldiers; they were killed and left as evidence of the Polish "invasion." While the full invasion of Poland was under way, Hitler announced to the world that "this action is for the present not to be described as war, but merely as engagements which have been brought about by Polish attacks" (Shirer, 1959, p.793). The Americans may have used a similar tactic in Vietnam. Alleged attacks on American destroyers by North Vietnamese PT boats in the Bay of Tonkin were used as the rationale for the start of air attacks against targets in North Vietnam.

The apparent need to justify coercive actions implies that failure to do so often leads to negative consequences. We saw earlier that arbitrary frustrations lead to swift and equitable retaliation, while justified harmdoing does not bring retribution (Pastore, 1952; Mallick & McCandless, 1966). An observer's prior impression of an actor may also affect the way behavior is labeled. Fauconnet (quoted in Heider, 1944, p. 363) emphasizes the primacy effect of prior impressions of the labeling of a person: "Persons dreaded for their brutality are the first ones to be suspected of a violent crime; despised persons of a mean act; and those who arouse disgust of an unclean act. Peo-

ple with bad reputations are accused and convicted on the basis of evidence which one would consider insufficient if an unfavorable prejudice did not relate them to the crime in advance. On the contrary, if the accused has won our favor we demand irrefutable proof before we impute to him the crime." The studies carried out by Dion (1972) and Landy and Aronson (1969) reported in Chapter 11 (IV, F) showed that an attractive person who harmed other persons was considered less apt to do it again and was assigned less punishment than an unattractive transgressor.

An actor can justify his coercive actions by derogating the victim. Davis and Jones (1960) found that subjects derogated another person to justify their earlier hostility to him. Glass(1964) showed that a harmdoer's self-esteem was important in determining whether or not the victim would be derogated. In a teacher-learner paradigm in which subjects administered shocks to a confederate, the high self-esteem subjects derogated the victim, whereas the low self-esteem subjects did not. Derogation of the learner justified why he had to be shocked; his lack of intelligence made it necessary to use corrective shocks to help him learn.

If an actor cannot rationalize his behavior to observers, he may engage in one or another of the post-transgression responses discussed in Chapter 6. He may express guilt, self-criticism, or remorse, or he may engage in self-punitive behavior. Schwartz, Kane, Joseph, and Tedeschi (1975) found that the expression of remorse is an effective post-transgression strategy in mitigating punishment. Subjects read about a brief incident in which two boys find a rope under a park bench and use it to trip a little girl. Variations in the description used in different groups indicated that the little girl tripped but did not fall, that she fell and skinned her knee, or that she fell and hurt herself so badly she could not get up again. In one set of descriptions, boy A expressed remorse for what they had done ("We shouldn't have done that, we might have hurt her"), while in the other set of descriptions boy A expressed a lack of remorse ("That was a lotta fun"). The remorseful boy was perceived as less aggressive, evaluated more positively, considered less apt to repeat the harmful action in the future, and was assigned a lesser punishment than the boy who showed a lack of remorse. Thus, post-transgression responses can affect observers' judgments about the intentions of an actor and the way they label his behavior, which, in turn, lessen the amount of retribution he suffers.

C. Perceived Aggression and the Scientific Study of Coercive Power

It is important to recognize the difference between the behavior of an actor and its labeling by observers. This distinction was clearly noted by Bandura and Walters (1963): "Strictly speaking, of course, it is not 'aggressive' responses that are learned, but only classes of responses that are labeled as aggression on the basis of social judgments that themselves must be learned. An adequate learning approach to the problem of aggression must consider both how responses usually labeled as aggressive are acquired and maintained and how a child learns to make the social judgments that enable him to discriminate an aggressive from a non-aggressive response" (p.114). As we have just seen, the labeling of responses as aggressive has negative consequences for an actor.

The determinants of perceived aggression include attributions, social norms, and personal values. These social factors are rarely taken into account in studies of so-called "aggression." In fact, most naive observers would not label behavior studied in the laboratory as aggressive because the subjects are usually provoked into taking defensive or retaliatory action, and defensive actors are not perceived as aggressive

(Brown & Tedeschi, 1976). Most of the research on aggression can be reconceptualized as studies of coercive power under the major subtopics of reciprocity and revenge, arousal and harmdoing, the offensive use of coercion, and modeling.

In a series of studies, Tedeschi and his students have shown that naive observers do not label behavior in the same way as social psychologists. An examination of the essay evaluation paradigm developed by Berkowitz was carried out by Kane, Joseph, and Tedeschi (1976). Students were asked to read one of four descriptions of an experiment. In the descriptions person A evaluated an essay written by person B by shocking him once (for an excellent essay) or 7 times (for a poor essay). B was then given the opportunity similarly to evaluate A and either shocked him twice or six times.

A was perceived as more aggressive when he delivered 7 shocks rather than 1, but B was not perceived as aggressive when delivering 6 shocks rather than 2 if he had received 7 shocks from A. B was perceived as aggressive if he returned 6 shocks when he had received only 1. Thus, disproportionate retaliation led observers to label person B as aggressive, but proportionate retaliation did not. In contrast, Berkowitz always considers the subject (B) to be more "aggressive" the more shocks he delivers to the confederate (A) no matter how many shocks the confederate had first administered. Thus, while naive observers take into account the social context and meaning of behavior in terms of norms and values, the social psychologist focuses on the responses of subjects independent of their social meanings.

In a similarly naive analysis of the reaction-time game, Stapleton, Joseph, Efron, and Tedeschi (1974) asked observers to rate the behavior of "players." A pattern of escalating intensity settings was seen as aggressive or nonaggressive, depending on whether the second player's settings were higher or lower than the first player's settings. The player who set the higher intensities was perceived as offensive and aggressive. Equivalent reciprocity was not perceived as aggressive: disproportionate retaliation was.

The results of these two studies show that naive observers, unlike social scientists, tend to view an actor's coercive behavior on a relative basis and in terms of the context that gives it social meaning. Social scientists tend to view an actor's behavior absolutely and without regard to the provocations or justifications for it. A focus on factors internal to the individual such as learning, frustration-aggression, and tension release has caused the experimental social psychologist to ignore the difference between behavior that is legitimate and that which is antinormative. And though aggression is often defined as the intent to do harm, no theory of attribution has ever been tied to any theory of aggression. Furthermore, experimenters never establish the motives of subjects in the laboratory. Future theories are likely to make more clear the distinction between the types of coercive behavior performed by an actor and the conditions under which observers will label him as aggressive.

V. CHAPTER SUMMARY

Biological approaches to the study of harmdoing distinguish between predatory and agonistic behavior. The predatory and agonistic behavior of many animals is instinctual. Territorial instincts, dominance hierarchies, and reflex-like attack behavior in response to pain by subhuman animals appear to have a hereditary basis. "Go" and "stop" centers for predatory and agonistic behavior have been found in the brain, and biochemical factors have been implicated in facilitating or inhibiting such behavior. But there is no evidence that men have predatory or agonistic instincts or fighting reflexes. There is no internal biological energy that must be released in destructive and harmful behavior. The harm that men

do is a result of accident or learning and not of their phylogenetic history.

Three basic learning approaches have been taken toward understanding the harmdoing behavior of men: frustration-aggression theory, instrumental learning theory, and social learning theory. These approaches differ with regard to what is learned and how it is learned. Frustration-aggression theory presents a model in which frustration produces aggressive energy which must be released through aggressive responses. The responses performed by the organism are ordinarily directed at the source of frustration. If a response is successful in removing the frustration and in discharging aggressive energy, it is reinforced and is likely to occur the next time a frustration occurs. However, an individual may learn to inhibit an aggressive response if it has been punished in the past; a substitute response (displacement) will be performed under the pressure of the internal aggressive energy. Draining this energy through aggressive responses or through witnessing aggression is referred to as catharsis. It is considered useful to classify responses as aggressive because of their presumed equivalence so that one can substitute for another in producing catharsis. Unfortunately, the concepts of this theory are ambiguous and the accumulated evidence shows almost no support for a process of catharsis. There is evidence for a displacement-like effect, but the phenomena are interpretable as instances of other social psychological processes.

The instrumental learning view asserts that aggressive responses are learned just like any other responses. Research has shown reinforcement effects in strengthening and suppressing aggressive responses that are like those found with other responses. According to social learning theory, observers can learn to imitate the aggressive responses of a rewarded model. Both of these approaches run into difficulty with the definition of aggression. Instrumental learning theory defines aggression as harmdoing behavior and assumes that learning one kind of aggressive behavior (e.g., verbal insults) affects the probability that an individual will perform another kind of aggressive behavior (e.g., physical assault). While social learning theory recognizes that it is necessary to define aggression in terms of an intent to do harm in order to distinguish accidental from planned effects, there is a total disregard for the intent of subjects in laboratory experiments. It has not been demonstrated that observers will imitate the "bad" behavior of models. Furthermore, there is an acknowledgment that an actor who does harm for a legitimate purpose will not be considered aggressive; that is, intent to do harm is not in itself sufficient to define aggressive behavior.

A social psychological approach tries to interpret and explain harmdoing in terms of its social context and meaning. Behavior that has been labeled as aggressive can be classified into types of coercive power, including various kinds of threats and punishments (see Chapter 7). These coercive means can be used offensively for purposes of gain, power, or security, as was discussed in Chapter 9, or they can be used defensively after an individual has been attacked by someone else.

Most laboratory research has focused on the use of noxious stimulation as a form of retaliation. The norms of reciprocity and equity regulate the amount of retaliation delivered by persons as they make the punishment fit the provocation. The exceptions to the rule include a proscription not to harm females and an inhibition regarding retaliation against powerful and attractive persons. People with a generally coercive influence style may not follow the social norms regarding the regulation of harmdoing behavior. In general, if a harmed person can be convinced that the harmdoer had legitimate and justifiable reasons for his action, no retaliatory behavior will occur.

Common observation shows that men often get enraged and seem to lose control over their behavior. The effects of physiological arousal on the use of coercion have been intensively studied. Insult, attack, the observation of violence, and erotic stimulation have all been shown to produce arousal and subsequent amplification of the frequency and intensity of retaliatory behavior against a person who previously provoked the aroused individual. Whatever the sources of the accumulated arousal state of the individual, he may attribute a high state of anger to himself when provoked by another person, and his subsequent retaliatory behavior may be out of all proportion to the amount of provocation. But arousal effects are restricted to the retaliatory use of coercion and do not instigate unprovoked attacks on others.

Modeling experiments and studies that employ films to produce arousal states or to investigate the possibility of catharsis have contributed to concern about the possible deleterious effects of watching violence on television. Correlational studies have found no relation, a weak positive relation, and a weak negative relation between the amount of violence viewed on television and the aggressive behavior of children. Because of the lack of control over extraneous variables that are endemic to this kind of research, no firm conclusions can be reached. Experiments have shown modeling effects on the defensive use of coercion against live targets, but have yet to demonstrate convincingly the imitation of the offensive use of coercion. No catharsis effect has been found as a result of watching violence on television. The content of programs can make a norm of reciprocity or equity salient to an individual and cause him to seek retribution against someone who is believed to have previously harmed him. Watching a great deal of violence may desensitize an individual so he no longer is morally and emotionally repelled by antisocial actions. Television programs may legitimize an individual's sense of grievance and injustice and provide him with models showing how he can seek redress.

A coercive action will be perceived as aggressive when an observer attributes malevolent or selfish intent to an actor, when the action is offensive and antinormative in character, and when the effects are considered detrimental to the interest of the target person. When coercive actions are defensive in character, an actor will not be perceived as aggressive, as long as his reaction is proportional to the provocation. The label of aggressiveness is usually associated with blame and a belief that the actor deserves to be punished. Actors usually try to rationalize their coercive actions to avoid being labeled as aggressive. The failure to distinguish between the coercive behavior of an actor and the label of aggressiveness applied by observers has often produced difficulties and ambiguities for social psychologists in their attempts to understand harmdoing behavior.

SUGGESTED READINGS

Bandura, A. *Aggression: A social learning analysis.* Englewood Cliffs, N.J.: Prentice-Hall, 1973. Presents a sustained argument for a social learning theory of aggression that emphasizes modeling. There is discussion of the effects of television violence and student demonstrations, and ways to control aggression.

Comstock, G. A., and Rubinstein, E. A. *Television and social behavior.* 5 volumes. Washington, D.C.: U.S. Department of Health, Education, and Welfare, 1972. A technical report to the Surgeon General's Scientific Advisory Committee on Television and Social Behavior that represents a broad inquiry into the topic by many able social scientists.

Daniels, D. N., Gilula, M. F. and Ochberg, F. M. (Eds.) *Violence and the struggle for existence.* Boston: Little, Brown, 1970. A stimulating and informative series of papers by members of the psychiatry department at Stanford University examining contemporary theories and public issues regarding violence.

Johnson, R. M. *Aggression in man and animals.* Philadelphia: Saunders, 1972. An excellent introduction to the biological and learning approaches to aggression.

Megargee, E. I., and Hokanson, J. E. (Eds.) *The dynamics of aggression.* New York: Harper & Row, 1970. A collection of some of the classic studies of human aggression.

Singer, J. L. (Ed.) *The control of aggression and violence.* New York: Academic Press, 1971. A collection of original papers that devotes a good deal of attention to practical problems in controlling aggression.

PART 5

The Person in Groups and Society

The presence of other people can motivate a person to work harder or it can cause him to become anxious and interfere with the quality of his performance. Both of these effects of being observed by an audience have been shown in laboratory studies. Think of a time when you were required to make a presentation before an audience. How did you feel? What effect did the audience have on your performance? The presence of others may also produce pressures on an individual to conform to the judgments and opinions of everyone else in the group. People usually don't want to leave the impression that everyone else is out of step but them. Why people conform is a question that has been the subject of much research as well as much social philosophizing. We shall see that the same factors that produce conformity may cause an individual in group decision-making situations to act in a more extreme manner than others in his group.

In order to solve problems that are too complex for a individual to solve by himself, small groups must organize the activities of their members. Purposive groups must establish communication channels, must exert some pressure on members to perform their specific functions, and should have a leader to propose ideas, direct action, and bargain with other groups. The type of task facing the group, the skills and motivations among its members, and the effectiveness of its leader are among the oldest problems studied by social scientists. In Chapter 13 we will describe the social psychologist's answers to the effects an audience has on an individual's performances, the nature and causes of conformity, the differences in decisions made by individuals and groups, the intricacies of group problem-solving, and the factors that contribute to effective leadership. Although a great deal of research on these topics has also been carried out by industrial and governmental groups, sociologists, management scientists, and economists, we will not venture into their levels of analysis.

Men often are embedded in collectivities so large that they cannot possibly get to know all the names or even talk to other members and yet they act in a coordinated way. Large crowds enter and leave auditoriums, arenas, and stadiums with minor amounts of inconvenience. Mobs spontaneously form to lynch a victim or to create a riot. When faced with a common danger people may panic. These phenomena are not easily studied in the laboratory. Much of the speculation about these mass phenomena to be discussed in Chapter 14 is in the form of prescientific theories and consist of generalizations of processes and mechanisms that have been learned through the study of interpersonal interaction.

The subject matter in Chapter 14 not only stretches beyond the social psychologist's available techniques of research but also is often outside his unique level of analysis. The effects of the mass media, the social conventions that lead the person to label others as deviant, criminal, or insane, or the way in which collective behavior leads to economic development, mass movements, and revolutions are complex events that include sociological, political, economic, religious, and geographical, as well as social psychological factors. We will tentatively explore the kinds of contributions social psychologists might make to such phenomena. The importance of these phenomena to contemporary life cannot be overemphasized, but it must be recognized that the methods used to study them are flawed, nonexistant, or inadequate.

CHAPTER 13

Influence in Groups

CHAPTER PREVIEW

A small group is characterized by a need to coordinate behavior to achieve a common goal. Processes and structures emerge in the group context that have consequences for the behavior of individuals. These group-related factors do not affect the individual we have considered so far in this book. We have considered many processes that take place in the smallest possible human group, the dyad, such as influence tactics, reciprocity, and bargaining. In addition, the process of coalition formation, considered by many social scientists to be the most fundamental process occurring in groups, has been examined. However, we have not considered these processes in the context of the enduring, purposive, and organized interrelationships of persons in small groups.

Social scientists are not in agreement about the defining characteristics of "a small group." Certainly there must be at least two persons to make a group, and their dyadic interactions involve influence, bargaining, and exchange. However, students of small group behavior point out that only when there are three or more persons in a group can coalition formation, mediation and arbitration, and deviance occur. If the group becomes large, the intensive involvement and interaction that are typical of a small group are impossible. In large aggregations, many people become spectators rather than active participants. Thus, the size of a small group may be considered as greater than two and as having an upper limit determined by a change in the interaction pattern from intense involvement to mere observation.

Perhaps the most important aspect of a small group is that its members engage in coordinated activity to achieve a *common goal*. The members are mutually interdependent and the fate of each is contingent on the success or failure of the group's ventures. A common goal makes the members cohesive. The degree of *cohesiveness* of a group is largely determined by its success in achieving its goals and the importance of those goals to its members. A group that has no important goals or few successes usually dissolves within a short period of time.

Communication among members is an essential feature of groups. Communication serves the purposes of orientation, goal-setting, coordination, information dispersal, maintenance of social relationships, and the allocation of rewards. An aggregation of individuals waiting for a train at a subway station shares a common goal, but cannot be considered a group.

Success in achieving group goals usually requires the development of a group structure. The most important aspect of such a structure is the regulation of behavior by social norms. The formation of norms governing the behavior of members provide for the differentiation of roles, emergence and support of a leader, and the adoption of rules of inclusion and exclusion for membership. *Norms* governing the functioning of the group, the distribution of authority, and the behavior of group members may be formally adopted or implicitly established through custom. The group may adopt a constitution and a set of by-laws, and established customs regarding manner of dress, permissible use of language, and so forth. *Role differentiation* allows the group to use its members' talents and skills to solve problems efficiently and effectively; a lack of coordination or a poor fit between the members' skills and their assignments can contribute to group failure. Authority may be given to a *leader* or leaders who make decisions in behalf of the group. The adequacy of the leader is a central concern of group members. *Rules of inclusion and exclusion* clearly establish boundaries between one group and others. People refer to themselves as members of groups, incorporate membership into their self-identities, and experience a type of we-feeling with respect to other members.

In summary, groups are characterized as involving at least three persons, who communicate with one another to coordinate their activities in the pursuit of common goals. The structure of a group typically consists of role differentiation, leadership, a set of norms, and rules of membership.

Actually, few studies are carried out with groups having all these characteristics. Some of the earliest studies in the history of social psychology focused on individual behavior in public settings; the mere presence of others was found to affect behavior. Groups tend to put pressure on their members to conform to collective standards of thought and behavior. Research on conformity and deviance often is undertaken with people who act similarly but do not share a common goal. Of course, it is often

necessary for groups to make collective decisions, and it has become clear that the decisions individuals make in groups are different from those they make when they are alone. In studies of this process investigators typically organize aggregations of strangers into undifferentiated and leaderless groups whose only goal is to arrive at consensus on a decision. The study of group problem-solving (rather than decision-making) is much more concerned with role differentiation, communication and leadership structure, the distribution of abilities in the group, and the nature of the task facing the group. Thus, which characteristics will be built into laboratory groups will depend on the research interests of the investigator. This chapter will examine the principles governing the individual's performance in the presence of other people, social conformity, group decision-making, problem-solving, and leadership.

I. THE EFFECTS OF THE PRESENCE OF OTHERS

Early in the history of social psychology it was demonstrated that individuals behaved differently in the presence of others than when alone. An aspiring orator might wax grandiloquent in front of his bedroom mirror but quake, mumble and falter in front of a live audience. On the other hand, many athletes claim that their performances are improved by the presence of a large number of boisterous fans. In addition to these audience effects, the presence of coactors working simultaneously but independently on the same type of task may affect an individual's performance. Audience and coaction effects on the individual depend on the nature of the task, self-confidence, and other factors.

A. Audience Effects

In an early demonstration of an audience effect on performance, Travis (1925) trained subjects in a task in which the objective was to hold a flexible pointer in contact with a target spot on a rotating disc. The training was carried out over several days, and the subjects were alone except for the experimenter. When the task had been well learned, each subject was asked to perform in front of a passive audience of from four to eight persons. More than 80 percent of the subjects performed better in front of the audience than alone. This effect is referred to as *social facilitation,* because the presence of the audience spurred the individual to better performance.

Many studies confirm the social facilitation effect of an audience on the performance of well-rehearsed, simple, motor behavior. However, audiences impair the learning of new and complex conceptual tasks. Pessin (1933) found that subjects made more errors in learning nonsense syllables before an audience than when alone, and Husband (1931) found interference in learning a finger maze when an individual was observed by spectators.

Zajonc (1965) has suggested a parsimonious way of explaining these contradictory effects. Individuals who work in the presence of others are assumed to be more aroused than those who work alone. Arousal, in turn, increases the probability that a person will act in simple or well-learned ways. That is, arousal increases the likelihood of dominant behavior. When a task is familiar, as in the pursuit rotor study, the arousing audience facilitates performance. However, when the task has not been well learned, the most available responses of the individual are likely to be wrong for achieving success; hence, the presence of an audience impairs performance. Zajonc has suggested that a student ought to study by himself in an isolated cubicle, but after mastering the material, he should prefer to be tested in the company of other students or before an audience.

Jones and Gerard (1967, p. 607) agreed that the presence of an audience may produce arousal, but they also proposed that the audience may distract the individual and interfere with his ability to concentrate on complex tasks. They cited Pessin's finding of an equal degree of impairment in learning nonsense syllables by subjects who were bombarded with distracting stimuli (a buzzer and a flashing light) and those who performed in front of an audience. Both groups performed less well than a group of subjects who learned while alone.

One obvious concern of an individual is that an audience will evaluate him. Recent research has found social facilitation effects only when the audience is evaluative. Cottrell, Wack, Sekerak, and Rittle (1968) found no social facilitation of dominant responses when subjects performed in the presence of a blindfolded audience. Similarly, Henchy and Glass (1968) found social facilitation effects when subjects believed the audience was evaluating their performance but not in the opposite condition. Social facilitation or impairment of performance may be attributable at least partly to the individual's concern with impression management. When subjects believe they are being evaluated, they attempt to demonstrate that they are skillful, resourceful, and worthy persons, and because of the anxiety generated by the attempt to show their merits, they succeed only when their responses are well rehearsed.

Visible audience reactions affect an individual's performance. Sports writers generally believe that an enthusiastic crowd gives the home team an advantage. Laird (1923) found that heckling was disruptive of performance. He had fraternity pledges engage in several simple tasks, such as speed of tapping and standing still without swaying. They either performed in front of a passive audience (made up of fraternity members) or were exposed to heckling. The pledges exposed to a hostile audience showed a substantial decrement in performance.

Negative reactions from an audience can shake the confidence of a speaker. Gross,

Riemer, and Collins (1973) provided feed-back to subjects that an audience consi-dered their speeches to be either sincere or insincere. The subjects were then asked to indicate how confident they were of the opinions expressed in their speeches. Sub-jects who believed their sincerity had been accepted were more confident about their opinions than those whose sincerity had been challenged.

The overall picture that can be drawn from the above research is twofold: (1) when the task facing an individual is simple, and a good performance depends on the degree of motivation or effort he puts into it, the presence of an evaluative audience produces social facilitation; and (2) an individual's concern for presenting a posi-tive image of himself in front of an evalua-tive audience may cause anxiety and dis-tract him sufficiently to impair his perfor-mance on a complex motor or conceptual task.

B. Coaction Effects

The first experiment ever done in social psychology was concerned with the social facilitation produced by coactors. Triplett (1897) compared the times achieved in three types of bicycle competition: *unpaced,* in which a single rider raced against time on a given course; *paced,* in which a "rabbit" set the pace for a lone rider; and *competitive,* in which a number of riders raced each other. The fastest times occurred in competition and the slowest times occurred in the un-paced races.

F. H. Allport (1924) carried out a further series of experiments comparing individu-als working alone with subjects working in groups of four or five around a table on such tasks as crossing out vowels in written material, doing simple multiplication prob-lems, making word associations, and generating arguments to refute epigrams drawn from classical literature. The sub-jects working in groups were not allowed to make comparative appraisals, and competi-tion between them was minimized. Subjects in the coacting groups worked more vigor-ously and completed a greater quantity of each of the tasks than subjects who worked alone. However, the quality of the argu-ments was poorer in the coacting than in the alone condition.

Rivalry has also been associated with so-cial facilitation. Dashiell (1930) had subjects work on the same kinds of tasks used by Allport, in one of three conditions: (1) in front of a passive audience, (2) together with coactors, knowing that their perfor-mances would not be compared, or (3) to-gether with coactors, knowing that their performances would be compared. Rivalry produced faster but less accurate perfor-mance than the other two conditions.

The concern of actors about comparative evaluation in coacting groups was demon-strated by Allport. Subjects were asked to judge the pleasantness or unpleasantness of odors either while alone or in groups. More moderate judgments were made in groups; bad odors were judged as less ob-noxious and fragrant ones as less pleasant. According to Allport, the subjects avoided making extreme judgments to minimize the chance of being at odds with the group, of making deviant judgments, and hence inviting unfavorable appraisals by others. As we shall see later in this chapter when group decision-making is discussed, there are times when subjects will make more ex-treme judgments in groups than when alone; this will happen when they believe they can create a favorable impression by doing so.

Cottrell (1972) has speculated about the socialization experiences that lead to the social facilitation effects of audiences and coaction settings. The child very quickly learns that significant reinforcements, in-cluding praise and blame, come from other persons. Because others are associated with these reinforcements they acquire arousal-instigating properties that raise the performer's drive level. The raised drive level facilitates simple and well-learned behavior and impairs the performance of complex and new tasks. Similarly, rivals are also associated with rewards (winning) and punishments (losing) and hence become arousal-producing stimuli.

It is entirely consistent with this line of thought to expect persons to differ in the amount of social facilitation they will display. There are individual differences in concern about praise and blame and in the degree of confidence one feels in competitive or evaluative situations. As we noted in Chapter 6 (VI, C) there are also sex differences in concern with social evaluation; females, on the average, tend to be more concerned than males. Hunt and Hillery (1973) observed that females worked much harder in a coaction setting than when alone, while there was only a slight social facilitation effect among males.

In summary, the effects of audiences and coacting groups support the view that the presence of others arouses a person and motivates him to work harder than when he is alone. A desire to create a favorable impression in the eyes of witnesses underlies the arousal. When a person is aroused he performs better on simple tasks which have been well learned, but less accurately and innovatively on complex and new tasks. Concern for praise or blame is probably rooted in the socialization process and in the frequent past association of social evaluation with rewards and punishments.

II. SOCIAL CONFORMITY

What do you think about when the topic of social conformity is raised? Fads and fashions? An example of this kind of uniformity strikes a foreigner in London who observes businessmen trudge off to work each morning. Black suits, bowler hats, and swinging umbrellas are common. By labeling this uniformity of dress as social conformity, it is implied that these men have a choice among different styles and select those believed to be acceptable to others. If a tourist

were in Peking and saw everyone dressed in plain blue Mao jackets, the label of conformity might be inappropriate, since no other style of clothing may be available.

A person's behavior may match the behavior of others by coincidence. If an individual acts on the basis of his private assessment of a situation and without consideration of the reactions of others to his choice, it cannot be said he is a conformist even when his behavior is consistent with group expectations and brings approval from other members. For example, an American who wears black suits and bowler hats no matter where he is may appear eccentric in Chicago but as a conformist on the streets of London. In such a case, there has been no change in his behavior in response to real or imagined pressure from others.

Social conformity occurs at all levels of social organization, and it can be studied effectively in small groups. We will examine a number of theoretical and empirical approaches toward social conformity as a general orientation to the topic. We will then turn to situational factors that influence the amount of conformity displayed by persons. Finally, we will consider conformity from the point of view of social influence and examine message factors and source and target characteristics as they contribute to conforming behavior.

A. Theoretical and Empirical Approaches

We have noted the difficulty social psychologists often have in defining the phenomena they study (e.g., interpersonal attraction, love, and aggression). Many investigators have similar difficulty in providing an acceptable abstract definition of social conformity. Often the researcher simply goes ahead on the basis of "I know it when I see it." Nevertheless, attempts have been made to provide a theoretical orientation to social conformity, which, in turn, has spawned a number of different experimental paradigms for its study.

Sherif, Asch, and Crutchfield have all devised methods that have been repeatedly used by other investigators.

1. Orienting Definition of Conformity

Kiesler and Kiesler (1969) have defined conformity as a "change in behavior or belief toward a group as a result of real or imagined group pressure" (p. 2). This definition explicitly assumes that an individual's behavior in a group may be different than when he is alone, and that his behavior change is in a direction he believes to be accepted and approved by the relevant group. What may be perceived as conformity from the vantage point of one observer may be considered deviance from the viewpoint of another. A bohemian or hippie may be considered deviant in both dress and behavior when he is compared to "straight" society, but he may be perceived as a strict conformist in the context of his membership group. Sometimes it is difficult to ascertain whether deviant behavior is an assertion of independence from the pressures of one group or conformity to another. A hippie may dress as he does more because it distresses his parents than to obtain acceptance from other hippies.

2. Theoretical Models of Conformity

Crutchfield (1955) proposed a tripartite classification of the ways in which an individual may respond to group pressure. He may yield by *conforming;* he may maintain his *independence* by doing what he would do in the absence of pressure; or he may react by doing just the opposite of what the group desires *(anti-conformity).* Figure 13.1a depicts Crutchfield's conception of the individual's response alternatives when exposed to group pressure. The triangle suggests that independence is on a different dimension from conformity and anti-conformity. The latter two forms of behavior are responsive to the norms or expectations of the group; one represents

yielding and the other reactance to group pressure. Independence is action that simply disregards the expectations of the group.

In an experiment that measured the degree of conformity, anti-conformity, and independence of subjects over four different tasks, Stricker, Messick, and Jackson (1970) found that anti-conformity and independence were unrelated to one another rather than opposed in the way suggested by Crutchfield's model. Conformity was found to be negatively correlated with both anti-conformity and independence. From these results, the model shown in Figure 13.1b was constructed. As can be seen, conformity is contrasted with both anti-conformity and independence, indicating that if an individual does not conform, he can be expected either to display an anticonformity effect or to ignore the group norm.

Still another model was proposed by Willis (1965). As can be seen in Figure 13.1c, Willis emphasizes two dimensions of response to group pressure: conformity-anticonformity and independence-variability. The addition of variability changes Crutchfield's triangle to a diamond, and serves to clarify the meaning of independence. A response falling at the midpoint of the independence-variability dimension represents total dependence on (or orientation to) the norm to which a person conforms or anticonforms. Movement either left or right of the midline indicates less dependence on the norm. At the extreme right the person is guided by his own beliefs, attitudes, values, and plans, and, although he may be aware of norms that are relevant to his behavior, he is not influenced by them. The independent person is capable of resisting normative pressure without either giving in to perceived group demands or by showing reactance to them.

The variable person, at the extreme left of the diamond, also resists group pressure, but he is characterized by indecision;

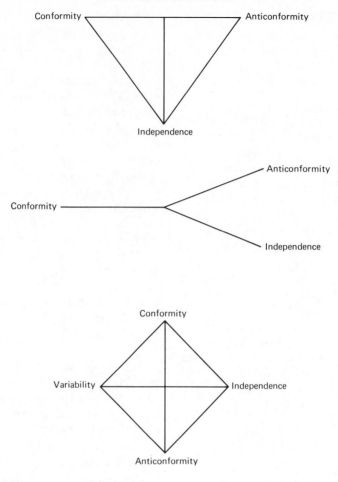

Figure 13.1. The Crutchfield, Stricker, et al, and Willis models of conformity.

he has no beliefs and commitments of his own, and simply changes his behavior and opinions whenever a choice arises. It is difficult to think of an example, since a person usually either follows the lead of others or has a plan of his own. Complete unpredictability is usually associated with mental illness.

The variability of behavior can be assessed only when an individual is given many choices of basically the same type. Then his lack of consistency either with respect to internal dispositions or in reaction to group pressure can be discerned. Thus the triangle and arrow models are applicable to single instances of behavior, while the

diamond model is relevant to multiple observations of a single person in similar group situations. All three models agree that an individual may respond either positively or negatively to group pressure; moreover, what looks like conforming or nonconforming behavior may be neither, but may instead be only coincidentally related to normative demands. This coincidental behavior may represent either independence or variability.

3. Standard Experimental Paradigms for Studying Conformity

Probably no experimental procedure used in the study of behavior in small groups is better known than *Asch's line-matching task* (1956). In a typical study, a subject is asked to announce orally his judgment about which of the three lines on a comparison card matches the single line on a standard card (see Figure 13.2). In his original study of conformity, Asch had a single subject join a group of seven confederates. The group members were seated so they could all view the cards, which were placed about three feet apart on a blackboard ledge. All eight persons announced their judgments in a pre-established order with the subject coming next to last; the confederates' judgments were prearranged.

Eighteen pairs of cards were presented to the group. On six of the trials, including the first two, the confederates made correct matches; but on 12 of the 18 trials, beginning with the third, the confederates made incorrect but unanimous judgments. Hence on 12 occasions the subjects were faced with two facts: (1) six persons had publicly indicated agreement in their judgments, and (2) the judgments were apparently wrong. The latter fact is known because when the subjects made the line judgments alone they made the correct match on 95 percent of the trials. Faced with this dilemma, almost 80 percent of the subjects agreed with the incorrect judgments of the confederates at least once, and the average subject conformed four or five times out of the 12 critical trials.

During post-experimental interviews, the subjects said they had been torn between conforming to avoid the possible disapproval or rejection of the group and their desire to make correct judgments. Independent judgments required the subjects to follow faithfully the experimenter's instructions to "call them as you see them." But the unanimous judgments by the other group members had the effect of shaking the subject's confidence in his own judgment and raised the question of whether everyone was out of step but he. Thus to make an independent judgment incurred the risk of being wrong. On the other hand, if the subject conformed to the group he had to go against his own private judgment and risk the experimenter's disapproval, but could avoid standing alone and suffering the reproach of the other group members. As we will see in a later section, which of these concerns will weigh heaviest on a subject depends on a number of situational, interpersonal, and personality factors.

The Asch situation presents subjects with a choice of conformity or independence. In a recent study of Japanese college students, Frager (1970) observed anticonformity in the line-matching task. On the trials when the confederates made unanimous and correct judgments, some subjects indicated disagreement with the group by choosing an incorrect comparison line. These subjects apparently wanted to signal their re-

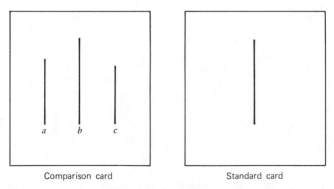

Comparison card   Standard card

Figure 13.2. An example of the line-judgment task used in the Asch procedure for studying social conformity.

sentment of the group's attempts to pressure them to conform on the critical trials. Frager found through his contacts with other researchers that American students almost never display anticonformity in this experimental task. He noted that the middle class stresses tradition and conventionality more in Japan than in America, but the Japanese student is given more freedom to rebel against institutional pressures.

The procedures used by Asch are somewhat clumsy and inefficient, primarily because of the need to hire so many confederates. Crutchfield (1955) and Gerard (Deutsch & Gerard, 1955) independently devised a research paradigm that eliminates all confederates and makes it possible to test several subjects simultaneously. The subjects are seated side by side, with each separated from his neighbor by partitions. In each booth (formed by the partitions) the subject faces a set of switches that are used to indicate his judgments, and a bank of lights that provide feedback about the choices of other subjects on each trial (see Figure 13.3). The stimulus material is projected on a screen that may be viewed by each subject through the front of his booth. The subjects are instructed that judgments are to be made sequentially, but each subject is told he will respond last. The experimenter then proceeds to turn on all of the feedback lights, one at a time, to simulate choices by other subjects. When all of the simulated members of the group have made their choices, the subjects make their own choices; each believes he is the last to make a judgment, but in fact they all respond simultaneously. The projected stimuli may be line lengths to be judged, dots to be counted, multiple choice questions, statements of opinion, and so forth. On opinion items, measures of anticonformity can be readily obtained.

The Sherif (1936) autokinetic situation (described in Chapter 3, IV, A), which has been used to study the development of individual frames of reference and group

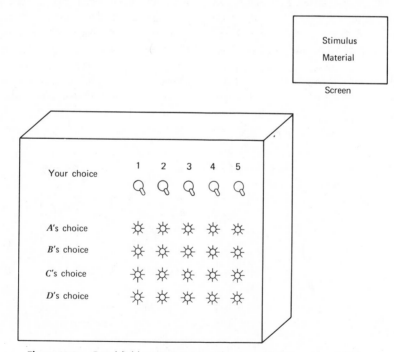

Figure 13.3. Crutchfield apparatus as seen by one subject in one booth. Four other subjects in separate booths have a similar panel before them.

norms has also been used to study conformity to group pressure. The autokinetic phenomenon involves illusory rather than real movement; as a consequence, it represents a more ambiguous task than the comparisons of line lengths made in the Asch task. In the Sherif situation, the subjects cannot ascertain whether their judgments are right or wrong and they become informationally dependent on the group for judgmental standards. The judgments of confederates in this situation represent informational influence, whereas the unanimous incorrect judgments of the confederates in the line comparison task represent normative influence (Deutsch & Gerard, 1955; see Chapter 3, IV, B).

The judgments of the group members provide information about the standards to be used by the individual in making his own decisions in the autokinetic situation. The persistence of the standards provided by the unanimous judgments of group members was demonstrated by Jacobs and Campbell (1961). A standard provided by an initial set of confederates was transmitted over eleven generations of laboratory subjects, each generation consisting of thirty trials with four persons calling out their estimates of the amount of movement by the light. At the end of each generation, one person left and a new subject took his place. In the first generation, there were three confederates who made judgments of "15 to 16 inches" and one naive subject. For the second generation, one confederate left and was replaced by a second naive subject; by the fourth generation there were no confederates left, and by the fifth generation the original naive subject had been replaced. The standard set by the original generation still had some effect on judgments for several more generations.

B. The Effect of Situational Factors on Conformity

Pressures to conform to the group may involve normative or informational influence or both. Those factors that make an individual informationally dependent on the group produce pressure on him to conform. The difficulty or ambiguity of his task serve to undermine his confidence in his own judgment and cause him to rely on the standards provided by others. Normative pressure on an individual takes the form of explicit or tacit threats of rejection, which may involve reproach, condemnation, and social ostracism. The degree of conformity displayed by an individual who is exposed to normative influence depends on whether he is under surveillance by group members and how he values group approval or rejection. Public behavior is affected by normative pressure, whereas private judgments are not.

The ambiguity associated with the autokinetic experimental situation encourages subjects to perceive the judgment of the confederates as helpful in making their own, whereas with line comparisons, the judgment of others serves as a source of confusion, conflict, and concern about being deviant. In either case, the size of the majority in the group affects the probability and extent of conformity by an individual.

1. Task Difficulty

Moscovici and Faucheux (1972) have analysed conformity situations in terms of information dependence and attribution theory. According to Kelley's (1967) theory, one of the factors in making attributions regarding features of the environment is the consensus of others. Without stable information, an individual must rely on this consensus about the dimensions of the stimulus. When a task is very difficult or its solution is ambiguous, he often does not have sufficient information to make stable attributions about the stimulus. Under these conditions, he becomes more susceptible to the informational influence of the group.

The ambiguity of a task is directly related to the amount of conformity displayed by subjects. About 80 percent of all subjects conform in the autokinetic situation (Sherif & Sherif, 1956). When subjects listened to metronome clicks and were asked to report their count for a given time period, about 60 percent yielded to group pressure (Shaw, Rothschild, & Strickland, 1957). About 50 percent of the subjects conformed when the task was to estimate the relative areas of various geometric figures, such as circles, triangles, and squares (Nickols, cited in Shaw, 1971). Conformity occurs about one-third of the time in the nonambiguous Asch situation.

Any experimental manipulation that reduces an individual's confidence in his own judgment and opinions increases the probability he will conform. Conolley (1964, cited in Gerard & Conolley, 1972) reduced the differences among the comparison lines in the Asch task, making the judgments more difficult. The more difficult the discrimination, the more the subjects yielded. When the cards were removed from sight before the first person made his judgment, adding an element of memory to the situation, there was more yielding (Deutsch & Gerard, 1955). Coleman, Blake, and Mouton (1958) reported that conformity was related to the difficulty of the factual questions posed to subjects. Consistent with the analysis of the stability of attributions by Moscovici and Faucheux, it has been found that the more competent a person rated himself, the less conforming he was to group pressures (Goldberg & Lubin, 1958; Mausner, 1954; Snyder, Mischel, & Lott, 1960).

The evidence from all these studies supports the conclusion that the informational influence of the group is diminished in direct relation to the confidence the individual has in his own judgments. This confidence may derive either from the ease or clarity of the task or from his prior experience of competence.

2.   Public Versus Private Responses

The Sherif and Asch settings require face-to-face confrontations among subjects and confederates, while the Crutchfield-Gerard apparatus does not provide visual and auditory contact. In the latter situation, the subject preserves some degree of anonymity; hence his concern about incurring disfavor for going against majority opinion should be reduced. The anonymous subject is also unlikely to gain approval from the group for comformity. Consistent with these effects of normative influence, Deutsch and Gerard (1955) obtained greater conformity to line judgments in the Asch face-to-face situation than in the more private booth setting. Similar private-public differences were found by Argyle (1957) and by Mouton, Blake, and Olmstead (1956), who required subjects in the public condition to identify themselves by name prior to making their judgments.

Allen (1965) has cautioned that the public-private differences in conformity may result from the fact that a group's pressures are convincing and influential and not from its normative pressures alone; the increased persuasiveness of face-to-face interaction may facilitate informational influence. In the public condition, an individual can be certain that the others confront the same stimuli he does. Also, face-to-face interaction allows the subject to observe the facial expressions and listen to the sincerity of the voices of other group members. These social cues may reduce his suspicion about whether there are other people actually present in the experimental situation.

3.   The Size of the Majority

When a subject is put in the Asch situation with only one confederate, little conformity to the confederate's incorrect judgment occurs. Variations in the size of the majority have shown that three confederates produced as much conformity as 16 (Asch, 1951). Apparently, an individual believes his judgments are as good as those of any other single peer, but when he is confronted with consistent judgments by several others, his confidence in what constitutes a correct response is shaken. When there are only two people, a difference between them does not establish one of them as deviant, but opposition to the unanimous judgment of three people makes an individual appear highly idiosyncratic.

Gerard, Wilhelmy, and Conolley (1968) found some increase in conformity up to eight group members, the largest group they tested. However, they used the separate booth situation and seven unseen confederates may be more convincing than three when there is no deviant image to worry about. Rosenberg (1961), on the other hand, found a leveling off of conformity in groups of four in the separate booths situation. These minor differences between studies are probably inconsequential; the psychological impact of informational and normative influence is significant, and the number of persons necessary to exert maximum influence is at least three and changes slightly with variations in the situation.

C. Tacit Communication and Social Conformity

The typical experiment in social conformity may be interpreted as a special case of the social influence processes presented in Part III of this book. Compliance in a conformity situation can take one of two forms: *private acceptance,* where the target person privately as well as publicly accepts the group's judgment as correct, and *public conformity,* where the target maintains a private belief that the group is in error but publicly acquiesces to its pressure (Allen, 1965; Festinger, 1953b; Kiesler, 1969).

Private acceptance depends on all those factors that produce attitude and value change and affect the social comparison process. Public conformity is a kind of behavioral compliance and depends on the probability and value of rewards and punishments associated with conforming and nonconforming behavior. Anticipated sanctions may be merely assumed by an individual or tacitly communicated by a group. Tacit communication may take the

form of implicit threats of disapproval and punishment for nonconformity, or promises of approval and rewards for conformity. The credibility of the communications and the value of the contingent reinforcements affect conformity in much the same way they affect compliance to explicit threats and promises (see Chapter 8). Public conformity to normative influence is likely to occur only when an individual believes he is under surveillance, since rewards and punishments cannot affect him if there is no one to witness his responses.

1. The Credibility of Tacit Messages

In conformity studies, the subjects are fully aware they are participating in an experiment and are usually concerned with how the experimenter will evaluate them (see Chapter 2, V, F). If all the other people in the situation make identical judgments and have not been disapproved or corrected by the experimenter, the subject may believe the best way to get the experimenter's approval is to do what the others have done. The group members may serve as models who tacitly communicate warnings or recommendations through the judgments they make, which indicate the appropriate responses to obtain a favorable evaluation.

In a study interpretable in terms of the credibility of the majority's judgments, Endler (1966) provided subjects with feedback about the truth or falsity of their judgments. Rewarding a subject for an independent judgment or punishing him for agreeing with the majority informs him that the majority was in error, while rewarding conformity and punishing independence affirms the reliability of the judgments made by the majority. Manipulating credibility in these ways, Endler created six experimental conditions.

In the first condition, the subjects were positively reinforced 100 percent of the time for conforming and punished 100 percent of the time for disagreeing with the majority; the group was always right and therefore possessed 100 percent credibility. In the second condition, feedback was provided only after every other judgment under the same reinforcement contingencies; here the group majority again had 100 percent credibility, but subjects had only half as many opportunities to observe them as in the first condition and may not have been as confident of their infallibility. No reinforcing feedback was given in the third condition; the subjects had no information about the group's credibility.

In the fourth condition, the subjects received feedback after every other trial and were consistently punished for agreeing with the group and rewarded for making independent judgments; the majority had 0 percent credibility, but the subjects had no information about their accuracy on half the trials. The subjects received feedback on every trial in the fifth condition and were reinforced as in the fourth; they were thus informed that the majority was always wrong. In the sixth condition, the subjects made judgments alone, with neither group pressure nor feedback.

The results are shown in Table 13.1. As can be seen, the data support the hypothesis of a direct relationship between the credibility of a group's judgments and conformity by individuals. The degree of conformity was ordered from high to low over conditions one through six. The general tendency for females to be more con-

forming than males will be discussed in section E. 3 below.

In a variation of this study, Allen and Crutchfield (1963) provided subjects with feedback about the accuracy of the majority's judgments and opinions. When the subjects were told the majority was correct, they conformed more than noninformed subjects on items of perception and vocabulary. However, the personal opinions expressed by the subjects were not affected by information about the credibility of the majority. Thus, judgments of external referents were changed by group pressures, but subjective preferences were not.

Asch (1951) found that the credibility of the majority was undermined if one confederate always made correct judgments and thereby destroyed the unanimity of the incorrect judgments. Supportive dissent by only one other person in a group eliminates all the pressure to conformity; subjects under such conditions make no more errors than when judging alone. The presence of an ally reduces a subject's fear about public ridicule and negative evaluation by the experimenter and/or gives him more confidence in the veridicality of his own perceptions.

Lack of consensus among members of the group can take other forms as well. Asch (1955) reported that subjects made independent judgments when one confederate departed from the majority by being even more in error. Furthermore, Shaw, Rothschild, and Strickland (1957) showed that subjects maintained independence when one confederate merely said that he was unable to make judgments. The example of a dissenter who is neither punished nor disapproved stiffens an individual's resolve to go his own way and resist pressure to conform. An example of dissent in a democratic society should provide each person with enough courage to withstand the pressure to conform to the majority. Perhaps this is why the majority is always tempted to try to silence and punish dissen-

Table 13.1 Average Conformity Scores for Males and Females under Different Reinforcement Conditions.[a]

Experimental condition	Sex of subject	
	Males	Females
1. Conform, 100%	9.50	13.00
2. Conform, 50%	7.50	10.50
3. No feedback	6.60	6.10
4. Independence, 50%	4.20	4.60
5. Independence, 100%	2.90	3.50
6. Control	2.10	2.50

[a] After Endler, 1966.

ters (see Schachter's study of dissent, Chapter 3, IV, B, 1).

2. The Value of Outcomes

The value of reinforcements is directly related to the amount of conformity displayed by subjects (Jones, Wells, & Torrey, 1958). Conformity may be considered an exchange process in which an individual tenders his compliance in return for reinforcements. Burdick and McBride (cited in Festinger, 1957) found that explicit promises of reward and threats of punishment were effective in inducing subjects to agree with group consensus regarding curfew regulations. Nord (1969) suggested that an individual incurs a loss of self-esteem when he seeks the approval of group members. The importance of the approval must compensate for this or he will not yield to group pressure.

The loss of self-esteem can be increased by inducing subjects to make a prior commitment before eliciting public judgments from them. The observer (experimenter) would then know the individual's private beliefs and would also know if he changes his judgments to conform to group pressure. A private-public inconsistency would cause an observer to view him as trying to ingratiate himself, and such behavior is usually viewed negatively.

Deutsch and Gerard (1955) examined the effects on conformity of prior commitment. They had subjects make line judgments in one of four conditions. In a public commitment condition, each subject wrote his judgment on a signed paper that was to be turned in at the end of the experiment. These written judgments were made prior to the usual public judgments made by confederates and subjects. In a private commitment condition, each subject wrote his choice on an unsigned piece of paper that was ultimately dropped in a waste basket. In a most private commitment condition, each subject wrote his selection on a "magic pad," which is a layer of cellophane covering a piece of graphite; by pressing on the

cellophane with a stylus one can write on the pad, and when the cellophane is raised, the writing is erased. A control group followed the no commitment, public response procedures typically used by Asch.

In general, the greater the public commitment made by subjects and the greater their possible loss of self-esteem for conforming, the less likely they were to conform. When a subject wrote his private judgments on paper, he remained independent of group pressure. Although the investigators expected more conformity when the unsigned paper was to be thrown away, the subjects apparently viewed both paper conditions, as public commitment; perhaps they thought the unsigned paper might be recovered and the handwriting might be recognized. Subjects conformed most frequently in the no commitment (control) condition, but they also conformed to the erroneous judgments of the majority in the magic pad condition. The latter subjects could be reasonably sure no one would discover their private judgment before public judgments were made; hence, they could conform without being concerned about being perceived as ingratiating by the experimenter.

Technically, the participants in laboratory conformity situations do not comprise a group because they share no real collective goal. Kane and Tedeschi (1973) have shown that, in addition to loss of self-esteem, conformity to group pressure when no collective goal is sought may bring the individual the social costs associated with disapproval by the group. Subjects were led to believe they were serving as confederates in a replication of one of Asch's studies, and were instructed to make unanimous judgments of the same type made by Asch's confederates. After the instructions were completed, another supposed subject was brought in from a waiting room. This subject was actually a confederate and either conformed frequently or remained independent over the 18 trials. The real subjects were asked to give their impressions of the "critical subject" at the end of the experiment. The conformist was perceived as weak and was evaluated negatively, while the independent person was perceived as strong and was evaluated very positively. As Schachter's (1951) study demonstrated, a dissenter is usually disapproved and rejected in a real group, whereas a conformist is approved and accepted. The implication is that the degree of conformity observed in typical laboratory experiments is less than would occur in real groups, which are characterized by cohesiveness, communication, and common objectives.

D.   Group Characteristics and Conformity

Conformity may be considered a special case of compliance by an individual to tacit communication from a collective source—the group. The principles of social influence considered in Chapters 8 and 9 can be applied to understanding both the informational and normative pressures leading to conformity. The chief differences between the study of compliance and conformity are that the communications involved in conformity are usually implicit rather than explicit and are sent by a group rather than by an individual. The individual may also act in anticipation of the group's expectations rather than as a reaction to directly communicated pressure. These anticipatory reactions may be interpreted as ingratiation attempts designed to win favor from group members.

The attractiveness, competence, and status of a group affect conformity in the same ways these source characteristics affect influence in dyadic relationships.

1.   Attractiveness of the Group

The referent power or attractiveness of a group is often operationalized as a measure of the cohesiveness of the group, which consists of a combined score representing the tendency for its members to stick to-

gether. Cohesiveness may result from a variety of factors. Steiner (1972) suggests that people remain in groups because "they enjoy the activities, desire the wages or other tangible payoffs they hope to receive, wish to satisfy ego needs, avoid boredom, alleviate uncertainty and fear, or escape the more oppressive social restrictions imposed by other groups. Perhaps all of the reasons people remain in groups can be subsumed under the term 'attraction' but an abstract label should not obscure the fact that many different bonds may be holding members together" (p. 161).

There is a direct relationship between how attractive a group is and how much an individual will conform to its norms, standards, and expectations. After reviewing the available evidence, Kiesler and Kiesler (1969) have concluded that this is "as solid a generalization as one can arrive at in social psychology" (p. 66). Two field studies have confirmed this psychological principle; there was more uniformity of opinion and conformity to the standards of groups in university housing units when high rather than low cohesiveness characterized relations within them (Festinger, Schachter, & Back, 1950), and observation of cliques of school teachers found a strong relationship between group cohesiveness and conformity (Rasmussen & Zander, 1954).

Back (1951) produced high or low cohesiveness by three different experimental manipulations. In one set of conditions he told subjects either they would or they would not find their partner congenial; positive or negative first impressions produce high or low cohesion. In a second set of conditions, the amount a pair could win by the successful performance of a task was either high or low; degree of cohesion is directly related to the importance of the group's goals. In a third set of conditions, some subjects were led to believe they had been paired because both had special competencies with respect to the experimental task, while others were given no information about why they had been paired; high cohesion is established through mutual respect. In all sets of conditions, greater cohesiveness produced more conformity. Hence, the more attractive the group, the more apt the individual was to conform to it, whatever the basis of group cohesiveness.

One more example should establish the firmness of the relationship of attraction and conformity. We saw in Chapter 11 that similarity is a basis for attraction; hence, we might expect similarity to result in conformity to a group. Linde and Patterson (1964) found that similarity in physical disability or health may have this effect. They constructed face-to-face groups of persons who were disabled and confined to wheel chairs and of persons without disabilities. In the Asch situation, the naive subjects were more conforming when there was similarity in their physical attributes and those of the confederates. Disabled subjects conformed more when the confederates were also in wheelchairs; and able-bodied subjects conformed more when faced with the unanimous judgments of a majority of confederates who did not have obvious disabilities.

2. Competence Within the Group

Two factors that may affect an individual's perception of his competence relative to other group members have already been discussed—the ambiguity of the task and the prior history of success of group members in performing it. Kelman (1950) manipulated the self-confidence of subjects directly by providing them with experiences of success or failure before exposing them to group pressure in the autokinetic situation. Relative to prior failure, experience of success lowered "suggestibility." Mausner (1954) had subjects make judgments in the Asch situation with a confederate who either had been previously successful or had failed. The subjects conformed more frequently when the confederate was perceived as competent. In general, the evidence supports the general proposition that the less the confidence of an individual or the more competent the group, the more conformity he will display.

Croner and Willis (1961) have shown that the competence of group members must be relevant to the task at hand. A person may not yield to an expert when the issue is irrelevant to the latter's area of competence. Two separate experiments were carried out. In the first, subjects completed a paper-and-pencil test and were informed they had either succeeded or failed. A subject who was supposedly highly competent on the test was then paired with an incompetent subject, and they made line comparisons. The comparison lines were actually identical; hence, the task was very ambiguous. Each subject alternated, giving his oral judgment first or second. No effect of competence on conformity was found.

In the second experiment, the pretest given to the subjects consisted of making judgments about the relative areas of 36 irregularly drawn figures—a task of perception related to line judgment. The subjects were told that they had performed well or not, and were coupled in competent-incompetent pairs. Incompetent subjects displayed more conformity subsequently in the line judgment task than competent subjects. The combined results of these two studies support the conclusion that the competence of a source affects conformity only when the basis of his expertise is clearly related to the particular task facing the group. Thus, a particular individual may have great influence on a group on some issues and be ignored on others.

3. Status Within the Group

In Chapter 8 we defined *status* as the perception that another person deserves deference because of the legitimate authority associated with his role position. Status relationships are embedded in group structures. Unlike the more direct influence exerted in the use of coercive power, status derives its effectiveness from the members of the group who "enforce" compliance to the requests of a high status source (Blau, 1964). High status members of the group are perceived as powerful and able to generate significant rewards for conformity and punishments for deviance; they may also appear more competent and self-confident than lower status persons. These factors combine, so that a low status individual feels great pressure to conform to high status members of a group.

The fact that the member of the group with highest status (the leader) also is under great pressure to conform is often ignored. Hollander (1958) has noted that a leader has two contrary demands placed on him. He is expected to show initiative in approaching group problems *and* to conform to the group's norms and values. To initiate change, he must often deviate from the accepted ways of doing things in the group. To understand how the leader's dilemma is resolved, Hollander proposed an accountancy notion of debits and credits. Each individual gains credits from the group by conforming to their expectations or by making important contributions to solving their problems. The high status person is someone who has accumulated more credits than other members. The value of these credits is that they may be expended for proposals and actions contrary to the group's norms, procedures, and wishes. The more credits possessed by an individual, the more deviance by him will be tolerated by the group. Hollander called these hypothetical credits *idiosyncrasy credits*.

A new member of a group begins with no credits. He needs to conform, to avoid deviation or anticonformity, until he has enough credits to prevent rejection by the group. A long-standing and loyal member accrues idiosyncrasy credits and can engage in deviant action without rejection, but he expends some of his credits by his behavior. Consider the new college graduate who is a management trainee in a large corporation. Although his title gives him some arbitrary status, any attempt he makes to institute

immediate changes in the procedures followed by sales and office personnel is apt to be resisted by the more experienced workers because he has not yet made himself an accepted member of the group. He must observe the group norms and follow the accepted ways of doing things for a time before he can be successful in proposing changes. Early conformity permits later deviation. This is why leaders are often the most conspicuously conforming members of groups.

Hollander (1960) has provided evidence in support of his theory. He combined subjects into five-man groups and gave each group fifteen trials in which to perform a complex task. On each trial the subjects had to provide a single decision representing the group's solution. Before beginning the experiment, group members decided the order in which they would report their individual choices, adopted a majority rule for the group's collective decision, and generated a rule for dividing any group winnings. A confederate, who by his task-relevant contributions obviously possessed competence, was in each group, and his conformity to the procedural rules of the group was manipulated. He deviated either from the very first trial, only after five trials, or after 10 trials had been completed. The measurement of his influence consisted of the number of trials on which his correct solution was accepted as the group's choice.

Naturally, it took a while before it became evident that the confederate was offering superior suggestions; his influence grew with time in all conditions of the experiment. However, his influence was greater when he had conformed to the group's rules during the first few trials. His suggestion that the group should abandon the majority rule was more acceptable when he had conformed early than when he had not. Thus the group found the superior suggestions of the competent confederate relatively more acceptable if he had first demonstrated his willingness to conform to their standards of conduct.

Persons who have reason to worry about

their acceptability in a desirable group will conform to increase their acceptability. This ingratiation hypothesis was investigated by Dittes and Kelley (1956). Subjects were asked to engage in group discussion to get acquainted prior to a group problem-solving task. They were then asked to indicate whether they wanted to exclude anyone before going on to the next two tasks, which, if solved, would lead to monetary prizes. False feedback was provided, indicating to the subjects that they were either high, average, low, or very low in acceptability to other group members. Since the two groups of low subjects indicated on subsequent ratings that they did not value the group, their nonconforming behavior could not be interpreted in terms of the hypothesis guiding the study. However, both the high and the average subjects rated the group as having value for them. Those who were told of their average acceptability were more conforming in both problem-solving tasks than were those who believed they were highly acceptable. According to the theory of idiosyncrasy credits, the highly acceptable subjects could more afford to remain independent of the group than the less acceptable.

The same processes occur in real-life groups. Harvey and Consalvi (1960) asked boys at a training school for delinquents to rank the desirability of the four or five other members of their small cliques. Each member was then asked to make 20 private judgments about the distance between a pair of lights. The apparatus was rigged so the members of each clique believed they were all perceiving the same stimulus, but in fact the critical subject in each clique saw lights that were 48 inches apart while all other members saw lights that were 12 inches apart. The subjects were then asked to make 20 public judgments with other members of their clique. The procedure required each member to call out his estimate, and the critical subject always made his judgment last. The degree of conformity of these subjects was measured by the difference in their public and their private estimates. Across experimental conditions the critical subject was the member of the group who was ranked highest, next highest, or lowest.

As can be seen in Table 13.2, the highest ranked subjects were least yielding, while the second ranked subjects were most yielding. The highest ranked person is secure and has idiosyncrasy credits to expend; the lowest ranked person has little to lose through further deviance, and, in fact, yielded little more than the highest. Deviance is most risky for the second-ranked person, who is most concerned about maintaining and improving his position in the group.

E. Target Characteristics and Conformity

While a wide range of personality factors have been related to yielding in conformity situations, the evidence has been inconsistent, and no conclusion can be reached about whether there is a "conforming per-

Table 13.2 Subjects' Mean Judgments of the 48-inch Stimulus Before and During Group Members' Influence.[a]

Status of the critical subject	Average judgments of subjects		
	Before influence	During influence	Difference
Highest	47.70	32.08	15.62
Second highest	56.67	17.52	39.15
Lowest	46.87	27.20	19.68

[a] After Harvey and Consalvi, 1960, p. 185.

sonality." The relationship between authoritarianism and conformity is illustrative of the inconsistencies found by researchers. Beloff (1958), Crutchfield (1955) Nadler (1959), and Wells, Weinert, and Rubel (1956) have reported positive correlations between authoritarianism and conformity; others have found no relationship (Gorfein, 1961; Hardy, 1957; Weiner & McGinnies, 1961); in still other studies, authoritarianism has been correlated with conformity only when lack of confidence also existed (Berkowitz & Lundy, 1957) or when group members had greater relative competence than the critical subjects (Millon & Simkins, 1957). In general, those traits that reflect lack of self-confidence or a concern about acceptance by others are directly related to conforming behavior.

1. Need for Approval

The California F scale is commonly used to measure authoritarianism. Many of the items on the scale that indicate authoritarianism also have been identified as measuring *acquiescence,* the readiness of subjects to agree with statements ("yea-saying"). Positive relationships between authoritarianism and conformity may simply indicate that those who acquiesce to questions asked of them also conform to group pressure on other tasks in experimental settings. Such acquiescence may be a manifestation of an individual's concern about being evaluated and his desire for approval. Moeller and Applezweig (1957) found that subjects identified on a paper-and-pencil test as having a high need for social approval and low self-approval were more conforming in the Asch situation than persons with the opposite profile. Strickland and Crowne (1962) have reported a similar positive correlation between conformity and need for approval.

2. Anxiety and Self-Esteem

Apprehension about evaluation or being accepted by a group may be associated with an individual's readiness to conform to

pressure. Smith and Richards (1967) compared subjects who obtained high scores on a measure of anxiety with those who obtained low scores; the highly anxious subjects were more conforming. Breger and Rutz (1963) found indirect support for this relationship. They provided two groups of subjects with information about conformity procedures and findings before exposing them to group pressure. One of these informed groups was also given a lecture on anticonformity and deviance prior to making public judgments. The lecturer advocated the independence of personal values and resistance to group pressure.

The subjects who heard the anticonformity lecture conformed more frequently than did the other preinformed subjects or a control group of subjects who had not been told about conformity research. Breger and Rutz interpreted these results in terms of the anxieties generated about the negative consequences of anticonformity made salient to them by the lecture, which pointed out why it was difficult to stand up for one's beliefs and values against the group. Apparently the subjects were more impressed with the costs associated with nonconformity than with the gains to be achieved by independence.

Persons of low intelligence and self-esteem are more conforming than those of high intelligence and self-esteem (Berenda, 1950; Berkowitz & Lundy, 1957; Crutchfield, 1953; deCharms & Rosenbaum, 1960; Nakamura, 1958). Thus, anxiety and low self-esteem, personality traits associated with lack of self-confidence and a concern about the evaluations of others, make an individual vulnerable to group pressures. These same traits are associated with susceptibility to influence (Janis & Field, 1959). Successful persuasion and conformity may reflect identical processes.

3. Sex and Conformity

Sex differences in conformity have been reliably reported. Females have often been found to be more conforming than males

(Asch, 1956; Beloff, 1958; Crutchfield, 1955; Tuddenham, 1958; see also Table 13.1). One explanation for this difference is in terms of gender identity and sex-role prescriptions. In American society the female sex role stresses cooperation and concern about social approval and self-presentation, factors related to conformity. The male sex role stresses independence and achievement motivation, factors associated with nonconformity. It may be too early to say whether the Women's Liberation movement will have a significant impact on traditional sex role learning and values, but there are clear signs that independence and rebelliousness, typically associated with the male role, is becoming acceptable behavior for females.

Another explanation for sex differences in conformity is related to the fact that most social psychologists are male. Presumably, they devise male-oriented tasks for subjects to perform. Females, having less experience with such tasks, are more uncertain and informationally dependent than males and therefore are more conforming. Sistrunk and McDavid (1971) devised both male and female items and, in a series of four replications at different schools, submitted them to males and females. The sex-relatedness of items was rated by another group of subjects prior to the main experiment. Social pressure was brought to bear on the subjects in the form of information that "200 college students" had responded in a certain manner. They were then asked to indicate agreement or disagreement with each questionnaire item. Males conformed more than females on female-related items, while females conformed more on male-related items. The standard sex effect, therefore, may be attributed to specially contrived circumstances in which females are more informationally dependent than males.

III.   GROUP DECISION MAKING

Committees and boards are a prominent characteristic of modern organizational life. In complex organizations, important policy decisions are seldom the product of a single individual; usually they represent the collective wisdom of a group. Although the prevalence of group decisions has probably increased throughout history, they were made by community elders, tribal councils, and other social and political groups in pre-industrial societies. As industrial growth occurred in the United States, more and more people were employed in white-collar managerial positions in large bureaucracies. The embeddedness of individuals in organizations is believed by many observers to rob them of initiative and to stultify innovation.

Whyte (1956) argued that big businesses place great pressure on their employees to conform. The gray flannel suit became the uniform of this managerial class, just as bowler hats and umbrellas characterized the London business class. An image was painted of an "organization man" as afraid to take a chance, as alienated, and as refusing to risk departure from the "company way" of doing things.

Group decision-making is a process of choosing among goals and policies, and such choices always entail an element of risk. The Board of Directors of a business may make a decision about investments or marketing, a family may discuss the possibility of a job change by the principal wage earner, a team of coaches may formulate strategy for the next football game, and a national security committee may plan diplomatic and military tactics. These are goal-directed decisions that involve a choice among many alternative actions. Research has shown that individuals make different decisions in groups than when acting alone. Intensive investigation of this difference has resulted in a number of theories to explain the phenomenon, including diffusion of responsibility, familiarization, leadership, and theories of rhetoric, value, and social process.

Highly cohesive, long-standing groups strive for consensus in decision-making. They actively avoid argumentation, and they try to simplify the problem, to consider only a few alternatives. Janis (1972) refers to these group phenomena as *groupthink* and has provided a series of post hoc analyses of international policy decisions to illustrate how it works. A number of ways to avoid the pitfalls of groupthink have been proposed.

A. The Risky Shift

The well-known tendency for persons to conform to group pressures made it seem reasonable to assume, as Whyte did, that groups will make more conservative decisions than individuals. Given the prevailing view of individuals as organization men, social psychologists were surprised when Stoner (1961) demonstrated that individuals recommend greater risks when making decisions in groups than when alone, a phenomenon usually referred to as the *risky shift*. Stoner's experimental procedures have been used by many researchers and hence we shall describe them in some detail.

Each subject (for Stoner, graduate students in industrial management) was given a Choice-Dilemmas Questionnaire (CDQ) to complete by himself. The CDQ was developed by Kogan and Wallach (1964) as a tool for studying individual differences in risk-taking. The original instrument contained 12 hypothetical situations, including, for example, the following three items:

1. Mr. A, an electrical engineer, who is married and has one child, has been working for a large electronics corporation since graduating from college 5 years ago. He is assured of a lifetime job with a modest, though adequate, salary and liberal pension benefits upon retirement.

On the other hand, it is very unlikely that his salary will increase much before he retires. While attending a convention, Mr. A is offered a job with a small, newly founded company which has a highly uncertain future. The new job would pay more to start and would offer the possibility of a share in the ownership if the company survived the competition of the larger firms.

Imagine that you are advising Mr. A. Listed below are several probabilities or odds of the new company's proving financially sound. PLEASE CHECK THE LOWEST PROBABILITY THAT YOU CONSIDER ACCEPTABLE TO MAKE IT WORTHWHILE FOR MR. A. TO TAKE THE NEW JOB.

___The chances are 1 in 10 that the company will prove financially sound.

___The chances are 3 in 10 that the company will prove financially sound.

___The chances are 5 in 10 that the company will prove financially sound.

___The chances are 7 in 10 that the company will prove financially sound.

___The chances are 9 in 10 that the company will prove financially sound.

___Place a check here if you think Mr. A. should *not* take the new job no matter what the probabilities.

4. Mr. D. is the captain of College X's football team. College X is playing its traditional rival, College Y, in the final game of the season. The game is in its final seconds, and Mr. D's team, College X, is behind in the score. College X has time to run one more play. Mr. D, the captain, must decide whether it will be best to settle for a tie score with a play which would be almost certain to work; or, on the other hand, should he try a more complicated and risky play which could bring victory if it succeeded, but defeat if not.

9. Mr. J is an American captured by the enemy in World War II and placed in a prisoner-of-war camp. Conditions in the camp are quite bad, with long hours of hard physical labor and a barely sufficient diet. After spending several months in this camp, Mr. J notes the possibility of escape by concealing himself in a supply truck that shuttles in and out of camp. Of course, there is no guarantee that the escape would prove successful. Recapture by the enemy could well mean execution.

All 12 items were accompanied by alternative choices similar to those shown for item 1.

When the subjects had each completed a CDQ, they were gathered into small groups and asked to discuss each item. They were told that the experimenter was interested in ascertaining whether the CDQ items stimulated good group discussion, and were asked to reach a group consensus on the recommendation they would make to the central character in each item. To compare individual with group decision-making, Stoner added together the probabilities associated with the alternatives recommended by the subjects when they were alone and obtained an average; this average was then compared to the probability associated with the consensus choice. In Stoner's study, groups made more risky decisions than individuals. Subsequent studies have shown that this finding is very reliable; the risky shift has been found among men and women, college students and professional personnel, and citizens of many different Western nations (cf. Pruitt, 1971b).

The discovery of the risky shift provoked excitement among social scientists, who saw implications that were just as unsettling as Whyte's had been. Do foreign policy groups—the National Security Council, the Joint Chiefs of Staff, etc.—throw caution to the winds when they meet to consider possible military action? Would they risk military intervention as a group when none of them would do so if they made the decision alone and in the privacy of their offices? Would a surgeon be inclined not to risk surgery on the basis of his own diagnosis but go ahead and recommend it on the basis of the same facts when consulting with a group of other surgeons?

Practical questions undoubtedly stimulated many experiments on the risky shift, but as Pruitt (1971b) has pointed out, the evidence probably has greater theoretical than practical import. As we shall see, conservative shifts also occur in group decision-making, and group shifts occur on matters that are irrelevant to risk. A number of competing theories have been developed to explain these shifts in choice, and evidence has been gathered for and against each theory.

1. Diffusion of Responsibility Theory

A person who makes a decision by himself assumes sole responsibility for the consequences of his choice. But when a number of people reach a consensus, it is difficult to attribute responsibility to any single person. Each group member is more willing to gamble when making a collective rather than an individual decision. Wallach, Kogan, and Bem (1964) advanced the hypothesis that the risky shift occurs because of the diffusion of responsibility in a group for any negative consequences that might occur as a result of the group's choice.

In a test of the responsibility diffusion hypothesis, Wallach, et al gave subjects the task of solving problems of varying difficulty with actual monetary rewards determined by the level of difficulty selected. The greater the difficulty of a problem, the greater the risk of failing to solve it. Three conditions were produced: each subject chose the level of difficulty that he would attempt (Control), the group selected a problem for a designated member to attempt (Group Decision), or one individual was by chance designated to select the difficulty level of the problem for the group (Individual Decision). In the control condition each individual was responsible for his own outcome, but in the other conditions the individual's success or failure determined whether all members of the group would win the money. When subjects' individual decisions determined the outcome for all group members a conservative shift occurred. They chose less difficult problems than did control subjects. A risky shift occurred (more difficult problems were chosen) when responsibility for success or failure belonged to the whole group.

It could be presumed that anxiety about being responsible for the possible negative consequences of a decision is what causes an individual to make conservative choices. A highly anxious person would be afforded shelter if responsibility is diffused in a group. People with very little anxiety should gain comparatively little courage, comfort, or shelter in a group because they are willing to take risks as individuals. According to this reasoning, highly anxious persons should make greater shifts in a risky direction than nonanxious persons. Kogan and Wallach (1967a) found support for this deduction from the responsibility diffusion hypothesis. All subjects were pretested for chronic anxiety levels and ushered through the Stoner procedures. All the subjects made risky shifts, but those with high anxiety levels showed a greater shift than those with low anxiety.

Responsibility diffusion should be greater when the consensual nature of a group's decisions are stressed as compared with a situation in which the group discusses an issue but each individual makes his own decision. Wallach and Kogan (1965) had subjects make private decisions on the Choice Dilemma Questionnaire and then assigned them to one of two conditions: (1) the usual group decision-making situation in which consensus was to be reached, or (2) a group discussion of items without an attempt to reach consensus and then a second private set of judgments on the CDQ by each subject. Both conditions produced a risky shift and there was no difference between them—a clear disconfirmation of the responsibility diffusion hypothesis. There was no shift in a third condition in which consensus was reached without discussion.

Wallach and Kogan took their evidence seriously and revised their theory to account for the data. According to the revised theory, group discussion is the essential element and leads to the development of *affective bonds* between members. The causal chain of events can be summarized: "(1) group discussion creates affective

bonds; (2) affective bonds permit diffusion of responsibility; (3) diffusion of responsibility reduces fear of failure; (4) reduced fear of failure produces the risky shift" (Dion, Baron, & Miller, 1970, p. 312).

A direct relationship between affective bonds and the risky shift has been found. Pruitt and Teger (1969) obtained a positive correlation between measures of group cohesion and shifts toward risk. In a more indirect affirmation of this relationship, Kogan and Wallach (1967a) found that defensive persons, who would presumably avoid close affective bonds with others for fear of exposing their personal weaknesses, shifted less than relatively less defensive persons. On the other hand, Dion, Miller, and Magnan (1971) directly manipulated affective bonds and found the opposite relationship. The greater the bonds, the less the risky shift. In one condition group members were led to expect they would be very congenial; in a second condition the subjects were informed they were quite different from one another and probably would not be congenial. The highly cohesive groups did not shift toward risk, whereas the less cohesive groups did. Nevertheless, Dion et al. interpreted their findings as supporting the responsibility diffusion hypothesis. According to their interpretation, persons who are attracted to one another in a group are less likely to assign to other group members the blame for the negative consequences of group decisions than are members of groups with less cohesion.

In addition to the mixed character of the evidence, Pruitt (1971b) has summarized some damaging criticisms of responsibility diffusion theory. He notes that several items on the CDQ reliably produce shifts toward caution. Whether a risky or conservative shift occurs in a group apparently depends on the nature of the decision to be made. For example, subjects choose less risky alternatives in groups than when alone on Item 12, which reads:

12. Mr. M is contemplating marriage to Miss T, a girl whom he has known for a little more than a year. Recently, however, a number of arguments have occurred between them, suggesting some sharp differences of opinion in the way each views certain matters. Indeed, they decide to seek professional advice from a marriage counselor as to whether it would be wise for them to marry. On the basis of these meetings with a marriage counselor, they realize that a happy marriage, while possible, would not be assured.

Pruitt notes that the reasoning involved in diffusion of responsibility theory applies only to shifts toward risk; it cannot explain conservative shifts where there is no responsibility to diffuse. Secondly, individual decisions made six weeks after group discussion still reflect a shift toward risk even though the group is no longer part of the decision process and cannot assume any of the responsibility for the decision. A third criticism involves the fact that the hypothetical problems of the CDQ have no real consequences for group members, and it is difficult to understand why subjects should be concerned about being blamed for outcomes which never actually occur. Finally, risky shifts occur without any group interaction; learning what other persons have chosen merely by listening to a taped discussion (Kogen & Wallach, 1967b), listening to a live discussion or watching it through a one-way mirror (Lamm, 1967), or simply having all group members hold up cards showing their choices (Teger & Pruitt, 1967) all have produced shifts toward risk. How can people shift the burden of blame to others who are not involved in their decision-making? These criticisms of responsibility diffusion theory have been sufficiently convincing to cause social psychologists to seek alternative explanations of choice shifts in groups.

2. Familiarization Theory

Experience with risky situations may reduce an individual's fear of negative conse-

quences. A person may hesitate when he first faces a hazard such as jumping off a diving board or driving along a narrow mountain road, but familiarization with the situation may reduce his original fear or cause him to reconsider the alternative outcomes (see the discussion of desensitization in Chapter 6, Box 6.2). The hazards associated with a risky situation may be salient at first, but with closer examination the favorable outcomes associated with taking the risk may loom larger. Bateson (1966) has suggested that familiarization with the CDQ problems, which is promoted by group discussions, accounts for the risky shift.

Bateson compared subjects who engaged in group discussion with others who were asked to write arguments for and against the available alternatives. The subjects in both conditions evidenced a shift toward risk in the same amount. Flanders and Thistlethwaite (1967) found similar support for familiarization theory.

Despite the commonsense appeal of Bateson's analysis and the supporting evidence from two studies, the familiarization theory has not fared well. A series of experiments have failed to find a shift toward risk among subjects who were familiarized with the CDQ items (Bell & Jamieson, 1970; Fraser, 1970; St. Jean, 1970; Teger, Pruitt, St. Jean, & Haaland, 1970). There are a number of theoretical limitations to the familiarization theory, also. It does not account for shifts toward caution and provides no means for explaining why group cohesion and other factors influence the shift to risk.

3. Leadership and Rhetoric Theories

During group discussions and decision-making a single individual may have great influence over other members. If this group leader also is someone who tends to take great risks, then the risky shift may be due simply to social influence (Collins & Guetzkow, 1964; Marquis, 1962). In groups that shifted toward risk, the subjects who made risky decisions while alone were perceived by other members to be the most influential during group discussions (Wallach, Kogan, & Bem, 1962; Wallach, Kogan, & Burt, 1965). Conversely, the most cautious individuals were identified as most influential in groups that shifted toward caution (Brown, 1965; Rabow, Fowler, Bradford, Hofeller, & Shibuya, 1966). This evidence is not compelling, however, because it poses a chicken-and-egg problem. Which comes first, the perception of influence or the choice shifts of group members? It is just as plausible to suggest that the subjects perceived the most extreme person as a leader because of their own shifts as it is to state that the most extreme person was the cause of the shifts.

Direct tests of the leadership hypothesis have typically led to negative results. Vidmar (1970) set up groups composed entirely of persons who had made nonrisky choices when alone and still obtained a risky shift. Since there was no early risk advocate in the groups, it is not apparent who should be identified as the leader. In a similar disconfirmation of leadership theory, Hoyt and Stoner (1968) formed discussion groups made up of persons with homogeneous risk-taking scores. With no disparity in risk-taking preferences among group members, no leader could emerge yet a risky shift was manifested.

A study reported by Teger and Pruitt (1967) suggests that more than one process is involved in the risky shift. One group of subjects exchanged information about their choices on the CDQ by holding up cards with their choices marked on them. After this information exchange each subject was asked to make a second independent decision. A second group engaged in group discussion before making individual decisions. The information-exchange condition produced a small risky shift, while the discussion condition produced a rather substantial shift. Thus, both information about how other people choose and discussion itself appear to affect choice shifts.

Kelley and Thibaut (1969) have suggested that risky arguments are more persuasive than conservative arguments. They maintain that there "are two related aspects of the risky position that may give the proponent of such a position a disproportionate weight in open discussion: (1) the 'rhetoric of risk' is more dramatic, and (2) the conflicts and uncertainties entailed in accepting the riskier alternative might lead the proponent of such alternatives to state his arguments with heightened intensity and amplitude. In short, he may have the advantage of a more potent language, more intensively produced" (p. 82). Although the rhetoric-of-risk notion has some common-sense appeal, it remains untested. How it would explain shifts to caution is not clear.

4. Value Theory

The economic ideology of capitalism extols the virtues of risk-taking. Investment, innovation, and many other decisions depend upon the willingness of entrepreneurs to risk losing their venture capital. Noting that American culture generally values risk-taking, Brown (1965) has proposed a cultural value theory of the risky shift. According to this theory, when an individual is first presented with the CDQ, he makes his choices match with what he considers to be the average amount of risk other subjects are likely to choose. Later, when placed in a group setting, he gains information about the values of the other members. He and the others "discover that they are failing to realize the ideal of riskiness that they may have thought they were realizing. Consequently, they feel impelled to move in a risky direction both in accepting the decision of the group and in changing their private opinions. Subjects at or above the group mean feel no such impulsion; they are relatively risky just as they meant to be. The result would be, of course, a shift in the group decision toward greater risk than the mean of the individual decisions" (p. 701).

The components of Brown's theory can

be quickly summarized as including a cultural value assigned to risk and caution, gathering information about the decisions of other group members, making social comparisons, and a concern for acceptance (or impression management) that results in shifts toward the value manifested by the decisions of the other members. A wide variety of experimental approaches have provided support for this theory.

If risk has value, then those who display risky decision making should gain social approval. Madaras and Bem (1968) tested this hypothesis by creating fictitious individuals who allegedly had made either risky or cautious decisions on risk-oriented items. Subjects were asked to rate these individuals on a semantic differential scale. Those who took risks were evaluated more positively than cautious decision-makers. Although this experiment did not include an evaluation of decision-makers under conditions where caution is the relevant cultural value, the theory predicts that cautious people would be evaluated more positively in these circumstances.

Pruitt (1969) has observed what he has called the *"Walter Mitty effect."* Walter Mitty is a James Thurber character who is very meek and timid and frequently indulges in daydreaming. His fantasies are centered on performing heroic deeds requiring enormous courage. In an experiment, Pruitt had subjects make independent decisions on the CDQ and asked them also to rate the degree of risk or caution associated with each alternative. Some subjects made their ratings first and then their decisions, and others followed the opposite procedure. Although both groups made equally risky decisions, those who made their decisions first rated them as more risky. Thus they had a tendency, as does Walter Mitty, of making rather conservative decisions but imagining themselves to be high risk takers.

Higbee (1971) also found a Walter Mitty effect when his subjects played a game of strategy. They repeatedly reported they would take greater risks in the future than they had in the past. Higbee referred to this phenomenon as the "just-wait-until-next-time" effect. It seems apparent that people place a value on the *appearance* of being risk-takers, presumably because of the high value placed on risk in our culture.

Choosing a risky alternative may be an impression management strategy undertaken to elicit social approval from a group that values risk. In this case, people will believe that their judgments are more risky than those made by the average person. Investigations have supported this hypothesis. Subjects were asked to make independent decisions and then to estimate the average decision that others would make. They guessed that others would make more cautious decisions than their own on items that usually produce a risky shift and more risky decisions on items that typically produce a conservative shift. (Fraser, 1970; Levinger & Schneider, 1969; Wallach & Wing, 1968). Even when Ferguson and Vidmar (1971) had subjects participate in group discussions, they still perceived themselves as more extreme than other group members. On a post-experimental questionnaire, the subjects showed a preference for being among the most risky members of the group on risk-oriented items and among the most conservative on caution-oriented items.

Risk-taking conveys the impression of expertise. Subjects view high risk takers as more competent than cautious decision-makers (Jellison & Riskind, 1970). Furthermore, when asked to designate the decision they most admired in an experimental situation, subjects chose decisions riskier than their own (Lamm, Schaude, & Trommsdorff, 1971; Levinger & Schneider, 1969).

When the strands of evidence are put together, a picture emerges revealing that people admire risk-taking, view themselves as more courageous than others, and perceive their own decisions as riskier than they really are. The reverse of this picture is true when a value is placed on caution. The facilitative function played by group discussion in choice shifts suggests that at least two processes are at work. The discovery of the choices made by others allows an individual to make social comparisons. But unlike conformity situations, in which subjects are apprehensive about standing in isolation, group decision-making involving risk encourages a person to seek notice by taking a more extreme position than other group members. By so doing, he proclaims what he values and presumably earns the favorable evaluation of others for doing so.

5. Social Processes Theory

Each of the above theories has focused on the risky or conservative nature of decision-making in terms of the probability of negative consequences flowing from the alternative chosen. It has become clear that similar social processes operate in group discussions of issues not related to risky decisions. Individuals shift toward a more extreme position in group discussions of political attitudes (Moscovici & Zavalloni, 1969), the educational institution they are attending (Doise, 1969), the selection of consumer products (Johnson & Andrews, 1971), dilemmas placing values in conflict (Myers & Bishop, 1971), and in a person perception task (Moscovici, Zavalloni, & Weinberger, 1972). Any issue relevant to the group's values provides an opportunity for an individual to proclaim his worth by expressing opinions strongly supporting those values.

Informational and normative influence produce about the same effects on group decision-making as in traditional social conformity studies. Baron, Dion, Baron, and Miller (1971) provided a clear demonstration of normative influence. One week after making their independent decisions on CDQ items, subjects were assembled into groups, were given their original questionnaires with their answers on them, and were asked to discuss four items. They were asked to try to reach a unanimous decision, but it was not required.

The groups were composed of one naive subject, who was either risky or conservative in making his original decisions, and three confederates who argued for either extremely risky or extremely conservative choices that were at least two scale positions different from the subject's prior decisions. The items discussed were either all risk-oriented or all caution-oriented. Control groups provided information about how far individuals shifted when taking the CDQ twice without contact with each other. Risky and conservative subjects comparable to those in the experimental groups served as controls for both risk-oriented and caution-oriented items.

As can be seen from the summary of results shown in Table 13.3, the artificial group consensus provided by the three confederates had a powerful effect in producing shifts in the subjects. When the group placed a high value on risk, the subjects moved toward a more risky decision, and when the group valued caution, they moved toward a more conservative decision. The group pressure made all the difference; the risky or conservative nature of the items as reflected in previous research made none. However, the subjects were clearly attentive to the more general cultural value associated with the content of the item. They rated groups that put pressure on them in a direction opposite to the cultural value of the items as less intelligent, less democratic, and less satisfactory than groups that had the "right" values.

Informational influence can also have a strong impact on choice shifts. Bennett and Lindskold (1973) ascertained the average risk taken by a group of students on the CDQ. A second group was provided with false norms; they were told that a control group of college students like themselves had made an average decision choice two levels higher than was really the case. When the subjects were then asked to make independent decisions, their choices were much more risky than those of the control subjects. Vinokur and Burnstein (1974) have tried to show that the risky-shift is simply a

Table 13.3   The Effects of Artificially Created Consensus Regarding the Value of Risk or Caution on the Choice Shifts of Subjects and Ratings of the Consensus Groups. [a]

Experimental conditions	Shift [b] towards risk	Group Ratings [c]		
		Intelligent	Democratic	Satisfactory
Risk-oriented items				
Risky consensus	7.14	24.28	23.57	23.57
Risky control	1.29			
Cautious consensus	−6.11	21.50	19.62	22.62
Cautious control	.89			
Caution-oriented items				
Risky consensus	6.80	20.20	18.80	21.40
Risky control	−1.75			
Cautious consensus	−6.66	22.80	22.10	24.50
Cautious control	1.52			

[a] After Baron, Dion, Baron, and Miller, 1971.
[b] High scores indicate an increase in risk and negative scores indicate a decrease.
[c] High scores indicate more favorable ratings.

matter of group problem solving in which persuasion is a major factor. They have demonstrated that the frequency and persuasiveness of pro-risk and pro-caution arguments during discussions are directly related to the type of shift displayed by a group. Furthermore, they ascertained that only a few group members knew the relevant arguments prior to group discussions. In one of their experiments Vinokur and Burnstein had individual subjects read 20 pro-caution or pro-risk arguments previously provided by other subjects who rated their persuasibility. The subjects displayed a shift that was consistent with the type of arguments thay had read and which correlated with the rated persuasiveness of the arguments. It was therefore concluded that group shifts are a product of relevant and persuasive information.

Ebbesen and Bowers (1974) prepared tapes of discussions in which the proportion of risky and conservative arguments was varied (.10, .30, .50, .70, or .90). After subjects made independent choices on the CDQ, they listened to one of the taped discussions and made independent choices a

second time. The type and magnitude of the shift they displayed was directly related to the predominance of a particular kind of argument in the overheard group discussion. As can be seen in Figure 13.4, when the group made predominantly conservative arguments, the subjects shifted toward caution, and when tapes contained predominantly risky arguments, the subjects shifted toward risk. When the proportion of arguments was 50-50 and the subjects could detect no preference in the group for one or the other value, no choice shift occurred.

6.   Choice Shifts Outside the Laboratory

Risky and conservative shifts have been shown in groups when subjects were given hypothetical choices or were asked to discuss abstract or theoretical issues, but research has not shown a risky shift in real life situations (Cartwright, 1973). The research on choice shifts has limited generalizability because of its total reliance on a single specialized experimental instrument (the CDQ). The study of choice shifts in gambl-

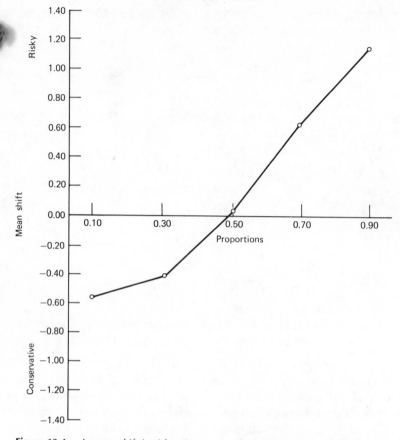

Figure 13.4. Average shift in risk estimates as a function of the proportion of risky arguments that subjects heard. (After Ebbeson and Bowers, 1974.)

ing situations with real monetary consequences has produced inconsistent results. An attempt to engineer a risky shift at a race track failed. Bettors were offerred a free $2 ticket if they would make their choices jointly with two other persons; rather than picking long shots, the groups picked favorites—safer bets than the ones they had just made as individuals (McCauley, Stitt, Woods, & Lipton, 1973). Perhaps this shift toward caution represented a concern for impression management. The bettors could look good in front of the experimenter if their horse won, and of course the favorite was most likely to win.

The research on choice shifts may be disappointing to social philosophers, since it does not really bear upon Whyte's concern about the effects of mass society on the independence and innovativeness of the individual. Nor can it be said that the Joint Chiefs of Staff are likely to make riskier decisions than would one officer by himself. On the other hand, individuals do spend a great deal of time in groups discussing issues or problems, and these discussions are often of a hypothetical nature in which the individual can use tactics of self-presentation. The role of cultural values, normative and informational influence, direct persuasion, and an individual's attempt to present himself favorably to group members have been rather clearly illustrated.

B. Groupthink

Laboratory studies of group decision-making usually involve a number of strangers collected on an ad hoc basis by an experimenter to solve a problem he selects. The situation is different in nonlaboratory situations. Janis (1972) has analysed a set of important governmental decisions on foreign policy and has found that long-standing, cohesive groups tend to arrive at decisions in a characteristic way which he calls *groupthink*. A major concern of cohesive groups is to maintain their consensus, and striving to do so impairs their decision-making, reality testing, and moral judgment. Janis reached this conclusion after examining American planning for the Bay of Pigs invasion of Cuba, the American decision to invade North Korea, the U.S. failure to read signals warning of the Japanese sneak attack against Pearl Harbor at the start of World War II, and the escalation of the Vietnam war.

1. Symptoms of Groupthink

Janis has compiled a list of symptoms of the groupthink syndrome, shown in Table 13.4. These symptoms can be illustrated in the context of the Bay of Pigs disaster. President Kennedy's highly intellectual set of advisors were basking in the euphoria of invulnerability; everything had gone right since the opening of the Kennedy drive in 1956 to capture the 1960 Presidential election. It seemed that nothing could stop them from succeeding in implementing their plans, so they tended to ignore glaring defects in their thinking. The group had an assumed air of consensus. Several of the President's senior advisors had strong doubts about the Bay of Pigs planning, but the group atmosphere inhibited them from voicing criticism. Thinking became simplified into black-and-white, either-or terms. The advisors viewed themselves as strong and intelligent good guys, while the other side was made up of weak and stupid bad guys. In their quest for group consen-

Table 13.4   The Groupthink Syndrome.[a]

---

1. An illusion of invulnerability, shared by most or all the members, which creates excessive optimism and encourages taking extreme risks;

2. Collective efforts to rationalize in order to discount warnings which might lead the members to reconsider their assumptions before they recommit themselves to their past policy decisions;

3. An unquestioned belief in the group's inherent morality, inclining the members to ignore the ethical or moral consequences of their decisions;

4. Stereotyped views of enemy leaders as too evil to warrant genuine attempts to negotiate, or as too weak and stupid to counter whatever risky attempts are made to defeat their purposes;

5. Direct pressure on any member who expresses strong arguments against any of the group's stereotypes, illusions, or commitments, making clear that this type of dissent is contrary to what is expected of all loyal members;

6. Self-censorship of deviations from the apparent group consensus, reflecting each member's inclination to minimize to himself the importance of his doubts and counterarguments;

7. A shared illusion of unanimity concerning judgments conforming to the majority view (partly resulting from self-censorship of deviations, augmented by the false assumption that silence means consent);

8. The emergence of self-appointed mindguards—members who protect the group from adverse information that might shatter their shared complacency about the effectiveness and morality of their decisions.

---

[a] After Janis, 1972, pp. 197–198.

sus, a stereotyped view of the situation was adopted in place of the more complex, differentiated assessment demanded by the available (if unsought and undigested) facts.

The group protected itself against possible criticism and a breach of consensus in a number of ways. Attorney General Robert Kennedy and Secretary of State Dean Rusk served as "mindguards," who suppressed the views of opponents by recourse to either of two arguments: (1) the decision to go ahead had already been made and everyone should help the President instead of distracting him with dissension; and (2) no check of the assumptions underlying the planning could be made because it would compromise the secrecy required for its successful implementation.

The way the meetings were conducted served to suppress dissent. When a point of criticism was raised, the President encouraged the CIA planners of the invasion to respond immediately to it. In a specific instance recounted by Janis, Senator Fulbright raised strong objections to the plan and correctly predicted some of the adverse effects the invasion would have on American foreign relations. Rather than discuss Fulbright's criticisms, the President returned to taking a straw vote of his advisors on the plan. The group maintained its consensus to support the plan, and Arthur Schlesinger, Jr., one advisor who was known to be in agreement with Fulbright, was not even called upon for his vote because time had run out.

An attempt to maintain consensus produces a number of defects in the planning process: (1) only a few courses of action are considered; (2) once it is discovered that the majority of a group prefers a particular course, the drawbacks and risks associated with that course are given insufficient attention; (3) plans initially rejected are not reconsidered to explore possible less obvious gains and ways of reducing costs that earlier seemed prohibitive; (4) the group spends more time considering arguments

favoring the consensus than arguments against it and for alternative plans; and (5) optimism about the adopted plan causes the group to overlook the preparation of contingency plans to deal with setbacks that may occur as a result of bureaucratic inertia, political sabotage, inefficiency, or other accidents that may endanger its success.

According to Janis, these defects in planning are illustrated by the six assumptions made by the Advisory group in devising the Bay of Pigs invasion of Cuba in April, 1961: (1) the cover story that the invasion was carried out by Cuban expatriates would be accepted and the U.S. government would not be implicated in the operation; the lid blew off of this cover story very quickly; (2) the Cuban Air Force was ineffectual and could easily be destroyed; on the contrary, it was very effective; (3) the 1400-man invasion brigade had high morale and could carry out the operation without American ground support; actually, the high morale was a result of reliance on a United States guarantee to make the invasion successful; (4) the Cuban Army was not prepared to withstand an invasion; it turned out that they were fully mobilized and well trained; (5) uprisings would emerge in the Cuban underground to support the invasion and contribute to Castro's demise; the extent of underground activities was overestimated and the support for Castro in the Cuban population was grossly underestimated; and (6) the invaders could join guerillas in the Escambray Mountains if the main operation failed; the simple scanning of a map would have led to the realization that 80 miles of swamps and jungle stood between the invaders and the mountains. Thus, all of the assumptions proved to be incorrect.

2. Avoiding Groupthink

Sobered by the Bay of Pigs fiasco, the same group of advisors engaged in a very different kind of planning process 18 months later when they were faced with the Cuban missile crisis. The Soviet Union was installing ballistic missiles with nuclear warheads within 90 miles of the continental United States, and our government had to decide what to do about it. Now all members of the group were encouraged to question all ideas and facts, no matter who presented them. They were not restricted to their roles as spokesmen for various departments of government or special interests. Their discussions were not formally organized with an agenda, and subcommittee meetings away from the consensus-producing environment of the Cabinet Room were encouraged. Sessions were held outside the always forbidding presence of the President to encourage a broad airing of views. Early commitment to any single plan was discouraged, while alternative courses of action were presented and debated. There was an explicit and conscious attempt to develop as many alternatives as possible. (This kind of strategy for creative planning by a group is similar to the technique known as *brainstorming*, which is discussed in Box 13.1.)

There was no organized subgroup among the advisors advocating or defending a prepared course of action as in the Bay of Pigs discussions. The Joint Chiefs of Staff were not given a stronger voice than any other group simply because of the obvious military aspects of the situation. Consideration was given to American moral commitments under the Monroe Doctrine. Robert Kennedy argued against a sneak attack on Cuba on moral grounds, likening such an action to the Japanese attack on Pearl Harbor. Specific attention was directed toward developing a non-stereotyped view of the enemy and scenarios were considered from the Soviet Union's point of view. The advisors wanted to avoid placing the Soviet Union in an humiliating position where that nation either had to fight or lose face. The ultimate decision to stand firm militarily but without provoking World War III and to promise not to invade Cuba in exchange for the Soviet withdrawal of missiles worked. This

planning took place over the course of several days and some of the participants have indicated that had the decision been made in a shorter period of time, pressures on the group might have promoted the defects associated with groupthink. Crisis decision-making is characterized by groupthink because of the short time period within which a plan must be devised, adopted, and implemented.

3. Research Evaluation of Groupthink

The analysis of groupthink provided by Janis is a creative synthesis of historical records and laboratory studies of small group behavior, as well as research on human behavior under conditions of stress. The procedures followed in his analysis are necessarily incomplete and selective with respect to the available evidence. Nevertheless, his hypotheses and analyses have strong commonsense appeal and deserve careful investigation.

One difficulty facing the laboratory researcher is that he is usually restricted to the use of ad hoc groups assembled from classes of college students. The cohesion of longstanding groups and the intricacies of political decision networks, characteristics considered by Janis as essential for groupthink, are difficult to duplicate in a laboratory setting. Nevertheless, simulations of international crisis situations in the laboratory have produced manifestations of groupthink, including a narrowing of the alternatives considered, a stereotyping of the enemy by lower status decision-makers, and an increase in the frequency of consensus by group members (Druckman, 1968; Guetzkow, 1968; Hermann, 1965). Natural observation and field research will be needed to supplement laboratory studies in developing a network of evidence to evaluate groupthink theory.

IV. GROUP PROBLEM-SOLVING

Most of the work done in modern technological societies is carried out through

Box 13.1   BRAINSTORMING

An advertising man (Osborn, 1957) heralded the promise of free-wheeling group discussions for generating creative alternatives and perspectives. He argued that a group could produce more unique ideas than an individual if the proper atmosphere was created. To create this atmosphere the following rules should be followed: (1) participants should express all their ideas without concern for their quality or fear about the reactions of others, (2) no idea should be evaluated until all ideas have been advanced, and (3) each participant should freely elaborate on the ideas presented by others (Shaw, 1971, p. 71). The view that shedding all constraints on the elaboration of ideas and removing all concern about being right, wrong, or just plain crazy will allow the generation of usefully creative ideas. This sounds good in theory but has not received very encouraging empirical support.

Taylor, Berry, and Block (1958) reported findings that are characteristic of the available research. They gave brainstorming instructions to subjects in four-person groups and compared the ideas they generated with those developed by individuals working alone. The output of the subjects who worked alone was combined to make up nominal four-person groups; that is, four persons who worked alone were randomly selected and their ideas were combined as if they had been in a group. The problems provided to the subjects were designed to be somewhat bizarre or were such that a wide variety of suggestions would be appropriate. For example, the subjects were asked to list the benefits and difficulties that would occur if all persons born after 1960 had an extra thumb on each hand, to propose steps that could be taken to deal with the effects of population growth on public school enrollment, and to develop means to promote European tourism in the United States. Contrary to Osborn's claims, the production of ideas and unique proposals was greater in the nominal groups than in the real groups.

There is some support for the presumption that apprehension about the reception of strangers to one's novel ideas inhibits creativity. Cohen, Whitmyer, and Funk (1960) found that pairs of subjects who were trained in creative thinking and pairs who had chosen to work with one another generated more creative ideas than nominal pairs, inexperienced pairs, and pairs who had not chosen to work with one another. Thus, when experience or choice of partners makes a person relatively comfortable in the performance of a task, brainstorming may facilitate the development of new ideas.

---

the coordinated activities of a number of people. Placing a man on the moon or directing traffic at a major international airport requires extraordinary cooperation among many individuals. Steiner (1972) has described what must happen if a group is to transform its resources and skills into a product. Actions must "include the intellective and communicative behaviors by which members evaluate, pool, and assemble their resources; decide who shall do what, when; assign differential weights to one another's contributions; and extol one another to participate fully in the group's task-oriented activities" (p. 8).

Measures of the success of a group may involve its productivity, how well it meets some theoretical criteria, or how favorably its output compares with that of other similar groups. Sometimes a single individual may achieve as much or more than a group of people. The effectiveness of a problem-solving group may depend on the nature of the task, the number of persons in it and the pooled skills available, the internal organization of communications, and the effectiveness of the group's leader.

A. A Typology of Group Tasks

Some tasks are *divisible* into a set of subtasks, each of which can be carried out by a separate individual. In the production of a book, writing, editing, setting type, printing, designing the jacket, advertising, and shipping are usually separate activities, and different people specialize in performing each of them. *Unitary* tasks must be carried out by a single person even when they might in the abstract be subdivided. Theoretically, you and one of your classmates can divide the reading of this book; but such a division of labor will detract from each person's understanding of what is read, especially if you were to read every other page.

When a unitary task is assigned to a group, the product will depend on the performance of a single individual, but the group must decide which member's product will be accepted. Steiner (1972) refers to such a task as *disjunctive* because it requires an "either-or" decision by the group regarding whose contribution to accept as its own. Disjunctive tasks usually involve judgments evaluating which of several solutions is the best.

When more than one individual contributes to a group product, the nature of the task has implications for how the various activities will be combined. Some tasks require that the contributions of group members be additive, while other tasks combine activities in a conjunctive manner. An *additive* task requires that all members engage in essentially the same behavior, and group productivity is the sum of their efforts. At that point on an assembly line where each worker performs essentially the same operation, the output that feeds into the next stage of production is additive.

Sometimes an additive task requires the coordination of responses. In a tug-of-war, the total force exerted on a rope depends on the coordinated efforts of team members. Presumably, four people should be able to pull four times as forcefully as a single person. However, Dashiell (1935) reported that Ringlemann found a loss of efficiency in rope pulling proportional to the number of people involved. The amount of pull of each member of a team was separately measured, and then teams of two, three, and eight persons were observed. Given the individual measures of the members, the teams should have exerted pulls of 126, 189, and 504 kilograms; but the actual amount of pull for the teams was 118, 160, and 248 kilograms, respectively.

In a *conjunctive task,* the outcome of a chain of responses is dependent on the weakest link or the least competent member of the group; each individuals's contribution is crucial to the quality of the product. The quality of chamber music depends on the least proficient member of the quartet. A football team probes to discover the weaknesses of its opponent. Attempting to reach consensus in a group may result in a policy that represents the lowest common denominator. The distinction between disjunctive and conjunctive tasks is important. The quality of the group's performance is dependent on the most competent member in a disjunctive task, but depends on the skills of the least competent member in a conjunctive task.

B.   The Size of a Group and Its Productivity

Increases in the size of a group should be directly related to its productivity on an additive task. Usually, however, there is some limit to the number of persons that can add to the effectiveness of performance. The concerted campaign of the Chinese people to rid themselves of flies was limited by the number of such insects in that part of the world. Snow removal may be limited by the number of shovels available and the elbow room needed by each shoveler to work effectively. The limit to the number of people that can work on an additive task is fixed by the goal set for the group, the tools available, and the losses in efficiency that occur as a result of the growing need for coordination.

The motivation of individuals may decline when the number of persons in a group is large. In small groups each individual's performance is highly visible to other members. Wicker (1969b) found that members of small churches contributed more time to their organizations' programs than did members of large churches. The latter were also less critical of low participation. One reason for this reduction of motivation is that members of large groups are less likely to gain social approval for their contributions. In addition, investigators have found that members of large groups feel they have less influence in determining outcomes than do members of smaller groups (cf. Golembiewski, 1962).

Many of the early studies in social psychology were directed to finding the answer to whether groups could perform unitary judgmental tasks better than individuals. A classic study of this type was carried out by Shaw (1932), who compared single individuals with four-person groups on a set of three intellectual problems. The kinds of tasks given to the subjects were called "eureka" puzzles because once the solution is perceived, it is self-evidently true. For the group this is a disjunctive task, since a solution depends on the first person

who has the eureka experience. The so-called Tartaglia Problem was one of the three puzzles Shaw gave to subjects: "Three missionaries and three cannibals are on the A side of a river. Get them across to the B side by means of a boat that holds only two at a time. All the missionaries and one cannibal can row. Never, under any circumstances or at any time, may the missionaries be outnumbered by the cannibals."[1]

Groups solved more of these puzzles than did individuals. Shaw accounted for this result by observing that members of groups check against errors and help to reject incorrect solutions before they are offered as the group product. Rejections of incorrect solutions typically originate from other members rather than from the person proposing the solution.

In comparing the efficiency of individuals and groups, Taylor and Faust (1952) asked how many man-hours are required to solve a task. If each single subject in Shaw's experiment had had as much time to solve the puzzles as was taken collectively by the four-person groups, perhaps individuals would have been as or more successful. In a test of relative efficiency, Taylor and Faust had individuals, dyads, and four-person groups participate in a series of games of Twenty Questions. The number of questions required to answer each solution, the number of wrong guesses, and the time utilized were recorded. Groups made fewer errors and asked fewer questions than individuals, but the four-person groups were no better than the dyads. When the number of minutes taken to find solutions was used as a measure of efficiency, individuals were clearly superior to groups. Efficiency decreased as the number of persons working on this essentially unitary and disjunctive task was increased.

Stroop (1932) observed that groups

[1]   The answer is; (a) M1 and C1 cross, M1 returns; (b) M1 and C2 cross, C2 who rows, returns; (c) C2 and M2 cross, C2 returns; (d) C2 and C3 cross, C2 returns once again; (e) C2 and M3 cross and everyone is now on the other side.

make more judgments than individuals in a given period of time. If an individual were given the same number of opportunities to make judgments as occurs in a group, he might be just as accurate in solving a task. To test this hypothesis, subjects were asked to make comparative judgments of lifted weights. Comparisons between the average judgment of one person making five judgments and the judgments of five-person groups revealed little difference. Similar comparisons for 10, 20, and 50 persons in groups and an equal number of judgments by individuals showed that either increasing the size of the group or the number of judgments by individuals increased accuracy and to the same degree. These findings imply that a judgment by a single individual with superior ability may be better than the judgment of a group. Of course, the nature of a disjunctive task is that the quality of a group judgment will be determined by its most competent member.

Adding members to a group increases the probability that at least one member will possess the competence to solve a disjunctive task. However, this positive relationship between group size and efficiency depends on the distribution of skills in the group. When a wide range of abilities are represented in a group that must face a series of different disjunctive tasks, increases in size should contribute to group success. When additions to membership provide no further skills or resources or when the task requires little competence, increases in size will not contribute to group productivity (Steiner, 1972).

Since conjunctive tasks depend on the contribution of the least competent member, increases in group size are apt to detract from the quality of performance. Of course, this generalization is restricted by the nature of the task and the distribution of skills among group members. When the task is easy or everyone in the group is equally competent, increases in group size will not detrimentally affect performance. But when the abilities of group members vary widely, it is more probable that productivity will suffer by the addition of new members.

Coordination is critical to success when a task is divisible and various functions are distributed among group members. Steiner (1972) has indicated how increases in size complicate the coordination problem: "The number of ways in which available persons can be matched with a given number of subtasks necessarily increases very dramatically. If two persons are available to be matched with two subtasks, only two different patterns of specialization are possible. By chance alone, the group has a .5 probability of selecting the better of the two, and the simplicity of the situation is likely to permit members to make a better-than-chance decision. If three persons are available, there are six different ways of assigning at least one individual to each of two subtasks, and if the group contains four members there are 20 different ways of doing it" (p. 83). The problem of coordination can be the chief reason for losses in efficiency as an organization experiences growth.

C. Communication Patterns and Group Problem-Solving

The coordination of actions and the sharing of information that are characteristic of group problem-solving require communication among group members. While many work situations provide opportunities for face-to-face communications, modern technology has provided means of exchanging information indirectly, including the telephone, intercom systems, closed circuit television, computer linkages, radio, and so on. Each of these systems, along with old-fashioned memoranda and letters, provide ways to coordinate work activities. The efficiency of coordination depends on who communicates to whom and when.

The structure of communication channels can have large effects on group processes. To study these effects, Bavelas (1948) suggested a procedure by which various networks could be constructed. In a five-man group, for example, the members could be physically separated and a means of communicating installed, with different channels created by the pattern of connections between the members. Figure 13.5 shows several of the communication networks that are widely used in research. In the all-channel network, everyone can freely communicate to everyone else. In the wheel, four persons can communicate only to a central person (C), while the latter can communicate to everyone else. The accuracy, speed, and quality of task performance in each of these communication structures has been assessed.

Before the members of a group can solve a problem, they must discover what information they collectively possess. In an investigation of information exchange, Leavitt (1951) provided each member of a five-person group with a card that had five of six possible symbols on it. Each person's card had a different symbol omitted, so only one symbol was common to every card.

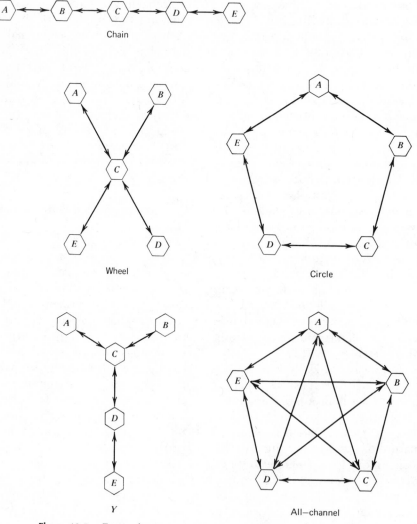

Figure 13.5. Types of communication networks in five-member groups.

The task given to the group was to discover which symbol all members had in common. They could communicate with one another only within the communication structure imposed by the experimenter. Four networks were created: circle, chain, Y, and wheel. There was no restriction on how often a person could communicate so long as he remained within channels. The task was considered solved when all members of a group discovered the correct symbol. Fifteen such tasks were solved by groups within each type of communication network. The dependent variables included the length of time it took to complete the task, the number of messages transmitted, the number of incorrect solutions reported by groups, and how much the subjects enjoyed the tasks. In addition, all the subjects were asked if their group had a leader and, if so, who it was.

The wheel network required fewer communications and produced fewer errors than did the other structures, while the worst performance occurred in the circle. Leavitt (1951) summarized the findings very succinctly: "Patternwise, the picture formed by the results is of differences almost always in the order *circle, chain, Y, wheel*. We may grossly characterize the kinds of differences that occur in this way: the circle, one extreme, is active, leaderless, unorganized, erratic, and yet is enjoyed by its members. The wheel, at the other extreme, is less active, has a distinct leader, is well and stably organized, is less erratic, and yet is unsatisfying to most of its members" (p. 46).

The task presented to subjects in all networks was conjunctive; each member had information that was needed for solving the group task. The task might also be considered disjunctive in the wheel network because information was channeled to the central member of the group who had to solve the problem and communicate his solution to the other members. The task was not completed until all members agreed with the central member's solution.

Whereas the wheel imposed a structure on the group, any structure could emerge in the circle. When no agreement was reached concerning who was to be the *keyman,* the one who collected the information and arrived at the solution, every member had to reach his own solution and seek agreement from all other members. The development of organization in the circle was complicated by the fact that at least two stages of communication were required to establish a keyman. In the wheel, each peripheral member could communicate his symbols directly to the central person, but in the circle, some members were once removed from the keyman no matter who he turned out to be. Thus peripheral group members and the keyman had to communicate through intermediaries. The need to use intermediaries provided an extra coordination problem for the members of the circle network and created delays in the transmissions of messages.

1. Task Complexity and Network Efficiency

The complexity of the task, the amount of information possessed by group members, and the competence of the keyman affect the relative efficiency of the various communication networks. Research has shown that when a task involves a simple coordination problem, a centralized network such as the wheel is more efficient, but decentralized networks (circle or all-channel) are superior in solving complex tasks (cf. Shaw, 1964).

Shaw (1954) explained this superiority of the circle over the wheel as due to the saturation of information in the latter network. The keyman in the wheel suffers from an information overload when the task is complex, and he may not always be the most competent member of the group. In the circle each person can communicate to two others, providing each with more opportunities to discover what others consider to be relevant and important and imposing more checks on errors made in transmission. The keyman in the wheel must be innovative and must be able to judge innovative proposals by group members or creative solutions may not be found. In a decentralized network, innovative suggestions by any member are more likely to be evaluated by the entire group. Since innovation and error detection are relatively insignificant in simple coordination tasks, centralized networks are more efficient in solving them.

2. Networks and Member Satisfaction

The morale of members of a group is directly related to the degree of responsibility and involvement they have in contributing to the solution of group tasks (Trow, 1957; Shaw, 1954). In a centralized network, the keyman is typically satisfied with his role while peripheral members tend to be dissatisfied. All members tend to have high morale in decentralized groups. Gilchrist, Shaw, and Walker (1954) varied the contribution that a peripheral member could make in centralized networks by giving him more or less information relevant to the task solution. The more information he could contribute, the greater his satisfaction with his position in the group. Coch and French (1958) found a similar effect on morale in a factory; when workers were involved in making decisions about changes in procedures or work assignments, morale and acceptance were much higher than when changes were simply imposed upon them by higher authority. Findings such as this one served as a foundation for the "human relations" approach to supervision in industry as opposed to traditional supervisory practice. Production is increased when workers have a voice in policy making and when they can gain psychological satisfaction through their work.

3. The Development of Organization Within Network Structures

After an organizational pattern is established in a group, the communication net-

work may lose its initial impact on the efficiency of task performance. Guetzkow and Simon (1955) observed the performance of circle, wheel, and all-channel groups over a lengthy set of trials. Organizational structures were given sufficient time to develop, and the early superior performance of wheel groups disappeared after 20 trials. According to Guetzkow and Simon, "these findings hint that the wheel groups, with the least difficult organizational problem, organized earliest; and that the all-channel groups, with the more difficult job, organized more slowly, but were eventually performing as well as the wheel groups; that the circle groups had difficulty in organizing, not reaching the optimal performance within the 20 trials allowed" (p. 242).

V. LEADERSHIP IN GROUPS

The special role of the leader in organized groups has received widespread research attention. Despite many decades of study, many of the fundamental questions remain unanswered. We will consider competing definitions of leadership, the evidence regarding the personal characteristics of leaders, the way they acquire and maintain authority, and the factors that contribute to their effectiveness.

A. Definitions of Leadership

Identifying a leader in a group seems like an easy task, but serious attempts to define leadership have run into complications. According to Bass (1960, p. 87), over 130 definitions were offered in the literature prior to 1949. These definitions can be grouped into several categories, based on (1) the degree of influence a single individual has over other group members, (2) the kinds of activities that must be performed by a keyman in a group, and (3) the acquisition and maintenance of authority in a group.

A *social influence* perspective considers leadership to be a matter of degree. Everyone in a group may be considered to be a leader at one time or another, depending on who influences whom and when. A group may not be constituted with one leader and many followers; instead, the members may each take their turn at exercising influence. This way of viewing leadership encourages a distinction between *formal* and *informal* leaders. A table of organization may stipulate that a particular role, such as supervisor or foreman, gives its incumbent authority over members of the group, whereas in actual practice, someone other than the formal authority may wield a great deal of influence. Formal and informal leaders may support one another or they may have conflicting objectives.

Behavioral definitions of leadership focus on what a leader does. For example, as Hemphill (1952) states: "To lead is to engage in an act which initiates structure in the interaction of others as part of the process of solving a mutual problem" (p. 15). Clarifying group goals, suggesting alternative possibilities for action, decision-making, recruiting support for a course of action, and coordinating the behavior of group members constitute the set of actions considered important in the study of leadership. According to such a definition, any member of the group who engages in any of these activities is performing an act of leadership.

The *authority* approach focuses on the possession of power resources by an individual. A person who performs a gatekeeper function in the flow of information, who occupies a keyman role in the communication structure of the group, or who possesses scarce and important information relevant to group goals will have an advantage over other members in acquiring authority. Political scientists have emphasized the control exercised over information by authorities. Schattschneider (1960) argued that the definition of the al-

ternatives open to decision is the supreme instrument of power. Similarly, Lasswell (1966) considered the giving and receiving of orientation as the fundamental characteristic of the leader-follower relationship. The leader can define the nature of issues, goals, and alternatives. As the result of his control over information and the legitimacy he has acquired, the authority (or leader) not only can prescribe what ought to be (the goals of the group) but what is (the alternatives available to the group). Consider the power of the President of the United States. The mere fact that he says something is good enough for many loyal Americans to believe that it must be so.

B. Traits of Leaders

The definition of leadership in terms of influence or power is a relatively recent development. The early study of leadership was guided by theories of history and by the requirements of a technocratic society. On the one hand, some researchers followed Carlyle's (1888) view that historical circumstances were created by great men, and set out to find the invariant characteristics that set leaders apart from others. This search was encouraged by the practical demands of industry and the military for executives to direct the activities of their bureaucracies. Some way of identifying people with leadership potential was desired by personnel officers throughout the world. On the other hand, many investigators became disillusioned by the lack of evidence linking personality characteristics with leadership performance. They leaned toward Tolstoy's theory presented in the novel *War and Peace* that all men are the pawns of historical forces and that the course of events produces leaders. They began a search for the situational factors affecting leadership behavior (a discussion of these views was presented earlier in Box 4.4).

The intensive search for the characteristics of effective leaders has yielded few consistent findings (cf. Gibb, 1969). A social influence perspective suggests some factors, like self-confidence, that may be linked to the frequency with which an individual exercises influence (see Chapters 8 and 9), and positive correlations have been found between measures of self-confidence and leadership status (Gibb, 1947). However, self-confidence is usually based on a person's experiences of success; hence, a leader's status and his self-confidence may stem from the same base—his competence. Perhaps a competent person becomes more confident after he acquires authority.

General assertiveness is often associated with leadership, and it is difficult to see how a person could become a leader if he were too shy to offer suggestions and propose goals to his group. Several studies have found positive correlations between extraversion or talkativeness and leadership status (Caldwell & Wellman, 1926; Goodenough, 1930; Norfleet, 1948). Bass (1949) and Bales (1953) have also observed that the amount of a person's participation in the group is positively related to his emergence as a leader.

Assertiveness and talkativeness may be related to leadership because of a belief by group members that quantity of participation is equivalent to quality of contribution. Riecken (1958) manipulated both the participation rate and the usefulness of information in four-man groups. The experimenter identified high and low participants while the groups discussed two human relations problems. Then a third problem was discussed, and in some groups a correct hint to the difficult solution was given to a high participant by the experimenter, while in the other groups the hint was given to a low participant.

Regardless of the merit of their suggestions, the high participants were perceived as contributing more to the solution than the low participants. The solution offered by the high participant with the hint was accepted two-thirds of the time, but only one-third of the time when it was contributed by the low participant. Unfortu-

nately, it is difficult to draw the conclusion that the rate of participation and not the value of the contribution led to the perception of emergent leadership. The way in which the information was presented to the group by the high and low participants was not controlled. The least talkative person may have been ineffective in making a suggestion—in making it clear, in advocating it, and in gaining credit for the idea.

Gintner and Lindskold (1975) reported a clarifying study in which a confederate provided information so the style of its presentation could be controlled. Subjects met in four-person groups to discuss two modern paintings; their task was to describe correctly what the artists were trying to communicate. In a high expertise condition, the confederate introduced herself as an art major and advanced strong, accurate, and perceptive opinions regarding the two paintings. In the low expertise condition, she identified herself as undecided about her college major, and during the discussions she made only rather obvious points. The amount of talking by the high and low expertise confederates was also manipulated; in each condition, she either talked more than any other group member (actually 52 percent of the total talk) or less than two of the other three members (actually 20 percent of the total talk). The subjects were asked to nominate a leader for their groups, to rate the effectiveness of the other members in guiding the discussion, and to indicate who contributed the best ideas.

The results are shown in Table 13.5. When the confederate was an expert, her rate of talking did not affect the number of leadership nominations she received nor the high ratings she got for guiding the group discussion and contributing the best ideas. However, when she was not an expert, her amount of talking did affect the measures; when the volume of her contribution was high, she gained ratings that were almost as positive as those obtained by the expert. It may be concluded that the

Table 13.5 Average Number of Leadership Nominations and Ratings of the Confederate. [a]

	Amount of talking			
	High		Low	
Dependent measure	Expert	Not expert	Expert	Not expert
Number of leadership nominations	2.67	1.67	2.67	0.17
Who guided discussion	11.33	10.17	10.50	4.67
Who contributed best ideas	11.83	8.17	11.67	4.67

[a] After Gintner and Lindskold, 1975.

perceived value of a member's contributions determines his selection as a leader, but if there is no competent person in a group, assertiveness alone will gain support.

Other traits have occasionally been found to be associated with leaders. They have been found to be taller than nonleaders (cf., Stogdill, 1948), but the correlation is weak and does not always appear. Even when height is placed at a premium, as on basketball teams, there seems to be no regular choice of the tallest man as captain or floor leader. Intelligence has sometimes been associated with leadership (cf. Mann, 1959), but here again the relationship is not stable. Sometimes general intelligence may be crucial, but in many groups there is a tendency to prefer someone of average intelligence over persons of either low or very high intelligence.

After reviewing all the evidence regarding the traits of leaders, Gibb (1969) concluded that there has been a general failure to find any definitive relationship between personality and leadership. As has been the case in other areas of research in social behavior, it is not known why personality factors contribute so little to our understanding of social psychological phenomena. Perhaps the relevant traits still have not been identified; perhaps our measures of the relevant traits are inadequate; or perhaps an interactionist view combining traits and situations needs to be worked

out. Whatever the reasons for the inconsistent and weak relationships discovered, there is very little encouragement for any theory of leadership based on the presumed characteristics of Great Men.

C. Acquisition and Maintenance of Authority

The chief basis of a leader's influence is his status in the group. Once he has acquired legitimate status and authority, subordinates comply with his demands and requests even in the absence of additional inducements and even when compliance is costly (Blau, 1964, p. 200). The exercise of authority does not require the direct use of threats, promises, rewards, or punishments.

Legitimate authority may be said to have the property of "requiredness"; a subordinate feels he *ought* to perform the behavior requested of him. Friedrich (1963) has defined legitimate authority in terms of its potential for "reasoned elaboration." By this he means that subordinates are willing to act without understanding the reasons for the leader's requests because they believe he could elaborate the reasons if there were time to do so. A surgeon in the middle of an operation cannot take the time to explain to his nurse why each command should be promptly obeyed; the nurse suspends her own judgment and complies to his commands because she believes that given enough time, he could elaborate all trust is therefore involved in granting legitimate authority to a leader.

1. The Acquisition of Authority

How does a formal leader acquire legitimate authority? The rules governing the members of a group or organization prescribe the proper channels of communication and decision and identify who should accept what directives from which other people (Goffman, 1963). A table of organization in formal groups specifies various positions of authority and usually specifies the range and limits of authority of each office. The authority of the occupant derives from his office and not from his personal characteristics. For this reason, Gamson (1968) has distinguished between authority and influence; the latter derives from the skills, tactics, and personal characteristics of the individual. Of course, a leader uses both his authority and his influence in obtaining compliance.

A person may be appointed to a position of authority or may emerge as a leader through democratic procedures. Business executives are not usually elected to office and are sometimes referred to as "heads" rather than leaders. Their legitimacy derives from the rewards and satisfactions their subordinates receive from the institution. The loyalty shown to an appointed head can be lost through practices that are considered unfair, such as demanding behavior that is considered beyond the scope of his authority (e.g., attempting to dictate political preferences) or enforcing an inequitable distribution of rewards.

A head can also expand the scope of his own authority. A supervisor may use his position to obtain rewards for his staff, such as unauthorized coffee breaks, thereby creating a feeling of obligation among his subordinates who may then comply with a wider range of his demands to pay off the social obligation incurred. Elected leaders can similarly affect the scope of their authority by the way they fill their offices.

Hollander's (1964) theory of idiosyn-

cracy credits (discussed in more detail earlier in this chapter—II, D, 3) considers the acquisition of authority as a matter of exchange. A leader earns his position through conformity to the normative structure of the group and by contributing significantly to the achievement of group goals. As a reward for his contributions, the emergent leader is given credits to expend in future idiosyncratic behavior without jeopardizing his authority. An overexpenditure of credits results in a loss of legitimate authority.

2. Gaining Endorsement

The endorsement of a leader refers to the satisfaction of group members with his policies and practices, and reflects how willing they are to have him serve as their spokesman and continue in his position of power over them. In a series of studies, Hollander and Julian (1970) examined factors that affect a group's endorsement of its leader. In the first study, the perceived competence of the leader and his motivation in solving the group's tasks were shown to be important in gaining endorsement.

Over 600 students were presented with written descriptions of a hypothetical leader and rated their endorsement of him. The source of the leader's authority was described as elected or appointed or was not mentioned. In addition, he was portrayed as competent or incompetent or no mention was made of the quality of his performance. Finally, his motivation was varied: he was described as motivated to solve the task, or as interested in the members of the group, or no mention was made of his motivation.

The source of the leader's authority had no effect on the degree of endorsement he received. He received more endorsement when he was competent than when he was not, and he was given more endorsement when he was perceived as motivated by the task or his interest in other members than when his motivation was not known.

According to exchange theory, a leader

should gain more endorsement when he is instrumental in helping a group achieve its goals, and he should lose endorsement when he is instrumental in the group's failure. Hollander and Julian tested this hypothesis by assembling students into four-person groups and directing them to devise a defense for a friend who had been accused of cheating on an examination. Following a 20-minute discussion, a group spokesman was chosen to present his brief at the inquiry; thereafter, he returned to the group with the inquiry board's verdict.

The competence of the spokesman, the source of his authority, and his success or failure in representing the group were manipulated. Subjects were identified as high or low on competence by assessing the frequency of their contributions to the group discussion. The spokesman was either appointed by the experimenter or elected by a rigged ballot. The result was that four types of spokesmen were created: appointed and elected leaders of high and low competence. To manipulate the spokesman's success or failure in representing the group's interests verdicts of "acquitted" or "guilty" were returned. After hearing the verdict the members rated how willing they would be to have the spokesman represent the group again.

The spokesman received more endorsement when he was competent rather than incompetent and when he was successful rather than unsuccessful in gaining the acquittal verdict. The appointed spokesman received high endorsement when he was either competent *or* successful. The elected spokesman received endorsement only when he was both competent *and* successful. Hollander and Julian interpreted these results as supporting "the general position that election builds higher expectation for success or higher demands by group membership on the leadership role" (p. 55). Elected leaders have a less secure basis of authority than do appointed heads, possibly because members assign greater responsibility to their leaders under

election conditions. Also, it is sometimes easier to change leaders when a democratic process is involved than when the structure of authority is less responsive to member control.

The idiosyncrasy credit theory implies that a leader may gain greater confidence and attempt more vetoes of group decisions, the more endorsement credits he accumulates. An elected leader may be presumed to come into office with some credits, since voters have expressed endorsement in choosing him. A head, however, must secure credits from his subordinates after his appointment. It can be predicted, therefore, that elected leaders will at first deviate more frequently from group consensus than appointed heads. Furthermore, it follows that the greater the endorsement of a leader, whether he is appointed or elected, the less need he has to justify his actions. An insecure leader must elaborate on the reasons for his actions to followers because they will not suspend their judgment and place their trust in him. Hollander and Julian tested and confirmed these hypotheses in a third experiment.

3. Normativity and Legitimate Authority

Michener and Burt (1974) have distinguished between endorsement and normativity in analysing the legitimate power of leaders. *Normativity* refers to the rules that define the scope and limits of authority of the occupant of a position. Three components are considered to be important in assessing normativity: (1) the group's consensus about the rules, (2) the magnitude of the sanctions possessed by the leader, and (3) the range of activities he is given authority to direct or control.

Any given norm may have more or less support in a particular group. We have seen that conformity is less apt to occur when there is a breach in the ranks of the majority; when one other person does not go along with the rest in the Asch situation, a subject is encouraged to act independently. A group almost always has expectations about the kinds of behavior a leader can command, and when there is little consensus about it, deference and compliance are likely to be low. For example, during the prohibition era in the U.S., it was against the law to sell, buy, or drink alcoholic beverages. However, many people did not believe the government had the right to dictate their private habits, and the law was frequently violated.

Failure on the part of a leader to use his power fairly may lead group members to form a coalition to replace him. In a laboratory demonstration of such revolutionary uprisings Michener and Lyons (1972) placed subjects in three-person groups to solve very difficult spatial judgment problems. All subjects were informed that one of the others would be assigned a high status role because of high ability demonstrated on a preliminary test. They were then physically separated and subsequent interaction took place through the exchange of notes. Actually, the experimenter played the role of the high status person who could decide on how to weigh the advice of group members in rendering a group judgment and on the allocation of winnings earned for accurate judgments. In every case the high status member took the heaviest role in making decisions and also took a disproportionate amount of the winnings for herself. This sequence of activities occurred over three consecutive problem solutions.

After each trial the two low status persons were provided the opportunity to communicate with each other. The messages received by subjects were actually sent by the experimenter and expressed continued strong support or opposition to the high status member. By the rules laid down by the experimenter at the beginning the two low status persons could agree to redistribute the winnings if they were sufficiently opposed to the actions of the high status person.

Messages received from the other group member expressing opposition to the high status person eroded subjects' support of the existing system and contributed to the development of a revolutionary coalition. The opposition messages stimulated coalitional behavior for two reasons. First, they made it obvious that a potential coalition was available for redistributing the winnings, and second, they probably influenced the perceived injustice of the high status member's allocation of the winnings. Thus as compared to subjects who received messages supporting the high status member, those who received opposition messages believed the distribution of winnings was more unfair. In another study Michener and Lawler (1975) found that endorsement for a leader was affected both by his success in achieving group goals and by his commitment to important moral ideals, such as those involved in allocating rewards to group members.

A source of influence is more likely to gain compliance, the greater the magnitude of the sanctions he controls (see Chapter 8, I, A). A leader's use of sanctions must be kept within the bounds of the norms governing the group to be effective. A supervisor may demand that a subordinate report to work on time by threatening a reduction in pay, a transfer, or even dismissal; but resistance rather than compliance is apt to occur should he threaten to seize the subordinate's personal property. The effects of the normativity of sanctions on the probability and degree of compliance by subordinates have not been experimentally examined. Historical accounts of revolutions frequently describe rulers who used their power in ways that violated the accepted norms of the people.

The range of activities that can be controlled by an authority is also circumscribed by rules that govern the group. The President, Congress, and the Judiciary are each assigned certain powers by the U. S. Constitution. In a parallel way, a supervisor is limited by the rules of his organization and the norms of his group, and he cannot make demands that are outside what is permitted by those rules. For example, he will be resisted if he demands that a subordinate buy a particular kind of family automobile. Nevertheless, this excessive use of power does occur, as the example in Box 13.2 illustrates.

Box 13.2   THE ABUSE OF AUTHORITY: HENRY FORD AND THE FIVE-DOLLAR DAY

One of the most interesting chapters in the history of industrial development in 20th-century America is provided by Henry Ford and the Ford Motor Company. The production line approach to the assembly of automobiles has affected the lives of millions of persons around the world since about 1900. Although a great deal of justifiable criticism has been aimed at the stultifying and alienating effects of work on the assembly line, some positive things can be said for Ford and some of his innovations.

Henry Ford possessed a rather Puritanical set of values and took a paternalistic approach in attempting to guide the lives of his workmen. He ran a well-maintained plant, complete with health and safety devices; but also he provided no place for the workmen to sit, and whistling, singing, and talking were forbidden (although this rule was not strictly enforced). Smoking was not permitted, and an employee guilty of excessive drinking was bound to be fired. Yet Ford hired many handicapped persons and ex-convicts, and English-language lessons were provided for the large number of immigrant workers.

In about 1913, Ford felt that the lives of his workmen would be improved—that they would be more decent persons—if their wages were much improved over the $2.70 to $3.30 per day then paid. Thus, on January 5, 1914, it was announced that workmen would go on three eight-hour shifts, and that they would be paid a basic wage of $5 per day. This announcement set the industry on its ear. Even Ford's top advisors thought he was being completely foolish. But Ford, of course, received a lot of praise for his humanitarian steps, even though he might also be criticized by his competitors for "pampering" his employees, for disturbing the "traditional" reliance on market forces to set wage rates in the industry, and for attempting to force them out of business by raising their labor costs.

Ford wanted to improve the lives of his workmen by this move, and he was not going to leave the improvement up to chance. In order to qualify for $5 per day, each workman had to pass an inspection. A crew of 150 investigators (each with interpreter, driver, and car) visited the workers in their homes to inquire regarding their religion, citizenship and citizenship intentions, number and age of dependents, ownership of home and size of mortgage, their debts, the amount of their savings, whether they had life insurance, who their doctor was, what they did for recreation, whether their habits were temperate, what kind of home conditions existed, whether they took in boarders, etc., etc. If the workers fell short on any of these measures, they could make the necessary corrections and become eligible for the higher wage. If they did not pass muster in 6 months, they were usually fired.

Actually very few men were fired. They wanted the benefits strongly enough to give at least the outward appearance of meeting Ford's standards. Certainly, however, most of them did not like his intervention in their lives. Some twenty years later, when labor unrest grew during the depression of the 1930's, Ford and his personnel director, Harry Bennett (a tough ex-sailor and ex-prize-fighter), used spies to weaken labor organization activity in their plants. In these years, more than 4000 men were fired, usually on trumped up charges and really because they showed sympathy to the union movement. Finally, pitched battles broke out and eventually organized labor moved into the Ford Motor Company. The paternalistic and coercive labor practices of Ford, Harry Bennett, and other officials who attempted control beyond the normal bounds of authority were eventually insufficient to suppress legitimate labor activity (see Nevins, 1954; Nevins and Hill, 1962).

Michener and Burt have argued that the three components of normativity are the bases of legitimate authority. They believe endorsement merely provides the leader with information by which he can judge his own performance and allows him to adapt to changing group conditions. His success in achieving group goals, his fairness in distributing rewards, and his conformity to group norms affect the endorsement of a leader, but according to Michener and Burt, they do not add to his authority. Hence subordinates should comply no more frequently with a popular than with an unpopular leader.

In support of this theory, Raven and French (1958a,b) found just as much compliance to a supervisor's commands whether or not he had been fair in distributing rewards in the group. However, it should be remembered that Hollander and Julian found that strongly endorsed leaders were encouraged to deviate from group decisions more often than weakly endorsed leaders. Thus, while endorsement may not gain more compliance for a leader, he may be encouraged to exercise more power. The overwhelming election victories of Lyndon Johnson and Richard Nixon may have encouraged them to make unpopular decisions in both foreign and domestic policies. But both of these presidents were probably less effective after they received strong endorsement at the polls than before, and presumably their loss of effectiveness can be attributed to normativity rather than endorsement. President Johnson pursued an unpopular and unsuccessful war in Vietnam, an action that ultimately lost for him the consensual support of the American people. President Nixon lost effectiveness because of the Watergate scandal, which consisted of a series of actions violating the norms considered appropriate to the activities of the executive branch of government.

D. Leadership Style and Effectiveness

Within the constraints of the rules and norms of his group, a leader has opportunity to fulfill the duties of his position using a variety of styles. Some leaders seem to be primarily task-oriented, while others give greater emphasis to maintaining group cohesion and are more sensitive to the feelings and needs of individual members. Leadership style may create a group atmosphere that has wide-ranging effects on behavior and morale. Fiedler (1964) has proposed that the effectiveness of various leadership styles is contingent on the situation, the nature of the task, and the power of the leader. The assessment of effectiveness thus requires an analysis of the specific behavior of the leader.

1. The Structure of Leadership Behavior

The most comprehensive examination of the behavior of leaders was undertaken at Ohio State University. A definition of leadership as the "behavior of an individual when he is directing the activities of a group toward a shared goal" (Halpin & Winer, 1952, p. 6) served as the basis for these studies. Subjects were asked to respond to questionnaires asking them what characteristics they considered most important in a leader. The responses were submitted to factor analysis, and the two most important factors identified were called *consideration* and *initiating structure*.

Among the kinds of behavior subsumed under "consideration" were warmth of personal relationships, openness in explaining actions, receptivity to communication from subordinates, mutual trust between leader and followers, and a democratic style that permitted group members to participate in decision-making. "Initiating structure" included behavior directed toward organizing and coordinating group activities, such as clarifying operating procedures and assigning group members to specific subtasks.

Two minor factors contributed to the picture of what makes an effective leader. *Production emphasis* represented the degree to which the leader focused on getting a job done. Such behavior emphasizes standards and schedules and is typified in pep talks and other motivating strategies. *Social sensitivity* was reflected by the leader's awareness of the feelings of group members. A leader with social sensitivity does not castigate or blame subordinates who make mistakes, does not make scapegoats out of others, and shows his concern about being liked by his followers. These two factors have been referred to as "job-centered" and "employee-centered" orientations.

Research subsequent to the Ohio State studies has established that consideration and initiation of structure are the two major dimensions of leadership behavior (Fleishman, Harris, & Burtt, 1955; Halpin, 1955). These two leadership functions do not always appear in a single individual but may be contributed by different group members (Fleishman & Peters, 1962; Halpin, 1956). When subjects are asked, following group discussion, who they perceive as the leader, they identify the person who made the most suggestions; but when they are asked who they like best, it is often the person who was the second most frequent contributor to group discussion (Bales, 1953). Thus the *task leader* need not be the same person as the *socioemotional leader* in a group.

2. Group Atmosphere

In a classic social psychological study, Lewin, Lippitt, and White (1939) investigated the effects of leadership styles on the behavior of group members. Clubs composed of 10- and 11-year-old boys were created, and three different "social climates" were established by the adult leader as the boys worked on carving models from soap. In democratic groups, the leader fostered group decisions on objectives and procedures, was friendly, and provided help when the boys sought it. In authoritarian groups, the leader gave orders, assigned the boys to tasks, and made decisions and changes without consulting them. In the laissez-faire groups, the leader was passive, merely handing out tools, not attempting to lead or coordinate group activities.

These styles produced dramatically different effects among the boys. In the authoritarian groups, the boys produced the greatest number of models; they were passive in the presence of the leader but engaged in misbehavior when he was out of the room. These boys took little pride in their work, often destroying their models after completing them. The boys in the laissez-faire groups were quite discontented about their work and with their Club; their output was lower than that of the boys in the other two conditions. Democratic leadership promoted a moderate amount of productivity, below that of the authoritarian groups, but the quality of their models was higher. The boys in the democratic groups kept working when the adult leader was absent; they were proud of their work, their morale was high, and they were generally friendly and cooperative with one another.

These effects of leadership styles have not been found consistently, however. While Hare (1962) found greater productivity under autocratic leadership, Kahn and Katz (1953) reported greater productivity under democratic styles. Perhaps the authoritarian or democratic tradition of the group makes it receptive to one or the other style. In India, where the development of democratic traditions is relatively recent, Meade (1967) found that elementary school boys performed less well in a democratic group than their counterparts in America. In an effort to explain these conflicting findings, Fiedler (1971) has developed a theory detailing how situational factors interact with leadership styles in affecting group productivity.

3. Fiedler's Contingency Theory

Fiedler assumes two kinds of styles: *task orientation* and *relationship orientation,* which are similar to the two factors of initiating structure (i.e., emphasis on production) and consideration (i.e., social sensitivity). Leadership style is measured by asking respondents to think of all the people they have ever worked with and then describe the one who was the most inadequate. This description of a *least preferred coworker* (LPC) is made up of a set of semantic differential scales such as "friendly-unfriendly" and "cooperative-uncooperative." A high score indicates a relatively favorable attitude toward the LPC while a low score shows a relatively negative attitude. Fiedler infers

that a strong negative feeling toward a least preferred coworker is attributable to his poor past performances, while a positive attitude toward a least preferred coworker indicates the generally benign character of the person. Thus, a person who gives a low rating to his LPC is considered to be task-oriented, while the high LPC person is considered to be relationship-oriented.

The effectiveness of a particular leadership style depends on three situational factors: (1) *Leader-follower relations:* when a leader is accepted and endorsed, the situation is obviously more favorable to him than when he is distrusted and rejected. (2) *Task structure:* it is easier to lead a group that has a well-defined task than one with a vague or poorly structured task; for example, a production group will usually have more task structure and be easier to lead than a policy-making group. (3) *The power position of the leader:* the more authority a leader has and the greater the resources available to him, the more effective he can be. In some groups he may be able to hire and fire, while in others he may be limited to persuasive means of control.

If each of these three situational factors can be considered as high or low, the eight different combinations (referred to by Fiedler as *octants*) shown in Figure 13.6 can be formed. Octant I, for example, describes the leader-follower relationship as good, the task as highly structured, and power of the leader as strong. Given the favorable conditions in an octant I situation, a leader who is task-oriented (low LPC) and focuses on task completion should be quite effective, whereas a relationship orientation (high LPC) would contribute little because of the already high morale of the group members (i.e., high endorsement).

The most important situational factor contributing to favorable leadership conditions, according to Fiedler, is the leader-follower relationship. When it is good, only one other situational factor needs to be favorable for a low LPC leader to perform fairly effectively; these patterns are found in octants II and III. A low LPC leader is

Octants

	I	II	III	IV	V	VI	VII	VIII
Leader-follower relations	Good	Good	Good	Good	Poor	Poor	Poor	Poor
Task structure	High	High	Low	Low	High	High	Low	Low
Leader position power	Strong	Weak	Strong	Weak	Strong	Weak	Strong	Weak
Overall favorableness of the situation	Extremely high	High	High	Moderately high	Moderately high	Low	Low	Extremely low

Figure 13.6. Fiedler's typology of leadership situations (after Fiedler, 1971).

also predicted to be more effective than a high LPC leader in totally unfavorable circumstances (octant VIII); the leader needs to be directive and forceful in initiating structure and pursuing the performance of the task when all situational factors are low.

High LPC leaders are most effective, according to this theory, when situational factors are moderately favorable or moderately unfavorable. For example, when leader-follower relations are good but the task is unstructured and the power position is weak (octant IV), or when the leader-follower relations are poor but the task is structured and the power position of the leader is strong (octant V), the high LPC leader can be effective. In the first case, he can use his relationship orientation together with his acceptance and endorsement to organize group activities through persuasion; and in the second case, he can use his relationship orientation to win acceptance and endorsement. The predicted relationships between style of leadership in interaction with the favorability of the situation and the effectiveness of the group are shown in compressed form in Figure 13.7.

Most of the research testing Fiedler's contingency theory is correlational in nature. Group leaders are asked to complete the LPC scale, and the situational factors of the group setting are assessed by the investigator. These measures are then tested for their relationships to some criterion of the

effectiveness or productivity of the group. Fiedler (1964) reported a series of studies that provide some support for his theory. In bomber crews, which (like many military units) have well-structured tasks and provide a strong power base to the leader (Octant I), low LPC leaders were found to be more effective than high LPC leaders. High LPC leaders were more effective in military crews in which leader-follower relations were poor (octant V). When all situational factors were unfavorable (octant VIII), low LPC chairmen of the Boards of Directors of small, cooperatively-owned companies were successful. High LPC Board Chairmen were more effective when the only favorable situational factor was the leader-follower relationship (octant IV).

Despite these positive findings, serious questions have been raised about the adequacy of contingency theory. Graen, Alvares, Orris, and Martella (1970) have noted that even the supportive studies find only a weak relationship between LPC scores and measures of group effectiveness under various situational conditions; many studies find no relationship at all. For example, Graen, Orris, and Alvares (1971) assembled three-man groups and gave them structured or unstructured tasks. One member of each group was appointed as the leader. The leader's power was manipulated by providing special task-relevant information and by giving him

	Situational factors		
Leadership style	Very favorable	Intermediate favorable	Very unfavorable
Relationship-oriented leaders (high LPC)	Ineffective	Effective	Ineffective
Task-oriented leaders (low LPC)	Effective	Ineffective	Effective

Figure 13.7. The relationships between situational factors and leadership styles and the effectiveness of the task performance of the group as predicted by Fiedler's contingency theory of leadership (after Fiedler, 1971).

experimenter-sanctioned decision-making authority (high position power) or by providing no special information and giving him little decision-making authority (weak position power). Leader-follower relations were assessed by a questionnaire following each group session. The results showed no relationship between leader LPC scores and group effectiveness under any of the manipulated situational conditions.

Contingency theory ignores many of the factors that operate in the social influence process. For example, one could ask whether high LPC leaders actually use more persuasion, promises, and social reinforcement or whether low LPC leaders use more threats, manipulative tactics, and social punishments. If leadership style reflects preferences for various modes of influence, it might be asked what reactions these tactics elicit from group members. Does the use of threats undermine the normativity of the leader's status in the long run but facilitate task performance in the short run? Until social influence theory is integrated with the kinds of factors considered by contingency theory, questions such as these will remain unanswered.

VI. CHAPTER SUMMARY

People often act in front of an audience or in the company of others. Their concern for gaining a positive evaluation from others creates physiological arousal, which may either facilitate or impair performance. When a person is highly aroused, social facilitation occurs on simple tasks that have been overlearned, but he may work too rapidly on complex tasks requiring novel responses and the quality of performance may suffer.

Conformity consists of yielding to social pressure in groups and may take the form of private acceptance or public compliance. Group pressure may be experienced as informational or normative influence. A person may conform in anticipation of a

group's expectations as an ingratiation tactic. A group may tacitly communicate threats of disapproval, sanction or exclusion for deviant behavior, or promises of approval, rewards or inclusion for conforming behavior. Much conformity behavior takes the form of an exchange involving a loss of self-esteem by an individual in return for the social approval of a group.

Situational factors such as task difficulty, public or private responding, and group size affect the degree of conformity. Ambiguity and complexity in the assigned task make an individual informationally dependent upon the group. A requirement that he make a public response places an individual under surveillance, thereby encouraging him to conform to avoid sanctions or to achieve rewards. The size of a group has an effect on an individual because he becomes concerned about being out of step and because a majority opinion shakes his confidence in a deviant judgment.

Both private acceptance and public compliance are affected by the credibility of a group's tacit communications and the values associated with compliance and noncompliance. The group's credibility can be undermined so far as a member is concerned by information from an authority that it is wrong, by feedback about the accuracy of his own judgment, and by the presence of dissenters. The greater the costs of conformity, whether material or in terms of self-esteem, the less apt an individual is to conform. On the other hand, the greater the rewards for conforming, material or social, the more likely it is he will conform.

The attractiveness, competence, and status of the group are positively related to the degree of conformity displayed by individual members. Group cohesiveness and attractiveness may be based on mutual goals, personal friendships, mutual respect, or other relationships; but whatever the cause of cohesiveness, the greater it is, the more conforming group members will be. Any special competence of the group produces conformity only when it is relevant to group goals. With regard to status, Hollander's theory of idiosyncrasy credits suggests that a leader (high status person) can be deviant if he has established himself as a loyal member by his prior conformity or as an effective resource person in realizing group goals. Low status persons may have little investment in a group and hence may be unlikely to conform. Middle status persons are most conforming because they do not have enough credits to risk deviance and have a strong investment in the group.

Research on the types of personality traits that characterize the conforming person have been somewhat inconsistent. However, a constellation of factors associated with sensitivity to the normative and informational pressures of groups including such traits as acquiescence, low self-esteem, anxiety, and concern for social approval, has been found to induce conformity by members.

Several theories have been advanced to explain why individuals make different decisions involving risk when alone than when contributing to group decisions. A theory of responsibility diffusion assumes that greater risks are taken in groups because of the reduction in the fear of being blamed for any negative outcome. However, the evidence has not provided convincing support for the theory.

Familiarization and leadership theories have proven inadequate in explaining the risky shift phenomenon. There is a wealth of evidence, however, to support the theory that people in groups express more extreme opinions and choices on matters related to important and approved cultural values, (whether the values support risk, caution, or whatever), than they do when alone. A desire for approval by the group causes a person to present himself as feeling at least as strongly as anyone else with respect to values held by the group. Of course, the more cohesive and attractive the group, the more motivated a member will

be to make a good impression and the greater the choice shift he will display. Groups impose normative and informational influence on their members. They are the source of pressures to conform, and the evidence indicates that the same pressures produce extremity of behavior in the direction of cultural values.

The analysis of groupthink has focused on the impairment of effective planning in cohesive groups. When a group feels it is right, good, and together in its thinking, its members may ignore evidence, avoid criticizing each other, seek to bolster an early decision, and work to protect their leader from questioning. A highly cohesive group is so subject to normative pressure for consensus that it cannot benefit from the relevant, persuasive, and factual information and arguments possessed by or easily available to group members. A willingness to explore alternatives and avoid early commitments, and an atmosphere in which criticism is not considered as disloyalty or a personal attack, is required to overcome the defects of groupthink.

The efficiency of a group in problem-solving depends to a large degree on the type of task it must carry out. Unitary tasks depend on individual actions; when they are given to groups, they take a disjunctive form and the group's performance will depend on its most competent member. Performance on additive tasks usually reveals a loss of efficiency compared to what might be expected by a simple summing of the ability of each contributing member. If an additive task is conjunctive and hence requires the coordinated efforts of group members, the loss of efficiency may be due to problems of coordination and, if the group is large, it may be attributable to decreasing member motivation.

The relation of group size to productivity depends on several factors. When a task is additive, the objectives of the group, the availability of tools, and the requirements of work space and coordination among workers determine the optimal group size. In general, increases in group membership are inversely related to proficiency in performing conjunctive tasks and directly related to the probability of performing well on disjunctive tasks. When unitary judgments are required by the nature of the task, groups may be superior to single individuals because of error correction; but when an individual expends the same number of man-hours as the collective investment of group members, he is often superior in performing eureka (insight) tasks.

The structure of communications within a group is a vital factor determining how well it will perform. A centralized communication network imposes a keyman on the group and relegates all other members to peripheral roles. A group with a centralized network is efficient in solving simple tasks, but unless the keyman is a very superior person, he is likely to be saturated with an overload of information in complex tasks. A decentralized network allows the development of alternative organizational structures within the group. Until an organization takes form, the group is likely to be inefficient in solving problems, but an organized group with a decentralized network provides opportunities for all members to make innovative suggestions and to check for errors. As a consequence, decentralized groups are more efficient in solving complex problems, and once organized, are just as efficient as centralized groups in solving simple problems. The morale of the member is highest when he is most involved in helping his group solve its tasks.

Leadership has been defined as an individual's influence over other members of a group or as the possession of informational or other important resources. Leadership may also be defined in terms of behavior that contributes to accomplishing group objectives, such as clarifying goals, organizing resources, and coordinating activities. Central to a leader's position and effectiveness is the legitimacy he is granted by the group.

Leaders do not possess distinctive personality characteristics that cause them to be selected by group members or that make them particularly effective. Assertiveness may convey the impression of competence, but when obvious and relevant competence is possessed by a group member, it is a more effective determinant of leadership selection than mere talkativeness. A correlation between intelligence and leadership may often occur, but this relationship may be more the result of a failure to select persons of low and very high intelligence than of a systematic increase in leadership skills as a function of I.Q.

Leadership status may be acquired through formal appointment or democratic election. The general support or endorsement of a leader by group members is a consequence of his ability to achieve success in the pursuit of group goals. A strongly endorsed leader may deviate from the preferences of the group more easily than one who is weakly endorsed. By conforming to important group norms and by facilitating the achievement of group goals, a leader acquires idiosyncrasy credits that he can use for purposes of innovation and deviation. The level of endorsement for a leader apparently does not affect the readiness of followers to comply with his requests and demands.

The basis of legitimacy is in the normativity of the group, which involves the degree of consensus about rules and norms, the amount of sanctions possessed by the leader, and the degree of deference considered appropriate to his authority. When all three of these factors are high and the leader acts within the limitations of the group's norms and expectations, subordinates are most likely to comply with his demands and requests. Violations of norms and of the scope of authority given to a leader will cause followers to form revolutionary coalitions against him.

Different leadership styles create different group atmospheres. Autocratic, democratic, and laissez-faire styles have produced differences in member productivity, social interaction, morale, and quality of work. Factor analyses have shown that leadership styles can be categorized into two basic types: (1) task leaders, who emphasize production and the initiation of structure in the work group, and (2) socioemotional leaders, who show consideration and social sensitivity toward their subordinates as persons. Fiedler has proposed that leadership effectiveness is a function of: (1) task and relationship orientation as leadership styles, and (2) the situational factors of leader-follower relations, task structure, and the amount of power possessed by the leader. The evidence for contingency theory is mixed. Future theorizing about leadership must take social influence processes into account in attempting to understand the factors contributing to effectiveness.

SUGGESTED READINGS

Gibb, C. A. Leadership. In G. Lindzey and E. Aronson (Eds.), *The handbook of social psychology*. Vol. 4. (2nd ed.) Reading, Mass.: Addison-Wesley, 1969. Pp. 205–282. A comprehensive review of the available theories and evidence regarding leadership.

Kiesler, C. A., and Kiesler, S. B. *Conformity*. Reading, Mass.: Addison-Wesley, 1969. A short but thorough examination of scientific work on the topic.

Janis, I. L. *Victims of groupthink*. Boston: Houghton Mifflin, 1972. An illustrative examination of the principles of groupthink that reviews a half dozen important policy decisions made in recent history.

Shaw, M. E. *Group dynamics: The psychology of small group behavior*. (2nd ed.) New York: McGraw Hill, 1976. A comprehensive survey of the group dynamics literature covering most of the topics examined in this chapter.

Steiner, I. D. *Group processes and productivity*. New York: Academic Press, 1972. Reviews the processes involved in group problem solving and their effects on group productivity.

Collective Behavior

CHAPTER PREVIEW

When large numbers of persons act together with a common orientation, we
speak of collective behavior. The persons
may actually be congregated, as in a football
stadium, or they may be physically separated, as when they watch a television
broadcast of a football game. The common
orientation of the many persons involved
may be based on momentary needs or the
desire to produce permanent social change.
For example, once a football game is over
and the crowd melts away, the members remain relatively unchanged, but economic
development and violent revolution produce permanent and irreversible changes
in an entire society. Collective behavior
may also take active or passive forms. It is
one thing to put the rope around the victim's neck during a lynching party and it
is another merely to observe these events
on a television newscast. Audiences are
passive collectivities.

Crowds are characterized by dimensions
such as size, density, polarization, boundaries, and shape. Essentially, a *crowd* is a
large number of people who are physically
in one another's presence and have a common focus of attention. Blumer (1957)
notes the short life, the spontaneity, and the
lack of any intricate organization of crowds.
He points to the potential constructive and
destructive possibilities of crowd behavior:
"The crowd has profound possibilities of
dissolving individual organization, freeing
individuals from the arresting hold of given
group values and thus preparing them to
disregard, attack, or undermine the values
in given areas of the established social
order. Second, the crowd is a means of
energizing group action by arousing strong
collective feelings as in the case of en-
thusiasm, courage, and glee" (p. 131). Some
forms of crowd action are riots, lynchings,
panics, and queues.

A mass public is a second distinct way of
classifying aggregate activities. Blumer
(1946) defined a mass public as a large

number of anonymous persons who can be
differentiated in terms of class, occupation,
ethnic identification, political affiliation, religious background, etc. The distinguishing
characteristic of a mass public is that a large
number of people who are not physically in
each other's presence adopt a common
focus of attention, behavior, opinion, attitude, or perception. Four basic areas of
mass behavior have received attention from
social psychologists: (1) the mass media, (2)
public opinion, (3) fashions, fads, and
crazes, and (4) deviant behavior.

Collective behavior sometimes leads to
relatively permanent social change. Modern technology has contributed to worldwide revolutionary alterations in human
ways of life. Every nation wants to participate in economic development, to provide
more of the necessities and comforts of life
to its citizens. The conditions for innovation and the diffusion of new techniques,
habits, and values often depend on important psychological factors. Dislocations and
the loss of orientation that stem from
changes in the conditions of life often produce social movements. The organized
groups involved in social movements may
have religious, cultural, political, and
economic purposes. Violent attempts to
overthrow constituted political authorities
have become common in our revolutionary
age. The causes, creation, and prevention
of revolutions are of great interest to
groups and governments throughout the
world.

In this chapter our discussion of crowds,
mass publics, and the factors contributing
to social change is based primarily on
natural observation and speculation, with
only a sprinkle of experimental evidence
here and there. The phenomena are by
their very nature almost impossible to study
in a laboratory. The degree of confidence
we have in our knowledge regarding these
collective forms of behavior is therefore not
great. Much of what psychology and sociology have contributed to an understanding
of these collective phenomena does not

consist of scientific laws or empirical generalizations that are true or false, but conceptual distinctions that may sharpen our perceptions beyond what is available through common sense.

I. CROWD BEHAVIOR

Brown (1954) developed a taxonomy of crowds based on whether they are active or passive (see Table 14.1). An *audience* is a relatively passive crowd that may have congregated for the specific purpose of witnessing an event or may have formed spontaneously to observe an unplanned event. The collectivity may have the common intention of listening to a lecturer, and their actions in queuing up to get tickets, entering the auditorium, and driving into and out of the parking lot are only incidental to their main focus on hearing what is said. Similarly, when passersby stop to witness an accident, they incidentally form a crowd because they share a common focus on a happening.

Table 14.1   A Taxonomy of Crowds. [a]

I.   Audiences (passive)
   A.   Intentional
      1.   Information-seeking
      2.   Recreational
   B.   Casual
II. Mobs (active)
   A.   Expressive
   B.   Acquisitive
   C.   Escape
      1.   Escape in organized crowds
      2.   Panics in unorganized crowds
   D.   Aggressive
      1.   Riots
      2.   Lynchings
      3.   Terrorization
---

[a] After Brown, 1954.

Crowds may gather without a common focus of attention. Large numbers of people gather at public beaches on hot summer days, presumably to catch a few cool breezes, swim in the cooling ocean, and enjoy the company of friends. The presence of a large crowd may be annoying and detract from the pleasure of the experience, but on the other hand, in every crowd a considerable amount of time is spent in watching people. People take care in dressing for the beach, the opera, and the rock festival because they are aware they will engage in much mutual social comparison. At any such gathering there are usually opportunities for casual interaction for meeting new and old friends, and for the accumulation of valuable information. Attitudes may be aired, evaluated, and revised. Business deals may be initiated, discussed, and completed. Thus, members of a crowd may be gathered in the same physical location but may have a great diversity of purposes.

Brown distinguishes between a passive and an active crowd by referring to the latter as a *mob*. The presence of others is important for generating, facilitating, or hindering the purposes of each person in a mob. Milling about distinguishes the active crowd from the passive audience. Milling permits movement into and out of the focus of attention (e.g., the speaker's rostrum), promotes information exchange and the transmission of rumors, fosters contagion of emotions, and facilitates modeling of the active behavior of leaders.

According to Brown, a mob may have any of four purposes: expressive, acquisitive, escape, or aggressive. Expressions of joy or discontent may be manifested by large crowds in Mardi Gras celebrations or at political demonstrations. Acquisitive mobs may form to acquire aid in time of crisis or to obtain bargains or souvenirs at sales. A crowd may calmly organize to escape from danger or it may deteriorate into disorganized and terror-stricken panic. Finally, mobs may form for the purpose of doing physical or psychological damage to property or to other people. We will discuss riots and lynchings below, but will defer the topic of terrorization until we take up revolution and wars of national liberation.

A. Characteristics of Audiences

A practical problem facing businessmen and agents of social control is the prediction of the size and growth of an audience. The construction of new theaters and stadiums depends on the estimates and projections that are made. The number of policemen and security agents sent to a particular location also is contingent on someone's guess about the potential size of the audience.

The *polarization* of the crowd refers to the degree to which its members focus their attention on a single object or event. The degree of polarization is affected by both the size and density of the audience, as well as the attractiveness of the focal event. From the individual's perspective, lack of polarization reduces the information or enjoyment he is apt to receive from his experience. Interrelated with the other characteristics of the crowd (and defined by them) are the boundaries and shape of the audience.

1. Predicting the Size of an Audience

Two factors that determine the size of an intentional audience are the drawing power of the focal event and the physical capacity of the lecture hall, theater, stadium, or arena. Unintentional audiences at unadvertised events also vary in size as a function of drawing power and the number of passersby. The more distinctive, dangerous, or gruesome the event, the more people will be attracted to it. There may be a limit to crowd size imposed by the ability to get a good view of the event. Milgram and Toch (1969) reported that a television producer arranged for two cars to hit each other on a rather quiet street in Rome. Despite the quiet, a crowd soon gathered; however, after approximately 100 people had congregated, no further increases in crowd size occurred.

The size of a group is dependent on both the number of persons available to join the group and the "break-away" rate. Coleman and James (1961) argued that the tendency

of persons to leave a group depends on the amount of time necessary for them to satisfy their curiosity. If a strange fish washes up on the beach, people will gather to examine it and then they will leave; the period of time necessary to make the examination determines the break-away rate. The growth and dissolution of a crowd therefore depends on the number of available interested persons, the nature of the focal event, and the break-away rate.

The size of a gathering may stimulate a person to join a casual audience. Milgram, Bickman, and Berkowitz (1969) arranged for stimulus crowds of sizes 1, 2, 3, 5, 10 and 15 persons to stop on a busy New York sidewalk and look up at a sixth floor window in a skyscraper. There was nothing distinctive about the window. A person unseen took motion pictures of a 50-foot stretch of the sidewalk during the 60 seconds of each trial. The proportions of the available persons who entered the critical area and joined the stimulus crowd either by looking up or by stopping were recorded.

As can be seen in Figure 14.1, more people looked up while continuing to walk than stopped to join the crowd, but crowd size affected both kinds of behavior. The simple behavior of looking upward increased with crowd size, reaching its limit when five persons constituted the group. The proportion of people stopping was a linear function of crowd size. Apparently, the number of people obviously looking at a particular event allows the passerby to make an inference about whether the event will be of interest to him too.

Both crowd development and crowd size are determined by the anticipated rewards associated with the satisfaction of curiosity, the acquisition of information, or the enjoyment of entertainment. The decision to join a passive crowd is based on an individual's calculation of the probable rewards less the probable costs associated with the focal event. A lawyer rushing to court cannot afford to stop to look up to satisfy his curiosity. Similarly, a decision to

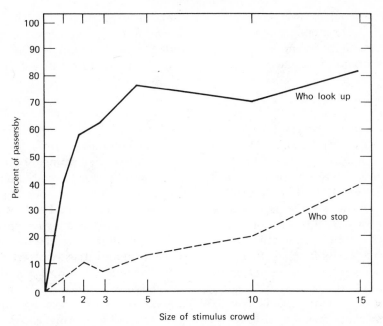

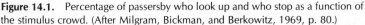

Figure 14.1. Percentage of passersby who look up and who stop as a function of the stimulus crowd. (After Milgram, Bickman, and Berkowitz, 1969, p. 80.)

join an intentional audience at a meeting, lecture, or show is based on a consideration of the other activities that could be undertaken instead.

2. Effects of Crowd Size

The noise and excitement engendered by an expressive large crowd can stimulate an individual to perform actions he otherwise would not do. Argyle (1959) found that the proportion of persons who make a public conversion at revival meetings increased with the size of the audience in attendance. Miller and Dollard (1941) described this effect of the audience on its members in terms of circular stimulation. One person notices the behavior of a second, and the stimuli given off by the latter's response serve to intensify the first person's response. A person's applause may be amplified by the "bravos" shouted by neighboring members of the audience, and the shouts of appreciative neighbors may, in turn, become more strident as the first person's applause grows louder.

It is not clear why one person's behavior should stimulate or intensify that of another person. According to Miller and Dollard, it is a matter of learning: "Children have learned that when others are running toward the same goal, it is advisable to speed up, if the goal is to be reached. They are frequently rewarded, in such situations, for running faster when they see others run. The response of running faster when others run is therefore fixed to the stimulus of seeing the other person run" (pp. 227–228). Furthermore, the presence of a large crowd may imply tacit approval of the activities or values expressed in the focal event. A person may make a decision for Christ during a Billy Graham crusade because of the implication that such an action is right and deserving of approval by a very large number of people. But Inkeles (1963) believes that this learning theory is inadequate to explain novel or unique behavior such as a public commitment to devote one's life to religion. He even doubts its application to the running behavior of children, who are often taught at school *not* to run just because other children are observed to be running. Yet if interstimulation does not produce novel responses, naive observation still suggests that the en-thusiasm and size of a crowd can engender and heighten the excitement experienced by its members. Bombardment by intense stimuli arouses emotional reactions.

3. Crowd Density

The pressure and jostling associated with a dense crowd may engulf a person and stimulate him. The discomfort of a hot and crowded situation (see Griffitt & Veitch, 1971, in Chapter II, I, B) may produce negative arousal and lead the person under certain conditions to act in a hostile way to total strangers. The penetration of an individual's space bubble (Hall, 1966) may cause irritation or fear, depending on the circumstances. The closeness of the surrounding persons, including personal contact and vocal expressiveness, distract the individual and often physically interfere with his ability to see or hear what is going on.

Stokols (1972) has indicated that in analysing human behavior in crowds a distinction should be made between density and crowding. He suggests that density should be considered in physical terms of spatial limitation, while crowding should be considered in experiential terms and "can be characterized as a motivational state directed toward the alleviation of perceived restriction and infringement, through the augmentation of one's supply of space, or the adjustment of social and personal variables so as to minimize the inconvenience imposed by spatial limitation" (p. 276).

An observer may perceive a populated space as crowded in terms of numbers, but the physical density may not generate a sense of crowdedness in the occupants. People who live in densely populated areas do not feel crowded if there are no requirements for behavioral coordination and the social atmosphere is friendly and cooperative. Draper (1973), for example, found that the Kung Bushmen live in campsites that are tightly packed by Western standards with no indication of stress.

She reported greater crowding (with comfort) among females than males—a phenomenon found also in our culture (Ross, Layton, Erickson, & Schopler, 1973; Sommer, 1969).

4. Polarization of Crowds

A polarization index for a crowd at a given time can be determined by dividing the number of persons actually attending to the focal event by the number of people present (Milgram & Toch, 1969). Most events of one or more hours duration have peaks and valleys of interest to members of the audience. Size and density affect polarization. The larger the crowd, the more difficult it may be to see or hear the focal event. Density interferes with polarization because of the conflicting cues presented by the crush of neighboring persons. When members of a crowd are attending to a number of nonfocal events, they are difficult to control.

5. Boundaries of the Audience

The boundary of an audience in an open space is related to gradients of polarization. The boundary has more significance for outsiders than for those in the audience. Milgram and Toch (1969) offer the illustration of an aggregate of people at a fairgrounds on a busy day. Crowds gather around various exhibits, break off and flow back into the Midway, only to join other crowds along the way. At a given distance from an exhibit polarization falls off to near zero. This zero point marks the boundary of the crowd, even though some persons may be pushing through the fringe as they move along.

The boundaries of audiences are more or less permeable. A fairground crowd has a highly permeable boundary because it is relatively easy to sift in and out of it. Some crowds are impermeable and refuse to allow anyone to penetrate their boundaries. For example, a crowd of idolizing fans may congregate around a stage to wait for a performer to toss them a few souvenirs. The members will strongly resist anyone who tries to push in front of them.

Experimental studies of the boundaries of small groups have been done in an attempt to examine this phenomenon under highly controlled conditions. It is clear that people learn to respect the boundaries of a group and not to violate them. Knowles (1973) placed stimulus persons in a passageway 10 feet wide. In one condition he had two persons engage in a conversation across the hallway; each stood with his back 30 inches from the wall and facing one another but separated by five feet of space. In a second condition, four people engaged in a conversation, with pairs facing each other across the hall and spaced as in the first condition. In a control situation, two wastebarrels were placed on either side of the hallway instead of people. The status of the group members was also manipulated; the persons engaged in conversation were either students dressed in casual attire or they were older students conversing with an instructor, who was formally dressed in business clothes.

Passersby were obviously aware of the group boundaries and were reluctant to violate them. When the wastebarrels were placed in the hallway, 75 percent of the passing students walked between them. When two people held a conversation across the space in the hall, 30 percent of the passersby walked between them, and most walked through the smaller space in back of them. When four people held a conversation, only 20 percent of the passing students penetrated the group's boundaries. Many of the penetraters excused themselves verbally or with gestures, such as ducking their heads and hurrying through. The status of the group members also affected the willingness of passersby to penetrate the group's boundary. Irrespective of the size of the group, fewer persons (18 percent) passed through the high status group than through the low status group (30 percent).

Lindskold, Albert, Baer, and Moore (1976) found that passersby respect the boundaries both of conversing groups and of audiences. Groups of four confederates were placed to create a five-foot passageway (as in Knowles' study) in the middle of a 13-foot sidewalk at six different locations in the downtown area of Athens, Ohio. Three conditions were created: (1) in the conversational groups, the confederates talked to one another across the open space of the sidewalk; (2) in the audience condition all four confederates faced toward a store and looked into its window; and (3) in the control condition the four confederates engaged in independent activities, such as looking into a purse, reading a paper, or checking the operation of a camera.

Significantly fewer passersby went through the passageway formed by the audience than passed through the same physical space in the control condition; still fewer people penetrated the boundaries of the conversational group. Among the passersby who went around the audience, very few chose the store side and almost all went to the curb side; in the other two conditions, there was no preference for the store or curb sides in going around the group. Thus, the boundary of the audience included the object of their attention as well as their own bodies. Apparently there are implicit norms about passing in front of a person gazing in a store window, just as at a museum it would be considered impolite to walk in front of someone looking at a painting.

B. Characteristics of Mobs

The milling that typically occurs in active crowds provides an opportunity for information to be transmitted quickly to a large number of people which facilitates the transformation of a passive audience into an angry mob. Aggressive mobs may engage in vigilante action toward a hapless victim, or they may attack a mob of other people in a riot. One factor considered important in producing aggressive mobs is the loss of individuality by each person as he becomes embedded in the crowd; he sheds the inhibitions associated with his normal behavior because he is less responsible for what happens and less likely to be punished for his actions. Information transmitted through a mob may create fear and cause it to panic as it attempts to escape danger. One kind of acquisitive mob that has been studied is the queue. Standing in line to obtain food, tickets to events, or to register for school or voting is a common feature of modern life. Each of these kinds of mobs has important effects on its members.

1. Rumors

Emotions may spread throughout a crowd through nonverbal means. However, much of the information that is necessary for each person to define what is happening and what norms should govern his conduct is transmitted through a chain of verbal communication. The distortions of communication characteristic of rumors may cause a mob to define the situation incorrectly and spur them on to inappropriate action.

The role of rumor in defining a situation was described in Chapter 3 (III, C, 3); it is only necessary here to stress its role in crowd behavior. Allport and Postman (1947) have proposed that rumor intensity is a function of interest *times* ambiguity, and both of these factors are maximized in large crowds. The members of the crowd have a keen interest in what is going on about them, and it may be difficult to ascertain the cause of a disturbance in the schedule of expected events. The failure of an actor to reappear, a melée at the other end of the stadium or arena, the presence of a large number of policemen, or any other unexpected events may be the basis of rumors rapidly transmitted. Depending on the nature of the rumor and the circumstances extant in the situation, the crowd may become a lynch mob, engage in a riot, seek to

make an orderly escape from the facility or area, flee in disorganized panic, or sit bemused by the story transmitted to them.

2. Deindividuation

A person who is embedded in a crowd has his identity concealed. His individuality is merged with that of others and his anonymity releases him from the normal inhibitions of civilized life. According to Zimbardo (1969b), the deindividuated person exhibits uncivilized and aggressive behavior int he mob.

Because it is difficult to study deindividuation systematically in the context of a mob, Zimbardo (1969b) has attempted to produce this phenomenon in laboratory groups. He stressed the individuality of some female subjects by having them wear name tags and by greeting each of them by name, while those in another group were deindividuated by dressing them in large baggy lab coats and by placing hoods over their heads. Groups of four individuated or deindividuated subjects were then given the task of administering 20 painful shocks to a victim who was actually a confederate of the experimenter. The rationale provided to the subjects for shocking the victim was that the experimenter wanted to determine if there was greater empathy for a victim when subjects administered shocks compared to when they merely observed the victim being shocked. The confederate victim was described as a warm, kind person or as an obnoxious and prejudiced person.

Each subject had a key to depress when provided with a signal to shock the victim. The subjects were assembled in groups of four, and although each believed she was a shocker, each was told that there were two shockers and two observers in the group. A shock was delivered to the victim when one key was depressed, and when both were pressed, the intensity was said to be greater than when only one was used. The subjects were told that the experimenter would not know which shocker depressed the key (when only one did so) because both keys led to a common terminal. The duration of shocks administered to the victim could also be varied by the length of time the key was depressed.

The strong cues indicating the experimenter's desire for delivering shocks was displayed by the fact that on the average the subjects gave shocks 17 out of the 20 times the signal was given. Although there were no differences in the frequency or intensity of shocks delivered by deindividuated and individuated subjects, the former did give shocks of longer duration than the latter, averaging .90 seconds rather than .47 seconds. The time intervals involved here are extremely short and do not justify a conclusion that deindividuated subjects acted in a strongly antisocial way.

An alternative explanation can be offered for these results. The difference may be attributed to the extra effort of individuated subjects to gain credit for both complying to the experimenter's wishes by shocking frequently and by being nice by releasing the key quickly to minimize the pain for the victim. The deindividuated subjects may have been more concerned with complying with the experimenter's demands and less concerned about being socially disapproved of by the victim.

Deindividuated persons can avoid embarrassment for what they say or do. Becker-Haven and Lindskold (1975) have found that pairs of hooded persons come to the aid of a victim more rapidly than do pairs of identifiable (individuated) persons. Perhaps the hooded subjects were less concerned with appearing foolish should their interpretation of the emergency situation turn out to be wrong (see Chapter 10, IV).

An examination of the Human Relations Area files of over 200 cultures allowed Watson (1973) to compare cultures where people prepared for warfare by deindividuating themselves with those that did not. Deindividuation was accomplished by face and body painting and wearing masks and other special garments. Most of the cultures with deindividuation rituals scored high on measures of torture and human sacrifice. Cultures with individuated warriors were less brutal, took prisoners for slaves rather than killing them, and often terminated battles before all the enemy had been killed. However, one should be careful not to conclude that there is a cause-effect relationship from this correlational study.

The study of deindividuation has not produced sufficiently persuasive results to draw any firm conclusions about its social psychological effects. The notion that persons who lose their identity in a small group also lose their inhibitions regarding normatively proscribed behavior, if proven reliable, would be important for understanding the behavior of mobs.

3. Lynching

The origin of the word "lynching" is associated with the Revolutionary War in this country (Cutler, 1905). Colonel Charles Lynch organized a local court in a small Virginia town, to punish Tories who were harassing the Continental forces. The nearest established court was over 200 miles away. This extra-legal vigilante court dealt scrupulously and fairly (but not harshly) with the Tories and never invoked the death penalty. Thus "lynch law" was originally the "relatively mild extra-legal justice administered by community leaders to repair the inadequacies of the civil courts" (Brown, 1954, p. 847). However, over time lynching came to mean extra-legal killings by mobs, usually as retribution for alleged crimes of violence. Tables 14.2 and 14.3 provide a record of the number of lynchings against whites and blacks over a 70-year period, including the alleged crimes that presumably motivated mob justice.

Although lynchings occurred sporadically on the Western frontier before the establishment of law there, most of them have taken place in the Southeastern Unit-

Table 14.2   Number of Lynchings of Whites and Blacks by Decades, from 1882 to 1949.[a]

Decade	Blacks	Whites	Total
1882–1889	534	669	1203
1890–1899	1111	429	1540
1900–1909	791	94	885
1910–1919	563	53	616
1920–1929	281	34	315
1930–1939	120	11	131
1940–1949	30	2	32
Totals	3430	1292	4722

[a] After Brown, 1954, p. 848.

ed States. Beginning at the end of the 19th century, most of the victims were Negroes and the perpetrators were often members of a secret organization, the Ku Klux Klan. A frequent pattern was mutilating or killing a Negro accused of raping a white woman. The charge of rape was often a pretense and the lynching was directed at the Negro people rather than at a particular black person; little effort was directed toward establishing the guilt of the accused. Racial, economic, and cultural factors were all involved in motivating this pattern of mob behavior. Poor whites perceived the emancipation of the slaves as a threat to their jobs and wealthy whites resented losing their slaves (Raper, 1933). Concern for the "purity" of the white race and protection of the plantation way of life encouraged the whites to take actions to keep the "Nigras" in their place. Lynching was a form of terrorization directed toward maintaining white supremacy in the South.

When the Klan rode through the night, its members were protected from outsiders by their hoods, but within the group strong norms and expectations effectively gained conformity from everyone. Harsh penalties could occur if a member failed to demonstrate his loyalty to the group. Atrocities were committed, not because of man's base and brutish nature, but because the penalty for not participating was high and the likelihood of apprehension and conviction by legal authorities was low. In addition, many members believed their actions were justified. The atrocities committed by a lynch mob, on a battle field, or on a prison march are often considered just punishment for the victim because of his perceived brutality and inhumanity. Lynchings represented a very complex set of social psychological, economic, and cultural factors, including deindividuation, conformity pressure, the use of coercion to protect privileges, and the restoration of equity (revenge).

4.   Riots

The major characteristic of a riot is the spontaneous and violent clash of two unorganized mobs. The history of the United States is peppered with riots (Hofstadter & Wallace, 1970). During the Civil War,

Table 14.3   Alleged reasons given for lynchings occurring between 1882 and 1951.[a]

Causes	Number of lynchings	Percent of lynchings
Homicides	1937	41.0
Felonious assault	204	4.3
Rape	910	19.2
Attempted rape	288	6.1
Robbery and theft	232	4.9
Insult to white person	84	1.8
Other	1075	22.7
Totals	4730	100.0

[a] After Brown, 1954.

around 2000 people were killed in the New York draft riots—the most destructive of human life in our history. Riots almost always involve a complex set of factors, including economic, political, and ethnic differences between a dominant and a segregated and subordinate group.

From 1940 to the present there has been an extraordinary growth of population in the urban areas of America, and particularly in the concentration of blacks and other minority groups in the central areas of the cities. For example, in the three years from 1940 to 1943, the city of Detroit added 62,000 blacks to its ghettos, while some 490,000 whites also migrated to the city (Lee & Humphrey, 1943). Many of the migrants from both racial groups came from the South, bringing with them attitudes and resentments that were further fired by the dislocations and frustrations of the new environment. Yet over 74% of the 5,000 black and white participants who were arrested for rioting near the Detroit River on 20 June 1943, were not recent immigrants.

The prelude to riots generally involves a series of events which heighten tension and conflict between contending groups. Before the New York draft riots, blacks had predominated in the occupations of longshoremen, brick makers, hod carriers, barbers, waiters, and domestic servants. Irish immigrants quickly took over many of these jobs, leaving blacks with no option but to take strikebreaking jobs when they became available. Animosities were further inflamed by the Emancipation Proclamation and an unpopular civil war. In every riot there is a precipitating event that trips off the violence. In 1863, a Conscription Act was passed which allowed men to escape the draft by paying $300 to the government. Of course, the poor could not avoid conscription and were afraid of losing their jobs while they were away. The riot began as an assault on the draft headquarters, but gradually became directed at blacks. During the course of the three days

of rioting, the mobs defeated a number of militia units. Only when Union troops were called in from Gettysburg was the riot finally quelled (Hofstadter & Wallace, 1970).

The riots of the middle 1960s were often precipitated by incidents involving the police. The ghetto riots in Harlem, Philadelphia, and Watts began when persons on the street intervened while policemen were making arrests, and confrontations ensued. These riots were generally confined to attacks against the police, looting stores owned predominately by whites, and the destruction of property by fire. The grievances and the sense of injustice associated with these riots were often symbolic. Resentment against the police among ghetto residents is associated with alleged cases of police brutality, harassment, and abuse; the police are also symbols of established authority which is believed to maintain two different systems of justice, one for the white man and another for the black man. Radical elements often accuse the police of acting as agents of the white society to keep blacks in a state of oppression and servitude. The assassination of Martin Luther King, Jr., also sparked property riots around the nation as blacks were enraged by this presumed attempt to halt the civil rights movement to promote racial equality.

Analyses have revealed that criminal elements are often the instigators of riots but that many ordinarily law-abiding citizens may join the mob action. Rumors often play an important part in luring people into the fray. For example, in the Detroit riot of 1943, a frequently heard rumor was that a Negro baby had been thrown from a bridge by white hoodlums. In white areas, the same rumor circulated but with the race of the baby and the hoodlums reversed. Long-held grievances were combined with anger regarding the alleged atrocity and people socialized to believe in the efficacy of violence for solving problems joined the mob in search of revenge. Of course, in property riots there is also the motive to acquire material goods.

The probability of riots can be reduced by a combination of preventive measures. Greater representation of members of minority groups on the police force, a reduction in job discrimination, and effective political representation are associated with a low incidence of riots (Lieberson & Silverman, 1965). The provision of supervised recreational activities for adolescents, the enlistment of gang members into community organizations, training the police to avoid confrontation and the polarization of hostilities, and meetings among community officials, law enforcement representatives, and members of neighborhoods that allow grievances to be aired—all these help to defuse volatile situations. Constructive remedial actions to remove the original sources of irritation, where legitimate, must follow or else people will lose confidence in the social agents and the social system as a whole.

5. Panic

Mobs motivated by a need to escape or defend themselves may coordinate their behavior in an orderly retreat or may display unruly and noncooperative panic behavior. Prior training and preparation for various contingencies allow a military commander to conduct an orderly retreat under very trying circumstances. Unpredictable and dangerous events for which no preparations have been made and no rehearsed responses are available may cause panic. During World War II, air raids that occurred at regularly spaced intervals produced less panic than unpredictable raids (Janis, 1951).

Two disasters illustrate the dysfunctional nature of panic behavior. In the Iroquois Theater fire in Chicago in 1903 over 500 people were killed in less than 10 minutes, and an almost equally disastrous panic occurred at the Coconut Grove nightclub in Boston in 1942 as people piled up trying to

get out of the doorway of the burning building. In both these incidents, only slight damage was actually done to the buildings; the large number of fatalities was caused by trampling and asphyxiation resulting from the panic and not from the fire.

LaPiere (1938) believed a crowd would follow whatever behavior was exemplified by a leader. If the first few people in a crowd rush for the exits at the shout of "fire," their behavior is contagious and panic ensues; but a display of leadership can lead the crowd to queue up and leave a burning building calmly and efficiently. Rushing for the exit in a mad dash to escape may actually be the most rational thing a person can do when everyone else seems ready to do the same; the only chance one may have is to beat the others to the door. A leader can provide the necessary cues for organizing an orderly escape if he emerges quickly enough and is firm in his directions. Fire drills in schools are conducted to promote the automatic acceptance of organization in an emergency and to forestall the possibility of panic.

Panic behavior is difficult to study because it is unethical to deliberately create such situations, and their occurrence is sufficiently unpredictable to make field study improbable. Researchers have attempted to abstract certain analytical aspects from panic situations and simulate them in the laboratory. For example, Mintz (1951) tried to capture the logic of a panic situation by having subjects stand around a large bottle with a small neck. Each subject held a string that was attached to a cone inside the bottle. The cones were small enough to pass separately through the neck of the bottle, but two cones would jam the opening and cause a pile-up so that no other cones could get out.

At the beginning of the experiment, water was siphoned into the bottle through a side valve. The subjects' task was to get their cones out of the bottle before they got wet. The subjects could win from 10 to 25 cents or avoid a loss of from one to 10 cents by successfully removing their cones from the bottle. The greater the value of the consequences, the more likely it was that the subjects would jam the neck with their cones. In addition, the development of cooperative norms through prior instruction contributed to success, while competitive instructions caused more intense and counterproductive "panics."

Kelley, Contry, Dahlke, and Hill (1965) simulated a panic situation in a different way. Subjects were given the task of coordinating their actions to avoid a shock that could be delivered through electrodes attached to two of their fingers. A subject could attempt to escape by pushing a switch, which illuminated a light on the panels of the other subjects. The escape mechanism, shutting off the shock, required three seconds to operate, and it would not work if two or more subjects pressed their switches during any three-second period. The percentage of subjects who escaped shocks decreased as the severity of the threatened shock increased. The subjects showing the greatest fear of being shocked were least able to avoid it by coordinating their behavior with others; they were not capable of waiting for others to escape before attempting to escape themselves.

Schultz (1969) posed a conflict for female subjects by facing them with an electric shock and then providing them with two ways of escaping: (1) they could wait for the escape route to be unjammed and cooperate with others so that all could escape, or (2) they could escape immediately through an alternate route, but only by sacrificing the other subjects in the group to immediate exposure to shock. The choice of individual escape was considered a panic response. A series of manipulations, including the size of the group, variations in time pressure, panic by other members of the group, and deindividuation of the subjects, had no effect on the incidence of panic responses. However, between 25 and 50 percent of all subjects "panicked" during

the experiments. Some individual differences were also found. Females who were only children panicked sooner and more often than later-borns, and those who scored higher in anxiety, dependency, femininity, and sensitiveness on a personality test were more willing to sacrifice others to save themselves than were women with the opposite characteristics.

These laboratory simulations appear to produce results that are much the same as those observed in real panics. Without the coordination provided by rehearsal, planning, and organization, people cannot anticipate what others will do and hence tend to make self-protective responses even when they require the sacrifice of others. In many crowds, the lack of strong identification with other group members makes the sacrifice of others to save oneself an easier choice.

6. Queues

A crowd of persons attempting to acquire a desired commodity, such as tickets to an entertainment event, can be classified as an acquisitive mob. Violent stampedes for gold and land in the West and the disruption of traffic and the defiance of the police by bargain hunters at department store sales are other examples of acquisitive mobs (Turner & Killian, 1972, p. 85). Many of these crowds are so orderly and passive that they hardly deserve the name of mob; members form a queue and wait their turns.

Mann (1970) studied the fans who turned out to wait in lines for tickets to championship soccer games in Australia. They often camped out overnight in the gueues, and a short-lined, minature social system was created. Cooperation and orderliness rather than competition and selfishness were dominant at the annual event; conviviality, drinking, card-playing, and communal living characterized the behavior of the good-natured crowd.

The critical factor governing the social system of the queue is the time spent waiting. The norm of equity dictates that those who spend the most time waiting are entitled to being served first when the ticket window opens. Time is the investment offered in exchange for having a greater chance of purchasing a ticket or of obtaining a better seat. Norms formed in the queue permit individuals to take a leave of absence from it. Members of a small party may take turns manning a particular position, and especially toward the end of the line, persons who come alone can stake their claim by leaving a box, chair, or sleeping bag in their place. At one point, when a pick-up game of football was being played, Mann (1970) observed that the queue actually consisted of one-third people and two-thirds inanimate objects.

Physical violence and cutting into line are usually avoided, perhaps because the resulting disintegration of the queue would lead everyone to lose his position in line. If someone cuts into line, it is the job of the person immediately behind to eject him. If he does not, then the cutter has won himself a place. Cutting is usually attempted only toward the end of the line, where the queuers have less investment at stake and there is less risk of an altercation.

Mann (1970) has also reported some informal studies of queue formation as a function of the type of situation and the number of people waiting. When there are fewer than 10 persons in a queue at a bus stop, newcomers may not join the line; for example, observations indicated that with only six in the queue, most new arrivals stood apart from it. When about 10 persons were planted in a queue at a bus stop, new arrivals joined at the end of the line. As the number of people waiting grows, presumably the risk of not getting a seat increases; the bus is likely to pull up to the beginning of the line, and the newcomer takes a place to protect his position. Apparently, the probable cost of not waiting in line strongly contributes to the newcomer's adherence to the developing norm to queue up.

C. Theories of Crowd Behavior

The analysis of behavior in active crowds has not progressed very rapidly. Theories typically consist of metaphors (e.g., collective or group mind), analogies (e.g., father-son relationship), and generalizations from social psychological principles that have been found to govern interpersonal relationships (e.g., informational and normative influence). For the most part these theories of crowd behavior are either untested or untestable, and hence are unsatisfactory scientific explanations. Nevertheless, it may be useful to describe several representative theories to illustrate the difference between the careful development and evaluation of scientific hypotheses of the type considered throughout this book and the more speculative approach that is required when the events considered are not amenable to the techniques of laboratory science.

A 19th century French social philosopher, Gustav LeBon, proposed a theory of mobs which viewed them as if they were organisms ruled by a single collective mind. A person in the mob loses his individual will to act, abdicates his sense of social responsibility, is susceptible to suggestion, and acts in an animalistic or barbaric manner. Freud agreed with much of LeBon's theory, but suggested that a powerful leader with whom the crowd identifies is required to direct and control the mob. The leader gains compliance from members of the crowd and releases them from the control of their individual consciences.

Turner and Killian (1972) explain mob behavior in terms of norms that emerge spontaneously in a crowd and supersede existing standards of conduct. Informational and normative influence are then presumed to produce compliance with the new norms by crowd members. Finally, Smelser (1963a) has offered a multiple-causation model of collective behavior referred to as value-added theory.

Although there are other theories of mob behavior, these four capture the flavor of this kind of speculation. Of course, when discussing lynching and riots, we suggested a conflict model of economic, political, or cultural competition in which mob action constituted one way of trying to resolve the conflicts. We will have more to say about conflict models of collective behavior when discussing social movements and revolutions later in this chapter.

1. LeBon's Theory of the Collective Mind

According to a "law" formulated by LeBon (1895), a crowd is believed to form a single being with a collective mind. The members represent the cells of the corpus (body) of the crowd. Each individual comes under the control of his spinal cord, like lower animals without brains. Thus, the crowd is considered to have one collective brain and many spinal cords. The individual is therefore controlled by the group mind and his own primitive urges; he surrenders his self-control and no longer reasons for himself. Instincts and passions govern the behavior of crowd members, and "superior" men become no different from ordinary men. As a consequence, crowds are impulsive, irritable, incapable of higher sentiments and morality, irresponsible, suggestible, dictatorial, intolerant, fanatical, and dominated by the despotic and hypnotic control of their leaders.

This theory of a collective or group mind was based on three basic processes: (1) anonymity and the loss of responsibility of crowd members, (2) social contagion, and (3) suggestibility. Joining a crowd gives an individual the "sentiment of invincible power"; he loses his sense of responsibility, drops his civilized inhibitions, and lets go the reins of his most destructive animal instincts. This process is synonymous with deindividuation. Each sentiment and act performed in a crowd is contagious and quickly infects every member like a raging disease. The later ideas of interstimulation

and circular reaction (Miller & Dollard, 1941) were based on the notion of social contagion. The individual is extremely suggestible to the demands of a leader in a crowd; he is not conscious of his actions and, in a hypnotic-like trance, obeys commands like an automaton.

It is now clear that the idea of a crowd mind is a metaphor without scientific foundation. The idea that people in a mob become irrational expresses the distrust and hostility of LeBon toward mobs. Katz (1940) challenged this view by stating that "there is no difference between the logic of men in crowds and their logic elsewhere" (p. 160). LeBon's view of crowds was colored by his elitist political attitudes. He believed that "Civilizations as yet have only been created and directed by a small intellectual aristocracy, never by crowds" (1903, p. 19). He was concerned about the increasing tendency of governments to become more democratic and dependent on the masses. There was also a distinct racist and sexist tone to his thinking. Consider the following statement: "It will be remarked that among the special characteristics of crowds there are several—such as impulsiveness, irritability, incapacity to reason, the absence of judgment and of the critical spirit, the exaggeration of the sentiments, and other besides—which are almost always observed in beings belonging to inferior forms of evolution—in women, savages, and children, for instance" (1903, pp. 35–36).

Despite these defects, LeBon's ideas tend still to represent present-day conventional wisdom concerning mob behavior. However, there is little evidence to substantiate the basic processes he postulated as operating to mobilize and activate crowd behavior. Men have no instincts, many traditional views regarding hypnosis have been challenged (see Box 14.1), and the evidence for deindividuation is not very substantial. The reason for the persistence of LeBon's influence is that several of his ideas have found empirical support. Research on conformity and obedience suggests the

Box 14.1   SOCIAL PSYCHOLOGY AND HYPNOSIS

Hypnosis has long been a source of fascination, perhaps because of its long association with faith healing. It was known as "the temple sleep" during the age of Egyptian high priestesses, Mesmerism during the 19th century, and hypnosis in the 20th century. Freud was trained in the techniques of hypnosis prior to developing his psychoanalytic theory and the phenomenon convinced him of the existence of the unconscious.

Early theories attributed trance-like states to magnetism emanating from the stars (astrology) or to special forces originating within the hypnotist. James Braid attributed the trance state to the subject's concentration on a single idea to the exclusion of all others and in response to the operator's suggestions. Inhibitions, which are presumably associated with contradictory ideas, are thereby eliminated and the subject simply obeys the commands of the operator. While there has been an intensive search for the physiological factors that might account for the state of hypnosis, none has yet been found (Hilgard, 1973; Spanos & Barber, 1974).

Role and influence theories have been recently developed to explain hypnosis. Role theory states that the subject assumes the role of hypnotized person and commits himself to being influenced by the operator (Sarbin & Coe, 1972). The role of hypnotized person is very much like that of a good subject in psychological laboratories (see Chapter 2), who does whatever is asked of him, including putting his hand in acid or petting a deadly snake. Barber (1969) considers hypnosis to be a special case of social influence. People who are properly motivated to be compliant will assume the attitudes and perform the behavior asked of them, including acting out the role of a trance state, whether or not they have been "hypnotized." The central idea behind these views is that the subject is highly motivated to cooperate with the hypnotist. As White (1941) characterized hypnotic behavior, it manifests "meaningful, goal-directed striving, its most general goal being to behave like a hypnotized person as this is continuously defined by the operator and understood by the subject" (p. 503).

Although role-playing and influence theories are often considered by their advocates to be conflicting, the evidence generally supports both. Researchers seem to agree that a necessary, though not sufficient, condition for hypnotic effects is a positive attitude toward hypnosis and a willingness to cooperate on the part of the subject. In addition, good subjects are those who have a developed capacity for imaginative involvement. They are capable of shutting out competing sensations and thoughts, much like a person who concentrates so hard on what he is studying that he fails to hear people talking to him. Diamond (1972) has reported that subjects best learn hypnotic behavior from a model who not only performs such behavior but who also describes his imaginings while responding. The strong success of modeling in helping phobic patients (see Box 6.1) is also associated with a model who expresses what he is thinking and doing.

mechanisms by which a leader may gain control over members of a crowd, and social facilitation effects support the existence of something like social contagion.

2. Freud's Theory of the Crowd

Freud (1914, 1922, 1930) was familiar with and adopted many of LeBon's ideas regarding crowd behavior. The concept of a collective mind and the belief that individuals surrender personal control to the mob were ideas consistent with psychoanalytic theory. The ego and superego controls of an individual may be reduced or removed in a crowd, particularly when a strong leader suggests, commands, or supports behavior consistent with the instinctual urges of the id. Primitive instincts, which are normally held in check by the threatened sanctions of civilized society, are released in the context of a mob.

According to Freud, the most important factor in crowd behavior is the relationship between the members and their leader, which he presumed to be similar to a father-son relationship. The little boy initially falls in love with his mother, but soon finds that his rival (the father) blocks the fulfillment of his erotic aspirations. Because the mother rebuffs the child's advances and obviously prefers the father as a mate, the boy gives up his incestuous desires and repudiates his wish to murder his father. These renunciations, forming the resolution of the Oedipus complex, are fundamental to the development of a conscience (or superego) reflecting the values of the parents. The father becomes the ego-ideal and has a powerful influence over the development of the child's superego. In turn, the boy's superego is the master of his ego and controls much of his behavior.

The development of love for the leader in a crowd cannot be fulfilled because he cannot reciprocate the love of all the members. Hence, the libidinal bond to the leader is unreciprocated. The result is that the group member sets the leader up as an ego-ideal and identifies with him, surrendering the superego function to him. The conscience of the leader supersedes the consciences of his followers. His influence resembles the control of the hypnotist over his subject. The narcissistic love for self is canceled out by the libidinal bond with the leader and the crowd acts with the unity of a collective being.

Freud's theory is one of crowd unity under the directives of a leader who fulfills the role of parent-surrogate. The leader's power is based on the love felt for him and the fear in which he is held. Individuals have a tendency to identify with a potential aggressor (see the discussion of power and modeling in Chapter 6), but a love-hate relationship may maintain an ambivalence toward a leader. The Italians loved Mussolini, but they also manifested their hatred by desecrating his body. It is the leader who organizes and leads the mob, provides a directive function for their actions, and releases them from the superego inhibitions that usually regulate their behavior.

Historical observation leaves little doubt that leaders can incite mob action and that followers often sacrifice themselves out of loyalty and devotion. Unfortunately, it is not possible to test Freud's theory empirically because the language he used is metaphorical. There are no empirical indicators of processes like the id, ego, and superego. There is solid evidence for the underlying idea that people do have ambivalent relations with those who both nurture and discipline (or control) them. However, the frequent observation of mobs that are either virtually leaderless or which act against the pleadings of their leaders (Milgram & Toch, 1969) contradicts Freud's view of the leader's role in mob behavior.

3. Emergent Norm Theory

Turner and Killian (1972) criticize the collective mind and unified crowd assumptions of LeBon and Freud. Not all members of a crowd blindly follow the dictates of those around them or of a leader. Some persons leave the mob, some stay and observe but do not participate, others try to stop objectionable activities. Some members inadvertently get caught up in the mob's activities, as when a bystander is attacked during a riot and then must protect himself by fighting back. The belief that a mob is homogeneous and acts in a unanimous fashion is contrary to observation.

Turner and Killian distinguish between three major processes postulated by various theorists as basic to crowd behavior: contagion, convergence, and the emergence of norms. The automatic transmission of feeling states and response dispositions through a semi-hypnotized and receptive crowd characterizes social *contagion,* the major factor in LeBon's theory. *Convergence* refers to the homogeneity of attitudes and actions of crowd members; people act collectively because they are like-minded. Freud's theory of crowd behavior could be interpreted in terms of the convergence of members toward the leader. Unlike the contagion and convergence theories, emergent norm theory does not assume the homogeneity or unanimity of action or feeling in a crowd. According to Turner and Killian, members of a crowd act rationally and yield to the new expectations of others in the crowd for much the same reasons they do in group conformity and risky shift studies. An event occurs, an interpretation is quickly communicated through the crowd (informational influence), and shared expectations are developed regarding behavior. Normative pressures are then brought to bear on members to comply with the emergent norms in the situation. Mob action is the result of this communication, emergent norm, influence, and compliance sequence. Hence, the behavior of people in a crowd is no different than in any other type of interpersonal situation. While these generalizations drawn from principles of interpersonal behavior, and designed to explain what happens in a crowd seem

plausible, they remain untested in the context of the collectivity. Unfortunately, other speculations explaining crowd behavior seem to be equally plausible.

4. Smelser's Value-Added Theory

Smelser (1963a) has advanced a systematic sociological theory of collective behavior that attempts to account for mobs, social movements, and revolutions. It is referred to as *value-added theory* because there are six conditions that are necessary before collective action will take place, and these conditions must occur in sequence—each added to the other in exactly the right order. The six conditions required are structural conduciveness, structural strain, a generalized belief, a precipitating factor, mobilization for action, and lack of social control.

Structural conduciveness is a situational factor or social condition that makes collective action possible. The frequency with which riots took place in urban ghettos during the 1960s was partly due to the fact that people living there tend to spend a great deal of time on the streets and in front of their homes. The availability of a large number of people provides a necessary condition for collective action, but it is not sufficient to cause an incident. In general, people who are to act together must be in contact with one another, must be unable to achieve what they wish without some kind of joint action, must have some means of acting jointly, and must have an institution or group in the social system to act against.

Structural strain refers to a conflict situation. The collectivity must be in conflict with some other aspect of the social system. Perceived deprivation or persecution, unredressed grievances or injustice, economic competition, and other sources of conflict may cause a collectivity to strain against societal institutions and groups believed to be responsible for the problem. Riots by blacks in the ghettos were obviously aimed at destroying the symbols of oppressive white authority—stores, buildings, and police. Similarly, lynchings of Negroes in the South dramatically increased after the Civil War and the Emancipation Proclamation, events which produced a strain in the established relationships between whites and blacks for more than a century.

A *generalized belief* must develop among members of the collectivity regarding the causes for the structural strain and the means by which it may be eliminated. If blame for the strain cannot be focused, no collective action can occur. A lynch mob shares a belief in the culpability of the victim. The rumor of hoodlums dropping a baby off a bridge was an important generalized belief focusing blame in the 1943 Detroit race riot. A developed ideology serves the same function in social movements and wars of national liberation.

A *precipitating event* is needed to trigger the collective behavior. The arrest of citizens in the ghettos was often the precipitating event for property riots against the symbols of white authority, as was the assassination of Martin Luther King, Jr. A murder or rape may be the event tripping off the actions of a lynch mob, although little effort may be exerted in assuring that the victim is the guilty party. A panic is precipitated by the shout of "fire" or the smell of smoke.

A precipitating event in one situation may not set off collective behavior in another. Many arrests are made in the ghetto without provoking riots; murders and rapes occur without subsequent lynchings; and crowds frequently make orderly escapes from dangerous situations. *Mobilization for action* is required for collective action to occur. Some direction or leadership must be given to the milling and disorganized crowd before it can take coordinated action. Criminal elements have often led race riots, and lynchings may be organized by leaders of the KKK.

The manner, strength, and timing with which *social controls* are implemented may be crucial for determining whether a mobilized mob or an organized revolutionary group will be able to carry out its activities. Law enforcement officials winked at the KKK in the South and hence made it possible for the lynchings to take place. It was common knowledge that a white person wouldn't get arrested for killing a Negro and people would joke about bounties of $5 and $10 for each black killed. It was extremely difficult to maintain social control in ghettos during property riots. As a consequence, police often adopted the strategy of containing the riot within geographical limits by surrounding it; within this cordoned area no attempts to make arrests or to interfere with looting were made. Quick, sure, and tight social controls can nip a mob action in the bud, but it is not always possible to institute them, and the authorities must be careful not to exercise more force than necessary to establish order. Overreaction by an authority may simply cause an increase in the sense of injustice felt by the mob and lead to escalation rather than containment of the conflict.

Smelser's value-added theory is a useful way to organize the determinants of collective behavior; however, the outline is too sketchy in detail to qualify as a scientific theory. How does one measure structural conduciveness or strain? How much strain does there have to be as a precondition for collective action? How does a crowd get mobilized for action? Although these questions remain unanswered, Smelser's scheme does have intuitive appeal because of the multidimensionality of his causal analysis.

II. MASS BEHAVIOR

Mass phenomena include public opinion, mass culture, voting, leisure time activities, viewing the mass media, fads and fashions, and crazes and cults. These phenomena have been studied by economists, political scientists, and sociologists. Social psychologists have generally confined their attention to the effects of the mass media, fads, fashions, crazes, and deviance.

A.   The Mass Media

Daniel Boorstin (1961), an American historian, has referred to recent advances in communication technology as the Graphic Revolution. There can be little question that the Graphic Revolution has had a tremendous impact on the world. A foreign ambassador in the 19th century was given a great deal of authority in dealing with foreign governments because it took several months to communicate directly with his home office. A treaty ending the war of 1812 was concluded two weeks before the terrible defeat of the British militia at New Orleans, but the news had not yet reached the combatants. Today, a voice transmitting a lecture over radio travels at the speed of light and can be received halfway around the world before it reaches your ear in the classroom where the voice travels at the speed of sound. Instantaneous communication has transformed entertainment, the average person's knowledge of the world, and the ability of governments to accumulate and wield power. It has provided new opportunities for propagandists and advertisers to promote their ideas and commodities, and much else.

Three important functions served by the mass media are: (1) to provide information, (2) to create and support public opinion, and (3) to entertain. These three effects are not independent of one another.

1.   Information Dispersal

The news media disperse information to consumers about events. The local newspaper provides information about the sale of commodities, the motion picture playing at the local theater, the television schedule, the weather, accidents, and deaths, local, state, and national politics, and international events. Magazines tend to treat events in more depth and to specialize in the kinds of events they cover. Television allows an individual to view events immediately after or while they happen. Movie documentaries and television specials add the visual dimension to a magazine format. And, of course, books have traditionally conveyed the most penetrating and thorough analyses of events and ideas.

The transistor radio, television, and the movies have brought the entire world into the experience of even the wholly illiterate person. Each man can now directly witness events all over the world through the images presented to him in his own living room. The information gained may create beliefs, expectations, values, and desires having a profound effect on domestic and international affairs. Audiovisual aids have become standard means of communicating history, language, and culture to students. The ability to recreate past eras brings them to life again on the movie and television screens.

Of course, the media provide a monitoring function that allows people to prepare for hurricanes, tornados, floods, and other natural or man-made disasters. The reliance placed in the mass media was demonstrated by the fear and panic generated by Orson Welles' famous radio broadcast of *The War of the Worlds* on Halloween night in 1938. In an investigation of this event Cantril (1940) found that listeners all over the United States had been frightened to the point of panic by the program. Some people ran to save loved ones or called friends or neighbors to warn them of the danger of the invasion of the Martians, which was vividly described in an alleged eye-witness account of the landing of a space vehicle and its subsequent emission of death gases. Praying, crying, and preparations to take flight characterized the behavior of many listeners.

2.   The Creation and Support of Public Opinion

The substitution of mediated reality for direct experience by watching and listening to the electronic media confuses fact and fantasy. Events can be contrived for the very purpose of creating supportive opinions or gaining notice. Propagandists have become concerned about projecting an image of their product, whether it is a soft drink, an automobile, or a presidential candidate. What matters is not what is actually the case, but what people believe; so images are manipulated in order to create the effect desired. An image is a fascimile or representation of the external form of an object, especially of a person. The mass media are quite aware of their power to affect the beliefs and attitudes of people. For example, *The Philadelphia Bulletin* advertised that "You buy belief when you buy *The Bulletin*" (Boorstin, 1961).

The impact of the mass media will depend upon a person's state of information dependence. In a study of adolescents, Gerson (1964) found that the respondents who were least well integrated in their homes and schools were more dependent on models and advice in the media for ideas about dating. The mere fact that an event or person has been singled out by the mass media confers status, prestige, and legitimacy (Lazarsfeld & Merton, 1948). Who would ever have heard of Stokely Carmichael, Rap Brown or other self-appointed leaders of black protest movements during the 1960s without the exposure given to them by the media? Their lack of historical importance is suggested by the fact that just a few short years later many people do not recognize their names. Persons caught up in the eye of publicity tend to gain an exaggerated sense of their own importance (Waples, Berelson, & Bradshaw, 1940; Davison, 1956). An event that might have been relatively isolated in a former age takes on momentous importance under the glare of television lights and the flash bulbs of newspaper photographers. Civil rights incidents, demonstrations against war, rent strikes, and shootouts can be transformed from local happenings to events of national significance by mass media coverage.

In Chapter 12 we saw that the media can reinforce an individual's sense of injustice, provide him with models of how to respond, and indicate the degree of support he has from other members of his society. On the other hand, news reports revealing a discrepancy between private behavior and public protestations of value can provide consensual support for maintaining hypocritical attitudes and deviant behavior (Williams, 1947).

Because public opinion is a way of judging the endorsement of plans, decisions, and policies (and by extension, of political leaders), it has become important to manipulate it and to monitor it continually. President Lyndon Johnson was notorious for carrying the latest public opinion polls around in his pocket. The latest polls are front page news because members of society can look in the social mirror the polls represent and make social comparisons. If we can generalize from the research on conformity and the risky shift, it can be said that the very act of reporting public opinion may change or support it. Once people know the public values, they may shift toward them. The study of public opinion and its effects on the political decision process has been increasingly emphasized by political scientists (cf. Hennessy, 1970; Rosenau, 1961).

3. Entertainment

The shift from rural to urban living, from work on the farm to the factory or office, and from scarcity to relative affluence has given people in industrialized countries much more leisure time than they had in the past. It may be suggested that in the United States one manifestation of this release from work is that the number of local art museums has increased by four times since the 1930s and the number of symphony orchestras has doubled since 1950 (Brooks, 1966).

By far the greatest growth in the area of entertainment has been associated with the electronic media, which have created an entirely new form of mass culture. The development of phonograph records stimulated the transmission of songs and made their singers popular (and rich). A parade of crooners, rock, folk, and country singers, big bands, jazz ensembles, and rock groups have hit the limelight only to fade within a few short years under its hot glare. Radio and television have both destroyed and promoted sports activities. Boxing was first helped by both media, but the availability of a fight a week in the fan's living room kept him away from all the little clubs that fed into the pugilistic apprenticeship system and literally killed the fight game. Now most of the world champions are from other countries, whereas less than two decades ago almost all of them were from the United States. The popularity of professional football and basketball is directly attributable to their promotion on television. The development of new leagues, like the American Basketball Association and the World Hockey League, cannot occur without lucrative television contracts to give them financial solvency. A recent example is the World Football League which survived only from 1974 to mid-season of 1975 without a network television contract.

The electronic media often have an effect on the structure of the events they transmit. During his first tour of the United States in 1925, Igor Stravinski signed a contract with a gramaphone company to record some of his music. He wrote *Serenade in A* so that each of its four movements would exactly fill one side of a 10-inch record. Most team sports that have wide television coverage now have a series of "referee's time outs" that provide one-minute time slots for commercial messages.

Entertainment provides an audience with stimulation, breaks up boredom, and provides a momentary escape from the problems of the everyday world. Men need

continual change and environmental stimulation or they suffer from mental malfunctioning (see Chapter 3, I, A). There is plenty of action on the most popular TV programs. Why people choose to watch particular programs is not known. The amount of information and reassurance provided by an entertainment probably is related to its popularity. Crime, disaster, and illness are frequent events in our society, but the average person does not have much personal experience with them. The individual who is concerned about law and order may be somewhat insecure and may need reassurance that the police are kind and efficient in protecting private citizens. A person worried about his health may be fascinated with programs about thoughtful and skillful doctors. And it is nice to know that should false charges ever be made against you, a competent lawyer will be certain to prove your innocence and perhaps capture the real culprit to boot.

Television drama cannot become too real or it becomes frightening and objectionable. Series that try to dramatize real life social problems seldom are commercially successful. Reassurance requires fantasy and caricature, because real life has many unhappy endings. A doctor may lose his patient through carelessness, false diagnosis, or because the problem is not soluble in the light of current knowledge. Many crimes are unsolved, some criminals are never caught or else are not rehabilitable; lawyers make mistakes of procedure and substance and hurt their client's interests. These lapses into real life would lose a program its sponsors.

The average television viewer wants programs that reflect a comfortable, progressive, and safe world and maintain his myths about society. Boorstin has referred to television as "chewing gum for the eyes." He believes it is not dangerous as long as we are aware of its lack of nourishment. The fantasy is fostered by making sure that victims never suffer very much pain, that heroes never experience guilt for killing the villains, and that blood and gore are never really seen by the viewer; the characters are all one-dimensional. Undoubtedly, the mass media transmit values and provide models having widespread effects on public conduct. But social scientists know very little about these effects. The controversy regarding the effect of television violence on viewers, discussed in Chapter 12, III, C, which is the best researched area of mass media effects, reveals the complexity of the problem and the difficulty of drawing any firm conclusions. Perhaps even more important is a question that has received almost no attention from the scientific community. How does passive viewing of television for great amounts of time affect a person's general life style?

B. Fashions, Fads, and Crazes

Fairchild's (1944) *Dictionary of Sociology* defines fashion as "relatively short-lived, socially approved, continuous variations in dress, furniture, music, art, speech, and other areas of culture" (p. 117). Styles in women's clothing have been interpreted in terms of erogenous zones, satiation, and utility (see Box 11.1). Other motivations and attitudes have been postulated as underlying changes of fashion. The individual's wish for adventure and novelty, exhibitionism, his desire to display symbols of success, status, and prestige, rebellion against the standards of the majority society, compensation for inferiority, and a strong need for power have all been proposed by students of fashion (Barr, 1934; Flugel, 1930; Sherif & Cantril, 1947; Veblen, 1934). Unfortunately, not even the designers themselves can tell us why a particular fashion is adopted while so many other possibilities are rejected.

Fads are more sporadic and short-lived than fashions. According to Sargent and Williamson (1958). "A fad may be local or national in scope but it is always temporary and unpredictable. Sometimes what begins

as a fad may end up as a fashion, custom, or hobby. For example, bobbed hair, slacks, blue jeans, and bingo started as fads and have continued in more permanent form" (p. 471). Fads characteristically flare up and spread rapidly, then just disappear. Elephant jokes, hula hoops, swallowing gold fish, and jamming into telephone booths are some examples of the fads of our own college years.

A number of factors make Americans particularly susceptible to fashions and fads (and to crazes and social movements, as we shall see). The spread of fads through social contagion is most prevalent in urban areas, particularly among the young. The mobility of the population, their receptivity to change, the wealth that allows people to buy gadgets and trifles, the encouragement of notoriety in the mass media, and many other factors facilitate these intermittent social experiments.

Sargent and Williamson suggested that a fad must seem novel or new and must be broadly consistent with the times and with widespread values, and is vastly accelerated by publicity and advertising. "Streaking" in the nude in public places was one of the popular fads of 1974. It erupted in California (where it is warm), spread to college campuses in the Southern United States, and finally hit northern campuses and cities in the spring. Streakers sped across television screens, basketball courts, highways, and jumped out of airplanes. They sometimes wore ties or socks or hats. Males streaked through female dormitories and females retaliated. Streakers were everywhere and then just as suddenly as it began, it was over. In the year of Richard Nixon's fateful resignation and grave conflict in the Middle East, the streakers' sense of humor, freedom, and rebelliousness against the grim morality of the political scene provided some contrast and relief. Although some arrests were made, the authorities generally winked at the fad.

A craze refers to the total involvement of a mass of people in a particular activity.

Crazes sometimes take the form of mania or mass hysteria. Strong emotions are elicited but after a time, commitment to the cause or activity wanes. The processes of suggestion and social contagion appear to be implicated in this form of mass behavior.

A craze occurred in Mattoon, Illinois, during the first twelve days of September, 1944. A "phantom anesthetist" allegedly struck a number of victims. On September 1, a woman reported to the police that someone had opened her bedroom window and sprayed her with a gas that made her ill and partially paralyzed her legs. Two dozen similar cases were reported thereafter. Of the four victims attended by a physician, all were diagnosed as cases of hysteria. No known gas could produce the effects associated with the spray allegedly used by the phantom anesthetist. No unambiguous sightings of prowlers were reported to the local or state police even though many of the townspeople combed the community. It must be presumed that the victims' dogs were also gassed, since none of them had barked at the alleged attacker (Johnson, 1945).

The local newspaper in Mattoon was somewhat sensational in its coverage of these events. Police records revealed a marked upsurge of prowler reports during the craze; but once skepticism became more widespread and the victims were labeled as hysterical, prowler reports fell to zero for several weeks. Johnson concluded that psychological suggestibility and not a mysterious gas was responsible for these events.

The feverish runs on the banks in the 1930s; the teenage manias associated with Frank Sinatra, Elvis Presley, James Dean, the Beatles, and David Cassidy; and the spread of dance manias are just some of the crazes that have spread and created great excitement, anger, or despair among large masses of people. Fear, disappointment, rebelliousness, and any number of other factors can predispose people to suggestion and to manifest a behavior carried by social contagion.

Kerckhoff, Back, and Miller (1965) found that social contagion may begin among social outsiders and then spread rapidly among groups of friends. During one week in the summer of 1962, sixty-two employees at a clothing manufacturing plant complained of symptoms such as fainting, severe pain, nausea, and disorientation. Although the affected persons believed their symptoms were caused by insect bites, neither a physician or an entomologist could find any sign of bites or insects, or of chemicals which could qualify as causes of the outbreak. Interviews established that the epidemic had begun among employees who were relative social isolates with predispositions to hysterical complaints. These isolates tended to accept the report of the epidemic from its originator because they had no friends to use for social comparison purposes. After several persons were "infected," the contagion spread faster as persons who were socially integrated became sources of influence among their friends. As the epidemic became widespread, social integration became less of a factor and a general "crowd response" (consensus) rendered more and more people susceptible to this form of mass delusion.

C. Mass Reactions to Deviance

The orderly coexistence of a mass of people depends on their shared expectations and norms governing behavior. Interdependence requires that each person fulfill his obligations for all to gain their objectives. Of course, social rules do not guarantee that every person will gain the rewards he desires and not every rule is so clear and unambiguous that he knows what to do in order to conform to it. The very existence of a norm or rule creates the possibility of someone defying it. Behavior that is contrary to the rules of the group is perceived as *deviance*.

Deviance has both constructive and destructive effects on the organization and coordinated interdependence that characterizes much of modern life (Cohen, 1966). Among its constructive effects are innovation and rule clarification. No rules can anticipate every possible situation, and there may be a better solution to the problem at hand than is allowed or prescribed by the existing norms. To implement a better method of solving tasks, someone must violate the group's norms. Rule clarification often results from deviant behavior. As Cohen points out, "just what is included within each term of the rule; the exact limits of its applicability; its qualifications and reservations; the intensity of feeling associated with it; whether it is a pious sentiment or an injunction to be taken seriously—all these can seldom be communicated in a few words, or even in a complicated formula. It is a hard fact of life that these things are learned, to a great extent, only by testing the limits (or witnessing what happens when others test the limits) of propriety and *discovering* whether one has overstepped the bounds" (p. 8). One of the chief functions of courts of law (especially the appellate courts) is to provide interpretations of rules in the course of their confrontations with deviance.

Cohen also points to three destructive effects of deviance. First, it may represent a breakdown of the intricate social coordination of the behavior of many people. For example, vandals may disable a fleet of trucks and cause failure by a supplier to deliver paper which, in turn, would prevent newspapers from printing their daily editions; further effects would reverberate throughout the social system. Second, deviance constitutes a break in the unanimity of a group and may encourage other people to withdraw their cooperation from ongoing activities. Perhaps its most important destructive effect is that it undermines the willingness of people to make commitments and invest resources, skills, and effort on the assumption that others can be relied on to play their parts in bringing interdependent and reciprocal benefits to them all.

The collapse of reciprocal expectations removes the motivation to take positive unilateral action and causes people to view their own initiatives as "pointless, wasted, and foolish, and the future as hazardous and uncertain" (Cohen, p. 5). The consequence is a change in the structure of the organization, institution, group, crowd, or mass.

Aberrant behavior, nonconformity, and rebellion represent three forms of deviance. The deviant who engages in aberrant behavior violates the rules but does not dispute their validity and makes no attempt to alter them; he is intent on gaining his own objectives and avoiding any penalty. The nonconformist flouts the rules openly as a means of drawing attention to their imperfections and in order to change or replace them. Civil disobedience involves a deliberate and public violation of law which is intended to draw attention to an injustice associated with the law; the nonconformist often seeks to be arrested so he can test the law in a proper court. Whereas the aberrant person seeks to avoid apprehension, trial, and punishment, the nonconformist does not break the law for personal profit and may wish to be arrested and tried. The rebel denies the system of authority on which the entire set of rules depends. He is not concerned with this or that rule, but with the entire social order. Unlike the nonconformist, who is basically a reformist, the rebel is a revolutionary.

Still another type of deviance may be added to our list—the mentally ill. The mentally ill person either manifests unconcern for the norms, rules, and laws governing a situation or else claims to be incapable of controlling his own behavior. In either case, his behavior does not appear to have any instrumental purpose and it is difficult to understand why he does what he does.

Shared values and expectations not only define what is deviant behavior, but also prescribe what should be done about it. Social control measures include prevention or deterrence, justice, vengeance, reform, compensation or reparation, and rehabilitation. As a means of social control, the legal system seldom works the same way for all indicted persons. The wealthy and better educated make more positive self-presentations and can hire more skilled attorneys than the poor. A former Vice-President and an Attorney General of the United States convicted of crimes that would have brought stiff penalties if they had lower status never actually spent a day in jail. Of course, those who wield political power enact the laws, and interpret and enforce them. The law is responsive to the interests, groups, and classes represented by those who hold office. The legal system represents a series of compromises reached through conflict and bargaining between different interest groups in society. A law almost always favors one group over another because each right implies a responsibility. For example, the right of blacks to eat in a restaurant deprives the proprietor of the right to choose freely among his potential customers. The legal system is a conglomeration of interpretations, favors, exceptions, and deliberate omissions. As Nieburg (1969) points out, "The doctrine that every good citizen obeys every law is an ideology of the status quo" (p. 67).

Whether a deviant form of behavior will be considered eccentric, sinful, illegal, "sick," or an act of high idealism and martyrdom, leadership, and genius depends on who it helps and hurts, the magnitude of its consequences, and the way it is rationalized. What is considered illegal in one society or age may be labeled "sick" in another. At least until the advent of the recent Gay Liberation Movement, the police in most cities in the United States harassed homosexuals, sometimes booking them on loitering or vagrancy charges. Yet homosexuality is positively valued in some societies and may be practiced there by every "normal" person (Ford & Beach, 1952). Many people in contemporary society classify homosexuality as a disease that happens to be very difficult to treat. Members of the Gay Liberation Movement have decided they would rather be considered morally bad than to carry the stigma of being labeled as mentally ill. Their success in getting the American Psychiatric Association to remove homosexuality from their list of "mental illnesses" demonstrates a relationship between social power and what is considered deviant.

Power as a factor in defining and treating "mental illness" is one of the most fashionable topics in current sociology and clinical psychology. Admission to and discharge from a mental hospital involves power. The very fact that a patient enters a hospital may be evidence that he is the loser in a long and perhaps violent struggle with his family (Laing & Esterson, 1964) or perhaps a winner if he desired entry to escape from an unbearable world (Goffman, 1961). Psychiatric screening is typically a perfunctory process in which the patient's condition is only one of a number of factors which decide the outcome (Hollingshead & Redlich, 1958). Just being a mental patient represents for most people a loss of status and power.

There is growing recognition that so-called psychiatric symptoms represent an individual's idiosyncratic attempts to deal with other people. A symptom may be an effort to control a relationship or may constitute a subtle and ambiguous form of communication (Haley, 1963; Szasz, 1961). Haley has described a number of examples of the control that "sickness" gives the patient over others: "A patient with an alcoholic wife once said that he was a man who liked to have his own way but his wife always won by getting drunk. His wife, who was present in the therapy session, became indignant and said she won nothing but unhappiness by her involuntary drinking. Yet obviously she did win something by it. In this case she won almost complete control of her relationship with her husband.

He could not go where he wanted because she might drink; he could not leave her alone because of what she might do when drunk; and he could not make any plans but had to let her initiate whatever happened. She might suffer distress and humiliation and even provoke her husband to beat her, but *she* provoked those situations and thereby controlled what was to happen" (p. 15). Similarly, dizzy spells, anxiety attacks, compulsive washing of the hands, and other symptoms may allow a person to control the behavior of another. Paradoxically, the patient is likely to deny the social control motivation of his "symptoms."

Hysterical symptoms, according to Szasz, are subtle or indirect communications, similar to hints, that are directed by the patient to significant others. The hints communicated through the manifestation of hysterical symptoms such as paralysis, blindness, hiccoughing, sneezing, itching, and other physical malfunctions having no physiological basis, have three advantages over direct and explicit verbal messages: (1) the message can be denied should it have unforseen consequences; (2) it provides a way of communicating a message the effect of which is feared (the patient may be concerned about losing the love of a person but feel the need to communicate some critical message to him); and (3) it may lead another person to initiate a desired action without being specifically requested to do so. Compliance with a request does not reveal the same degree of love as a seemingly more spontaneous and unilateral action, and the latter may be helped along by a hint indicating receptivity.

If mental illness can be interpreted in terms of power conflicts, therapy can be viewed as a means of social control. The therapist may have a great deal of power over the patient. Behavior therapies rely on both coercive and reward power; other forms, such as psychoanalysis, rely on information control. The psychoanalyst encourages the patient to view the world through the categories of psychoanalytic theory or, as Szasz interprets it, to convert the indirect language of symptoms back into an explicit language. Nondirective therapy capitalizes on the manipulation of social reinforcement (care and affection) to foster modeling and the imitation of the therapist by the patient. During the therapeutic process, the patient gives up his unattainable goals, changes his strategies, adjusts his interpretations of events, adopts new aspirations, or else he remains unchanged or becomes depressed and dissatisfied as a result of the lack of therapeutic success.

Clinical psychologists and psychiatrists dislike acknowledging their control over the patient; they prefer to picture themselves as merely allowing him to cause changes in himself. "Allows" turns out on examination to mean "causes." The therapist's lack of clear awareness about how he is using power may vitiate the effectiveness with which he employs his techniques. The clinician is a technician, and as such he is expected to produce results. In general, his avowed aim is to change perceptions, motives, beliefs, goals, and behavior; otherwise, he has no social function. Although there is no rigorous study to tell us whether the collective activities of clinicians serve the economic, social or political interests of any particular segment of society, it may be conjectured that for the most part (there are significant exceptions) they serve the same social control functions as agents of the legal system. In the Soviet Union, blatantly political purposes are served when ideological deviates are adjudicated as mentally ill rather than tried for breaking the law.

Of course, mental patients are not entirely powerless. Many use the mental hospital as a refuge against the conflicts and agonies they experience in the outside world. Braginsky, Braginsky, and Ring (1969) reported that at a large mental hospital in New England the predominant motivation of most patients was to remain there and enjoy life as much as possible. Patients on the open wards used ingratiation and impression management tactics to get what they wanted. For example, patients who signed their names to a questionnaire about their opinions of the hospital expressed more favorable attitudes than did anonymous patients.

In a study of impression management, three interview conditions were created for long-term schizophrenic patients living on the open ward who had been in the hospital for more than two years: (1) A Discharge set in which they were told, "I think the person you are going to see is interested in examining patients to see whether they might be ready for discharge;" (2) An Open Ward set, in which they were informed the interviewer was interested in deciding whether they should remain on the preferred open ward or transferred to the undesirable closed ward; and (3) A Mental Status set, in which they were told the interviewer was interested in seeing how they were feeling and getting along in the hospital (Braginsky & Braginsky, 1967).

Patients in the Open Ward condition presented themselves in the interview as less mentally ill and in less need of hospital control than did those in either the Discharge or Mental Status conditions. Clearly, the patients subtlely manipulated the information presented to the interviewer so as to create a healthy or sick impression with the apparent goal of maintaining their position in the open ward. When the interview had implications for release, the patients presented themselves as "sick," but when they might have been placed on the closed ward, they presented themselves as relatively "well." Braginsky, Braginsky, and Ring concluded that "Mental patients, for all their pathology, are in most respects, most of the time, just like the rest of us; they want to live in a mental hospital in the same way that ordinary persons want to live in their own community" (p. 73).

III. SOCIAL CHANGE

In the first 75 years of the 20th century, man has made more advances in his control over the physical and biological environment than in all his previous millions of years on earth. He has conquered time and space. He has been to the moon and is sending space probes to the other planets. Signals disclosing the cosmic events of 200 million years ago can be picked up by radio telescopes. Jet planes can carry passengers over the Atlantic Ocean in 6 hours, a trip that took the Pilgrim fathers 106 days to make. In a more ominous development, rockets have been placed underground, on aircraft, and in submarines below the polar icecaps that can deliver nuclear destruction to hundreds of millions of people in less than one hour.

The shrinkage of the world through modern transportation and electronic communication systems has changed human relationships. A few decades ago it was possible to ignore famines and diseases that killed millions of people; they always seemed remote and far away. But in 1959 the death of a hundred people from starvation in the Maldive Islands in the Indian Ocean was publicized by large headlines in the newspapers of Great Britain and provoked indignant editorials demanding remedial action by the British government. Sometimes these humanitarian concerns also serve the self-interest of the potential samaritans. For example, a louse brushed off the rags of a beggar in an Eastern country can transport typhus and pestilence to any Western capital within hours by aircraft. To fight the carriers of disease is in everyone's interest.

The combination of a population explosion and economic underdevelopment in two-thirds of the world creates a tinder-box promising many revolutionary explosions for the remainder of this century. Consider the plight of Brazil, the largest nation in Latin America. Given its rate of population increase, it will need 21 times its present Gross National Product by the year 2000 just to maintain the present per capita income of less than 200 dollars per year. A good indicator of the gap between the rich and the poor of the world is the fact that all the energy produced in India in 1953 for a population of over 450 million people would not have been sufficient to light up New York City in that year (Hoffman, 1962). And it is in the poor countries that the energies of the people are sapped by malnutrition and illness.

Naturally, all the people of the world want good health, plenty of enriching food to eat, nice clothes and homes to live in, and the consumer products so common in the industrialized countries of the West. But this desire for social change is relatively new. As we shall see, many people cling to tradition and have attitudes and values that cause them to resist change. Innovation is the key to economic development. Naturally, we cannot here explain all the complications and problems associated with economic development, but we will examine some of the social psychological factors that are associated with this process.

Social change produces dislocations, inequities, and strain on the social system. Perceived injustice and a need to find meaning in one's life in response to a changing social order are elements that give rise to social movements. Of course, not all social change is attributable to planned activity or to social movements but the latter are almost always a function of social change. According to Toch (1965), a *social movement* is "an effort by a large number of people to solve collectively a problem that they feel they have in common" (p. 5). The United States has been alive with social movements over the past two decades. The civil rights movement, the Women's Liberatio

movement, the Gay Liberation movement, the anti-war movement, the John Birch Society, and McCarthyism are only some of the more renowned collective activities during this recent period. The social psychological factors that contribute to the emergence of a social movement, attract persons to it, maintain the fervor of its members and lead to their disaffection, have been topics of much speculation among social philosophers.

Ideological movements, particularly those involving political aspirations, sometimes lead to largescale violence within a society. These civil wars have become a matter of concern for the superpowers of an interdependent yet competitive world. The United States, the Soviet Union, France, and England have all sponsored and supported with men and arms client groups in foreign nations in so-called wars of national liberation. In these wars, a revolutionary group typically has confronted a government strongly supported by an industrialized Western government. Recent confrontations of this type have occurred in the Philippines, Indonesia, Malaysia, Cuba, Vietnam, Laos, Cambodia, Zaire (formerly the Belgian Congo), and Algeria. Revolutionaries have relied on guerrilla warfare to defeat the superior weapons technology and economic power of the sponsor nations. A use of violence for psychological purposes and a reliance on indoctrination and propaganda characterizes guerrilla warfare.

Economic development, social movements, and wars of national liberation are related to one another; each represents significant change in the lives of masses of people. The degree to which social psychology can contribute to an understanding of these problems should not be exaggerated; economic, political, and geographical factors are probably more important than social psychological ones. Most of what is known about these phenomena is in the form of speculation and conjecture. Very few social psychology textbooks discuss them at all because the phenomena tend to fall outside the social psychologist's level of analysis and because little of a scientific nature is known about them.

The substitution of intuitive analysis and historical speculation for scientific rigor serves as a contrast to the careful experimental work that the social psychologist prefers to carry out. As we indicated in Chapter 2, the more complex the social event to be explained and the more practically relevant it is to everyday human affairs, the less accessible it usually is to scientific analysis and empirical study. However, the significance of problems of population control, worldwide starvation, and constant warfare is sufficiently great that we feel it would be morally irresponsible for us to ignore them simply because little of scientific merit is known about them. Whatever analogies, metaphors, or generalizations scientists can bring to bear on these problems may be of help to the policy makers who must ultimately cope with them by using as many strands of information as they can pull together. Therefore, we end this book by discussing some of the social psychological aspects of social change.

A. Economic Development

Two out of every three people in the world—a total of 2 billion persons—living in almost 100 countries have a yearly income below $300. These poor countries are called "underdeveloped" because they are believed to have valuable but unused resources, including labor. Nearly all of them are in or near the tropics. Enke (1963) offers three reasons why a tropical climate may stultify economic growth: (1) Human motivation to work is lowered because a tropical environment is not challenging; many kinds of food, such as coconuts, bananas, and sweet potatoes are available for the picking and the warm weather makes it unnecessary to use fuel, clothing,

or shelter. (2) The prevalence of disease together with the malnutrition prevalent in overpopulated areas reduce the energy of the people and shorten their lives. (3) The soil, sun, humidity, insects, and fungi of the tropics and near-tropics are unfavorable for higher organized agricultural production.

Economic development is as much a political and social process as it is an economic one. The first stirrings of development may be considered pre-economic and involve changes in attitudes, values, and habits, The mobilization of collective energies and changes in institutions are required. Heilbroner (1963) points out that those who have power in a society tend to resist these changes for fear of losing their privileges in a changed social structure.

Schumpeter (1934) asserted that innovation is the key to economic development. His analysis of the growth in the economies of the advanced countries during the 19th century showed how vital innovation was. The exploitation of raw materials, the production of new types of goods, penetrating new markets, and inventing new ways of organizing production are necessary economic innovations if development is to take place. Perhaps even more important are the changes required of the peoples of the poor countries. The inventions, technology, and perhaps the investment capital of the wealthier countries could be used to help the poor nations of the world develop their economies. But the customs and habits of the people often produce resistance and hostility toward innovation. Although the wealth and consumer items of the West are desired by poor people everywhere they are often unwilling to give up important noneconomic values to acquire them.

Technical experts often view the native population as stubborn or ignorant and tend to assume that Western values are superior to those in the economically backward countries. These indigent peoples have lived precariously for centuries without experiencing much change, and they survived—a not insignificant achievement. Before they are willing to change their customs, they must have hard proof that innovation will improve their lot. And the experts are not always right. Consider what happened in Turkey. Experts convinced some young peasants to remove the stones from their land; at harvest time, the fields of the old men had a better crop because the stones helped to preserve moisture in a very dry climate (Hoffman, 1962).

Technical assistance may be offered in a way to preserve significant cultural values despite the adoption of an innovation. The cow is a sacred animal in India and in parts of Africa. Cattle often trample upon and eat the crops of peasants, who for religious reasons will not chase or molest them. One remedy is to introduce crops that cows do not like to eat, as Holmes did in India (*Time,* 1951). However, in some pastoral societies, the very conception of cattle in economic terms would be destructive of important cultural values and of personal feelings of security. For example, the Nuer of Africa name themselves after their cattle, enjoy watching them as a leisure time activity, compose songs for them, and develop personal attachments to them (Evans-Pritchard, 1940). Yang (1945) found that people in a Chinese village treated their cattle as members of the household and even set days aside for celebrating their birthdays.

Attitudes toward children, the family, physical labor, saving money, and hygiene (or the lack thereof) are all related to the problem of economic development. Population increases often cancel economic growth; family planning is required just to get off the treadmill of penury. But most societies have a positive attitude toward fertility and a negative attitude toward death. Who could expect people to forego having children when a childless old age can mean starvation? Children represent a form of social security in many poor countries. For many people having and raising a family is the most important value in life. The con-

trol of death has been more important in generating the population explosion than rising birth rates. The advanced nations have displayed humanitarianism in providing the latest in medical technology to underdeveloped countries. Saving lives through modern medicine may therefore have the net effect of keeping more people locked in the chains of poverty and of greatly increasing the aggregate amount of misery there is in the world.

Most of our grandmothers and grandfathers worked very long and hard during their lives, most likely at physical labor. The average westerner still expects to work away from home for a relatively fixed number of hours per week in exchange for money. Not everyone in the world has developed these expectations. Many people in poor countries work only long enough to acquire the bare necessities of life. They may work regularly only during the time for cutting sugar cane or picking coffee beans; the remainder of the year they are underemployed. Whereas giving a bonus in American factories increases the morale as well as the productivity of workers, a similar bonus elsewhere in the world may lead the worker to absenteeism. Why should he work when he has already received the amount of money he needs? Positive work attitudes, a conception of time whereby one is responsible to be at a particular place every day for exactly the same period, achievement motivation, and a desire for more than the bare necessities of life are requirements for economic development.

The development of an economic infrastructure of dams, roads, schools, hospitals, railroads, port facilities, and airports requires investment capital. Where is the capital to be obtained? The average peasant earns less than $300 per year. But sometimes the peasants control a great deal of wealth. In India, for example, family heirlooms are hoarded away for the weddings of the children and savings are spent for elaborate funerals. The cost of these ceremonies in rural India represents over 7 per cent of per capita income. If a comparable sum had been spent on productive capital assets, they would have been increased by 50 pecent (Smelser, 1963b). A change in cultural values would produce a major effect on economic development.

Hygiene is important because sickness drains the energy of people away from productive activities. Life expectancy in poor countries is typically less than 40 years, and as many as one-third of the able-bodied men and women are sick with a fever at all times. These societies are quite young; the majority of the people are juveniles, who consume without producing very much, especially since in some nations as many as 50% of them die before becoming productive adults (Heilbroner, 1963). The World Health Organization, a special agency of the United Nations, has been effective in combating the great killer diseases, such as malaria and typhus, by implementing insect control measures and innoculation campaigns. But changing the execretory habits of people has been more difficult to accomplish. Latrines and toilets are seldom available or used by poor people. It is said that the odor emanating from Bombay can be detected thirty miles away (Naipaul, 1964); the residents commonly eliminate on the surface of the ground. Rains wash the parasites from the excreta into the water supplies and cause dysentery and other intestinal disorders. Children walking over such areas in their bare feet are exposed to hookworms. But changing the habits developed over many centuries is not a simple matter.

Innovation and change are not easy to accept for people who have lived on the precipice of disaster all their lives; they have little margin for error, and what worked for their ancestors is their safest course of action. Patience, ingenuity, and understanding are necessary to help people acquire the attitudes and habits they need in economic development. It is no longer a matter of choice; without development many peoples are doomed to disaster. Modeling, persuasion from a highly credi-

ble expert source, and legitimization of change by the authorities or in association with sacred symbols encourage people to adopt innovations. The great agricultural revolution that took place in the United States was due in great measure to enlightened governmental policies developed and implemented by the Departments of the Interior and Agriculture. The availability of cheap land encouraged people to move West and settle there. The experimental farms and agricultural agents associated with the land grant colleges (founded by Abraham Lincoln), provided models and experts. Farmers were convinced by both example and persuasion to adopt innovations that greatly increased their productivity.

The use of important cultural symbols may help legitimize the adoption of innovations. For example, the radio and telephone were adopted in Saudi Arabia only after the people first heard verses of the *Koran* spoken over them. Similarly, the installation of a pump in a village in Lebanon was legitimized by quoting a passage from the *Koran* stating that cleanliness was required from every faithful Moslem (Mead, 1955).

It must be recognized that economic change always brings social and cultural change; people are stimulated to new desires and aspirations. But economic development is usually a slow process and is never guaranteed to be successful. The new expectations of people may therefore be frustrated; and discontent, instability, and tension may be created. These negative psychological states may be manifested by an increased dependency on the benevolence of others, an inner emigration from reality into such activities as alcoholism, drug addiction, and nativistic cults, or in social movements and revolutions.

B.   Social Movements

Social movements attract recruits from among those who share a common perception of injustice, crisis, or need, and who feel they can do something about it. A number of factors differentiate the social movement from other less organized and more spontaneous forms of collective behavior. The movement usually has a core of leaders who plan its activities; it has an organization that coordinates the behavior of its members; and its ideology provides a basis for interpreting events, formulating goals and values, and propagandizing. The course of a social movement is apt to be erratic and unpredictable; its success or failure often depends on events that no one can forsee or plan beforehand. The history of utopian communities reveals the unanticipated problems that arise for even well-planned and highly organized movements (see Box 14.2).

In general, Smelser's value-added theory of collective behavior provides an adequate analysis of the conditions that breed social movements. Situational conduciveness and system strain are the circumstances in which a precipitating event may trigger collective action. A generalized belief or ideology is required to recruit membership and to maintain it, and leadership is necessary to mobilize the mass into an organized group. The reactions of social control agents to innovative collective action may be successful in removing the leadership, discouraging the membership and leading them to defect; but sometimes if they create additional strain, they may help the movement attract more members and radicalize the actions taken by the group.

1. Conduciveness and Strain

Economic, cultural, and political conditions may create enough system strain to give birth to a social movement. Hofstadter (1963) has interpreted the political and religious movements of the far right (e.g., the John Birch Society, McCarthyism, the Ku Klux Klan) as defenses against the intrusions of a literate, urban, and modern culture on rural and small town America. Sci-

entists were preaching evolution; reformers were trying to desegregate the races; "socialist" practices, such as the TVA and social security, were adopted by an ever more powerful central government; and modern theologians were criticizing the Bible and demythologizing religion. These attacks on a traditional way of life were often construed as part of a conspiracy that came to be attributed to international communism. Patriotic symbols could be enlisted against "traitors" who were responsible for cultural heresies. One manifestation of this reinterpretation of every ill as a conspiracy against America was the McCarthyism of the 1950s.

The United States had been drawn into a war in Korea and had suffered many casualties. China came into the war and rebuffed General MacArthur's attempt to capture all of North Korea, and a long stalemate followed without real advantage to either side. This lack of success was linked to treason by a senator from Wisconsin, Joseph McCarthy. He charged in a series of speeches in February, 1950, that Communists had infiltrated the State Department. Most of the Asian experts in the State Department were accused of engineering the takeover of China by Mao Tse Tung. McCarthy labeled a host of educators, scientists, goeernment officials, and entertainers as communists, fellow travelers of communists, or dupes of communists. He would point to a brief case or wave papers in the air indicating that there was hard evidence for his charges, but seldom did anyone ever get to see these papers.

McCarthy became chairman of the Senate Permanent Investigations Committee and used this position in a campaign of blacklisting and witch-hunting. Although serving as a "destroying angel," he did not put himself forth as a candidate for positive fascist leadership. McCarthy Clubs were established across the nation (Toch, 1965, p. 60–63), and the patriotic chord he struck attracted responsive followers from all

Box 14.2   COMMUNES AND UTOPIAS

Communes reflect the efforts of like-minded persons to structure a new social environment rather than to change the existing social system. The idea is to create conditions of self-government in a perfect society—a utopia. Questions of the private possession of property and freedom of religious practice have been the central concerns of most communes. The settling of the Americas in the 17th century by Europeans was carried out for these very same reasons. As early as 1680, members of certain religious sects went into the wilderness of North America to establish communal societies (Kantner, 1970).

By the 19th century there was a veritable stream of utopias in America. Some of them drew their inspiration from the writings of a Frenchman, Francois Charles-Marie Fourier (1772-1837), whose view of man held that happiness and virtuous behavior could occur only when individuals are released from the restraints of society and allowed freely to develop and express themselves. To realize their promise, men should abandon individualism and competition and construct a society emphasizing cooperative and united industry. Fourier proposed that society should be divided into rather small groups called phalanges, numbering about 1600 persons, which would be subdivided into work groups so that each person could perform the task he liked best and could move to other tasks to avoid boredom. Private property was not to be abolished, and families were to live together in separate apartments. However, the rich and poor were to be closely intermingled to avoid the sharp distinction between them in the existing world.

Although Fourier's plan was never successfully put into effect during his lifetime, 41 phalanges were formed in the decade of the 1840's. The best known was Brook Farm, which numbered Charles Dana, Nathaniel Hawthorne, Ralph Waldo Emerson, Amos Bronson Alcott, and William Henry Channing among its members and visitors. Brook Farm suffered a series of financial problems and never recovered from the losses suffered when its large central building (the Phalanstery) burned down the very night a dance was held to celebrate its completion.

The Oneida Community was founded in Putney, Vermont, in 1842 by John Humphrey Noyes, a minister who had been convinced through his study of the Bible that the second coming of Christ occurred in 70 A.D. On his reappearance, Christ absolved Christians of the necessity of sin. Noyes and his followers pooled their property, renounced religious practices, and instituted "complex marriage" in which each member had sexual access to all others, with the consent and approval of the leaders. They attempted to practice eugenics; sexual union was not to be productive unless arranged by the leaders. Males were skilled in the practice of coitus interruptus, and only Noyes and a select few were permitted to impregnate females.

Noyes and his followers were forced to leave Putney in 1847 and migrated to Oneida, New York, where they were extremely successful economically. In 1880, Noyes and a few others left for Canada, and the

Oneida Community dissolved as a communistic enterprise and became a stock company—by then well-known for its silverware.

In present-day communes, there is a strong current of concern for interpersonal warmth, intimacy, and genuineness as a contrast to the depersonalizing influence of industrial urban life. The desire to recover the simplicity of living close to nature has a different meaning than it did 130 years ago, when people were not far removed from the chores of farming and household crafts. However, in some modern communes, the members earn income in the outside world, which makes the commune only an extended family rather than an independent, self-sufficient, cooperative enterprise. Many modern attempts at forming communes have been early failures because of the lack of an organizing ideology that would enhance the commitment of the members. Such anarchistic communities are designed to let each person "do his own thing" with little order and control. The resultant financial problems and inability to get necessary work done bring about failure, despite genuine and earnest attempts to develop intimate and sensitive interpersonal relations (Kantner, 1970). The more successful present-day communes (e.g., Twin Oaks, modeled after Skinner's *Walden Two)* tend to have very complicated systems of apportioning work and penalizing shirkers (Kincade, 1973). The Jesus People communes are interesting in that they typically involve an oppressed role for the women at a time when the larger society is much concerned with women's liberation (Harder, Richardson, & Sommonds, 1972).

---

walks of life. Soon, school boards and colleges were firing teachers and professors; Hollywood blacklisted writers, directors, and movie stars; the "commies" were driven out of government, and left-wing businessmen were ruined. However, McCarthy went too far when he challenged the patriotism of the military, particularly at a time when an unquestioned hero was president of the nation (Dwight David Eisenhower). The Congressional hearings of 1954 in which McCarthy confronted representatives of the U.S. Army, were televised, and the senator was discredited before a national audience. Subsequently, he was censured by his Senate colleagues. Nevertheless, blaming all evil on communism simplified for many people the complex national and international problems of the postwar era. As a symbol linking patriotism with anti-communism McCarthyism has had a lasting impact on the policies of the United States and still appeals to many Americans.

Religious movements throughout history have usually emerged from some crisis situation—a drought, a flood, or other natural or human-made disaster. The successful evangelical movements in the United States in the middle of the 19th century took place in the midst of a severe economic depression (Brodie, 1946). The ideology of a movement must give people hope, either of progress in this life or of salvation in the hereafter. Political movements seldom occur when people are resigned to their fates. The starving peoples of Brazil or Haiti do not take collective action to improve their lot in life because they do not believe anything can be done to solve their problems. Persons must experience a sense of relative deprivation before they will take collective action.

The principle that relative deprivation depends upon the reference group with which social comparisons are made was demonstrated in the classic study by Stouffer, et.al. of promotions and morale in the

Army and Air Force (described in Chapter 2, I, B, 1). In a debate at Oxford University, William Buckley compared blacks in America with Africans and noted how well off the former were. James Baldwin responded that the relevant comparison was with other Americans, and that relative to whites in the U.S., blacks were deprived of health, occupational opportunity, and political freedom.

Jones and Gerard (1967) reported a personal observation of the discontent associated with relative deprivation in the military. A group of volunteers was engaged in a program of training in Japanese language and culture at a midwestern university. These soldiers were relatively free of the usual military constraints, were allowed to live in the city, and could use their time after classes as they saw fit. Compared to the great majority of G.I.s, they had it made. Yet the group suffered great discontent, low morale, and caused a variety of incidents culminating in disciplinary action. The reason for this dissatisfaction was that the group did not compare itself to other soldiers, especially not those doing battle at the front; instead, the comparison group they used was composed of civilians. Compared with civilians, these soldiers felt relatively deprived of their freedom.

The combination of relative deprivation and rising expectations provides the conditions for the emergence of a social movement. There must, of course, be social change for these two conditions to occur. People do not suddenly adopt new comparison groups or experience relative deprivation when nothing around them ever changes; acceptance of fate is not replaced by hope of change until some improvement in the conditions of life has already occurred or has been demonstrated as possible. The Supreme Court decision in 1954 regarding school integration had the effect of legitimizing comparisons between white and black (segregated) schools and hence fostered the experience of relative deprivation where it did not already exist among

blacks; also, the decision encouraged blacks to seek equality on busses, at recreation centers and beaches, in restaurants and clubs, and in occupations and at the polling booths.

2. Precipitating Events

When social conditions are conducive to the emergence of a social movement, an event that might earlier have seemed ordinary or inocuous may precipitate collective action. On December 1, 1955, Mrs. Rosa Parks boarded a bus in Montgomery, Alabama, and took a seat in the section reserved for Negroes at the back. The white driver ordered her and three other blacks to move further back so that some standing whites could be seated. Because her feet were sore and she did not want to give up her seat to a white man, Mrs. Park refused to move. She was quietly led off the bus by the police and arrested. The whole incident lasted only about five minutes, and the other passengers simply murmured or giggled (Toch, 1965, p. 199). This kind of incident had occurred repeatedly in Montgomery, but this time there was a group of civil rights leaders, led by Martin Luther King, who reacted by distributing leaflets calling for a black boycott of all buses on December 5th. On that day, 99 percent of the blacks in Montgomery either walked to work or drove in carpools. From this small beginning, a revolutionary social movement swept through the United States and has permanently changed the structure of our society, as well as the self-concepts of millions of people.

The Civil Rights movement was filled with precipitating events that gave momentum to the struggle and attracted followers and sympathizers to the cause. The arrest of Dr. King, his letter from the Birmingham city jail, the pictures of black women being attacked by burly white policemen and by dogs, the defiant actions of the governors of Alabama and Mississippi, and the police arrests in Northern urban areas, all had the effect of accelerating and intensifying the movement. At each stage of its development, reinforcement was provided by new civil rights legislation and favorable court decisions.

3. Ideology and Organization

An ideology consists of a relatively coherent set of fundamental beliefs and values that characterizes a group and serves to explain spiritual, economic, political, and/or social events. An ideology can be an important integrative social force. It would be impossible to coordinate the behavior of large masses of people without shared myths and legends. There are many different kinds of belief systems sufficiently cohesive to be considered ideologies—economic, political, religious, racial, and so on. These *isms* explain the meanings of events and may suggest or command actions that should be taken by the collectivity to achieve it goals. We are all familiar with the Marxist interpretation of every conflict as due to economic processes, and particularly to class antagonisms. But Marxist ideology also explains the meanings and social functions of art, literature and religion, sets up a utopian goal optimistically considered to be inevitable, and forecasts the shriveling away of all government. This ideology is so powerful in guiding men's perceptions of the world that in the Soviet Union, the censorship of art and literature, the failure to eliminate recalcitrant social problems (like drunkenness), and the growth of centralized power can all be interpreted as support for the ideological system. The ability to make words mean whatever you want them to mean was illustrated by the differences between nations in their definitions of socialism and capitalism that we described in Box 3.3.

An ideology cannot be successfully propagated and adopted until social conditions have made a population susceptible to it. Which ideology is accepted by a receptive audience is determined to some extent by the charisma of its propagator. In the middle of the 19th century in New York state there were many people wandering about claiming to be prophets or even the reincarnation of Jesus Christ. Although many of these wanderers were considered to be frauds or worse, several were accepted as true prophets. For example, Joseph Smith of Palmyra claimed to have received the Book of Mormon from the angel Moroni. This spellbinding man had a magnetic effect on a sizeable group of people and the Mormon religion was founded on his revelations and prophesies.

The marriage of conditions, ideology, and leadership is illustrated by the founding of the Nation of Islam, commonly known as the Black Muslim movement. By 1930 the automobile industry in Detroit had been hard hit by the depression. A large number of illiterate blacks who had fled the poverty and terror of the South for the opportunities of the production lines lived in the inner city. They were without work, lived in the filth and degradation characteristic of the urban slum, were dependent on the welfare doled out by abusive social workers after long waits in queues, and were inclined to blame the white man as the cause of their plight. At this time, W. D. Fard, a peddler of silks, arrived in the city and founded a new version of Islam. After he mysteriously disappeared in 1934, leadership passed to Elijah Muhammad. He preached black pride and promoted literacy, abstention from liquor and other stimulants, frugality, industry, and cleanliness. The Muslim convert must adopt new habits, a new conception of himself, and a new name. Appeals to self-esteem include the doctrine that blacks were the first people on earth and that God intended them to adopt their original religion, Islam. Antagonism toward the white "devils" is promoted white culture and racial integration were (until recently) explicitly rejected. While black pride and self-reliance are stressed as in accord with Allah's will, their rewards are expected to

Black Muslims have been successful in converting convicts, of "curing" them of dope addiction and alcoholism, of rehabilitating them and instilling new pride in being black. Despite their avowed hostility towards whites, there have been few racial incidents associated with this group (Cameron, 1966; Milgram & Toch, 1969).

Organization requires money and means of communicating to members. Taxing or tithing members, seeking contributions from sympathizers, and providing entertainment to benefit the movement are some ways of acquiring funds. In some cases, radical social movements have carried out robberies and kidnappings to obtain money for organizational purposes. Newsletters, newspapers, small magazines, leaflets, chain letters, radio and television broadcasts, and telephone calls may be used to communicate to followers.

4. Social Control

The enemies of a social movement may attempt to curtail or destroy it in a number of ways. The most direct approach is to attack, arrest, or kill its members. Systematic campaigns have been carried out at various times to kill Christians, Moslems, Jews, and members of other religious groups in attempts to stop the proliferation of these ideologies. The leadership of the Black Panthers was decimated by police bullets; thousands were arrested in the Civil Rights and anti-war movements; and the police have clubbed, kicked, shot, and hosed demonstrators from all these movements. Another way to attack a social movement is to discredit its leaders and members as "kooks," "radicals," and phonies. Sometimes the ideas associated with a social movement seem "far-out" as, for example, with the cryonics movement described in Box 14.3

We have noted the tendency to associate all evil with Communism. To label a leader of a disliked or feared social movement as

an enemy of America is an attempt to turn all "patriotic citizens" against the movement. Photographs were circulated of Martin Luther King, Jr. sitting in the same audience as two known communists, and written materials pointed out that Dr. King was acquainted with the reds; ergo, Dr. King was clearly a communist. No matter how many well-dressed middle class people there were in an anti-war demonstration during the 1960s, the mass media always seemed to focus on the long-haired "freaks" in the crowd. Discrediting emphasizes the differences between the people in the movement and those outside it. The credibility of the claims of the insurgents is thereby undermined and the suceptibility of nonmembers to recruitment is lessened.

Social control measures must be rationalized within the legitimate norms and laws of the established order. A failure to rationalize actions, overreacting by using more force than is necessary to contain a collective action, or restraining or punishing the wrong people, may create new grievances among the population and provide the movement with new membership. To be effective, social control techniques must be applied firmly and in a timely fashion, but they must also be legitimate and scaled to fit the nature of the situation.

5. Membership: Recruitment and Defection

When persons experience fear and anxiety, they seek affiliation to make social comparisons (see Chapter 3, IV, C). The dislocation resulting from social change, the alteration in status of large groups of people through economic depression and development or natural disaster, and the consequent fears and anxieties of people create information dependence. People want events to be predictable and they want to know how to meet their basic needs. When the world becomes uncertain, the individual's search for an interpretation of the changes that are occur-

Box 14.3   THE CRYONICS MOVEMENT—FROZEN IMMORTALITY

A small number of persons have acted recently to do something about the problem of their own mortality (Bryant & Snizek, 1973). They come from many walks of life, but they have several things in common. They are typically atheists with above-average intelligence, possess an interest in science, technology and science fiction, believe their lives to be worthwhile and meaningful, and tend to show a sense of mastery over their own lives through such actions as flying their own planes and building bombshelters.

In 1962, Robert Ettinger published his book, *The Prospect of Immortality*. In it he speculated that the dead could be frozen to preserve them until science found a way to revive them and cure them of their fatal illness. Eventually, even aging could perhaps be stopped. Admittedly, there is not much evidence to support a belief that these technological advances can be made in the near future. However, if there is any chance at all that they will occur, the thing to do is be frozen now and take advantage of the advances when they come along. In other words, he argued you only gain by Cryonics; you could not lose, except for the $10,000 original cost and the $1,200 per year required from your estate to keep your body temperature at —320° F.

The first cryonic voyager was a 73-year-old retired professor of psychology, who, having died of cancer, was frozen on January 12, 1967, in Los Angeles. There are now about 15–20 "corpsicles." However, the number of living persons who have accepted cryonics as the solution to mortality has fallen off drastically. No formal meetings of the New York Cryonics Society were held from 1971 to 1974. Rather than being in the forefront of exciting scientific advances, cryonics enthusiasts are viewed as on the lunatic fringe, and most of the remaining members have a financial stake in the movement. The quick rise and fall of the movement probably expressed a passing hope for sudden scientific advance. When it did not come, the financial cost and embarrassment of ridicule became too great to attract and sustain membership.

---

ring may be fulfilled by adopting an ideology and joining a social movement. The ideology provides a world-view and the other members of the movement provide consensus for it. In addition, the movement offers the individual an object of emotional and value identification.

Arthur Koestler (1959), a former communist, has commented about his information dependence and conversion to communism in the 1930s: "To say that one had 'seen the light' is a poor description of the mental rapture which only the convert knows (regardless of what faith he has been converted to). The new light seems to pour from all directions across the skull; the whole universe falls into a pattern like the stray pieces of a jigsaw puzzle assembled by magic at one stroke. There is now answer to every question; doubts and conflicts are a matter of the tortured past" (p. 19). Once a person is in the movement he is subject to the usual group pressures to conform.

The process of conversion to a social movement may be preceded by a long period of indecision, dissatisfaction, and despair. Disaffection with a movement may be similarly slow. The erosion of belief in an ideology is likely to be associated with a lack of significant success by the movement, increases in cost to the members, and a realization that it is frequently contradicted by the evidence. Finally, some crisis event occurs and brings the accumulated doubts into focus and the person defects.

The individual who joins a social movement may be very idealistic, and he may choose to defect because he objects to certain practices and actions associated with it. The Communist Party may have seemed the best socialist organization to join in the 1930s, but the Moscow trials by Stalin's regime of dissidents were such a travesty on ideals of fairness and justice that many members defected because of strong personal commitment to their own values. Of course, a member may defect for personal reasons, too. Dislike of other members or lack of trust in the leaders or a desire for financial security or social approval may lead a person to withdraw from a movement. Some nudists defect from the group when their children become increasingly modest on reaching adolescence (Toch, 1965, p. 162).

C. Revolutions

A social movement that uses violent means to overthrow and replace a legitimate government is referred to as a *revolution*. A war of national liberation is a revolution against colonial domination. When a country has been ruled by a foreign power for many years a native civil service is usually formed to serve the emissaries of the colonial power. Even when a country is given its freedom the native population may feel that indirect economic colonialism remains. The privileged natives (the ex-civil servants) may have taken on the language, the religion, and the values of the foreign power and denigrate the native customs as old-fashioned, barbarian, and uncivilized.

Fanon (1963) suggests that the privileged class in a recently freed nation often perpetrates an internal form of colonialism that is no better than the external form. An internal revolution in such a case may be referred to as a war of national liberation.

Internal wars follow the same pattern as other types of social movements. Social change produces system strain, dislocation, a sense of injustice, and a readiness by a large number of people to take violent forms of collective action. A precipitating incident allows a charismatic leader to organize the revolutionary movement, which challenges the agents of social control. Nieburg (1969) has listed the functions that violence and threats of violence can serve in a revolutionary group: " 'propaganda of the act'; as a demonstration of group unity or individual commitment, or as a test of these qualities in rival groups; as a demand for attention from a larger audience; as a claim, assertion, and testing of legitimacy; as an act of enforcing and maintaining authority; as a provocation falsely blamed on innocent groups in order to justify actions against them, as retaliation or reprisal in a bargaining relationship that moves toward settlement; as a method of terror; as a way of forcing confrontation on other issues; or as a way of avoiding such confrontation by diverting attention; as an expression and measure of group or individual commitment; as a test of the manhood and loyalty of new recruits; as a method of precipitating revolutionary conditions; and so on" (p. 14).

An insurgent movement requires recruits, shelter, food, and information from the domestic environment, and cadres, weapons, ammunition, publicity, and financing often provided by foreign sources. The mix between the contributions from internal and external sources has historically been variable (Leites & Wolf, 1970). For example, the Vietcong were indigent South Vietnamese who were in rebellion against their government. Although their cadres were trained by the

North Vietnamese, early in the war (about 1960) they were using primitive weapons, such as bows and arrows, spears, and hand-made guns, in their attacks against forces possessing superior weapons. As a result of their successful attacks, they acquired the weapons of their victims (Browne, 1965; Fall, 1964; Shaplen ,1965). It was only later in the war that the North Vietnamese supplied both weapons and manpower; and still later the Chinese and Russians increased their support of economic and military aid to North Vietnam. On the other side, first the French and then the United States set up client governments, installing and replacing heads of state more or less at will, none of whom would have survived without economic and military support from external sources.

To obtain support from the local population, a revolutionary group relies on both persuasive and coercive tactics. Handbooks have been published by such revolutionaries as Mao Tse Tung and Che Gueverra about how to conduct a guerrilla campaign to overthrow a government. According to Thornton (1964), there are five phases to a successful revolution: preparatory, terrorism, guerrilla warfare, conventional warfare, and consolidation.

1. Preparation and Terrorism

A small nucleus of hard-core revolutionaries is organized in small cadres during the preparatory phase of the movement. They try to avoid notice and do not openly proclaim their movement until they feel adequately prepared. The *phase of terrorism* launches the movement and, over time, may gain support from a significant portion of the population and establish a small geographical base. As Thornton points out, "The insurgents need to achieve maximum public attention and support for their struggle. If they are unable to achieve them by means of political tactics, they may choose terror for their weapon. This period is the classic one for the employment of agitational terror in all its functions—provocation, disorientation, elimination of rivals, and propaganda" (p. 93).

The terrorist phase has both psychological and political purposes. The revolutionaries seek to sever the bond tying the masses to the incumbent government. Terrorism produces disorientation among the masses by removing their confidence in the government's ability to protect them. The symbolic nature of terrorism is enhanced when attacks are made against the symbols of the state and against the normative structures that regulate the relationships among people in the society. For example, in South Vietnam the insurgents are said to have carried out an intensive terrorist campaign in the early phases of the war by assassinating thousands of people in small villages throughout the country. Assassination is a terrorist act when it has symbolic value; the specific person killed is historically less important than the meaning of the act in terms of overthrowing the established order. The Vietcong killed absentee landowners, tax collectors, and their agents in the small villages; political cadres, often native to the village, were left behind to rationalize the action and to indoctrinate people in the villages, gaining their tacit or active support for future operations. Thus the victim is identified with a group that will feel threatened by the assassination, such as a government elite, the police or members of hostile political or economic groups.

It is important that a terrorist act should demonstrate discrimination. It should not be so discriminating as to become predictable or it will lose its ability to frighten and immobilize people. On the other hand, total indiscrimination would not allow a selection of targets, would rob the act of its symbolic meaning, and would reduce its disorienting effect on the masses. This disorientation makes people informationally dependent and receptive to the propaganda and indoctrination of the political cadres in the insurgent movement. Acts of terrorism display the weakness of government and assert the strength of the insurgents. They also stimulate the energies of the members of the terrorist organization; an increase in motivation results from the exhilaration that comes from effectively striking a blow against the enemy.

2. Guerrilla Warfare

According to Thornton, guerrilla warfare is the third phase of revolution and is characterized by an expansion of the conflict. This warfare is conducted from a geographical base in which a revolutionary government is established. A reduction in terrorism must take place to show the increased fortunes of the insurgents. Now quick thrusts are made by well-disciplined military units against the infrastructure of the society, including airfields, communications centers, oil depots, transportation links, arsenals, police stations, and military bases. These guerrilla attacks are intended to disrupt the normal functioning of the society. The aim is to create dissatisfaction with the government because of its inability to maintain a smoothly running society and to protect the populace. Guerrilla activities are as much directed toward winning the hearts and minds of the people as they are toward undermining the incumbent government.

During the guerrilla phase of a revolution, it is important for the insurgents to have the support of a significant part of the population. Pomeroy (1964) claims that the failure of the Huk movement in the Philippines was due to the fact that the guerrillas were too impatient and did not devote enough time and energy to indoctrinating the people. Without the support of the people, the guerrilla is like a fish out of the sea. It only takes one or two people to divulge his whereabouts when he is hiding from government counter-insurgency forces. The guerrillas must be hidden, fed, and cared for by sympathizers.

Guerrilla tactics are designed to win sympathizers. For example, in Vietnam the

insurgents attacked government forces and then silently withdrew from the villages, which the counter-insurgency forces would then systematically destroy with overwhelming firepower. The unfortunate effect of this counter-attack (from the government's point of view) was that the guerrillas were not hurt, the village was destroyed, and the villagers developed an everlasting hostility toward the government. The actions of the government forces, including bombing villages with napalm, amounted to an indiscriminate campaign of terror which had the effect of alienating the populace and making them susceptible to the carefully planned propaganda campaigns of the political cadres of the Vietcong.

It is difficult to wage counter-insurgency against guerrilla warfare. The first problem is locating the enemy. In Vietnam the guerrillas included children and both young and old men and women. The guerrillas surfaced at night, but during the day they worked in the fields as did all the other peasants. Unless there were informants or intelligence agents available to reveal their identities, it was impossible to know who in a village was the enemy. Fear, frustration, and anger led the counter-insurgency forces to use indiscriminate force in the capture and killing of innocent persons.

3. Conventional Warfare and the Consolidation of Victory

If recruitment has been brisk and the guerrilla program has worked well, the revolution may then employ conventional military units in direct confrontation with government forces. This *conventional warfare* constitutes the fourth phase of a revolution. The focus is on destroying the forces of the government rather than holding territory. The revolutionaries attempt to control when, where, and for how long any military engagement will take place. Their strategy is to trap smaller governmental units and run to fight again another day. This tactic was frequently employed by the Americans in their revolutionary war and by the American Indians against conventional military units. Larger and larger battles occur until either the government seeks a political solution or the revolutionaries are defeated. If the latter happens, there may be a de-escalation back either to guerrilla warfare or to terrorism by the revolutionaries as they recycle the phases of their struggle. This happened several times in the course of the Vietnam war over a 25-year period.

If the revolutionaries are victorious they must establish a government. The last phase of a successful revolution, then, is *consolidation*. Visible reforms are necessary to convey to the people that the idealism which served as the ideology of the revolution still guides the policies of the new government. Consolidation is difficult because of the breakdown in norms and shared expectations that was produced by the revolution. Economists are not in agreement about whether revolution ever improves the material life of a people. However, the impressive achievements of the Chinese people since their revolution in 1949 could not have occurred under the corrupt leadership of Chiang Kai-Shek (Tuchman, 1971).

IV. CHAPTER SUMMARY

A crowd is formed from a mass of people when they are in physical contact with one another and have a common focus of attention or a collective purpose. Passive crowds are audiences who may intentionally seek information or entertainment or who may casually happen on an event that arouses curiosity. The size of an audience depends on the drawing power of the focal event and the capacity of the available physical facilities. The size of a casual crowd is a function of the number of people available and the break-away rate. The greater the size of the crowd and the more excited and aroused the members become, the more difficult it is for authorities to control them. Unless an individual has experience in dense crowds, he may become hostile as he is jostled about and his personal space is penetrated by others.

Active crowds are referred to as mobs, and may have aggressive, expressive, avoidance or acquisitive purposes. Milling, the transmission of information, interstimulation and circular reaction, and the spread of rumors are characteristic processes in mobs. The embeddedness of an individual in the crowd causes him to become anonymous and reduces his sense of responsibility for what he does.

Lynch mobs are generally rationalized in terms of the alleged crimes of the victims and serve the function of terrorism against a suborindate group of people so as to deter activities directed toward social, economic, and cultural change. Riots are preceded by a set of conditions that make it possible for a precipitating event to trigger violence; they represent unorganized and unplanned coercive attempts to solve social conflicts by collective effort. Attempts to escape a perceived danger may cause members of a crowd to coordinate their activities or they may stampede in panic. A panic is most likely when the precipitating event is unpredictable and dangerous, and the members of the crowd have made no preparations and have rehearsed no responses. Research has consistently indicated that a rather sizeable number of people are prepared to sacrifice others to save themselves rather than attempt to coordinate their behavior to maximize the safety of the entire group. A queue is an acquisitive mob that is usually orderly, develops its own norms, and for the most part consists of congenial members who conform to the expectations of the crowd.

No satisfactory scientific theory of crowd behavior has been devised. LeBon believed the crowd formed a single collective mind and that individual members abdicated all reason as they reverted to primitive, instinctual, destructive, and animal states. This process was fostered by the social contagion of feelings and actions. The highly suggestible state of mind of crowd members is much like a person acting under hypnosis, who automatically performs any response suggested to him.

Freud agreed with much of LeBon's analysis but proposed somewhat different mechanisms for the organization of the crowd. Members form a libidinal attachment to a leader and set him up as an ego-ideal. The leader's relationship to the crowd is analogous to the superego's relationship to the ego—one of command and obedience. The members of the crowd are likely to identify with the leader also because of his power to harm them (identification with the aggressor). Hence, there is an ambiguous love-hate relationship with the leader. The merging of the crowd around the leader is considered the basic factor in mob behavior.

Modern theories of collective behavior tend to take social, economic, and cultural factors into account in addition to psychological processes. Turner and Killian have proposed an emergent norm theory in which it is assumed that members of a crowd develop shared mutual expectations that are sanctioned; mob behavior is therefore considered to be a form of conformity to normative pressures. Smelser's value-added theory proposes that structural conduciveness and strain and a generalized belief prepare a population for collective activity; some event precipitates collective behavior if there is enough organization to coordinate the action of crowd members and insufficient social control to deter or contain it.

Mass behavior refers to a collective focus on events, a shared definition of events, a consistency in action or habit, or a coincidence of motivations and values. The revolution in the mass media, particularly in their electronic forms, has had a tremendous impact on the lives of ordinary people all over the world. Even the most illiterate of men are instantaneously informed about events occurring in the most remote spots on earth. The information provided by the media may be important in regulating everyday life, providing people with interpretations of what is happening in the world and profoundly affecting their system of values and expectations for the future Those who have easy access to or control over the mass media may manipulate the images presented to their audiences for economic, social, political, and cultural gain. As a consequence, a rather homogeneous public opinion may be formed, indicating the degree of endorsement the propagandists receive from the audience. The mere fact that persons and events receive attention in the media is sufficient to lend importance, status, and prestige to them. The media provide entertainment that mixes fantasy and reality together in a manner that is reassuring and comforting to the audience and supports the myths and values of the society.

The collective acceptance of styles in clothing, furniture, automobiles, music, art, and other consumer items constitutes a fashion. The social needs of people for attention, approval, love, esteem, prestige, and status make them responsive to changes in fashion. Conformity in accepting a fashion is usually from the top down; that is, people of importance model a particular style and then others imitate by adopting the same style. Why a particular style is fashionable at any point in time is not known. Once fashions begin, the usual social pressures to conform are experienced by group members, and they either enthusiastically imitate the available models or grumble while reluctantly conforming.

Fads are "quickie" versions of fashions. A fad spreads quickly, especially when it receives publicity; and when the newness or novelty wears thin, it disappears. The motivation of participants is often a matter of adventure, seeking attention, and rebellion. Crazes reflect more intense emotional involvement and greater commitment by the participants than do fashions and fads. Suggestibility, mass hysteria, and social contagion are exaggerated and obvious features of crazes, but probably operate to some extent in fashions and fads as well. The affluence, freedom, social mobility, accent on youth, and receptivity to change of people in American society makes them particularly susceptible to these mass phenomena.

The invisible and silent coordination that is required of large masses of people in order to have safe, predictable, and reciprocally prosperous lives requires that they share expectations, norms, and rules. Deviance from these shared expectations can be constructive in finding new solutions for problems, and establishing the limits of applicability of the norms and rules. The destructive effects of deviance include the breakdown of coordination, the encouragement given to other persons to withdraw their cooperation, and a reduction in the expectation of reciprocal behavior that allows unilateral cooperative initiatives to be taken in interpersonal relationships.

Deviance may take the form of aberrant behavior, nonconformity, rebellion, and mental illness. Society usually attempts to protect itself from such behavior by means of social controls aimed at preventing, punishing, or curtailing deviant conduct. A legal system is developed to apprehend, punish, and rehabilitate those who break rules. Not everyone is treated alike by the legal system; it is responsive to the power of special interests, groups, classes, and parties.

In past centuries, some forms of deviant behavior were considered a moral problem; people labeled as mentally ill were considered to be possessed by the devil, sometimes had their tongues cut out, and were burned at the stake. In the past 100 years, almost all forms of deviance have more and more frequently been treated as medical problems. A person who disregards the expectations of others and appears unable to control himself is considered to have diminished responsibility for his actions and is labeled as mentally ill. Such a person is generally the loser in a power struggle, although his symptoms may be successful in exercising control over others. Symptoms may also be tacit communications transmitted to other people, asking for help, love, or other behavior from them, or transmitting criticism and hostility toward them. Patients may manifest symptoms as a means of escaping from agonizing life situations into the relative quiet and safety of the mental hospital. These ways of exercising power and influence may appear different in content but the processes are the same as those employed by all of us. Therapists use every means of influence to convince their patients to change attitudes, goals, values, means, and behavior. The clinical psychologist and psychiatrist can be viewed as social control agents serving in parallel with the agents of the legal system.

Life for many people in the world is miserable and short. Only through economic development can people be given enough food, medical care, clothing, and shelter to meet their needs. The innovation and application of new technology that accompanies development produces changes in the attitudes, values, behavior of, and relations among people. These social changes create uncertainty, disorientation, and anxiety; hence, people often resist innovation and cultural diffusion. Economic development depends on innovation, investment income, literacy, changes in the motivations and attitudes of people, and population control. Peasants in underdeveloped countries have adopted the habits and values of their ancestors because they worked in their struggle for survival. Development may require a change in attitudes toward work, perspectives of time, values toward children and the family, and in the status and class relationships of large groups of people. These changes can be effectively implemented by presenting people with successful models and experts who make their recommendations in the context of the values of the given society, and by associating innovation with the legitimizing symbols of the culture and the political regime.

The dislocations and expectations produced by social change create conditions conducive to the emergence of a social movement. In the context of system strain, a precipitating event may trigger collective action. The presence of a charismatic leader allows the propagation of an ideology that serves as a rallying point around which a social movement can be organized. Membership is attracted from disaffected members of the society, for whom the movement represents an answer to needs for information and re-orientation of perspective, for self-identity and renewal, redress for a sense of injustice, and hope of solving personal and social problems. Embarrassment and costs may cause a person to defect from a movement. Although social control agents may attempt to curtail or destroy a social movement, they must be careful to legitimize and rationalize their actions; otherwise, they may create even more dissatisfaction and make more people susceptible to the movement.

A revolution is a social movement that employs violence as a means to overthrow a legitimate government. Analyses suggest that successful revolutions go through five phases. The preparatory phase is devoted to the development of a revolutionary nucleus. A somewhat discriminating terrorist campaign is then waged to weaken the support given to government, to attack the symbols of hated groups, to demonstrate the strength of the movement, and to publicize the movement and attract recruits. When the terrorist campaign has gained at least the tacit support of a large number of people, attracted sufficient recruits, and given the revolutionaries a geographical base of operation, they will escalate their

activities into guerrilla warfare. The targets of guerrilla activities are the vital centers of the economic, social ,and political life of the nation. By disrupting the functioning of society, they weaken the incumbents' ability to govern and make themselves indispensable to the people. Gathering strength, the revolutionaries engage the government forces in conventional warfare. Victory requires a consolidation phase in which a revolutionary government is established and at least some of the reforms promised are implemented.

SUGGESTED READINGS

Eckstein, H. (Ed.) *Internal war.* Glencoe, Ill., Free Press, 1964. A collection of papers that presents some illuminating insights into the causes and tactics of revolutions and wars of national liberation.

Heilbroner, R. L. *The great ascent: The struggle for economic development in our time.* New York: Harper Torchbooks, 1963. A short but excellent summary of the immense problems facing underdeveloped countries. For the introductory reader.

Hofstadter, R. and Wallace, M. *American violence: A documentary history.* New York: Vintage, 1971. Lucid and brief accounts of violent incidents—political, economic, racial, religious, anti-radical, police, and personal—written by eminent American historians.

LeBon, G. *The crowd.* New York: Viking, 1960. This is a classic. Quaint and entertaining, and still influential among social scientists.

Rubington, E., and Weinberg, M. S. *Deviance: The interactionist perspective.* 2nd ed. New York: Macmillan, 1973. A collection of sociological papers that examine many aspects of deviance, including the labeling of people, the consequences of such labeling for both the person labeled and the one doing the labeling, and the public control of deviance.

Toch, H. *The social psychology of social movements.* Indianapolis: Bobbs-Merrill, 1965. A discussion of mass movements that is chock-full of entertaining examples.

Wells, A. (Ed.) *Mass Media and society.* Palo Alto, Calif.: National Press Books, 1972. A series of papers that examine the structure of media industries, how they are regulated, and related public issues.

References

Abel, H., and Sahinkaya, R. Emergence of sex and race friendship preferences. *Child Development*, 1962, *33*, 939–943.

Abelson, R., and Miller, J. Negative persuasion via personal insult. *Journal of Experimental Social Psychology*, 1967, *3*, 321–333.

Abelson, R. P., and Rosenberg, M. J. Symbolic psychologic: A model of attitudinal cognition. *Behavioral Science*, 1958, *3*, 1–13.

Abrams, R. H. Residential propinquity as a factor in marriage selection: Fifty-year trends in Philadelphia. *American Sociological Review*, 1943, *8*, 288–294.

Adams, S. Inequity in social exchange. In L. Berkowitz (Ed.), *Advances in experimental social psychology*. Vol. 2. New York: Academic Press, 1965.

Adorno, T. W., Frenkel-Brunswik, E., Levinson, D. J., and Sanford, R. N. *The authoritarian personality*. New York: Harper, 1950.

Ajzen, I., and Fishbein, M. The prediction of behavioral intentions in a choice situation. *Journal of Experimental Social Psychology*, 1969, *5*, 400–416.

Alker, H. A. Is personality situationally specific or intrapsychically consistent? *Journal of Personality*, 1972, *40*, 1–16.

Allen, V. L. Uncertainty of outcome and post-decision dissonance reduction. In L. Festinger (Ed.), *Conflict, decision and dissonance*. Stanford, Calif.: Stanford University Press, 1964.

Allen, V. L. Situational factors in conformity. In L. Berkowitz (Ed.), *Advances in experimental social psychology*. Vol. 2. New York: Academic Press, 1965.

Allen, V. L., and Crutchfield, R. S. Generalization of experimentally reinforced conformity. *Journal of Abnormal and Social Psychology*, 1963, *67*, 326–333.

Allport, F. H. *Social psychology*. Boston: Houghton, 1924.

Allport, G. W. *Personality: A psychological interpretation*. New York: Holt, 1937.

Allport, G. W. *The nature of prejudice*. Reading, Mass.: Addison-Wesley, 1954.

Allport, G. W. The historical background of modern social psychology. In G. Lindzey and E. Aronson (Eds.), *The handbook of social psychology*. Vol. 1. (2nd ed.) Reading, Mass.: Addison-Wesley, 1968.

Allport, G. W., and Postman, L. *The psychology of rumor*. New York: Holt, 1947.

Altmann, S. A. The structure of primate communication. In S. A. Altmann (Ed.), *Social communication among primates*. Chicago: University of Chicago Press, 1967.

Anderson, N. H., and Hubert, S. Effects of concomitant verbal recall on order effects in personality impression formation. *Journal of Verbal Learning and Verbal Behavior*, 1963, *2*, 379–391.

Anderson, N. H. Application of an additive model to impression formation. *Science*, 1962, *138*, 817–818.

Anderson, N. H. Averaging versus adding as a stimulus combination rule in impression formation. *Journal of Experimental Psychology*, 1965, *70*, 394–400.

Anderson, N. H. Integration theory and attitude change. *Psychological Review*, 1971, *78*, 171–206.

Anderson, N. H., and Barrios, A. A. Primacy effects in personality impression formation. *Journal of Abnormal and Social Psychology*, 1961, *63*, 346–350.

Anderson, N. H., and Jacobson, A. Effect of stimulus inconsistency and discounting instructions in personality impression formation. *Journal of Personality and Social Psychology*, 1965, *2*, 531–539.

Anderson, R. E. Status structures in coalition bargaining games. *Sociometry*, 1967, *30*, 393–403.

Angell, R. C., Dunham, V. S., and Singer, J. D. Social values and foreign policy attitudes of Soviet and American elites. *Journal of Conflict Resolution*, 1964, *8*, 329–491.

Ardrey, R. *The territorial imperative*. New York: Atheneum, 1966.

Argyle, M. Social pressure in public and private situations. *Journal of Abnormal and Social Psychology*, 1957, *54*, 172–175.

Argyle, M. *Religious behavior*. Glencoe, Ill.: Free Press, 1959.

Argyle, M., and Kendon, A. The experimental analysis of social performance. In L. Berkowitz (Ed.),

Advances in experimental social psychology. Vol. 3. New York: Academic Press, 1967.

Armsby, R. E. A reexamination of the development of moral judgments in children. *Child Development,* 1971, *42,* 1241–1248.

Aronfreed, J. The origin of self-criticism. *Psychological Review,* 1964, *71,* 193–218.

Aronfreed, J. The socialization of altruistic and sympathetic behavior: Some theoretical and experimental analyses. In J. Macaulay and L. Berkowitz (Eds.), *Altruism and helping behavior: Social psychological studies of some antecedents and consequences.* New York: Academic Press, 1970.

Aronfreed, J., and Paskal, V. *The development of sympathetic behavior in children: An experimental test of a two-phase hypothesis.* Unpublished manuscript, University of Pennsylvania, 1966.

Aronfreed, J., and Reber, A. Internalized behavioral suppression and the timing of social punishment. *Journal of Personality and Social Psychology,* 1965, *1,* 3–17.

Aronson, E. *The social animal.* San Francisco: W. H. Freeman, 1972.

Aronson, E., and Carlsmith, J. M. Effect of the severity of threat on the devaluation of forbidden behavior. *Journal of Abnormal and Social Psychology,* 1963, *66,* 584–588.

Aronson, E. The theory of cognitive dissonance: A current perspective. In L. Berkowitz (Ed.), *Advances in experimental social psychology.* Vol. 4. New York: Academic Press, 1969.

Aronson, E., and Carlsmith, J. M. Experimentation in social psychology. In G. Lindzey and E. Aronson (Eds.), *Handbook of social psychology.* Vol. 2 (2nd ed.) Reading, Mass.: Addison-Wesley, 1968.

Aronson, E., and Cope, V. My enemy's enemy is my friend. *Journal of Personality and Social Psychology,* 1968, *8,* 8–12.

Aronson, E., and Golden, B. W. The effect of relevant and irrelevant aspects of communicator credibility on opinion change. *Journal of Personality,* 1962, *30,* 135–146.

Aronson, E., and Linder, D. Gain and loss of esteem as determinants of inter-personal attraction. *Journal of Experimental Social Psychology,* 1965, *1,* 156–171.

Aronson, E., and Mills, J. The effect of severity of initiation on liking for a group. *Journal of Abnormal and Social Psychology,* 1959, *59,* 177–181.

Aronson, E., Turner, J., and Carlsmith, J. Communicator credibility and communication discrepancy as determinants of opinion change. *Journal of Abnormal and Social Psychology,* 1963, *67,* 31–36.

Aronson, E., Willerman, B., and Floyd, J. The effect of a pratfall on increasing interpersonal attractiveness. *Psychonomic Science,* 1966, *4,* 227–228.

Asch, S. E. Forming impressions of personality. *Journal of Abnormal and Social Psychology,* 1946, *41,* 258–290.

Asch, S. E. Effects of group pressure on the modification and distortion of judgments. In H. Guetzkow (Ed.), *Groups, leadership, and men.* Pittsburgh: Carnegie Press, 1951.

Asch, S. E. *Social psychology.* Englewood Cliffs, N. J.: Prentice-Hall, 1952.

Asch, S. E. Opinions and social pressure. *Scientific American,* 1955, *193* (5), 31–35.

Asch, S. E. Studies of independence and conformity: A minority of one against a unanimous majority. *Psychological Monographs,* 1956, *70* (9, Whole No. 416).

Atkins, A. L., Deaux, K. K., and Bieri, J. Latitude of acceptance and attitude change: empirical evidence for a reformulation. *Journal of Personality and Social Psychology,* 1967, *6,* 47–54.

Azrin, N. H., Hutchinson, R. R., and Hake, D. F. Pain-induced fighting in the squirrel monkey. *Journal of the Experimental Analysis of Behavior,* 1963, *6,* 620.

Azrin, N. H., Hutchinson, R. R., and Hake, D. F. Attack, avoidance, and escape reactions to aversive shock. *Journal of the Experimental Analysis of Behavior,* 1967, *10,* 131–148.

Bachrach, P., and Baratz, M. S. Decisions and nondecisions: An analytical framework. *American Political Science Review,* 1963, *57,* 632–642.

Back, K. W. Influence through social communication. *Journal of Abnormal and Social Psychology,* 1951, *46,* 9–23.

Bacon, M. K., Child, I. L., and Barry, H. III. A cross-cultural study of correlates of crime. *Journal of Abnormal and Social Psychology,* 1963, *66,* 291–300.

Bales, R. F. The equilibrium problem in small groups. In T. Parsons, R. F. Bales, and E. A. Shils (Eds.), *Working papers in the theory of action.* Glencoe, Ill.: Free Press, 1953.

Bales, R. F. Task roles and social roles in problem-solving groups. In E. E. Maccoby, T. M. Newcomb, and F. L. Hartley (Eds.), *Readings in social psychology.* (3rd ed.) New York: Holt, 1958.

Bandler, R. J., Madaras, G. R., and Bem, D. J. Self-observation as a source of pain perception. *Journal of Personality and Social Psychology,* 1968, *9,* 205–209.

Bandura, A. *Principles of behavior modification.* New York: Holt, Rinehart, & Winston, 1969.

Bandura, A. *Social learning theory.* Morristown, N. J.: General Learning Press, 1971.

Bandura, A. *Aggression: A social learning analysis.* Englewood Cliffs, N. J.: Prentice-Hall, 1973.

Bandura, A., Blanchard, E. B., and Ritter, B. Relative efficacy of desensitization and modeling approaches for inducing behavioral, affective, and attitudinal changes. *Journal of Personality and Social Psychology,* 1969, *13,* 173–199.

Bandura, A., Grusec, J. E., and Menlove, F. L. Observational learning as a function of symbolization and incentive set. *Child Development*, 1966, *37*, 499–506.

Bandura, A., and Huston, A. C. Identification as a process of incidental learning. *Journal of Abnormal and Social Psychology*, 1961, *63*, 311–318.

Bandura, A., and Kupers, C. J. Transmission of patterns of self-reinforcement through modeling. *Journal of Abnormal and Social Psychology*, 1964, *69*, 1–9.

Bandura, A., and McDonald, F. J. Influence of social reinforcement and the behavior of models in shaping children's moral judgments. *Journal of Abnormal and Social Psychology*, 1963, *67*, 274–281.

Bandura, A., and Menlove, F. L. Factors determining vicarious extinction of avoidance behavior through symbolic modeling. *Journal of Personality and Social Psychology*, 1968, *8*, 99–108.

Bandura, A., Ross, D., and Ross, S. Transmission of aggression through imitation of aggressive models. *Journal of Abnormal and Social Psychology*, 1961, *63*, 575–582.

Bandura, A., Ross, D., and Ross, S. A. A comparative test of the status envy, social power, and secondary reinforcement theories of identificatory learning. *Journal of Abnormal and Social Psychology*, 1963, *67*, 527–534. (a)

Bandura, A., Ross, D., and Ross, S. Imitation of film-mediated aggressive models. *Journal of Abnormal and Social Psychology*, 1963, *66*, 3–11. (b)

Bandura, A., and Walters, R. H. *Adolescent aggression.* New York: Ronald, 1959.

Bandura, A., and Walters, R. H. *Social learning and personality development.* New York: Holt, Rinehart, & Winston, 1963.

Banikiotes, P. G., Russell, J. M., and Linden, J. D. Interpersonal attraction in simulated and real interactions. *Journal of Personality and Social Psychology*, 1972, *23*, 1–7.

Barber, T. X. *Hypnosis: A scientific approach.* New York: Van Nostrand Reinhold, 1969.

Barber, T. X., and Silver, M. J. Fact, fiction, and the experimenter bias effect. *Psychological Bulletin Monograph Supplement*, 1968, *70*, 1–29.

Barker, R. G. *Ecological psychology: Concepts and methods for studying the environment of human behavior.* Stanford: Stanford University Press, 1968.

Baron, R. A. Magnitude of victim's pain cues and level of prior anger arousal as determinants of adult aggressive behavior. *Journal of Personality and Social Psychology*, 1971, *17*, 236–243. (a)

Baron, R. A. Aggression as a function of magnitude of victim's pain cues, level of prior anger arousal, and aggressor-victim similarity. *Journal of Personality and Social Psychology*, 1971, *18*, 48–54. (b)

Baron, R. A. The aggression—inhibiting influence of heightened sexual arousal. *Journal of Personality and Social Psychology*, 1974, *30*, 318–322.

Baron, R. A., and Eggleston, R. J. Performance on the "aggression machine": Motivation to help or harm? *Psychonomic Science*, 1972, *26*, 321–322.

Baron, R. A., and Kepner, C. R. Model's behavior and attraction toward the model as determinants of adult aggressive behavior. *Journal of Personality and Social Psychology*, 1970, *14*, 335–344.

Baron, R. S., Dion, K. L., Baron, P. H., and Miller, H. Group consensus and cultural values as determinants of risk taking. *Journal of Personality and Social Psychology*, 1971, *20*, 446–455.

Barr, E. A psychological analysis of fashion motivation. *Archives of Psychology*, 1934, No. 171.

Barrett, W. *Irrational man: A study in existential philosophy.* Garden City, N. Y.: Doubleday, 1958.

Bartlett, F. C. *Remembering.* Cambridge, England: Cambridge University, 1932.

Bartos, O. J. Concession-making in experimental conditions. *General Systems*, 1966, SSRI Reprint No. 6, 145–156.

Bartos, O. J. Determinants and consequences of toughness. In P. Swingle (Ed.), *The structure of conflict.* New York: Academic Press, 1970.

Bass, B. M. An analysis of the leaderless group discussion. *Journal of Applied Psychology*, 1949, *33*, 527–533.

Bass, B. M. The leaderless group discussion. *Psychological Bulletin*, 1954, *51*, 465–492.

Bass, B. M. *Leadership, psychology, and organizational behavior.* New York: Harper & Row, 1960.

Bass, B. M. Amount of participation, coalescence, and profitability of decision-making discussions. *Journal of Abnormal and Social Psychology*, 1963, *67*, 92–94.

Bass, B. M., and Wurster, C. R. Effects of company rank on LGD performance of oil refinery supervisors. *Journal of Applied Psychology*, 1953, *37*, 100–104. (a)

Bass, B. M., and Wurster, C. R. Effects of the nature of the problem on LGD performance. *Journal of Applied Psychology*, 1953, *37*, 96–99. (b)

Bateson, N. Familiarization, group discussion, and risk-taking. *Journal of Experimental Social Psychology*, 1966, *2*, 119–129.

Battle, E. S., and Rotter, J. B. Children's feelings of personal control as related to social class and ethnic group. *Journal of Personality*, 1963, *31*, 482–490.

Bavelas, A. A mathematical model for group structures. *Applied Anthropology*, 1948, *7*, 16–30.

Bayton, J. A. McAlister, L. B., and Hamer, J. Race-class stereotypes. *Journal of Negro Education*, 1956, *25*, 75–78.

Bazelon, D. T. *The paper economy.* New York: Random House, 1963.

Bazelon, D. T. Untitled. Address to the American Association of Correctional Psychologists' Conferences on "Psychology's Roles and Contributions in Problems of Crime, Delinquency and Correction." Lake Wales, Florida, January 20, 1972. (Mimeo)

Beattie, R. H., and Kenney, J. P. Aggressive crimes. *Annals of the American Academy of Political and Social Science*, 1966, *364*, 73–85.

Becker, H. S. *Outsiders: Studies in the sociology of deviance.* New York: Free Press, 1963.

Becker, H. S. Marihuana: A sociological overview. In H. Gadlin and B. E. Garskof (Eds.), *The uptight society: A book of readings.* Belmont, Calif.: Brooks/Cole, 1970.

Becker-Haven, J. F., and Lindskold, S. Deindividuation, self-concern, and bystander intervention. Unpublished manuscript, Ohio University, 1975.

Beckman, L. J. Effects of students' performance on teachers' and observers' attributions of causality. *Journal of Educational Psychology*, 1970, *61*, 76–82.

Beez, W. V. Influence of biased psychological reports on teacher behavior and pupil performance. *Proceedings of the 76th Annual Convention of the American Psychological Association*, 1968. 605–606.

Bell, P. R., and Jamieson, B. D. Publicity of initial decisions and the risky shift phenomenon. *Journal of Experimental Social Psychology*, 1970, *6*, 329–345.

Beloff, H. Two forms of social conformity: Acquiescence and conventionality. *Journal of Abnormal and Social Psychology*, 1958, *56*, 99–104.

Bem, D. J. An experimental analysis of self-persuasion. *Journal of Experimental Social Psychology*, 1965, *1*, 199–218.

Bem, D. J. Self-perception: An alternative interpretation of cognitive dissonance phenomena. *Psychological Review*, 1967, *74*, 183–200. (*a*)

Bem, D. J. Self-perception: The dependent variable of human performance. *Organizational Behavior and Human Performance*, 1967, *2*, 105–121. (*b*)

Bem, D. J. The epistemological status of interpersonal simulations: A reply to Jones, Linder, Kiesler, Zanna, and Brehm. *Journal of Experimental Social Psychology*, 1968, *4*, 270–274.

Bem, D. J. *Beliefs, attitudes and human affairs.* Belmont, Calif.: Brooks/Cole, 1970.

Bem, D. J. Self-perception theory. In L. Berkowitz (Ed.), *Advances in experimental social psychology*, Vol. 6. New York: Academic Press, 1972.

Bem, D. J., and McConnell, H. K. Testing the self-perception explanation of dissonance phenomena: On the salience of premanipulation attitudes. *Journal of Personality and Social Psychology*, 1970, *14*, 23–31.

Bennett, C. R., and Lindskold, S. The comparative and reflected appraisal process in group risk taking. Unpublished manuscript, Ohio University, 1973.

Bennis, W. G., Berkowitz, M., Affinito, M., and Malone, M. Authority, power, and the ability to influence. *Human Relations*, 1958, *11*, 143–155.

Benzer, S. Genetic dissection of behavior. *Scientific American*, 1973, *229* (6). 24–37.

Berenda, E. W. *The influence of the group on the judgments of children.* New York: King's Crown Press, 1950.

Berger, P. L., and Luckmann, T. *The social construction of reality: A treatise in the sociology of knowledge.* Garden City, N. Y.: Doubleday, 1966.

Berger, S. M. Conditioning through vicarious instigation. *Psychological Review*, 1962, *69*, 450–466.

Berkowitz, H., and Zigler, E. Effects of preliminary positive and negative inter-actions and delay conditions on children's responsiveness to social reinforcement. *Journal of Personality and Social Psychology*, 1965, *2*, 500–505.

Berkowitz, L. *Aggression: A social psychological analysis.* New York: McGraw-Hill, 1962.

Berkowitz, L. Some aspects of observed aggression. *Journal of Personality and Social Psychology*, 1965, *2*, 359–369.

Berkowitz, L. The frustration-aggression hypothesis revisited. In L. Berkowitz (Ed.), *Roots of aggression: A re-examination of the frustration-aggression hypothesis.* New York: Atherton Press, 1969.

Berkowitz, L. The "weapons effect," demand characteristics, and the myth of the compliant subject. *Journal of Personality and Social Psychology*, 1971, *20*, 332–338.

Berkowitz, L. Social norms, feelings, and other factors affecting helping and altruism. In L. Berkowitz (Ed.), *Advances in experimental social psychology.* Vol. 6. New York: Academic Press, 1972.

Berkowitz, L., and Conner, W. H. Success, failure, and social responsibility. *Journal of Personality and Social Psychology*, 1966, *4*, 664–669.

Berkowitz, L., Corwin, R, and Heironimus, M. Film violence and subsequent aggressive tendencies. *Public Opinion Quarterly*, 1963, *27*, 217–229.

Berkowitz, L., and Cottingham, D. R. The interest value and relevance of fear-arousing communications. *Journal of Abnormal and Social Psychology*, 1960, *60*, 37–43.

Berkowitz, L., and Daniels, L. R. Responsibility and dependency. *Journal of Abnormal and Social Psychology*, 1963, *66*, 429–436.

Berkowitz, L., Green, J. A., and Macaulay, J. R. Hostility of the scapegoat. *Journal of Abnormal and Social Psychology*, 1962, *64*, 293–301.

Berkowitz, L., Green, J. A., and Macaulay, J. R. Hostility catharsis as the reduction of emotional tension. *Psychiatry*, 1962, *25*, 23–31.

Berkowitz, L., and LePage, A. Weapons as aggression-eliciting stimuli. *Journal of Personality and Social Psychology*, 1967, *7*, 202–207.

Berkowitz, L., and Levy, B. I. Pride in group performance and group-task motivation. *Journal of Abnormal and Social Psychology*, 1956, *53*, 300–306.

Berkowitz, L., and Lundy, R. M. Personality characteristics related to susceptibility to influence by peers or authority figures. *Journal of Personality*, 1957, *25*, 306–316.

Berkowitz, L., and Rawlings, E. Effects of film violence: An inhibition against subsequent aggression. *Journal of Abnormal and Social Psychology*, 1963, *66*, 405–412.

Berlo, D. K., Lemert, J. B., and Mertz, R. Dimensions of evaluations of sources. Unpublished manuscript, Department of Communications. Michigan State University, 1966.

Berlyne, D. E. *Conflict, arousal, and curiosity.* New York: McGraw-Hill, 1960.

Berlyne, D. E. *Structure and direction in thinking.* New York: Wiley, 1965.

Berlyne, D. E. Curiosity and exploration. *Science*, 1966, *153*, 25–33.

Bernstein, I. S., and Mason, W. A. Group formation by rhesus monkeys. *Animal Behavior*, 1963, *11*, 28–31.

Berscheid, E., Dion, K., Walster, E., and Walster, G. W. Physical attractiveness and dating choice: A test of the matching hypothesis. *Journal of Experimental Social Psychology*, 1971, *7*, 173–189.

Berscheid, E., and Walster, E. When does a harm-doer compensate a victim? *Journal of Personality and Social Psychology*, 1967, *6*, 435–441.

Berscheid, E., and Walster, E. Physical attractiveness and heterosexual attraction. In L. Berkowitz (Ed.), *Advances in experimental social psychology.* Vol. 7. New York: Academic Press, 1974.

Bettleheim, B. Individual and mass behavior in extreme situations. In E. E. Maccoby, T. M. Newcomb, and E. L. Hartley (Eds.), *Readings in social psychology.* (3rd ed.) New York: Henry Holt, 1958.

Bickman, L. The effect of social status on the honesty of others. *Journal of Social Psychology*, 1971, *85*, 87–92. (a)

Bickman, L. The effect of another bystander's ability to help on bystander intervention in an emergency. *Journal of Experimental Social Psychology*, 1971, *7*, 367–379. (b)

Bickman, L., and Henchy, T. *Beyond the laboratory: Field research in social psychology.* New York: McGraw-Hill, 1972.

Bieri, J. Cognitive complexity-simplicity and predictive behavior. *Journal of Abnormal and Social Psychology*, 1955, *51*, 263–268.

Bieri, J., Orcutt, B. A., and Leaman, R. Anchoring effects in sequential clinical judgments. *Journal of Abnormal and Social Psychology*, 1963, *67*, 616–623.

Biondo, J., and MacDonald, A. P. Internal-external locus of control and response to influence attempts. *Journal of Personality*, 1971, *39*, 406–419.

Birdwhistell, R. L. The kinesic level in the investigation of the emotions. In P. H. Knapp (Ed.), *Expression of the emotions in man.* New York: International University Press, 1963.

Birdwhistell, R. L. Some relationships between American kinesics and spoken American English. In A. G. Smith (Ed.), *Communication and culture.* New York: Holt, Rinehart, & Winston, 1966.

Birdwhistell, R. L. Some body motion elements accompanying spoken American English. In L. Thayer (Ed.), *Communication: Concepts and perspectives.* Washington, D. C.: Spartan Books, 1967.

Birney, R. C., Burdick, H., and Teevan, R. C. *Fear of failure.* New York: Van Nostrand-Reinhold, 1969.

Bitterman, M. E., and Kniffin, C. W. Manifest anxiety and "perceptual defense." *Journal of Abnormal and Social Psychology*, 1953, *48*, 248–252.

Bixenstine, V. E., and O'Reilly F. F. Jr. Money versus electric shock as payoff in a Prisoner's Dilemma Game. *Psychological Record*, 1966, *16*, 251–264.

Bixenstine, V. E., Potash, H. M., and Wilson, K. V. Effects of levels of cooperative choice by the other player on choices in a Prisoner's Dilemma game. Part I. *Journal of Abnormal and Social Psychology*, 1963, *66*, 308–313.

Bjerstedt, A. A field-force model as a basis for predictions of social behavior. *Human Relations*, 1958, *11*, 331–340.

Bjorkman, M. On the ecological relevance of psychological research. *Scandinavian Journal of Psychology*, 1969, *10*, 145–157.

Blalock, H. M. Jr. *Causal models in the social sciences.* Chicago: Aldine, 1971.

Blau, P. M. *Exchange and power in social life.* New York: Wiley, 1964.

Block, J. H. Conceptions of sex role: Some cross-cultural and longitudinal perspectives. *American Psychologist*, 1973, *28*, 512–526.

Blumenthal, M., Kahn, R. L., Andrews, F. M., and Head, K. B. *Justifying violence: Attitudes of American men.* Ann Arbor, Mich.: Institute for Social Research, 1972.

Blumer, H. Collective behavior. In J. B. Gittler (Ed.), *Review of Sociology.* New York: Wiley, 1957.

Blumer, H. Collective behavior. In A. M. Lee (Ed.), *New outline of the principles of sociology.* New York: Barnes & Noble, 1946.

Boelkins, R. C., and Heiser, J. F. Biological bases of aggression. In D. N. Daniels, M. F. Gilula, F. M. Ochberg (Eds.), *Violence and the problem of human existence.* Boston: Little Brown, 1970.

Bonney, M. E. Choosing between the sexes on a sociometric measurement. *Journal of Social Psychology*, 1954, *39*, 99–114.

Bookbinder L. J. Perception of others, self-perception, and response sets in high and low authoritarians. *Perceptual and Motor Skills*, 1963, *17*, 694.

Boorstin, D. J. *The image: Or what happened to the American dream.* New York: Atheneum, 1961.

Boring, E. G. *A history of experimental psychology.* (2nd ed.) New York: Appleton-Century-Crofts, 1950.

Bornstein, M. H. Color vision and color naming: A psychophysiological hypothesis of cultural difference. *Psychological Bulletin,* 1973, *80,* 257–285.

Bossard, J. Residential propinquity as a factor in marriage selection. *American Journal of Sociology,* 1932, *38,* 219–224.

Boulding, K. E. Am I a man or a mouse—or both? In A. Montagu (Ed.), *Man and aggression.* New York: Oxford University Press, 1968.

Bowers, J. W. Language intensity, social introversion and attitude change. *Speech monographs,* 1963, *30,* 345–352.

Bowers, J. W., and Osborn, M. M. Attitudinal effects of selected types of concluding metaphors in persuasive speech. *Speech Monographs,* 1966, *33,* 147–155.

Bowers, K. S. Situationism in psychology: An analysis and a critique. *Psychological Review,* 1973, *80,* 307–336.

Braginsky, B., and Braginsky, D. Schizophrenic patients in the psychiatric interview: An experimental study of their effectiveness at manipulation. *Journal of Consulting Psychology,* 1967, *31,* 543–547.

Braginsky, B. M., Braginsky, D. D., and Ring, K. *Methods of madness: The mental hospital as a last resort.* New York: Holt, Rinehart, & Winston, 1969.

Bramel, D. A dissonance theory approach to defensive projection. *Journal of Abnormal and Social Psychology,* 1962, *64,* 121–129.

Bramel, D. Selection of a target for defensive projection. *Journal of Abnormal and Social Psychology,* 1963, *66,* 318–324.

Bramel, D. Interpersonal attraction, hostility, and perception. In J. Mills (Ed.), *Experimental social psychology.* New York: Macmillan, 1969.

Breger, L., and Rutz, C. *The role of ego defense in conformity.* Paper read at Western Psychological Association, Santa Monica, California, April, 1963.

Brehm, J. W. Post-decision changes in the desirability of alternatives. *Journal of Abnormal and Social Psychology,* 1956, *52,* 384–389.

Brehm, J. W. *A theory of psychological reactance.* New York: Academic Press, 1966.

Brehm, J. W., and Cohen, A. R. Choice and chance-relative deprivation as determinants of cognitive dissonance. *Journal of Abnormal and Social Psychology,* 1959, *58,* 383–387.

Brehm, J. W., and Mann, M. Effect of importance of freedom and attraction to group members on influence produced by group pressure. *Journal of Personality and Social Psychology,* 1975, *31,* 816–824.

Brehm, J. W., Stires, L. K., Sensenig, J., and Shaban, J. The attractiveness of an eliminated choice alternative. *Journal of Experimental Social Psychology,* 1966, *2,* 301–313.

Brigham, J. C., and Cook, S. W. The influence of

attitude on judgments of plausibility: A replication and extension. *Educational and Psychological Measurement,* 1970, *30,* 283–292.

Broadbent,, D. E. *Perception and communication.* New York: Pergamon Press, 1958.

Brock, T. C. Communicator-recipient similarity and decision change. *Journal of Personality and Social Psychology,* 1965, *1,* 650–654.

Brock, T. C., and Becker, L. A. Ineffectiveness of overheard counter-propaganda. *Journal of Personality and Social Psychology,* 1965, *2,* 654–660.

Brock, T. C., and Becker, L. A. "Debriefing" and susceptibility to subsequent experimental manipulations. *Journal of Experimental Social Psychology,* 1966, *2,* 314–323.

Brock, T. C., and Becker, L. A. Volition and attraction in everyday life. *Journal of Social Psychology,* 1967, *72,* 89–97.

Brock, T. C., and DelGiudice, C. Stealing and temporal orientation. *Journal of Abnormal and Social Psychology,* 1963, *66,* 91–94.

Brodie, F. M. *No man knows my history: The life of Joseph Smith, the Mormon Prophet.* New York: Knopf, 1946.

Brody, R. A. Some systematic effects of the spread of nuclear-weapons technology: A study through simulation of a multi-nuclear future. *Journal of Conflict Resolution,* 1963, *7,* 663–753.

Bronfenbrenner, U. The mirror image in Soviet-American relations: A social psychologist's report. *Journal of Social Issues.* 1961, *17* (3), 45–56.

Brooks, J. *The great leap: The past twenty-five years in America.* New York: Harper & Row, 1966.

Brown, B. R. The effects of need to maintain face in interpersonal bargaining. *Journal of Experimental Social Psychology,* 1968, *4,* 107–122.

Brown, D. G. Sex-role preference in young children. *Psychological Monographs,* 1956, *70,* No. 14 (Whole No. 421).

Brown, D. G. Inversion and homosexuality. *American Journal of Orthopsychiatry,* 1958, *28,* 424–429.

Brown, M., Feldman, K., Schwartz, S., and Heingartner, A. Some personality correlates of conduct in two situations of moral conflict. *Journal of Personality,* 1969, *37,* 41–57.

Brown, P., and Elliott, R. Control of aggression in a nursery school class. *Journal of Experimental Child Psychology,* 1965, *2,* 103–107.

Brown, R. *Social psychology.* New York: Free Press, 1965.

Brown, R. C. Jr., Helm, B., and Tedeschi, J. T. Interpersonal attraction and social reinforcement. *Journal of Social Psychology,* 1973, *91,* 81–85.

Brown, R. C. Jr., Smith, R. B., III, and Tedeschi, J. T. *First impressions and their effect on interpersonal expectancies.* Unpublished manuscript, Georgia State University, 1974.

Brown, R. C. Jr., and Tedeschi, J. T. Determinants of perceived aggression. *Journal of Social Psychology*, 1976.

Brown, R. W. Mass phenomena. In G. Lindzey (Ed.), *Handbook of social psychology*. Vol. 2. Cambridge, Mass.: Addison-Wesley, 1954.

Brown, R. W., and Lenneberg, E. H. A study in language and cognition. *Journal of Abnormal and Social Psychology*, 1954, *49*, 454–462.

Browne, M. W. *The new face of war*. New York: Bobbs-Merrill, 1965.

Bruner, J. S. Going beyond the information given. In *Contemporary approaches to cognition*. Cambridge, Mass.: Harvard University, 1957.

Bruner, J. S., and Postman, L. J. On the perception of incongruity: A paradigm. *Journal of Personality*, 1949, *18*, 206–223.

Bruner, J. S., Shapiro, D., and Tagiuri, R. The meaning of traits in isolation and combination. In R. Tagiuri, and L. Petrullo (Eds.), *Person perception and interpersonal behavior*. Stanford, Calif.: Stanford University Press, 1958.

Brunswick, E., and Kamiya, J. Ecological cue-validity of "proximity" and of other Gestalt factors. *American Journal of Psychology*, 1953, *66*, 20–32.

Bryan, J. H., Redfield, J., and Mader, S. Words and deeds about altruism and the subsequent reinforcement power of the model. *Child Development*, 1971, *42*, 1501–1508.

Bryan, J. H., and Schwartz, J. Effects of film material upon children's behavior. *Psychological Bulletin*, 1971, *75*, 50–59.

Bryan, J. H., and Test, M. Models and helping: Naturalistic studies in aiding behavior. *Journal of Personality and Social Psychology*, 1967, *6*, 400–407.

Bryan, J. H., and Walbek, N. H. The impact of words and deeds concerning altruism upon children. *Child Development*, 1970, *41*, 747–757.

Bryant, C. D., and Snizek, W. E. The iceman cometh: The cryonics movement and frozen immortality. *Society*, 1973, *11*, 56–61.

Burnham, J. R., and Hartsough, D. M. *Effects of experimenters' expectancies on children's ability to learn to swim*. Paper presented at the meeting of the Midwestern Psychological Association, Chicago, May, 1968.

Burnstein, E., and Worchel, P. Arbitrariness of frustration and its consequences for aggression in a social situation. *Journal of Personality*, 1962, *30*, 528–540.

Burton, R. V. Generality of honesty reconsidered. *Psychological Review*, 1963, *70*, 481–499.

Buss, A. H. *The psychology of aggression*. New York: Wiley, 1961.

Buss, A. H. Instrumentality of aggression, feedback, and frustration as determinants of physical aggression. *Journal of Personality and Social Psychology*, 1966, *3*, 153–162.

Buss, A. H. Aggression pays. In J. L. Singer (Ed.), *The control of aggression and violence*. New York: Academic Press, 1971.

Buss, A. H., Booker, A., and Buss, E. Firing a weapon and aggression. *Journal of Personality and Social Psychology*, 1972, *22*, 296–302.

Buss, A. H., and Gerjuoy, I. R. Verbal conditioning and anxiety. *Journal of Abnormal and Social Psychology*, 1958, *57*, 249–250.

Butler, R. A. Incentive conditions which influence visual exploration. *Journal of Experimental Psychology*, 1954, *48*, 19–23.

Byrne, D. Response to attitude similarity-dissimilarity as a function of affiliation need. *Journal of Personality*, 1962, *30*, 164–177.

Byrne, D. Attitudes and attraction. In L. Berkowitz (Ed.), *Advances in experimental social psychology*. Vol. 4. New York: Academic Press, 1969.

Byrne, D. *The attraction paradigm*. New York: Academic Press, 1971.

Byrne, D., and Blaylock, B. Similarity and assumed similarity of attitudes between husbands and wives. *Journal of Abnormal and Social Psychology*, 1963, *67*, 636–640.

Byrne, D., and Buehler, J. A. A note on the influence of propinquity upon acquaintanceships. *Journal of Abnormal and Social Psychology*, 1955, *51*, 147–148.

Byrne, D., Clore, G. L., Jr., and Worchel, P. Effect of economic similarity-dissimilarity on interpersonal attraction. *Journal of Personality and Social Psychology*, 1966, *4*, 220–224.

Byrne, D., Ervin, C. R., and Lamberth, J. Continuity between the experimental study of attraction and real-life computer dating. *Journal of Personality and Social Psychology*, 1970, *16*, 157–165.

Byrne, D., and Lamberth, J. Cognitive and reinforcement theories as complementary approaches to the study of attraction. In B. I. Murstein (Ed.), *Theories of attraction and love*. New York: Springer, 1971.

Byrne, D., and Nelson, B. A. Attraction as a linear function of proportion of positive reinforcements. *Journal of Personality and Social Psychology*, 1965, *1*, 659–663.

Byrne, D., Young, R. K., and Griffitt, W. The reinforcement properties of attitude statements. *Journal of Experimental Research in Personality*, 1966, *1*, 266–276.

Caldwell, O. W., and Wellman, B. L. Characteristics of school leaders. *Journal of Educational Research*, 1926, *14*, 1–13.

Calhoun, J. B. Population density and social pathology. *Scientific American*, 1962, *206*, 139–148.

Calvin, A. D. Social reinforcement. *Journal of Social Psychology*, 1962, *59*, 15–19.

Cameron, P., Frank, F., Lifter, M., and Morrissey, P. Cognitive functionings of college students in a general psychology class. Paper presented at the 76th annual meeting of the American Psychological Association, San Francisco, September, 1968.

Cameron, W. B. *Modern social movements: A sociological outline.* New York: Random House, 1966.

Campbell, A., Converse, P. E., Miller, W. E., and Stokes, D. E. *The American voter.* New York: Wiley, 1960.

Campbell, D. T. Factors relevant to validity of experiments in social settings. *Psychological Bulletin,* 1957, *54,* 297–312.

Campbell, D. T. Reforms as experiments. *American Psychologist,* 1969, *24,* 409–429.

Campbell, D. T., and Stanley, J. C. Experimental and quasi-experimental designs for research on teaching. In N. L. Gage (Ed.), *Handbook of research on teaching.* Chicago: Rand McNally, 1963.

Canon, L. K. Self-confidence and selective exposure to information. In L. Festinger (Ed.), *Conflict, decision, and dissonance.* Stanford: Stanford University Press, 1964.

Cantril, H. *The invasion from Mars.* Princeton: Princeton University Press, 1940.

Caplan, N., and Nelson, S. D. On being useful: The nature and consequences of psychological research on social problems. *American Psychologist,* 1973, *28,* 199–211.

Caplow, T. A theory of coalitions in the triad. *American Sociological Review,* 1956, *21,* 489–493.

Caplow, T. Further development of a theory of coalitions in the triad. *American Journal of Sociology,* 1959, *64,* 488–493.

Carlsmith, J. M., Collins, B. E., and Helmreich, R. L. Studies in forced compliance: The effect of pressure for compliance on attitude change produced by face-to-face role playing and anonymous essay writing. *Journal of Personality and Social Psychology,* 1966, *4,* 1–13.

Carlson, E. R. Attitude change through modification of attitude structure. *Journal of Abnormal and Social Psychology,* 1956, *52,* 256–261.

Carlson, N. J., and Black, A. H. Traumatic avoidance learning: The effect of preventing escape responses. *Canadian Journal of Psychology,* 1960, *14,* 21–28.

Carlyle, T. *Critical and miscellaneous essays.* Vol. 5. London: Chapman and Hall, 1888.

Carmichael, L., Hogan, H. P., and Walter, A. A. An experimental study of the effect of language on the reproduction of visually perceived form. *Journal of Experimental Psychology,* 1932, *15,* 73–86.

Carmichael, L., Roberts, S. O., and Wassel, N. Y. A study of the judgment of manual expressions as presented in still and motion pictures. *Journal of Social Psychology,* 1937, *8,* 115–142.

Carson, R. C. *Interaction concepts of personality.* Chicago: Aldine, 1969.

Carter, L. F., and Schooler, K. Value need and other factors in perception. *Psychological Review,* 1949, *56,* 200–207.

Cartwright, D. Achieving change in people: Some applications of group dynamics theory. *Human Relations,* 1951, *4,* 381–393.

Cartwright, D. Influence, leadership, control. In J. G. March (Ed.), *Handbook of organizations.* Chicago: Rand McNally, 1965.

Cartwright, D. Determinants of scientific progress: The case of research on the risky shift. *American Psychologist,* 1973, *28,* 222–231.

Cartwright, D. C., and Zander, A. *Group dynamics: Research and theory.* New York: Harper & Row, 1953.

Cassirer, E. *An essay on man.* New Haven, Yale U. Press, 1944.

Cater, D. *The fourth branch of government.* New York: Vintage, 1959.

Cavior, N. *Physical attractiveness, perceived attitude similarity, and inter-personal attraction among fifth and eleventh grade boys and girls.* Doctoral dissertation, University of Houston, 1970.

Cavior, N., and Dokecki, P. R. *Physical attractiveness self-concept: A test of Mead's hypothesis.* Paper presented at the 79th Annual Convention of the American Psychological Association, Washington, D. C., 1971.

Chaffee, S. H., and McLeod, J. M. *Adolescents, parents, and television violence.* Paper presented at the 79th Annual Meeting of the American Psychological Association, Washington, D. C., 1971.

Chambliss, W. J. The deterrent influence of punishment. *Crime and Delinquency,* 1966, *12,* 70–75.

Chapman, I. W., and Volkmann, J. A social determinant of the level of aspiration. *Journal of Abnormal and Social Psychology,* 1939, *34,* 225–238.

Chasdi, E. H., and Lawrence, M. S. Some antecedents of aggression and effects of frustration in doll play. In D. McClelland (Ed.), *Studies in motivation.* New York: Appleton-Century-Crofts, 1955.

Chertkoff, J. M. The effects of probability of future success on coalition formation. *Journal of Experimental Social Psychology,* 1966, *2,* 265–277.

Chertkoff, J. M. A revision of Caplow's coalition theory. *Journal of Experimental Social Psychology,* 1967, *3,* 172–177.

Chertkoff, J. M. Sociopsychological theories and research on coalition formation. In S. Groennings, E. W. Kelley, and M. Leiserson (Eds.), *The study of coalition behavior: Theoretical perspectives and cases from four continents.* New York: Holt, Rinehart, & Winston, 1970.

Chertkoff, J. M., and Conley, M. Opening offer and frequency of concession as bargaining strategies. *Journal of Personality and Social Psychology,* 1967, *7,* 181–185.

Chomsky, N. *Language and mind.* New York: Harcourt, Brace, & World, 1968.

Christie, R. Authoritarianism re-examined. In R.

Christie, and M. Jahoda (Eds.), *Studies in the scope and method of "The Authoritarian Personality."* New York: Free Press, 1954.

Christie, R., and Jahoda, M. (Eds.) *Studies in the scope and method of "The Authoritarian Personality."* New York: Free Press, 1954.

Cialdini, R. B., Levy, A., Herman, C. P., and Evenbeck, S. Attitudinal politics: The strategy of moderation. *Journal of Personality and Social Psychology,* 1973, *25,* 100–108.

Clark, K. B., and Clark, M. P. Racial identification and preference in Negro children. In E. E. Maccoby, T. M. Newcomb, and E. L. Hartley (Eds.), *Readings in social psychology.* (3rd ed.) New York: Holt, 1958.

Clarke, D. E. M. (Translator) *The Havamal, with Selections from other poems in the Edda.* Cambridge, England: The University Press, 1923.

Clausewitz, K. von. *War, politics, and power.* Chicago: Regnery Co., 1962.

Clifford, R. A. *The Rio Grande flood: A comparative study of border communities in disaster.* Washington, D. C.: National Academy of Sciences—National Research Council, 1956.

Cline, V., Croft, R., and Courrier, S. Desensitization of children to television violence. *Journal of Personality and Social Psychology,* 1973, *27,* 360–365.

Coch, L., and French, J. R. P. Jr. Overcoming resistance to change. In E. E. Maccoby, T. M. Newcomb, and E. L. Hartley (Eds.), *Readings in social psychology.* (3rd ed.) New York: Holt, Rinehart & Winston, 1958.

Cohen, A. K. *Deviance and control.* Englewood Cliffs, N. J.: Prentice-Hall, 1966.

Cohen, A. R. Social norms, arbitrariness of frustration, and status of the agent of frustration in the frustration-aggression hypothesis. *Journal of Abnormal and Social Psychology,* 1955, *51,* 222–226.

Cohen, A. R. Upward communication in experimentally created hierarchies. *Human Relations,* 1958, *11,* 41–53.

Cohen, A. R. Some implications of self-esteem for social influence. In C. I. Hovland and I. L. Janis (Eds.), *Personality and persuasibility.* New Haven, Conn.: Yale University Press, 1959.

Cohen, A. R. Cognitive tuning as a factor affecting impression formation. *Journal of Personality,* 1961, *29,* 235–245.

Cohen, A. R., Brehm, J. W., and Latané, B. Choice of strategy and voluntary exposure to information under public and private conditions. *Journal of Personality,* 1959, *27,* 63–73.

Cohen, D. J., Whitmyre, J. W., and Funk, W. H. Effect of group cohesiveness and training upon group thinking. *Journal of Applied Psychology,* 1960, *44,* 319–322.

Cohen, E. A. *Human behavior in concentration camps.* New York: Grosset & Dunlap, 1953. Translated from the Dutch by M. H. Braaksma.

Cohen, R. Altruism: Human, cultural, or what? *Journal of Social Issues,* 1972, *28,* 39–57.

Coleman, J. F., Blake, R. R., and Mouton, J. S. Task difficulty and conformity pressures. *Journal of Abnormal and Social Psychology,* 1958, *57,* 120–122.

Coleman, J. S., and James, J. The equilibrium size distribution of freely-forming groups. *Sociometry,* 1961, *24,* 36–45.

Collins, B. E. Attribution theory analysis of forced compliance. *Proceedings, 77th Annual convention, American Psychological Association,* 1969, *4,* 309–310.

Collins, B. E. *Social psychology.* Reading, Mass.: Addison-Wesley, 1970.

Collins, B. E. Four components of the Rotter Internal-external scale: Belief in a difficult world, a just world, a predictable world, and a politically responsive world. *Journal of Personality and Social Psychology,* 1974, *29,* 381–391.

Collins, B. E., and Guetzkow, H. *A social psychology of group processes for decision-making.* New York: Wiley, 1964.

Conn, L. K., Edwards, C. E., Rosenthal, R., and Crowne, D. Perception of emotion and responses to teachers' expectancy by elementary school children. *Psychological Reports,* 1968, *22,* 27–34.

Cook, M. *Interpersonal perception.* Baltimore, Md.: Penguin, 1971.

Cook, S. W., and Selltiz, C. A. Multiple-indicator approach to attitude measurement. *Psychological Bulletin,* 1964, *62,* 36–55.

Cook, T. D., Bean, J. R., Calder, B. J., Frey, R., Krovetz, M. L., and Reisman, S. R. Demand characteristics and three conceptions of the frequently deceived subject. *Journal of Personality and Social Psychology,* 1970, *14,* 185–194.

Cooley, C. H. *Human nature and the social order.* New York: Scribner, 1902.

Cooley, C. H. *Social organization.* New York: Scribner, 1909.

Coombs, R. H., and Kenkel, W. F. Sex differences in dating aspirations and satisfaction with computer-selected partners. *Journal of Marriage and the Family,* 1966, *28,* 62–66.

Cooper, E., and Dinerman, H. Analysis of the film "Don't be a Sucker": A study of communication. *Public Opinion Quarterly,* 1951, *15,* 243–264.

Cooper, J., and Jones, E. E. Opinion divergence as a strategy to avoid being miscast. *Journal of Personality and Social Psychology,* 1969, *13,* 23–30.

Cooper, J., and Jones, R. A. Self-esteem and consistency as determinants of anticipatory opinion change. *Journal of Personality and Social Psychology,* 1970, *14,* 312–320.

Cooper, J., and Worchel, S. Role of undesired consequences in arousing cognitive dissonance. *Journal of Personality and Social Psychology,* 1970, *16,* 199–206.

Corah, N. L., and Boffa, J. Perceived control, self-observation, and response to aversive stimulation. *Journal of Personality and Social Psychology*, 1970, *16*, 1–4.

Corey, S. M. Professed attitudes and actual behavior. *Journal of Educational Psychology*, 1937, *28*, 271–280.

Cottrell, F. *Energy and society.* New York: McGraw-Hill, 1955.

Cottrell, N. B. Social facilitation. In C. G. McClintock (Ed.), *Experimental social psychology.* New York: Holt, Rinehart, & Winston, 1972.

Cottrell, N. B., and Wack, D. L. Energizing effects of cognitive dissonance upon dominant and subordinate responses. *Journal of Personality and Social Psychology*, 1967, *6*, 132–138.

Cottrell, N. B., Wack, D. L., Sekerak, G. J., and Rittle, R. H. Social facilitation of dominant responses by the presence of an audience and the mere presence of others. *Journal of Personality and Social Psychology*, 1968, *9*, 245–250.

Cowan, P. A., Langer, J., Heavenrich, J., and Nathanson, M. Social learning and Piaget's cognitive theory of moral development. *Journal of Personality and Social Psychology*, 1969, *11*, 261–274.

Cowan, P. A., and Walters, R. H. Studies of reinforcement of aggression: Part I: Effects of scheduling. *Child Development*, 1963, *34*, 543–551.

Cox, D. F., and Bauer, R. A. Self-confidence and persuasibility in women. *Public Opinion Quarterly*, 1964, *28*, 453–466.

Cozby, P. C. Self-disclosure, reciprocity, and liking. *Sociometry*, 1972, *35*, 151–160.

Crandall, V. C., Katkovsky, W., and Crandall, V. J. Children's beliefs in their own control of reinforcements in intellectual-academic achievement situations. *Child Development*, 1965, *36*, 91–109.

Crandall, V. J., Katkovsky, W., and Preston, A. A conceptual formulation of some research on children's achievement development. *Child Development*, 1960, *31*, 787–797.

Crockett, W. H. Cognitive complexity and impression formation. In B. A. Maher (Ed.), *Progress in experimental personality research.* Vol. 2. New York: Academic Press, 1965.

Crockett, W. H., and Meidinger, T. Authoritarianism and interpersonal perception. *Journal of Abnormal and Social Psychology*, 1956, *53*, 378–380.

Cronbach, L. J. Processes affecting scores on "understanding of others" and "assumed similarity." *Psychological Bulletin*, 1955, *52*, 177–193.

Croner, M. D., and Willis, R. H. Perceived differences in task competence and asymmetry of dyadic influence. *Journal of Abnormal and Social Psychology*, 1961, *62*, 705–708.

Crosbie, P. V. Social exchange and power compliance: A test of Homans' proposition. *Sociometry*, 1972, *35*, 203–222.

Cross, J. F., and Cross, J. Age, sex, race and the perception of facial beauty. *Developmental Psychology*, 1971, *5*, 433–439.

Crowley, P. M. Effect of training upon objectivity of moral judgment in grade school children. *Journal of Personality and Social Psychology*, 1968, *8*, 228–232.

Crowne, D. P., and Marlowe, D. *The approval motive: Studies in evaluative dependence.* New York: Wiley, 1964.

Crowne, D. P., and Strickland, B. R. The conditioning of verbal behavior as a function of the need for social approval. *Journal of Abnormal and Social Psychology*, 1961, *63*, 395–401.

Crutchfield, R. S. Correlates of individual behavior in a controlled group situation. *American Psychologist*, 1953, *8*, 338. (Abstract).

Crutchfield, R. S. Conformity and character. *American Psychologist*, 1955, *10*, 191–198.

Cutler, J. E. *Lynch-law.* London: Longmans Green, 1905.

Dabbs, J. M., Jr., and Leventhal, H. Effects of varying the recommendations in fear-arousing communication. *Journal of Personality and Social Psychology*, 1966, *4*, 525–531.

Dahl, R. A. *Who governs?* New Haven, Conn.: Yale University Press, 1961.

Dahl, R. A., and Lindblom, C. E. *Politics, economics, and welfare.* New York: Harper, 1953.

Darley, J. M., and Berscheid, E. S. Increased liking as a result of the anticipation of personal contact. *Human Relations*, 1967, *20*, 29–39.

Darley, J. M., and Latané, B. Bystander intervention in emergencies: Diffusion of responsibility. *Journal of Personality and Social Psychology*, 1968, *8*, 377–383.

Darley, J. M., Teger, A. I., and Lewis, L. D. Do groups always inhibit individuals' responses to potential emergencies? *Journal of Personality and Social Psychology*, 1973, *26*, 395–399.

Darlington, R. B., and Macker, C. E. Displacement of guilt-produced altruistic behavior. *Journal of Personality and Social Psychology*, 1966, *4*, 442–443.

Darwin, C. *The expression of emotions in man and animals.* London: J. Murray, 1872.

Dashiell, J. F. An experimental analysis of some group effects. *Journal of Abnormal and Social Psychology*, 1930, *25*, 190–199.

Dashiell, J. F. Experimental studies of the influence of social situations on the behavior of individual human adults. In C. Murchison (Ed.), *Handbook of social psychology.* Worcester, Mass.: Clark University Press, 1935.

Davis, J. M., and Farina, A. Humor appreciation as social communication. *Journal of Personality and Social Psychology*, 1970, *15*, 175–178.

Davis, K. E., and Jones, E. E. Changes in interpersonal perceptions as a means of reducing cognitive dissonance. *Journal of Abnormal and Social Psychology*, 1960, *61*, 402–410.

Davison, W. P. Political significance of recognition via mass media—an illustration from the Berlin blockade. *Public Opinion Quarterly*, 1956, *20*, 327–333.

Deaux, K. Anticipatory attitude change: A direct test of the self-esteem hypothesis. *Journal of Experimental Social Psychology*, 1972, *8*, 143–155.

deCharms, R. *Personal causation: The internal effective determinants of behavior.* New York: Academic Press, 1968.

deCharms, R., Carpenter, V., and Kuperman, A. The "origin-pawn" variable in person perception. *Sociometry*, 1965, *28*, 241–258.

deCharms, R., and Rosenbaum, M. E. Status variables and matching behavior. *Journal of Personality*, 1960, *28*, 492–502.

DeFleur, M. A., and Westie, F. R. Verbal attitudes and overt acts: An experiment on the salience of attitudes. *American Sociological Review*, 1958, *23*, 667–673.

Delgado, J. M. R. Emotional behavior in animals and humans. *Psychiatric Research Report*, 1960, *12*, 259–271.

DeNike, L. D. The temporal relationship between awareness and performance in verbal conditioning. *Journal of Experimental Psychology*, 1964, *68*, 521–529.

deRivera, J. H. *The psychological dimension of foreign policy.* Columbus, Ohio: Charles Merrill, 1968.

Deutsch, M. The pathetic fallacy: An observer error in social perception. *Journal of Personality*, 1960, *28*, 317–332. (*a*)

Deutsch, M. Trust, trustworthiness, and the F-scale. *Journal of Abnormal and Social Psychology*, 1960, *61*, 138–140. (*b*)

Deutsch, M. Socially relevant science: Reflections on some studies of inter-personal conflict. *American Psychologist*, 1969, *24*, 1076–1092.

Deutsch, M., Canavan, D., and Rubin, J. The effects of size of conflict and sex of experimenter upon interpersonal bargaining. *Journal of Experimental Social Psychology*, 1971, *7*, 258–267.

Deutsch, M., and Collins, M. *Interracial housing: A psychological evaluation of a social experiment.* Minneapolis, Minn.: University of Minnesota Press, 1951.

Deutsch, M., and Gerard, H. B. A study of normative and informational social influence on individual judgment. *Journal of Abnormal and Social Psychology*, 1955, *51*, 629–636.

Deutsch, M., and Krauss, R. M. The effect of threat upon interpersonal bargaining. *Journal of Abnormal and Social Psychology*, 1960, *61*, 181–189.

Deutsch, M., and Krauss, R. M. Studies of interpersonal bargaining. *Journal of Conflict Resolution*, 1962, *6*, 52–76.

Deutsch, M., and Lewicki, R. J. The effects of "locking oneself in" during a game of "chicken." *Journal of Conflict Resolution*, 1970, *14*, 367–378.

Deutsch, M., and Solomon, L. Reactions to evaluations by others as influenced by self-evaluations. *Sociometry*, 1959, *22*, 93–112.

DeWolfe, A. S., and Governale, C. N. Fear and attitude change. *Journal of Abnormal and Social Psychology*, 1964, *69*, 119–123.

Diamond, M. J. The use of observationally presented information to modify hypnotic susceptibility. *Journal of Abnormal Psychology*, 1972, *79*, 174–180.

Dietrich, J. E. The relative effectiveness of two modes of radio delivery in influencing attitudes. *Speech Monographs*, 1946, *13*, 58–65.

Dillehay, R. C. On the irrelevance of the classical negative evidence concerning the effect of attitudes on behavior. *American Psychologist*, 1973, *28*, 887–891.

Dinsmoor, J. A., and Campbell, S. L. Escape-from-shock training following exposure to inescapable shock. *Psychological Reports*, 1956, *2*, 43–49.

Dion, K. K. Physical attractiveness and evaluation of children's transgressions. *Journal of Personality and Social Psychology*, 1972, *24*, 207–213.

Dion, K., Berscheid, E., and Walster, E. What is beautiful is good. *Journal of Personality and Social Psychology*, 1972, *24*, 285–290.

Dion, K. L., Baron, R. S., and Miller, N. Why do groups make riskier decisions than individuals? In L. Berkowitz (Ed.), *Advances in experimental social psychology.* Vol. 5. New York: Academic Press, 1970.

Dion, K. L., Miller, N., and Magnan, M. A. Cohesiveness and social responsibility as determinants of group risk taking. *Journal of Personality and Social Psychology*, 1971, *20*, 400–406.

Dittes, J. E. Attractiveness of group as function of self-esteem and acceptance by group. *Journal of Abnormal and Social Psychology*, 1959, *59*, 77–82.

Dittes, J. E., and Kelley, H. H. Effects of different conditions of acceptance upon conformity to group norms. *Journal of Abnormal and Social Psychology*, 1956, *53*, 100–107.

Doise, W. Intergroup relations and polarization of individual and collective judgments. *Journal of Personality and Social Psychology*, 1969, *12*, 136–143.

Dollard, J. Under what conditions do opinions predict behavior? *Public Opinion Quarterly*, 1949, *12*, 623–632.

Dollard, J., Doob, L. W., Miller, N. E., Mowrer, O. H., and Sears, R. R. *Frustration and aggression.* New Haven: Yale University Press, 1939.

Dominick, J. R., and Greenberg, B. S. *Attitudes toward violence: The interaction of TV exposure, family attitudes and social class.* Michigan State University, Violence in the Media Report #2, 1970.

Dornbusch, S. M., Hastorf, A. H., Richardson, S. A., Muzzy, R. E., and Vreeland, R. S. The perceiver and the perceived: Their relative influence on the categories of interpersonal perception. *Journal of Personality and Social Psychology,* 1965, *1,* 434–440.

Dorr, D., and Fey, S. Relative power of symbolic adult and peer models in the modification of children's moral choice behavior. *Journal of Personality and Social Psychology,* 1974, *29,* 335–341.

Douvan, E. Independence and identity in adolescence. *Children,* 1957, *4,* 186–190.

Dowling, J. H. Individual ownership and the sharing of game in hunting societies. *American Anthropologist,* 1970, *70,* 502–507.

Downs, R. M., & Stea, D. (Eds.) *Image and environment: cognitive mapping and spatial behavior.* Chicago: Aldine, 1973.

Draper, P. Crowding among hunter-gatherers: The !Kung bushman. *Science,* 1973, *182,* 301–303.

Driscoll, R., Davis, K. E., and Lipetz, M. E. Parental interference and romantic love: The Romeo and Juliet effect. *Journal of Personality and Social Psychology,* 1972, *24,* 1–10.

Droppleman, L. F., and Schaefer, E. S. Boys' and girls' reports of maternal and paternal behavior. Paper read at the 69th Annual Meeting of the American Psychological Association, August, 1961, New York City.

Druckman, D. Dogmatism, prenegotiation experience, and simulated group representation as determinants of dyadic behavior in a bargaining situation. *Journal of Personality and Social Psychology,* 1967, *6,* 279–290.

Druckman, D. Ethnocentrism in the inter-nation simulation. *Journal of Conflict Resolution,* 1968, *12,* 45–68.

Duchacek, I. W. *Nations and men: An introduction to international politics* (2nd ed.) New York: Holt, Rinehart, & Winston, 1971.

Dulaney, D. E. The place of hypotheses and intentions: An analysis of verbal control in verbal conditioning. In C. W. Eriksen (Ed.), *Behavior and awareness: A symposium of research and interpretation.* Durham, N. C.: Duke University Press, 1962.

Dusenberry, D., and Knower, F. H. Experimental studies of the symbolism of action and voice. I. A study of the specificity of meaning in facial expression. *Quarterly Journal of Speech,* 1938, *24,* 424–436.

Dutton, D. G. *Social perception as a function of own self-discrepant role performance and acceptance or rejection of self-discrepant role.* Unpublished master's thesis, University of Toronto, 1967.

Dutton, D. G., and Arrowood, A. J. Situational factors in evaluation congruency and interpersonal attraction. *Journal of Personality and Social Psychology,* 1971, *18,* 222–229.

Eagly, A. E., and Telaak, K. Width of the latitude of acceptance as a determinant of attitude change. *Journal of Personality and Social Psychology,* 1972, *23,* 388–397.

Ebbesen, E. B., and Bowers, R. J. Proportion of risky to conservative arguments in a group discussion and choice shift. *Journal of Personality and Social Psychology,* 1974, *29,* 316–327.

Edel, A. Social science and value: A study in interrelations. In I. L. Horowitz (Ed.), *The new sociology.* New York: Oxford University Press, 1964.

Efron, D. *Gesture and environment.* New York: King's Crown, 1941.

Ehrlich, D., Guttman, I., Schonback, P., and Mills, J. Post-decision exposure to relevant information. *Journal of Abnormal and Social Psychology,* 1957, *54,* 98–102.

Ehrlich, H. J., and Graeven, D. B. Reciprocal self-disclosure in a dyad. *Journal of Experimental Social Psychology,* 1971, *7,* 389–400.

Eisenstadt, S. N. Processes of communication among new immigrants. *Public Opinion Quarterly,* 1952, *16,* 42–58.

Ekman, P., and Friesen, W. V. The repertoire of nonverbal behavior: Categories, origins, usage, and coding. *Semiotica,* 1969, *1,* 49–97.

Ekman, P., and Friesen, W. V. Constants across cultures in the face and emotion. *Journal of Personality and Social Psychology,* 1971, *17,* 124–129.

Elder, G. Appearance and education in marriage mobility. *American Sociological Review,* 1969, *34,* 519–533.

Ellis, A. Rational psychotherapy. *Journal of General Psychology,* 1958, *59,* 35–49.

Ellison, J. W. Computers and the Testaments. In *Computers for the humanities.* New Haven: Yale University Press, 1965.

Ellsworth, P. C., and Carlsmith, J. M. Effects of eye contact and verbal context on affective responses in a dyadic interaction. *Journal of Personality and Social Psychology,* 1968, *10,* 15–20.

Ellsworth, P. C., Carlsmith, J. M., and Henson, A. The stare as a stimulus to flight in human subjects: A series of field experiments. *Journal of Personality and Social Psychology,* 1972, *21,* 302–311.

Ellul, J. *Propaganda: The formation of men's attitudes.* New York: Knopf, 1965.

Encyclopedia Brittanica, Inc. Chicago, William Benton, 1967, Vol. 7.

Endler, N. S. Conformity as a function of different reinforcement schedules. *Journal of Personality and Social Psychology,* 1966, *4,* 175–180.

Enke, S. *Economics for development.* Englewood Cliffs, N. J.: Prentice-Hall, 1963.

Epstein, S. Authoritarianism, displaced aggression and social status of the target. *Journal of Personality and Social Psychology,* 1965, *2,* 585–589.

Epstein, S. The self-concept revisited: Or a theory of a theory. *American Psychologist,* 1973, *28,* 404–416.

Epstein, S., and Taylor, S. P. Instigation to aggression as a function of degree of defeat and perceived aggressive intent of the opponent. *Journal of Personality,* 1967, *35,* 265–289.

Epstein, Y. M., and Hornstein, H. A. Penalty and interpersonal attraction as factors influencing the decision to help another person. *Journal of Experimental Social Psychology,* 1969, *5,* 272–282.

Epstein, Y. M., Suedfeld, P., and Silverstein, S. J. The experimental contract: Subjects' expectations of and reactions to some behaviors of experimenters. *American Psychologist,* 1973, *28,* 212–221.

Erdelyi, M. H. A new look at the new look: Perceptual defense and vigilance. *Psychological Review,* 1974, *81,* 1–25.

Erikson, E. H. *Childhood and society.* New York: Norton, 1950.

Eron, L., Walder, L. O., and Lefkowitz, M. M. *Learning of aggression in children.* Boston: Little, Brown, 1971.

Eron, L., Walder, L. O., Toigo, R., and Lefkowitz, M. M. Social class, parental punishment for aggression and child aggression. *Child Development,* 1963, *34,* 849–867.

Etzioni, A. The Kennedy Experiment. In E. I. Megargee and J. E. Hokanson (Eds.), *The dynamics of aggression: Individual, group, and international analyses.* New York: Harper & Row, 1970.

Evan, W. M., and Zelditch, M., Jr. A laboratory experiment on bureaucratic authority. *American Sociological Review,* 1961, *26,* 883–893.

Evans, R. I., and Rozelle, R. M. *Social psychology in life.* (2nd ed.) Boston: Allyn & Bacon, 1973.

Evans-Pritchard, E. E. *The Nuer.* Oxford: Clarendon Press, 1940.

Exline, R. V., and Winters, L. C. Affective relations and mutual glances in dyads. In S. Tomkins and C. Izard (Eds.), *Affect, cognition and personality.* New York: Springer, 1965.

Fairchild, H. P. (Ed.), *Dictionary of sociology.* New York: Philosophical Library, 1944.

Faley, T. E., and Tedeschi, J. T. Status and reactions to threats. *Journal of Personality and Social Psychology,* 1971, *17,* 192–199.

Fall, B. B. *The two Vietnams.* (Rev. ed) New York: Praeger, 1964.

Fannin, L. F., and Clinard, M. B. Differences in the conception of self as a male among lower and middle class delinquents. *Social Problems,* 1965, *13,* 205–214.

Fanon, F. *The wretched of the earth.* New York: Grove, 1963.

Faunce, D., and Beegle, J. A. Cleavages in a relatively homogeneous group of rural youth: An experiment in the use of sociometry in attaining and measuring integration. *Sociometry,* 1948, *11,* 207–216.

Feather, N. T. Attribution of responsibility and valence of success and failure in relation to initial confidence and task performance. *Journal of Personality and Social Psychology,* 1969, *13,* 129–144.

Feather, N. T., and Simon, J. G. Attribution of responsibility and valence of outcome in relation to initial confidence and success and failure of self and other. *Journal of Personality and Social Psychology,* 1971, *18,* 173–188.

Federal Bureau of Investigation. *Uniform Crime Reports.* Washington, D. C.: U. S. Government Publications Office, 1968.

Feld, S. Need achievement and test anxiety in children and maternal attitudes and behaviors toward independent accomplishments: A longitudinal study. Paper read at the 67th annual meeting of American Psychological Association, Cincinnati, 1959.

Feldman, R. E. Response to compatriot and foreigner who seek assistance. *Journal of Personality and Social Psychology,* 1968, *10,* 202–214.

Feldman, S. D. The presentation of shortness in everyday life—height and heightism in American society: Toward a sociology of stature. Paper presented before the meetings of the American Sociological Association, 1971.

Ference, T. P. Feedback and conflict as determinants of influence. *Journal of Experimental Social Psychology,* 1971, *7,* 1–16.

Ferguson, D. A., and Vidmar, N. Effects of group discussion on estimates of culturally appropriate risk levels. *Journal of Personality and Social Psychology,* 1971, *20,* 436–445.

Feshbach, S. The drive-reducing function of fantasy behavior. *Journal of Abnormal and Social Psychology,* 1955, *50,* 3–11.

Feshbach, S. The stimulating versus cathartic effects of a vicarious aggressive activity. *Journal of Abnormal and Social Psychology,* 1961, *63,* 381–385.

Feshbach, S. Dynamics and morality of violence and aggression: Some psychological considerations. *American Psychologist,* 1971, *26,* 281–292.

Feshbach, S., and Singer, R. D. The effects of fear arousal and suppression of fear upon social perception. *Journal of Abnormal and Social Psychology,* 1957, *55,* 283–288.

Feshbach, S., and Singer, R. *Television and aggression: An experimental field study.* San Francisco: Jossey-Bass, 1971.

Festinger, L. Wish, expectation, and group standards as factors influencing level of aspiration. *Journal of Abnormal and Social Psychology,* 1942, *37,* 184–200.

Festinger, L. Informal social communications. *Psychological Review,* 1950, *57,* 271–280.

Festinger, L. Architecture and group membership. *Journal of Social Issues,* 1951, *7,* 152–163.

Festinger, L. Group attraction and membership. In D. Cartwright and A. Zander (Eds.), *Group dynamics.* New York: Row, Peterson, 1953. (*a*)

Festinger, L. An analysis of compliant behavior. In M. Sherif and M. O. Wilson (Eds.), *Group relations at the crossroads.* New York: Harper, 1953. (*b*)

Festinger, L. A theory of social comparison processes. *Human Relations,* 1954, *7,* 117–140.

Festinger, L. *A theory of cognitive dissonance.* Stanford, Calif.: Stanford University Press, 1957.

Festinger, L. *Conflict, decision, and dissonance.* Stanford, Calif.: Stanford University Press, 1964.

Festinger, L., and Carlsmith, J. M. Cognitive consequences of forced compliance. *Journal of Abnormal and Social Psychology,* 1959, *58,* 203–210.

Festinger, L., Riecken, H. W., and Schachter, S. *When prophecy fails.* Minneapolis: University of Minnesota, 1956.

Festinger L., Schachter, S., and Back, K. *Social pressures in informal groups: A study of human factors in housing.* New York: Harper & Row, 1950.

Festinger, L., and Thibaut, J. Interpersonal communication in small groups. *Journal of Abnormal and Social Psychology,* 1951, *46,* 92–99.

Fiedler, F. E. A contingency model of leadership effectiveness. In L. Berkowitz (Ed.), *Advances in experimental social psychology.* Vol. 1. New York: Academic Press, 1964.

Fiedler, F. E. Validation and extension of the contingency model of leadership effectiveness: A review of empirical findings. *Psychological Bulletin,* 1971, *76,* 128–148.

Fillenbaum, S. Prior deception and subsequent experimental performance: The "faithful" subject. *Journal of Personality and Social Psychology,* 1966, *4,* 532–535.

Fine, R. E., and Lindskold, S. Subjects' experimental history and subject based artifact. *Proceedings* of the 79th Annual Convention of the American Psychological Association, 1971, *6,* 289–290.

Finlay, D. J., Holsti, O. R., and Fagen, R. R. *Enemies in politics.* Chicago: Rand McNally, 1967.

Firth, R. Rumor in a primitive society. *Journal of Abnormal and Social Psychology,* 1956, *53,* 122–132.

Fischer, P. W. F. Sharing in preschool children as a function of amount and type of reinforcement. *Genetic Psychology Monographs,* 1963, *68,* 215–245.

Fishbein, M. An investigation of the relationships between beliefs about an object and attitude toward that object. *Human Relations,* 1963, *16,* 233–239.

Fisher, R. Fractionating conflict. In R. Fisher (Ed.), *International conflict and behavioral science: The Craigville papers.* New York: Basic Books, 1964.

Fisher, R. *International conflict for beginners.* New York: Harper & Row, 1969.

Fishkin, J., Keniston, K., and MacKinnon, C. Moral reasoning and political ideology. *Journal of Personality and Social Psychology,* 1973, *27,* 109–119.

Fishman, C. G. Need for approval and the expression of aggression under varying conditions of frustration. *Journal of Personality and Social Psychology.* 1965, *2,* 809–816.

Fitzgerald, M. P. Self-disclosure and expressed self-esteem, social distance and areas of the self-revealed. *Journal of Psychology,* 1963, *56,* 405–412.

Flanders, J. P., and Thistlethwaite, D. L. Effects of familiarization and group discussion upon risk taking. *Journal of Experimental Social Psychology,* 1967, *5,* 91–97.

Flanders, J. P., and Thistlethwaite, D. L. Effects of informative and justificatory variables upon imitation. *Journal of Experimental Social Psychology,* 1970, *6,* 316–328.

Flavell, J. H. *The development of role-taking and communication skills in children.* New York: Wiley, 1968.

Fleishman, E. A., Harris, E. F., and Burtt, H. E. *Leadership and supervision in industry.* Columbus: Ohio State University Press, 1955.

Fleishman, E. A., and Peters, D. R. Interpersonal values, leadership attitudes and managerial success. *Personnel Psychology,* 1962, *15,* 127–143.

Flugel, J. C. *The psychology of clothes.* London: Leonard and Virginia Woolf, 1930.

Ford, C. S., and Beach, F. A. *Patterns of sexual behavior.* New York: Harper & Row, 1952.

Form, W. H., and Nosow, S. *Community in disaster.* New York: Harper, 1958.

Forte, R. A., Haake, C. S., Schmidt, E. K., and Lindskold, S. Political preference and views regarding the Vietnam peace announcement. Unpublished manuscript. Ohio University, 1974.

Foulkes, D., and Foulkes, S. H. Self-concept, dogmatism, and tolerance of trait inconsistency. *Journal of Personality and Social Psychology,* 1965, *2,* 104–110.

Frager, R. Conformity and anticonformity in Japan. *Journal of Personality and Social Psychology,* 1970, *15,* 203–210.

Frank, J. D. Experimental studies of personal pressure and resistance. *Journal of General Psychology,* 1944, *30,* 23–64.

Frank, J. D. *Sanity and survival: Psychological aspects of war and peace.* New York: Vintage, 1967.

Frank, P. G. *Modern science and its philosophy.* New York: Collier, 1961.

Fraser, C. *Group risk-taking and group polarization.* Paper presented at the European Association of Social Psychology Conference, Konstanz, 1970.

Freedman, J. L. Attitudinal effects of inadequate justification. *Journal of Personality,* 1963, *31,* 371–385.

Freedman, J. L. Long-term behavioral effects of cognitive dissonance. *Journal of Experimental Social Psychology,* 1965, *1,* 145–155. (*a*)

Freedman, J. L. Confidence, utility, and selective exposure: A partial replication. *Journal of Personality and Social Psychology*, 1965, *2*, 778–789. (*b*)

Freedman, J. L. Role playing: Psychology by consensus. *Journal of Personality and Social Psychology*, 1969, *13*, 107–114.

Freedman, J. L., Carlsmith, J. M., and Sears, D. O. *Social psychology*. Englewood Cliffs, N. J.: Prentice-Hall, 1970.

Freedman, J. L., Carlsmith, J. M., and Suomi, S. The effect of familiarity on liking. Unpublished paper. Stanford, Calif.: Stanford University, 1969.

Freedman, J. L., and Sears, D. O. Warning, distraction, and resistance to influence. *Journal of Personality and Social Psychology*, 1965, *1*, 262–266.

Freeman, J. T. Set or perceptual defense. *Journal of Experimental Psychology*, 1954, *48*, 283–288.

French, J. R. P., Jr., and Raven, B. The bases of social power. In D. Cartwright (Ed.), *Studies in social power*. Ann Arbor: University of Michigan Press, 1959.

French, J. R. P., Jr., and Snyder, R. Leadership and interpersonal power. In D. Cartwright (Ed.), *Studies in social power*. Ann Arbor: University of Michigan Press, 1959.

Freud, S. *Psychopathology of everyday life*. London: Unwin, 1914.

Freud, S. *Group psychology and the analysis of the ego*. London: Hogarth Press, 1922.

Freud, S. *Civilization and its discontents*. London: Hogarth, 1930.

Freud, S. *Beyond the pleasure principle*. Translated by James Strachey. New York: Liveright, 1950.

Friedman, N. *The social nature of psychological research*. New York: Basic Books, 1967.

Freidrich, C. J. *Man and his government*. New York: McGraw-Hill, 1963.

Friend, K. E. *An information processing approach to small group interaction in a coalition formation game.* Unpublished Doctoral dissertation, Carnegie-Mellon University, 1973.

Frieze, I., and Weiner, B. Cue utilization and attributional judgments for success and failure. *Journal of Personality*, 1971, *39*, 591–605.

Fromm, E. *The art of loving*. New York: Harper & Row, 1956.

Fromm, E. *The anatomy of human destructiveness*. New York: Holt, Rinehart, and Winston, 1973.

Fulbright, J. W. *The arrogance of power*. New York: Random House, 1966.

Gaes, G. G., Rivera, A. N. and Tedeschi, J. T. Cognitive dissonance vs. impression management: A study using the Bogus Pipeline. Unpublished manuscript, State University of New York at Albany, 1975.

Gahagan, J. P. *Effects of promise credibility, outside options and social contact on interpersonal conflict.* Unpublished doctoral dissertation, University of Miami (Fla.), 1969.

Gamson, W. A. A theory of coalition formation. *American Sociological Review*, 1961, *26*, 373–382.

Gamson, W. A. Experimental studies of coalition formation. In L. Berkowitz (Ed.), *Advances in experimental social psychology*. Vol. 1. New York: Academic Press, 1964.

Gamson, W. A. *Power and discontent*. Homewood, Ill.: Dorsey Press, 1968.

Garfinkel, H. Studies of the routine grounds of everyday activities. *Social Problems*, 1964, *11*, 225–250.

Geen, R. G., & O'Neal, E. C. Activation of cue-elicited aggression by general arousal. *Journal of Personality and Social Psychology*, 1969, *11*, 289–292.

Geer, J. H., and Turteltaub, A. Fear reduction following observation of a model. *Journal of Personality and Social Psychology*, 1967, *6*, 327–331.

Gelfand, D. M. The influence of self-esteem on the rate of verbal conditioning and social matching behavior. *Journal of Abnormal and Social Psychology*, 1962, *65*, 259–265.

Gentry, W. D. Effects of frustration, attack, and prior aggressive training on overt aggression and vascular processes. *Journal of Personality and Social Psychology*, 1970, *16*, 718–725.

Gerard, H. B. The effect of different dimensions of disagreement on the communication process in small groups. *Human Relations*, 1953, *6*, 249–271.

Gerard, H. B. Emotional uncertainty and social comparison. *Journal of Abnormal and Social Psychology*, 1963, *66*, 568–573.

Gerard, H. B., and Conolley, E. S. Conformity. In C. G. McClintock (Ed.), *Experimental social psychology*. New York: Holt, Rinehart, & Winston, 1972.

Gerard, H. B., and Greenbaum, C. W. Attitudes toward an agent of uncertainty reduction. *Journal of Personality*, 1962, *30*, 485–495.

Gerard, H. B., and Mathewson, G. C. The effects of severity of initiation on liking for a group: A replication. *Journal of Experimental Social Psychology*, 1966, *2*, 278–287.

Gerard, H. B., and Rabbie, J. M. Fear and social comparison. *Journal of Abnormal and Social Psychology*, 1961, *62*, 586–592.

Gerard, H. B., Wilhelmy, R. A., and Conolley, E. S. Conformity and group size. *Journal of Personality and Social Psychology*, 1968, *8*, 79–82.

Gerson, W. M. Social structure and mass media socialization. Discussed by O. N. Larsen, Social effects of mass communication. In R. E. L. Faris (Ed.), *Handbook of modern sociology*. Chicago: Rand McNally, 1964.

Gerth, H., and Mills, C. W. *Character and social structure*. New York: Harcourt, Brace, & World, 1953.

Gewirtz, J. Three determinants of attention seeking in young children. *Monographs of the Society for Research in Child Development*, 1954, *19*, No. 2. (Whole No. 59)

Gewirtz, J. L., and Baer, D. M. Deprivation and satiation of social reinforcers as drive conditions. *Journal of Abnormal and Social Psychology*, 1958, *57*, 165–172.

Gibb, C. A. The principles and traits of leadership. *Journal of Abnormal and Social Psychology*, 1947, *42*, 267–284.

Gibb, C. A. Leadership. In G. Lindzey and E. Aronson (Eds.), *The handbook of social psychology*. Vol. 4. (2nd ed.) Reading, Mass.: Addison-Wesley, 1969.

Gibbs, J. P. Crime, punishment, and deterrence. *Southwestern Social Science Quarterly*, 1968, *48*, 515–530.

Gide, A. *The counterfeiters*. New York: Modern Library, 1927.

Gilbert, G. M. Stereotype persistence and change among college students. *Journal of Abnormal and Social Psychology*, 1951, *46*, 245–254.

Gilbert, G. M. A survey of "referral problems" in metropolitan child guidance centers. *Journal of Clinical Psychology*, 1957, *13*, 37–42.

Gilchrist, J. C., Shaw, M. E., and Walker, L. C. Some effects of unequal distribution of information in a wheel group structure. *Journal of Abnormal and Social Psychology*, 1954, *49*, 554–556.

Gillin, J. C., and Ochberg, F. M. Firearms control and violence. In D. N. Daniels, M. F. Gilula, and F. M. Ochberg (Eds.), *Violence and the struggle for existence*. Boston: Little, Brown, 1970.

Gintner, G., and Lindskold, S. Rate of participation and expertise as factors influencing leader choice. *Journal of Personality and Social Psychology*, 1975, *32*, 1085–1089.

Glass, D. C. Changes in liking as a means of reducing cognitive discrepancies between self-esteem and aggression. *Journal of Personality*, 1964, *32*, 531–549.

Glassco, J. A., Milgram, N. A., and Youniss, J. Stability of training effects on intentionality in moral judgment in children. *Journal of Personality and Social Psychology*, 1970, *14*, 360–365.

Glueck, S., and Glueck, E. *Unraveling juvenile delinquency*. New York: Commonwealth Fund, 1950.

Goethals, G. R., Reckman, R. F., and Rothman, R. E. Impression management as a determinant of attitude statements. Unpublished Manuscript, Williams College, Williams, Mass., 1973.

Goffman, E. On cooling the mark out: Some aspects of adaptation to failure. *Psychiatry*, 1952, *15*, 451–463.

Goffman, E. *The presentation of self in everyday life*. Garden City, N. Y.: Doubleday, 1959.

Goffman, E. *Asylums*. New York: Doubleday, 1961.

Goffman, E. *Behavior in public places*. New York: The Free Press of Glencoe, 1963.

Goffman, E. *Strategic interaction*. Philadelphia: University of Pennsylvania Press, 1969.

Goffman, E. *Relations in public*. New York: Basic Books, 1971.

Goldberg, S. C., and Lubin, A. Influence as a function of perceived judgment error. *Human Relations*, 1958, *11*, 275–280.

Goldstein, M., and Davis, E. E. Race and belief: A further analysis of the social determinants of behavioral intentions. *Journal of Personality and Social Psychology*, 1972, *22*, 346–355.

Golembiewski, R. T. *The small group: An analysis of research concepts and operations*. Chicago: University of Chicago Press, 1962.

Golightly, C., and Byrne, D. Attitude statements as positive and negative reinforcements. *Science*, 1964, *146*, 798–799.

Goodenough, F. L. Interrelationships in the behavior of young children. *Child Development*, 1930, *1*, 29–47.

Goodstadt, B. E., and Hjelle, L. A. Power to the powerless: Locus of control and the use of power. *Journal of Personality and Social Psychology*, 1973, *27*, 190–196.

Goranson, R. E., and Berkowitz, L. Reciprocity and responsibility reactions to prior help. *Journal of Personality and Social Psychology*, 1966, *3*, 227–231.

Gore, P. M. Individual differences in the prediction of subject compliance to experimenter bias. Unpublished doctoral dissertation, Ohio State University, 1962.

Gore, P. M., and Rotter, J. B. A personality correlate of social action. *Journal of Personality*, 1963, *31*, 58–64.

Gorer, G. Man has no "killer" instinct. In A. Montagu (Ed.), *Man and aggression*. New York: Oxford University Press, 1968.

Gorfein, D. Conformity behavior and the "Authoritarian Personality." *Journal of Social Psychology*, 1961, *53*, 121–125.

Gottschalk, L. *Understanding history: A primer of historical method*. (2nd ed.) New York: Knopf, 1969.

Gouaux, C. Induced affective states and interpersonal attraction. *Journal of Personality and Social Psychology*, 1971, *20*, 37–43.

Gouldner, A. W. The norm of reciprocity: A preliminary statement: *American Sociological Review*, 1960, *25*, 161–178.

Gouldner, A. W. Anti-Minotaur: The myth of a value-free sociology. In I. L. Horowitz (Ed.), *The new sociology*. New York: Oxford, 1964.

Graen, G., Alvares, K., Orris, J. B., and Martella, J. A. Contingency model of leadership effectiveness: Antecedent and evidential results. *Psychological Bulletin*, 1970, *74*, 285–296.

Graen, G., Orris, J. B., and Alvares, K. M. Contingency model of leadership effectiveness: Some experimental results. *Journal of Applied Psychology*, 1971, *55*, 196–201.

Green, D. Dissonance and self-perception analyses of "forced compliance": When two theories make competing predictions. *Journal of Personality and Social Psychology*, 1974, *29*, 819–828.

Greenberg, M. S., Block, M. W., and Silverman, M. A.

Determinants of helping behavior: Person's rewards versus other's costs. Unpublished manuscript. Univ. of Pittsburg, 1971.

Greenberg, M. S., and Shapiro, S. F. Indebtedness: An adverse aspect of asking for and receiving help. *Sociometry*, 1971, *34*, 290–301.

Greenspoon, J. The reinforcing effect of two spoken sounds on the frequency of two responses. *American Journal of Psychology*, 1955, *68*, 409–416.

Greenstein, F. I. *Personality and politics*. Chicago: Markham, 1969.

Greenwald. H. J., and Oppenheim, D. B. Reported magnitude of self-misidentification among Negro children—artifact? *Journal of Personality and Social Psychology*, 1968, *8*, 49–52.

Griffitt, W. Interpersonal attraction as a function of self-concept and personality similarity-dissimilarity. *Journal of Personality and Social Psychology*, 1966, *4*, 581–584.

Griffitt, W. Personality similarity and self-concept as determinants of interpersonal attraction. *Journal of Social Psychology*, 1969, *78*, 137–146.

Griffitt, W. Environmental effects on interpersonal affective behavior: Ambient effective temperature and attraction. *Journal of Personality and Social Psychology*, 1970, *15*, 240–244.

Griffitt, W., and Guay, P. "Object" evaluation and conditioned affect. *Journal of Experimental Research in Personality*, 1969, *4*, 1–8.

Griffitt, W., and Veitch, R. Hot and crowded: Influence of population density and temperature on interpersonal affective behavior. *Journal of Personality and Social Psychology*, 1971, *17*, 92–98.

Gronlund, N. E. Relationship between the sociometric status of pupils and teachers' preferences for or against having them in class. *Sociometry*, 1953, *16*, 142–150.

Gross, A. E., Riemer, B. S., and Collins, B. E. Audience reactions as a determinant of the speaker's self-persuasion. *Journal of Experimental Social Psychology*, 1973, *9*, 246–256.

Gruder, C. L. Determinants of social comparison choices. *Journal of Experimental Social Psychology*, 1971, *7*, 473–489.

Gruner, C. R. An experimental study of satire as persuasion. *Speech Monographs*, 1965, *32*, 149–153.

Grusec, J. E., and Brinker, D. R. Reinforcement for imitation as a social learning determinant with implications for sex-role development. *Journal of Personality and Social Psychology*, 1971, *21*, 149–158.

Grusec, J., and Mischel, W. The model's characteristics as determinants of social learning. *Journal of Personality and Social Psychology*, 1966, *4*, 211–215.

Grusec, J. E., and Skubiski, S. L. Model nurturance, demand characteristics of the modeling experiment, and altruism. *Journal of Personality and Social Psychology*, 1970, *14*, 352–359.

Guetzkow, H. Some correspondence between simulations and "realities" in international relations. In M. A. Kaplan (Ed.), *New approaches to international relations*. New York: St. Martin's Press, 1968.

Guetzkow, H., and Simon, H. A. The impact of certain communication nets upon organization and performance in task-oriented groups. *Management Science*, 1955, *1*, 233–250.

Gullahorn, J. T. Distance and friendship as factors in the gross interaction matrix. *Sociometry*, 1952, *15*, 123–134.

Gump, P. V., Schoggen, P., and Redl, F. The camp milieu and its immediate effects. *Journal of Social Issues*, 1957, *13*, 40–46.

Gunn, J. *The joy makers*. New York: Bantam, 1961.

Guze, S. B., Tuason, V. B., Gatfield, P. D., Steward, M. A., and Picken, B. Psychiatric illness and crime with particular reference to alcoholism: A study of 223 criminals. *Journal of Nervous and Mental Disease*, 1962, *134*, 512–521.

Haan, N. Activism as moral protest: Moral judgments of hypothetical moral dilemmas and an actual situation of civil disobedience. In L. Kohlberg and E. Turiel (Eds.), *The develoment of moral judgment and action*. New York: Holt, Rinehart & Winston, 1972.

Haan, N., and Block, J. H. Further studies in the relationship between activism and morality: I: The protest of pure and mixed moral states. Unpublished manuscript, Berkeley, Calif.: Institute of Human Development, 1969.

Haan, N., Smith, M. B., and Block, J. Moral reasoning and young adults: Political-social behavior, family background, and personality correlates. *Journal of Personality and Social Psychology*, 1968, *10*, 183–201.

Haas, R. G. Persuasion or moderation? Two experiments on anticipatory belief change. *Journal of Personality and Social Psychology*, 1975, *31*, 1155–1162.

Haefner, D. P. Some effects of guilt-arousing and fear-arousing persuasive communications on opinion change. *American Psychologist*, 1956, *11*, 359 (Abstract)

Haire, M., and Grunes, W. F. Perceptual defenses: Processes protecting an organized perception of another personality. *Human Relations*, 1950, *3*, 403–412.

Hakel, M. D. Significance of implicit personality theories for personality research and theory. *Proceedings of the 77th annual meeting of the American Psychological Association*, 1969, *4*, 403–404.

Halberstam, D. *The making of a quagmire*. New York: Random House, 1965.

Haley, J. *Strategies of psychotherapy*. New York: Grune & Stratton, 1963.

Hall, C. S., and Lindzey, G. *Theories of personality.* (2nd ed.) New York: Wiley, 1970.

Hall, E. T. *The silent language.* Garden City, N. Y.: Doubleday, 1959.

Hall, E. T. *The hidden dimension.* Garden City, N. Y.: Doubleday, 1966.

Halle, L. J. *The society of man.* New York: Harper & Row, 1965.

Halpin, A. W. Evaluation through the study of the leader's behavior. *Educational Leadership*, 1956, *14*, 172–176.

Halpin, A. W. The leader behavior and leadership ideology of educational administrators and aircraft commanders. *Harvard Educational Review*, 1955, *25*, 18–32.

Halpin, A. W., and Winer, B. J. *The leadership behavior of the airplane commander.* Columbus: Ohio State University Research Foundation, 1952.

Hamblin, R. L. Leadership and crisis. *Sociometry*, 1958, *21*, 322–335.

Hamilton, D. L., Thompson, J. J., and White, A. M. Role of awareness and intentions in observational learning. *Journal of Personality and Social Psychology*, 1970, *16*, 689–694.

Hanratty, M. A., Liebert, R. M., Morris, L. W., and Fernandez, L. E. Imitation of film-mediated aggression against live and inanimate victims. *Proceedings of the 77th Annual Convention of the American Psychological Association*, 1969, *4*, 457–458.

Harder, M. W., Richardson, J. T., and Simmonds, R. B. Jesus people. *Psychology Today*, 1972, *6*, 45–50, 110–113.

Hardy, K. R. Determinants of conformity and attitude change. *Journal of Abnormal and Social Psychology*, 1957, *54*, 289–294.

Hare, A. P. *Handbook of small group research.* Glencoe, N. Y.: Free Press, 1962.

Harnett, D. L., and Cummings, L. L. Bargaining behavior in an asymmetric triad: The role of information, communication, and risk-taking propensity. Mimeographed manuscript, Indiana University, 1968.

Harsanyi, J. C. Measurement of social power, opportunity costs, and the theory of two-person bargaining games. *Behavioral Science*, 1962, *7*, 67–80.

Hartmann, D. *The influence of symbolically modeled instrumental aggression and pain cues on the disinhibition of aggressive behavior.* Unpublished doctoral dissertation. Stanford University, 1965.

Hartmann, D. P. Influence of symbolically modeled instrumental aggression and pain cues on aggressive behavior. *Journal of Personality and Social Psychology*, 1969, *11*, 280–288.

Hartshorne, H., and May, M. A. *Studies in the nature of character.* Vol. 1. *Studies in deceit.* New York: Macmillan, 1928.

Hartup, W. W., and Zook, E. A. Sex role preferences in three- and four-year-old children. *Journal of Consulting Psychology*, 1960, *24*, 420–426.

Harvey, O. J., and Consalvi, C. Status and conformity to pressure in informal groups. *Journal of Abnormal and Social Psychology*, 1960, *60*, 182–187.

Hastorf, A. H., and Cantril, H. They saw a game. *Journal of Abnormal and Social Psychology*, 1954, *49*, 129–134.

Heider, F. *The psychology of interpersonal relations.* New York: Wiley, 1958.

Heilbroner, R. L. *The worldly philosophers.* (Rev. ed.) New York: Simon & Schuster, 1961.

Heilbroner, R. L. *The great ascent: The struggle for economic development in our times.* New York: Harper & Row, 1963.

Heilman, M. E. Threats and promises: Reputational consequences and transfer of credibility. *Journal of Experimental Social Psychology*, 1974, *10*, 310–324.

Heinicke, C., and Bales, R. Developmental trends in the structure of small groups. *Sociometry*, 1953, *16*, 7–38.

Helm, B., Bonoma, T. V., and Tedeschi, J. T. Reciprocity for harm done. *Journal of Social Psychology*, 1972, *87*, 89–98.

Helm, B., Brown, R. C., Jr., and Tedeschi, J. T. Esteem and the effectiveness of a verbal reinforcer. *Journal of Social Psychology*, 1972, *87*, 293–300.

Helm, B., Nacci, P., and Tedeschi, J. T. Interpersonal perception and coalition decisions: The role of attraction and esteem. *Journal of General Psychology*, 1976.

Helmreich, R. L., and Collins, B. E. Studies in forced compliance: Commitment and magnitude of inducement to comply as determinants of opinion change. *Journal of Personality and Social Psychology*, 1968, *10*, 75–81.

Hemphill, J. K. Theory of leadership. Unpublished staff report. Ohio State University, Personnel Research Board, 1952.

Hemphill, J. K. Why people attempt to lead. In L. Petrullo, and B. M. Bass (Eds.), *Leadership and interpersonal behavior.* New York: Holt, Rinehart, & Winston, 1961.

Henchy, T., and Glass, D. C. Evaluation apprehension and the social facilitation of dominant and subordinate responses. *Journal of Personality and Social Psychology*, 1968, *10*, 446–454.

Hendrick, C., and Constantini, A. F. Effects of varying trait inconsistency and response requirements on the primacy effect in impression formation. *Journal of Personality and Social Psychology*, 1970, *15*, 158–164.

Hendrick, C., and Taylor, S. P. Effects of belief similarity and aggression on attraction and counteraggression. *Journal of Personality and Social Psychology*, 1971, *17*, 342–349.

Henle, M., and Hubbell, M. B. "Egocentricity" in adult conversation. *Journal of Social Psychology*, 1938, *9*, 227–234.

Hennessy, B. C. *Public opinion*. (2nd ed.) Belmont, Calif.: Wadsworth, 1970.

Hermann, C. F. *Crises in foreign policy-making: A simulation of international politics*. Ph.D. dissertation. Evanston, Ill.: Department of Political Science, Northwestern University, 1965.

Hersh, S. M. *My Lai 4: A report on the massacre and its aftermath*. New York: Vintage Books, 1970.

Hertzler, J. O. *A sociology of language*. New York: Random House, 1965.

Hetherington, E. M. A developmental study of the effects of sex of the dominant parent on sex-role preference, identification, and imitation in children. *Journal of Personality and Social Psychology*, 1965, *2*, 188–194.

Hewitt, L. E. Student perceptions of traits desired in themselves as dating and marriage partners. *Marriage and Family Living*, 1958, *20*, 344–349.

Hicks, D. J. Imitation and retention of film-mediated aggressive peer and adult models. *Journal of Personality and Social Psychology*, 1965, *2*, 97–100.

Higbee, K. L. Expression of "Walter Mitty-ness" in actual behavior. *Journal of Personality and Social Psychology*, 1971, *20*, 416–422.

Hilgard, E. R. Human motives and the concept of self. *American Psychologist*, 1949, *4*, 374–382.

Hilgard, E. R. The domain of hypnosis: With some comments on alternative paradigms. *American Psychologist*, 1973, *28*, 972–982.

Hill, G. E. The ethical knowledge of delinquent and nondelinquent boys. *Journal of Social Psychology*, 1935, *6*, 107–114.

Hill, J. P., and Kochendorfer, R. A. Knowledge of peer success and risk of detection as determinants of cheating. *Developmental Psychology*, 1969, *1*, 231–238.

Himmelweit, H., Oppenheim, A., and Vince, P. *Television and the child: An empirical study of the effects of television on the young*. London: Oxford University Press, 1958.

Hjelle, L. A. Susceptibility to attitude change as a function of internal-external control. Paper presented at the convention of the Eastern Psychological Association. Atlantic City, April, 1970.

Hobbes, T. *Leviathan*. (Reprint of first (1651) ed.), Oxford, England: Clarendon, 1909.

Hochberg, J. E. *Perception*. Englewood Cliffs, N. J.: Prentice-Hall, 1964.

Hoffer, E. *The true believer*. New York: New American Library, 1951.

Hoffman, P. G. *World without want*. New York: Harper & Row, 1962.

Hoffman, P. J., Festinger, L., and Lawrence, D. H. Tendencies toward group comparability in competitive bargaining. *Human Relations*, 1954, *7*, 141–159.

Hofling, C. K., Brotzman, E., Dalrymple, S., Graves, N., and Pierce, C. M. An experimental study in nurse-physician relationships. *Journal of Nervous and Mental Diseases*, 1966, *143*, 171–180.

Hofstadter, R. *Anti-intellectualism in American life*. New York: Knopf, 1963.

Hofstadter, R., and Wallace, M. *American violence: A documentary history*. New York: Knopf, 1970.

Hogan, R., and Dickstein, E. Moral judgment and perceptions of injustice. *Journal of Personality and Social Psychology*, 1972, *23*, 409–413.

Hokanson, J. E., and Burgess, M. The effects of three types of aggression on vascular processes. *Journal of Abnormal and Social Psychology*, 1962, *64*, 446–449.

Hokanson, J. E., Burgess, M., and Cohen, M. F. Effects of displaced aggression on systolic blood pressure. *Journal of Abnormal and Social Psychology*, 1963, *67*, 214–218.

Hokanson, J. E., and Shetler, S. The effect of overt aggression on physiological arousal. *Journal of Abnormal and Social Psychology*, 1961, *63*, 446–448.

Hollander, E. P. Conformity, status, and idiosyncrasy credit. *Psychological Review*, 1958, *65*, 117–127.

Hollander, E. P. Competence and conformity in the acceptance of influence. *Journal of Abnormal and Social Psychology*, 1960, *61*, 365–369.

Hollander, E. P. *Leaders, groups, and influence*. New York: Oxford, 1964.

Hollander, E. P. *Principles and methods of social psychology*. (2nd ed.) New York: Oxford University Press, 1971.

Hollander, E. P., and Julian, J. W. Studies in leader legitimacy, influence, and innovation. In L. Berkowitz (Ed.), *Advances in experimental social psychology*, Vol. 5. New York: Academic Press, 1970.

Hollander, E. P., and Webb, W. B. Leadership, followership, and friendship: An analysis of peer nominations. *Journal of Abnormal and Social Psychology*, 1955, *50*, 163–167.

Hollingshead, A. B., and Redlich, F. C. *Social class and mental illness: A community study*. New York: Wiley, 1958.

Holmberg, A. M. *The Siriono: A study of the effect of hunger frustration on the culture of a semi-nomadic Bolivian Indian tribe*. Ph.D. thesis, Yale University, 1946. (Cited in M. Sherif and C. W. Sherif, *Social Psychology*. New York: Harper & Row, 1969.)

Holmes, D. S. Compensation for ego threat: Two experiments. *Journal of Personality and Social Psychology*, 1971, *18*, 234–237.

Holmes, D. S. Aggression, displacement and guilt. *Journal of Personality and Social Psychology*, 1972, *21*, 296–301.

Holzner, B. *Reality construction in society.* Cambridge, Mass.: Schenkman, 1968.

Homans, G. C. *Social behavior: Its elementary forms.* New York: Harcourt, Brace, & World, 1961.

Hook, S. *The hero in history.* Boston: Beacon, 1955.

Hoppe, F. Erfolg und Misserfolg. *Psychologische Forschung,* 1931, *14,* 1–62.

Horai, J., Naccari, N., and Fatoulaah, E. The effects of physical attractiveness and expertise on opinion agreement and liking. *Sociometry,* 1974, *37,* 601–606.

Horai, J., and Tedeschi, J. T. The effects of threat credibility and magnitude of punishment upon compliance. *Journal of Personality and Social Psychology,* 1969, *12,* 164–169.

Hornberger, R. H. The differential reduction of aggressive responses as a function of interpolated activities. Paper read at the 67th annual meeting of the American Psychological Association, Cincinnati, 4 September, 1959.

Hovland, C. I. The role of primacy and recency in persuasive communication. In E. E. Maccoby, T. M. Newcomb, and E. L. Harley (Eds.), *Readings in social psychology.* (3rd ed.) New York: Holt, 1958.

Hovland, C. I., Campbell, E. H., and Brock, T. C. The effects of 'commitment' on opinion change following communication. In C. I. Hovland (Ed.), *Order of presentation in persuasion.* New Haven: Yale University Press, 1957.

Hovland, C. I., Harvey, O. J., and Sherif, M. Assimilation and contrast effects in reactions to communication and attitude change. *Journal of Abnormal and Social Psychology,* 1957, *55,* 244–252.

Hovland, C. I., Janis, I. L., and Kelley, H. H. *Communication and persuasion.* New Haven, Conn.: Yale University Press, 1953.

Hovland, C. I., Lumsdaine, A. A., and Sheffield, F. D. *Experiments on mass communication.* Princeton, N. J.: Princeton University Press, 1949.

Hovland, C. I., and Mandell, W. An experimental comparison of conclusion-drawing by the communicator and by the audience. *Journal of Abnormal and Social Psychology,* 1952, *47,* 581–588.

Howes, D. H., and Solomon, R. L. A note on McGinnies' "Emotionality and perceptual defense." *Psychological Review,* 1950, *57,* 229–234.

Howes, D. H., and Solomon, R. L. Visual duration threshold as a function of word probability. *Journal of Experimental Psychology,* 1951, *41,* 401–410.

Hoyt, G. C., and Stoner, J. A. F. Leadership and group decisions involving risk. *Journal of Experimental Social Psychology,* 1968, *4,* 275–285.

Hoyt, M. F., Henley, M. D., and Collins, B. E. Studies in forced compliance: The confluence of choice and consequences on attitude change. *Journal of Personality and Social Psychology,* 1972, *23,* 205–210.

Hull, C. L. *A behavior system.* New Haven: Yale University Press, 1952.

Hunt, P. J., and Hillery, J. M. Social facilitation in a coaction setting: An examination of the effects over learning trials. *Journal of Experimental Social Psychology,* 1973, *9,* 563–571.

Hurwitz, J. I., Zander, A. F., and Hymovitch, B. Some effects of power on the relations among group members. In D. Cartwright and A. F. Zander (Eds.), *Group dynamics.* (3rd ed.) New York: Harper & Row, 1968.

Husband, R. W. Analysis of methods in human maze learning. *Journal of Genetic Psychology,* 1931, *39,* 258–277.

Huston, T. L. Ambiguity of acceptance, social desirability, and dating choice. *Journal of Experimental Social Psychology,* 1973, *9,* 32–42.

Huxley, J. *Evolution in action.* New York: Mentor Books, 1953.

Hyman, H. H. *Interviewing in social research.* Chicago: University of Chicago Press, 1954.

Hyman, H. H., and Sheatsley, P. B. "The Authoritarian Personality"—A methodological critique. In R. Christie, and M. Jahoda (Eds.), *Studies in the scope and method of "The Authoritarian Personality."* New York: Free Press, 1954.

Ingersoll, R. Creed. In J. Bartlett's *Familiar quotations.* (14th ed.) E. M. Beck (Ed.). Boston: Little, Brown, & Co., 1968, p. 249.

Inkeles, A. Sociology and psychology. In S. Koch (Ed.), *Psychology: A study of science.* Vol. 6. New York: McGraw-Hill, 1963.

Insko, C. A. Primacy versus recency in persuasion as a function of the timing of arguments and measures. *Journal of Abnormal and Social Psychology,* 1964, *69,* 381–391.

Insko, C. A., Arkoff, A., and Insko, V. M. Effects of high and low fear-arousing communications upon opinions toward smoking. *Journal of Experimental Social Psychology,* 1965, *1,* 256–266.

Insko, C. A., and Schopler, J. Triadic consistency: A statement of affective-cognitive-conative consistency. *Psychological Review,* 1967, *74,* 361–376.

Isen, A. M., and Levin, P. F. Effect of feeling good on helping: Cookies and kindness. *Journal of Personality and Social Psychology,* 1972, *21,* 384–388.

Itard, J. M. G. *The wild boy of Aveyron.* New York: Appleton-Century-Crofts, 1962. (Originally published, 1894.)

Iwao, S. Internal versus external criticism of group standards. *Sociometry,* 1963, *26,* 410–421.

Izard, C. E. The effect of role-played emotion on affective reactions, intellectual functioning and evaluative ratings of the actress. *Journal of Clinical Psychology*, 1964, *20*, 444–446.

Izard, C. E. The emotions and emotion constructs in personality and culture research. In R. B. Cattell (Ed.), *Handbook of modern personality theory*. Chicago: Aldine, 1969.

Izzett, R. R. Authoritarianism and attitudes toward the Vietnam war as reflected in behavioral and self-report measures. *Journal of Personality and Social Psychology*, 1971, *17*, 145–148.

Jacobs, R. C., and Campbell, D. T. The perpetuation of an arbitrary tradition through several generations of a laboratory microculture. *Journal of Abnormal and Social Psychology*, 1961, *62*, 649–658.

Jacoby, J. Interpersonal perceptual accuracy as a function of dogmatism. *Journal of Experimental Social Psychology*, 1971, *7*, 221–236.

Jakubczak, L. F., and Walters, R. H. Suggestibility as dependency behavior. *Journal of Abnormal and Social Psychology*, 1959, *59*, 102–107.

James, G., and Lott, A. J. Reward frequency and the formation of positive attitudes toward group members. *Journal of Social Psychology*, 1964, *62*, 111–115.

James, W. *Principles of psychology*. New York: Holt, 1890.

James, W. *Psychology*. New York: Holt, 1892.

James, W. H., Woodruff, A. B., and Werner, W. Effects of internal and external control upon changes in smoking behavior. *Journal of Consulting Psychology*, 1965, *29*, 184–186.

Jamias, J. F., and Troldahl, V. C. Dogmatism, tradition, and general innovativeness. Unpublished manuscript, 1965.

Janis, I. L. *Air war and emotional stress*. New York: McGraw-Hill, 1951.

Janis, I. L. *Victims of groupthink*. Boston: Houghton-Mifflin, 1972.

Janis, I. L., and Feshbach, S. Effects of fear-arousing communications. *Journal of Abnormal and Social Psychology*, 1953, *48*, 78–92.

Janis, I. L., and Field, P. B. Sex differences and personality factors related to persuasibility. In C. I. Hovland, and I. L. Janis (Eds.), *Personality and persuasibility*. New Haven: Yale University Press, 1959.

Janis, I. L., and Hoffman, D. Facilitating effects of daily contact between partners who make a decision to cut down on smoking. *Journal of Personality and Social Psychology*, 1971, *17*, 25–35.

Jecker, J. D. The cognitive effects of conflict and dissonance. In L. Festinger (Ed.), *Conflict, decision, and dissonance*. Stanford: Stanford University Press, 1964.

Jegard, S., and Walters, R. A study of some determinants of aggression in young children. *Child Development*, 1960, *31*, 739–747.

Jellison, J. M., and Riskind, J. A social comparison of abilities interpretation of risk-taking behavior. *Journal of Personality and Social Psychology*, 1970, *15*, 375–390.

Jellison, J. M., and Zeisset, P. T. Attraction as a function of the commonality and desirability of a trait shared with another. *Journal of Personality and Social Psychology*, 1969, *11*, 115–120.

Johnson, D. L., and Andrews, I. R. Risky-shift phenomenon tested with consumer products as stimuli. *Journal of Personality and Social Psychology*, 1971, *20*, 382–385.

Johnson, D. M. The "phantom anesthetist" of Mattoon: A field study of mass hysteria. *Journal of Abnormal and Social Psychology*, 1945, *40*, 175–186.

Johnson, H. H., and Izzett, R. R. Relationship between authoritarianism and attitude change as a function of source credibility and type of communication. *Journal of Personality and Social Psychology*, 1969, *13*, 317–321.

Johnson, R. C., Ackerman, J. M., Frank, H., and Fionda, A. J. Resistance to temptation and guilt following yielding and psychotherapy. *Journal of Counseling and Clinical Psychology*, 1968, *32*, 169–175.

Johnson, R. N. *Aggression in man and animals*. Philadelphia: W. B. Saunders, 1972.

Johnson, T. J., Feigenbaum, R., and Weiby, M. Some determinants and consequences of the teacher's perception of causation. *Journal of Educational Psychology*, 1964, *55*, 237–246.

Johnston, J. M. Punishment of human behavior. *American Psychologist*, 1972, *27*, 1033–1054.

Jones, E. E. Authoritarianism as a determinant of first-impression formation. *Journal of Personality*, 1954, *23*, 107–127.

Jones, E. E. *Ingratiation: A social psychological analysis*. New York: Appleton-Century-Crofts, 1964.

Jones, E. E., and Davis, K. E. From acts to dispositions: The attribution process in person perception. In L. Berkowitz (Ed.), *Advances in experimental social psychology*. Vol. 2. New York: Academic Press, 1965.

Jones, E. E., Davis, K. E., and Gergen, K. J. Role playing variations and their informational value for person perception. *Journal of Abnormal and Social Psychology*, 1961, *63*, 302–310.

Jones, E. E., and deCharms, R. Changes in social perception as a function of the personal relevance of behavior. *Sociometry*, 1957, *20*, 75–85.

Jones, E. E., and Gerard, H. B. *Foundations of social psychology*. New York: Wiley, 1967.

Jones, E. E., Gergen, K. J., Gumpert, P., and Thibaut, J. W. Some conditions affecting the use of ingratiation to influence performance evaluation. *Journal of Personality and Social Psychology*, 1965, *1*, 613–625.

Jones, E. E., Gergen, K. J., and Jones, R. G. Tactics of ingratiation among leaders and subordinates in a status hierarchy. *Psychological Monographs*, 1963, *77*, (3, Whole No. 566).

Jones, R. E., and Harris, V. A. The attribution of attitudes. *Journal of Experimental Social Psychology*, 1967, *3*, 1–24.

Jones, E. E., and Nisbett, R. E. *The actor and the observer: Divergent perceptions of the causes of behavior.* Morristown, N. J.: General Learning Press, 1971.

Jones, E. E., Rock, L., Shaver, K. G., Goethals, G. R., and Ward, L. M. Pattern of performance and ability attribution: An unexpected primacy effect. *Journal of Personality and Social Psychology*, 1968, *10*, 317–340.

Jones, E. E., and Sigall, H. The bogus pipeline: A new paradigm for measuring affect and attitudes. *Psychological Bulletin*, 1971, *76*, 349–364.

Jones, E. E., Wells, H. H., and Torrey, R. Some effects of feedback from the experimenter on conformity behavior. *Journal of Abnormal and Social Psychology*, 1958, *58*, 207–213.

Jones, E. E., Worchel, S., Goethals, G. R., and Grumet, J. F. Prior expectancy and behavioral extremity as determinants of attitude attribution. *Journal of Experimental Social Psychology*, 1971, *7*, 59–80.

Jones, R. A., Linder, D. E., Kiesler, C. A., Zanna, M., and Brehm, J. W. Internal states or external stimuli: Observers' attitude judgments and the dissonance theory–self-persuasion controversy. *Journal of Experimental Social Psychology*, 1968, *4*, 247–269.

Jones, S. C., Knurek, D. A., and Regan, D. T. Variables affecting reactions to social acceptance and rejection. *Journal of Social Psychology*, 1973, *90*, 269–284.

Jordan, N. Behavioral forces that are a function of attitudes and of cognitive organization. *Human Relations*, 1953, *6*, 273–287.

Jourard, S. M. Self-disclosure and other cathexis. *Journal of Abnormal and Social Psychology*, 1959, *59*, 428–431.

Jourard, S. M. *The transparent self: Self-disclosure and well-being.* Princeton, N. J.: Van Nostrand, 1964.

Jung, J. Current practices and problems in the use of college students for psychological research. *Canadian Psychologist*, 1969, *10*, 280–290.

Kaats, G. R., and Davis, K. E. The dynamics of sexual behavior of college students. *Journal of Marriage and the Family*, 1970, *32*, 390–399.

Kagan, J., Hosken, B., and Watson, S. Child's symbolic conceptualization of the parents. *Child Development*, 1961, *32*, 625–636.

Kagan, J., Moss, H. A., and Sigel, I. E. Psychological significance of styles of conceptualization. *Monographs of the Society for Research on Child Development*, 1963, *28* No. 2 (Whole No. 86).

Kahn, H. *On thermonuclear war.* Princeton, N. J.: Princeton University Press, 1960.

Kahn, H. *Thinking about the unthinkable.* New York: Horizon Press, 1962.

Kahn, H. *On escalation: Metaphors and scenarios.* New York: Praeger, 1965.

Kahn, R., and Katz, D. Leadership practices in relation to productivity and morale. In D. Cartwright and A. Zander (Eds.), *Group dynamics: Research and theory.* Evanston, Ill.: Row, Peterson, 1953.

Kalven, H., Jr., and Zeisal, H. *The American Jury.* Boston: Little, Brown, 1966.

Kanareff, V., and Lanzetta, J. T. The acquisition of imitative and opposition responses under two conditions of instruction-induced set. *Journal of Experimental Psychology*, 1958, *56*, 516–528.

Kanareff, V. T., and Lanzetta, J. T. Effects of success-failure experiences and probability of reinforcement upon the acquisition and extinction of an imitative response. *Psychological Reports*, 1960, *7*, 151–166.

Kane, T., Joseph, J. M., and Tedeschi, J. T. Person perception and the Berkowitz paradigm for the study of aggression. *Journal of Personality and Social Psychology*, 1976, In press.

Kane, T., and Tedeschi, J. T. Impressions of conforming and independent persons. *Journal of Social Psychology*, 1973, *91*, 109–116.

Kanfer, F. H., and Duerfeldt, P. H. Age, class standing, and commitment as determinants of cheating in children. *Child Development*, 1968, *39*, 545–557.

Kanfer, F. H., and Marston, A. R. Determinants of self-reinforcement in human learning. *Journal of Experimental Psychology*, 1963, *66*, 245–254.

Kantner, R. M. Life in a commune. *Psychology Today*, July, 1970, *4*, 78, 53–57.

Kaplan, A. *The conduct of inquiry.* San Francisco: Chandler, 1964.

Kaplan, F. M., and Singer, E. Dogmatism and sensory alienation: An empirical investigation. *Journal of Consulting Psychology*, 1963, *27*, 486–491.

Karlins, M., Coffman, T. L., and Walters, G. On the fading of social stereotypes: Studies in three generations of college students. *Journal of Personality and Social Psychology*, 1969, *13*, 1–16.

Kates, S. L. First-impression formation and authoritarianism. *Human Relations*, 1959, *12*, 277–286.

Katz, A. M., and Hill, R. Residential propinquity and marital selection: A review of theory, method, and fact. *Marriage and Family Living*, 1958, *20*, 27–35.

Katz, D. The psychology of the crowd. In J. P. Guilford (Ed.), *Fields of psychology.* New York: Van Nostrand, 1940.

Katz, D. The functional approach to the study of attitudes. *Public Opinion Quarterly*, 1960, *24*, 163–204.

Katz, D., and Braly, K. W. Racial prejudice and racial stereotypes. *Journal of Abnormal and Social Psychology*, 1933, *30*, 175–193.

Katz, E., and Lazarsfeld, P. F. *Personal influence.* Glencoe, Ill.: Free Press, 1955.

Katzenbach, N. *The challenge of crime in a free society: A report by the President's Commission on Law Enforcement and Administration of Justice.* New York: Avon, 1968.

Kaufmann, H. Similarity and cooperation received as determinants of cooperation rendered. *Psychonomic Science*, 1967, *9*, 73–74.

Kaufmann, H. The unconcerned bystander. *Proceedings of the 76th Annual Convention of the American Psychological Association*, San Francisco, 1968, *3*, 387–388.

Kaufmann, H. *Aggression and altruism*. New York: Holt, Rinehart, & Winston, 1970.

Kazdin, A. E., and Bryan, J. H. Competence and volunteering. *Journal of Experimental Social Psychology*, 1971, *7*, 87–97.

Kelley, H. H. The warm-cold variable in first impressions of persons. *Journal of Personality*, 1950, *18*, 431–439.

Kelley, H. H. Communication in experimentally created hierachies. *Human Relations*, 1951, *4*, 39–56.

Kelley, H. H. Attribution theory in social psychology. In D. Levine (Ed.), *Nebraska symposium on motivation*. Lincoln, Nebraska: University of Nebraska Press, 1967.

Kelley, H. H. The processes of causal attribution. *American Psychologist*, 1973, *28*, 107–128.

Kelley, H. H., and Arrowood, A. J. Coalitions in the triad: Critique and experiment. *Sociometry*, 1960, *23*, 231–244.

Kelley, H. H., Contry, J. C., Dahlke, A. E., and Hill, A. H. Collective behavior in a simulated panic situation. *Journal of Experimental Social Psychology*, 1965, *1*, 20–54.

Kelley, H. H., and Ring, K. Some effects of "suspicious" versus "trusting" training schedules. *Journal of Abnormal and Social Psychology*, 1961, *63*, 294–301.

Kelley, H. H., and Stahleski, A. J. Social interaction basis of cooperators' and competitors' beliefs about others. *Journal of Personality and Social Psychology*, 1970, *16*, 66–91. (a)

Kelley, H. H., and Stahleski, A. J. Errors in perception of intentions in a mixed-motive game. *Journal of Experimental Social Psychology*, 1970, *6*, 379–400. (b)

Kelley, H. H., and Stahelski, A. J. The inference of intentions from moves in the Prisoner's Dilemma game. *Journal of Experimental Social Psychology*, 1970, *6*, 401–419. (c)

Kelley, H. H., and Thibaut, J. W. Group problem solving. In G. Lindzey and E. Aronson (Eds.), *Handbook of social psychology*. Vol. 4. (2nd ed.) Reading, Mass.: Addison-Wesley, 1969.

Kellogg, R., and Baron, R. S. Attribution theory, insomnia, and the reverse placebo effect: A reversal of Storms and Nisbett's findings. *Journal of Personality and Social Psychology*, 1975, *32*, 231–236.

Kellogg, W. N., and Kellogg, L. A. *The ape and the child*. New York: McGraw-Hill, 1933.

Kelly, G. A. *The psychology of personal constructs*. New York: Norton, 1955.

Kelman, H. C. Attitudes are alive and well and gainfully employed in the sphere of action. *American Psychologist*, 1974, *29*, 310–324.

Kelman, H. C. Effects of success and failure on 'suggestibility' in the autokinetic situation. *Journal of Abnormal and Social Psychology*, 1950, *45*, 267–285.

Kelman, H. C. Human use of human subjects: The problem of deception in social psychological experiments. *Psychological Bulletin*, 1967, *67*, 1–11.

Kelman, H. C., and Barclay, J. The F scale as a measure of breadth of perspective. *Journal of Abnormal and Social Psychology*, 1963, *67*, 608–615.

Kelman, H. C., and Lawrence, L. Violent man: American response to the trial of Lt. William L. Calley. *Psychology Today*, 1972, *6*, 41–45, 78–81.

Kendon, A. Some functions of gaze direction in social interaction. *Acta Psychologia*, 1967, *26*, 22–63.

Keniston, K. *The uncommitted: Alienated youth in American society*. New York: Harcourt, Brace, & World, 1965.

Kennan, G. F. The sources of Soviet conduct. *Foreign Affairs*, 1947, *25*, 568–582.

Kennan, G. F. *Memoires: 1950–1963*. Boston: Little, Brown, 1972.

Kerckhoff, A. C., Back, K. W., and Miller, N. Sociometric patterns in hysterical contagion. *Sociometry*, 1965, *28*, 2–15.

Keys, A., Brozek, J., Henschel, A., Mickelsen, O., and Taylor, H. L. *The biology of human starvation*. (2 vols.) Minneapolis: University of Minnesota, 1950.

Kiesler, C. A. Group pressure and conformity. In J. Mills (Ed.), *Experimental social psychology*. New York: Macmillan, 1969.

Kiesler, C. A., and Kiesler, S. B. Role of forewarning in persuasive communications. *Journal of Abnormal and Social Psychology*, 1964, *68*, 547–549.

Kiesler, C. A., and Kiesler, S. B. *Conformity*. Reading, Mass.: Addison-Wesley, 1969.

Killian, L. M. Social movements. In R. E. L. Farris (Ed.), *Handbook of modern sociology*. Chicago: Rand McNally, 1964.

Kinkade, K. Commune: A Walden–Two experiment. *Psychology Today*, 1973, *6*, 35–42, 90–93.

Kipnis, D. Interaction between members of bomber crews as a determinant of sociometric choice. *Human Relations*, 1957, *10*, 263–270.

Kipnis, D. The effects of leadership style and leadership power upon the inducement of an attitude change. *Journal of Abnormal and Social Psychology*, 1958, *57*, 173–180.

Kipnis, D. The powerholder. In J. T. Tedeschi (Ed.), *Perspectives on social power*. Chicago: Aldine, 1974.

Kipnis, D., and Consentino, J. Use of leadership powers in industry. *Journal of Applied Psychology*, 1969, *53*, 460–466.

Kipnis, D., and Misner, R. P. Police actions and disorderly conduct. Mimeographed manuscript, Temple University, 1972.

Kipnis, D., and Vanderveer, R. Ingratiation and the use of power. *Journal of Personality and Social Psychology*, 1971, *17*, 280–286.

Kirkham, J. S., Levy, S., and Crotty, W. J. (Eds.), *Assassination and political violence*. New York: Praeger, 1970.

Kissinger, H. *Nuclear weapons and foreign policy*. New York: Harper, 1957.

Kite, W. R. Attributions of causality as a function of the use of reward and punishment. Unpublished doctoral dissertation, Stanford University, 1964.

Kleiner, R. The effects of threat reduction upon interpersonal attraction. *Journal of Personality*, 1960, *28*, 145–155.

Klineberg, O. Emotional expression in Chinese literature. *Journal of Abnormal and Social Psychology*, 1938, *33*, 517–520.

Kluckhohn, C., and Leighton, D. *The Navaho*. Cambridge, Mass.: Harvard University Press, 1946.

Knowles, E. S. Boundaries around group interaction: The effect of group size and member status on boundary permeability. *Journal of Personality and Social Psychology*, 1973, *26*, 327–331.

Knox, R. E., and Inkster, J. A. Postdecision dissonance at post time. *Journal of Personality and Social Psychology*, 1968, *8*, 319–323.

Koch, H. L. The relation in young children between characteristics of their playmates and certain attributes of their siblings. *Child Development*, 1957, *28*, 175–202.

Koestler, A. The initiates. In R. Crossman (Ed.), *The god that failed*. New York. Bantam, 1959.

Kogan, N., and Wallach, M. A. *Risk-taking: A study in cognition and personality*. New York: Holt, 1964.

Kogan, N., and Wallach, M. A. Group risk taking as a function of members' anxiety and defensive levels. *Journal of Personality*, 1967, *35*, 50–63. (*a*)

Kogan, N., and Wallach, M. A. The risky-shift phenomenon in small decision-making groups: A test of the information-exchange hypothesis. *Journal of Experimental Social Psychology*, 1967, *3*, 75–85. (*b*)

Kohlberg, L. The development of children's orientations toward a moral order: I. Sequence in the development of moral thought. *Vita Humana*, 1963, *6*, 11–33.

Kohlberg, L. Development of moral character and moral ideology. In M. Hoffman and L. Hoffman (Eds.), *Review of child development research*. Vol. 1. New York: Russell Sage Foundation, 1964.

Kohlberg, L. *Stage and sequence: The cognitive-proach to moralization*. Chicago: Aldine, 1968.

Kohlberg, L. Stage and sequence: The cognitive-developmental approach to socialization. In D. A. Goslin (Ed.), *Handbook of socialization theory and research*. Chicago: Rand McNally, 1969. (*a*)

Kohlberg, L. *The relations between moral judgment and moral action: A developmental view*. Paper presented at the Institute of Human Development, Berkeley, 1969. (*b*)

Komorita, S. S., and Brenner, A. R. Bargaining and concession-making under bilateral monopoly. *Journal of Personality and Social Psychology*, 1968, *9*, 15–20.

Komorita, S. S., and Chertkoff, J. M. A bargaining theory of coalition formation. *Psychological Review*, 1973, *80*, 149–162.

Konečni, V. J. Some effects of guilt on compliance: A field replication. *Journal of Personality and Social Psychology*, 1972, *23*, 30–32.

König, R. A. *A la mode: On the social psychology of fashion*. New York: Seabury, 1973.

Kopera, A. A., Maier, R. A., and Johnson, J. E. Perception of physical attractiveness: The influence of group interaction and group coaction on ratings of the attractiveness of photographs of women. Presented at the 79th Annual Convention of the American Psychological Association, Washington, D. C., 1971.

Kraus, S., El-Assal, E., and DeFleur, M. L. Fear-threat appeals in mass communications: An apparent contradiction. *Speech Monographs*, 1966, *33*, 23–29.

Krauss, R. M. Structural and attitudinal factors in interpersonal bargaining. *Journal of Experimental Social Psychology*, 1966, *2*, 42–55.

Krebs, D. L. Altruism: An examination of the concept and a review of the literature. *Psychological Bulletin*, 1970, *73*, 258–302.

Krebs, R. *Some relations between moral judgment, attention, and resistance to temptation*. Unpublished doctoral dissertation, University of Chicago, 1967.

Krech, D., Crutchfield, R. S., and Ballachey, E. L. *Individual in society: A textbook of social psychology*. New York: McGraw-Hill, 1962.

Kremers, J. *Scientific psychology and naive psychology*. Groningen, Netherlands: Nordhoff, 1960.

Krout, M. H. The social and psychological significance of gestures (a differential analysis). *Journal of Genetic Psychology*, 1935, *47*, 385–412.

Kruglanski, A. W. Attributing trustworthiness in supervisor-worker relations. *Journal of Experimental Social Psychology*, 1970, *6*, 214–232.

Kuhlman, C. E., Miller, M. J., and Gungor, E. Interpersonal conflict reduction: The effects of language and meaning. In L. Rappoport and D. A. Summers (Eds.), *Human judgment and social interaction*. New York: Holt, Rinehart, & Winston, 1973.

Kuhn, A. *The study of society: A unified approach*. Homewood, Ill.: Irwin, 1963.

Kutner, B., Wilkens, C., and Yarrow, P. R. Verbal attitudes and overt behavior involving racial prejudice. *Journal of Abnormal and Social Psychology*, 1952, *47*, 649–652.

Laing, R. D., and Esterson, A. *Sanity, madness, and the family*. New York: Basic Books, 1964.

Laird, D. A. Changes in motor control and individual variations under the influence of "razzing." *Journal of Experimental Psychology*, 1923, *6*, 236–246.

Lambert, W. W., and Lambert, W. E. *Social psychology*. Englewood Cliffs, N. J.: Prentice-Hall, 1964.

Lamm, H. Will an observer advise high risk taking after hearing a discussion of the decision problem? *Journal of Personality and Social Psychology*, 1967, *6*, 467–471.

Lamm, H., Schaude, E., and Trommsdorff, G. Risky shift as a function of group members' value of risk and need for approval. *Journal of Personality and Social Psychology*, 1971, *20*, 430–435.

Lana, R. E. Pretest sensitization. In R. Rosenthal, and R. L. Rosnow (Eds.), *Artifact in behavioral research*. New York: Academic Press, 1969.

Landy, D., and Aronson, E. The influence of the character of the criminal and his victim on the decisions of simulated jurors. *Journal of Experimental Social Psychology*, 1969, *5*, 141–152.

Landy, D., and Mettee, D. Evaluation of an aggressor as a function of exposure to cartoon humor. *Journal of Personality and Social Psychology*, 1969, *12*, 66–71.

Landy, D., and Sigall, H. Beauty is talent: Task evaluation as a function of the performer's physical attractiveness. *Journal of Personality and Social Psychology*, 1974, *29*, 299–304.

Langfeld, H. S. The judgment of emotion by facial expression. *Journal of Abnormal and Social Psychology*, 1918, *13*, 172–184.

Lansky, L. M., Crandall, V. J., Kagan, J., and Baker, C. T. Sex differences in aggression and its correlates in middle-class adolescents. *Child Development*, 1961, *32*, 45–58.

Lanzetta, J. T., and Hannah, T. E. Reinforcing behavior of "naive" trainers. *Journal of Personality and Social Psychology*, 1969, *11*, 245–252.

LaPiere, R. T. Attitudes versus actions. *Social Forces*, 1934, *13*, 230–237.

LaPiere, R. T. *Collective behavior*. New York: McGraw-Hill, 1938.

Lasswell, H. D. Conflict and leadership: The process of decision and the nature of authority. In A. S. de Reuck and J. Knight (Eds.), *Ciba Foundation symposium: Conflict in society*. Boston: Little, Brown, Co., 1966.

Lasswell, H. D. and Kaplan, A. *Power and society*. New Haven, Conn.: Yale University Press, 1950.

Latané, B. The urge to help. Paper presented at the 75th annual meeting of the American Psychological Association, Washington, D. C., September, 1967.

Latané, B., and Darley, J. M. Bystander "apathy." *American Scientist*, 1969, *57*, 244–268.

Latané, B., and Darley, J. Social determinants of bystander intervention in emergencies. In J. Macaulay and L. Berkowitz (Eds.), *Altruism and helping behavior*. New York: Academic Press, 1970.

Latané, B., and Rodin, J. A. A lady in distress: Inhibiting effects of friends and strangers on bystander intervention. *Journal of Experimental Social Psychology*, 1969, *5*, 189–202.

Lawson, R. *Frustration: The development of a scientific concept*. New York: Macmillan, 1965.

Lazarsfeld, P. F., and Merton, R. K. Mass communication, popular taste and organized social action. In L. Bryston (Ed.), *The communication of ideas*. New York: Harper, 1948.

Lazarus, R. S., Speisman, J., Mordkoff, A., and Davison, L. A laboratory study of psychological stress produced by a motion picture film. *Psychological Monographs*, 1962, *76*, No. 34 (Whole No. 553).

Lazarus, R. S., Yousem, H., and Arenberg, D. Hunger and perception. *Journal of Personality*, 1953, *21*, 312–328.

Leavitt, H. J. Some effects of certain communication patterns on group performance. *Journal of Abnormal and Social Psychology*, 1951, *46*, 38–50.

LeBon, G. *Psychologie de foules*. Paris: Odeon (Trans., *The crowd*, London: Unwin, 1903), 1895.

Lee, A. McC., and Humphrey, N. D. *Race riot*. New York: Dryden Press, 1943.

Lefcourt, H. M. Recent developments in the study of locus of control. In B. A. Maher (Ed.), *Progress in experimental personality research*. Vol. 6. New York: Academic Press, 1972.

Leites, N., and Wolf, C. Jr. *Rebellion and authority: an analytic essay on insurgent conflicts*. Chicago, Markham, 1970.

Lemert, J. B. Dimensions of source credibility. Paper presented at the meeting of the Association for Education in Journalism, August, 1963.

Lemert, J. B. Status conferral and topic scope. *Journal of Communication*, 1969, *19*, 4–13.

Lenneberg, E. H. *Biological foundations of language*. New York: Wiley, 1967.

Lepper, M. R., Zanna, M. P., and Abelson, R. P. Cognitive irreversibility in a dissonance reduction situation. *Journal of Personality and Social Psychology*, 1970, *16*, 191–198.

Lerner, M. J., Dillehay, R. C., and Sherer, W. C. Similarity and attraction in social contexts. *Journal of Personality and Social Psychology*, 1967, *5*, 481–485.

Lerner, M. J., and Matthews, G. Reactions to suffering of others under conditions of indirect responsibility. *Journal of Personality and Social Psychology*, 1967, *5*, 319–325.

Lesser, G. S., and Abelson, R. P. Personality correlates of persuasibility in children. In C. I. Hovland and I. L. Janis (Eds.), *Personality and persuasibility*. New Haven: Yale University Press, 1959.

Lessing, E. E. Racial differences in indices of ego functioning relevant to academic achievement. *Journal of Genetic Psychology*, 1969, *115*, 153–167.

Leventhal, H. Fear communications in the acceptance of preventive health practices. *Bulletin of the New York Academy of Medicine,* 1965, *41,* 1144–1168.

Leventhal, H., and Singer, D. L. Cognitive complexity, impression formation and impression change. *Journal of Personality,* 1964, *32,* 210–226.

Leventhal, H., and Singer, R. P. Affect arousal and positioning of recommendations in persuasive communications. *Journal of Personality and Social Psychology,* 1966, *4,* 137–146.

Leventhal, H., Singer, R. P., and Jones, S. Effects of fear and specificity of recommendation upon attitudes and behavior. *Journal of Personality and Social Psychology,* 1965, *2,* 20–29.

Leventhal, H., Watts, J. C., and Pagano, F. Effects of fear and instructions on how to cope with danger. *Journal of Personality and Social Psychology,* 1967, *6,* 313–321.

Levinger, G., & Breedlove, J. Interpersonal attraction and agreement: A study of marriage partners. *Journal of Personality and Social Psychology,* 1966, *3,* 367–372.

Levinger, G., and Schneider, D. J. Test of the "risk is a value" hypothesis. *Journal of Personality and Social Psychology,* 1969, *11,* 165–169.

Levinger, G. and Snoek, J. D. *Attraction in relationship: A new look at interpersonal attraction.* New York: General Learning Corporation, 1972.

Lewin, K. Frontiers in group dynamics. *Human Relations,* 1947, *1,* 5–41. (a)

Lewin, K. Group decision and social change. In T. M. Newcomb, and E. L. Hartley (Eds.), *Readings in social psychology.* New York: Holt, 1947. (b)

Lewin, K. Group decision and social change. In E. E. Maccoby, T. M. Newcomb, and E. L. Hartley (Eds.), *Readings in social psychology.* (3rd ed.) New York: Henry Holt, 1958.

Lewin, K., Lippitt, R., and White, R. K. Patterns of aggressive behavior in experimentally created 'social climates.' *Journal of Social Psychology,* 1939, *10,* 271–299.

Lieberman, B. Experimental studies of conflict in some two-person and three-person games. In J. Criswell, H. Solomon, and P. Suppes (Eds.), *Mathematical methods in small group processes.* Stanford: Stanford University Press, 1962.

Lieberman, B. i-trust: A notion of trust in three-person games and international affairs. *Journal of Conflict Resolution,* 1964, *8,* 271–280.

Lieberman, S. The effect of changes in roles on the attitudes of role occupants. *Human Relations,* 1956, *9,* 385–402.

Lieberson, S., and Silverman, A. R. The precipitants and underlying conditions of race riots. *American Sociological Review,* 1965, *30,* 887–898.

Liebert, R. Television and social learning: Some relationships between viewing violence and behaving aggressively. In J. P. Murray, E. A. Rubinstein, and G. A. Comstock (Eds.), *Television and social behavior. Vol. II: Television and social learning.* Washington, D. C.: U. S. Government Printing Office, 1972.

Liebert, R. M., and Baron, R. A. Short term effects of televised aggression on children's aggressive behavior. In J. P. Murray, E. A. Rubinstein, and G. A. Comstock (Eds.), *Television and social behavior. Vol. II: Television and social learning.* Washington, D. C.: U. S. Government Printing Office, 1972.

Liebert, R. M., Neale, J., and Davidson, E. *The early window: Effects of television on children and youth.* New York: Pergamon Press, Inc., 1973.

Liebert, R. M., Odom, R. D., Hill, J. G., and Huff, R. L. Effects of age and rule familiarity on the production of modeled language constructions. *Developmental Psychology,* 1969, *1,* 108–112.

Liebert, R. M., Smith, W. P., Kieffer, M., and Hill, J. H. The effects of information and magnitude of initial offer on interpersonal negotiation. *Journal of Experimental Social Psychology,* 1968, *4,* 431–441.

Lifton, R. J. *Thought reform and the psychology of totalism: A study of "brainwashing" in China.* New York: Norton, 1961.

Lincoln, A., and Levinger, G. Observers' evaluations of the victim and the attacker in an aggressive incident. *Journal of Personality and Social Psychology,* 1972, *22,* 202–210.

Linde, T. F., and Patterson, C. H. Influence of orthopedic disability on conforming behavior. *Journal of Abnormal and Social Psychology,* 1964, *68,* 115–118.

Linder, D. E., Cooper, J., and Jones, E. E. Decision freedom as a determinant of the role of incentive magnitude in attitude change. *Journal of Personality and Social Psychology,* 1967, *6,* 245–254.

Lindskold, S., Albert, K. P., Baer, R., and Moore, W. C. Territorial boundaries of interacting groups and passive audiences, *Sociometry,* 1976, in press.

Lindskold, S., and Bennett, R. Attributing trust and conciliatory intent from coercive power capability. *Journal of Personality and Social Psychology,* 1973, *28,* 180–186.

Lindskold, S., Bonoma, T. V., Schlenker, B. R., and Tedeschi, J. T. Some factors affecting the effectiveness of reward power. *Psychonomic Science,* 1972, *26,* 68–70.

Lindskold, S., and Tedeschi, J. T. Self-confidence, prior success, and the use of power in social conflicts. *Proceedings of the 78th Annual Convention of the American Psychological Association,* 1970, *5,* 425–426.

Lindskold, S., and Tedeschi, J. T. Reward power and attraction in interpersonal conflict. *Psychonomic Science,* 1971, *22,* 211–213. (a)

Lindskold, S., and Tedeschi, J. T. Self-esteem and sex as factors affecting influenceability. *British Journal of Social and Clinical Psychology,* 1971, *10,* 114–122. (b)

Lipetz, M. E. The effects of information on the assessment of attitudes by authoritarians and nonauthoritarians. *Journal of Abnormal and Social Psychology*, 1960, *60,* 95–99.

Lippitt, R., Polansky, N., Redl, F., and Rosen, S. The dynamics of power. *Human Relations*, 1952, *5,* 37–64.

Long, B. H., and Ziller, R. C. Dogmatism and predecisional information search. *Journal of Applied Psychology*, 1965, *49,* 376–378.

Lorenz, K. *On aggression*. New York: Harcourt, Brace, & World, 1966.

Lott, A. J., Aponte, J. F., Lott, B. E., and McGinley, W. H. The effect of delayed reward on the development of positive attitudes toward persons. *Journal of Experimental Social Psychology*, 1969, *5,* 101–113.

Lott, A. J., Bright, M. A., Weinstein, P., and Lott, B. E. Liking for persons as a function of incentive and drive during acquisition. *Journal of Personality and Social Psychology*, 1970, *14,* 66–76.

Lott, A. J., and Lott, B. E. The power of liking. In L. Berkowitz (Ed.), *Advances in experimental social psychology*. Vol. 6. New York: Academic Press, 1972.

Lott, B. E., and Lott, A. J. The formation of positive attitudes toward group members. *Journal of Abnormal and Social Psychology*, 1960, *61,* 297–300.

Lott, D. F., and Sommer, R. Seating arrangements and status. *Journal of Personality and Social Psychology*, 1967, *7,* 90–94.

Lovaas, O. I. Effect of exposure to symbolic aggression on aggressive behavior. *Child Development*, 1961, *32,* 37–44.

Luce, R. D., and Raiffa, H. *Games and decisions: Introduction and critical survey*. New York: Wiley, 1957.

Luchins, A. S. Social influence on perception of complex drawings. *Journal of Social Psychology*, 1945, *21,* 257–273.

Luchins, A. S. Definiteness of impression and primacy-recency in communications. *Journal of Social Psychology*, 1958, *48,* 275–290.

Lull, P. E. The effectiveness of humor in persuasive speeches. *Speech Monographs*, 1940, *7,* 26–40.

Lumsdaine, A. A., and Janis, I. L. Resistance to 'counterpropaganda' produced by one-sided and two-sided 'propaganda' presentations. *Public Opinion Quarterly*, 1953, *17,* 311–318.

Lutzker, D. R. Internationalism as a predictor of cooperative behavior. *Journal of Conflict Resolution*, 1960, *4,* 426–430.

Lynn, D. B. Sex-role and parental identification. *Child Development*, 1962, *33,* 555–564.

Maccoby, E. E., and Wilson, W. C. Identification and observational learning from films. *Journal of Abnormal and Social Psychology*, 1957, *55,* 76–87.

MacKinnon, D. W. Violation of prohibitions. In H. Murray (Ed.), *Explorations in personality*. New York: Oxford University, 1938.

MacKinnon, W. J., and Centers, R. Authoritarianism and urban stratification. *American Journal of Sociology*, 1956, *61,* 610–620.

Madaras, G. R., and Bem, D. J. Risk and conservatism in group decision making. *Journal of Experimental Social Psychology*, 1968, *4,* 350–366.

Maisonneuve, J., Palmade, G., and Fourment, C. Selective choices and propinquity. *Sociometry*, 1952, *15,* 135–140.

Malinowski, B. *Argonauts of the western Pacific*. New York: Dutton, 1922.

Mallick, S. K., and McCandless, B. R. A study of catharsis of aggression. *Journal of Personality and Social Psychology*, 1966, *4,* 591–596.

Mandler, G. Emotion. In *New directions in psychology*. New York: Holt, Rinehart, & Winston, 1962.

Mann, J. H. The effect of interracial contact on sociometric choices and perceptions. *Journal of Social Psychology*, 1959, *50,* 143–152.

Mann, L. The social psychology of waiting lines. *American Scientist*, 1970, *58,* 390–398.

Marañon, G. Contribution a l'etude de l'action emotive de l'adrenaline. *Review Francaise D'endocrinologie*, 1924, *2,* 301–323.

March, J. G. An introduction to the theory and measurement of influence. *American Political Science Review*, 1955, *49,* 431–451.

March, J. G. Measurement concepts in the theory of influence. *Journal of Politics*, 1957, *19,* 202–226.

Marquis, D. G. Individual responsibility and group decisions involving risk. *Industrial Management Review*, 1962, *3,* 8–23.

Marshall, S. L. A. *Men under fire*. New York: Morrow, 1947.

Marwell, G., and Schmitt, D. R. Dimensions of compliance-gaining behavior: An empirical analysis. *Sociometry*, 1967, *30,* 350–364.

Masling, J. Role-related behavior of the subject and psychologist and its effects upon psychological data. In D. Levine (Ed.), *Nebraska symposium on motivation*. Lincoln, Neb.: University of Nebraska Press, 1966.

Mausner, B. The effect of prior reinforcement on the interaction of observer pairs. *Journal of Abnormal and Social Psychology*, 1954, *49,* 65–68.

Mauss, M. *The gift*. Translated by I. Cunnison. New York: Norton, 1967.

Mayo, C. W., and Crockett, W. H. Cognitive complexity and primacy-recency effects in impression formation. *Journal of Abnormal and Social Psychology*, 1964, *68,* 335–338.

McArthur, L. A. The how and what of why: Some determinants and consequences of causal attribution. *Journal of Personality and Social Psychology*, 1972, *22,* 171–193.

McCauley, C., Stitt, C. I., Woods, K., and Lipton, D.

Group shift to caution at the race track. *Journal of Experimental Social Psychology*, 1973, *9*, 80–86.

McClearn, G. E., and Rodgers, D. A. Genetic factors in alcohol preference of laboratory mice. *Journal of Comparative and Physiological Psychology*, 1961, *54*, 116–119.

McClelland, D. C., Atkinson, J. W., Clark, R. A., and Lowell, E. L. *The achievement motive*. New York: Appleton-Century-Crofts, 1953.

McClintock, C. G., Gallo, P. S., and Harrison, A. Some effects of variations in other strategy upon game behavior. *Journal of Personality and Social Psychology*, 1965, *1*, 319–325.

McClintock, C. G., Harrison, A. A., Strand, S., and Gallo, P. Internationalism-isolationism, strategy of the other player, and two-person game behavior. *Journal of Abnormal and Social Psychology*, 1963, *67*, 631–636.

McClosky, H. Conservatism and personality. *American Political Science Review*, 1958, *42*, 27–45.

McCord, W., McCord, J., and Howard, A. Familial correlates of aggression in nondelinquent male children. *Journal of Abnormal and Social Psychology*, 1961, *62*, 79–93.

McDaniel, J. W., O'Neal, E., and Fox, E. S. Magnitude of retaliation as function of the similarity of available responses to those employed by attacker. *Psychonomic Science*, 1971, *22*, 215–217.

McDougall, W. *Introduction to social psychology*. London: Methuen & Co., 1908.

McGinnies, E. Emotionality and perceptual defense. *Psychological Review*, 1949, *56*, 224–251.

McGinnies, E. Studies in persuasion: IV. Source credibility and involvement as factors in persuasion with students in Taiwan. *Journal of Social Psychology*, 1968, *74*, 171–180.

McGinnies, E., Comer, P. B., and Lacey, O. L. Visual recognition thresholds as a function of word length and word frequency. *Journal of Experimental Psychology*, 1952, *44*, 65–69.

McGinnies, E., and Donelson, E. Knowledge of experimenter's intent and attitude change under induced compliance. College Park: Department of Psychology, University of Maryland, 1963. (Mimeo)

McGuire, W. J. Inducing resistance to persuasion: Some contemporary approaches. In L. Berkowitz (Ed.), *Advances in experimental social psychology*. Vol. 1. New York: Academic Press, 1964.

McGuire, W. J. Some impending reorientations in social psychology: some thoughts probed by Kenneth Ring. *Journal of Experimental Social Psychology*, 1967, *3*, 124–139.

McGuire, W. J. The nature of attitudes and attitude change. In G. Lindzey and E. Aronson (Eds.), *Handbook of social psychology*. Vol. 3. (2nd ed.) Reading, Mass.: Addison-Wesley, 1969.

McGuire, W. J. The yin and yang of progress in social psychology: seven koan. *Journal of Personality and Social Psychology*, 1973, *26*, 446–456.

McGuire, W. J., and Millman, S. Anticipatory belief lowering following forewarning of a persuasive attack. *Journal of Personality and Social Psychology*, 1965, *2*, 471–479.

McGuire, W. J., and Papageorgis, D. The relative efficacy of various types of prior belief-defense in producing immunity against persuasion. *Journal of Abnormal and Social Psychology*, 1961, *62*, 327–337.

McGuire, W. J., and Papageorgis, D. Effectiveness of forewarning in developing resistance to persuasion. *Public Opinion Quarterly*, 1962, *26*, 24–34.

McGuire, W. J., and Ryan, J. Receptivity as a mediator of personality relationships. Unpublished manuscript, University of Minnesota, 1955.

McIntyre, J., and Teevan, J. Television violence and deviant behavior. In G. A. Comstock and E. A. Rubinstein (Eds.), *Television and social behavior. Vol. III. Television and adolescent aggressiveness*. Washington, D.C.: U. S. Government Printing Office, 1972.

McKeon, R. (Ed.), *Introduction to Aristotle*. New York: The Modern Library, 1947.

McLeod, J., Atkin, C., and Chaffee, S. Adolescents, parents, and television use: Adolescent self-report measures from Maryland and Wisconsin samples. In G. A. Comstock and E. A. Rubinstein (Eds.), *Television and social behavior. Vol. III: Television and adolescent aggressiveness*. Washington, D. C.: U. S. Government Printing Office, 1972.

McMartin, J. A. The taxicab as a mobile laboratory for the study of social influence. Paper presented at the annual meeting of the Western Psychological Association, Portland, Oregon, April, 1972.

Mead, G. H. *Mind, self and society*. Chicago: University of Chicago Press, 1934.

Mead, M. *Sex and temperament in three primitive societies*. New York: Morrow, 1935.

Mead, M. (Ed.), *Cultural patterns and technical change*. New York: The United Nations Educational, Scientific, and Cultural Organization, 1955 (reprinted by Mentor Books).

Meade, R. D. An experimental study of leadership in India. *Journal of Social Psychology*, 1967, *72*, 35–43.

Megargee, E. I. Undercontrolled and overcontrolled personality types in extreme antisocial aggression. In E. I. Megargee and J. E. Hokanson (Eds.), *The dynamics of aggression*. New York: Harper & Row, 1970.

Mehrabian, A. Inference of attitudes from the posture, orientation, and distance of a communicator. *Journal of Consulting and Clinical Psychology*, 1968, *32*, 296–308.

Mehrabian, A. Significance of posture and position in the communication of attitude and status relationships. *Psychological Bulletin*, 1969, *71*, 359–372.

Mehrabian, A. *Nonverbal communication.* Chicago: Aldine, 1972.

Mehrabian, A., and Williams, M. Nonverbal concomitants of perceived and intended persuasiveness. *Journal of Personality and Social Psychology,* 1969, *13,* 37–58.

Meichenbaum, D. H., Bowers, K. S., and Ross, R. E. A behavioral analysis of teacher expectancy effect. *Journal of Personality and Social Psychology,* 1969, *13,* 306–316.

Melges, F. T., and Harris, R. F. Anger and attack: A cybernetic model of violence. In D. N. Daniels, M. F. Gilula, and F. M. Ochberg (Eds.), *Violence and the struggle for existence.* Boston: Little, Brown, 1970.

Mencken, H. L. *The Vintage Mencken.* New York: Vintage Books, 1955.

Merton, R. K. Patterns of influence: A study of interpersonal influence and communications behavior in a local community. In P. F. Lazarsfeld and F. N. Stanton (Eds.), *Communications research 1948–1949.* New York: Harper, 1949.

Mettee, D. R. Changes in liking as a function of the magnitude and affect of sequential evaluations. *Journal of Experimental Social Psychology,* 1971, *7,* 157–172.

Meyer, T. P. Effects of viewing justified and unjustified real film violence on aggressive behavior. *Journal of Personality and Social Psychology,* 1972, *23,* 21–29.

Michener, H. A., and Burt, M. R. Legitimacy as a base of social influence. In J. T. Tedeschi (Ed.), *Perspectives on social power.* Chicago: Aldine, 1974.

Michener, H. A., and Lawler, E. J. Endorsement of formal leaders: an integrative model. *Journal of Personality and Social Psychology,* 1975, *31,* 216–223.

Michener, H. A., and Lyons, M. Perceived support and upward mobility as determinants of revolutionary coalitional behavior. *Journal of Experimental Social Psychology,* 1972, *8,* 180–195.

Midlarsky, E., and Bryan, J. H. Training charity in children. *Journal of Personality and Social Psychology,* 1967, *5,* 408–415.

Milgram, S. Behavioral study of obedience. *Journal of Abnormal and Social Psychology,* 1963, *67,* 371–378.

Milgram, S. Some conditions of obedience and disobedience to authority. *Human Relations,* 1965, *18,* 57–76.

Milgram, S. The experience of living in cities: A psychological analysis. *Science,* 1970, *167,* 1461–1468.

Milgram, S., Bickman, L., and Berkowitz, L. Note on the drawing power of crowds of different size. *Journal of Personality and Social Psychology,* 1969, *13,* 79–82.

Milgram, S., and Toch, H. Collective behavior: Crowds and social movements. In G. Lindzey and E. Aronson (Eds.), *Handbook of social psychology.* Vol. 4. (2nd ed.) Reading, Mass.: Addison-Wesley, 1969.

Miller, G. A. The magical number seven, plus or minus two: Some limits on our capacity for processing information. *Psychological Review,* 1956, *63,* 81–97.

Miller, G. A., Galanter, E., and Pribram, K. H. *Plans and the structure of behavior.* New York: Holt, Rinehart & Winston, 1960.

Miller, G. R., and Hewgill, M. A. Some recent research on fear-arousing message appeals. *Speech Monographs,* 1966, *33,* 377–391.

Miller, N., and Butler, D. Social power and communication in small groups. *Behavioral Science,* 1969, *14,* 11–18.

Miller, N., and Campbell, D. T. Recency and primacy in persuasion as a function of the timing of speeches and measurement. *Journal of Abnormal and Social Psychology,* 1959, *59,* 1–9.

Miller, N. E., and Bugelski, R. Minor studies in aggression: The influence of frustration imposed by the in-group on attitudes expressed toward the out-groups. *Journal of Psychology,* 1948, *25,* 437–442.

Miller, N. E., and Dollard, J. *Social learning and imitation.* New Haven: Yale University Press, 1941.

Millis, W., and Real, J. *The abolition of war.* New York: Macmillan, 1963.

Millon, T., and Simkins, L. D. *Suggestibility of authoritarians and egalitarians to prestige influence.* Paper read at the 65th annual meetings of The American Psychological Association in New York, 1957.

Millon, T., and Simkins, L. D. Suggestibility of authoritarians and egalitarians to prestige influence. Paper read at the 65th Annual Convention of The American Psychological Association in New York, 1957.

Mills, J. Changes in moral attitudes following temptation. *Journal of Personality,* 1958, *26,* 517–531.

Mills, J. Comment on Bem's "Self-perception: An alternative interpretation of cognitive dissonance phenomena." *Psychological Review,* 1967, *74,* 535.

Mills, J., and Aronson, E. Opinion change as a function of the communicator's attractiveness and desire to influence. *Journal of Personality and Social Psychology,* 1965, *1,* 173–177.

Mills, J., and Jellison, J. M. Effect on opinion change of how desirable the communication is to the audience the communicator addressed. *Journal of Personality and Social Psychology,* 1967, *6,* 98–101.

Mills, J., and Jellison, J. M. Effect on opinion change of similarity between the communicator and the audience he addressed. *Journal of Personality and Social Psychology,* 1968, *9,* 153–156.

Minton, H. L. Power and personality. In J. T. Tedeschi (Ed.), *The social influence processes.* Chicago: Aldine, 1972.

Mintz, A. Non-adaptive group behavior. *Journal of Abnormal and Social Psychology,* 1951, *46,* 150–159.

Mischel, W. Theory and research on the antecedents of self-imposed delay of reward. In B. A. Maher (Ed.), *Progress in experimental personality research.* Vol. 3. New York: Academic Press, 1966.

Mischel, W. *Personality and assessment.* New York: Wiley, 1968.

Mischel, W., and Gilligan, C. Delay of gratification, motivation for the prohibited gratification, and responses to temptation. *Journal of Abnormal and Social Psychology,* 1964, *69,* 411–417.

Moeller, G. H., and Applezweig, M. H. A motivational factor in conformity. *Journal of Abnormal and Social Psychology,* 1957, *55,* 116–120.

Montagu, A. *Man and aggression.* New York: Oxford University Press, 1968.

Monteverde, F., Paschke, R., and Tedeschi, J. T. The effectiveness of honesty and deceit as influence tactics. *Sociometry,* 1974, *37,* 583–591.

Moore, S., and Updegraff, R. Sociometric status of preschool children related to age, sex, nurturance-giving, and dependency. *Child Development,* 1964, *35,* 519–524.

Morgan, W. R., and Sawyer, J. Bargaining, expectations, and the preference for equality over equity. *Journal of Personality and Social Psychology,* 1967, *6,* 139–149.

Morgenthau, H. *Politics among nations.* (5th ed.) New York: Knopf, 1969.

Morland, J. K. A comparison of race awareness in northern and southern children. *American Journal of Orthopsychiatry,* 1966, *36,* 22–31.

Morris, D. *The naked ape.* New York: McGraw-Hill, 1967.

Morris, D. *The human zoo.* New York: McGraw-Hill, 1969.

Moscovici, S. Communication processes and the properties of language. In L. Berkowitz (Ed.), *Advances in experimental social psychology.* Vol. 3. New York: Academic Press, 1967.

Moscovici, S., and Faucheux, C. Social influence, conformity bias, and the study of active minorities. In L. Berkowitz (Ed.), *Advances in experimental social psychology.* Vol. 6. New York: Academic Press, 1972. 149–202.

Moscovici, S., and Zavalloni, M. The group as a polarizer of attitudes. *Journal of Personality and Social Psychology,* 1969, *12,* 125–135.

Moscovici, S., Zavalloni, M., and Weinberger, M. Studies on polarization of judgments: II. Person perception. *European Journal of Social Psychology,* 1972, *2,* 92–94.

Mosteller, F., and Wallace, D. L. *Inference and disputed authorship: The Federalist.* Reading, Mass.: Addison-Wesley, 1964.

Mouton, J. S., Blake, R. R., and Olmstead, J. A. The relationship between frequency of yielding and the disclosure of personal identity. *Journal of Personality,* 1956, *24,* 339–347.

Moyer, K. E. A preliminary physiological model of aggressive behavior. In J. P. Scott and B. E. Eleftheriou (Eds.), *The physiology of fighting and defeat.* New York: Plenum Press, 1971.

Muir, D., and Weinstein, E. The social debt: An investigation of lower-class and middle-class norms of social obligation. *American Sociological Review,* 1962, *27,* 532–539.

Murstein, B. I. Physical attractiveness and marital choice. *Journal of Personality and Social Psychology,* 1972, *22,* 8–12.

Mussen, P., Rutherford, E., Harris, S., and Keasey, C. B. Honesty and altruism among preadolescents. *Developmental Psychology,* 1970, *3,* 169–194.

Mussen, P. H., and Rutherford, E. Effects of aggressive cartoons on children's aggressive play. *Journal of Abnormal and Social Psychology,* 1961, *62,* 461–464.

Myers, A. Team competition, success, and the adjustment of group members. *Journal of Abnormal and Social Psychology,* 1962, *65,* 325–332.

Myers, D. G., and Bishop, G. P. Enhancement of dominant attitudes in group discussion. *Journal of Personality and Social Psychology,* 1971, *20,* 386–391.

Nacci, P. Displacement: drive-reduction or equity restoration? Unpublished doctoral dissertation, State University of New York at Albany, 1975.

Nacci, P., and Tedeschi, J. T. A social psychological interpretation of the displacement of aggression literature. Unpublished manuscript. State University of New York at Albany, 1975.

Nadler, E. B. Yielding, authoritarianism, and authoritarian ideology, regarding groups. *Journal of Abnormal and Social Psychology,* 1959, *58,* 408–410.

Nagel, E. *The structure of science.* New York: Harcourt, Brace & World, 1961.

Naipaul, V. S. *An area of darkness.* New York: Macmillan, 1964.

Nakamura, C. Y. Conformity and problem-solving. *Journal of Abnormal and Social Psychology,* 1958, *56,* 315–320.

Nemeth, C. Effects of free versus constrained behavior on attraction between people. *Journal of Personality and Social Psychology,* 1970, *15,* 302–313.

Nevins, A. *Ford: The times, the man, the company.* New York: Schribners, 1954.

Nevins, A., and Hill, F. E. *Ford: decline and rebirth 1933-1962.* New York: Schribners, 1962.

Newcomb, T. M. *Personality and social change: Attitude formation in a student community.* New York: Dryden, 1943.

Newcomb, T. M. *Social psychology.* New York: Dryden, 1950.

Newcomb, T. M. Attitude development as a function of reference groups: The Bennington study. In E. E. Maccoby, T. M. Newcomb, and E. L. Hartley (Eds.), *Readings in social psychology*. (3rd ed.) New York: Holt, Rinehart, & Winston, 1958.

Newcomb, T. M. Individual systems of orientation. In S. Koch (Ed.), *Psychology: A study of a science*. Vol. 3. New York: McGraw-Hill, 1959.

Newcomb, T. M. *The acquaintance process*. New York: Holt, Rinehart, & Winston, 1961.

Newcomb, T. M. Interpersonal balance. In R. P. Abelson, et al. (Eds.), *Theories of cognitive consistency: A sourcebook*. Chicago: Rand McNally, 1968.

Newcomb, T. M., Koenig, K. E., Flacks, R., and Warwick, D. P. *Persistence and change: Bennington College and its students after twenty-five years*. New York: Wiley, 1967.

Nickerson, D., and Newhall, S. M. A psychological color solid. *Journal of the Optical Society of America*, 1943, *33*, 419–422.

Nieburg, H. L. *Political violence: The behavioral process*. New York: St. Martin's Press, 1969.

Nielsen, G. *Studies in self confrontation*. Copenhagen: Munksgaard, 1962.

Nisbett, R. E., Caputo, C., Legant, P., and Marecek, J. Behavior as seen by the actor and as seen by the observer. *Journal of Personality and Social Psychology*, 1973, *27*, 154–164.

Nisbett, R. E., and Schachter, S. Cognitive manipulation of pain. *Journal of Experimental Social Psychology*, 1966, *2*, 227–236.

Nord, W. R. Social exchange theory: An integrative approach to social conformity. *Psychological Bulletin*, 1969, *71*, 174–208.

Norfleet, B. Interpersonal relations and group productivity. *Journal of Social Issues*, 1948, *4*, 66–69.

Norman, W. T. Toward an adequate taxonomy of personality attributes: Replicated factor structure in peer nomination personality ratings. *Journal of Abnormal and Social Psychology*, 1963, *66*, 574–583.

Nothman, F. H. The influence of response conditions on recognition thresholds for tabu words. *Journal of Abnormal and Social Psychology*, 1962, *65*, 154–161.

Novak, D. W., and Lerner, M. J. Rejection as a consequence of perceived similarity. *Journal of Personality and Social Psychology*, 1968, *9*, 147–152.

Nye, F. I. *Family relations and delinquent behavior*. New York: Wiley, 1958.

O'Connor, R. D. Relative efficacy of modeling, shaping, and the combined procedures for modification of social withdrawal. *Journal of Abnormal Psychology*, 1972, *79*, 327–334.

Ofshe, L., and Ofshe, R. *Utility and choice in social interaction*. Englewood Cliffs, N. J.: Prentice-Hall, 1970.

Orne, M. T. On the social psychology of the psychological experiment: With particular reference to demand characteristics and their implications. *American Psychologist*, 1962, *17*, 776–783.

Orne, M. T. Demand characteristics and the concept of quasi-controls. In R. Rosenthal and R. L. Rosnow (Eds.), *Artifacts in behavioral research*. New York: Academic Press, 1969.

Orne, M. T., and Evans, F. J. Social control in the psychological experiment: Antisocial behavior and hypnosis. *Journal of Personality and Social Psychology*, 1965, *1*, 189–200.

Osborn, A. F. *Applied imagination*. New York: Scribners, 1957.

Osgood, C. E. *An alternative to war or surrender*. Urbana: University of Illinois Press, 1962.

Osgood, C. E. Semantic differential technique in the comparative study of cultures. *American Anthropoligist*, 1964, *66*, 171–200.

Osgood, C. E., Suci, G. J., and Tannenbaum, P. H. *The measurement of meaning*. Urbana: University of Illinois Press, 1957.

Osgood, C. E., and Tannenbaum, P. H. The principle of congruity in the prediction of attitude change. *Psychological Review*, 1955, *62*, 42–55.

Oskamp, S., and Hartry, A. A factor-analytic study of the double standard in attitudes toward U. S. and Russian actions. *Behavioral Science*, 1968, *13*, 178–188.

Oskamp, S., and Perlman, D. Effects of friendship and disliking on cooperation in a mixed-motive game. *Journal of Conflict Resolution*, 1966, *10*, 221–226.

Overmier, J. B., and Seligman, M. E. P. Effects of inescapable shock upon subsequent escape and avoidance responding. *Journal of Comparative and Physiological Psychology*, 1967, *63*, 28–33.

Packard, V. D. *The hidden persuaders*. New York: David McKay, 1957.

Page, M. M. Demand awareness, subject sophistication, and the effectiveness of a verbal "reinforcement." *Journal of Personality*, 1970, *38*, 287–301.

Page, M. M., and Scheidt, R. J. The elusive weapons effect: Demand awareness, evaluation apprehension and slightly sophisticated subjects. *Journal of Personality and Social Psychology*, 1971, *20*, 304–318.

Pallack, M. S. Effects of expected shock and relevant or irrelevant dissonance on incidental retention. *Journal of Personality and Social Psychology*, 1970, *14*, 271–280.

Palmore, E. B. The introduction of Negroes into white departments. *Human Organization*, 1955, *14*, 27–28.

Palola, E. G., Dorpat, T. L., and Larsen, W. R. Alcoholism and suicidal behavior. In D. J. Pittman, and C. R. Snyder (Eds.), *Society, culture, and drinking patterns*. New York: Wiley, 1962.

Parsons, R. Family structure and the socialization of the child. In T. Parsons and R. F. Bales (Eds.), *Family*, socialization, and interaction process. New York: Free Press, 1955.

Parsons, T. The social system. Glencoe, Ill.: Free Press, 1951.

Parsons, T. On the concept of influence. Public Opinion Quarterly, 1963, 27, 37–62.

Passini, F. T., and Norman, W. T. A universal conception of personality structure? Journal of Personality and Social Psychology, 1966, 4, 44–49.

Pastore, N. The role of arbitrariness in the frustration-aggression hypothesis. Journal of Abnormal and Social Psychology, 1952, 47, 728–731.

Pavlov, I. P. The work of the digestive glands. London: Griffin, 1902.

Peirce, C. S. The fixation of belief. In M. H. Fisch (Ed.), Classic American philosophers. New York: Appleton-Century-Crofts, 1951. (Originally published in Popular Science Monthly, 1877.)

Pepitone, A. Motivational effects in social perception. Human Relations, 1949, 3, 57–76.

Pepitone, A. Social psychological processes in the generation of violence. Paper read at the meeting of the American Association for the Advancement of Science, Philadelphia, December, 1971.

Pepitone, A., and Kleiner, R. The effects of threat and frustration on group cohesiveness. Journal of Abnormal and Social Psychology, 1957, 54, 192–199.

Pepitone, A., McCauley, C., and Hammond, P. Change in attractiveness of forbidden toys as a function of severity of threat. Journal of Experimental Social Psychology, 1967, 3, 221–229.

Pepitone, A., and Sherberg, J. Intentionality, responsibility, and interpersonal attraction. Journal of Personality, 1957, 25, 757–766.

Pessin, J. The comparative effects of social and mechanical stimulation on memorizing. American Journal of Psychology, 1933, 45, 263–270.

Peterson, P. D., and Koulack, D. Attitude change as a function of latitudes of acceptance and rejection. Journal of Personality and Social Psychology, 1969, 11, 309–311.

Petrunkevitch, A. The spider and the wasp. In Twentieth-Century Bestiary, New York: Simon & Schuster, 1955.

Phares, E. J. Expectancy changes in skill and chance situations. Journal of Abnormal and Social Psychology, 1957, 54, 339–342.

Phares, E. J. Differential utilization of information as a function of internal-external control. Journal of Personality, 1968, 36, 649–662.

Piaget, J. The language and thought of the child. New York: Harcourt, Brace, 1926.

Piaget, J. The origins of intelligence in children. New York: International Universities Press, 1952.

Piaget, J. The moral judgment of the child. (Orig. Pub. 1932) New York: Free Press, 1966.

Piaget, J., and Inhelder, B. The child's conception of space. London: Routledge & Paul, 1956.

Piccolino, E. B. Depicted threat, realism, and specificity, variables governing safety poster effectiveness. Unpublished doctoral dissertation, Illinois Institute of Technology, 1966.

Piliavin, I. M., Hardyck, J. A., and Vadum, A. C. Constraining effects of personal costs on the transgressions of juveniles. Journal of Personality and Social Psychology, 1968, 10, 227–231.

Piliavin, J. A., Piliavin, I. M., Lowenton, E. P., McCauley, C., and Hammon, P. On observer's reproductions of dissonance effects: The right answers for the wrong reasons? Journal of Personality and Social Psychology, 1969, 13, 98–106.

Piliavin, I. M., Rodin, J., and Piliavin, J. A. Good samaritanism: An underground phenomenon? Journal of Personality and Social Psychology, 1969, 13, 289–299.

Piliavin, I. M., Vadum, A. C., and Hardyck, J. A. Delinquency, personal cost, and parental treatment: A test of a cost-reward model of juvenile criminality. Journal of Criminal Law, Criminology, and Police Science, 1969, 60, 165–172.

Pilisuk, M., Potter, P., Rapoport, A., and Winter, J. A. War hawks and peace doves: Alternate resolutions of experimental conflicts. Journal of Conflict Resolution, 1965, 9, 491–508.

Pisano, R., and Taylor, S. P. Reduction of physical aggression: The effects of four strategies. Journal of Personality and Social Psychology, 1971, 19, 237–242.

Plant, W. T., Telford, C. W., and Thomas, J. A. Some personality differences between dogmatic and non-dogmatic groups. Journal of Social Psychology, 1965, 67, 67–75.

Platt, E. S. Internal-external control and changes in expected utility as predictors of the change in cigarette smoking following role playing. Paper presented at the meeting of the Eastern Psychological Association, Philadelphia, April, 1969.

Plotnick, R., and Delgado, M. M. R. Aggression and pain in unrestrained rhesus monkeys. Paper presented at the AAAS symposium on the physiology of fighting and defeat, Dallas, Texas, December, 1968.

Podell, J. E., and Knapp, W. M. The effect of mediation on the perceived firmness of the opponent. Journal of Conflict Resolution, 1969, 13, 511–520.

Polanyi, M. The tacit dimension. Garden City, N. Y.: Doubleday, 1966.

Pomeroy, W. J. Guerrilla and counter-guerrilla warfare. New York: International Publishers, 1964.

Postman, L., Bronson, W. C., and Gropper, G. L. Is there a mechanism of perceptual defense? Journal of Abnormal and Social Psychology, 1953, 48, 215–224.

Postman, L., Bruner, J. S., and McGinnies, E. Personal values as selective factors in perception. *Journal of Abnormal and Social Psychology*, 1948, *43*, 142–154.

Powell, F. A. Open- and closed-mindedness and the ability to differentiate source and message. *Journal of Abnormal and Social Psychology*, 1962, *65*, 61–64.

Powell, F. A., and Miller, G. R. Social approval and disapproval cues in anxiety-arousing communications. *Speech Monographs*, 1967, *34*, 152–159.

Premack, D. Language in chimpanzee? *Science*, 1971, *172*, 808–822.

Price, K. O., Harburg, E., and Newcomb, T. M. Psychological balance in situations of negative interpersonal attitudes. *Journal of Personality and Social Psychology*, 1966, *3*, 265–270.

Proshansky, H. M., Ittleson, W. H., and Rivlin, L. G. *Environmental psychology*. New York: Holt, Rinehart, & Winston, 1970.

Pruitt, D. G. *Problem solving in the Department of State*. University of Denver Social Science Foundation and Department of International Relations. Modern Series in World Affairs, November, 1964.

Pruitt, D. G. Definition of the situation as a determinant of international action. In H. C. Kelman (Ed.), *International behavior: A social psychological analysis*. New York: Holt, Rinehart, & Winston, 1965.

Pruitt, D. G. Reciprocity and credit building in a laboratory dyad. *Journal of Personality and Social Psychology*, 1968, *8*, 143–147.

Pruitt, D. G. The "Walter Mitty" effect in individual and group risk-taking. *Proceedings of the 77th Annual Convention of the American Psychological Association*, 1969, *4*, 425–426.

Pruitt, D. G. Indirect communication and the search for agreement in negotiation. *Journal of Applied Social Psychology*, 1971, *1*, 205–239. (a)

Pruitt, D. G. Choice shifts in group discussion: An introductory review. *Journal of Personality and Social Psychology*, 1971, *20*, 339–360. (b)

Pruitt, D. G. Methods for resolving differences of interest: A theoretical analysis. *Journal of Social Issues*, 1972, *28*, 133–154.

Pruitt, D. G., and Drews, J. L. The effect of time pressure, time elapsed, and the opponent's concession rate on behavior in negotiation. *Journal of Experimental Social Psychology*, 1969, *5*, 43–60.

Pruitt, D., and Gahagan, J. P. Campus crisis. In J. T. Tedeschi (Ed.), *Perspectives on social power*. Chicago: Aldine, 1974.

Pruitt, D. G., and Johnson, D. F. Mediation as an aid to face saving in negotiation. *Journal of Personality and Social Psychology*, 1970, *14*, 239–246.

Pruitt, D. G., and Teger, A. I. The risky shift in group betting. *Journal of Experimental Social Psychology*, 1969, *5*, 115–126.

Psathas, G., and Stryker, S. Bargaining behavior and orientation in coalition formation. *Sociometry*, 1965, *28*, 124–144.

Pudovkin, V. I. *Film technique and film acting*. London: Vision, 1954.

Pyle, E. *Here is your war*. New York: Harcourt, Brace & World, 1945.

Rabow, J., Fowler, F. H. Jr., Bradford, D. L., Hofeller, M. S., and Shibuya, Y. The role of social norms and leadership in risk-taking. *Sociometry*, 1966, *29*, 16–27.

Radloff, R. Opinion evaluation and affiliation. *Journal of Abnormal and Social Psychology*, 1961, *62*, 578–585.

Radloff, R., and Helmreich, R. *Groups under stress: Psychological research in SEALAB II*. New York: Appleton-Century-Crofts, 1968.

Ransford, H. E. Isolation, powerlessness, and violence: A study of attitudes and participation in the Watts riot. *American Journal of Sociology*, 1968, *73*, 581–591.

Raper, A. *The tragedy of lynching*. Chapel Hill: University of North Carolina Press, 1933.

Raser, J. R. Personal characteristics of political decision-makers: A literature review. *Papers, Peace Research Society* (International), 1966, *5*, 161–182.

Rasmussen, C., and Zander, A. Group membership and self-evaluation. *Human Relations*, 1954, *7*, 239–251.

Raven, B. H. Social influence and power. In I. D. Steiner and M. Fishbein (Eds.), *Current studies in social psychology*. New York: Holt, 1965.

Raven, B. H., and French, J. R. P. Group support, legitimate power and social influence. *Journal of Personality*, 1958, *26*, 400–409. (a)

Raven, B. H., and French, J. R. P. Legitimate power, coercive power, and observability in social influence. *Sociometry*, 1958, *21*, 83–97. (b)

Regan, D. T. Effects of a favor and liking on compliance. *Journal of Experimental Social Psychology*, 1971, *7*, 627–639.

Rettig, S. An exploratory study of altruism. *Dissertation Abstracts*, 1956, *16*, 2229–2230.

Rettig, S., and Pasamanick, B. Differential judgment of ethical risk by cheaters and noncheaters. *Journal of Abnormal and Social Psychology*, 1964, *69*, 109–113.

Richardson, L. F. *Statistics of deadly quarrels*. Pittsburgh: Boxwood, 1960.

Riecken, H. W. The effect of talkativeness on ability to influence group solutions of problems. *Sociometry*, 1958, *21*, 309–321.

Riker, W. The nature of trust. In J. T. Tedeschi (Ed.), *Perspectives on social power*. Chicago: Aldine, 1974.

Ring, K., and Kelley, H. H. A comparison of augmentation and reduction as modes of influence. *Journal of Abnormal and Social Psychology*, 1963, *66*, 95–102.

Ritchie, E., and Phares, E. J. Attitude change as a function of internal-external control and communicator status. *Journal of Personality*, 1969, *37*, 429–443.

Rittle, R. H., and Cottrell, N. B. Cognitive bias in the perception of interpersonal relations. *Psychonomic Science*, 1967, *9*, 551–552.

Rivera, A. N., Gaes, G. G., and Tedeschi, J. T. Determinants of perceived altruism. Unpublished manuscript, State University of New York at Albany, 1975.

Robinson, B. W. Summary of symposium, the physiology of fighting and defeat. Presented at the American Association for the Advancement of Science, Dallas, Texas, December, 1968.

Robinson, J. P., and Bachman, J. G. Television viewing habits and aggression. In G. A. Comstock and E. A. Rubinstein (Eds.), *Television and social behavior. Vol. III: Television and adolescent aggressiveness*. Washington, D. C.: U. S. Government Printing Office, 1972.

Roethlisberger, F. J., and Dickson, W. J. *Management and the worker*. Cambridge, Mass.: Harvard University Press, 1939.

Rogers, R. W., and Thistlethwaite, D. L. Effects of fear arousal and reassurance on attitude change. *Journal of Personality and Social Psychology*, 1970, *15*, 227–233.

Rokeach, M. Belief versus race as determinants of social distance: Comment on Triandis' paper. *Journal of Abnormal and Social Psychology*, 1961, *62*, 187–188.

Rokeach, M. *Beliefs, attitudes, and values*. San Francisco: Jossey-Bass, 1968.

Rokeach, M., and Kliejunas, P. Behavior as a function of attitude-toward-object and attitude-toward-situation. *Journal of Personality and Social Psychology*, 1972, *22*, 194–201.

Rokeach, M., and Rothman, G. The principle of belief congruence and the congruity principle as models of cognitive interaction. *Psychological Review*, 1965, *72*, 128–142.

Rokeach, M., Smith, P. W., and Evans, R. I. Two kinds of prejudice or one? In M. Rokeach (Ed.), *The open and closed mind*. New York: Basic Books, 1960.

Rosen, S., and Tesser, A. On reluctance to communicate undesirable information: The MUM effect. *Sociometry*, 1970, *33*, 253–263.

Rosenau, J. N. *Public opinion and foreign policy*. New York: Random House, 1961.

Rosenbaum, M. E., and Franc, D. E. Opinion change as a function of external commitment and amount of discrepancy from the opinion of another. *Journal of Abnormal and Social Psychology*, 1960, *61*, 15–20.

Rosenbaum, M. E., and Levin, I. P. Impression formation as a function of source credibility and order of presentation of contradictory information. *Journal of Personality and Social Psychology*, 1968, *10*, 167–174.

Rosenbaum, M. E., and Zimmerman, I. M. The effect of external commitment on responses to an attempt to change opinions. *Public Opinion Quarterly*, 1959, *23*, 247–254.

Rosenberg, L. A. Group size, prior experience, and conformity. *Journal of Abnormal and Social Psychology*, 1961, *63*, 436–437.

Rosenberg, M. J. Cognitive structure and attitudinal affect. *Journal of Abnormal and Social Psychology*, 1956, *53*, 367–373.

Rosenberg, M. J. When dissonance fails: On eliminating evaluation apprehension from attitude measurement. *Journal of Personality and Social Psychology*, 1965, *1*, 18–42.

Rosenberg, M. J. The conditions and consequences of evaluation apprehension. In R. Rosenthal, and R. W. Rosnow (Eds.), *Artifacts in behavioral research*. New York: Academic Press, 1969.

Rosenberg, M. J., Hovland, C. I., McGuire, W. J., Abelson, R. P., and Brehm, J. W. *Attitude organization and change*. New Haven, Conn.: Yale University Press, 1960.

Rosenfeld, H. M. Effect of an approval-seeking induction on interpersonal proximity. *Psychological Reports*, 1965, *17*, 120–122.

Rosenhan, D. L. Learning theory and prosocial behavior. *Journal of Social Issues*, 1972, *28*, 151–164.

Rosenhan, D., and White, G. M. Observation and rehearsal as determinants of prosocial behavior. *Journal of Personality and Social Psychology*, 1967, *5*, 424–431.

Rosenkrantz, P. S., and Crockett, W. Some factors influencing the assimilation of disparate information in impression formation. *Journal of Personality and Social Psychology*, 1965, *2*, 397–402.

Rosenzweig, S. The experimental situation as a psychological problem. *Psychological Review*, 1933, *40*, 337–354.

Rosenthal, R. Interpersonal expectations: Effects of experimenter's hypothesis. In R. Rosenthal, and R. L. Rosnow (Eds.), *Artifacts in behavioral research*. New York: Academic Press, 1969.

Rosenthal, R. *On the social psychology of the self-fulfilling prophecy: Further evidence for Pygmalion effects and their mediating mechanisms*. New York: MSS Modular Publications, Inc., 1974.

Rosenthal, R., and Fode, K. L. The effect of experimenter bias on the performance of the albino rat. *Behavioral Science*, 1963, *8*, 183–189.

Rosenthal, R., and Jacobson, L. *Pygmalion in the classroom: Teacher expectation and pupil intellectual development*. New York: Holt, Rinehart, & Winston, 1968.

Rosenthal, R., and Rosnow, R. L. The volunteer subject. In R. Rosenthal and R. L. Rosnow (Eds.), *Artifacts in behavioral research*. New York: Academic Press, 1969.

Ross, L., Rodin, J., and Zimbardo, P. G. Toward an attribution therapy: The reduction of fear through induced cognitive-emotional misattribution. *Journal of Personality and Social Psychology*, 1969, *12*, 279–288.

Ross, M., Layton, B., Erickson, B., and Schopler, J. Affect, facial regard, and reactions to crowding. *Journal of Personality and Social Psychology*, 1973, *28*, 69–76.

Ross, M., and Shulman, R. F. Increasing the salience of initial attitudes: Dissonance versus self-perception theory. *Journal of Personality and Social Psychology*, 1973, *28*, 138–144.

Rotter, J. B. *Social learning and clinical psychology.* Englewood Cliffs, N.J.: Prentice-Hall, 1954.

Rotter, J. B. Generalized expectancies for internal versus external control of reinforcement. *Psychological Monographs*, 1966, *80*, (1, Whole No. 609), 1–28.

Rotter, J. B. Beliefs, social attitudes, and behavior: A social learning analysis. In R. Jessor and S. Feshbach (Eds.), *Cognition, personality and clinical psychology.* San Francisco: Jossey-Bass, 1967. (*a*)

Rotter, J. B. A new scale for the measurement of interpersonal trust. *Journal of Personality*, 1967, *35*, 651–655. (*b*)

Rubin, Z. Measurement of romantic love. *Journal of Personality and Social Psychology*, 1970, *16*, 265–273.

Rubin, Z. *Liking and loving.* New York: Holt, Rinehart, & Winston, 1973.

Rubin, Z., and Zajonc, R. B. Structural bias and generalization in the learning of social structures. *Journal of Personality*, 1969, *37*, 310–324.

Rule, B. G., and Hewitt, L. S. Effects of thwarting on cardiac response and physical aggression. *Journal of Personality and Social Psychology*, 1971, *19*, 181–187.

Saegert, S., Swap, W., and Zajonc, R. B. Exposure, content and interpersonal attraction. *Journal of Personality and Social Psychology*, 1973, *25*, 234–242.

St. Jean, R. Reformulation of the value hypothesis in group risk taking. *Proceedings of the 78th Annual Convention of the American Psychological Association*, 1970, *5*, 339–340.

Saitz, R. L., and Cervenka, E. J. *Columbian and North American gestures: An experimental study.* Bogota, Columbia: Centro Colombo Americano, 1962.

Sampson, E. E., and Insko, C. A. Cognitive consistency and performance in the autokinetic situation. *Journal of Abnormal and Social Psychology*, 1964, *68*, 184–192.

Samuel, W. On clarifying some interpretations of social comparison theory. *Journal of Experimental Social Psychology*, 1973, *9*, 450–465.

Sandler, J., and Quagliano, J. Punishment in a signal avoidance situation. Paper read at the Southeastern Psychological Association Meeting, Gatlinburg. Tenn., 1964.

Sapolsky, A. Effect of interpersonal relationships upon verbal conditioning. *Journal of Abnormal and Social Psychology*, 1960, *60*, 241–246.

Sarason, I. G. Interrelationships among individual difference variables, behavior in psychotherapy, and verbal conditioning. *Journal of Abnormal and Social Psychology*, 1958, *56*, 339–344.

Sarbin, T. R., and Coe, W. C. *Hypnosis: A social psychological analysis of influence communication.* New York: Holt, Rinehart, and Winston, 1972.

Sargent, S. S., and Williamson, R. C. *Social psychology: An introduction to the study of human relations.* (2nd ed.) New York: Ronald Press, 1958.

Schachter, S. Deviation, rejection, and communication. *Journal of Abnormal and Social Psychology*, 1951, *46*, 190–207.

Schachter, S. *The psychology of affiliation.* Stanford, Calif.: Stanford University Press, 1959.

Schachter, S. The interaction of cognitive and physiological determinants of emotional state. In L. Berkowitz (Ed.), *Advances in experimental social psychology.* Vol. 1. New York: Academic Press, 1964.

Schachter, S. Cognitive effects on bodily functioning: Studies of obesity and eating. In D. C. Glass (Ed.), *Neurophysiology and emotion.* New York: Rockefeller University Press and the Russell Sage Foundation, 1967.

Schachter, S., and Burdick, H. A field experiment on rumor transmission and distortion. *Journal of Abnormal and Social Psychology*, 1955, *50*, 363–372.

Schachter, S., Goldman, R., and Gordon, A. Effects of fear, food deprivation, and obesity on eating. *Journal of Personality and Social Psychology*, 1968, *10*, 91–97.

Schachter, S., and Gross, L. P. Manipulated time and eating behavior. *Journal of Personality and Social Psychology*, 1968, *10*, 98–106.

Schachter, S., and Singer, J. E. Cognitive, social and physiological determinants of emotional state. *Psychological Review*, 1962, *69*, 379–399.

Schachter, S., and Wheeler, L. Epinephrine, chlorpromazine, and amusement. *Journal of Abnormal and Social Psychology*, 1962, *65*, 121–128.

Schaps, E. Cost, dependency, and helping. *Journal of Personality and Social Psychology*, 1972, *21*, 74–78.

Schattschneider, E. E. *The semi-sovereign people.* New York: Holt, Rinehart, & Winston, 1960.

Schein, E. H. The Chinese indoctrination program for prisoners of war: A study of attempted "brainwashing." In E. E. Maccoby, T. M. Newcomb, and E. L. Hartley (Eds.), *Readings in social psychology.* (3rd ed.) New York: Holt, Rinehart, & Winston, 1958.

Schein, E. H., Schneier, I., and Barker, C. H. *Coercive persuasion.* New York: Norton, 1961.

Schelling, T. C. *The strategy of conflict.* New York: Oxford University Press, 1960.

Schelling, T. C. *Arms and influence.* New Haven: Yale University Press, 1966.

Schlenker, B. R. Liking for a group following an initiation: Impression management or dissonance reduction? *Sociometry,* 1975, *38,* 99–118.

Schlenker, B. R., Bonoma, T. V., Tedeschi, J. T., and Pivnick, W. P. Compliance to threats as a function of the wording of the threat and the exploitativeness of the threatener. *Sociometry,* 1970, *33,* 394–408.

Schlenker, B. R., Brown, Jr., R. C., and Tedeschi, J. T. Attraction and expectation of harm and benefits. *Journal of Personality and Social Psychology,* 1975, *32,* 664–670.

Schlenker, B. R., Helm, B., and Tedeschi, J. T. The effects of personality and situational variables on behavioral trust. *Journal of Personality and Social Psychology,* 1973, *25,* 419–427.

Schlenker, B. R., Nacci, P., Helm, B., and Tedeschi, J. T. Reactions to coercive and reward power: The effects of switching influence modes on target compliance. Unpublished manuscript, University of Florida, 1974.

Schlenker, B. R., and Tedeschi, J. T. Interpersonal attraction and the exercise of reward and coercive power. *Human Relations,* 1972, *25,* 427–439.

Schlosberg, H. The description of facial expressions in terms of two dimensions. *Journal of Experimental Psychology,* 1952, *44,* 229–237.

Schlosberg, H. Three dimensions of emotion. *Psychological Review,* 1954, *61,* 81–88.

Schneider, D. J. Tactical self-presentation after success and failure. *Journal of Personality and Social Psychology,* 1969, *13,* 262–268.

Schopler, J., and Bateson, N. The power of dependence. *Journal of Personality and Social Psychology,* 1965, *2,* 247–254.

Schopler, J., and Compere, J. S. Effects of being kind or harsh to another on liking. *Journal of Personality and Social Psychology,* 1971, *20,* 155–159.

Schopler, J., and Layton, B. D. Attributions of interpersonal power. In J. T. Tedeschi, (Ed.), *Perspectives on social power: The Albany Symposium.* Chicago: Aldine, 1974.

Schopler, J., and Thompson, V. D. Role of attribution processes in mediating amount of reciprocity for a favor. *Journal of Personality and Social Psychology,* 1968, *10,* 243–250.

Schramm, W., Lyle, J., and Parker, E. *Television in the lives of our children.* Stanford, Calif.: Stanford University Press, 1961.

Schroder, H. M., Driver, M. J., and Streufert, S. *Human information processing: Individuals and groups functioning in complex social situations.* New York: Holt, Rinehart, & Winston, 1967.

Schultz, D. P. The human subject in psychological research. *Psychological Bulletin,* 1969, *72,* 214–228.

Schumpeter, J. A. *The theory of economic development.* Cambridge, Mass.: Harvard University Press, 1934.

Schwartz, E. F. Statistics of juvenile delinquency in the United States. *Annals of the American Academy of Political and Social Science,* 1949, *261,* 9–20.

Schwartz, G., Kane, T., Joseph, J., and Tedeschi, J. T. The effects of remorse on reactions to a harm-doer. Unpublished manuscript, State University of New York at Albany, 1974.

Schwartz, S. H. Normative explanations of helping behavior: A critique, proposal, and empirical test. *Journal of Experimental Social Psychology,* 1973, *9,* 349–364.

Schwartz, S. H., and Clausen, G. T. Responsibility, norms, and helping in an emergency. *Journal of Personality and Social Psychology,* 1970, *16,* 299–310.

Schwartz, S. H., and Tessler, R. C. A test of a model for reducing measured attitude-behavior discrepancies. *Journal of Personality and Social Psychology,* 1972, *24,* 225–236.

Scodel, A. Induced collaboration in some non-zero-sum games. *Journal of Conflict Resolution,* 1962, *6,* 335–340.

Scodel, A., and Freedman, M. L. Additional observations on the social perceptions of authoritarians and nonauthoritarians. *Journal of Abnormal and Social Psychology,* 1956, *52,* 92–95.

Scodel, A., and Mussen, P. Social perceptions of authoritarians and nonauthoritarians. *Journal of Abnormal and Social Psychology,* 1953, *48,* 181–184.

Scott, J. P. *Aggression.* Chicago: University of Chicago Press, 1958.

Scott, J. P. The social psychology of infrahuman animals. In G. Lindzey, and E. Aronson (Eds.), *The handbook of social psychology.* Vol. 4. (2nd ed.) Reading, Mass.: Addison-Wesley, 1969.

Scott, J. P. Biology and human aggression. *American Journal of Orthopsychiatry,* 1970, *40,* 568–576.

Scott, J. P., and Fuller, J. L. *Genetics and the social behavior of the dog.* Chicago: University of Chicago Press, 1965.

Sears, P. S. Doll play aggression in normal young children: Influence of sex, age, sibling status, father's absence. *Psychological Monographs,* 1951, *65,* (6, Whole No. 323), 1–42.

Sears, R. R., Maccoby, E. E., and Levin, H. *Patterns of child rearing.* Evanston, Ill.: Row, Peterson, 1957.

Seeman, M. Powerlessness and knowledge: A comparative study of alienation and learning. *Sociometry,* 1967, *30,* 105–123.

Seligman, M. P., and Maier, S. F. Failure to escape traumatic shock. *Journal of Experimental Psychology,* 1967, *74,* 1–9.

Seligman, M. P., Maier, S. F., and Greer, J. H. Alleviation of learned helplessness in the dog. *Journal of Abnormal Psychology*, 1968, *73*, 256–262.

Selltiz, C., and Cook, S. W. Racial attitude as a determinant of judgments of plausibility. *Journal of Social Psychology*, 1966, *70*, 139–147.

Sensenig, J. and Brehm, J. W. Attitude change from an implied threat to attitudinal freedom. *Journal of Personality and Social Psychology*, 1968, *8*, 324–330.

Severin, F. T. *Discovering man in psychology: A humanistic approach.* New York: McGraw-Hill, 1973.

Shaplen, R. *The lost revolution.* New York: Harper & Row, 1965.

Shaw, M. E. A comparison of individuals and small groups in the rational solution of complex problems. *American Journal of Psychology*, 1932, *44*, 491–504.

Shaw, M. E. Some effects of unequal distribution of information upon group performance in various communication nets. *Journal of Abnormal and Social Psychology*, 1954, *49*, 547–553.

Shaw, M. E. Communication networks. In L. Berkowitz (Ed.), *Advances in experimental social psychology.* Vol. 1. New York: Academic Press, 1964.

Shaw, M. E. *Group dynamics: The psychology of small group behavior.* New York: McGraw-Hill, 1971.

Shaw, M. E., and Costanzo, P. R. *Theories of social psychology.* New York: McGraw-Hill, 1970.

Shaw, M. E., Rothschild, G. H., and Strickland, J. F. Decision processes in communication nets. *Journal of Abnormal and Social Psychology*, 1957, *54*, 323–330.

Sheard, M. H., and Flynn, J. P. Facilitation of attack behavior by stimulation of the midbrain of cats. *Brain Research*, 1967, *4*, 324–333.

Sherif, M. *The psychology of social norms.* New York: Harper & Row, 1936.

Sherif, M., and Cantril H. *Psychology of ego-involvements.* New York: Wiley, 1947.

Sherif, M., and Sherif, C. W. *An outline of social psychology.* (Rev. ed.) New York: Harper & Row, 1956.

Shirer, W. L. *The rise and fall of the Third Reich.* New York: Simon & Schuster, 1959.

Shortell, J., Epstein, S., and Taylor, S. P. Instigation to aggression as a function of degree of defeat and the capacity for massive retaliation. *Journal of Personality*, 1970, *38*, 313–328.

Shortell, J. R., and Miller, H. B. Aggression in children as a function of sex of subject and of opponent. *Developmental psychology*, 1970, *3*, 143–144.

Shubik, M. On the study of disarmament and escalation. *Journal of Conflict Resolution*, 1968, *12*, 83–101.

Shure, G. H., Meeker, R. J., and Hansford, E. A. The effectiveness of pacifist strategies in bargaining games. *Journal of Conflict Resolution*, 1965, *9*, 106–117.

Sigall, H., and Aronson, E. Opinion change and the gain-loss of interpersonal attraction. *Journal of Experimental Social Psychology*, 1967, *3*, 178–188.

Sigall, H., and Aronson, E. Liking for an evaluator as a function of her physical attractiveness and nature of the evaluations. *Journal of Experimental Social Psychology*, 1969, *5*, 93–100.

Sigall, H., and Landy, D. Radiating beauty: Effects of having a physically attractive partner on person perception. *Journal of Personality and Social Psychology*, 1973, *28*, 218–225.

Sigall, H., and Page, R. Current stereotypes: A little fading, a little faking. *Journal of Personality and Social Psychology*, 1971, *18*, 247–255.

Silverman, I. Differential effects of ego threat upon persuasibility for high and low self-esteem subjects. *Journal of Abnormal and Social Psychology*, 1964, *69*, 567–572.

Silverman, I., and Kleinman, D. A response deviance interpretation of the effects of experimentally induced frustration on prejudice. *Journal of Experimental Research in Personality*, 1967, *2*, 150–153.

Simmel, G. The number of members as determining the sociological form of the group. *American Journal of Sociology*, 1902, *8*, 1–46, 158–196.

Simmel, G. *The sociology of Georg Simmel.* Translated by Kurt H. Wolff. New York: Glencoe Press, 1950.

Singer, J. D. Threat-perception and the armament-tension dilemma. *Journal of Conflict Resolution*, 1958, *2*, 90–105.

Singer, J. D. International influence: A formal model. *American Political Science Review*, 1963, *57*, 420–430.

Singer, J. L. The influence of violence portrayed in television or motion pictures upon overt aggressive behavior. In J. L. Singer (Ed.), *The control of aggression and violence: Cognitive and physiological factors.* New York: Academic Press, 1971.

Sistrunk, F., and McDavid, J. W. Sex variable in conforming behavior. *Journal of Personality and Social Psychology*, 1971, *17*, 200–207.

Skinner, B. F. *The behavior of organisms: an experimental analysis.* New York: Appleton-Century, Inc., 1938.

Skinner, B. F. Are theories of learning necessary? *Psychological Review*, 1950, *57*, 193–216.

Skinner, B. F. *Science and human behavior.* New York: Macmillan, 1953.

Smelser, N. *Theory of collective behavior.* New York: Free Press, 1963. (*a*)

Smelser, N. J. *The sociology of economic life.* Englewood Cliffs, N. J.: Prentice-Hall, 1963. (*b*)

Smith, C. R., Williams, L., and Willis, R. H. Race, sex, and belief as determinants of friendship acceptance. *Journal of Personality and Social Psychology*, 1967, *5*, 127–137.

Smith, K. H., and Richards, B. Effects of a rational

appeal and of anxiety on conformity behavior. *Journal of Personality and Social Psychology*, 1967, *5*, 122–126.

Smith, R. Restraints on American foreign policy. *Daedalus*, 1962, *91*, 705–716.

Smith, R. B., III., Brown, R. C. Jr., and Tedeschi, J. T. Connotative impressions and predictions of interpersonal behavior. Unpublished manuscript, Georgia State University, 1974.

Smith, W. P. Reward structure and information in the development of cooperation. *Journal of Experimental Social Psychology*, 1968, *4*, 199–223.

Smith, W. P., and Leginski, W. A. Magnitude and precision of punitive power in bargaining strategy. *Journal of Experimental Social Psychology*, 1970, *6*, 57–76.

Snyder, A., Mischel, W., and Lott, B. E. Value, information, and conformity behavior. *Journal of Personality*, 1960, *28*, 333–341.

Snyder, G. H. *Deterrence and defense, toward a theory of national security*. Princeton, N. J.: Princeton University Press, 1961.

Snyder, M., and Ebbesen, E. B. Dissonance awareness: A test of dissonance theory versus self-perception theory. *Journal of Experimental Social Psychology*, 1972, *8*, 502–517.

Snyder, M., and Rothbart, M. Communicator attractiveness and opinion change. *Canadian Journal of Behavioral Science*, 1971, *3*, 377–387.

Solomon, L. The influence of some types of power relationships and game strategies upon the development of interpersonal trust. *Journal of Abnormal and Social Psychology*, 1960, *61*, 223–230.

Sommer, R. *Personal space: The behavioral basis of design*. Englewood Cliffs, N. J.: Prentice-Hall, 1969.

Soskin, W. F., and John, V. P. The study of spontaneous talk. In R. G. Barker (Ed.), *The stream of behavior*. New York: Appleton-Century-Crofts, 1963.

Southwick, C. H. An experimental study of intragroup agonistic behavior in rhesus monkeys (*Macaca mulatta*). *Behavior*, 1967, *28*, 182–209.

Spanos, N. P., and Barber, T. X. Toward a convergence in hypnosis research. *American Psychologist*, 1974, *29*, 500–511.

Spence, J. T., and Spence, K. W. The motivational components of manifest anxiety: Drive and drive stimuli. In C. D. Spielberger (Ed.), *Anxiety and behavior*. New York: Academic Press, 1966.

Spielberger, C. D., DeNike, L .D., and Stein, L. S. Anxiety and verbal conditioning. *Journal of Personality and Social Psychology*, 1965, *1*, 229–239.

Staats, A. W., and Staats, C. K. Attitudes established by classical conditioning. *Journal of Abnormal and Social Psychology*, 1958, *57*, 37–40.

Staines, G. L. The attributional dilemma in social problems: Person versus situation. Unpublished manuscript. University of Michigan, 1972.

Stapleton, R. E. *Interpersonal attraction as a function of observer effects and performance*. Unpublished Doctoral Dissertation, State University of New York at Albany, 1975.

Stapleton, R. E., Joseph, J. M., Efron, B., and Tedeschi, J. T. An empirical reevaluation of the concept of aggression: Labeling behaviors in the competitive reaction time game. Unpublished manuscript, State University of New York at Albany, 1974.

Stapleton, R. E., Nacci, P., and Tedeschi, J. T. Interpersonal attraction and the reciprocation of benefits. *Journal of Personality and Social Psychology*, 1973, *28*, 199–205.

Stapleton, R. E., Nelson, B. L., Franconere, V. T., and Tedeschi, J. T. The effects of harm-doing on interpersonal attraction. *Journal of Social Psychology*, 1975, *96*, 109–120.

Staub, E. A. A child in distress: The influence of nurturance and modeling on children's attempts to help. *Developmental Psychology*, 1971, *5*, 124–132.

Stein, D. D., Hardyck, J. A., and Smith, M. B. Race and belief: An open and shut case. *Journal of Personality and Social Psychology*, 1965, *1*, 281–290.

Stein, K. B., Sarbin, T. R., Chu, C., and Kulik, J. A. Adolescent morality: Its differential structure and relation to delinquent conduct. *Multivariate Behavioral Research*, 1967, *2*, 199–210.

Steiner, I. D. Perceived freedom. In L. Berkowitz (Ed.), *Advances in experimental social psychology*. Vol. 5. New York: Academic Press, 1970.

Steiner, I. D. *Group process and productivity*. New York: Academic Press, 1972.

Steiner, I. D., and Field, W. L. Role assignment and interpersonal influence. *Journal of Abnormal and Social Psychology*, 1960, *61*, 239–246.

Steiner, I. D., and Johnson, H. H. Authoritarianism and "tolerance of trait inconsistency." *Journal of Abnormal and Social Psychology*, 1963, *67*, 388–391.

Steiner, I. D., and Rogers, E. D. Alternative responses to dissonance. *Journal of Abnormal and Social Psychology*, 1963, *66*, 128–136.

Stephenson, G. M., and White, J. H. An experimental study of some effects of injustice on children's moral behavior. *Journal of Experimental Social Psychology*, 1968, *4*, 460–469.

Steuer, F. B., Applefield, J. M., and Smith, R. Televised aggression and interpersonal aggression of preschool children. *Journal of Experimental Child Psychology*, 1971, *11*, 442–447.

Stevenson, H. W. Social reinforcement of children's behavior. In L. P. Lipsitt and C. C. Spiker (Eds.), *Advances in child development*. Vol. II. New York: Academic Press, 1965.

Stevenson, H. W., and Stewart, E. C. A developmental study of racial awareness in young children. *Child Development*, 1958, *29*, 399–410.

Stewart, R. H. Effect of continuous responding on the order effect in personality impression formation. *Journal of Personality and Social Psychology,* 1965, *1,* 161–165.

Stogdill, R. M. Personal factors associated with leadership: A survey of the literature. *Journal of Psychology,* 1948, *25,* 35–71.

Stokols, D. On the distinction between density and crowding: Some implications for future research. *Psychological Review,* 1972, *79,* 275–277.

Stolz, H. R., and Stolz, L. M. *Somatic development of adolescent boys.* New York: Macmillan, 1951.

Stoner, J. A. F. *A comparison of individual and group decisions involving risk.* Unpublished master's thesis, Sloan School of Management, Massachusetts Institute of Technology, 1961.

Storms, M. D. Videotape and the attribution process: Reversing actors' and observers' points of view. *Journal of Personality and Social Psychology,* 1973, *27,* 165–175.

Storms, M .D., and Nisbett, R. E. Insomnia and the attribution process. *Journal of Personality and Social Psychology,* 1970, *16,* 319–328.

Stouffer, S. A., Suchman, E. A., DeVinney, L. C., Star, S. A., and Williams, R. M., Jr. Adjustment during army life. In *Studies in social psychology in World War II.* Vol. 1. *The American soldier.* Princeton, N. J.: Princeton University Press, 1949.

Streufert, S., and Fromkin, H. L. Cognitive complexity and social influence. In J. T. Tedeschi (Ed.), *The social influence processes.* Chicago: Aldine, 1972.

Stricker, L. J., Messick, S., and Jackson, D. N. Conformity, anticonformity, and independence: Their dimensionality and generality. *Journal of Personality and Social Psychology,* 1970, *16,* 494–507.

Strickland, B. R. The prediction of social action from a dimension of internal-external control. *Journal of Social Psychology,* 1965, *66,* 353–358.

Strickland, B. R., and Crowne, D. P. Conformity under conditions of simulated group pressure as a function of the need for social approval. *Journal of Social Psychology,* 1962, *58,* 171–181.

Strickland, L. H. Surveillance and trust. *Journal of Personality,* 1958, *26,* 200–215.

Stroebe, W., Insko, C. A., Thompson, V. D., and Layton, B. D. Effects of physical attractiveness, attitude similarity, and sex on various aspects of interpersonal attraction. *Journal of Personality and Social Psychology,* 1971, *18,* 79–91.

Stroop, J. R. Is the judgment of the group better than that of the average member of the group? *Journal of Experimental Psychology,* 1932, *15,* 550–562.

Sullivan, H. S. *The interpersonal theory of psychiatry.* New York: Norton, 1953.

Summers, G. F., and Hammonds, A. D. Effects of racial characteristics of investigator on self-enumerated responses to a Negro prejudice scale. *Social Forces,* 1966, *44,* 515–518.

Sweeney, E. J. Sex differences in problem solving. Stanford University, Department of Psychology, Technical Report, 1953, No. 1.

Swets, J. A. Is there a sensory threshold? *Science,* 1961, *134,* 168–177.

Swingle, P. G. *Social psychology in natural settings.* Chicago: Aldine, 1973.

Szasz, T. S. *The myth of mental illness: Foundations of a theory of personal conduct.* New York: Harper & Row, 1961.

Taffel, C. Anxiety and the conditioning of verbal behavior. *Journal of Abnormal and Social Psychology,* 1955, *51,* 496–501.

Tannenbaum, P. H. The congruity principle revisited: Studies in the reduction, induction, and generalization of persuasion. In L. Berkowitz (Ed.), *Advances in experimental social psychology.* Vol. 3. New York: Academic Press, 1967.

Tannenbaum, P. H., and Gengel, R. W. Generalization of attitude change through congruity principle relationships. *Journal of Personality and Social Psychology,* 1966, *3,* 299–304.

Tarde, G. *The laws of imitation.* Translated. New York: Holt, 1903.

Taylor, A. J. P. *The origins of the second world war.* Greenwich, Conn.: Fawcett, 1961.

Taylor, D. W., Berry, J. P., and Block, C. N. Does group participation when using brainstorming facilitate or inhibit creative thinking? *Administrative Science Quarterly,* 1958, *3,* 23–47.

Taylor, D. W., and Faust, W. L. Twenty questions: Efficiency in problem solving as a function of size of group. *Journal of Experimental Psychology,* 1952, *44,* 360–368.

Taylor, R. L., and Weiss, A. E. American presidential assassination. In D. H. Daniels, M. F. Gilula, and F. M. Ochberg (Eds.), *Violence and the struggle for existence.* Boston: Little, Brown, 1970.

Taylor, S. P. Aggressive behavior and physiological arousal as a function of provocation and the tendency to inhibit aggression. *Journal of Personality,* 1967, *35,* 297–310.

Taylor, S. P., and Epstein, S. Aggression as a function of the interaction of the sex of the aggressor and the sex of the victim. *Journal of Personality,* 1967, *35,* 474–486.

Tedeschi, J. T. Attributions, liking, and power. In T. Huston (Ed.), *Foundations of interpersonal attraction.* New York: Academic Press, 1974.

Tedeschi, J. T., Bonoma, T. V., and Schlenker, B. R. Influence, decision, and compliance. In J. T. Tedeschi (Ed.), *The social influence processes.* Chicago: Aldine-Atherton, Inc., 1972.

Tedeschi, J. T., Horai, J., Lindskold, S., and Faley, T. The effects of opportunity costs and target compliance on the behavior of a threatening source. *Journal of Experimental Social Psychology*, 1970, *6*, 205–213.

Tedeschi, J. T., Lindskold, S., Horai, J., and Gahagan, J. Social power and the credibility of promises. *Journal of Personality and Social Psychology*, 1969, *13*, 253–261.

Tedeschi, J. T., and O'Donovan, D. Social power and the psychologist. *Professional Psychology*, 1971, *2*, 59–64.

Tedeschi, J. T., Schlenker, B. R., and Bonoma, T. V. Cognitive dissonance: Private ratiocination or public spectacle? *American Psychologist*, 1971, *26*, 685–695.

Tedeschi, J. T., Schlenker, B. R., and Bonoma, T. V. *Conflict, power, and games: The experimental study of interpersonal relations.* Chicago: Aldine, 1973.

Tedeschi, J. T., Schlenker, B. R., and Bonoma, T. V. Compliance to threats as a function of source attractiveness and esteem. *Sociometry*, 1975, *38*, *81*–98.

Tedeschi, J. T., Smith, R. B., III, and Brown, R. C. Jr., A reinterpretation of research on aggression. *Psychological Bulletin*, 1974, *81*, 540–563.

Tedeschi, R. E., Tedeschi, D. H., Muchs, A., Cook, L., Mattis, P. A., and Fellows, E. J. Effects of various centrally acting drugs on fighting behavior of mice. *Journal Pharmacological Experimental Therapy*, 1959, *125*, 28–34.

Teevan, R. C., and McGhee, P. Childhood development of fear of failure motivation. *Journal of Personality and Social Psychology*, 1972, *21*, 345–348.

Teger, A. I. The effect of early cooperation on the escalation of conflict *Journal of Experimental Social Psychology*, 1970, *6*, 187–204.

Teger, A. I., and Pruitt, D. G. Components of group risk taking. *Journal of Experimental Social Psychology*, 1967, *3*, 189–205.

Teger, A. I., Pruitt, D. G., St. Jean, R., and Haaland, G. A re-examination of the familiarization hypothesis in group risk-taking. *Journal of Experimental Social Psychology*, 1970, *6*, 346–350.

Teleki, G. The onmivorous chimpanzee. *Scientific American*, 1973, *228*, 32–42.

Television and growing up: The impact of televised violence. Report to the Surgeon General, United States Public Health Service from the Surgeon General's Scientific Advisory Committee on Television and Social Behavior. Washington: U. S. Department of Health, Education, and Welfare, 1972.

Terwilliger, R. F. *Meaning and mind.* New York: Oxford University Press, 1968.

Tesser, A., Gatewood, R., and Driver, M. Some determinants of gratitude. *Journal of Personality and Social Psychology*, 1968, *9*, 233–236.

Textor, R. B. *A cross-cultural summary.* New Haven: Human Resources Area Files Press, 1967.

Thibaut, J. W., and Coules, J. The role of communication in the reduction of interpersonal hostility. *Journal of Abnormal and Social Psychology*, 1952, *47*, 770–777.

Thibaut, J. W., and Kelley, H. H. *The social psychology of groups.* New York: Wiley, 1959.

Thibaut, J. W., and Riecken, H. W. Some determinants and consequences of the perception of social causality. *Journal of Personality*, 1955, *24*, 113–133. (a)

Thibaut, J. W., and Riecken, H. W. Authoritarianism, status, and the communication of aggression. *Human Relations*, 1955, *8*, 95–120. (b)

Thibaut, J. W., and Strickland, L. H. Psychological set and social conformity. *Journal of Personality*, 1956, *25*, 115–129.

Thomas, E. H., Webb, S., and Tweedie, J. Effects of familiarity with a controversial issue on acceptance of successive persuasive communications. *Journal of Abnormal and Social Psychology*, 1961, *63*, 656–659.

Thomas, W. I. *Primitive behavior: An introduction to the social sciences.* New York: McGraw-Hill, 1937.

Thorndike, E. L. *The elements of psychology.* New York: A. G. Seiler, 1905.

Thornton, T. P. Terror as a weapon of political agitation. In H. Eckstein (Ed.), *Internal war.* Glencoe: The Free Press, 1964.

Tilker, H. A. Socially responsible behavior as a function of observer responsibility and victim feedback. *Journal of Personality and Social Psychology*, 1970, *14*, 95–100.

Tillich, P. *The courage to be.* New Haven: Yale University Press, 1952.

Time. Plows and sacred cows. January 22, 1951, p. 74.

Time. A gun-toting nation. August 12, 1966, *15*.

Tinbergen, N. *Social behavior in animals, with a special reference to vertebrates.* London: Methuen, 1953.

Tinbergen, N. The curious behavior of the stickleback. In *Twentieth-Century bestiary.* New York: Simon & Schuster, 1955.

Tinklenberg, J. R., and Stillman, R. C. Drug use and violence. In D. N. Daniels, M. F. Gilula, and F. M. Ochberg (Eds.), *Violence and the struggle for existence.* Boston: Little, Brown, 1970.

Toch, H. *The social psychology of social movements.* Indianapolis, Indiana: Bobbs-Merrill, 1965.

Toch, H. H. *Violent men: An inquiry in to the psychology of violence.* Chicago: Aldine, 1969.

Toffler, A. *Future shock.* New York: Random House, 1970.

Tolman, E. C. *Purposive behavior in animals and men.* New York: Century, 1932.

Tolman, E. C. Principles of performance. *Psychological Review*, 1955, *62*, 315–326.

Tornatzky, L., and Geiwitz, P. J. The effects of threat

and attraction on interpersonal bargaining. *Psychonomic Science*, 1968, *13*, 125–126.

Torrance, E. P. Some consequences of power differences on decision making in permanent and temporary three-man groups. *Research Studies*, State College of Washington, 1954, *22*, 130–140.

Tracy, J. J., and Cross, H. J. Antecedents of shift in moral judgment. *Journal of Personality and Social Psychology*, 1973, *26*, 238–244.

Travis, L. E. The effect of a small audience upon eye-hand coordination. *Journal of Abnormal and Social Psychology*, 1925, *20*, 142–146.

Triandis, H. C. A note on Rokeach's theory of prejudice. *Journal of Abnormal and Social Psychology*, 1961, *62*, 184–186.

Triandis, H. C., and Fishbein, M. Cognitive interaction in person perception. *Journal of Abnormal and Social Psychology*, 1963, *67*, 446–453.

Triplett, N. The dynamogenic factors in pacemaking and competition. *American Journal of Psychology*, 1897, *9*, 507–533.

Trotsky, L. *History of the Russian revolution.* (Translated by Max Eastman) Vol. 1. New York: Simon & Schuster, 1932.

Trow, D. B. Autonomy and job satisfaction in task-oriented groups. *Journal of Abnormal and Social Psychology*, 1957, *54*, 204–209.

Truax, C. L., Wargo, D. G., Frank, J. D., Imber, S. C., Battle, C. B., Hoehn-Saric, R., Nash, E. H., and Stone, A. R. Therapist empathy, genuineness, and warmth and patient therapeutic outcome. *Journal of Consulting Psychology*, 1966, *30*, 395–401.

Tryon, R. C. Genetic difference in maze learning ability in rats. *Yearbook of the National Society for Studies in Education*, 1940, *1*, 111–119.

Tuchman, B. *The guns of August.* New York: Dell, 1962.

Tuchman, B. W. *Stilwell and the American experience in China 1911–45.* New York: Macmillan, 1971.

Tuddenham, R. D. *Studies in conformity and yielding: VII, some correlates of yielding to a distorted group norm.* Technical Report No. 8, ONR Contract NR 170–159. University of California, Berkeley, 1958.

Tuddenham, R. D. *Studies in conformity and yielding: A summary and interpretation.* Final Report, Office of Naval Research, Contract NR 170-159, University of California, Berkeley, California, 1961.

Turiel, E. An experimental test of the sequentiality of developmental stages in the child's moral judgments. *Journal of Personality and Social Psychology*, 1966, *3*, 611–618.

Turner, R., and Killian, L. M. *Collective behavior.* (2nd ed.) Englewood Cliffs, N. J.: Prentice-Hall, 1972.

Ullman, C. A. *Identification of maladjusted school children. Public Health Monograph, No. 7.* Washington, D. C.: U. S. Government Printing Office, 1957.

Ulrich, R. E., and Azrin, N. H. Reflexive fighting in response to aversive stimulation. *Journal of the Experimental Analysis of Behavior*, 1962, *5*, 511–520.

Underwood, B., Moore, B. S., and Rosenhan, D. L. The effect of mood on children's giving. Unpublished manuscript, Stanford University, 1972.

United Nations Department of Economic and Social Affairs. *Capital punishment.* New York: UNESCO, 1962.

U. S. Department of Transportation. *Alcohol and public safety report.* Washington, D. C.: U. S. Government Printing Office, 1968.

Vail, J. P., and Stuadt, V. M. Attitudes of college students toward marriage and related problems: Dating and mate selection. *Journal of Psychology*, 1950, *30*, 171–182.

Valins, S., and Nisbett, R. E. *Attribution processes in the development and treatment of emotional disorders.* Morristown, N. J.: General Learning Press, 1971.

Vallance, T. R. Social science and social policy: Amoral methodology in a matrix of values. *American Psychologist*, 1972, *27*, 107–113.

Veblen, T. *The theory of the leisure class.* New York: Modern Library, 1934.

Verplanck, W. S. The control of the content of conversation: Reinforcement of statements of opinion. *Journal of Abnormal and Social Psychology*, 1955, *51*, 668–676.

Vidmar, N. Group composition and the risky shift. *Journal of Experimental Social Psychology*, 1970, *6*, 153–166.

Vidulich, R. N., and Kaiman, I. P. The effects of information source status and dogmatism upon conformity behavior. *Journal of Abnormal and Social Psychology*, 1961, *63*, 639–642.

Vinacke, W. E., and Arkoff, A. Experimental study of coalitions in the triad. *American Sociological Review*, 1957, *22*, 406–414.

Vinacke, W. E., Crowell, D. C., Dien, D., and Young, V. The effect of information about strategy on a three-person game. *Behavioral Science*, 1966, *11*, 180–189.

Vinokur, A., and Burnstein, E. Effects of partially shared persuasive arguments on group-induced shifts: *Journal of Personality and Social Psychology*, 1974, *29*, 305–315.

von Frisch, K. *The dancing bees.* New York: Harcourt, Brace, 1955.

Wagner, C., and Wheeler, L. Model, need, and cost effects in helping behavior. *Journal of Personality and Social Psychology*, 1969, *12*, 111–116.

Walker, E. L., and Heyns, R. W. *An anatomy for conformity.* Englewood Cliffs, N. J.: Prentice-Hall, 1962.

Wallace, J., and Sadalla, E. Behavioral consequences

of transgression: I. The effects of social recognition. *Journal of Experimental Research in Personality*, 1966, *1*, 187–194.

Wallach, M. A., and Kogan, N. The roles of information, discussion, and consensus in group risk taking. *Journal of Experimental Social Psychology*, 1965, *1*, 1–19.

Wallach, M. A., Kogan, N., and Bem, D. J. Group influence on individual risk taking. *Journal of Abnormal and Social Psychology*, 1962, *65*, 75–86.

Wallach, M. A., Kogan, N., and Bem, D. J. Diffusion of responsibility and level of risk taking in groups. *Journal of Abnormal and Social Psychology*, 1964, *68*, 263–274.

Wallach, M. A., Kogan, N., and Burt, R. Can group members recognize the effects of group discussion upon risk taking? *Journal of Experimental Social Psychology*, 1965, *1*, 379–395.

Wallach, M. A., and Wing, C. W., Jr. Is risk a value? *Journal of Personality and Social Psychology*, 1968, *9*, 101–106.

Waller, W. The rating and dating complex. *American Sociological Review*, 1937, *2*, 727–737.

Walls, R. T., and Smith, T. S. Development of preference for delayed reinforcement in disadvantaged children. *Journal of Educational Psychology*, 1970, *61*, 118–123.

Walster, E. The temporal sequence of post-decision processes. In L. Festinger (Ed.), *Conflict, decision, and dissonance.* Stanford: Stanford University Press, 1964.

Walster, E. The effect of self-esteem on liking for dates of various social desirabilities. *Journal of Experimental Social Psychology*, 1970, *6*, 248–253.

Walster, E. Passionate love. In B. I. Murstein (Ed.), *Theories of attraction and love.* New York: Springer, 1971.

Walster, E., and Abrahams, D. Interpersonal attraction and social influence. In J. T. Tedeschi (Ed.), *The social influence processes.* Chicago: Aldine, 1972.

Walster, E., Aronson, E., and Abrahams, D. On increasing the persuasiveness of a low prestige communicator. *Journal of Experimental Social Psychology*, 1966, *2*, 325–342.

Walster, E., Aronson, V., Abrahams, D., and Rottman, L. Importance of physical attractiveness in dating behavior. *Journal of Personality and Social Psychology*, 1966, *4*, 508–516.

Walster, E., Berscheid, E., and Barclay, A. M. A determinant of preference among modes of dissonance reduction. *Journal of Personality and Social Psychology*, 1967, *7*, 211–216.

Walster, E., Berscheid, E., and Walster, G. W. New directions in equity research. *Journal of Personality and Social Psychology*, 1973, *25*, 151–176.

Walster, E., and Festinger, L. The effectiveness of

'overheard' persuasive communications. *Journal of Abnormal and Social Psychology*, 1962, *65*, 395–402.

Walters, R. H., and Brown, M. Studies of reinforcement of aggression: III. Transfer of responses to an interpersonal situation. *Child Development*, 1963, *34*, 536–571.

Walters, R. H., Leat, M., and Mazei, L. Inhibition and disinhibition of responses through empathetic learning. *Canadian Journal of Psychology*, 1963, *17*, 235–243.

Walters, R. H., and Ray, E. Anxiety, social isolation, and reinforcer effectiveness. *Journal of Personality*, 1960, *28*, 358–367.

Walton, R. E., and McKersie, R. B. *A behavioral theory of labor negotiations.* New York: McGraw-Hill, 1965.

Waly, P., and Cook, S. W. Effect of attitude on judgments of plausibility. *Journal of Personality and Social Psychology*, 1965, *2*, 745–749.

Waples, D., Berelson, B., and Bradshaw, F. R. *What reading does to people.* Chicago: University of Chicago Press, 1940.

Ward, C. D. Ego-involvement and the absolute judgment of attitude statements. *Journal of Personality and Social Psychology*, 1965, *2*, 202–208.

Warner, L. G., and DeFleur, M. L. Attitude as an interactional concept: Social constraint and social distance as intervening variables between attitudes and action. *American Sociological Review*, 1969, *34*, 153–169.

Warr, P. B., and Sims, A. A study of cojudgment processes. *Journal of Personality*, 1965, *33*, 598–604.

Waterman, C. K. The facilitating and interfering effects of cognitive dissonance on simple and complex paired associates learning tasks. *Journal of Experimental Social Psychology*, 1969, *5*, 31–42.

Waterman, C. K., and Katkin, E. S. The energizing (dynamogenic) effect of cognitive dissonance on task performance. *Journal of Personality and Social Psychology*, 1967, *6*, 126–131.

Watson, R. I., Jr. Investigation into deindividuation using a cross-cultural survey technique. *Journal of Personality and Social Psychology*, 1973, *25*, 342–345.

Webb, E. J., Campbell, D. T., Schwartz, R. D., and Sechrest, L. *Unobtrusive measures: Nonreactive research in the social sciences.* Chicago: Rand McNally, 1966.

Weber, M. *The protestant ethic and the spirit of capitalism,* New York: Scribner, 1958.

Weber, S. J., and Cook, T. D. Subject effects in laboratory research: An examination of subject roles, demand characteristics, and valid inference. *Psychological Bulletin*, 1972, *77*, 273–295.

Wedge, B. M. *Visitors to United States and how they see us.* Princeton: Van Nostrand, 1965.

Weiner, B., Frieze, I., Kukla, A., Reed, I., Rest, S. A., and Rosenbaum, R. M. Perceiving the causes of success and failure. In E. E. Jones, D. E. Kanouse, H. H. Kelley, R. E. Nisbett, S. Valins, and B. Weiner (Eds.), *Attribution: Perceiving the causes of behavior.* Morristown, N. J.: General Learning Press, 1971.

Weiner, H., and McGinnies, E. Authoritarianism, conformity, and confidence in a perceptual judgment situation. *Journal of Social Psychology,* 1961, *55,* 77–84.

Weiss, R. F., Weiss, J. J., and Chalupa, L. M. Classical conditioning of attitudes as a function of source consensus. *Psychonomic Science,* 1967, *9,* 465–466.

Weiss, W. Opinion congruence with a negative source of one issue as a factor influencing agreement on another issue. *Journal of Abnormal and Social Psychology,* 1957, *54,* 180–186.

Weiss, W. Effects of the mass media of communication. In G. Lindzey and E. Aronson, (Eds.), *Handbook of social psychology.* Vol. 5. (2nd ed.) Reading, Mass.: Addison-Wesley, 1969.

Welker, W. I. An analysis of exploratory and play behavior in animals. In D. W. Fiske and S. R. Maddi (Eds.), *Functions of varied experience.* Homewood, Ill.: Dorsey, 1961.

Wells, W. D. Television and aggression: A replication of an experimental field study. University of Chicago: Mimeographed manuscript, 1972.

Wells, W. D., Weinert, G., and Rubel, M. Conformity pressure and authoritarian personality. *Journal of Psychology,* 1956, *42,* 133–136.

Westermarck, E. A. *The origin and development of the moral ideas.* Vol. 2. London: Macmillan, 1906.

Wheeler, L., Shaver, K. G., Jones, R. A., Goethals, G. R., Cooper, J., Robinson, J. E., Gruder, C. L., and Butzine, K. W. Factors determining choice of a comparison other. *Journal of Experimental Social Psychology,* 1969, *5,* 219–232.

White, B. J., Alter, R. D., and Rardin, M. Authoritarianism, dogmatism, and usage of conceptual categories. *Journal of Personality and Social Psychology,* 1965, *2,* 293–295.

White, G. M. The elicitation and durability of altruistic behavior in children. *Research Bulletin,* 67–27. Princeton, N. J.: Educational Testing Service, 1967.

White, L. A. *The science of culture: A study of man and civilization.* New York: Farrar, Straus, 1949.

White, R. K. Images in the context of international conflict: Soviet perceptions of the U. S. and the U. S. S. R. In H. C. Kelman (Ed.) *International behavior: A social-psychological analysis.* New York: Holt, Rinehart & Winston, 1965.

White, R. K. "Socialism" and "capitalism:" An international misunderstanding. *Foreign Affairs,* 1966, *44,* 216–228.

White, R. W. A preface to the theory of hypnotism. *Journal of Abnormal and Social Psychology,* 1941, *36,* 477–505.

White, R. W. Motivation reconsidered: The concept of competence. *Psychological Review,* 1959, *66,* 297–333.

White, W. S. Trying to find the shape—if any—of the news in Washington. *Harper's Magazine,* August, 1958. 76–80.

Whittaker, D., and Watts, W. A. Personality characteristics of a nonconformist youth subculture: A study of the Berkeley non-student. *Journal of Social Issues,* 1969, *25,* 65–89.

Whorf, B. L. *Language, thought, and reality.* Cambridge, Mass.: MIT Press, 1956.

Whyte, W. H. Jr., *The organization man.* New York: Simon & Schuster, 1956.

Wicker, A. W. Attitudes versus actions: The relationship of verbal and overt behavioral responses to attitude objects. *Journal of Social Issues,* 1969, *25,* 41–78. *(a)*

Wicker, A. W. Size of church membership and members' support of church behavior settings. *Journal of Personality and Social Psychology,* 1969, *13,* 278–288. *(b)*

Wicklund, R. A. Prechoice preference reversal as a result of threat to decision freedom. *Journal of Personality and Social Psychology,* 1970, *14,* 8–17.

Wiener, M., Devoe, S., Rubinow, S., and Geller, J. Nonverbal behavior and nonverbal communications. *Psychological Review,* 1972, *79,* 185–214.

Wilke, H., and Lanzetta, J. T. The obligation to help: The effects of amount of prior help on subsequent helping behavior. *Journal of Experimental Social Psychology,* 1970, *6,* 488–493.

Willerman, B., and Swanson, L. Group prestige in voluntary organizations: A study of college sororities. *Human Relations,* 1953, *6,* 57–77.

Williams, R. M. The reduction of intergroup tensions. *Social Science Research Council Bulletin,* No. 57, 1947.

Willis, R. H. Conformity, independence, and anticonformity. *Human Relations,* 1965, *18,* 373–388.

Wilson, E. O. Animal communication. In *Communication.* San Francisco: Freeman, 1972.

Winch, R. F., Ktsanes, T., and Ktsanes, V. The theory of complementary needs in mate selection: An analytic and descriptive study. *American Sociological Review,* 1954, *19,* 241–249.

Windes, R. R., Jr. A study of effective and ineffective Presidential campaign speeches. *Speech Monographs,* 1961, *28,* 39–49.

Winterbottom, M. The relation of need for achievement to learning experiences in independence and mastery. In J. W. Atkinson (Ed.), *Motives in fantasy, action, and society.* Princeton, N. J.: Van Nostrand, 1958.

Wishner, J. Reanalysis of "impressions of personality." *Psychological Review,* 1960, *67,* 96–112.

Wispé, L. G., and Drambareen, N. C. Physiological need, work frequency, and visual duration thresholds. *Journal of Experimental Psychology*, 1953, *46*, 25–31.

Wispé, L. G., and Freshley, H. B. Race, sex, and sympathetic helping behavior: The broken bag caper. *Journal of Personality and Social Psychology*, 1971, *17*, 59–65.

Wolfgang, M. E., and Ferracuti, F. *The subculture of violence*. London: Tavistock, 1967.

Wolfgang, M. E., and Strohm, R. B. The relationship between alcohol and criminal homicide. *Quarterly Journal of Studies in Alcohol*, 1956, *17*, 411–425.

Womack, W. M., and Wagner, N. N. Negro interviewers and white patients. *Archives of General Psychiatry*, 1967, *16*, 685–692.

Worchel, P., and McCormick, B. L. Self-concept and dissonance reduction. *Journal of Personality*, 1963, *31*, 588–599.

World Almanac. New York: Newspaper Enterprise Association, 1974.

Wrightsman, L. S, Personality and attitudinal correlates of trusting and trustworthy behaviors in a two-person game. *Journal of Personality and Social Psychology*, 1966, *4*, 328–332.

Wrightsman, L. S. Wallace supporters and adherence to "law and order." *Journal of Personality and Social Psychology*, 1969, *13*, 17–22.

Wyer, R. S., Jr., and Lyon, J. D. A test of cognitive balance theory implications for social inference processes. *Journal of Personality and Social Psychology*, 1970, *16*, 598–618.

Wylie, R. C. *The self concept: A critical survey of pertinent research literature*. Lincoln, Nebraska: University of Nebraska Press, 1961.

Yang, M. *Chinese village*. New York: Columbia University Press, 1945.

Yarrow, L. The effects of antecedent frustration on projective play. *Psychological Monographs*. 1948, *62*, (6, Whole No. 293).

Yarrow, M. R., and Scott, P. M. Imitation of nurturant and nonnurturant models. *Journal of Personality and Social Psychology*, 1972, *23*, 259–270.

Yaryan, R. B., and Festinger, L. Preparatory action and the belief in the probable occurrence of future events. *Journal of Abnormal and Social Psychology*, 1961, *63*, 603–606.

Yutang, L. *The wisdom of China and India*. New York: Random House, 1942.

Zajonc, R. B. *Cognitive structure and cognitive tuning*. Unpublished doctoral dissertation. University of Michigan, 1954.

Zajonc, R. Social facilitation. *Science*, 1965, *149*, 269–274.

Zajonc, R. B. Cognitive theories in social psychology. In G. Lindzey and E. Aronson (Eds.), *Handbook of social psychology*. Vol. 1. (2nd ed.) Reading, Mass.: Addison-Wesley, 1968. *(a)*

Zajonc, R. B. Attitudinal effects of mere exposure. *Journal of Personality and Social Psychology*, 1968, *9*, (Monograph), 1–27. *(b)*

Zajonc, R. B., and Marin, I. C. Cooperation, competition, and interpersonal attitudes in small groups. *Psychonomic Science*, 1967, *7*, 271–272.

Zajonc, R. B., and Sherman, S. J. Structural balance and the induction of relations. *Journal of Personality*, 1967, *35*, 635–650.

Zander, A., and Havelin, A. Social comparison and interpersonal attraction. *Human Relations*, 1960, *13*, 21–32.

Zeigarnik, B. Uher das behalten von erledigter und unerledigter Handlungen. *Psychologische Forschung*, 1927, *9*, 1–85.

Ziegler, F. J., Rodgers, D. A., and Prentiss, R. J. Psychological response to vasectomy. *Archives of General Psychiatry*, 1969, *21*, 46–54.

Zigler, E., and Child, I. L. Socialization. In G. Lindzey and E. Aronson (Eds.), *Handbook of social psychology*. Vol. 3. (2nd ed.) Reading, Mass.: Addison-Wesley, 1969.

Zillman, D. Excitation transfer in communication-mediated aggressive behavior. *Journal of Experimental Social Psychology*, 1971, *7*, 419–434.

Zillman, D., Katcher, A. H., and Milvavsky, B. Excitation transfer from physical exercise to subsequent aggressive behavior. *Journal of Experimental Social Psychology*, 1972, *8*, 247–259.

Zimbardo, P. G. *The cognitive control of motivation: The consequences of choice and dissonance*. Glenview, Ill.: Scott, Foresman, 1969. *(a)*

Zimbardo, P. G. The human choice: Individuation, reason and order versus deindividuation, impulse and chaos. In W. J. Arnold and D. Levine (Eds.), *Nebraska symposium on motivation*. Lincoln: University of Nebraska Press, 1969. *(b)*

Zimbardo, P. G., and Formica, R. Emotional comparison and self-esteem as determinants of affiliation. *Journal of Personality*, 1963, *31*, 141–162.

Zimbardo, P., Haney, C., Banks, W., and Jaffe, D. The psychology of imprisonment: Privation, power, and pathology. Unpublished manuscript, Stanford University, 1972.

Zimbardo, P. G., Weisenberg, M., Firestone, I., and Levy, B. Communicator effectiveness in producing public conformity and private attitude change. *Journal of Personality*, 1965, *33*, 233–256.

Zimring, F. Is gun control likely to reduce violent killings? Unpublished study, Center for Studies in Criminal Justice, University of Chicago Law School, 1968.

Zinnes, D. A. Coalition theories and the balance of

power. In S. Groennings, E. W. Kelley, and M. Leiserson (Eds.), *The study of coalition behavior: Theoretical perspectives and cases from four continents.* New York: Holt, Rinehart, & Winston, 1970.

Zipf, S. G. Resistance and conformity under reward and punishment. *Journal of Abnormal and Social Psychology,* 1960, *61,* 102–109.

Zuckerman, M. Psychological responses and exposure to erotica. Paper presented at the 79th annual meeting of the American Psychological Association, Washington, D. C., September, 1971.

Author Index

Subject Index